A Historical Dictionary
of the
U.S. Merchant Marine
and
Shipping Industry

A HISTORICAL DICTIONARY
OF THE
U.S. MERCHANT MARINE
AND
SHIPPING INDUSTRY

Since the Introduction of Steam

RENÉ DE LA PEDRAJA

GREENWOOD PRESS

Westport, Connecticut • London

Library of Congress Cataloging-in-Publication Data

De la Pedraja Tomán, René.
   A historical dictionary of the U.S. merchant marine and shipping
industry : since the introduction of steam / René De la Pedraja.
     p. cm.
   Includes bibliographical references and index.
   ISBN 0–313–27225–5 (alk. paper)
   1. Merchant marine—United States—History—Dictionaries.
2. Shipping—United States—History—Dictionaries. I. Title.
HE745.D39   1994
387.7'03—dc20   93–39354

British Library Cataloguing in Publication Data is available.

Library of Congress Catalog Card Number: 93–39354
ISBN: 0–313–27225–5

First published in 1994

Greenwood Press, 88 Post Road West, Westport, CT 06881
An imprint of Greenwood Publishing Group, Inc.

Printed in the United States of America

The paper used in this book complies with the
Permanent Paper Standard issued by the National
Information Standards Organization (Z39.48–1984).

10 9 8 7 6 5 4 3 2 1

To Beatriz

CONTENTS

PREFACE

Readers have before them a road map through merchant shipping. This historical dictionary presents in alphabetical order the basic historical facts about the U.S. merchant marine and shipping since the introduction of steam until today. The focus has been on the institutions and the persons involved in merchant shipping, in both government and private business. Inevitably the nuts and bolts of the subject have taken prominence, yet, to avoid a bland compilation of dry facts, the dictionary, whenever possible, has tried to present, or at least to suggest, the passion and high drama of the struggles for survival in one of the riskiest and most volatile businesses in the world.

No comparable reference work exists for merchant shipping, a subject made particularly difficult by the lack of a single overriding institution, as has been the case with the U.S. Navy and the U.S. Army. The failure to grasp the nature of merchant shipping has led to excessive compartmentalization, so that its individual components generally are portrayed independently of its other aspects. For the first time this historical dictionary attempts to integrate the entire subject, making easier the task of all those who are searching for additional information on merchant shipping. Certainly in my case, the availability of this dictionary would have saved considerable time and effort when writing my previous book, *The Rise and Decline of U.S. Merchant Shipping in the Twentieth Century* (1992). The historical dictionary provides the reader with brief accounts of the following topical groupings within merchant shipping: companies; labor organizations (see Appendix C); major legislation and court cases; key individuals, both private and government; agencies (see Appendix B); ships; and shipping terms.

The reader has the right to expect accounts of the above, but this historical dictionary goes beyond the conventional and breaks new ground by including for the first time capsule accounts on conferences* (over two dozen are discussed) and business groups (see Appendix C).

The chronology in Appendix A provides an overview of the field and suggests the many linkages not only inside merchant shipping itself but also with other events of historical significance. The bibliographic essay offers useful suggestions to the reader on how to obtain additional information for individual topics within merchant shipping and complements the references that appear after the individual entries.

While the book remains a reliable reference for experts in the field, the historical dictionary also has the more difficult goal of introducing merchant shipping to persons who are just becoming interested in the subject or who desire to explore other aspects of the vast world of merchant shipping. Consequently, the book has minimized the use of technical and specialized terms and, when absolutely indispensable, has defined them in separate entries. While a number of excellent dictionaries on shipping terms provide the specialist with very extensive lists, here the historical approach has been the most useful vehicle to introduce the meaning of the most basic terms.

Originally the historical dictionary was intended to be just a summary of standard books whose contents supposedly contained all that was needed. This optimistic assessment proved unfounded, and soon I found myself engaged in extensive searching in newspapers, magazines, and government publications. The unpublished documents in archives proved once again essential to provide a complete summary, while in order to provide the most up-to-date information, correspondence and conversations with persons in existing institutions have helped fill in most of the gaps. I still would have liked to include a dozen more entries on companies and executives, but not at the price of delaying the publication of this sorely needed dictionary, already of considerable length.

While the selection of what institutions, persons, and topics to include was ultimately mine, I have tried to follow certain definitions and restrictions. For business and labor leaders, Greenwood Press has published two other works, the *Biographical Dictionary of American Business Leaders* by John N. Ingham and the *Biographical Dictionary of American Labor* by Gary M. Fink, both extremely useful in solidifying the initial selection, to which I have added many other individuals. To keep the size within manageable proportions, this dictionary continues from my previous book the emphasis on the deep-sea ocean trade, and consequently this work rarely touches upon developments in the rivers, lakes, bays, and sounds of the United States. However, intercoastal* and coastwise* shipping have received extensive attention in this historical dictionary.

Vessels owned by U.S. firms but flying foreign flags have been, since the nineteenth century, an important and often crucial element in the U.S. merchant marine, so this dictionary, just like my previous book, takes them into account. The inclusion of the foreign-flag operations of U.S. companies not only allows a discussion of famous cases like the *Titanic*,* which, although flying the British flag, was owned by a U.S. corporation, the International Mercantile Marine,* but, more important, avoids the tunnel vision that results from considering exclusively firms whose ships were all under U.S. registry.*

Originally this historical dictionary planned to cover only the twentieth century, but as the research progressed, an underlying theme appeared that not only gave unity to the entries but almost dictated what should be included. This theme was the gradual struggle to develop and apply with increasing efficiency mechanical forms of energy to vessels, a process that has provided a continuity between the first steamboat,* the *Clermont* in 1807, and the diesel* containerships of today. Even the introduction of containers,* the second most important event in merchant shipping since steam power, was possible only with mechanical energy and was the most successful of the many efforts to improve the efficiency of vessels. The reader wishing to understand the dynamics of merchant shipping can profitably begin by turning to the entries on marine propulsion* and containers* and afterward glancing at the chronology in Appendix A. Once the fundamental significance of the engineering advances that produced marine propulsion is understood, the rest of the story boils down to discussing how society, the economy, and the government came to grips with the new technology for moving ocean vessels. Consequently, I decided to start this dictionary with the introduction of steam and then to construct the business, individual, labor, and government histories around the fundamental changes in marine propulsion. At times it might seem hard to visualize that so many changes would haven taken place because of the adoption of a new system of marine propulsion. One example is the clearest illustration: while in the age of sailing vessels the government gave almost complete freedom to shipowners, with the introduction of steam, the government began gradually to take a closer look, beginning with inspections, later with subsidies, then with regulation, and in some cases even with government ownership. While the exact role of government in merchant shipping remains a topic of valid controversy, by the early twentieth century marine propulsion created the consensus that government has a major role to play, a position recently restated with powerful force in the Oil Pollution Act of 1990.*

The coverage of the main events in the U.S. merchant marine becomes fairly comprehensive in this historical dictionary once the introduction of steel hulls and the triple-expansion engine* in the 1880s largely replaced sailing vessels. The dictionary, however, does not ignore the earlier period from 1807 to 1880, when the real dynamics of merchant shipping first appeared, as shipowners struggled with the recurrent decisions over adopting, modifying, rejecting, improving, or partially accepting the newest advances in marine propulsion. Hence, while the engineers struggled to improve the new technology, the shipowner had to make the final decision, and with so many shipowners existing during most of the history of the United States, a wide variety of outcomes has usually been the result. Thus while the first steps toward new technology, such as replacing the side-wheels with the propeller,* may seem quaint to some today, the issues and the stakes were no less different than the equally momentous decisions of adopting containers, or the LASH* system. The shipowners, in spite of being driven by the profit motive, did not always select what was in their best interests and sometimes made completely wrong decisions. As a result, initially government and later labor by the end of the nineteenth century stepped in to have an impact on how the United States accepted and managed the new technology and its implications. The ongoing process provides a fascinating spectacle of interaction among technology, economics, government, and labor; this historical dictionary has tried to continue the coverage at least until December 1992 and has been able to include some events for 1993.

Some final suggestions should help the user make the most from this dictionary. After looking under the alphabetical list of entries, the reader should not hesitate to consult the index, into whose elaboration considerable time and effort have gone to try to make it friendly to use so that the reader can extract every last bit of information on a particular topic. Appendix B provides a clear guide to the government agencies, while Appendix C on labor unions and business groups similarly illustrates those topics. Careful perusal of Appendix A not only gives the reader an overview but also provides leads to approach a particular item. As for the entries themselves, those on individual companies contain the largest numbers of references to other entries, because they are generally accompanied by lists of executives, ships, and, sometimes, subsidiaries. Every time a word that has a separate entry first appears in an entry, an asterisk (*) follows the word. Numerous cross-references inside the entries and even in the alphabetical entries direct the user to other related bodies of information. In an attempt to help the reader through a corporate maze, whenever possible the dictionary has referred to companies by the name most frequently used, which usually was also the easiest to remember. This simplification helps the reader, while for the specialist the entries note major name changes.

Like my previous book on merchant shipping, this book has not received any guidance or financial backing from private companies, business groups, or organized labor and ultimately remains the product of an independent academic scholar. Many individuals proved useful in the long and arduous task of gathering information, and I must begin by thanking the persons who answered my inquiries on many specific points. The staffs at libraries and archives were courteous and friendly, and William Kooiman at the San Francisco National Maritime Museum went beyond reasonable bounds to meet my requests. At the National Archives in Washington, D.C., I must single out Angie Vandereedt for her skill and care in tracking down in record time the obscure references to the many boxes and documents I needed. Once again Helen Toman provided the gracious hospitality of her home, which made possible my extended stay for research in Washington, D.C. Robin Higham convinced me to write this dictionary on the grounds the project ''would keep me out of trouble,'' and it certainly did—it kept me out of just about everything else! He has my thanks for his constant encouragement, and I am also grateful to Mildred Vasan, senior editor at Greenwood Press, for her sponsorship of this project and for her appreciation of this very complex field. The History Department at Canisius College allowed me flexibility with my teaching hours so that I could maximize the writing time for this project, and Canisius College also assigned me a student, Melissa Fuller, as my research assistant, without whose help in gathering the information this dictionary would still not be finished.

As with my other publications, this book was possible only because of the trust and support that in countless ways my wife, Beatriz, has always shown to my intellectual career, and to her I dedicate the book. My son, Jaroslav, continued to direct criticism at some of my worst sentences, thereby shaking me out of any complacency, while he also drew the diagrams in the book. To all the persons who have supported me, I am immensely grateful, but the responsibility for any errors or omissions remains with the author.

A Historical Dictionary
of the
U.S. Merchant Marine
and
Shipping Industry

A

ABLE-BODIED SEAMAN. Able-bodied seaman has been the key ''rating'' or skill status for sailors on the deck crew. Prior to the passage of the La Follette Seamen's Act* in 1915, officers often abused their right to assign whatever duties they thought fit to the crew members. Although the rating of able-bodied seaman (AB) was implicitly recognized, no formal qualifying system existed as was the case for officers. The La Follette Seamen's Act for the first time stipulated that to obtain the rating of able-bodied seaman, a person had to pass certification exams and have three years' sailing experience. Compliance with other provisions of the law proved impossible: shipowners ignored the requirement that 65 percent of the deck crew had to be ABs, while they likewise sidestepped the requirement that 75 percent of the crew understand the language of the officers by teaching the Oriental crews a few words in English.

The rise of the powerful maritime labor movement has assured since the late 1930s full compliance with the laws on ABs. Since World War II the standard requirements to become an AB in U.S.-flag ships have been to pass Coast Guard* tests and to serve aboard ships for three years. The higher the percentage of ABs in the deck crew, the smoother and more effective becomes the operation of the ship.

References: Joseph P. Goldberg, *The Maritime Story: A Study in Labor-Management Relations* (Cambridge: Harvard University Press, 1958); James C. Healey, *Foc'sle and Glory Hole: A Study of the Merchant Seaman and His Occupation* (New York: Merchant Marine Publishers Association, 1936); Betty V. H. Schneider, *Industrial Relations in the West Coast Maritime Industry* (Berkeley: University of California, 1958); Hyman Weintraub, *Andrew Furuseth: Emancipator of the Seamen* (Berkeley: University of California Press, 1959).

ACCESSORY TRANSIT COMPANY, 1850–1860. Cornelius Vanderbilt*
created the Accessory Transit Company to provide passenger service from New
York to San Francisco via Nicaragua after the California gold rush had begun.
The first ship of the company departed for Nicaragua from New York on 27
December 1850. Because Nicaragua was farther to the north than Panama, Vanderbilt believed that the Nicaragua route was much faster than the trek through
the steamy path in the Isthmus of Panama. Vanderbilt, a man of large ambitions,
originally had wanted to build a canal across Nicaragua, but when British investors balked at the proposal, he fell back upon the more modest business of
carrying passengers aboard his ocean steamers and across the overland route in
Nicaragua. In accordance with a contract from the Nicaraguan government, the
Accessory Transit Company built docks and hotels and improved the navigation
of the San Juan River; lake steamers ferried the passengers across Lake Nicaragua, while the company placed a layer of asphalt and broken rock on the last
twelve-mile stretch to the Pacific Ocean so that passengers would have a smooth
coach ride. Initially the company carried across any passenger who had reached
Nicaragua, but starting in January 1852 the company restricted the route only
to passengers who had come to Nicaragua aboard the company's fleet of steamers. The competition by Vanderbilt cut into the business of the Pacific Mail
Steamship Company* (PMSS) and United States Mail Steamship Company,*
which used the Panama route, but in spite of all of their efforts to discredit
the Nicaragua route and the Accessory Transit Company, the increase in the
number of passengers allowed all the companies to raise their fares, so that
Vanderbilt made huge profits from the operation. In 1852 he added service
from New Orleans, and normally he kept five steamers plying the Pacific
Ocean and at least three in the New York to Nicaragua run. The company
continued to deliver on its slogan of "Through ahead of any other line," and
many passengers seeking faster arrival time naturally patronized the Accessory
Transit Company.

  Vanderbilt was having such great success that he decided to return to Europe
on a vacation and to promote interest among investors again in his Nicaragua
canal project. As part of complex arrangements, he resigned the presidency in
September 1852, trusting to resume direct control once he returned from his
grand European tour. His associates Charles Morgan* and Cornelius K. Garrison
quietly began buying Accessory Transit Company—soon to justify its Wall
Street nickname of "Sick" Company—and in July 1853 Morgan became its
president and severed all payments to Vanderbilt. When the latter returned in
September and learned the news, he promptly fired off a note: "Gentlemen: You
have undertaken to cheat me. I won't sue you, for the law is too slow. I'll ruin
you. Yours truly, Cornelius Vanderbilt" (Folkman 1972). He started in February
1854 the Independent Opposition Line to operate steamers on the Atlantic and
Pacific sides for service via Panama, and by drastically slashing rates he attracted
large numbers of passengers. By September the Accessory Transit Company,

the PMSS, and United States Mail were in dire straits, and they agreed to buy out the Independent Opposition Line at prices set by Vanderbilt, who appeared to have extracted enough revenge.

The Accessory Transit Company resumed operations but continued to face occasional rate wars with PMSS. Vanderbilt, however, was still determined to regain his company and was quietly buying up all the stock he could find, until in January 1856 he was elected president after having forced Morgan to resign. Morgan and his associates had in fact anticipated the move and had done everything they could to drive the stock prices as high as possible, while quietly disposing of their own stock and even going heavily "short" or selling at a high price stock they later expected to purchase at a low price. Prior to the stock market transactions, Morgan and Garrison had made a deal with the American adventurer William Walker, who was temporarily in control of the Nicaraguan government, to cancel the contract of the Accessory Transit Company on February 1856. When news of this cancellation finally reached New York, the price of the stock collapsed, and Morgan and his associates made a killing by covering their "short" position; it was estimated that they had increased a hundred times their original investment. With these profits Morgan and Garrison started their own line of steamers to Nicaragua, in the hope of driving out Vanderbilt completely from the up-till-then profitable Nicaragua route.

Vanderbilt was outraged when he discovered the maneuvers of his rivals and decided to take reprisals. He supported a military campaign in Central America that closed the Nicaragua route and drove Walker from power by May 1857. However, Vanderbilt's efforts to obtain a new contract from Nicaragua for the Accessory Transit Company ran into complications. Morgan and Garrison had been too closely connected with the adventurer Walker to stand any chance of receiving the contract, so they wisely sold their fleet of steamers in the Nicaragua route to Vanderbilt in 1858. Vanderbilt by now was having doubts about the Nicaragua route itself, especially after the completion of the Panama railroad in 1855 provided the easiest and fastest land link for the ocean voyage between New York and San Francisco. In 1859 Vanderbilt obtained a U.S. mail contract and verbal assurances from the Nicaraguan government that he could return his steamers to the route and use the properties of the Accessory Transit Company, but when he heard about Walker's preparations for another military expedition to Central America, Vanderbilt, on the advice of the postmaster general, sent his steamers via Panama. Passenger service across Nicaragua had stopped in December 1858, and the properties of the Accessory Transit Company remained in limbo until 1860, when the Nicaraguan government awarded the contract to a successor firm, the Central American Transit Company.*

Principal Executives

Cornelius Vanderbilt	1850–1853; 1856–1860
Charles Morgan	1853–1856

References: *Dictionary of National Biography*, vol. 19; David I. Folkman, Jr., *The Nicaragua Route* (Salt Lake City: University of Utah Press, 1972); John H. Kemble, *The Panama Route, 1848–1869* (Berkeley: University of California Press, 1943).

ACTION ON THE NORTH ATLANTIC, **1943.** The movie *Action on the North Atlantic* about the merchant marine in World War II effectively portrays the sacrifices and contributions seafarers made during that war. The movie covers the ordeals of one Liberty* ship sailing from Halifax, Nova Scotia, to Murmansk, Russia, the most deadly sea route. Humphrey Bogart played the role of chief mate, and as the main protagonist just his presence sufficed to guarantee the movie's success. The film, compiled from actual experiences of merchant seamen, graphically revealed the gruesome toll German submarines took upon the convoy, with merchant ships and seamen literally blasted out of the water. Although navy personnel handled the weapons aboard the Liberties, the merchant seamen promptly replaced wounded navy sailors to keep gunfire going against the Germans. The movie included moving episodes, such as the burial at sea, and had such poignant scenes as the cadet from Kansas who had always dreamed about sailing on ships. The film communicated to a large public not only the crucial role played by merchant shipping in the war but also the tremendous sacrifices made by highly skilled and dedicated seafarers. The film has remained a minor classic, and to make it more appealing to late twentieth-century viewers, Turner Networks issued a colorized version in 1988. Undoubtedly *Action on the North Atlantic* is the film American seafarers most treasured and is in stark contrast to the notorious *Dead Ahead: The Exxon Valdez Disaster.**

Reference: Jay R. Nash and Stanley R. Ross, *The Motion Picture Guide, 1927–1983* (Chicago: Cinebooks, 1986).

ADMIRAL LINE, 1920–1938. The Admiral Line was the largest company in the coastwise* trade of the Pacific Coast. The Admiral Line was the creation of Hubbard F. Alexander,* who around 1910 gave this trade name to the separate steamship companies he operated out of Tacoma, Washington. He adopted the slogan "Safety, Courtesy, and Food" to attract passengers and gradually started to outdistance the older rival, the Pacific Coast Steamship Company,* which he merged with the Admiral Line in 1916. One reason for the early success of Alexander was the arrangement he made in 1910 with the Metropolitan Steamship Company* to coordinate its sailing schedules with those of the Admiral Line. In this way Alexander neutralized the otherwise fearful competition from the *Harvard** and the *Yale,** the swift turbine* ships of the Metropolitan Steamship Company, and he confirmed the Admiral Line's supremacy in July 1916, when he leased these two ships, which remained under his control until 1918, when they were requisitioned by the government for wartime duty.

The Admiral Line operated coastwise service along the Pacific Coast and to Alaska, but Alexander sensed that World War I provided the opportunity to enter the foreign trade routes. In 1917 he sent ships as far as Singapore to test the market, and amazed at the profits, he chartered* vessels to begin regular sailings in 1918. Later that year, the Admiral Line stopped private chartering when the Shipping Board offered government-owned vessels at incredibly favorable terms as "managing operator."* By the spring of 1920 the Admiral Line was operating eighteen government-owned freighters, but because the Shipping Board insisted they be handled through a separate company, Alexander created the Admiral Oriental Mail Line in late 1920. Unfortunately for Alexander, Robert Dollar* and his son R. Stanley Dollar* engineered a swift power play that took away the Admiral Mail Line from the Admiral Line in September 1922.

Henceforth the Admiral Line remained limited to its coastwise service along the Pacific Coast, including Alaska. Alexander proceeded to expand by purchasing many vessels, not only freighters (whose names began with the word *Admiral*) but also fast combination cargo-passenger liners like the *Dorothy Alexander*. His most spectacular acquisition came early in 1922, when, after intense lobbying, he obtained for the Admiral Line the express liner the *Great Northern*,* renamed the *H. F. Alexander*, which placed the company far ahead of its competitors. The Admiral Line supported the creation of the Coastwise Conference* in 1925, but indiscriminate price cutting and even rate wars continued to plague shipping along the Pacific Coast. Nevertheless, the Admiral Line was riding the boom of the 1920s and enjoyed a substantial rise in its income.

Since 1919 the Dollars had quietly purchased stock in the Admiral Line, until by 1921 they owned more shares than Alexander, although they still lacked a controlling interest. The Dollars were on the Board of Directors and continued to exercise a strict vigilance over Alexander, which he resented. When the Great Depression struck, the Admiral Line was the first of the coastwise firms to feel the blow, and Alexander immediately realized nothing could be done to save the company and resigned the presidency on 1 August 1930. J. Harold Dollar became the second president of the company, but he could do nothing to stop the collapse of the company, which lost $2 million in 1929–1931 and more than $1 million just in 1932. The Admiral Line began to sell off ships and assets to keep at bay the creditors, but when J. Harold Dollar died of cancer on 7 April 1936, the hopelessness of the situation became evident; the company was on the verge of collapse in March 1937 and suspended the last of its operations in June 1938. The demise of the Admiral Line, the largest company in coastwise trade, meant the end to any hopes of permanently reviving shipping along the Pacific Coast after World War II.

Principal Executives

Hubbard F. Alexander	1910–1930
J. Harold Dollar	1930–1936

Some Notable Ships

Harvard and *Yale*	1916–1918

H. F. Alexander; formerly,	1922–1936
Great Northern	
Dorothy Alexander	1922–1936
Emma Alexander; formerly,	1923–1936
*Congress** and *Nanking*	

References: Giles T. Brown, *Ships That Sail No More: Marine Transportation from San Diego to Puget Sound, 1910–1940* (Lexington: University of Kentucky Press, 1966); John Niven, *The American President Lines and Its Forebears, 1848–1984* (Newark: University of Delaware Press, 1987).

ADMIRAL ORIENTAL MAIL LINE. See American Mail Line.

ADVISORY COMMISSION ON CONFERENCES IN OCEAN SHIPPING (ACCOS), 1991–1992. The antitrust immunity of conferences* has traditionally aroused considerable criticism, and as a result Congress agreed to include in the Shipping Act of 1984* a provision for the review of the act five and a half years later. The Advisory Commission on Conferences in Ocean Shipping (AC-COS) duly convened on 10 April 1991; eight of its members were from Congress, while the president of the United States appointed the remaining nine from the private sector.

The Federal Maritime Commission* (FMC) provided a large volume of empirical data (required by the act) for the review, and ACCOS itself also held field hearings in five cities and conducted over 120 interviews. No matter how vigorous the pace, the differences in opinion evident in the opening meeting on 10 April 1991 grew until they were ''reaching cataclysmic proportions.'' The members of Congress, whose political skills could have fashioned some agreement, ''rarely [showed] their faces,'' (Advisory Commission 1992) and their staff aides rarely spoke out. The shippers* charged that the ocean carriers had gained control of ACCOS to give a clean bill of health to the Shipping Act of 1984. Within the eternal shipper-carrier rivalry no consensus was possible, and finally ACCOS presented only the main facts in its report of 10 April 1992 but made no recommendations.

In minority opinions members of Congress, in particular, Walter B. Jones,* defended the lack of recommendations on the grounds that ''the statute is working well, and it has been successful in achieving its goals and purposes.'' A commissioner who represented a foreign-flag line claimed victory: ''If the process ended in a draw, we would win'' (Advisory Commission 1992). Congress had joined with ACCOS in agreeing to postpone any further action on conferences for years, if not decades, to come, so that the regulatory provisions of the Shipping Act of 1984 survived intact. The big shadow overlooking the commission's work was the virtual demise of the U.S.-flag shipping, and since AC-COS failed to propose any solutions, this unanswered question will have to be addressed at some time by the U.S. government.

References: Advisory Commission on Conferences in Ocean Shipping, *Report to the President and the Congress* (Washington, DC: Government Printing Office, 1992); *American Shipper*, January–April 1992.

AFL-CIO MARITIME COMMITTEE. See Maritime Trades Department.

AFL-CIO MARITIME TRADES DEPARTMENT. See Maritime Trades Department.

ALASKA HYDRO-TRAIN, 1963–present. Alaska Hydro-Train, a subsidiary of the Crowley Maritime Corporation,* has been one of the companies providing ocean transportation between mainland United States and Alaska. Alaska Hydro-Train evolved from the Puget Sound Alaska Van Lines, a service Crowley Maritime Transport originally established in 1961 to carry just containers* and Roll-on/Roll-off* (Ro/Ro) cargoes. As its title indicated, the company specialized since 1964 in transporting railcars to Alaska, much in the same manner that Seatrain* had done for Cuba for decades. As the Alaska highway system expanded, the need for Roll-on/Roll-off* (Ro/Ro) service emerged, and in 1984 the company began to transport truck trailers and all types of vehicles. In 1992 the fleet had in service two double-deck combination barges and three single-deck railcar barges.

References: "Crowley Maritime Corporation," Special Supplement of the *Journal of Commerce*, 1988; *Pacific Maritime Magazine*, May 1992.

ALASKA MARINE HIGHWAY, 1960–present. The Alaska Marine Highway has been carrying passengers and vehicles among Seattle, Washington; Prince Rupert, British Columbia; and many ports in Alaska. In 1960 Alaska voters, dissatisfied with the irregular and partial services provided by private operators, approved bond issues so that the Department of Public Works of the state government of Alaska could order vessels to establish the Alaska Marine Highway. The service began in 1963 with three car ferries and has continued without interruption. Of the original three liners, the *Malaspina* and the *Matanuska* have remained after having been rebuilt and lengthened to 408 feet in 1972 and 1978, respectively. Another vessel, the *Columbia*, was ordered in 1974 and has been the flagship of the fleet, which comprised a total of nine vessels in 1987. The blue ferryliners, as they have been popularly called, have operated on two separate itineraries: one linking the southeastern ports of Alaska with British Columbia and Seattle, Washington, and another linking the communities along the Gulf of Alaska. "The friendly blue ferryliners are the workhorses of the coastal waters, faithfully carrying passengers, vehicles, and freight from one port town to the next" (State of Alaska 1988). For communities vitally dependent on ocean transportation, the state of Alaska, just like Puerto Rico, had concluded that direct government ownership and operation were the only real and long-term solution. The investment has paid off, and today the Alaska Marine Highway has survived as one of the rare cases of U.S.-flag passenger (as distinct from cruise) service still in operation and as the only substantial U.S.-flag passenger service to a foreign port.

Some Notable Ships

Malaspina	1962–present
Matanuska	1962–present
Columbia	1974–present

References: Frederick E. Emmons, *American Passenger Ships: The Ocean Lines and Liners, 1873–1983* (Newark: University of Delaware Press, 1985); State of Alaska, *Alaska and Canada's Yukon* (1988); Sarah Bird Wright, *Ferries of America* (Atlanta: Peachtree, 1987).

ALASKA STEAMSHIP COMPANY (ASC), 1895–1970. The Alaska Steamship Company (ASC) provided service not only inside that region but in particular between Alaska and West Coast ports. The company began operations in 1895 with a small wooden schooner as a competitor to the Pacific Coast Steamship Company,* whose high rates had angered the local population. The Alaska gold rush provided a boom to the ASC, which, unlike many other small outfits that appeared to meet the sudden demand for water transportation, survived and became the most important water carrier for the region. In 1905 the Guggenheim copper conglomerate bought the ASC and in 1907 merged it with the Northwestern Commercial Company (1904–1907), the only other sizable company in that trade. The ASC at last appeared to have attained a near monopoly position in the trade between the West Coast and Alaska, but unlike Matson Navigation Company* in Hawaii, the company never developed close links with local businesses and consequently retained throughout its history a bad reputation among the population of the territory.

Resentment at the ASC encouraged many Alaskans to patronize other companies, such as the Alaska Coast Company, which in 1907, when it was purchased by Hubbard F. Alexander,* operated three small steamers between Seattle and Alaska. In 1914 Alexander merged the Alaska Coast Company into the Admiral Line,* which became the most formidable competitor of the ASC for nearly twenty years. However, the Admiral Line was never able to destroy the ASC, which often invaded the West Coast coastwise* trade during the winter months, when, given the seasonal nature of the Alaska cargo movements, many of its ships were otherwise idle. To end the ruinous competition, in March 1933 the Admiral Line made an agreement to withdraw from the Alaska route, and in exchange the ASC agreed not to reenter the coastwise trade in the West Coast. The ASC now had another chance to improve its relations with the population of the territory, but foolishly neglected the opportunity and preferred instead to make extra profits by letting shipping rates rise; to protect themselves, most of the salmon canneries, the shippers* of 85 percent of the south-bound cargoes, purchased and operated their own fleets with a total of nineteen vessels.

When the United States entered World War II, the government requisitioned the ships of the ASC and of the canneries. With the end of the conflict, the government returned the combination cargo-passenger vessels to the ASC, which also chartered* thirteen vessels from the U.S. Maritime Commission,* but the canneries decided not to return immediately to ocean transportation. Since 1944 the ASC and the Northland Transportation Company (1923–1947) were both in the hands of the same owners, the G. W. Skinner Company, which decided to fuse the two shipping companies in 1947 as the ASC. With the spread of air travel, the ASC gradually abandoned passenger service, until its remaining cargo-passenger vessel made the last passenger voyage on 24 September 1954. The cargo services continued to antagonize Alaskans who believed "that the Alaska Steamship Company by a virtual monopoly has controlled the freight rates on commodities shipped to Alaska" (*Congressional Record,* 6 March 1964).

The ASC could never shake itself from the charge of being responsible for the high cost of living in the forty-ninth state, and under pressure from the state government, the Federal Maritime Commission* (FMC) suspended a general rate increase proposed by the ASC in April 1966. This refusal to raise rates was a serious blow to the ASC, which needed capital to complete the conversion to containers.* ASC limped along until 1970, when its principal assets were purchased by the Dillingham Corporation of Honolulu, but by then other companies, most notably Sea-Land* and Alaska Hydro Train,* were carrying the majority of the cargo moving between mainland United States and Alaska.

References: Giles T. Brown, *Ships That Sail No More: Marine Transportation from San Diego to Puget Sound, 1910–1940* (Lexington: University of Kentucky Press, 1966); *Congressional Record,* 4 May 1960, 6 March 1964; Frederick E. Emmons, *American Passenger Ships: The Ocean Lines and Liners, 1873–1983* (Newark: University of Delaware Press, 1985); *New York Times,* 13 April 1966; U.S. Maritime Commission, *Decisions,* vol. 3 (Washington, DC: Government Printing Office, 1963); *Wall Street Journal,* 15 October 1970.

ALCOA CAVALIER, ALCOA CLIPPER, **and** *ALCOA CORSAIR,* **1947–1960.** The Alcoa Steamship Company,* in an effort to increase voyage revenues and keep possible competitors away from its trade to South America, decided to expand its cargo services to include passenger travel. In 1941 the company ordered three cargo-passenger liners, but they were not yet completed when the U.S. Navy requisitioned them for World War II. At the end of the war, Alcoa did not want the ships back and preferred to take advantage of the Ship Sales Act* to buy three unfinished Victory* hulls for operation under the U.S. flag. The three ships, named the *Alcoa Cavalier,* the *Alcoa Clipper,* and the *Alcoa*

Corsair, were completed with a new design that provided a swimming pool and other first-class facilities for ninety-eight passengers.

Alcoa Cavalier and the sister ships entered the company's regular service in 1947. The ships carried general cargo and tourists southward from New Orleans and returned with the travelers and bauxite from South America. As an aluminum company, the primary responsibility of the three ships remained bringing the bauxite from Suriname; nevertheless the three ships attracted an average of seventy passengers per voyage, and sometimes a single tourist group fully booked one of the vessels.

By the late 1950s airline competition was making deep inroads into the passenger business of the three ships, while the cost of operating U.S.-flag vessels had become prohibitive. The *Alcoa Cavalier*, the *Alcoa Clipper*, and the *Alcoa Corsair* stopped passenger service in 1960, and the next year all three were laid up; to haul the bauxite, the company henceforth relied only on foreign-flag bulk* carriers.

References: Frank O. Braynard, *Famous American Ships* (New York: Hastings House, 1956); Frederick E. Emmons, *American Passenger Ships: The Ocean Lines and Liners, 1873–1983* (Newark: University of Delaware Press, 1985).

ALCOA STEAMSHIP COMPANY, 1917–present. The Alcoa Steamship Company has been the subsidiary in charge of ocean transportation for the Aluminum Company of America (Alcoa). The steamship company has passed through three stages: (1) foreign-flag operations through separate lines from 1917 to 1940; (2) U.S.-flag operations from 1940 to 1969; (3) flags-of-convenience* ships from the 1960s to the present. Throughout all these stages the overriding concern of the fleet has been to deliver the bauxite from the British and Dutch Guianas to the parent company's plants in the United States and Canada. Alcoa has been one of the "industrial" carriers or proprietary companies,* like the steel and banana corporations.

Early in the twentieth century Alcoa had relied on other steamship companies to carry the bauxite, but wartime shipping shortages forced the company to purchase its first ship, the *Mohegan*, a steamer of wood hull, in 1917. The *Mohegan*, built for the Great Lakes, was far from satisfactory for ocean voyages and was sold in December 1918. Shortly afterward the company ordered two new steamships (the *George B. Mackenzie* and *John R. Gibbons*) and two specially designed barges. Each vessel was supposed to tow behind one of the barges, but this early experiment with towing barges across the sea (see Crowley Marine Corporation*) did not live up to expectations because "the barges had a habit of breaking loose and wandering off by themselves, as well as breaking their anchorage during the southbound leg of the voyage" (Alcoa Steamship Company 1976). In 1921 the vessels were sold, but these setbacks did not deter Alcoa from staying in ocean shipping; on the contrary the company had discovered the advantages of operating its own fleet, and henceforth control of a steamship subsidiary became a permanent part of Alcoa's corporate strategy.

The 1921 recession halted bauxite shipments from South America, but once it was over, Alcoa again reconstituted its own fleet of foreign-flag vessels leased under time charter.* This arrangement avoided the financial disadvantages of having to own vessels temporarily idled by lack of cargo and gave Alcoa the flexibility to increase or decrease the fleet size in response to cargo needs. Shipping with South America was divided among three subsidiaries: the Aluminum Line served the Gulf of Mexico; the American Caribbean Line served the East Coast; and the Ocean Dominion Steamship Corporation covered Canada. Alcoa did not purchase or receive for operation government-owned vessels after World War I, and its refusal to ship cargo in the American Antilles Line and in the Colombian Steamship Company* destroyed the former and weakened the latter. As the Colombian Steamship Company recounted its 1925 offer to Alcoa "to transport their ore north of Hatteras at the indicated cost to them of their transportation of last year, we have been unsuccessful in securing a pound of freight" (Record Group 32).

Alcoa knew the reckless experiment of the Shipping Board* in subsidizing over a hundred ill-conceived lines could not be lasting and preferred to rely on its own foreign-flag services. However, the outbreak of World War II in 1939 forced the company to order fourteen C-1* ships under the U.S. Maritime Commission's* construction program for operation under the U.S. flag, because foreign-flag vessels had disappeared from the chartering market. In 1940 Alcoa combined the three lines into the Alcoa Steamship Company, which in reality had existed and operated in corporate headquarters since the early 1920s but without the formal corporate shell.

With U.S. entry into the conflict, the War Shipping Administration* (WSA) requisitioned most of Alcoa's fleet, but since the bauxite had to keep coming for the war effort, the WSA made the company general agent for decrepit old vessels as well as some new ships from the construction program. Alcoa Steamship Company ended the war with ten C-1s (four had been sunk) and took advantage of the Ship Sales Act* to acquire three C-2* vessels and three unfinished Victory* hulls in 1946.

The three Victories were redesigned and finished with accommodations for ninety-six passengers in addition to the cargo. Alcoa Steamship hoped that by entering the passenger business, this would give the company an edge on any rival who might lure away some cargo, thereby reducing income per voyage. In 1947 the *Alcoa Cavalier,** the *Alcoa Clipper*, and the *Alcoa Corsair* established a regular service between New Orleans and South America. Prior to 1940 with a chartered foreign-flag fleet, the company had enjoyed an ample margin of safety to maneuver out of shipping losses, but after the war under the higher operating costs of U.S. registry* and once the postwar shipping shortages were over, the company's safety margin against losses became slim indeed.

Nonetheless, a highly motivated and dedicated management team was determined to make the U.S.-flag operations operate successfully. Under pressure from the parent company, the steamship subsidiary debated building an aluminum ship, but the proposals remained in the study stage. To reduce handling costs, Alcoa Steamship Company began to provide container* service in 1949 with 275-cubic-foot boxes (about one-fourth the size of a standard 20-foot container, or TEU*), and in 1966 the company began to provide regular service for containers in the standard sizes of 20 feet and 40 feet, or FEU.*

In spite of these and other efforts, the mounting costs of U.S.-flag operations could not be hidden from the parent company, which by 1960 had quietly begun to acquire ships flying flags of convenience. The passenger service ended in 1960, and the three ships were later sold. In 1963 Alcoa Steamship was able to take advantage of the Vessel Exchange Act to trade in its old C-1s for the slightly newer C-2s. The company was still operating seven U.S.-flag C-2s in 1968, but these vessels had also become overage and because of the container revolution had become obsolete for the transport of general cargo. The last U.S.-flag vessel of the company was sold in 1969.

By the late 1960s large bulk* ore carriers had emerged as the cheapest way to transport the bauxite from South America, and with general cargo no longer essential to cover costs, Alcoa Steamship gradually reduced its general cargo services. The company has owned part of its fleet and chartered additional vessels as they were needed, in the pattern of the pre–World War II fleet. All ships since 1969 have been foreign flag.

Some Notable Ships

Alcoa Cavalier	1947–1960
Alcoa Clipper	1947–1960
Alcoa Corsair	1947–1960
George B. Mackenzie	1919–1921
John R. Gibbons	1919–1921

References: *Alcoa News*, February 1982; Alcoa Steamship Company, company press release, 1976; *American Shipper*, April 1986; Maritime Administration, *Foreign Flag Merchant Ships Owned by U.S. Parent Companies*, 1988–1992; Record Group 32, National Archives, Washington, DC; President's Advisory Commission on the Merchant Marine, Harry S. Truman Presidential Library, Independence, Missouri.

ALEXANDER, HUBBARD F., 14 August 1879–17 February 1952. Hubbard F. Alexander was the founder of the Admiral Line* and its president during most of the company's existence. He was born in Colorado Springs, Colorado, on 14 August 1879, and later his parents brought him to Tacoma, Washington, where he studied in a private school. The panic of 1893 wiped out his parents' fortune and left his father an invalid, and to help support the family he began working as a longshoreman in the docks, until in five years he had risen to become the head of the stevedoring firm. With money he saved he bought an old vessel, and using his first ship as collateral, he borrowed enough to buy the Alaska Pacific Company, whose three small ships steamed between Seattle and

Alaska. Through aggressive marketing Alexander was gradually able to break into the coastwide* trade of the Pacific Coast, and as a born gambler, he delighted in taking great risks in the hope of making quick profits.

Alexander began calling his steamship ventures the Admiral Line, and its great opportunity to leap ahead of its rivals came with the entry of the Metropolitan Steamship Company* in 1910. Alexander convinced Metropolitan to coordinate sailing schedules with the Admiral Line, thereby gradually squeezing out the other rival companies in the Pacific coastwise trade. In 1916 Alexander merged the Admiral Line with the Pacific Coast Steamship Company,* the oldest and largest coastwise company, and as the undisputed shipping tycoon of the West Coast, his rags-to-riches career fascinated the public.

Alexander was eager to expand into the transpacific trade and in 1917 sent ships as far as Singapore to test the market; the results were so favorable that he began a regular transpacific service with chartered* ships. In 1918 the Shipping Board* offered for operation government-owned vessels on incredibly lucrative terms, and soon the Admiral Line was operating eighteen freighters on the transpacific service. However, the Shipping Board insisted that a separate company handle the foreign trade as managing operator,* and so Alexander organized the Admiral Oriental Mail Line in late 1920.

Alexander was overextended, he had heavy loan obligations outstanding, and the stock of the Admiral Line had dropped precipitously in price. Since 1919 Robert Dollar* and his sons had begun buying shares quietly through dummy firms, until by 1921 the Dollars owned more stock than Alexander himself in the Admiral Line, although the family still did not have a controlling interest. As members of the Board of Directors, the Dollars began to squeeze Alexander in his company, while through additional lobbying at the Shipping Board, they secured the transfer of the Admiral Oriental Mail Line (later known as American Mail Line*) to the Dollar Line.*

Alexander took very bitterly the loss of his transpacific service and chafed at being under the vigilance of the Dollars, but with no other alternative left, he remained president of the Admiral Line and was still far from powerless. He had masterminded two acquisitions of his own in Washington, D.C., in 1922: first, that of the *Northern Pacific* and, even more spectacularly, that of the *Great Northern*,* which he rather immodestly renamed the *H. F. Alexander*. He concentrated on the Admiral Line, whose expansion in services brought a dramatic increase in company revenues. Unfortunately his company was one of the first to suffer the impact of the Great Depression, and correctly despairing of any solution, he left the presidency of the Admiral Line on 1 August 1930.

Alexander remained on the Board of Directors and was able to watch closely how the Admiral Line declined and finally fell into bankruptcy in November 1936. The desire to return to coastwise navigation never left him, and as late as 1948 he proposed to revive Pacific coastwise shipping through a 50 percent subsidy, but naturally nothing came of the plan. He died in Tacoma, Washington, on 17 February 1952.

References: Giles T. Brown, *Ships That Sail No More: Marine Transportation from San Diego to Puget Sound, 1910–1940* (Lexington: University of Kentucky Press, 1966); *National Cyclopedia of American Biography*, vol. 17; John Niven, *The American President Lines and Its Forebears, 1848–1984* (Newark: University of Delaware Press, 1987).

ALEXANDER, JOSHUA W., 22 January 1852–27 February 1936. Joshua Alexander was the chairman of the Merchant Marine and Fisheries* Committee of the House of Representatives in 1911–1919 and formed with Schuyler Otis Bland,* Herbert C. Bonner,* and Walter B. Jones* the group of congressmen who had the greatest impact on the merchant marine during the twentieth century. Alexander was born in Cincinnati, Ohio, on 22 January 1852, and in 1863 his mother took him to Missouri, where he graduated from Culverton-Stockton College and later practiced law. Alexander soon became actively involved in local and state politics and eventually was elected to the House of Representatives in 1906. He was fortunate to rise quickly through the seniority system to become chairman of the Merchant Marine and Fisheries Committee in 1911.

In accordance with the free trade principles of the Democratic party, Alexander pushed for a free ship* bill and managed to have its essential provisions included in the Panama Canal Act of 1912.* One of his major accomplishments was to conduct the massive ''Investigation of Shipping Combinations'' in 1912–1914 (generally referred to as the Alexander Committee*). This exhaustive inquiry into conferences* laid the groundwork for many legislative proposals and set the tone for additional hearings his congressional committee conducted after the outbreak of World War I in 1914. Alexander's greatest accomplishment was the passage of the Shipping Act of 1916*, which not only established for the first time government regulation of ocean transportation but also created the Shipping Board.* However, Alexander did not attain his initial goal of including in the act provisions for a permanent government-owned fleet, and this setback was at the root of so many of the failures and scandals of later decades.

By 1919 Alexander sensed his career within Congress and his political survival had begun to take divergent paths: after the passage of the landmark Shipping Act of 1916, any later legislation necessarily paled, while as a representative from a landlocked state his maritime accomplishments were increasingly irrelevant to his political future in Missouri. Alexander decided to make a grateful exit from Washington and on 15 December 1919 accepted the offer to become the last secretary of commerce of Woodrow Wilson. Alexander served as secretary until 4 March 1921 and then returned to his law practice in Missouri, continuing, of course, to play a role in state politics as one of the elders. He died in Gallatin, Missouri, on 27 February 1936.

References: Jeffrey J. Safford, *Wilsonian Maritime Diplomacy, 1913–1921* (New Brunswick, NJ: Rutgers University Press, 1978); U.S. Congress, *Biographical Directory of the United States Congress, 1774–1989* (Washington, DC: Government Printing Office, 1989); U.S. Congress, House, Committee on Merchant Marine and Fisheries, *Investigation of Shipping Combinations*, 4 vols. (Washington, DC: Government Printing Office, 1913); Paul M. Zeis, *American Shipping Policy* (Princeton, NJ: Princeton University Press, 1938).

ALEXANDER COMMITTEE, 1912–1914. The Alexander Committee is the name given to the first congressional investigation into conferences* and takes its name from Joshua Alexander,* who, as the chairman of the Merchant Marine and Fisheries Committee* of the House of Representatives, conducted the inquiry. The 1901 Report of the Royal Commission on Shipping Rings to the British Parliament had not removed Americans' fears of monopoly practices in ocean transportation. Congress now wanted the Alexander Committee "to make a complete and thorough investigation of the methods and practices of the various ship lines, both domestic and foreign, engaged in carrying our over-sea or foreign commerce and in the coastwise and inland commerce . . . and to investigate whether any such ship lines have formed any agreements, understandings, working arrangements, conferences, pools, or other combinations among one another, or with railroads or other common carriers'' (U.S. Congress 1913).

The Alexander Committee began its work in late 1912 and opened public hearings in January 1913; the published proceedings amounted to three thick volumes, while a fourth volume consisted of reports from U.S. consular officers. Out of the mass of evidence and many witnesses heard, the Alexander Committee reached the fundamental conclusion that the conferences in almost all the trades had controlled, if not reduced, competition. However, the committee did not believe that the conferences should be prosecuted under the Sherman Antitrust Act, because they provided stability in rates and regularity in sailings and services. Although the conferences tended toward monopoly, the committee also concluded that without their stabilizing presence many carriers could not survive; hence conferences were necessary to maintain at least a level of competition.

The Alexander Committee felt certain practices of the conferences, in particular, the fighting ship* and the deferred rebate,* were totally objectionable and must be banned. For the rest of the conference activities, the committee recommended regulation as the best way to encourage competition and to diminish the monopolistic tendencies. The Interstate Commerce Commission* (ICC) was already regulating the railroads and inland transportation, so the Alexander Committee proposed extending its jurisdiction to cover the steamship companies. The committee wanted the mandatory filing of all conference agreements with the ICC, without whose approval they would lack validity; to handle the increased work load, the Alexander Committee also proposed adding more commissioners to the ICC.

The steamship companies were outraged by the conclusions and recommendations of the Alexander Committee, and they blocked any action on its proposals. The outbreak of World War I, however, created such a tremendous crisis in ocean transportation that public pressure for action became overwhelming. Finally Congress was convinced to include most, but not all, of the recommendations of the Alexander Committee in the Shipping Act of 1916.*

References: Samuel A. Lawrence, *United States Merchant Shipping Policies and Politics* (Washington, DC: Brookings Institution, 1966); U.S. Congress, House, Committee on Merchant Marine and Fisheries, *Investigation of Shipping Combinations*, 4 vols.

(Washington, DC: Government Printing Office, 1913); Paul M. Zeis, *American Shipping Policy* (Princeton, NJ: Princeton University Press, 1938).

ALEXANDRE LINE, 1867–1888. The Alexandre Line established the first regular steamship service between New York City and the Atlantic ports of Mexico. In 1874 the Alexandre Line (by then formally styled the New York, Havana, and Mexican Mail Steamship Line) received a mail subsidy from the Mexican government. Initially the service was only to Veracruz on vessels of wooden hulls, but gradually the routes extended to Progreso, Tampico, and other Caribbean ports in Mexico as well as in Cuba, and in 1877 the first iron steamship entered service, and others soon followed. Trade with Mexico was definitely increasing, but the profitability of the voyages ultimately depended on the mail subsidy.

When the Mexican government failed to renew the contract in 1887, the Alexandre Line attempted to solve the crisis by trying to seek cargo in Cuba, thereby clashing with the more powerful and entrenched Ward Line.* Unlike Cuba, Mexico did not generate enough cargo to support by itself a steamship line, while the most profitable alternative was to combine the service from New York to Mexico and Cuba in one line. Consequently in 1888 the Ward Line purchased the Alexandre Line, whose Mexican freight nicely complemented the profitable Cuban cargoes.

References: Frederick E. Emmons, *American Passenger Ships: The Ocean Lines and Liners, 1873–1983* (Newark: University of Delaware Press, 1985); Frank J. Taylor, "Early American Steamship Lines," in Society of Naval Architects and Marine Engineers, *Historical Transactions 1893–1943* (Westport, CT: Greenwood Press, 1981); U.S. Congress, *Report of the Merchant Marine Commission*, 3 vols., Report No. 2755, 58th Congress, 3d Session, 1905.

ALGIC. The *Algic* was a government-owned freighter operated by the American Republics Line, whose managing agent (an euphemism for managing operator*) for the U.S. Maritime Commission* was C. H. Sprague & Co. of Boston. The American Republics Line provided cargo services between the Atlantic coasts of the United States and South America. Out of many other freighters in this run, the *Algic* acquired notoriety because of the alleged mutiny by its crew. When the *Algic* reached Montevideo, Uruguay, in September 1937, a longshoremen's strike was in progress, and the National Maritime Union* (NMU) crew refused to cooperate with scab longshoremen to unload the cargo. The crew sympathized with the strike and also claimed that working with the scabs was unsafe. The captain of the ship was outraged, and in response to his complaints Joseph P. Kennedy,* the chairman of the U.S. Maritime Commission, telegraphed authorization on 10 September to arrest the seamen if they did not carry out the orders. Upon the ship's return to Baltimore, the fourteen ringleaders were arrested and convicted on charges of mutiny, even though the charge of mutiny was applicable only in the high seas and not when attempting to unload near a port.

Obviously much more was at issue than the isolated actions of the *Algic* seamen. For some shipowners, the *Algic* case was one last opportunity to use the mutiny statues to crush the newly emerging seamen's unions. For the American Federation of Labor, the *Algic* case was a cheap way to strengthen its own maritime unions and weaken the NMU of the rival Congress of Industrial Organization. For Joseph P. Kennedy the *Algic* was a way to show shipowners that he was not soft with labor and signaled the government's willingness to take strong action against any breach of discipline.

The internationalist tradition within the NMU had been responsible for the spontaneous sympathy of the *Algic* crew with the striking longshoremen in Montevideo, but henceforth the NMU became more careful about defying orders in foreign ports or in the high seas. Internationalist actions inspired in the multi-ethnic membership of the NMU and the Communist party influence continued until World War II, but the NMU preferred U.S. ports as the proper locale. Within U.S. borders the union could bring to bear a whole range of influences, opinions, witnesses, and resources to mobilize public opinion and the government, but abroad, the NMU's control was much more constrained. After World War II, sympathy strikes in behalf of foreign workers virtually disappeared as the Communist party was pushed out of the NMU, while ''beefs''* and ''job action''* provided powerful enough means to achieve union purposes inside U.S. ports.

References: Bruce Nelson, *Workers on the Waterfront: Seamen, Longshoremen, and Unionism in the 1930s* (Urbana: University of Illinois Press, 1990); *New York Times*, 11 September 1937; William L. Standard, *Merchant Seamen: A Short History of Their Struggles* (New York: International Publishers, 1947); U.S. Congress, House, Committee on Merchant Marine and Fisheries, *Amending Merchant Marine Act, 1936* (Washington, DC: Government Printing Office, 1938).

AMERICA, **1940–1964.** United States Lines* (USL) built the *America* as a partial replacement for the *Leviathan** on the strategy that the *America*, in combination with the *Manhattan** and the *Washington*, could provide effective competition to European liners in the North Atlantic. Unlike the other two vessels, the *America* was fitted with steam turbines* rather than the more expensive turboelectric drive but at twenty knots was below the speed travelers had grown accustomed to expect. Although the second biggest passenger liner ever built in the United States, the *America* was still smaller than the European liners and, with accommodations for only 515 passengers in first class, 371 in cabin, and 159 in tourist class, did not have the appropriate size for the highly competitive North Atlantic traffic.

USL briefly operated *America* in 1940 and 1941 before the ship was taken over and then purchased by the U.S. Navy as a transport. After World War II, USL chartered* the *America* to handle the peak postwar demand for passenger travel, but the liner already was known as a "problem ship." The government had totally rebuilt the ship but in the process had reduced the passenger accommodations by 150 persons, making even harder earning any substantial profits. Nonetheless, there were no other U.S.-flag liners available at bargain prices, and in 1948 USL bought the ship for operation in unison initially with the *Washington** and afterward with the *United States,** once the latter was completed in 1952.

The *America* had never been a completely satisfactory ship, and its substantially higher operating costs stood in sharp contrast to those of the *United States*. USL pressed the government for a large subsidy outlay to defray the cost of a replacement for the *America*, but the construction of the *United States* had been so expensive and controversial that, although Congress authorized the expenditures on a new passenger liner, the Eisenhower administration refused to include the subsidies in the annual budget. By 1960 the inroads of jet travel to Europe finally convinced USL that passenger travel aboard ships was largely obsolete and, rather than seeking a replacement, sought ways to dispose of the *America*. USL first obtained from the Maritime Administration* permission to reduce the number of money-losing voyages by the liner, whose last trips were in late 1963. The next year Greek shipowners bought the ship for operation in the cruise business. The career of the *America* under new names and under a shifting combination of foreign owners has been full of colorful episodes, and as of this writing it continues.

References: René De La Pedraja, *The Rise and Decline of U.S. Merchant Shipping in the Twentieth Century* (New York: Twayne, 1992); Frederick E. Emmons, *American Passenger Ships: The Ocean Lines and Liners, 1873–1983* (Newark: University of Delaware Press, 1985); *New York Times*, 11 July 1948; Files of the Maritime Administration, Washington, DC; *Time*, 17 July 1978.

AMERICA-FRANCE LINE. See Cosmopolitan Shipping Company.

AMERICAN ANTILLES LINE. See Colombian Steamship Company.

AMERICAN BANNER LINES, 1957–1960. American Banner Lines was the last steamship venture of Arnold Bernstein,* who created this line in 1957 to provide inexpensive but comfortable passage to Europe for middle-class tourists. He bought a Mariner* freighter, which he extensively refitted to carry up to 900 passengers, only 40 in first class and the rest in tourist class. The refurbished ship, the *Atlantic*, whose cabins all had their own showers and toilets for greater privacy, was entirely air-conditioned for the comfort of the passengers. The *Atlantic* sailed from New York on her maiden voyage in June 1958 and, besides the passengers, carried containers* with express cargo. Bernstein had a good business idea, but he was too late in his timing: for the line to be successful, a second sister ship had to be ordered, but the company's financial backers refused to make the investment because jet airline service had begun to Europe in October 1958. In November 1959 the *Atlantic* suspended service, and shortly after, American Export Lines* purchased the vessel. Bernstein himself resigned as president of American Banner Lines in 1960, and the company became inactive.

Principal Executive

Arnold Bernstein	1957–1960

A Notable Ship

Atlantic	1959–1960

References: Frederick E. Emmons, *American Passenger Ships: The Ocean Lines and Liners, 1873–1983* (Newark: University of Delaware Press, 1985); *National Cyclopedia of American Biography*, vol. 56; *New York Times*, 19 April 1957.

AMERICAN BUREAU OF SHIPPING (ABS), 1898–present. In the United States the American Bureau of Shipping (ABS) has been the classification society* that has set safety standards and has inspected vessels to rate or "classify" their seaworthiness. The bureau replaced the American Shipmasters' Association,* which, besides classifying ships, had also certified the officers. The new bureau limited itself to surveying and rating the vessels in order to determine their correct classification for insurance purposes.

In 1901 Lloyd's Register of Shipping, the British classification society, sent a committee to the United States to try to absorb ABS, but the takeover attempt failed. In 1908 ABS acquired the United States Standard Steamship Owners, Builders, and Underwriters Association, a classification society established in 1889 to survey iron and steel ships. The coverage of U.S. ships became virtually complete in 1916, when the ABS acquired the *Great Lakes Register*, thereby extending its activities into the inland waters. Also in 1916 the bureau was reorganized as a nonprofit organization, with the initial expenses covered by shipowners, shipbuilders, and insurance underwriters.

Prior to the 1916 reorganization, Lloyd's Register of Shipping had made one last attempt to take over the American Bureau of Shipping, but nationalist feeling, as explained by one underwriter, saved the ABS: "I would regret, and I think it would be a sad day for this country if we had to depend absolutely on London for insurance." To prevent another hostile takeover, the Jones Act* of 1920 gave official standing to the American Bureau of Shipping, which Congress recognized as the only classification society for all vessels owned, financed, subsidized, or contracted in any way by the government. The act also authorized the federal government to name two representatives to the governing board of the bureau; since 1942 one has been from the U.S. Coast Guard,* and since 1950 the other has been from the Maritime Administration.* The impact of the Jones Act was dramatic, and the percentage of U.S. vessels classified by the ABS climbed from barely 8 percent in 1916 to 80 percent in 1921.

The bureau has remained self-supporting by charging fees for the work of its surveyors and engineers and for whatever other special tests the shipbuilders or operators may require. However, in the late 1930s, as the number of U.S.-flag ships declined sharply, the bureau struggled to cover its operating expenses, and its survival was in doubt. Until World War II the classification of vessels rarely extended beyond U.S.-flag ships, but already during the war bureau offices followed the battle lines in Europe. The purchase by foreigners of many vessels under the Ship Sales Act of 1946* extended the jurisdiction of the ABS over many foreign-flag ships whose mortgages were held by the U.S. government, and out of this core of work the ABS gradually went on to open foreign branches to survey vessels in overseas areas until, in effect, it became an international classification society comparable to Lloyd's.

By the late 1980s the volume of worldwide business had swamped the New York office, and, to avoid unnecessary delays, the bureau embarked upon a decentralization plan called ABS 2000, which opened new regional offices in London and Singapore to handle Asia, Africa, and Europe. In 1986 headquarters moved from New York City to a new building the bureau bought in Paramus, New Jersey. However, the institution still faced in the 1980s the problem of survival, because unlike Lloyd's and Bureau Veritas, classification societies whose revenue came at least 50 percent from non-marine services, ABS earned less than 10 percent of its income from nonmarine activities. Diversification away from shipping seemed the answer, and as early as the 1930s ABS had participated in testing the bridges in San Francisco Bay, including the Golden Gate. In 1970 ABS created the subsidiary ABSTECH to seek major contracts for land-based work, but without too much success. ABS dissolved ABSTECH in 1991 and replaced it with ABS Industrial Verification, a for-profit subsidiary that hopefully will be more successful in finding nonmarine work.

ABS remained one of the least-noticed maritime institutions and was in effect a tightly knit group of engineers bonded by professional links and often family ties as well. A major tidal wave hit when Frank Iarossi,* the former president of Exxon Shipping Co., became president of ABS in April 1990. To handle North and South America, Iarossi chose Houston as the third and last regional office, a move that angered many employees, one-third of whom preferred severance pay rather than make the transfer. Even more controversial was the new president's decision to move back to New York City into what some considered extravagant offices in the World Trade Center: not only did ABS pay rent for the new location, complete with a sumptuous fireplace—already famous in the novel and later the movie *The Bonfire of the Vanities*—but the Paramus building was left largely unoccupied.

The need to be closer to New York City clients appeared to justify having the World Trade Center as headquarters, but soon Iarossi faced accusations of poor judgment, manipulation, and intolerance to other views. On a different level he "used bureau dollars to make political contributions, asked his wife to work for the organization and hired his daughter" (*Houston Chronicle*, 12 April 1992). Iarossi's rivals staged a coup on 8 January 1992 to remove him as president of the ABS, although he could remain as chairman of the Board of Directors. Iarossi rose to the challenge and launched his own countercoup on 5 February 1992, whereby the Board of Directors by secret ballot reinstated him as president. Five respected members of the Board of Directors resigned in protest, but Iarossi soon filled the vacancies. The shipping community was left in shock: "It hurts to open up the innards of an institution that people thought was run like a monastery" (*American Shipper*, May 1992).

By April Iarossi had leased out the Paramus building, thereby restoring the prospects for another profitable year. The opinion remained that as long as Iarossi could show a favorable balance at the end of the year, his less orthodox tactics would be overlooked. The terrorist explosion of 26 February 1993 forced ABS to abandon its offices in the World Trade Center for several months, and it was not clear whether recrimination would follow over the initial decision to leave Paramus for the World Trade Center.

Principal Executives

Anton A. Raven	1899–1916
Stevenson Taylor	1916–1926
Charles A. McAllister	1926–1932
J. Lewis Luckenbach	1932–1950
Walter L. Green	1950–1957
David P. Brown	1957–1963
Arthur R. Gatewood	1963–1964
Andrew Neilson	1964–1970
Robert T. Young	1970–1977
William N. Johnston	1977–1986
Richard T. Soper	1986–1990
Frank J. Iarossi	1990–present

References: American Bureau of Shipping, *History 1862–1991*; American Shipper, May 1992; E. K. Haviland, "Classification Society Registers from the Point of View of a Marine Historian," *American Neptune* 30 (1970): 9–39; *Houston Chronicle*, 12 April 1992; J. Lewis Luckenbach, "American Bureau of Shipping 1862–1943," in the Society of Naval Architects and Marine Engineers, *Historical Transactions 1893–1943* (Westport, CT: Greenwood Press, 1981); *New York Times*, 31 January 1954; U.S. Congress, *Report of the Merchant Marine Commission*, 3 vols., 58th Congress, 3d Session, Report No. 2755, 1905.

AMERICAN COMMITTEE FOR FLAGS OF NECESSITY (ACFN), 1959–1973.

The American Committee for Flags of Necessity (ACFN) was the first trade organization created to represent the companies with ships registered under flags of convenience.* Prior to 1959, shipowners had been satisfied with membership in the American Steamship Owners Association* (ASOA) and its successor, the American Merchant Marine Institute* (AMMI), but a 1958 campaign by the National Maritime Union* (NMU) and the Seafarers' International Union* (SIU) against "runaway flags"* forced the targeted companies to take special countermeasures. Companies seeking subsidies for their U.S-flag ships did not want to have AMMI defending foreign-flag operations, so a separate group was necessary. In January 1959 some U.S. companies that owned ships registered under flags of convenience created the American Committee for Flags of Necessity. Erling Naess, a Norwegian shipowner with considerable U.S. interests, became the president, and he hired a top-level legal and lobbying staff to defend vigorously the companies.

Labor staged boycotts against ships flying flags of convenience beginning in December 1958, and in the initial years management failed to obtain injunctions against union picketing. In the *Peninsular and Occidental* case, the National Labor Relations Board ruled that unions had the right to organize crewmen aboard flags-of-convenience ships, a decision it upheld and extended in the *West India Fruit* case of May 1960. ACFN managed to convince the Eisenhower administration to support the position of the owners, but the incoming Kennedy administration reversed the policy and filed a brief in behalf of the unions. ACFN carefully prepared its appeal and decided to bring before the Supreme Court a United Fruit Co.* case in which there was a close relationship between the country with the flag of convenience registry and the company. The resulting *Incres-Hondureña** decision of February 1963 was a major setback for the unions, because the Supreme Court ruled that even though Congress could extend labor jurisdiction to ships flying flags of convenience, it had not done so, and hence boycotts and pickets were illegal until Congress passed the appropriate legislation.

Incres-Hondureña was the decisive victory for ACFN, whose tactics had been vindicated, but its chief spokesman in 1964 still feared hostile actions by the executive branch of government: "His understandable interest in the deliberations of the Maritime Advisory Committee with respect to 'flags of necessity' contained overtones of panic. . . . I tried to assure Mr. McAllister that the 'flags of necessity' ships would be neither sunk nor brought under the American flag before the end of the year, which seemed to relieve some of his anxiety about the pressure of time'' (White House Central Files). In 1962 a group of companies created the American Maritime Association* (AMA), which ACFN regarded as under the control of organized labor; the ACFN devoted considerable efforts to counter AMA's hostility to flags of convenience. Not all the companies using flags of convenience belonged to ACFN, but certainly the largest did, as was reflected in the 1963 membership:

Alcoa Steamship Co.*	National Bulk Carriers Inc.
American Oil Co.	Paco Tankers, Inc.
Atlantic Refining Co.	Richfield Oil Corp.

Bernuth, Lembcke Co.

Cities Service Oil Co.

Gotass-Larsen, Inc.

Gulf Oil Corp.

Marine Transport Lines

Naess Shipping Co.

Socony Mobil Oil Co.

Standard Oil of California

Standard Oil of New Jersey*

Texaco

Tidewater Oil Co.

In 1974 ACFN became the Federation of American-Controlled Shipping* (FACS).

Principal Executive

Philip J. Loree   1964–1973

References: Rodney P. Carlisle, *Sovereignty for Sale: The Origins and Evolution of the Panamanian and Liberian Flags of Convenience* (Annapolis, MD: Naval Institute Press, 1981); John J. Collins, *Never Off Pay: The Story of the Independent Tanker Union, 1937–1962* (New York: Fordham University Press, 1964); *Congressional Quarterly 1974*; Gale Research, *Encyclopedia of Associations*, 1964–1973; White House Central Files, and Records of the Executive Departments, Lyndon B. Johnson Presidential Library, Austin, Texas.

AMERICAN DIAMOND LINE. See Black Diamond Steamship Corporation.

AMERICAN EXPORT ISBRANDTSEN LINES. See American Export Lines.

AMERICAN EXPORT LINES (AEL), 1919–1977. American Export Lines (AEL) was the most important U.S.-flag steamship company in the trade between the East Coast of the United States and the Mediterranean; at other times in its history the company operated major services to Western Europe and even as far as India. The company was organized in 1919 by a group of businessmen as the Export Steamship Corporation, but by the mid-1920s the word *American* had been added to emphasize its links with the United States, and henceforth it was known as the American Export Lines. AEL was one of the over 200 new firms that appeared to take advantage of the offer of government vessels whose operating expenses were covered by the Shipping Board.* In spite of the very generous arrangements, AEL, like many other "managing operators*" of the Shipping Board, was soon in difficulties, and this gave Henry Herbermann* the opportunity to purchase the company with borrowed money in 1920. Herbermann, a product of the New Jersey waterfront, owned trucking, warehouse, and lighterage firms and had always wanted to own his own steamship company. He plunged with great energy into the work of making AEL a profitable venture, and good luck initially accompanied his career. In 1921 the

Shipping Board negotiated an agreement that reserved 50 percent of Egyptian cotton cargoes for U.S. vessels, essentially those of AEL. In 1924, when the Shipping Board began to consolidate the Mediterranean services, AEL was still showing losses, but fortunately for Herbermann, the line of Clifford D. Mallory* had similar losses and had also allowed its ships to deteriorate, so that the Shipping Board decided to take the ships and services away from Mallory and give them to Herbermann.

He pulled his biggest coup in 1925, when the Shipping Board put on sale the eighteen government-owned freighters used by AEL, and Herbermann placed the ridiculously low bid of $1 million for the fleet, which had cost over $33 million to build. The Shipping Board, under pressure to get the government out of merchant shipping, accepted the bid, and AEL was now firmly entrenched in the U.S.-Mediterranean trade. Gradually the company expanded into passenger service and ordered special combination-cargo vessels, named the ''Four Aces''* as shorthand for *Excalibur, Exochorda, Exeter*, and *Excambion*, all of which were in service in 1931.

The onset of the Great Depression was hardly the most propitious time for new passenger services, and in any case the design of the Four Aces had been badly bungled, because the ships were too slow for passenger service and their fuel consumption was too expensive for carrying freight. The Great Depression naturally reduced passenger, as well as cargo, volumes, but since AEL had been receiving very generous mail subsidies since 1928, it could ride out the crisis in the same way as the remaining well-managed steamship companies had managed to do.

Unfortunately, Herbermann's rapid rise had made him more conscious of social status rather than business performance, and besides giving himself a large salary and huge expense accounts to splash money around, he expanded his staff and engaged in activities designed to bolster his image. He became so determined to show off the flag of his company that he began sending ships to ports even when there was not enough cargo to justify the trip, but with his fleet depleted, he had to buy additional ships to maintain the regular schedule of the subsidized routes. Soon the company fell behind on the mortgage payments on the Four Aces and even on the previous loans taken out to purchase the original eighteen freighters. The Shipping Board began to pressure Herbermann to change his manner of operations, but for years he refused to receive John E. Slater as an outside consultant. The repeated warnings of the government went unheeded, and the Shipping Board reluctantly began its own long cumbersome internal proceedings prior to foreclosing on AEL.

With the government about to foreclose on AEL, the New York Shipbuilding Company, one of the creditors, took control of AEL in 1934 and demoted Herbermann to the position of vice president; to try to save AEL, New York Shipbuilding brought in a new talented transportation engineer, William H. Coverdale.* However, his first task was to find a buyer for AEL, because New York Shipbuilding had no intention of remaining the owner for long, and in any case the government did not want the same company to control a shipyard and a steamship line. Lehman Brothers, a Wall Street firm, contacted a group of investors that included Coverdale himself, Charles Ulrich Bay, and John E. Slater, who banded together to buy AEL for $1.5 million in May 1935, a real business coup.

The new owners kept Coverdale as president, and he, with the assistance of his vice president, Slater, turned the company around. The excessive expenses associated with Herbermann's management were eliminated, while the bloated staff was slashed. Coverdale concentrated on rationalization of the routes to make sure the shipping services again earned profits; the fleet had become too big for the existing routes, so he sold six vessels and returned the fleet to its previous size of eighteen ships. With the increased earnings Coverdale was able to pay off the company's mortgages and other loans, so that AEL was in a very sound position by the start of World War II and even purchased from the U.S. Maritime Commission* the American Pioneer Line service to India in 1939.

The remarkable comeback of AEL was so strong that Coverdale decided to enter the new field of aviation in 1937, through a new subsidiary, American Export Airlines. The airline company pioneered nonstop transatlantic passenger service and was a very profitable venture. American Export Airlines lasted until 1945, when intense lobbying by Pan American Airlines convinced the Civil Aeronautics Board to prohibit the ownership of scheduled airline services by steamship companies.

With U.S. entry into World War II, the fleet of AEL was requisitioned, but once peace returned, the company proceeded to reconstitute its fleet with surplus vessels. Three of the Four Aces had been lost during the war, and as replacements, AEL preferred to buy four navy attack transport ships and convert them to combination passenger-cargo liners. All four were completed in 1948 and were likewise called the Four Aces, keeping the same names of the first generation, namely, *Excalibur*, *Exochorda*, *Exeter*, and *Excambion*. AEL also renewed its fleet of freighters with surplus vessels so as to resume its traditional subsidized routes from New York to the Mediterranean, now extended to include calls in the Indian subcontinent. When Coverdale died in 1949 and was replaced as president by Slater, AEL was solidly established to stay in business for at least fifteen years, the remaining useful life of the World War II surplus vessels it had acquired for its fleet.

Because of AEL's experience with airlines, the company was among the first to realize that airplanes meant major reductions in ocean passenger traffic, and Slater himself as early as 1944 and again in 1946 had warned about the risks of investing in passenger liners. However, the conversion of navy transports into the second generation of Four Aces had allowed the company to earn profits out of the demand for passenger travel in the postwar years and, worse, convinced AEL to order in 1948 the construction with government subsidies of two express passenger liners, the *Constitution** and *Independence*, which began service between New York and Italy in 1951. The initial profitability of the two superliners led the company to regret the construction of the second generation of Four Aces: "We will never build a combination passenger-cargo ship again; it will be either passenger ships or cargo vessels from now on" (*New York Times*, 5 October 1952). AEL, like so many other U.S. steamship companies, had fallen prey to the passenger ship myth, and its belief in the continued profitability of ocean passenger travel was so strong that as late as 1956, right before the introduction of the passenger jet airliners, AEL was still thinking of ordering a third liner to make profitable the operation of the *Constitution* and the *Independence*.

Although Charles Ulrich Bay had emerged as the stockholder with the controlling interest in AEL, he had allowed the management team of Coverdale and Slater to handle the company's affairs. Upon his death in 1955, his wife, Josephine Bay Paul,* began to exercise a stricter control, and she soon had replaced Slater in the presidency with John F. Gehan, formerly a vice president. With her keen business sense she knew the company was in trouble, and to try to straighten things out she also brought into AEL Frazer A. Bailey* as general manager for two years. The decisive catalyst for change came, however, when she married C. Michael Paul in January 1959, and the next month she assumed the chairmanship of the Board of Directors, the first and last woman ever to occupy such a high executive position in a steamship company. Her major decision was the purchase of the passenger liner *Atlantic* at a giveaway price from the bankrupt American Banner Line* in November 1959.

From early in their marriage the Pauls had decided to dispose of AEL, and after playing one bidder against another, on 3 October 1960 she sold her stock to Jakob Isbrandtsen,* who was desperate to qualify for subsidies to keep his father's steamship empire alive. Isbrandtsen retained most of the existing management team in place, and although he formally changed the company's name to American Export Isbrandsten Lines, the original name of American Export Lines remained the term in general use. More important than the name was Isbrandtsen's decision to saddle the company with the huge loan he had taken out precisely to buy AEL; initially Isbrandtsen met the loan payments on time, and his good credit history allowed him to borrow even more to pursue his strategy for AEL, namely diversification into land activities. In the manner of other steamship companies like Lykes Brothers,* Isbrandtsen was now buying business on land, and he placed them in a new holding company, American Export Industries, which he created in 1964 with AEL as one of the main subsidiaries. He soon claimed that nonshipping activities were generating more income than AEL itself, but in any case the success of the diversification strategy ultimately depended on meeting the high loan payments with the income the new investments were supposed to generate. In a long-overdue move, in 1969 he laid up the *Independence*, the last of the three passenger liners AEL was still operating in the North Atlantic.

The Vietnam War gave a boost to AEL, but the beneficial effects were more than canceled by the refusal of the Maritime Administration* (MARAD) to subsidize the operation of the new containerships the company was building for service on the North Atlantic. The belief that with the new technology of containers* a U.S.-flag steamship company could at last compete against foreign lines was so strong that even Isbrandtsen himself concluded he could succeed, and rather than limit his shipping operations to those ships needed for the Vietnam War, he decided to operate his new containerships in the North Atlantic. Early in 1970 a rate war broke out that lasted until June 1971, and as the company continued to bleed losses, the creditors intervened to remove Isbrandtsen, the majority stockholder, from the presidency of American Export Industries and hence from AEL.

The banks imposed a management team whose main duty was to safeguard the loans, in particular by having AEL sell off assets in order to meet its loan payments. The sale at a huge loss of the laid-up passenger liners, *Atlantic*, *Constitution*, and *Independence*, brought in little cash, unlike the sale of five tankers, which did bring in money but deprived the company of sure income earners and even worse of the opportunity to profit from the onset of the energy crisis in 1973. The sale of the Staten Island marine terminal to the city of New York in March 1974 brought in over $47 million and appeared to have bailed out AEL, whose containerships at last started to earn profits. The crushing debt burden was too much for AEL, whose loan repayments continued to fall due, and, after attempts to merge with other steamship companies were blocked by the vigilant antitrust division of the Department of Justice, AEL had no choice but to file for bankruptcy on July 1977. No comeback like in the 1930s was possible, and although the history of AEL came to an end, its impact was still not over, because Farrell Line,* in a bold expansion move, purchased at bankruptcy court the remainder of AEL's fleet. See Farrell Line.

Principal Executives

Henry Herbermann	1920–1935
William H. Coverdale	1934–1949
John E. Slater	1934–1956
John F. Gehan	1939–1959
Frazer A. Bailey	1957–1959
Josephine Bay Paul	1959–1960
Jakob Isbrandtsen	1960–1971
John M. Will	1959–1971

Some Notable Ships

Four Aces (*Excalibur*, *Exochorda*, *Exeter*, *Excambion*)	1931–1941; 1948–1964

Atlantic	1960–1967
Constitution	1951–1968
Independence	1951–1969

References: René De La Pedraja, *The Rise and Decline of U.S. Merchant Shipping in the Twentieth Century* (New York: Twayne, 1992); Frederick E. Emmons, *American Passenger Ships: The Ocean Lines and Liners, 1873–1983* (Newark: University of Delaware Press, 1985); *New York Times,* 5 October 1952, 2 September 1954, 22 March 1956, 3 January 1960; *Moody's Transportation Manual 1957, 1964, 1974; Ships and Sailing,* July 1951; *Who Was Who,* vols. 4, 7.

AMERICAN-HAWAIIAN STEAMSHIP COMPANY (AHSS), 1899–1956.
American-Hawaiian was engaged in the intercoastal* and foreign trade, although, as its name implied, originally it had provided the majority of the steamship service between the United States and the Hawaiian islands. After the annexation of the Hawaiian islands to the United States on 7 July 1898, George S. Dearborn,* who owned a fleet of sailing vessels, decided to establish a modern steamship service between New York City and Hawaii. He sold his sailing ships and raised additional capital from other investors, most notably, Lewis Henry Lapham, until Dearborn was able to organize the American-Hawaiian Steamship Company on 7 March 1899. Dearborn became the president of the company, and his general manager until 1914 was Captain William D. Burham. American-Hawaiian ordered new steamships from the shipyards, and the success of the venture was assured when Dearborn secured from the Big Five (the main business conglomerates in the islands) contracts to bring the sugar to the U.S. mainland. Service was supposed to begin in 1900, but the Boxer Rebellion in China forced the U.S. Navy to requisition the vessels for emergency duty, and not until January 1901 did the service begin that promised to be a long-term source of prosperity to the company's U.S.-flag ships protected under the cabotage* laws.

In one of several innovations, starting with their first voyage, the steamships used the Straits of Magellan rather than the longer route followed by sailing vessels around Cape Horn. Resupply of fuel was another problem in the long voyage from New York to Hawaii, because only in Chile was low-quality coal available, and as an alternative, American-Hawaiian supported the efforts of Valdemar Frederick Lassoe, its chief engineer, to developed an oil burner for the steamships. The oil burner was first fitted in the *Nebraskan,* which completed its first voyage from the Pacific to New York in 1904; the results so impressed the U.S. Navy that it launched a program to convert warships from coal to oil.

In January 1907 American-Hawaiian took advantage of the opening of the Tehuantepec Railroad across Mexico to divide its ships into two fleets: one operated on the Pacific Ocean, while the other fleet handled the cargo on the Atlantic between New York and Tehuantepec. This arrangement lasted until 1914, when revolutionary turmoil in Mexico shut down the Tehuantepec Railroad, while the opening of the Panama Canal on 15 August 1914 provided a cheaper and better alternative. However, landslides closed the Panama Canal between 13 September 1915 and 15 April 1916, forcing American-Hawaiian to use the Straits of Magellan one last time.

The position of the company in the Hawaiian trade could not have been more secure, yet when World War I began in 1914, Dearborn gradually succumbed to the temptation of chartering* out most of his fleet in order to profit from the record-high rates in the North Atlantic. In 1916 American-Hawaiian announced that it would no longer handle the sugar crop of the islands; not surprisingly the Hawaiians felt betrayed, and as reprisals they made sure that American-Hawaiian would never be able to return. Henceforth the Matson Navigation Company,* enjoying the full support of the Big Five, emerged as the principal ocean carrier of the islands. Once the wartime profits ended, American-Hawaiian realized it had foolishly abandoned long-term stability for the sake of short-term gains; the company kept its original name, in the hope of returning one day to Hawaii, but more as a reminder of the prosperous days when it had been the largest U.S.-flag merchant fleet.

In 1920, after the government returned the vessels requisitioned during World War I, American-Hawaiian decided to operate its fleet in the intercoastal trade, mainly between New York and California. When Dearborn died in April 1920, W. Averell Harriman became the principal stockholder and assigned the management of the company to his United American Lines.* The attempted merger proved more complex than expected, and soon Harriman realized that the troubled American-Hawaiian needed its own separate organization, and to that effect he appointed Cary W. Cook as its president on 20 March 1923. As a condition for accepting the job, Cook had specified that the company's headquarters be moved from New York City to San Francisco, not only because that was where he lived but also because he felt the future of the company was in the Pacific. Cook put American-Hawaiian back on a solid footing and also began the negotiations with the Grace Line,* which wanted to sell its six vessels on the unprofitable intercoastal service. The purchase was concluded in June 1925 by Roger D. Lapham,* who succeed Cook as president that same month. The intercoastal route already enjoyed sailings every five days, but as a further step to consolidate the company's position, Lapham acquired one of its competitors, the Williams Line, in early 1929.

The intercoastal trade was proving to be rather unstable and subject to sharp rate wars, so Lapham correctly concluded the company needed to enter into other trade routes. His most important move was the creation of the Oceanic & Oriental Navigation Company in 1928 to take over a line of Shipping Board* vessels; American-Hawaiian and Matson each had a 50 percent stake in the venture, and while Matson managed the government ships on the Australia/New Zealand route, American-Hawaiian managed those ships sailing to China, Indochina, Japan, and the Philippines. When the Great Depression struck, American-Hawaiian was hard hit because the intercoastal trade so closely reflected the collapse of the American economy; Lapham considered a merger with the Dollar Line* in 1930, but the negotiators failed to find a satisfactory arrangement. However, in 1936, American-Hawaiian did purchase four steamers from the Dollar Line, which was desperately trying to avoid bankruptcy.

The government requisitioned the ships of American-Hawaiian and of all other lines during World War II. Once the war was over, the company did not want the surviving ships back, which in any case were overage, and instead preferred to bareboat* charter government vessels for the intercoastal trade and for a service to the Far East, at least until the postwar shipping situation became clearer. Roger's son, Lewis A. Lapham,* became the president of the company in 1947, and he moved headquarters back to New York City from San Francisco. The company was wisely keeping its options open, but the Korean War panicked American-Hawaiian into buying six surplus ships on the mistaken assumption that high freight rates would continue indefinitely. The ships had barely been brought when the intercoastal service took a downward plunge, and with each voyage piling up losses, the company had no choice but to suspend the intercoastal service in March 1953.

The question of what to do with the fleet vexed the stockholders, who reached the conclusion that the only hope left was to shift to foreign flags. Because the company had exclusively operated under the U.S. flag, the stockholders decided to bring in as an investor the billionaire Daniel Ludwig,* whose experience with foreign-flag operations was renowned. Ludwig decided to use the company for his own plans, and in 1955, after a bitter takeover battle, he gained full control and sold off the ships and most of the assets of American-Hawaiian, whose steamship career really ended at this point.

Ludwig, however, for purpose of tax advantages, kept American-Hawaiian involved in real estate ventures and also embroiled the company during ten years in sundry schemes, first to build Roll-On/Roll-Off* vessels, then containerships, and finally nuclear-powered vessels. By 1968 the last of these schemes had failed, and Ludwig proceeded to liquidate American-Hawaiian as a first step toward making an extremely lucrative deal with Sea-Land.*

Principal Executives

George S. Dearborn	1899–1920
William D. Burham	1899–1914
Cary W. Cook	1923–1925
Roger D. Lapham	1925–1944
John E. Cushing*	1938–1947
Edward P. Farley	1944–1955
Lewis A. Lapham	1947–1953

References: Thomas C. Cochran and Ray Ginger, "The American-Hawaiian Steamship Company, 1899–1919," *Business History Review* 28 (1954): 342–365; René De La Pedraja, *The Rise and Decline of U.S. Merchant Shipping in the Twentieth Century* (New

York: Twayne, 1992); *New York Times*, 26 November 1948, 28 February 1953; *Pacific Marine Review*, November 1926; Roger D. Lapham Oral History, Bancroft Library, University of California, Berkeley; *San Francisco Examiner*, 7 May 1930; Jerry Shields, *The Invisible Billionaire: Daniel Ludwig* (Boston: Houghton Mifflin, 1986).

AMERICAN INSTITUTE OF MERCHANT SHIPPING (AIMS), 1969– present. The American Institute of Merchant Shipping (AIMS) has been the trade group representing companies owing U.S.-flag vessels, principally tankers and dry cargo ships and sometimes liner* companies as well. As U.S.-flag steamship companies declined in the 1960s, the need to pool their dwindling resources behind one trade organization convinced executives to create AIMS out of the merger of the American Merchant Marine Institute* (AMMI), the Committee of American Steamship Lines* (CASL), and the Pacific American Steamship Association* (PASA). The key to success was to forge a common maritime policy among the disparate groups, and for that purpose AIMS was divided into a Liner Council, a Tanker Council, and a Dry Cargo and Coastal Council; each group had ample opportunity to formulate within its own council its views, which supposedly were then reconciled into a common policy by the executive board of AIMS.

Cooperation was the rule during the initial years, but in 1977 the liner operators felt frustrated because AIMS was not lobbying Congress hard enough for subsidies. In January 1978 the Liner Council bolted AIMS and created its own organization, the Council of American-flag Ship Operators* (CASO), in effect a revival of the earlier CASL. To facilitate consultation on points of mutual interest, during many years CASO and AIMS occupied nearby floors in the same office building, but formal cooperation was impossible because of the differing nature of their membership.

For the members of CASO, legislation was a matter of life and death, because without subsidies or government cargoes. U.S.-flag ships could not be profitably employed for any length of time in the foreign trade. Instead the members of AIMS were multinational corporations whose primary business was not shipping, but rather oil, food, chemicals, or other bulk commodities. The multinationals were forced by law to use U.S. ships in the coastwise* and intercoastal* trades, when in reality most preferred to rely on their large foreign-flag fleets. AIMS was thus a residual organization that had to exist to represent their U.S.-flag vessels, but the companies' heart and money were generally in the foreign-flag shipping operations. The Federation of American-Controlled Shipping* (FACS), which defended the right to own and operate foreign-flag vessels, and the American Petroleum Institute, the organization for the oil industry, were the preferred lobbying bodies for corporations like Exxon* and Mobil. The membership of AIMS in 1978 consisted of twenty-three companies owning oil and gas tankers, dry bulk vessels, and chemical carriers. After the collapse of the United Shipowners of America* (USA) in 1990, all but one of its member companies joined AIMS.

Principal Executives

Ralph E. Casey*	1969
James J. Reynolds	1970–1980
Thomas J. Lengyel	1985–1987
Ernest J. Corrado	1987–present

References: *American Shipper*, February 1978, March 1987, August 1991; *Congressional Record*, 8 September 1971; Gale Research, *Encyclopedia of Associations*, 1970, 1980, 1985–1993; *New York Times*, 19 January 1969.

AMERICAN LINE, 1873–1884. The Pennsylvania Railroad established the American Line in 1873 to try to attract cargoes to Philadelphia for loading aboard the company's trains. The railroad was forced to organize its own steamship line in order to compete against New York railroads: while New York City could count on adequate foreign-flag lines to bring abundant cargoes to the port, unless deliberate action was taken, few ships would call in Philadelphia. The strategy of the Pennsylvania Railroad was sound except for one crucial point: the company decided not to operate foreign-flag vessels. Instead, under the more expensive U.S. flag, the services of the American Line were a drain on the railroad, which finally decided to sell the American Line to the Red Star Line* of the International Navigation Company in 1884. Henceforth the American Line ceased to operate as a separate entity and was directed first by the Red Star Line of the International Navigation Company and after 1902 by the International Mercantile Marine* (IMM).

References: William S. Lindsay, *History of Merchant Shipping and Ancient Commerce*, 4 vols. (New York: AMS Press, 1965); Winthrop L. Marvin, *The American Merchant Marine* (New York: Scribner's, 1902).

AMERICAN MAIL LINE (AML), 1920–1954. The American Mail Line (AML) provided service between Seattle, Washington, and the Far East. The AML began as an attempt by the coastwise* Admiral Line* to open a transpacific service during World War I. In 1917 its owner, Hubbard F. Alexander,* sent ships as far as Singapore to test the market, and in 1918 he began regular sailings; the large profits convinced him to charter* additional ships from private companies for the transpacific service. The Shipping Board* now stepped into the picture and in late 1918 offered government-owned ships under incredibly favorable terms, so that the Admiral Line did not renew its private charters as they expired and instead by the spring of 1920 was operating seventeen government-owned vessels.

In the winter of 1920 the Shipping Board decided to allocate five of the new "535s" (freighters so named because of their length) to the Admiral Line, but on the condition that they be operated in a new line separate from the Admiral Line's coastwise service. Consequently, to run the new 535s and the other government freighters, Alexander organized the Admiral Oriental Mail Line in the late 1920; Ancil F. Haines, who had been in charge of the Admiral Line's transpacific service, became the general manager of the new line. Soon after this, the Shipping Board decided to name the 535s after American presidents, with these five called the *President Jackson*, the *President McKinley*, the *President Grant*, the *President Madison*, and the *President Jefferson*; this pattern of naming ships was later adopted by the Dollar Line* for its ships as well.

As a "managing operator"* for the government, Alexander was earning incredible profits, yet he did not effectively handle these funds so that the financial condition of both the Admiral Line and the Admiral Oriental Mail Line was not too solid. The Dollar family seized upon this weakness to take away in a swift power play the Admiral Oriental Mail Line from Alexander in September 1922. Soon after, the Dollars began to call the Admiral Oriental Mail Line by the new name of American Mail Line (AML), which they formally adopted in 1926.

The AML gradually merged with the Dollar Line, although to placate Seattle inhabitants who resented the loss of local influence, the Dollars tried to keep AML distinct at least in name. In April 1926 R. Stanley Dollar* made one of his greatest deals when he bought the five 535s from the Shipping Board at giveaway prices, whereupon AML transferred its home office from Seattle to San Francisco. He was less successful with the seven government-owned freighters of the AML: Seattle and Tacoma interests were outraged at the loss of local control over the line, and in 1928 they created the rival Tacoma Oriental Steamship Company* to purchase the seven freighters from the Shipping Board. However, by 1931 Stanley had likewise gained control of the Tacoma Oriental Steamship Company, which he operated as a subsidiary of the AML.

The history of the AML during its first two decades was largely undistinguishable from that of the Dollar Line. Just like the latter, it requested its first moratorium on loan payments in 1931. Ample mail subsidies bailed out the AML, only to have the Dollar family drain for its benefit even more funds from the firm. The passage of strict safety regulations after the *Morro Castle** disaster forced the company to abandon passenger service in October 1937, because the cost of remodeling the ships was too high. Finally, in June 1938, the company suspended operations altogether and went into bankruptcy proceedings.

Public ownership advocates wanted the government to take over the AML, in the same way as the U.S. Maritime Commission* had transformed the Dollar Line into the American President Lines* (APL), and from the viewpoint of coordinated services for the Pacific Coast, the logic for one single owner was overwhelming. However, the Dollar family refused to give up its stock in the AML, while Seattle groups had coalesced to create the Pacific Northwest Oriental Line, whose main goal was to regain local control by buying the ships of the bankrupt AML. Finally, as a compromise solution, tobacco magnate and former sailor Richard J. Reynolds bought the Dollars' stock and agreed to invest funds to rebuild the AML; furthermore, once he was convinced that the company was well managed, he promised not to interfere in its operations. Reynolds was impressed by the new general manager, A. R. Lintner, and gave him freedom to rebuild the company. World War II profits allow Lintner to pay off the old debts and rebuild the AML, which continued to thrive during the postwar shipping boom.

In June 1951 Reynolds sold his controlling share of the AML stock to the Murchison group of Texas investors. In June 1954 the Murchison group offered to sell the shares, and Ralph K. Davies obtained a loan from the Bank of America to finance their purchase. Since Davies already owned a controlling interest in APL, it seemed that AML had once again become a part of the larger San Francisco company. However, continued pressure from Seattle interests, antitrust court challenges, and the entrenched opposition of the AML bureaucracy blocked attempts to merge or even to combine some operations with American President Lines. Ownership was not enough to consolidate the two companies, but finally economic forces became too strong: AML ''plus APL was going to be better than the sum of the two components. And if they remained as individuals, one of them was going to go down the drain'' (Niven 1987). By the end of 1973 APL quietly absorbed AML, whose existence came to a close.

Principal Executives

Ancil F. Haines	1920–1937
A. R. Lintner	1940–1959
Worth B. Fowler	1959–1968
Robert E. Benedict	1968–1973

Some Notable Ships

President Grant	1921–1936
President Jackson	1921–1938
President Jefferson	1921–1938
President McKinley	1921–1938
President Madison	1922–1938

References: René De La Pedraja, *The Rise and Decline of U.S. Merchant Shipping in the Twentieth Century* (New York: Twayne, 1992); Frederick E. Emmons, *American Passenger Ships* (Newark: University of Delaware Press, 1985); John Niven, *The American President Lines and Its Forebears, 1848–1984* (Newark: University of Delaware Press, 1987); E. Mowbray Tate, *Transpacific Steam: The Story of Steam Navigation from the Pacific Coast of North America to the Far East and the Antipodes, 1867–1941* (New York: Cornwall Books, 1986).

AMERICAN MARITIME ASSOCIATION (AMA), 1961–present. The American Maritime Association (AMA) has been the trade organization that has represented mainly the tankers in the domestic trades of the United States and also some of the nonsubsidized companies. One of the key labor demands in the Seamen's Strike of 1961* was a halt to the trend by some U.S. companies to increasingly use flags of convenience* for their new ships in order to take advantage of lower wages, taxes, and other benefits. The group of U.S.- flag-tanker and nonsubsidized carrier companies represented by the labor negotiator J. Max Harrison* shared the concern of the Seafarers' International Union* (SIU) and agreed to create and finance a "Joint Committee for the Maritime Industry" under combined leadership by labor and management. The Joint Committee was later declared illegal, and to satisfy the contract demand the companies created the AMA with Harrison as its first president. Labor influence remained strong in the new organization; the Washington office was filled mainly with former union officials, and the first executive vice president was a former president of an SIU affiliate. The strong labor links made AMA a natural channel to negotiate new contracts, and unlike most of the other maritime trade groups that gradually have delegated industrial relations to specialized management entities, AMA has remained active and very successful in collective bargaining.

The backbone of AMA has been the independent tanker owners who in the 1960s financed lavishly the organization to make their case heard by the government. In the 1960s and 1970s AMA fought to obtain construction differential subsidies* for the ships in the domestic trades and to expand the cargo-preference* laws to require a greater use of U.S.-flag ships in foreign trade. AMA's strong support for cargo-preference legislation made it an attractive membership choice for the few U.S.-flag tramp owners (such as American Foreign Steamship Group) who had survived the collapse of the American Tramp Shipowners' Association* in 1970. Quite naturally, AMA was in the forefront of the legislative battles of 1973–1980 to secure for U.S.-flag tankers a percentage of foreign oil imports. The thirteen member companies in 1974 were:

Sea-Land*

Overseas Shipholding Group* (with nine subsidiaries)

Hudson Waterways Corporation (with five subsidiaries)

Ogden Marine Inc. (with ten subsidiaries)

Waterman Steamship Corporation*

Victory Carriers Group (with five subsidiaries)

Calmar Steamship Company* (with two subsidiaries)

American Foreign Steamship Group (with three subsidiaries)

Sea Transport Corporation

Ecological Shipping Corporation

Vantage Steamship Corporation

Transport Commercial Corporation

Isco, Inc.

In the 1980s AMA shifted its efforts toward keeping tankers built with subsidies or in foreign shipyards out of the trades protected by the cabotage* privileges, and in particular AMA strove to preserve for U.S.-flag ships the
transportation of oil from Alaska to the East Coast. The instability in membership, typical of the independent tanker companies and tramp firms, which disappear, change names, merge, or break into smaller units, has continued.

Principal Executive

J. Max Harrison   1961–1965

References: *American Shipper*, July 1978, March 1983; Gale Research, *Encyclopedia
of Associations*, 1983–1993; Samuel A. Lawrence, *United States Merchant Shipping Pol-
icies and Politics* (Washington, DC: Brookings Institution, 1966); Michael Raoul-Duval
Papers, Gerald Ford Presidential Library, Ann Arbor, Michigan; *National Cyclopedia of
American Biography*, vol. 55; White House Central Files, John F. Kennedy Presidential
Library, Boston.

AMERICAN MERCHANT LINE, 1918–1937. The American Merchant Line
was one of over 200 shipping firms created by the Shipping Board* after World
War I. The American Merchant Line provided cargo service and limited passenger service principally between London and New York. J. H. Winchester &
Co. was the initial managing operator* for the government-owned vessels. In
1929 mounting losses forced the Shipping Board to transfer the service and sell
the vessels to the financial speculator Paul W. Chapman, who planned to operate
them in conjunction with the passenger liners of the United States Lines* (USL),
which he had just recently purchased from the Shipping Board. Chapman went
broke, and the Shipping Board resumed control over the American Merchant
Line and USL in July 1931 in order to find a more solid buyer. The best bid
came from the International Mercantile Marine* (IMM), which purchased USL
and American Merchant Line in October 1931. After transferring the four remaining freighters to USL in 1937, IMM formally abolished the American Merchant Line in 1937.

References: René De La Pedraja, *The Rise and Decline of U.S. Merchant Shipping in
the Twentieth Century* (New York: Twayne, 1992); Mark H. Goldberg, *The Hog Islanders: The Story of 122 American Ships* (Kings Point, NY: American Merchant Marine
Museum, 1991); *Nautical Gazette*, 30 April 1927; *New York Times*, 7 February 1937.

AMERICAN MERCHANT MARINE INSTITUTE (AMMI), 1938–1968.
The American Merchant Marine Institute (AMMI) was the main trade organization for steamship companies and was the successor to the American Steamship Owners' Association* (ASOA). The main task of AMMI was to try to
rehabilitate steamship companies whose image had been badly tarnished by the
revelations of the Black Committee.* The new organization placed the stress on
U.S.-flag ships, unlike the old ASOA, whose members had been deeply involved
in foreign-flag operations; likewise, AMMI expected its lobbying and publicity

functions to be eased by the shift from the more privileged name of "Steamship Owners" to the more popular "Merchant Marine."

In structure, AMMI ratified a change that ASOA had reluctantly accepted, namely, the creation of a full-time presidency held by an individual who was not holding simultaneously an executive position in a company. ASOA's practice of rotating its chairmanship among present or past presidents of the steamship companies had broken down in 1934 when R. J. Baker assumed temporarily the rank of president of ASOA until a better-known candidate could be found. Only in 1938 did the companies finally agree to hire Frank J. Taylor* as the last president of ASOA, who shortly after became the first president of the newly created AMMI; more continuity was provided by Baker, who remained as secretary-treasurer until the late 1940s. Almost all the large and older steamship companies in the East Coast belonged to AMMI, whose headquarters was in New York City. Throughout its life, AMMI performed the additional function of negotiating labor contracts with the unions of dockworkers and seamen.

In 1944 AMMI joined in the creation of the National Federation of American Shipping* (NFAS) and became its most important affiliate. When NFAS collapsed in 1953, AMMI absorbed the former's offices and functions. AMMI immediately decided to bolster its lobbying efforts and hired Herbert R. O'Conor, a former senator from Maryland, and Francis T. Greene, who had just resigned as general counsel of the Maritime Administration,* as vice presidents in charge of the Washington office. However, the attempted merger in December 1953 of AMMI with the Pacific American Steamship Association* (PASA) failed, although both groups decided to maintain joint offices in Washington, D.C., for lobbying purposes. Another major setback came when the subsidized lines refused to transfer their membership from the defunct NFAS to the AMMI and instead created their own independent group, the Committee of American Steamship Lines* (CASL) in 1954.

AMMI thus remained principally an organization for tanker companies, bulk* carriers, and unsubsidized liner* companies. As the number of U.S.-flag ships and U.S. steamship companies continued to decline in the 1950s and 1960s, the need for a consolidation with other trade groups appeared advisable, at the very least so that shipowners could speak with a less divided voice. The member companies agreed to end AMMI on 31 December and to merge its offices and resources with those of PASA and CASL to create a new group, the American Institute of Merchant Shipping* (AIMS) on 1 January 1969.

Principal Executives

Frank J. Taylor	1938–1951
Walter E. Maloney	1950–1955
Ralph E. Casey*	1956–1968

References: *New York Times*, 27 June 1938, 21, 30 September, 29 December 1953, 8 May 1958; Propeller Club, *American Merchant Marine Conference: Proceedings*, 1961–1962; *Who's Who in the Maritime Industry 1946*.

**AMERICAN MERCHANT MARINE LIBRARY ASSOCIATION, 1921–
present.** The American Merchant Marine Library Association (AMMLA) was
created in May 1921 to supply portable libraries to U.S. merchant vessels. The
forerunner of AMMLA had been the Social Service Bureau created in February
1918 by the Shipping Board* to provide a wide variety of entertainment and
social distractions to seamen. With the end of the war, the government discontinued the Social Service Bureau on 31 December 1919, but its head, Mrs. Henry
Howard, wife of the chief of the Recruiting Service of the Shipping Board,
decided that the function of providing books to vessels should continue. With
the support of steamship executives, she created the American Merchant Library
Association, which also received large stocks of books from the American Library Association. The Shipping Board provided annual subsidies, which, however, had to be complemented with fund-raisers and book drives to keep the
libraries stocked with recent titles.

Headquarters has been in New York City, where its main library was located,
but the principal function of dispatching the portable libraries has taken place
largely at supply centers scattered across U.S. ports. "Libraries for the ships are
placed in specially built cases, each containing approximately 80 books. Fifty
volumes of fiction, 20 of travel, history, biography, literature, and 10 of technical
books comprise an average library. For a very large vessel or one making an
extended voyage, two cases are supplied" (American Merchant Marine Library
Association 1923).

In 1936 the abolishment of the Shipping Board Bureau* meant the end of its
subsidy. Executives met at the India House* and decided to increase their contributions to AMMLA, "especially at this time, in view of the activities of social
revolutionary elements who are circulating large quantities of propaganda on
American vessels" (Record Group 32). After World War II, maritime unions
took the lead in supporting AMMLA, while in recent decades corporate sponsors
have once again become prominent. AMMLA extended its services to Coast
Guard* vessels, and it became an affiliate of the United Seamen's Service* in
1973.

References: American Merchant Marine Library Association, *Report January 1923*,
and *70th Annual Report 1991*; Record Group 32, National Archives, Washington, DC;
Marion G. Sherar, *Shipping Out* (Cambridge, MD: Cornell Maritime Press, 1973).

AMERICAN NEW YORK, **1984–present**. The *American New York* was the
first of the twelve Econships* built by United States Lines (USL)* in Korean
shipyards. USL preferred to call the ships "the *American New York* class," but
the term *Econships* remained the usual designation. Each one was named after
a state (e.g., *American New Jersey*, *American Alabama*, *American Maine*), and
all of them were at the time the largest containerships afloat. On 22 July 1984
the *American New York* finished its maiden voyage from the Far East, and by
1985 the shipyard had delivered enough Econships to inaugurate the round-the-

world* service. When the shipyard delivered the last ships in early 1986, USL was able to offer weekly sailings to shippers* on the round-the-world service. In spite of these and other inducements, the Econships were a financial failure and drove USL into bankruptcy in November 1986. The *American New York* and her sister ships remained on the auction block nearly two years, and although eventually purchased by Sea-Land,* they have not yet found an adequate place in world shipping.

References: A. J. Ambrose, ''US Lines' Big 12,'' *Jane's Merchant Shipping Review 1984*; *American Shipper*, September 1984; René De La Pedraja, *The Rise and Decline of U.S. Merchant Shipping in the Twentieth Century* (New York: Twayne, 1992).

AMERICAN PRESIDENT LINES (APL), 1938-present. The American President Lines (APL) has been the largest U.S. merchant shipping company in the transpacific trade and for over thirty years also operated a westbound round-the-world* service. APL was born out of bankruptcy of its direct predecessor, the Dollar Line,* whose owners, in particular, R. Stanley Dollar,* had consistently siphoned off the company's resources into their private pockets. The bankruptcy and collapse of the Dollar Line were averted only by timely government intervention in August 1938, when at last the Dollar family agreed to sell its 93 percent stock share in the Dollar Line to the U.S. Maritime Commission,* which promptly changed the company's name to American President Lines. Dollar had escaped the creditors and believed, along with most businessmen, that APL would soon shrivel, if not collapse, under inefficient government operation.

William McAdoo, the first head of APL, plunged into the task of rescuing the new government-owned company and, after a large loan from the Reconstruction Finance Corporation, put APL into shape in time for World War II. McAdoo's successor, Henry F. Grady, continued the task of rebuilding APL, which after the end of World War II emerged as a revitalized force, although hampered occasionally by charges of unfair government competition from private companies. Nevertheless, APL's future appeared secure as a tightly managed firm run by the government with the exclusive purpose of guaranteeing quality service to shippers* and without having to worry either about satisfying stockholders with enough profits or about the even more divisive takeover fights. As APL quietly reinvested its earnings into fleet expansion, reestablished its prewar routes, including the round-the-world service, and paid off the last creditors of the old Dollar Line in 1945, the success of the reorganized company could no longer be hidden, and Stanley Dollar decided to make his last move to make personal profit at the government's expense. He initiated the Dollar Line Case* in 1945 with a lawsuit demanding that the government return the now profitable company, and the long, complex legal struggle culminated on 29 October 1952 in a settlement whereby the government sold its stock in APL, keeping half of the proceeds and giving the other half to the Dollar family, whose family fortune was restored by this incredible coup.

APL had now returned to private ownership under the control of oilman Ralph

K. Davies, who did not, however, become head of APL, but kept as president George Killion,* who had been instrumental in orchestrating the complex arrangements that brought APL under the control of Davies. A long and ultimately negative period had begun during which APL drifted because of the personal characteristics of Killion and Davies. Killion had never really been interested in merchant shipping and had engineered his appointment as president in 1948 as a way to return to California in a big way, and because he did want to retain the presidency for reasons of status, he had supported Davies in his bid for APL. By the late 1950s Killion developed an enormous interest in the film industry and had become a director of Metro-Goldwyn-Mayer, leaving little time for APL. Davies, a difficult person to deal with, had spread his time unevenly between his oil company, APL, and later two new acquisitions as well, American Mail Line* (AML) and Pacific Far East Line* (PFEL). Tremendous good luck had placed in Davies's hand the means to create a veritable shipping and oil empire, yet his failure to create clear lines of command and responsibility was so blatant that he was unable even to impose the consolidation of his three companies. The shortcomings of Killion as APL head became evident even to Davies, but he still kept Killion on, partly out of a sense of gratitude for the latter's support in the APL acquisition, partly because Killion's political contacts in Washington were useful for a company now receiving operating differential subsidies.*

APL necessarily drifted, and a whole set of blunders and missed opportunities characterized its activities in the 1950s and 1960s. When the Maritime Administration* (MARAD) offered for sale the Mariners,* the last vessel type designed and constructed at government expense, even Killion could see the advantages of buying the Mariners, but afterward management could not easily clear a path into the future of the company. A first decision had to be taken with regard to passenger services: Davies wanted, for prestige reasons, to build two large passenger liners whose operation he insisted would be profitable. Congress approved the appropriations in 1958, and only President Dwight D. Eisenhower's refusal to include the sums in the budget for these two white elephants spared the company some of the misfortunes that befell USL. However, existing ships still had passenger accommodations, and Davies, out of nostalgia, could not bring himself to suspend these services and for years toyed with the idea of operating cruise ships under the U.S. flag, even when confronted with evidence that such an attempt was doomed to fail. Only after Davies's death did APL at last dare to end its passenger service in April 1973, but not before the passenger ship myth had wasted years and distracted the company from crucial matters.

Any future of APL rested with cargo, but the company had badly bungled the transition to containers.* Impressed by Matson Navigation Company's* start with containers in the Hawaii trade, APL received its first two ships for containers, the Searacers,* in 1961 but, afraid that the transpacific trade was not yet ready for this novel form of transportation, had designed each ship half for containers and the other half for the traditional break-bulk* cargo. Not surprisingly, the ships were failures, because the two different cargo-handling systems got in each other's way to increase expenses and time, but rather than taking the bold step of shifting to full containerships for the next generation of ships, in 1965–1966 APL hid itself from reality and ordered the Master Mariners that carried only break-bulk cargo and were essentially a faster and slightly bigger version of the Mariners. The firing of Killion as president in 1966 did not suffice to win full approval for containerships, and only in 1970 did Davies finally accept the need to convert most of the existing vessels to containers and, in the future, to order only new containerships.

As APL hurried to make up for the time lost in the adoption of containers, a succession of presidents after Killion tried to repair the damage of the previous decades. The old finger piers in San Francisco were totally inadequate to handle the growing volume of containers, and finally in 1973 APL decided to move across the bay to a new terminal under construction by the city of Oakland. The move to Oakland not only broke with San Francisco, the traditional headquarters of the company and its predecessor companies in the transpacific trade, but also had the long-term significance of linking directly APL's new container terminal with the major railroad systems for the first time, not just with Southern Pacific, as had been the case in San Francisco.

With its new container terminal in Oakland, APL decided to concentrate on the transpacific service and began to reduce its other routes. The first to be canceled was the Atlantic/Straits service, whereby ships had sailed from New York via the Panama Canal to the Philippines and other ports near Singapore; this service was barely profitable and finally ended in 1976. The round-the-world service had tremendous emotional attachment, because it had been running since 1924 and had catapulted the Dollar Line into prominence, so the company was most hesitant to cancel this very prestigious route, but its hand was forced by the closing of the Suez Canal in 1967. APL had routed the ships around the Cape of Good Hope in Africa, but because these ships could not then detour to pick up cargo in the Mediterranean, the costs rapidly climbed. As a temporary substitute, the company established a feeder service to bring containers from the ports of the Indian subcontinent for transfer to the other transpacific ships of APL. When the Suez Canal reopened in 1975, APL resumed the full round-the-world service, which soon turned into a major money loser, and faced with no other choice, the company ended the service in 1977.

APL was still in serious difficulties, and the possibility of its sale was under serious consideration in 1977. However, three studies commissioned by the company suggested that if a drastic break was made, APL could become profitable again. A new president, Bruce Seaton,* promptly instituted a series of measures that finally saved APL from its past mistakes. Since 1970 Seaton had been a financial expert at the oil company that owned APL, and thoroughly familiar with the balance sheet problems of APL, he was ready to introduce changes; ironically, Seaton, who had repeatedly urged that APL be sold off as bad investment, now had the daunting task of trying to make the company into a paying proposition. He realized that the operating differential subsidy the company received, although essential for the company's survival, was not enough to keep the firm prosperous. Seaton vastly expanded the landbridge* concept under APL, and in a first step the company created an organization to own and control the railroad cars carrying containers from Oakland to New York. APL no longer just handed over the containers but, having learned the lesson from the winter of 1977 that paralyzed rail and highway traffic in many parts of the United States, retained full operational control over the containers, whose movement across the United States was closely monitored. APL pioneered in the introduction of new computer applications to handle the vast number of containers, so that the company could track each one from the start of its voyage in Japan to its final delivery in New York City. In a technological innovation, APL in 1984 introduced double-stack* trains, so that the railroad cars carried containers piled two high rather than just one as before. The cost of moving containers across the United States dropped dramatically with the double-stack trains, and APL claimed that the all-water route across the Panama Canal was obsolete, and certainly the merchant shipping competitors who did not switch quickly to double-stack trains were driven out of transpacific shipping.

The concentration on running railroad cars across the continent led some shippers to question the company's commitment to ocean business, yet Seaton was ready with an ambitious and well thought out program for enlarging the fleet. The new ships, called the C9s, revealed innovations, starting with the use of diesel* engines instead of the fuel-guzzling steam turbines* that the United States had insisted on using for its merchant marine. The C9s had a speed of 23.5 knots and a capacity for 2,900 twenty-foot containers or TEUs.* In still another vessel innovation, APL ordered post-Panamax* containerships, the C10s, also diesel-powered, with a speed of twenty-four knots and a capacity of 3,900 TEUs. The width of 129 feet did not allow the vessels to pass the Panama Canal but resulted in substantial benefits in reducing costs and increasing container capacity. The C10s were built in the subsidized German shipyards, and in special arrangements with the U.S. government, the company continued to receive its operating differential subsidy.

APL appeared to have prospered at a time when few other U.S.-flag companies had survived, yet technological innovations had never managed to disperse completely the dark clouds on the horizon of the company's existence. In 1983, after a bitter takeover battle over its parent oil company, APL was spun off and established as an independent company and the only U.S. steamship company with shares publicly traded in the stock market. Since no single person or individual has ever owned a controlling interest, the risk of a bloody takeover fight has been since 1983 a lurking danger. The company has taken all the precautions available to prevent a hostile takeover, although at times it looked as if a speculator was testing the waters for a possible raid. If the price of the company's shares fell too much in the stock market, prospective investors were scared away and takeover artists were attracted, so the company has authorized management to rebuy stock, a practice carried out on numerous occasions. At the same time, should the company fail to declare satisfactory dividends, the drop in stock prices would put tremendous pressures on the company; if the experience of other steamship companies that have diversified into land business was any indication, the pressure to sell off the ships and concentrate on the profitable railcar operations could become irresistible.

In January 1992 Seaton retired and left to his hand-picked successor, John M. Lillie, the task of trying to steer a course for APL that guaranteed not only its survival but also its profits. While the expiration of the operating differential subsidy agreement on 31 December 1997 will give the company complete freedom to build cheaper ships abroad, the loss of the subsidy will deprive APL of one of its reliable income flows. The Gulf War provided a substantial but passing stimulus to APL, and its president, Lillie, recognized the challenges ahead when he wrote ''that APL could no longer rely only upon technological innovation'' (American President Companies 1991). Among new measures, APL has begun to explore links with foreign competitors to reduce expenses and in December 1991 entered into a ''slot exchange and coordinated sailing agreement with Orient Overseas Container Line'' (ibid.), which so far has worked satisfactorily.

Management felt confident about the future of the company, and ordered six new containerships, three each from shipyards in Korea and Germany. When delivered in 1995, the ships will fly flags of convenience,* but the competitive pressures were so strong, that APL could not afford to wait until 1995 and filed application on 16 July 1993 to remove from U.S. registry* seven of its fifteen containerships. The company agreed to delay its application for transfer out of U.S. flag in order to give time for the Bill Clinton administration to shape a new maritime policy, but unless large subsidies are approved, the fleet of APL will soon operate under foreign flags.

Principal Executives

William G. McAdoo	1938–1940
Henry F. Grady	1940–1947
George Killion	1947–1966
Ralph Davies	1952–1971
Raymond W. Ickes	1966–1968
Worth B. Fowler	1968–1973
Norman Scott	1973–1977
Chandler Ide	1971–1974
W. Bruce Seaton	1977–1992
John W. Lillie	1990–present

References: American President Companies, *Annual Reports*, 1988–1992, *Quarterly Reports*, 1988–1993, and *Fact Book*, 1987; René De La Pedraja, *The Rise and Decline of U.S. Merchant Shipping in the Twentieth Century* (New York: Twayne, 1992); John

Niven, *The American President Lines and Its Forebears, 1848–1984* (Newark: University of Delaware Press, 1987).

AMERICAN SCANTIC LINE. See Moore-McCormack.

AMERICAN SHIPMASTERS' ASSOCIATION, 1860–1898. To certify that qualified officers sailed aboard seaworthy vessels, the American Shipmasters' Association was organized in 1860 and incorporated in 1862. The association had been created "under the auspices of the Atlantic Mutual and several other insurance companies with a membership comprising marine underwriters, merchants, shipowners, shipmasters, shipbuilders, representatives of the U.S. government and others" (Haviland 1970). In order to assign insurance premiums, the companies needed an independent organization to rank officers and classify vessels. The immediate motive behind the establishment of the association had been the suspension of certification by the Steamboat Inspection Service* in 1860, and although the latter resumed licensing in 1870, the association continued to administer exams on seamanship and navigation to masters and mates until 1900. In that year the federal government, through the Steamboat Inspection Service, assumed full authority over certifying ships' officers, a function the Coast Guard* has performed since 1942.

In 1867 the association turned to the task of surveying and rating vessels, in part because American shipowners felt that Lloyd's of London was unjustly degrading U.S. ships to an inferior rating and hence had to pay higher insurance premiums. Once the association had assumed the functions of a classification* society, it began to distribute the ratings of individual ships in monthly leaflets and in January 1869 issued the first bound volume of the *Record of American and Foreign Shipping*; this annual publication has continued to appear until the present. American insurance companies cooperated with the association in drafting and updating the *Rules* for classification of wooden and iron vessels. In 1898 the name of the American Shipmasters' Association was changed to the American Bureau of Shipping.*

Principal Executives

John D. Jones	1862–1871 and 1881–1886
Horace J. Moody	1879–1881
Theodore B. Bleecker, Jr.	1871–1879 and 1886–1898

References: American Bureau of Shipping, *History 1862–1991*; E. K. Haviland, "Classification Society Registers from the Point of View of a Marine Historian," *American Neptune* 30 (1970):9–39; James C. Healey, *Foc's'le and Glory-Hole: A Study of the Merchant Seaman and His Occupation* (New York: Merchant Marine Publishers Association, 1936); J. Lewis Luckenbach, "American Bureau of Shipping 1862–1943," in the Society of Naval Architects and Marine Engineers, *Historical Transactions 1893–1943* (Westport, CT: Greenwood Press, 1981); Winthrop L. Marvin, *The American Mer-*

chant Marine (New York: Scribner's, 1902); U.S. Congress, House, Committee on Merchant Marine and Fisheries, *American Merchant Marine in the Foreign Trade*, 51st Congress, 1st Session, Report No. 1210, 1890.

AMERICAN SHIPPING AND INDUSTRIAL LEAGUE, 1886–1891. The American Shipping and Industrial League was the first business group organized to promote the U.S. merchant marine. By the 1880s the collapse of U.S. shipping was a palpable reality, and to try to secure government support, as well as to keep the British from dumping their obsolete compound engine* ships in the American market, shipowners and shipbuilders united to create this organization in New Orleans in 1886; later it held conventions in Boston, New York, and Chicago. The idea of reviving the merchant marine struck a responsive cord in many Americans, and the organization claimed to have registered over 100,000 citizens as members in both the East and West coasts. The activities of the American Shipping and Industrial League were so closely identified with the national interest of the country that a congressman, Gospel Wheeler, became its chairman.

More significantly, the league mobilized almost unanimous support from chambers of commerce, and trade groups, as well as agricultural and manufacturing interests. Congress responded to the clamor, and the Merchant Marine and Fisheries Committee* of the House launched an extensive investigation under John M. Farquhar in 1890. As a result of its findings, the committee proposed two bills, one that gave a generous subsidy to all U.S. vessels (either of steam or sail) that were engaged in the foreign trade and another that allowed the Post Office to grant subsidies only to steamers. Both bills passed in the Republican Senate, but the plan to subsidize all vessels seemed too wasteful for the Democratic House, which rejected the extremely expensive scheme. Instead a modified subsidy bill for steamers that were built in the United States passed the next year as the Ocean Mail Act of 1891.*

Existing steamship lines and shipyards benefited from the Ocean Mail Act of 1891, but no wholesale revival of the U.S. merchant marine took place, while the failure to subsidize sailing vessels hastened their inevitable disappearance. The American Shipping and Industrial League concluded that no further legislative relief was possible and shortly after disbanded. The powerful tactic of uniting shipowners and shipbuilders in the same organization was not attempted again until the National Merchant Marine Association* in 1919.

References: John G. B. Hutchins, *The American Maritime Industries and Public Policy, 1789–1914* (Cambridge: Harvard University Press, 1941); U.S. Congress, House, Committee on Merchant Marine and Fisheries, *American Merchant Marine in the Foreign Trade*, 51st Congress, 1st Session, Report No. 1210, 1890; U.S. Congress, Merchant Marine Commission, *Report*, 3 vols., 58th Congress, 3d Session, Report No. 2755, 1905.

AMERICAN SOUTH AFRICAN LINE, 1922–1948. The American South African Line was the original name for the steamship company that since 1947 has been known as the Farrell* Line. In 1919 the Shipping Board* supported the establishment of direct service to South Africa by the U.S. & Australian Steamship Company, whose activities, however, came to an end in 1922. Shippers* clamored for an alternative service, and the Shipping Board that same year created the South African Line and made Clifford D. Mallory* the managing operator* of the government-owned ships. Mallory failed to maintain the vessels in proper condition, and as a result in October 1924 the Shipping Board chose as a replacement the Bull Line* to manage the line, also renamed the American South African Line. When the Shipping Board decided to sell the vessels of this service, the Bull Line declined to make an offer, so that the high bid by the Farrell family gave them control over the route and the vessels of the American South African Line. Henceforth the histories of the family and the company were inseparable.

James A. Farrell, Jr.,* fresh out of Yale University, became the first and only president of the company, which continued to enjoy the protection of his father, James A. Farrell, Sr., then president of United States Steel Corporation. Leigh C. Palmer,* a former president of the Emergency Fleet Corporation,* joined the company to help make the service to Africa a successful venture. The company received generous mail subsidies under the provisions of the Merchant Marine Act of 1928* and also qualified for a government loan to order a combination cargo-passenger liner. The new ship, the *City of New York*, began service in 1930 and had accommodations for sixty passengers.

This company was one of a number of shipping ventures of the Farrell and the Lewis families, whose relations suffered a permanent rift in 1933, and they proceeded to separate completely their mutual investments. While the Farrell family was confirmed as sole owner of the American South African Line, the Lewis family now gained full control of the Robin Line,* whereupon its president, Arthur R. Lewis, Jr.,* decided to enter the African trade in 1935. When the Robin Line applied for membership in the U.S.A.-South Africa Conference,* James A. Farrell, Jr., blocked the application, and the ensuing rate war, because of its personal overtones, became one of the most bitter in the history of the U.S. merchant marine. The rate war finally ended in 1935, but the losses had been so great that the American South African Line was on the verge of bankruptcy and was saved only by the outbreak of World War II, which sent rates soaring sky-high on the Atlantic.

John J. Farrell,* the elder brother, who meanwhile had headed the Argonaut Line,* decided to bring the ships of his intercoastal* fleet into American South African Line in 1940. James remained as president, while John became chairman of the board. The transition to joint management of the firm was eased by James's service in naval intelligence during World War II. After the war the company acquired surplus vessels to renew its fleet, but because this was now the only shipping venture of the Farrell family, the brothers decided to change its name to the Farrell Line in April 1948.

Principal Executives

James A. Farrell, Jr.	1925–1948
Leigh C. Palmer	1925–1948
John J. Farrell	1940–1948

Notable Ship

City of New York	1930–1942

References: Robert G. Albion, *Seaports South of Sahara: The Achievements of an American Steamship Company* (New York: Appleton-Century Crofts, 1959); James P. Baughman, *The Mallorys of Mystic; Six Generations in American Maritime Enterprise* (Middletown, CT: Wesleyan University Press, 1972).

AMERICAN STEAMSHIP ASSOCIATION, 1905–1919. The American Steamship Association was the trade organization created in 1905 to represent originally just the coastwise* steamship companies of the East Coast and grew out of attempts by merchant-shipowners to create organizations to deal with labor in the nineteenth century. The word *steamship* was included to distinguish the association from the Atlantic Carriers' Association, which as late as 1905 represented the owners of sailing vessels. The main task of the American Steamship Association was to make the members' views heard by government. In common with the early trade organizations that had little or no full-time staff, the chairmanship was rotated among the company presidents, while an executive committee composed of company presidents retained full powers. In 1913 the American Steamship Association expanded its membership to include all lines on the Atlantic coast, and forty-two companies had joined by 1917.

World War I brought a dramatic expansion in the U.S.-flag merchant marine and soon forced the American Steamship Association to deal with industrial relations. The International Seamen's Union* (ISU) had organized many seamen, and the American Steamship Association became the bargaining unit for the member companies. The Shipping Board* was also seeking a formal channel of liaison with the association, which in order to expand its activities and create new committees, amended its constitution and by-laws in November 1919, in the process changing its name to the American Steamship Owners' Association.

References: Clarence E. Bonnett, *History of Employers' Associations in the United States* (New York: Vantage Press, 1957); Record Group 32, National Archives, Washington, DC; Benjamin M. Squires, "Associations of Harbor Boat Owners and Employees in the Port of New York," *Monthly Labor Review* 7 (1918):45–62; U.S. Congress, Merchant Marine Commission, *Report*, 3 vols., 58th Congress, 3d Session, Report No. 2755 (Washington, DC: Government Printing Office, 1905).

AMERICAN STEAMSHIP COMPANY, 1863–1867. The American Steamship Company, like the North American Lloyd Line,* was another example of

U.S. attempts to reenter steamship service in the North Atlantic after the end of the Civil War. The American Steamship Company had the additional goal of increasing the biweekly sailings that the city of Boston had been limited to during the previous twenty years and that were in sharp contrast to New York's daily steamship departures. In 1863 Boston investors incorporated the American Steamship Company, whose activities began as soon as the Civil War ended. The company avoided the mistake of acquiring used American ships from the pre–Civil War period and instead ordered from the shipyards two new wooden steamships, no longer side-wheelers* but driven by propellers. The first vessel, the *Ontario*, steamed from Boston in August 1867 and promised good performance for the future. However, to achieve a profitable operation at that time the company needed to operate four ships in the line, and the American Steamship Company had never been able to raise enough capital for the venture. In any case, the company ran out of money even before the second vessel was completed and soon after had to cease operations and liquidate its assets.

References: Winthrop L. Marvin, *The American Merchant Marine* (New York: Scribner's, 1902); David B. Tyler, *Steam Conquers the Atlantic* (New York: D. Appleton-Century, 1939).

AMERICAN STEAMSHIP OWNERS' ASSOCIATION (ASOA), 1919–1938. The American Steamship Owners' Association was the trade organization that represented the large liner* companies in the Atlantic Coast of the United States and was the successor to the previous American Steamship Association.* Because of snobbishness, the new upstart firms spawned by the Shipping Board* were not admitted, so they had to form a separate group, the U.S. Ship Operators' Association.* Unlike on the Pacific Coast, where the Pacific American Steamship Association* (PASA) represented companies in the foreign trade and the Shipowners' Association of the Pacific Coast (SAPC) the coastwise* firms, the American Steamship Owners' Association comprised both coastwise and foreign trade companies. A separate coastwise organization had not been necessary because of the considerable overlap with the foreign trade, and the main corporate expression of both the coastwise and West Indies trade was in the hands of the same firm, the Atlantic, Gulf, and West Indies Steamship Lines* (AGWI), which was quite satisfied with membership in ASOA.

The adding of the word *owners* to the name of the association in 1919 reflected a shift toward a harsh antilabor policy. The International Seamen's Union* (ISU) won the 1919 strike, but ASOA, which was the bargaining agent for the companies, learned from this first skirmish, while rank-and-file labor developed an exaggerated sense of power. In January 1921 ASOA took the offensive and convinced the Shipping Board (the owner of 70 percent of the vessels) to demand a reduction in wages of about 35 percent because of the collapse of the postwar shipping boom. The ISU tried to delay the outcome by negotiating a package of work conditions to soften the blow, but not even a pathetic appeal by Andrew Furuseth,* head of the ISU, to pro-business president Warren G.

Harding could keep the Shipping Board from imposing the wage cuts aboard government-owned vessels on 1 May. The ISU went on a strike that collapsed completely, and while the government stuck to its announced conditions, ASOA could not resist taking advantage of the strike failure to slash wages even more. Maritime labor remained powerless until the mid-1930s, and ASOA had no difficulty imposing whatever conditions it wanted upon the submissive shell of the ISU affiliates, which had degenerated at best into company unions.

Relations with the government proved more difficult than with labor for ASOA. Within the business group, power remained in an executive committee of company presidents who did not give Winthrop L. Marvin,* the head of the permanent staff, sufficient freedom to advance the organization's interests, while the part-time presidency was rotated among company executives. Not unexpectedly, the association obtained little from the federal government, but the opportunity to end the dual role for company presidents came in 1924 when Alfred G. Smith retired as president of the Ward Line* (one of the AGWI subsidiaries). Smith had become quite attached to shipping, and he welcomed his election in 1924 to a three-year term as the first full-time president of ASOA as the way to remain within the field. Unfortunately Smith's health was poor, and even before the expiration of his term in February 1927, he was no longer active in the affairs of the organization.

The task of choosing a replacement for Smith was complicated by rumblings within the association, while the sudden death of Winthrop L. Marvin on 3 February 1926 compounded the need to restore direction to ASOA. Marvin's position was filled by R. J. Baker, who became a source of continuity in ASOA and its successor organization for the next twenty years. A reorganization plan established committees for passenger, cargo, tanker, and coastwise owners because each of these groups was no longer satisfied with occasional representation in the executive committee. Behind this shift was the gradual decline of the IMM, which no longer had a majority share of the tonnage, and also the appearance of more specialized trades. In 1927 ASOA chose as its next president H. B. Walker, who, in the manner of Smith, had recently retired from the presidency of a company (the Old Dominion Line). Walker successfully maneuvered among the increasingly hostile factions, but his death on 23 June 1932 left ASOA bereft of leadership to face the onslaught of the Black Committee.*

Although no clear malfeasance was proven, the role of ASOA as an accomplice in milking treasury funds for the private steamship companies did remain in the public's mind. The secretary-treasurer, R. J. Baker, became acting president in 1932 and was elected president in 1934. In spite of the Great Depression, membership continued to grow, because the U.S. Ship Operator's Association* had disbanded in the early 1930s, when its member firms purchased vessels and thus qualified to join the American Steamship Owners' Association, whose dues were two and a half cents per gross ton of their vessels. The member companies in 1935, including some of their known subsidiaries, were:

Alaska Steamship Co.*

American Line Steamship Corp.

American Scantic Line (subsidiary)

American South African Line*

American Sugar Transit Corp.

American-West African Line

Argonaut Steamship Line*

Atlantic Refining Co.

Atlantic & Caribbean Steam Navigation Co.

Atlantic, Gulf & West Indies Lines*

Black Diamond Steamship Corp.*

Boat Owning & Operating Co.

A. H. Bull Steamship Co.*

Calmar Steamship Corp.*

Chile Steamship Co.

Cities Service Transportation Co.

Clyde-Mallory Lines (subsidiary)

Colombian Steamship Co.*

Colonial Navigation Co.

Dollar Steamship Lines*

Eastern Steamship Lines*

Grace Line*

Gulf Pacific Mail Lines

Gulf Refining Co.

H. N. Hartwell & Son, Inc.

Hudson River Steamboat Co.

International Freighting Corp.

Isthmian Steamship Co.*

Luckenbach Steamship Co.*

Lykes Bros.-Ripley Steamship Co. (subsidiary)

Lykes Bros. Steamship Co.*

Malacca Steamship Co.

Maltran Steamship Co.

Matson Navigation Co.*

Merchants & Miners Transportation Co.*

Moore-McCormack Co.*

Mystic Steamship Co.

New York & Cuba Mail Steamship Co. (subsidiary)

New York & Puerto Rico Steamship Co. (subsidiary)

Newark Terminal & Transportation Co.

Norfolk & Washington, D.C., Steamboat Co.

Ore Steamship Corp.

Peninsular & Occidental Steamship Co.*

Pennsylvania Shipping Co.

Petroleum Navigation Co.

Pocahontas Steamship Co.

Sabine Transportation Co.

Seatrain*

Seminole Co.

Sinclair Navigation Co.

Socony-Vacuum Oil Co.

South Atlantic Steamship Co.

Southern Steamship Co.

C. H. Sprague & Son, Inc.

Standard Oil Co. of California

Standard Shipping Co. (see Esso*)

Starin New Haven Line

Sun Oil Co.

Texaco

Tide Water Associated Transport Corp.

M. J. Tracy Inc.

Union Oil Co.

Union Sulphur Co.

United Fruit Co.*

United States Lines*

U.S. Tank Ship Corp.

Williams Steamship Corp.

Wilson Line

In December 1935 the cracks within ASOA became public when the Black Diamond Line withdrew, and other companies followed. The organization was torn by factions and in its weakened state failed to present forcefully shipowners' views at the critical moment when Congress was drafting the Merchant Marine Act of 1936.* At last a reorganization plan adopted in February 1938 promised to revitalize ASOA. The special committees for tanker, coastwise, intercoastal offshore, and collier owners remained, but now each one selected two of the ten members in the Board of Directors. The old rotating chairmanship was finally abolished, and the new president, Frank J. Taylor,* became the sole spokesman for ASOA, which now planned a strong lobbying effort in Washington, D.C., to deal with the flood of New Deal measures. No sooner had Taylor taken office that he realized that ASOA needed drastically to improve its public image, still under a cloud since the revelations of the Black Committee; his first step was to drop the old privileged name of ASOA, and in its place Taylor picked the more appealing American Merchant Marine Institute* in June 1938.

Principal Executives

Winthrop L. Marvin	1919–1926
Alfred Gilbert Smith	1923–1927
H. B. Walker	1927–1932
R. J. Baker	1926–1938
Frank J. Taylor	1938

References: Arthur Emil Albrecht, *International Seamen's Union of America: A History of Its History and Problems*, Bulletin of the Bureau of Labor Statistics, Miscellaneous Series No. 342 (Washington, DC: Government Printing Office, 1932); *Congressional Record*, 19 February 1929; *Nautical Gazette*, February 1925–June 1927; Record Group 32, National Archives, Washington, DC; *New York Times*, 3 February 1920, 9, 18 February 1938; Propeller Club, *American Merchant Marine Conference, Proceedings*, 1952; U.S. Congress, House, Committee on Merchant Marine and Fisheries, *To Develop an American Merchant Marine* (Washington, DC: Government Printing Office, 1935); *Who's Who in the Maritime Industry 1946*.

AMERICAN TRAMP SHIPOWNERS' ASSOCIATION (ATSA), 1953– circa 1970.

The owners of tramp* vessels created the American Tramp Shipowners' Association in January 1953. ATSA replaced the previous Committee for Promotion of Tramp Shipping Under American Flag in Foreign Commerce,* but continuity was provided by the latter's chairman, F. Riker Clark, who remained as head of the organization until 1954. Headquarters were in New York City, and the association also opened a permanent office in Washington, D.C., to conduct lobbying campaigns. To support these activities, ATSA levied dues based on a "per vessel" basis, unlike the predecessor committee which had relied on voluntary contributions of money and time from its members. Apparently not all agreed to pay, and in 1953 the association represented seventy firms with eighty-eight vessels, slightly less than the committee had counted as members in 1952.

Under Clark, the association published the pamphlet *Tramp Shipping and the American Merchant Marine*, the first time that the American public had the chance to receive full information directly from the tramp owners. James B. Stuart assumed the presidency of the ATSA in 1955, which he led through many battles to preserve the cargo preference* laws, but his successes did not stop many members from beginning to shift their operations to foreign-flag ships.

By 1958 membership in ATSA had dropped to twenty-six firms owning about seventy vessels, and the new executive secretary, James C. Anderson, desperately tried to lobby for subsidies as a way to keep the rest of the U.S.-flag tramps from either going bankrupt or changing to flags of convenience.* The refusal of the government to grant subsidies—partly because of the opposition of the Committee of American Steamship Lines* (CASL)—led the next chairman of ATSA, Earl J. Smith, to refocus attention on keeping the subsidized lines from competing with the U.S.-flag tramp vessels.

The association made one last attempt to obtain subsidies in 1965, and while the government was receptive to spreading around the existing sums to a large number of firms, the firms in CASL bitterly resisted any attempt to "share" any of their subsidies. Shortly after, the tramps found in the Vietnam War a better solution for their problems. Ships were run past their age limits, and after earning several times their original value, they were scrapped and the profits invested in business on land. Some few owners did buy ships to operate under flags of convenience, but it was clear that the end of the Vietnam War also meant the end of almost all U.S.-flag tramps. These facts were so clear that no further activities were necessary from ATSA, which faded in the last years of the 1960s. The few U.S.-flag tramp owners who survived in the domestic trades found more than adequate trade representation in the American Maritime Association,* an organization for nonsubsidized companies.

Principal Executives

F. Riker Clark	1953–1954
James B. Stuart	1954–1956
James C. Anderson	1956–1961
Earl J. Smith	1962–1965
M. Klebanoff	1968–1970

References: René De La Pedraja, *The Rise and Decline of U.S. Merchant Shipping in the Twentieth Century* (New York: Twayne, 1992); Gale Research, *Encyclopedia of Associations*, 1956–1970; Wytze Gorter, *United States Shipping Policy* (New York: Council on Foreign Relations, 1956); *New York Times*, 14 January 1953; Propeller Club, *American Merchant Marine Conference Proceedings*, 1954–1956.

AMERICAN TRAMP SHIPOWNERS' INSTITUTE, 1946–1949. When the more prestigious Ship Operators and Owners' Association* refused to accept the smaller tramp* firms, they had no choice but to create their own organization, the American Tramp Shipowners' Institute, in February 1946. The new organization, however, was not open to all: "According to our constitution and by-laws, unless a company was engaged in this business on or before December 7, 1941, they aren't eligible for membership now. We have had a number of applications from people who came up during the war" (President's Advisory Committee 1947). The age of a firm filtered down to the lowest levels of the steamship business as a hierarchical principle, in effect excluding the "war babies" from the new institute. In May 1947 the American Tramp Shipowners' Institute represented only ten companies, each with an average age of twenty-five years. This weak organization only served to divide the voice of the tramps, because the government could never really know whether the American Tramp Shipowners' Institute or the Ship Operators and Owners' Association really spoke for the constituency. Quite naturally the Ship Sales Act of 1946* and its implementation by the U.S. Maritime Commission* did not meet the needs of the tramps. To defend more effectively their interests, the members dissolved the American Tramp Shipowners' Institute in November 1949 and created in its place the Committee for Promotion of Tramp Shipping Under American Flag in Foreign Commerce.*

References: *Business Week*, 19 January 1952; René De La Pedraja, *The Rise and Decline of U.S. Merchant Shipping in the Twentieth Century* (New York: Twayne, 1992); *New York Times*, 17 November 1949; President's Advisory Committee on Merchant Marine, Harry S. Truman Presidential Library, Independence, Missouri; Records of Commissioner John M. Carmody, Record Group 178, National Archives, Washington, DC.

AMERICAN TRANSPORT LINES. See Crowley American Transport.

AMERICAN WEST AFRICAN FREIGHT CONFERENCE, 1945–present. The American West African Freight Conference has covered the trade from the Atlantic and Gulf coasts of the United States and Atlantic Canada to the ports in West Africa, the Azores, and the Canary Islands. The conference largely superseded the U.S.A.-South Africa Conference,* which was inactive by the early 1960s. The member companies were twelve in 1970, nineteen in 1980, and seven in 1993. Unlike the majority of trade routes in the world, which have separate conferences for the inbound and outward movements (e.g., Transpacific Westbound Rate Agreement*), the American West African Freight Conference has been the rare case that controlled the trade in both directions. Of seven members in 1990 only one, Farrell Lines,* was U.S.-flag.

References: Robert G. Albion, *Seaports South of Sahara: The Achievements of an American Steamship Service* (New York: Appleton-Century Crofts, 1959); Federal Maritime Commission, *Carrier Agreements in the U.S. Oceanborne Trades*, September 1990; Gale Research, *Encyclopedia of Associations*, 1970, 1980, 1993.

ARAGO **DECISION.** (*Robertson v. Baldwin*). In 1896 the International Seamen's Union* (ISU) under Andrew Furuseth* had led a successful campaign to pass the Maguire Act,* which outlawed the imprisonment of seamen who deserted in the coastwise* trade. The ISU then turned to the much more difficult campaign to obtain from Congress a prohibition against the arrest of American and foreign seamen in the foreign trade, a highly inhuman practice that was fast disappearing. The *Arago* case appeared to provide a shortcut to obtain by judicial action what Congress was reluctant to grant. Four sailors signed Shipping Articles* in San Francisco to sail to Chile via Oregon, but in their last U.S. port, they left the ship, claiming they had never left the coastwise trade. The outraged captain decided to make an example of their desertion and had them arrested: certainly the spectacle of dragging them in chains through the streets sent a chilling effect through many seamen.

Appeals by the ISU soon brought the case before the Supreme Court, in part because the union decided to base its case not just on the Maguire Act but also on the Thirteenth Amendment, which supposedly had outlawed all involuntary servitude in the United States. In a startling reversal on 25 January 1897, the Supreme Court ruled in the *Arago* decision that seamen were not covered by the Thirteenth Amendment, because their Shipping Articles were different from other contracts, and that a seaman could "surrender his personal liberty." The court's reasoning was condescending in the extreme. "Seamen are treated by Congress, as well as by the Parliament of Great Britain, as deficient in that full and intelligent responsibility for their acts which is accredited to ordinary adults, and as needing the protection of the law in the same sense in which minors and wards are entitled to the protection of their parents and guardians" (Standard 1947).

Organized labor condemned the *Arago* decision as nothing less than the "Second Dred Scott Decision," which had legalized slavery throughout the United States right before the Civil War. This potentially explosive issue was, however, ably diffused by management. It was wasteful for the steamship companies to arrest deserters from ships when the docks were full of men almost begging for any opening. As the personalized labor relations between captains and their crews gave way to the impersonal hiring practices of the companies in the twentieth century, the spectacle of dragging sailors in chains to their ships not only caused unnecessary expense but easily risked a public relations disaster in the form of adverse publicity.

The right of management to imprison the sailors remained only as a legal threat hanging in the background, and to eliminate this last reminder of the seaman's former servitude, Furuseth conducted a campaign of nearly twenty

years to obtain its repeal. Finally in 1915 Woodrow Wilson signed the La Follette Seamen's Act,* which ended the arrest of any seamen for desertion in all
the ports of the United States, a law that effectively negated the *Arago* decision
of 1897.

References: James C. Healey, *Foc'sle and Glory Hole: A Study of the Merchant
Seaman and His Occupation* (New York: Merchant Marine Publishers Association,
1936); Stephen Schwartz, *Brotherhood of the Sea: A History of the Sailors' Union of
the Pacific, 1885–1985* (New Brunswick, NJ: Transaction Books, 1986); William L.
Standard, *Merchant Seamen: A Short History of Their Struggles* (New York: International, 1947); Hyman Weintraub, *Andrew Furuseth: Emancipator of the Seamen* (Berkeley: University of California Press, 1959).

ARGENTINA, BRAZIL, AND URUGUAY. See Good Neighbor Fleet.

ARGONAUT LINE, 1922–1940. The Argonaut Line was a company organized
in 1922 to provide intercoastal* service. John J. Farrell* was the owner and
president of the company he had created at the urging and with the support of
his father, James A. Farrell, Sr. As president of United States Steel Corporation,
the father provided not only guidance but also steel cargoes to keep the ships
of his son's line running profitably, and occasionally he also chartered* some
of its ships for the steel corporation.

John J. gradually built up the fleet of the Argonaut Line through purchases
of surplus vessels from the Shipping Board* at rock-bottom price, thereby min-
imizing the original investment costs. Operations in the intercoastal trade initially were very profitable but were hard hit by the Great Depression. In the late
1930s the intercoastal trade suffered from wide fluctuations, and the fleet of the
Argonaut Line was fast reaching block obsolescence. To stay in the trade required making a large capital outlay in new ships, but before John J. had to
make a decision, the outbreak of World War II provided an easy solution. Ocean
freight rates in the Atlantic skyrocketed, and the American South African Line*
of his brother James A. Farrell, Jr.,* needed more ships to replace the voyages
formerly made by the British lines. The two brothers reached an agreement to
fuse the Argonaut Line, with its fleet and assets, into the American South African Line in 1940. John J. became the chairman of the Board of Directors,
while James A., Jr., remained as president, and the American South African
Line functioned harmoniously under this joint management.

Principal Executive

John J. Farrell   1922–1940

Reference: Robert G. Albion, *Seaports South of Sahara: The Achievements of an
American Steamship Company* (New York: Appleton-Century Crofts, 1959).

ARLEDGE, HARDIN B., 1880s?–1940s? Hardin B. Arledge was one of the
major lobbyists of steamship companies before World War II. Undoubtedly others existed, but because no registration was required at that time for lobbying,

even their identities have remained obscure, if not unknown. After World War II, long lists of lobbyists' names were published regularly, but information about their activities has remained no less elusive, except when brought out in sensational trials like that of Lyn Nofziger in 1988. The chance survival of the records of the Waterman Steamship Corporation* revealed Arledge's real role as an influence mover and power broker in Washington, D.C., in the years between the two world wars. Little is known about Arledge himself, who may have been an attorney and in any case wrote effectively resolutions and other government documents. He developed strong friendships with senators and congressmen and soon had inside links within the Shipping Board* and other executive branch offices. He became a lobbyist for the steamship companies of the Gulf of Mexico, most notably the Delta Line,* Lykes Brothers,* and Waterman Steamship Corporation. He also had the more general function of reconciling farm groups to shipping subsidies and maintained an extensive network of contacts with organizations of the Middle West states.

Essentially the companies paid him substantial fees, and in return he obtained results, whether information or favorable arrangements. Most important, he was a thorough professional lobbyist who left no incriminating evidence behind. Occasionally some of his written statements were so well argued that they appeared in the *Congressional Record*, but his real work took place behind the scenes as he quietly influenced key officials and lawmakers, many of whom were his close friends. His supreme accomplishment came during the Black Committee* hearings, when the Senate investigators, by focusing only on written evidence and confessions, totally failed to realize his significance, so that Arledge escaped after only a perfunctory hearing while his reputation among his clients was enhanced. He weathered nicely the initial changes of the New Deal and appeared to have bored effectively into the new bases of power in the Democratic administration. As Waterman Steamship Corporation and Lykes Brothers heightened their rivalry in the 1930s, Arledge's position as lobbyist for both was bound to become untenable, but his activities faded from view by the early 1940s, so that both the end and the beginning of his incredibly successful lobbying career remained lost in an obscurity he also wanted for all his lobbying efforts.

Glimpses into high-powered lobbying are rare indeed, but it appears that Arledge has not lacked worthy successors; the trial of former presidential aide Lyn Nofziger in early 1988 revealed how this time not a company, but a labor union, the Marine Engineers' Beneficial Association* (MEBA), still needed a skilled lobbyist to promote a particular maritime policy within the government.

References: *Congressional Record*, 5 January 1928; René De La Pedraja, *The Rise and Decline of U.S. Merchant Shipping in the Twentieth Century* (New York: Twayne, 1992); *New York Times*, 12 February 1988; Waterman Steamship Corporation Records, Mobile Public Library, Mobile, Alabama.

AROUND-THE-WORLD SERVICE. See Round-the-World Service.

ASIA NORTH AMERICA RATE AGREEMENT (ANERA), 1985–present.

In 1985 merchant shipping companies combined nine former conferences* into the Asia North America Rate Agreement (ANERA), one of the superconferences* made possible by the Shipping Act of 1984.* ANERA set rates for the lines and negotiated service contracts* for the cargo moving eastward from Asia to any port in the United States. However, the cargoes moving eastbound from Japan remained under the jurisdiction of two separate bodies, the Transpacific Freight Conference of Japan (TPFCJ), which covered the trade to the West Coast of the United States, and the Japan Atlantic and Gulf Conference* (JAG), which covered the trade to the Atlantic and Gulf ports of the United States.

After initial debate the member companies decided to have a strong executive, and Dougald Dick, head of one of the dissolved conferences, became the first chief of ANERA. Upon his retirement in 1987, ANERA decided to have the head of the conference stationed in Asia, initially in Hong Kong, thereby depriving the New York office of most powers. The shift to Asia has fueled charges that ANERA has fallen under the control of Asian lines, which might neglect the interests of U.S. shippers, but Federal Maritime Commission* (FMC) investigations have failed to uncover anything significant.

The withdrawal of a Hong Kong firm in 1988 was expected to trigger a wave of resignations, but the remaining lines decided to stay within the conference, whose membership in 1989–1990 comprised the following:

American President Lines*	Neptune Orient Lines
Kawasaki Kisen Kaisha	Nippon Liner System
Mitsui O.S.K. Lines	Nippon Yusen Kaisha
A. P. Moller-Maersk Line	Sea-Land*

In 1990 ANERA extended its coverage to include cargoes moving to the United States from Bangladesh, Burma, India, Pakistan, and Sri Lanka.

References: Advisory Commission on Conferences in Ocean Shipping, *Report to the President and the Congress* (Washington, DC: Government Printing Office, 1992); *American Shipper*, June, November 1984, June 1987, January 1990; Federal Maritime Commission, *Section 18 Report on the Shipping Act of 1984*, September 1989; *Journal of Commerce*, 30 December 1988, 10 March 1989.

ASSOCIATION OF AMERICAN SHIPOWNERS (AASO), 1942–1962.

This trade association was founded in 1942 by the coastwise* and intercoastal* shipowners whose vessels had been requisitioned by the government for wartime service. These shipowners correctly concluded that while the government could be expected to provide some help to companies engaged in the foreign trade routes, those in the coastwise and intercoastal service had to organize effectively to protect themselves from government indifference and railroad competition. The first goal of AASO was to press for favorable chartering* contracts from the War Shipping Administration* (WSA) for the requisitioned ships. As the end of World War II approached, the association joined with other merchant

shipping groups to organize the National Federation of American Shipping*
(NFAS) in the hope that a united front would improve the chances of obtaining
replacement ships from the government in the most favorable terms. The Ship
Sales Act of 1946* and its implementation persuaded the coastwise and intercoastal shipowners that their interests were being neglected in favor of the subsidized companies engaged in foreign trade, and in protest the association
withdrew from the NFAS in March 1948, an action that also foreshadowed the
latter's eventual demise.

By the early 1950s no amount of lobbying by a weak organization could
convince the government to revive coastwise and intercoastal shipping. The
railroads continued to enjoy regulatory advantages at the Interstate Commerce
Commission* (ICC), while Congress and the executive branch mandated a huge
spending program on highways to benefit the trucking industry. By April 1953
the membership of ASOA had declined to the following twelve companies:

American-Hawaiian Steamship Co.*	Pacific-Atlantic Steamship Co.
A. H. Bull & Co.*	Seatrain Lines*
California Eastern Line	Shepard Steamship Co.
Eastern Steamship Lines*	States Marine Corp.*
Luckenbach Steamship Co.*	States Steamship Co.*
Oliver J. Olson & Co.	Weyerhauser Steamship Co.*

Of these twelve companies, American-Hawaiian and California Eastern Line
had already suspended operations, and soon most of the others likewise abandoned their service. Along with other employer groups, the association did engage in talks with the Committee of American Maritime Unions* (CAMU) in
1954 but did not figure prominently in later maritime policy debates. By the
late 1950s ASOA was left virtually without members and finally closed its office
by 1962.

Principal Executive

George W. Morgan   1944–1955

References: CIO Files of John L. Lewis, Part I, Correspondence with CIO Unions;
Gale Research, *Encyclopedia of Associations*, 1956–1964; *New York Times*, 14 March,
23 April 1948; U.S. Congress, Senate, Committee on Interstate and Foreign Commerce,
Merchant Marine Studies (Washington, DC: Government Printing Office, 1953); *Who's
Who 1966–1967*.

ATLANTIC AND PACIFIC STEAMSHIP COMPANY, 1859–1864. The Atlantic and Pacific Steamship Company provided service between New York and
California and was the last ocean venture of Cornelius Vanderbilt.* When Marshall O. Roberts, the manager and owner of United States Mail Steamship Company,* realized that his mail contract would not be renewed, he hurried to
organize a new company with additional investors. The collapse of the Central

American Transit Company* had left Vanderbilt with excess ships, which he decided to place, along with those of Roberts, into the Atlantic and Pacific Steamship Company. The Vanderbilt ships were little more than "floating pig sties" because of the atrocious and deplorable treatment given to the passengers: "Not one of the whole company from the Commodore down, have the slightest regard for even the most ordinary comfort of the unfortunate passengers who are forced to travel on their ships" (Kemble 1943).

The new company was soon locked in a bitter rate war with the Pacific Mail Steamship Company* (PMSS), and the latter, besides providing splendid service, in anticipation of the clash had also opened its own line between New York and Panama so as to compete with the Atlantic and Pacific Steamship Company on both oceans. After a very bitter struggle, whose very low fares increased the volume of passenger traffic, the companies reached in February 1860 an agreement whose basic condition was that the Atlantic and Pacific Steamship Company henceforth operated only in the Atlantic side, while the PMSS confined itself to the Pacific; the passengers could complain about having been condemned to wretched service only on the Atlantic side. In 1864 Vanderbilt sold the Atlantic and Pacific Steamship Company, by then often referred to as "the Panama Line," to the Atlantic Mail Steamship Company of Daniel B. Allen. The next year Allen sold out to the PMSS, which regained full control over the New York-California route.

References: Robert G. Albion, *The Rise of New York Port, 1815–1860* (New York: Scribner's 1939); John H. Kemble, *The Panama Route 1848–1869* (Berkeley: University of California Press, 1943); Wheaton J. Lane, *Commodore Vanderbilt: An Epic of the Steam Age* (New York: Alfred A. Knopf, 1942).

ATLANTIC AND PACIFIC STEAMSHIP COMPANY, 1912–1925. Expectations of high profits from the imminent opening of the Panama Canal* convinced the merchant house of W. R. Grace & Co. to begin intercoastal* service through a new company, the Atlantic and Pacific Steamship Company (not to be confused with the 1859–1864 company of the same name owned by the Cornelius Vanderbilt*). W. R. Grace & Co. needed a separate company and could not use its British-flag subsidiary, the New York and Pacific Steamship Company,* because under the cabotage* laws, only U.S.-flag vessels could carry cargoes between the East and West coasts of the country.

The parent company was so eager to participate in the expected profits that it did not order new steamers but bought four already under construction in the William Cramp shipyard of Philadelphia. The haste proved unnecessary, because unexpected landslides delayed the opening of the Panama Canal, so that when the first steamers entered service in early 1913, they could not remain idle running up expenses, so the Atlantic and Pacific Steamship Company had no choice but to put them into intercoastal service around South America through the Straits of Magellan until the Panama Canal at last opened on 15 August 1914. The intercoastal service appeared to be profitable, with lumber from Puget

Sound making the majority of the eastbound cargoes, while metal and manu-factured products were shipped westward.

The profits of the trade attracted the International Mercantile Marine* (IMM), and it created a special subsidiary, the Panama-Pacific Line, which began op-eration in the intercoastal route in May 1915. When a major landslide closed the Panama Canal in September 1915, the Atlantic and Pacific Steamship Com-pany redeployed its vessels into other routes, so that even after the Panama Canal reopened permanently on 15 April 1916, the company's ships did not return to this route. After World War I when the Grace Line* reentered the intercoastal service, it decided to use the remnants of the fleet of the Pacific Mail Steamship Company* (PMSS), which had been purchased in December 1915, and not the fleet of the Atlantic and Pacific Steamship Company. In 1916 W. R. Grace & Co. had taken the decision to consolidate its steamship subsid-iaries into one operating company, the Grace Line, but for reasons not entirely clear, the Atlantic and Steamship Company was allowed to operate separately until 1925, even though almost all its ships had been merged with the Grace Line's other services.

References: Lawrence A. Clayton, *Grace: W. R. Grace & Co. The Formative Years* (Ottowa, IL: Jameson Books, 1985); William Kooiman, *The Grace Ships, 1869–1969* (Point Reyes, CA: Komar, 1990).

ATLANTIC, GULF & WEST INDIES STEAMSHIP LINES (AGWI), 1908–1955. Bondholders incorporated the Atlantic, Gulf & West Indies Steam-ship Lines (AGWI) on 25 November 1908 to replace the Consolidated Steamship Lines,* which had gone bankrupt along with the rest of Charles W. Morse's Wall Street ventures. The subsidiaries of Consolidated now became subsidiaries of AGWI under their traditional names: Clyde Line,* Mallory Line,* New York & Puerto Rico Steamship Company,* Southern Steamship Co., and Ward Line* (New York & Cuba Mail Steamship Co.). Henry R. Mal-lory,* the former owner of the Mallory Line prior to its sale to the Consolidated Steamship Lines, became the president of AGWI and of each of the subsidiary companies; the latter in reality were run with great independence by vice pres-idents. Harry H. Raymond* was the vice president for the Clyde and Mallory lines, while Franklin D. Mooney was the vice president for the New York & Puerto Rico Steamship Company.

A recurrent debate at AGWI almost from its inception was to what degree the activities of the subsidiaries should be centralized in the parent company. Mallory had established a centralized treasury for all the subsidiaries so that he could make sure the repayment schedules for the debts were met, and he care-fully scrutinized orders for new vessel construction, but otherwise he left all other operational affairs in the hands of the subsidiaries. When he retired in 1915, Galen Stone, a banker who had been vice president of AGWI, became president but left his former position vacant as an indication that the former decentralization would continue. Stone also allowed each of the vice presidents of the subsidiaries to assume the title of president.

Rivalry among the subsidiaries for support from the parent company did bring a much needed dose of competition into the firm, which otherwise enjoyed a near monopoly position in the many coastwise* and Caribbean routes. AGWI used its influence among shipbuilders, ship brokers,* and shippers* to try to keep competitors out and, when threatened by powerful foreign lines, reached understandings to divide the market. AGWI was the counterpart to the International Mercantile Marine* (IMM), although, unlike the latter, it rarely used foreign-flag ships because so many of its routes were in the trades reserved for U.S.-flag ships.

The outbreak of World War I in 1914 gave AGWI the opportunity to charter* some of its vessels for transatlantic service, and after some false starts, these charters became extremely lucrative. With the entry of the United States into the war in 1917, the government requisitioned at very favorable rates almost all the ships of AGWI and ended the financial problems of the holding company, which accumulated huge profits. After the war the Shipping Board* agreed to sell replacement vessels to AGWI and even made the firm a "managing operator,"* but AGWI's reputation as a monopolistic competitor precluded continued government support. As one subterfuge, AGWI in 1923 created a disguised subsidiary, the Colombian Steamship Company,* so that, through this real subsidiary, the parent company could safely continue to receive large subsidies from the Shipping Board.

The Colombian Steamship Company maneuver functioned well until the 1930s but barely compensated a major investment disaster. With the huge cash reserves from the war, AGWI had decided in 1919 to diversify into the international oil business. The company bought tankers, began construction on a pipeline between Paris and Le Havre, purchased stock in Colombian oil fields, and created another subsidiary, the Atlantic Gulf Oil Corporation, to manage three producing oil wells in Mexico. Before profits could start flowing, the whole oil venture turned sour, and although details were sketchy, some actions, such as blocking the construction of the Paris pipeline, could be explained only by the intervention of another powerful company like Standard Oil of New Jersey* (today, Exxon). During 1921–1922 AGWI was in serious difficulties because of its oil ventures, but shipping and the subsidies of the Colombian Steamship Company rescued the parent company, which eventually disposed of its unsuccessful oil ventures. However, embarrassment was not avoided, and from 1923 to 1925 the spectacle of having the Ward Line in receivership sounded the first public warnings about the solidity of AGWI.

Banker Stone had pushed a merger with IMM as the best way to strengthen AGWI, but at his death in 1926, the new head H. H. Raymond, dropped the merger plans. Instead, he and his successor, Franklin D. Mooney, revived the old centralization proposals and in 1934 combined the Clyde, Mallory, and New York & Puerto Rico steamship companies into the single subsidiary of Agwilines; only the Ward Line continued to operate separately, but the trade names of all remained in use for advertising.

Mounting losses—a million each year in 1932–1934—threatened AGWI with bankruptcy. Coastwise cargo continued to decline because of rail and truck transport, while in the protected Puerto Rico trade the competition by Bull Line* had become fiercer because of the entry of Waterman Steamship Corporation,* while Seatrain's novel form of carrying railcars had also deeply cut into the Ward Line's cargoes to Havana. AGWI needed to reduce services and find cash quickly to pay off mounting debts; the wreck of the *Morro Castle** in 1934 very conveniently disposed of an ill-suited ship, whose insurance payments provided the company with the much needed cash infusion.

AGWI reached the outbreak of World War II with fifteen combination passenger and cargo vessels and twenty-four freighters, but it had found the operating differential subsidies* of the Merchant Marine Act of 1936* barely adequate to compete against foreign-flag ships. The entry of the United States into World War II brought most of the company's fleet under government control, and although the rates were generous, AGWI did not emerge from World War II swimming in profits, as had been the case after World War I. The resumption of postwar operations was plagued with difficulties; for example, the U.S. Maritime Commission* refused to absorb the cost of fitting two C-2* ships for passenger accommodations, thereby weakening the service to Puerto Rico. Attempts to reenter coastwise service were abandoned because revenue did not cover costs.

In December 1948 the financial group of Graham-Newman Corporation bought a controlling interest in AGWI, and the new owner, Jerome A. Newman, debated whether to revive or downsize the steamship company. A first decision came in March 1949, when AGWI sold its assets in the Dominican Republic and Puerto Rico, including the ships and routes, to the Bull Line, which now assumed and promptly discontinued the old trade names of Clyde-Mallory Lines and New York & Puerto Rico Steamship Company. Although Newman denied rumors that he planned to liquidate AGWI altogether, the sale of assets continued, and the company was down to the six freighters of the Ward Line by 1952.

Negotiation of a subsidy agreement with the Maritime Administration* (MARAD) in August 1951 retroactive to 1 January 1948 convinced Newman not to abandon the steamship business yet. To maintain close relations with the government, AGWI in August 1953 hired as president of the Ward Line Earl W. Clark, who had been deputy administrator in 1950–1953 of MARAD and who replaced the retiring Charles H. C. Pearsall. Whether to dissolve or to operate under subsidies was the question the AGWI owners had been trying to decide; with subsidies, however, the proceeds from the sale to the Bull Line could not be distributed among the stockholders, who in a meeting of 14 October 1953 voted to begin the liquidation of the company.

Thomas J. Stevenson, a steamship executive, obtained the backing of private investor Richard Weininger to purchase the Ward Line on 1 January 1954. However, AGWI still owned part of the debt of the Ward Line, and to complete the acquisition, Stevenson and Weininger bought a majority control of AGWI in March 1955. AGWI, along with most of its subsidiaries, now ceased to exist, but the hectic career of the Ward Line was still not over. See Ward Line.

Principal Executives

Henry R. Mallory	1908–1915
Galen L. Stone	1908–1926
Harry H. Raymond	1908–1935
Franklin D. Mooney	1908–1938
Charles C. H. Pearsall	1938–1953
Edgar S. Bloom	1941–1950
Jerome A. Newman	1948–1955
Earl W. Clark	1953

Some Notable Ships

Morro Castle* and *Oriente*	1930–1941
Havana 1907–1917; 1928–1935; later, *Yucatan*	1935–1940
Borinquen; later, *Puerto Rico*	1931–1949
Coamo	1926–1941
Carolina; formerly, *La Grande Duchesse*	1906–1918

Main Subsidiaries

Clyde Line	1906–1932
Clyde-Mallory Lines	1932–1949
Mallory Line	1906–1932
New York and Puerto Rico Steamship Company	1906–1949
Ward Line	1906–1954

References: James P. Baughman, *The Mallorys of Mystic: Six Generations in American Maritime Enterprise* (Middletown, CT: Wesleyan University Press, 1972); Mallory Family Papers, G. W. Blunt White Library, Mystic Seaport, Connecticut; Gordon Thomas and Max M. Witts, *Shipwreck: The Strange Fate of the Morro Castle* (New York: Dorset Press, 1972); U.S. Senate, Special Committee on Investigation of Air Mail and Ocean Mail Contracts, *Hearings*, 9 vols. (Washington, DC: Government Printing Office, 1933–1934).

ATLANTIC TRANSPORT COMPANY, 1881–1934. In 1881 the Baltimore & Ohio Railroad and Bernard N. Baker* organized the Atlantic Transport Company to provide steamship service between Baltimore and London; later the Pennsylvania Railroad also backed the enterprise. The original goal of the Atlantic Transport Company was to generate cargo for the railroads in Baltimore, a port that, just like Philadelphia, was struggling to overcome the supremacy of New York City. This new steamship company operated only British-flag ships, because it had learned the lesson from the experience of the American Line* that U.S.-flag ships were too expensive to build and operate. In 1890 the company extended its service to Philadelphia but dropped this call after six years when the Atlantic Transport Company bowed to the inevitable and concentrated its ships on the New York-London route already started in 1892.

The destination port for transatlantic cargoes had by then become largely New York City, and with both Atlantic Transport Line and the Red Star Line,* the other United States-owned firm, serving that same port, the possibility of consolidating both firms in order to face the ever fiercer foreign competition became a recurrent issue in the late 1890s. Baker knew he needed more capital to build a new generation of ships for his Atlantic Transport Line, but when British investor John R. Ellerman, the owner of the Leyland Line, proposed in late 1899 to merge with the Atlantic Transport Line, Clement A. Griscom* of the Red Star Line blocked the merger. However, Ellerman's action triggered a series of bigger and bolder moves that finally culminated in the creation of the International Mercantile Marine* (IMM) in 1902, one of whose subsidiaries became the Atlantic Transport Company.

Although IMM retained the name and flag of the Atlantic Transport Company, after 1902 its activities were inseparable from those of its corporate parent. Once IMM had taken the decision in the 1920s to dispose of its profitable British-flag operations, the Atlantic Transport Company became a liability; after the sale of the last of its vessels, IMM liquidated the Atlantic Transport Company in 1934.

Principal Executive

Bernard N. Baker   1881–1902

References: Frederick E. Emmons, *American Passenger Ships: The Ocean Lines and Liners, 1873–1983* (Newark: University of Delaware Press, 1985); Thomas R. Navin and Marian V. Sears, ''A Study in Merger: Formation of the International Mercantile Marine Company,'' *Business History Review* 28 (1954): 291–328; Vivian Vale, *The American Peril: Challenge to Britain on the North Atlantic, 1901–1904* (Manchester, England: University Press, 1984).

B

BAILEY, FRAZER A., 23 September 1888–2 May 1960. Frazer A. Bailey was president of Matson Navigation Company in 1945–1947 and of the National Federation of American Shipping* (NFAS) in 1947–1953. Bailey was born in Spotsylvania County, Virginia, on 23 September 1888 and attended public schools prior to entering the Newport News Shipbuilding & Dry Dock Co. as a clerk in 1904. He climbed rapidly and became general manager four years later. In 1910 Captain William Matson* called him to become secretary to the president, and his constant dedication and long hours of work soon made Bailey indispensable for the smooth running of the company. In 1930 he became vice president, and when William P. Roth* retired, Bailey became the president on 16 March 1945.

His decades of preparation would seem to make Bailey the ideal choice to head Matson Navigation Company, but unfortunately he faced new issues for which no prior experience existed. Bailey, like Roth, wanted Matson to enter commercial aviation, but the company's airplane operations had to be abandoned when the Civil Aeronautics Board prohibited steamship companies from offering airline service. Bailey also had many difficulties when the company began to ship sugar in bulk* rather than sacks as before. But ultimately what ended Bailey's career in Matson was his decision to try to rejuvenate the three big passenger liners, the *Mariposa,* *Monterey,* and *Lurline,* in the small shipyard the company had operated at government urging World War II. Not even the large shipyards had dared tackle such a huge job all at once, and soon the conversion began to devour mounting sums. Finally the company stopped work on two ships, and only the *Lurline* was finished, but Bailey was blamed for the mistake and was eased out of his job.

Fortunately for Bailey, the National Federation of American Shipping was looking for a president, and he accepted the position. Bitter dissensions had been tearing apart NFAS, but Bailey tried almost everything to save this co-alition of the merchant shipping industry. Finally the task proved impossible, and when NFAS collapsed in 1953, he retired. In 1957 the widow and heir of Charles Ulrich Bay called Bailey out of retirement to become the managing director of American Export Lines* (AEL) and charged him with the task of attempting to find a new direction for that drifting steamship company. Bailey held the position for two years and then permanently retired; he died in San Francisco on 2 May 1960.

References: *Business Week*, 23 February 1957; *National Cyclopedia of American Biography*, vol. 47; William L. Worden, *Cargoes: Matson's First Century in the Pacific* (Honolulu: University of Hawaii Press, 1981).

BAKER, BERNARD N., 11 May 1854–20 December 1918. Bernard N. Baker, a shipping executive, was born in Baltimore on 11 May 1854. In his late twenties he established the Baltimore Storage & Lighterage Company, and then in 1881 he and the Baltimore & Ohio Railroad organized the Atlantic Transport Company* to provide steamship service between Baltimore and London. Baker remained head of Atlantic Transport Company until he sold the firm to the International Mercantile Marine* (IMM) in 1900. His involvement in merchant shipping did not end then, and he prepared to organize with Albert Ballin of Hamburg-America an intercoastal* line, but World War I canceled these plans. As a result of the war Baker pressed the government to support the merchant marine, and he labored strongly to obtain passage of the Shipping Act of 1916,* which, among other things, created the Shipping Board.* Baker was appointed an original member of the Shipping Board in January 1917 but promptly re-signed when he failed to be named its chairman. Ill health plagued him in his last years, and he died on 20 December 1918.

References: Thomas R. Navin and Marian V. Sears, ''A Study in Merger: Formation of the International Mercantile Marine Company,'' *Business History Review* 28 (1954): 291–328; William N. Thurston, ''Management- Leadership in the United States Shipping Board 1917–1918,'' *American Neptune*, 32 (1972): 155–170; Vivian Vale, *The American Peril, Challenge to Britain on the North Atlantic, 1901–1904* (Manchester, England: University Press, 1984); *Who Was Who, 1897–1942*, vol. 1.

BALTIMORE MAIL LINE, 1930–1938. The Baltimore Mail Line, the only steamship company created as a result of the Merchant Marine Act of 1928,* provided fast cargo service from Baltimore to Hamburg, Havre, London, and Southhampton. The Baltimore Mail Line was also significant as the last attempt of a U.S. port city to increase its volume of cargo by the establishment of its own steamship line.

In late 1929 a group of private investors approached the Baltimore Trust Corporation in order to organize a steamship company in Baltimore. The Pennsylvania Railroad and the Baltimore & Ohio Railroad were the main backers, because they wished to tap into some of the cargo that normally flowed through New York. The investors raised $3 million and went to Washington for government help. The Shipping Board* was more than glad on 21 March 1930 to sign a ten-year mail contract under the generous provisions of the Merchant Marine Act of 1928.* The Baltimore Trust Corporation, without any experience in running a steamship company, did not want to make the mistakes of a starter firm and wisely asked the Shipping Board to recommend the best operator on the North Atlantic; the Shipping Board suggested the Roosevelt Steamship Company,* which entered into an agreement with the Baltimore Trust Corporation to operate the Baltimore Mail Line. Roosevelt Steamship, in order to keep a possible rival under control, also agreed to the request of the original investors to acquire a 25 percent stock interest in the new line. The Baltimore Mail Line bought five ships and lengthened and totally rebuilt them, and the ships' speed of 16.5 knots gave Baltimore perhaps the best freighter fleet on the East Coast.

The Baltimore Mail Line inaugurated service to Europe on 1 July 1931 and, in spite of the deadening effect of the Great Depression, managed to draw substantial amounts of cargo to the port of Baltimore, even in the face of competition from German lines. Although the Roosevelt Steamship Company* became in 1930 a subsidiary of the International Mercantile Marine* (IMM), accustomed to overcharge for managing services, in the case of the Baltimore Mail Line no gauging occurred: "This line has been scrutinized by the Black Committee,* by the Post Office, by every authority on the face of the earth. . . . We do not pay any high salaries, any salaries that amount to anything. Nobody has gotten any money out of it. There has been no criticism of the line" (U.S. Congress 1938).

The line covered expenses but did not earn profits and never paid dividends to the stockholders; more than anything else, the Baltimore Mail Line was the rare case of successful pooling of government and private resources to achieve a service otherwise unattainable by either. For example, although the railroads were not willing to assume all the expenses of the line, they were more than willing to forgo dividends on their stock investment in the Baltimore Line because of the larger cargo volumes they received to haul inland on their tracks. The successful operation of the Baltimore Mail Line abruptly ended when the Merchant Marine Act of 1936* canceled the existing mail contracts and ordered the new U.S. Maritime Commission* to substitute instead operating differential subsidies.* The Baltimore Mail Line duly requested the minimum subsidy needed to avoid losses, but on 5 December 1937 the U.S. Maritime Commission denied the application, because under the narrow and rigid clauses of the Merchant Marine Act of 1936 the government did not have the authority to grant the amount the line had requested.

The uproar in Maryland created a political crisis of the first dimension, and to make things worse, the Baltimore Trust Corporation had gone bankrupt during the Great Depression. The creditors and former depositors were hoping to recuperate the bank's stock in the Baltimore Mail Line, but without the government subsidy the bank's stock was totally worthless. Admiral Emory Land,* recently appointed to head the U.S. Maritime Commission, was left to try to pick up the pieces on the Baltimore Mail Line, which was being made to pay for the abuses other companies had committed with their mail contracts. The Baltimore Mail Line had the strongest case for appeals to the courts because of the abrupt cancellation of its mail contract, and to avoid more embarrassing political fallout, in 1938 Admiral Land engineered an arrangement whereby the vessels of the Baltimore Mail Line went into the intercoastal* service, and to bail out the former stockholders, the company was purchased by, and then merged into, IMM. The U.S. Maritime Commission agreed to take government-owned ships out of lay-up and place them in operation in the route between Baltimore and Europe, but these slower vessels could never equal the service of the previous five fast freighters.

Before any better arrangements could be worked out, the outbreak of World War II in September 1939 began a series of changes that eventually made unnecessary shipping services to the European continent, and soon the Baltimore Mail Line political crisis was overtaken by the rush of other pressing wartime issues. The demise of the Baltimore Mail Line was the first uncontestable evidence that even for well-run steamship companies, the operating differential subsidy was an unworkable mechanism to maintain U.S.-flag merchant ships in the high seas, but this early warning was ignored, and for over fifty years the U.S. government vainly tried to apply the Merchant Marine Act of 1936.

References: U.S. Congress, House, Committee on Merchant Marine and Fisheries, *Baltimore Mail Line* (Washington, DC: Government Printing Office, 1938); U.S. Maritime Commission, *Decisions*, vol. 3 (Washington, DC: Government Printing Office, 1963).

BAREBOAT CHARTER. A bareboat charter has consisted of chartering (renting or leasing) a vessel from the owner without provisions, fuel, or crews; the charterer received the ship "bare" and assumed all other expenses for its operation. The bareboat charter of steamships in the United States was rare until the late nineteenth century and even up to World War I was not very common in U.S. merchant shipping, because shipowners not in the liner* trades preferred to operate their own vessels as tramps.* After World War I the more attractive alternatives of purchasing surplus ships at giveaway prices or becoming a managing operator* for the Shipping Board* sharply reduced the demand for bareboat charters in U.S. merchant shipping. Instead, after World War II the U.S. Maritime Commission* adopted the policy of chartering government surplus vessels on a bareboat basis, so that bareboating from the government became a very widespread practice among U.S. liner companies in the immediate postwar years.

In bareboating two interests intersected: the investor who did not want to operate the vessel and the operator who could not or did not want to own the vessel. In world commerce, bareboating also has opened to private operators and shippers* a wide field of opportunities for maximizing profits and reducing costs, because they could bareboat a vessel in one port and then obtain the fuel, provisions, and the crew from whatever countries were most convenient. In the simplest case, the shipper* who did not want to pay the tramps for a shipload could try to save on transportation costs by operating a vessel he bareboated. See Charter, Tramps.

References: Grover G. Huebner, *Ocean Steamship Traffic Management* (New York: D. Appleton, 1920); Lane C. Kendall, *The Business of Shipping*, 5th ed. (Centreville, MD: Cornell Maritime Press, 1986); William J. Miller, *Encyclopedia of International Commerce* (Centreville, MD: Cornell University Press, 1985).

BARKER, JAMES R., 3 August 1935–present. James R. Barker was the head of Moore-McCormack* from 1971 to 1982 and remained in charge of Moore-McCormack Resources until 1987. He was born in Cleveland, Ohio, on 3 August 1935, and his father was a company executive. Barker's early education was in the public schools of Ohio, and he later graduated from Columbia University in 1957. From early childhood he was interested in ships, and as soon as he was old enough, he took summer jobs aboard the Great Lakes vessels; after graduation from Columbia he joined the Coast Guard* and became the executive officer for the captain in a vessel, an experience that completed his education in handling ships, crews, and captains. He then went to Harvard Business School, where he received his master's in business administration in 1963. His first job was at Pickands, Mather & Co., an iron and coal producer that had its own fleet of Great Lakes vessels. In 1967 he joined the consulting firm of Paul Cherington, his former professor at Harvard Business School, and remained a consultant with Cherington until Barker was offered the position of head of Moore-McCormack.

Actually the job offer had materialized out of his work for the consulting firm, in particular, the contract with Moore-McCormack, which, facing mounting losses, had hired Barker to identify the problems and find solutions. Management of Moore-McCormack was so impressed with the consultant's grasp of the problems that he was asked to implement the solutions he had proposed, and in February 1971 he assumed the position of head of the steamship company. His formula was straightforward, essentially to reduce investment in shipping and diversify into other land activities. He reduced shipping services and sold off surplus vessels, and with the proceeds he invested in natural resources, the field he considered most suitable for the future of the company. He reorganized the company into Moore-McCormack Resources in 1974 as a holding company and demoted Moore-McCormack Line into a small subsidiary of the new parent company. In one of the biggest purchases, Barker bought his first employer, Pickands, Mather & Co., in 1972, whose acquisition also brought the Interlake Steamship Company, a fleet of Great Lakes ore carriers.

Because of legal requirements, he had to spend some of the money of Moore-McCormack on new vessels, and he wisely decided to order three new tankers for operation in the domestic trade. When the energy crisis of 1973 struck,

Barker had very favorably positioned the company to reap profits, but dazzled by the opportunities of what appeared to be a long-term period of high oil prices, he plunged Moore-McCormack too deeply into miscellaneous energy ventures. As a result, Barker neglected the South American trade of Moore-McCormack, although for the African route he did purchase the Farrell* service to East and South Africa in 1980.

When the energy bubble started to collapse that year, Barker found himself rushing to sell off assets of Moore-McCormack Resources to cover the losses from the energy ventures. The conversion to containers* in Latin America promised to be long as well as complex, and Barker decided to avoid the whole problem and raise some much needed cash by selling off Moore-McCormack Line to United States Lines* (USL) in December 1982. Barker, who had been hired in 1971 to save the steamship company, had finished selling off most of the steamship services, and after 1982 he concentrated on saving the natural resource ventures of the parent company, Moore-McCormack Resources.

Finally, in early 1987 Barker was eased out of the chairmanship of Moore-McCormack Resources, but he arranged for the parent company to spin off all its bulk* carriers (including the Great Lakes vessels) to form a new company, the Mormac Marine Group, under his control. Mormac Marine Group's bulk carriers consisted mainly of the Interlake Steamship Company and the three tankers he had ordered in 1973. Barker has remained involved with these bulk carriers until the present.

References: *American Shipper*, March 1987; René De La Pedraja, *The Rise and Decline of U.S. Merchant Shipping in the Twentieth Century* (New York: Twayne, 1982); *Forbes*, 15 December 1986; *Journal of Commerce*, 2 June 1988; *National Cyclopedia of American Biography*, current vol. M; *New York Times*, 2 September 1973; *Who's Who in America*, 1992–1993.

BAY, JOSEPHINE. See Paul, Josephine Bay.

BEEFS. Beefs have been the grievances or complaints of seamen and longshoremen against management. The beefs have been a central part of labor-management relations since the establishment of strong seamen's unions, particularly, the National Maritime Union* (NMU) in the late 1930s. Seamen first aired and approved the grievances in the ships' committees,* at least one of which functioned in every union ship. The beefs often had to do with the food served on board, hence the name "beef," but gradually they spread to cover almost anything in the ship, whether relations with officers, defective machinery, or sleeping quarters. The ship's committee through the union's ship delegate tried to solve the grievance by dealing with the shipboard officers, but if not satisfied, the ship's union delegate took the beef to the patrolman* as soon as the ship reached port. Even in the best-run and cared for ships, it was normal to have a dozen beefs after each voyage, and when properly used, they did serve as a valuable tool to alert management to new or endemic problems.

In the hands of unscrupulous labor leaders who wanted to remain popular with the rank and file, sham or fake grievances called ''bum beefs'' became a source of endless problems for the steamship companies. Often the original beef was lost sight of, and the struggle degenerated into interunion rivalry, with each labor leader trying to appear more concerned for the sailors than the competing rival. Delays in sailing were frequent because of work stoppages (euphemistically referred to as job action*) even when a formal strike had never taken place. Management generally concluded that capitulating to all the union demands was the only alternative, a policy, however, that did not always end the problem, especially when the real issue behind the bum beef had been interunion rivalry. Even in the first decade of the twentieth century, when companies had absolute control over their labor force, they preferred to operate foreign-flag ships, and after World War II, the constant beefs from the sailors certainly did nothing to endear shipowners to U.S.-flag operations.

References: Joseph H. Ball, *The Government-Subsidized Union Monopoly* (Washington, DC: Labor Policy Association, 1966); National Maritime Union, *This Is the NMU* (New York: William P. Gottlieb, 1954).

BENSON, WILLIAM S., 25 September 1855–20 May 1932. William S. Benson was the first chief of naval operations and, after retirement from the navy, played a major role in trying to set the postwar goals for the Shipping Board.* William S. Benson was born to a southern plantation family near Macon, Georgia, on 25 September 1855, but as a child he suffered with his family the ravages of the Civil War. After graduation from Alexander High School in Macon, he gained admission into the U.S. Naval Academy on 23 September 1872 and was among the first southerners to have entered after the Civil War. Until 1920 Benson pursued a very successful naval career, and eventually he reached the highest position in the navy, chief of naval operations. President Woodrow Wilson was impressed with how Benson had handled the navy during World War I and now asked Benson to became chairman of the Shipping Board.

Admiral Benson assumed the chairmanship on 13 March 1920 and proceeded to restore direction to an agency left largely drifting since the resignation of Edward N. Hurley* in July 1919. The Emergency Fleet Corporation* (EFC) of the Shipping Board owned a huge fleet of surplus vessels, but under the Shipping Act of 1916* the EFC's authority to exist expired five years after the end of World War I. To solve the problem, Benson quickly teamed up with Republican senator Wesley Jones* to secure passage of the Jones Act* on 5 June 1920; the new law lifted the five-year limitation on the EFC and also gave the Shipping Board a mandate to use the surplus ships for the purpose of creating a strong, privately owned U.S.-flag merchant marine. In another provision, the Jones Act also increased the number of commissioners from five to seven, and this brought about the unfortunate consequence that Admiral Benson and the other existing commissioners had to be reappointed and reconfirmed by the Senate. For some unexplained reason neither Benson nor the Woodrow Wilson administration pushed through these nominations. Once the Republicans won in the November elections, the lame-duck session of the Congress took no action on confirmation, so Benson's recess appointment expired when the Warren Harding administration took office on 4 March 1921.

The new Republican president personally admired Admiral Benson and secured his appointment as a commissioner to the Shipping Board, but not as its chairman. The series of coincidences that deprived Admiral Benson of the six-year chairmanship of the Shipping Board must be considered one of the worst missed opportunities in the history of the Shipping Board, whose agenda subsequently was dominated by private speculators out to milk the government of funds and ships. During his brief stint as chairman, Benson had constantly kept the attention focused on the benefits and necessity of a merchant marine, but in the Republican administration his voice was gradually drowned out by the growing influence of the Thomas O'Connor*-Edward Plummer clique.

By speeches and publications like his book *The Merchant Marine*, the admiral tried to keep alive interest in merchant shipping, but soon public attention was captivated by the power struggles and the emerging scandals in the Shipping Board. For Benson it was a bitter moment to see his ideas for a strong merchant marine sacrificed for the benefit of a few slick operators out to make a quick profit, and he was glad when his term as commissioner expired in June 1928. He returned to a well-earned retirement in his home on Washington, D.C., where he spent the last years of his life until his death on 20 May 1932.

References: René De La Pedraja, *The Rise and Decline of U.S. Merchant Shipping in the Twentieth Century* (New York: Twayne, 1992); Mary Klachko, *Admiral William S. Benson: First Chief of Naval Operations* (Annapolis, MD: Naval Institute Press, 1987); Jeffrey J. Safford, *Wilsonian Maritime Diplomacy, 1913–1921* (New Brunswick, NJ: Rutgers University Press, 1978).

BENTLEY, HELEN D., 28 November 1923–present. Helen D. Bentley became the first female advocate of merchant shipping and was also the first woman to head the Federal Maritime Commission* (FMC); since 1985 she has been a member of Congress. She was born in Ruth, Nevada, on 28 November 1923 and graduated from the University of Missouri School of Journalism in 1944. She became the maritime reporter for the *Baltimore Sun* in 1945, and after she wrote important articles such as a four-part series on the slump of the merchant marine, she was promoted to maritime editor in 1953. From 1950 to 1964 she also produced the weekly television documentary, "The Port That Built a City and a State," which made her a familiar name and face in Maryland. Bentley belonged to that first generation of women who became actively involved in maritime affairs but who initially faced skepticism from an industry traditionally an all-male bastion. Not until 1966 did the Propeller Club* accept her and five other women* to full membership, not just to its female auxiliary. As proof of her determination to participate fully in a man's world, she was the only woman who traveled aboard the tanker *Manhattan** on its historic crossing through the Northwest Passage.

Bentley's entry into national prominence came with her appointment as the first female chairman of the FMC in 1969, a move widely welcomed by both management and labor. She vigorously defended American steamship companies and did "an impressive job in revitalizing a moribund bureaucracy at the FMC" (Presidential Handwriting File). President Gerald Ford decided to reappoint her for an unprecedented second term as chairman of the FMC, but unfortunately in 1975 she came under public questioning because she had allowed policy-level officials in the FMC to continue owning stock in companies engaged in merchant shipping. She admitted "that she had acted foolishly in a couple of matters over the years that could prove particularly damaging to her" and was "concerned by a current investigation of Jack Anderson" (ibid.). Even though the FBI cleared her of any criminal wrongdoing, her friend Senator Daniel Inouye "specifically advised her to resign" (ibid.), which she did on the expiration of her term as chairman on 1 July 1975.

She became an international business consultant, and with her name recognition in Maryland, soon she was involved in local politics. She made two unsuccessful attempts to run for Congress until her campaign promise to dredge Baltimore harbor won her election as representative in 1985. The incumbent she defeated had blocked action on environmental grounds, and after she took office she had the harbor dredged. She has remained in Congress, serving from the start in the Merchant Marine and Fisheries Committee;* indeed, it has been felt that without her dynamism and interest, the House might have abolished this committee. In Congress she has been the most outspoken defender of the old and rapidly disappearing maritime policy based on the alliance between big labor and big business to secure government subsidies. Clearly Bentley has been the woman in the twentieth century who has most taken to heart the commitment to the merchant marine.

References: *American Shipper*, May 1974, April 1991; Michael Barone and Grant Ujifusa, *Almanac of American Politics 1992* (Washington, DC: National Journal, 1991); *Congressional Record*, Appendix Part 14, March 1950; *Journal of Commerce*, 24 August 1988; *New York Times*, 23 October 1975; Presidential Handwriting File, Gerald Ford Presidential Library, Ann Arbor, Michigan; U.S. Congress, *Biographical Directory of the United States Congress, 1774–1989* (Washington, DC: Government Printing Office, 1989); *Weekly Compilation of Presidential Documents*, 11 August 1969; *Who's Who in America*, 1992.

BERNSTEIN, ARNOLD, 23 January 1888–6 March 1971. Arnold Bernstein was a German shipping executive who became a U.S. citizen in 1939. He was born in Breslau, Germany, on 23 January 1888, and after completing secondary education, he entered his father's merchant business. He served in the German army during World War I and was highly decorated as a combat hero. After the war Bernstein bought surplus vessels to become a steamship executive; in 1925 he pioneered the transport of unboxed automobiles aboard specially designed garage ships in the Baltic Sea, and starting in 1926 he carried thousands of automobiles from U.S. factories to Europe.

When the Great Depression hit Europe, the volume of cars declined, but then Bernstein decided to design ships to carry cars below and passengers in the upper decks. His three ships offered only tourist-class facilities and provided a comfortable but inexpensive option to the middle-class passengers who could not afford first class in the more luxurious transatlantic liners. Bernstein's ships were a success, and in 1935 he bought from International Mercantile Marine* (IMM) its Belgian-flag Red Star Line,* thereby gaining two more cargo-passenger ships.

The Nazi government in Germany in 1937 arrested Bernstein because he was Jewish. The Nazis confiscated his assets and sold his ships to other lines (Holland-America bought the Red Star Line). Bernstein was well known in international circles, and his continued arrest was embarrassing to the Nazis, who, in exchange for a ransom payment, agreed to release him in 1939. A friend had managed to save some funds from the New York office of the shipping firm, and with these meager resources Bernstein resumed his career by chartering* cargo vessels. Once World War II was over, he made several attempts to reestablish his prewar passenger service, and came very near to success with the American Banner Lines* in 1957–1960. After this last venture he retired, and he died in Florida on 6 March 1971.

References: Frederick E. Emmons, *American Passenger Ships: The Ocean Lines and Liners, 1873–1983* (Newark: University of Delaware Press, 1985); Kermit Roosevelt Papers, Library of Congress, Washington, DC; *National Cyclopedia of American Biography*, vol. 56; *New York Times*, 25 November 1937, 19 April 1957.

BETHLEHEM STEEL CORPORATION. See Calmar Steamship Company.

BIG STRIKE. In San Francisco in 1934 there took place one of the momentous struggles of American workers and the single most significant maritime strike in U.S. history. Shipowners had refused to recognize the International Longshoremen's Association* (ILA) and the union hiring hall,* provoking bitter discontent among longshoremen who now hoped to participate in some of the reforms offered by the New Deal of Franklin D. Roosevelt. The rank and file revolted and removed the conservative leadership of the ILA in the West Coast and voted by a very large margin to strike unless the shipowners accepted the union demands. The strike began on 9 May 1934, and soon the picket lines were joined by the sailors and many shoreside workers; even the teamsters refused to carry "scab" merchandise. The shipowners brought the pliable ILA president Joseph Ryan* from New York City to try to end the strike, but when he was booted out, they decided to employ force. On 3 July, 700 policemen crashed the picket lines to open a path for the scab cargo, and on 5 July or Bloody Thursday, the police used force to clear the pickets at the cost of two dead strikers, thirty with bullet wounds and forty-three seriously injured. National Guard troops set up barbed wire and left armored personnel carriers along the previous picket lines, and the strike appeared to be over.

The maritime workers' determination was unbroken, and they began to receive signs of working-class solidarity, beginning with the huge funeral procession on 9 July for the two victims of Bloody Thursday. If such wanton force could be used freely against the maritime workers, what would keep owners from unleashing similar attacks on other labor unions? On 16 July locals in San Francisco and Oakland turned to that rarely used measure, the general strike, and soon over 100,000 workers had walked off their jobs in solidarity with the maritime struggle. The general strike scared employers throughout the area and panicked the conservative union leaders of the American Federation of Labor (AFL), who regarded this "communist" movement as a danger to their meager gains in previous decades. With the full support of the employers, the conservative leaders of the AFL infiltrated the general strike movement by "boring from within" in a few days, more effectively and rapidly than any communists had ever accomplished in decades. The AFL leaders ended the general strike four days later, and shortly after the teamsters agreed to carry any cargo, thereby leaving the maritime unions isolated and exposed to more concentrated attacks.

To soften up the maritime unions still highly defiant, the employers and concerned local citizens carried out a devastating campaign of publicity, terrorism, and vigilante actions. Unions halls were raided, labor leaders were arrested, and rank and file were beaten and terrorized through brutal assaults. Particular fury was reserved for the communist-led Marine Workers' Industrial Union* (MWIU), which, although very small, was highly vociferous. Maritime unity collapsed when the longshoremen voted to accept the government's offer of arbitration. The sailors felt betrayed, and after some futile protests, the Sailors' Union of the Pacific* (SUP) decided to return to work on 31 July, the same day the longshoremen had set for the resumption of normal activities. The Big Strike was over, thanks to federal government mediation, and although neither employers nor workers could claim a clear victory, maritime labor had learned how powerful joint strike action could be, a lesson that shortly was put into practice with the creation of the Maritime Federation of the Pacific* (MFP).

References: Charles P. Larrowe, *Harry Bridges: The Rise and Fall of Radical Labor in the U.S.* (New York: Lawrence Hill, 1972); Bruce Nelson, *Workers on the Waterfront: Seamen, Longshoremen, and Unionism in the 1930s* (Urbana: University of Illinois Press, 1990); Stephen Schwartz, *Brotherhood of the Sea: A History of the Sailors' Union of the Pacific* (New Brunswick, NJ: Transaction Books, 1986).

BILL OF LADING. A bill of lading was the document issued by an ocean carrier, whether liner* or tramp,* to a shipper* as a receipt listing the latter's merchandise and stating where the goods were received and their place of destination. The bill of lading, as a contract between shipper and carrier, has been the basic document in ocean transportation, and as a contract between shipper and carrier, the government has stipulated its characteristics, obligations, and liabilities in the Carriage of Goods by Sea Act* (COGSA). In practice the shippers fill out the printed forms provided by the ocean carriers, and if the latter sign the document, then the bill of lading has become a valid contractual agreement. Proprietary* companies, since they own the cargo traveling aboard their ships, naturally dispense with bills of lading.

References: Lane C. Kendall, *The Business of Shipping*, 5th ed. (Centreville, MD: Cornell Maritime Press, 1986); William J. Miller, *Encyclopedia of International Commerce* (Centreville, MD: Cornell Maritime Press, 1985).

BLACK COMMITTEE, February 1933–June 1936. The Black Committee, so named because it was headed by Senator Hugo Black, exposed the blatant way in which private individuals had drained funds from the Shipping Board* in the name of promoting the merchant marine. The inquiry, called the "Special Committee on Investigation of Air Mail and Ocean Mail Contracts," focused on how the mail contracts authorized by the Merchant Marine Act of 1928* had been abused.

The Black Committee preempted the jurisdiction of the Commerce Committee* in the Senate and reflected the concern of the Senate leadership that existing legislative committees had been so manipulated by private groups that no meaningful inquiry could take place unless entirely different people were in charge, a conclusion that was also valid for the Merchant Marine and Fisheries Committee* of the House, whose jurisdiction was likewise preempted at other key moments in the twentieth century.

The Black Committee exposed many of the abuses and detailed some of the practices by which shipowners had enriched themselves with public funds. However, not all the culprits were exposed, perhaps because they had ample time to destroy incriminating evidence, and not all the companies were attacked, perhaps because the Black Committee felt it had made a more than sufficient case for reform, and further revelations could only be demoralizing for the maritime industry. Key lobbyists like Hardin B. Arledge* escaped with their reputations enhanced.

Most significantly, the members of Black Committee were divided over the recommendations, with its majority and minority opinions making fascinating reading. Essentially, the majority opinion argued that if enough safeguards were built into a new government program, the policy of subsidizing private shipowners was a feasible way to maintain U.S.-flag merchant shipping. The dissenting opinion forcefully argued that if public funds were to be used, then they should be channeled into a fleet owned and operated by the government, rather than by private individuals. If shipowners continued to receive subsidies, the dissenting opinion feared two results: either private individuals would make profits out of public funds, or conversely, if the subsidies were too rigidly doled out in very measured doses, then the private fleets would gradually decline and wither—as eventually happened in the last decades of the twentieth century. In spite of the prescience of the dissenting opinion, the majority opinion of the Black Committee prevailed, and Congress passed the Merchant Marine Act of 1936,* which inaugurated a new subsidy program for private shipowners, but only under very stringent and rigid requirements.

References: René De La Pedraja, *The Rise and Decline of U.S. Merchant Shipping in the Twentieth Century* (New York: Twayne, 1992); Samuel A. Lawrence, *United States Merchant Shipping Policies and Politics* (Washington, DC: Brookings Institution, 1966); Walter Stubbs, *Congressional Committees, 1789–1982* (Westport, CT: Greenwood Press, 1985); U.S. Congress, Special Committee on Investigation of Air Mail and Ocean Mail Contracts, *Hearings*, 9 vols. (Washington, DC: Government Printing Office, 1933–1934); Paul M. Zeis, *American Shipping Policy* (Princeton, NJ: Princeton University Press, 1938).

BLACK CROSS NAVIGATION AND TRADING COMPANY, 1924–1925.

The Black Cross Navigation and Trading Company was the second shipping venture of Marcus Garvey, the black leader and head of the Universal Negro Improvement Association (UNIA). After the failure of the Black Star Line,* Garvey had been convicted and jailed on charges of mail fraud, but as soon as he was out on bond in 1924 pending his final appeal, he organized the Black Cross Navigation Company to encourage trade between blacks throughout the world and also to carry American colonists back to Africa. As in his first venture, he relied on appeals to the black masses for stock subscriptions, and with these funds he tried to buy a surplus vessel from the Shipping Board,* but when the latter declined because of a previous negative experience with Garvey, he then purchased the *General G. W. Goethals* from the Panama Railroad Steamship Company.* The vessel, renamed the *Booker T. Washington*, was delivered in time for the annual convention of the UNIA, and Garvey scored a tremendous publicity success as the UNIA conventioneers paid fifty cents each to tour the docked vessels, and even his enemies were amazed at how he had managed to bounce back and inspire more blacks to subscribe additional shares.

The *General G. W. Goethals*, although old, was the best vessel Garvey had ever bought and with proper care could provide at least five more years of service. Unfortunately Garvey had not learned anything about vessel management from his previous bungled attempts, and after the vessel sailed on her first voyage for the West Indies in January 1925 to engage in the banana business, she never returned, at least not for the Black Cross Navigation and Trading Company. Discipline aboard the ship collapsed, and without funds to cover port expenses, creditors seized the *Booker T. Washington* as collateral for debts. When Garvey's final appeal was denied, he went to jail on 8 February 1925, and then the Black Cross Navigation and Trading Company promptly collapsed. The *Booker T. Washington* was auctioned to pay for debts, and the ship, once again under its original name of the *General G. W. Goethals*, performed satisfactorily for the Munson Steamship Company* until laid up in 1933. Garvey himself, although pardoned by President Calvin Coolidge in 1927, was deported to Jamaica and never again attempted to establish a steamship company.

References: John H. Clarke, ed., *Marcus Garvey and the Vision of Africa* (New York: Random House, 1974); David Cronon, *Black Moses: The Story of Marcus Garvey and the Universal Negro Improvement Association* (Madison: University of Wisconsin Press, 1969); Frederick E. Emmons, *American Passenger Ships: The Ocean Lines and Liners, 1873–1983* (Newark: University of Delaware Press, 1985).

BLACK DIAMOND STEAMSHIP CORPORATION, 1918-mid-1950s. The Black Diamond Steamship Corporation provided cargo service in the New York-Rotterdam/Antwerp route; from 1919 to the early 1930s the line was called the American Diamond Line, but in reality the ships were operated by the Black Diamond Steamship Corporation.

J. E. Dockendorff* was a general agent in New York City who charged commissions on imports and exports; in 1914 his firm was on the verge of receivership, but the wartime boom allowed him to recoup his fortunes and try to make really big profits. The tremendous shipping shortage induced him to buy a ship from the Shipping Board* in May 1918, but because the ship was unsuitable for operation in transatlantic service, the Shipping Board obligingly agreed to two exchanges until finally in September 1919 he was satisfied with a third ship, the *New Britain*. The high purchase price was the only real investment he ever made in shipping, and with the exorbitant cargo rates prevailing in the 1919–1920 period, he quickly recovered his initial outlay on the ship. The business was so lucrative that he agreed to operate the American Diamond Line, which the Shipping Board had created to carry cargo between New York and the European ports of Rotterdam and Antwerp. By 1921 Black Diamond was operating over twenty government-owned vessels on the American Diamond Line. The "managing operator"* arrangements went beyond the wildest dream of any businessman: J. E. Dockendorff siphoned off the profits to keep the company in the red, while the government absorbed the resulting losses.

Many other operators became careless and failed to run the ships properly or on time, and gradually after 1920 the Shipping Board began to end these arrangements. Dockendorff, however, sensed that if Black Diamond provided adequate service and secured ample cargo, the Shipping Board would leave the line alone for many years, as actually happened. Unfortunately the business was so lucrative that other operators who had learned the trick of how to manipulate the Shipping Board wanted to take away the American Diamond Line from the Black Diamond, which "was continually on the defensive" (U.S. Senate 1933–1934). The operator most determined to wrest the line away from Black Diamond was the Cosmopolitan Shipping Company,* which already operated the America-France line for the Shipping Board. Cosmopolitan began its campaign in 1919, "one of the most unique and extraordinary cases in the annals of the Shipping Board history" (ibid). Black Diamond fought back with its own attorneys and lobbyists, who were effective but very expensive.

Black Diamond at last realized that to make huge profits government largesse

was not enough and that costs had to be reduced. After the Strike of 1921*
Black Diamond—like the rest of U.S. steamship firms—could pay seamen what
it wanted. To take care of foreign competition, a rate war in 1928 convinced
the Holland-America Line and Lloyd Belge to enter a pool agreement that guaranteed Black Diamond 33 percent of the revenue earned in the New York-
Rotterdam/Antwerp route; the only dark cloud in the horizon was the appearance
of newcomer Arnold Bernstein,* whose Red Star Line* had fought its way into
the pool.

In 1929 the Shipping Board opened bids for the purchase of the American
Diamond Line and the America-France Line; Black Diamond put in its bid for
the former, but to everyone's surprise Cosmopolitan made an offer only for the
latter, thereby ending the ten-year rivalry between these two firms. A bigger
struggle materialized, however, because United States Lines* (USL) did make
an offer for American Diamond, and the ensuing complex and bitter bureaucratic
battle included appeals all the way to President Herbert Hoover. The Shipping
Board finally put aside all bids and decided to apply the policy of giving preference to the existing operators; consequently in 1931 Black Diamond purchased
the American Diamond and that same year received a splendid mail contract
subsidy.

In order to qualify for the purchase in 1931, Black Diamond had to reveal
substantial assets, but except for the *New Britain* there were none because Dockendorff had drained away the profits into his other firms, while "drawing out
salaries, entertainment, and expenses, and having representatives in Washington
who cannot be aiding in the operation of a shipping line" (ibid.). This strategy
sharply contrasted with that of Waterman Steamship Corporation,* one of the
few firms that had plowed the profits and the subsidies back into shipping. Black
Diamond was undeterred and calmly borrowed from the New York Central
Railroad and from the financial group of A. Iselin & Co. enough to build up an
asset base. The investors were convinced by the rosy prospects of the purchase,
because the government subsidy guaranteed that each year at least $1 million
would be "velvet": in financial circles *velvet* meant clear profit and "was manna
descended from Heaven into their pockets" (ibid.).

These and other revelations caused many embarrassing moments to Black
Diamond during the Black Committee* hearings of 1933–1934, but the company
did not lose its mail subsidy until Congress passed the Merchant Marine Act of
1936.* Henceforth the government granted only operating differential subsidies*
under excessively rigid standards; Black Diamond continued to operate efficiently and extended the pool agreement, but the drastically reduced subsidies
made the company more vulnerable. Labor costs skyrocketed as the National
Maritime Union* (NMU) organized sailors, while Arnold Bernstein remained a
thorn, and to make things worse, Cosmopolitan planned to enter the An-
twerp/Rotterdam route with chartered* Norwegian ships in 1939.

The outbreak of World War II kept Cosmopolitan from entering the route,
because shortly after, the U.S. government proclaimed a "Neutrality Zone,"

into which U.S.-flag ships could not enter, a small comfort because "Black Diamond was one of the companies hardest hit by the limitations imposed by neutrality" (*New York Times*, 17 December 1939). By December 1939 Black Diamond had chartered its eight U.S.-flag vessels to other U.S. companies for operation in neutral trades, while the company itself chartered twelve foreign-flag vessels to continue service in the New York-Rotterdam/Antwerp route. When the United States entered World War II in December 1941, the control of merchant shipping passed to the U.S. government.

Sometime during World War II, Black Diamond sold all its ships, so that when peace returned, the company requested ships on bareboat* charter from the U.S. Maritime Commission.* Waterman Steamship Corporation and USL objected, because they had invested large sums in the purchase of their own large fleets and did not want to compete against the government-owned ships of Black Diamond. Lawsuits prevented Black Diamond from chartering government ships, and instead it turned to private owners to charter ships in 1947 at the high postwar rates. Black Diamond realized that the best way to sidestep the opposition of USL and Waterman was to purchase ships from the government, but once again the company was without assets.

Black Diamond decided to repeat the old Shipping Board trick of getting the government to pay the price of the ships by means of subsidies, but this time USL and Waterman rushed to block Black Diamond's 1947 request for subsidy on the grounds that they were operating profitably without subsidies, a valid argument in the still-disrupted shipping market of the immediate postwar years.

In the early 1950s Black Diamond was operating a fleet of chartered Norwegian-flag vessels and faced sharp competition from USL and Waterman Steamship. In January 1953 Black Diamond resigned from the North Atlantic Westbound Freight Conference (see North Atlantic Continental Freight Conference*), and the ensuing rate war seriously crippled the line, which in the mid-1950s ceased to operate vessels.

Principal Executives

J. E. Dockendorff   1918–1934

Michael J. Hanlon   1928–1948

References: *New York Times*, 14 August, 28 September, 17 December 1939, 5 September 1947, 22 October 1947, 3, 4 January 1953; U.S. Senate, Special Committee on Investigation of Air Mail and Ocean Mail Contracts, *Hearings*, 9 vols. (Washington, DC: Government Printing Office, 1933–1934).

BLACK STAR LINE, 1919–1921. The Black Star Line was the bold attempt of the black leader Marcus Garvey to create a steamship company whose primary mission was to link, through trade and travel, all peoples of African origin. Marcus Garvey established the Universal Negro Improvement Association (UNIA) in Jamaica in 1914 and subsequently shifted his activities to a new organization with the same name he incorporated in New York in 1917; the West Indian presence remained strong throughout his movement's existence, and when he made his first appeal for stock subscriptions for his Black Star Line in 1919, West Indians throughout the Caribbean immediately responded; after translations into Spanish, so did blacks in Cuba and other Hispanic countries of the Caribbean. A master propagandist, Garvey soon captivated many American blacks, who fell under the spell of what they often called "The Back to Africa Movement," and although he made plans to carry American colonists back to Africa, his main goal in creating the Black Star Line was to better the economic fortunes of blacks throughout the world by mutual trading.

Until the middle of the twentieth century ownership of steamship companies gave a social status that in itself was reason enough for Garvey to want to break into the formerly all-white ranks of steamship owners. While established companies certainly did not want the competition from the Black Star Line (incorporated in June 1919) at a time when the Shipping Board* was in the process of creating nearly 200 new "managing operators,"* Garvey's later charges that white companies contributed to his downfall can be taken only as very effective rhetoric. If anything, the established companies watched with amusement bordering on laughter the antics of Garvey, while white but shady ship brokers* and agents joined with no less unscrupulous blacks to fleece the Black Star Line for all it was worth.

Garvey's initial attempt to raise capital through stock subscriptions was sound, provided he wisely invested the money into profitable shipping operations. Of the three vessels in his fleet, one, the *Shadyside*, was an 1873 side-wheeler that he intended to use as an excursion boat, but she lost money on voyages in the summer of 1920. After just five months' service, the company had to tie up at the dock the *Shadyside*, which sprang a leak and slowly sank to the bottom of the Hudson River. The second vessel was the *Kanawha*, an overage millionaire's yacht with no possible use for either passenger or cargo services and in disastrous condition. After spending huge sums in refitting and constantly repairing the yacht, the *Kanawha* made some accident-filled trips until her final breakdown and abandonment in Antilla, Cuba, as a useless hulk in August 1921.

Any chances of success for the Black Star Line rested with the *Yarmouth*, bought in September 1919 and the only real merchant ship in the fleet. The *Yarmouth* had been built in Scotland in 1887 and had the same age as Garvey himself; skilled navigator Hugh Mulzac understated the reality when he said that "the *Yarmouth* was not a vessel to set a sailor's heart aflame" (Mulzac 1963). The British-flag vessel needed massive repairs as well as a total overhaul of the hull and could not have been worth more than $25,000, yet in a period when ship prices had collapsed because the Shipping Board was dumping government vessels on the market, Garvey had been suckered into paying $165,000; as the white ship broker explained, "If this fellow has got so much money, we are going to sell him this ship and make as much out of it as we can" (Cronon 1969). The operation of the vessel was marked by one complication after another, and Garvey never understood the significance of hauling cargo and passengers according to fixed schedules, because for him the ships "represented the triumph of propaganda over business" (ibid.). The ship was detoured from the scheduled run and raked up constant losses in the three voyages the *Yarmouth* made. Rather than a sound investment with the stockholders' money, Garvey had fallen into a version of the old promoters' scam, a mounting "pyramid" game that required him to receive more stock subscriptions in order to pay for the mounting debts of the Black Star Line's voyages. He ran out of money before he could buy a modern steamship from the Shipping Board, a transaction that had been delayed but not stopped by false charges from the FBI that Garvey headed a communist organization; Garvey, the perpetual showman, later countered these charges by accusing the Bolsheviks of launching attacks on his line. In late 1921 the creditors caught up with the company, and the *Yarmouth* was auctioned off for $1,625, not even 1 percent of her original purchase price.

In circulars and speeches, Garvey misrepresented the company and announced to blacks eager to believe in any signs of black success the existence of a large fleet, including ships that did not exist, while in UNIA propaganda the *Yarmouth*, whose name had never been formally changed, was always referred to as the *Frederick Douglass*. In January 1922 the government arrested Garvey on charges of defrauding people through the mails, and while admittedly the federal prosecutors failed to prove their case conclusively, the most cursory examination of UNIA and Black Star Line materials revealed outlandish claims and false information that, whether intentionally or not, deceived thousands of trusting blacks. Many had sold furniture and prize possessions and even mortgaged or sold their homes to buy the worthless Black Star Line stock, and while many continued to see Garvey as a hero, the hard fact remained that he had scammed thousands out of their hard-earned money, and the government had the obligation to prevent similar frauds in the steamship business. After many delays a very long trial began in May 1923, and the jury found Garvey guilty of mail fraud in June 1923. He was jailed, and his steamship career appeared to be over, but while out on bail in September 1923 pending appeal, now as a martyred victim, his reputation was enhanced, and he plunged into the task of renewing his campaign for stock subscriptions, this time for the Black Cross Navigation and Trading Company.*

References: John H. Clarke, ed., *Marcus Garvey and the Vision of Africa* (New York: Random House, 1974); David Cronon, *Black Moses: The Story of Marcus Garvey and the Universal Negro Improvement Association* (Madison: University of Wisconsin Press, 1969); Hugh Mulzac, *A Star to Steer By* (New York: International, 1963).

BLAND, SCHUYLER OTIS, 4 May 1872–16 February 1950. Schulyer Otis Bland formed with Joshua Alexander,* Herbert C. Bonner,* and Walter B. Jones* the group of congressmen who had the greatest impact on the merchant marine during the twentieth century. Bland was born on 4 May 1872 near

Gloucester, Gloucester County, Virginia. He attended private schools, graduated from the College of William and Mary, and afterward began to practice law in Newport News, Virginia, in 1900. As an attorney, he witnessed the return of the Great White Fleet to Newport News after it had left on a world voyage in 1907 and was outraged to see that the impressive display of naval power depended on the merchant ships of England, Italy, and Norway for its resupply. Bland determined to do something to restore the U.S.-flag merchant fleet, a popular cause in Newport News, whose shipbuilding activities were crucial to the local economy. Bland was elected to Congress as a Democrat in 1918 and served continuously until his death; he joined the Merchant Marine and Fisheries Committee,* whose chairman he became in 1933, and except for a brief interruption by the Republican party in 1947–1948, he remained its chairman until his death.

Among Bland's most notable accomplishments was the Merchant Marine Act of 1936,* whose father he was considered by many fellow congressmen. The fact that he came from a shipbuilding district accounted for the strange hybrid arrangement in the act, which attempted to promote simultaneously both U.S.-flag shipping and domestic shipyards, but with the well-known results that gradually each one has helped smother the other over the decades. While still holding office, Bland died in Bethesda, Maryland, on 16 February 1950, but his death did not leave the maritime industry without a strong political figure, because waiting in the wings was his successor, Herbert C. Bonner.

References: Samuel A. Lawrence, *United States Merchant Shipping Policies and Politics* (Washington, DC: Brookings Institution, 1966); U.S. Congress, *Biographical Directory of the United States Congress, 1774–1989* (Washington, DC: Government Printing Office, 1989); U.S. House, Committee on Merchant Marine and Fisheries, *Independent Federal Maritime Administration* (Washington, DC: Government Printing Office, 1967).

BLOOMFIELD STEAMSHIP COMPANY, 1946–1968? The Bloomfield Steamship Company was one of the handful of new shipping firms that appeared after the end of World War II. The strategy was to take advantage of low prices for surplus vessels, and just like after World War I, the new firms had a regional base, specifically Houston in the case of the Bloomfield Steamship Company. The founder, Ben M. Bloomfield, had gained support from Texas investors and also obtained a 20 percent stock subscription from Farrell Line,* the main U.S.-flag firm in the African trade; he was trying to repeat the success of Thomas E. Cuffe, who had created the Pacific Far East Line* (PFEL) in 1946. There was another similarity: Cuffe was a former executive of American Presidents Line* (APL), while Bloomfield was a former executive of Lykes Brothers Steamship Co.* But there was a crucial difference: APL was then under government ownership and could not take any action against PFEL to avoid the remotest charges of unfair government competition against private business, but family-owned Lykes Brothers was under no such restriction and, as a matter of fact, had a rich tradition of cornering and eventually crushing any rival firms in the Gulf of Mexico.

In 1946 Lykes blocked the subsidy application of Bloomfield for a service between the Gulf of Mexico and Africa, and the company, unable to resist the pressure from Lykes, decided in 1947 to sell its three surplus C-2s* and the remaining 80 percent of the stock to Farrell, whose resources and government contacts matched those of Lykes Brothers. Undaunted by this setback, Bloomfield obtained new Texas backers to reestablish his company in 1951, and the new Bloomfield Steamship Company bought five Victory* and three Liberty* vessels, for operation this time in the routes between the Gulf of Mexico and ports in Europe and the Mediterranean. Lykes Brothers was as determined as ever to keep the rival out of the Gulf, but as long as the Korean War shipping boom lasted, the company prospered. In 1954 management of Bloomfield Steamship passed to States Marine Corporation,* which, through a process not altogether clear, eventually gained control of Bloomfield, whose name continued to be used until 1968.

Principal Executive

Ben M. Bloomfield   1946–1954

References: Robert G. Albion, *Seaports South of Sahara: The Achievements of an American Steamship Company* (New York: Appleton-Century Crofts, 1959); Committee of American Steamship Lines, *Progress of the U.S. Liner Fleet*, Washington, D.C., December 1964; Federal Maritime Board, *Decisions*, vol. 4, *1952–1956* (Washington, DC: Government Printing Office, 1963); *New York Times*, 25 February 1951, 1 April 1968; U.S. Maritime Commission, *Decisions*, vol. 3, *1947–1952* (Washington, DC: Government Printing Office, 1963).

BLUE BOOK UNION or LONGSHOREMEN'S ASSOCIATION OF SAN FRANCISCO AND THE BAY DISTRICT, 1915–1933. The Blue Book Union was the company union for longshoremen in the San Francisco Bay area. Thomas Herring created the union in 1915, when his bid to capture the International Longshoremen's Association (ILA) presidency from Thomas V. O'Connor* failed. The "Blue Book Union," as it was called because of the color of each worker's membership book, languished during World War I and was eclipsed by a rival organization, the "Red Book Union." The defeat of the longshoremen in the bitter 1919 strike destroyed the Red Book Union and gave management the opportunity to transform the languishing Blue Book Union into the company union for all longshoremen. All had to belong and pay dues to the newly renamed Longshoremen's Association of San Francisco and the Bay District, and without its notorious blue book nobody could work on the waterfront. The repugnant "shape-up"* continued undisturbed, because the blue book was just a prerequisite but did not guarantee employment. Any attempt by longshoremen to use the grievance machinery of the union resulted in blacklisting.

In effect, the Blue Book Union had become an extension of the companies' personnel department.

Workers hated the Blue Book Union as a parasite; nevertheless other labor leaders cooperated with it, and one American Federation of Labor official went so far as to praise the company union ''for correcting a number of prevailing evils'' (Nelson 1990) in the waterfront. As the labor movement revived with the coming of the New Deal, the Blue Book Union was one of the first casualties in the waterfront. Angry longshoremen ripped to shreds their despised blue books in 1933, the first inkling of the Big Strike,* which erupted the next year.

References: Giles T. Brown, *Ships That Sail No More: Marine Transportation from San Diego to Puget Sound, 1910–1940* (Lexington: University of Kentucky Press, 1966); Charles P. Larrowe, *Harry Bridges: The Rise and Fall of Radical Labor in the U.S.* (New York: Lawrence Hill, 1972); Bruce Nelson, *Workers on the Waterfront: Seamen, Longshoremen, and Unionism in the 1930s* (Urbana: University of Illinois Press, 1990); William W. Pilcher, *The Portland Longshoremen: A Dispersed Urban Community* (New York: Holt, Rinehart, and Winston, 1972).

BONNER, HERBERT C., 16 May 1891–7 November 1965. Herbert C. Bonner formed with Joshua Alexander,* Schuyler Otis Bland,* and Walter B. Jones* the group of congressmen who had the greatest impact on the merchant marine during the twentieth century. Bonner was born in Washington, North Carolina, on 16 May 1891. He received only a modest education and served in World War I as a sergeant. After trying his luck with various odd jobs, he became an aide to Democrat Lindsay C. Warren, who, after his election to Congress, took Bonner with him to Washington. Bonner served fifteen years as Warren's aide, and when the latter was appointed U.S. comptroller general, Bonner ran for Warren's seat and won the election. Bonner remained in the House until the end of his life and throughout that period was also a member of the Merchant Marine and Fisheries Committee,* whose chairman he became in 1955.

The larger size of the House allowed Bonner to specialize more in the merchant marine than was the case with senators, like Warren G. Magnuson,* who had to distribute their time to other issues as well; Bonner's interest in the merchant marine had come through his links with shipowners, unlike Magnuson, whose interest came from the support of organized labor, in particular, the maritime unions. Among Bonner's greatest accomplishments was the passage of the Cargo Preference Act of 1954,* but afterward opposition from shippers* and farmers did not allow him to expand cargo preference; as a matter of fact, during the rest of his congressional career he was on the defensive, fighting off attempts to repeal or nullify earlier gains of the maritime industry.

Through legislation, Bonner made permanent the Merchant Marine Academy* and also saved the state maritime colleges* from sure extinction. He obtained the legislation for the construction of the *Savannah,* the first nuclear-powered vessel, but he insisted on having Congress approve any subsequent nuclear vessels. The revelations of the Celler Committee* subjected the merchant marine to many serious charges, and Bonner had to wield considerable political capital to contain the damage. However, he decided not to stop Reorganization Plan No. 7, which created a separate Federal Maritime Commission* (FMC) charged with preventing the abuses denounced by the Celler Committee.

By 1962 maritime policy seemed to have reached a dead end, or at least so it seemed to Bonner, who exclaimed at a hearing that he was tired of having "to bail out" U.S.-flag shipping. No new initiatives appeared, and Bonner had lost considerable interest in the field by the time of his death on 7 November 1965. The constantly frustrating task of seeking subsidies and defending the privileges of the private U.S.-flag merchant marine now fell to Edward A. Garmatz,* who replaced Bonner as chairman of the Merchant Marine and Fisheries Committee. More significantly, the vacancy in the congressional district caused by Bonner's death was filled in a special election by Walter B. Jones,* who eventually became the real successor to Bonner in the defense of the merchant marine.

References: *Current Biography*, 1956; Samuel A. Lawrence, *United States Merchant Shipping Policies and Politics* (Washington, DC: Brookings Institution, 1966); *New York Times*, 3 July 1955; U.S. Congress, *Biographical Directory of the United States Congress, 1774–1989* (Washington, DC: Government Printing Office, 1989).

BOWERS, JOHN M., 1924 or 1925–present. John M. Bowers has been the president of the International Longshoremen's Association* (ILA) since 1987. He was from New York City and was the fourth generation of his family to work in the docks. He distinguished himself in 1954, when the ILA was threatened by destruction, and he became president of his local. He later joined the camp of Thomas William Gleason* and backed the latter's candidacy for ILA president in 1963. Bowers routinely isolated himself by taking unpopular positions, and his candid descriptions often caused resentment, but precisely this unpopularity made him attractive to Gleason, who did not have to worry about Bowers's turning into a rival for power. From 1963 until 1987 Bowers was the executive vice president of the ILA and in effect held the number two position behind Gleason. Bowers distanced himself from the racketeering and corruption that proliferated in the ILA during Gleason's presidency and was the logical choice to succeed Gleason upon his retirement in 1987. When the International Longshoremen and Warehousemen's Union* (ILWU) affiliated with the American Federation of Labor and Congress of Industrial Organizations (AFL-CIO) in 1988, Bowers hoped this action would eventually lead to the return of the ILWU to the ILA, but the ILWU has continued to defend its independence in the West Coast.

References: *American Shipper*, January, May 1991; Maud Russell, *Men Along the Shore: The ILA and Its History* (New York: Brussel and Brussel, 1966); *Who's Who in Labor, 1976* (New York: Arno Press, 1976).

BRAZIL. See Good Neighbor Fleet.

BREAK-BULK CARGO or GENERAL CARGO. Break-bulk cargo or general cargo has been the term traditionally used to describe freight stowed in the holds and decks of merchant vessels. Break-bulk cargo has existed since the beginning of ocean navigation thousands of years ago, but the term was coined to differentiate general cargo from the bulk* shipments that began in the late nineteenth century. In bulk shipments the commodities, usually coal, oil, ores, wheat, and other grains, were poured directly into the hold of specially designed ships. However, if the liquids and grains were carried in barrels or inside other packages, then it was not a bulk shipment but rather break-bulk cargo.

Loading and unloading the ship were only two of the many labor-intensive steps in handling break-bulk cargo as it moved from point of origin to the final destination. Mechanization and the application of nonhuman energy had become more widespread, with winches and cranes commonplace by the early twentieth century, and forklift trucks appeared around 1935, but no radical change had occurred in the handling of the cargo. Furthermore, improvements in rail and truck systems meant that the volume of cargo reaching the warehouses continued to mount and made manifest the bottleneck that existed in loading the ships. While most merchandise could afford to wait short periods in the warehouse, shipowners always lost money every hour their ships were docked, but handling break-bulk cargo was such a slow process that ships on the average spent half their time in port.

The widespread introduction of containers* since the late 1960s dramatically reduced the volume of break-bulk cargo, while the introduction of Roll-on/Roll-off* (Ro/Ro) vessels further reduced the volume of break-bulk cargo. Because the shipowners who still provided break-bulk service charged rates considerably higher than for container cargoes, shippers* have a permanent and powerful incentive to abandon break-bulk cargo whenever possible.

However, break-bulk cargo has not disappeared completely from U.S. shipping. Heavy equipment and oversize machinery continued to require conventional freighters, while many countries of the underdeveloped world use them because they cannot afford the investment in the port and transportation machinery needed to handle containers. Because labor costs have been so high in the industrialized countries, not even in the trade with the underdeveloped world could the merchant shipping companies afford to use break-bulk freighters, and instead they employ that older generation of containerships still fitted with their own cranes, so they can discharge the containers on the docks of an underdeveloped country and load the containers for the return voyage. Rather than vanishing completely, break-bulk cargo has become one more small specialized field in the vast area of ocean transportation, a far cry from the time in the nineteenth century when break-bulk cargoes formed the backbone of merchant shipping.

References: Advisory Commission on Conferences in Ocean Shipping, *Report to the President and the Congress* (Washington, DC: Government Printing Office, 1992); Lane C. Kendall, *The Business of Shipping*, 5th ed. (Centreville, MD: Cornell Maritime Press, 1986).

BREMEN LINE or OCEAN STEAM NAVIGATION COMPANY, 1846–1857. The Bremen Line, formally titled the Ocean Steam Navigation Company, was the first U.S.-flag steamship company to provide regularly scheduled service across the Atlantic. British lines had taken the lead with side-wheel* steamers, and when the English government decided to subsidize their operations, the U.S. government in response awarded generous mail contracts, starting in 1845, to try to establish U.S.-flag service. Edward Mills and his fellow promoters received the mail contract for a line to Bremen and Havre, and they hoped that the mail contract would attract more investors. However, because Mills was relatively unknown in shipping circles, the company's stock sold so slowly that he could begin operations only through a generous loan raised from the still independent German states.

The company's first ship, the *Washington,* was launched in New York on 31 January 1847; the side-wheel wooden steamer carried 120 passengers in first and second class but had very little space for cargo. The *Washington* sailed on 1 June and was followed by the *Hermann** ten months later, but the ships turned out to have been poorly designed and much slower than any of their rivals; in spite of several alterations, they proved to be "disastrous . . . to our professional reputation as constructors and engineers" (Tyler 1939). Profoundly disappointed with the performance of the Bremen Line, the U.S. government decided to award a separate mail contract to Edward K. Collins,* whose line was expected to provide the fastest and best service across the Atlantic. The Bremen Line had never been able to gather enough funds to start the service to Havre, and in 1849 the postmaster general took away the unfulfilled part of the mail contract and assigned it to a separate company, which became known as the Havre Line.*

Nevertheless, the Bremen Line managed to survive in the route for ten years and even paid dividends to stockholders in 1853 and 1854. The company needed to order new ships to match those of its rivals, but investors remained skeptical, while the Germans, who had been decisive in launching the line, had become disillusioned with its performance and were saving their capital to establish their own German line. In the spring of 1857 the Vanderbilt European Line* entered the New York-Bremen route with new fast ships and soon captured most of the business in that trade. In June 1857 the Bremen Line's mail contract expired, and without funds to order new vessels, the company halted service in July and proceeded to liquidate itself; the sale price of the *Washington* and *Hermann* was one-tenth of their original value, and stockholders recovered about a third of their original investment.

Notable Ships

Washington	1847–1857
Hermann	1847–1857

References: Robert G. Albion, *The Rise of New York Port, 1815–1860* (New York: Scribner's, 1939); Wheaton J. Lane, *Commodore Vanderbilt: An Epic of the Steam Age* (New York: Alfred A. Knopf, 1942); William S. Lindsay, *History of Merchant Shipping* *and Ancient Commerce,* 4 vols. (New York: AMS Press, 1965); David B. Tyler, *Steam Conquers the Atlantic* (New York: D. Appleton-Century, 1939).

BRENT, THEODORE, 30 March 1874–8 June 1953. Theodore Brent was the president of the Delta Line* in 1943–1953. He was born in Muscatine, Iowa, on 30 March 1874 and studied in public schools. In 1896 he began working for a railroad in Kansas City, Missouri, and stayed working in different Midwest railroad companies until World War I. In 1914 he moved to New Orleans, and this city became his home for the rest of his life. He left the railroads for shipping in New Orleans and helped organize several ventures in ocean transportation. He went to Washington, D.C., as one of the original commissioners of the Shipping Board,* but less than six months after his appointment, he resigned on 26 July 1917. Back in New Orleans, he became the general manager of the Federal Barge Lines in 1920–1927, and during 1928–1931 he was president of the Redwood Steamship Line, which provided intercoastal* service between New Orleans and the Pacific Coast of the United States. In 1932–1943 he was president of another company he had founded, the Coast Transportation Company.

In 1943, upon the death of Norman O. Pedrick, he became the president of the Delta Line, on whose Board of Directors he had served since the foundation of the company in 1919. After the end of World War II, he presided over the acquisition of surplus vessels so that the Delta Line could restore its prewar services. Brent was always involved in multiple steamship ventures and was one of the individuals who contributed to bringing plentiful and reliable steamship service to New Orleans. He died in that city on 8 June 1953.

References: Paul V. Betters and Darrell H. Smith, *The United States Shipping Board: Its History, Activities and Organization* (Washington, DC: Brookings Institution, 1931); Gilbert M. Mellin, ''The Mississippi Shipping Company,'' Ph.D. diss., University of Pittsburgh, 1955; *National Cyclopedia of American Biography,* vol. 46.

BRIDGES, HARRY, 28 July 1901–30 March 1990. Harry Bridges, the president of the International Longshoremen and Warehousemen's Union* (ILWU) from 1937 to 1977, was one of the most controversial labor leaders of the United States. He was born in Melbourne, Australia, on 28 July 1901 of a middle-class family and attended a Catholic parochial school until the age of fourteen. His father was a real estate agent, and Bridges's first job was collecting rents, a task he disliked, while another job as a clerk he found boring. Stories by Jack London fueled his curiosity about the sea and he began shipping out as a sailor. His fascination with the sea and the waterfront never abated, but he became disgusted with the way shipowners treated the workers, and he eagerly participated in the 1917 general strike in Australia. In 1920 Bridges made San Francisco his base for shipping out as a seaman. Participation in the Sailors' Union of the Pacific* (SUP) was automatic, because membership books in the SUP and the Australian seamen's union were interchangeable at that time. When the strike of 1921* erupted, he was already a picket captain. The failure of the strike turned him against the conservative policies of Andrew Furuseth,* and in protest he joined the Industrial Workers of the World (Marine Transport Workers Industrial Union No. 510) but soon became disillusioned with its poor organization and lack of a political program.

In 1922, like many seamen, he left the sea and became a longshoreman but soon clashed with the antilabor policies of the Blue Book Union,* the company union in the San Francisco Bay Area. Bridges was constantly hopping from one dock to another, because if he worked longer than a day or two, the representatives of the Blue Book Union would locate him and have him fired. In 1932 the Blue Book Union had tightened its net, and he was fired after working only a couple of hours on the dock, but by then, before Bridges was permanently destroyed, great changes were coming to the waterfront.

Bridges had refused to join the communist-led Marine Workers' Industrial Union* (MWIU) because from very early he had discovered the profoundly conservative nature of most American workers but saw nothing wrong with making tactical alliances with the communists in the manner of John L. Lewis, the first president of the Congress of Industrial Organizations (CIO). Bridges and other longshoremen took over the *Waterfront Worker* in 1932 from the MWIU and converted the procommunist paper to one that advocated a strong union within the American Federation of Labor (AFL).

The *Waterfront Worker* fueled the labor effervescence, and the first casualty was the Blue Book Union, which collapsed in 1933. Bridges's itinerant work pattern had made him familiar to most longshoremen, but even more significantly he had the rare capacity to capture their real problems and needs in words they easily understood. He was a product of the rank and file who throughout his career never strayed far from the concerns of the longshoremen. His leadership success was all the more remarkable because he avoided tuxedo unionism* and refused to surround himself with squads of armed thugs in the manner of Joseph Ryan, the rival on the East Coast. With all these qualities, Bridges's rise during the Big Strike* of 1934 and his emergence as the real leader of the longshoremen on the West Coast were almost foreordained.

The International Longshoremen's Association* (ILA) under Joseph Ryan in theory had jurisdiction over the West Coast, but traditionally its membership had been concentrated on the East Coast and the Gulf of Mexico. Bridges made one last attempt to obtain ILA support for the 1936 strike but failed, and a split was inevitable. He continued to try until the end to remain within the AFL, but then abruptly in June 1937 Bridges decided that the only alternative was to join the newly founded CIO under Lewis. The longshoremen had extended the organizing drive to the warehousemen, and in August 1937 the CIO issued a charter to create the new ILWU, with Bridges as the first president.

The ILWU was in part a substitute for the Maritime Federation of the Pacific* (MFP), already in the throes of disintegration because Bridges had wrongly believed that Harry Lundeberg* was the right person to lead the seamen. Lundeberg converted the SUP into a personal fiefdom and pulled out of the MFP, in effect starting a bitter and violent struggle between Lundeberg and Bridges that raged for the next twenty years. Bridges had antagonized not only Lundeberg but also the employers, who feared his supposed radicalism. Tremendous political pressure was applied to try to deport Bridges from 1939 to 1955, when at last his right to U.S. citizenship was vindicated (see *Bridges* case*).

After World War II Bridges resumed his efforts to re-create a common front on the waterfront, and his ILWU joined with the National Maritime Union* (NMU) and other labor unions to create the short-lived Committee for Maritime Unity* (CMU). The strike of 1948 began a long period of quiet on the docks, as the employers finally realized that the charges of Bridges's communism were untrue and that, as a matter of fact, he was a stabilizing force on the waterfront— provided the longshoremen's wages and conditions were well attended. Bridges himself began to mellow and became more conservative, eventually switching his party registration from Democrat to Republican, in stark contrast to the fiery and radical-sounding speeches of his earlier years.

The newfound understanding between Bridges and the employers allowed him to negotiate successfully in 1960 the Mechanization and Modernization Agreement* (M&M) to take care of the jobs lost because of the introduction of containers.* Labor peace was broken in 1971–1972, when the workers were on strike for 135 days to gain increases in wages and other benefits, but the M&M agreement remained in force. The Vietnam War brought huge volumes of cargo to the docks and postponed the loss of jobs on the waterfront, but Bridges still felt the need to warn the country of the injustice of that war, and the ILWU passed resolutions but did not engage in strike actions to halt the flow of war materiel. Wisely Bridges concluded that the antiwar movement was a task for a new generation, although later in 1972 he helped to establish the organization Labor for Peace as a way to protest the AFL's blind support of the Vietnam War.

Bridges and his close associate, the secretary-treasurer, Louis Goldblatt,* retired in 1977. Bridges died in San Francisco on 30 March 1990, but even after his death his name continued to be haunted by false accusations about his supposed communist links.

References: Gary M. Fink, ed., *Biographical Dictionary of American Labor*, 2d ed. (Westport, CT: Greenwood Press, 1984); Charles P. Larrowe, *Harry Bridges: The Rise and Fall of Radical Labor in the U.S.* (New York: Lawrence Hill, 1972); *Who's Who in the Maritime Industry 1946;* Bruce Nelson, *Workers on the Waterfront: Seamen, Longshoremen, and Unionism in the 1930s* (Urbana: University of Illinois Press, 1990).

BRIDGES CASE, 1934–1955. The *Bridges* case was the collective name given to the three trials and numerous legal proceedings in which the U.S. government attempted to deport or arrest Harry Bridges,* the Australian-born president of the International Longshoremen and Warehousemen's Union* (ILWU). When Bridges emerged as the radical leader of the West Coast longshoremen in the Big Strike* of 1934, employers and the government tried to neutralize this labor movement by having Bridges deported. A chronology reveals best the many steps in the *Bridges* case:

1934	The Immigration Service attempted to deport Bridges as "an undesirable alien" (Larrowe 1972), but lack of evidence halted the proceedings. However, some of the unsubstantiated remarks and contradictory evidence gathered in this attempt continued to surface in the later trials.
1936	The Labor Department repeated the deportation investigation to try to see if anything had been overlooked in the previous proceedings, only to conclude that Bridges could not be deported.
1939	A Supreme Court decision on a related case encouraged the Immigration Service to reopen the deportation case and consequently began the first hearings. President Franklin D. Roosevelt appointed James M. Landis, the dean of Harvard Law School, to preside over the courtroom. After eleven weeks of sessions, Dean Landis found Bridges innocent of any accusations of membership in the Communist party and hence could not be deported. The Landis hearings exhausted the compilation of evidence, and nothing new of significance surfaced at the later trials.
1940	A combination of employers and conservative union leaders secured passage through the House of Representatives of a bill that ordered the deportation of Harry Bridges, but the bill died in the Senate.
1941	Congress changed the immigration laws to allow bringing Bridges to trial. Bridges was ordered deported, but execution of the sentence was delayed pending a long appeal procedure.
1945	The Supreme Court reversed the deportation order against Bridges, who immediately asked for naturalization and was granted U.S. citizenship. The *Bridges* case, which had evoked tremendous sympathy from American labor, appeared to be over.

1949–1950	Cold War hysteria allowed Harry Lundeberg* and other labor enemies of Harry Bridges to reopen the case on the grounds of ''perjury,'' essentially that Bridges had falsely denied his membership in the Communist party when he applied for U.S. citizenship. Bridges was found guilty and served twenty-one days in jail before his release, pending appeal of the order stripping him of U.S. citizenship.
1953	The Supreme Court reversed the conviction. Opponents of Bridges brought a civil suit to try to prove that Bridges had been a communist.
1955	At a civil trial, the judge dismissed the charges against Bridges because the government had failed in all the previous proceedings and trials to present convincing evidence that Bridges had ever been a communist. The *Bridges* case was at last over.

Two other aspects of the *Bridges* case bear mentioning. First, during its twenty-one years, the *Bridges* case served as a rallying point for generations of longshoremen who automatically sympathized with Bridges as a victim of a persecution they all suffered in one way or another. The accusations, rather than weakening Bridges's grip on the longshoremen, actually increased his stature. Second, while before 1945 employers had taken the lead in urging the deportation of Bridges, after 1949 they came to testify as character witnesses on behalf of Bridges, and on the other hand, rival union leaders now led the struggle to arrest and deport Bridges. Thus, what had begun as an attempt, like the Modesto Boys* case, to destroy a labor organization had degenerated into interunion rivalry.

References: CIO Files of John L. Lewis, Correspondence with CIO Unions, Microfilm, University Publications of America; Charles P. Larrowe, *Harry Bridges: The Rise and Fall of Radical Labor in the U.S.* (New York: Lawrence Hill, 1972).

BROKER, SHIP. See ship broker.

BRYSON, HUGH, 4 October 1914–circa 1990. Hugh Bryson was the most controversial president of the National Union of Marine Cooks and Stewards* (NUMCS), the labor union that represented the seagoing workers who prepared and served the food, as well as performing housekeeping chores on board. Bryson was born on 4 October 1914 in an Illinois farm, where he was raised by his parents, who were farmers. Self-driven, Bryson completed high school and attended business college in 1932, but in the midst of the Great Depression he could neither complete college nor find a job at his educational level. He drifted to California, where he found sporadic employment in the steward's department of ships, and joined the NMCSA. He was overqualified for the job but was popular among the cooks and stewards, who soon chose him to be their ship's delegate. A string of union positions on land followed after 1938, until he became editor of the *Voice*, the official periodical of the union, in 1944. His election as president of the union in 1946 capped his labor career. Bryson had risen so rapidly under the labor revival of the New Deal because of his personality and the shortage of labor leaders with his educational level and because as a bachelor he could devote full time to union activities (only in 1945 did he marry Abigail Alvarez).

Bryson's career did not have a happy ending, however. He had joined the Communist party, and with the onset of the Cold War, his union increasingly felt the brunt of anticommunist attacks. To obtain some protection, in 1950 he sought to move closer to the perpetual maverick of the labor movement, John L. Lewis. The anticommunist attacks continued, and in 1953 a federal grand jury indicted him of having falsely denied his membership in the Communist party. Shortly afterward he was removed from all union offices and in 1955 was convicted in the San Francisco Federal District Court and served time in federal prison. Bryson's career as a labor leader was over, but not as a writer, and after his release, he published in 1961 the *History of the Study of Ideological Conflict in the American Labor Movement, 1865–1900*. He afterward "went into real estate deals" in southern California, where he died around 1990.

References: CIO FILES of John L. Lewis, Correspondence with CIO Unions, Microfilm, University Publications of America; William Kooiman letter to author, 11 February 1993; Gary M. Link, ed., *Biographical Dictionary of American Labor*, 2d ed., (Westport, CT: Greenwood Press, 1984); Jane Cassels Record, "The Rise and Fall of a Maritime Union," *Industrial and Labor Relations Review* 10 (1956):81–92; *Who's Who in Labor, 1946*.

BULK. The term *bulk* has referred to commodities, usually coal, oil, ores, wheat, and other grains, that were shipped unpacked in the holds of specially designed ships. The companies that needed to carry the bulk cargoes either operated their own fleets, in which case the owners were called proprietary* companies, or else chartered tramp* vessels. See break-bulk cargo.

BULL, ARCHIBALD HILTON, 14 January 1847–13 February 1920. Archibald H. Bull was the founder and first president of both the New York and Puerto Rico Steamship Company* and the Bull Line.* He was born in New York City on 14 January 1847 and attended public schools. Bull began his business career as an office boy in 1863, and already in 1873 he began to operate a line of sailing vessels between New York and the Spanish colony of Puerto Rico. Later he added steamers to the route, and in 1885 he agreed to amalgamate with his competitors into the New York and Puerto Rico Steamship Company, whose president he became. In 1900 he was maneuvered not only into the sale of his stock in the New York and Puerto Rico Steamship Company, but also into the commitment not to run steamers in the Puerto Rican route for ten years. With the proceeds from the sale he incorporated in 1902 a new firm, the Bull Line,* to operate in the coastwise* trade of eastern U.S. ports and to run only sailing vessels to Puerto Rico. His spectacular success caught the attention of Wall Street magnate Charles W. Morse, who was trying to buy up individual companies to create a coastwise shipping cartel. "Mr. Bull, you have the opportunity of your lifetime . . . name your price and sell out." Bull thought otherwise: "I have a son in business with me and another son I am educating for the business, and if I were to sell out I would leave these boys with plenty of money and no business, and I prefer to leave them with plenty of business and no money" (U.S. Congress, 1913).

In 1910 he returned to Puerto Rico with steamers, and after facing ferocious competition from both the New York and Puerto Rico Steamship Company and the Insular Line,* he bought the latter and thereby assured the Bull Line a long-term place in the shipping of that island. He remained president of the company until his death on 13 February 1920, when he was replaced by his son Ernest Miller Bull.*

References: *National Cyclopedia of American Biography.* vol. 32; U.S. Congress, House, Committee on Merchant Marine and Fisheries, *Investigation of Shipping Combinations*, 4 vols. (Washington, DC: Government Printing Office, 1913).

BULL, EDWARD MYRON, 31 March 1904–4 June 1953. E. Myron Bull was the president of the Bull Line* in 1943–1953. He was born in Cranford, New Jersey, on 31 March 1904, and his father was Ernest Miller Bull.* E. Myron graduated from Cornell University in 1926 and received his law degree from Yale in 1929. Initially he worked for law firms, but in 1933 he joined the Bull Line as general counsel and vice president. When his father died in 1943, E. Myron became the head of the company; as a third-generation president, E. Myron was a very rare case in the history of U.S. merchant shipping.

The task of the return to peacetime operations fell squarely on E. Myron. To restore the company's service to Puerto Rico, he took advantage of the Ship Sales Act of 1946* and purchased thirteen vessels to replace those lost during the war. When the Bull Line attempted to revive the prewar coastwise* service, however, competition from the railroads produced only heavy losses. Henceforth the Bull Line limited its activities to trade between Puerto Rico and the U.S. mainland.

E. Myron decided to consolidate his grip on the Puerto Rico trade by buying out his only competitor, the Clyde-Mallory Line (a subsidiary of the Atlantic, Gulf & West Indies Steamship Lines* [AGWI]) in 1949. This was a wise move, but with the purchase came the combination passenger-cargo ship *Borinquen*, which was losing money. Rather than sell the ship, E. Myron fell prey to the passenger-ship myth and poured huge sums of money into her conversion into a first-class passenger liner renamed the *Puerto Rico*, which also carried express freight. The *Puerto Rico* sailed in August 1949, but heavy losses forced the layup of the ship in March 1953. E. Myron Bull never recovered from the staggering failure of the passenger service, and on 4 June 1953, when he was only forty-nine, he died of a heart attack. The losses also were a blow to the Bull family, and three years later it had no choice but to sell off the Bull Line.

References: John S. Blank, "Fifty Years to the Indies," *Ships and the Sea*, July 1952, pp. 50–57. René De La Pedraja, *The Rise and Decline of U.S. Merchant Shipping in the Twentieth Century* (New York: Twayne, 1992); *National Cyclopedia of American Biography*, current vol. G; *New York Times*, 5 June 1953.

BULL, ERNEST MILLER, 2 October 1875–6 October 1943. Ernest Miller Bull was the president of the Bull Line* in 1920–1943. He was born in Elizabeth, New Jersey, on 2 October 1875, and his father was Archibald H. Bull.* Ernest Miller graduated from Cornell University in 1898 and became the first vice president of the Bull Line when his father created the company in 1902. When his father died in 1920, Ernest became president.

As head of the company, Ernest Miller faced two new situations. First was the operation of the two Shipping Board* lines, one to West Africa and another to the Black Sea ports. Except for occasional calls in the Dominican Republic, the Bull Line had not previously ventured into the foreign trade routes, so consequently the experiment with these subsidized foreign services proved short-lived. The Shipping Board withdrew the Black Sea ports line in August 1924 and the West Africa line in 1928. Second, Ernest Miller faced in 1923 a more direct danger when the Puerto Rico-American Line appeared to provide service from Baltimore to the island. After intense competition, the new steamship company sold itself to the Bull Line in 1925.

No more rivals challenged the Bull Line's position in Puerto Rico, and its fleet gradually increased until the company owned thirty-two in 1941. When the United States entered World War II, all the company's vessels were requisitioned. On 6 October 1943 Ernest Miller died, and he was succeeded in the presidency by his son E. Myron Bull.*

References: *Mast Magazine*, November 1949; *Nautical Gazette*, 30 May 1925; *National Cyclopedia of American Biography*, vol. 32.

BULL LINE or A. H. BULL STEAMSHIP COMPANY, 1902–1963. Archibald H. Bull,* the founder of the New York & Puerto Rico Steamship Co.,* had been forced in 1900 to sell his shares in the company and had bound himself not to run steamers to Puerto Rico for ten years. He could not stay away from the steamship business, and in 1902 he incorporated the Bull Steamship Company to operate steamers on the coastwise* trade between Florida and New York and sailing vessels to Puerto Rico. In 1910 he placed steamers in the Puerto Rico service and soon was locked in bitter competition with the Insular Line* and with the New York & Puerto Rico Steamship Co., the latter since 1907 a subsidiary of the powerful Atlantic, Gulf & West Indies Steamship Lines.* In 1914 the Bull Line bought the Insular Line, while the New York & Puerto Rico

Steamship Co. and the Bull Line learned to coexist as the two U.S.-flag firms that largely monopolized the Puerto Rico service until 1949.

The Shipping Board* requisitioned Bull Line's fleet for service during World War I. With the return of peace, the firm purchased seven surplus vessels to resume its service to Puerto Rico. The Shipping Board also made the Bull Line one of the "managing operators"* to run government vessels. Bull received two routes, one to West Africa and another to Black Sea ports. In 1922 the Shipping Board added Constantinople to the Black Sea route, but in August 1924, as part of the process of consolidating routes, the Shipping Board assigned the Constantinople and Black Sea ports to the American Export Lines.* The Shipping Board left the Bull Line as managing operator of the West African service until 1928.

The appearance of the the Puerto Rico–American Steamship Company in 1923 challenged Bull's grip on the island's trade. This new firm provided service from Baltimore and was partially funded by Puerto Rican merchants and shippers.* The service proved unprofitable, and the owners of the Puerto Rico–American Steamship Company agreed to merge with the Bull Line in May 1925.

When the Shipping Board took the West African service away from the Bull Line in 1928, the company was back to its prewar pattern of operating ships to Puerto Rico and to other ports on the East Coast of the United States, with only an occasional foreign call at the Dominican Republic. When World War II began, the company owned a fleet of thirty-two freighters, twenty of which were lost during the war when the government requisitioned all the vessels. With the return of peace, the Bull Line bought thirteen vessels under the Ship Sales Act of 1946* for operation in the Puerto Rican route. The company tried to return to the coastwise service, but heavy losses in those routes because of competition from the railroads forced the company to abandon what had been one of its two prewar foundations.

With nowhere else to turn, the Bull Line decided to invest heavily in the Puerto Rico service. The company received three ships in 1949, when it bought the New York and Puerto Rico Steamship Co. from AGWI. This purchase not only gave the Bull Line (now with twenty-three vessels) a near-monopoly share of the Puerto Rican steamship business but also brought a passenger liner into the service, the *Borinquen*, now renamed the *Puerto Rico*. The ship had been a money loser for AGWI, but Bull Line decided that with a major overhaul the *Puerto Rico* could become profitable. After undergoing "one of the greatest streamlinings any ship has ever received" (Blank 1952), the *Puerto Rico* became "a completely first-class passenger ship" (Tennant 1949) for 199 passengers in seventy-four staterooms, unlike the *Borinquen*, which had carried 370 passengers in 101 cabins. The new staterooms held three passengers, but to increase their attractiveness, the line considered them filled when occupied by two persons of the same family. The *Puerto Rico* sailed in August 1949, but in spite of swimming pools and many new amenities, airline competition proved too strong and the ship's last voyage to Puerto Rico was in March 1953. Subsequently the Bull Line sold the vessel, but only after having taken a very heavy loss in the whole passenger venture.

The passenger ship had diverted the Bull Line from containers,* and by the time the company regularly began to use large steel vans in 1955, it was too late to remedy past mistakes. The new heir of the company, W. A. Kiggins, Jr., decided to sell the Bull Line while it was worth something, and taking advantage of the momentary surge in shipping during the Suez crisis, he sold the firm to American Coal Shipping in 1956. In 1961 a new competitor in the Puerto Rico service, Sea-Land,* wanted to buy the Bull Line, but the threat of antitrust action led American Coal Shipping to accept the offer from the Greek shipping magnate Manuel K. Kulukundis. Through these transfers the name and house flag of Bull Lines had continued in use, but when Kulukundis's companies went into bankruptcy proceedings in 1963, the history of the Bull Line ended completely.

Notable Ship

Puerto Rico; formerly,	1949–1951
Borinquen	

Principal Executives

Archibald H. Bull	1902–1920
Ernest M. Bull	1920–1943
E. Myron Bull	1943–1953
W. A. Kiggins, Jr.	1953–1956
Manuel E. Kulukundis	1961–1963

References: James P. Baughman, *The Mallorys of Mystic: Six Generations in American Maritime Enterprise* (Middletown, CT: Wesleyan University Press, 1972); John S. Blank, "Fifty Years to the Indies," *Ships and the Sea*, July 1952, pp. 50–57; René De La Pedraja, *The Rise and Decline of U.S. Merchant Shipping in the Twentieth Century* (New York: Twayne, 1992); President's Advisory Committee on the Merchant Marine, Harry S. Truman Presidential Library, Independence, Missouri; Record Group 32, National Archives, Washington, DC; *New York Times*, 5 March and 17 June 1953, 13 December 1956, 14 December 1959, 29 March and 22 April 1961; John K. Tennant, "Bull Line," *Mast Magazine* November 1949, pp. 4–10; *Wall Street Journal*, 20 March 1963.

BUNKERS and BUNKERING. *Bunkers* originally referred to the space reserved in tanks or holds for the carriage of the ship's coal. Soon the word took the additional meaning of the fuel itself, and hence came the verb form *bunkering*, or loading the bunkers; in the nineteenth century the term *bunkers* was synonymous with the word *coal*. All space used for bunkers reduced the earning capacity of the vessel, and thus the shipowner tried to keep the bunker area to a minimum in order to maximize income, but when the ship was regularly on service to coal-poor regions, the owner often found it advisable to load larger bunkers to save money and also to avoid any interruptions in the vessel's schedule because of coal shortages.

During the nineteenth century loading the ships' bunkers with coal was one of the most time-consuming and labor-intensive duties; if necessary the whole crew was put to work on the task, in addition to the shore gangs. Starting in the 1910s oil began to replace coal as the principal fuel for steamers, and the transition was virtually complete by World War II. Besides easier handling, oil reduced considerably the space needed for bunkers and also for the crew because fewer persons were needed to feed the fuel to the engines. Since 1945 bunkers and bunker fuel have been synonyms for the oil consumed aboard steamers and diesel ships.

BUREAU OF MARINE INSPECTION AND NAVIGATION (BMIN), 1932–1946. The Bureau of Marine Inspection and Navigation (BMIN) had as its principal duties the shipping and discharge of seamen, the enrollment and inspection of vessels in U.S. registry,* and the certification of deck and engine officers. The BMIN emerged from the consolidation authorized by Congress on 30 June 1932 of the Steamboat Inspection Service* and the Bureau of Navigation and Steamboat Inspection, whose name was changed by Congress to BMIN on 27 May 1934. The burning and subsequent shipwreck of the *Morro Castle** off Asbury Park, New Jersey, on 8 September 1934 exposed major flaws in the procedures for certifying vessels and personnel, and not surprisingly the pressure for changes in the BMIN mounted.

The idea gained ground that civilian control by boards and other consultative methods was unsuited for the rigors of maritime duty and that only a strict military system could guarantee lives and property on the seas. The opportunity to begin the overhaul came with the U.S. entry into World War II, when the executive order of 28 February 1942 placed BMIN under the Coast Guard,* with the exception of vessel documentation, which returned to the Bureau of Customs of the Treasury Department. The old entrenched civilian bureaucracy refused to accept new changes in navigation but, because of the extreme shortage of qualified personnel, the Coast Guard had to content itself with putting uniforms on the former civilians who still refused to change their ways. The uniformed bureaucrats and the labor unions expected the return to civilian control after the war, when "out of a clear sky on 16 May 1946 Reorganization Plan No. 3" (*Congressional Record*, 26 July 1946) abolished the BMIN, whose functions were permanently assumed by the Coast Guard. A bill to halt this transfer passed in the House but failed in the Senate, thus nearly 100 years of civilian supervision over vessels and seafarers came to a final end in the United States.

References: *Congressional Record*, 26 July 1946; Frank F. Farrar, *A Ship's Log Book* (Saint Petersburg, FL: Great Outdoors Publishing Co., 1988); Robert L. Scheina, "U.S. Coast Guard," in Donald R. Whitnah, ed., *Government Agencies* (Westport, CT: Greenwood Press, 1983); H. C. Shepheard, "History of United States Navigation and Vessel

Inspection Laws,'' in Society of Naval Architects and Marine Engineers, *Historical Transactions, 1893–1943* (Westport, CT: Greenwood Press, 1981); U.S. National Archives, *Guide to the National Archives of the United States* (Washington, DC: Government Printing Office, 1974); *U.S. Statutes at Large*, vol. 47 (1932).

BUREAU OF NAVIGATION, 1884–1932. The Bureau of Navigation, the second agency of the U.S. government created to supervise the merchant marine, was primarily concerned during its existence with the shipping and discharge of seamen and with the enrollment of vessels in U.S. registry,* including their sale, transfer, and change of names. The Bureau of Navigation had its origin in the position of shipping commissioners that was created by an act of Congress of 7 June 1872 to handle the discharge and hiring of seamen and thereby relieve the judicial system of a large number of cases. Federal Circuit courts appointed the shipping commissioners, who operated as officers of the court and were under the supervision of the federal judges. The shipping commissioners received no salary and instead charged the owners fees for shipping and discharging the seamen.

The need to place the shipping commissioners under the executive, rather than the judicial, branch became pressing, and on 26 June 1884 Congress transferred the authority over the shipping commissioners to the secretary of the treasury, and in another act on 5 July 1884 formally established within the Department of Treasury the Bureau of Navigation, to be headed by the commissioner of navigation appointed by the president with the consent of the Senate. The new bureau also assumed all the functions previously performed by other bureaus of the Department of the Treasury relating to the enrollment of merchant vessels under U.S. registry,* such as their sale, transfer, mortgage, and change of names, as well as the collection of tonnage duties. The Bureau of Navigation also published annually the list of merchant vessels under the U.S. flag.

Shipping commissioners continued to receive fees from shipowners for the discharge and hiring of seamen until Congress, by an act of 19 June 1886, abolished this practice, so conducive to collusion. As a dependency of the Treasury Department, the Bureau of Navigation continued to function smoothly until it was transferred to the newly created Department of Commerce and Labor on 14 February 1903, and when the latter split into two on 4 March 1913, the Bureau of Navigation remained within the Department of Commerce. However, the transfer from the Treasury Department proved to be unwise, because the activities of the bureau ''involved close relations with the collectors of customs and cooperation at times with the customs division, special agents, and other branches of the Treasury service'' (Short 1923). Only twelve ports had shipping commissioners, while in the rest of the ports customs officers handled the shipping and discharge of seamen. Without the personnel or resources to enforce the laws, ''the Bureau of Navigation is, in fact, hardly more than the direct agency of the Secretary of Commerce for supervising the enforcement of the navigation laws by officers of the Customs Service'' (Thorpe 1925).

The Bureau of Navigation appeared to have found a meaningful, independent function when it received from the Department of Commerce, in 1910, the task of ensuring that all vessels had wireless or radio-telegraphs properly installed and maintained in good working condition. A Radio Service was organized and was responsible for much of the bureau's growth in later years, but when the Radio Service was removed in 1927, the bureau contracted. A partial substitute function for the bureau was the new task of enforcing the load lines* in accordance with the Act of 2 March 1929 and the International Load Line Convention of 1930.

The La Follette Seamen's Act of 1915* had added some additional functions to the Bureau of Navigation, whose duties increasingly blurred with those of another agency, the Steamboat Inspection Service.* In an economy move dictated by the Great Depression, Congress on 30 June 1932 ordered the consolidation of these two agencies into the Bureau of Navigation and Steamboat Inspection, whose name was changed by Congress on 27 May 1936 to the Bureau of Marine Inspection and Navigation.*

References: H. C. Shepheard, "History of United States Navigation and Vessel Inspection Laws," in Society of Naval Architects and Marine Engineers, *Historical Transactions, 1892–1943* (Westport, CT: Greenwood Press, 1981); Lloyd M. Short, *The Bureau of Navigation: Its History, Activities, and Organization* (Baltimore: Johns Hopkins University Press, 1923); George C. Thorpe, *Federal Departmental Organization and Practice: The Executive Departments, Bureaus and Independent Establishments of the United States Government* (Kansas City, MO: Vernon Law Book, 1925); *U.S. Statutes at Large*, vol. 47 (1962); Carroll H. Woody, *The Growth of the Federal Government, 1915–1932* (New York: McGraw-Hill, 1934).

C

C-1. The C-1 was one of the standard types of vessels (C stand for *cargo*) that the U.S. Maritime Commission* designed right before World War II for construction in series, and as in the other types, the shipowners could still select various models within the same basic design. The commission was trying to repeat the successful experience of the Shipping Board* with the production of similar vessel designs for World War I, in particular the Hog Islander,* and wanted to achieve savings in time and money (or "economies of scale") by mass-producing the same type of vessel. At all costs the commission wanted to avoid the normal practice of steamship companies of ordering small numbers of custom-made vessels suited only to particular trades. With the standard ship types, the U.S. Maritime Commission also aimed to take the lead in marine architecture, by designing a vastly superior ship that would surpass all other vessels then in existence.

The C-1 was the smallest of the three original vessel designs, and answered the need for a small, highly versatile vessel that could operate either as a tramp* or on trade routes where speed was not a premium. Within the C-1 there were four types, all of which were 418 feet long, or 42 feet less than the C-2, and a beam of 60 feet or 3 feet less than that of the C-2. The four-C-1 types varied in deadweight* tons from 6,200 to 8,000. The C-1 at 14 knots was supposed to be slower than the C-2 at 15.5 knots, however, in practice the C-1 was routinely logging 16 knots, making the speed difference inconsequential. Although many shipowners had wanted to install only the simpler steam turbines* on the C-1s, shortages of turbines forced the commission to place diesel* engines in many of the C-1s built during the war. The U.S. Maritime Commission built a total of 173 C-1s, and only 16 were lost during the war. Under the provisions of the Ship Sales Act of 1946,* U.S. shipowners bought 23 C-1s and foreign owners bought 48, the rest going into the National Defense Reserve Fleet.*

References: John A. Culver, *Ships of the U.S. Merchant Fleet* (Weymouth, MA: Denison Press, 1965; William Kooiman, *The Grace Ships, 1869–1969* (Point Reyes, CA: Komar, 1990); Carl D. Lane, *What the Citizen Should Know About the Merchant Marine* (New York: W. W. Norton, 1941); Frederick C. Lane, *Ships for Victory: A History of Shipbuilding Under the U.S. Maritime Commission in World War II* (Baltimore: Johns Hopkins University Press, 1951); L. A. Sawyer and W. H. Mitchell, *From America to United States*, 4 vols. (Kendal, England: World Ship Society, 1979–1986).

C-1-M. The needs of the war in the Pacific against Japan forced the U.S. Maritime Commission* to create a different type of vessel based on its earlier C-1* design. The vast distances in the Pacific and the many shallow harbors and bays required a short, versatile vessel with low fuel consumption and an ability to travel long distances without refueling. At the same time, the U.S. Maritime Commission wanted to avoid at all costs the disastrous experience of the Liberty* ships and wanted instead a sturdy vessel that would have many years of profitable commercial service once the war was over. With a length of 320 feet (nearly 100 feet less than the C-1, the next biggest vessel size) and a beam of 50 feet (10 feet less than the C-1), the C-1-M was the smallest of the cargo types of the U.S. Maritime Commission. All the vessels used a diesel* engine, the only one capable of providing the required economies of space and fuel for this vessel of 5,000 deadweight* tons whose speed was 11 knots.

The U.S. Maritime Commission delivered 239 of the C-1-M vessels. Foreign buyers found the vessels attractive because of the low operational cost, while in the United States the C-1-Ms were candidates for conversion to a variety of functions, ranging from floating plants, to barges and to the first LNG* ship. Generally, however, U.S. shipowners considered the C-1-M too small and never felt comfortable with the diesel that required the training of a new engine crew.

References: John A. Culver, *Ships of the U.S. Merchant Fleet* (Weymouth, MA: Denison Press, 1965); William Kooiman, *The Grace Ships, 1869–1969* (Point Reyes, CA: Komar, 1990); Frederick C. Lane, *Ships for Victory: A History of Shipbuilding Under the U.S. Maritime Commission in World War II* (Baltimore: Johns Hopkins University Press, 1951); L. A. Sawyer and W. H. Mitchell, *From America to United States*, 4 vols. (Kendal, England: World Ship Society, 1979–1986).

C-2. The C-2 was one of the standard types of vessels (C stands for *cargo*) that the U.S. Maritime Commission* designed right before World War II for construction in series, and as in the other types, the shipowners could still select various models within the same basic design. The World War I experience of the Shipping Board,* which has successfully built standard ship types, in particular the Hog Islander,* inspired the U.S. Maritime Commission, which wanted to save time, resources, and money by mass-producing the same type of vessel, in contrast to the preference of the individual steamship companies for ordering small numbers of specially designed freighters. With the standard ship types, the commission also wanted to gain for the United States the lead in marine architecture, by designing and imposing on world trade ships vastly superior to any vessel then in operation.

The C-2 represented a definite advance over the vessels of World War I, and not surprisingly, among American shipowners the C-2 was the most popular ship type. With a speed of 15.5 knots, the C-2s were faster and more economical than the World War I vessels, and in a major break with tradition, the crew quarters were moved from the forecastle* to amidships; for the first time seafarers enjoyed decent and ample living space, a previously unheard-of luxury. The C-2s had a length of 460 feet and a beam of 63 feet; the diesel* version was 8,700 deadweight tons and the steam turbine* version was 9,800 deadweight tons. Many other improvements and innovations made the C-2 the pride of the American merchant marine, and the U.S. Maritime Commission considered the C-2s its finest vessel design. After the war U.S. companies purchased many of these vessels under the Ship Sales Act of 1946,* and the C-2 remained their favorite freighter until the late 1950s. Because they had been built so sturdily, many remained in service until the 1970s, and some were even converted to carry containers,* like the *Mayagüez.*

References: John A. Culver, *Ships of the U.S. Merchant Fleet* (Weymouth, MA: Denison Press, 1965); Carl D. Lane, *What the Citizen Should Know About the Merchant Marine* (New York: W. W. Norton, 1941); Frederick C. Lane, *Ships for Victory: A History of Shipbuilding Under the U.S. Maritime Commission in World War II* (Baltimore: Johns Hopkins University Press, 1951); L. A. Sawyer and W. H. Mitchell, *From America to United States*, 4 vols. (Kendal, England: World Ship Society, 1979–1986).

C-3. The C-3 was one of the standard types of vessels (C stands for *cargo*) that the U.S. Maritime Commission* designed right before World War II for construction in series, and as in the other types, the shipowners could still select various models within the same basic design. The commission was trying to repeat the successful experience of the Shipping Board* with the production of similar vessel designs for World War I, in particular the Hog Islander,* and wanted to achieve savings in time and money (or economies of scale) by mass-producing the same type of vessel. At all costs the commission wanted to avoid the normal practice of steamship companies of ordering small numbers of custom-made vessels suited only to particular trades. With the standard ship types, the U.S. Maritime Commission also aimed to take the lead in marine architecture, by designing a vastly superior ship that would surpass all other vessels then in existence.

The most successful design had been that of the C-2,* but the commission realized that a vessel with a larger capacity and faster speed was also required in many trade routes. The C-3 had a length of 492 feet, 32 more than the C-2, and had a beam of 70 feet, 7 more than the C-2. The steam C-3s were of 12,500 deadweight* tons, compared with the 9,800 deadweight tons on the steam C-2s. In speed, the C-3s were a knot faster than the 15.5 knots of the C-2s, but in practice many of the C-3s had even higher speeds than their supposed 16.5 knots. For marine propulsion,* the C-3s were fitted as available with either diesel* engines or steam turbines;* the diesel C-3s had 500 less deadweight tons than the steam version. The U.S. Maritime Commission sold most of the C-3s after the war under the provisions of the Ship Sales Act of 1946.* U.S. companies preferred the more familiar turbine vessels, while foreign buyers eagerly snapped up the diesel C-3s, whose low-cost operation made them formidable competitors in the world's trade routes.

References: John A. Culver, *Ships of the U.S. Merchant Fleet* (Weymouth, MA: Denison Press, 1965); Mark H. Goldberg, *Caviar & Cargo: The C-3 Passenger Ships* (Kings Point, NY: American Merchant Marine Museum, 1992); Carl D. Lane, *What the Citizen Should Know About the Merchant Marine* (New York: W. W. Norton, 1941); Frederick C. Lane, *Ships for Victory: A History of Shipbuilding Under the U.S. Maritime Commission in World War II* (Baltimore: Johns Hopkins University Press, 1951); L. A. Sawyer and W. H. Mitchell, *From America to United States*, 4 vols. (Kendal, England: World Ship Society, 1979–1986).

CABOTAGE. Cabotage has been the policy of reserving the trade along a country's coast to the ships of its registry. Cabotage and cargo preference* have been the two most widely used methods of supporting a nation's merchant marine without the actual payment of subsidies. Cabotage, which comes from the Spanish *cabo* or cape, originally meant navigation between capes, and gradually took on the wider meaning of merchant shipping along the coast of one country. Cabotage dated back to mercantilist practices of the seventeenth century, such as the Navigation Acts, and has remained a fairly widespread practice among the nations of the world.

The United States has pushed to the limits the meaning of the concept. In 1817 Congress adopted its first law excluding foreign ships from the trade between U.S. ports, and subsequent legislation has confirmed and amplified this exclusive privilege. Since 1920 the dominant law in cabotage has been the Jones Act.* The United States applied the principle of cabotage not only to trade along the coast, generally referred to as "coastwise,"* but also to trade between the East and West coasts, generally referred to as "intercoastal."* After the annexation of territories in the Pacific Ocean and the Caribbean, Congress extended the cabotage privileges to all trade between the United States and its new overseas possessions.

There have been exemptions, however, most notably the Philippines, which in spite of annexation to the United States in 1898, was never covered by the cabotage privilege. During World War I, the Shipping Board* allowed the entry of foreign vessels into the coastwise and intercoastal trades, and the existing laws have authorized the government to wave the cabotage privileges in times of emergency. The Virgin Islands, because of their particular status as a free port, have remained exempt from cabotage since 1936, so foreign ships may freely carry cargoes between the islands and the U.S. mainland. Last, the United States has never extended cabotage to include voyages by foreign ships leaving and returning at the same port, so that since the 1960s foreign cruise ships freely return to their U.S. port of departure. These "voyages to nowhere," as they were dubbed during Prohibition* years, became quite popular in the 1920s as thousands flocked to foreign-flag ships to enjoy both the beauties of the ocean and alcoholic beverages.

Since the 1980s proposals to repeal the cabotage laws of the United States have surfaced, because shippers* were eager to obtain the lower rates that foreign vessels could offer if allowed into the coastwise and intercoastal trades, but the precipitous decline of the U.S. merchant marine makes any abandonment of the cabotage principles highly unlikely.

References: Ernst G. Frankel, *Regulation and Policies of American Shipping* (Boston: Auburn House, 1982); Gerald R. Jantscher, *Bread upon the Waters: Federal Aids to the Maritime Industries* (Washington, DC: Brookings Institution, 1975); Clinton H. Whitehurst, Jr., *The U.S. Shipbuilding Industry: Past, Present, and Future* (Annapolis, MD: Naval Institute Press, 1986); Paul M. Zeis, *American Shipping Policy* (Princeton, NJ: Princeton University Press, 1938).

CALIFORNIA, OREGON, **and** *PANAMA*, 1848–1870. The wooden side-wheelers *California, Oregon,* and *Panama,* were the first three steamers of the Pacific Mail Steamship Company* (PMSS), which had been founded in April 1848 by William Henry Aspinwall. PMSS ordered these ships from New York City shipyards, and they were finished by the end of 1848. The ships had been built, and indeed PMSS itself had been created, in response to the U.S. Navy's offer to subsidize a mail service between the Pacific side of Panama and the Columbia River in the Oregon territory. In accordance with the mail contract, the steamers incorporated military features so that in time of emergency they could easily be converted to naval auxiliaries. As usual for this time, the wooden vessels were fully rigged for sail should the single-expansion engine* break down or run out of coal. The 200-foot-long ships had been designed primarily to carry cargo, although they also had passenger accommodations initially just for sixty persons; later the company added space for steerage* class as well.

News of the discovery of gold in California had unleashed a gold rush fever in New York City in December 1848, so that by the time the three ships rounded South America on the way to California, crowds of passengers were waiting to board the ships in Peru and in Panama. The *California,* also the first U.S. steamer to cross the Straits of Magellan, was the first of the three to reach San Francisco on 28 February 1849, and immediately the passengers, crew, and officers ran to the gold fields; only the timely intervention of the U.S. Navy saved the nearly deserted ship from being wrecked. The *California* soon was joined by the *Oregon* and the *Panama* in the regular run between the Pacific Coast of Panama and Oregon, and for years the California gold rush guaranteed the ships overflowing loads of cargo and passengers. PMSS ordered better and larger ships for the trade and sold the *Oregon* and the *Panama* in 1861, the *California* in 1870. PMSS, whose initial investment had appeared risky, had latched onto one of the most lucrative routes of world shipping, and not surprisingly the extraordinary profits from the venture with the first three ships launched the long career of this remarkable steamship company.

References: Erik Heyl, *Early American Steamers*, 6 vols. (Buffalo, NY: 1953–1969); John H. Kemble, *The Panama Route, 1848–1869* (Berkeley: University of California Press, 1943).

CALIFORNIA, PENNSYLVANIA, and *VIRGINIA, 1928–1938*. These three combination cargo-passenger liners were the first ships in the world with turboelectric drive (see marine propulsion*). The International Mercantile Marine* (IMM) ordered these three large ships (overall length of 601 feet and beam of 80) for the intercoastal* service; besides carrying cargo, the liners each carried 384 persons in first class and 363 in tourist class. The demand for intercoastal passenger travel had greatly increased because of the Supreme Court decision that limited Prohibition* to the territorial waters of the United States; hence liners like the *California*, *Pennsylvania*, and *Virginia* served alcoholic beverages while on the high seas or when calling in foreign ports like Havana. The *California* entered service in January 1928, the *Virginia* in December 1928, and the *Pennsylvania* in October 1929, and initially they made profitable voyages for IMM. However, with the onset of the Great Depression, the three vessels started to show losses in 1931, and when Prohibition was repealed on 5 December 1933, a powerful incentive to travel aboard the liners disappeared. The ships at a speed of eighteen knots were very slow for passenger liners and certainly did not justify the huge investment in turboelectric drive, which quickly went out of favor with shipowners.

Only generous mail subsidies under the Merchant Marine Act of 1928* kept these ships in service, but when Congress in the Merchant Marine Act of 1936* ordered the cancellation of the mail contracts and their replacement by operating differential subsidies,* IMM strove to transfer the ships out of the intercoastal trade, which no longer qualified for subsidies, and into the New York–South America route still eligible to receive the new operating differential subsidy. IMM attempted to buy the bankrupt Munson Steamship Company* to obtain the latter's South American routes for the *California*, *Pennsylvania*, and *Virginia*, but fears of a monopoly convinced the U.S. Maritime Commission* to block the acquisition. IMM was left stuck with the three liners, which since March 1936 had also become entangled in labor disputes led by Joseph Curran,* the future creator and leader of the National Maritime Union.* IMM decided to cut its losses and in 1938 sold the three ships to the U.S. Maritime Commission, which shortly after, chartered them to Moore-McCormack* for operation as the Good Neighbor Fleet.*

References: René De La Pedraja, *The Rise and Decline of U.S. Merchant Shipping in the Twentieth Century* (New York: Twayne, 1992); Frederick E. Emmons, *American Passenger Ships: The Ocean Lines and Liners, 1873–1983* (Newark: University of Delaware Press, 1985); National Maritime Union, *On a True Course: The Story of the National Maritime Union AFL-CIO* (New York: NMU, 1968).

CALMAR STEAMSHIP COMPANY, 1927–1976. Bethlehem Steel Corporation, the second largest steel company in the United States and at one time also the second largest in the world, operated this subsidiary to provide service in the intercoastal* trade. Bethlehem Steel had been operating ore carriers since before World War I through another subsidiary, the Ore Steamship Company, but Bethlehem was forced to enter the intercoastal trade because United States Steel (the nation's largest steel company), through its Isthmian Line* subsidiary, was underquoting steel prices in the West Coast. The Calmar Steamship Company, originally in a combined operation with Moore-McCormack,* carried steel products westward and returned with lumber from the Pacific for the East Coast. Unlike Ore Steamship Company, which was a pure proprietary* company because it carried only the cargoes of Bethlehem Steel, Calmar was a proprietary carrier only in the westbound leg, while in the eastbound voyages it was a common or public carrier because it solicited cargo from shippers,* generally lumber companies.

In the late 1940s Calmar was one of five steamship companies Bethlehem operated with considerable overlap in management; for example H. W. Warley was the president for all five, and at that time one of them, Ore Steamship, owned eight 24,000-deadweight*-ton carriers, while Calmar purchased eight Liberty* ships for the intercoastal route. In making extensive alterations in the Liberty ships in the late 1940s, Calmar verified once more the World War II discovery that containers* slashed expenses and time in port, but it did not adopt them because the cargo Bethlehem Steel's ships normally carried—ores, steel, and lumber—was least suited for containers. Calmar maintained its intercoastal service until 1976, when it halted operations. However, Bethlehem was still not out of merchant shipping and continued to own bulk* ships through another subsidiary, the Interocean Shipping Company. Interocean Shipping still owned two carriers in 1985 but sold the last one in 1986, when apparently other corporate priorities ended Bethlehem Steel's direct investment in merchant shipping.

References: Maritime Administration, *Foreign Flag Merchant Ships Owned by U.S. Parent Companies*, 1983, 1985, 1986, and 1992; *Nautical Gazette*, 3 September 1927; President's Advisory Committee on the Merchant Marine, Harry S. Truman Presidential Library, Independence, Missouri.

CARGO PREFERENCE or PREFERENCE CARGOES. In world shipping cargo preference has meant the practice of requiring that a certain percentage, amount, or type of cargo has to move aboard the ships of a specific country. Cargo preference, most frequently applied as a percentage requirement, has been a very powerful tool to support the expansion of merchant fleets in the world, for example, those in Latin America. In the United States, cargo preference has taken a more narrow definition and in practice has referred only to the requirement that a certain percentage of U.S.-government cargoes have to travel aboard U.S.-flag ships. Thus while the essence of foreign cargo preference laws has been to require the use of ships of one country even if the shippers* did not want to, the United States has always hesitated to introduce this element of compulsion. The nearest the United States ever came to having a cargo preference law in the world model was the Energy Transportation bill of 1974, which required that 30 percent of oil imports be carried aboard U.S.-flag tankers, but President Gerald Ford vetoed that bill, which never became law. Consequently, all other cargo preference acts of the United States have applied only to official cargoes, including those financed by, or otherwise connected to, the government.

The Military Transportation Act of 1904,* still in force, was the first cargo preference law of the United States, while the most important statute was the Cargo Preference Act of 1954.* In these laws the United States established minimum requirements for carrying government cargoes aboard U.S.-flag ships, and many foreign countries likewise reserved their government cargoes for their own fleets. However, the United States appears to be one of the few, if not the only country, that also required that part of the government cargoes travel aboard *privately* owned ships, a distinction introduced by the Cargo Preference Act of 1954. This last requirement was specifically introduced by the steamship companies to limit the activities of the Military Sealift Command* (MSC). In general this has meant considerably higher costs because the ships of the MSC have traditionally enjoyed lower operating costs than the privately owned fleet. (See also Wilson-Weeks Agreement.) While other countries of the world have generally given a wider scope than the United States to cargo preference, the practice of this mercantilist principle shows no sign of disappearing in the coming decades.

References: René De La Pedraja, *The Rise and Decline of U.S. Merchant Shipping in the Twentieth Century* (New York: Twayne, 1992); Ernst G. Frankel, *Regulation and Policies of American Shipping* (Boston: Auburn House, 1982); Gerald R. Jantscher, *Bread upon the Waters: Federal Aids to the Maritime Industries* (Washington, DC: Brookings Institution, 1975).

CARGO PREFERENCE ACT OF 1954. The Cargo Preference Act of 1954 has been the principal statute governing cargo preference* in the United States. This law, approved on 26 August 1954, required that at least 50 percent of all government-owned or financed cargoes move aboard *privately* owned U.S.-flag vessels. Most countries have laws reserving government cargoes for ships of their nationality, but the 1954 act broke new ground by specifying that the ships be privately owned; the law complemented, but did not repeal, the other major cargo preference statute, the Military Transportation Act of 1904.* The Cargo Preference Act also raised to the level of law the principles of the Wilson-Weeks Agreement* of just two months before; the latter had sharply limited the fleet of the Military Sea Transportation Service* (MSTS), but as only an agreement between two cabinet departments, could have easily been repealed by an administration that was not as staunchly pro-private business as that of Dwight D. Eisenhower.

The U.S. Navy was strongly opposed to the measure because the higher costs of privately owned ships meant a bigger drain on the navy's budget; indeed as originally drafted, the bill would have also eliminated the MSTS. Agricultural groups did not want to lose access to foreign-flag ships in order to keep the price of exported grains competitive, while most government agencies testified against the bill. Pro-business sentiment was so strong during the Eisenhower administration, however, that opponents grudgingly accepted the compromise of requiring only 50 percent of government cargoes to travel aboard privately owned U.S.-flag ships. The impact of this law has been immense, because the Department of Defense, as the biggest shipper* in the United States, provided ample government cargoes to both liner* companies and tramp* vessels. However, this extreme generosity has dulled the fighting spirit of many of the companies, which never were able to compete in world shipping beyond the protective mantle of the U.S. government's programs.

A section in the Food Security Act of 1985 raised the percentage of cargoes that must be shipped aboard U.S.-flag vessels from 50 to 75 percent for certain agricultural exports, but strong opposition from farm groups has made difficult the enforcement of this higher percentage, and compliance with the original 50 percent requirement was never universal.

References: René De La Pedraja, *The Rise and Decline of U.S. Merchant Shipping in the Twentieth Century* (New York: Twayne, 1992); Ernst G. Frankel, *Regulation and Policies of American Shipping* (Boston: Auburn House, 1982); Samuel A. Lawrence, *United States Merchant Shipping Policies and Politics* (Washington, DC: Brookings Institution, 1966); Maritime Administration, *Annual Report 1986; U.S. Statutes at Large,* vol. 68 (1954), vol. 99 (1985).

CARRIAGE OF GOODS BY SEA ACT (COGSA). The Carriage of Goods by Sea Act (COGSA) of 16 April 1936 has been until the present the official law governing an ocean carrier's liability for any damages to the merchandise transported aboard ships in accordance with bills of lading.* COGSA codified in U.S. legislation the concepts of the Hague Rules of 1924, the most important of which were placing a $500 limit on liability per package and the establishment of seventeen "carrier defenses," which effectively placed the burden of proof on the shipper* and not on the shipowner.

Not surprisingly, shippers have been unhappy with COGSA and have pressured for the adoption of the Hamburg Rules of 1978, which removed almost all of the seventeen carrier defenses and shifted the burden of proof to the shipowner. Merchant shipping companies themselves have recognized the need for some change, because the $500 liability became a ridiculously low sum in recent decades, while the introduction of containers* has meant that no matter how many bags were inside a container, the one container counted as a single package. Shipowners favor the Visby Amendments of 1968, which raised carrier liability per package to a significant figure and treated each bag inside a container as an individual package for purposes of liability. In 1989 the Matson Navigation Company* decided to increase the liability of each package inside a container to $1,000, and although this company did not publicly adopt the Visby Agreements, Sea-Land* did in 1991. However, ratification by Congress of the Visby Amendments seems unlikely until shippers drop their demands for the adoption of the Hamburg Rules.

References: *American Shipper*, September 1991; William J. Miller, *Encyclopedia of International Commerce* (Centreville, MD: Cornell Maritime Press, 1985); Transportation Research Board, *Intermodal Marine Container Transportation: Impediments and Opportunities* (Washington, DC: National Research Council, 1992).

CASEY, RALPH E., 25 May 1911–? Ralph E. Casey was the president of the American Merchant Marine Institute* (AMMI) from 1956 to 1969. Casey was born in Boston on 25 May 1911 and studied at Boston Latin School. He was among the most highly educated persons in shipping, because besides graduating from Harvard College in 1932 and from Harvard Law School in 1934, he also received a postgraduate degree in economics and labor law at Georgetown University in 1941. In 1939 he joined the General Accounting Office and left it in 1955 to become chief counsel of the Merchant Marine and Fisheries Committee* of the U.S. House of Representatives.

On 1 May 1956 he assumed the office of president of AMMI, and he was a good example of high government officials who subsequently moved to higher-paying jobs in the private sector. During his long tenure Casey effectively handled relations with Congress and the agencies of the executive branch. His last major task was to conduct the consolidation negotiations that ultimately resulted in the merger of AMMI, the Pacific American Steamship Association,* and the Committee of American Steamship Lines* (CASL) into the new American Institute of Merchant Shipping* (AIMS) on 1 January 1969. Casey headed the new organization for a few months and then entered private practice. In early 1971 he returned to his old job as chief counsel of the Merchant Marine and Fisheries Committee, a position he held until the middle of 1972, when he was replaced by Ernest J. Corrado, a future president of AIMS. Apparently Casey went into retirement after 1972, but he may have remained as an adviser to AIMS or other shipping groups.

References: *New York Times*, 19 January 1969; Propeller Club, *American Merchant Marine Conference Proceedings*, 1961, 1962.

CELLER COMMITTEE, 1959–1960. The Celler Committee was the name given to the investigation that Congressman Emanuel Celler of New York conducted into conferences.* Celler was the chairman of the Committee of the Judiciary and of its Antitrust Subcommittee, which for years had been conducting an ongoing study on ''Monopoly Problems in Regulated Industries.'' The Celler Committee had accustomed the public to a pattern of recurrent revelations and was on the lookout for new industries to target when the Supreme Court in the Isbrandtsen Case* struck down dual rates.* Shippers,* who had always resented the conference system, were afraid that steamship companies would use the Isbrandtsen decision crisis to ram through legislation legalizing once and for all dual rates; shippers felt the Merchant Marine and Fisheries

Committee* was not receptive enough and instead turned to Emanuel Celler, whose antitrust subcommittee was eagerly looking to deliver to a waiting public the next installment in the ongoing drama of monopoly revelations.

Exceeding the zeal of the Black Committee* in 1933–1936, the Celler Committee began a witch-hunt never before or since seen in merchant shipping. While the Black Committee had the specific task of finding out how companies had converted subsidies into private profit, the Celler Committee was free to roam broadly to pursue any supposed antitrust violations. Using its subpoena powers, the Celler Committee searched repeatedly through the files of many U.S. steamship companies and printed large amounts of correspondence and other internal documents of the corporations. It seemed that the innards of the merchant shipping business had been poured out for public inspection, and with tremendous glee the committee paraded before the public any signs of possible collusions to deprive shippers of the lowest rates. Foreign competitors were delighted to see this spectacle of Congress's crucifying in public the American companies then entering a very vulnerable period in their existence. One U.S. executive pointed out the discrepancy: "The records of our dear Japanese friends are not available to us, and presumably not to this committee. I wish they were. That is one of the things that worries us greatly, that we are called before public bodies, made to explain our conduct. But apparently they are not. Perhaps they will be" (U.S. Congress, House, Committee on the Judiciary 1960). The suggestion that the Celler Committee was not being even-handed rankled the members, but, after many fruitless efforts, all they could obtain from foreign companies were some records from the New York office of Holland-America, certainly not enough to dispel the claim that the whole inquiry was nothing but a persecution of American firms.

Herbert C. Bonner* had resented that his Merchant Marine and Fisheries Committee had been bypassed, and he proceeded to hold his own hearings, called the *Steamship Conference Study.* Unlike in the Celler Committee, steamship companies were not condemned beforehand, and the evidence gathered in Bonner's committee began to limit the damage caused by the Celler Committee. The House approved a bill following closely upon the Celler Committee's harsh recommendations, but the Senate, relying more on Bonner's *Steamship Conference Study,* approved a softer bill, which even legalized dual rates under strict conditions. When the House bowed before the Senate version, the political damage from the Celler Committee appeared to have been contained.

The consequences of the Celler Committee did not go away, however. The hearings had been the worst public relations disaster for merchant shipping since the Black Committee, and the public image of the U.S. merchant marine was tarnished for decades to come, while that of foreign competitors escaped virtually intact. Second, the pressure for separating regulation from the other functions of the Maritime Administration* (MARAD) became irresistible, and the findings of the Celler Committee led to Reorganization Plan of 1961, which created a separate agency, the Federal Maritime Commission* (FMC), to regulate conferences. By the late 1960s the FMC was firmly in the hands of the shippers, and it interpreted the existing legislation in such a way as to weaken the conference system; for example, dual rates virtually disappeared, so that through the actions of this regulatory agency the antitrust goal of the Celler Committee was largely achieved.

References: René De La Pedraja, *The Rise and Decline of U.S. Merchant Shipping in the Twentieth Century* (New York: Twayne, 1992); Samuel A. Lawrence, *United States Merchant Shipping Policies and Politics* (Washington, DC: Brookings Institution, 1966); U.S. Congress, House, Committee on the Judiciary, *Monopoly Problems in Regulated Industries: Ocean Freight Industry*, 7 vols. (Washington, DC: Government Printing Office, 1960); U.S. Congress, House, Committee on Merchant Marine and Fisheries, *Steamship Conference Study*, 3 vols. (Washington, DC: Government Printing Office, 1959).

CENTRAL AMERICAN TRANSIT COMPANY, 1860–1868. The Central American Transit Company provided passenger service between New York and California via Nicaragua. The company owned fleets of steamers on the Atlantic and Pacific sides and also maintained roads, hotels, docks, and river steamers to transport the passengers smoothly across Nicaragua to the vessels waiting on the other ocean. The company had been organized in 1860 to restore the passenger service that had been interrupted when its predecessor, the Accessory Transit Company,* lost its contract with the Nicaraguan government in 1857.

The Central American Transit Company found the roads and properties in the country in deplorable condition, and only in October 1862 was the company able to begin transporting passengers across Nicaragua in an irregular intermittent manner, while the resumption of regular passenger service did not come until August 1864. The company was in danger of bankruptcy in 1865, and in order to raise capital for new steamers, the North American Steamship Company was organized as a separate company, but in reality it operated as a disguised subsidiary with the same officers as those of the Central American Transit Company. Unfortunately the average time to go from New York to San Francisco via Nicaragua increased from the twenty-one days under the Accessory Transit Company to twenty-nine days, because of unforeseen events such as the silting of the harbor on the Atlantic and the drying up of the river normally used for navigation. Dredging was out of the question, while the only real solution, the construction of a railway across Nicaragua, was too expensive for investors, who knew how cost overruns had raised the price of the Panama railroad. With transport time across Nicaragua taking at least nine days more than the twenty days via Panama, the Central American Transit Company could attract passengers only by offering lower fares. Travelers were enticed, but the erosion of the financial base was driving the company again to bankruptcy by 1867. The Nicaraguan government meanwhile had used a private claim to secure the cancellation of the original contract, and in anticipation of legal seizures of its properties, the Central American Transit Company had begun to shift the steamers of the North American Steamship Company to the Panama route in November 1867. The company suspended sailings to Nicaragua in April 1868, and in November the North American Steamship Company made the last trips to Panama, prior to the bankruptcy of both companies.

References: David I. Folkman, Jr., *The Nicaragua Route* (Salt Lake City: University of Utah Press, 1972); John H. Kemble, *The Panama Route, 1848–1869* (Berkeley: University of California Press, 1943).

CENTRAL GULF LINES, 1947–present. The Central Gulf Lines was the only one of the steamship companies created in the immediate years after World War II to have survived until the present. The company was incorporated originally as the Central Gulf Steamship Corporation (the present name was adopted in 1972) by Niels F. Johnsen* in April 1947. The company's fleet began with the purchase of a Liberty* vessel renamed the *Green Wave* in honor of Tulane University, the alma mater of his two sons; Johnsen established the pattern of including in the names of all the company's U.S.-flag ships the word *green*, such as in *Green Bay*, *Green Harbour*, and *Green Valley*. In 1949 the company purchased Victory* vessels to begin liner* service and in 1958 inaugurated a liner service from the Gulf and East coasts of the U.S. to the Red Sea, Persian Gulf, India, and Pakistan. With the outbreak of the Vietnam War, the company extended its routes to that country, and the vessels carried mainly military cargoes. Crowded port facilities in Vietnam led the company to develop the LASH* technology, so that a ship carrying barges could lower them into the water, a good way to unload cargo for transport in river systems. Central Gulf Lines began operations with the world's first two LASH vessels in 1969–1970 and ordered three more, which were delivered in 1974–1975. The experience of Central Gulf Lines with this type of vessels was unique, because almost all the other steamship companies suffered irreparable losses and even collapse because of the attempt to operate with LASH vessels. As Erik Johnsen* explained, "LASH barges have 'particular advantages' and success depends upon proper selection of routes and feeder operations" (*American Shipper* 1978).

In 1971 Central Gulf Lines was merged with Trans Union Corporation, which in 1979 spun off the International Shipholding Company; this latter firm held the assets of Central Gulf Lines and its foreign subsidiaries. In principle Central Gulf Lines handled the U.S.-flag vessels, while International Shipholding Company was the holding company for Central Gulf Lines as well as for the foreign-flag subsidiaries. In the 1980s the company began a break-bulk* service to Central America from Gulf ports and in 1987 received two Pure Car Carriers (PCCs) for carrying automobiles between Japan and North America; these two PCCs were under the U.S. flag, while two subsequent ones were under foreign flags. The company wisely did not want to be overexposed in the international market and signed in 1981 and twenty-two-year contract to transport coal from mines in Kentucky and Indiana to a Florida electric utility. In the 1970s the company had operated two bulk* carriers and in 1990 returned to moving bulk cargoes with the purchase of one 148,000-deadweight*-ton bulk carrier. The company has also chartered vessels to the Military Sealift Command* (MSC).

On 30 March 1989 International Shipholding Company purchased Waterman Steamship Corporation,* which was barely recovering from Chapter 11 bankruptcy protection proceedings and was in danger of disappearance. In a major policy change, the Maritime Administration* (MARAD) approved the sale without forcing International Shipholding Corporation to divest itself or foreign-flag holdings, while Waterman Steamship continued to receive the operating differential subsidy.* International Shipholding, whose stock had been traded over the counter since 1979, issued new shares to finance the Waterman acquisition and pay off the latter's debts. In 1990 International Shipholding bought some of its shares and initiated a program to repurchase additional shares "when and if it considers advisable to do so" (International Shipholding Corporation 1990). The Gulf War provided ample business for the company, even including the PCCs. In January 1992 the stock of International Shipholding "made the big leap from being traded over the counter to being listed on the New York Stock Exchange" (*American Shipper* 1992). Central Gulf Lines has been the rare U.S.-flag company that survived without receiving any subsidies prior to 1989, thanks to a combined strategy of meeting niches in the market and also operating a parallel fleet of foreign-flag vessels.

Principal Executives

Niels F. Johnsen	1947–1970
Niels W. Johnsen*	1956–present
Erik F. Johnsen	1956–present

References: *American Shipper*, September 1978, January 1992; *Florida Journal of Commerce*, June 1967; International Shipholding Corporation, *Annual Reports*, 1987–1990; *Journal of Commerce*, 28 April 1988.

CHARTER or CHARTERING. To charter simply means to rent or lease a vessel, and the charterer is the person or firm renting the vessel. Charters generally specified at least two main conditions: the duration and the services the owner of the vessel provided the charterer. Concerning duration, the contract could specify a voyage charter or a set time period, ranging from weeks, to months, to long-term charters of five and ten years in the case of bulk* carriers. Concerning services the owner provided, they ranged from bareboat* charter, in which, as its name implied, the charterer received the vessel "bare," to tramp* operation, whereby the charterer simply specified the destination of the cargo and the shipowner covered all other expenses, including fuel, supplies, provisions, and crew. Chartering has been useful not only to shippers* but also to merchant shipping companies that could expand and contract their fleet size to meet temporary changes in demand without having to bear the fixed costs of vessel ownership.

References: Grover G. Huebner, *Ocean Steamship Traffic Management* (D. Appleton, 1920); Lane C. Kendall, *The Business of Shipping*, 5th ed. (Centreville, MD: Cornell Maritime Press, 1986); William J. Miller, *Encyclopedia of International Commerce* (Centreville, MD: Cornell University Press, 1985).

***CHINA II* or *CHINA*, 1889–1923.** To replace the *City of Tokyo** lost in 1885, Pacific Mail Steamship Company* (PMSS) ordered the *China II*, its only British-built ship, which entered service in 1889. The *China II* was also noteworthy as the only vessel PMSS ordered for the transpacific trade during the years 1875–1902. The ship was built with a steel hull and was the first in the PMSS fleet to have the triple-expansion engine* and could steam as fast as nineteen knots. The normal traveling speed of fifteen knots easily surpassed the company's other ships powered by the compound engine,* and on its first voyage the ship established a westbound record. The *China II* was also the first PMSS ship to be lighted by electricity, but because it still retained its full complement of sails in four masts (rarely used), the ship captured the final fleeting moments of the transition to modern steamers.

As a foreign-built vessel (the only one of PMSS in its entire career), the *China II* did not qualify for U.S. registry* and flew the British flag until 1897, when the ship was registered under the Hawaiian flag. As part of the arrangements for the annexation of Hawaii in 1898, all Hawaiian-flag ships became eligible for U.S. registry, and therefore by this indirect procedure method the *China* (the *II* was dropped by the late 1890s) was able to fly the U.S. flag after 1898.

When PMSS decided to abandon merchant shipping in August 1915, the company sold the *China*, along with the newer *Korea, Siberia,* *Manchuria,** and *Mongolia,** to a subsidiary of the International Mercantile Marine* (IMM). Upon closer inspection, IMM concluded that the *China* was too old, too small, and too slow to operate in the North Atlantic and attempted to resell her, preferably to a Pacific company so as not to risk losing the ship in the long voyage to the Atlantic.

The Japanese line Toyo Kisen Kaisha was willing to buy, but only at a very low price. The Chinese-American community was shocked at the suspension of PMSS service to the Far East and decided to incorporate its own company, the China Mail Steamship Company* (CMSS), which bought the *China* from IMM in October 1915. Former officials of PMSS and the traditional Chinese crews continued to operate the vessel for CMSS. The company vastly enlarged passenger accommodations, so that the *China*, which had been refitted in 1901 to carry 139 passengers in first class, 41 in second, and 347 in steerage,* carried in the first voyage for CMSS the record number of 272 in first, 41 in second, and 569 in steerage. The *China* remained a very popular ship with Chinese-American travelers, while Chinese merchants kept its holds full of cargo. However, when CMSS went bankrupt in April 1923, the *China* went out of service and was subsequently broken up.

References: Frederick E. Emmons, *American Passenger Ships: The Ocean Lines and Liners, 1873–1983* (Newark: University of Delaware Press, 1985); John H. Kemble, "A Hundred Years of the Pacific Mail," *American Neptune* 10 (1950):123–143; Robert J. Schwendinger, *Ocean of Bitter Dreams: Maritime Relations Between China and the United States, 1850–1915* (Tucson: Westernlore Press, 1988); E. Mowbray Tate, *Transpacific Steam: The Story of Steam Navigation from the Pacific Coast of North America to the Far East and the Antipodes, 1867–1941* (New York: Cornwall Books, 1986).

CHINA MAIL STEAMSHIP COMPANY (CMSS), 1915–1923. When the Pacific Mail Steamship Company* (PMSS) announced in April 1915 that its final sailing would be on 25 August 1915, Chinese-American merchants in San Francisco, who were already feeling the pinch of shipping shortages and rising rates because of World War I, decided to fill the gap with their own U.S.-flag firm, the China Mail Steamship Company. Investors from China eagerly backed the project, and the experienced Chinese crews from the former Pacific Mail ships were looking for employment. However, the Chinese government could give only its blessings, because it had already placed its guarantees behind an ill-fated Sino-American venture, the Pacific & Eastern Steamship Company,* which ultimately achieved nothing except waste time and money.

The first and hardest task of CMSS was to find ships, terribly scarce because of World War I. International Mercantile Marine* (IMM) had bought the five largest steamers of PMSS, but on closer examination IMM concluded that one, appropriately named *China** (built in 1889), was too small for transatlantic service. The company also feared that the ship might not be able to make the trip to the Atlantic and decided to sell her in the Pacific Coast. CMSS promptly purchased the vessel, which was operated by its previous Chinese crews and the former PMSS officers. The U.S.-flag *China* was an instant success, and all passenger accommodations were permanently overfilled, while Chinese merchants on both sides of the Pacific kept the holds overflowing on every voyage.

CMSS needed more ships, but in wartime 1917 only the burned-down hulk of the abandoned steamer *Congress** was on the market. CMSS paid the huge sum of $600,000 for the purchase and spent $2.5 million to virtually rebuild the ship in one of the largest conversions of any U.S. shipyard. Rechristened the *Nanking*, the U.S.-flag ship first sailed on 3 July 1918 and, like the *China*, was also a complete success. In 1919 CMSS bought a third ship, the *Asia*, but because of racial prejudices, the company stood no chance of purchasing any of the government surplus vessels, much less receiving the lucrative managing operator* contract from the Shipping Board.*

Without either subsidies or government-owned ships, CMSS was at a serious disadvantage when competing against the steamship companies operated by white Americans; nevertheless the strong commercial networks of the Chinese sufficed to keep the line profitable. During the war other steamship companies had tolerated CMSS, but now they wanted to drive out this competitor, which, because it flew the U.S. flag, could not be dismissed as merely an Oriental firm.

In spite of the fact that 51 percent of the stock was owned by U.S. citizens, Matson Navigation Company* and other lines obtained a ruling from federal courts keeping the U.S.-flag ships of CMSS out of the California-Hawaii route, which was reserved to U.S.-flag vessels only when all the owners were white Americans. A ferocious campaign to destroy CMSS focused on the narcotics traffic that supposedly flourished on its ships, and the company was forced to post enormous bonds to sail its vessels; these bonds ultimately so weakened the company that in March 1923 CMSS ceased operations, and its vessels were sold. The Dollar Steamship Company,* never above using unscrupulous tactics, had the most to gain from the demise of CMSS, and soon after, the Dollar Steamship Company became the dominant U.S. force in transpacific shipping.

Some Notable Ships

China	1915–1923
Nanking; formerly *Congress*; later, *Emma Alexander*	1918–1923

References: Giles T. Brown, *Ships That Sail No More: Marine Transportation from San Diego to Puget Sound, 1910–1940* (Lexington: University of Kentucky Press, 1966); Frederick E. Emmons, *American Passenger Ships* (Newark: University of Delaware Press, 1985); Robert J. Schwendinger, *Ocean of Bitter Dreams: Maritime Relations Between China and the United States, 1850–1915* (Tucson: Westernlore Press, 1988); E. Mowbray Tate, *Transpacific Steam: The Story of Steam Navigation from the Pacific Coast of North America to the Far East and the Antipodes, 1867–1941* (New York: Cornwall Books, 1986).

CITY OF HONOLULU, **1922.** The Los Angeles Steamship Company* (LASSCO) established regular service between Los Angeles and Hawaii in the fall of 1922 with vessels bought from the Shipping Board.* The *City of Los Angeles*, a former German liner, inaugurated the service on 11 September and was followed by the *City of Honolulu* (the former German liner *Friedrich der Grosse*) on 23 September. The *City of Honolulu* reached Hawaii safely, but on 12 October during the return voyage and 600 miles from the coast of California, a fire broke out in the early hours of the morning. The flames spread rapidly, and at 6:00 A.M. the captain sent an SOS; although the fire appeared to be under control, the vessel began to list heavily to the port side and the captain decided to abandon ship. While the orchestra played, the efficient crew lowered the boats with all the passengers, and by 10:00 A.M. the last of the crew had safely departed the *City of Honolulu*. Fortunately the sea was calm and smooth, no lives were lost, and by mid-afternoon the first rescue ships arrived. The *City of Honolulu* remained adrift for five days, until the U.S. government decided to sink her as a menace to navigation.

References: Frederick E. Emmons, *American Passenger Ships: The Ocean Lines and Lines, 1873–1983* (Newark: University of Delaware Press, 1985); Milton H. Watson, *Disasters at Sea* (Northamptonshire, England: Patrick Stephens, 1987); William L. Worden, *Cargoes: Matson's First Century in the Pacific* (Honolulu: University Press of Hawaii, 1981).

CITY OF HONOLULU II, **1927–1930.** Undaunted by the loss of the first *City of Honolulu** in 1922, the Los Angeles Steamship Company* (LASSCO) continued to provide service between Hawaii and Los Angeles. In 1926 LASSCO bought from the Shipping Board* another ex-German liner, the *Prinzess Alice*, which the company renamed the *City of Honolulu*, in spite of what had befallen the first vessel with this name. After extensive renovation work, the *City of Honolulu II* made the first voyage on the Los Angeles-Hawaii route in June 1927 and operated successfully, at least in the initial years.

On 25 May 1930, while the ship was docked in Honolulu harbor, a fire broke out, and although all available fire-fighting equipment was rushed to the scene, the ship continued to blaze for twelve hours and was judged a total loss by the company. Later, however, the ship was able to reach California under her own power but never returned to service and was laid up and finally scrapped in 1933.

References: Frederick E. Emmons, *American Passenger Ships: The Ocean Lines and Liners, 1873–1983* (Newark: University of Delaware Press, 1985); Milton H. Watson, *Disasters at Sea* (Northamptonshire, England: Patrick Stephens, 1987); William L. Worden, *Cargoes: Matson's First Century in the Pacific* (Honolulu: University Press of Hawaii, 1981).

CITY OF NEW YORK, CITY OF SAN FRANCISCO, **and** *CITY OF SYDNEY*, **1875–1910.** The Pacific Mail Steamship Company* (PMSS) ordered the *City of New York* and the sister ships, the *City of San Francisco* and the *City of Sydney*, to inaugurate in 1875 a new PMSS route from San Francisco to Australia. The three ships were iron steamers with screws and compound engines* but were smaller than the much larger *City of Tokyo** and *City of Peking*, which the PMSS operated between San Francisco and the Far East.

The Australian route offered little cargo, and consequently PMSS shifted the *City of San Francisco* to the route between Panama and San Francisco. On 16 May 1877 the *City of San Francisco* was wrecked on Tartar Shoal, near Acapulco, Mexico, but without any loss of life. When PMSS abandoned the Australia service in 1885, it transferred the *City of Sydney* and the *City of New York* to its other routes. The former continued in service until it was laid up in 1910, but on 26 October 1893 the latter ran into the rocks of Point Bonita right inside San Francisco Bay. The captain did not want to delay his sailing for Yokohama in spite of poor visibility, and after passing Alcatraz island, heavy fog and a strong tide drove the ship aground near the northern shore. All passengers and most of the cargo were safely removed, but the ship was declared a total loss. Unfortunately the *City of New York* was not the last ship the PMSS lost in San Francisco Bay, and a worse fate befell the *City of Rio de Janeiro** in 1901.

References: Frederick E. Emmons, *American Passenger Ships: The Ocean Lines and Liners, 1873–1983* (Newark: University of Delaware Press, 1985); John H. Kemble, ''A Hundred Years of the Pacific Mail,'' *American Neptune* 10 (1950):123–143; E. Mowbray

Tate, *Transpacific Steam: The Story of Steam Navigation from the Pacific Coast of North America to the Far East and the Antipodes, 1867–1941* (New York: Cornwall Books, 1986).

CITY OF PEKING. See *City of Tokyo.*

CITY OF RIO DE JANEIRO, 1878–1901. The *City of Rio de Janeiro*, completed in 1878, was one of five ships the shipbuilder John Roach constructed in his vain attempt to make the United States and Brazil Mail Steamship Company* a successful venture. The *City of Rio de Janeiro* was an iron screw steamer with a compound engine* and capable of twelve knots, and although she was not big for the time, just like her sister vessels, she was too large for the barely incipient trade between the United States and Brazil. Roach and his partners took heavy losses in the United States and Brazil Mail Steamship Company, and when the service was suspended in 1881, Pacific Mail Steamship Company* (PMSS) bought the *City of Rio de Janeiro* at a giveaway price.

The *City of Rio de Janeiro* performed well in the transpacific service for nearly twenty years. In the morning of 22 February 1901, the captain of the *City of Rio de Janeiro* was anchored outside San Francisco Bay, waiting for the fog to clear in order to enter the bay; the visibility improved, but fifteen minutes later the fog returned, and the captain, rather than anchoring again, decided to make a run for the Golden Gate. At 5:20 A.M. the *City of Rio de Janeiro* struck the rocks below the Golden Gate; of the 210 passengers, officers, and crew on board, 122 lost their lives, while strong tides swept out to sea the wreck, which was never found.

References: Frederick E. Emmons, *American Passenger Ships: The Ocean Lines and Liners, 1873–1983* (Newark: University of Delaware Press, 1985); John H. Kemble, "A Hundred Years of the Pacific Mail," *American Neptune* 10 (1950):123–143; Leonard A. Swann, *John Roach, Maritime Entrepreneur: The Years as Naval Contractors, 1862–1886* (Annapolis: U.S. Naval Institute Press, 1965); E. Mowbray Tate, *Transpacific Steam: The Story of Steam Navigation from the Pacific Coast of North America to the Far East and the Antipodes, 1867–1941* (New York: Cornwall Books, 1986).

CITY OF SAN FRANCISCO. See *City of New York.*

CITY OF SYDNEY. See *City of New York.*

CITY OF TOKYO and *CITY OF PEKING*, 1875–1908. In 1875 the *City of Tokyo* and the *City of Peking* became the first screw steamers with iron hulls to provide regular service between San Francisco and the Far East. Earlier in 1873 the Pacific Mail Steamship Company* (PMSS) had received similar steamers for the route between Panama and San Francisco but continued to operate wooden side-wheelers with single expansion* engines in the transpacific trade. PMSS added more steamers with screws and iron hulls to this route but did not completely replace the wooden side-wheelers until the early 1880s.

The *City of Tokyo* and the *City of Peking* "were the largest American passenger vessels in active service'' (Tate 1986) in 1875. They had iron hulls and single screws, and their compound engines* could attain a maximum speed of fourteen knots. They still had a full set of back-up masts to rely on sails in case of engine failure. Carrying Chinese passengers had become extremely profitable for PMSS, and each ship had space for 1,500 Chinese in steerage* class and accommodations for 150 first-class passengers.

The *City of Peking* remained in the fleet of PMSS until 1908, when it was laid up and subsequently broken up. The *City of Tokyo*, however, was lost at the entrance to Tokyo Bay on 24 June 1885. Visibility was very poor, and an unknown current drove the ship against the rocks. The passengers disembarked safely, and some of the cargo was removed in the hope of refloating the ship, but before the plans could be carried out, a typhoon appeared and destroyed the *City of Tokyo*.

References: Frederick E. Emmons, *American Passenger Ships: The Ocean Lines and Liners, 1873–1983* (Newark: University of Delaware Press, 1985); John H. Kemble, ''A Hundred Years of the Pacific Mail,'' *American Neptune* 10 (1950):123–143; Cedric R. Nevitt, ''American Merchant Steamships,'' in Society of Naval Architects and Naval Engineers, *Historical Transactions, 1893–1943* (Westport, CT: Greenwood Press, 1981); E. Mowbray Tate, *Transpacific Steam: The Story of Steam Navigation from the Pacific Coast of North America to the Far East and the Antipodes, 1867–1941* (New York: Cornwall Books, 1986).

CLASSIFICATION or CLASSIFICATION SOCIETIES. Classification, performed by a classification society, established uniform standards to determine the seaworthiness of vessels and also certified that a vessel met the structural and mechanical conditions needed to safeguard the lives and cargoes aboard. Based on considerations such as design, materials, age, maintenance, and other occurrences in the life of the vessel, the classification society placed the ship within a specific class and by means of periodic surveys determined whether that particular class status remained valid. This function was crucial to determine what insurance rates the shipowner must pay, and as the ship deteriorated because of age or other factors, the shipowner usually faced higher insurance premiums because of the lower classification. If a vessel has a very low classification, many countries will forbid its entry into their ports; in the United States the Coast Guard* has this authority to exclude unsafe vessels.

Although the American Shipmasters' Association* existed since 1862, during the nineteenth century Lloyd's of London was the classification society for most U.S. ships and for the majority of the world's shipping. Not until the passage of the Merchant Marine Act of 1920* did the American Bureau of Shipping* (the successor to the American Shipmasters' Association) become the principal classification society for the U.S. merchant marine.

Originally only a handful of classification societies existed in the world, but in the 1980s their number exploded to over fifty, as many countries sought to share in their prestige and supposed profits. Since the shipowner, rather than the insurance company, paid the classification society, the result has been that "these societies pander to shipowners who can shop around for the least stringent society or change societies to avoid making recommended repairs" (*American Shipper*, January 1991). The blame fell also on the insurance companies, because some will not require the repairs recommended by the classification society for fear of losing the customer. The flags-of-convenience* system contributed to the problem, because shipowners could also choose as the registry for their vessels a country that had little or no safety requirements. Governments in the industrialized countries could prohibit the entry into their ports of vessels that lack the standards set by the stringent classification societies, but public pressures have diverted official attention to environmental concerns and away from the issue of the safety of the ships themselves. See also American Bureau of Shipping.*

References: American Bureau of Shipping, *History 1862–1991*; *American Shipper*, January, May 1991; E. K. Haviland, "Classification Society Registers from the Point of View of a Marine Historian," *American Neptune* 30 (1970):9–39.

CLYDE, WILLIAM P., 11 November 1839–18 November 1923. William P. Clyde was born in Claymont, Delaware, on 11 November 1839 and was the son of the Scottish immigrant Thomas Clyde, who had established the Clyde Line* in 1844. William became the president of the company in 1861, and although he participated in several other business ventures, the center of his activities remained the Clyde Line.

Before the Civil War the Clyde Line was running a fleet of over forty steamers in the foreign trade, but by 1890 their number had dropped to only five in the Dominican Republic–New York route. However, the coastwise* trade between New York City and ports in South Carolina and Florida increased and remained the core of the company's operations. In the search for faster vessels, Clyde was a pioneer, and his constant quest to reduce travel time put his line ahead of competitors. He ordered the *Geo. W. Clyde* in 1871, the first vessel built in the United States with the compound engine,* and in his drive to increase the speed of the vessels, he was also among the first to adopt the triple-expansion* and the quadruple-expansion engines (see marine propulsion). In 1888 he ordered the *Iroquois*, the first all-steel commercial ship in the United States.

The outlandish purchase offers of Wall Street speculator Charles W. Morse convinced Clyde to sell the line in February 1906. The collapse of Morse's financial empire took Clyde partially out of retirement to cooperate in the establishment of the Atlantic, Gulf & West Indies* (AGWI) in 1908. He kept an office on Broadway near the steamship firms and continued to follow shipping matters until his death in New York City on 18 November 1923.

References: *Dictionary of American Biography*, vol. 20; *New York Times*, 19 November 1923; U.S. Congress, House, Committee on Merchant Marine and Fisheries, *American Merchant Marine in the Foreign Trade*, Report No. 1210, 51st Congress, 1st Session, 1890.

CLYDE LINE, 1844–1906. Thomas Clyde established in 1844 the line that bore his name to provide steamship service from Philadelphia to other East Coast ports. The line prospered, and during the Civil War its ships were chartered* by the federal government. The Clyde Line began to run ships to Galveston in 1865, but after a good start, increasing competition convinced the firm to abandon the Galveston run in 1876 and to concentrate on its other services. In 1872 the Clyde Line moved from Philadelphia to New York and in 1873 opened a new service to Havana. The competition from the Ward Line* was too strong, and by the 1880s the Clyde Line limited its West Indies service to the Dominican Republic. In addition, coastwise* service along the East Coast remained the backbone of the Clyde Line's operations, in particular fast service linking New York to Charleston and Jacksonville.

To stay ahead of the competing coastwise lines, the Clyde Line was always eager to try new, untested technologies that promised more speed. In 1844 the line placed in service the *John S. McKim*, the first propeller* vessel built and designed in the United States. The line ordered the *Geo. W. Clyde* in 1871, the first ship to use the compound engine* in the United States, and it was also among the first to introduce the triple-expansion engine* in 1886 with the *Cherokee*. In 1888 the company ordered the first all-steel commercial ship in the United States, the *Iroquois* (since the 1880s most of the company's ships were named after North American Indian tribes). In 1895 the company took the next step and ordered the quadruple-expansion engine for the *Comanche*, which then set the record that stood for many years of forty-one hours, thirty minutes' steaming time from New York to Charleston.

During the Spanish-American War the U.S. Army chartered many vessels of the Clyde Line. In February 1906 William P. Clyde* sold the Clyde Line to Charles W. Morse, who was in the process of creating a cartel of coastwise firms. When Morse incorporated the Consolidated Steamship Lines* in January 1907, the Clyde Line became one of its main subsidiaries. When the Consolidated Steamship Lines collapsed in 1908, its subsidiaries, including the Clyde Line, became a part of the Atlantic, Gulf & West Indies Steamship Lines (AGWI).* The Clyde Line ceased to operate as an independent entity, but its trade name continued to be used until 1932, when AGWI changed it to Clyde-Mallory. When AGWI sold Clyde-Mallory to the Bull Line* in 1949, the Clyde name was dropped altogether.

Some Notable Ships

Geo. W. Clyde	1872–1926
Iroquois	1888–1918
Comanche	1895–1925
Lenape	1913–1917

Principal Executives

Thomas Clyde	1844–1861
William P. Clyde	1861–1906

References: James P. Baughman, *The Mallorys of Mystic: Six Generations in American Maritime Enterprise* (Middletown, CT: Wesleyan University Press, 1972); Frederick E. Emmons, *American Passenger Ships: The Ocean Lines and Liners, 1873–1983* (Newark: University of Delaware Press, 1985); Erik Heyl, *Early American Steamers*, 6 vols. (Buffalo: Erik Heyl, 1953–1969); Frank J. Taylor, "Early American Steamship Lines," in Society of Naval Architects and Marine Engineers, *Historical Transactions 1893–1943* (Westport, CT: Greenwood Press, 1981).

COAST GUARD, 1915–present. Since 1942 the Coast Guard has been the government agency charged with enforcing safety standards aboard merchant vessels. The Coast Guard has performed these functions by inspecting vessels of U.S. registry* to certify that they are seaworthy and by licensing the officers on U.S.-flag vessels. The Coast Guard also has the power to prohibit the entry into U.S. waters of ships it regards as unsafe or a menace to other vessels, property, or the environment. These functions were originally performed by the civilian Bureau of Marine Inspection and Navigation* (BMIN) until it was transferred to the Coast Guard on 28 February 1942 as part of the emergency measures of World War II; the Coast Guard itself had come automatically under the jurisdiction of the Navy Department upon U.S. entry into World War II on 7 December 1941.

Although the Coast Guard has traced its roots to the Revenue Cutter Service, which dated back to the foundation of the republic, it acquired its present name in the reorganization authorized by Congress on 28 January 1915. The Coast Guard has generally followed a military type of organization, with the personnel divided into officers and crew, and distributed in accordance with a system of ranks patterned on that of the navy, whose influence was great in the formative history of the Revenue Cutter Service; as the latter's name indicated, its work consisted primarily in enforcing the decisions of the Customs Service, which, like the Revenue Cutter Service, was a dependency of the Treasury Department.

Above all, the essential characteristic of the Coast Guard has been that of a federal maritime police, whose primary duty has been to enforce all laws and regulations in the waters under U.S. jurisdiction. Because the Coast Guard has had the ships and the skilled personnel to actually enforce the laws in the ports and on the seas, since 1915 it found itself increasingly performing services for the Bureau of Navigation* and the Steamboat Inspection Service.* The Oil Pollution Act of 7 June 1924 brought the government into a new field of activity, and the Coast Guard received the responsibility for enforcing its provisions. Nonetheless, the duties as a federal police remained paramount, and in the 1920s and until the repeal of Prohibition* in 1933, the prevention of liquor smuggling was its single largest activity, consuming 37 percent of its budget.

A grant from the Works Progress Administration in 1933 allowed the Coast

Guard to escape drastic budget cuts after the repeal of Prohibition, at least until the approach of World War II guaranteed sufficient funds for an enlarged organization. A healthy and vigorous Coast Guard contrasted with the sluggish and somnolent BMIN, which had never been able to overcome the negative image caused by the *Morro Castle** shipwreck. Once the United States entered World War II, the capability of the BMIN to handle in its usual leisurely routine the crash expansion of the American Merchant Marine was open to serious questions, so that by executive order of 28 February 1942 the president transferred that bureau to the Coast Guard for the duration of the war. Maritime labor leaders denounced this measure as a first step in the ''militarization'' of seafarers and confidently expected the return of the BMIN back to civilian control in the Department of Commerce once the war was over. However, organized labor was unable to block Reorganization Plan No. 3 of 16 May 1946, which abolished the old BMIN and transferred its functions permanently to the Coast Guard (with the exception of vessel documentation, which in 1942 had been returned to the Bureau of Customs in the Treasury Department and was not assigned to the Coast Guard until 4 February 1967).

Ever since, the Coast Guard has continued to administer the laws affecting vessels and seafarers, and the Maritime Administration* (MARAD) has been in charge of programs to promote U.S.-flag merchant shipping, while the Federal Maritime Commission* (FMC) has regulated the ocean trades. The Coast Guard, which had been during its entire previous history in the Treasury Department, was transferred to the newly created Department of Transportation on 1 April 1967.

Within its merchant marine duties, public opinion and additional legislation have emphasized the Coast Guard's role in preventing oil spills. In the wake of the *Argo Merchant* and *Sansinena** disasters, Congress passed the Port and Tanker Safety Act of 1978* to strengthen and broaden the Tank Vessel Act of 1936 and the Ports and Waterways Safety Act of 1972. The Coast Guard was thus endowed with ample powers to inspect vessels and enforce requirements, but the *Exxon Valdez** shipwreck showed that even more drastic measures were needed to prevent catastrophic oil spills. In August 1990 Congress in the Oil Pollution Act* (OPA) mandated for the first time double hulls* for all tankers, foreign or domestic, operating or entering U.S. waters by the year 2010. The enforcement of this extreme measure, which among other provisions had a complex transition period for gradually phasing out the older high-risk tankers, became a new responsibility for the Coast Guard, which has been drafting and establishing the rules and regulations to implement the double-hull requirements of the OPA. But the Coast Guard has remained above all a military police force, and just like in the years of Prohibition, since the 1970s the interdiction of drugs from other countries has been its single most important activity.

References: *American Shipper*, April 1991; Charles L. Daaring and Wilfred Owen, *National Transportation Policy* (Washington, DC: Brookings Institution, 1949); Robert L. Scheina, ''U.S. Coast Guard,'' in Donald R. Whitnah, ed., *Government Agencies*, (Westport, CT: Greenwood Press, 1983); H. C. Shepheard, ''History of United States

Navigation and Vessel Inspection Laws,'' in Society of Naval Architects and Marine Engineers, *Historical Transactions, 1893–1943* (Westport, CT: Greenwood Press, 1981); U.S. National Archives, *Guide to the National Archives of the United States* (Washington, DC: Government Printing Office, 1974); Carroll H. Woody, *The Growth of the Federal Government, 1915–1932* (New York: McGraw-Hill, 1934).

COAST SEAMEN'S UNION (CSU), 1885–1891. In the United States the Coast Seamen's Union was the first permanent sailors' union, and it still exists today under the name of its direct successor, the Sailors' Union of the Pacific* (SUP). The CSU was established in San Francisco in March 1885 to represent the 3,500 coastwise* sailors aboard sailing vessels, and soon 2,200 had joined as members. Earlier attempts to create an organization for sailors had ended in failure, but the CSU survived serious setbacks, most notably the disastrous 1886 strike against shipowners. Andrew Furuseth* nursed the wounded union back to strength when he took over as secretary in 1887. Furuseth insisted on the need to have a union newspaper, and in 1887 the *Coast Seamen's Journal* appeared. Membership, which had dropped to under 1,000 after the strike, returned to over 2,000 in 1889, and the union treasury was in sound condition. Furuseth took two actions that had a lasting effect on the CSU and its successor, the SUP. First, he led a successful struggle to eliminate socialist influence from the CSU, thereby keeping the union free of any particular ideological or partisan affiliation. Second, he ended the divisive conflict between sailors of steam vessels and those of sailing ships; after lengthy negotiations, he combined the Steamship Sailors' Protective Union* with the CSU to create the SUP on 29 July 1891.

References: Stephen Schwartz, *Brotherhood of the Sea: A History of the Sailors' Union of the Pacific, 1885–1985* (New Brunswick, NJ: Transaction Books, 1986); Hyman Weintraub, *Andrew Furuseth: Emancipator of the Seamen* (Berkeley: University of California Press, 1959).

COASTWISE. The word *coastwise* has referred to the ocean trade along the coasts of the United States, specifically from Maine to Texas and from Puget Sound to San Diego. The cabotage* privileges have reserved this trade for U.S.-flag ships built in the United States. The term *coastwise* sometimes has been loosely used to refer as well to the trade of mainland United States with Puerto Rico in the Atlantic and with Hawaii and Alaska in the Pacific, but generally the expression *offshore domestic trade* has been more widespread. No confusion has existed over the difference with intercoastal* trade, which has referred only to the cargoes moving between the East and West coasts of the United States. The cabotage privileges originally applied first to the coastwise trade of the United States, and as the country expanded geographically across the North American continent and overseas, the new terms of *intercoastal* and *offshore domestic* appeared to differentiate more clearly the various types of domestic ocean shipping.

The coastwise trade of the United States was fairly vigorous until the 1930s, when the companies providing the shipping services began to face mounting difficulties. The requisition of most vessels in the coastwise trade for World War II was a blow from which most companies never recovered. Although some hardy survivors resumed modest coastwise service with the return of peace, by the early 1960s the United States had virtually abandoned coastwise shipping for the sake of the more costly rail and truck transportation.

References: Giles T. Brown, *Ships That Sail No More: Marine Transportation from San Diego to Puget Sound, 1910–1940* (Lexington: University of Kentucky Press, 1966); René De La Pedraja, *The Rise and Decline of U.S. Merchant Shipping in the Twentieth Century* (New York: Twayne, 1992); John G. B. Hutchins, *The American Maritime Industries and Public Policy, 1789–1914* (Cambridge: Harvard University Press, 1941); Gerald R. Jantscher, *Bread upon the Waters: Federal Aids to the Maritime Industries* (Washington, DC: Brookings Institution, 1975).

COASTWISE CONFERENCE, 1925–1940. The Coastwise Conference was the only conference* that ever existed on the Pacific Coast to establish rates and services for its coastwise* trade and possibly was also the only coastwise conference in U.S. history because for the East Coast no formal conference has been identified so far, although near-conference arrangements did exist. Because the Admiral Line* practically monopolized the coastwise trade along the Pacific Coast for decades, no conference emerged until 1925, when a rate war caused by the entry of new competitors ended in the creation of a "traffic bureau"— the original name for the conference—to set rates and sailings. The members were the Los Angeles Steamship Company* (LASSCO), the Admiral Line,* Nelson Steamship Company, McCormick Steamship Company,* and the Los Angeles-San Francisco Navigation Company. The entry of a new company in the winter of 1929 sparked a round of rate cuts, and by June a full-blown rate war had erupted, but by the fall the companies had agreed to respect conference rates, just a few days before the October stock market crash.

On 12 April 1930 the Los Angeles-San Francisco Navigation Company withdrew from the conference, and because it "used slow, wooden vessels on irregular runs with high insurance rates" (Brown 1966) began to quote lower prices, and more new companies appeared offering low rates. The Coastwise Conference almost dissolved in January 1931, and it finally collapsed in December 1931 as the former member lines turned to indiscriminate rate cutting to meet the prices of the new rivals. The Admiral Line described well the plight of the conference lines when confronted by these "outsiders":* "With large capital invested and the necessity of maintaining regular service, we are subject to attack by irresponsible operators using cheap, slow, antiquated tonnage, with practically no investment and insufficient responsibility to meet their liabilities in case of accident or disaster. . . . When the trade is poor these irresponsibles drop out and leave the companies with large investments to continue. Then when business revives the irresponsibles come out of their holes and attack again" (ibid.).

The impact of the Great Depression so hurt the companies that nine of them decided to reestablish the Coastwise Conference on 1 March 1932 to raise rates, but the entry of intercoastal* companies like American-Hawaiian* and the Grace Line* forced the conference on 22 May 1933 to reduce the rates again. Henceforth the rates at last stabilized along the coast, and the conference raised them in December 1934 only to cover the wage demands won by longshoremen in the Big Strike.* Long before the labor threat appeared, however, the coastwise companies were in deep crisis, and as the Interstate Commerce Commission* (ICC) explained, ''At the bottom of the troubles lies too much and uncontrolled competition'' (ibid.). The experience of the coastwise companies showed how destructive competition could be and left the companies in such a weakened state that they later could not face the challenges of the railroad and other forms of transportation. The intercoastal companies like Grace had virtually abandoned the coastwise service by 1938, and although the coastwise companies continued to operate through the 1930s, they lacked the funds to replace their ships, which were increasingly old and obsolete. By 1940 the Coastwise Conference was defunct, because only Pope and Talbot* was providing regular sailings, and even that last company suspended service in December 1941.

References: Giles T. Brown, *Ships That Sail No More: Marine Transportation from San Diego to Puget Sound, 1910–1940* (Lexington: University of Kentucky Press, 1966); Edwin T. Coman, Jr., and Helen M. Gibbs, *Time, Tide, and Timber: A Century of Pope and Talbot* (New York: Greenwood Press, 1968); William Kooiman, *The Grace Ships, 1869–1968* (Point Reyes, CA: Komar, 1990).

COLLIER. Colliers were steamships designed to haul coal. Colliers—many of which were tramp vessels*—existed since the late nineteenth century, when, after the introduction of the triple-expansion engine,* they gradually replaced sailing vessels of iron hulls. In the United States coastwise* firms like Sprague Steamship Company owned fleets of colliers to transport coal on regular schedules from Hampton Roads, Virginia, to New York and New England. During World War II the U.S. Maritime Commission* built one type of Liberty* ship for hauling coal, and many of these Liberty colliers remained in use for decades. However, gradually after the war the colliers were replaced (and the word fell out of use) by bulk* carriers designed to carry a variety of cargoes, including coal, but also ores and grains. The most versatile vessels to emerge were the oil/bulk/ore carriers or OBOs.*

COLLINS, EDWARD K., 5 August 1802–22 January 1878. Edward K. Collins was the founder and only president of what was perhaps the most famous steamship company of the United States in the nineteenth century, the Collins Line.* He was born in Truro, Cape Cod, Massachusetts, on 5 August 1802 and came from a family that for generations had been involved with the sea. When he was fifteen, he moved to New York City, where he lived for the rest of his life, and after working as a clerk in a merchant house, he joined his father's commission business in 1821. The father was also operating sailing vessels for his own and others' cargoes, and gradually the young Collins shifted the focus of shipping operations away from Europe toward the Gulf of Mexico, in particular to take advantage of the new opportunities afforded by the opening of Latin America to world trade after its independence. Once the boom in Mexican silver trade had spent itself by 1837, Collins had already built up since 1832 a separate line of vessels sailing between New Orleans and New York. He was, however, too ambitious to remain only in the Gulf trade, and in 1836 he began a transatlantic service of sailing vessels, which soon was called the Dramatic Line, not just because the ships were named after actors but also because the speed, decoration, fine food, and wine of the vessels made the trips memorable for travelers. All the time Collins continued to operate as a merchant, so that always a considerable amount of the cargo aboard his ships belonged to his firm. By the early 1840s he was among the wealthiest men in New York City, and his reputation as one of the most successful shipowners in the United States seemed securely confirmed.

Collins's keen business eye sensed that the introduction of the steamship offered new opportunities for profit, while the United States resented the early lead Great Britain had taken in the establishment of successful steamship service across the Atlantic. Collins sensed he was the man of the hour and lobbied extensively until at last he obtained the subsidies without which the operation of the early steamers was virtually impossible. He now disposed of his lines of sailing ships and abandoned his profitable trade in merchandise with the Gulf of Mexico, leaving him without any backup activities. Unfortunately for Collins, he had also promised to operate the fastest steamers on the North Atlantic, at a time when the single-expansion* engines of side-wheelers* provided limited propulsion. His only possible solution was to place more engines in each ship, with the result that the coal consumption of each vessel, already excessively high because of the tremendous wastefulness of the single-expansion engine, became phenomenal.

On 27 April 1850 the Collins Line began service between New York and Liverpool with the *Atlantic*, the first of its wooden side-wheel steamers, and later in the year was joined by three more steamers. In 1851 the Collins Line duly set new speed records for crossing the Atlantic, and a grateful nation through the Congress increased the amount of the subsidies. This raise in the payments was actually indispensable for the Collins Line to operate at high speeds, because the huge coal consumption and the need for repairs after almost every voyage piled up incredibly large expenses that could not be defrayed otherwise. Furthermore, Collins had set a very high standard of food and drink in each of his vessels to attract the cream of the traveling public, but this splurge in luxuries necessarily increased the expenses of the line.

Collins was successful in the initial years, but adversity appeared with the loss of the *Arctic* in 1854 with considerable loss of life, including his wife, daughter, and one of his sons. This was a personal blow to Collins, but he was urged to continue by the support of his two remaining sons, yet in 1856 a second disaster came when the *Pacific* disappeared at sea without any trace. Meanwhile a mounting campaign against the huge subsidies culminated in the repeal in August 1857 of the additional subsidies granted by Congress, and the company had no choice but to cease operations in February 1858.

Envy of rivals and resentment of the South, which wanted subsidies for its own ports and not just New York, had contributed to the political coalition that brought the repeal, but it just did not make sense to subsidize a line lavishly so that wealthy passengers could travel in greater speed; in a sense, the repeal of the Collins Line's subsidy paralleled the decisions in the 1960s not to build more transatlantic liners and not even to finance the construction of a supersonic jet plane. The British had poured their funds in the 1850s not into the sea, as really was the case with the Collins Line, but into technical improvements that gradually increased the performance of the steamships, with items like iron hulls, propellers,* higher steam pressures, and eventually the compound engine.*

Collins never returned to the sea after the disastrous venture of the Collins Line, which had never paid a dividend during its existence, and he himself saw his previously large fortune substantially diminished and had to live the rest of his life under more modest circumstances in relative obscurity. The development of iron and coal properties in Ohio sustained him in his later years, and although he was never able to overcome the stigma of his titanic failure, he lived a more tranquil and less stressful life for the rest of his days now that he no longer had to worry about the gigantic steamships on the Atlantic. He died in New York City on 22 January 1878.

References: *Dictionary of American Biography*, vol. 4; Edward W. Sloan, "The Roots of a Maritime Fortune: E. K. Collins and the New York-Gulf Coast Trade, 1821–1848," *Gulf Coast Historical Review* 5 (1990):104–113.

COLLINS LINE, 1847–1858. The Collins Line was the most famous American steamship service of the nineteenth century, because of both its dramatic history and the no less striking career of its founder, Edward K. Collins.* When the U.S. government decided to challenge British supremacy on the Atlantic by granting mail subsidies to encourage the creation of U.S.-flag firms, Collins, one of the most successful owners of sailing fleets, was among the first applying for a mail contract. Intense lobbying, in the tradition of the period, determined who would receive the contracts; Collins was not favored in the first round of awards, but after splurging on lavish entertainment, he won his first subsidy contract from the postmaster general in November 1847. Collins ordered the construction of four steamers whose design provided the best comfort then possible for the passengers. Nonetheless, what had managed to clinch Collins's bid for the mail contract was his catering to the public's demand for speed; Americans had been disappointed in the lackluster performance of the Bremen Line's* *Washington* and wanted a U.S.-flag ship to take the speed records away from the British.

On 27 April 1850, the *Atlantic*, the first of the Collins Line side-wheel* steamers, inaugurated the service between New York and Liverpool, and later in the year was joined by the *Pacific*, *Arctic*, and *Baltic*. In 1851 the *Baltic* and the *Pacific* set the new record of nine days, eighteen hours, traveling at an average of thirteen knots; the enthusiastic public acclaimed this triumph, and Congress rewarded the line by increasing its annual subsidy. The increase in the mail contract was absolutely vital, because the fast speed of the ships had been attained only by putting more single-expansion engines* in each vessel, thereby dramatically increasing coal consumption and using most of the additional space in the large ships to store coal for the trip rather than income-earning cargo. In the period of the single-expansion engine, vessels could not operate without some subsidy or government privileges, and the fast Collins liners needed even larger subsidies to offset their unusually high operating expenses; it was rumored that the ships, when they returned to New York, had to undergo secret extensive repairs to offset the wear and strain of running the engines to the maximum in the voyage.

Collins, a master of entertainment, made sure the passengers were well dined and wined during the voyages, and soon the traveling public preferred the fast Collins liners over the more drab Cunard vessels, whose English grub many found wanting. For four years the Collins Line operated successfully in the North Atlantic, until on 27 September 1854 the *Arctic* collided with the small French steamer *Vesta* (saved because of a watertight bulkhead) and hours later sank with the loss of 318 lives, including the wife, son, and daughter of Collins. A second disaster came in January 1856, when the *Pacific*, after leaving Liverpool in an apparent race with a British steamer, disappeared without any trace; the most informed opinion suggests that she hit an iceberg and sank rapidly with the loss of all on board. Undaunted by these business and personal disasters, Collins, with the help of his two remaining sons, pushed forward and ordered a replacement, the *Adriatic*, and chartered* ships to maintain the scheduled service. The new ship, as well as the rest of his fleet, was now fitted with watertight compartments to prevent another disaster like the *Arctic*.

Ultimately survival of the company depended upon the large subsidies, but their excessive amount led Americans, like Cornelius Vanderbilt,* to offer to provide the same service with smaller subsidies. Likewise, the South resented that the subsidies were monopolized by the northern port of New York, and on 3 March 1855 President Franklin Pierce vetoed a bill that would have guaranteed the large subsidy to the Collins Line; henceforth the government needed only a six months' notice to reduce the amount of the subsidy by nearly half. In August 1857 Congress voted to give the six months' notice, and from that moment the days of the Collins Line were numbered. Whatever hope might have existed of attracting private funds vanished when the panic of 1857 struck in October, and the general paralysis of business activities ruled out any help for the collapsing Collins Line. The *Adriatic* made its first voyage in November but had barely completed its second voyage when the Collins Line halted all operations in February 1858. On 1 April all the properties of the Collins Line were put at public auction, bringing to an end the very dramatic career of the only U.S.-

flag steamship company that managed to compete successfully against foreign lines in the nineteenth century.

Principal Executive

Edward K. Collins

Some Notable Ships

Arctic	1850–1854
Pacific	1850–1856
Atlantic	1850–1858
Baltic	1850–1858
Adriatic	1857–1858

References: Robert G. Albion, *The Rise of New York Port, 1815–1860* (New York: Scribner's, 1939); Winthrop L. Marvin, *The American Merchant Marine* (New York: Scribner's, 1902); David B. Tyler, *Steam Conquers the Atlantic* (New York: D. Appleton-Century, 1939).

COLOMBIAN STEAMSHIP COMPANY, 1923–1938. The Colombian Steamship Company, a disguised subsidiary of the Atlantic, Gulf & West Indies Steamship Lines* (AGWI), provided service from the East Coast of the United States to Colombia and other Caribbean ports. Another AGWI subsidiary was managing operator* for government vessels, but as the Shipping Board* reduced its budget, AGWI could not count on continued subsidies and hence decided in 1923 to create a separate corporation, the Colombian Steamship Company, to run the service under an official of unquestionable loyalty, Charles H. C. Pearsall. To further allay Shipping Board fears, the Colombian Steamship Company bought the five ships in the service, making the new company the first one to comply with the announced government policy of selling the ships to private owners. The company also received as managing operator the American Antilles Line, whose two government-owned ships it promised to buy at a later date.

The American Antilles Line continued to suffer heavy losses, and the Shipping Board no longer wanted to subsidize its operations. Meanwhile Colombian Steamship negotiated an agreement that limited the Panama Steamship Line* (owned by the U.S. Army) to Port-au-Prince, leaving the rest of the ports in Haiti to the American Antilles Line. However, negotiations with Alcoa Steamship Company* failed to reach any agreement on bauxite cargoes, and in 1926 the Shipping Board discontinued the American Antilles Line, although Colombian Steamship bought one of the two steamers on that line from the government.

In 1927 Colombian Steamship invested heavily in barges and tugs in the Magdalena River to try to generate cargo for its ships calling at Colombian ports. The company also purchased a Colombian-flag steamship, which operated in that country's coastwise* trade. Unfortunately the investment in Colombia proved a disaster: the company took a loss of nearly $1 million and suspended all river operations on 1 January 1929.

To offset the losses in Colombia, the company adroitly lobbied to secure from the Shipping Board the appointment as managing operator for the American-Brazil Line for the period from February 1928 to August 1931. Before the subsidies from the American-Brazil Line ran out, Colombian Steamship was awarded in 1930 the even more lucrative mail contract. Colombian Steamship paid off the old debts and operated a profitable service once again but did face the additional obligation of having to order two faster vessels. The still-hidden parent company, AGWI, did not want to invest its funds into this disguised subsidiary, but fortunately an arrangement was worked out with United Fruit Company,* which in exchange for unknown trade and route privileges, agreed to lend $1,350,000. With these sums Colombian Steamship ordered the construction of the fast seventeen-knot *Colombia* and *Haiti*, which entered into service in 1932. In addition to cargo facilities, each had accommodations for 101 first-class and 24 tourist-class passengers.

The Black Committee* hearings in 1933 exposed both the AGWI ownership of Colombian Steamship as well as the huge sums the Shipping Board had poured into what had been essentially a channel to draw subsidies into the coffers of the parent corporation. When the Merchant Marine Act of 1936* canceled the mail contracts, Colombian Steamship's last claim to exist as a separate company vanished, but first AGWI had to negotiate with United Fruit Company over the disposition of the earlier loan. The terms of the agreement were not revealed, but it was known that chartered* ships were returned to United Fruit, while *Colombia* and *Haiti* were incorporated into AGWI's other lines. Finally in early 1938, the Colombian Steamship Company ceased to operate.

Principal Executives

Charles H. C. Pearsall	1923–1938
H. H. Raymond*	1923–1935

Some Notable Ships

Colombia and *Haiti*	1932–1938

References: Frederick E. Emmons, *American Passenger Ships: The Ocean Lines and Liners, 1873–1983* (Newark: University of Delaware Press, 1985); Mark H. Goldberg, *Going Bananas: 100 Years of American Fruit Ships in the Caribbean* (Kings Point, NY: American Merchant Marine Museum, 1993); *Nautical Gazette*, 26 June 1926, 14 January 1928; Record Group 32, National Archives, Washington, DC; U.S. Senate, Special Committee on Investigation of Air Mail and Ocean Mail Contracts, *Hearings*, 9 vols. (Washington, DC: Government Printing Office, 1933–1934).

COLORADO, **1864–1879.** When the *Colorado* sailed from San Francisco on 1 January 1869, the wooden side-wheeler inaugurated the first regular transpacific steamship service in history. For centuries sailing ships had plowed the

Pacific, but the shifting nature of winds and currents prevented any semblance of regularity for voyages, which necessarily lasted months. The introduction of steamers into the Pacific Coast removed the technical obstacles to fast regular service, but steamer voyages remained a rarity because no investor wanted to risk huge sums in any permanent endeavor across the vast Pacific Ocean. All this changed when Congress awarded Pacific Mail Steamship Company* (PMSS) a generous mail subsidy to make twelve round trips a year between San Francisco and Yokohama/Hong Kong.

PMSS ordered the *Great Republic*,* *China*, *Japan*, and *America* from New York shipyards, but because these four new steamers were not ready in time to meet the contract starting date, the company took its largest vessel on the San Francisco-Panama line, the *Colorado*, in order to inaugurate the run. When completed in 1864, the *Colorado* was one of the largest vessels built in the United States up to that time; with a length of 340 feet, the ship had fifty-two staterooms for first-class passengers and space for nearly 1,500 persons in steerage* class. As a side-wheeler with a wooden hull and single expansion* engine, the technology was on the verge of becoming obsolete, and, as was usual, she still carried sails in case the engine broke down or ran out of coal. Nevertheless, after being refitted for the long transpacific run, the *Colorado* reached Yokohama in twenty-two days and continued to make round-trip voyages on the route. When the *Great Republic* departed for the Far East on 3 September 1867, PMSS was able to announce sailings every six weeks; after the *Japan* entered service in August 1868, the company no longer needed the *Colorado* to maintain the six-week schedule and returned the vessel to the San Francisco-Panama run in early 1869. That year PMSS announced monthly sailings from San Francisco to the Far East and, to maintain the schedule, kept the *Colorado* as a ''spare'' ship, which occasionally made transpacific voyages to replace any of the other steamers out of commission, but the *Colorado* mainly operated in the coastwise* trade. In 1878 PMSS laid up the *Colorado*, which was sold for scrapping the next year.

References: Erik Heyl, *Early American Steamers*, 6 vols. (Buffalo, NY: 1953–1969); John H. Kemble, ''A Hundred Years of the Pacific Mail,'' *American Neptune* 10 (1950): 123–143; John Niven, *The American President Lines and Its Forebears, 1848–1984* (Newark: University of Delaware Press, 1987); E. Mowbray Tate, *Transpacific Steam: The Story of Steam Navigation from the Pacific Coast of North America to the Far East and the Antipodes, 1867–1941* (New York: Cornwall Books, 1986).

COLUMBIA, **1880–1907.** The first vessel to have electric lights was the *Columbia*. The ship was under construction in a Pennsylvania shipyard for the Oregon Railway and Navigation Company* when the financier Henry Villard, a man of ''bold ideas,'' decided to install electric lights on the otherwise unremarkable ship (compound engine,* single screw, and fourteen-knot speed). Villard contacted the inventor Thomas A. Edison, under whose direction four generators, powered by two steam engines, were installed to light 115 lamps.

The *Columbia* steamed for Oregon in May 1880 with all lamps brightly lit, and this successful application of electricity gradually convinced owners to install electric lights in their ships. The practice had become so prevalent that in 1891 the American Bureau of Shipping* published the first issue of the *Rules for the Installation of Electric Lighting and Power Apparatus on Shipboard.* The original system aboard the *Columbia* lasted for fifteen years and was replaced only in 1895. On 20 July 1907 a lumber schooner rammed the *Columbia*, which had been steaming at fourteen knots through fog; unlike the schooner, which stayed afloat because of its cargo, the *Columbia* sank in eight minutes. "Most of the passengers were asleep below and of the 189 aboard, 88 were drowned" (Emmons 1985), including the captain.

References: American Bureau of Shipping, *History 1862–1991*; Frederick E. Emmons, *American Passenger Ships: The Ocean Lines and Liners, 1873–1983* (Newark: University of Delaware Press, 1985); Matthew Josephson, *Edison: A Biography* (New York: McGraw-Hill, 1959); E. H. Rigg and A. J. Dickie, "History of the United States Coastwise Steamers," in Society of Naval Architects and Marine Engineers, *Historical Transactions, 1893–1943* (Westport, CT: Greenwood Press, 1981).

COMMERCE COMMITTEE OF THE U.S. SENATE, 1825–present. The Commerce Committee of the U.S. Senate has handled the legislation affecting the U.S. merchant marine, and whenever the chairman was particularly interested in the subject, he could have a decisive impact on shaping government policies toward the merchant marine. The Commerce Committee has undergone name modifications throughout its history and since 1977 has been known as the Committee on Commerce, Science and Transportation. Previous versions of its name have been Commerce Committee (1825–1947 and 1961–1977) and Committee on Interstate and Foreign Commerce (1947–1961), while a separate Committee on Interstate Commerce existed from 1887 to 1947, when it was merged with the Commerce Committee.

A subcommittee has handled merchant marine affairs since the 1940s, and for many years it was headed by Warren G. Magnuson,* who later also became a chairman of the Commerce Committee. Major accomplishments of the Commerce Committee have been legislation like the Merchant Marine Act of 1920* and exhaustive examinations like the *Merchant Marine Study and Investigation* of 1950. However, this Senate committee, with a smaller and more diverse membership than its counterpart in the House, the Merchant Marine and Fisheries Committee,* has generally not devoted as much sustained attention as the latter to ocean transportation. At the same time, senators generally have needed to appeal to a broader constituency to assure their reelection than has been the case with representatives, and thus since the 1950s the decline of the U.S. merchant marine convinced even staunch supporters like Magnuson not to squander too much time and effort on a dwindling industry.

Notable Chairmen

Wesley L Jones*	1919–1930
Warren G. Magnuson	1955–1978

References: Congressional Quarterly Service, *Congress and the Nation, 1945–1964* (Washington, DC: Congressional Quarterly, 1965); René De La Pedraja, *The Rise and Decline of U.S. Merchant Shipping in the Twentieth Century* (New York: Twayne, 1992); Samuel A. Lawrence, *United States Merchant Shipping Policies and Politics* (Washington, DC: Brookings Institution, 1968); Walter Stubbs, *Congressional Committees, 1789–1982: A Checklist* (Westport, CT: Greenwood Press, 1985); Paul M. Zeis, *American Shipping Policy* (Princeton, NJ: Princeton University Press, 1938).

COMMITTEE FOR MARITIME UNITY (CMU), 1946–1947. During World War II the Congress of Industrial Organizations (CIO) Maritime Committee (see Maritime Trades Department) had limited itself to preparing policy statements, but once the war was over, it was clear to Harry Bridges,* the president of the International Longshoremen's and Warehousemen's Union* (ILWU) that in the face of inflation, unified action from the maritime unions was necessary to preserve their wartime gains. Bridges invited the CIO maritime unions to a Washington, D.C., conference in December 1945, at whose meetings the labor leaders agreed to set up the Committee for Maritime Unity (CMU), which was formally founded on 6 May 1946 with the motto "one out, all out." Founding members were the National Maritime Union* (NMU), the Marine Engineers' Beneficial Association,* the National Union of Marine Cooks and Stewards,* and the Marine Firemen, Oilers, Watertenders, and Wipers* (MFOWW), as well as others, but real control lay in Bridges of the ILWU and Joseph Curran* of the NMU, who became cochairmen.

The CMU briefly made real the industrial dream of maritime workers' combining to achieve their common goals, and initially the results were very favorable: after a successful strike, Bridges negotiated a 40 percent increase in longshoremen's wages, because "the employers began to give ground" (Larrowe 1972) as soon as they heard of the establishment of the CMU. A second strike in the fall of 1946 failed to achieve all union demands, and in protest, the MFOWW withdrew, but not without blasting the communists in the CMU. Curran resented Bridges's ascendancy, and he too resigned in December 1946, taking the NMU out of the moribund CMU, which was formally dissolved in February 1947. Bridges made one last effort to revive the CMU when he proposed in December 1947 to fuse the NMU and the ILWU, a proposal promptly rejected by Curran. Joint strike action by seamen and dockworkers against the employers ended in the twentieth century with the collapse of the CMU. However, the seamen tried one more time to coordinate a single front among themselves in the Conference of American Maritime Unions* (CAMU) in 1954–1955.

Principal Labor Leaders

Harry Bridges	1946–1947
Joseph Curran	1946–1947

References: Richard O. Boyer, *The Dark Ship* (New York: Little, Brown, 1947); Joseph P. Goldberg, *The Maritime Story: A Study in Labor-Management Relations* (Cambridge: Harvard University Press, 1958); Charles P. Larrowe, *Harry Bridges: The Rise* *and Fall of Radical Labor in the United States* (New York: Lawrence Hill, 1972); William L. Standard, *Merchant Seamen: A Short History of Their Struggles* (New York: International, 1947).

COMMITTEE FOR PROMOTION OF TRAMP SHIPPING UNDER AMERICAN FLAG IN FOREIGN COMMERCE, 1949–1953. This committee, whose name sounded like the nightmare of a public relations agent, was created in 1949 to represent all the U.S.-flag tramp* firms. The predecessor organization, the American Tramp Shipowners' Institute,* had remained a closed, chummy group, so that most tramp outfits felt left out and without an effective voice to influence government decisions. Companies that had previously belonged to the more exclusive but rapidly disintegrating Ship Operators and Owners' Association* found in the new committee an acceptable alternative. F. Riker Clark, president of American Foreign Steamship Corp., emerged as the chairman of the committee, which he ran in the pattern of those company executives who doubled up as heads of their respective trade organizations.

The initial concern of the committee was to find alternate cargoes to compensate for the decline of government shipments to Europe. The outbreak of the Korean War in 1950 revived the ailing tramp sector, but by 1952 the boom was over, and the committee under Clark once again was fighting a rear guard action to preserve every bit of government cargoes for the U.S.-flag tramps. In November 1952 the committee secured a signal victory when it convinced the Maritime Administration* to take eight government-owned ships out of charter* and return them to the mothballed National Defense Reserve Fleet.* In 1952 the committee represented 116 vessels belonging to seventy-eight tramp firms, although many of the latter were subsidiaries of a smaller number of parent firms. Lobbying the government had become an essential task for the tramp owners, who decided to replace the rather informal committee with a more solid organization, the American Tramp Shipowners' Association.*

Principal Executive

F. Riker Clark   1949–1953

References: *New York Times*, 23 June 1952, 19 January 1953; Papers of Robert L. Dennison, Harry S. Truman Library, Independence, Missouri.

COMMITTEE OF AMERICAN STEAMSHIP LINES (CASL), 1954–1968. The Committee of American Steamship Lines (CASL) was the trade organization of the subsidized U.S.-flag steamship companies. The liner* firms, whose executives had begun to meet informally since 1950, had a vested stake in the complex subsidy procedures of the Merchant Marine Act of 1936.* After the collapse of the National Federation of American Shipping* (NFAS), the liner companies created CASL as an independent entity in 1954 for the central purpose of defending their government subsidies; another purpose was to make it as difficult as possible for other firms to qualify to receive the shrinking pie of subsidies. The members of CASL (without listing their subsidiaries) were in 1964:

American Export Isbrandtsen Lines*	Matson Navigation Company*
American President Lines*	Moore-McCormack Lines*
Bloomfield Steamship Company*	Pacific Far East Line*
Delta Line*	Prudential Lines*
Farrell Line*	States Steamship Lines*
Grace Line*	United States Lines*
Lykes Brothers Steamship Co.*	

As a lobbying organization, CASL became very effective and gained most of its requests from Congress and the Maritime Administration.* The presidents of the thirteen member companies rotated the chairmanship among themselves and also met four times each year during three days to shape common policies and plan their strategy toward the government and the public. CASL prepared and distributed publications and contracted studies to bolster its case for subsidies.

During 1964–1965 CASL did consider proposals to subsidize other companies so they could bring their foreign-flag fleets under the U.S. flag, but the staggering price tag doomed such an idea. Consequently, CASL remained what it had been since its foundation, an exclusive club for the U.S.-flag subsidized liner companies. After 1964 Vietnam War cargoes rescued the steamship companies otherwise struggling to survive, but the decline was too real to be ignored. When Grace Line, a strong supporter of CASL, decided to withdraw completely from merchant shipping, the remaining members began to worry about the future of their trade association. Other companies were in an even more precarious situation, and to try to seek help from the government, unity among the different sectors of shipping was the only way to become more effective. CASL, the American Merchant Marine Institute* (AMMI), and the Pacific American Steamship Association* (PASA) were dissolved in December 1968 and merged into a new organization, the American Institute of Merchant Shipping (AIMS) on 1 January 1969.

Principal Executives

Alexander Purdon	1954–1960
Albert E. May	1961–1968

References: Robert G. Albion, *Seaports South of Sahara: The Achievements of an American Steamship Service* (New York: Appleton-Century-Crofts, Inc., 1959); Committee of American Steamship Lines, *Progress of the U.S. Liner Fleet*, December 1964; Gale Research, *Encyclopedia of Associations*, 1956–1964; White House Central Files, Lyndon B. Johnson Library, Austin, Texas; *New York Times*, 1 July 1954, 1 October 1968.

COMMITTEE ON MERCHANT MARINE AND FISHERIES. See Merchant Marine and Fisheries, Committee on.

COMPOUND ENGINE, 1865–1890s. The introduction of the compound engine in the late 1860s at last made steamships economical; their expensive operation was impossible before without massive government subsidies. Modern ocean transportation began to appear with the compound engine and not with its predecessor, the single-expansion engine.* Besides other problems, the fundamental disadvantage of the single-expansion engine was its enormous waste of steam, so that the huge consumption of coal meant high costs without a corresponding improvement in performance. Early in the nineteenth century engineers knew that the compound engine was the solution, but it required steam pressures at least three times higher than the twenty pounds per square inch possible in the single-expansion engine (atmospheric pressure at sea level is fifteen pounds per square inch). Fatal explosions of boilers and pipes postponed the introduction of the compound engine until the late 1860s, when at last steels able to withstand the higher pressures became available.

In the compound engine, a second larger cylinder was added to the one cylinder of the single-expansion. High-pressure steam went first into the small cylinder, and its exhaust steam then went to the larger low-pressure cylinder. The results were dramatic: the consumption of coal per horsepower dropped from four pounds for the single-expansion engine to two pounds or less in the compound engine. Furthermore, because this more efficient engine had a higher number of revolutions, the shaft could be connected directly to the propeller without having to waste energy in gearing up, as with the single-expansion engine; now that the more powerful engine was directly connected to the propeller, a faster ship speed also became possible. The first ship to use the compound engine was the British *Agamemnon* in 1865, while the first U.S. ship to use the compound engine (albeit imported from England) was the *George W. Clyde* in 1871. The American shipowner William P. Clyde stated that the compound engine "has done more to revolutionize the carrying trade of the world and to fasten still more closely England's hold upon it than, perhaps, any other single instrumentality" (U.S. Congress 1890).

The implications of the compound engine were momentous enough for ocean transportation. Steamships could now travel 8,000 miles and more without refueling, and long ocean crossings became routine. If less coal was loaded on shorter routes, then the released space increased the cargo-carrying capacity of the vessel. Ships with single-expansion engines had very small holds, but now with compound engines ships could start to haul large cargoes across the sea. With extra space available aboard ships, the cramped cabins of first-class travelers gave way to roomy accommodations and ample public spaces, so that the companies could begin to promote ocean travel to attract large numbers of passengers. However, bulk* cargoes of low value such as mineral ores and logs still traveled cheaper by sailing vessels. As a matter of fact, the fuel consumed by the steamships came from bunkering* stations supplied by iron sailing vessels, because shipowners preferred to save the cargo holds of the steamships for higher-paying cargoes.

The ships with compound engines could still cut costs by unfurling sails (standard equipment in case of mechanical failure) to gain some speed, and in any case they complied with their stated arrival times, unlike the sailing vessels, whose schedules ultimately hinged on the whims of nature. From another perspective, the compound engines accelerated the pace of overseas trade, as shippers* of the 1870s began to expect as normal guaranteed delivery schedules, as well as larger cargo capacities and even faster speeds. See also Marine Propulsion.

References: Gerald S. Graham, "The Ascendancy of the Sailing Ship 1850–1885," *Economic History Review* 9 (1956): 74–88; William S. Lindsay, *History of Merchant Shipping and Ancient Commerce*, 4 vols. (New York: AMS Press, 1965); John F. Nichols, "The Development of Marine Engineering," in Society of Naval Architects and Marine Engineers, *Historical Transactions, 1893–1943* (Westport, CT: Greenwood Press, 1981); Edward W. Sloan III, "The Machine at Sea: Early Transatlantic Steam Travel," in Benjamin W. Labaree, *The Atlantic World of Robert G. Albion* (Middletown, CT: Wesleyan University Press, 1975); U.S. Congress, House, Committee on Merchant Marine and Fisheries, *American Merchant Marine in the Foreign Trade*, Report No. 1210, 51st Congress, 1st Session, 1890.

CONFERENCE OF AMERICAN MARITIME UNIONS (CAMU), 1954–

1955. The collapse of the Committee for Maritime Unity* (CMU) ended hopes of a strike alliance between seamen and dockworkers, but the seamen's unions felt that coordination among themselves was still attainable. The end of the Korean War, with the accompanying drop in jobs for sailors, provided the initial impetus for organizing the Conference of American Maritime Unions (CAMU) in January 1954. Harry Lundeberg* of the Sailors' Union of the Pacific* (SUP) and Joseph Curran* of the National Maritime Union* (NMU) agreed "to forego our animosities" (*New York Times*, 20 January, 1954) and jointly assumed the chairmanship. Given the bitter personal hostility that existed between the men, the initial agenda of CAMU was kept simple and limited to congressional proposals, but no legislative victories materialized. Turf wars soon erupted among the member unions, and the surprise climax came in March 1955: in response to attacks on his union, "Lundeberg walked out of the CAMU conference within 20 minutes of the time it convened" (Schneider, 1958), in effect burying the organization, which was doomed from the start.

Principal Labor Leaders

Harry Lundeberg   1954–1955

Joseph Curran   1954–1955

References: Joseph P. Goldberg, *The Maritime Story: A Study in Labor-Management Relations* (Cambridge: Harvard University Press, 1958); *New York Times*, 20 January, 1954; Betty V. H. Schneider, *Industrial Relations in the West Coast Maritime Industry* (Berkeley: University of California Press, 1958).

CONFERENCES. Conferences have been voluntary associations created by liner* companies to set rates, sailings, and services and possibly also to arrange agreements for the pooling of revenues and cargo. Conferences became necessary when the introduction of the compound engine* at last made steamships competitive with sailing vessels. If too many steamships were in the trade route, rates for cargo declined, and the resulting rate war meant the ruin of most owners and the emergence of a single monopoly firm in the trade route. The Calcutta Conference, the first conference in the world, appeared in 1875 to establish uniform rates and assign to each carrier a number of voyages and cargo shares from a common pool in the trade between India and England. Gradually other companies followed suit until conferences became a permanent presence in almost all the sea-lanes of the world. The introduction of the triple-expansion engine* reconfirmed the need for conferences, because with faster speeds and lower vessel operating costs, individual companies were easily tempted to risk partial rate wars.

Western European countries and Japan accepted the conferences as an indispensable mechanism to prevent monopoly in the ocean trade. The United States, however, considered the conferences already to be monopolistic conspiracies, whose operation was forbidden under the Sherman Antitrust Act of 1890. Because over 90 percent of U.S. trade with foreign countries traveled aboard foreign-flag vessels (whether American-owned or not), the conferences were able to sidestep most antitrust actions until the passage of the Shipping Act of 1916.*

The Shipping Act of 1916 incorporated the findings and most of the recommendations of the Alexander Committee.* The Shipping Act of 1916 granted antitrust immunity to conferences, but only after they had been stripped of objectionable practices and provided the government closely regulated them. The act prohibited conferences from using the deferred rebate,* fighting ships,* and other monopolistic practices, although it was contradictory on dual or contract rates;* the act also created the Shipping Board* to regulate the conferences, which henceforth were to be "open" to any company wishing to join or even rejoin. The number of conferences in the U.S. trade routes climbed to over 100 in the 1920s.

While the rest of the world left conferences alone to manage ocean transportation (except for occasional exhaustive investigations), the Shipping Act of 1916 and its successor, the Shipping Act of 1984,* established the principles under which conferences in the U.S. foreign trade routes have generally operated. Although the later act was more sympathetic to conferences than the earlier one, both reflected a profound U.S. fear of monopolistic practices. Only in the United States have conferences been required to be "open" to any company that wished to join, while the excessive regulation and the outlawing of many discriminatory practices have gradually weakened the conferences in the U.S. trade routes during the twentieth century. The Shipping Act of 1984 did not bring conferences all the relief they expected, and the liner companies had to

wage a determined struggle in 1992 to keep the Advisory Commission on Conferences in Ocean Shipping* from erasing the earlier gains.

In an effort to survive, liner companies used the new authorization contained
in the Shipping Act of 1984 to create "superconferences."* Instead of the over
100 conferences that had existed since the 1920s, the liner companies reduced
them to less than 20 by 1992. Whether under one form or another, conferences
will remain a permanent part of ocean transportation, at least until a totally
different technology replaces the existing methods of marine propulsion.*

References: Advisory Commission on Conferences in Ocean Shipping, *Report to the
President and the Congress* (Washington, DC: Government Printing Office, 1992); René
De La Pedraja, *The Rise and Decline of U.S. Merchant Shipping in the Twentieth Century*
(New York: Twayne, 1992); Federal Maritime Commission, *Section 18 Report on the
Shipping Act of 1984*, September 1989; Lane C. Kendall, *The Business of Shipping*, 5th
ed. (Centreville, MD: Cornell Maritime Press, 1986).

CONGRESS; later, *NANKING;* later, *EMMA ALEXANDER,* **1913–1936.**
The Pacific Coast Steamship Company* ordered the *Congress* from the New
York Shipbuilding Company, and when the ship arrived in San Francisco on 6
October 1913 she was the largest coastwise* liner in service in the United States.
The *Congress* carried 416 persons in first class and 120 in second class, and
although not a slow vessel, neither was she particularly fast for a passenger liner
because her triple-expansion engines* could make fifteen knots at most. When
the next year James Hill placed two fast turbine* liners, the *Great Northern**
and the *Northern Pacific*, in the same coastwise service, it was clear that the
Congress could not compete, and not surprisingly the poor voyage results from
the *Congress* were one more reason that convinced the owners of the Pacific
Coast Steamship Company to sell out to the Admiral Line* of Hubbard F.
Alexander* in early September 1916.

Before the *Congress* could join the fleet of the Admiral Line, the vessel caught
fire at sea off Coos Bay, Oregon, on 14 September 1916, and after attempts to
put out the flames failed, the captain headed the ship toward land and anchored
near the shore to allow the passengers and crew to disembark aboard the lifeboats. No loss of life occurred, and the fire was allowed to burn itself out,
leaving the *Congress* "a smoldering skeleton" (Brown 1966). The engines of
the *Congress* by a miracle escaped damage, and the vessel was able to return
from Coos Bay to Seattle on her own power. The Admiral Line was able to sell
the engines and boilers at a profit, thanks to the scarcity of marine equipment
during the World War I shipping shortage, and then abandoned the gutted,
burned-out hulk of the *Congress* for scrapping at a later date.

The China Mail Steamship Company* (CMSS) was desperately trying to operate a transpacific service between California and China but simply could not
find vessels to buy because of the critical shortage caused by World War I. The
CMSS ran into the abandoned *Congress* and, after buying the burned-out hulk,
spent a small fortune reconstructing the ship in what was called "the largest

reconditioning job ever performed in an American shipyard'' (Tate 1986). CMSS refitted the vessel, now renamed the *Nanking*, to carry 123 passengers in first class, 100 in second class, and 554 in steerage.* The *Nanking* began service in the first days of July 1918 and served the CMSS until April 1923, when the company went bankrupt largely because of extensive persecution by private and government officials who did not want an enterprise owned by persons of Chinese origin to succeed.

On 18 November 1923 the Admiral Line purchased the *Nanking* and reconditioned the vessel to carry only 442 passengers, none in steerage class and all in better and roomier accommodations to meet the demands of travelers seeking maximum comfort. Under the new name of *Emma Alexander*, the vessel provided coastwise passenger and express freight service until 1936, when the Admiral Line went bankrupt, and the *Emma Alexander* was laid up. The British purchased the very old vessel in 1942 for one last tour of duty during World War II; with the return to peace the ship was sunk at sea in 1946.

References: Giles T. Brown, *Ships That Sail No More: Marine Transportation from San Diego to Puget Sound, 1910–1940* (Lexington: University of Kentucky Press, 1966); Frederick E. Emmons, *American Passenger Ships* (Newark: University of Delaware Press, 1985); Robert J. Schwendinger, *Ocean of Bitter Dreams: Maritime Relations Between China and the United States, 1850–1915* (Tucson: Westernlore Press, 1988); E. Mowbray Tate, *Transpacific Steam: The Story of Steam Navigation from the Pacific Coast of North America to the Far East and the Antipodes, 1867–1941* (New York: Cornwall Books, 1986).

CONSOLIDATED STEAMSHIP LINES, 1907–1908. Wall Street financier Charles W. Morse created the Consolidated Steamship Lines as a holding company for coastwise* companies on the eastern seaboard of the United States. Morse wanted to do for the coastwise lines what J. P. Morgan had tried to do for the transatlantic lines with the International Mercantile Marine* (IMM), namely, to combine into a near monopoly or cartel the main steamship firms, thereby reducing operating costs while increasing profit margins. Morse had begun to buy individual steamship companies in 1900, and by 2 January 1907, when he incorporated the Consolidated Steamship Lines, he had acquired the Clyde Line* and the Mallory Line* and also had reorganized several smaller firms into the Eastern Steamship Company.* He completed his impressive acquisitions with the purchase of the New York and Puerto Rico Line* in March 1907 and the Ward Line* in April of the same year.

The owners of the component lines had been extremely reluctant to part with their properties, and Morse could convince them to sell only by paying prices at least twice the real worth of their stock. Morse had an apparently inexhaustible source of money: he borrowed money to purchase a company and then used its assets as collateral to buy another company. Unfortunately for Morse, he could not buy every coastwise company, because at least twelve belonged to the railroads, which not only refused to sell but launched their steamship firms into a fierce competition against the Consolidated Steamship Lines. Morse had ordered fourteen new steamships, but the payments to the shipyards cut deeply into revenue, and soon several of the subsidiaries began to show heavy losses. Consolidated Steamship Lines asked for funds from Morse's financial institutions, but rumors of the difficulties spread fast, and on 23 October 1907 a run on his bank began. Soon his financial empire collapsed, and the run spread to other banks, triggering the panic of 1907; Morse himself ended in the federal penitentiary.

The former owners of the subsidiaries staged "a swift power play" (Baughman 1972) a few days later and regained control of the companies by promising to assume the debt obligations of the individual subsidiaries but not of Consolidated Steamship Lines. By the end of December the former owners, along with bankers, created a Bondholders' Protective Committee to try to deal with the impending bankruptcy of Consolidated Steamship Lines. At the foreclosure sale on 25 November 1908 the Bondholders' Protective Committee made the only offer for Consolidated Steamship Lines, which was accepted by the court. That same day the Atlantic, Gulf & West Indies Steamship Lines* (AGWI) was incorporated as the new holding company to replace Consolidated Steamship Lines.

References: James P. Baughman, *The Mallorys of Mystic: Six Generations in American Maritime Enterprise* (Middletown, CT: Wesleyan University Press, 1972); U.S. House, Committee on Merchant Marine and Fisheries, *Investigation of Shipping Combinations*, 4 vols. (Washington, DC: Government Printing Office, 1913).

CONSTITUTION **and** *INDEPENDENCE,* **1951–present.** The *Constitution* and the *Independence* were the two large express passenger liners the American Export Lines* (AEL) built for service between New York and Italy. The company ordered the ships in 1948; the Quincy, Massachusetts, shipyard of Bethlehem Steel delivered them in 1950; and the two ships entered service in 1951. Transatlantic ocean travel had not yet slackened in the late 1940s, and AEL believed there was still room for these large (length of 683 feet and beam of 89 feet) liners before the jet airplane appeared, but the company calculated wrong, and the steam turbine* ships of twenty-three-knot speed were money losers almost from the start. AEL still did not realize that ocean passenger travel was nearly obsolete and was even considering ordering a third liner in the hope of achieving a profitable operation with the combination of three vessels, but in time AEL relented and decided to make do with the purchase in November 1959 of a refitted Mariner,* the *Atlantic*, from the bankrupt American Banner Lines.*

As passenger travel declined, AEL gradually disposed of its other passenger vessels, including the *Atlantic* and the Four Aces,* but still hoped to keep the express liners in service by means of an intensive advertising campaign and by scheduling more off-season cruise voyages to the Caribbean. Nevertheless, losses continued to mount, and AEL had no choice but to lay up the *Constitution* in 1968 and the *Independence* the next year. After constant efforts to find a good buyer failed, AEL had to accept the ridiculously low sum of $2 million from Hong Kong shipping magnate C. Y. Tung for both vessels in 1974. The two liners lay idle in Hong Kong and were saved from the inevitable trip to the scrap yard only when American Hawaiian Cruises gambled on trying to run the vessels in the interisland tourist trade of Hawaii. The ships were under the Panamanian flag of convenience,* but a special act of Congress allowed their return to U.S. registry* after extensive refitting in U.S. shipyards. The *Independence* first entered Hawaiian islands service in 1980, and success guaranteed the entry of the *Constitution* in 1982. American Hawaiian Cruises extensively remodeled the ships to accommodate the demands of modern tourist travel, and as "the only American 'passengers only' cruise ships" (Emmons 1985), these magnificent liners have continued to ply the Hawaiian waters until the present.

References: René De La Pedraja, *The Rise and Decline of U.S. Merchant Shipping in the Twentieth Century* (New York: Twayne, 1992); Frederick E. Emmons, *American Passenger Ships: The Ocean Lines and Liners, 1873–1983* (Newark: University of Delaware Press, 1985).

CONSTRUCTION DIFFERENTIAL SUBSIDY (CDS), 1936–1981. The construction differential subsidy (CDS) was one of the two subsidies created by the Merchant Marine Act of 1936* to maintain a strong U.S.-flag presence in the foreign trade routes and, like the companion operating differential subsidy* (ODS), established the concept of parity or equality of costs between the United States and foreign countries. Since the introduction of iron and steam vessels in the second half of the nineteenth century, shipbuilding costs have been lower abroad than in the United States, and the purpose of the construction differential subsidy was to equalize the sales prices so that the American shipowner would not be penalized for buying vessels built in U.S. shipyards. The concept of parity was simple enough, that the U.S. government would cover the difference or the "differential" between the higher U.S. and the lower foreign costs, but the application of the concept has been far from simple.

The 1936 Merchant Marine Act limited the CDS to vessels for the liner* trade, and although in 1952 Congress opened the CDS to vessels in the bulk* trade, in practice the CDS went only to companies also receiving the ODS. The Maritime Administration* (MARAD) tried constantly to determine the exact price difference between ships built abroad and those in the United States, but by the time it had obtained the figures, they were out of date, and the agency usually could not estimate with any precision the even more significant figure of *costs*, rather than just prices. Furthermore, the CDS was a subsidy to the shipyard and not to the shipowner, so that even if the government covered the entire difference in price, other, apparently nonmonetary factors made the American shipowners reluctant to order from U.S. shipyards. While foreign shipyards guaranteed delivery times and were eager to work out the best possible arrangements for special and rush orders, U.S. shipyards showed no similar cooperative spirit and took twice as long to deliver the ships, sometimes not even in satisfactory condition, so that costly litigation became normal. Concerning technology, U.S. shipyards were in a paradoxical situation: although leading the world in the construction of very advanced vessels like liquified natural gas carriers, they had lost the capacity to introduce the latest innovations into containerships. The inability to produce and install slow-speed diesels* in the United States for many decades was a crucial technological shortcoming.

Finally, U.S. shipyard prices rose from at least twice those of foreign shipyards in the 1950s to three times as high as building abroad in the 1990s. The growing disparity in prices meant even larger outlays from the federal government, which, groaning under deficit problems, decided in 1981 to suspend the CDS program. Since companies receiving ODS were obligated by their contracts to order vessels through the CDS program, the government granted a special temporary dispensation so that thirty-two new ships could be built abroad and still qualify for the ODS. The CDS failed to maintain a strong shipyard base or a strong U.S.-flag merchant fleet, and although the program ranked as a very expensive failure, no adequate substitute to attain the original goals has yet been found.

References: Commission on Merchant Marine and Defense, *Public Hearings, July-December 1988*; René De La Pedraja, *The Rise and Decline of U.S. Merchant Shipping in the Twentieth Century* (New York: Twayne, 1992); Ernst G. Frankel, *Regulation and Policies of American Shipping* (Boston: Auburn House, 1982); Gerald R. Jantscher, *Bread upon the Waters: Federal Aids to the Maritime Industries* (Washington, DC: Brookings Institution, 1975); Samuel A. Lawrence, *United States Merchant Shipping Policies and Politics* (Washington, DC: Brookings Institution, 1966); Transportation Research Board, *Intermodal Marine Container Transportation: Impediments and Opportunities* (Washington, DC: National Research Council, 1992).

CONTAINERS. In the history of merchant shipping, two events stand out: the introduction of the compound engine* in the 1870s and, a hundred years later, the adoption of containers. The compound engine, soon replaced by the even more efficient triple-expansion engine,* created the modern merchant shipping industry. The status quo in merchant shipping did not experience its first revolution until the advent of containers, which practically eliminated break-bulk cargo* from the trade routes of the industrialized nations.

The container is a big steel box of two basic sizes: a smaller one of twenty by eight by eight feet (6 by 2.5 by 2.5 meters) and measured in TEUs* or twenty-foot equivalent units, and a larger one of forty by eight by eight feet (12.5 by 2.5 by 2.5 meters) and measured in FEUs* or forty-foot equivalent units. World shipping adopted overwhelmingly the twenty- and forty-foot units, although a few U.S. companies continued to use containers of other sizes; for specialized cargoes containers of different dimensions were also available.

Carrying cargo in boxes and crates dated back centuries, but because the packaged items were treated just like break-bulk cargo, no savings in time or money occurred. The history of the containers properly begins with Seatrain,* which in 1929 began to carry railroad cars from the United States to Havana: through ingenious methods the cars were placed on specially built rails aboard the ship, which could carry almost a hundred cars per trip. Opposition from Cuban longshoremen, who refused to handle the cars unless at least part of the cargo was unloaded and then reloaded on other railroad cars, deprived this method of some of its advantages. Seatrain continued to provide the service until 1960, and although it did not pursue the concept further, the company left a pioneering legacy for the later development of both containers and Roll-on/Roll-off* vessels.

During World War II, the War Shipping Administration* (WSA) was over-whelmed with the handling of the vast amount of military cargoes and, to try to speed up cargo deliveries, began to fill whole vessels with crates of the same size. The results were so favorable in time and costs that the WSA decided to adopt the new containers for all cargo movements, but before it could order the conversion to containers, World War II ended, and the tradition-bound merchant shipping business was more than ready to return to the practices prevailing before the war.

The WSA distributed its findings in several publications, but to no avail, because the highly conservative shipping industry refused to budge. However, in the late 1950s, three firms at last began to experiment with containers. The first was the company later known as Sea-Land,* which, under the direction of Malcom McLean,* offered the first commercial container service in April 1957 on top of a T-2* tanker and later that year placed in service the first full container vessel. The second company, Matson Navigation Company,* began carrying containers on top of its vessels in 1958 and in 1960 placed its first full contai-nerships in the route between San Francisco and Hawaii. Both Sea-Land and Matson were operating within the domestic trades of the United States, where they were protected from foreign competition, but the Grace Line* first intro-duced containers into the foreign trades in 1960. Grace had carefully studied the economic and technical, but not the historical, aspects of containers, so that the outcome was predictable: longshoremen in Venezuela, just like those dec-ades earlier in Cuba, refused to handle the containers. The whole Grace exper-iment was a costly flop and effectively set back the introduction of containers into foreign trades almost a decade.

Not until February 1966 did containers appear in the North Atlantic when Moore-McCormack* offered the service, followed a few months later by Sea-Land, while United States Lines* (USL) had under construction a fleet of spe-cially designed containerships, the Lancers.* Many executives, including Mc-Lean, believed that because U.S. firms had taken such a lead in container technology, subsidies were no longer required to compete against the European and Japanese lines, just starting to order their own containerships.

By the early 1970s containers were handling the majority of the cargo moving between ports in Western Europe, the United States, and the Far East. The benefits to shipowners were dramatic: before, one-half of the freighter's time was spent in port, but now only one-fifth of a containership's time was spent in port. By 1960 labor costs in port with break-bulk vessels had reached 80 percent of voyage expenses, but now this percentage dropped dramatically. The containership had more time to steam between ports, its real function, so that the cargo was now delivered faster without having to incur the additional expenses of steaming at higher speeds.

However, to obtain the maximum benefits from containerization required radically different port facilities, and until these were built in the 1970s and 1980s, the early generations of containerships had to carry huge cranes, which necessarily lowered the efficiency of the ships. The old warehouses and the traditional finger piers in the world's docks became obsolete overnight, because the containers required vast spaces on land as marshaling yards and rows of tall and extremely heavy cranes alongside the ships' moorings. Most companies and port authorities opted for abandoning their traditional sites and constructing new facilities in less-urbanized areas. The price tags ran into the billions of dollars and often included extensive dredging and major overhauls of the ports. The huge cost of port transformation—often overlooked in discussions on the benefits of containerization—finally freed the ships to be purely "floating boxes" whose only function was to carry the maximum number of containers aboard.

Containers returned vessels to their original function of crossing the seas, rather than serving as floating warehouses next to the piers, as had been the rule with break-bulk cargo. Even more significantly, containers rescued ocean transportation from being drowned by competition from railroads, trucks, and airplanes. Containers came too late to save coastwise* and intercoastal* shipping and gave only a momentary edge to U.S.-flag-lines against foreign competitors, but containers did bring efficiency and reliability, along with low costs, back to ocean transportation. Shippers* had come to dread sending merchandise by ocean transportation, because of pilfering, damage, high costs, and delays, while the shipowners found it humanly impossible to keep track of the freight handled so many times by so many individuals. Instead each container had its own registration and was classified by the American Bureau of Shipping,* and the movements of the containers, just like those of the ships themselves, were easily followed with the help of the computers. While a company's fleet rarely had numbered more than fifty vessels, containers soon multiplied into the tens of thousands, whose movements could be tracked only through computers; indeed, the latter became inseparable from containers in merchant shipping, a business that pioneered in the widespread adoption of computers in the United States.

The introduction of containers in the 1960s marked nothing less than the beginning of the "container revolution," whose ramifications still continue at the end of the twentieth century. Besides the radical transformation of operations by ships and ports, containers have had a major impact beyond the water. First and foremost has been the spread of intermodalism,* a practice that consisted in switching the same container among different forms of transportation—barge, rail, truck, and ship. The containers were loaded at the factory and then traveled by whatever means were most convenient to the nearest port for loading aboard the vessel. The shipper could arrange his own transportation for taking the container to the port; but the freight forwarder* was also willing to provide "portal-to-portal" service so that the shipper simply handed over the cargo to the freight forwarder at the factory, and the freight appeared at its destination without having to deal with anybody else.

In the early years of intermodalism, the goal had always been to reach the nearest port, but in 1971 Seatrain broke new ground and created the concept of a permanent landbridge* between the East and West coasts of the United States. Under the landbridge concept, Seatrain transferred the containers from its ships to specially chartered flatcars for travel across the United States, and during the whole trip the cargo remained the responsibility of the company. The landbridge normally saved ten days from the all-water route of thirty days from Tokyo to New York City via the Panama Canal,* and although the latter was cheaper, shippers in a rush to deliver their merchandise flocked to the landbridge. Soon other companies followed the lead of Seatrain, most notably American President Lines* (APL), whose introduction of double-stack trains* in 1984 dramatically lowered the costs and even further increased the appeal of the landbridge. In double-stack trains, the containers were piled two high on top of the flatcars, and although other companies soon imitated the practice, by then APL, the pioneer in double-stack trains, had managed to carve out a sizable market. Mc-Lean, at that time the owner of United States Lines, failed to realize the significance of the landbridge, and instead he made his fatal move to try to revive intercoastal shipping via the Panama Canal.

As steamship companies perfected the arrangements that allowed containers to move smoothly and without any interruption from origin to destination, industrialists could now adopt "just-in-time" production methods, by which the parts or raw materials reached the factory at the exact moment they were needed for manufacture. Containers and intermodalism made unnecessary huge inventories, and factory managers could count on the scheduled arrival of whatever inputs were needed. In conclusion, containers, the greatest revolution in ocean transportation since the introduction of the compound engine, have had a massive impact on the entire transportation system, and they have also had a significant influence on the adoption of computers and of new techniques in manufacturing.

References: Advisory Commission on Conferences in Ocean Shipping, *Report to the President and the Congress* (Washington, DC: Government Printing Office, 1992); American Bureau of Shipping, *History 1862–1991*; René De La Pedraja, *The Rise and Decline of U.S. Merchant Shipping in the Twentieth Century* (New York: Twayne, 1992); *Journal of Commerce*, 12 December 1988, 12 December 1989; Lane C. Kendall, *The Business of Shipping*, 5th ed. (Centreville, MD: Cornell Maritime Press, 1986); Transportation Research Board, *Intermodal Marine Container Transportation: Impediments and Opportunities* (Washington, DC: National Research Council, 1992).

CONTROLLED CARRIERS ACT or OCEAN SHIPPING ACT OF 1978.
Congress passed this law in an effort to curb predatory practices on the part of state-owned shipping lines, specifically FESCO, the Soviet shipping company of the Far East. Many Americans had long resented the existence of state enterprises in shipping, and the Cold War provided the opportunity to retaliate. By the Controlled Carriers Act, the Federal Maritime Commission* (FMC) could take reprisals against those state-owned firms, whose excessively low rates qualified as ''noneconomic'' behavior. The act was an attempt to impose a particular mercantile mentality on world shipping and narrowly defined *noneconomic* to mean ''for profits on capital invested only''; consequently, if a state carrier attempted to earn foreign currency by quoting lower rates, this action was not considered an ''economic'' activity. In the irrational Cold War climate, state-owned companies provided a convenient scapegoat for the failures of many U.S. steamship companies in the 1970s.

Since FESCO was undercutting American companies as well as lines of other nationalities, the law could not be drafted exclusively against the Soviet Union and instead sought to create a general standard by which to control state-owned firms. However, a closer analysis revealed that the merchant fleets of major allies, such as France and Italy, were state-owned, forcing the drafters of the bill to exempt from its provisions those countries that enjoyed most-favored-nation status. Thus, ironically, the act, rather than striking a deadly blow against state ownership, ended up doing what was highly repugnant to most Americans, namely, formally recognizing state ownership as an acceptable way to maintain a country's merchant marine.

Did FESCO feel the brunt of reprisals? By the time the FMC concluded its normally cumbersome and lengthy proceedings, FESCO had ceased to call on U.S. ports. Subsequent developments have confirmed the inefficacy of the Controlled Carriers Act, and in one major loophole, state-owned firms could evade reprisals by placing their ships under flags of convenience.* Congress passed the Foreign Shipping Practices Act of 1988 in order to try to stop business practices harmful to U.S. shipowners, but the FMC has been no more successful with the 1988 act than it was with the 1978 law. Both the legislative and regulatory approaches to foreign competition proved generally ineffective, except against weak Third World countries. The Controlled Carriers Act remained not only a legacy of the Cold War but also an example of how the United States insisted on trying to impose its economic principles on the rest of the world.

References: Advisory Commission on Conferences in Ocean Shipping, *Report to the President and the Congress* (Washington, DC: Government Printing Office, 1992); René De La Pedraja, *The Rise and Decline of U.S. Merchant Shipping in the Twentieth Century* (New York: Twayne, 1992); Ernst G. Frankel, *Regulation and Policies of American Shipping* (Boston: Auburn House, 1982).

COORDINATED CARIBBEAN TRANSPORT (CCT), 1961–1986. The Co-ordinated Caribbean Transport (CCT) provided Roll-on/Roll-off* (Ro/Ro) serv-ice between the United States and ports in Central and South America. United States Freight Company established CCT as a subsidiary, which began service to Guatemala with landing ship tanks (LSTs) in 1961. With a new vessel ac-quired in 1968 from German yards and placed under the Panamanian flag, CCT was able to extend its Ro/Ro service to Honduras in 1969, to Ecuador in 1974, and to Peru in 1981. The really booming market, however, was Venezuela, and in 1971 CCT placed a U.S.-flag Ro/Ro vessel in that trade, and in 1981 increased the sailings to one every ten days. The company also pioneered the practice of placing refrigerated trailers at remote farms in Venezuela, thereby gathering the cargoes that subsequently traveled on CCT's Ro/Ro vessels.

Three private Venezuelan carriers felt the competition and pressured the Ve-nezuelan government to enforce strictly the cargo-preference* laws starting in 1980, and by the summer of 1982 the campaign to drive shippers* away forced CCT to face losses for the first time. The company began proceedings in the Federal Maritime Commission* (FMC) to try to obtain sanctions against the Venezuelan government, but the long struggle was necessarily tiring. Interna-tional Controls Corporation, the owners of CCT by the mid-1980s, lacked the resources to expand the fleet and decided to sell CCT to Crowley Maritime Corporation in October 1986. See Crowley Caribbean Transport.

References: *American Shipper*, June 1981, November 1986, December 1992; ''Crow-ley Maritime Corporation,'' Special Supplement, *Journal of Commerce*, 1988; *Florida Journal of Commerce*, February 1968.

COSMOPOLITAN SHIPPING COMPANY, 1916–late 1980s? The Cosmo-politan Shipping Company provided cargo service from New York to French ports in the years between the two world wars. The company was established in 1916 to own and charter* ships in response to the tremendous shipping short-age caused by World War I. In 1919 the company, along with over 200 other firms, became one of the ''managing operators''* of government-owned vessels whose voyages were splendidly subsidized by the Shipping Board.* In 1923 the Shipping Board confirmed Cosmopolitan as the operator of the America-France Line, which provided cargo service between New York and French ports. Since 1919 Cosmopolitan had also tried to combine its services with those of the American Diamond Line, which served the New York-Rotterdam/Antwerp route, but its managing operator, the Black Diamond Steamship Corporation,* bitterly resisted the takeover attempt. Cosmopolitan and Black Diamond engaged in a ten-year struggle for control of the American Diamond Line, but finally in 1930 Black Diamond emerged victorious, while Cosmopolitan retained the America-France Line.

In 1939 the U.S. Maritime Commission* removed the America-France Line from Cosmopolitan, which then chartered Norwegian-flag freighters to replace the government-owned vessels. When the United States entered World War II,

Cosmopolitan operated government vessels for the War Shipping Administration* under general agency agreements.

After the War Shipping Administration was dissolved on 1 September 1946, its last head, Captain Granville Conway, became president of Cosmopolitan. The company operated from New York two lines, one to France, Belgium, and Holland and the other—the Southern Cross—down the east coast of South America, with Buenos Aires the last port of call. In 1946 the company had chartered fifteen surplus ships from the U.S. Maritime Commission* and had under charter eleven foreign-flag ships as well. By 1953, when Cosmopolitan resigned from the North Atlantic Westbound Freight Association,* the company operated exclusively Norwegian-flag vessels. In the late 1950s Cosmopolitan operated a stevedoring subsidiary and also served as New York agent for other merchant shipping companies. As late as the mid-1980s Cosmopolitan continued to operate chartered foreign-flag ships but did not own vessels of its own.

References: *New York Times*, 13 August 1939, 31 August and 8 November 1946, 25 August 1947, 3 January 1953, 14 January 1954, 8 July 1959; U.S. Senate, Special Committee on Investigation of Air Mail and Ocean Mail Contracts, *Hearings*, 9 vols. (Washington, DC: Government Printing Office, 1933–1934).

COTTON CLUB, 1947–present. The Cotton Club, based in Washington, D.C., has been the group of foreign diplomats who represented their countries' shipping interests. Membership was limited to "the traditional maritime powers of Europe with the single Asian addition of Japan . . . there is no intention of admitting anyone else" (*American Shipper*, November 1987). The Cotton Club began in 1947 as an informal gathering among shipping attachés to discuss the transportation of Marshall Plan cargoes to Europe but quickly became a formal group extremely useful to the member nations. By the 1980s regular meetings were held twice a month, with lengthy minutes of the discussions. In November 1987 the Cotton Club celebrated its 1,000th meeting. Another function of the Cotton Club has been to serve as a forum for invited speakers who themselves were powerful figures in the U.S. merchant marine. The Cotton Club has no fixed site, and meetings rotate among the various embassy buildings; the cohesion and seriousness with which foreign countries have treated shipping matters in the United States were in sharp contrast with the fragmented and often contradictory policies the U.S. government has pursued toward foreign shipping since World War II.

References: *American Shipper*, November 1987; Papers of Robert L. Dennison, Harry S. Truman Library, Independence, Missouri.

COUNCIL OF AMERICAN-FLAG SHIP OPERATORS (CASO), 1978–1987. The Council of American-Flag Ship Operators (CASO) represented the U.S.-flag subsidized companies. CASO originally had been the Liner Council of the American Institute of Merchant Shipping* (AIMS), but when the tanker companies in AIMS failed to back requests for more government funds, the eight subsidized companies decided in March 1977 to separate, and in January 1978 they created their own trade group, whose founding members were:

American Export Lines*   Moore-McCormack Lines*

American President Lines*   Prudential Lines*

Farrell Lines*   States Steamship Lines*

Lykes Brothers Steamship*   United States Lines*

CASO hired a small staff in Washington, D.C., and the chairmanship of the organization was rotated among the presidents of the steamship companies. Even before CASO began to function, the refusal of Sea-Land,* Central Gulf,* Delta,* and Waterman Steamship* to join crippled the organization, whose membership was reduced to seven in November 1978 because of the bankruptcy of States Steamship Lines.

The first chairman, W. J. Amoss, Jr., who was also the president of Lykes Brothers, stated that "CASO primarily will be concerned with the promotion and maintenance of a United States merchant marine owned, operated, built, and manned by United States citizens" (*American Shipper*, February 1978). CASO soon changed its mind about building the ships in the United States, and in the early 1980s defended the right to construct U.S.-flag vessels in the cheaper foreign shipyards, a change in position that cost the National Maritime Council* (NMC), the umbrella organization for shipping, the support of the shipyards. CASO continued to represent the interests of the U.S.-flag subsidized lines during the legislative struggles of 1978–1984, but not even the passage of the Shipping Act of 1984* could arrest the downward trend in U.S.-flag operations. The bankruptcy of United States Lines in 1986 deprived CASO of its largest paying member, and the few surviving companies agreed to join with the non-subsidized companies to create a new trade organization, the United Shipowners of America* (USA), in 1987.

Principal Executive

Albert E. May   1978–1987

References: *American Shipper*, February, November 1978, September 1983, April 1984; Gale Research, *Encyclopedia of Associations*, 1983–1988.

COVERDALE, WILLIAM HUGH, 27 January 1871–10 August 1949. William H. Coverdale was the president of American Export Lines* (AEL) in 1934–1949 and was responsible for the remarkable comeback of the company from bankruptcy. Coverdale, whose father was an architect, was born in Kingston, Ontario, Canada, on 27 January 1871; he studied in public schools and graduated as an engineer from Geneva College in 1891. After graduation he began working with the Pennsylvania Railroad, in whose employ he stayed until 1900, when he became a consulting engineer for transportation companies. He became a naturalized citizen of the United States in 1904. His consulting experience extended to steamship companies, and he became the head of the Canada Steamship Lines in 1922, so that when AEL faced bankruptcy, the investors who tried to save the company called on the expert Coverdale to become its new president, replacing Henry Herbermann.*

Coverdale promptly slashed costs, reduced the staff, and put the company to work in a very regular pattern. Above all, he trimmed the fleet and consolidated sailings in the existing routes, so the steamship services again began to earn profits, and gradually AEL dug its way out of the accumulated debts. Coverdale brought John E. Slater* a fellow engineer from their consulting firm, to become vice president, and with their careful work AEL made one of the very rare, if not unique, comebacks for a pre–World War II steamship company.

Under Coverdale AEL became profitable and even purchased from the government another route, the American Pioneer Line to India, in 1939. As a transportation engineer, Coverdale sensed the significance of aviation and in 1937 organized a separate subsidiary, American Export Airlines. AEL's venture into aviation was very successful and ended only in 1945, when, under pressure from Pan American Airlines, the Civil Aeronautics Board prohibited steamship lines from operating airlines. After World War II, Coverdale supervised the restoration of the prewar shipping services to the Mediterranean and to India, by means of the purchase of surplus vessels. To replace the Four Aces,* the combination passenger-cargo liners lost in the war, AEL converted four navy attack transports into a second generation of Four Aces with the same names as the prewar vessels. He had thus not only made a major comeback in the 1930s but also positioned AEL for solid growth in the late 1940s. The only mistake came when Coverdale allowed Slater to proceed with the plans for two new express passenger lines. In 1948 AEL ordered the *Constitution** and the *Independence*, which were completed only in 1951, after Coverdale's death on 10 August 1949. He was replaced as president of AEL by his fellow engineer, Slater.

References: René De La Pedraja, *The Rise and Decline of U.S. Merchant Shipping in the Twentieth Century* (New York: Twayne, 1992); *National Cyclopedia of American Biography*, vol. 39; *Who's Who in the Maritime Industry, 1946.*

CRIMPS (or CRIMPING SYSTEM). Crimps were agents who supplied sailors to captains who needed crews. Essentially the crimps were middlemen or brokers who, from the nineteenth century to World War I, were the source of seafaring laborers. The crimps operated on two fronts. First they convinced sailors who had just reached port to desert their ships (forfeiting their wages and personal belongings on board) and come to boardinghouses, with all expenses paid out of advances from their future jobs. Then the crimps found jobs (or "berths") for the sailors in outbound ships; the sailors soon discovered that the faster they ran up debts at the boardinghouse, the faster the crimps found them another job. The crimps themselves could own or have a stake in the boardinghouses or simply be pure intermediaries, and in either case they solved the captain's problem of finding a crew in an unknown port and without having to waste precious shore time. The sailors themselves were trapped in a perpetual cycle of debt, desertions, and forfeited wages, but the system at the same time kept the seamen employed without having to worry about room, board, clothing, drink, or having to find a job. Boardinghouse keepers were repaid with full occupancy, and payment was guaranteed by the captains, while the crimps charged a commission for finding, keeping, and supplying the sailors. Also, the crimping system avoided the need of having to "shanghai"* sailors.

Until 1900, when wooden sailing vessels, long voyages, and a captain's financial stake in the ship were still widespread, the crimping system had a certain internal logic that obtained results no matter how much the seamen were exploited. With the appearance of modern steamship companies at the turn of the century, the usefulness of the crimps diminished. The companies had shoreside offices and personnel available at all times, while the captain no longer had a financial stake in the vessel and was simply one more salaried employee. At the same time, both the captain and the company became more concerned about the best possible performance aboard and were no longer willing to accept whatever the crimps offered but wanted the freedom to choose among the better and more experienced seamen. For modern corporations to be successful, job performance had to be very productive, and to have shoreside personnel distracted from their essential tasks in order to sober up drunken sailors or release them from jail was time-consuming and unproductive. Hence companies did not oppose the campaign of the Sailors' Union of the Pacific* and Andrew Furuseth* to end the crimping system, because the corporations wanted more choice on who they picked but without the responsibility for their personal problems. World War I with its huge demand for sailors dealt a heavy blow to the crimping system, and after the disastrous 1921 strike,* the "shape-up,"* long traditional among longshoremen, had become the standard way to recruit all those seamen who had not worked out special relationships with individual companies or ships' captains.

References: Beth McHenry and Frederick N. Myers, *Home Is the Sailor: The Story of an American Seaman* (New York: International, 1948); Bruce Nelson, *Workers on the Waterfront: Seamen, Longshoremen, and Unionism in the 1930s* (Urbana: University of Illinois Press, 1990); Stephen Schwartz, *Brotherhood of the Sea: A History of the Sailors' Union of the Pacific, 1885–1985* (New Brunswick, NJ: Transaction Books, 1986); Hyman Weintraub, *Andrew Furuseth: Emancipator of the Seamen* (Berkeley: University of California Press, 1959).

CROMWELL LINE, 1858–1902. Georgia investors and H. B. Cromwell created this line to provide service between Savannah and New York, but with the outbreak of the Civil War the U.S. Navy took over the small fleet of the company. In 1862 federal forces recaptured New Orleans, and the Cromwell Line was one of the firms that saw a business opportunity and later that same year began a New York–New Orleans service. During the Civil War New Orleans turned into a "competitive jungle" for steamship companies, but when peace returned, only three companies remained in the New York–New Orleans trade, and by 1875 two had withdrawn, leaving "the field to the Cromwell line, which, it is understood, has not realized anything very handsome from the monopoly of the business'' (Baughman 1968).

In 1875 Charles Morgan* burst into the New York-New Orleans trade with four new vessels, and immediately a ferocious rate war broke out with the Cromwell Line and with the Mallory Line* on the Galveston-New York route. Only the death of Charles Morgan ended the rate war in 1878, and the three surviving lines decided to distribute the market among themselves. The Morgan and Cromwell Lines agreed to split in half the trade of New Orleans with New York, while the Mallory Line retained a monopoly on the Galveston-New York route. The agreement remained in force until the early years of the twentieth century, and although the short-lived Lone Star Line tried to break into the trade in 1897–1899, the challenger was crushed by the combined opposition of the three existing lines. In 1885 Southern Pacific Railroad purchased the Morgan Line* and in later years gained a majority control of the Cromwell Line. In 1902 the Southern Pacific Railroad Company transferred to its shipping subsidiary the remaining vessels of the Cromwell Line, whose name and existence came to an end.

References: James P. Baughman, *Charles Morgan and the Development of Southern Transportation* (Nashville: Vanderbilt University Press, 1968); James P. Baughman, *The Mallorys of Mystic: Six Generations in American Maritime Enterprise* (Middletown, CT: Wesleyan University, 1972); Frederick E. Emmons, *American Passenger Ships: The Ocean Lines and Liners, 1873–1983* (Newark: University of Delaware Press, 1985).

CROWLEY, THOMAS B., 1914–present. Thomas B. Crowley, the owner of the nation's largest tug and barge business, expanded into merchant shipping with Latin America and in recent years has headed one of the largest privately held maritime enterprises in the world. He was born in San Francisco in 1914 and attended Stanford University for two years, but when a teacher refused to admit that a textbook contained factual errors, he concluded that such an education was useless and left without completing a bachelor's degree. In 1933 he went to work with his father, Thomas Crowley, the owner of a small tug and barge outfit in San Francisco Bay, and learned the business through a long apprenticeship; gradually after 1950 he started to take over from his father, who retired at age seventy-five. Perhaps more than any other shipping executive, he concentrated his whole life on the company; as a shy, private man he did little socializing, and, as he explained, ''I don't drink, smoke, or tell dirty jokes.''

The company, Crowley Maritime Corporation,* was still fairly small in 1972 but was poised for growth because of Alaska oil and had already entered ocean transportation through the establishment of the subsidiary Alaska Hydro-Train* in 1964. Crowley had already plunged the company into seeking contracts in other parts of the United States, in particular Hawaii, Alaska, and the Caribbean, and he eventually began to carry specialized equipment to other parts of the world. Crowley Maritime grew by accretion as it added one type after another of specialized vessel or equipment to the existing services. Eventually the corporation had as many as 100 subsidiaries of Crowley Maritime, although these later were consolidated into more manageable units. Crowley has run his extensive transportation empire through a management committee, whose members, besides himself, have included Leo Collar for operations, James B. Rettig for engineering, and J. Alec Merrian for finance.

Crowley's attempts to enter ocean transportation between Puerto Rico and mainland United States culminated in his acquisition of Trailer Marine Transport* (TMT) in 1974. TMT not only became one of the major carriers in that trade but went on to expand service to the Dominican Republic, other Caribbean islands, and even Colombia. In the domestic trades protected by the cabotage* laws, Crowley's operations were profitable, but when he purchased the nearly bankrupt Delta Line* in December 1982, his first plunge into liner* operations in foreign routes failed. United States Lines* (USL) agreed to purchase Delta in December 1984, but soon USL itself went bankrupt in November 1986. Crowley sensed a good opportunity, and he was able to reacquire the modern ships of the former Delta Line, which he placed in a new subsidiary, Crowley American Transport.* In 1986 he also purchased the Coordinated Caribbean Transport* (CCT), which he kept as a separate entity but renamed Crowley Caribbean Transport* (CCT).

Already in the late 1980s ocean shipping and, in particular, the Latin American trades had become the principal source of income for the Crowley Maritime Corporation, whose operations continued under the direction of Crowley himself. In 1987 Leo Collar became the president, while Crowley remained as chairman of the board and chief executive officer. In 1991 Collar retired and was replaced by James B. Rettig, who retired in 1993. Crowley's son, Thomas B. Crowley, Jr., has been rising through the ranks of the corporation and may well become the third Crowley generation to head this major maritime enterprise.

References: *American Shipper*, January 1984, October 1987, May 1992, September 1993; ''Crowley Maritime Corporation,'' Special Supplement of *Journal of Commerce*, 1988, 5 August 1992; *Pacific Maritime Magazine*, May 1992.

CROWLEY AMERICAN TRANSPORT or AMERICAN TRANSPORT LINES, 1987–present. When Crowley Maritime Corporation* reacquired the containerships of the Delta Line* in 1986, Thomas B. Crowley* decided to create for them a new subsidiary in February 1987, the American Transport Lines (Amtrans). Crowley Maritime Corporation poured more resources into Amtrans until the latter was operating six ships on routes to Venezuela and the east coast of South America and to Europe via the Azores islands. Because the ships were fitted with diesel* engines, they were much more economical to operate than the expensive steamships of the former Delta Line, and since some were built in foreign shipyards under special permits from the U.S. government, Amtrans has enjoyed considerable success. Two chartered* ships provided the service to Europe, which depended considerably on U.S. military cargo; and the company canceled the service to Europe in 1991 when the ships were diverted to service in the Gulf War. In 1991 Amtrans was renamed Crowley American Transport and has concentrated its efforts on the Latin American routes.

References: *American Shipper*, April, August 1987, May 1992; "Celebrating a Century of Service," *Journal of Commerce*, 5 August 1992; "Crowley Maritime Corporation," Special Supplement of the *Journal of Commerce*, 1988.

CROWLEY CARIBBEAN TRANSPORT (CCT), 1986–present. Crowley Caribbean Transport (CCT) has been providing Roll-on/Roll-off* (Ro/Ro) service from the United States to Central and South America. Crowley Maritime Corporation* purchased the Coordinated Caribbean Transport* in October 1986 and gave the new subsidiary the name of Crowley Caribbean Transport, a minimal change since the company has usually been referred to as CCT. Crowley Maritime Corporation also poured resources into CCT to increase its capacity as well as the number of its sailings. In 1988 CCT operated eight Ro/Ro vessels to Costa Rica, Panama, Honduras, Guatemala, Ecuador, and Peru, as well as to Haiti and the Dominican Republic. CCT also sent barges towed by powerful tugs to Honduras, Guatemala, and Panama on regular schedules, in this way repeating some of the successful transportation methods Crowley Maritime Corporation had already utilized with Trailer Marine Transport* (TMT) in Puerto Rico.

References: *American Shipper*, May 1992; "Crowley Maritime Corporation," Special Supplement, *Journal of Commerce*, 1988; *Pacific Maritime Magazine*, May 1992.

CROWLEY MARITIME CORPORATION, 1892–present. Crowley Maritime Corporation, the nation's largest tug and barge business, has become, since the late 1980s, one of the largest U.S.-flag merchant shipping companies. Thomas Crowley established Crowley Maritime Corporation in 1892, but back then it was just one of many small outfits operating rowboats between ships and the shore in the San Francisco Bay Area. Crowley was among the first to buy gasoline launches for this service, and slowly he expanded his fleet. A big opportunity came with the San Francisco earthquake of 1906, when he safely stored money, bonds, and records in a barge in the middle of the bay until the bankers could rebuild their destroyed vaults and buildings. The goodwill he gained allowed him to expand his barge operation, and in May 1917 he formed a partnership to purchase, as a speculation, the North Pacific Steamship Company, a coastwise firm whose three small and old vessels they sold, apparently at a nice profit, in early 1918. Through judicious transactions and careful service, Crowley expanded his barge and tug fleet until it became the largest in the San Francisco Bay Area by World War II.

In 1933 his son Thomas B. Crowley* began to work in Crowley Maritime Corporation, and after a long apprenticeship he gradually took over from his father. The younger Crowley expanded business beyond the San Francisco Bay Area and soon saw a great opportunity in Alaska. Crowley Maritime Corporation established a subsidiary, Alaska Hydro-Train,* in 1963 to haul railroad cars between Alaska and the U.S. mainland. Even greater opportunities came from taking barges to the oil fields of Alaska, and Crowley Maritime Corporation expanded into many areas of transportation where specialized equipment was needed.

Crowley had seen the advantages of operating in the Alaska trade protected by the cabotage* laws of the United States and decided to repeat the earlier success in Puerto Rico. After several abortive attempts to shift tugs and barges no longer needed for the Alaska route into Puerto Rico, Crowley Maritime Corporation acquired Trailer Marine Transport* (TMT) in 1974 and went on to make this subsidiary one of the major carriers in the Puerto Rico-U.S. trade. Crowley Maritime Corporation purchased the Delta Line* in 1982, but this first experience with a liner* service in the foreign trade turned out badly, and Crowley sold it in 1984 at a loss, but not without first having learned some valuable lessons. In 1986 Crowley Maritime Corporation reacquired the good containerships of the former Delta Line and placed them in a new subsidiary, the American Transport Lines (renamed Crowley American Transport* in 1991), which has continued to operate successfully in the trade to Argentina and Brazil from the United States. A further acquisition in 1986, Coordinated Caribbean Transport* (CCT), gave Crowley Maritime Corporation control of Roll-on/Roll-off* (Ro/Ro) services to Central and South America.

To manage more effectively its sprawling maritime business, in late 1991 the corporation decided upon a new structure. The reorganization placed all the liner services under the direction of Crowley American Transport, while all the contract services business was placed under Crowley Marine Services; this twofold division reflected the profound requirements and characteristics of both types of ocean services. Crowley Maritime Corporation has built its remarkable expansion upon the policy of acquiring the best technology available in order to provide a superior service to customers. The company has also been a pioneer in pushing the limits of barge services in the oceans, opening up a new dimension to merchant shipping. By retaining a large base of domestic business in the United States, the company enjoys a diversified base to counter the inevitable shifts in ocean transportation, but with two-thirds of the company's income coming from ocean shipping since the late 1980s, most of that from volatile Latin America, the avoidance of serious setbacks depends on the constant attention of executives, who must constantly navigate a very careful course for the billion-dollar corporation.

Principal Executives

Thomas Crowley	1892–1940s
Thomas B. Crowley	1948–present
Leo Collar	1948–1991
James B. Rettig	1948–1993

Notable Subsidiaries

Alaska Hydro-Train	1963–present
Trailer Marine Transport (TMT)	1974–present
Delta Line	1982–1984
Crowley Caribbean Transport (CCT)	1986–present
Crowley Transport Lines*	1987–present

References: *American Shipper*, April, August 1987, May 1992, September 1993; Giles T. Brown, *Ships That Sail No More: Marine Transportation from San Diego to Puget Sound, 1910–1940* (Lexington: University of Kentucky Press, 1966); "Celebrating a Century of Service," *Journal of Commerce*, 5 August 1992; "Crowley Maritime Corporation," Special Supplement, *Journal of Commerce*, 1988; René De La Pedraja, *The Rise and Decline of U.S. Merchant Shipping in the Twentieth Century* (New York: Twayne, 1992); *Pacific Maritime Magazine*, May 1992.

CURRAN, JOSEPH EDWIN ("JOE"), 1 March 1906–14 August 1981. Joseph E. Curran was one of the most powerful of maritime labor leaders, ruling the National Maritime Union* (NMU) with an iron hand as president from 1937 to 1973. Born in New York City on 1 March 1906 of Irish Catholic parents, his education stopped when he was expelled from a parochial school in the fifth grade, apparently for poor attendance; in any case, he had lost interest in schooling. A succession of irregular jobs followed, the last one as office boy when he was fifteen at the Gold Medal Flour Company near the New York City waterfront. Watching ships enter and leave the harbor made the lure of the sea irresistible, and in 1922, at age sixteen, he joined the crew of an "old rust bucket" to France; like generations of young men before him, he hoped to find in the sea a better chance for success than on land. After seventeen hard years as a seaman, all his boyhood illusions vanished, and he realized that there was no romance, and even less wealth in the backbreaking work. Conditions aboard the vessels were deplorable, but when he tried to organize seamen, he found himself in various company blacklists and chronically unemployed. In 1935, in order to be hired on the *California** on the intercoastal* route between New York and California, he had to join the International Seamen's Union* (ISU), which had degenerated into little more than a company union; when the ship arrived in California, the crew members discovered that wages for sailors were higher on the West Coast than on the East Coast, as stated in the contract with the ISU. Incensed at this differential, Curran on 1 March 1936 convinced the sailors on the *California* to strike. In previous strikes the shipowners had simply hired a new crew and steamed away; in this one Curran decided to keep the striking crew aboard while the ship remained in port. The shipowners hollered "mutiny," but Secretary of Labor Frances Perkins offered to protect Curran and his crew from reprisals if they sailed back to New York. The momentary publicity was essential both to bring Curran for the first time before a national audience and to gain for him a reputation among fellow sailors.

When the *California* returned to New York City, Curran, along with sixty-five crew members, was discharged and blacklisted. Outrage at the company reprisals led other crews to strike in sympathy, and soon over ninety ships were tied up in the spontaneous "spring strike." The strike went on for nine weeks, but hostility from employers and corrupt leaders of the ISU was too strong, and in late May the strike ended. For Curran, without education or a skill, this was the make-or-break point: either he overcame the employer hostility, or he was finished once and for all aboard any vessel. There was no turning back, but he could advance only if he found trusted and powerful allies. Curran's pleas for help were ignored, except by the Communist party, which immediately stepped forward with its vast organizational skills and accumulated experience on the waterfront. Curran agreed to create a communist-controlled Seamen's Defense Committee, and soon preparations were under way for a second challenge. In October 1936 the "fall strike" began after a tempestuous session at Cooper Union Hall in New York City, where Curran and his followers defied the ISU leadership represented by the corrupt "Emperor" David Grange.* Bitter fighting raged as ISU officials repeatedly tried to crush the strikers, and at least twenty-five seamen were killed in brutal reprisals, but finally the shipowners agreed to grant most of the strikers' demands, provided that the old ISU leadership remained as the representative for the seamen. Curran decided to end the fall strike on 24 January 1937 and to prepare for the next round not against the shipowners but against the ISU.

Invaluable as the communists had been in the fall strike, Curran had resented having to share power with them, and to break their grip, he wanted to make an alliance with Harry Lundeberg* to create a new, nationwide union that would include Lundeberg's Sailors' Union of the Pacific (SUP).* Lundeberg feared that his smaller SUP would be gobbled up in any larger grouping, and he rebuffed Curran, whose only allies remained the communists and who still lacked his own union.

The answer to Curran's problems was John L. Lewis, whose newly founded Congress of Industrial Organizations (CIO) was looking for affiliations to counter the rival American Federation of Labor (AFL). The CIO decided to create and support a new seamen's union under Curran, who now was free to formally establish the National Maritime Union* (NMU) on 5 May 1937. The new union was an instant success on the East and Gulf coasts and claimed 47,325 members by the end of 1937.

Curran pursued three goals as president of the NMU. The first was to drive the communists from his union, a task that he gradually achieved by 1946. Ideology did not matter to Curran, who eagerly welcomed former communists as long as they supported his personal rule. Long after the communists had been driven out of the union, Curran continued the anticommunist campaign as a valuable way to achieve his second goal, namely, establish himself as the undisputed ruler of his union. Power became centralized in his hands, and even ships' committees* lost the right to elect their own union delegate aboard each ship. To perpetuate himself as president, pro forma elections sufficed to keep him and his slate in office as long as he wanted. The last goal was personal enrichment: by teaming up with treasurer M. Hedley Stone,* a former communist, Curran obtained free and secret access to union funds; Curran retired in 1973 a millionaire, a remarkable rags-to-riches story.

In 1953 Curran suffered a heart attack, and thereafter he reduced his contacts to a small group of insiders, always afraid to bring him bad news; even when in good health, Curran became visibly upset when contradicted or challenged on the smallest of points. Not surprisingly Curran lost touch with the rank and file, who began to see in Curran the reincarnation of the old-time bosses of the ISU. As early as World War II, defections had begun to the Seafarers' International Union* (SIU), and the need to block this rival union was another reason Curran agreed to join with Harry Bridges* in the creation of the short-lived Committee for Maritime Unity* (CMU) in 1946–1947. The Conference of American Maritime Unions* (CAMU) of 1954–1955, another attempt to end Curran's rivalry with Lundeberg's SIU, ended in a noisy failure. Seamen continued to desert Curran's union, so that when the AFL and the CIO merged in 1955, Curran did not receive the presidency of the Maritime Trades Department,* but as a consolation he was allowed to control a rump group, the AFL-CIO Maritime Committee, which duplicated the functions of the Maritime Trades Department.

The erosion of NMU membership continued because of both the rivalry with the SIU and the decline of U.S.-flag steamship companies, but Curran refused to change his tactics. Finally he retired in 1973 and died in Boca Raton, Florida, on 14 August 1981. The task of trying to restore the NMU to its former prominence fell to his hand-picked successor, Shannon J. Wall.*

References: Richard O. Boyer, *The Dark Ship* (New York: Little, Brown, 1947); *Current Biography 1945*; Gary M. Fink, ed., *Biographical Dictionary of American Labor*, 2d ed. (Westport, CT: Greenwood Press, 1984); Walter Galenson, *The CIO Challenge to the AFL: A History of the American Labor Movement 1935–1941* (Cambridge: Harvard University Press, 1960); Helen Lawrenson, *Stranger at the Party: A Memoir* (New York: Random House, 1975); Bruce Nelson, *Workers on the Waterfront: Seamen, Longshoremen, and Unionism in the 1930s* (Urbana: University of Illinois Press, 1990); *New York Times*, 15 August 1981; *Who's Who in the Maritime Industry 1946*.

CUSHING, JOHN E., 20 November 1887–22 April 1956. John E. Cushing was born in San Rafael, California, on 20 November 1887, and after attending public schools, he graduated from Stanford University in 1908. He spent his whole career in ocean transportation, starting with his first job in a shipping agency. He shifted among different employers until he became the traffic manager of the American-Hawaiian Steamship Company* (AHSS) in 1923. Cushing devoted the bulk of his career to that company, through whose ranks he rose until he became president in 1938.

With the end of World War II, AHSS faced some very difficult choices, and the company was starting to face losses in the intercoastal* service, the core of its operations. Cushing felt that AHSS needed a major overhaul if it was to survive, but with very divided opinions among the directors who owned the bulk of the stock, Cushing was not free to take forceful action.

As a seasoned steamship executive, Cushing was greatly respected and was an attractive candidate for Matson Navigation Company,* on the lookout for a replacement to Frazer A. Bailey.* Matson needed a transitional president who would keep the company on a steady course until a younger, dynamic person was found for the presidency. Cushing, then nearing retirement age, was the perfect candidate, and he accepted the better conditions Matson offered to become its president on 8 May 1947. After familiarizing himself with the company, Cushing concluded that the next president should be the Matson executive in Hawaii, Randolph Sevier.* Cushing first brought Sevier to San Francisco as vice president in 1948 and then transferred the presidency to him on 30 June 1950. Cushing went into retirement but remained active on a number of boards in San Francisco until his death on 22 April 1956.

References: *Dictionary of American Biography* vol. 46; *Nation's Business*, April 1952, pp. 45–47; Jerry Shields, *Daniel Ludwig: The Invisible Billionaire* (Boston: Houghton Mifflin, 1986); William L. Worden, *Cargoes: Matson's First Century in the Pacific* (Honolulu: University Press of Hawaii, 1981).

D

DAKOTA, **1905–1907.** The *Dakota* and the *Minnesota** were the twin passenger-cargo ships of the Great Northern Steamship Company* (GNSS), whose owner was the railroad magnate James J. Hill. The *Dakota*, with 22,250 deadweight* tons, length of 622 feet, beam of 73, and accommodations for 200 first-class passengers and at least 1,800 persons in steerage* class, was among the biggest ships of its time, but her maximum speed of thirteen knots was slow for a passenger liner. Hill insisted on such huge ships in order to achieve "economies of scale" or lower operating costs; he believed low rates would attract large volumes of cargo and make the shipping venture profitable. The GNSS had ordered the two vessels in 1900, but the *Dakota* was not completed until 1905 and departed on her first voyage from Seattle to the Far East only on 20 September 1905.

On 3 March 1907 the *Dakota* was on her seventh voyage when she struck a reef off the coast of Japan on a clear day in broad daylight. A later commission of inquiry held the captain solely responsible for this wreck, because he had underestimated the distance to the shore and had done nothing to verify his position; for the rest of his life the captain could find work only as a night watchman. All the passengers and crew disembarked safely, but the luggage and the cargo of wheat flour were lost. The liner broke in half and was salvaged for scrap metal. The wreck of the *Dakota* was one of the largest losses up to that time for the insurance underwriters, who afterward decided to raise the premiums on the sister ship *Minnesota*.

References: Don L. Hofsommer, "The Maritime Enterprises of James J. Hill," *American Neptune* 47 (1987):193–205; W. Kaye Lamb, "The Transpacific Ventures of James J. Hill," *American Neptune* 3 (1943):185–204; E. Mowbray Tate, *Transpacific Steam: The Story of Steam Navigation from the Pacific Coast of North America to the Far East* *and the Antipodes, 1867–1941* (New York: Cornwall Books, 1986); Milton H. Watson, *Disasters at Sea* (Northamptonshire, England: Patrick Stephens, 1987).

DEAD AHEAD: THE EXXON VALDEZ DISASTER, 1992. While *Action on the North Atlantic** had portrayed the U.S. merchant marine at its heroic and selfless best, the movie *Dead Ahead: The Exxon Valdez Disaster* depicted the merchant marine at one of the lowest points in its history. The movie belongs to the new genre of "docudrama," whereby the director tries to reconstruct as closely as possible the actual historical events, in this case the shipwreck of the tanker *Exxon Valdez** and the subsequent oil spill. Bungling ineptness, cover-ups, and political expediency predominate among all levels of the merchant marine, whether the drunkenness of the captain, the laxity of the Coast Guard,* or the greed of Exxon* executives, all ages away from the gallant service of the merchant marine in World War II. What made the *Exxon Valdez* shipwreck particularly damming for the U.S. merchant marine was that it belied the supposedly higher safety and performance standards of U.S.-flag ships: now it was no longer possible to shift the blame to foreign-flag ships or to those using flags of convenience,* as had been the case in previous oil spills. Although *Dead Ahead* was not shown in movie theaters, the film, as a production of Home Box Office (HBO), was repeatedly transmitted during many prime-time viewing hours through this premium channel of cable television with 17 million subscribers. While the actual events of the shipwreck cannot be denied, the movie's exclusive focus on that one voyage necessarily neglected the tens of thousands of successful but otherwise uneventful trips and failed to take into account the fatigue and stress tanker crews routinely suffer. The movie has inflicted tremendous and possibly irreparable damage on the image of the U.S. merchant marine.

DEADWEIGHT TONS. Deadweight tons is the *weight* of the cargo, fuel, and supplies needed to make a vessel fully loaded; in other words, it is the weight difference—expressed in long tons of 2,240 pounds—between a completely empty and a fully loaded vessel. Deadweight tons is the most frequently used term to refer to cargo ships, although other measurements exist that are useful for specialized purposes. For example, gross tonnage refers to the *volume* of *all* the enclosed space within the ship, and net tonnage to the *volume* of only the enclosed spaces used to carry paying cargo (omitting areas for engines, crews, ship's fuel, and supplies). The purposes of this historical dictionary have been more than adequately met by referring to tankers and cargo vessels only in deadweight tons, a practice that should also help to avoid confusion.

However, deadweight tons have two limitations. First, for ships primarily used as passenger liners, deadweight tons do not adequately reflect the ship's capacity. Most authors generally use gross tons for passenger liners, yet this dictionary believes it simpler and more meaningful just to state the number of persons a passenger vessel carried. Second, since the beginning of the container* age in the 1960s, the twenty-foot equivalent unit* (TEU) and the forty-foot-equivalent unit* (FEU) have emerged as more precise measures for stating the capacity of containerships to carry cargo, and consequently this dictionary has not hesitated to use these terms for containerships.

DEARBORN, GEORGE S., 28 March 1858–28 May 1920. George S. Dearborn was the president of American-Hawaiian Steamship Company* (AHSS) for over twenty years. He was born in Brooklyn, New York, on 28 March 1858, his father owned a shipping agency, and his uncles were masters of vessels. George Dearborn completed his formal education at age sixteen, but even before, he frequented the waterfront and visited his father's offices. Quite naturally George became a shipping agent, and already in 1882 he had drawn up plans for an intercoastal* steamship service, but skepticism from financial backers kept him from carrying out the project until 1899. Besides his agency business, Dearborn gradually acquired a fleet of sailing vessels. He continued to press for steamship service between New York and California, but only the annexation of Hawaii in 1898 and the subsequent extension of the cabotage* laws to those islands finally convinced investors to back Dearborn's project.

The result was the incorporation of the AHSS on 7 March 1899. Dearborn, who had sold his fleet of sailing vessels and placed the proceeds in the new company, became its first president. He wisely surrounded himself with highly capable executives, whom he kept working together in a very effective team. Captain William D. Burham became the general manager of the company until his retirement in 1914, while the brilliant Valdemar Frederick Lassoe was in charge of all engineering and technical matters; Lewis H. Lapham, a major stockholder, supervised the financial affairs of the company.

Dearborn obtained contracts from the Big Five (the main conglomerates in Hawaii) to carry the sugar crop of the islands to the U.S. mainland and planned to begin service in 1900 with the new fleet of steamships he had ordered, but when the government requisitioned the vessels for duty during the Boxer War, he had to postpone the start of the service until January 1901. Initially the company sent vessels around South America through the Straits of Magellan, and in January 1907 the company considerably shortened the route by transferring cargoes from the Atlantic to the Pacific across the Tehuantepec Railroad in Mexico. Finally in August 1914 the company's ships used the newly opened Panama Canal* for the trade between Hawaii and New York.

During his presidency Dearborn took many momentous decisions but was also responsible for the greatest blunder in the company's history, namely, the abandonment during World War I of the Hawaii route in order to charter* the fleet at record high prices for service in the North Atlantic. Hawaii was outraged when American-Hawaiian suspended its service to the islands in 1916, and this gap allowed Matson Navigation Company* the space to grow and replace AHSS. Dearborn himself started to sense he had made a mistake, but there was nothing he could do to regain the lost paradise of the Hawaiian trade. As the ships returned from service at the end of World War I, he redeployed the fleet into the intercoastal trade between California and New York, but the laborious struggle to build up that trade was a task left for a later president when Dearborn died in Rye, New York, on 28 May 1920.

References: Lincoln Concord, "History of the American-Hawaiian Steamship Company," unpublished manuscript; René De La Pedraja, *The Rise and Decline of U.S. Merchant Shipping in the Twentieth Century* (New York: Twayne, 1992); Roger D. Lapham Oral History, Bancroft Library, University of California, Berkeley.

DEFERRED REBATE or DEFERRED RATE REBATE. The deferred rebate has been an effective mechanism of conferences* to keep shippers* from bolting to nonconference lines and also to reward loyal shippers who have large amounts of cargo. As a matter of fact, shippers had originally requested the deferred rebate as one way to obtain discounted rates. In the deferred rebate the shipper who agreed to carry all his cargo on vessels of the conference will receive a rebate or partial refund, usually after six months or a year. If during the prescribed time period the shipper decided to take advantage of the lower rates of another line, he lost the rebate. Deferred rebates have been legal and widespread throughout the world, but in the United States they have been seen as a restraint on competition, so that both the Shipping Act of 1916* and that of 1984* have outlawed their use within trade routes subject to U.S. jurisdiction.

References: Advisory Commission on Conferences in Ocean Shipping, *Report to the President and the Congress* (Washington, DC: Government Printing Office, 1992); Federal Maritime Commission, *Section 18 Report on the Shipping Act of 1984*, September 1989.

DELTA LINE, 1919–1985. The Delta Line provided U.S.-flag steamship service between the Gulf of Mexico and the east coast of South America. Incorporated on 24 March 1919 in New Orleans as the Mississippi Shipping Company, the original name reflected the founders' aim of increasing the trade of South America with the Mississippi valley. Coffee merchants were the main backers of the line, because they wanted to import through New Orleans the Brazilian coffee that otherwise went through New York City. Although the name of the company was not formally changed to Delta Line (or Delta Steamship Line) until 1962, since decades before, the Delta Line appellation was in widespread usage.

The Delta Line was one of several hundred steamship companies that began service after World War I using government-owned vessels under managing operator* contracts; the Shipping Board* paid the private companies to operate these vessels, so the proposition was risk-free. The Delta Line sent its first ship to Brazil in August 1919, and although coffee cargoes were plentiful, southbound the ships were sailing rather empty. The general manager, Norman O. Pedrick, realized that government largesse could not be expected to last forever and that the line had to pay its way, so he obtained the approval of the Shipping

Board to send the ships as far south as Argentina in September 1920 because the latter country was importing large amounts of U.S. products. Henceforth the ships of the Delta Line sailed south with cargoes for Argentina and then returned loaded with coffee from Brazil, a pattern of operation that lasted into the 1960s.

The Delta Line had also obtained government vessels for a line to Northern Europe in June 1920, although in April 1921 the Shipping Board shifted the company to the route between the Gulf of Mexico and Le Havre, Antwerp, and Ghent. For some years it appeared that the European route would become as important for the Delta Line as it had become for Moore-McCormack,* but in a power struggle inside the Shipping Board, Delta Line lost the European route to Lykes Brothers Steamship Company* in August 1930.

Lykes Brothers had been successful against the Delta Line because the latter had been engaged since 1926 in a very bitter struggle against the Munson Steamship Company.* When the Shipping Board consolidated Gulf services, the Munson Line tried to take away the South American route from Delta Line in 1926 but failed. When the Shipping Board put the vessels in the route on sale to private buyers in 1929, Munson made a bid more than twice as high as Delta's, and only by strenuous lobbying did the Delta Line gain time to present a second bid that equaled Munson's original offer. When the postmaster general made a call for bids for the very lucrative mail contracts under the Merchant Marine Act of 1928,* Munson made one last try, and although it succeeded in delaying the outcome, the Delta Line finally emerged victorious with the mail contract in July 1930.

The tremendous amount of energy spent in the struggle with Munson and also with Lykes Brothers left the door open for German and Japanese lines, as well as tramps,* to take the choice northbound coffee cargoes during the Great Depression and the 1930s. Fortunately for the Delta Line, its main competitor was Lloyd Brasileiro, the state-owned line of Brazil, which generally preferred to avoid fierce clashes. With the outbreak of World War II, only Lloyd Brasileiro and the Delta Line were left providing service in the route, and with U.S. entry into the global conflict the latter's ships were requisitioned for wartime duty.

After World War II the Delta Line resumed operation with surplus vessels in South America and in 1947 expanded its services to include a new route to West Africa. The company returned to trade patterns similar to those of the prewar period and received operating differential subsidies.* By the 1960s the question of vessel replacement had become pressing, while frequent foreign-flag services to New Orleans assured more than ample shipping space for coffee cargoes from Brazil. The owners decided to sell their investment, and Transcontinental Bus System acquired over 50 percent of the Delta stock by August 1967 and over 97 percent by 1968, by which time it had changed its name to TCO Industries and subsequently merged into Holiday Inns in January 1969. By this roundabout process Delta became a subsidiary of Holiday Inns, and morale in the steamship company was boosted when it was learned that the parent company was willing to invest funds in a new fleet.

Unfortunately the management of Delta bungled the vessel replacement program, and, instead of acquiring container* vessels, ordered in 1973 three LASH* ships as those most suited to the rudimentary port facilities in South America. By 1977 Delta was losing money, but management still did not realize that the LASH vessels were the source of the company's problems and managed one last time to convince Holiday Inns to purchase the Latin American service of the Prudential Line,* in the hope that by consolidating these separate services, Delta would once again earn profits.

The financial results for 1978 were disappointing, and in a management shake-up, Holiday Inns brought in as president of Delta Andrew E. Gibson,* a former head of the Maritime Administration* (MARAD). Gibson began the long-delayed conversion of freighters to containerships, but his main task was to try to find a way to unload the LASH vessels on the U.S. government; he did not achieve this goal with either the Jimmy Carter or Ronald Reagan administrations. Holiday Inns meanwhile had tired of the steamship business and decided to cut its losses by selling Delta to Thomas B. Crowley* in December 1982.

Crowley, the nation's largest operator of barges and tugs, had seen the Delta acquisition as a way to broaden his maritime enterprises, but very soon he regretted having purchased "old junk ships with large crews" (De La Pedraja 1992). Crowley tried to do what should have been done years before, namely, outfit Delta with the right fleet. He arranged a complex swap with MARAD whereby he turned in old freighters in exchange for two older containerships well suited for the Latin American ports, and he also disposed of other older ships. He ordered economical diesel* containerships to replace oil-guzzling turbine* ships, and the new highly automated vessels also reduced the crew from forty-five men to eighteen.

Three of the new containerships were still under construction when Crowley, tired of mounting losses, decided to bail out from the fast track of merchant shipping. In December 1984 Malcom McLean,* president of United States Lines* (USL), agreed to purchase Delta Line in exchange for stock in USL, and the sale was completed in early 1985. Delta Line was absorbed into USL, but the attempt to operate Delta's remaining ships failed after a few months, thereby ending not only the corporate existence but the services Delta Line had provided during its long career.

Principal Executives

Norman O. Pedrick	1919–1942
Theodore Brent*	1943–1953
John W. Clark	1959–1979
Andrew E. Gibson	1979–1982
Thomas B. Crowley	1982–1985

References: *American Shipper*, May 1979; *Business Week*, 3 December 1984; René De La Pedraja, *The Rise and Decline of U.S. Merchant Shipping in the Twentieth Century* (New York: Twayne, 1992); William Kooiman, *The Grace Ships, 1869–1969* (Point

Reyes, CA: Komar, 1990); *Moody's Transportation Manual, 1969*; *Wall Street Journal*, 21 August 1967, 17 June 1968.

DEMPSTER, PAUL, 12 October 1928–present. Paul Dempster was the president of the Sailors' Union of the Pacific* (SUP) 1978–1990. He was born in Honolulu, Hawaii, on 12 October 1928 and joined the union in 1948. His climb to the top of the union hierarchy began in February 1966, when he became a tanker business agent. By the time Dempster assumed the presidency of the SUP in 1978, its power had sharply declined, and it was ruled from above by the Seafarers' International Union* (SIU). In his first year in office, Dempster witnessed the bankruptcy of three U.S.-flag steamship companies, thereby seriously curtailing the number of jobs available to sailors. The decline of the U.S. merchant shipping industry has continued, making the survival of the SUP the most crucial task for President Dempster. In 1990 he was replaced as president by Gunnar Lundeberg.

Reference: Stephen Schwartz, *Brotherhood of the Sea: A History of the Sailors' Union of the Pacific, 1885–1985* (New Brunswick, NJ: Transaction Books, 1986).

DIESEL ENGINE. In the 1890s the German engineer Rudolf Diesel patented the basic engine design that bears his name. In the diesel, when fuel was injected into the very hot compressed air of the cylinder, the fuel ignited and exploded, thereby pushing down the piston that produced motion in the crankshaft. The process was repeated in each of the cylinders, of which as many as eleven could be installed in marine diesels. The diesel was the first internal combustion engine found suitable for ocean transportation, but first many technical obstacles had to be overcome, and the first diesel merchant vessel did not sail until 1911. Putting diesels into submarines during World War I led to further technical advances, and in the 1920s European lines began to order these engines, whose performance gradually improved. In comparison with the guzzling steam turbines,* even the earliest of diesels reduced fuel consumption by half.

In spite of this undoubted energy efficiency, barely ten diesel ships existed in the United States in 1924. To end the technological lag, the Shipping Board* launched a program to make widespread the new engine in the U.S. merchant marine; as a first step, the board paid for the conversion of twelve vessels, most of which were assigned to sail in the long route between New York and Australia of the American Pioneer Line. However, diesel engines were more expensive to purchase than turbines* or triple-expansion* engines, so U.S. steamship companies were reluctant to make the large initial investment. Furthermore, the manufacturers of steam engines had a vested interest in stopping the spread of the rival technology, so that the Shipping Board quietly had to drop its plan to shift the U.S. merchant marine to diesels. Critics denounced in 1936 "our slavish adherence to only constructing steamship vessels" as "part of our disadvantage in competition with other maritime nations" but by then it was too late to reverse the trend (Official File).

When the United States entered World War II, the government began a crash program to produce a huge fleet of ships, but the constant bottlenecks in the production of diesels meant that most ships launched during the war used steam power. After the war only steamships were built, and the United States lost the capacity to manufacture the slow-speed diesels, the type best suited for marine propulsion because the engine turned the propeller shaft directly, without the wasteful reduction gear of the steam turbine.

In the 1950s diesels became nearly universal in world shipping except in the United States, which continued to build and use only the fuel-wasteful steam turbines. The energy crisis of 1973 finally forced the United States to accept diesels, because short of returning to the still inexpensive coal, no other alternative was left. American President Lines* ordered the first three diesel containerships in 1978, and when Sea-Land* received its ten new D-9 containerships, the diesels so bolstered the company's competitive position that it launched a rate war in the Transpacific Freight Conference of Japan.* However, for most U.S. companies it was already too late, because the failure to adopt the diesel engine had been one more factor that contributed to erode their financial base, so that very few survived to make the transition to diesel containerships. See also marine propulsion.

References: *American Shipper*, May 1974, May, June, October 1980; Edwin P. Harnack, ed., *All About Ships & Shipping*, 11th ed. (London: Faber and Faber Ltd., 1964); Lane C. Kendall, *The Business of Shipping*, 5th ed. (Centreville, MD: Cornell Maritime Press, 1986); John F. Nichols, "The Development of Marine Engineering," E. H. Rigg and A. J. Dickie, "History of the United States Coastwise Steamers," both in Society of Naval Architects and Marine Engineers, *Historical Transactions, 1893–1943* (Westport, CT: Greenwood Press, 1981); Official File, Franklin D. Roosevelt Presidential Library, Hyde Park, New York; T. W. Van Metre, *Tramps and Liners* (New York: Doubleday, Doran, 1931).

DOCKENDORFF, J. E., 20 March 1866–2 April 1934. J. E. Dockendorff was a merchant and the president of the Black Diamond Steamship Corporation.* He was born on 20 March 1866 in Lima, Peru, of a merchant family temporarily engaged in trade with South America, but he spent almost all his life in New York City. Among other commercial achievements, he "was one of the largest independent importers of aluminum in the U.S." (*New York Times*, 3 April 1934).

He entered shipping in 1918, when he purchased the first ship for the Black Diamond Steamship Corporation,* and he remained its president and main owner until his death on 2 April 1934. See Black Diamond Steamship Corporation.

References: *New York Times*, 3 April 1934; U.S. Senate, Special Committee on Investigation of Air Mail and Ocean Mail Contracts, *Hearings*, 9 vols. (Washington, DC: Government Printing Office, 1933–1934).

DOLLAR, ROBERT ("CAPTAIN"), 20 March 1844–16 May 1932. Robert Dollar, a successful lumberman, was also the founder and first president of the

Dollar Line.* He was born in Falkirk, Scotland, on 20 March 1844 and studied at a local school until age twelve, when he began to work, and shortly after his father, a lumberman, took the whole family to Ottawa, Canada. Robert Dollar worked in lumber mills, eventually becoming a foreman, and in his spare time he read widely, learned French, and eventually married. He started his own lumbering firm in Canada, but only with moderate success, and later transferred his operations to the forests of northern Michigan. In 1888 he moved to California and soon had bought large tracts of timber land the government had put on sale; lumbering remained the backbone of his business success and provided not only the profits but also the opportunities to expand into other ventures.

Dollar originally had no intention of entering the steamship business, but when he saw that shipowners did not pick up his timber when he needed their services, he had no choice but to purchase his first steam schooner to guarantee the pickup and delivery of his logs. The profits from hauling the lumber surprised him, and soon he had a fleet of steamers carrying cargoes from the Pacific Northwest to California, and as long as the Dollar Line relied primarily on its lumber cargoes, the steamship company remained profitable. With the annexation of the Philippines in 1898, Dollar saw a great opportunity to enter the transpacific trade, up to that time largely monopolized by the Pacific Mail Steamship Company* (PMSS). In 1902 he sent his first ship across the Pacific, but the vessel had been preceded by Dollar himself, who was busily drumming up business. Dollar instituted the habit of making frequent personal tours in the Far East to secure business, discover opportunities for making a profit, and inspect the offices and installations of the company. His services were particularly valuable, because while the Dollar Line had no difficulty filling the westbound ships with his lumber, the difficulty was to find return cargoes for the eastbound trip, a challenge that has continued to face a forest firm like Weyerhaeuser* in the last decades of the twentieth century. In the years before World War I, Dollar solved the problem by shipping to the United States a variety of low-value bulk* products and also by scheduling as closely as possible the vessels' sailings around the shippers'* needs. As further advantages, his ships, except those in the coastwise* trade, were under the British flag, he used Oriental crews, and also earned profits by carrying Chinese in steerage* class.

After the late 1910s, advancing age forced him to relinquish to his sons the greater part of the management of the Dollar Line, yet he remained active and was involved in numerous key decisions, as the *Memoirs* he wrote amply revealed. As a solution to the recurrent problem of finding return cargo, he had matured in the 1910s the idea of a round-the-world* service, which was formally inaugurated on 5 January 1924. In another important move, he had advised his sons to purchase shares of the Admiral Line,* until the Dollar family became the single largest stockholder. Another important acquisition was the American Mail Line,* whose Far East service from Tacoma, Washington, had posed a potential challenge to the Dollar Line. With so many successes, Dollar allowed himself to be swept by the glamour of passenger services, and already the ships in the round-the-world service carried 87 first-class passengers, while four were subsequently remodeled to carry 175 passengers. The decisive break with cargo as the main activity came when the Merchant Marine Act of 1928* offered lucrative mail contracts to operate express liners; the Dollar Line ordered the *President Hoover** and the *President Coolidge*,* two modern turboelectric liners, each carrying 988 passengers. Robert Dollar was extremely impressed by these gigantic ships, which seemed the ultimate in marine construction, but their delivery in 1931 posed the problem of how these ships could remain profitable in the midst of the Great Depression. His death in San Rafael, California, on 16 May 1932 spared Robert of having to cope with the mounting problems of the Dollar Line, a task that now fell squarely upon his son Robert Stanley Dollar.*

References: René De La Pedraja, *The Rise and Decline of U.S. Merchant Shipping in the Twentieth Century* (New York: Twayne, 1992); Robert Dollar, *Memoirs*, 4 vols. (San Francisco: Schwabacher and Frey, 1927); John Niven, *The American President Lines and Its Forebears, 1848–1984* (Newark: University of Delaware Press, 1987); Gregory C. O'Brien, "The Life of Robert Dollar, 1844–1932," Ph.D. diss., Claremont Graduate School, 1968.

DOLLAR, ROBERT STANLEY, 6 July 1880–28 September 1958. R. Stanley Dollar was the second and last president of the Dollar Line.* He was born in Bracebridge, Ontario, Canada, on 6 July 1880 and was the son of Robert Dollar,* who was then starting his own lumbering firm. When he was eight, his parents moved to California, and after graduating from high school, he began to work, because his father, like many other self-made men, did not believe in college, and allowed his sons to attend the Healds Business School only to learn practical business skills like typing and bookkeeping. In 1900, when Robert Dollar incorporated the Dollar Steamship Company or Dollar Line, Stanley became one of its officers, rising to vice president. Since the late 1910s Stanley was in charge of the Dollar Line and most of the family business, although he did not take the title of president until his father's death in 1932.

Unfortunately, Stanley had not inherited his father's sharp business sense, and his successes in shipping came mostly through highly advantageous deals with the government. In pure business deals he made such colossal blunders as the attempt to increase the Dollar Line's share of Hawaiian trade, which resulted in a costly capitulation to Matson Navigation Company* in April 1930. The two main deals that kept the Dollar Line profitable were the maneuvers that culminated in the acquisition of the American Mail Line* and the intense lobbying and even a hefty bribe for the purchase of the route and five liners the Grace Line* was operating for the Shipping Board.* By these two acquisitions Stanley had eliminated two formidable rivals from the transpacific service, and emboldened by his emerging monopoly, he pushed ahead with the plans to increase the passenger services of the Dollar Line.

The inauguration of the round-the-world* service on 5 January 1924 had marked the formal entry of the Dollar Line into the passenger business, but the big jump came with the Merchant Marine Act of 1928.* The Dollar Line received lucrative mail contracts under the provision of the act, and with this support and construction loans from the Shipping Board, Stanley decided to order two modern turboelectric liners, the *President Hoover** and the *President Coolidge.** Each carried express cargo and 988 passengers but could not be profitable because, among other reasons, they entered into service in 1931, in the midst of the Great Depression. Stanley was accustomed to drain from the company large sums of money as expense accounts, fees, and huge salaries, and the Great Depression did not in the least stop his wasteful practices, and soon the Dollar Line was on the verge of bankruptcy. The company was not able to meet even its easy repayments to the Shipping Board, and soon the other creditors of the Dollar Line wished to foreclose but were delayed by the lack of any real assets to seize. Stanley pleaded innocence, asked for more time, and largely left in the hands of the new U.S. Maritime Commission* the struggle to try to save the company's Far East services through reorganization plans. Confronted with the inevitable bankruptcy, Stanley at the urging of his private creditors finally consented on 15 August 1938 to sell the 93 percent stock interest of the Dollar family in the Dollar Line to the U.S. Maritime Commission, which then assumed all debt obligations.

Not even the U.S. Maritime Commission had enough money to save the Dollar Line, which was promptly renamed the American President Lines* (APL), and only a huge loan from the Reconstruction Finance Corporation allowed the government to rehabilitate APL and pay off all its old debts. As soon as the last of the creditors had been repaid in full in 1945, Stanley reappeared to pull off one last coup against the government: arguing that he had only "loaned" his stock but never really meant to sell it, he now wanted the government to return the company back to the Dollar family. The legal struggle over Stanley's preposterous claim resulted in the Dollar Line case,* which was not finally settled until 29 October 1952. The very favorable financial settlement allowed the Dollar family to overcome financial difficulties of the 1940s and to regain ready cash to revitalize its lumber and other interests.

Enormously rich, Stanley still missed the excitement of running a steamship firm, and with some of the funds from the Dollar Line settlement, he purchased a block of stock in Moore-McCormack* in April 1953 and became a member of its Board of Directors. He remained as one of the grand old men of the shipping industry until his death in San Francisco on 28 September 1958.

References: René De La Pedraja, *The Rise and Decline of U.S. Merchant Shipping in the Twentieth Century* (New York: Twayne, 1992); *National Cyclopedia of American Biography*, vol. 37; John Niven, *The American President Lines and Its Forebears, 1848–1984* (Newark: University of Delaware Press, 1987); *New York Times*, 16 April 1953, 3 July 1955.

DOLLAR LINE or DOLLAR STEAMSHIP COMPANY, 1900–1938. The Dollar Line was the main U.S. steamship company in the transpacific trade between the two world wars. Robert Dollar,* the owner of a lumber company, had acquired in the 1890s a fleet of schooners to carry wood from his sawmills in the Pacific Northwest to the markets in central and southern California. Shipping was proving as profitable as the lumber business, and to expand both, he decided after the Spanish-American War of 1898 to enter transpacific shipping; significantly, a government cargo to the just acquired Philippines paid handsomely the first voyage to the Far East. He now formally organized the Dollar Steamship Company on 15 August 1900 and gradually acquired more vessels for his growing transpacific business.

Any activities took place under the shadow of the Pacific Mail Steamship Company* (PMSS), a giant in transpacific shipping that Dollar could never dream of overtaking. The Dollar Steamship Company had no margin for error, because any false step meant that PMSS and the rapidly rising Japanese lines would capture all the business. Like PMSS, the Dollar Line utilized Chinese crews, but unlike the U.S.-flag PMSS, only the coastwise* lumber schooners were under U.S. registry,* while the rest of the ships flew the British flag and hence purchased cheaper ships from British shipyards (except for the *China*,* all PMSS vessels had been built in U.S. shipyards). The only reason the Dollar Line was able to compete at all was that its own lumber guaranteed outward cargoes; the challenge was to find return cargoes to make the voyages profitable. Dollar traveled constantly in the Far East as a drummer for additional eastbound cargo and if necessary entered into business deals himself. His two most important coups were the contracts he landed to ship Chinese pig iron to California and Japanese oak timber for the Southern Pacific Railroad; the latter was particularly embarrassing for PMSS since the railroad was its parent company.

Nonetheless, by the start of World War I the Dollar Line remained essentially a tramp* operator, whose main cargoes were bulk,* low-value merchandise not suitable for the larger and faster passenger-cargo liners of the PMSS. Dollar united with Rennie Schwerin* of PMSS to try to block the La Follette Seamen's Act,* but upon its passage in 1915, PMSS sold most of its vessels and abandoned the transpacific trade, leaving a huge void that the Japanese lines avidly attempted to fill. In one sudden move, PMSS, the competitor that blocked the expansion of the Dollar Line, had disappeared. Dollar, however, was extremely careful, and rather than rashly expand, he decided to reap enormous profits with the record-high rates prevalent during World War I and to wait until the return of peace to acquire ships.

In 1920 the Dollar Steamship Company purchased five British-flag steamers, which it began to send home via the Suez and Panama* canals; although these voyages lost money, the trade potential was there, and in January 1921 Dollar announced plans for the creation of a permanent round-the-world* service. As a freighter service the route offered a solution to the endemic problem of finding sufficient eastbound cargoes, because now the ships could easily skim the cream from the cargoes going from Asia and the southern Mediterranean to the East Coast of the United States.

Instead of staying with this solid proposition, Robert's son, R. Stanley Dollar,* now decided to plunge into the more glamorous but riskier passenger business, a move that required a series of power plays. Ordering new vessels did not make sense, because the Shipping Board* had for disposal many new passenger-cargo vessels. As a matter of fact, the Shipping Board had already assigned five of the 535s (vessels so named because of their length) to the Admiral Line* for operation between Seattle and the Far East. Stanley had been quietly buying shares of the Admiral Line until he was a larger stockholder than its president, H. F. Alexander,* while in Washington both Dollars lobbied vigorously to have the Admiral Oriental Mail Line* (the subsidiary of Admiral Line) transferred to their control. Finally in September 1922 the Shipping Board and the Dollars delivered their ultimatum: to remain as president of the Admiral Line, Alexander had to give up the Admiral Oriental Mail Line to the Dollars. The Admiral Oriental Mail Line gradually became known as the American Mail Line* (AML), while the Admiral Line itself was combined with the Dollar Line in November 1922. Operation of the 535s gave the Dollar Line experience in passenger operations and prepared them to begin a modest passenger service in the round-the-world service. From 1923 to 1925 the company bought seven 502s vessels (likewise named because of their length), which were modestly fitted to carry eighty-seven first-class passengers; should the passenger service flop, the service was profitable just with the cargo.

All these vessels were renamed after American presidents, and on 5 January 1924 the *President Harrison** sailed on the first voyage of the round-the-world service. More than adequate cargoes and passengers convinced the Dollar Line to bid on the five government-owned 535s that the Grace Line* operated through its subsidiary, the Pacific Mail Steamship Company* (PMSS). Intense lobbying and at least one hefty bribe convinced the Shipping Board to reject Grace's bid and instead to sell the ships to the Dollar Line in April 1925. All that was left to complete the Dollar Line's grip on transpacific shipping was to purchase from the Shipping Board the five 535s it operated through its American Mail Line subsidiary, and this was accomplished in April 1926. Henceforth the AML and the Dollar Line operated as one large company, with the ships shifted among the different services as required. The Dollar family had finally acquired a near monopoly on U.S. shipping in the Pacific Coast.

The Japanese and other foreign lines, however, were improving their passenger-cargo services, and with newer ships under construction they threatened to seriously undermine the position of the Dollar Line in the Far East. Fortunately the Merchant Marine Act of 1928* authorized extremely generous mail subsidies, and the Dollar Line soon had signed a very lucrative contract, which, however, required the construction of faster and more modern liners. Money for the new vessels was no problem because a separate construction fund of the Shipping Board allowed the Dollar Line to borrow 75 percent of the shipyard price. Under such favorable conditions the Dollar Line planned to order six new liners, but the onset of the Great Depression meant that the only ships delivered were the *President Hoover** in 1930 and the *President Coolidge** in 1931.

By 1931 the Dollar Line was in deep financial problems, and Stanley had requested a two-year moratorium on the repayment of the debt to the Shipping Board. Stanley made a number of blunders in running the company, and he lacked his father's keen business sense. Furthermore, the Dollar family members had grown accustomed to drain funds from the company to enrich themselves by a variety of subterfuges, not the least of which were outrageously high salaries. The financial crisis of the Dollar Line became progressively worse, but when the newly created U.S. Maritime Commission* attempted to rescue the company by a reorganization plan, the loss of the *President Hoover* off the coast of Formosa in December 1937 doomed this first rescue effort.

A subsidiary of the AML, the Tacoma Oriental Steamship Company,* had ceased operations in 1936 and went into bankruptcy the next year, while the AML itself had suspended its last operations in June 1938 and likewise went into bankruptcy; would the Dollar Line be the next victim? Stanley found himself trapped and had to choose between the two alternatives he found personally repulsive: either government ownership or bankruptcy. With private creditors ready to foreclose, finally in August 1938 he sold the Dollar family stock to the U.S. Maritime Commission, which now renamed the Dollar Line the American President Lines.* Stanley himself was down but not out, and the *Dollar Line* case* soon saw him make an astonishing comeback.

Principal Executives

Robert Dollar	1900–1930
R. Stanley Dollar	1915–1938

Some Notable Ships

President Harrison	1923–1941
President Coolidge	1931–1941
President Hoover	1931–1937

President Johnson and *President Fillmore*—see *Manchuria** and *Mongolia.**

References: René De La Pedraja, *The Rise and Decline of U.S. Merchant Shipping in the Twentieth Century* (New York: Twayne, 1992); John Niven, *The American President Lines and Its Forebears, 1848–1984* (Newark: University of Delaware Press, 1987); Gregory C. O'Brien, "The Life of Robert Dollar, 1844–1932," Ph.D. diss., Claremont Graduate School, 1968.

DOLLAR LINE CASE. The *Dollar Line* case referred to a series of trials and appeals over control of American President Lines* (APL), whose original name had been the Dollar Line.* The defendant was the U.S. government, which claimed that it had purchased the Dollar Line, while the plaintiff was R. Stanley

Dollar,* the leader of the Dollar family interests. In 1938 the Dollar Line was in bankruptcy and about to be foreclosed by creditors who wanted their money back, an action that necessarily would have interrupted the shipping services to the Far East. The U.S. government decided that with the worsening international situation, the country could not afford any interruption in steamship services, particularly to bring back Americans from war-threatened areas in the Far East. The U.S. Maritime Commission,* after all attempts to bail out the Dollar Line had failed during previous years, decided to acquire the 93 percent stock interest the Dollar family had in the Dollar Line, and as payment the U.S. Maritime Commission assumed all the debts and personal obligations of the Dollar family in the line. The creditors, in particular the Anglo-California Bank, forcefully pressed for this solution, because now they would recover all of their money, not just a small fraction, as would have been the case if the Dollar Line had ended up in bankruptcy court.

On 15 August 1938 the U.S. Maritime Commission formally took control of the now renamed APL and began not only to pay off the debts but to rebuild the deteriorated fleet, which was able to contribute vital services during World War II. The last of the old debts were paid in 1945, but in spite of this success, the U.S. Maritime Commission decided to sell off the profitable company in order to avoid charges of promoting government ownership and operation. Charles U. Bay, the majority stockholder of American Export Lines,* submitted the highest purchase bid, but before he could take possession of the company, R. Stanley Dollar filed a lawsuit on 6 November 1945 and soon obtained a restraining order against the proposed sale.

Charles Bay never obtained control of the APL, while Dollar entangled the government in recurrent trials in which he attempted to prove unsuccessfully that he had put up the 93 percent stock only as collateral until the government canceled all the debts of the company, whereupon he had all the right in the world to demand that the government return the stock. By means of appeals, publicity, and campaign contributions to politicians, he was able to keep the *Dollar Line* case in front of the public, and he loved to portray himself as the small businessman victimized by an oppressive government. His claims were so preposterous that the government did not take them seriously for some years, and when at last the Justice Department decided to handle the case as a political struggle, it was too late—the damage had already been done to the Democratic administration of Harry S. Truman. The family fortunes of the Dollar family, noted for excessive spending habits, had taken a turn for the worse by 1950, and rather than wanting APL back, in reality Stanley just wanted a cash infusion. As an alternative to continuing the dragged-out judicial process, an out-of-court settlement was finally arranged in March 1952, whereby the government agreed to call for bids on APL and to sell the company to the highest bidder; of the proceeds from the sale, half went to the federal government and the other half to the Dollar family. The bids were opened on 29 October

1952, and the new owner of APL was oilman Ralph K. Davies; the second highest bidder had been the Matson Navigation Company,* which wanted to neutralize this potential rival for the Hawaiian trade, while the Dollar family, with no real desire or means to return to the APL, had entered the lowest bid. Half the proceeds from the sale sufficed to restore the fortune of the Dollar family, whose last attempt to drain funds from the government had been remarkably lucrative.

References: René De La Pedraja, *The Rise and Decline of U.S. Merchant Shipping in the Twentieth Century* (New York: Twayne, 1992); John Niven, *The American President Lines and Its Forebears, 1848–1984* (Newark: University of Delaware Press, 1987).

DOUBLE BOTTOM and DOUBLE HULL. A double bottom has simply been a second watertight steel deck or level in a ship. Initially the double bottoms were installed only under the engine room, in order to sustain better the weight of the machinery and also to provide a handy place to store the fresh water for the boilers. Gradually experience showed that having two separate levels of steel also provided additional protection for persons, cargo, and the ship itself. Too many early marine disasters were caused by rocks or other objects ripping the bottom of the hull, and a second bottom did reduce considerably the risks of shipwreck. However, if the gash took place above the double bottom, as apparently was the case in the *Titanic*,* then the double bottom was useless. Placing a second or "double" hull in the sides of the ship as well as in the bottom afforded the greatest margin of safety, but only made worse the main drawback of the double bottom: the space was wasted without carrying any cargo. Consequently, double hulls were used mainly in warships rather than in commercial vessels.

Double bottoms became widespread in steamships by the early twentieth century, partly because the companies avoided the problem of idle capacity by using the large space between the two bottoms to store fresh water, fuel, and other liquids, thereby releasing areas above the inner bottom for additional, revenue-earning cargo. In the 1970s, however, the focus of attention shifted from saving the ship to protecting the environment. With the small T-2* tankers, the oil spills had been of modest proportions, but tankers grew in size since the 1960s, and the huge oil spills now meant massive environmental damage. As tankers became longer and wider, the useless space left between the two bottoms increased geometrically, far outstripping the need to store fresh water, but if oil was pumped into the space, then why not dispense with the double bottom altogether? The economic pressure to fill every space in the tanker with oil finally convinced the government to accept the oil companies' claim that highly sophisticated navigational equipment had made double bottoms superfluous.

The *Exxon Valdez** disaster proved otherwise, and Congress, in the Oil Pollution Act of 1990,* outlawed all single-hull tankers from U.S. waters after the year 2015. Companies must begin converting their larger tankers to double hulls starting in 1995, and the smaller and newer vessels will have until 2015 to conform or be replaced.

In one prime-time television commercial of 1992, the Du Pont corporation announced, against a backdrop of deliriously happy birds and dolphins, that its subsidiary Conoco had completed the construction of tankers with double hulls. Conoco committed itself to operating a fleet of all double-hull tankers, but other companies have continued to regard such a measure as too drastic. The main attractiveness of the double hull has remained its capacity to save the ship and the persons on board, but a double hull cannot prevent an oil spill in high-speed collisions like that of the *Exxon Valdez.*

References: *American Shipper*, February, April, October 1992; Edwin P. Harnack, ed., *All About Ships & Shipping*, 11th ed. (London: Faber and Faber Ltd., 1964); *Houston Chronicle*, 12 January 1992; Cedric R. Nevitt, "American Steamship Lines," and E. H. Rigg and A. J. Dickie, "History of the United States Coastwise Steamers," both in Society of Naval Architects and Marine Engineers, *Historical Transactions, 1883–1943* (Westport, CT: Greenwood Press, 1981).

DOUBLE HULL. See Double Bottom.

DOUBLE-STACK TRAINS, 1984–present. Double-stack trains have consisted of loading one container atop another on a railroad flatcar. When American President Lines* (APL) introduced this innovation quietly in 1984 and without any fanfare so as not to tip off the competition, costs dropped dramatically in comparison with the previous practice of sending only one container atop the flatcar. The landbridge* concept for moving cargo from the Far East to the East Coast of the United States by railroad took a decisive lead, and although APL prematurely rushed to claim that the all-water route by the Panama Canal* was obsolete, there was no doubt that double-stack trains had tremendously changed the nature of ocean transportation and affected the railroads as well. The other competitors were caught by surprise and rushed to imitate APL by introducing their own double-stack trains. The only real barriers to the spread of this service has been the need to enlarge physical facilities such as tunnels and overpasses to handle the height of the double-stack trains, whose presence has become fundamental to U.S. transportation.

References: American President Lines, *Fact Book*, 1987; *American Shipper*, December 1991; *Journal of Commerce*, 25 January 1988; Lane C. Kendall, *The Business of Shipping*, 5th ed. (Centreville, MD: Cornell Maritime Press, 1986).

DROZAK, FRANK P., 24 December 1927–11 June 1988. Frank P. Drozak was the president of the Maritime Trades Department* (MTD) of the American Federation of Labor-Congress of Industrial Organizations (AFL-CIO) and of the Seafarers' International Union* (SIU) from 1980 to 1988. Drozak's early career remained under the long shadow of Paul Hall,* but as the latter's health began to deteriorate, Drozak gradually emerged as the heir apparent. In 1972 Drozak became the executive vice president of SIU, and in February 1980 he was elected president of the MTD to replace the ailing Hall. By then Drozak was also in full control of the SIU, but formal elevation to the presidency came only with Hall's death on 22 June 1980.

Drozak faced a daunting task: automation and the collapse of U.S.-flag steamship companies had made seafaring employment an endangered species. The new president realized that the traditional policy of gouging the companies for the benefit of the seamen had become counterproductive, and he decided instead to work together with the companies to try to salvage what was left of the U.S.-flag shipping services.

One way to help companies and also to strengthen labor was to merge the many sailors' unions into a few organizations. Management benefited by negotiating with a single union for the entire ship, rather than before, when separate agreements were signed for the deck, engine, and bridge crews; not only was this simpler, but also "whipsawing*" was avoided. Maritime unions had seen their membership shrink dramatically, but they had remained top-heavy with bureaucracy, so consolidation was expected to reduce costs. Drozak's plans bore fruition when District 2 of the Marine Engineers' Beneficial Association* merged with SIU in early 1988, and the example was followed by other maritime unions. Cancer cut Drozak's career short, and he died on 11 June 1988. He was succeeded by Michael Sacco.

References: *Maritime Newsletter*, March 1980, June-July 1988; *Who's Who in Labor, 1976*.

DUAL-RATE CONTRACTS or LOYALTY CONTRACTS. Shippers* who signed dual-rate contracts ("contract system") with conferences* or with a company in exchange for using that conference or company for all or a certain percent of their cargo during a specified time period received a lower rate than shippers who did not sign the contract ("noncontract system"). The dual-rate contract and the deferred rebate* have been the most powerful mechanisms used by conferences and companies to tie effectively a shipper to their ocean carriers and have remained legal outside the United States. The Shipping Act of 1916* prohibited both the deferred rebate and the dual-rate contract in the U.S. foreign trade routes, but conflicting clauses within that act convinced the Shipping Board* to accept the existence of dual rates. Under this interpretation conferences signed thousands of dual-rate contracts with shippers until 1958.

In the *Isbrandtsen* case* of 1958 the Supreme Court declared dual rates illegal, and although Congress attempted to make them legal again in 1961, it failed to provide a general antitrust immunity, and consequently "there has been a chilling effect on the number filed with the Federal Maritime Commission"* (Advisory Commission 1992). As the U.S.-flag merchant fleet continued to decline precipitously, the need for the revival of some form of dual-rate contracts became more pressing, and although they remained illegal in the United States, the Shipping Act of 1984 transmuted the old dual-rate contracts into the new legal form of service contracts* as a compromise alternative.

References: Advisory Commission on Conferences in Ocean Shipping, *Report to the President and the Congress* (Washington, DC: Government Printing Office, 1992); Federal Maritime Commission, *Section 18 Report on the Shipping Act of 1984*, September 1989.

E

EASTERN STEAMSHIP LINES, 1901–1954. The Eastern Steamship Lines provided service along the northern East Coast of the United States and, after 1917, also to Yarmouth, Nova Scotia. The company was the creation of Wall Street financier Charles W. Morse, who consolidated six New England coastwise* companies to form the Eastern Steamship Company on 8 October 1901. Morse correctly sensed that coastwise lines could survive only if they combined into larger and more efficient units, but unfortunately the collapse of his financial empire in 1907 plunged Eastern Steamship Company into receivership. On 4 December 1911 a new firm, Eastern Steamship Lines, was organized to continue operations under the ownership of the New York, New Haven, and Hartford Railroad Company. At the same time, the Metropolitan Steamship Company,* with the two express liners *Yale** and *Harvard** of the New York-Boston run, was merged with Eastern Steamship Lines, and so was the Maine Steamship Company (1868–1911), which had provided service between Portland, Maine, and New York City.

These acquisitions made Eastern Steamship Lines the largest coastwise fleet on the East Coast, with the exception of the Merchants and Miners Transportation Company,* but Eastern Steamship Lines continued to show losses and was back in receivership in November 1914. Shortly after, under court order, the railroad disposed of its stock in the steamship company, another reorganization took place on 30 January 1917, and the new owners proceeded to sell off assets and ships in order to pay off the accumulated debt. By 1921 the company's fortunes had turned around, and a stock issue brought in much needed capital. Eastern Steamship Lines, whose routes were north of Norfolk, expanded its services and also chartered its ships in the winter for service to Florida. The company also continued to acquire smaller firms, most notably in

1923 the Old Dominion Steamship Company, which had provided service from Norfolk and other ports in Virginia to New York City since 1868. The boom times of the 1920s convinced Eastern Steamship to replace its old fleet with a total of eight new turbine* steamers, and the first two, the *Yarmouth* and the *Evangeline*, entered service in 1927. The last two turbine steamers, the *St. John* and the *Acadia*, were ordered after the government had awarded the company in 1928 a very lucrative mail contract for service to Nova Scotia.

The timing for the *St. John* and the *Acadia* could not have been worse, because they were delivered in 1932, in the midst of the Great Depression. The company began to abandon its routes one after another, and when the government canceled the lucrative mail contract shortly after 1936, the survival of the company was in doubt. Eastern Steamship Lines began to sell its ships, and those not sold when World War II began were requisitioned for emergency duty by the government. After the return of peace, Eastern Steamship Lines reestablished only summer sailings to Yarmouth, Nova Scotia, with the *Evangeline* and the *Yarmouth* refitted as cruise ships. In 1954 the company suspended operations and, after selling its remaining assets, liquidated itself in 1956.

Some Notable Ships

Yarmouth and *Evangeline*	1927–1954
Saint John and *Acadia*	1932–1941

References: Frederick E. Emmons, *American Passenger Ships: The Ocean Lines and Liners, 1873–1983* (Newark: University of Delaware Press, 1985); Frank F. Farrar, *A Ship's Log Book* (St. Petersburg, FL: Great Outdoors, 1988); *Moody's Transportation Manual, 1952, 1955, 1956; Nautical Gazette,* 5 October 1929.

ECONSHIPS, 1984–present. Econships has been the name generally used to refer to the twelve large containerships (the largest in the world at the time they were launched) built for United States Lines* (USL). The first ship was the *American New York,** whose maiden voyage was completed in July 1984, followed by the *American New Jersey*, the *American Maine*, and the *American Alabama*; the remaining ships likewise bore names for the states of California, Illinois, Kentucky, Nebraska, Oklahoma, Utah, Virginia, and Washington. By early 1986 the vessels offered shippers* weekly sailings from the United States on the round-the-world* service. Each Econship was of 57,800 deadweight* tons and had a capacity for 2,129 forty-foot equivalent units (FEUs)* or 4,380 twenty-foot equivalent units (TEUs).* With a length of 950 feet and a beam of 106 feet, these Panamax* class ships barely squeezed through the Panama Canal.* USL finally adopted for the Econships the more economical diesel* rather than turbine* engines, a long overdue change in U.S. merchant shipping. Because of their advances in marine propulsion and size, many believed the Econships to have "the lowest unit costs of any American-flag containership afloat and maybe the lowest in the world" (*American Shipper*, September 1984).

Malcom P. McLean,* the owner of USL, had staked the entire future of the company on the low-cost operation of the Econships. Analysts calculated that to cover costs the ships needed to travel only 50 percent full, while any cargo load over 80 percent meant large profits. To ensure the lowest price possible to shippers, McLean had designed the ships to travel at the very slow speed of sixteen knots, and when questioned whether shippers might prefer more expensive but faster means of transport, he replied that the Econships on the round-the-world service "would suck up cargo like a vacuum" (De La Pedraja 1992).

McLean's gamble proved a disaster because he simply could not keep enough cargo aboard the ships all the time. With small loads the ships began to pile up losses, and by November 1986 USL had been driven into bankruptcy; McLean himself was later removed from control of the company after having taken a tremendous financial beating. The Econships had turned out to be "moving bathtubs" that were too large to operate profitably except in a few high-volume routes in the world. The Econships remained on the auction block for nearly two years, because other lines did not want to get stuck with these "floating elephants" and preferred instead to order faster containerships with lower operating costs of the Post-Panamax* generation, as American President Lines* (APL) did for the transpacific trade. This later company was also a major beneficiary of the failure of the Econships, because APL could proceed to increase its double-stack* service from the Far East to the East Coast of the United States without fear of any serious competition from the all-water route via the Panama Canal.

The danger that the Econships would become "killer" ships if they fell into the hands of foreign competitors finally prompted Sea-Land* to buy them in February 1988. The new owner tried to rename them the "Atlantic Class," but more than a name change was needed to make the Econships profitable in the overtonnaged trade of the North Atlantic. The company had to enter into complex and shifting arrangements to charter* space aboard the vessels and even the ships themselves to European lines. Later in 1989 Sea-Land sold four of the Econships to obtain desperately needed cash and then continued to operate those same four vessels on long-term charters. The ships were too slow to meet the normal sailing schedules, but the company hoped that by carrying only 3,400 rather than 4,400 TEUs, the faster ship speed thereby would make possible a modestly profitable operation. The operating costs per container, of course, increased, and it was not clear how the Econships could remain competitive once Post-Panamax vessels entered the North Atlantic trade routes. The Econships, one of the greatest blunders committed by American steamship executives, have never really found a satisfactory place in ocean transportation.

References: A. J. Ambrose, "US Lines' Big 12," *Jane's Merchant Shipping Review 1984*; *American Shipper*, September 1984; René De La Pedraja, *The Rise and Decline of U.S. Merchant Shipping in the Twentieth Century* (New York: Twayne, 1992); *Journal of Commerce*, 27 October, 22 December 1987, 4, 5 February, 16 May 1988, 7 March 1989; Transportation Research Council, *Intermodal Marine Container Transportation: Impediments and Opportunities* (Washington, DC: National Research Council, 1992); *U.S. News & World Report*, 14 December 1987.

ELECTRICITY. After the successful inauguration of electric lamps on the *Columbia** in 1880, other companies rushed to install electric lighting aboard their ships. By the start of the twentieth century the use of electric lights aboard ships had become so universal as to be taken for granted. Electricity has powered navigational aids, radios, and also amenities for the passengers and crew but has had a very limited impact on marine propulsion.* For freighters the additional expense of installing generators and motors to the steam turbine* was not justified and also meant higher operating costs. Large combination passenger-cargo liners like the *President Coolidge** and the *President Hoover** employed turboelectric propulsion in an attempt to lure tourists by higher speeds and less vibration, but the financial results proved disappointing, and by the late 1930s shipowners had rejected turboelectric propulsion as inferior to the steam engine.

During the crash building program of World War II, some T-2* tankers were built with turboelectric drive, but, soon after, all countries returned to the traditional forms of marine propulsion. Turboelectric drive appeared to revive with the launching of the *Savannah,** the first nuclear-powered merchant vessel, but the operating results were a commercial failure. In the 1980s the navy began to intensively research electric propulsion for vessels, but the budget cutbacks after the end of the Cold War seemed to have ended any hope for technological breakthroughs in this area. Electricity, indispensable for lighting and many other functions aboard ships, failed to find a satisfactory role in the marine propulsion of the twentieth century.

References: American Bureau of Shipping, *History 1862–1991*; Commission on Merchant Marine and Defense, *Third Report: Appendices* (Washington, DC: Government Printing Office, 1988); John F. Nichols, "The Development of Marine Engineering," E. H. Rigg and A. J. Dickie, "History of the United States Coastwise Steamers," both in Society of Naval Architects and Marine Engineers, *Historical Transactions, 1893–1943* (Westport, CT: Greenwood Press, 1981); T. W. Van Metre, *Tramps and Liners* (New York: Doubleday, Doran, 1931).

EMERGENCY FLEET CORPORATION (EFC), 1917–1927. The Emergency Fleet Corporation (EFC) was in charge of the World War I shipbuilding program and also of the operation of the vessels of the Shipping Board.* The Shipping Act of 1916* had authorized the Shipping Board to create its own subsidiary corporations, should the need so arise, but limited their existence to a period no longer than five years after the end of World War I. Initially the Shipping Board did not feel any subsidiary was necessary, but the U.S. entry into World War I quickly convinced the board to create the Emergency Fleet Corporation on 16 April 1917. The Shipping Board, itself barely organized in early 1917, as the nation's first agency charged with the promotion of the merchant marine, lacked any experience to draw upon, and, consequently, the relations between the Shipping Board and the EFC were punctuated by clashes, even though their functions were often so overlapping as to make imperceptible the separation between both institutions.

The chairman of the Shipping Board, William Denman, was an admiralty lawyer whose abilities to handle the vast shipbuilding program were as yet untried, and, as a precaution, the Woodrow Wilson administration brought in Major General George Goethals, the builder of the Panama Canal,* as head of the EFC in April 1917. Soon a bitter clash erupted between these men, and only by accepting their resignations was President Wilson finally able to end the Goethals-Denman controversy. President Wilson now appointed as chairman the millionaire Edward N. Hurley,* who at last made the EFC operate effectively under the direction of Charles Piez; the job was so vast, however, that Wilson in April 1919 called in another millionaire, Charles M. Schwab, to relieve Piez of some of the nonshipbuilding duties.

With Hurley at the Shipping Board and the Piez-Schwab team at the EFC, the construction program finally took off at full speed. Although the Shipping Board had requisitioned all keels under construction in U.S. shipyards, awarding new contracts proved counterproductive, first because the existing yards were already booked solid, and second, because too many opportunities for private graft appeared. While carefully monitoring the private shipyards, the EFC decided to concentrate its efforts in the creation of new government shipyards, the largest of which was Hog Island near Philadelphia. From Washington, D.C., Piez and Schwab could not supervise effectively the new shipyards, and they decided to move the EFC headquarters to Philadelphia, where it stayed while the shipbuilding program lasted. The EFC, which had become the largest industrial enterprise of the war, performed the massive task of building a shipyard base and launching a huge fleet of merchant vessels. The EFC became so effective that the U.S. government was able to promise already in March 1918 enough tonnage to transport and supply the eighty divisions needed by the Allies for the final offensive in the spring of 1919.

The unexpected collapse of Germany on 11 November 1918 left the EFC in a lurch because most of its vessels were still under construction but were no longer needed for the war. Charles M. Schwab felt his job was over, and he resigned on 2 December 1918; but what should Hurley tell Piez to do? Hurley, with the support of the Wilson administration, decided to complete almost the entire shipbuilding program, with the result that nearly three times more vessels were completed in peacetime than during the war. Before Armistice Day the EFC had delivered 470 ships; after the war the deliveries were 757 ships in 1919, 406 in 1920, and 68 in 1921, until the program finally ended in 1922 with the last three vessels. Gradually the EFC returned the private shipyards to full control by their owners and also began to demobilize the government shipyards; in a foolish move, the EFC took the initial steps toward the sale by its successor, the Merchant Fleet Corporation,* of the lands of the Hog Island shipyard, whose facilities were sorely missed in World War II.

While the EFC was wrapping up its shipbuilding program, the Shipping Board was grappling with the bigger question of what to do with all these surplus ships. Eventually EFC received the task of either operating itself the ships, most notably in the case of United States Lines* while it belonged to the Shipping Board or, more likely, supervising the vessels to make sure they were properly cared for and maintained by the managing operators.* During the war the EFC had operated all ships under U.S. control in accordance with the orders of the Shipping Control Committee of the Shipping Board, but with the return to peace, the wartime controls ended, and as private companies regained their requisitioned vessels or took advantage of low prices to purchase surplus vessels, the EFC tried to abandon most direct government operation of vessels. The goal of the Shipping Board was to place as many as possible of the surplus vessels in the hands of the managing operators, who wanted to establish U.S.-flag lines in most of the routes in the world. The EFC generally passed the same information and reports on to the bureaus of the Shipping Board, and often where the EFC ended and the Shipping Board began was unclear.

Hurley resigned as chairman of the Shipping Board on 31 July 1919, and then Admiral William S. Benson,* together with Senator Wesley Jones,* attempted to define the future of the EFC, slated to expire five years after the end of World War I. The Jones Act* of 1920 removed the five-year limit on the EFC, which now could continue to function as the operating arm of the Shipping Board without any time limitations. Unfortunately the EFC piled up huge losses starting in 1922, and to try to stem the mounting deficit, President Calvin Coolidge secured the appointment of Admiral Leigh C. Palmer* as head of the EFC in January 1924. Admiral Palmer quickly discovered that the problem was not with the EFC itself but with the practices of some commissioners of favoring private companies at government expense in some very suspicious deals. The commissioners saw nothing wrong with running government deficits to pay for private profits, but when Admiral Palmer began to stop the juicy deals, the board in a swift power play removed him from office in October 1925. President Coolidge for a moment considered abolishing the board, but the pro-business climate was too strong in the 1920s, so that the EFC, now under the full grip of the Thomas O'Connor*-Edward Plummer clique at the Shipping Board, continued to enrich certain managing operators who knew how to influence the commissioners. To reaffirm its authority, the Shipping Board assumed direct control over the EFC in 1927 and, in a related move, also changed its name to the Merchant Fleet Corporation,* since the old name of Emergency had become outdated.

Notable Executives

General George Goethals	1917
Charles Piez	1917–1919
Charles M. Schwab	1918
Admiral Leigh C. Palmer	1924–1925
Captain Elmer E. Crowley	1925–1927

References: Paul V. Betters and Darrell H. Smith, *The United States Shipping Board. Its History Activities and Organization* (Washington, DC: Brookings Institution, 1931); René De La Pedraja, *The Rise and Decline of U.S. Merchant Shipping in the Twentieth*

Century (New York: Twayne, 1992); Record Group 32, National Archives, Washington, DC; William N. Thurston, "Management-Leadership in the United States Shipping Board 1917–1918," *American Neptune* 32 (1972):155–170; Carroll H. Woody, *The Growth of the Federal Government, 1915–1932* (New York: McGraw-Hill, 1934).

EMMA ALEXANDER. See *Congress.*

EMPIRE CITY LINE, 1848–1852. The Empire City Line was one of the steamship services created to meet the huge demand for passenger travel after the discovery of gold in California in 1848. Charles Morgan* had just established a New York-New Orleans service that same year with calls in Charleston and Havana, but without a mail subsidy he had obtained poor results, and now with the start of the California gold rush he transferred his steamers to the Empire City Line he created with John T. Howard for service between New York and Panama. The new firm faced bitter competition from the Pacific Mail Steamship Company* (PMSS) and the United States Mail Steamship Company,* but the demand for passenger space for California was so great that Morgan was able to reap huge windfall profits during the initial years. However, by 1850 the boom was receding and the competition from PMSS and the United States Mail Steamship Company was intensifying, so Morgan sold out his interest in Empire City Line at a profit to PMSS in 1850; his associate John T. Howard tried to keep the Empire City Line operating, but it disappeared in 1852.

References: James P. Baughman, *Charles Morgan and the Development of Southern Transportation* (Nashville: Vanderbilt University Press, 1968); David I. Folkman, Jr., *The Nicaragua Route* (Salt Lake City: University of Utah Press, 1972); John H. Kemble, *The Panama Route, 1848–1869* (Berkeley: University of California Press, 1943).

ENERGY INDEPENDENCE, 1983–present. The high oil prices after the energy crisis of 1973 convinced many countries to try to avoid an excessive reliance on oil. In an attempt to return to coal-burning ships, shipowners in the United States, Australia, and Spain built or converted eight ships during 1982–1983. The biggest at 38,200 deadweight* tons was *Energy Independence*, the first coal-burning ship built in the United States since 1921. For propulsion the ship used a steam turbine,* while new mechanisms automated the process of feeding a steady supply of coal to keep boiling the water in the boiler. The fact that the ship was used to carry coal by the New England Collier Company no doubt contributed to the success of this experimental vessel, which has remained in service. However, ship designers and shipowners were not convinced, and the diesel* engine remained the preferred mode of propulsion. The energy crisis had sufficed to eliminate oil-burning steam turbines from U.S.-flag ships but had not lasted long enough to force a return to coal-burning steam engines.

References: Lane C. Kendall, *Business of Shipping*, 5th ed. (Centreville, MD: Cornell University Press, 1986); Maritime Administration, *Vessel Inventory Report, 1992.*

ENGINES. See Marine Propulsion.

ESSO. See Standard Oil Company of New Jersey.

EXPORT STEAMSHIP CORPORATION. See American Export Lines.

EXXON. See Standard Oil Company of New Jersey.

EXXON VALDEZ later *EXXON MEDITERRANEAN*, **1986–present.** The *Exxon Valdez* became the most notorious U.S.-flag ship in recent times when this tanker ran aground in Prince William Sound, off Valdez, Alaska, in the first morning hour of 24 March 1989. The resulting oil spill, the worst in the nation's history, caused immense environmental damage, and in the ensuing legal settlement, Exxon* agreed to pay over $1 billion during a ten-year period. The *Exxon Valdez*, a tanker of 209,200 deadweight* tons built in 1986, was the largest U.S.-flag ship owned by Exxon Shipping Company, the ocean transportation subsidiary of Exxon. The company put Joseph Hazelwood, a graduate of the New York Maritime College at Fort Schuyler, in command of its flagship vessel, apparently because he was well liked and "treats everyone like a gentleman" (*Journal of Commerce*, 6 April 1989) and evoked affection from fellow officers and the crew. The company knew the captain had alcohol problems and earlier had put him in a rehabilitation program, but neither the company nor the Coast Guard,* which issued the captain's license, bothered to find out that he had been convicted of drunken driving and three times his automobile driver's license had been revoked. Being an officer aboard tankers has become even more stressful than it has always been (see Independent Tanker Unions*), and the company, obsessed since the 1960s with the fear of massive environmental damage precisely like that of the *Exxon Valdez*, had added more requirements and regulations, and the mounting pressure upon the officers actually increased, rather than reduced, the possibility of an oil spill.

Captain Hazelwood had been drinking the night of the accident, gave several contradictory commands to his subordinates, and abandoned the bridge after leaving command of the tanker to Third Mate Gregory Cousins, who did not have the required pilot's licence to navigate in Prince William Sound. To try to avoid icebergs, the tanker veered off the normal sealane; the equipment aboard that warned of the danger had previously malfunctioned and thus was ignored, while the Coast Guard radar on land was no longer tracking the vessel. At 12:04 A.M. on 24 March the vessel, which had been moving at a fast speed, radioed, "We're hard aground," and the tanker began to leak 11 million gallons of oil into the sea. Measures to contain the oil spill revealed that prior preparations for such an emergency were grossly inadequate, and soon Exxon had a major public relations disaster. The Coast Guard, a victim of budget cutbacks, also received criticism, and the fact that the vessel was under U.S. registry* prevented transferring the blame to foreigners or the flags of convenience,* as had happened with previous disasters such as the *Torrey Canyon* or the *Sansinema*.* The company refloated and repaired the ship which later returned to service. Declining oil cargoes from Alaska as well as the desire to bury this episode in the past convinced the company in early 1990 to shift the tanker to southern Europe for operation under the new name of *Exxon Mediterranean*. The public outcry was so huge, however, that Congress passed the Oil Pollution Act of 1990* to mandate in the future not only strict background checks and licensing requirements for the personnel in the bridge but also double-hulls* for all tankers entering U.S. waters. The notoriety of the oil spill became so great that in 1992 Home Box Office even produced a movie, *Dead Ahead: The Exxon Valdez Disaster,** a docudrama that relived in painful detail for over 10 million households one of the low points in the history of the U.S. merchant marine.

References: *Business Week*, 20 May 1991; Home Box Office, *Dead Ahead: The Exxon Valdez Disaster*, 1992; *Journal of Commerce*, 5, 6 April, 23 June 1989, May-June 1990; Maritime Administration, *Vessel Inventory Report 1987; Time*, 10 April 1989.

F

FAR EAST CONFERENCE (FEC), 1920–1984. The Far East Conference established the rates and the sailings for the member companies serving the trade from the Atlantic and Gulf ports of the United States to the Far East (the countries bordering on the Pacific Coast from Siberia to Indochina, including Japan, Formosa, and the Philippine islands). European lines had established a previous conference* in 1905, but it did not survive the shipping crisis of World War I. To avoid wasteful and chaotic competition (rates fluctuated sometimes on a daily basis), the Shipping Board* forced the managing operators* of government ships to create the Far East Conference in 1920. Without the participation of foreign lines, the FEC proved ineffective, and to remedy the situation, the Shipping Board encouraged and approved their entry into an enlarged conference on 1 September 1922. A separate group of conferences, most notably the Japan-Atlantic & Gulf Conference* (JAG), controlled the rates and sailings for the cargoes moving eastward to the East and Gulf coasts of the United States.

The FEC managed the route harmoniously until the appearance of Hans Isbrandtsen* as an outsider* in 1928. Isbrandtsen had requested admission to the FEC on the condition that he be allowed to quote rates 10 percent lower, but when his application was rejected, he reacted angrily and for the rest of his life waged single-handedly a ferocious campaign against conferences. At first he had sent only old ships from New York to the Far East, but in 1931, when he placed new ships on the route, he began a furious rate war. Quite naturally the member companies of the FEC, already suffering under the impact of the Great Depression, fought to retain their cargoes. Japanese lines cleverly used the rate war to expand their share of cargoes, and soon after, Japanese military aggressions in the Far East disrupted the FEC, whose member lines had largely ceased regular operations even before U.S. entry into World War II on 7 December 1941.

The War Shipping Administration* assumed full control of all ships, and the FEC remained inactive until peace returned to the Pacific Ocean. When the U.S. occupation of Japan gave U.S. companies privileged access to all Japanese cargoes, the need to establish uniform rates brought the FEC back into operation in 1946. The next year Isbrandtsen's ships had also returned to Japanese ports, and in 1949 his ships had established an eastbound round-the-world service* from New York via the Suez Canal to Japan and then continuing across the Pacific and the Panama Canal back to New York. As an eastbound service across the Pacific, Isbrandtsen's actions fell within the jurisdiction of two other associations, the Transpacific Freight Conference of Japan, and the JAG, so that, fortunately for the FEC, it escaped the brunt of Isbrandtsen's attacks.

The membership of the FEC comprised the following lines in 1964:

American President Lines*

Fern-Ville Lines, joint service

Isthmian Line*

Japan Line

Kawasaki Kisen Kaisha

Lykes Bros. Steamship Co.*

Maritime Co. of the Philippines

Mitsui O.S.K. Lines

A. P. Moller-Maersk Line, joint service

Nippon Yusen Kaisha

States Marine Corp.,* joint service

United Philippine Lines

United States Lines*

Wilhelmsens Dampskibsaktieselskab, joint service

Yamashita-Shinnihon Steamship Co.

The spread of the landbridge* was reducing cargoes on this route, and many companies threatened to abandon the FEC in mid-1977, but the crisis passed, and not until the end of 1984 did the member lines dissolve FEC. Its trade route, along with those of six other outbound conferences, went into the Transpacific Westbound Rate Agreement* (TWRA) in 1985, one of the superconferences* that emerged after the passage of the Shipping Act of 1984.*

References: *American Shipper*, June and November 1984; René De La Pedraja, *The Rise and Decline of U.S. Merchant Shipping in the Twentieth Century* (New York: Twayne, 1992); Federal Maritime Commission, *Section 18 Report on the Shipping Act of 1984*, September 1989; U.S. Congress, House, Committee on Merchant Marine and Fisheries, *Review of Dual-Rate Legislation, 1961–1964* (Washington, DC: Government Printing Office, 1964); U.S. Congress, House, Committee on Merchant Marine and Fisheries, *Steamship Conference Study*, 3 vols. (Washington, DC: Government Printing Office, 1959).

FARLEY, EDWARD PHILIP, 18 October 1886–5 March 1956. Edward Philip Farley, steamship executive of the American-Hawaiian Steamship Company* (AHSS), was also an official in the Emergency Fleet Corporation* (EFC) and the Shipping Board.* Farley was born on 18 October 1886 in Madison, Wisconsin, and attended the University of Wisconsin. He moved to Chicago and in 1909 became a yacht and ship broker* and gradually built up holdings in several Great Lakes steamship companies. When World War I broke out, he joined the army as a captain but was soon transferred to the EFC, where he rose to high position, and in 1919 he attended the Versailles Peace Conference as an adviser to Edward N. Hurley,* the chairman of the Shipping Board. In 1921 Farley became the vice president of the EFC, and in June 1923 he replaced Albert D. Lasker* as chairman of the Shipping Board. Because another member of the board already represented Chicago, the Senate refused to confirm his nomination, to prevent any one region from dominating the Shipping Board, and finally he requested the withdrawal of his nomination in December 1923 and then returned to private business.

Farley now reopened his ship brokerage firm, but in New York City and not in Chicago. His main investment became the AHSS, and he served on its Board of Directors, starting in 1926. When Roger D. Lapham* resigned from the company in order to serve as mayor of San Francisco in 1944, Farley became the chairman of the board and exercised the greatest influence on the company. In 1947, however, Roger's son, Lewis A. Lapham,* became president of the company in order to watch over his family's investment in the company.

Until 1951 the company remained profitable because it was operating on the intercoastal* and Far East routes vessels on bareboat* charter from the government, but when the company decided to purchase six surplus ships in 1951, AHSS began to suffer such heavy losses on each of its intercoastal voyages that the company was forced to suspend the service in March 1953. It is not clear whether Farley was in the faction of stockholders who supported or in the faction of those who opposed the sale of the company to billionaire Daniel Ludwig; in any case Ludwig gained control of AHSS, and in 1955 Farley resigned as chairman. He died the next year in New York City on 5 March 1956.

References: *National Cyclopedia of American Biography*, vol. 42; *New York Times*, 11 February 1955; Jerry Shields, *The Invisible Billionaire: Daniel Ludwig* (Boston: Houghton Mifflin, 1986).

FARRELL, JAMES A., JR., 13 January 1901–15 September 1978. James A. Farrell, Jr., was the president of the American South African Line* and the Farrell Line,* whose ownership he shared with his elder brother, John J. He was born in Brooklyn, New York, on 13 January 1901 and graduated from Yale University in 1924. The next year he became the president of the American South African Line, one of the shipping ventures organized under the direction of his father, James A., Sr., who during thirty years was president of the United States Steel Corporation. James A., Jr., carefully developed the trade with Africa, while his brother as president and principal owner of the Argonaut Line* concentrated on the intercoastal* trade. In 1940 a slump in the intercoastal trade and booming rates in the Atlantic convinced the brothers to merge their two companies, and while James A., Jr., remained as president, John J. became chairman of the board. During World War II, James A., Jr., served in Naval Intelligence and afterward returned to the presidency. Because the American South African Line was by then the only shipping venture of the family, the brothers decided to change the name of the company, which henceforth was known as the Farrell Line.

James A., Jr., remained as president of Farrell Line until 1963, when he became the chairman of the board. When the heirs of the Robin Line* decided to sell out and abandon shipping in 1957, this action prompted the owners of the Farrell Line to explore the option; after careful examination, James A., Jr., who was determined to remain in the business, easily reached unanimous agreement with his brother and the other stockholders not to abandon shipping. James A., Jr., wanted to expand, and in 1965 the Farrell Line bought from United States Lines* (USL) its service between Australia and the East Coast, which was complemented in 1975 by the purchase from Pacific Far East Lines* (PFEL) of its service between Australia and the West Coast. This last acquisition stretched the company's resources, but James A., Jr., could not resist the temptation of acquiring at bargain price in bankruptcy court the fleet of American Export Lines* (AEL) in March 1978. He wished to leave behind the largest U.S.-flag merchant fleet, but when he died later that year in 15 September, the real legacy was a crushing burden that both his heirs and those of his brother, John J., struggled to overcome.

References: Robert G. Albion, *Seaports South of Sahara: The Achievements of an American Steamship Service* (New York: Appleton-Century-Crofts, 1959); *American Shipper*, October 1978; James A. Farrell, Jr., *Sea Lanes South of Sahara: The Story of Farrell Lines Incorporated* (New York: Newcomen Society, 1963); *New York Times*, 10 December 1950.

FARRELL, JOHN J., 28 April 1890–22 April 1966. John J. Farrell was a steamship executive and shipowner. He was born on 28 April 1890 in Brooklyn, New York, studied at Yale University, and served as a captain in World War I. The key person shaping his life was his father, James A. Farrell, Sr., who during thirty years was the president of the United States Steel Corporation and in 1928 also became its chairman of the board. The father had developed a strong interest in shipping, and he wisely guided his two sons, John J. and James A., Jr.,* as they entered the steamship business. The elder Farrell involved his two sons in at least a half-dozen shipping ventures, the most important of which were the Argonaut Line,* the Robin Line,* and the American South African Line.* John J. became the principal stockholder and president of the Argonaut Line when it was organized in 1922, although he also participated in the ownership and management of the other Farrell shipping activities.

The Argonaut Line operated mainly on the intercoastal* trade of the United States, although occasionally its ships were chartered* out or transferred to operate in the other routes of the Farrell family. The decline of intercoastal cargoes and booming rates in the Atlantic convinced John J. to abolish the Argonaut Line and transfer its vessels to the American South African Line in 1940. This could have created a personality clash, because the latter company had been headed by the younger brother, James A. Jr., but because the latter, shortly after, went to serve in Naval Intelligence for the duration of the war, John J., now as chairman of American South African Line and ably assisted by Vice President Leigh C. Palmer,* was able to make an effortless transition into the management of the company.

When James A., Jr., returned to his position as president of the company after the war, the two brothers formed a harmonious management team. Since 1940 the American South African Line was the only steamship service left in the hands of the family, and to reflect its new status, the brothers adopted the name of Farrell Line for the company in April 1948. When the owners of the Robin Line* decided to sell their shipping assets in 1957, the Farrell family considered carefully the option of withdrawing, but after careful examination, John J. reached agreement with his brother to remain in the business. In 1963 John J. retired as chairman of the board, but he remained as chairman of the Executive Committee of the Board of Directors and from that position participated in the decision to buy the Australian service of United States Lines in 1965. He died the next year on 22 April 1966; Mary, one of his two daughters, had married the lawyer George F. Lowman, who later became chairman of the board of the Farrell Line.

References: Robert G. Albion, *Seaports South of Sahara: The Achievements of an American Steamship Service* (New York: Appleton-Century-Crofts, 1959); *New York Times*, 10 December 1950, 23 April 1966; *Who Was Who*, vol. 4.

FARRELL LINE, 1948–present. The Farrell Line was the name of the former American South African Line,* which was the main U.S.-flag service between Africa and the United States. The Farrell Line had renewed its cargo fleet with war surplus vessels, but it sorely missed the *City of New York*, the combination passenger-cargo liner that had been sunk during wartime service in 1942. The rate war in the U.S.A.-South Africa Conference* had left the company too weak to think of ordering a new passenger liner, but it was able to swing a deal with the U.S. Maritime Commission* whereby the company received at a giveaway price the *Deltargentino* and *Delbrasil*, two combination passenger-cargo ships left abandoned after wartime service, on the condition that the two vessels return properly fitted to passenger service. Renamed the *African Enterprise* and the *African Endeavor*, the two vessels, each with accommodations for 80 passengers, began service to Africa in 1949 and were so profitable that the Farrell Line planned in 1953 to build two larger liners, with air-conditioning and accommodations for 140 passengers. The company delayed before placing the orders, and when competition from aviation began to take away the majority of passengers starting in 1955, Farrell quietly shelved its plans and in 1959, when the *African Endeavor* and the *African Enterprise* were near the end of their service lives, laid them up.

Cargo services were satisfactory, in part because the company had made special modifications in the surplus vessels of World War II, such as extra fuel tanks to avoid the need to refuel with expensive oil in Africa. The Robin Line,* which had engaged in a ferocious rate war in 1935–1937, still refused to join the U.S.A.-South Africa Conference but avoided destructive competition over cargoes. The German line Hansa did not return to the trade, while the British lines withdrew from the U.S.-South Africa trade in 1955, leaving the Farrell Line free to build up a profitable volume of cargo. An operating differential subsidy* from the government further solidified the company's position.

The Farrell Line remained a family-owned firm, and the two brothers, John J. Farrell* as chairman of the board and James A. Farrell, Jr.,* as president, held about 60 percent of the stock; the brothers had retained this tight grip over the company by plowing back profits into the company, thereby eliminating the need to make the public offerings of stock that necessarily would have diluted the family ownership.

Two events occurred in 1957 that appeared to bring the existence of the Farrell Line to a successful close. The operating differential subsidy contract expired, and while renewal with the Maritime Administration* could be taken for granted, the opportunity existed to sell the ships now that they were not restricted by the provisions of a subsidy contract. Second, the new owners of the Robin Line took advantage of the temporary boom in ship prices after the 1956 Suez crisis to sell out to Moore-McCormack* in early 1957. The owners of the Robin Line made a tidy profit and now could put their money into safe investments on land; should the Farrell brothers follow the Robin Line example and sell out? In retrospect they should have left the sea, but the brothers thought otherwise, and after an all-day meeting on 25 November 1957, they decided to stay in shipping and to renew the subsidy contract.

The rudimentary facilities in most African ports made vessel replacement less urgent and less costly for Farrell Line than it was for companies serving Western European and Far Eastern ports. However, the Farrell brothers had tired of serving only the narrow African trade and wished to expand into the wider world, and to that effect the Farrell Line acquired the Australia-U.S. East Coast service of United States Lines (USL) in 1965. Farrell developed a strong hold in this trade and decided to expand in 1975 by purchasing the West Coast-Australia service of the Pacific Far East Line* (PFEL) in 1975.

The Farrell Line now provided all of the U.S.-flag service to Australia and to Africa, but James A. Farrell, Jr., still craved a bigger role in world shipping. In 1969 Farrell Line had proposed consolidating with Moore-McCormack, but the attempted takeover failed. The big break came in 1978, when the bankruptcy of American Export Line* put the ships of this company on the auction block at giveaway prices; with this purchase, the Farrell Line became the second biggest U.S.-flag merchant fleet with forty-four ships and at last satisfied its owners' ambition for status and prestigious routes. Farrell continued with its own construction program for containers* and also assumed the obligation of completing the orders American Export had placed with the shipyards. For one brief moment Farrell Line appeared to have successfully climbed into the ranks of the largest shipping companies, not only in the United States but also in the world.

The dream was short-lived, however, because the company had financed the purchase of American Export with a loan from the Chase Manhattan Bank, and meeting the installment payments became a permanent burden. Doubts about the wisdom of such frenzied expansion led to a shake-up in management, and George F. Lowman, whose wife was the daughter of John J. Farrell, now became the chief executive officer and named to the presidency James P. Horn, the former president of American Export. Horn promptly canceled the Far East route of Farrell Line, because the break-bulk* freighters of that run simply could not compete against containerships. In 1980 rumors circulated that the company was in danger of bankruptcy, but Lowman and Horn cut routes and sold ships to try to stop the mounting losses.

The family firm had with difficulty stretched its management talents to cover the Australian routes, but the task of integrating American Export into Farrell Line went beyond what a tightly controlled family could do. Unable to take the step into a large impersonal corporation to handle wideflung sea routes, Farrell Line, driven by the pressure of the creditors, was not only selling off its assets but instinctively returning to a smaller size more easily managed by a family. Farrell dropped the routes to Europe and then those to South and West Africa, and just in 1980 the company sold or traded into the government sixteen vessels.

Lowman appointed Richard V. Parks as the new president in 1981, and by then the company was operating only eleven ships in the African and Australian routes. Farrell Line had counted on four new containerships to make the Australian route a big money-earner, but the ships had been badly designed and had, among other drawbacks, fuel-expensive steam turbines* so that the route was losing $10 million a year until the company finally sold the four containerships in 1983. Somehow the company drew on hidden inner strength to stagger through, but in 1989 it was so small that Lykes Brothers Steamship Company* attempted to purchase Farrell Line. The sale did not take place, and shortly after, Farrell withdrew from the service to West Africa, the last remnant of the links with Africa that had been the origin of the company as well as the core of its activities for decades. The service in the early 1990s was limited to the Mediterranean and the Persian Gulf. In contrast to the fleet of forty-four ships in 1978, the Farrell Line operated only four ships in the trade from the U.S. East Coast to the Mediterranean and the Persian Gulf in 1991.

Principal Executives

Leigh C. Palmer*	1925–1955
James A. Farrell, Jr.	1925–1978
John J. Farrell	1940–1965
C. Carlton Lewis	1966–1970
Thomas J. Smith	1970–1979
George F. Lowman	1978–present
James P. Horn	1979–1981

Richard V. Parks	1981–present
Some Notable Ships	
African Endeavor; formerly, *Delbrasil*	1949–1959
African Enterprise; formerly, *Delargentino*	1949–1959

References: Robert G. Albion, *Seaports South of Sahara: The Achievements of an American Steamship Company* (New York: Appleton-Century Crofts, 1959); *American Shipper,* February 1978, August, September 1979, March 1981, March 1983, March 1991; *Business Week,* 26 May 1980, 14 December 1981; René De La Pedraja, *The Rise and Decline of U.S. Merchant Shipping in the Twentieth Century* (New York: Twayne, 1992); *Mast Magazine,* October 1949; *New York Times,* 21 February 1953, 15 October 1966, 22 January 1981.

FEDERAL MARITIME BOARD (FMB), 1950–1961. Reorganization Plan 21 of 1950 created the Federal Maritime Board (FMB) and the Maritime Administration* (MARAD) to replace the discredited U.S. Maritime Commission.* While the FMB decided all issues affecting government assistance and regulation of ocean transportation, MARAD implemented the decisions and performed all other administrative duties not specifically reserved to the FMB. The Reorganization Plan began but did not complete the transition from management by a board to control by a single executive officer, and the FMB emerged as a compromise between both methods of government. Unlike the U.S. Maritime Commission, which had been a completely independent agency, the FMB was under the Department of Commerce and was supposed to "be subject to general policy guidance by the Secretary of Commerce" (Public Papers 1950), but the decisions of the FMB could not be appealed to the secretary of commerce. The three members of the FMB were appointed by the president with the consent of the Senate, and its chairman was also the head of the newly created MARAD. Supposedly these combinations of the best of different methods of administration would make the FMB a success.

On the contrary, the results were disappointing in the extreme. As an economy measure, the same staff served MARAD and FMB, without any clear separation. The FMB had lost its independent status, but because FMB decisions could not be appealed to the secretary of commerce, it had not gained any guidance or input from the executive branch. The quality of most appointees to the board was deplorable and that of proposed members was no better: "The cries that the West Coast or the Gulf or New England want 'representation' on the Board do not come from the general public. These cries come only from greedy shipping interests who want to get their own 'stooges' on the Maritime Board, to serve their selfish interests" (Confidential File). Reports emphasized that the FMB had neglected its regulatory functions, but the real concern was that shippers* felt that as long as the same agency continued to handle both the promotion and the regulation of the merchant marine, shipowners and not shippers always had the last word. The FMB, just like the U.S. Maritime Commission and the Shipping Board* before, had two different constituencies, the shipowners and the shippers, and because the latter felt neglected, they pressured for their own separate agency. Major revelations were necessary to shock Congress into action, and these the Celler Committee* effectively provided. Reorganization Plan Number 7 of 1961 abolished the FMB and replaced it with two separate bodies, the Federal Maritime Commission* (FMC) for the shippers, who at last could begin to gain control of their own agency, and the Maritime Subsidy Board* (MSB) for the shipowners.

References: Confidential File, Dwight D. Eisenhower Presidential Library, Abilene, Kansas; René De La Pedraja, *The Rise and Decline of U.S. Merchant Shipping in the Twentieth Century* (New York: Twayne, 1992); Samuel A. Lawrence, *United States Merchant Shipping Policies and Politics* (Washington, DC: Brookings Institution, 1966); *Public Papers of the Presidents, Harry S. Truman, 1950.*

FEDERAL MARITIME COMMISSION (FMC), 1961–present. The Federal Maritime Commission was established on 12 August 1961 as a separate government institution to defend shippers* through its power to approve or reject rates and agreements that conferences* and steamship companies must file with the agency and make public. The FMC has been an independent regulatory agency, composed of five commissioners. The president with the consent of the Senate appointed the commissioners for terms of five years (originally four years until 1965) and also designated one to be the chairman. The FMC has jurisdiction over the foreign trade routes of the United States and domestic offshore shipping (basically Guam, Hawaii, Puerto Rico, and Alaska), but for the latter some overlap has occurred with the authority of the Interstate Commerce Commission* (ICC). With the increasing prevalence of intermodal* transportation since the late 1970s, many ocean carriers have faced double regulation at the hands of the FMC and the ICC. The FMC has authority only over the liner* trades and has no jurisdiction to regulate tankers, ore and bulk* carriers, or tramp* vessels of any country.

The creation of the FMC culminated nearly forty years of controversy over whether a separate agency was needed to protect the shippers. The Shipping Act of 1916* placed the regulatory powers over ocean transportation in the hands of the Shipping Board,* which also was charged with the promotion of a strong merchant marine. The Shipping Board and its successors used these powers to protect U.S.-flag steamship companies and shippers from foreign lines. However, in the inevitable quarrels between American shippers and U.S.-flag steamship companies, the Shipping Board tried to strike a balance, and not surprisingly shippers felt neglected and began to clamor for a separate agency as their true defender.

The regulatory structure did not change significantly when the U.S. Maritime Commission* replaced the Shipping Board in 1936. In 1950, when the Maritime

Administration* (MARAD) replaced the U.S. Maritime Commission, regulatory functions went to the Federal Maritime Board,* whose chairman was also the head of MARAD. Shippers still did not feel adequately protected, and Isbrandtsen's morbid hatred of the conference system provided the opportunity for a major assault on the deficient regulation of ocean shipping. Shippers had particularly resented the practices of conferences, and when the Supreme Court in the *Isbrandtsen* case* struck down the dual-rate* contracts, shippers convinced Congressman Emanuel Celler of the Antitrust Subcommittee of the House to hold extensive hearings on the monopoly abuses of conferences and the lax regulation by MARAD.

Steamship companies tried to head off the danger by a separate set of hearings in the Merchant Marine and Fisheries Committee,* which traditionally was more favorable to the ocean carriers, but the more sensational revelations of the Celler Committee convinced Congress to approve the Reorganization Plan of 1961, which at last provided shippers with their long-sought independent agency, the Federal Maritime Commission.

The shippers' insistence on a separate regulatory agency could be understood only in reference to the difference between subsidies before and after World War II. During the Shipping Board era, subsidies to create and support U.S.-flag steamship companies had lowered freight rates and provided shippers with a variety of unusual services, as well as the opportunity to choose among many American and foreign lines in most trade routes. Thus the shippers were pacified not so much by the actions of the Division of Regulation of the Shipping Board but by the tangible and substantial benefits they received from the policy of subsidizing so many competing U.S.-flag lines. Instead, after World War II, the mounting billions of dollars in subsidies to U.S.-flag lines, rather than lowering, appeared to be keeping rates high, and regulatory relief now seemed the most promising way to obtain some benefits for American shippers, especially because budget constraints excluded subsidizing the shippers directly.

MARAD continued with its traditional duty of trying to defend the U.S.-flag steamship companies, while the new FMC necessarily had to attack and weaken the U.S. merchant marine. In its initial years the FMC was still under the influence of the steamship companies, but since the late 1960s the shippers' interests clearly dominated the commission. Thus maritime policy joined the list of classic contradictions within the federal bureaucracy: what one agency was trying to build, another was trying to destroy. The FMC was supposed to make no distinctions between U.S. and foreign lines, but until the passage of the Shipping Act of 1984* and the Foreign Shipping Practices Act of 1988, U.S. steamship companies bore the brunt of regulatory enforcement. Within the United States the FMC could subpoena records and witnesses, and once enough evidence had been gathered, the FMC imposed a variety of sanctions, usually fines, but the most serious were restrictions or, if necessary, a prohibition on certain practices;

against foreign lines the trump card was the authority to forbid the entry of their ships into U.S. ports.

In formal proceedings that the FMC itself admitted "will take a long period of time"—and "more than five years" was not unheard of—a veritable lawyers' paradise had been created (*American Shipper*, September 1978). The FMC staff was never large enough to handle the flood of cases, while the shippers and liner companies were forced to hire large legal teams to conduct and monitor the proceedings. But until 1984 the cost fell heavier on the steamship companies, because the burden of proof rested squarely on them. The result was a gradual weakening of the conference system, in particularly through the virtual elimination of the dual-rate system in the U.S. foreign trade routes. Not surprisingly, the hostility of the FMC contributed to the bankruptcy of many U.S. steamship companies in the 1970s and 1980s, for the commission an inevitable if unfortunate consequence of its duty of protecting the shippers at all costs.

As far as protecting American shippers from possible abuses by foreign lines and, in particular, conferences controlled by foreign lines, the results were mixed and revealed a double standard. Since the creation of the FMC, the leading maritime nations of the world have stoutly refused to recognize any U.S. jurisdiction over their steamship companies, on the principle that this was a matter affecting the very sovereignty of each individual state; their position was that the FMC could take measures only as a result of bilateral negotiations and not of unilateral action. The key to the FMC proceedings was obtaining the requisite documentation from the accused ocean carriers, but the leading maritime nations have refused to release any information; England went so far as to pass a law in 1964 ordering its companies not to turn over records to a foreign government. The leading maritime nations coordinated their policies at meetings such as the Cotton Club* and generally were able to stop action against their ocean carriers, usually by combining sharp legal action with the lack of evidence.

Only the ultimate reprisal of closing U.S. ports to the ships of the offending carrier or nation could work, but both the need to maintain close relations with countries otherwise friendly to the United States and the overriding concern of the FMC as the defender of shippers not to unduly disrupt the services available to the latter have prevented anything but token reprisals against major maritime powers. In the case of the Soviet Union, when its Far East Shipping Company was engaged in predatory rate cutting in the 1970s, the FMC, bogged down as usual in proceedings, failed to respond promptly and furthermore required additional legislation, specifically the Controlled Carriers Act of 1978,* to take effective action, but by then the Soviet shipping threat was rapidly vanishing. However, for countries of the Third World, the FMC has enjoyed the advantage of drawing on the economic and political might of the United States to secure compliance with its orders and thereby favor U.S. shippers. Thus, to mention some cases, in the Philippines, Venezuela, and Ecuador, the FMC has threatened

retaliation until the individual countries backed down; in one of its most revealing moves, the case of the Philippines in 1984, the FMC obtained the repeal
of the cargo preference decree that ironically had boosted the business of U.S.-
flag companies. Ineffective against the maritime powers, while more like a big
bully in the case of underdeveloped countries, the interventions of the FMC on
behalf of shippers have caused considerable diplomatic friction with other countries, in contrast with the practice of the Shipping Board, the U.S. Maritime
Commission, and the Federal Maritime Board of avoiding international confrontations.

Meanwhile, by the 1970s the shippers were finding in the extreme competition
among foreign lines a more than adequate mechanism to obtain the lowest rates
with the best service. What was left of U.S.-flag companies joined with foreign
lines to mount a counterattack on the FMC, while the deregulation fever that
seized the United States by the late 1970s spawned proposals to simply abolish
the FMC as a useless bureaucratic jungle. After some long and vicious legislative battles, whose congressional proponents vowed never to repeat again, the
Shipping Act of 1984* emerged as a workable compromise that attempted to
harmonize the unique American contributions to business practices with the
harsh realities of world shipping. The new law reformed and updated the Shipping Act of 1916,* the principal law enforced by the FMC. The 1984 act at last
shifted the burden of proof away from conference and carrier agreements to the
challengers—including the FMC—and also broadened the antitrust immunity of
conferences, including interconference agreements. The act strengthened the
self-policing functions of conferences and encouraged ''independent'' action by
individual carriers on rates as the best way to check any conference abuses. The
dual-rate system in its classic form remained illegal but, under the variation of
a ''service contract,''* became an accepted tool in the foreign trade of the United
States.

Since the passage of the Shipping Act of 1984, the FMC has maintained a
proper balance between the interests of the shippers and those of shipowners.
Besides functioning as a very useful clearinghouse on aspects such as rates and
tariffs, the FMC has continued to police conference agreements and to perform
its quasi-judicial duties. The Advisory Commission on Conferences in Ocean
Shipping of 1992 did not study the FMC itself but throughout the pages of its
report assumed that the FMC would continue to perform its meaningful functions. However, in 1992 proposals to dismantle the FMC surfaced again, but
they did not completely disappear even in the first year of the new Bill Clinton
administration. Vice President Al Gore's National Performance Review (a commission on government reform) considered a July 1993 draft that called for
stripping the FMC of almost all its functions, presumably as a first step toward
its elimination. This return to the Republican deregulatory fever of the early
1980s was at the very least bizarre for a Democratic administration, and the
pro-shipper bias was so blatant that Transportation Secretary Federico Peña had
to step in to quash the proposal that was not included in the final published

version of the National Performance Review. Although FMC has survived this attack on its well-functioning regulatory functions over world shipping, the future of the agency still remains threatened until the Clinton administration either defines a maritime policy or reserves its reformist impulses for other areas of the U.S. economy.

Chairmen

Thomas E. Stakem	1961–1963
Admiral John Harllee	1963–1969
Helen D. Bentley*	1969–1975
Karl E. Bakke	1975–1977
Richard J. Daschback	1977–1981
Alan ("Punch") Green, Jr.	1981–1985
Edward V. Hickey, Jr.	1985–1988
Elaine L. Chao	1988–1989
James J. Carey	1989–1990
Christopher Koch	1990–1993
William D. Hathaway	1993–present

References: *American Shipper,* December 1976, September 1978, December 1978, February 1984, September 1991, May 1992, October 1993; René De La Pedraja, *The Rise and Decline of U.S. Merchant Shipping in the Twentieth Century* (New York: Twayne, 1992); Ernst G. Frankel, *Regulation and Policies of American Shipping* (Boston: Auburn House, 1982); *Journal of Commerce,* 26 October 1988; Samuel A. Lawrence, *United States Merchant Shipping Policies and Politics* (Washington, DC: Brookings Institution, 1966); *Newsweek,* 27 September 1993; President's Advisory Council on Executive Organization, *A New Regulatory Framework: Report on Selected Independent Regulatory Agencies* (Washington, DC: Government Printing Office, 1971).

FEDERATION OF AMERICAN-CONTROLLED SHIPPING (FACS), 1974–present. The Federation of American-Controlled Shipping (FACS) has represented U.S. companies whose ships were registered under flags of convenience.* FACS replaced the American Committee for Flags of Necessity* (ACFN) in 1974; in structure, membership, and goals, FACS was simply a name change: the old title "Flags of Necessity" was no longer widely accepted and was becoming counterproductive, while the new title "American-Controlled" reflected on a more popular level the latest lobbying slogan of "effective control." Almost all the large independent tanker owners have been members, as well as most of the major oil companies in the United States. The following companies belonged to FACS in 1984:

Alcoa Steamship Company*	Gulf Oil
Amoco Marine Transportation	Lubrizol Corp.

Arco Marine, Inc.

Bethlehem Steel (See Calmar)

Castle and Cooke (Dole since 1991)

Charter Shipping Agents, Inc.

Chevron Shipping Co.

Conoco Division/Duont

Cosmopolitan Shipping Co.*

Dow Chemical Co.

Exxon*

getty Oil

Grand Bassa Tankers, Inc.

Marathon Oil Co.

Marine Transport Lines

Navios Ship Management Serivces

Phillips Petroleum Co.

Reomar, Inc.

Reynolds Metals Co.

Skaarup Shipping Corp.

States Marine Corp.*

Sun Transport

Texaco

Union Oil Co. of California

Utah International

FACS's biggest challenge came during the energy crisis of 1973–1980. In 1974 a bill passed the House and Senate that would have required 30 percent of U.S. oil imports to be carried aboard U.S.-flag vessels. President Gerald Ford vetoed this cargo preference* legislation, but the bill had managed to reach his desk only because of a rift within FACS membership as well as divisions in the powerful oil lobby represented by the American Petroleum Institute. In 1977 a once again unified FACS skillfully maneuvered to defeat in the House a more modest bill that would have required U.S.-flag tankers to carry only 9.5 percent of oil imports.

FACS remained alert for new signs of cargo preference proposals or any other attempts to otherwise restrict flags of convenience, but the decline of maritime labor kept any serious challenges from materializing. The system of flags of convenience was more than adequate for the U.S. companies, but occasionally in the 1980s FACS could intervene to make some improvements. Until the 1980s, only Panama and Liberia offered true flags of convenience because the registry of Honduras existed for only one U.S. company, United Fruit,* and many executives worried over the lack of additional options. The bloody Liberian coup of 1980 convinced many to look for alternatives, even though the registry of Liberia continued to operate without any disruptions. Small island states soon realized there was big money to be made with little effort by registering ships under their flags, and nearby Bahamas led the way in 1980 with their ship registry, which soon became attractive to U.S. companies. The task of FACS in 1987 was to convince the U.S. government to accept Bahamian registry as part of the ''effective control'' fleet up till then limited to Honduras, Liberia, and Panama. The Maritime Administration* (MARAD) agreed, thereby making U.S.-owned ships registered under the Bahamas flag eligible for U.S. war-risk insurance. This approval was timely and allowed many jumpy owners to abandon the Panamanian registry during the risky years of confrontation between the United States and Panamanian dictator Manuel Noriega. FACS has continued to defend and promote effectively the interests of U.S. companies whose ships have been registered under flags of convenience.

Principal Executives

Eugene A. Yourch   1978–1987

Philip J. Loree   1974–present

References: Rodney P. Carlisle, *Sovereignty for Sale: The Origins and Evolution of the Panamanian and Liberian Flags of Convenience* (Annapolis, MD: Naval Institute Press, 1981); René De La Pedraja, *The Rise and Decline of U.S. Merchant Shipping in the Twentieth Century* (New York: Twayne, 1992); Ernst G. Frankel, *Regulation and Policies of American Shipping* (Boston: Auburn House, 1982); Gale Research, *Encyclopedia of Associations*, 1983–1992; Gale Research, *Business Organizations and Agencies Directory 1980*; William J. Miller, *Encyclopedia of International Commerce* (Centreville, MD: Cornell Maritime Press, 1985); Clinton H. Whitehurst, Jr., *The U.S. Merchant Marine: In Search of an Enduring Maritime Policy* (Annapolis, MD: Naval Institute Press, 1983).

FEU. FEU or forty-foot equivalent units has been a measurement for containers* forty-feet long. The most common container size has been twenty-feet long, and hence TEUs* or twenty-foot equivalent units has been the most frequently used measurement for containers. However, the next most common length for containers has been forty feet, and consequently companies like American President Lines* (APL) that used mostly these longer containers reported their volumes in terms of FEUs.

References: American President Lines, annual and quarterly reports, 1987–1992.

FIGHTING SHIPS. The fighting ships have been used deliberately by a merchant shipping company or a conference* to try to drive a competing line out of a particular trade route. The fighting ships quoted lower rates and provided special services that finally convinced the shippers* to abandon the vessels of the targeted line. The Shipping Act of 1916* and that of 1984* prohibited fighting ships, but during brief periods of fierce competition the practices of some U.S. companies have come very close to the definition of fighting ships.

FLAGS OF CONVENIENCE. This has been the most widespread term used since the 1970s to refer to the practice by companies (usually European or U.S.) to register their ships initially under the flags of Honduras, Liberia, Panama, and most recently Bahamas in order to benefit from labor, tax, and other advantages. The practice has become very widespread, and since 1980 a growing number of small island states (e.g., Malta, Vanatu) have jumped into the business and opened their own registry systems so that today the shipowner can choose from over fifty flags. The latest attraction of the newer flags of convenience registries is skimping on safety standards for ships. The expression *flags of convenience* has gradually replaced the two exaggerated terms *flags of necessity** and runaway flags,* used respectively by the vessel owners and the maritime labor unions. See also Federation of American-Controlled Shipping.

FLAGS OF NECESSITY. An exaggerated term used in the 1960s by the U.S. companies to refer to the practice of registering their ships under the flags of Honduras, Liberia, and Panama. The term *flags of necessity* was intended to counter the no less emotion-charged *runaway flags,** the latter expression popularized by the labor unions. The companies since the 1970s have opted for the more moderate terms of *American-controlled* or *effective control* when referring to their foreign-flag operations. See also flags of convenience; Federation of American-Controlled Shipping.

FORECASTLE. The forecastle (pronounced ''foksel'') was the raised front portion of a ship, so named because in medieval sailing ships it stood out as a ''castle'' in contrast to the other castle (''poop'') in the stern or rear of the ship. Aboard sailing ships the forecastle held the sleeping quarters of the sailors and was generally the worst and most crowded part of the vessel. With the shift to steam and steel, naval designers saw no reason to change the location of the sailors' quarters and as a matter of fact could not resist placing steam tubes, toilets, and any other ill-smelling or dangerous facilities near or right in the forecastle. In general the areas not suitable for cargo were reserved by ship designers for crew space. When weather permitted, the sailors ate on deck, but more commonly they ate in the forecastle, which Andrew Furuseth* described as ''too large for a coffin and too small for a grave'' (Nelson 1990); however, not even he or other leaders of the International Seamen's Union* (ISU) even dreamed of requesting the unheard-of luxury of a sailors' mess hall.

Lousy was a moderate term for the food that the sailors described as ''stuff that seagulls wouldn't eat'' (ibid.). Sailors lashed out at the cooks and stewards who served the miserly portions when in reality the blame was with the shipowners, who provided inferior and scarce rations; in this way poor food served to keep both groups divided and at each other's throats.

The forecastle represented the worst in living accommodations, and while equally bad *working* conditions could easily be found on land, shoreside workers returned home every day, while sailors had to live aboard. The emergence of militant unionism in the late 1930s began to improve conditions on the forecastles, which, however, could not be ripped out in existing ships and for decades remained a visible reminder of what shipowners were capable of doing to extract the last cent out of their workers. Automation and mechanization of ships began to reduce crew size, so that existing quarters could easily be made more comfortable. During the last fifty years radical changes in ship design, which started with the C-2* vessels, have made unnecessary using the forecastle as sailors' quarters. In many ships the forecastle has disappeared altogether, and in others moving the propulsion machinery to the rear of the ship has released space for cargo and ample crews' quarters. As vessels have become longer and bigger, superstructures or "islands" have risen in height to provide ample visibility to maneuver the ship from the bridge, in the process creating lots of space under the bridge for crews' quarters. Sailors now generally have private rooms, mess halls, and recreation rooms, and aboard U.S.-flag ships or those owned by U.S. companies, the forecastle of notorious fame is nothing but a nearly forgotten nightmare. In many Third World countries, however, the crews sailing on obsolete ships continue to suffer the atrocious conditions associated with living in the forecastle.

References: James C. Healey, *Foc'sle and Glory Hole: A Study of the Merchant Seaman and His Occupation* (New York: Merchant Marine Publishers Association, 1936); Bruce Nelson, *Workers on the Waterfront: Seamen, Longshoremen, and Unionism in the 1930s* (Urbana: University of Illinois Press, 1990); Marion G. Sherar, *Shipping Out* (Cambridge, MD: Cornell Maritime Press, 1973).

FOUR ACES, 1931–1941 and 1948–1964. Four Aces was the name given to the four combination cargo-passenger liners of the American Export Lines* (AEL). Actually, there were two generations of the Four Aces making a total of eight ships, with the names of the first four ships repeated for the last four. The first generation of the Four Aces (1931–1941) comprised the *Excalibur*, the *Exorchorda*, the *Exeter*, and the *Excambion*, each with accommodations for 125 first-class passengers and a speed of sixteen knots. The design of the ships was basically that of modified freighters and reflected the gradual entry by accretion into the passenger business. The result was that the first Four Aces were adequate neither as freighters nor passenger liners: the use of the fuel-wasteful turbine* engines was justified only to attain speeds over twenty knots, but at sixteen knots the Four Aces were too slow for passenger travel yet too expensive for operation as freighters. This blunder contributed to the company's troubles in the 1930s, but fortunately the ships were requisitioned for service in World War II. Three of the Four Aces were sunk in combat, and AEL did not want the fourth back, arguing that the ship was too old and that profitable operation was possible only by having four in service at the same time.

Instead AEL agreed to convert four surplus navy attack transports into the second generation of Four Aces, and these two were given the names of *Excalibur*, *Exorchorda*, *Exeter*, and *Excambion*. They were about the same size but had a slightly faster speed of eighteen knots, and with improvements in double-reduction gear the company hoped that their turbine engines would be less wasteful than those of the first generation. The hopes proved unfounded, and by the 1950s these ships began to show losses; the company had already concluded in 1952 to operate either passenger or cargo ships in the future, but no more combination ships. In 1960 the *Exorchorda* and *Excambion* were laid up and replaced by the modern passenger liner *Atlantic*, which the company had purchased from the defunct American Banner Line.* The *Excalibur* and the *Exeter* remained in service until December 1964, and the next year they were sold to foreign buyers, bringing to an end the Four Aces, whose continuing losses helped drive AEL toward its later bankruptcy.

References: René De La Pedraja, *The Rise and Decline of U.S. Merchant Shipping in the Twentieth Century* (New York: Twayne, 1992); Frederick E. Emmons, *American Passenger Ships: The Ocean Lines and Liners, 1873–1983* (Newark: University of Delaware Press, 1985); *New York Times*, 1 December 1947, 12 May 1948, 5 October 1952, 22 August 1965.

FRANKLIN, JOHN M., 18 June 1895–2 June 1975. John M. Franklin was the president of United States Lines* (USL) and during thirty years was considered the dean of American steamship executives. Franklin was born in Cockeysville, Maryland, on 18 June 1895, the son of the president of the International Mercantile Marine* (IMM), Philip A. S. Franklin.* John attended private schools and graduated from Harvard in 1918. He joined the U.S. Army and served in France in World War I and rose to the rank of captain. In 1922 he married Emily Hammond and had three children, Emily, John, and Laura. After the war Franklin began his shipping career, and in 1927 he became a vice president of the Roosevelt Steamship Company.*

Franklin's real goal, however, was to continue the control his father had acquired over IMM. Franklin belonged to a group of friends that included Kermit Roosevelt,* Vincent Astor, James A. Farrell, Jr.,* and Basil Harris,* who in June 1930 subscribed the bulk of a new stock issue by IMM, in effect gaining control of the company. Franklin and his father maneuvered decisively until they took over the U.S.-flag company USL in 1931. Also in that year Franklin was elected vice president of IMM and, following his father's retirement in 1936, became president. While his father's career had relied on the profitable foreign-flag operations to assure the survival of IMM, Franklin had the more difficult task of shifting the company to the more costly U.S.-flag ships. By 1936 Franklin had disposed of IMM's last foreign-flag ships and furthermore had made USL the center of his operations. He agreed to sign new subsidy contracts under the terms of the Merchant Marine Act of 1936,* and consequently USL could receive a new liner, the *America*,* in 1940. In 1943, when IMM, by then just a corporate shell, was abolished, the transition to a purely U.S.-flag operation was complete.

During World War II Franklin served in the Army Transport Service, eventually rising to the rank of major general; most significantly, he had been instrumental in securing for the War Shipping Administration* authority to operate in the most efficient manner. After the war he returned to the presidency of USL and conceived the plan of building the fastest passenger liner in the world. Franklin pursued this plan with determination and secured approval for larger than usual subsidies on grounds of national defense to cover the expected losses from the operation of such a fast ship. The new superliner, the *United States*,* sailed on its maiden voyage in July 1952, and the ship's record for fastest transatlantic crossing still stands today.

By the early 1960s, with increasing competition from jet planes, the investment in passenger liners resulted only in mounting losses, while for the cargo services the company faced the no less challenging task of trying to replace the surplus vessels of World War II. Franklin hoped to leave these problems to his successor, but only his son-in-law, William B. Rand, wanted to continue the family tradition in the company. Franklin in 1960 became chairman of the board, and eventually Rand became president of USL. Unfortunately for the company, the marriage of Rand to Franklin's daughter collapsed, and Rand was removed from the presidency in late 1966. Franklin himself retired as chairman of the board in 1967, thereby ending the control his family had enjoyed over the largest merchant fleet in the United States for over fifty years. Franklin died on 2 June 1975.

References: *Current Biography 1949*; René De La Pedraja, *The Rise and Decline of U.S. Merchant Shipping in the Twentieth Century* (New York: Twayne, 1992); *Nautical Gazette*, 19 March 1927; *New York Times* 22 June 1960, 22 June 1967.

FRANKLIN, PHILIP A. S., 1 February 1871–14 August 1939.

Philip A. S. Franklin (or P.A.S. Franklin, as he preferred to be known) was the president of the International Mercantile Marine* (IMM) and remained the dean of steamship executives for over twenty years. He was born in Ashland, Maryland, on 1 February 1871, and he attended public schools. An uncle and a brother were admirals in the U.S. Navy, although his father was a civil engineer. In 1889 Franklin began to work as an office boy for Bernard M. Baker* of the Atlantic Transport Company,* and Baker remained his immediate supervisor during many years.

When the Atlantic Transport Company entered the IMM, Franklin became a vice president of the new shipping combine. Gradually he began to prepare his advance and took maximum advantage of the sinking of the *Titanic** and the outbreak of World War I to consolidate his position. When the IMM went into bankruptcy at the end of 1914, Franklin convinced the creditors to appoint him president of the combine, and soon under his direction he used the record wartime profits to bail out the company. In 1916 the stockholders confirmed Franklin as president of the IMM, a position he held until his retirement in 1936.

When the United States entered World War I, Franklin became the chairman of the Shipping Control Committee of the Shipping Board.* As virtual dictator of ship movements, he controlled the pool of all merchant vessels under U.S. control, and he efficiently allocated cargo space for the wartime needs. However, he needlessly antagonized many: "He is the type of man who wants everybody to cooperate with him, but lacks the spirit of cooperation himself" (Edward N. Hurley Papers). Likewise he shunned publicity and photographs, so that the harshness of both his public and private image doubtlessly contributed to some of the difficulties the IMM faced after the war. For example, he was not able to counter the clever campaign by the Hearst newspapers to keep the Shipping Board from assigning the *Leviathan** and other surplus vessels to the IMM.

Even while World War I was raging, Franklin had made attempts to dispose of the foreign-flag vessels of the IMM. Americans insisted on viewing the shipping combine, in spite of its majority American ownership, as nothing more than a British front to undermine the U.S. merchant marine. In 1926 Franklin sold off the British-flag White Star Line,* the largest foreign subsidiary of IMM, and he continued to look for ways to dispose of the remaining foreign-flag vessels at reasonable prices. However, Franklin's most momentous decision was not the selling of the foreign-flag vessels but rather the attempt to acquire a U.S.-flag merchant fleet. Instead of investing the proceeds from the sales into profitable and sure businesses on land, Franklin fell into the trap of trying to operate the expensive U.S.-flag vessels. He and his son John engaged in the complex maneuvers that finally resulted in the takeover of the United States Lines* (USL), which became in October 1931 the main subsidiary of the IMM.

The daunting task of trying to make profitable the U.S.-flag operations of the IMM vexed Franklin during his last years at IMM, and although he found no adequate solution, the problem increasingly was left on the shoulders of John, who replaced Franklin as president in 1936. Franklin remained as chairman of the Board of Directors, but already ill health forced him to resign in 1938, and he died of Parkinson's disease on 14 August 1939 in his Long Island estate.

References: René De La Pedraja, *The Rise and Decline of U.S. Merchant Shipping in the Twentieth Century* (New York: Twayne, 1992); *Dictionary of American Biography*, Supplement 2; Edward N. Hurley Papers, Notre Dame University Archives; Thomas R. Navin and Marian V. Sears, "A Study in Merger: Formation of the International Mercantile Marine Company," *Business History Review* 28 (1954):291–328.

FREE SHIPS. Free Ships was the expression that conveniently summarized the proposal of allowing the registration under the U.S. flag of ships built abroad. The slogan was widely used by the Democratic party as a rallying cry against the protectionist policies of the Republican party. The agitation for free ships began in the last decades of the nineteenth century and came to an end only with World War I. See Registry, U.S.

FREIGHT FORWARDERS or OCEAN FREIGHT FORWARDERS. The freight forwarders have made the arrangements to move the cargo of the shippers.* Large companies with their own traffic departments generally dealt directly with the ocean carrier, but small and medium-sized shippers hired freight forwarders to move the cargo at the lowest rates possible. Only since the passage of the Shipping Act of 1984* have some small- and medium-sized shippers started to move their merchandise through shippers' associations.*

The freight forwarder has been a middleman who obtained the rate information, secured the necessary space, prepared the documentation, including the bill of lading,* and tracked the movement of the shipper's cargo. The ocean freight forwarders, who number nearly 2,000, stand between the at least 100,000 potential shippers and the approximately 100 liner* companies (not counting the tramps*). The freight forwarders have not been necessarily in a position of weakness with respect to the ocean lines, and the latter paid the former a service charge or commission of at least 1.25 percent on the price the shipper paid to carry the merchandise; in times of rate wars the percentage could go higher as competing lines attempted to secure a greater share of the available cargoes.

With the introduction of containers* in the 1960s, many freight forwarders (in particular, the subcategory known as freight brokers, which dated back at least to the 1920s) discovered that they could obtain for their shippers significantly lower rates (specifically, quotations for "freight of all kinds" or FAK) if they consolidated small lots into what a container could carry. Most freight forwarders added this new service to their traditional functions, but in the United States those who specialized mainly in the consolidation of lots into full container loads were called Non-Vessel Operating Common Carriers* (NVOCCs), a distinction the rest of the world has not made.

References: Advisory Commission on Conferences in Ocean Shipping, *Report to the President and the Congress* (Washington, DC: Government Printing Office, 1992); *American Shipper*, January 1977; Federal Maritime Commission, *Section 18 Report on the Shipping Act of 1984*, September 1989; Grover G. Huebner, *Ocean Steamship Traffic Management* (New York: D. Appleton, 1920); *Nautical Gazette*, 4 July 1931; Transportation Research Board, *Intermodal Marine Container Transportation: Impediments and Opportunities* (Washington, DC: National Research Council, 1992).

FURUSETH, ANDREW, 12 March 1854–22 January 1938. Andrew Furuseth was the first national labor leader of the seamen, and for decades he controlled the Sailors' Union of the Pacific* (SUP) and the International Seamen's Union* (ISU). He was born on 12 March 1854 in Norway of a poor family and had to begin working when he was only eight, but more significantly he managed to attend school until he was sixteen and developed a passion for reading. He was nineteen when he began shipping aboard sailing vessels, and he sailed across the seas until 1880, when he reached the West Coast of the United States. He continued to sail in the coastwise* trade until 1891, when he became a full-time union official.

Even before 1891 union activities had taken him increasingly away from the sea, and as a literate and articulate seaman, his climb was rapid. He served as secretary of the SUP in 1887–1889 and again held this position—the highest ranking in the union—from 1891 until 1936. When the ISU was founded in 1899, he was the real power in the organization and from 1908 to his death served as its president. Furuseth's position was West Coast czar of the seamen appeared secure, but beginning in 1894, he began to devote more time to lobbying in Washington, D.C., for legislation favorable to the seamen. In dealing with Congress, his dual role as leader and representative of the two main seamen's unions in the United States gave him an unusual advantage, and he was able to translate this position into favorable legislation, most notably the Maguire Act* (1895), the White Act (1898), and the La Follette Seamen's Act of 1915.* This last act had taken years of lobbying effort and was finally passed thanks to the decisive backing of his close friend Senator Robert M. La Follette. The Seamen's Act abolished imprisonment for desertion and signified to sailors nothing less than attaining the personal freedom that as near-slaves they had previously lacked.

The passage of the La Follette Seamen's Act was Furuseth's greatest success and earned him the title of "emancipator of the seamen," but because many of its other provisions remained dead letter, he spent most of the rest of his life in a vain attempt to secure its full implementation. Furuseth now faced a crucial decision: he could remain a full-time lobbyist in Washington, D.C., or he could return to the West Coast to resume the personal direction of the ISU and the SUP, but he could not hold both jobs. The result was that after 1910 he spent most of the time in Washington, D.C., and left the running of the unions to subordinates who were less motivated and competent. The temporary World War I boom brought a temporary surge in the ISU, but the disastrous strike of 1921* weakened seamen's unions, particularly the ISU. In the 1920s, graft, loafing, and racketeering became the rule in the ISU, while Furuseth lost touch with the seamen in the SUP.

Furuseth himself led a Spartan life, and his honesty and unceasing devotion to the seamen made him a legend. He avoided personal publicity, and only at the direct intervention of his friend La Follette did he finally consent to have a photograph taken. Furuseth dressed, talked, and behaved like a seaman, and without a family or a wife, he devoted all his time to union activities. His personal values were in stark contrast to those of a later generation of labor leaders, most notably Joseph Ryan* and Joseph Curran.*

On the negative side, Furuseth was intolerant of differing views, and he labeled dissenters in the unions first as wobblies and later as communists. What made his end somewhat tragic was that he remained attached to craft organization in an age when technology had depersonalized the employer-worker relations. To the end he believed that a skill "puts the mechanic nearest the gods" and he proclaimed that "work is worship—to labor is to pray" (Nelson 1990). Quite naturally he opposed alliances with other workers, and his opposition to cooperation with the longshoremen remained an obsession.

Furuseth could not understand the upheavals of maritime workers in the 1930s, and finally insurgents removed him as secretary of the SUP in 1936. He authorized the creation of a rival union to attempt to lure back the sailors, but by then he was too weak, and after a year's illness he died on 22 January 1938.

References: *Dictionary of American Biography*, Supplement 2; Gary M. Fink, ed., *Biographical Dictionary of American Labor*, 2d ed., (Westport, CT: Greenwood Press, 1984); Bruce Nelson, *Workers on the Waterfront: Seamen, Longshoremen, and Unionism in the 1930s* (Urbana: University of Illinois Press, 1990); Hyman Weintraub, *Andrew Furuseth: Emancipator of the Seamen* (Berkeley: University of California Press, 1959).

G

GAMBLE, MILLARD G., 24 May 1894–5 November 1974. Millard G. Gamble headed the tanker operations of the Standard Oil Company* of New Jersey, or Esso, from 1945 to 1959. He was born in Louisville, Georgia, on 24 May 1894, and after attending the Louisville Academy, he graduated from the U.S. Naval Academy in 1915. He served in World War I and advanced to the rank of lieutenant commander. In 1919 he resigned from the navy to join the Standard Oil Company of New Jersey, where he stayed until his retirement. He climbed through the ranks of the company and became assistant general manager of the marine department in 1942 and then its manager in 1945. He in effect had become the replacement to the highly flamboyant Robert L. Hague,* but Gamble always operated in a very orderly manner through formal channels as befitted a former naval officer. Gamble described his job in the marine department as that of "a man walking ahead on a fast moving treadmill and having difficulty holding his own" (Larson 1971). In January 1950, the parent company, in one of its recurrent reorganizations, decided to centralize its tanker operations in a separate entity, Esso Shipping company, and appointed Gamble as president of this new subsidiary. He held this position until 1958, when the parent company decided to reabsorb Esso Shipping. Gamble also served as an adviser to the Board of Directors of Esso until 1958, when he retired from the company. Afterward he remained involved as a consultant in many projects affecting tankers until his death on 5 November 1974.

References: Henrietta M. Larson, Evelyn H. Knowlton, and Charles S. Popple, *New Horizons, 1927–1950* (New York: Harper & Row, 1971); *National Cyclopedia of American Biography*, Current vol. I; *Who's Who, 1966–1967*.

GARMATZ, EDWARD A., 7 February 1903–22 July 1986. Edward A. Garmatz, a congressman from Maryland, bravely attempted to halt the decline of the U.S. merchant marine. Garmatz was born on 7 February 1903 in Baltimore, Maryland, and after education in public schools and the Polytechnic Institute, worked in the electrical business until 1942, when he became involved in local politics. In July 1947 he was elected as a Democrat to the House of Representatives and served continuously until January 1973. After the death of Herbert C. Bonner* in 1965, Garmatz became the chairman of the Merchant Marine and Fisheries Committee* and also of its Subcommittee on Merchant Marine.

Garmatz was actively involved in the discussions on maritime policy during the Lyndon B. Johnson administration, but no legislative results were forthcoming. Instead under the presidency of Richard Nixon, Garmatz secured passage of the Merchant Marine Act of 1970,* which created a new program for subsidizing bulk* carriers. Garmatz decided not to run for reelection in 1972, and he went to work for the Masters, Mates, and Pilots* union, whose headquarters are in the Baltimore area. His involvement in maritime affairs flared into public view in 1977, when he was indicted of having received bribes from steamship executives while he was chairman of the Merchant Marine and Fisheries Committee; later, when it was discovered that the evidence against him had been fabricated, all charges were dropped. Garmatz died in Baltimore on 22 July 1986.

References: Ernst G. Frankel, *Regulation and Policies of American Shipping* (Boston: Auburn House, 1982); Samuel A. Lawrence, *United States Merchant Shipping Policies and Politics* (Washington, DC: Brookings Institution, 1966); *New York Times*, 2 August 1977, 10 January 1978; U.S. Congress, *Biographical Directory of the United States Congress, 1774–1989* (Washington, DC: Government Printing Office, 1989).

GENERAL CARGO. See break-bulk cargo.

GIBSON, ANDREW E., 1922–present. Andrew E. Gibson was the head of the Maritime Administration* (MARAD) in 1969–1972 and was the president of Delta Line in 1979–1982. Gibson was born in Boston in 1922 and graduated from the Massachusetts Maritime Academy in 1942. He served in the merchant marine during World War II and in 1945 at age twenty-two became the youngest captain of an ocean freighter in recent history. After the war he returned to college and graduated cum laude from Brown University in 1951. Gibson worked with the Grace Line* from 1953 to 1967 and rose to become senior vice president for operations. A staunch Republican, he was picked by the Richard Nixon administration to head MARAD in 1969.

Gibson wanted the closest relationships among all maritime groups, and he decided to institutionalize the strong personal links he cultivated by creating the National Maritime Council* (NMC) in 1970. MARAD provided facilities and the time of government employees to make NMC into an effective coordinating voice for maritime labor, shipowners, and shipyards. Gibson also carefully cultivated relations with Congress, and taking advantage of the Nixon administration's willingness to support new legislation, he managed to secure approval for the Merchant Marine Act of 1970,* which, in a new development, extended the subsidy programs to bulk* carriers. Gibson was extremely well received by the maritime industry as one of their own, but the Nixon administration, after its reelection victory in November 1972 and as part of a wholesale reshuffling of personnel in most government agencies, decided not to keep Gibson at his post.

Gibson worked as a consultant for merchant shipping companies until 1979, when Holiday Inns asked him to become the president of its subsidiary, the Delta Line.* Gibson had to try to repair the previous error of ordering LASH* vessels rather than containerships, and Holiday Inns hoped he could sell or trade them to the government. Meanwhile Gibson began the long-delayed conversion of freighters into containerships, but as costs continued to mount, Holiday Inns finally tired of the whole steamship venture and sold Delta Line to Thomas B. Crowley* in December 1982. Crowley brought new officials into Delta to see if they would have better success than Gibson, who returned to consulting work and has continued to advise private entrepreneurs about ocean transportation.

References: *American Shipper*, March 1984; *Baltimore Sun*, 19 April 1970; *Congressional Record*, 7 February 1973; René De La Pedraja, *The Rise and Decline of U.S. Merchant Shipping in the Twentieth Century* (New York: Twayne, 1992); *Weekly Compilation of Presidential Documents*, 26 October 1970.

GLEASON, THOMAS WILLIAM ("TEDDY"), 8 November 1900–24 December 1992. Thomas William Gleason was the president of the International Longshoremen's Association* (ILA) for twenty-four years. He was born in New York City on 8 November 1900 and went to Catholic parochial school until the seventh grade. Both his father and grandfather had been longshoremen, and he began working in the docks alongside his father, suffering like all the rest of the indignities of the ''shape-up.''* When the Great Depression struck, jobs became very scarce on the waterfront, and the employers took the opportunity to reduce wages in 1931. Gleason and his men walked out, whereupon they were blacklisted; in a more heroic version, he claimed that he was blacklisted because he denounced a criminal ring among the scab laborers, but given the proliferation of illegal activities in the ILA during his presidency, the claim is more revealing of his obsession to deny any wrongdoing on the waterfront. The blacklist was real, however: he and his family were evicted for failure to pay rent, and only by the sale of their furniture did they scrape enough to pay for a room where he slept on the floor while his wife and two children were in the one bed they had saved. Somehow he managed to eke out a living through odd jobs, and the blacklisting was a turning point in his life because it shaped his determination to pursue a union career if he ever was allowed to return to the docks.

The New Deal and its pro-labor legislation opened the waterfront to Gleason, and in the ILA he ''was the spark plug of Local 1346 almost from its founding'' (Russell 1966). He held his first union post in 1934 and rose to become president of his local; Gleason's talents caught the attention of Joseph Ryan,* who promoted him to the rank of ILA organizer in 1947. Ryan believed that Gleason would eventually be his successor, but differences in policies led Ryan to fire Gleason on three different occasions; each time the turbulent union politics secured his reinstatement, and Gleason continued to admire Ryan decades after the latter had fallen from power and died. Gleason's growing power within the ILA certainly hastened Ryan's fall, but a combination of outside forces with internal pressures finally toppled Ryan in 1953. Gleason, however, had not yet consolidated his position to grab the presidency at once, and he threw his support behind Captain William Bradley as a transitional president. Captain Bradley lasted ten years in office, and only the timely offer of continuing his salary avoided a messy election fight in 1963, when at last Gleason was acclaimed president of the ILA, whose membership reached 60,000.

The new president immediately promised to return to the strong leadership style of Ryan. Gleason restored centralized control to the ILA, and soon all decisions affecting the locals were in his hands and those of his loyal subordinates. Gleason perpetuated himself in office through a rigid grip on the election machinery, and he turned the ILA into his personal empire, where only his voice was supreme. While Ryan had ultimately served as a tool for employers, Gleason was the first ILA president to realize that he could hold a power base independent of both the union membership and the employers, in effect being accountable to no one. He bought off the rank and file by the extremely generous wages and concessions he secured from the employers, while he disguised his autocratic control by a constant and virulent anticommunism. Employers did not like his excessive power, but most had no desire to negotiate with a chaotic group of leaders and preferred the convenience of dealing with an ILA president whose word was the final law on the waterfront.

With unchecked power and accountable only to themselves, ILA officials indulged in racketeering, extortion, and embezzlement; the drive for personal wealth had replaced the earlier idealism, whose only echo were the periodic denunciations of the communist dictatorships. Gleason's image began to deteriorate by the late 1970s as a long list of ILA indictments and convictions became public knowledge, but without affecting his tight grip on the union. Only old age made Gleason end his reign in 1987, when he handed over power to his longtime associate and vice president, John Bowers.* Gleason died in New York City on 24 December 1992.

References: *American Shipper*, September 1987; *Current Biography 1965*; Gary M. Fink, ed., *Biographical Dictionary of American Labor*, 2d ed. (Westport, CT: Greenwood Press, 1984); Maud Russell, *Men Along the Shore: The ILA and Its History* (New York: Brussell and Brussell, 1966); *Who's Who in Labor 1976*.

GLOBAL BULK TRANSPORT. See States Marine Corporation.

GOLDBLATT, LOUIS, 5 June 1910–17 January 1983. Louis Goldblatt was the secretary-treasurer of the International Longshoremen and Warehousemen's

Union* (ILWU) from 1943 to 1977, in which position he was the right-hand man of Harry Bridges.* He was born in New York City of a working-class family on 5 June 1910 and grew up in this city. He began to study at the City College but then transferred to the University of California, where he received a B.A. degree from Berkeley. He went on to graduate school and needed only the thesis to complete his Ph.D. requirement, but lack of money forced him in the midst of the Great Depression to seek employment first in the motion picture studios and later as a warehouseman in San Francisco. He immediately began to organize workers and lost many of his jobs because of his union activities. The dedication to union activities soon caught the attention of Harry Bridges, who put Goldblatt in charge of Congress of Industrial Organizations (CIO) efforts in northern California in 1937. Goldblatt continued to climb rapidly within the CIO hierarchy in California until 1942, when Bridges brought him back to the ILWU as organizer for Chicago and New York. In 1943 Goldblatt was elected secretary-treasurer, in effect the number two position at the ILWU. In 1946–1947 Goldblatt was also the secretary of the brief-lived Committee for Maritime Unity* (CMU).

   Goldblatt was one of the few labor leaders who publicly denounced the unjust internment of Japanese-Americans during World War II, a position that helped immensely the ILWU's organizing drive in Hawaii. Goldblatt remained the intellectual within the union but with few opportunities to express his writing abilities; however, he did write the text for *Men and Machines*, the photo book that explained the Mechanization and Modernization* Agreement of 1960.

   Goldblatt's relationship with Bridges was complex, but their combined efforts provided the type of leadership the ILWU required. Among many examples, the Bridges case* gave Goldblatt the opportunity to defend his chief from the many deportation attempts and still keep the union running smoothly. In 1977 both Goldblatt and Bridges retired. Goldblatt died on 17 January 1983.

   References: Gary M. Fink, ed., *Biographical Dictionary of American Labor*, 2d ed. (Westport, CT: Greenwood Press, 1984); Charles P. Larrowe, *Harry Bridges: The Rise and Fall of Radical Labor in the U.S.* (New York: Lawrence Hill, 1972); *Who's Who in Labor, 1976.*

GOOD NEIGHBOR FLEET, 1938–1958. The Good Neighbor Fleet referred to the three passenger-cargo liners operated by Moore-McCormack* in service between New York City and the east coast of South America. The origins of the Good Neighbor Fleet dated to a visit of President Franklin D. Roosevelt to Buenos Aires in 1936; the president was shocked to see that old World War I freighters provided the U.S.-flag passenger service to the United States, while in contrast modern European passengers liners provided regular service to Europe. Roosevelt directed the newly formed U.S. Maritime Commission* to create a fast, reliable service between the United States and South America, so that Latin Americans would no longer have to travel to Europe first to obtain quality accommodations for New York.

   When the International Mercantile Marine* (IMM) discontinued intercoastal* service, its three large turboelectric liners, the *California,** Pennsylvania*, and *Virginia*, came on the market and after several transactions were purchased by the U.S. Maritime Commission which spent over $1 million to modernize the three vessels. When the commission put the ships up for sale or charter,* no purchase bids appeared, but Moore-McCormack offered to charter the ships for operation in combination with its regular cargo vessels. Left with only the alternative of direct government operation or chartering to this company, the commission agreed, and on 8 September 1938 the Good Neighbor Fleet inaugurated its regular service to the east coast of South America. In keeping with the spirit of Roosevelt's goal of developing closer relations with Latin America, the company called the service the Good Neighbor Fleet and changed the names of the three vessels to *Argentina, Brazil*, and *Uruguay*.

To attract tourists as distinct from regular passengers, the company "embarked somewhat extravagantly on professional floor show entertainers and various 'amusement activities' designed to occupy the time of the indolent" (Record Group 59). After an initial failure to provide enough personnel able to understand Spanish or Portuguese, the company began to teach the languages to the crew. While company and government propaganda praised the smashing success of the new passenger service, it was "highly unpopular in Brazil and Uruguay. In Brazil especially it could apparently be held in scarcely less esteem had the company chosen its representatives with a view to selecting those most calculated to achieve unpopularity in that country" (ibid.). The general impression in Brazil was that the service "is endeavoring to extract as much money as possible in the shortest period of time from shippers* and travellers" (ibid.).

As owner of the vessels, the government soon called them for service during World War II, but with the return of peace Moore-McCormack took the vessels in charter again, and they resumed passenger service in 1948. Having the government own the vessels gave tremendous flexibility to the company, which could return them if traffic volume drastically declined, but because the demand for passenger travel remained booming, Moore-McCormack decided to order two new replacement vessels for the Good Neighbor Fleet, the *Argentina* and the *Brasil*, both of which the company owned outright. Only two ships were needed, because their faster speed of twenty-three knots made unnecessary the third ship. The *Argentina* and *Brasil* began sailing in 1958, but by then the goal of winning the Cold War had taken precedence over closer hemispheric relations, and the company quietly dropped the term of Good Neighbor Fleet as an anachronism from a bygone era.

References: Robert C. Lee, *Mr. Moore, Mr. McCormack—and the Seven Seas!* (New York: Newcomen Society, 1957); *New York Times*, 23 August 1938, 10 October 1948, 10 December 1957; Record Group 59, National Archives, Washington, DC; U.S. Maritime Commission, *Decisions*, vol. 3 (Washington, DC: Government Printing Office, 1963).

GRACE, J. PETER, 25 May 1913–present. J. Peter Grace has been the head of the conglomerate W. R. Grace & Co. since 1946, and he made the fundamental decisions that affected its shipping subsidiary, the Grace Line.* He was born in Manhasset, New York, on 25 May 1913, the son of the president of W. R. Grace & Co., Joseph Peter, and the grandson of the founder of the firm, William R. Grace.* His initial education was in Catholic schools, and he graduated from Yale University in 1936. He promptly began working for W. R. Grace & Co., gradually climbing to positions of greater responsibility. Upon the retirement of his father in 1946, J. Peter became the head of the company.

He soon realized that the company, in spite of growth and constant profits, had stagnated in previous decades and was really in a potentially vulnerable position. He concluded that W. R. Grace & Co. was overextended in Latin America, particularly in Peru and Chile, and needed to find other alternate sources of income. Grace decided to begin liquidating investments in Latin America and to shift the focus of the company's activities to the United States; after considerable research and study, he concluded that the future of the company lay in the chemical industry, and starting in 1952 he proceeded to buy chemical plants and related ventures.

His decision to shift operations to the United States had serious implications for the Grace Line, whose ships traditionally relied on a percentage of cargo belonging to the parent company. With less proprietary* cargo, the Grace Line now had to compete more vigorously to keep its ships full, but precisely in the 1950s strong Latin American companies appeared to take cargoes away. The management of Grace Line strove to keep the competitive edge by opening a route to the Great Lakes in 1959 and beginning container* service to Venezuela in 1960. Both of these initiatives turned out to be costly flops, and henceforth the Grace Line management conducted a holding action, trying to persuade Grace that there still was a future in U.S.-flag merchant shipping.

Losses in 1967 convinced Grace to sell the line, and although profits returned in 1968, this did not change his mind; as a matter of fact, the favorable profit statement was expected to lure unwary buyers. Unfortunately no eager buyers appeared, and he had to take the extreme decision of cutting the price by half, so as to put the Grace Line at last within the financial grasp of ambitious buyers. Finally Prudential Lines* agreed to purchase the Grace Line, and the sale was completed in February 1969. Grace considered his decision inevitable and the only right one to maintain the parent company in a sound basis, and henceforth he concentrated all his energies in the running of his growing conglomerate.

References: René De La Pedraja, *The Rise and Decline of U.S. Merchant Shipping in the Twentieth Century* (New York: Twayne, 1992); William Kooiman, *The Grace Ships 1869–1969* (Point Reyes, CA: Komar, 1990); *National Cyclopedia of American Biography*, Current vol. I.

GRACE, WILLIAM R., 10 May 1832–21 March 1904. William R. Grace was a merchant and shipowner who founded the company that bears his name. He was born in Ireland on 10 May 1832, and after completing his education and acquiring practical business experience in his native land under his father's guidance, he emigrated to Peru, where the guano boom was in progress. Although he did not engage in the export of that organic fertilizer, he concentrated on mercantile activities and soon specialized in supplying the many ships that called on the very busy port of Callao in Peru. In order to bring merchandise to Peru, he formed partnerships to charter* sailing vessels, and soon he wanted to own his own fleet.

In 1866 he moved with his family to New York, where he established his residence for the rest of his life. He fostered carefully his trade and investments in Peru, and in 1890 he secured valuable concessions from the Peruvian government in exchange for help in meeting the country's crushing foreign debt. To carry merchandise to Peru he had relied on charters of individual vessels, but with increased volumes of cargo he established in 1882 the first regular line of sailing vessels between New York and Peru to carry not only his merchandise but also that of other merchants. The advantages of steam in this very long route were clear, and in 1892 he organized the New York and Pacific Steamship Company* to provide scheduled steamer service between Peru and New York around the tip of South America. The fleet of steamers built and registered in Britain began service in 1893 and immensely increased the business his trading house conducted with Peru and Chile. Increased volume of trade meant continued expansion for the fleet of W. R. Grace & Co., whose long and prosperous career had begun. Grace did not limit his activities to commerce and shipping but also served two terms as the first Roman Catholic mayor of the city in 1881–1886, and throughout his life he remained involved in issues affecting the relations between the United States and Latin America. After a long bout with pneumonia, he died in New York City on 21 March 1904. Management of the company passed into the hands of his brother Michael and his son Joseph.

References: Lawrence A. Clayton, *Grace: W. R. Grace & Co.: The Formative Years, 1850–1930* (Ottawa, IL: Jameson Books, 1985); René De La Pedraja, *The Rise and Decline of U.S. Merchant Shipping in the Twentieth Century* (New York: Twayne, 1992); *Dictionary of American Biography*, vol. 7; William Kooiman, *The Grace Ships 1869–1969* (Point Reyes, CA: Komar, 1990).

GRACE LINE, 1916–1969. The Grace Line, the steamship subsidiary of the parent company W. R. Grace, was the main carrier providing service between the United States and the west coast of South America and operated many routes as well to Central America and the Caribbean. The Grace Line actually dated back to 1893, when the parent company established regular steamship service between Peru and New York under the name of New York and Pacific Steamship Company* (a line of sailing vessels on that same route dated back to 1882). This subsidiary, generally known as the "Merchants' Line," was a London-based corporation that operated ships built and registered in Britain. The line was a proprietary* company because during those early decades the bulk of the cargo was owned by the parent firm, W. R. Grace & Co.

W. R. Grace & Co. did not feel the need to operate the more expensive U.S.-flag ships until the construction of the Panama Canal* opened the possibility of profits in the intercoastal* service protected by the cabotage* laws. The company established another subsidiary for its U.S.-flag vessels, the Atlantic and Pacific Steamship Company,* in 1912 and in 1915 further complicated matters by acquiring the remnants of the fleet of the Pacific Mail Steamship Company* (PMSS), which continued to operate under its own name as a separate organization. In 1916 the parent company created the Grace Steamship Company, almost immediately known as the Grace Line, to begin the consolidation of the different steamship ventures into one single entity, and although the process of combining names was not fully completed until ten years later, after 1916 the Grace Line handled the shipping affairs of the parent company and began to give to almost all the company's ships names that began with the word *Santa*.

For services from New Orleans to the Pacific Coast of South America, the Grace Line decided to establish a separate firm with local investors, the New Orleans and South American Steamship Company* (NOSA), from 1918 to 1935, in order to secure easier access to the vessels of the Shipping Board.* After World War II the Grace Line reconstituted the New Orleans service, but the danger of fierce competition from Lykes Brothers Steamship Company* forced the creation of a joint venture between both companies in 1947, the Gulf and South American Steamship Company.*

The New Orleans route had been the only new successful venture of the Grace Line after World War I, because attempts to enter the transpacific trade with India, and even a short-lived round-the-world* service had proven abortive. The trade between the United States and the Pacific Coast of South America remained the essential base for the Grace Line, although it continued to operate the intercoastal service. The success of International Mercantile Marine* (IMM) when it placed the *California,* *Virginia*, and *Pennsylvania* on the intercoastal run in 1928 convinced the Grace Line to order four new vessels for this trade, and the first, the *Santa Rosa*, entered into service in 1932, and besides cargo, the ship had accommodations for 225 first-class passengers. During Prohibition* years ocean trips were particularly attractive to many persons because the vessels served alcohol as soon as they cleared U.S. territorial waters, and the Grace Line expected both a booming cargo and passenger business on its four new vessels. The Great Depression and the later repeal of Prohibition dashed the hopes for the intercoastal voyages. Already in 1934 the Grace Line obtained government approval for an arrangement with IMM to alternate sailings in order to maintain a weekly schedule and to avoid destructive competition. The demand did not improve, and in January 1938 the Grace Line withdrew permanently from the intercoastal service.

The Grace Line expanded in the Caribbean, because the U.S. Maritime Commission* under Joseph P. Kennedy* wished to consolidate existing services in the Caribbean. In October 1937 the Grace Line acquired the Red D Line,* whose owners had wisely refused to continue operation under the reduced subsidies of the Merchant Marine Act of 1936.* Venezuela, which had been the center of the Red D Line's activities, now became a permanent port of call for the Grace Line. In February 1938 the Grace Line purchased the Colombian Steamship Company,* whose main trade was with Colombia, but which also made calls in Jamaica, Haiti, and other Caribbean ports. Thus, when World War II began and the U.S. government requisitioned the vessels of the company, the Grace Line had already established a strong position in the Caribbean to complement its traditional services in the Pacific coast of South America.

After World War II the Grace Line resumed its services to South America and the Caribbean, but at least for the new president of the parent company, J. Peter Grace,* it was not going to be business as usual again. To Grace it seemed that W. R. Grace & Co. was overexposed in Latin America, not only because of the Grace Line but also more dangerously because of the investments and trade in South America, particularly in Peru. Grace felt it was time to move the company's activities back to the United States; after considerable study, he concluded that chemicals were the best opportunity for the parent company, and starting in 1952 he started to invest heavily in the chemical industry until by 1963 the chemical division of W. R. Grace earned 70 percent of the parent company's profits.

As the parent company quietly disposed of its holdings in Latin America, the percentage of proprietary cargo moving in the company's ships declined, putting the Grace Line at a more vulnerable position. In the 1950s new Latin American shipping companies, in particular Grancolombiana, appeared to challenge the previous predominance of the Grace Line. In an attempt to outflank its new competitors, the Grace Line pioneered service from the Great Lakes to South American upon the opening of the St. Lawrence Seaway in April 1959, but the service turned out to be a flop, and even after a subsidy cost the company several million dollars in losses. In another attempt to beat its Latin American competitors with new technology, the Grace Line introduced the first commercial container* service in a foreign trade route when the *Santa Eliana** sailed for Venezuela in January 1960. The service never really had a chance, because longshoremen in Venezuela refused to handle the vessel for fear of losing their jobs to machinery. Grace Line's fiasco with containers contributed more than anything else to postpone the introduction of containers into world shipping until the late 1960s, and even in Latin America their adoption is far from complete today.

The Cuban Revolution confirmed J. Peter Grace's decision to abandon Latin America as too risky, but Grace Line continued to try everything possible to stay in the steamship business. Wilfred J. McNeil, the president of the line, hoped that by acquiring additional routes he could shape a combined profitable service and in May 1966 purchased the Pacific Republics Line of Moore-McCormack.* However, opposition from Latin American shipping companies convinced the Grace Line to back down and operate only a more modest service between the U.S. Pacific Coast and the east coast of South America through the Straits of Magellan.

Devaluations in Latin America in 1967 reduced the profits of the parent company, and W. R. Grace & Co. decided to find a buyer for the Grace Line. The asking price was too high, and only after slashing by half the real value of the company did the Grace Line come within the reach of Spyros S. Skouras, the owner of the Prudential Lines.* The sale was completed in December 1969, and the Grace Line came to an end. The sale of the Gulf and South American Steamship Company* to Lykes Brothers required longer negotiations and was completed only in June 1971, but long before then W. R. Grace & Co. had broken its links with ocean shipping.

Principal Executives

William R. Grace*	1892–1904
Joseph P. Grace	1906–1946
J. Peter Grace	1946–1969
R. Ranney Adams	1945–1953
Cassius S. Mallory	1953–1955
Lewis A. Lapham*	1955–1959
Wilfred J. McNeil	1959–1967

Some Notable Ships

Santa Rosa and *Santa Paula*	1932–1958
Santa Lucía	1932–1942
Santa Elena	1933–1943
Santa Rosa and *Santa Paula*	1958–1969
Santa Eliana; later *Mayagüez**	1947–1964
Santa Leonor	1945–1964
Santa Magdalena, Santa Mariana and *Santa María*	1963–1969
Santa Mercedes	1964–1969

Principal Subsidiaries

New York and Pacific Steamship Company	1892–1921
Atlantic and Pacific Steamship Company	1912–1925
New Orleans and South American Steamship Company (NOSA)	1918–1935
Gulf and South American Steamship Company	1947–1971
Pacific Mail Steamship Company (PMSS)	1915–1925

References: Lawrence A. Clayton, *Grace: W. R. Grace & Co. The Formative Years* (Ottowa, IL: Jameson Books, 1985); René De La Pedraja, *The Rise and Decline of U.S. Merchant Shipping in the Twentieth Century* (New York: Twayne, 1992); William Kooiman, *The Grace Ships, 1869–1969* (Point Reyes, CA: Komar, 1990).

GRANGE, DAVID E. ("EMPEROR"), 1890s–1940s? From the strike of 1921* to the formation of the National Maritime Union* (NMU) in 1937, David E. Grange, or "Emperor" Grange, was the president of the Marine Cooks, Stewards, and Waiters' Union of the Atlantic and Gulf" (MCSWU). Within the International Seamen's Union* (ISU), the predominantly black MCSWU was the only labor affiliate that accepted persons of African origin; the segregation and tokenism were complete because on the Pacific Coast even the Marine Cooks and Stewards' Union* did not accept blacks until after the demise of the ISU.

Grange, himself, like many other pre–World War II black leaders, was from the British West Indies. He became the second highest official in the MCSWU, and when the strike of 1921 began, he had already concluded that the road to personal advancement lay through cooperation with the steamship companies, which generously rewarded his loyalty with monthly "subsidies." The failure of the strike disgraced the previous president Henry P. Griffin, and the eager Grange now climbed to hold the number one position. In the early 1920s there was a strong German-speaking element in the union, but gradually under Grange persons of African origin became the majority in the union. He quickly turned the MCSWU into his private kingdom, and soon members were addressing him as the "Emperor," who was always immaculately dressed in the finest clothes, "with a red rose in his lapel and a gun in his shoulder holster" (Nelson 1990). The money from union dues vanished mysteriously, and he ran the union for his convenience; if anyone raised objections in the rare union meeting, Grange bragged the he "shoved a gun in the offender's guts and beat his head in" (ibid.).

The more flamboyant aspects of Grange's leadership could not hide the fact that he did deliver better conditions for the cooks, stewards, and waiters than those available without the MCSWU; apparently the steamship companies realized how useful it was to have in their pockets a union president, and in 1924 they preferred to support him rather than a brief-lived company union, the Eastern and Gulf Marine Cooks and Stewards' Association. Grange's power base remained strong throughout the 1920s, but the growing militancy on the waterfront led to challenges in the mid-1930s. He fought back with thugs, violence, and intimidation, but the last straw was a constitution that he unilaterally adopted on 31 January 1935. As befitted the "Emperor," the new constitution created a lifetime presidency, and he now had absolute power to suspend and expel any other member or officer of the union.

The 1936 strikes on the East Coast finally destroyed Grange's "empire." He continued to send his speeches to the International Mercantile Marine* (IMM) for management's approval, but no words of his could stop the upheaval when his "subsidies" from the shipping companies were exposed. Large sums of union funds were missing, and through court action he was removed from office. Grange concluded that the way to regain his position was to crush the 1936 strikes, and he gathered scabs with whom he tried to crash the picket lines. Grange's last known action was his police arrest on the charge of "attacking a seaman and brandishing a gun in his face" (ibid.). The Emperor's later actions and whereabouts have remained unknown.

References: Bruce Nelson, *Workers on the Waterfront: Seamen, Longshoremen, and Unionism in the 1930s* (Urbana: University of Illinois Press, 1990); Record Group 32, National Archives, Washington, DC; William L. Standard, *Merchant Seamen: A Short History of Their Struggles* (New York: International, 1947).

GREAT NORTHERN (later, *H. F. ALEXANDER* and *NORTHERN PACIFIC*), 1915–1946. The *Great Northern* and the *Northern Pacific* were the two fast liners of the Great Northern Pacific Steamship Company.* In 1913 the company ordered the ships to compete against coastal railroads in the San Francisco-Portland Oregon route. High speed was essential, and these ships, powered by steam turbines,* traveled at twenty-three knots and reached Flavel, Oregon, after steaming 26.5 hours from San Francisco. The ships carried 856 first-class passengers and express cargo. The *Great Northern* inaugurated the route on 23 March 1915, and when she was joined by the *Northern Pacific* on 19 April, the company claimed they provided a service as fast as the coastal railroad. In spite of three scheduled departures from San Francisco each week, traffic on the route was so light that the company shifted the *Great Northern* to the San Francisco-Hawaii vacation run in the winter, and already in early 1916 the company was thinking of selling the ships.

In September 1917 the Shipping Board* requisitioned both liners for military use during World War I. With the return of peace, the Admiral Line* purchased the *Northern Pacific* for express service between Seattle and California, but two days after the sale, the vessel burned and was a complete wreck off Cape May, Delaware, on 9 February 1922. Immediately Hubbard F. Alexander,* the owner of the Admiral Line, lobbied to obtain the sister ship. However, the U.S. Navy had previously commissioned the *Great Northern* as the U.S.S. *Columbia* and was so impressed by the high speed of the vessel and ample space compared with a warship that the *Columbia* became the flagship of the Atlantic Fleet, "the first time in modern naval history that a merchant vessel had been assigned this type of duty" (Brown 1966). The navy resisted giving up the vessel, but in a shameful example of sacrificing national defense for the sake of private profit, Alexander lobbied directly with President Warren Harding to secure the sale of the vessel at a giveaway price in March 1922.

Rather immodestly, Alexander renamed the liner after himself as the *H. F. Alexander*, which became the flagship of the Admiral line. The ship was refitted in the latest comfort and as usual carried only first-class passengers, whose number was reduced for greater space and luxury to 583. The ship could now make twenty-four knots and provided luxury express service between Seattle and San Francisco. At first the ship was profitable, but gradually the spreading use of the automobile reduced the number of travelers. The Admiral Line tried other routes, such as New York-Florida in the winter—with the added advantage of liquor legally served on board during the Prohibition* years—and even chartered* the ship in attempts to cover costs. The Great Depression found the Admiral Line unprepared to withstand this economic shock, and the repeal of Prohibition eliminated the many passengers who had sought alcohol on board. The company began to pile up losses and laid up the *H. F. Alexander* in September 1936. The vessel was once again recalled for service in World War II as the troopship *George S. Simonds*; in 1946 the ship was laid up, and she was scrapped in 1948.

References: Frank O. Braynard, *Famous American Ships* (New York: Hastings House, 1956); Giles T. Brown, *Ships That Sail No More: Marine Transportation from San Diego to Puget Sound, 1910–1940* (Lexington: University of Kentucky Press, 1966); Frederick E. Emmons, *American Passenger Ships: The Ocean Lines and Liners, 1873–1983* (Newark: University of Delaware Press, 1985); *Nautical Gazette*, 12 October 1925; Cedric R. Nevitt, ''American Steamship Lines,'' in Society of Naval Architects and Marine Engineers, *Historical Transactions, 1883–1943* (Westport, CT: Greenwood Press, 1981).

GREAT NORTHERN PACIFIC STEAMSHIP COMPANY, 1913–1917.
James J. Hill, the railroad magnate, had been deeply disappointed with his first maritime venture, the Great Northern Steamship Company* (GNSS), yet he did not hesitate to establish a second ocean firm, the Great Northern Pacific Steamship Company, in 1913. His goal was to break the monopoly of the Southern Pacific Railway on passenger travel between Portland, Oregon, and Los Angeles, California, by running two express passenger ships fast enough to compete against the Southern Pacific Railway. To avoid slow travel up the Columbia River, Hill extended the terminus of his railroad from Portland to Flavel on the coast of Oregon, so that passengers could board the liners for a fast trip to San Francisco, where waiting trains took the travelers on the final leg to Los Angeles.

Hill ordered the *Great Northern** and the *Northern Pacific*, each with accommodations for 856 first-class passengers, from the reputable William Cramp shipyard, rather than from an inexperienced outfit, as had been the case with the GNSS. Speed was the essential characteristic for these twenty-three knot ships, which had triple screws and steam turbines* for propulsion and bows like knives that sliced through the water. The company spared no effort to provide luxury facilities aboard the ships, which it dubbed the ''twin palaces of the Pacific.''

The two liners entered service in the spring of 1915, and the company claimed they were as fast as the coastal railroad. Three times a week one of the ships left San Francisco to arrive 26.5 hours later in Flavel; express cargo was carried, as well as the first-class passengers. Initially bookings were satisfactory, but by December 1915 only 100 passengers were traveling, and freight was skimpy.

The company decided to use the *Great Northern* during the winter to carry vacation travelers to Hawaii from San Francisco in the hope of increasing the volume of traffic on the remaining *Northern Pacific*, and although this strategy was temporarily successful, by early 1916 Hill's executives were already talking about selling the ships. The Great Northern Pacific Steamship Company, just like the GNSS, had failed to earn a profit on its own, but in the same manner as the GNSS, the parent company offset the losses with the additional business for the railroad.

In 1917 freight and passenger traffic increased, but before management could take a final decision about the steamship service, the Shipping Board* requisitioned the two vessels and paid roughly their order price in September 1917. Railroad executives were relieved to be out of the alluring but generally disappointing steamship business and never again revived the Great Northern Pacific Steamship Company, which disappeared.

Notable Ships

Great Northern

Northern Pacific

References: Frank O. Braynard, *Famous American Ships* (New York: Hastings House, 1956); Giles T. Brown, *Ships That Sail No More: Maritime Transportation from San Diego to Puget Sound, 1910–1940* (Lexington: University of Kentucky Press, 1966); Don L. Hofsommer, "The Maritime Enterprises of James J. Hill," *American Neptune* 47 (1987):193–205.

GREAT NORTHERN STEAMSHIP COMPANY (GNSS), 1900–1917. The Great Northern Steamship Company (GNSS) provided service between Seattle and ports in the Far East. James J. Hill incorporated the GNSS in 1900 to generate cargo for the Seattle terminus of his Great Northern Railway. Hill ordered the construction of two monster ships, the *Dakota** and the *Minnesota*,* and had they been completed in time, they would have been the largest vessels in the world. Construction problems delayed the delivery of these ships until 1905, while their slow speed forced the company to charter* in addition five freighters in order to provide some semblance of regular service to the Far East. Like Malcom McLean* eighty years later, Hill made the mistake of assuming that low rates sufficed to attract cargo for his ships, in spite of their slow speed.

The *Dakota*, barely on its seventh voyage, struck a reef off the coast of Japan in 1907 and was a total loss. Hill by then had grown tired of the constant frustrations of his steamship company and refused to replace the *Dakota*, and by 1908 he had withdrawn all the chartered vessels. He was stuck with the *Minnesota*, a veritable white elephant, whose gigantic cargo holds and slow speed made the ship unsuitable for any route in the world. However, by employing Chinese crews and making four voyages each year, the *Minnesota* covered most of its operating costs, while the cargo brought to Seattle generated railroad profits for the parent company.

The passage of the La Follette Seamen's Act* threatened the use of Chinese crews and convinced GNSS to suspend operations. Record-earning profits in the North Atlantic persuaded the International Mercantile Marine* to buy the huge ship in January 1917, and after her transfer to the Atlantic Ocean by March, GNSS for all practical purposes disappeared, although it continued to exist on paper for at least another ten years.

Notable Ships

Dakota	1905–1907
Minnesota	1905–1917

References: Thomas C. Buckley, "Railroader Afloat: James J. Hill as Ship Builder and Operator," 1993, forthcoming article; René De La Pedraja, *The Rise and Decline of U.S. Merchant Shipping in the Twentieth Century* (New York: Twayne, 1992); Don L. Hofsommer, "The Maritime Enterprises of James J. Hill," *American Neptune* 47 (1987): 193–205; W. Kaye Lamb, "The Transpacific Ventures of James J. Hill," *American Neptune* 3 (1943):185–204.

GREAT REPUBLIC, CHINA, JAPAN, and AMERICA, 1867–1884. New York shipyards delivered these four wooden side-wheelers* to the Pacific Mail Steamship Company* (PMSS), starting with the *Great Republic* on 2 August 1867 and ending with the *America* in 1869. PMSS had ordered these ships to provide the monthly sailings from San Francisco to Yokohama/Hong Kong, required by the mail subsidy contract with the U.S. government. Since these ships were not ready in time to meet the contract starting date of 1 January 1867, the PMSS began the transpacific voyages with the *Colorado*,* which later in the year was joined by the *Great Republic*, and the *China*; when the *Japan* arrived, the *Colorado* was pulled out of service and maintained as a "spare" ship for use in time of emergencies. When the shipyard delivered the last ship, the *America*, PMSS could go the next step and establish a schedule of monthly sailings from San Francisco in 1869.

These ships mainly carried passengers; for example, the *Great Republic* had accommodations for 250 persons in cabin staterooms and 1,200 in steerage* class, while the *China* had accommodations for 500 persons in cabin staterooms and 800 in steerage class. These ships were noteworthy not only because they established the first regularly scheduled steamship service across the Pacific Ocean but also because they were "the largest wooden sidewheelers ever built for oceanic service" (Niven 1987). At a time when iron hulls, screws, and compound engines* had become standard, the technology of these ships (still fitted with back-up sails) harked back to the pre–Civil War era, and indeed they were obsolete even before they were ordered. PMSS rejected the newer technologies on the grounds that modern repair facilities were lacking in the Pacific Coast, while, on the other hand, the expertise to repair single-expansion engines* and the wooden paddles was readily available and allowed meeting on time the scheduled sailings in the mail contract. In 1872 Congress decided that more modern ships were needed in the transpacific service, and PMSS, in response to a larger mail subsidy, ordered the first screw steamers of iron hulls, the *City of Tokyo** and the *City of Peking.**

The four side-wheelers remained in service to meet the new mail requirement of sailings every two weeks (not always observed) from San Francisco, but gradually their ranks began to thin. The first to go was the *America*: on the night of 24 August 1872 a fire was discovered while anchored in Yokohama Harbor, but the low steam pressure in the boiler was insufficient to operate the pumps, and the ship burned down. Most passengers escaped by jumping in the water, but at least nineteen drowned because they had overloaded themselves with silver coins.

Those aboard the *America* were fortunate compared with those on the *Japan* on 17 December 1874. The ship had begun the homeward portion of the voyage and had just sailed a few hundred miles out of Hong Kong. Fire was discovered in one of the bunkers,* and although twenty-one hoses pumped water furiously, the blaze spread rapidly through the wooden hull of the ship. By the time the captain ordered the *America* abandoned, it was too late to evacuate some crew members and almost all the steerage* passengers, who could only jump in the water. About 400 died in this disaster, and the blame was later placed on the chief engineer for carelessness.

PMSS transferred the *Great Republic* from the transpacific to the coastwise* service in 1870 and then sold the obsolete side-wheeler to P. B. Cornwall in 1878. The next year, on 19 April 1879, the *Great Republic* ran aground near the Columbia River sandbar and was totally destroyed by the pounding seas. The *China* remained with the PMSS until 1883, when Henry Villard bought the vessel and then sold her again in 1884. That same year the new owner burned the wooden *China* to recover the metal in her hull for scrap. Although the careers of the four side-wheelers had ended somewhat ingloriously, nothing could deny the fact that they had made world history by establishing the first regularly scheduled steamship service between North America and the Far East.

References: Erik Heyl, *Early American Steamers*, 6 vols. (Buffalo, NY, 1953–1969); John H. Kemble, "A Hundred Years of the Pacific Mail," *American Neptune* 10 (1950): 123–143; John Niven, *The American President Lines and Its Forebears, 1848–1984* (Newark: University of Delaware Press, 1987); E. Mowbray Tate, *Transpacific Steam: The Story of Steam Navigation from the Pacific Coast of North America to the Far East and the Antipodes, 1867–1941* (New York: Cornwall Books, 1986).

GREAT WHITE FLEET. See United Fruit Company.

GRISCOM, CLEMENT ACTION, 15 March 1841–10 November 1912. Clement A. Griscom, a steamship executive who was one of the wealthiest men in the United States, was born in Philadelphia on 15 March 1841. Of an old, established family, his business abilities soon made him a partner in the importing firm of Peter Wright & Sons of Philadelphia. He convinced the firm to purchase its own fleet of ships to carry its cargo, and the success of this first venture aroused his interest in shipping and marine architecture. When the Pennsylvania Railroad decided in 1872 to establish the International Navigation Company to operate a Belgian-flag service between Antwerp and Philadelphia, he participated in the enterprise and became vice president of the new company, soon better known by the name of its main subsidiary, the Red Star Line.* When the Pennsylvania Railroad sold its stock in the company, Griscom became the principal stockholder and president of the Red Star Line in 1888. The company by then also operated two other subsidiaries, one running under the British flag and the other under the American flag; among his masterful moves, Griscom secured special congressional permission to transfer two British-built ships, the *City of New York* and the *City of Paris*, to U.S. registry,* on the condition that he build in the United States two new liners. Griscom constructed the *St. Louis** and the *St. Paul*, but in spite of including several innovations in naval architecture, the vessels proved to be money-losers.

By 1883 the majority of the company's ships served New York City rather than Philadelphia, and Griscom concluded that profitable operation required a merger with the only other U.S. firm serving New York, the Atlantic Transport Company* of Bernard N. Baker.* In 1900 at last the merger between the two companies took place, but only as part of a broad arrangement that resulted in the creation of the International Mercantile Marine* (IMM) in 1902. During the first two years of the shipping combine's existence, Griscom was the president of IMM, and in 1904 he became chairman of the board, a position he held until his death on 10 November 1912.

References: *Dictionary of American Biography*, vol. 8; Lloyd C. Griscom, *Diplomatically Speaking* (New York: Literary Guild, 1940); Thomas R. Navin and Marian V. Sears, "A Study in Merger: Formation of the International Mercantile Marine Company," *Business History Review* 28 (1954):291–328; Vivian Vale, *The American Peril, Challenge to Britain on the North Atlantic, 1901–1904* (Manchester, England: University Press, 1984).

GULF AND SOUTH AMERICAN STEAMSHIP COMPANY, 1947–1971.

In 1946 the Grace Line* resumed service from New Orleans to the Pacific coast of South America in what was an effort to restore the routes of the pre–World War II subsidiary, the New Orleans and South American Steamship Company* (NOSA). Lykes Brothers Steamship Company* had already consolidated a very strong position for itself in the Gulf of Mexico and did not welcome any rivals. Grace Line was too powerful to be kept out of the Gulf for long, but Lykes Brothers with its strong regional links could impede profitable operations; rather than have a head-on clash, cooler heads prevailed in both companies, and they agreed to set up a joint venture, the Gulf and South American Steamship Company, in June 1947. Each company held a 50 percent share in the joint venture, while should one company decide to withdraw, the other had first claim on the acquisition of the other's half. The initial outlay consisted of each partner's providing two vessels for the route. No particular staff was needed, because the regular Lykes organization handled the New Orleans and Gulf end of the business, while the Grace offices did the same in the Pacific coast of South America. The partnership worked to the advantage of both and was not ended until W. R. Grace, the parent company of the Grace Line, decided to abandon merchant shipping altogether. The Grace Line was sold to Prudential Lines* in December 1969, but the sale of the 50 percent share in Gulf and South American Steamship to Lykes Brothers took longer and was not completed until June 1971. Although Lykes Brothers frequently transferred the vessels of this service to other routes, it maintained under its own name the service to South America from New Orleans until the company finally laid up the vessels in 1983.

References: Lawrence A. Clayton, *Grace: W. R. Grace & Co.: The Formative Years, 1850–1930* (Ottowa, IL: Jameson Books, 1985); William Kooiman, *The Grace Ships, 1869–1969* (Point Reyes, CA: Komar, 1990); *Wall Street Journal*, 15 June 1971.

GULF ASSOCIATED FREIGHT CONFERENCES, 1932–1964. This was a coordinating body that administered the affairs of five conferences.* Since 1932 the three original members had been the Gulf/French Atlantic Hamburg Range Freight Conference, the Gulf-Mediterranean Ports Conference, and the Gulf/United Kingdom Conference. The Gulf/Scandinavian and Baltic Sea Ports Conference joined in 1936, and the Gulf/South and East African Conference, in 1947. The chairman of the Gulf Associated Freight Conferences was at New Orleans, and he was also the head of the five separate conferences. The American lines active in this conference were:

Bloomfield Steamship Co.*	Central Gulf Lines*
Isthmian*	Lykes Bros. Steamship Co.*
States Marine Corp.*	Waterman Steamship Corp.*

On the average, at least a dozen foreign lines belonged to the Gulf Associated Freight Conferences. A rate war precipitated by the resignation of Bloomfield Steamship Company, States Marine Corporation, and Lykes Brothers Steamship Company led to the collapse of the conference in 1964. Nevertheless, the conference was reconstituted the next year as the Gulf European Freight Association.*

References: *Congressional Record*, 17 March 1964; Gale Research, *Encyclopedia of Associations 1968*; U.S. Congress, House, Committee on Merchant Marine and Fisheries, *Steamship Conference Study* 3 vols. (Washington, DC: Government Printing Office 1959).

GULF EUROPEAN FREIGHT ASSOCIATION, 1965–1989. After the collapse of the Gulf Associated Freight Conferences* in 1964, the lines that survived the rate war created the Gulf European Freight Association in 1965 to set rates on outbound traffic moving from the Gulf of Mexico to continental northern Europe, including Scandinavia. Membership in the conference,* which set rates on cargo moving from the Gulf of Mexico to continental Northern Europe, hovered around six lines. The two American lines most active in this conference were Lykes Brothers Steamship Company,* a solid backer throughout the conference's history, and Sea-Land,* a member in the 1980s. As part of the restructuring of the conferences in the Atlantic, the Gulf European Freight Association merged into a new superconference,* the U.S.A.-North Europe Rate Agreements* (USANERA) in 1989.

References: Gale Research, *Encyclopedia of Associations*, 1968, 1973, 1980–1988; *Journal of Commerce*, 2 June 1989.

GULF INTERCOASTAL CONFERENCE, 1923–1936. The Gulf Intercoastal Conference established uniform rates for the lines operating between the Gulf of Mexico and the Pacific Coast, but it did not pool revenues and only rarely established frequency of sailing, in contrast to the United States Intercoastal Conference.* This latter conference covered the trade between the ports of the Pacific Coast and the Atlantic and originally had also covered Gulf ports until two member lines concluded that a separate organization was needed and hence in 1923 organized the Gulf Intercoastal Conference, which, however, collapsed in 1925. Luckenbach Steamship Company,* Transmarine Corporation, Gulf Pacific, and Redwood Steamship Company reconstituted the Gulf Intercoastal Conference in August 1927, but it collapsed again in March 1928, when Redwood employed "rate cutting tactics" to begin "a very vicious rate war ... which greatly depleted the treasuries of all the four lines operating in the trade" (U.S. Shipping Board 1942). The rate war ended and the conference was reorganized in February 1929, but stability did not return to the trade until Gulf Pacific purchased the Redwood Steamship Company in October 1930. In 1933 the conference had established a weekly schedule of sailings, and in 1934 it refused to admit the Nelson Steamship Company on the grounds this carrier did not have the capability to maintain service during at least one year. With the passage of the Intercoastal Shipping Act of 1933, regulatory proceedings became much more important to the conference, whose members eventually concluded that their interests were better served by joining the Intercoastal Steamship Freight Association* in 1936.

References: *Journal of Commerce*, 7 April 1934; U.S. Shipping Board, *Decisions*, vol. 1 (Washington, DC: Government Printing Office, 1942).

GULF SHIPPING CONFERENCE, 1923–1932. The Gulf Shipping Conference was a coordinating body that administered the affairs of the Gulf/French Atlantic Hamburg Range Freight Conference, the Gulf-Mediterranean Ports Conference, and the Gulf/United Kingdom Conference. The chairman, whose offices were at New Orleans, was also the head of the three individual conferences. The Shipping Board* had encouraged the creation of the Gulf Shipping

Conference to try to harmonize the activities of the many new managing operators* in this trade. In 1932 the Gulf Shipping Conference became the Gulf
Associated Freight Conferences.*

Reference: U.S. Congress, House, Committee on Merchant Marine and Fisheries,
Steamship Conference Study, 3 vols. (Washington, DC: Government Printing Office,
1959).

H

HAGUE, ROBERT LINCOLN, 2 March 1880–8 March 1939. Robert L. Hague directed the tankers of Standard Oil Company of New Jersey* for twenty years, during most of which the fleet was the largest in the world. He was born in Lincoln, Rhode Island, on 2 March 1880; his father was an Episcopal cleric. Hague studied at the Worcester Polytechnic Institute, but before graduating he left for the sea. He returned to land to work in a railroad but went back to the sea in 1904 to work aboard the ships of the American-Hawaiian Steamship Company until he became the firm's chief engineer. In 1909 he joined the Standard Oil Company of California and soon was in charge of its fleet. From 1918 to 1920 he put in wartime service with the Emergency Fleet Corporation* of the Shipping Board.*

In July 1920 Standard Oil Company of New Jersey selected him to head its fleet of tankers, the job he held until his death. At a time when the company was building up its layers of corporate hierarchy, Hague remained a maverick and ran the fleet on his own in an autocratic manner. The member of the Board of Directors who supposedly supervised him was always swamped with the many other problems of the vast corporation, and since the tankers were always ready when needed at the lowest cost, the board members decided not to tamper with Hague's system of proven results. Actually, Hague combined large-scale delegation of authority with a profound distrust of hierarchy. He gave the foreign subsidiaries of Standard Oil a free hand to operate their ships but kept a sharp eye on transfers between fleets as well as the charter* and purchase of vessels. In one major case, he argued strongly for the transfer of the Danzig-flag tankers to a Western Hemisphere registry that eventually became the Panamanian flag of convenience.*

Hague loved to mingle with the tanker crews, and when a problem arose with machinery, rather than convene a meeting, he preferred as an engineer to go and see for himself and talk to the ship's personnel. His close contact with the men allowed Standard Oil to escape the worst labor problems during the 1920s because he finally convinced management to pay decent wages and treat the employees as persons. As the 1930s advanced, he came to accept the necessity for labor unions but correctly sensed that the tanker personnel did not want the National Maritime Union* (NMU). He worked to create the Independent Tanker Unions* as the best solution for both the personnel and Standard Oil.

During his lifetime Hague was considered the world's expert on marine transportation of oil, and he constantly encouraged technical innovations. One of his major contributions was to convince Standard Oil in 1938 to order twelve new tankers ("Cimarron" class) in 1938; the government covered the additional expense of their construction, at a time when such tankers lacked a commercial justification, yet their high speed of eighteen knots proved invaluable to the navy during World War II and pointed the way to further evolutions in tanker design, including the T-2.* Hague also founded the *Register of Tank Vessels of the World*, whose publication has since continued under various titles.

In spite of apparently total immersion in tanker affairs, he had another, personal side. His social activities were on a lavish scale, and he took a deep interest in the theater, which he supported through many contributions. He ran through three divorces and at the time of his death was separated from his fourth wife, a soprano at the Metropolitan Opera. From the Shipping Board days he developed a close friendship with Clifford D. Mallory,* whose tanker fleet Hague routinely chartered for Standard Oil starting in 1923; however, the distance between the nouveau-riche Hague and the puritanical-old-wealth Mallory was too great to bridge their social circles. Hague died of cirrhosis in New York City on 8 March 1939.

References: James P. Baughman, *The Mallorys of Mystic: Six Generations in American Maritime Enterprise* (Middletown, CT: Wesleyan University Press, 1972); John H. Collins, *Never Off Pay: The Story of the Independent Tanker Union, 1937–1962* (New York: Fordham University Press, 1964); *Dictionary of American Biography*, supp. 2; George S. Gibb and Evelyn H. Knowlton, *The Resurgent Years, 1911–1927* (New York: Harper and Brothers, 1956); Henrietta M. Larson, Evelyn H. Knowlton, and Charles S. Popple, *New Horizons, 1927–1950* (New York: Harper and Row, 1971).

HALL, PAUL, 21 August 1914–22 June 1980. Paul Hall was the president of the Seafarers' International Union* (SIU) and the Maritime Trades Department* (MTD) from 1957 until his death in 1980. He was born in Alabama on 21 August 1914, and after attending public schools, he went to work in the engine crew of ships in the 1930s. He was one of the original members of the SIU, which the American Federation of Labor (AFL) had created in 1938 to replace the totally discredited International Seamen's Union* (ISU) and to provide as well an alternative to the communist-infiltrated National Maritime Union*

(NMU). Thus from the first day anticommunism and anti-NMU became the two main currents in Hall's union career.

Hall continued to sail aboard freighters in the initial years of World War II, but his active participation in union affairs landed him the job of patrolman* in Baltimore, and soon after he was put in charge of all organizing in the Atlantic and Gulf coasts. His tremendous success in bringing the crews of new wartime operators into the SIU led to his election as New York port agent in 1944. At this time the SIU was under the control of Harry Lundeberg,* who was impressed by Hall's remarkable organizing successes and later, in 1948, appointed him chief officer of the Atlantic and Gulf districts as well as the first vice president of the SIU. Five years later Lundeberg began to distrust his new supporter, and to block him, the SIU president attempted an alliance with the former enemy Joseph Curran* of the NMU. The resulting Conference of American Maritime Unions* (CAMU) collapsed in 1955. Hall could not be removed from his position as heir apparent, and upon Lundeberg's death in 1957, Hall assumed the presidency of SIU and MTD. Lundeberg had also been the sole officer of the Sailors Union of the Pacific,* his real power base, and now Hall secured the election of a staunch ally, Morris Weisberger,* to that sensitive post.

Hall pursued relentlessly his central goal of undermining the NMU. The opening wedge came from the purges, corruption, and dictatorship that crept into the NMU starting in the 1950s, destroying its earlier prestige. In the 1960s disillusioned NMU members considered hopeless the task of reforming their union and gradually succumbed to the promises of the SIU. The NMU originally had a larger membership, but by 1971 SIU with 80,000 members exceeded the 50,000 of the NMU, which continued to shrink.

The rivalry between Hall and Curran never became as bitter as Lundeberg's intense hatred for all rivals. Hall and Curran attempted to cooperate on issues of mutual importance, for example, in trying to stop the growing use of "flags of convenience"* by U.S. firms. The two men created the International Maritime Workers Union* to organize crews on foreign-flag ships owned by U.S. companies, but intense rivalry forced them to dissolve the new union in 1961. Attempts at harmonizing mutually beneficial actions between both unions continued to resurface over the latent hostility between Hall and Curran, but both remained opposed to any merger of their unions.

Hall's opposition to corruption was well known even from the early 1950s, when he had led the American Federation of Labor's (AFL) attempt to destroy racketeering in the International Longshoremen's Association. Although he tolerated the use of violence and beatings, he kept the ISU clean of corruption, the mob, and other illegal activities. Hall's opposition to communism was notorious, and even after Curran had purged the communists from the NMU, he continued to use the communist charge to smear Curran and his clique. In spite of Hall's frequent denunciations of any dealings with communists, he agreed to the sale of wheat to Russia in the early 1960s because the requirement that half the wheat travel in U.S.-flag ships meant many jobs for seamen. Hall was an early and strong supporter of the Vietnam War, and his union benefited enormously from the large increase in wartime shipping to Vietnam; in one of the more interesting scams, the shortage of American seamen during that war was compensated by hiring alien seamen, who were required to make unusually large contributions to SIU.

Hall generally threw the political weight of the SIU behind the Democratic candidates, but he did back the Republican, Richard M. Nixon. Outside of the maritime sector, Hall carefully cultivated relations with union patriarch George Meany and wanted to be the successor to Meany as president of the AFL-CIO (American Federation of Labor-Congress of Industrial Organizations). Because he was a very effective speaker, Hall was greatly in demand by other union groups to deliver a good, rousing speech. At least within organized labor, Hall had earned the right to be the voice for the seamen of the United States.

Poor health plagued the last years of his union career, and he was forced to delegate a larger number of duties to Frank P. Drozak,* the heir apparent. In February 1980 Drozak replaced the ailing Hall as president of the MTD, but Hall remained, at least in title, president of the SIU until his death on 22 June 1980.

References: Joseph H. Ball, *The Government-Subsidized Union Monopoly* (Washington, DC: Labor Policy Association, 1966); *Congressional Record*, 30 October 1969; *Current Biography 1966*; Gary M. Fink, ed., *Biographical Dictionary of American Labor*, 2nd ed. (Westport, CT: Greenwood Press, 1984); *Maritime Newsletter*, July 1980.

HARRIS, BASIL, 31 October 1889–18 June 1948. Basil Harris, a very wealthy individual, was a financial backer and high executive of the Roosevelt Steamship Company,* the International Mercantile Marine* (IMM), and the United States Lines* (USL). Harris was born in Pullman, Illinois, on 31 October 1889; his father was a high official in the Pullman Car Co. and became one of the founders of the American Tobacco Company. After studying in the exclusive, private Lawrenceville School in New Jersey, Harris graduated from Princeton University in 1912. Afterward he began working for the American Tobacco Company but became bored with that work and resigned in 1921 to take up what he considered the much more exciting task of running a steamship company.

Harris's entry into merchant shipping was remarkable in many ways: as a very wealthy individual, first of all he did not have to work, and second, he could have found other, more quiet, and certainly more profitable activities. He was fascinated by the high drama of merchant shipping, and without the financial worries of normal shipowners, he could enjoy its excitement to the fullest. His business choice was reinforced by personal reasons, because he had formed a permanent friendship with Kermit Roosevelt,* Vincent Astor, James A. Farrell, Jr.,* and John Franklin,* a group from a high social background, all fascinated, like Harris, with merchant shipping.

From 1921 to 1930 Harris worked closely as a vice president with Roosevelt and Franklin at the Roosevelt Steamship Company, and when the group of friends took over IMM in 1930, Harris became a vice president, a position he held until 1942. In 1939–1940 he took a brief leave of absence to serve as assistant secretary of the treasury under Henry Morgenthau. While Franklin was serving in the army during World War II, Harris occupied the presidency of USL until 1945, when Franklin returned to regain his previous position. That year Harris became the chairman of the board of USL, a position he held until his death in New York City on 18 June 1948. Harris was one of the few wealthy men with prior prestige and status who took a personal interest in merchant shipping, an industry that has suffered because it rarely has been able to attract persons of such high caliber, prestige, and means.

References: Cunard Records, University of Liverpool; René De La Pedraja, *The Rise and Decline of U.S. Merchant Shipping in the Twentieth Century* (New York: Twayne, 1992); *National Cyclopedia of American Biography*, vol. 38; *Who's Who in the Maritime Industry, 1946*.

HARRISON, J. MAX, 10 December 1914–4 April 1966. J. Max Harrison was a specialist in labor relations who stood out because of his valuable contributions to labor-management harmony. Harrison, whose father was a skilled worker, was born in Excel, Alabama, on 10 December 1914. He studied in public schools in Excel and then graduated from Auburn University in 1941. He played for three years professional football with the New York Giants and then stayed in that city to work for the office of the Waterman Steamship Corporation,* which was still owned by businessmen of Mobile, Alabama. Until 1949 he worked as labor relations director for Waterman in Mobile and New York City, and thereafter he opened his own consulting firm for labor relations. He eventually became the representative for most of the shipping companies in the Gulf of Mexico and many on the East Coast as well. Harrison had gained the trust not only of the shipowners but also of labor leaders and was gradually able to build bridges between both groups.

The Seamen's Strike of 1961* showed that even better links were needed between labor and management, and Harrison, who had previously proposed the establishment of a new institution, now insisted on the creation of the American Maritime Association* (AMA) as one of the conditions for the settlement of the Seamen's Strike of 1961. In 1962 this new employer group was formally organized, and it represented mainly the independent tanker companies. AMA was heavily staffed with former union officials and often defended positions similar to those espoused by the big maritime unions, although in practice AMA had the greatest similarity with the Independent Tanker Unions* (ITUs). Under Harrison the AMA, because of its innovative approach, became a very effective vehicle or bridge to work out labor-management differences. In 1965 Harrison was forced to retire because of ill health, and he died soon after in Mobile, Alabama, on 4 April 1966.

References: John J. Collins, *Never Off Pay: The Story of the Independent Tanker Union, 1937–1962* (New York: Fordham University Press, 1964); Samuel A. Lawrence, *United States Merchant Shipping Policies and Politics* (Washington, DC: Brookings Institution, 1966); *National Cyclopedia of American Biography*, vol. 55.

HARVARD. See *Yale and Harvard.*

HAVRE LINE, 1849–1861. The Havre Line provided U.S.-flag steamship service between New York and Havre, France. Mortimer Livingston obtained the mail contract for this route when the earlier Bremen Line* failed to fulfill its obligation to provide service to Havre. Livingston, who already operated a line of sailing packets on that same route, easily built up the trade for the side-wheel* steamers of the Havre Line. By 1851 the Havre Line was operating two steamers, the *Humboldt* and the *Franklin*, which made the Atlantic crossing in twelve days compared with ten days for the smaller steamers of the Bremen Line. The loss of the *Humboldt* in 1853 and of the *Franklin* in 1854 disrupted the activities of the Havre Line, but Livingston, undaunted, ordered two new steamers, the *Arago* and the *Fulton*, which reestablished regular service across the Atlantic in 1855. Because of the shipping experience and careful management of Livingston, the company survived the expiration of the mail contracts in 1857, unlike the Bremen Line, which folded in that year. However, the Havre Line could not escape the effects of the Civil War: shortly after the outbreak of that conflict in 1861 it had ceased operations, while the federal government took over the *Arago* and the *Fulton* as war transports.

Principal Executive

Mortimer Livingston

Notable Ships

Franklin	1850–1854
Humboldt	1851–1853
Arago	1855–1861
Fulton	1855–1861

References: Robert G. Albion, *The Rise of New York Port, 1815–1860* (New York: Scribner's, 1939); Winthrop L. Marvin, *The American Merchant Marine* (New York: Scribner's, 1902); David B. Tyler, *Steam Conquers the Atlantic* (New York: D. Appleton-Century, 1939).

HAWAIIAN STEAMSHIP COMPANY. See Textron.

HAWAIIAN TEXTRON. See Textron.

HERBERMANN, HENRY, 1878–23 October 1935. Henry Herbermann was the president of American Export Lines* (AEL) in 1920–1934. He was born in 1878 in Jersey City, New Jersey, and after some years in elementary school, he promptly started to work on the New Jersey waterfront, initially with the Pennsylvania Railroad. After eight years he established his own business with borrowed money to provide trucking, warehousing, and lighterage services. Soon he developed the ambition of acquiring his own steamship company, and the opportunity came in 1920 when the Export Steamship Corporation was on the verge of collapse, and the Shipping Board* was looking for a new managing operator* for this firm. Herbermann quickly secured the appointment from the Shipping Board, and with great dedication and hard work he plunged into the task of making the company, soon renamed the American Export Lines* (AEL), into a growing and paying concern.

AEL ran government-owned ships from New York to the Mediterranean and the Black Sea and was in competition with other Shipping Board operators, most notably, Clifford D. Mallory.* On 27 August 1924 the Shipping Board, dissatisfied with the performance of Mallory, transferred the ships he operated to AEL, and Herbermann was now confirmed as the main operator of U.S.-flag vessels between New York and the Mediterranean. In a major coup, he was able to purchase for a very low price the eighteen Shipping Board freighters on this route in 1924, and he appeared to have securely consolidated his fortune and that of AEL.

In the late 1920s Herbermann could not resist entering passenger service, and he ordered four new vessels, dubbed the "Four Aces,"* which were in service by 1931. He hoped to gain additional prestige by operating these combination ships, which, besides carrying freight, had accommodations for 100 passengers, but he had blundered badly in ordering ships that at sixteen knots were too slow for passenger service between Italy and New York. He neglected his cargo business and insisted on sending a vessel to ports just to show the AEL name even if there was not enough cargo. The Great Depression reduced even more the income from cargo and passengers, but because AEL was receiving massive mail subsidies under the Merchant Marine Act of 1928,* Herbermann expected to survive the hard times.

However, since the early 1930s he splashed his money around, paid himself large salaries, ran up huge bills in his lavish expense accounts, and borrowed substantial sums from AEL as personal loans. He also increased the size of his staff in order to be surrounded by a retinue commensurate with the status he felt he deserved. Not surprisingly, AEL fell behind on the mortgage repayments for the Four Aces, while the loans taken out for the purchase of the original eighteen freighters were also in arrears. Bankruptcy was inevitable, but before that happened the Black Committee* grilled Herbermann in public hearings about his exorbitant waste of taxpayers' money.

Herbermann's reputation was permanently ruined, and shortly after, the second mortgage holders forced him to resign as president of AEL in April 1934, in order to prevent the Shipping Board, the holder of the first mortgages, from foreclosing on the company. However, the new management team of William H. Coverdale* felt it advisable to keep Herbermann as vice president of the company. When Herbermann died suddenly of a heart attack in his office on 23 October 1935, his life insurance of over half a million went to AEL and helped to offset the considerable damage he had previously inflicted on the company. He was perhaps the most visible of the new generation of steamship executives who emerged under the support of the Shipping Board. Herbermann's career showed that even in the rare cases of rags-to-riches success stories, the plot continued to unfold into the later stages of embarrassment, bankruptcy, and ultimate failure at the end.

References: René De La Pedraja, *The Rise and Decline of U.S. Merchant Shipping in the Twentieth Century* (New York: Twayne, 1992); *Fortune*, March 1931, September 1937; Record Group 32, National Archives, Washington, DC.

HERMANN, **1848–1869.** The *Hermann* was one of the two side-wheel* steamers the Bremen Line* built for operation in the North Atlantic. The ship was poorly designed, and even though the company altered its machinery several times, the *Hermann* remained too slow to compete against the ships of rivals. After the dissolution of the Bremen Line in 1857, the *Hermann* was sold for service on the Pacific Coast.

In preparation for the inauguration of transpacific service, the Pacific Mail Steamship Company* (PMSS) bought the *Hermann* in 1866. After a very thorough overhaul, the ship sailed on 1 March 1867 to Yokohama, but unlike the rest of the fleet (*Great Republic,* China, Japan, and America*), it did not make a return voyage and instead remained stationed in Yokohama as a "spare" ship to cover any gap in the sailings by the other vessels. On 13 February 1869 *Hermann* struck an uncharted rock off the coast of Japan on Point Kwatzu, Honshu, and was lost; at least 275 persons perished as they desperately attempted to reach the safety of the shore.

References: Robert G. Albion, *The Rise of New York Port, 1815–1860* (New York: Scribner's, 1939); John H. Kemble, "A Hundred Years of the Pacific Mail," *American Neptune* 10 (1950):123–143; John H. Kemble, *The Panama Route 1848–1869* (Berkeley: University of California Press, 1943); E. Mowbray Tate, *Transpacific Steam: The Story of Steam Navigation from the Pacific Coast of North America to the Far East and the Antipodes, 1868–1941* (New York: Cornwall Books, 1986); David B. Tyler, *Steam Conquers the Atlantic* (New York: D. Appleton-Century, 1939).

H.F. ALEXANDER. See *Great Northern.*

HIRING HALL, UNION. Since the late 1930s the union hiring hall has been the normal way to hire the overwhelming number of maritime workers, whether seamen or longshoremen. After the violent strikes of the late 1930s, the unions won the right to establish the hiring halls to replace the degrading shape-up.* Exceptions have remained, in particular, among tanker crews, whose continuous employment with the same company and often the same ship made the hiring hall superfluous for the independent tanker unions.* Likewise, companies have refused to surrender the right to appoint the captain, chief engineer, and their assistants, but management agreed to chose only from union members.

Union hiring halls for longshoremen generally have had a threefold classification system. The first rank, usually called the "A-men," consisted of the permanent union members, whom the foremen must hire first before turning to the next level. From the 1930s to the 1970s, demand for longshoremen exceeded the supply of A-men, so almost every day foremen had to complete their work gangs by calling on the "B-men," or persons who had applied for status as full union members but who had to wait a probationary period of from a few months to several years; supposedly as the ranks of A-men were depleted by age, death, retirement, or other personal reasons, experienced B-men were ready to climb to A-status. The ranks of B-men were changing, as some men concluded that the wait was too long or the work too hard and permanently dropped out to pursue other employment opportunities on land. Hence in peak periods, on weekends, holidays, and on generally less favorable days, foremen might not find enough B-men to complete the work gang and then turned to the "C-men," or casuals who just walked off the street, and many more quickly came by spreading the word that the hiring hall was short of men. Working as a casual was a good way to earn some extra money, and if the individual was desperate for a job, a quick glance told him what his chances were: the blackboards in the front of the hall listed the ships in port with their labor demands. When the foremen entered, the men lined up behind painted lines, the last line being the C-men, and only when the A and B lines were empty did some of the casuals stand a chance of being hired.

Hiring halls for seamen were built around the same basic structure but with some important modifications. After World War II, the glut of skilled seamen wiped out the class of casuals, so that all who sailed had to have at the very least valid Coast Guard* certification, ending a long-existing avenue of advancement for unskilled workers. Thus, the nineteenth-century tradition of just signing up for a ship and learning through on-the-job practice came to an end; any prospective seafarer henceforth had to make the effort to attend a training school or one of the maritime academies. Seamen's hiring halls also had to take account of additional factors: while longshoremen were back at home every day, sailors could be gone on voyages for weeks and months. Also, while longshoremen at major ports could count on an ever-growing number of ships docking for cargo handling, seamen were limited to the U.S.-flag ships, whose numbers relentlessly declined after World War II.

Not only might a seaman be months abroad in a voyage, but once he returned to port, he might need to wait months for a new opening. The solution was the rotary shipping system: as soon as their voyage finished, seamen went to the hiring hall and had their cards stamped with the date and time. After this official registration, they were then at the bottom of the list, because according to the rotary shipping system, first priority went to those seamen who had been waiting longest for a job. This allowed the jobs to be evenly distributed, with no one individual ever blacklisted or passed up. These arrangements were for seamen who were interested in as much regular employment as the ships' voyages allowed; seamen who took a semester off for any reason fell into a second category; that is, they were not assigned to ship until all the regulars had first shipped out. A third category consisted of experienced seamen with Coast Guard papers who, however, were members of other maritime unions, and in the very bottom were men approved by the Coast Guard but without any experience on U.S.-flag ships.

The union hiring halls occasionally have come in for criticism, but when compared with the shape-up that they replaced, the advantages were obvious. Employers knew the union guaranteed an adequate and skilled labor force, while workers were spared the slave market atmosphere of the notorious shape-up.

References: Joseph H. Ball, *The Government-Subsidized Union Monopoly: A Study of Labor Practices in the Shipping Industry* (Washington, DC: Labor Policy Association, 1966); John J. Collins, *Never Off Pay: The Story of the Independent Tanker Union, 1937–1962* (New York: Fordham University Press, 1964); Charles P. Larrowe, *Harry Bridges: The Rise and Fall of Radical Labor in the United States* (New York: Lawrence Hill, 1972); Hugh Mulzac, *A Star to Steer By* (New York: International, 1963); National Maritime Union, *This Is the NMU* (New York: William P. Gottlieb, 1954); Bruce Nelson, *Workers on the Waterfront: Seamen, Longshoremen, and Unionism in the 1930s* (Urbana: University of Illinois Press, 1990); William W. Pilcher, *The Portland Longshoremen: A Dispersed Urban Community* (New York: Holt, Rinehart and Wilson, 1972); William L. Standard, *Merchant Seaman: A Short History of Their Struggles* (New York: International, 1947).

HOG ISLANDER. Hog Islander was the name given to one of the ship types built by the Shipping Board* for World War I. The Shipping Board established a huge shipyard at Hog Island near Philadelphia in 1917, and in a lapse of public relations, allowed the unfortunate expression of Hog Islander to stick as the name for the ships themselves. The original program called for the construction of 110 freighters and 70 troop transports. The idea behind the Hog Islander was to mass produce a single vessel design, thereby achieving tremendous savings in labor and material; the Shipping Board applied the same principle in the Pacific Coast to build a similar type vessel, "Wests," so-called because their compound names all began with the word "West."

The Hog Islanders were designed with straight lines and flat surfaces to ease construction; the stern or rear of the ship was square, and the sides of the ship were straight, while the deck and bottom of the ship were flat. "She looked like a shallow flower box with a pot in the middle, called the homelist of all the merchantmen" (Lane 1941). The Hog Islander freighters were around 7,800 deadweight* tons, had an overall length of 410 feet and a beam of 46 feet, and with triple-expansion engines* normally traveled at 10 knots and had a maximum speed of 11.5 knots. The troop transports, with over 8,000 deadweight tons, an overall length of 448 feet and a beam of 58 feet, were larger, but above all the troopships, with a maximum speed of 16 knots, were faster than the freighters.

The first keel was laid at Hog Island in February 1918, and the first ship, the

Quistconck, was launched on 5 August 1918. Many of the Hog Islanders had Indian names; for example, the *Quistconck* supposedly meant ''hog's place'' in the language of the Delaware Indians. During its years of operation the yard completed 122 Hog Islanders, 110 as freighters, and only 12 as troop transports (after Armistice Day the Shipping Board canceled the orders for the additional 58 troop transports). The shipyard delivered the last of the 122 Hog Islanders on 21 January 1921, and then ceased to operate. The Shipping Board sold the land to the city of Philadelphia in 1930 and eventually the site became the city airport. These sturdy and economical ships, whether sold or handed over to managing operators,* became the core units of most U.S.-flag steamship companies until the mid-1930s. Conversions and alterations lengthened the commercial life of the Hog Islanders, and many survived to provide gallant service in World War II.

References: Robert G. Albion, *Seaports South of Sahara: The Achievements of an American Steamship Service* (New York: Appleton-Century Crofts, 1959); John Bunker, *Liberty Ships, the Ugly Ducklings of World War II* (Annapolis, MD: Naval Institute Press, 1972); Mark H. Goldberg, *The ''Hog Islanders'': The Story of 122 American Ships* (Kings Point, NY: American Merchant Marine Museum, 1991); Edward N. Hurley, *The Bridge to France* (Philadelphia: J. B. Lippincott Co., 1927); Carl D. Lane, *What the Citizen Should Know About the Merchant Marine* (New York: W. W. Norton, 1941).

HUDSON, ROY BANNERMAN, 9 April 1904–1982. Roy Bannerman Hudson was the national secretary of the Marine Workers Industrial Union* (MWIU), the communist union for the waterfront. He was born on 9 April 1904 in Tonepah, Nevada. His parents were of Anglo-Saxon descent. After he finished eighth grade, he left home and joined the navy in 1919. He served aboard ships first in the navy until 1923 and afterward as a merchant seaman. The poor treatment given to sailors soon led him to join the Marine Transport Workers of the International Workers of the World (IWW), but soon he gave up on that moribund organization. His enthusiasm for uniting sailors was revived by the more effective structure of the Communist party, which he joined around 1929. He soon became a party organizer, and in 1931 he visited the Soviet Union. In 1932 he replaced Harry Hynes as national secretary of the MWIU and became its main public figure. Hudson held the position until the dissolution of the MWIU in 1935.

Many of the MWIU organizers went on to hold high posts in the newly created National Maritime Union* (NMU), but the union's president, Joseph Curran,* feared Hudson as a dangerous rival and blocked his entry. As a close ally of Earl Browder, Hudson returned to the hierarchy of the Communist party in 1937, becoming the main liaison with the trade unions and rising to vice president of the party in 1943. A failure to quickly switch sides in 1945, when Browder fell from power, ended Hudson's career in the communist hierarchy. Subordinate party positions followed (including a brief return to the San Francisco waterfront in 1948), but Hudson was finally expelled from the party in 1951 and had to support himself as a housepainter. In spite of his expulsion, he

HURLEY, EDWARD NASH

refused to testify against communists before the Un-American Activities Committee of the U.S. House of Representatives.

References: Bernard K. Johnpoll and Harvey Klehr, eds., *Biographical Dictionary of the American Left* (Westport, CT: Greenwood Press, 1986); Bruce Nelson, *Workers on the Waterfront: Seamen, Longshoremen, and Unionism in the 1930s* (Urbana: University of Illinois Press, 1990); William L. Standard, *Merchant Seamen: A Short History of Their Struggles* (New York: International, 1947).

HURLEY, EDWARD NASH, 31 July 1864–14 November 1933. Edward N. Hurley, a millionaire businessman, was the chairman of the Shipping Board* during World War I and was responsible for the remarkable expansion of the U.S. merchant marine during that conflict. Hurley, whose parents were Irish immigrants, was born in Galesburg, Illinois, on 31 July 1864. Until he finished his public school education at Galesburg, he lived with his family and worked as a farmhand and in the railroad shops during the summers, but quickly he realized there were few opportunities for advancement in his hometown. In December 1981 he moved to Chicago, where he held different jobs and became an engineer to run a locomotive, but later he found he could make more money as a traveling salesman selling railroad supplies. He revealed his interest in public affairs when he briefly worked in 1889–1890 for local political bodies but found more rapid advancement in setting up his own businesses. He organized a very successful Pneumatic Tool Industry in the United States and also in Europe, and after selling the rights to this business in 1902, he retired at an early age and bought a large farm in Wheaton, Illinois. But he was too restless to remain for long in this quiet, secluded farm life, especially because he was alone since the death of his first wife in 1900.

By 1905, when he remarried, Hurley started to come out of his shell, and the next year he reentered business as president of the local bank in Wheaton. Later, in 1906 he organized the most successful of his many businesses, the Hurley Machine Company, to manufacture electrical house appliances. By 1914 his firm was running very smoothly, and he felt the desire to enter public service; the Woodrow Wilson administration found in him a valuable supporter and called on Hurley to fill a variety of jobs, in particular, the chairmanship of the Federal Trade Commission. President Wilson was so impressed that he decided to shift Hurley to the more prestigious and challenging task of chairman of the Shipping Board,* then just recovering from the Denman-Goethals controversy. Hurley plunged eagerly into the new job, and soon he had established clear lines of authority between the Shipping Board and its subsidiary, the Emergency Fleet Corporation* (EFC), thereby guaranteeing that the shipbuilding program could proceed without interruption.

At the same time, Hurley was responsible for operating not only those vessels coming off the ways in the shipyards but also all the other vessels under U.S. control, whether the vessels repositioned from private owners or the German vessels confiscated upon U.S. entry into World War I. Hurley surrounded himself by the best available talent and called on P.A.S. Franklin* to head the Shipping Control Committee to allocate in the most efficient way possible the cargo space of all vessels under U.S. control. Hurley also pushed the huge training program necessary to find enough officers and seamen to man the increasing number of vessels under U.S. control. Thanks to Hurley's untiring efforts, the U.S. government was able in March 1918 to guarantee to the Allies the tonnage required to transport and supply eighty American divisions for the final offensive in the spring of 1919.

The unexpected collapse of Germany on 11 November 1918 suddenly left the Shipping Board with more vessels than it would ever need for the war. Hurley had to make a decision: the EFC had delivered for service only 470 ships and launched an additional 276, but what to do with the additional 1,419 keels already laid? In his only mistaken decision while on the Shipping Board, Hurley decided to complete most of the original shipbuilding program as the best way to create a strong U.S.-flag merchant marine. Between 1919 and 1922, when the last three ships were delivered, the EFC completed 1,234 vessels, but what to do with this huge surplus became the monstrous burden that ultimately crushed the Shipping Board in the 1920s. Indeed, the failure to curtail the shipbuilding program meant that the Shipping Board squandered away the time and the funds more wisely used to support the consolidation of U.S.-flag steamship lines.

In 1919 Hurley participated in special missions to Europe and was one of the representatives chosen by President Wilson to participate in the Paris Peace Conference. Hurley devoted less and less time to the Shipping Board, whose demobilization loomed more daunting than the dramatic wartime buildup. On 31 July 1919 Hurley resigned as chairman and returned to Chicago. Although he served in different government commissions, he devoted the bulk of his time to writing and, in particular, to publicizing the importance of foreign trade and the merchant marine for the future of the United States. His book *The New Merchant Marine* tried to sustain public interest in ocean transportation, while his *The Bridge to France*, one of the rare memoirs on merchant shipping, was an exciting and clear account of his dramatic years on the Shipping Board. He always viewed the merchant marine as an integral part of U.S. foreign trade and was also an early proponent of business education to improve the performance of companies. In 1930 he made a large donation to Notre Dame University to construct the building (which still stands) for the Edward N. Hurley College of Foreign and Domestic Commerce. He died in Chicago on 14 November 1933.

References: René De La Pedraja, *The Rise and Decline of U.S. Merchant Shipping in the Twentieth Century* (New York: Twayne, 1992); Edward N. Hurley Papers, University of Notre Dame Archives, Notre Dame, Indiana; Edward N. Hurley, *The Bridge to France* (Philadelphia: J. B. Lippincott, 1927); Jeffrey J. Safford, *Wilsonian Maritime Diplomacy, 1913–1921* (New Brunswick, NJ: Rutgers University Press, 1978).

I

IAROSSI, FRANK (1937?–present). Frank Iarossi was the president of Exxon Shipping Company, and is the president of the American Bureau of Shipping* (ABS). He served in the Coast Guard, and in 1968 joined the tanker division of Exxon.* He climbed through the corporate ranks, and managed the tanker construction program of Exxon in Japan in 1972–1976. He was appointed president of Exxon Shipping Company in 1982, and in that position he had to handle the *Exxon Valdez** shipwreck and oil spill of 24 March 1989. Iarossi became almost a household word thanks to Home Box Office (HBO), whose *Dead Ahead: The Exxon Valdez Disaster** portrayed Iarossi as the principal protagonist in the docudrama.

As even the movie *Dead Ahead* showed, and in spite of later company denials, Exxon sought to make him take the blame for both the oil spill and the subsequent public relations disaster. Iarossi decided to continue his career in a less hostile environment, and in April 1990 he accepted the appointment as president of the (ABS), the classification* society in the United States. However, his tenure at ABS has been anything but tranquil, and soon he was at the center of controversies over the decision to relocate ABS headquarters to the World Trade Center and his brief hiring of his wife and daughter. The Board of Directors staged a coup on 8 January 1992 to remove Iarossi as president, but he plotted his own countercoup on 5 February 1992, and managed to remain in office. The terrorist explosion of 26 February 1993 forced ABS to abandon its offices in the World Trade Center for several months, but it appears that as long as Iarossi can deliver a favorable balance at the end of the year, his position at ABS will remain secure.

References: *American Shipper*, May 1992; Home Box Office, *Dead Ahead: The Exxon Valdez Disaster*, 1992; *Houston Chronicle*, 12 April 1992; *Journal of Commerce*, 5 March 1990.

INCRES-HONDUREÑA **CASES.** In the *Incres-Hondureña* cases, the Supreme Court of the United States decided that under existing legislation, the National Labor Relations Board (NLRB) had no jurisdiction over ships owned by U.S. corporations but flying flags of convenience*; in effect, by this decision the Supreme Court removed the last doubts about the right of U.S. companies to own and operate vessels under the flags of convenience. In 1961 the NLRB had determined that ships of the United Fruit Company* flying the flag of Honduras were under U.S. jurisdiction, because the determining factor was not the flag itself but rather the ''contact'' between the ships and the U.S. company; in the *Hondureña* case the vessels were owned and under the direct control of United Fruit, a U.S. corporation, and henceforth under U.S. jurisdiction.

The labor unions, in particular, the National Maritime Union* (NMU), had greeted the decision as a blow against what labor leaders derisively called runaway* flags. The shipowners grouped in the American Committee for Flags of Necessity* (ACFN) filed appeals, and the Supreme Court agreed to hear the case simultaneously with the related *Incres* cases about an Italian-owned firm that operated through American management in New York flags-of-convenience ships. The NMU counted on success in the appeal, because President John F. Kennedy had made a campaign promise to Joe Curran* to try to stop the runaway flags. The arguments against the flags of convenience system were weak, however, and the government pleaded with the Supreme Court to limit itself to these two cases without granting any blanket approval.

The Supreme Court, in a unanimous decision on 18 February 1963, effectively grasped the essence of the problem and stated that the NLRB had not been given any power by Congress to impose U.S. labor legislation on ships flying foreign flags. The *Incres-Hondureña* cases had called the attention of the Supreme Court precisely because an independent commission had outstripped its legislative mandate and went on to create laws on its own. The Supreme Court clearly recognized that Congress had the right to extend jurisdiction to foreign ships, and although the judges directed the parties in the cases to present their arguments to Congress, no further legislation was ever forthcoming, so that the *Incres-Hondureña* cases marked the end of the attempts to halt the flags of convenience system by recourse to the courts.

References: Rodney P. Carlisle, *Sovereignty for Sale: The Origins and Evolution of the Panamanian and Liberian Flags of Convenience* (Annapolis, MD: Naval Institute Press, 1981); Commission on Merchant Marine and Defense, *Public Hearings, February-July 1987*; Erling Naess, *The Great PanLibHon Controversy* (Epping, England: Gower Press, 1972).

INDEPENDENCE. See *Constitution.*

INDEPENDENT TANKER UNIONS (ITUs), 1937–present. *Independent tanker unions* (ITUs) has been a collective, catchall name given to those locals that have not affiliated with any of the major maritime labor organizations (or

"Big Labor"), such as the Seafarers' International Union* (SIU), the National Maritime Union* (NMU), or other member organizations of the AFL-CIO. The major oil companies, in particular, Standard Oil of New Jersey* (today Exxon) and Mobil, but also others like Texaco and Getty Oil, have been the employers for the members of the ITUs, although a few small employers have not been engaged in the petroleum business. Unlike the national unions of Big Labor, which have complex bureaucracies and deduct large sums as mandatory dues from the workers' paychecks, the ITU members themselves conduct the local-level bargaining with the companies. The ITUs' only assistance has been outside consultants, and during nearly forty years they relied on Fordham University professor John J. Collins as their adviser.

As the wave of unionization spread in the late 1930s, deck officers and engineers in the tanker unions realized that unless they created their own union, the powerful organization drives of the NMU and the SIU would soon force them to join organizations not to their liking. The tanker industry with its short turnaround time at port and its employment year-round was very different from the liner* and tramp* operations, so that the officers and engineers had developed very close links with the parent corporations, most of whom were proprietary companies.* The seafaring personnel felt their best interests for individual advancement lay in developing close and special ties with their parent company, rather than being lumped together in the NMU or other unions with the seafarers of every other steamship company; likewise, the hiring hall,* the concession Big Labor had obtained after very bitter struggles, was meaningless to the employees of the major oil companies who were guaranteed year-round employment.

Officers and engineers began to create their own ITUs in 1937–1938, and in one of his last contributions to the tanker industry, Robert L. Hague* convinced the management of Standard Oil Company that it was in the interest of the firm to support the ITUs, and soon most of the major oil companies followed suit. The ITUs did not remain just for officers and engineers, but the unlicensed personnel also created their own ITUs, for example, Esso (later Exxon) Seamen's Organization and Getty Tanker Men's Association. The violent hostility of Texaco to labor organizations allowed the NMU to organize the seamen, but when the company diminished its opposition to organized labor, the officers then managed to create their own ITU.

The national unions denounced the ITUs as company unions and have tried many times unsuccessfully to lure the membership away by promises of better contracts. In reality the terms obtained from management have been comparable, and membership has not affiliated with the national unions because the locals would lose power and the members would "pay and pay and pay" to support the large union bureaucracy. Instead the ITUs keep control at the local level and thus allow the democratically elected executive committee of each local to negotiate patiently arrangements beneficial both to the personnel as well as the firm. In 1946 careful bargaining obtained from Esso the concept of extended vacations, a major breakthrough for all maritime unions, but in other cases the

NMU jumped ahead when it obtained a twenty-year retirement plan without any age requirement. This competition between the national unions and the ITUs conclusively proved that the latter were not company unions but has had unfortunate consequences, because the resulting whipsawing* has meant the extension across the industry of conditions and requirements that, while valid and proper in the setting of one large company, proved at best unworkable and often ruinous to other firms handling only ocean transportation.

In general, however, the ITUs have been a successful and durable method in labor-management relations and have some resemblances to the policies that J. Max Harrison* introduced in the American Maritime Association.* The members of the ITUs have often also been stockholders in the major oil companies, whose fate they follow and support with a close interest. Transfers to land jobs and promotions to management ranks have been frequent, so that the ITU could often be just one more step in an individual's career advancement strategy. The lines between labor and management have been deliberately blurred by the common overriding interest of both sides to achieve the best results for the firm, and the esprit de corps that has characterized the major oil companies quite naturally has been fully shared by the ITUs.

Since the 1960s the ITUs have been among the strongest backers of cargo-preference* legislation to require that at least a percentage of imported oil travel aboard U.S.-flag ships. Although that battle was lost, the ITUs remained concerned about their members' psychological, and not just physical, welfare; in a major example, when Exxon developed "top management phobia" over the possibility of oil spills and pollution by the tankers, the Exxon Tanker Officers' Association constantly intervened to try to relieve the tremendous pressure brought upon the membership so as to avoid the stressful situations that, rather than preventing, could in fact cause unsafe behavior, as finally happened with the *Exxon Valdez.** The ITUs, given the special characteristics of the oil industry, have been able to meet the real needs of their members more effectively than the national unions, whose characteristics have largely been shaped in other trade routes. The ITUs also showed how ingenious approaches to labor-management relations could avoid the crippling strikes and disruptive stoppages that from the 1930s to the 1980s plagued the U.S. merchant marine. While it has not been clear how far the example of the ITUs could be taken beyond the special conditions of the oil industry, it certainly has been an experience that needs to be taken into account.

References: Joseph H. Bail, *The Government-Subsidized Union Monopoly: A Study of Labor Practices in the Shipping Industry* (Washington, DC: Labor Policy Association, 1966); John J. Collins, *Bargaining at the Local Level* (New York: Fordham University Press, 1974); John J. Collins, *Never Off Pay: The Story of the Independent Tanker Union, 1937–1962* (New York: Fordham University Press, 1964).

INDIA HOUSE, 1914–present. In New York City the India House has been the main social club for executives in merchant shipping and other areas of foreign trade. India House at 1 Hanover Square is located in the financial district of New York, and bankers were prominent among the founders. Shipowners had felt the need for a club, and at least since 1900 most belonged to the "Jolly Mariners' Club," which rented space on the upper floor of the Bush Terminal Building in Broad Street and was under the general direction of George S. Dearborn.* In May 1914 Willard Straight, an associate of J. P. Morgan & Co., in union with James A. Farrell, the president of United States Steel, convoked thirty-nine business leaders to a dinner in which they agreed to establish a club of appropriate standing and prestige, which they called the India House. The name was chosen because it evoked the proverbial wealth of the Indies, "since Renaissance times . . . a synonym for all that is rare and precious" (*Descriptive Catalogue* 1973). Farrell convinced his close friend Dearborn to bring into the new India House the members of the Jolly Mariners' Club, which then dissolved. Meanwhile Straight selected and rented the building that during several decades, also held the offices of the National Foreign Trade Council. In 1918 Straight purchased the property and left provision in his will for its sale at reasonable terms to the India House, which in 1921 acquired the property, which has remained its residence ever since. The building itself was declared a New York Landmark in 1965, and it houses an impressive collection of marine art, ship models, and many other objects that its members—beginning with Straight—have donated over the century.

Originally just a lunch club for already famous business leaders, after World War I membership in the India House became a sign that an individual had arrived in the world of merchant shipping. Cozy and comfortable as an informal meeting place for executives to talk about mutual concerns over a meal or drinks, the India House provided a more intimate gathering than was possible in the Propeller Club,* whose main purpose was to provide a neutral meeting ground for representatives from management, labor, government, and the general public. The India House did participate in policy affairs when it joined the outcry against the La Follette Seamen's Act* in 1915, and it has served as a meeting place for executives who gather to discuss issues such as the Merchant Marine Library Association,* but in practice the India House has left public controversies to the business associations and has remained a reserved exclusive club.

References: Lincoln Colcord, "History of the American-Hawaiian Steamship Co.," unpublished manuscript; Herbert Croly, *Willard Straight* (New York: Macmillan, 1924); *Descriptive Catalogue of the Marine Collection at India House*, 2nd ed. (Middletown, CT: Wesleyan University Press, 1973); Robert Dollar, *Memoirs*, 3rd ed., 4 vols. (San Francisco: Privately printed, 1927); Joseph P. Goldberg, *The Maritime Story* (Cambridge: Harvard University Press, 1958); Record Group 32, National Archives, Washington, DC; *Who Was Who in America*.

INDUSTRIAL CARRIERS. See proprietary companies.

INSULAR LINE, 1904–1914. The Insular Line provided service between mainland U.S. ports and the island of Puerto Rico. Puerto Rico had been annexed to the United States as a result of the Spanish-American War, and the extension of the cabotage* laws to that island excluded the foreign lines from the service to the U.S. mainland and in effect gave the New York and Puerto Rico Steamship Company* a monopoly on the steamer service. W. E. Peck & Co., a steamship agency, concluded that the volume of trade justified the existence of another steamship company. A number of Puerto Rican merchants invested in this venture, which was shortly after named the Insular Line.

In 1911 Archibald H. Bull,* who until 1900 had been one of the owners of the New York and Puerto Rico Steamship Company, reentered the Puerto Rican service with steamers. Soon a ferocious rate war erupted, as the three companies struggled to remain in a trade that could support at most only two. The rivalry became so intense that brawls between rival crews became frequent, and messengers were ambushed to rip up the bills of lading.* The clashes came to an end in 1914, when the smaller Insular Line was purchased by Bull Line.*

References: John S. Blank, ''Fifty Years to the Indies,'' *Ships and the Sea*, July 1952, pp. 50–57; René De La Pedraja, *The Rise and Decline of U.S. Merchant Shipping in the Twentieth Century* (New York: Twayne, 1992); U.S. House, Committee on Merchant Marine and Fisheries, *Investigation of Shipping Combinations*, 4 vols. (Washington, DC: Government Printing Office, 1913).

INTER-AMERICAN FREIGHT CONFERENCE (IAFC), 1967–present.

The Inter-American Freight Conference (IAFC) became in 1967 the successor to the River Plate and Brazil Conferences* and has grouped the most important conferences* in the trade between the United States and Latin America. IAFC has been a common name for seven separate conferences, each of which is further identified by its respective ''section.'' Two sections in New York City control the trade moving southward from the East and Gulf coasts: IAFC Section A controls the trade going to Brazil, and IAFC Section D controls the trade to Argentina, Paraguay, and Uruguay. Section B, in Buenos Aires, controls the trade moving north from Argentina, Paraguay, and Uruguay to U.S. ports in the Atlantic and Gulf, while Section C, in Rio de Janeiro, does the same for the trade going north from Brazil. Because the separate sections or conferences share offices and staff in New York City, not surprisingly a proposal surfaced in 1992 to combine the seven separate units into one superconference.*

The ocean trade between the United States and Latin America has been ''characterized by pooling agreements and cargo preference* programs'' (Federal Maritime Commission, September 1989). The collapse of United States Lines* (USL), which had planned to enter this trade in a big way, brought IAFC to a state of confusion, as other companies rushed to try to fill the apparent void left by USL. Even Sea-Land* entered but never operated a regular service and soon dropped out. When the member companies discovered in 1987 that the chairman of the IAFC in New York City had been bribing a clerk in the Federal Maritime Commission* (FMC) to backdate conference tariffs not filed in time, the ensuing Federal Bureau of Investigation (FBI) inquiry created considerable embarrassment. A new and efficient chairman soon restored the IAFC to normal operations. Of the twenty-three companies offering service in these routes in 1990, fourteen were members of IAFC, and only one—Lykes Brothers Steamship Co.*—was U.S.-flag, but it too has been considering the possibility of shifting to flags of convenience.* The trade controlled by IAFC "has had extremely high rates, some of the highest in the world" (*American Shipper* 1992), and in April 1992 the conference finally agreed to quote the lower "freight of all kinds" (FAK) rates to Non-Vessel Operating Common Carriers (NVOCCs), who, by consolidating "less than container loads" (LCL), were expected to offer shippers* lower prices and hence stimulate the volume of trade moving in those routes.

References: Advisory Commission on Conferences in Ocean Shipping, *Report to the President and the Congress* (Washington, DC: Government Printing Office, 1992); *American Shipper*, May 1987, June 1992; Federal Maritime Commission, *Carrier Agreements in the U.S. Oceanborne Trades*, September 1990; Federal Maritime Commission, *Section 18 Report on the Shipping Act of 1984*, September 1989; *Journal of Commerce*, 7 Sept 1988.

INTERCOASTAL. The term *intercoastal* has referred to the trade between the East and West coasts of the United States. In accordance to the cabotage* privilege, only U.S.-flag vessels built in the United States may ply the intercoastal and coastwise* trade. Although intercoastal voyages began earlier, the recognition of the U.S. claim to the Oregon territory in 1846 may be taken as the official date for the start of the intercoastal trade, whose real boost, however, came in 1848 with the discovery of gold in California. Intercoastal trade traveled through three main routes: around the Cape Horn in the tip of South America and via the Panama or the Nicaragua routes. In the latter two cases the passengers and the merchandise coming from New York made a short land trip through the isthmus to continue the voyage on waiting steamers on the Pacific side. The completion of the Panama Railroad in January 1855 made this route the fastest means of travel between both coasts of the United States, but a substantial volume of traffic, particularly for bulk* commodities, continued to go around South America.

In 1907 the Tehuantepec Railroad through Mexico became the fastest route for intercoastal travel, but it was almost completely eclipsed in August 1914 by the opening of the Panama Canal,* which at last allowed vessels to travel directly between both coasts of the United States without having to take the long trip around South America. Intercoastal shipping using the Panama Canal remained important until World War II, when most vessels in that trade were requisitioned by the U.S. government. After the war the intercoastal trade attempted a comeback, but ferocious competition from the railroads gradually eliminated almost all the liner* companies, except for fleets of proprietary* companies. By treaty the United States has promised to withdraw from the Panama Canal in the year 2000, and the resulting political uncertainty may well mean the virtual disappearance of the already nearly moribund intercoastal shipping.

References: René De La Pedraja, *The Rise and Decline of U.S. Merchant Shipping in the Twentieth Century* (New York: Twayne, 1992); David I. Folkman, Jr., *The Nicaragua Route* (Salt Lake City: University of Utah Press, 1972); John H. Kemble, *The Panama Route, 1848–1869* (Berkeley: University of California Press, 1943.

INTERCOASTAL STEAMSHIP FREIGHT ASSOCIATION, 1936–1980.
The Intercoastal Steamship Freight Association covered the trade between the Atlantic and Pacific coasts of the United States, including the Gulf of Mexico. The association replaced two previous conferences,* the Gulf Intercoastal Conference,* which covered trade between the Pacific and Gulf of Mexico ports of the United States, and the United States Intercoastal Conference,* which covered trade between the Atlantic and Pacific ports of the United States. As a matter of fact, this last conference had disbanded in 1934, and only the passage of the Intercoastal Shipping Act of 1933 gradually convinced the lines in the intercoastal trade of the need to create a new association to present their case before the regulatory agencies and Congress, as well as to perform the traditional conference functions of setting rates, schedules, and sailings.

The Intercoastal Steamship Freight Association managed to operate effectively until February 1939, when American-Hawaiian Steamship Company* and Luckenbach Steamship Company* quit the conference and plunged the trade into the earlier pattern of vicious rate wars and chronic instability. The shippers* had tired of waiting for the U.S. Maritime Commission* to wield its new powers to impose stability upon the trade, and in desperation they united with the railroads to seek the transfer of jurisdiction over coastwise* and intercoastal trades (but not including offshore areas like Puerto Rico, Hawaii, and Alaska) to the Interstate Commerce Commission* (ICC). The Transportation Act of 1940 codified the change, and since then coastwise and intercoastal shipping has remained under the jurisdiction of the pro-railroad ICC.

The U.S. government gradually requisitioned the entire intercoastal fleet for duty in World War II, so that the Intercoastal Steamship Freight Association did not have to deal with the railroad-controlled ICC until after the war was over. The temporary post-war shipping shortage helped to keep the intercoastal lines afloat, but by 1950 the boom was over. In order to drive the ships out, the railroads had expanded their schedules, kept their rates low, and blocked the requests of the Intercoastal Steamship Freight Association for rate increases so that the lines could not raise enough capital to buy new ships.

By the late 1950s intercoastal trade was rapidly disappearing, and it gradually dwindled to ships of proprietary* carriers that usually carried only their own cargoes or at best offered shippers services in only one direction. By the 1960s the Intercoastal Steamship Freight Association was largely inoperative. However, because some firms occasionally provided limited services and also because schemes to place new vessels in the intercoastal trade continued to surface, the association lingered on in the vain hope of a revival, until it quietly folded by 1980.

Principal Executive

Harry S. Brown   1936–1959

References: René De La Pedraja, *The Rise and Decline of U.S. Merchant Shipping in the Twentieth Century* (New York: Twayne, 1992); Gale Research, *Encyclopedia of Associations*, 1959, 1980; *New York Times*, 23 February 1939; Ronald A. Shadburne, "Coastwise and Intercoastal Shipping," *Annals of the American Academy of Political and Social Science* 230 (1943):29–36; U.S. House, Committee on Merchant Marine and Fisheries, *Amending Merchant Marine Act, 1936* (Washington, DC: Government Printing Office, 1938).

INTERMODALISM. As containers* became widespread in the late 1960s, steamship companies began to explore the possibilities of moving containers directly from the ships to other forms of transportation. At the heart of intermodalism was using two or more types of transportation, such as railroads, ships, trucks, and barges, to move the containers. The goal was to provide the shipper* with "door-to-door" service rather than just between ports. One of the pioneers was American Export Lines,* which unfortunately had to assume the start-up costs of introducing intermodalism. In 1971 Seatrain* broadened intermodalism to include the "landbridge"* concept, by which containers unloaded from its ships moved by train between the West and East coasts of the United States. In the 1970s intermodalism became firmly established in the United States, Western Europe, and the Pacific rim countries of the Far East.

The ideal of intermodalism was "portal-to-portal" service, whereby the merchant shipping company picked up the containers at the factory or business of the shipper* and then delivered them to their final destination. Besides its own ships, the merchant shipping company used a combination of trucks and railroads to move the containers. The shipper, of course, was free to make his own arrangements to deliver the containers to the port, and for small volumes the shipper might prefer to deal with a freight forwarder* rather than directly with the merchant shipping company.

No matter what particular legal arrangements were made to handle the merchandise, intermodalism ultimately depended on containers, which because of their uniform size could be easily transferred from one type of transportation to another. Thus the transportation map in the ideal intermodal world centered on rivers of containers flowing across the United States and beyond its borders, until the different forms of transportation meshed smoothly into a global network.

References: American President Lines, *Fact Book*, 1987; Commission on Merchant Marine and Defense, *Third Report: Appendices* (Washington, DC: Government Printing Office, 1988); Lane C. Kendall, *The Business of Shipping*, 5th ed. (Centreville, MD: Cornell Maritime Press, 1986); William J. Miller, *Encyclopedia of International Com-*

merce (Centreville, MD: Cornell Maritime Press, 1985); Transportation Research Board, *Intermodal Marine Container Transportation: Impediments and Opportunities* (Washington, DC: National Research Council, 1992).

INTERNATIONAL LONGSHOREMEN AND WAREHOUSEMEN'S UNION (ILWU). See Longshoremen and Warehousemen's Union, International.

INTERNATIONAL LONGSHOREMEN'S ASSOCIATION (ILA). See Longshoremen's Association, International.

INTERNATIONAL MARITIME WORKERS UNION (IMWU), November 1959–May 1961. This union was created to try to organize the seamen aboard ships that flew "flags of convenience"* but were owned by U.S. companies. The sponsors of the union were Paul Hall* of the Seafarers' International Union* (SIU) and Joseph Curran* of the National Maritime Union* (NMU). The International Transport Workers' Federation of London had finally accepted the position of the two U.S. unions that laborers should be organized not by their nationality but by that of the shipowners.

The organizing drive produced few results, while intense rivalry between the SIU and the NMU over the affiliation of the new union members led to the collapse of the IMWU in May 1961 and foreshadowed the Seamen's Strike of 1961.* The two unions continued separate organizing efforts among the foreign-flag affiliates, but this divided front was easily neutralized by management.

References: Rodney P. Carlisle, *Sovereignty for Sale: The Origins and Evolution of the Panamanian and Liberian Flags of Convenience* (Annapolis: Naval Institute Press, 1981); John J. Collins, *Never Off Pay: The Story of the Independent Tanker Union, 1937–1962* (New York: Fordham University Press, 1964).

INTERNATIONAL MERCANTILE MARINE (IMM), 1902–1943. During forty years the International Mercantile Marine was the largest U.S.-owned merchant fleet, although the majority of its vessels flew foreign flags, particularly British. IMM was the creation of Wall Street magnate J. P. Morgan, who merged two U.S. companies, International Navigation Company* and Atlantic Transport Company,* with two British companies, the Leyland and White Star lines, to form the new holding company in February 1902, although it did not formally incorporate itself as IMM until 1 October of that year. Morgan, however, was unable to acquire control of a last major British line, Cunard, and thus he could not complete his plan to establish a near monopoly over ocean routes in the North Atlantic. Consequently, IMM faced since 1902 strong competition from Cunard and from the two rapidly expanding German lines, Hamburg-America and North German Lloyd. Rate wars tore apart the conferences* on the Atlantic and reduced the income of IMM, which never paid dividends to stockholders before World War I.

When Cunard introduced the new *Lusitania* and *Mauretania* in 1907, IMM tried to meet the competition by building a trio of bigger and more luxurious ships. The first, the *Olympic*, initially caused quite a splash with the wealthy passengers, but the effort to increase the luxury features at the price of slower speed produced the disastrous *Titanic*,* which sank on its maiden voyage. The loss of the *Titanic* further weakened IMM, which because of this shipwreck could not earn the record profits other competing lines were enjoying in the boom year of 1912. Before the last of the trio, the *Britannic*, could make a single voyage, the British government requisitioned the vessel for service in World War I.

The disruption caused by the outbreak of World War I drove IMM into bankruptcy in 1914 and also provided P.A.S. Franklin* the opportunity to gain control of the company. He convinced the creditors to appoint him president on the promise he could restore financial soundness, and once the record high rates in ocean shipping rescued the company, he was confirmed as president of the company, a position he held until his retirement in 1936. In spite of Franklin's success, he realized that IMM ultimately depended on its British-flag vessels for profitable operation, but ownership of British ships had become politically unacceptable because of a very strong nationalist sentiment in the United States. Franklin tried to sell the IMM to the British, but at the request of the Woodrow Wilson administration, which feared losing all control over such a large merchant fleet, he dropped the deal.

However, after the war was over, the Shipping Board* generally avoided assigning surplus ships to IMM and instead preferred to create a large number of new firms. The Shipping Board refused to hand over the large captured German passenger liners, in particular the *Leviathan*,* to IMM, the only American company with the capacity and experience to handle such large ships on the North Atlantic. Of course, out of the profits of its foreign- flag ships, IMM could easily finance a new generation of British-flag ships built in foreign shipyards, but such a solution only antagonized the American public, which felt all along that the giant IMM was simply a front for British interests. Franklin resumed efforts to dispose of the foreign-flag vessels and sold the British-flag White Star Line, the largest subsidiary of IMM, to the Royal Mail Steam Packet Company in 1926, as a first major step toward relying only on U.S.-flag vessels. Shortly afterward he ordered the *California*,* *Pennsylvania*, and *Virginia* built in a U.S. shipyard, and when they were delivered in 1928–1929, he had them placed in the intercoastal* service of the Panama Pacific Line, one of the IMM subsidiaries.

Franklin would have been well advised to invest the proceeds from the White Star sale in less glamorous but safer land businesses or to restrict his ocean operations to the remaining foreign-flag subsidiaries of IMM, but the lure of running a U.S.-flag service across the Atlantic proved irresistible for him and his son John, who since 1930 was gradually replacing the aging father. The Shipping Board, too, had softened its rigid opposition to this combine and was seeking an accommodation with IMM. Meanwhile, in 1930 a new stock issued allowed a group headed by his son John Franklin* and including Kermit Roosevelt* and the financier Basil Harris* to gain control of IMM; however, P.A.S. Franklin remained president until his retirement in 1936, when John assumed full control over the company.

To remain a major force in the North Atlantic, IMM needed to find a U.S.-flag fleet, and the only available was United States Lines* (USL), which originally had been owned and operated by the Shipping Board. After a complicated series of transactions and negotiations, IMM acquired USL and the American Merchant Line* in October 1931; as part of the deal, IMM received the *Leviathan* as well as the *Manhattan** and *Washington*, two new liners still under construction in the shipyards. By 1936 IMM had disposed of the last of its foreign-flag ships and henceforth operated only vessels of U.S. registry.* This precaution, however, had failed to spare the company another wave of anti-British attacks, especially in September 1934, when it laid up the *Leviathan*, which by then was overage and could no longer compete against the faster liners in the Atlantic. By 1933 the *Manhattan* and the *Washington* were providing U.S.-flag passenger service across the Atlantic, but they were almost immediately outclassed by the larger and faster liners Cunard and German lines soon introduced.

IMM needed to order another set of liners, but because the company had disposed of its foreign-flag fleet, new ship orders were possible only with substantial financial support from the Shipping Board. Unfortunately for IMM, the Black Committee* hearings in 1933 exposed so many cases of milking public funds by private steamship companies that the Merchant Marine Act of 1936 abolished both the existing subsidies and the Shipping Board itself. Under the new construction differential subsidy,* IMM received enough support to order only one superliner, the *America*,* which was completed in 1940.

By then the center of activities had shifted from IMM to its subsidiary, USL. In spite of the changed subsidy circumstances, John Franklin, who became president in 1936, still insisted on running a U.S.-flag fleet. One after another of the subsidiaries of IMM were liquidated or sold off; for example, when the intercoastal service failed to qualify for a subsidy, IMM sold the *California, Pennsylvania*, and *Virginia* to the U.S. Maritime Commission* in 1938. Already in 1937 IMM had returned to its original function of a holding company, and as Franklin explained, "We are trying to merge everything into the USL as fast as we can" (U.S. Congress 1938). By 1940 IMM was little more than a paper shell, with all authority and control centralized in its subsidiary, USL. All that remained to emphasize the pure American character of the company was to replace the old name of International Mercantile Marine with the more acceptable one of United States Lines on 21 May 1943.

Principal Executives

Clement A. Griscom*	1902–1912
J. Bruce Ismay	1904–1912

Harold Sanderson	1912–1914
P.A.S. Franklin	1914–1936
John M. Franklin	1931–1943
Basil Harris	1931–1943

Some Notable Ships

Olympic	1911–1914
Titanic	1912
Britannic	1914
Leviathan	1931–1934
California, Pennsylvania, and Virginia	1928–1938
Manhattan and Washington	1932–1943
America	1940–1943

Principal Subsidiaries

American Merchant Line	1931–1937
American Pioneer Line	1930–1939
Atlantic Transport Line*	1902–1934
Baltimore Mail Line*	1930–1938
Leyland Line	1902–1933
Panama-Pacific Line	1914–1940
Red Star Line*	1902–1935
Roosevelt Steamship Co.*	1930–1940
United States Lines	1931–1943
White Star Line	1902–1926

References: Frank O. Braynard, *The World's Greatest Ship: The Story of the Leviathan*, 6 vols. (Sea Cliff, NY: F. O. Braynard, 1972–1978); Vincent P. Carosso, *The Morgans: Private International Bankers, 1854–1913* (Cambridge: Harvard University Press, 1987); René De La Pedraja, *The Rise and Decline of U.S. Merchant Shipping in the Twentieth Century* (New York: Twayne, 1992); Frederick E. Emmons, *American Passenger Ships: The Ocean Lines and Liners, 1873–1983* (Newark: University of Delaware Press, 1985); U.S. Congress, House, Committee on Merchant Marine and Fisheries, *Baltimore Mail Line* (Washington, DC: Government Printing Office, 1938).

INTERNATIONAL NAVIGATION COMPANY. See Red Star Line.

INTERNATIONAL SEAMEN'S UNION (ISU), 1899–1937. During its forty-year existence the International Seamen's Union (ISU) claimed to represent all the seamen in the United States. In practice, ISU had been created and was supported by the Sailors' Union of the Pacific* (SUP). ISU's attempts to escape the West Coast provincialism were never more than temporarily successful. Furthermore, bickering and jurisdictional disputes were all too frequent, because ISU was a federation of affiliated self-governing unions that were divided by craft (deck, engine room, and the cooks and stewards' departments) and in turn by regions (Atlantic, Great Lakes, and Pacific). Throughout its existence, ISU remained the main institutional arm of Andrew Furuseth.*

Membership rose from 3,300 in 1899 to 24,400 in 1907, but the financial panic of that year reduced job opportunities, and membership declined in subsequent years. The period of stagnation for the union appeared to be ending in 1911, but competition from the newly formed Marine Transport Workers' Industrial Union (MTWWIU) of the International Workers of the World (the "wobblies") prevented any permanent growth. Membership was only 19,000 in 1915, when Furuseth's years of able and persistent lobbying finally secured passage of the La Follette Seamen's Act,* the single most important accomplishment of the ISU.

The impact of World War I, particularly, U.S. entry, produced the period of greatest expansion for ISU, which saw membership climb from 49,500 in 1918 to 115,000 in 1920. This last extraordinary figure was attained because the postwar shipping shortage had driven wages up and allowed seamen to secure substantial raises by an easy and swift strike in 1919. The many new union members acquired an exaggerated idea of their power and could not imagine an end to the boom times. When a glut in shipping services materialized in January 1921, the Shipping Board* and the American Steamship Owners' Association* (ASOA) demanded a 15 percent reduction in wages, but the adamant workers preferred to strike in May 1921, with disastrous results. The strike was easily broken, and only on the West Coast did the SUP manage to preserve part of its former strength.

ISU membership plummeted from 50,000 in 1921 to 16,000 in 1923 and to barely 5,000 during the worst years of the Great Depression. In principle the union was finished, and since Furuseth was away most of the time lobbying in Washington, D.C., union offices fell into the hands of racketeers, loafers, and grafters. Embezzlement of union funds drove the ISU to bankruptcy in 1929, and it was saved only by a contribution from the British seamen's union.

From 1921 to 1926 the ISU faced competition once again from the wobblies, and barely had the union deflected that challenge, when a more formidable rival appeared in the Communist party, whose Marine Workers' Industrial Union* (MWIU) attracted many dedicated seamen. Both the wobblies and the communists were taking advantage of ISU's insistence on craft unions at a time when technology and the workers demanded an industrywide organization if unions were to survive. A major part if ISU's decline must be attributed to the nineteenth-century sailing ship mentality Furuseth imposed and to his rejection of alliances with any other workers' group. When the Big Strike* erupted on the West Coast in 1934, the ISU was caught totally surprised. Out of the 1934–1937 labor struggles a new generation of labor leaders emerged who only found resistance in the old ISU: when the new leaders gained control of the SUP, Furuseth went so far as to have it expelled from the ISU in 1936, in effect signing the death certificate for the federation, which had never existed before without its most powerful affiliate. Shortly after, Furuseth became too sick to take part in union affairs, but the remaining ISU officers failed to accept the new attitudes among the rank and file. In one of its rare direct takeovers of an affiliate, the American Federation of Labor intervened in late 1937 to revoke the charter of the defunct and bankrupt ISU and to create in its place a new successor union, the Seafarers' International Union* (SIU).

Principal Labor Leader

Andrew Furuseth   1899–1936

References: Arthur Emil Albrecht, *International Seamen's Union of America: A Study of Its History and Problems*, Bulletin of the Bureau of Labor Statistics, No. 342 (Washington, DC: Government Printing Office, 1932); CIO Files of John L. Lewis, Correspondence with CIO Unions, Microfilm, University Publications of America; Walter Galenson, *The CIO Challenge to the AFL: A History of the American Labor Movement, 1935–1941* (Cambridge: Harvard University Press, 1960); Bruce Nelson, *Workers on the Waterfront: Seamen, Longshoremen, and Unionism in the 1930s* (Urbana: University of Illinois Press, 1990); Stephen Schwartz, *Brotherhood of the Sea: A History of the Sailors' Union of the Pacific* (New Brunswick, NJ: Transaction Books, 1986); Hyman Weintraub, *Andrew Furuseth: Emancipator of the Seamen* (Berkeley: University of California Press, 1959).

INTERNATIONAL SHIPHOLDING CORPORATION. See Central Gulf Lines.

INTERSTATE COMMERCE COMMISSION (ICC), 1887–present. Congress created the Interstate Commerce Commission (ICC) in 1887 to regulate domestic surface transportation within the United States; nevertheless, in the early decades the ICC focused mainly on railroads. Because the ICC was concerned with transportation and because it was the first regulatory agency in U.S. history, the pressure to place ocean transportation under its jurisdiction grew to almost irresistible proportions. The Alexander Committee* of 1912–1914, after a thorough investigation of ocean conferences,* recommended that Congress grant the ICC full authority to regulate merchant shipping, but vigorous opposition from the shipowners delayed any legislation.

Lawsuits by the Department of Justice under the Sherman Antitrust Act of 1890 convinced the shipowners that they needed a regulatory agency to immunize the rate agreements of conferences from antitrust action. However, the Shipping Act of 1916* appeared to have deprived the ICC of any role, because the act assigned regulatory, as well as promotional, functions to the newly created Shipping Board* in 1916. The creation of a separate agency generally has been interpreted as a victory of shipowners over shippers,* but in reality the Shipping Board policed conference agreements closely and effectively, as the massive records of its Division of Regulation amply documented. The creation of over 200 new lines rather than regulation kept shippers happy during the

1920s, but as the number of lines drastically shrank by the early 1930s, shippers again felt unprotected and revived their earlier pleas to place regulation, their main defense against unfair rates, in the hands of the ICC.

The Franklin D. Roosevelt administration proposed the transfer of regulatory functions to the ICC, but when Congress passed the Merchant Marine Act of 1936,* it placed jurisdiction in a new agency, the U.S. Maritime Commission.* Shippers continued to lobby vigorously for at least partial protection, and in the Transportation Act of 1940 they managed to transfer jurisdiction over coastwise* and intercoastal* trade to the ICC. During World War II the War Shipping Administration* controlled coastwise and intercoastal trade, so not until after the abolishment of this agency in 1946 was the full impact of ICC jurisdiction felt. Normally beholden to the railroads, the ICC did not need merchant shipping for its bureaucratic survival, so that the agency became one more factor hastening the demise of domestic ocean transportation. The expansion of railroad and, later, truck traffic provided the ICC with more than ample cases to substitute those lost when coastwise and intercoastal traffic practically disappeared by the 1960s.

In two areas the ICC's jurisdiction has often overlapped with that of the Federal Maritime Commission* (FMC): the offshore domestic trades, particularly Hawaii and Puerto Rico, and, since the early 1970s, the intermodal* operations of ocean carriers, particularly the landbridge.* In 1992, Christopher Koch, the chairman of the FMC, proposed transferring jurisdiction over the offshore domestic trades to the ICC, but the opposition of Puerto Rican shippers, who preferred the more intensive scrutiny of the FMC, seemed to preclude such a transfer. The deregulation of the late 1970s made intermodal expansion easier, while the Shipping Act of 1984* granted such sweeping antitrust immunity to intermodal arrangements by ocean carriers that the ICC lost virtually all its remaining regulatory authority.

Antiregulatory fever reached such an extreme in 1981 that the Ronald Reagan administration proposed simply abolishing *both* the ICC and the FMC! However, not even the boldest of shippers seriously considered returning to the cutthroat competition of the nineteenth century, and the ICC survived. From the early to the late twentieth century the ongoing debate over the proper role of the ICC in ocean transportation has never found a satisfactory formula.

References: *American Shipper*, February 1981, March 1983, March 1992; Charles L. Dearing and Wilfred Owen, *National Transportation Policy* (Washington, DC: Brookings Institution, 1949); René De La Pedraja, *The Rise and Decline of U.S. Merchant Shipping in the Twentieth Century* (New York: Twayne, 1992); Samuel A. Lawrence, *United States Merchant Shipping Policies and Politics* (Washington, DC: Brookings Institution, 1966); Transportation Research Board, *Intermodal Marine Container Transportation: Impediments and Opportunities* (Washington, DC: National Research Council, 1992).

ISBRANDTSEN, HANS J., 7 September 1891–13 May 1953. Hans Isbrandtsen, the owner of Isbrandtsen Steamship Company,* had one of the most turbulent careers among steamship executives. He was born in Dragor, Denmark, on 7 September 1891 and came from a family strongly connected with the sea; his father, for example, was a shipowner. After completing education in the local schools, he soon began to work as a clerk in Danish shipping firms and also performed military service in the Danish navy. In 1915 he was already the manager of the steamers of Albert Jensen, and when the latter decided to transfer his fleet from Danish to U.S. registry,* he created a new firm, the American Transatlantic Company, and sent Isbrandtsen to New York City as its manager in 1915. The transactions for the transfer of the fleet were far from clear, and because the British suspected that American Transatlantic Company was little more than a German front, the company became the object of a tangled web of disputes between the United States and England, and thus from his first appearance on the American scene Isbrandtsen established the lifelong pattern of generally creating a storm of controversy around his activities.

The American Transatlantic Company was tremendously profitable, and although it was finally disbanded in 1918, Isbrandtsen's success convinced his cousin, Arnold P. Moller, to invest in the new firm of Hans Isbrandtsen, Inc. At a time when the Shipping Board* was creating over 200 new lines, Isbrandtsen concluded it was better for a foreigner to concentrate on operating warehouse and dock facilities as well as to expand his role as a merchant who bought and sold all types of commodities and cargoes. He increased his fortune and by the late 1920s felt that the ranks of new lines had thinned enough for him to enter safely, and consequently he created in a joint venture with his cousin, Moller, the Isbrandtsen Moller Steamship Company* (Ismolco) in 1928. Soon he was engaged in a bitter rate war against the members of the Far East Conference* and had become obsessed with destroying the conference* system at all costs; not surprisingly he earned a bad reputation among steamship executives, who resented his outsider* predatory tactics. The hostility died down on the eve of World War II, when there was enough cargo for all; however, sometime after the war began in 1939, he had a bitter clash with Moller, and the resulting vicious feud lasted until the end of his life.

Naturally Ismolco was dissolved, and in 1941 Isbrandtsen organized a new firm, the Isbrandtsen Steamship Company.* He had become a naturalized U.S. citizen in 1936 and now was ready to jump into merchant shipping as soon as surplus vessels became available after the war. Other companies delayed his application to purchase surplus vessels, but finally he bought ten vessels from the U.S. Maritime Commission* and gradually expanded his shipping routes until in 1949 he had established an eastward round-the-world* service from New York City via the Suez Canal. Isbrandtsen as usual managed to involve his ships in diplomatic complications, and blockade running, such as to Indonesia, became one of his favorite tactics. Although a very conservative individual, he angered conservatives by his insistence on continuing trade with communist China, because he felt that business, in the early nineteenth-century tradition, took precedence over ideological considerations.

He was determined as ever to destroy the conference system, and when the return of Japanese lines into world shipping triggered a rate war in 1952, Isbrandtsen jumped with enthusiasm in the battle against the Transpacific Freight Conference of Japan.* When U.S. companies introduced dual rates* as a way to compete against Isbrandtsen, he obtained injunctions, and the ensuing litigation culminated years later in the landmark Supreme Court decision in the *Isbrandtsen* case,* which outlawed dual-rate contracts. Meanwhile the conferences decided in March 1953 to suspend most of their common rates and to allow each company to quote whatever figures it thought best to challenge Isbrandtsen. Without knowing what their unpublished rates were, he could no longer know whether he was underquoting the other companies, and for the first time in his life he began to show losses. Realizing that he could compete against the conference system but not against individual companies that used his own tactics, he attempted to negotiate a solution, but it was too late, and in one of his last desperate trips to seek a way out, he suffered a heart attack and died on Wake Island on 13 May 1953. His son Jakob Isbrandtsen* took over as president and spent most of his steamship career trying to repair the damage his father had inflicted on the company.

A proponent of unbridled individualism who refused to accept the need for government or private institutions to guide and limit competitive forces, Hans Isbrandtsen did little more than raise havoc with U.S.-flag merchant shipping. His legacy was one of destruction, and by his constant undermining of the U.S.-flag shipping he contributed to its decline.

References: René De La Pedraja, *The Rise and Decline of U.S. Merchant Shipping in the Twentieth Century* (New York: Twayne, 1992); James Dugan, *American Viking: The Saga of Hans Isbrandtsen* (New York: Harper and Row, 1963); *National Cyclopedia of American Biography*, vol. 41.

ISBRANDTSEN, JAKOB, 1922–present. Jakob Isbrandtsen was the owner of the Isbrandtsen Steamship Company* in 1953–1962 and the head of American Export Lines* (AEL) in 1960–1971. Jakob was born in New York City in 1922; his father was the Danish immigrant Hans Isbrandtsen,* and his mother was an American. His father gave him a very strict and narrow upbringing. Hans refused to send Jakob to college and after graduation from high school put Jakob to work in the steamship company. It does not seem that Jakob's childhood was miserable, but his relentless exposure to the extremist and often contradictory positions of his father necessarily had to leave a mark on the son. World War II was a liberating experience for Jakob, who promptly volunteered to join the Coast Guard;* he eventually rose to become an officer and saw action in a number of attacks against islands in the Pacific Ocean.

The end of the war saw Jakob's return to the family business, and aware that one day he would inherit the steamship company, he tried to prepare himself. It is not known whether he disagreed with any of his father's business methods which, besides extremist were often anachronistic, and apparently the father, whose views were usually unchangeable, did not delegate any significant authority to his son. The unexpected death of Hans in Wake Island on 13 May 1953 caught Jakob apparently unprepared, and he did not end the rate war in the Pacific but let it continue until 1955, when the escalating losses finally forced him to abandon his father's campaign against conferences* and to seek an accommodation with other ocean carriers. As Jakob directly experienced the steamship business, the more he became convinced that his father's confrontational approach no longer earned profits and in any case was outmoded. He adopted what his father considered the ultimate heresy, namely, operation under government subsidies, but after thirty years of predatory tactics from his father, the steamship companies were not about to allow Jakob to bring Isbrandtsen Steamship Company under the operating differential* program of the Merchant Marine Act of 1936.* After years of battling, Jakob concluded that he would qualify for subsidies only if he purchased a company already authorized to receive subsidies. At this moment Josephine Bay Paul* had put up for sale her block of American Export Lines* (AEL) shares, and by playing counteroffers against Jakob, she was able to bid up the sale price.

Finally, on 3 October 1960 Jakob purchased the controlling interest of AEL, and in 1962 he obtained government approval to merge Isbrandtsen Steamship Company into AEL, a company that he wanted henceforth to be known as American Export Isbrandtsen Company, but in practice AEL remained the more usual name. To pay the high purchase price, Isbrandtsen had saddled AEL with a large debt, which only made worse the previous problems of that company. He felt that the only solution was to diversify away from shipping, and Isbrandtsen borrowed money to invest in other areas, in the hope that the profits from these new ventures would earn enough to pay off AEL's mounting debts. In 1964 he placed all his investments in a new holding company, American Export Industries, whose president he became. However, only when his new investments matured would they earn sizable profits, and meanwhile the subsidiary AEL remained the key to the success of the diversification, because he could meet the loan repayments only with income from merchant shipping.

Like other shipowners of the 1960s, Isbrandtsen faced the obstacle of vessel replacement, but he, more than anyone else, immediately realized the advantages not only of containers* but also of intermodalism.* Unfortunately for Isbrandtsen, the unsubsidized Sea-Land* claimed that the new container technology gave such a competitive edge to AEL that it no longer needed subsidies in the foreign trade routes and convinced in September 1969 the Maritime Subsidy Board* to halt government payments to AEL. For a company with a large debt burden and without subsidies it was impossible to introduce containerships and compete against foreign rivals, but Isbrandtsen was undaunted and made the fatal decision to push ahead.

As loan repayments continued to press upon the company, Isbrandtsen saw his field of action constantly reduced, and with creditors hounding at the door, the bankers removed him from the chairmanship of American Export Industries and from direct control of AEL in June 1971. He still remained the majority stockholder but could do little to stop the new management team from starting to sell off assets in order to meet the loan repayments. Meanwhile in 1974 he was charged with having siphoned off $20 million from Isbrandtsen Company, another corporation he had inherited from his father. His attempts to stop re-organization plans for AEL resulted only in delaying the inevitable, and finally in July 1977 American Export Industries and its subsidiary, AEL, filed for bankruptcy, ending whatever lingering hopes Isbrandtsen might still have harbored of ever returning to merchant shipping.

His woes were still not over, however, and the next year he found himself a victim of a scam involving stolen bonds, and only after a harrowing trial of two weeks and eight hours of deliberations by the jury was he declared innocent in July 1978. Since the late 1960s he had taken a very strong interest in the South Street Seaport Museum in Manhattan and in 1973 lent the money to acquire part of the land for the museum. As a trustee of the museum, he led the fight in 1985 to replace the chairman of the South Street Seaport Museum with an individual more attuned to preservation rather than to real estate matters.

References: René De La Pedraja, *The Rise and Decline of U.S. Merchant Shipping in the Twentieth Century* (New York: Twayne, 1992); James Dugan, *American Viking: The Sage of Hans Isbrandtsen* (New York: Harper and Row, 1963); *New York Times*, 27 July 1974, 1 April 1985; *Wall Street Journal*, 11 April, 11 July 1978.

ISBRANDTSEN CASE or *FEDERAL MARITIME BOARD V. ISBRANDTSEN*.

In this decision of 19 May 1958, the Supreme Court declared illegal dual-rate contracts* on the grounds that they violated antitrust laws as well as the prohibition in one clause of the Shipping Act of 1916.* The *Isbrandtsen* case ended once and for all the anomalous situation whereby the Shipping Board* and its successor agencies had used the very broad authority granted in the same law as an escape clause to tolerate dual-rate agreements. The somewhat conflicting clauses in the badly written Shipping Act of 1916 were partly responsible for this anomalous situation, but the urgent need to find some legal justification for dual-rate practices was the main driving force. Jakob Isbrandtsen* had developed a bitter and mortal hatred of all conferences,* and when they used dual-rates against him, he decided to challenge in court the doubtful legal validity of this practice.

By this decision the Supreme Court doomed dual-rates in the U.S. foreign trade, although they remained valid in the rest of the world. Congress gave a blanket amnesty to all U.S. steamship executives to avoid embarrassing prosecutions, but because of the revelations of the Celler Committee,* the 1961 amendments imposed additional restrictions on future dual-rate agreements. The Supreme Court itself, in the *Svenska** decision of 1968, made virtually impossible the approval of dual-rate contracts.

References: Advisory Commission on Conferences in Ocean Shipping, *Report to the President and the Congress* (Washington, DC: Government Printing Office, 1992); René De La Pedraja, *The Rise and Decline of U.S. Merchant Shipping in the Twentieth Century*

(New York: Twayne, 1992); Samuel A. Lawrence, *United States Merchant Shipping Policies and Politics* (Washington, DC: Brookings Institution, 1966).

ISBRANDTSEN-MOLLER STEAMSHIP COMPANY (ISMOLCO), 1928–1941. The Isbrandtsen-Moller Steamship Company was the first major steamship venture of Hans Isbrandtsen.* He had managed the American Transatlantic Company for the Danish shipowner Albert Jensen in 1915–1918, and after 1918 Isbrandtsen had concentrated on operating warehouse and dock facilities in New York City. With the profits he had accumulated, he set up with his cousin, Arnold P. Moller, owner of the Maersk Line, a joint venture called Isbrandtsen-Moller Steamship Company in 1928. Moller placed his old ships in this venture and accepted a promissory note from Isbrandtsen as his partner's share. Moller had graciously consented to offer very generous terms to his cousin as a way of increasing the cargo loadings; essentially Isbrandtsen had to make sure that the older ships of Maersk sailed with full cargoes from New York City to the Far East, but it was Moller's responsibility to do the same for the vessels during their return voyages from the Far East.

Isbrandtsen soon found that the old ships were too slow to attract much cargo, unless he quoted rates lower than those of the conferences.* When the Far East Conference* refused to accept his application to join unless he quoted the same rates as other conference members, Isbrandtsen developed a bitter and uncompromising hatred toward the entire conference system, which he attacked with crusading fervor for the rest of his life. His cousin Moller did not share this extremist view, so that the same ships of ISMOLCO were outside the conference when sailing westward from New York but returned eastward under the conference system. With the onset of the Great Depression competition for cargoes became keen, and in 1931 the outsider* tactics of Isbrandtsen had started a rate war that lasted until 1934. He made enough money to purchase more ships of his own to put in ISMOLCO's routes, but Moller failed to realize the change in status of Isbrandtsen, who had become a major shipowner in his own right. As a first sign of independence, Isbrandtsen created his own firm in 1939, the Isbrandtsen Steamship Company, to operate with new ships in areas not touched by ISMOLCO, whose management he carefully maintained. In 1940 upon the German invasion of Denmark, Isbrandtsen acted swiftly to save Danish ships, in particular, the Maersk vessels of his partner Moller, from seizure by the Germans. The Danish ships went on to become a sore diplomatic dispute whose solution was not settled until the 1950s, but somewhere during that episode a bitter clash erupted between the two cousins. In any case operation of IS-MOLCO had become impossible in the Far East because of the growing Japanese threat, but the clash between Isbrandtsen and Moller meant a bitter divorce to separate their assets in ISMOLCO when the latter was dissolved in 1941. Henceforth Isbrandtsen operated his ships out of the Isbrandtsen Steamship Company, but the permanent feud between both cousins remained a bitter legacy from the ISMOLCO venture.

References: René De La Pedraja, *The Rise and Decline of U.S. Merchant Shipping in the Twentieth Century* (New York: Twayne, 1992); James Dugan, *American Viking: The Saga of Hans Isbrandtsen* (New York: Harper and Row, 1963); *National Cyclopedia of American Biography*, vol. 41.

ISBRANDTSEN STEAMSHIP COMPANY, 1939–1962. The Isbrandtsen Steamship Company, established by maverick Hans Isbrandtsen,* was one of the largest unsubsidized U.S.-flag steamship companies in the United States. He established the company to serve other ports not covered by the Isbrandtsen-Moller Steamship Company* (ISMOLCO), the joint venture with his cousin, Arnold P. Moller. By late 1940 both had split up, and henceforth Isbrandtsen placed all his vessels in the Isbrandtsen Steamship Company. However, the new company did not operate for long, because with U.S. entry into World War II in December 1941, the company's five vessels were requisitioned by the government. In 1943 Isbrandtsen received vessels from the War Shipping Administration* (WSA) as one of over 100 operators under general agency agreements, but he was not able to resume commercial service until the return of peace.

Because of his vicious outsider* tactics during the rate war in the Pacific, Isbrandtsen faced serious opposition when he tried to buy surplus war vessels, but finally he purchased ten from the U.S. Maritime Commission,* and in 1947 he began sending his ships eastward from New York to Japan via the Suez Canal. In 1949 he instituted an eastern round-the-world* service and, along with the other U.S. steamship companies, made large profits hauling cargo to Japan while the Allied occupation of Japan lasted. However, Isbrandtsen was not satisfied and could not resist sending his ships to pick up cargoes in war-torn areas. The *Martin Berhman* was detained by Dutch warships during the Indonesian war for independence, while the *Flying Clipper* was involved in delivering explosives to Indochina via North Korea. Isbrandtsen also created many diplomatic incidents by his insistence on running the weak naval blockade the Nationalist Chinese had imposed upon communist China.

After the end of the Allied occupation of Japan, the competition for cargoes sharpened in the Far East, in particular, as the Japanese lines began a slow but determined reconstruction of their prewar fleets. A rate war broke out in 1952, and the Transpacific Freight Conference of Japan* vainly tried to stabilize conditions in the trade. As long as Isbrandtsen was making money, he was happy to see the wild competition continue, but when the Transpacific Freight Conference of Japan agreed in March 1953 to allow each company to set its own rates, Isbrandtsen Steamship Company began to lose money. He could compete against the conference system, but when other companies turned his own tactics against him, he had no choice but to seek an accommodation. The Japanese lines were considering making an arrangement, but his cousin, Moller, refused any compromise and wanted to settle his old scores with Isbrandtsen. In a desperate attempt to secure some sort of compromise, Isbrandtsen traveled across the Pacific, and when he stopped in Wake Island to change planes, he died of a heart attack on 13 May 1953.

His son Jakob now took over Isbrandtsen Steamship Company, but because his father had run affairs single-handedly for so long, the son took a long time to realize exactly what needed to be done to assure the survival of the company. Ending the rate war was a first step, and as losses continued to grow, in 1955 Jakob dropped the round-the-world service that had so antagonized other companies. However, the question of Japanese entry into the Pacific trade routes had not been settled, so the rate war dragged on until April 1958, further undermining the position of Isbrandtsen Steamship Company.

Jakob finally realized that his father's manner of operating was outmoded, and he applied for subsidies. So many companies had grudges against his father that they successfully blocked his applications, so that Jakob concluded that only by buying a company that already received subsidies would Isbrandtsen Steamship Company ever receive subsidies. In 1960 Josephine Bay Paul* wanted to sell her majority stockholdings in American Export Lines* (AEL), and Jakob, without any other apparent choice, was forced to raise his bid to compete against other offers for Paul's stock. The sale took place on 3 October 1960, but not until 1962 did the Maritime Administration* approve the merger of the Isbrandtsen Steamship Company into the new American Export Isbrandtsen Steamship Company, which, however, continued generally to be known as AEL. Jakob saddled AEL with the large loan he had taken out to pay for the purchase of Paul's stock, and this large burden placed AEL under serious strains.

References: René De La Pedraja, *The Rise and Decline of U.S. Merchant Shipping in the Twentieth Century* (New York: Twayne, 1992); James Dugan, *American Viking: The Saga of Hans Isbrandtsen* (New York: Harper and Row, 1963); *National Cyclopedia of American Biography*, vol. 41.

ISTHMIAN LINE, 1910–1956. The U.S. Steel Corporation owned the Isthmian Line, whose primary purpose was to carry the steel cargoes of the parent company. U.S. Steel organized Isthmian in London in 1910 to operate under the British flag its own vessels and others it chartered* as needed; the name was chosen in honor of the Panama Canal, whose inauguration in 1914 was expected to open opportunities to the new line. During its first years Isthmian operated more like a collection of tramp* vessels, because as a proprietary company,* vessels sailed to one port or another anywhere in the world where steel had to be carried. Isthmian Line was in reality the creation of James A. Farrell, Sr., the chief of the export subsidiary of U.S. Steel, who ahead of anyone else had realized that the key to steel exports lay in providing cheap and reliable ocean transportation. Farrell himself was later promoted to president of U.S. Steel, and from that position, which he occupied for decades, he continued to support the activities of the Isthmian Line.

When World War I broke out, Isthmian transferred its ships to U.S. registry,* but these were subsequently requisitioned by the U.S. government. During

World War I U.S. Steel established at the government's request huge shipyards, and after it had completed all the orders for the Shipping Board,* decided to build in its own shipyards and at its own cost a fleet of twenty-seven freighters for the Isthmian Line. Even this large number of vessels was not sufficient, and frequently the line chartered vessels as needed to meet all the needs of the parent company. Since the 1920s the Isthmian Line concentrated on providing regular sailings on established routes throughout the world but could still run tramp voyages to take a shipload of steel to some port. What made the line noteworthy was that in a period of massive subsidies from the Shipping Board, Isthmian Line operated successfully without the need for subsidies and was strong enough to engage in rate wars, for example, in the trade route between New York and India.

The War Shipping Administration* requisitioned the ships of the Isthmian Line during World War II, and after the return of peace Isthmian purchased as replacements twenty-four surplus C-3s.* The company earned high profits until the postwar shipping boom ended in 1948, and as rates collapsed, Isthmian found its profits shrinking. In a momentous decision, Isthmian applied for the first time in its history for subsidies in 1950, but even when awarded, these did not end the company's problems, and as one observer commented in 1951, "All is not well with the Isthmian Line" (*Ships and Sailing*, January 1951). The parent company was having serious doubts about keeping its fleet, partly because steel cargoes were declining as other countries set up their own steel mills and started to supply nearby countries as well. As a further embarrassment, the president of Isthmian Line was found by the New York State Crime Commission to have received a $10,000 gift from a mob-ridden stevedoring firm in 1953, and although he promptly resigned, the morale of the subsidiary necessarily was affected. U.S. Steel began looking for a buyer for its fleet, but several years passed until at last States Marine Corporation* purchased Isthmian in March 1956. States Marine kept alive the Isthmian name of its subsidiary for at least ten years, but it now formed an integral part of the new parent company's operations. There was no doubt that U.S. Steel made a good business decision in disposing of its obsolete fleet and thereby avoided altogether the problem of replacing its break-bulk* vessels with new containerships.

Principal Executive

John McAuliffe   1930–1947

References: Robert G. Albion, *Seaports South of Sahara: The Achievements of an American Steamship Company* (New York: Appleton-Century Crofts, 1959); René De La Pedraja, *The Rise and Decline of U.S. Merchant Shipping in the Twentieth Century* (New York: Twayne, 1992); *New York Times*, 17 December 1952, 11 February 1953, March 7, 1956; *Pacific Shipper*, 19 March 1956; *Ships and Sailing*, January 1951; U.S. Senate, Committee on Interstate and Foreign Commerce, *Merchant Marine Study and Investigation*, vol. 2 (Washington, DC: Government Printing Office, 1950); *U.S. Steel News*, January 1937; *Who Was Who*, vol. 4.

J

JAPAN-ATLANTIC & GULF CONFERENCE (JAG) and TRANS-PACIFIC FREIGHT CONFERENCE OF JAPAN (TPFCJ), 1926–present.
The two conferences,* Transpacific Freight Conference of Japan (TPFCJ) and Japan-Atlantic & Gulf Conference (JAG), both reorganized in 1926, have set rates and sailings for the trade moving eastward from Japan to the United States. Throughout their history, these two conferences have acted as one; for example, the same annual owners' meeting served for both, and often they shared the same staff. The merger of both into a single conference has been proposed occasionally, but more remarkable has been their failure to combine even after the Shipping Act of 1984* provided ample encouragement to create superconferences* in nearly all the trade routes of the United States.

Just as the United States has imposed since 1916 its regulatory framework upon ocean conferences, so Japan has insisted upon the existence of these two separate conferences. The pre–World War II situation was instructive: while the Japanese lines frequently preferred to operate outside the Far East Conference* (FEC) and the Pacific Westbound Conference* (PWC) in the trade coming from the United States, for eastbound cargoes the Japanese lines worked tightly within the conference system until they had virtually taken over the JAG and the TPFCJ by 1940. The close-knit links between Japanese shippers* and lines brought favorable results for the JAG and the TPFCJ, which were able to repulse the attempts by Hans Isbrandtsen* to enter the trade. Instead the divided American shippers and lines in the FEC and the PWC suffered tremendous instability because of Isbrandtsen's raids.

By 1940 the JAG and the TPFCJ had become largely superfluous as the whole Pacific area sank into World War II. Once the conflict was over the two conferences were reconstituted, but they really did not resume full activities until the U.S. occupation of Japan ended in 1951. Four Japanese lines began operations that year, followed by four more in 1952, but, because almost the entire Japanese merchant marine had been sunk during the war, initially they held a minority position within the two conferences. Without an effective Japanese control over JAG and TPFCJ, the door was open for Isbrandtsen to return and initiate one of the most bitter rate wars in the Pacific. The rate war finally ended in 1957 and convinced the Japanese that the U.S. regulatory system was incapable of maintaining order and stability in the eastbound trades, which were fundamental for Japan's campaign to become a world exporter.

Low rates were also important for Japan's export strategy; as late as 1967, rates still had not regained their pre-1953 level, and the Japanese lines agreed to raise them only when the stability of the trade was threatened. For example, in 1970–1971, when American President Lines,* Sea-Land,* and States Marine Corporation* operated as outsiders,* the JAG and the TPFCJ agreed to raise rates to restore order to the trade route. The Korean lines by 1974 had placed Korea under the jurisdiction of both conferences, which were then known as the Transpacific Freight Conference of Japan/Korea and the Japan/Korea Atlantic and Gulf Conference until 1985, when the Korean lines transferred jurisdiction to the Asia North America Rate Agreement* (ANERA). During the 1970s both the U.S. and Japanese lines sought to strengthen the two conferences against the vicious price-cutting by the Far Eastern Shipping Co. of the Soviet Union (FESCO), which was determined to earn hard currency by offering rates below operating costs. While the tight links in Japan among shippers, lines, and the government withstood the FESCO challenge, the U.S. lines saw the regulatory provisions fail miserably, and as a partial remedy, the U.S. Congress passed the Controlled Carriers Act of 1978,* giving broad power to the Federal Maritime Commission* (FMC) to take reprisals.

Before the FMC could apply the Controlled Carriers Act, FESCO diminished its sailings even before 1981, when the United States banned all Soviet ships from U.S. ports in response to the communist crackdown in Poland and the continuing occupation of Afghanistan. When Sea-Land withdrew in 1980, the JAG and the TPFCJ faced a new rate war, which ended only in 1983; one of Sea-Land's reasons for withdrawing had been to escape the block voting by the Japanese lines that refused to accept changes in the conference arrangements. Even after the return of Sea-Land to the fold in 1983, on the average Japanese lines were lifting around 60 percent of the conference cargo moving eastward, and to maintain their majority control over these two conferences, the Japanese did not consolidate them after the passage of the Shipping Act of 1984 into a superconference. For the Japanese lines, full control over two separate conferences was the best way to guarantee Japan's export strategy in the long run. The risks of takeover or destruction of either conference were minimized, while they closely coordinated their actions and followed the same policies with regard to the service contracts* authorized by the Shipping Act of 1984.

References: Advisory Commission on Conferences in Ocean Shipping, *Report to the President and the Congress* (Washington, DC: Government Printing Office, 1992); *American Shipper*, May 1974, December 1976, June 1977, October 1980, January 1983; René De La Pedraja, *The Rise and Decline of U.S. Merchant Shipping in the Twentieth Century* (New York: Twayne, 1992); Federal Maritime Commission, *Section 18 Report on the Shipping Act of 1984*, September 1989; Official File, Dwight D. Eisenhower Presidential Library, Abilene, Kansas; Federal Maritime Board, *Decisions*, vol. 4 (Washington, DC: Government Printing Office, 1963); Transpacific Westbound Rate Agreement records, San Francisco National Maritime Museum.

JOB ACTION. A job action or work stoppage occurred when maritime union workers—in spite of existing contracts—refused to work or threatened to stop working just when the vessel was about to sail. This was a practice dating back to the nineteenth century, when it was called "the oracle." In some extreme cases the job action became a "wildcat strike," or one not approved by the union leadership, but generally job action managed to avert illegal situations. Job action was particularly prevalent in the late 1930s as the maritime unions, particularly on the West Coast, strove to consolidate and expand gains like the union hiring hall.* After World War II, union leaders used job action against a single vessel or company as a way to demonstrate their power and to impose one-sided interpretations about the existing contracts. Job action soon degenerated into a weapon to keep out members of rival labor unions. Most job actions were quickly settled by a management that could not afford to have ships delayed for even two days, because that spelled the difference between a profitable voyage and large losses. As the number of U.S.-flag ships dwindled since the 1960s, job action gradually became a useless tactic.

References: Joseph H. Ball, *The Government-Subsidized Union Monopoly* (Washington, DC: Labor Policy Association, 1966); Charles P. Larrowe, *Harry Bridges: The Rise and Fall of Radical Labor in the U.S.* (New York: Lawrence Hill, 1972); Stephen Schwartz, *Brotherhood of the Sea: A History of the Sailors' Union of the Pacific, 1885–1985* (New Brunswick, NJ: Transaction Books, 1986).

JOHNSEN, NIELS F., 29 April 1895–1974. Niels F. Johnsen was the founder and first president of the Central Gulf Lines.* He was born on 29 April 1895 in Larvick, Norway, and after completing his education in his native country, he began work as a chartering clerk, eventually becoming an agent in New Orleans, where he settled and married a member of a prominent Louisiana family. In 1936 he began working for the States Marine Corporation,* eventually serving as one of its vice presidents in 1945–1956. His real interests, however, were in the first ship he had bought for the Central Gulf Steamship Corporation,* which he founded in April 1947. Gradually he expanded his fleet, and later with the help of his two sons, Erik and Niels W. Johnsen,* the father established on very secure grounds Central Gulf Lines as a U.S.-flag company that specialized in liner* service to the Red Sea, the Persian Gulf, and the Indian subcontinent.

By the late 1960s he gradually handed over control of the company to his two sons. He died in 1974.

References: International Shipholding Corporation, *Annual Report*, 1987; *The Story of Louisiana*, vol. 2 (New Orleans: J. F. Hyer, 1960).

JOHNSEN, NIELS W., 9 May 1922–present, and ERIK F., 17 August 1925– present. The Johnsen brothers formed a very successful management team, which replaced their Norwegian immigrant father, Niels E. Johnsen,* in the running of Central Gulf Lines.* Both Erik and Niels W. were born in New Orleans, and they attended Tulane University. They both served in different capacities during World War II, and with the end of the conflict, Erik finished his education at Tulane, while Niels began working as vice president of States Marine Corporation* in 1946 along with his father. Niels had been working with his father at Central Gulf Lines since its establishment in 1947, and Erik joined the firm in 1952. In the 1960s, as the father gradually withdrew from active involvement in the affairs of the company, Niels W. and Erik formed a splendid management team, which guided Central Gulf Lines into numerous successful ventures. Among other noteworthy accomplishments, they not only initiated LASH* service but were among the few companies to have mastered this demanding new technology. Niels and Erik have not limited themselves to the U.S.-flag operations of Central Gulf Lines but have also entered through the International Shipholding Corporation into the ownership of foreign-flag ships; this complementary mix of foreign and U.S. registry* has been a major reason for their continued success.

References: *American Shipper*, September 1978, March 1990; International Shipholding Corporation, *Annual Reports*, 1987, 1990; *Who's Who in America*, 1990–1993.

JOHNSON, NICHOLAS, 1934–present. Nicholas Johnson was the head of the Maritime Administration* (MARAD) in 1964–1966, and his tenure in office represented a last effort to overhaul government policies toward U.S. merchant shipping. Johnson was born in 1934 and was an attorney who had been a law clerk for Hugo Black, a justice on the Supreme Court. Johnson was teaching law at the University of California at Berkeley, but before settling down to the academic world, he decided to take a two-year leave of absence to acquire some real practice at the prestigious law firm of Covington and Burling. President Lyndon B. Johnson (no relation to Nicholas) routinely searched this law firm to find suitable candidates for government positions and discovered Nicholas Johnson. Nicholas had never before heard about MARAD, so although he did not hide his lack of interest in the position, the fact that all other possible candidates flatly refused to even consider an appointment to MARAD left the road wide open for Nicholas, who accepted the position without really knowing what he was getting into.

After quick Senate confirmation Johnson was sworn in as maritime administrator on 2 March 1964. During his years in office, he concentrated on two main issues. Because U.S.-flag shipping continued to decline, the need to revise government polices was evident, and Johnson developed new approaches to reduce subsidies and increase the productivity of the maritime industry. He quickly ran into a solid block of opposition from the subsidized companies, organized labor, business groups, the trade press, the admiralty lawyers, congressional backers, and others: "Any time you have tremendous financial stakes, involving millions of dollars for industries or for individual companies, a sub-government is formed, which takes over the policy formulation process from the President and from the Congress and holds it unto itself" (Nicholas Johnson Oral History). After two years of task forces, meetings, and planning sessions, all that Johnson attained was "complete frustration concerning the possibility of realizing his objective of decreasing shipping subsidies and decreasing union requirements on shipping" (ibid.).

Johnson's second attempt was to discover "whether it is possible to take an old-line agency that's somewhat less vibrant than such an assemblage of human beings might be, and breathe some life back into it" (ibid.). He experimented very successfully with all types of administrative techniques to improve the morale and quality of personnel at MARAD. Among the most important changes was his decision to keep MARAD employees more distant from the representatives of the maritime industry; Johnson considered this a matter of ethics and halted the wining and dining of MARAD employees by labor and business groups, although it was a constant uphill battle to keep the cozy arrangements of the "sub-government" from returning with greater vigor. This particular reform did not prove lasting, and already in 1971 another administrator, Andrew E. Gibson,* created the National Maritime Council* (NMC) to put MARAD employees in permanent and almost daily contact with maritime representatives. Johnson himself, although proud of his efforts to restore professionalism to MARAD, regretfully concluded that the attempt to breathe life to an old institution "requires such an extraordinary expenditure of human energy and time that it's not really worth it" (ibid.). Instead from his MARAD experience he concluded that "it's better simply to abolish it and create a new agency, which is what we intended to do" (ibid.).

By May 1966 Johnson felt that "he has served the purpose of being the center of controversy over maritime policy and that his usefulness in that regard is ending" (ibid.). Berkeley wanted him back to his old teaching post, and he gave notice of his intention to resign and end what "was really a weird experience" (ibid.). President Johnson, however, wished to retain young officials in the government to show that reform was possible within the system and convinced Nicholas to become a commissioner of the Federal Communications Commission on 18 June 1966. There was no doubt that a blind and rigid maritime industry, which still refused to accept containers,* had failed to realize that Nicholas Johnson's tour through MARAD was a last chance to save the rapidly declining U.S.-flag merchant shipping.

References: Confidential File, Lyndon B. Johnson Presidential Library, Austin, Texas; Samuel A. Lawrence, *United States Merchant Shipping Policies and Politics* (Washington, DC: Brookings Institution, 1966); Nicholas Johnson Oral History, Lyndon B. Johnson Presidential Library, Austin, Texas.

JONES, WALTER BEAMAN, 19 August 1913–15 September 1992. Walter B. Jones was chairman of the Merchant Marine and Fisheries Committee* in 1981–1992 and formed with Joshua Alexander, Schuyler Otis Bland,* and Herbert C. Bonner* the group of congressmen who had the greatest impact on the merchant marine during the twentieth century. Jones was born on 19 August 1913 in Fayetteville, North Carolina, where he attended public schools. He graduated from North Carolina State University in 1934 and afterward ran a local office supply business. In 1949–1953 he served as the mayor of his hometown; afterward he occasionally was elected to the North Carolina legislature. In 1966 he won the special election to fill the vacancy in the local congressional district caused by Bonner's death, and until September 1992 Jones remained continuously a member of Congress.

His district borders on the sea, and he harbored the aim to become chairman of the Merchant Marine and Fisheries Committee, the position Bonner had held for many years. In 1981 Jones became the chairman of that committee, and his first task was to try to regain respect for the committee, whose prestige had suffered badly because of the scandals and allegations concerning committee members. Soon Jones, in spite of his own bouts with disease, put the committee back on track and obtained his greatest achievement with the Shipping Act of 1984,* whose passage, "given the surrounding tempest" he felt was "somewhat of a minor miracle that a very successful law emerged" (Advisory Commission 1992). To keep Congress from abolishing the Merchant Marine and Fisheries Committee, he correctly emphasized environmental issues as a way to give the old committee a new mission for the future. When the *Exxon Valdez** oil spill occurred, the committee received some rare media publicity and was able to obtain easy passage for the Oil Pollution Act* (OPA), which unfortunately placed a tremendous burden on tanker companies. In 1991 Jones announced his retirement from Congress once his term expired in January 1993, but he died in Washington, D.C. on 15 September 1992, and "just four days before his death" (*American Shipper*, October 1992) he had asked Gerry Studds to assume the duties of chairman. Clearly Jones during his long tenure at the Merchant Marine and Fisheries Committee had a great impact on ocean transportation, and it remains to see who will carry on after him with the tremendous challenge of trying to maintain alive the U.S.-flag merchant marine.

References: Advisory Commission on Conferences in Ocean Shipping, *Report to the President and the Congress* (Washington, DC: Government Printing Office, 1992); *American Shipper*, October 1992; Michael Barone and Grant Ujifusa, *The Almanac of American Politics 1992* (Washington, DC: National Journal, 1991); U.S. Congress,

Biographical Directory of the United States Congress, 1774–1989 (Washington, DC: Government Printing Office, 1989).

JONES, WESLEY L., 9 October 1863–19 November 1932. Wesley L. Jones, the Republican senator from Washington, was the most passionate defender of the U.S. merchant marine in the Senate in the twentieth century. He was born on a farm near Bethany, Illinois, on 9 October 1863 and graduated from Southern Illinois College in 1885. The next year he was admitted to the bar, but his law practice had little success, and he moved to Washington state in 1889, and in 1917 he made Seattle his permanent residence. Already in Illinois he had made speeches for Republican presidential candidates, and he pursued politics eagerly in his adopted state of Washington. He was elected to the House of Representatives in 1898 and to the Senate in 1909, and he remained in the upper chamber until the end of his life.

He had taken an early interest in the merchant marine, and from 1919 to 1930 he was chairman of the Commerce Committee,* from which position he strongly supported the expansion of U.S.-flag shipping services. His first big measure was the Merchant Marine Act of 1920, often known as the Jones Act,* which if fully implemented, would have driven all foreign ships away from U.S. ports. Jones's fanatical support for a subsidized and privately owned merchant marine was shared by Admiral William S. Benson,* the chairman of the Shipping Board,* but opposition from shippers* and foreign governments left unenforced key clauses of the Jones Act, although the principal provisions on cabotage* were implemented.

Jones returned to the offensive for merchant shipping by passing through Congress the Merchant Marine Act of 1928,* which lavished generous mail subsidies on private steamship companies. The inevitable result was extravagance and waste on the part of private operators, and the act, initially known as the Jones-White Act, soon was recognized as a failure and a horrendous waste of taxpayers' money to favor a privileged few. Jones tried to distance himself from the Merchant Marine Act of 1928, and he hoped that his extreme support for Prohibition* would still win him one more senatorial, term, but the uproar over the ocean mail subsidies was too great, and he lost the election of 1932. The defeat was a shattering blow to a person like him, who was an inveterate workaholic and lacked any other entertainments or diversions. He continued to overwork himself with his last duties as senator, and he postponed a necessary operation, with the result that he died on 19 November 1932, apparently unable to visualize a life outside the Senate. His death deprived merchant shipping of its most effective voice in the Senate, and not until another senator from Washington, Warren G. Magnuson,* rose to prominence did the U.S. merchant marine find a comparable advocate.

References: René De La Pedraja, *The Rise and Decline of U.S. Merchant Shipping in the Twentieth Century* (New York: Twayne, 1992); *Dictionary of American Biography*, Suppl. 1; Jeffrey J. Safford, *Wilsonian Maritime Diplomacy, 1913–1921* (New Brunswick, NJ: Rutgers University Press, 1978); Paul M. Zeis, *American Shipping Policy* (Princeton, NJ: Princeton University Press, 1938).

JONES ACT or MERCHANT MARINE ACT OF 1920. The Jones Act of 5 June 1920, named after Republican senator Wesley Jones,* who rammed the bill through Congress without any debate, has been the popular term used to refer to the section of the Merchant Marine Act of 1920, which reserves the coastwise* and intercoastal* trade to U.S.-flag vessels built in the United States and owned by American citizens, although in reality the act covered other issues and generally sought to amend or complement the earlier Shipping Act of 1916.* The Jones Act reaffirmed the cabotage* privilege in existence since 1817, which had been suspended briefly only during World War I. The cabotage restrictions were extended to smaller territories like Guam, but opposition from shippers in the Philippines prevented the exclusion of foreign-flag ships from the trade of that archipelago. The federal government received the authority to suspend the act in times of emergency but in practice has granted only individual, temporary waivers, while separate legislation did allow American subsidiaries of foreign corporations to operate U.S.-built and manned vessels in the coastwise and intercoastal trades. Since the 1980s, shippers* have pressured for the repeal of the Jones Act in order that they could take advantage of the low rates offered by foreign steamship companies.

The Jones Act, in another of its lasting provisions, established the American Bureau of Shipping* (ABS) as the only official classification* society for all government agencies. The Jones Act also increased the number of commissioners in the Shipping Board from five to seven, and its chairman was now appointed by the president and not just elected by fellow board members, as had previously been the case. The Jones Act also strengthened the regulatory provisions already present in the Shipping Act of 1916. Another pending issue was the disposition of wartime surplus vessels, and here the Jones Act ratified the policy the Shipping Board had been following, in particular, that of giving preference to citizens of local communities who wished to establish their own lines. Looking toward the future replacement of vessels, the Jones Act established a Construction Loan Fund to stimulate shipbuilding in the United States.

The reason the Jones Act has been largely remembered as a cabotage* law was that its two most controversial provisions—preferential rail rates for cargoes carried on U.S.-flag ships and higher customs duties for cargoes traveling in vessels of foreign flags—never went into effect because of massive opposition from shippers* and foreign governments. The Jones Act or Merchant Marine Act of 1920 has been correctly referred to as an attempt to introduce the mercantilist principles of the seventeenth century into the task of creating and maintaining a strong U.S.-flag fleet in the twentieth century, but in practice the act gave the Shipping Board few new tools to try to promote and defend the American merchant marine.

References: Ernst G. Frankel, *Regulations and Policies of American Shipping* (Boston: Auburn House, 1982); Gerald R. Jantscher, *Bread upon the Water: Federal Aids to Maritime Industries* (Washington, DC: Brookings Institution, 1975); Jeffrey J. Safford, *Wilsonian Maritime Diplomacy, 1913–1921* (New Brunswick, NJ: Rutgers University Press, 1978); *U.S. Statutes at Large*, vol. 41; Clinton H. Whitehurst, Jr., *The U.S. Shipbuilding Industry: Past, Present, and Future* (Annapolis, MD: Naval Institute Press, 1986); Paul M. Zeis, *American Shipping Policy* (Princeton, NJ: Princeton University Press, 1938).

K

KEEFE, DANIEL JOSEPH, 27 September 1852–2 January 1929. Dan Keefe was the founder and first president of the International Longshoremen's Association* (ILA). Of Irish ancestry, he was born near Chicago on 27 September 1852 and finished only fourth grade in school. He began to work unloading lumber, and soon he had organized the workers on the Chicago waterfront, with himself as their leader, in 1882. Longshoremen locals spread throughout the Great Lakes, and to shape a common policy, they founded the ILA in Detroit in 1892.

The conservative Keefe, who always voted for the Republican party, was the recognized leader of the ILA during its first fifteen years. Keefe ruled the union like a dictator and demanded absolute compliance from the locals. He was a shrewd negotiator with the employers, and because he shared their conservative views, he was able to obtain modest concessions for the longshoremen. However, the benefits were often evident only to Keefe, and his performance smacked of company unionism, a less serious charge at that time because employers had repeatedly smashed defiant unions in New York City and other ports.

By 1908 Keefe was undistinguishable from the employers in dress and manners; the slim, trim boy of youth was now an obese figure and one of the first labor leaders to adopt ''tuxedo unionism.''* In 1908 he split with the American Federation of Labor when he refused to endorse the Democratic party candidate for president and instead backed William H. Taft, the Republican candidate. An upheaval was imminent within the ILA, and Keefe wisely decided to step down and accepted the post of commissioner-general of immigration on 1 December 1908.

Keefe realized after a few years that his job lacked any real decision-making power and finally resigned in 1913; during World War I he held a post within the Department of Labor. In 1921 he returned to maritime affairs as a labor disputes mediator for the Shipping Board.* He retired in 1925 and died in Illinois on 2 January 1929. His career served as a warning to future leaders that federal government jobs could not compare with union posts in power, duration, or income.

References: *Dictionary of American Biography*, vol. 10; Gary M. Fink, ed., *Biographical Dictionary of American Labor*, 2d ed. (Westport, CT: Greenwood Press, 1984); Maud Russell, *Men Along the Shore: The ILA and Its History* (New York: Brussel and Brussel, 1966).

KENNEDY, JOSEPH P., 6 September 1888–8 November 1969. Joseph P. Kennedy was the first chairman of the U.S. Maritime Commission,* and although he was best remembered as the father of President John F. Kennedy, as well as of Robert and Edward, his brief tenure in the U.S. Maritime Commission had a profound impact on merchant shipping. Joseph P. Kennedy was born on 6 September 1888 in Boston of Irish ancestors, and he soon became a wealthy businessman who, however, aspired to a wider political role for himself and his sons. He served a very successful term as chairman of the Securities and Exchange Commission prior to taking office on 19 April 1937 as the first chairman of the U.S. Maritime Commission. He had not been the first choice, and President Franklin D. Roosevelt had struggled for months to find a competent executive who would accept the job. The hesitation of many candidates was easy to understand: the Merchant Marine Act of 1936,* which had created the commission, had also imposed a 1 July deadline for the cancellation of the mail contracts granted under the Merchant Marine Act of 1928.* The holders of the contracts could be expected to file successful claims against what clearly was an ex post facto law, but then Kennedy was ready to file counterclaims because the private companies had committed gross abuses and other violations, including wasting large sums of money, under the mail contracts.

A sensible agreement between both parties seemed mutually advisable to avoid fruitless litigation, and in a burst of activity Kennedy settled the mail contracts at 1 percent of the value of the claims. He now awarded the operating differential subsidies* to about fifteen of the largest merchant shipping companies that he felt would be best able to withstand foreign competition. His accomplishment was considered near miraculous, yet when he realized that even under the new subsidy policy government funds were financing private profits, his earlier enthusiasm for private steamship companies waned. By the end of his term he had become a reluctant supporter of government ownership of shipping lines. In the specific case of the Dollar Line,* he had begun the process by which that bankrupt company, later renamed the American President Lines* (APL), passed under government ownership.

On the labor front, Kennedy clashed with the National Maritime Union* (NMU) over shipboard discipline, and he made his point forcefully in the *Algic** case. It seemed that every day a new complication arose in the merchant marine, and a tired Kennedy was talking about leaving this frustrating job already in late 1937. In any case, the chairmanship of the U.S. Maritime Commission had been for him only a temporary step until he obtained a more prestigious position. To his great pleasure, Roosevelt appointed him ambassador to Great Britain in February 1938, and Admiral Emory S. Land* succeeded him as chairman. During his tenure of barely ten months, Kennedy had concluded correctly that the Merchant Marine Act of 1936 was unworkable and should be repealed. However, his very own diligence in managing to put into force the provisions of that act made many believe that the operating differential subsidy program was workable, when in fact it insidiously undermined U.S.-flag merchant shipping companies during the rest of the twentieth century.

References: Michael R. Beschloss, *Kennedy and Roosevelt* (New York: Norton, 1980); René De La Pedraja, *The Rise and Decline of U.S. Merchant Shipping in the Twentieth Century* (New York: Twayne, 1992); Richard J. Whalen, *The Founding Father: The Story of Joseph P. Kennedy* (New York: New American Library, 1964).

KILLION, GEORGE, 15 April 1901–1980s? George Killion was the president of American President Lines* (APL) in 1947–1966. He was born in Steamboat Springs, Colorado, on 15 April 1901 and attended the University of Southern California and the University of California in 1921–1922. He worked for newspapers from 1922 until 1930, when he opened his own public relations firm in Oakland, which became his permanent residence. Killion, although a Democrat, held very conservative views; for example, he stated, ''I've often wondered if this wouldn't have been a better world if Mr. Hoover had been reelected to the presidency'' (Killion, Oral History). He worked at various public relations jobs until 1939, when his friendship with the new Democratic governor of California, Culbert L. Olson, brought him appointments to state government positions until the defeat of Governor Olson for reelection in 1942 by the Republican Earl Warren. Killion decided to perform wartime service and was commissioned a major; later he was assigned as assistant to Ralph K. Davies in the Petroleum Administration of the Interior Department. In 1944 Killion returned to civilian duties in the Democratic National Committee, whose treasurer he became in May 1945. By then Killion had seen enough of Washington, D.C., and wanted to return to California, and when Davies suggested that Killion seek the presidency of APL, after careful lobbying he secured his election to the presidency of APL in August 1947, elbowing out the in-house candidate, E. Russell Lutz, who had been supported by the outgoing president, Henry F. Grady.

For Davies, Killion was one of the pieces in the ongoing complex chess game to gradually acquire APL from the government. Davies was positioning himself to personally profit from the antigovernment conservative winds blowing after World War II, and his perseverance paid off when the long *Dollar Line* case* culminated on 29 October 1952 with his winning bid that gained for Davies ownership of APL. As a reward for Killion's constant help in undermining government ownership and bringing the coveted prize within Davies's reach, Killion remained as president of APL and with his conservative views made effortlessly the transition from government to private enterprise.

The lengthy maneuvers to acquire APL did not give way to bold aggressive management under private ownership. Even before the transfer, Killion had removed E. Russell Lutz, the shipping expert, from the management of the company, and the resulting vacuum in leadership was never quite filled. In the information handouts the press reproduced, Killion awarded himself high marks as a company executive, but in reality he soon had lost interest in the affairs of APL except for government and public relations. Davies himself, who devoted the majority of his time to his separate oil business, alternated between intervening in the affairs of APL and leaving Killion a free hand; quite naturally the company drifted, missed opportunities, and even committed blunders.

Davies, out of gratitude for Killion's help in the acquisition of APL, did not want to remove him as president, while the latter's political connections continued to be useful for the subsidized company. When the profits of APL started to decline in the 1960s, Killion himself devoted most of his time to the movie industry, eventually becoming a director of Metro-Goldwyn-Mayer. Davies, who did not change his own management style, the real cause of APL's problems, finally accepted the need to remove Killion as president in 1966. After Killion stepped down from the presidency, his career faded from national view, and he dropped into relative obscurity.

References: *Current Biography 1952*; George Killion, Oral History Interview, 1970, Herbert Hoover Presidential Library, West Branch, Iowa; *National Cyclopedia of American Biography*, vol. H; *New York Times*, 13 August 1947; John Niven, *The American President Lines and Its Forebears, 1848–1984* (Newark: University of Delaware Press, 1987).

KIRKLAND, JOSEPH LANE, 12 March 1922–present. Joseph L. Kirkland, who served in merchant ships during World War II, became in 1979 the president of the American Federation of Labor-Congress of Industrial Organizations (AFL-CIO), the highest labor position ever attained by a former member of the merchant marine. Kirkland, who was born in Camden, South Carolina, on 12 March 1922, graduated from the accelerated program at the Merchant Marine Academy* in 1942 and subsequently received his master's license. During 1941–1946, while he was a member of the Masters, Mates and Pilots Organization,* he acquired invaluable experience about rank-and-file concerns. In 1946 to complete his college education, he worked during the day drafting maps for the navy and took evening classes at Georgetown University. He earned a B.S. degree from the School of Foreign Service in 1948, but he did not begin a diplomatic career; instead he joined that same year the research staff of the American Federation of Labor (AFL). Because of his extraordinary speaking and writing abilities, he continued to climb rapidly through positions and survived unaffected the merger of the AFL with the Congress of Industrial Organizations (CIO) in 1955. The decisive jump for Kirkland was his appointment in 1961 as executive assistant to the president of the AFL-CIO, George Meany. Once Kirkland became secretary treasurer of the AFL-CIO in 1969, his position as successor to George Meany was guaranteed.

Strictly speaking, Kirkland's career was not that of the sailor who climbed to become head of the labor confederation but was typical of the college-educated individual who could advance more rapidly through the labor hierarchy than through the crowded corporate ladder of the post–World War II years. Through Kirkland maritime labor unions had a natural channel to Meany. Thus, in the 1960s and 1970s, when government and business were making crucial decisions about the future of U.S.-flag shipping services, the maritime labor unions could count on strong and uncompromising support from the AFL-CIO, for example, in the bitter battle over transferring or restructuring the Maritime Administration.* Paradoxically, Kirkland's advocacy of the maritime unions under Meany weakened, rather than strengthened, their position. The claims of maritime unions went unquestioned, and the AFL-CIO blindly pushed for mistaken remedies, in the process consuming precious political capital, which was sorely needed in other more critical labor battles.

References: *Current Biography 1980*; Gary M. Fink, ed., *Biographical Dictionary of American Labor*, 2d ed. (Westport, CT: Greenwood Press, 1984).

KOREA. See *Siberia* and *Korea*.

L

LA FOLLETTE SEAMEN'S ACT OF 1915. The La Follette Seamen's Act eliminated imprisonment as a punishment for deserting the crew of any ship in U.S. ports; the act also introduced detailed requirements for lifesaving equipment and procedures aboard ships. Passage of this law reflected nearly twenty years of efforts by Andrew Furuseth,* the president of the International Seamen's Union* (ISU), to secure congressional approval and earned him the title of the "Emancipator of Seamen." Under the bizarre *Arago** decision, the Supreme Court had ruled that sailors, along with American Indians, were not covered by constitutional guarantees and hence could be imprisoned for deserting their ships. Furuseth labored tirelessly to convince Congress to remedy this blatant discrimination, but without money and few votes to offer legislators, his efforts were fruitless. Fortunately for Furuseth, he became a lifelong friend of Senator Robert La Follette of Wisconsin, who assumed the task of guiding the Seamen's Bill through Congress as a charity case; when years later Furuseth tried to repay his friend by campaigning for La Follette's reelection, he learned that voters in Wisconsin knew little and cared less about seamen.

Senator La Follette made the bill more palatable to many legislators by tacking on lengthy requirements for life rafts, boats, preservers, drills, and other safety procedures. He then waited for a lull in shipowner vigilance and surprised opponents by swiftly securing approval from both houses of Congress by 27 February 1915, barely a week before the session of Congress closed. Besides the prohibition on arrests for desertions, the bill also forbade advance payment of sailors' wages to a third party (usually a "crimp"*), established requirements for the rating of able-bodied seamen,* and ordered improvements on safety and living conditions aboard, particularly in the notorious forecastle.*

When the bill reached President Woodrow Wilson, he was appalled by the infrahuman and slavelike conditions to which sailors were subjected, and his first impulse was to sign promptly. Secretary of State William J. Bryan dissuaded the president, on the grounds that passage of the bill would automatically repeal twenty-three navigation treaties, which required U.S. authorities to arrest deserting foreign seamen. The justice of the sailors' cause was too obvious, and rather than make an open rejection, Bryan, as a consummate politician, urged Wilson to wait until after Congress adjourned on 4 March, in effect killing the bill by a "pocket veto" but without an embarrassing rejection. Senator La Follette met on 2 March with President Wilson in a final attempt to obtain the bill's approval, and during their meeting Furuseth was allowed to come in and present the seamen's case, with Furuseth reportedly throwing himself on his knees, begging the president to liberate the seamen. On 4 March 1915, barely one hour before Congress adjourned, Wilson made up his mind and signed the bill, "because it seemed the only chance to get something like justice to a class of workmen who have been too much neglected by our laws" (Weintraub 1959).

Furuseth was overjoyed at having achieved his life's goal, and soon foreign crewmen began massive desertions from their ships, while the imprisonment of U.S. sailors for desertion became a historical relic. Nevertheless, enforcement of the salary, working, and living provisions in the La Follette Seamen's Act proved extremely difficult from the start, and once the sensitive Woodrow Wilson had been replaced in the White House by Republican incumbents, almost every administrative and judicial ruling went against the sailors: "During the open-shop era between 1921 and 1934, the law was for the most part a dead letter." However, the detailed requirements for protecting the lives of passengers and crew did make ocean travel safer and partially substituted for congressional failure to ratify the Safety of Life at Sea* (SOLAS) conventions.

References: James C. Healey, *Foc'sle and Glory Hole: A Study of the Merchant Seaman and His Occupation* (New York: Merchant Marine Publishers Association, 1936); Bruce Nelson, *Workers on the Waterfront: Seamen, Longshoremen, and Unionism in the 1930s* (Urbana: University of Illinois Press, 1990); Andrew Weintraub, *Andrew Furuseth: Emancipator of the Seamen* (Berkeley: University of California Press, 1959).

LANCERS. The Lancers were the first vessels in the world constructed as containerships from the keel up. They also inaugurated the second generation of containerships, because unlike the first generation, which had consisted of converted break-bulk* freighters or even T-2* tankers, the Lancers were the first vessels built expressly for carrying containers.* United States Lines* (USL) built eight Lancers, the first of which, the *American Lancer*, was delivered in May 1968 and gave the name to this class of ships. At a service speed of twenty-two knots, the Lancers were also the fastest containerships in the world, and their rapid turnaround time in port allowed the company to replace twenty-four of its break-bulk freighters with just the eight Lancers and still have a larger cargo-carrying capacity with only one-third of the former crews.

The Lancers meant such great savings in time and expenses that the company's hesitation to adopt the new technology was hard to explain. USL was in the midst of a vessel-replacement program and after extensive studies decided in 1964 to order modified break-bulk freighters with a capacity for 228 twenty-foot equivalent units* (TEU) containers; only when competitors introduced container service to the North Atlantic in 1966 did USL change its order to full containerships with a capacity of 638 TEUs. One year later, in May 1967, the company again changed its shipyard order to an even larger vessel, 700 feet long, 90 feet wide, and with a capacity of 1,178 TEUs. The cost of redesigning the original vessel was so high that USL decided to keep the marine propulsion of the original plant, instead of installing larger engines capable of driving the ship five or more knots faster. The company had also reasoned correctly that the real savings in time came not from racing at sea but from rapid loading and discharging in port. The highly successful Lancers revolutionized transportation in the North Atlantic because they provided shippers* savings in time and money that the first generation of converted containerships had never offered. However, the failure to install larger engines in the Lancers left an opening for Sea-Land* to mount a comeback by ordering as rivals another generation of containerships, the SL-7s.*

References: René De La Pedraja, *The Rise and Decline of U.S. Merchant Shipping in the Twentieth Century* (New York: Twayne, 1992); Henry S. Marcus, *Planning Ship Replacement in the Containerization Era* (Lexington, MA: Lexington Books, 1974); Transportation Research Board, *Intermodal Marine Container Transportation: Impediments and Opportunities* (Washington, DC: National Research Council, 1992).

LAND, EMORY SCOTT ("JERRY"), 9 January 1879–27 November 1971. Admiral Emory S. Land was chairman of the U.S. Maritime Commission* in 1938–1946 and head of the War Shipping Administration* (WSA) in 1942–1946; he easily ranked as one of the government officials who had the greatest positive impact on the U.S. merchant marine. Land was born in Canon City, Colorado, on 9 January 1879 and completed high school in that state prior to receiving an A.B. degree at the University of Wyoming in 1898. That same year he then qualified for an appointment to the U.S. Naval Academy, from which he graduated with honor in 1902. As part of his very successful naval career, he studied naval architecture at the Massachusetts Institute of Technology, where he received an M.S. and rose rapidly through the ranks because of his expertise and efficiency as a constructor. In addition, from 1923 to 1930 he was closely involved with efforts to develop aviation in the navy, partly because he was a cousin of Charles A. Lindbergh. He was promoted to rear admiral in 1932, and on 16 April 1937 President Franklin D. Roosevelt appointed him, with the consent of the Senate, to the U.S. Maritime Commission. Shortly after, Land considered retiring from the navy, and he received a handsome offer from Pan American Airlines to come to work at a much higher salary in private business. He admitted the job offer was quite a temptation, "but I've always had a sentimental interest, from 1907 on, in the merchant marine. I wasn't fool enough to think I could go over there and cure all the diseases, but I thought I'd like to give it a whirl'' (Land, Oral History).

The chairman of the U.S. Maritime Commission was Joseph P. Kennedy,* who did not serve a full year, and President Roosevelt picked Land to be the successor in February 1938. As chairman, Admiral Land was involved in all the crucial issues of the merchant marine. Kennedy had accomplished the transition from the mail contracts to the operating-differential subsidy,* but Land still had to take care of unsettled cases, such as the Baltimore Mail Line.* Kennedy had tackled but not solved the even more vexing issue of the bankruptcy of several companies, most notably the Dollar Line;* here Admiral Land finally concluded that the only alternative was for direct government ownership and operation of the bankrupt company, renamed the American President Lines* (APL). In anticipation of the world war, Admiral Land, the naval constructor, plunged with great enthusiasm into the task of designing and building the first C-1,* C-2,* and C-3* freighters, as well as the T-2* tankers. In a special arrangement with Standard Oil Company of New Jersey,* Land secured the company's cooperation to build a dozen fast tankers ("Cimarron" class) in 1938 to serve as resupply ships for the naval vessels.

With the outbreak of World War II in 1939, the U.S. Maritime Commission tried to deal with the disruptions caused by that conflict, but soon Admiral Land tired of the commission type of government and wanted a more executive body to make fast decisions. Right after U.S. entry into World War II, Admiral Land convinced President Roosevelt to create the WSA in February 1942. Land remained chairman of the U.S. Maritime Commission, whose concentration was on shipbuilding, and he also headed the WSA, whose primary task was the effective use and allocation of merchant ships; at the WSA Lewis W. Douglas, the deputy administrator in 1942–1943, was instrumental in creating the organization and procedures for the efficient functioning of the agency. Among the many tasks the WSA carried out during the war was the rapid expansion of training facilities for new seamen and officers; Land realized that this was a good moment to establish a permanent facility for training officers, and when the Walter Chrysler estate came on the market in Kings Point, Long Island, he decided to acquire the property as the seat for the new Merchant Marine Academy,* which was formally inaugurated in 1943.

Land surrounded himself with very able collaborators and kept the WSA and the U.S. Maritime Commission functioning at a high level of efficiency. The shipbuilding program was a tremendous success, and for the first time in its history, the United States boasted of the largest merchant fleet in the world. The WSA assigned the new ships to companies for operation under general agency agreements; this way the WSA avoided the precedent of the Shipping Board,* which had created a whole new bureaucracy to man and maintain the vessels in World War I; instead the WSA focused on the sufficiently difficult task of assigning the vessels in such a way as to attain the most efficient allocation of cargo space. When the war ended in 1945, Admiral Land immediately pressed for the sale of the fleet to the private companies, and one of his last actions was to try to convince President Harry S. Truman to obtain as soon as possible passage of the Ship Sales Act,* which Congress approved in March 1946, barely two months after Admiral Land resigned from all his government positions.

Admiral Land's rush to dispose of the wartime fleet did not turn out to be in the best interest of the country, and in any case he had left to others the task of maintaining a U.S.-flag merchant fleet. On 15 January 1946 he accepted another lucrative offer to join the aviation industry, this time as president of the Air Transport Association of America. After 1947 Admiral Land was in semi-retirement, although he continued as an adviser to the Electric Boat Company and the General Dynamics Corporation. In 1958 he published *Winning the War with Ships*, a slim memoir about his wartime activities; unfortunately it was not as complete, lively, or revealing as Edward N. Hurley's* much more valuable *Bridge to France* for the World War I years. Admiral Land continued to follow merchant marine issues and occasionally made appearances at the annual conventions of the Propeller Club.* He died on 27 November 1971.

References: Admiral Emory S. Land Oral History 1963, Columbia University Oral History Program; Admiral Emory S. Land Papers, Library of Congress, Washington, DC; Robert P. Browder and Thomas G. Smith, *Independent: A Biography of Lewis W. Douglas* (New York: Alfred A. Knopf, 1986); Rodney P. Carlisle, *Sovereignty for Sale: The Origins and Evolution of the Panamanian and Liberian Flags of Convenience* (Annapolis, MD: Naval Institute Press, 1981); *Public Papers of the Presidents of the United States, Harry S. Truman 1946* (Washington, DC: Government Printing Office, 1962); *Who's Who in the Maritime Industry 1946*.

LANDBRIDGE. Landbridge has been the name of one type of intermodal* transportation. In intermodalism, containers* unloaded from ships traveled in trucks, rails, or barges to a final destination, while in landbridge the containers moved only in railroad cars between the East and West coasts of the United States. In "pure" landbridge, the cargo moved by ship both before and after the land journey across the United States, as in the case of containers going from Japan to Europe. In "mini" landbridge, the cargo went by ship only once, either before or after the land journey, for example, cargo coming from Japan for New York. Finally, in "micro" landbridge, the cargo did not travel all the way between the two coasts, but instead reached a destination inside the United States, for example, containers coming from Japan for Chicago.

Since the completion of the transcontinental railroads in the nineteenth century, occasionally some merchandise moved from the eastern United States for export aboard vessels on the West Coast, but the large labor costs of handling the cargo precluded any stable traffic. Even when railroads like the Great Northern owned vessels as "feeder" services, the companies' goal had been to send cargo only from the Midwest to the Pacific ports and not from the East Coast. In the 1920s steamship companies did operate, as needed, the "silk express," whereby silk from Japan was discharged in Seattle and loaded into waiting railroads for shipment in express trains to New York City. This arrangement was possible, however, only for large shipments of high-value goods like silk, and until the introduction of containers, which drastically slashed labor costs, almost all cargo had no choice but to take the longer, slower, and cheaper route via the Panama Canal.*

In 1971 Seatrain* inaugurated mini landbridge service across the United States for cargo moving from the Far East to New York. Under the landbridge concept, Seatrain transferred the containers from its ships to specially chartered railroad flatcars for travel across the United States, and during the whole trip the cargo remained the responsibility of the company. The landbridge normally saved ten days from the all-water route of thirty days from Tokyo to New York City via the Panama Canal, and although the latter was cheaper, shippers* in a rush to deliver their merchandise flocked to the landbridge. Soon other companies followed the lead of Seatrain, most notably American President Lines* (APL), whose introduction of "double-stack" trains in 1984 even further increased the appeal of the landbridge. In double-stack trains, the containers were piled two high on top of the flatcars, and although this required some investments in the tracks, for example, to increase tunnel heights, the savings further reduced the difference between the rates for the landbridge and the all-water route.

Since so much of the container cargo has used the landbridge, the Panama Canal has become less vital to the United States, partially explaining the willingness of the Jimmy Carter administration to sign a treaty renouncing U.S. control over that waterway in the year 2000. Whatever the exact future of the Panama Canal, the landbridge, another consequence of the container revolution, has become a permanent part of shipping in the United States.

References: American President Lines, *Fact Book*, 1987; Lane C. Kendall, *The Business of Shipping*, 5th ed. (Centreville, MD: Cornell Maritime Press, 1986); William J. Miller, *Encyclopedia of International Commerce* (Centreville, MD: Cornell Maritime Press, 1985); Transportation Research Board, *Intermodal Marine Container Transportation: Impediments and Opportunities* (Washington, DC: National Research Council, 1992).

LANNON, AL, 3 October 1907–1990s? Al Lannon was a cofounder of the National Maritime Union* (NMU) and a communist waterfront organizer. He was born on 3 October 1907 in Brooklyn, New York, under the name of Francesco Albert Vetere and attended public school until 1923. He went to work as a seamen and adopted his new name of Al Lannon shortly afterward. He continued to sail until 1937 whenever he could obtain a shipboard job, but very early the degrading conditions on ships convinced him to join the Communist party. Lannon stood out as one of the more energetic organizers of the Marine Workers Industrial Union* (MWIU) of the Communist party. His biggest success came with the foundation of the NMU, whose constitution he helped draft. By preference an organizer rather than an administrator, he gave up his place in NMU the very year of its foundation in 1937. Instead, he tried to organize a rival union to challenge the International Longshoremen's Association,* and even after that failed attempt, he remained a waterfront organizer until 1942. He gradually drifted into the Communist party bureaucracy, but his big jump came in February 1946, when the demotion of Roy Hudson* allowed Lannon to become national maritime coordinator for the Communist party. In 1953 he was convicted because of the party membership and began to serve a prison term in 1955.

References: FBI Series, Dwight D. Eisenhower Presidential Library, Abilene, Kansas; Bruce Nelson, *Workers on the Waterfront: Seamen, Longshoremen, and Unionism in the 1930s* (Urbana: University of Illinois Press, 1990).

LAPHAM, LEWIS ABBOT, 7 March 1909–1990s? Lewis Lapham, a business executive, was closely connected with shipping until 1959, when he became a banker. Lapham was born in New York City on 7 March 1909 of a wealthy family, and his father, Roger D. Lapham,* was president of American-Hawaiian Steamship Company* (AHSS) until 1944. Lewis graduated from Yale University, and after six years as a reporter for the *San Francisco Examiner*, he began working for AHSS on the assumption that he would eventually succeed his father. His father resigned from the company in 1944 to become mayor of San Francisco, but Lewis did not immediately step in because he was participating in the war effort. After a stint as executive director of the Pacific American Steamship Association* (PASA), Lewis returned to AHSS and became president in 1947; one of his first actions was to move headquarters to New York City. When his family decided to sell their holdings in the company to Daniel Ludwig, Lapham resigned as president in 1953, but he still remained interested in shipping.

Lapham accepted an executive position in the Grace Line* and in 1955 became its president. He soon realized that Peter Grace,* the chairman, was determined to get out of merchant shipping, and Lapham himself concluded this was a wise example to follow, and in 1959 he resigned from the Grace Line. Later he made a major investment in the Bankers Trust Co. of New York, eventually becoming chairman of the executive committee of the Board of Directors. The Lapham family was among the fortunate few who managed to sell off their steamship investments while it was still profitable to do so and thus escaped the major losses that other investors later faced in the 1960s and 1970s.

References: *National Cyclopedia of American Biography*, Current vol. L; *New York Times*, 26 November 1948; Roger D. Lapham Oral History, Bancroft Library, University of California, Berkeley.

LAPHAM, ROGER D., 6 December 1883–16 April 1966. Roger D. Lapham was born in New York City on 6 December 1883 of a wealthy family. His father, Lewis Henry Lapham, had made a fortune in the leather manufacturing business and also became one of the largest stockholders in the oil company

Texaco. Lewis had invested widely in other enterprises as well, among which was the American-Hawaiian Steamship Company* (AHSS) of his brother-in-law George Dearborn. Among the different family investments, shipping called the attention of the young Roger, and he began working in the company in 1905, first as just a clerk and gradually climbing until he became treasurer before World War I.

The sudden resignation of Cary W. Cook in June 1925 led the Board of Directors to choose Roger D. Lapham as president of the company, a position he held until 1944. He concluded the purchase of the six Grace Line* vessels on the intercoastal* service, a transaction that Cook had begun. Lapham in 1929 wished to consolidate the company's grip on the intercoastal service, and to that effect he acquired a major competitor, the Williams Line. In a bolder move, AHSS and the Matson Navigation Company* organized as a joint venture the Oceanic and Oriental Navigation Company in 1928 in order to take over a line of Shipping Board* vessels; according to the agreement, AHSS managed the ships sailing to the Far East, while Matson handled those in the Australia/New Zealand route.

When the United States entered World War II, the War Shipping Administration* requisitioned the fleet of American-Hawaiian, and although the company continued to man and maintain the vessels assigned by the government for wartime service, operations had become largely routine, and Lapham decided to heed those who urged him to run for mayor of San Francisco. Lapham resigned from the company to serve as mayor in 1944–1948, and although he remained a stockholder, he never returned to an executive position. President Harry S. Truman put him in charge of economic aid to China in 1948–1949 and to Greece in 1950–1951. In the early 1950s he sold off the last of his American-Hawaiian stock. Lapham died on 16 April 1966.

References: *Current Biography 1948*, and *1966*; *Pacific Marine Review*, November 1926; Roger D. Lapham Oral History, Bancroft Library, University of California, Berkeley, 1957.

LASH or LASH VESSELS, 1969–late 1990s. The LASH or "Lighter Aboard Ship" was one of the new vessel designs that attempted to replace the break-bulk* freighters, whose obsolescence had become obvious, but finding the right replacement proved unexpectedly risky. Because many companies refused to fully accept containers,* the search for alternative ship designs led to many blunders, among which LASH was the most disastrous. A LASH vessel carried sixty-foot barges aboard, and its special lift or elevator in the rear lowered the barges into the water; if the ports lacked large cranes, the elevator could also load the barges aboard the vessel. Central Gulf Lines* introduced the first LASH vessel in 1969 and the second in 1970; soon other companies began to order their own LASH vessels to replace their old break-bulk freighters. The Vietnam War gave added impetus to the concept, because LASH vessels were well suited to unload merchandise directly into river systems such as the Mekong River in Vietnam.

Once the Vietnam War was over, the limitations of the LASH vessels gradually became evident through costly experience. Raising and lowering the vessels in rough weather often proved difficult, while port workers often struggled with the unfamiliar equipment and procedure. Finally it became painfully clear that a LASH vessel could not compete in costs against a containership and that only when the operation of the latter was physically impossible was the use of a LASH vessel justified. A number of companies, such as Pacific Far East Line* and Prudential Lines,* learned the drawbacks of LASH vessels too late to escape bankruptcy. Instead, Central Gulf Lines, the creator of the concept, was the only company that, through careful deployment, emerged as the only successful operator of LASH vessels, because it operated them as highly specialized vessels in very specific markets. Central Gulf used LASH vessels in particular between river systems such as the Mississippi and the Rhine and in areas where ports had not yet adopted the facilities to handle containers. However, the company has operated at the same time a variety of other vessels, helping offset any short-term setback with the LASH vessels. As of now the company has remained noncommittal over whether it will order in the mid-1990s replacements for its aging LASH vessels. Since no new LASH vessels have been ordered since the late 1970s, in all probability the LASH vessels will soon disappear and be remembered only as a passing but highly ruinous phenomenon.

References: American Bureau of Shipping, *History, 1862–1991; American Shipper*, November 1990; René De La Pedraja, *The Rise and Decline of U.S. Merchant Shipping in the Twentieth Century* (New York: Twayne, 1992); International Shipholding Corporation, *Annual Reports, 1987–1990*; William Kooiman, *The Grace Ships, 1869–1969* (Point Reyes, CA: Komar, 1990).

LASKER, ALBERT D., 1 May 1880–30 May 1952. Albert D. Lasker, an advertising tycoon, was the chairman of the Shipping Board* in 1921–1923. President Warren G. Harding wanted to bring businessmen into the federal government, and Lasker was one who agreed to come to Washington, D.C. Lasker had originally wanted a cabinet position and indignantly rejected Harding's offer of the job of commissioner of the Shipping Board. When Harding improved the offer to that of chairman of the Shipping Board, Lasker finally accepted, but on the condition that he would devote only two years to Washington.

In July 1921 Lasker assumed the chairmanship, and immediately he was saddled with the problem of what to do with the huge surplus fleet the government had built for World War I. The upkeep cost of this idle fleet was large, but even more staggering were the expenses run up by the managing operators;* the trick was to liquidate this huge investment and at the same time build a strong U.S.-flag merchant marine with the best ships. Lasker began the task with enthusiasm and promptly slashed the bloated bureaucracy of the Shipping Board and its subsidiary, the Emergency Fleet Corporation* (EFC). He discovered that these organizations were still operating on a wartime footing of three shifts of employees twenty-four hours every day; after a surprise visit in the middle of the night revealed hundreds of men sleeping on their desks with nothing else to do, the next day he fired 621, and he imposed other drastic personnel reductions as well. While he was firing the unnecessary employees, Lasker realized that superior talent was the key to success, and in order to keep the best steamship experts, he passed through Congress measures authorizing the Shipping Board to pay the heads of its different departments and bureaus the highest government salaries in the city (he himself was exempted from these pay raises). Lasker also devised means to keep passenger liners attractive to travelers during the initial years of Prohibition,* when alcoholic beverages were forbidden aboard U.S.-flag ships.

As far as the surplus fleet, Lasker believed the government should sell the ships in the hands of the managing operators, who would then qualify for subsidies he would try to obtain from Congress; if the managing operators did not buy all the vessels in their lines, then the government itself should operate the ships. When Congress failed to approve the subsidies, this was a bitter failure for Lasker, who then concluded that for many routes there was no other alternative but direct government ownership and operation. The managing operators, who were making huge profits from their contracts, could not accept this logic and wanted to preserve their comfortable arrangements for as long as possible; Lasker's last months in office were full of frustrations, and as soon as his two self-imposed years had passed (his term had not expired), he was extremely glad to resign in June 1923. The whole Washington experience left him bitter about government, and he turned down offers from President Calvin Coolidge to return to public service; later he looked back at his two years at the Shipping Board as the most unhappy of his life.

References: John Gunther, *Taken at the Flood: The Story of Albert D. Lasker* (New York: Harper, 1960); *New York Times*, 16 April 1923.

LAWRENSON, JACK, 22 October 1906–31 October 1957. Jack Lawrenson was a cofounder and vice president of the National Maritime Union* (NMU) and was one of the leaders who tried to stop Joseph Curran* from consolidating an iron grip on the NMU. Lawrenson was born in Dublin, Ireland, on 22 October 1906 and came to the United States as a merchant seaman in 1937 and actively participated in the movement that culminated in the foundation of the NMU. He married Helen Strough Brown in 1939 and subsequently became a U.S. citizen. He carried out a successful recruiting drive in the Great Lakes division of the NMU. His later duties included editorship of *The Pilot*, the official magazine of the NMU. Lawrenson had briefly been a communist but soon dropped out, and in the initial struggles between Curran and the communists, Lawrenson correctly sided against them. But Lawrenson, as a man of integrity and independence, wanted to preserve the open and democratic traditions of the NMU. Lawrenson could not become a supporter of Curran like M. Hedley Stone* and instead tried to detain the drift toward autocratic rule within the union. Curran denounced Lawrenson as a communist and had him threatened and attacked by armed thugs. In the manipulated union elections of 1949 he was defeated in his bid for reelection, and in any case Curran had previously deprived him of any meaningful functions within the union. Lawrenson started his own trucking and moving business in New York City, where he worked until he died on 31 October 1957.

References: Gary M. Fink, ed., *Biographical Dictionary of American Labor*, 2d ed. (Westport, CT: Greenwood Press, 1984); Joseph P. Goldberg, *The Maritime Story: A Study in Labor-Management Relations* (Cambridge: Harvard University Press, 1958); Helen Lawrenson, *Stranger at the Party: A Memoir* (New York: Random House, 1975).

LEVIATHAN, **1914–1934.** The *Leviathan* (originally the *Vaterland*) was the world's largest liner* during many years and had a turbulent career in the U.S. merchant marine. The huge ship was built in Germany for the Hamburg-America line, but the *Vaterland* completed only three transatlantic voyages for its original owner. The fourth voyage coincided with the outbreak of World War I, and the vessel was forced to seek refuge in New York harbor to escape capture by British ships. When the United States entered World War I in 1917, the navy seized the *Vaterland* (and the rest of the interned German vessels) and used the fast ship as a transport. The Shipping Board* asked Mrs. Woodrow Wilson, the wife of the president, to choose a new name for the vessel, and in the Bible she found the world "Leviathan"; the next president of the United States, Warren G. Harding considered renaming the vessel after himself, but the outbreak of a major scandal in his doomed administration soon killed the idea.

In 1919 the navy no longer needed the *Leviathan* for war purposes, and because the United States had received title to the *Leviathan* and to most of the interned German vessels, as reparations, the navy handed the ship over to the Shipping Board. A major overhaul was necessary before the ship could return to commercial service, while no less serious were the problems in the original design. The length of 950 feet, a novelty for the period, created such structural strain on the hull that at least one serious crack appeared, while the size and weight of the ship meant that even with steam turbines* and four propellers, the vessel's optimal speed of twenty-three knots was below that of competing transatlantic liners. Lastly, Hamburg-America in 1914 had based the expected profits on the transportation of persons in steerage* class, 936 of whom were stuffed into odd corners of the ship, and 944 into the slightly better third class; first class was for 876 passengers, and second for only 548. On 4 July 1923, when the *Leviathan* resumed commercial service, changes in the U.S. immigration laws had virtually halted the flow of steerage passengers, while in the nearly ten years that had elapsed since the ship was built, the changes in fashion and tastes necessarily made the ship look old-fashioned. Nevertheless, the overhaul of the ship, besides giving the naval architecture firm of Gibbs & Knox considerable experience, which later proved useful in the design of the *America** and the *United States*,* managed to introduce many amenities to attract passengers. The Supreme Court ruling that allowed alcohol to be served aboard during the Prohibition* years once the ship left the three-mile territorial limits of the United States was an additional incentive for ocean travelers.

Of existing American companies, only the International Mercantile Marine* (IMM) had the capability to operate the *Leviathan* in unison with its other passenger liners. However, when the Shipping Board attempted to sell the *Leviathan* to IMM, newspaper tycoon William Randolph Hearst launched a publicity and legal campaign that forced the cancellation of the sale. Left with no other alternative, the Shipping Board was forced to accept what has highly unpalatable to most of its commissioners, namely, direct government operation. The Shipping Board assigned the *Leviathan* to the government-owned United States Lines* (USL), which already operated other captured German steamers for which no buyers could be found.

Under government operation and ownership the *Leviathan* had its only years of successful operation, but instead of leaving well enough alone, private speculators began to pressure the Shipping Board to sell USL at a low price, including the *Leviathan*. IMM quite correctly calculated that only a low bid was justified for USL whose old ships did not have very long useful lives left, but Wall Street speculator Paul W. Chapman, in the spirit of the Roaring Twenties, presented a high bid that gained him control of USL in early 1929. Soon the *Leviathan* was losing money on each of its voyages, while the stock market crash and the onset of the Great Depression bankrupted USL, whose control had returned back to the Shipping Board to prevent foreclosure. After complicated transactions, IMM purchased USL, and at last IMM could operate the *Leviathan* in conjunction with its other passenger services, but by then it was too late to save the ship. The *Leviathan* continued to lose money, but extreme nationalistic pressures in the United States forced IMM to operate the ship in order to protect itself and the Shipping Board from charges that they were merely British fronts. The losses became unbearable, and finally in September 1934 the unlucky *Leviathan* was laid up; in 1938 the ship made the final voyage to Scotland for scrapping. While the *Leviathan* provided several opportunities to improve the American merchant marine, no consistent policy materialized, and consequently the *Leviathan* diverted time, energy, and resources from more worthwhile projects and turned out to be little more than a Trojan horse, which ultimately weakened the merchant shipping between the two world wars.

References: Frank O. Braynard, *The World's Greatest Ship: The Story of the Leviathan*, 6 vols. (Sea Cliff, NY: F. O. Braynard, 1972–1978); René De La Pedraja, *The Rise and Decline of U.S. Merchant Shipping in the Twentieth Century* (New York: Twayne, 1992); Frederick E. Emmons, *American Passenger Ships: The Ocean Lines and Liners, 1873–1983* (Newark: University of Delaware Press, 1985); U.S. House, Committee on Merchant Marine and Fisheries, *To Develop an American Merchant Marine* (Washington, DC: Government Printing Office, 1935).

LEWIS, ARTHUR R., JR., 6 March 1909–16 March 1954. Arthur R. Lewis, Jr., was born in New York City on 6 March 1909. His father was a shipping executive and business partner of the brothers John J. Farrell* and James A. Farrell, Jr.* Lewis attended private schools and graduated from Yale in 1932, and the next year he began working with his father. Sometime in the middle of 1933 a serious rift erupted between the Lewises and the Farrell brothers, and as a result, both families completely separated the assets previously combined in numerous shipping ventures. The Farrells received the Argonaut Line* and the American South African Line,* while the Lewises gained full control of the Seas Shipping Company, whose main subsidiary was the Robin Line.*

Out of personal and business reasons, Lewis decided in 1935 to attack the African trade of the Farrells, who fought back by refusing to admit the Robin Line into the U.S.A.-South Africa Conference.* Undaunted, Lewis plunged the Robin Line into one of the most furious rate wars between American steamship companies in the foreign trade routes. Rates fell way below operating costs, and both companies were driven to virtual bankruptcy, even after they ended the rate war in 1937. A timely subsidy from the U.S. Maritime Commission* in 1938 saved the Robin Line, whose fortunes were permanently restored by the high freight rates ensuing upon the outbreak of World War II.

After World War II Lewis kept the feud against the Farrells alive, but neither side wanted to risk another destructive rate war. For Lewis, shipping had become an obsession, and he imposed upon himself a crushing work schedule. He was persuaded to take a vacation in Fort Lauderdale, Florida, where he died unexpectedly of a heart attack on 16 March 1954. He left no children, and his heirs had no desire to continue in the exhausting shipping business and decided to sell their interests in the Robin Line to Moore-McCormack* in 1957.

References: Robert G. Albion, *Seaports South of Sahara: The Achievements of an American Steamship Service* (New York: Appleton-Century Crofts, 1959); *New York Times*, 17 March 1954.

LIBERTY SHIPS or LIBERTIES. In the World War II shipbuilding program, the Liberty was the most important and the most numerous ship type built by the U.S. Maritime Commission.* The Liberty was of 10,419 deadweight* tons and had a length of 442 feet and a beam of 57 feet. To speed up production at the yards, the fine lines of the C-2* gave way to blunt forms, while shortages in steam turbines* and diesel engines* forced the builders to install the simpler to manufacture triple-expansion engines,* which, although very economical, simply lacked the power to move swiftly such blunt vessels, whose nickname was the "ugly ducklings."

The U.S. Maritime Commission had opposed the construction of these vessels on the quite justified grounds that their slower speed would more than cancel any benefit from faster delivery, and this without counting the inevitable losses from enemy action. While the faster C-2s and C-3s* as well as the later Victory* vessels could outrun submarines, the Liberties were easy targets for German submarines unless heavily escorted. Finally in late 1943 Admiral Emory S. Land* obtained the decision to shift production from the Liberty to the Victory, but by then it was too late, so that Liberties continued to be launched until a total of 2,708 vessels were built during the wartime construction program. The question of what to do with these slow vessels after the war became a major problem for the U.S. merchant marine, and many unexperienced operators bought these vessels in the hope of reaping profits during the postwar shipping boom. As an emergency measure, some Liberties had been converted to bulk* and oil carriers during the war, but the attempt to operate them under peacetime conditions in those trades was a grave miscalculation. There were so many of the very cheap Liberties available after the war, and they had been so solidly built that many found places in odd corners of world shipping for decades of operation. Visitors today to the San Francisco National Maritime Museum can board the *Jeremy O'Brien*, a nearly perfectly preserved Liberty ship occasionally taken out on tours in the bay, and can try to imagine some of the scenes dramatically portrayed in the film *Action on the North Atlantic.**

References: John Bunker, *Liberty Ships, the Ugly Ducklings of World War II* (Annapolis, MD: Naval Institute Press, 1972); René De La Pedraja, *The Rise and Decline of U.S. Merchant Shipping in the Twentieth Century* (New York: Twayne, 1992); Frank F. Farrar, *A Ship's Log Book* (Saint Petersburg, FL: Great Outdoors, 1988); Frederic C. Lane, *Ships for Victory: A History of Shipbuilding Under the U.S. Maritime Commission in World War II* (Baltimore: Johns Hopkins University Press, 1951).

LINER or LINER SERVICE or LINE. The term *liner* (because it operated a "line" of ships between at least two points) has meant a merchant shipping company that provided regular service between ports in accordance with publicized schedules; in the case of passenger service, the word *liner* has also been often used to refer to the vessels themselves, such as "passenger liners" or just "liners" or more recently "cruise liners." The general rule has been that liner service must be available to any shipper* at the set rates announced by the company or the conference* in that route. Since the introduction of the compound engine* in the 1860s, the stability and reliability provided by liner service have been fundamental to the growth of foreign commerce. A shipper with enough cargo to fill a whole ship, however, was better off chartering a tramp* vessel, the direct opposite of liner services. While liner companies followed their scheduled routes, tramps chased around the world looking for cargoes. In practice break-bulk* cargo moved aboard liner services until the 1960s, and since then they have handled mainly containers;* tramps, on the other hand, have traditionally handled mostly bulk* cargoes of grains, ore, coal, and oil. All shipping services offered to shippers fall into either the liner or tramp category, the two branches of merchant shipping.

LITERATURE—NOVELS, SHORT STORIES, and PLAYS. Literature has contributed to shape the image many Americans held about the U.S. merchant marine, yet for the period since the introduction of steam power, fiction writers have largely neglected the merchant marine in their plots and stories. The much larger subject of the sea, which includes fishing, whaling, and man's eternal struggle against the ocean, has continued to attract the attention of some writers, but the stories dealing with persons and institutions in the merchant marine have declined until they have virtually disappeared.

During the first half of the nineteenth century, when, following the colonial pattern, the majority of the population still lived near the eastern seaboard of the United States, the major writers touched upon the merchant marine as part of their writings on the broader subjects of the sea. These authors lived in the age of sailing wooden vessels, which were particularly effective in tapping the creative impulses, and such giants as James Fenimore Cooper, Nathaniel Hawthorne, and Edgar Allan Poe wrote outstanding sea stories within their large production. With Richard Henry Dana and Herman Melville, the sea stories of the age of sail reached their highest development, in particular with the latter's *Moby Dick* (1851) and *Billy Budd* (1891), great classics of American literature.

Melville, like almost all American writers, never managed to make the transition from sail to steam in literature: while in 1851, when *Moby Dick* was published, the steam engine was still only a complement to the sails, by 1891, when he died after finishing *Billy Budd*, the disappearance of sailing vessels was so obvious to all that even writers such as Lincoln Colcord in the *Drifting Diamond* (1912), with perhaps a touch of nostalgia, rushed to describe a world rapidly vanishing before their eyes. The widespread introduction of the compound engine* by the late 1860s reduced sailing vessels (now built of iron) to bulk* cargoes, while the arrival of the triple-expansion* engine in 1881 meant the gradual replacement of the remaining sailing vessels. Because the transition from sail to steam lasted so long, a number of writers could avoid shifting to the age of steam in their works and instead concentrated on the agony of the last sailing vessels. With the popularity of Darwinist ideas about the survival of the fittest, the last sailing vessels, whose end was inevitable because of the triumph of steam, gave ample material for the study of the displacement and final extinction of one type of transportation. The classic studies about the degeneration and final collapse of the old sailing vessels were the two novels by Jack London, *The Sea-Wolf* (1904), which later was made into a very successful movie,* and, in particular, *The Mutiny of the Elsinore* (1914). This last novel, although marred by race theories London later rejected, was a powerful story about one of the last of the formerly great sailing ships, and because of its profound study of a dying order, has been described as "one of the best sea stories in our literature" (Bender 1988).

In both the *Sea-Wolf* and *The Mutiny of the Elsinore* the steamships hovered in the background as the winners in the struggle to survive and as harbingers of the future, but London himself never quite made the transition to study the new order that had emerged under steam power. Felix Riesenberg, an accomplished seaman himself, made the transition from sail to steam in one single novel, *Mother Sea* (1933). In *Mother Sea* the Darwinian struggle for survival and profits had finally driven the sailing vessels away from the ocean, but life went on, and the ships continued to ply their routes under steam power, and in this manner Riesenberg managed to dispel some of the pessimism of writers like London who described the end of an age but did not sketch out a new path for men at sea. In *Mother Sea* the Darwinian struggle was transformed into the hope of renewal and continued existence.

Riesenberg had captured better than anyone else the traumatic transition of individuals from two modes of life, one under sail and another under steam, but the relatively late date of his publication in 1933 was a sure indication that writers were starting to fall behind in the incorporation into their writings of the new situation in the merchant marine. In 1898, however, readers had no idea that the experiences of the merchant marine would no longer continue to enrich literature, because in that same year two great works on the steamship age appeared, the short story "The Open Boat" by the famous novelist Stephen Crane and *Futility: Or the Wreck of the Titan* by Morgan Robertson. "The Open Boat" immediately became one of the classic short stories of the sea, but it formed just an isolated part of the author's production and was written only because of the chance sinking that put the author adrift with part of the crew aboard a dinghy. The outstanding merit of "The Open Boat" should not hide the totally random circumstances that resulted in the publication of this story, which has inspired other stories that eventually fed into the Alfred Hitchcock movie,* *Lifeboat.*

Robertson, the son of a merchant captain, was enamored of the sea, became a sailor, and eventually rose to first mate. With his firsthand experience in all levels of the shipping business, he was able to write many short stories and novels about the sea. His most remarkable work was *Futility: Or the Wreck of the Titan*, in which he traced the career of a new passenger liner whose owners and officers were determined to break the speed records across the Atlantic. In an echo to the passing of sail, the steam liner cut in half a sailing vessel before the *Titan* herself, a product and a victim of Darwinian survival in the cutthroat business of shipping, sank after having collided with an iceberg. That Robertson was able to predict the disaster of the *Titanic** (whose specifications were strikingly similar to those of his *Titan*) fourteen years before it happened sufficed to make the book memorable, but the book also captured the spirit of unbounded optimism that seized many when experiencing the apparently unlimited potential of steam power: because the *Titan* was supposedly unsinkable, the ship carried few lifeboats, an eerie parallel to the later *Titanic* tragedy.

Robertson died in poverty in 1915, in spite of trying to make his later plots more market-oriented, and in 1912 Thornton J. Hains published his last book, *The White Ghost of Disaster: The Chief Mate's Yarn*, which gave a closer look at some of the corporate forces that drove men and vessels to destruction in the search for profits; afterward the tradition of great stories about the struggles of the modern steamship corporations and their ships gradually lost their appeal to most later writers. The British writer William McFee, who became a U.S. citizen in 1924, was himself an experienced chief engineer in both the British and U.S. merchant marines and tried to fill the gap with excellent stories, most notably *Casuals of the Sea* (1918) and *Swallowing the Anchor* (1925). McFee attained considerable fame, and more uniquely he was "the only writer to identify himself fully and proudly with steam" (Bender 1988). While most of the American writers since the age of sail had sympathized with the able-bodied* seaman on deck, McFee pointed out that a lot of that sympathy was not all that genuine, and he himself, more in the British tradition, brought an awareness of class and caste within the social order aboard ships, a dimension often missing in the more egalitarian American literature.

Just as novelists and short story writers were abandoning the merchant marine as subject matter for their plots, Eugene O'Neill, one of the greatest of American playwrights, made the merchant seamen the center of his literary efforts from 1914 to 1924. The lure of the sea as contained in books by Joseph Conrad and Jack London attracted O'Neill to the sea, and he shipped out as a seaman in British and U.S.-flag ships, until he discovered his true vocation as a playwright. Quite naturally he drew on his long, direct experience in merchant shipping for his early plays like *Bound East for Cardiff, The Long Voyage Home*, and *The Moon of the Caribbees*, these three later turned into a movie,* *The Long Voyage Home*. O'Neill continued to write other notable sea plays, such as *Ile, Anna Christie*, and *The Hairy Ape*. After 1924 O'Neill ceased to use the merchant marine as the main subject for his later plays, some of which, however, continued to have undertones of merchant shipping, in particular, his masterpiece *Mourning Becomes Electra*.

After O'Neill and McFee, the tradition of merchant shipping in literature became weak indeed, although the broader topic of man and the sea continued to inspire writers. John Steinbeck, who had studied marine biology, did use the sea in some of his writings, most notably *Sea of Cortez* (1941), but he never quite seized the opportunities for developing human plots around the ships. *The Old Man and the Sea* of Ernest Hemingway did not deal with merchant shipping and as a matter of fact unconsciously marked a return to the age of wood and sail, as if writers could find inspiration only by turning to the hallowed tradition in American literature of a vanished past rather than the present of steel and engines. World War II, of course, generated many naval novels and stories, and of these *Mister Roberts* (1946) by Thomas Heggen did deal with merchant shipping, in this case with the navy transport service. The book was an instant success, sold over a million copies, was adapted for the stage, and was eventually made into a movie. *Mister Roberts* dealt with the problems of men living in constant close proximity not of their own choice, a topic within merchant shipping that most writers have generally neglected.

While the sea has continued to inspire writers, the more specific topic of merchant shipping has gradually been lost in American literature. The opening of the West and the vast hinterland of the North American continent certainly captured the attention of many Americans, and some critics argue that the decline of U.S. merchant shipping in the late nineteenth century explained the loss of interest by writers in the merchant marine, but the shift from sail and wood to steam and steel seemed a more valid explanation. Writers who wished to explore merchant shipping under steam had to "retool" because the nautical and business knowledge of the age of sail no longer was applicable, while almost effortlessly, right before their eyes, many new topics appeared in the sprawling urban centers or in the cities of the West. The introduction of new forms of communications and transportation has also meant that as the twentieth century advanced, fewer writers themselves had the opportunity to experience merchant shipping—and if a smaller number of persons know about merchant shipping, presumably the market will not be able to sustain maritime novels. The neglect is regrettable, because for those who know how to look and write, from the corporate boardrooms to the lonely tramp* vessels, merchant shipping continues to offer fascinating plots just waiting to be tapped by the writer with the genius and abilities to produce great stories comparable to the classics of Herman Melville and Eugene O'Neill.

References: Bert Bender, *Sea-Brothers: The Tradition of American Sea Fiction from Moby-Dick to the Present* (Philadelphia: University of Pennsylvania Press, 1988); Max J. Herzberg, *The Reader's Encyclopedia of American Literature* (New York: Thomas Y. Corwell, 1962); Charles Lee Lewis, *Books of the Sea: An Introduction to Nautical Literature* (Westport, CT: Greenwood Press, 1972); Marion G. Sherar, *Shipping Out* (Cambridge, MD: Cornell Maritime Press, 1973).

LNG (LIQUIFIED NATURAL GAS) and LPG (LIQUIFIED PETROLEUM GAS) CARRIERS. Ocean vessels to carry liquified natural gas (LNG) and liquified petroleum gas (LPG) have given the United States a rare technological and commercial edge in one area of shipbuilding and merchant shipping. In LNG vessels, the gas was carried at very cold temperatures, while in LPG vessels the gas traveled under pressure; in the United States the LNG carriers have been the most common, exceeding in number and tonnage by a ratio of ten to one the LPG carriers. Until 1947 tankers had carried only oil ("crude") or refinery products, but not the natural gas which the companies had generally ignored or, worse, wasted. The C-1* freighter *Natalie O. Warren*, after conversion into the first LPG vessel, began to carry cargoes between Houston and New York in November 1947. The C-1-M* freighter, the *Methane Pioneer*, after conversion into the first LNG vessel, sailed on 31 January 1959 for England carrying natural gas from Louisiana. The United States has maintained a technological edge on the construction of these very expensive vessels, but as highly specialized ships, the LNG lacked the flexibility to carry other cargoes and, if they remained idle for long, immediately generated serious losses. In the mid-1980s a market slump idled many LNG vessels, whose owners defaulted in 1985–1988 on nearly half a billion dollars of loans guaranteed by the Maritime Administration.* Congress authorized a bailout to offset these huge losses that otherwise would have bankrupted the Maritime Administration. Even with the modest revival of the market in the early 1990s, the return of the LNGs with defaulted loans to commercial service has become a vexing task for the Maritime Administration.

References: American Bureau of Shipping, *History 1862–1991; American Shipper*, April 1990; Maritime Administration, *Tankers in the World Fleet 1982*, and *1992 Annual Report*; L. A. Sawyer and W. H. Mitchell, *From America to United States*, vol. 1 (Kendal, England, World Ship Society, 1979); Paul Stevens, ed., *Oil and Gas Directory* (New York: Nichols, 1988).

LOAD LINE. Experience had shown that overloading of vessels was one major cause of accidents at sea. An easy way was needed to restrain the natural desire of the shipowners to pack as much income-earning cargo into the vessel, and in the nineteenth century Samuel Plimsoll tried to convince the British government to require painting visible signs on the side of the ship. In 1931 the U.S. Congress ratified the International Load Line Convention, which required the following design to be easily visible on the side of the ship:

The lines marked the level to which a ship may settle in the water or how much of the hull must remain above the water as freeboard. The two highest ones stood for tropical fresh water (TF) and fresh water (F), the next four were for salt water: T for tropical, S for summer, W for winter, and WNA for winter in the North Atlantic. The circle with a line crossing its center and corresponding to the summer salt water level is called the Plimsoll mark in honor of its British advocate. One of the functions of classification* societies like the American Bureau of Shipping* has been to determine exactly the load lines for each ship, while enforcement since 1942 has been in the hands of the Coast Guard.* The shipowner could not be looking at the side to see how much more cargo could be loaded before exceeding the load line, so that the usual planning tool has been the deadweight* measurement (fuel, stores, and cargo of a ship). Each mark of the load line corresponded to a maximum number of deadweight tons, so that the shipowner knew exactly how many more deadweight tons he could load aboard the vessel without exceeding the load line applicable to the season and route of the specific voyage.

References: American Bureau of Shipping, *History 1862–1991; Jane's Merchant Ships, 1982*; Lane C. Kendall, *The Business of Shipping*, 5th ed. (Centreville, MD: Cornell Maritime Press, 1986); *New York Times*, 11 October 1959.

LONGSHOREMEN AND WAREHOUSEMEN'S UNION, INTER-NATIONAL (ILWU), 1937–present. The International Longshoremen and Warehousemen's Union (ILWU) since 1937 has been the labor organization representing all waterfront workers on the West Coast, as well as a majority of workers in Hawaii. The ILWU sprang partly from the particular conditions on the West Coast and also from the repeated failures of the International Long-shoremen's Association* (ILA) to establish any loyal following in that region. After the Big Strike* of 1934 Harry Bridges* emerged as the leader of the ILA branches on the West Coast, but when he tried to enlist the support of ILA president Joseph Ryan* for the 1936–1937 strike, he was rebuffed. Ryan offered a combination of company and tuxedo unionism* that the West Coast long-shoremen found repulsive, but since the American Federation of Labor (AFL) continued to back the ILA, Bridges turned for support to the Congress of Industrial Organizations (CIO), which authorized the creation of a new organization, the ILWU, in August 1937.

CIO affiliation was also necessary for the ILWU because the Maritime Federation of the Pacific* (MFP) had not only started to disintegrate but also spawned the extremely bitter rivalry between Bridges and Harry Lundeberg* of the Sailors Union of the Pacific* (SUP), a personal animosity whose intensity did not abate until Lundeberg's death in 1957. The ILWU and Lundeberg's new organization, the Seafarers' International Union* (SIU), waged bitter battles over the smaller maritime unions on the West Coast. Bridges warned in time the Marine Firemen, Oilers, Watertenders, and Wipers* (MFOWW) and the National Union of Marine Cooks and Stewards* (NUMCS) to join the ILWU before they were swallowed up by a hostile organization, but the smaller unions decided to retain their independence until it was too late. Once the Cold War began, Lundeberg cleverly manipulated the anti-communist hysteria to maneuver the MFOWW and the NUMCS into his SIU and away from Bridges's ILWU.

Lundeberg's Red-baiting was often successful because Bridges had a radical background and had at times cooperated with communist labor leaders, although he had never been a member. To neutralize Bridges and the ILWU, the employers and Lundeberg promoted a relentless effort to have the Australian Bridges deported from the United States, first on grounds of improper naturalization and later on charges of having falsely denied his alleged communist membership. The *Bridges* case* lasted from 1934 to 1955 and finally ended in Bridges's total vindication, although at the cost of considerable damage to the ILWU.

Most of the ILWU's organizing drives failed; for example, the "March Inland" in California was a flop, while the attempts to invade East Coast territory were literally beaten to insignificance by the strong-arm tactics of Lundeberg and the gangster-plagued ILA. However, the ILWU scored a major success in Hawaii when, under Jack Hall, all the workers in the docks as well as in the pineapple and sugar industries were organized as a branch of the ILWU in the 1940s. Hawaii was doubly remarkable because of the outstanding success of the union in overcoming racial barriers; indeed, this was the key to union strength, because the employers traditionally had pitted one race against another to keep wages and conditions low. The push toward racial harmony had begun with the Big Strike* of 1934 in San Francisco and gradually spread to other ports as the ILWU brought the locals under increasing pressure to accept persons of African and Asiatic ancestry. However, the traditional independence of locals allowed racist minorities in the Northwest and in southern California to delay the entry of blacks and other minorities until the 1960s.

The ILWU's progress in race relations was in sharp contrast to that of most other maritime unions, including Lundeberg's SIU, which remained a bastion of white supremacy. Even more striking was the ILWU's strong commitment to democratic practices, both at the central organization and at the locals. The ILWU leadership never sent thugs to beat the locals into obedience, while democratic processes remained the rule for elections and policies. As Bridges explained, "Our union is just as democratic as we can make it. Any guy can get up on the floor and call Harry Bridges all kinds of a bum, and I have got to take it" (Larrowe 1972). In some notable encounters, rank and file voted down Bridges's impassioned plea for a particular policy, but only after first giving him a spirited ovation. The ILWU's democratic tradition contrasted sharply with the iron rule by an oligarchy in most maritime unions.

The collapse of the MFP did not end ILWU's efforts to cooperate more closely with other unions. The ILWU offered to continue its no-strike pledge of World War II into the postwar period in order to help the reconstruction of war-torn Europe, but when employers rejected this olive branch, the ILWU with the National Maritime Union* (NMU) created the Committee for Maritime Unity* (CMU) in 1946. The brief-lived CMU secured high wages for the longshoremen and, more importantly, earned Bridges his reputation as a fair and reasonable negotiator. Employers learned to live with Bridges and the ILWU, and once the strike of 1948 was settled, labor peace reigned on the waterfront until 1971. The anticommunist hysteria was still in full force, however, and on the grounds of communist domination, the CIO expelled the ILWU on 29 August 1950. The ILWU survived as an independent union, and only in 1988, when organized labor faced the worst years since the 1920s, did the ILWU vote to affiliate with the AFL-CIO.

The Mechanization and Modernization Agreement* of 1960 was a milestone in the ILWU's life, because the union agreed to reduce the number of persons in the work gangs in exchange for large monetary payments. New technology, in particular, the containers,* had drastically reduced the need for labor on the waterfront, but the Vietnam War boom assured ample employment for longshoremen. Membership of the ILWU was around 65,000 men in 1971.

Bridges was eligible for retirement in 1965, but like many labor leaders, he was extremely reluctant to step down. Bridges made two bizarre moves in his last decade in the ILWU: first he proposed an alliance with tuxedo unionist Teddy Gleason* and his crime-ridden ILA in 1971, and later with the no less racket-prone Teamsters Union, but in both cases the rank and file rejected any efforts to abandon the traditional independence of the ILWU. Bridges finally retired in 1977 and was replaced as president by James R. Herman. In 1988 the ILWU voted to end its independent status and affiliated with the AFL-CIO, but this step has not meant any concrete moves toward a proposed merger with the ILA. In 1991 David Arian assumed the presidency of the ILWU.

Principal Labor Leaders

Harry Bridges	1937–1977
Louis Goldblatt*	1943–1977
James R. Herman	1977–1991
David Arian	1991–present

References: Walter Galenson, *The CIO Challenge to the AFL: A History of the American Labor Movement 1935–1941* (Cambridge: Harvard University Press, 1960); Howard Kimeldorf, *Reds or Rackets: The Making of Radical and Conservative Unions on the Waterfront* (Berkeley: University of California Press, 1988); Charles P. Larrowe, *Harry Bridges: The Rise and Fall of Radical Labor in the U.S.* (New York: Lawrence Hill, 1972); William W. Pilcher, *The Portland Longshoremen: A Dispersed Urban Community* (New York: Holt, Rinehart, and Winston, 1972); Maud Russell, *Men Along the Shore: The ILA and Its History* (New York: Brussel and Brussel, 1966).

LONGSHOREMEN'S ASSOCIATION, INTERNATIONAL (ILA), 1892– present. The International Longshoremen's Association has traditionally represented longshoremen in the Great Lakes, the East Coast, and Gulf. Numerous attempts to organize longshoremen in the New York Harbor area failed from 1864 to 1907, but instead in the Great Lakes, Dan Keefe* of Chicago rallied the men to create the ILA in Detroit in 1892. Locals spread rapidly throughout the country, but half of the reported 100,000 members in 1905 were in the Great Lakes. Keefe had succeeded where the rest had failed not only because of his dynamic personality but also because he realized that employers had the power to crush any union on the waterfront, so that disguised company unionism was the only possible alternative. Repeatedly Keefe would order locals to accept employer demands without a fight, because he knew the company would love to crush a strike. Extreme caution became ILA's policy, but all the time more longshoremen were effectively organized and placated with whatever crumbs Keefe could wiggle out of the employers. In 1908 Keefe resigned to accept a position in the federal government, and his most important legacy was the tradition of centralized power in the hands of an autocratic president.

Keefe's successor was Thomas V. O'Connor* of Buffalo, New York, who made that city the headquarters of the ILA. O'Connor was the most conservative of all ILA presidents, and under his leadership the ILA definitely turned into a company union meeting the needs of employers. O'Connor himself devoted most of his time and efforts to Buffalo and the Great Lakes, but he did authorize an organizing drive in New York City; starting in 1912, ILA's base began to shift from the Great Lakes to the East Coast. By 1915 O'Connor had become thoroughly disliked by longshoremen because of his policy of capitulating before employer demands. Discontent was so strong that he barely managed to fight off an ouster attempt by Thomas Herring of San Francisco. In disgust, Herring took his San Francisco local out of the ILA and established the separate Long-shoremen's Association of San Francisco and the Bay District in 1915, generally referred to as the "Blue Book Union."* O'Connor had become by then a pas-sive figure and made no attempt to gain other locals in the West Coast, a neglect that had consequences throughout the twentieth century. The wartime boom allowed O'Connor to hang on to the presidency until 1921, but seeing the end of the waterfront prosperity, he wisely accepted the appointment as commis-sioner of the Shipping Board* from President Warren Harding in 1921.

Authoritarian leadership had begun to erode under O'Connor and all but col-lapsed under his successor, Anthony Chlopek. Without centralized control, the locals negotiated their own contracts but frequently did not comply with their clauses. The locals and work gangs often engaged in wildcat strikes and other types of job action,* but in an uncoordinated way that hurt business without helping the labor movement. Employers began to remember longingly the good old days under Keefe when a disciplined labor force did not miss a beat, and finally after a bitter internal struggle, Joseph Ryan* emerged as the new ILA president in 1927.

Ryan had won the power struggle because he promised not to interfere with the independence of locals, whose officers continued to negotiate separate con-tracts in many cases. In exchange, Ryan gained freedom to use the presidency of the ILA without regard to the concerns of the locals. Soon Ryan degenerated into tuxedo unionism* as he paraded himself around in exquisitely tailored suits while he collected goon squads and thugs to enforce decisions. In order to "rehabilitate" former criminals, Ryan recruited actively among gangster ele-ments, and soon large parts of the New York waterfront were under mob control, either indirectly through Ryan or directly through the gangsters, who began to terrorize many of the locals. Ryan passed out large sums in cash to reward loyal followers and had become the undisputed boss of the waterfront on the East Coast, the Gulf, and the Great Lakes. Employers had the best of both worlds: they could negotiate cozy contracts with individual locals, but if the latter re-fused, steamship companies could always turn to Ryan to secure a favorable contract.

Ryan was so busy enjoying his empire that he neglected the West Coast, and consequently the Big Strike* in 1934 caught him by surprise; he had not even tried to fill the void left a few months before by the collapse of the Blue Book Union. In a desperate attempt to end the Big Strike,* employers rushed Ryan to San Francisco, but for the first time he was scared when he faced the furious determination of the striking workers. Their leader was Harry Bridges,* an Aus-tralian leftist who could be neither bought nor bullied. Ryan's mission in May 1934 was a failure and confirmed a permanent rift: the ILA remained in the

East, Gulf, and Great Lakes, while the West Coast became the domain of the newly created International Longshoremen and Warehousemen's Union* (ILWU) under Bridges.

Ryan continued to rule the ILA, but his abuses and arbitrary actions were eroding support. No longer concerned with rank-and-file feeling, he imposed a new contract in 1951, but its rushed approval triggered a wildcat strike against his leadership in October. Before he could regain full control over his union, government and judicial revelations further discredited him before the membership, and finally on 16 November 1953 he handed over the presidency to Captain William Bradley.

Ryan's resignation had been only the opening act in the concerted effort to destroy the ILA. The American Federation of Labor (AFL) had concluded that the ILA was rotten to the core and had to be replaced by a new organization, the International Brotherhood of Longshoremen (IBL). The AFL poured vast sums of money into the campaign and put Paul Hall,* the East Coast leader of the Seafarers' International Union (SIU), in charge of the campaign to destroy the ILA. David Beck of the Teamsters, another tuxedo unionist, also decided to attack the ILA in order to receive a share of the spoils. From March to May 1954 outright warfare raged on the waterfront, as each group sought to shore up its position for the crucial 25 May election to decide union representation. The ILA cause looked doomed, but the maverick of the labor movement, John L. Lewis, had his United Mine Workers support and fund the ILA. In spite of voting frauds and constant intimidation, the underdog ILA finally emerged the winner, but the AFL and the SIU kept up their attacks a few more years. Only in 1959 did the IBL finally merge with the ILA.

In 1956 the employers granted the union the dues checkoff, whereby the ILA received a percentage of each hour's wages received by the workers. This concession began to put the ILA on a solid financial basis, but many members still believed that under the more open and tolerant style of Captain Bradley the ILA had become soft in pressuring the employers. Thomas W. Gleason,* already a power behind the scenes, cleverly manipulated the discontent to mount a challenge against the incumbent for the ILA presidency in 1963. After a bitter fight, Captain Bradley decided the day before the election to withdraw from the race in exchange for the continuation of his salary, whereupon Gleason was acclaimed president at the ILA convention.

In his first statement the new president promised to return to the strong leadership style of Joseph Ryan. Gleason restored centralized control to the ILA, and soon all power was concentrated in his hands and those of his trusted subordinates. Gleason perpetuated himself in office through a rigid grip on the election machinery and turned the ILA into his personal empire. So much power brought Gleason the realization that he could be independent of *both* the union membership and the employers. Gleason disguised his autocratic control by a fanatical anticommunism. With the communist threat on the waterfront nonexistent, he directed his attacks against foreign communist governments. The ILA routinely participated in job actions* and threats of strikes against communist-flag ships, and even against ships of other countries that traded with communist Cuba. From very early Gleason strongly supported the Vietnam War.

Gleason's powerful grip did allow the ILA to drive a hard bargain with employers over the introduction of containers* into cargo-handling operations. Management's central demand was no longer to lower wages but rather to reduce the work gangs from their high of twenty men. A strike of December 1962-January 1963 was inconclusive, but a major strike in January 1965 finally resulted in a compromise "which made employers pay through the teeth for eliminating jobs" (Russell 1966). Featherbedding, high wages, and ample fringe benefits kept the membership satisfied under Gleason's iron rule but made some employers eager to seek nonunion docks to handle their containers at a fraction of the cost of Gleason's ILA. During the 1960s and 1970s, ILA membership hovered around 60,000 men, because larger cargo volumes had compensated for the jobs lost through containerization.

Racketeering, extortion, and embezzlement became widespread practices within the ILA, as the leaders used their unchecked power to accumulate personal fortunes. A long list of ILA convictions, not to mention indictments and many other charges, began to blacken the image of Gleason by the late 1970s, but his empire did not crumble at once, and only old age made Gleason end his reign in 1987. His hand-picked successor, John Bowers,* had been executive vice president for decades under Gleason, so no break occurred in policies.

Principal Labor Leaders

Daniel J. Keefe	1892–1908
Thomas V. O'Connor	1908–1921
Anthony Chlopek	1921–1927
Joseph P. Ryan	1927–1953
William V. Bradley	1953–1963
Thomas W. Gleason	1963–1987
John M. Bowers	1987–present

References: Howard Kimeldorf, *Reds or Rackets: The Making of Radical and Conservative Unions on the Waterfront* (Berkeley: University of California Press, 1988); Charles P. Larrowe, *Harry Bridges: The Rise and Fall of Radical Labor in the U.S.* (New York: Lawrence Hill, 1972); Maud Russell, *Men Along the Shore: The ILA and Its History* (New York: Brussel and Brussel, 1966).

LONGSHOREMEN'S ASSOCIATION OF SAN FRANCISCO AND THE BAY DISTRICT. See Blue Book Union.

LOS ANGELES STEAMSHIP COMPANY (LASSCO), 1920–1930. Until 1920 steamship service on the West Coast had remained concentrated in San Francisco and Seattle, to the virtual neglect of Los Angeles, in spite of the latter city's tremendous expansion. To remedy this deficiency, the Chamber of Commerce encouraged a group of local investors to incorporate the Los Angeles Steamship Company (LASSCO) on 10 June 1920. That same year LASSCO bought from the Shipping Board* the *Yale** and the *Harvard,** two combination passenger-cargo liners that, after extensive overhaul and upgrading, inaugurated the company's first line between Los Angeles and San Francisco. The company later added calls in San Diego and placed more ships in the run.

This highly successful coastwise* service convinced LASSCO to open a second line between Los Angeles and Hawaii. The Chamber of Commerce eagerly backed this idea and helped LASSCO lobby for the purchase of two ex-German passenger liners, the *Friedrich der Grosse* and the *Grosser Kurfurst*, from the Shipping Board in December 1921. Renamed, respectively, the *City of Honolulu** and the *City of Los Angeles*, the former on its first return voyage became a raging blaze and was abandoned without loss of life. As a replacement, LASSCO acquired other vessels from the Shipping Board, including two more ex-German passenger lines in August 1926, one of which was renamed the *City of Honolulu II.**

LASSCO was building up successfully the tourist trade to the Hawaiian islands, but Matson Navigation Company* did not accept being pushed to the side. In November 1927 Matson's new liner, *Malolo,** provided tough competition, and LASSCO's share of the passenger trade declined. To try to keep up, LASSCO had turned to short-term credits to refurbish extensively the old *City of Honolulu II*, only to have the ship burn down at the Honolulu pier in May 1930. By then the Great Depression had struck, and while Matson was ready to resume construction of three new liners at the signs of the first upturn, financially stretched LASSCO was stuck with an old fleet, and the Shipping Board had run out of vessels to sell at giveaway prices. LASSCO accepted in October 1930 a merger with Matson by means of an exchange of stock. However, the company had not been a failure, because afterward Matson, to prevent the appearance of another rival, always made sure its vessels made frequent calls in Los Angeles, and hence the original purpose of the venture had been achieved.

Notable Ships

Yale and *Harvard*	1920–1930
City of Honolulu I	1922
City of Honolulu II	1927–1930

References: Giles T. Brown, *Ships That Sail No More: Marine Transportation from San Diego to Puget Sound, 1910–1940* (Lexington: University of Kentucky Press, 1966); Frederick E. Emmons, *American Passenger Ships* (Newark: University of Delaware Press, 1985); Fred A. Stindt, *Matson's Century of Ships* (Modesto, CA: n.p., 1982).

LOYALTY CONTRACTS. See dual-rate contracts.

LUCKENBACH, EDGAR F., 19 January 1868–26 April 1943. Edgar F. Luckenbach was the president of the Luckenbach Steamship Company* during its most successful years. He was born in Kingston, New York, on 19 January 1868 and studied in public schools in Brooklyn. At an early age he went to work with his father, Lewis, who had established in 1850 a tugboat business, the origin of the Luckenbach Steamship Company. Edgar moved with his father to Philadelphia, where they prospered as operators of tugs and barges but later moved headquarters back to New York City and entered the business of salvaging wrecked ships. By the end of the nineteenth century the company owned iron-hulled sailing vessels, and when Edgar became president in 1906 upon the death of his father, the transition to steamers was well advanced. Edgar sensed a great opportunity in the Panama Canal,* prior to whose completion he acquired the financing to build a fleet of new steamships for the intercoastal* service in which his company was specializing. When the Panama Canal opened on 15 August 1914, Luckenbach Steamship was ready with its new steamers, and Edgar made sure the company acquired a strong position in the intercoastal trade.

After U.S. entry into World War I, the ships of the company were requisitioned for wartime service, and the last were not returned until 1920. Edgar was ready with a new program to maintain the lead of the company over other rivals, most notably the American-Hawaiian Steamship Company,* and his slogan became "the largest and fastest freighters in the intercoastal trade." In 1920 his son by his second marriage, J. Lewis Luckenbach, joined the company as vice president, and the father-and-son team appeared to be working very effectively until 1925, when the son resigned and subsequently went to work for the American Bureau of Shipping.* Although the company was prosperous, vicious rate wars were ruining all the steamship companies in the field, and because attempts to establish order through the United States Intercoastal Conference* failed, Edgar led the campaign to expand the authority of the federal government to set minimum rates (not just maximum rates, as before), an authority that the Interstate Commerce Commission* (ICC) administered since 1940. Edgar remained the president of Luckenbach Steamship Company until his death at Sands Point, New York, on 26 April 1943. However, neither of his two sons replaced him in the company because settlement of his estate proved particularly difficult, and to run the company the trustees appointed James Sinclair.

References: *National Cyclopedia of American Biography*, vol. 35; *New York Times*, 14 December 1958; *Pacific Marine Review*, April 1933; *Who's Who in the Maritime Industry, 1946.*

LUCKENBACH, EDGAR F., JR., 17 May 1925–9 August 1974. Edgar F. Luckenbach, Jr., was the president of Luckenbach Steamship Company* during its period of decline and eventual disintegration. He was born in New York City on 17 May 1925 and was the son of Edgar F. Luckenbach* by the latter's third marriage. Edgar, Jr., attended private schools, and when the United States entered World War II, he joined the navy as a sailor, refusing to use his connections to secure a plush desk job. He served until 1946, and the next year he was commissioned an ensign in the reserves. In 1947 he pursued his childhood dream of staging plays and opened his own theatrical production company in New York City; after producing a number of plays, his stage venture ended in 1950 when he returned to active duty in the navy because of the Korean War, and he eventually rose to the rank of captain in the reserves.

He worked as a marine insurance underwriter in 1952–1957 and then went to work with States Marine Corporation.* At last in 1959 he joined the Luckenbach Steamship Company, and the next year he replaced James Sinclair as the company's president. Edgar, Jr., tackled immediately the problem of the company's losses in its intercoastal* run, and he prepared to order new ships for containers* as the best way to meet the competition from the railroads. A government subsidy for the construction of the new ships was essential, but when it was not forthcoming, Edgar, Jr., had no choice but to suspend the intercoastal service, whose last sailing was on 22 March 1961.

Luckenbach Steamship Company now chartered* out its vessels in the foreign trade and eventually sold them. Edgar, Jr., widened his investment in other shoreside activities, such as stevedoring, the operation of terminals, steamship agency representation, and freight forwarding.* He still longed to return to the intercoastal service, and as a staunchly conservative Republican, he held high hopes that the election of Richard Nixon as president would mean the revival of the U.S. merchant marine. He announced his plans in October 1973 to build for the intercoastal trade the two largest lumber carriers in the world if his application for a construction subsidy was approved. These exciting plans ended suddenly when Edgar F. Luckenbach, Jr., was found dead in an East Side apartment of New York City on 9 August 1974. The one-bedroom apartment was occupied by two women, neither his relatives nor his wife; residents ''said they had frequently seen well-dressed middle-aged men entering the apartment'' (*New York Times*, 11 August 1974). The medical examiner termed the death ''suspicious,'' and in this mysterious way a shipping dynasty of three generations came to an end.

References: *Florida Journal of Commerce*, February 1969, October 1973; *National Cyclopedia of American Biography*, Current vol. L; *New York Times*, 14 December 1959, 11, 22 August 1974.

LUCKENBACH STEAMSHIP COMPANY, 1850–1974. In the twentieth century the Luckenbach Steamship Company was one of the most important firms in the intercoastal* trade between the East and West coasts of the United States. Lewis Luckenbach established the firm in New York City with a single tugboat, and later he moved the firm to Philadelphia. He pioneered in the use of oceangoing barges to carry coal from Norfolk to New England and against the opposition of insurance underwriters, began to tow barges in tandem, a practice that later became standard. ''With the towing and barging business definitely mastered, Lewis Luckenbach, accompanied by his son Edgar F. Luckenbach''* (*Pacific Marine Review*, April 1933) moved headquarters back to New York City, where they expanded into the business of salvaging wrecked ships. The salvage and repair of ships pointed toward vessel ownership, and starting with the *Tillie E. Starbuck*, the company began sending sailing ships of iron hull around Cape Horn to the West Coast and as far as Hawaii and the Far East. When Lewis died in 1906 and his son took over as head, the company was completing its shift to steamships.

With the construction of the Panama Canal* under way, Edgar Luckenbach sensed that the greatest opportunity for the company lay in the intercoastal trade, and to that effect he divided his ships into an Atlantic and Pacific fleet in 1908, with the cargoes carried across the isthmus by the Panama Railroad. The company obtained the financing to order the construction of a fleet of new steamers, and its ships were among the first to use the Panama Canal when it opened on 15 August 1914. Like almost all other steamship companies, the Luckenbach vessels were requisitioned in 1917 for duty during World War I, and the last one was not returned to the company until 1920.

The company's slogan became ''the largest and fastest freighters in the intercoastal trade,'' and with an average speed of twelve to fifteen knots, the ships were among the fastest and eventually served as inspiration to the U.S. Maritime Commission for its C-2* and C-3* vessels designs of the late 1930s. The *Andrea F. Luckenbach* and the *Lewis Luckenbach* when built were the largest under the U.S. flag. However, the company's treatment of seafarers was among the worst in the U.S. merchant marine and was exceeded only by the ''hell ships'' of the Munson Line.* In 1920 J. Lewis Luckenbach, the son of Edgar by his second marriage, joined the company as vice president and promptly began to reinvigorate and modernize his father's organization. The father-and-son team appeared to be working smoothly, but something happened in 1925, when the son resigned all his positions; however, Lewis's career in shipping was just starting, and in 1927 he joined the American Bureau of Shipping* (ABS) and eventually rose to the rank of president. Shortly after the outbreak of World War II in 1939, the government began to requisition the company's vessels until all were withdrawn from service. In 1943 Edgar died, but because the disposition of his contested estate dragged on for years, the trustees hired James Sinclair to run the company.

After the return of peace, the company sold its last old ships and purchased sixteen C-2 and C-3 surplus ships; while the postwar boom lasted, Luckenbach Steamship also operated chartered vessels on the foreign trade. Almost from the start the company was losing money on its intercoastal service and was kept afloat by the foreign trade, whose profits lasted until the postwar shipping shortage ended in 1949. Luckenbach was left with too many ships and could place them only in the unprofitable intercoastal service. Westbound the ships generally sailed full, but to supplement the lean eastbound cargoes the company's vessels began calling on Havana to try to complete their loads. The intercoastal service

324 LUDWIG, DANIEL K.

from the Gulf of Mexico to the West Coast was still showing losses, and in an attempt to solve the problem, in 1953 the company transferred the management of that route to States Marine Corporation,* which purchased the route and its nine freighters in 1959.

In 1960 Edgar F. Luckenbach, Jr.,* Edgar's son by his third marriage, assumed the presidency of the company and quickly decided that only decisive action could save the company. To remain competitive in the intercoastal trade, he began to negotiate for the construction of ships to carry containers,* but when it became clear that no government subsidies would be forthcoming for the construction costs, he discontinued the intercoastal service, whose last sailing from San Francisco to New York took place on 22 March 1961.

Luckenbach Steamship Company thereafter survived as a company engaged in a wide variety of shipping activities such as stevedoring, operation of terminals, steamship agency representation, and freight forwarder.* The company continued to charter* vessels, which apparently it operated in tramp* service; when Richard Nixon became president of the United States, Luckenbach had high hopes that the government at last would support the revival of intercoastal shipping. Luckenbach's tragic death in 1974 came as an unexpected blow to the company, whose breakup and eventual disappearance were inevitable. Under the same family control during three generations, the Luckenbach Steamship Company resembled the tradition of other families like the Mallorys* and the Bulls.*

Principal Executives

Lewis Luckenbach	1850–1906
Edgar F. Luckenbach	1906–1943
J. Lewis Luckenbach	1920–1925
James Sinclair	1943–1959
Edgar F. Luckenbach, Jr.	1960–1974

Notable Ships

Andrea L. Luckenbach and
Lewis Luckenbach

References: Frank F. Farrar, *A Ship's Log Book* (St. Petersburg, FL: Great Outdoors, 1988); *Florida Journal of Commerce*, February 1969, October 1973; *New York Times*, 15 October 1953; *Pacific Marine Review*, April 1933; *Pacific Shipper*, 23 September 1959, 27 February 1961; President's Advisory Committee on the Merchant Marine, Harry S. Truman Presidential Library, Independence, Missouri; U.S. Senate, Committee on Interstate and Foreign Commerce, *Merchant Marine Study and Investigation*, 7 vols. (Washington, DC: Government Printing Office, 1949–1950); *Who's Who in the Maritime Industry, 1946*.

LUDWIG, DANIEL K., 24 June 1897–27 August 1992. Daniel Ludwig, a billionaire, was a shipping executive and head of a worldwide conglomerate of business enterprises. He was born in South Haven, Michigan, on 24 June 1897 of a fairly prosperous family; his father, grandfather, and several uncles had been experienced captains or shipbuilders, and it was perhaps inevitable that the young Ludwig took interest in ships from early in his life. When his parents' marriage broke up around 1912, he left with his father for Port Arthur, Texas, and began to work for a ship chandler firm, while continuing his formal education at night school. After a year he returned to Michigan, where he obtained his engineer's license and worked for a company installing marine engines, but by the time he was nineteen years old, he quit and went into business on his own.

World War I had already started, and with the demand for ships skyrocketing, he could not have picked a better time to go into shipping. His biggest break came not during but after the war, when Prohibition* went into effect on 17 January 1920. He already owned barges he used to carry abroad molasses for distilling into alcoholic liquors, and he may have been involved in the actual rum-running into the United States. A close scrape with the law may have convinced him to abandon activities related to Prohibition, and in any case, with the profits he had made and the financial support from his father, Ludwig by 1923 shifted permanently to the carriage of oil. He hauled oil, but most of his profits came from buying, repairing, converting, and then selling ships, so that although he seemed to operate like a ship broker,* in reality he was drawing upon his engineering talents and his detailed knowledge of marine salvage to reap higher gains than a normal broker could make. Ludwig insisted on personally inspecting his ships and supervising all major repairs, and in 1926 while trying to convert a large freighter into a tanker, an explosion killed two crewmen and landed him on his back; he suffered agonizing pain in his spine for decades, and only in 1956 did he at last agree to corrective surgery. His first marriage in 1928 led to separation and divorce, but his second marriage in 1936 to G. Virginia (or Ginger, as she was usually called) proved lasting. His second wife was not an active participant in his business ventures, yet her name began to appear as a director in some of his many corporations; later she headed two cancer research institutes Ludwig had established with his wealth.

Up to World War II, he was involved mainly with merchant shipping and handled his activities through the American Tankers Corporation he had established in 1924, initially as an operating, and later as a holding, company. His favored approach was to buy a vessel from the Shipping Board* and later from the U.S. Maritime Commission,* refit her, and then resell her at a nice profit; if he could not find a buyer immediately, he would charter* the vessel, and since he had borrowed most of the money from the government, it was a great way to make large profits. Sometimes, however, when the deals became entangled or otherwise delayed, Ludwig suffered moments of anguish, but he always managed to keep the government from foreclosing on him until the right business opportunity once again restored his fortunes. By the late 1930s he was among those who to build a tanker pioneered the method of borrowing money from the banks against a long-term charter signed by an oil company: without having put up a cent of his money, American Tankers Corporation obtained a new tanker.

Ludwig studiously avoided the subsidy programs created by the Merchant Marine Act of 1936* and instead found in other arrangements with the government the way to make his profits. In anticipation of World War II, he acquired a shipyard near Norfolk, Virginia, in 1938 and until its closing in 1950 built a total of twenty ships in his Welding Shipyard. As an engineer Ludwig had taken great pride in constructing the biggest tankers, which were classified as oversize T-3, the largest of the tanker designs. In one of his easiest deals, he sold the *Hampton Roads*, a nearly finished tanker sitting in his ways to the government for $3 million and promptly rebought the tanker under the provisions of the Ship Sales Act of 1946*—which he had helped to write—for $1.3 million. During the war his ships had been requisitioned, but he still managed to make substantial profits by operating government vessels for the War Shipping Administration* (WSA) under the general agency agreements. With the return of peace, he received his former vessels, and with those he later acquired, he emerged as the fifth largest independent tanker operator in the United States, but his real goal was now to own the largest tanker fleet in the world.

The old American Tankers Corporation gradually faded from view, and its place was taken by National Bulk Carriers, which he organized on 1 June 1936. National Bulk Carriers evolved in a manner similar to that of the American Tanker Corporation, in that both began as ship-operating companies and gradually became holding companies. However, National Bulk Carriers reflected the lead Ludwig was taking in the transportation of bulk* cargoes as distinct from just oil, as before. Up to World War II, tankers, colliers,* and ore carriers had been mostly small vessels hauling their cargoes only in one direction and returning empty, but with the construction of versatile vessels capable of carrying most types of bulk cargoes, it was possible sometimes to obtain return cargoes or to combine different types of bulk cargoes to fill completely the same vessel. A new type of vessel was now necessary, the Ore/Bulk/Oil or OBO* ships, and Ludwig was at the forefront of their development, which also afforded him a valuable entry into the market for ores, coal, and grains for his rapidly diversifying international business conglomerate. In the OBO ships just like in the tankers, Ludwig strove to build the biggest vessels, because as he had verified during his shipbuilding experience in World War II, the bigger the ship, the lower the operating costs.

By 1947 Ludwig was the largest independent tanker operator in the United States (a position held before World War II by Clifford D. Mallory*), but Ludwig by then realized that the biggest profits in the tanker industry were in hauling oil from the Middle East to the United States and to other consuming centers. The Greek shipping tycoons Aristotle Onassis and Stavros Niarchos had purchased surplus U.S. vessels and placed them under flags of convenience,* and now Ludwig hurriedly had to play catch up as he rammed through the U.S. Maritime Commission the applications to shift his tankers from U.S. registry* to the Panamanian flag. The U.S. Maritime Commission, already greatly discredited, foolishly consented to these transfers, thereby contributing to the abolishment of this agency in 1950. In any case, Ludwig's transfers had helped coin the term *runaway** flag, which in his case was true, but not for the majority of U.S. corporations, whose ships had been built for operation only under the flags of convenience. His reputation with maritime unions was further deteriorated by the atrocious conditions on board his ships, and seafarers tried to avoid his tankers, while his fame for extreme stinginess was legendary.

In 1950 he closed his Welding Shipyard near Norfolk and moved shipbuilding to Kure, Japan, where the ways that had formerly built the battleships of the Japanese navy were big enough for the supertankers Ludwig had in mind. He retained a foothold in U.S.-flag shipping when he gained full control of American-Hawaiian Steamship* (AHSS) in 1955, and for another ten years played with proposals to revive its intercoastal* service with large new containerships generously subsidized by the federal government. AHSS never reentered shipping, but for Ludwig the tax advantages of the firm and the sale of its assets and real estate holdings proved a more than lucrative investment. During the AHSS venture Ludwig encountered Malcom McLean,* whose Sea-Land* was in deep financial problems; after some sparring, both men joined forces. Ludwig not only bailed out Malcom McLean by buying his stock but later also made a fivefold profit when he sold the McLean stock to R. J. Reynolds Tobacco. In spite of the profitable deals, Ludwig had by then ended his involvement in U.S.-flag operations and shifted completely toward the huge tankers under flags of convenience.

National Bulk Carriers as a holding company now left the actual operation of the tankers to a subsidiary, Universe Tankships. The closing of the Suez Canal in 1956 had stimulated the demand for giant tankers, and Ludwig built at his Kure shipyard bigger tankers and competed with Onassis and Niarchos to have the largest tanker in the world. National Bulk Carriers had meanwhile branched out into a myriad of international activities, starting with the construction of refineries and drilling for oil. Agriculture, financing, hotels, housing, and real estate became major new occupations for National Bulk Carriers, and the great size of this conglomerate allowed it to offset losses in one venture with spectacular gains in another part of the world. A major setback came, however, when Ludwig decided to tame the Brazilian Amazon, and in the worst business loss of his career and certainly the most embarrassing, the jungle destroyed his vast engineering projects.

Other ventures occasionally suffered losses, but the steady profits his huge tanker and bulk fleet kept grinding out allowed Ludwig to recover and to remain the richest of the American shipping executives. In politics he was a very conservative Republican and not only knew, but was a staunch supporter of, Richard Nixon and Ronald Reagan, whose photograph Ludwig displayed in his Manhattan apartment. Although still considered a billionaire in 1990, a number of his ventures of the 1980s had turned sour, including savings and loans associations that the federal government had to take over. He had been inactive in the last years because of poor health and died of heart failure in his Manhattan apartment on 27 August 1992.

References: René De La Pedraja, *The Rise and Decline of U.S. Merchant Shipping in the Twentieth Century* (New York: Twayne, 1992); John N. Ingham, *Biographical Dictionary of American Business Leaders* (Westport, CT: Greenwood Press, 1983); *New York Times*, 29 August 1992; Jerry Shields, *The Invisible Billionaire: Daniel Ludwig* (Boston: Houghton Mifflin, 1986).

LUNDEBERG, HARRY ("LUNCHBOX"), 25 March 1901–28 January 1957. Harry Lundeberg was the president of the Sailors' Union of the Pacific* (SUP) and the Seafarers' International Union* (SIU) for over twenty years. He was the real successor to Andrew Furuseth* and, like him, was a native of Norway, where he was born in Oslo on 25 March 1901. Lundeberg attended schools in Norway until he was fourteen and then, in the tradition of his family, shipped aboard a vessel. Two of his brothers died at sea, and he worked as a deckhand throughout the world's seas. In 1927 he joined the SUP in Seattle and in 1933 became a naturalized U.S. citizen. His literacy made him a natural candidate for full-time union work, and in 1934 he left the sea to become a union patrolman.* Initially he retained his parents' radicalism, and after he distinguished himself in the Big Strike,* he soon caught the attention of Harry Bridges, who chose Lundeberg to become the first president of the newly created Maritime Federation of the Pacific* (MFP). Lundeberg promised the MFP, "We'll fight the capitalists to a finish unless they give us our rights" (Nelson 1990), but soon after he began to move to the right and by 1937 had become the most conservative labor leader in the sailors' unions.

Lundeberg acquired a reputation for violence, and he used groups of thugs and goon squads to terrorize opponents; in a slugging clash with longshoremen, police caught him distributing baseball bats to sailors in 1938, but he later bragged that he fooled the police by claiming the communists had tried to frame him. After this street brawl, the disintegration of the MFP was inevitable, because any cooperation with the longshoremen under Bridges was out of the question. By then Lundeberg had lost any trace of his earlier radicalism and had moved so far to the right that he soon became a conservative Republican living in a fashionable neighborhood of San Francisco. He still dressed in the sailor's traditional garb and denounced tuxedo unionism,* but except for skipping the tuxedo, he was a throwback to the pro-business labor leaders of the early twentieth century.

Lundeberg decided to concentrate on building his own power base within the SUP by repeatedly challenging the supporters of Bridges, and the two became bitter enemies for the rest of their lives. When Lundeberg won the election for president of the SUP in January 1937, he had secured the bastion of power that he jealously guarded until his death. By 1937 the struggle for power and wealth had become the overriding consideration for Lundeberg, and on that criterion he decided the issue of whether to affiliate with the Congress of Industrial Organizations (CIO) or stay with the conservative American Federation of Labor (AFL). When the CIO encouraged the formation of the National Maritime Union* (NMU) in the Atlantic and Gulf, Lundeberg saw the new, larger union as a mortal threat that could swallow up his smaller SUP. The last straw came when the CIO chose Bridges as its West Coast regional director: Lundeberg tore up the ballots of sailors who had voted to affiliate with the CIO, and the SUP stayed within the AFL.

Lundeberg's labor enemies were all now in place: Bridges, Joseph Curran* of the NMU, and the CIO, all of whom he eventually lumped together as "communists." The AFL generously rewarded Lundeberg's support by creating for him the Seafarers' International Union (SIU) to replace the totally discredited International Seamen's Union* (ISU). Presidency of the SIU gave Lundeberg a national base to fight the NMU on its home grounds, but his penchant for violence did not abate: "Organizing in the Gulf, particularly in the seamen's field is no picnic, due to the fact that all kinds of tactics are used, such as goon squads, gun-play, black jacks, etc., which seems to be the order of the day. . . . This is indeed a strange way to organize, but . . . nowadays one must organize and deal with people as we find them—and according to circumstances" (ibid.). Actually, the attempts to build a new base for the SIU out of the wreckage of the ISU were largely unsuccessful until Paul Hall* became the chief organizer for the Atlantic and Gulf coasts. Lundeberg himself entered the highest hierarchy of the American labor movement: when the AFL and the CIO fused in 1955, he received the additional plum of president of the Maritime Trades Department* (MTD), but only after a furious power struggle against Curran.

The bitter rivalry between Lundeberg and Bridges poisoned the waterfront for over twenty years. Among other clashes, Lundeberg began in 1948 a bitter fight to gain control of the National Union of Marine Cooks and Stewards* (NUMCS) against the opposition of Bridges's longshoremen. Finally in 1955 Lundeberg brought the predominantly black union into the ISU, which reluctantly began to shed some of its white supremacist practices.

To the end Lundeberg maintained an iron grip over his main power base, the SUP, and he remained its only officer. However, during the 1950s his presidency of the ISU came increasingly under threat because of Paul Hall's extraordinary recruiting success in the Atlantic and Gulf against Curran's NMU. To head off the danger, Lundeberg began a reconciliation with the former archenemy Curran in June 1953, an effort that culminated with the establishment of the Conference of American Maritime Unions* (CAMU) in January 1954, whose two cochairman were Curran and Lundeberg. However, the feud between both men was too deep to be so easily healed, and CAMU collapsed in March 1955. The failure of CAMU meant that Paul Hall's power base continued to grow, so that when Lundeberg died on 28 January 1957, Hall became president of the SIU and the MTD, in effect becoming the real successor to Lundeberg, just as the latter had been the successor to Andrew Furuseth.

References: *Current Biography 1952*; *Dictionary of American Biography*, Supplement 6; Gary M. Fink, ed., *Biographical Dictionary of American Labor*, 2d ed. (Westport, CT: Greenwood Press, 1984); Bruce Nelson, *Workers on the Waterfront: Seamen, Longshoremen, and Unionism in the 1930s* (Urbana: University of Illinois Press, 1990); Betty V. H. Schneider, *Industrial Relations in the West Coast Maritime Industry* (Berkeley: University of California Press, 1958).

LURLINE, 1933–1963. The growing popularity of Hawaii as a tourist destination for mainland U.S. tourists convinced the Matson Navigation Company* to increase its fleet of passenger liners. To meet the higher than expected demand by wealthy travelers, Matson ordered the vessel built with accommodations for only 760 first-class passengers. The *Lurline* entered service in 1933, and in conjunction with the *Malolo*,* allowed Matson to provide weekly sailings in the San Francisco–Honolulu route. When the United States entered World War II, the government requisitioned the *Lurline*, but after the war she returned to Matson, which extensively refitted her so she could resume full passenger service between Hawaii and California in 1947. However, by the early 1950s the ship was starting to show losses, while the arrival of jet planes in the late 1950s reduced the number of first-class travelers. To cut losses, Matson decided to sell the *Lurline* in 1963 and to channel the passenger trade through its remaining liners. The name *Lurline* did not disappear immediately, however, because upon the sale of the ship, Matson changed the name of the *Matsonia** to the *Lurline*.

References: Frederick E. Emmons, *American Passenger Ships: The Ocean Lines and Liners, 1873–1983* (Newark: University of Delaware Press, 1985); Fred A. Stindt, *Matson's Century of Ships* (Modesto, CA: n.p., 1982); William L. Worden, *Cargoes: Matson's First Century in the Pacific* (Honolulu: University Press of Hawaii, 1981).

LYKES BROTHERS STEAMSHIP COMPANY, 1898–present. For nearly a century Lykes Brothers Steamship Company has been the most important ocean navigation firm in the Gulf of Mexico. The Lykes family began carrying lumber and cattle from its properties in the South to Cuba after the Spanish-American war in 1898, and with the acquisition of lands in the island, the link with Cuba became vital and lasted for nearly sixty years. Initially Lykes Brothers Steamship Company merely chartered* foreign-flag tonnage as needed to move its own cargoes to Cuba and gradually to other ports in the Caribbean. The decisive opportunity to expand dramatically came only when the Shipping Board* began to pay private companies to run government-owned ships, and Lykes Brothers jumped at the chance to become in October 1918 one of the first managing operators* in the Gulf of Mexico, and henceforth it operated U.S.-flag ships exclusively.

Lykes, just like Delta Line* and Waterman Steamship Corporation,* could count on strong regional support because shippers* for long felt that steamship services favored New York at the expense of the Gulf of Mexico. At least a dozen new firms appeared in the Gulf of Mexico, but Lykes soon concluded that only one could survive and decided to destroy or eliminate all the other rivals. Lykes Brothers crushed one opponent after another and absorbed firms such as United Steamship Company, Daniel Ripley and Company, the Tampa Interocean Steamship Company, and Dixie Steamship Company. Only the take-over attempt against Waterman Steamship Corporation* failed completely, while the attack against the Delta Line,* although repulsed, did gain for Lykes Brothers the European service of the Delta Line. Lykes Brothers in 1932 purchased at giveaway prices the fifty-two vessels on its routes from the Shipping Board, and although the transaction had been handled in such an unusual manner that the government later did not hand over nine of the ships, with the forty-three it had purchased Lykes Brothers permanently confirmed its position as the largest steamship company in the Gulf of Mexico prior to World War II.

The War Shipping Administration* (WSA) requisitioned the vessels for war-time duty, and after the conflict was over, Lykes Brothers took advantage of the favorable provisions of the Ship Sales Act of 1946* to purchase a new fleet. With these new vessels Lykes continued to operate in its traditional routes to the Caribbean and especially to Cuba and in the routes it had already established in the 1920s from the Gulf to the Mediterranean, Northern Europe, and the Far East. Once the postwar shipping shortage ended, foreign competition intensified, and Lykes, like most U.S.-flag companies, requested and received operating differential subsidies* from the Maritime Administration* (MARAD).

By the late 1950s the company's ships were nearing the end of their twenty-year life, and in order to raise funds for the vessel replacement program, Chairman Solon B. Turman decided to issue stock for the first time. He separated the shipping from the rest of the family businesses; the public bought about 10 percent of the stock in the new company in the 1950s, and by 1969 the Lykes family owned only about 55 percent of the stock. The careful plans to replace the World War II vessels with 1960s freighters were upset when U.S. opposition to the Cuban Revolution ended the trade with Cuba, leaving Lykes Brothers with an excess of vessels. Lykes was able to return the vessels on long-term charter back to MARAD and placed some of the excess vessels on a new service to Puerto Rico, with calls in other Caribbean ports; the profits from these ships were essential to continue the vessel replacement program, and the company gained enough time until U.S. involvement in the Vietnam War guaranteed for nearly ten years the full utilization of the company's fleet.

The ships initially ordered for the vessel replacement program were for the traditional break-bulk* cargo, but by the mid-1960s the wider use of new transportation methods like containers* convinced Lykes Brothers to experiment with a new design, the Seabees. These ships, of which three were ordered in 1966, were a hybrid between the barge carrier (similar to LASH*) and the Roll-on/Roll-off* (Ro/Ro) carrier and were particularly suited to handle extralarge and military equipment. The company operated the three Seabees until 1986, when they were sold to the navy for incorporation into the National Defense Reserve Fleet.* The advantages of containers soon became so clear that in 1970 the company ordered the conversion of nine break-bulk freighters, until eventually it had converted most of its fleet into containerships.

Lykes Brothers since 1962 had adopted the policy of diversification into non-shipping activities as a way to reduce the risks inherent in the highly volatile ocean transportation. The cash-rich company easily qualified to borrow large sums from the banks, and after several minor acquisitions, in February 1969 the company, under the leadership of Frank A. Nemec, bought Youngstown Sheet and Tube, then the eighth largest steel company in the United States. Lykes Brothers now became the steamship subsidiary, but complications soon appeared, and in 1978 LTV Corporation took over Youngstown Sheet and Tube, thereby gaining control of Lykes Brothers Steamship Company. However, LTV had no particular desire to remain in shipping and accepted an offer by the management of Lykes Brothers to repurchase the shipping subsidiary in November 1982, and the sale was completed in March 1983. Once again Lykes Brothers was an independent company devoted exclusively to ocean transportation.

Lykes Brothers had continued to look for new openings for its shipping services and in 1975 entered into the Great Lakes, which had lacked U.S.-flag service since 1968, when American Export Lines* abandoned its route. Lykes, however, wanted something bigger and since the 1960s had been carefully watching and trying to open trade with communist China as a way to obtain a commanding position in the Far East trade; the company's efforts eventually culminated in a 1979 agreement to open the ports of China and the United States to the ships of both countries. The China opening came just as Lykes Brothers had embarked on its most dramatic expansion ever, the establishment of trans-pacific service from the Far East to the West Coast. Lykes had reigned supreme in the Gulf of Mexico but had always wanted to become a major force in one of the other U.S. coasts, and the big opportunity came with the bankruptcy of States Steamship Lines* (SSS) in late 1978.

Lykes agreed to take over three of the Ro/Ro ships of SSS so that the latter could pay off its creditors; with these three ships and five of its other containerships, Lykes began in March 1979 its first regularly scheduled service between ports in the Far East and the West Coast. How Lykes could succeed where SSS had failed with the three Ro/Ros was never explained, but the company plunged with great enthusiasm into its West Coast venture. American President Lines* (APL) bitterly opposed the entry of this new rival and constantly fought back with every legal and economic tool at its disposal. In early 1984, however, APL backed off and accepted an arrangement that appeared to leave Lykes free to operate on the West Coast. In reality APL wanted to strike a crushing blow against its new rival by luring Lykes into a trap. Lykes had begun to sense that APL's new diesel* containerships could drive off all other U.S.-flag competition and had ordered its own diesel containerships, but these would be ready too late to affect the outcome of the battle in San Francisco. APL in one of its wisest decisions had earlier moved its operations to Oakland across the bay, while the city government of San Francisco now lured Lykes into new terminal facilities, which did not enjoy connections like those of Oakland to the major western railroads. Lykes's strategy was based on offering shippers* either all-water transportation from the Far East via the Panama Canal or microbridge service between the Gulf and West coasts, a variation of the landbridge,* but APL at Oakland was much better located to offer a cheaper and faster service to the Gulf.

Lykes did not realize how vulnerable its position was and tried to remain in the West Coast trade by adopting weekly sailings. APL with its highly efficient diesel containerships now reduced rates, and Lykes struggled to meet the cuts, and when APL introduced its double-stack* trains in 1984 for the landbridge service, it was only a matter of time before the rate war slowly drowned Lykes in losses.

Lykes Brothers, the victor in so many battles to crush or devour other competitors, for the first time stared at disaster in June 1986, when it suspended the sailings to the West Coast as the only way to save the company from bankruptcy. The debacle was so great that the company had even lost the ships in this costly foray into the Pacific Ocean; in a very bitter swap, Lykes chartered the four large containerships it was building in exchange for four smaller ships no longer suitable for APL's needs. Lykes had barely survived the transpacific venture and, in a seriously weakened condition, could not take advantage of the bankruptcy of United States Lines,* whose ships were acquired by Sea-Land,* thereby permanently dashing Lykes Brothers' chances of ever becoming a major force on either the East or West coasts. A weakened Lykes retreated into the Gulf of Mexico to try to survive in its traditional home grounds and in December 1990 became the first of the U.S.-flag subsidized companies to seek permission to operate foreign-flag ships, because otherwise the company could not replace its fleet of thirty ships, twenty-seven of which had been built in the 1960s.

Lykes Brothers needed at the same time to keep its operating differential subsidy* to compete against foreign lines, but the Merchant Marine Act of 1936* prohibited owning foreign-flag ships while receiving the subsidy. Efforts to change the legislation had met with little success, and in 1992 Lykes proposed a scheme to divide itself into two overlapping but separate companies, Louisiana Vessel Management (LVM) and Lykes, so that under complex arrangements Lykes would continue to benefit from the subsidies without owning the ships themselves. Critics called the plan a ''subsidy switcheroo'' (*American Shipper*, August 1993) and the company dropped the proposal in July 1993. Lykes will most likely have to shift to flags of convenience* if it wishes to survive.

Principal Executives

Joseph T. Lykes	1943–1960
Solon B. Turman	1951–1967
Frank A. Nemec	1965–1973
Joseph T. Lykes, Jr.	1962–1981

Charles P. Lykes	1983–1986
James Amoss, Jr.	1973–present
Eugene F. McCormick	1986–present
Tom L. Rankin	1989–present

References: *American Shipper,* February 1979, April 1983, April, December 1984, June 1986, February 1987, December 1990, October 1992, August 1993; *Business Week,* 21 July 1975; René De La Pedraja, *The Rise and Decline of U.S. Merchant Shipping in the Twentieth Century* (New York: Twayne, 1992); *Fortune,* 7 April 1969; *Journal of Commerce,* 4 August 1988; *New York Times,* 24 February 1979, 27 October 1981, 13 November 1982; *Wall Street Journal,* 15 November 1982.

M

MAGNUSON, WARREN G., 12 April 1905–20 May 1989. In the twentieth century Warren G. Magnuson was the second most effective defender of the U.S. merchant marine in the Senate after Wesley L. Jones;* both had been senators from Washington. Magnuson was born on 12 April 1905 in Moorhead, Minnesota, where he grew up, but in 1924 he was in Washington to continue his education, and he graduated from law school at the University of Washington in 1929. He practiced law but soon became involved in local politics. Running on a platform of total support for the New Deal, he was elected to the House of Representatives in 1936 and to the Senate in 1944.

He was a solid supporter of organized labor, and soon the maritime unions found in him the best Senate advocate for the U.S.-flag merchant marine. He joined the Commerce Committee* of the Senate and soon rose to head its Merchant Marine subcommittee; from this position he held numerous hearings and conducted a very exhaustive inquiry, the *Merchant Marine Study and Investigation* of 1949–1950, an invaluable source for postwar shipping problems. Magnuson worked closely with fellow Republican Senator John Marshall Butler and Representative Herbert C. Bonner* to secure passage of the Cargo Preference Act of 1954,* a new approach to the task of maintaining U.S.-flag ships in the foreign trade.

When, in addition, Magnuson assumed the chairmanship of the Commerce Committee in 1955, he was well positioned to push for more measures to favor U.S. shipping, but unfortunately the revelations of the Celler Committee* forced him and the maritime industry into a desperate struggle to preserve existing gains. A turning point for Magnuson was his near loss in the 1962 campaign, whereupon he totally changed his approach, staff, and policies in an attempt to regain touch with the voters back home in Washington. While he continued to support the merchant marine, he concentrated most of his efforts toward areas of broad appeal, such as health and consumer issues, in order to survive politically. The tremendous attention he had given the merchant marine in the 1950s had not produced many tangible results, and Magnuson concluded that by shifting his efforts to other issues, he could still have a significant impact. He was defeated for reelection in 1980, thereby depriving the maritime industry of its last sympathetic voice in the Senate. Magnuson returned to private law practice in Seattle, where he died on 20 May 1989.

References: *Congressional Record*, Appendix, 21 December 1950; *Current Biography*, 1945; Samuel A. Lawrence, *United States Merchant Shipping Policies and Politics* (Washington, DC: Brookings Institution, 1966); U.S. Congress, *Biographical Directory of the United States Congress, 1774–1989* (Washington, DC: Government Printing Office, 1989).

MAGUIRE ACT OF 1895. The Sailors' Union of the Pacific (SUP), under the prodding of Andrew Furuseth,* its president, abandoned its "no politics" rule and decided to support the candidacy of James G. Maguire as the Democratic party candidate from San Francisco to the U.S. Congress in 1892. Maguire was elected, but he did not forget his campaign promises and faithfully defended seamen's issues before Congress. Since the Shipping Commissioners' Act of 1872,* Congress had not passed laws defending seamen from the abuses of employers, but now in 18 February 1895, Maguire, working closely with Furuseth, obtained the enactment of the Maguire Act.

The law had three main provisions, the most important of which was that seamen in the coastwise* trade could not be arrested for deserting their ships. The Maguire Act also prohibited making advances from the sailors' future wages to the crimps* and exempted the seamen's personal clothes from confiscation to pay their bills. In practice employers generally ignored the Maguire Act, while the Supreme Court in the *Arago** decision overturned the key prohibition on the arrest of seamen for desertion. See Bureau of Navigation.

References: Arthur E. Albrecht, *International Seamen's Union of America: A Study of Its History and Problems*, Bulletin of the Bureau of Labor Statistics, No. 342 (Washington, DC: Government Printing Office, 1932); Hyman Weintraub, *Andrew Furuseth: Emancipator of the Seamen* (Berkeley: University of California Press, 1959).

MALLORY, CHARLES HENRY, 30 September 1818–21 March 1890. Charles Henry Mallory was born in Mystic, Connecticut, on 30 September 1818. His father, Charles, had built up a diversified maritime business ranging from sailmaking, shipyards, whaling, and commerce to operating clipper and other sailing vessels. When Charles Henry grew up, the shipyards became his special responsibility, and this gradually led him to take a greater interest in the operation of the vessels. Some of the Mallory ships began to make profitable voyages from New England to the Gulf of Mexico. The introduction of steam engines also gave the family the opportunity to manufacture some of the iron items needed for the new steam vessels. The Civil War meant boom times for the Mallory family as the Union chartered* all vessels of the firms and ordered more from the shipyards.

The end of the Civil War brought an abrupt end to the government contracts, and Charles Henry decided to focus on coastwise* ocean transportation as the most promising field. In 1866 he began regularly to run steamers to Galveston from New York City; to manage this new Mallory Line,* he opened an office in New York City, which gradually became the center of the Mallory family ventures. Charles, the father, and the brothers resisted the move away from Mystic and continued to cling to the small shipyards and the sailing vessels. The family finally abandoned the shipyards in 1876 and sold the last sailing vessel in 1885, because the steamship service to Galveston had been since 1866 the real money maker. Charles Henry accumulated a fortune and continued in the profitable coastwise trade until his death on 21 March 1890. His friend and close associate Captain Elihu Spicer, Jr., became the next president of the Mallory Line; upon the death of Captain Spicer in 1893, Henry Rogers Mallory,* a son of Charles Henry, became president of the firm.

References: James P. Baughman, *The Mallorys of Mystic: Six Generations in American Maritime Enterprise* (Middletown, CT: Wesleyan University Press, 1972); John N. Ingham, *Biographical Dictionary of American Business Leaders* (Westport, CT: Greenwood Press, 1983).

MALLORY, CLIFFORD DAY, 26 May 1881–7 April 1941. Clifford D. Mallory was born in New York City on 26 May 1881 and was the oldest son of Henry Rogers Mallory.* Clifford insisted on operating a family-owned steamship business, unlike his younger brother, Philip Rogers Mallory, who became a successful and wealthy manufacturer. Clifford had joined the Mallory Line* and, as he worked his way up through the ranks, expected eventually to replace his father as president. The sale of the Mallory Line to Charles W. Morse completely upset these plans, and even though his father emerged as head of the Atlantic, Gulf & West Indies Steamship Lines* (AGWI) in 1908, Clifford was never able to make the emotional transition from a family-owned firm to the impersonal publicly held corporation. Upon his father's retirement in 1915, Clifford became the vice president of two AGWI subsidiaries. He had also married Rebecca Sealy, daughter of a rich Texas family, and to most his situation seemed enviable: "He was financially and socially secure. His father was helping him build a beautiful home in Greenwich; he was an expert competitive yachtsman, belonged to the best clubs, and moved in the highest of society" (Baughman 1972). Yet he remained unsatisfied and in particular could not accept to see his father's former underlings running AGWI. U.S. entry into World War I was an excellent excuse to leave AGWI for government service, but he could never land a significant position and had to settle for assistant to the director of operations, a post way down in the Shipping Board* hierarchy.

After the war AGWI management pleaded with Clifford to return, partly to keep the Mallory name within the firm and also because he was acceptable to both the ''banker'' and ''steamship'' factions that had emerged in AGWI since his father's retirement. Clifford wanted to centralize power—presumably in his hands—in effect reviving the old family control under the new corporate shell, but this condition was unacceptable to AGWI management. Clifford now turned his back on AGWI and devoted the rest of his life to try to build from scratch another family-owned steamship firm.

The time seemed right, because the Shipping Board was willing to subsidize new companies splendidly, and in 1919 he was operating tramp* vessels for the government and the Mediterranean Line (running between Baltimore and Mediterranean ports) as a ''managing operator.''* The Shipping Board took a major loss on the tramp vessels and by early 1922 had recalled all of them, including those operated by Mallory. He was not unduly worried, because the Shipping Board had allowed him in January 1922 to transfer the Mediterranean Line service from cargo-poor Baltimore to New York City and in April 1922 had also made him the managing operator for the South African Line, which sailed from New York to the Union of South Africa as well as Mozambique. Clifford should have worried, because these changes now put him in direct competition with the American Export Lines,* a new aggressive outfit determined to corner the Mediterranean, and the Bull Line,* which saw in Africa an alternative to excessive specialization in the Puerto Rican trade. The two Shipping Board lines were a real gold mine, yet incredibly Clifford was bored by the day-to-day details, and his subordinates neglected the upkeep of the ships. The sloppy performance and the need to consolidate overlapping services convinced the Shipping Board to end Clifford's status as managing operator, and as expected, American Export received the Mediterranean Line while the Bull Line received the South African Line.

Clifford never admitted his incompetent handling and instead blamed the government for the failure of the two lines, and he went on to become a harsh critic of shipping subsidies. He was not out of the steamship business, however, because he had purchased seven surplus tankers from the Shipping Board in 1923–1924 and also because in 1926 he entered the coastwise* trade with U.S.-flag tramps that he began to acquire and that also made occasional voyages for bulk* cargoes to Eastern Canada, Mexico, and Cuba. The U.S.-flag tramps were kept employed and earned a modest profit, but his biggest break came with the tankers. Clifford cultivated strong links with the major oil companies, and in particular he became a close friend of Robert L. Hague,* who headed the shipping division of the Standard Oil Co. of New Jersey* (today, Exxon). Under the wing of Standard Oil, Clifford's business grew, until he owned the largest independent tanker fleet under the U.S. flag. The only setback was the Great Depression, which forced the layup from 1930 to 1935 of most of the tankers normally chartered to Standard Oil, but afterward ''phenomenal earnings'' returned.

By 1940 it appeared that Clifford had achieved his goal of a family-owned shipping firm, which one day he would pass on to his son, Clifford Day Mallory,

Jr. All the hassle, setbacks, and headaches of running a steamship firm had yielded, however, few financial returns, and Clifford's net worth had really not increased that much from the $.5 million in assets he had in1919. He was really lucky not to have gone broke in the risky steamship business, but his limited achievements contrasted with those of his younger brother, the industrialist Philip, who had become a millionaire many times over and whose wealth continued to multiply effortlessly. An inveterate enemy of subsidies, Clifford decided to use a tax dodge to increase his income. The scheme called for using the equity in his ships to buy bankrupt textile mills, thereby using the losses of the latter to reduce the income tax on the income from the former. In the middle of these complex and long transactions, Clifford died on 7 April 1941; since he had surrendered ownership over the ships, his son received a substantial monetary settlement but was excluded from control or ownership of the fleet. The ships and charters of Mallory went into Marine Transport Lines, a new company organized later in 1941. After three generations as steamship owners, the Mallory tradition came to an unforeseen end.

References: James P. Baughman, *The Mallorys of Mystic: Six Generations in American Maritime Enterprise* (Middletown, CT: Wesleyan University Press, 1972); *Who Was Who*, vol. 1.

MALLORY, HENRY ROGERS, 1848–4 March 1919. Henry Rogers succeeded his father, Charles Henry Mallory* as the head of the Mallory Line.* Henry Rogers was born in Mystic, Connecticut, the home of the Mallory family, in 1848. In January 1867 the growing business of the Mallory Line brought Henry Rogers to New York City, where he stayed to live during his business career. He worked for the Mallory Line and in 1893 became its president. His most important decision came in 1906,when he decided to sell the Mallory Line to Wall Street magnate Charles W. Morse.

The Mallory Line became a subsidiary of Consolidated Steamship Lines,* but the collapse of Morse's financial empire brought Henry Rogers out of retirement. Henry Rogers participated in the reorganization of Consolidated Steamship Lines into the Atlantic, Gulf & West Indies Steamship Lines* (AGWI), whose president he became in 1908. Under Mallory, AGWI paid off its debts and restored its prestige and profitability. He remained president until his retirement in May 1915 and died in Winter Park, Florida, on 4 March 1919.

References: James P. Baughman, *The Mallorys of Mystic: Six Generations in American Maritime Enterprise* (Middletown, CT: Wesleyan University Press, 1972); René De La Pedraja, *The Rise and Decline of U.S. Merchant Shipping in the Twentieth Century* (New York: Twayne, 1992).

MALLORY LINE, 1866–1907. The Mallory Line provided steamship service between New York and ports in the Gulf of Mexico. In 1866 Charles Henry Mallory* moved his office from Mystic, Connecticut, to New York City in order to supervise personally the line he had opened that same year between Galveston and New York City. The Mallory family had been engaged in shipbuilding, commerce, and banking and had also operated tramps* from Mystic, but Charles Henry's move to New York City marked the beginning of the family's specialization in coastwise* liner* operations. New steam and metal technologies required larger investments in steamships and shipyards, and by 1876 the Mallory family had abandoned shipbuilding in Mystic in order to concentrate on the operation of coastwise steamers. Among the older generation the love of wooden sailing ships died hard, and even though Charles Henry adopted steam for the bulk of the Mallory fleet, his father insisted on still using clipper ships, until their ruinous losses allowed Charles Henry to sell the last of their sailing ships in 1885.

The Galveston service soon was complemented with a run from New York City to New Orleans, while the laying of a telegraph cable between Havana and Key West allowed the vessels to routinely stop at Havana to complete their loads on the return voyage with cargoes bound for New York. In 1875 millionaire and railroad magnate Charles Morgan* decided to crash into the Gulf trade with his own ships, and a ferocious rate war ensued that lasted until Morgan's death in 1878. His heirs found the division of the routes a more sensible solution, and until 1902 the Morgan Line* left Galveston to the Mallory Line while the latter left New Orleans to the Morgan Line. In 1876 the Mallory Line began its weekly direct service to Florida from New York; the presence of other steamship companies like the Clyde Line* gave an appearance of intense competition, but in reality informal agreements allocated certain ports to each line, thereby avoiding ruinous rivalry.

The Mallory Line, after one last involvement in foreign trade, the disastrous United States and Brazil Mail Steamship Line* in 1878–1881, henceforth limited itself to the coastwise trade, the basis of its business. To protect their investment with corporate layers, the Mallory family incorporated the New York and Texas Steamship Company* in 1886; all maritime assets, including vessels, were owned by the new company, but the management and operation remained in the hands of the separate family firm, C. H. Mallory & Co, although in practice the new company and the steamship service generally remained known as the Mallory Line. Upon the death of Charles Henry Mallory in 1890, the presidency went to his close associate Captain Elihu Spicer, Jr., who died in 1893. For the rest of the Mallory Line's independent existence, Henry Rogers Mallory,* a son of Charles Henry, was the president.

The appearance of a new competitor, the Lone Star Line, in the New York-Galveston route unleashed a ferocious rate war from 1897 to 1899, and for the first time in its history, the Mallory Line faced a deficit in 1898. The Spanish-American War could not have come at a more opportune moment, and "proved to be the company's greatest windfall" (Baughman 1972). By chartering its vessels at high rates to the Quartermaster Corps, the Mallory Line restored its profitable condition and accumulated enough reserves to finish driving the Lone Star Line from the trade in 1899. To try to keep other rivals from appearing, the Mallory Line opened a New York-to-Mobile service with its older vessels in September 1902.

The cutthroat competition with the Lone Star Line had deeply affected the Mallory Line; the fears revived when the Morgan Line in August 1902 reneged on the 1878 informal agreement and opened a New York-Galveston service. Competition against the Morgan Line owned by the railroads was suicidal, but fortunately the new service, ''as a conciliatory gesture to the Mallory Line'' (ibid.), did not enter the passenger trade and carried cargo only. The Morgan Line had become a permanent threat that at any moment could swiftly crush the Mallory Line; at the same time only the better service from bigger and faster steamships could keep out other competitors, but the replacement cost for new vessels required ever larger investments. Just as high capital demands had finally driven Charles Henry Mallory to abandon shipbuilding and to concentrate on steamship operations, so in 1906 Henry Rogers Mallory concluded that the high capital demands made steamship operations too risky for a family-owned firm. He and his family decided to sell the Mallory Line in October 1906 to Charles W. Morse, a Wall Street magnate who supposedly had the vast amounts of capital necessary to build the next generation of steamships.

The Mallory Line became a subsidiary of Morse's Consolidated Steamship Lines* and, after the latter's bankruptcy, of the Atlantic, Gulf & West Indies Steamship Lines* (AGWI). The Mallory Line never again operated as an independent company, but the flag and trade name remained in use. Clifford Day Mallory,* the son of Henry Rogers, did operate from 1919 to 1941 a succession of lines, tankers, and tramps under the Mallory name, although legally he could not use the exact term *Mallory Line*. AGWI changed the name to Clyde-Mallory Line in 1932 and in 1949 sold Clyde-Mallory to the Bull Line, which ceased to use the old Mallory name.

Principal Executives

Charles Henry Mallory	1866–1890
Captain Elihu Spicer, Jr.	1890–1893
Henry Rogers Mallory	1893–1906

References: James P. Baughman, *The Mallorys of Mystic: Six Generations in American Maritime Enterprise* (Middletown, CT: Wesleyan University Press, 1972); Mallory Family Papers, G. W. Blunt White Library, Mystic Seaport, Connecticut.

MALOLO, **1927–1937; later, *MATSONIA*, 1938–1948.** When William P. Roth* decided to stimulate tourism to Hawaii, the construction of the *Malolo*, a specially designed liner, was central to the success of his strategy. The *Malolo* was the first luxury liner in the Hawaiian trade and surpassed anything previously seen in the islands. With a speed of twenty-one knots and accommodations for over 650 first-class passengers (no second or third class), the plush ship catered to the crème of the tourist trade. The long vessel (582 feet) allowed space for many ample lounges and other social areas, including a Pompeian-Etruscan swimming pool. When on land, the tourists stayed in the Royal Hawaiian Hotel, also built by Matson. The *Malolo* was a tremendous success and convinced Roth to order three more vessels, the *Mariposa,* Monterey,** and the *Lurline.**

However, the *Malolo* confirmed that the tourist trade to Hawaii was seasonal, with peak periods in winter and late summer, but for the rest of the year Matson had to find employment for the *Malolo* in special voyages to the Pacific Northwest or in convention trips to keep the vessel full. The most successful off-season voyage came in the fall of 1929, when only 325 passengers were allowed to participate in the ''millionaires' cruise'' of the Far East, which offered every imaginable luxury; however, the onset of the Great Depression prevented any repetition of this highly memorable cruise. In 1937 the *Malolo* underwent extensive upgrading, and to reflect these changes, she resumed service as the *Matsonia*. When the United States entered World War II, the government requisitioned the *Matsonia*, which returned briefly to service after the war but was sold to Greek interests in 1948. After operation by Greek cruise lines, the ship was scrapped in 1977–1978.

References: Frederick E. Emmons, *American Passenger Ships: The Ocean Lines and Liners, 1873–1938* (Newark: University of Delaware Press, 1985); Fred A. Stindt, *Matson's Century of Ships* (Modesto, CA: n.p., 1982); William L. Worden, *Cargoes: Matson's First Century in the Pacific* (Honolulu: University Press of Hawaii, 1981).

MANAGING OPERATORS, 1919–1936. *Managing operator* was the term coined by the Shipping Board* to refer to the private individuals who managed the government-owned vessels. What was remarkable about the arrangement was that the managing operators had no incentive to reduce losses on the operation of the ships, because the Shipping Board absorbed the losses, while the private individuals kept the profits. The intention of the Shipping Board, codified in the Jones Act,* was to encourage the entry of new firms into the steamship business, but a more wasteful way to accomplish this goal could hardly have been found. Soon the Shipping Board had over 200 managing operators running ships in overlapping routes, so that the government was subsidizing not only new firms but also ruinous competition between the new firms. Because the initial contracts for the managing operators were custom-made for specific circumstances and could lend themselves to charges of favoritism, the Shipping Board soon adopted standard agreements in one format, the Managing Operator 4, or M.O.4 contracts, as they were generally known. The M.O.4 contracts still retained the basic principle of transferring losses to the government, so that the managing operators had no incentive to reduce their costs.

The managing operators did provide U.S.-flag service to almost every port in the world, and shippers* were happy with a nearly personalized service, so that no outcry occurred about this outrageous way to create a merchant marine. Only because of shortage of funds did the Shipping Board begin to scale back the number of managing operators by gradually weeding out the most wasteful during the 1920s. In 1924 the Shipping Board modified the M.O.4 agreements and in 1931 replaced them with "lump-sum contracts," but without affecting the profits of the managing operators. The Shipping Board was really able to reduce expenditures only by consolidating or abolishing the lines of managing operators but could not dispose of some lines because of very effective lobbying by the managing operators, who had been represented by the U.S. Ship Operators' Association* since 1919. Congress, rather than heeding the warning signs, went on to approve the Merchant Marine Act of 1928,* which in many cases added mail subsidies. The Great Depression created political winds that at last forced a reexamination of the shipping policies, and the Black Committee* in 1933–1936 exposed so many abuses that the Merchant Marine Act of 1936* abolished the managing operators. However, the new U.S. Maritime Commission* had a hard time carrying out the legislative mandate and had to devise the transitional formula of renewable six-month contracts with "managing agents" in 1937 for the six remaining government-owned lines. Only the start of World War II finally ended the last offshoots of the managing operators, who had been a unique experiment in the history not just of American, but also world shipping.

References: Paul V. Betters and Darrell H. Smith, *The United States Shipping Board: Its History, Activities, and Organization* (Washington, D.C.: Brookings Institution, 1931); René De La Pedraja, *The Rise and Decline of U.S. Merchant Shipping in the Twentieth Century* (New York: Twayne, 1992); *New York Times*, 30 June 1937, 28 February 1939; Paul M. Zeis, *American Shipping Policy* (Princeton, NJ: Princeton University Press, 1938).

MANCHURIA **and** *MONGOLIA*, **1904–1952.** The success of the Pacific Mail Steamship Company* (PMSS) with the *Korea** and the *Siberia** convinced the company to order two more steamers, the *Manchuria* and *Mongolia*. When the ships were delivered in 1904, they were the largest in the Pacific Ocean, although later that same year in October the Great Northern Steamship Company* (GNSS) stole the record with its spectacular *Minnesota.** The *Manchuria* and *Mongolia* had quadruple-expansion engines (see marine propulsion) and twin screws like their predecessors the *Korea* and *Siberia* but were larger and longer. Whether by deliberate choice or engineering limitations, the *Manchuria* and *Mongolia*, at a speed of fifteen knots, were slower than the *Korea* and *Siberia*, whose speed records across the Pacific were not broken by the new vessels.

When PMSS decided to abandon merchant shipping in August 1915, the company sold the *Manchuria* and *Mongolia* to the International Mercantile Marine* (IMM) for operation in the latter's booming transatlantic routes. After World War I, the *Manchuria* and *Mongolia* were shifted among the various subsidiaries of IMM and served in both foreign and intercoastal* routes. In 1928 the Dollar Line* bought the *Manchuria* (renamed the *President Johnson*) and in 1929 the *Mongolia* (renamed the *President Fillmore*), but the onset of the

Great Depression soon forced the layup of these two obsolete vessels. Shipping shortages convinced the government to extensively overhaul the vessels for duty during World War II, but with the return of peace the *President Fillmore* was finally scrapped. Foreign speculators bought the *President Johnson* in 1946, but finally she too was scrapped in 1952.

References: Frederick E. Emmons, *American Passenger Ships: The Ocean Lines and Liners, 1873–1983* (Newark: University of Delaware Press, 1985); John H. Kemble, "A Hundred Years of the Pacific Mail," *American Neptune* 10 (1950):123–143; John Niven, *The American President Lines and Its Forebears, 1848–1984* (Newark: University of Delaware Press, 1987); E. Mowbray Tate, *Transpacific Steam: The Story of Steam Navigation from the Pacific Coast of North America to the Far East and Antipodes, 1867–1941* (New York: Cornwall Books, 1986).

MANHATTAN, **1962–1987.** The tanker *Manhattan* was until the early 1970s the largest merchant ship built in the United States and the largest U.S.-flag tanker. When the yard of Bethlehem Steel at Quincy, Massachusetts, delivered the *Manhattan* on 10 January 1962, the tanker of 106,500 deadweight* tons was also the largest merchant ship in the world; however, after the completion of this vessel the United States dropped out of the competition for largest ship sizes, and foreign shipyards permanently took the lead in the construction of the largest tankers of the world. The *Manhattan*, in spite of its size, enjoyed considerable maneuverability because of two propellers, and the two turbine* units drove the ship at seventeen knots, still a fast speed for merchant ships at that time. The vessel originally belonged to Manhattan Tankers Company, which was controlled by the Greek shipping tycoon Stavros Nirachos, but in 1962 the owners of the company became Joseph Kahn and Howard Pack, who had also acquired Seatrain* in 1965.

Although hauling oil was the main function of the tanker, in June 1964 the *Manhattan* sailed to the Soviet Union with the largest cargo of wheat ever loaded in a U.S. port. In 1969 Seatrain decided to use the *Manhattan* for an experimental voyage to try to open the Northwest Passage, so that oil could flow from the fields in north Alaska to the East Coast of the United States. Seatrain increased the tanker's weight to 112,900 deadweight tons and also fitted the *Manhattan* with icebreaking capabilities so that the ship could sustain operations under Arctic conditions. The ship sailed from Chester, Pennsylvania, on 24 August 1969, reached Alaska on 21 September, and returned to New York from the historic crossing on 12 November. Although the vessel suffered only superficial damage, Seatrain and the oil companies participating in the trial venture concluded that it was not economical to send oil through the Northwest Passage. After the bankruptcy of Seatrain in 1981, the ship remained in operation under the Manhattan Tankers Company until 1987.

References: John A. Culver, *Ships of the U.S. Merchant Fleet*, rev. ed. (Weymouth, MA: Denison Press, 1965); René De La Pedraja, *The Rise and Decline of U.S. Merchant Shipping in the Twentieth Century* (New York: Twayne, 1992); *Facts on File 1969*;

Maritime Administration, *Vessel Inventory Report 1987*, and *Tankers in the World Fleet as of January 1, 1988*; *New York Times*, 11 January, 2 February 1962.

MANHATTAN and *WASHINGTON*, 1932–1953. The *Manhattan* and the *Washington* were the two passenger liners of United States Lines* (USL) during the 1930s, and they were the first luxury liners built in the United States for service in the North Atlantic since the *St. Louis** and the *St. Paul** of 1895. USL, temporarily under the control of Paul W. Chapman, a financial speculator rather than a shipping executive, ordered the *Manhattan* and *Washington* as replacements for the larger but overage *Leviathan*;* Chapman expected the two smaller ships to provide a weekly sailing schedule across the North Atlantic, otherwise impossible with the single *Leviathan*. In a break with previous systems of marine propulsion,* the *Manhattan* and the *Washington* were fitted with turboelectric drive: the steam turbine* moved a generator, whose electricity powered electric motors.

Chapman soon went broke, and control of USL passed to the International Mercantile Marine* (IMM), which paid the final bills on the construction of the two new vessels. When completed, both ships had a capacity for 580 "cabin"-class passengers, 461 tourist, and 196 third-class; the *Manhattan* entered service in August 1932, and the *Washington* in May 1933. IMM had counted on the lucrative mail contracts of the Merchant Marine Act of 1928* to defray the high operating costs of the vessels, but when the Merchant Marine Act of 1936* canceled the mail contracts and substituted modest subsidies, the vessels became little more than white elephants. Recovery of the large initial investment on turboelectric drive proved impossible, while the *Manhattan* and the *Washington* were almost immediately outclassed by the larger and more luxurious Queens of Cunard, as well as by the new German liners *Europa* and *Bremen*.

The *Manhattan* and the *Washington* were resounding failures, and their poor performance contributed to the near bankruptcy of USL in the early 1940s; the only consolation was that the company did not make the same mistakes with the *America** in 1940. With the outbreak of World War II, the government requisitioned and then purchased the two vessels, taking a tremendous burden off the company. After the war the *Manhattan* never returned to commercial service and was laid up in 1946 (and scrapped in 1964). USL needed a running mate for the *America* to maintain minimal passenger schedules across the Atlantic and in 1948 chartered* the *Washington*, then with a capacity for 1,106 passengers, all of the same class. The government requisitioned the *Washington* for the Korean War in 1951, but by the time the wartime tour of duty ended in 1953, USL no longer needed the vessel because the new superliner *United States** had entered service in 1952. The *Washington* went into the National Defense Reserve Fleet* in 1953 and was scrapped in 1965.

References: Frank O. Braynard, *Famous American Ships* (New York: Hastings House, 1956); René De La Pedraja, *The Rise and Decline of U.S. Merchant Shipping in the Twentieth Century* (New York: Twayne, 1992); Frederick E. Emmons, *American Pas-*

senger Ships: The Ocean Lines and Liners, 1873–1983 (Newark: University of Delaware Press, 1985); Kermit Roosevelt Papers, Library of Congress.

MARINE COOKS AND STEWARDS, NATIONAL UNION OF (NUMCS), 1901–1955. The National Union of Marine Cooks and Stewards (NUMCS) was a craft union established in San Francisco in 1901 for the shipboard personnel who prepared and served food and also performed household chores abroad the ships; its original title was Marine Cooks and Stewards Association of the Pacific Coast. The founders were determined to ''relieve ourselves of the degrading necessity of competing with an alien and inferior race,'' and they created the new union ''for the purpose of replacing the Chinese and Japanese now on the coast by American citizens or by those who are eligible to citizenship'' (Nelson 1990). NUMCS affiliated with the International Seamen's Union* (ISU) and followed the guidance of Andrew Furuseth.* Along with the other affiliates of the ISU, the NUMCS prospered from 1901 until the disastrous strike of 1921.* The original 500 members in 1901 grew to 1,400 in 1903 and finally peaked at 2,600 in the boom year of 1920 but slumped during the 1920s.

The New Deal and dynamic new leadership revived the West Coast maritime unions, particularly after the successful 1934 strike. After the collapse of the ISU, the NUMCS affiliated with the Congress of Industrial Organizations (CIO). Within the NUMCS, the Communist party gained most of the leadership positions and, to increase its supporters, opened the whites-only union to blacks in 1934, so that by 1950 nearly half of the membership was black and another fifth belonged to other nonwhite minorities. The election of Hugh Bryson* to the presidency in 1944 consolidated communist control. In 1945 a new constitution changed the union's name to NUMCS and created a separate national office distinct from the San Francisco local; these two changes had become necessary because of the establishment of permanent locals in the Atlantic and Gulf coasts.

A faction of more than twenty members tried to wrest control of the NUMCS from Bryson, but after their expulsion, the ensuing lawsuits for compensation placed a crushing financial burden on the union, which also faced dangerous rivals. The Sailors' Union of the Pacific* (SUP) began a determined struggle in 1948 to gain control of the NUMCS, and the competition became particularly keen in 1950–1951, when the NMU also tried to absorb the cooks and stewards. The NUMCS leadership obtained the support of the International Longshoremen and Warehousemen's Union* (ILWU), but the conflicting union jurisdictions produced wildcat stoppages. To prevent any more delays in ships' sailings, particularly those of the Matson Navigation Company* to Hawaii, in June 1952 the federal circuit court created an employer-run hiring hall* to supply stewards and cooks for the ships. The loss of the hiring hall was accompanied by mounting financial difficulties because the courts had imposed the crippling awards payments in favor of the expelled dissidents. The independent union was doomed, but the struggle of who would gain control over the NUMCS was not yet finished.

The NUMCS remained loyal to Bryson, and the September 1952 election held by the National Labor Relations Board failed to hand over the union to the SUP. A bitter struggle raged between the SUP and the ILWU, but anticommunist accusations gradually tilted the balance toward the SUP. The NUMCS had been expelled from the CIO in 1950 because of communist infiltration, and the final blow came in 1953 when Bryson, who had been indicted because he had falsely denied his communist membership, was subsequently convicted in 1955. Nonetheless, one more electoral trick was still necessary to force the NUMCS into the SUP: a resolution from the National Labor Relations Board ordered the entire membership of the SUP and the NUMCS to vote in a single election to decide whether to affiliate with the ILWU or the SUP. Obviously, when the election was held in 1955, the larger membership of the SUP voted for their union, thereby bringing the cooks and stewards with them and ending the independent existence of the NUMCS.

Principal Labor Leaders

Gene Burke	1901–1944
Hugh Bryson	1944–1955

References: Bruce Nelson, *Workers on the Waterfront: Seamen, Longshoremen, and Unionism in the 1930s* (Urbana: University of Illinois Press, 1990): Jane Cassels Record, ''The Rise and Fall of a Maritime Union,'' *Industrial and Labor Relations Review* 10 (1956):81–92; Betty V. H. Schneider, *Industrial Relations in the West Coast Maritime Industry* (Berkeley: University of California Press, 1958).

MARINE COOKS, STEWARDS, AND WAITERS' UNION OF THE ATLANTIC AND GULF (MCSWU), 1901–1937. The Marine Cooks, Stewards, and Waiters' Union of the Atlantic and Gulf (MCSWU) was the craft union that existed in the Atlantic and Gulf coasts for cooks and stewards, the personnel who handled and prepared food and supplies aboard the ships. The MCSWU was an affiliate of the International Seamen's Union* (ISU), but unlike its West Coast counterpart, the Marine Cooks and Stewards' Union (later renamed the National Union of Marine Cooks and Stewards*), the MCSWU was predominantly for blacks, especially since the mid-1920s, after the German-speaking members had left the union. Thus, by the late 1920s, the ISU was a segregated labor federation, and the MCSWU was the sole black affiliate. For persons of African origin wishing jobs aboard ships, the only opportunity prior to World War II was to join this union and sail as a cook or steward, because even qualified blacks like Hugh Mulzac* were not allowed to hold any other shipboard position. After 1921 the MCSWU fell under the dictatorial control of ''Emperor'' David E. Grange.* A massive uprising against Grange during the 1936–1937 strikes put the union under new leaders, such as Ferdinand C. Smith,* who helped shape the organizational structure for the new National

Maritime Union* (NMU), into which the MCSWU incorporated itself. The original union had disappeared as an independent entity, in part because the American Federation of Labor and Grange had obtained a court injunction prohibiting the use of the name MCSA by the NMU, which henceforth represented the cooks, stewards, and waiters on the Atlantic and Gulf coasts.

Principal Labor Leaders

Henry P. Griffin	1903–1921
David E. Grange ("Emperor")	1921–1936

References: Hugh Mulzac, *A Star to Steer By* (New York: International, 1963); Bruce Nelson, *Workers on the Waterfront* (Urbana: University of Illinois Press, 1990); Record Group 32, National Archives, Washington, DC; William L. Standard, *Merchant Seamen: A Short History of Their Struggles* (New York: International, 1947).

MARINE ENGINEERS' BENEFICIAL ASSOCIATION (MEBA), 1875– present. The Marine Engineers' Beneficial Association (MEBA) has represented the engineers in the engine department of ships; it is also the oldest surviving union for seafarers. On 23 February 1875 locals convened in Cleveland, Ohio, to create the association, whose membership during the next thirty-five years came mainly from the Great Lakes. The shipboard engineers, along with the deck officers, have traditionally formed the maritime labor aristocracy, because of their power and authority over the rest of the crew. Not surprisingly, engineers have often confused their interests with those of management and were reluctant for decades to engage in any type of strike action, which in any case an 1865 law had declared illegal. During the first three decades of existence, MEBA concentrated mainly on safety, social, and educational issues. Originally called the Marine Engineers' Association, it added "beneficial" in 1883 to reflect mutual-aid functions like death benefits.

Legislative lobbying remained a high priority for MEBA, which one year after its foundation asked Congress to require all engineers to be U.S. citizens. The campaign against alien engineers appeared to be won in 1884, when Congress passed a law requiring all officers on U.S.-flag vessels to be U.S. citizens, but then in 1893 the secretary of the treasury stated that engineers were not "officers," and hence companies could hire aliens. Many Canadian engineers were taking advantage of this loophole to serve as engineers in U.S.-flag vessels of the Great Lakes until renewed lobbying finally convinced Congress in 1896 to designate engineers as part of the ship's officers. MEBA also continued its watchdog function over the Steamboat Inspection Service,* which licensed engineers to serve on vessels.

Membership in MEBA increased from 578 engineers in 1876 to 4,000 in 1897 and had reached nearly 11,000 in 1908. The locals came overwhelmingly from the Great lakes, and indeed the early history of MEBA paralleled that of the International Longshoremen's Association* (ILA). MEBA in 1909–1910 led a strike to try to counter the Lake Carriers' Association insistence on the open shop, but the union suffered a crushing defeat that effectively ended the Great Lakes locals and reduced total membership to 9,200 by 1913.

A beaten MEBA retreated to the Atlantic and Pacific Coast locals that still were alive, and as a first order of business it led a legislative effort to legalize strikes by engineers. MEBA had secured in 1903 the appointment of its former president, George Uhler, to become chief of the Steamboat Inspection Service, and while he held that office, the agency did not suspend any engineers because of participation in strikes. However, in 1913–1914 the government resumed the policy of revoking engineers' licenses as an antistrike tactic, and in response MEBA lobbied jointly with Andrew Furuseth* of the International Seamen's Union* (ISU) until Congress passed in 1915 the Hardy bill, which recognized the engineers' right to strike.

Internal debate had raged for years in MEBA over affiliation with the American Federation of Labor (AFL), a step the association was reluctant to take because of jurisdictional disputes with other unions representing engineers on land. Finally in January 1918, MEBA agreed to join the AFL out of fear that a rival organization, the Ocean Association of Marine Engineers (OAME), would usurp MEBA's jurisdiction. OAME, the first of several splinter groups, returned to MEBA in January 1919.

The expansion of the merchant marine following U.S. entry into World War I greatly favored MEBA, whose membership reached a high of 22,528 in January 1921. Because the shipping boom continued after the war, MEBA was able to extract substantial wage increases from the American Steamship Owners' Association* (ASOA) after a quickie strike in 1919. By 1921, however, cargo volume was declining, and ASOA went on the offensive to demand wage reductions. When ASOA and the Shipping Board* decided to impose lower wage schedules starting on 1 May 1921, MEBA and the ISU countered with the biggest seamen's strike in U.S. history, yet the employers felt confident of victory. Unemployment had spread in the United States, so shipowners could recruit all types of workers, including students, to man the ships. The Masters, Mates, and Pilots* (MM&P) declined to participate in the strike because their contracts did not expire until August 1, so only the lack of engineers kept the ships tied up. ASOA brought all possible pressure to bear to crush the engineers, many of whom had recently joined during the war and had no prior experience in labor militancy. The outcome of the strike of 1921* hinged on MEBA, but with a surplus of engineers, soon 3,500 were back at work and about 50 percent of the ships had returned to service. Perhaps failure was inevitable, but president William S. Brown capitulated too early and unilaterally ended MEBA's strike on 13 June without consulting the membership. At the very least Brown needed to coordinate the withdrawal with ISU, because he had left the sailors in the air, thereby intensifying the always deep suspicions between the unlicensed personnel and the engineers.

Brown had obtained nothing in return for the capitulation, and ASOA pressed home the attack and further slashed wages of engineers and all seamen in the hope of destroying MEBA and all other maritime unions. Anger at Brown's capitulation led to ouster attempts that failed, further increasing the demoralization of MEBA, whose membership collapsed to 11,000 by 1923, when the union withdrew from the AFL. In the face of the private employes' refusal to recognize MEBA and because only the Shipping Board continued to sign contracts with maritime unions like MEBA, a cornered Brown wrote, "We hope that the time will come when the United States government will operate every ship in the merchant marine of America" (Thor 1954).

Private employers set about destroying Brown's last hope and not only lobbied intensively to reduce the number of vessels operated by the Shipping Board but also sponsored rival company unions, most important, the American Society of Marine Engineers (ASME) for the San Francisco area in 1921. MEBA continued to decline during the 1920s, and the Great Depression further reduced MEBA's membership to 4,848 men in 1934, the lowest number since 1899. The union "was pitifully weak, dejected, and weary after 13 long years of retreat" (ibid.).

The Big Strike of 1934* totally reversed the union's fortunes. When longshoremen walked off their jobs in San Francisco on 9 May 1934, they were joined by seamen in the picket lines from the very first day. The Sailors' Union of the Pacific* (SUP) formally struck on 15 May, and MEBA, on the verge of extinction and with nothing to lose, voted to strike on 19 May, along with MM&P. Many engineers were still working at sea, but the majority joined the picket lines as soon as their ships docked. Indeed, the strike revealed hidden sources of strength for the union: "Some of these licensed officers had sailed in non-union ships between 1921 and 1934 while continuing to secretly maintain their union membership. Others were ex-union members who had been forced to join the ASME, but who were eager to regain their status as members of a legitimate union after the start of the strike." Before the Big Strike was over, ASME had collapsed, with almost all its members returning to MEBA. On 29 July the longshoremen and all seafarers, including MEBA, voted to return to work, thereby ending the successful Big Strike.

MEBA at last obtained recognition from employers, who signed an agreement on 22 April 1935. The agreement was not completely favorable to the engineers and in any case was only with the West Coast employers, the Pacific American Steamship Association* (PASSA), and the Shipowners' Association of the Pacific Coast* (SAPC). To complete and extend its gains, the four West Coast locals of MEBA joined with all the other maritime unions in the Maritime Federation of the Pacific* (MFP) that carried out the highly successful strike of 29 October 1936–4 February 1937. Participation in the strike gave MEBA locals in the Atlantic and Gulf a big boost, and they began to negotiate contracts with individual companies (the employers' organizations refused to negotiate as a unit with MEBA on the East Coast for years). Unlike the rest of the unions in the MFP, MEBA and MM&P failed to obtain a union-controlled hiring hall,* although the employers accepted that all engineers had to register with MEBA.

In October 1937 MEBA voted to affiliate with the Congress of Industrial Organizations (CIO) after the AFL failed to make a convincing appeal. World War II brought a renewed expansion, but tighter licensing requirements kept the number of engineers from ballooning as high as in World War I, so that the peak membership of 19,500 in 1948 was lower than the 22,500 of 1921. The period of easy prosperity was over for MEBA in 1949, not only because U.S.-flag steamship companies were in decline but also because still another rival appeared, the Brotherhood of Marine Engineers (BME). Harry Lundeberg,* head of the Seafarers' International Union* (SIU) and of the SUP, was the promoter of the BME, which was really his power play to take over MEBA, just as he was trying to do with the National Union of Marine Cooks and Stewards* (NUMCS) and the Marine Firemen, Oilers, Watertenders, and Wipers' Union of the Pacific Coast* (MFOWW).

BME initially attacked MEBA for accepting too many new members when the number of shipboard jobs was declining. MEBA continued to press for a hiring hall, but employers were unwilling to grant this privilege, already enjoyed by the unlicensed seamen of the SUP, SIU, and the National Maritime Union* (NMU). Finally employers agreed on a modified hiring hall for MEBA, whereby the company continued to appoint the chief engineer (who had to belong to MEBA), but the other engineering positions were filled by the union hiring hall. Some companies still wanted to retain the right to appoint all their engineers and found in BME the proper instrument. When Isbrandtsen Steamship Company* in 1949 and Isthmian Line* in 1951 refused MEBA's terms, they broke the strike by manning their ships with BME engineers.

After the death of Lundeberg in 1957, the challenge from the BME became less intense and gradually faded. After a series of struggles, MEBA returned to the Great Lakes in the early 1960s, over fifty years after the disastrous strike of 1909–1910 had driven the engineers' union out of that region. MEBA participated in the seamen's strike of 1961* along with the NMU, SIU, and MM&P, but henceforth it shunned strikes and concentrated its efforts on lobbying.

Jesse M. Calhoon became president in 1963 and aggressively led MEBA in its confrontations with employers and the government. When the oil embargo hit the United States in 1973, Calhoon commissioned and published a study, *The Energy Cartel: Who Runs the American Oil Industry*, which became a best-seller in 1974 and was the only time that a maritime union study reached mass circulation. Calhoon lobbied furiously to secure passage of cargo preference* legislation to require a percentage of oil imports to be carried on U.S.-flag tankers, but President Gerald Ford vetoed the bill on 30 December 1974, while embarrassing disclosures of campaign promises torpedoed similar bills during the Jimmy Carter administration. MEBA was also instrumental in writing the maritime policy statement in the 1988 George Bush presidential campaign.

In spite of all the lobbying, seafaring jobs continued to decline relentlessly. Membership in MEBA dropped to 9,500 in 1975, and the union itself was reorganized into two independent units: District 1 for the Atlantic, Gulf, and

Pacific coasts and District 2 for the Great Lakes, which merged with the Seafarers' International Union in 1988. In 1988 the NMU, once the world's largest seamen's union, was on the verge of collapse and agreed to fuse with District 1 of MEBA; reports also circulated that the MM&P was considering a merger with the engineers. The merger with NMU evoked bitter passions, and followers of retired president Calhoon united with former NMU members to unseat the MEBA president, C. E. ("Gene") DeFries, who was replaced in 1992 by Alexander C. ("Doc") Cullison. In spite of the intense power struggle, the new MEBA/NMU had attained equal importance with SIU as the voice of the rapidly disappearing U.S. seafarers. Furthermore, MEBA/NMU has copied the successful strategy of the SIU in organizing workers in nonmaritime areas, so that professional employees associations in Florida, California, and Alaska, as well as other groups such as the National Weather Service Employees Organization and the National Air Traffic Controllers' Association, are now represented by MEBA/NMU. The diversification into organizing workers on land paralleled a similar "coming ashore" by the merchant shipping companies themselves. The experience and talents MEBA painfully gained in its century-long struggle with the steamship companies–among the toughest of management groups–were in great demand on land since the 1980s, and MEBA/NMU has wisely and generously turned its talents to organizing new labor groups on land.

Principal Labor Leaders

George Uhler	1893–1903
William F. Yates	1907–1914; 1926–1930
A. Bruce Gibson	1915–1916
William S. Brown	1917–1926; 1935–1936
C. M. Sheplar	1930–1934
Samuel J. Hogan	1937–1949
Herbert L. Daggett	1950–1959
E. N. Altman	1960–1963
Jesse M. Calhoon	1963–1984
C. E. ("Gene") DeFries	1984–1992
Alexander C. ("Doc") Cullison	1992–present

References: *American Federationist*, May 1975; American Shipper, February, May 1991; Gary M. Fink, ed., *Labor Unions* (Westport, CT: Greenwood Press, 1977); Joseph P. Goldberg, *The Maritime Story: A Study in Labor-Management Relations* (Cambridge: Harvard University Press, 1958); *Journal of Commerce*, 31 March, October 1988; Marine Engineers' Beneficial Association, *Worthy of Our Heritage: A Brief History of America's Oldest Maritime Union* (1975); Betty V. H. Schneider, *Industrial Relations in the West Coast Maritime Industry* (Berkeley: University of California Press, 1958); Benjamin M. Squires, "Associations of Harbor Boat Owners and Employees in the Port of New York," *Monthly Labor Review* 7 (1918):45–62; Howard Andrew Thor, "A History of the Marine Engineers' Beneficial Association," M.A. thesis, University of California,

Berkeley, 1954; Hyman Weintraub, *Andrew Furuseth: Emancipator of the Seamen* (Berkeley: University of California Press, 1959).

MARINE FIREMEN, OILERS, WATERTENDERS, AND WIPERS' UNION OF THE ATLANTIC AND GULF (MFOWW), 1902–1937. On the Atlantic Coast and the Gulf of Mexico, the Marine Firemen, Oilers, Watertenders, and Wipers' Union (MFOWW) represented all workers in the engine room except for the engineers, who belonged to the Marine Engineers' Beneficial Association* (MEBA). During the age of coal steamships, the hard, backbreaking task of feeding coal to the furnaces and providing enough steam from the boilers fell to the marine firemen, oilers, watertenders, and wipers, who could easily be provoked into taking radical actions. In particular, these workers wanted their own labor organization that would understand what it meant to toil in the almost hell-like environment of the boilers and engine room. The International Seamen's Union* (ISU) initially had failed to recognize the need for a separate organization and had vainly tried to organize the deck personnel and marine firemen into one single union for the Atlantic Coast. In 1902 the ISU corrected its policy and finally allowed the firemen to have their own organization, the MFOWW, which became an affiliate of the ISU.

Internal differences plagued the MFOWW of the Atlantic from the start, and in particular its militancy found no place in the very conservative policies of the ISU. Ethnic discrimination by the MFOWW leadership against the rank and file (85 percent of whom were Spaniards) created a potentially explosive situation. In 1913, after the ISU failed to support adequately a MFOWW strike the previous year, almost all the Spaniards left to join the Marine Transport Workers' Union (MTWU) of the International Workers of the World (IWW), or wobblies.

The ISU tried to reconstitute the MFOWW in 1913 under the leadership of Oscar Carlson, but his blatant discrimination against Spanish speakers, whom he insisted on calling "dagos," reduced the union to 100 Anglo-Saxon workers. The shipping boom of World War I brought thousands of Americans into the sea and revived the previously moribund union. No less significant was the government persecution of the IWW at the end of World War I, which drove the Spanish firemen back into the ISU affiliate. The MFOWW saw membership climb to 20,000 in 1919 and to the record high of 38,000 in 1920. Marine firemen had started the highly successful strike of July 1919, but they went down to defeat in the disastrous strike of 1921,* which virtually destroyed all seamen's unions on the Atlantic and Gulf coasts for the next fifteen years.

Membership in the MFOWW collapsed to 10,000 in 1921 and continued to shrink afterward. In the 1920s the MFOWW became a company union, with Carlson the undisputed chief of his own fiefdom, although he never reached the extremes of arrogance as his ally "Emperor" David E. Grange,* the president of the Marine Cooks, Stewards and Waiters' Union of the Atlantic and Gulf* (MCSWU). With the renewal of union activity during the New Deal, the firemen were among the first to join the strikes of 1935–1937. Carlson, desperate to cling to his job, joined with ''Emperor'' Grange to hire thugs to crush a seamen's strike in Philadelphia in 1935, but that was not enough to stop the mounting upsurge. To keep the union under his control, Carlson appointed delegates to change the constitution of the MFOWW so that all power would henceforth be in the executive board. The rebel firemen were not able to stop the new constitution, but the outcry was so great that in the union election of 1936 the firemen by a two-to-one margin defeated Carlson and elected a new slate of officers. Carlson sought injunctions from the courts against the new officials and even tried to have the shipowners recognize him as the only bargaining agent for the union. The courts refused, so Carlson and the equally outcast ''Emperor'' Grange were left to try to run scabs through the picket lines during the fall strike of 1936. As soon as the National Maritime Union* (NMU) was created in May 1937, the MFOWW of the Atlantic and Gulf coasts merged into the new organization.

Principal Labor Leader

Oscar Carlson   1913–1936

References: Arthur E. Albrecht, *International Seamen's Union of America: A Study of Its History and Problems*, Bulletin of the Bureau of Labor Statistics, No. 342 (Washington, DC: Government Printing Office, 1932); James C. Healey, *Foc'sle and Glory Hole: A Study of the Merchant Seaman and His Occupation* (New York: Merchant Marine Publishers Association, 1936); Bruce Nelson, *Workers on the Waterfront: Seamen, Longshoremen, and Unionism in the 1930s* (Urbana: University of Illinois Press, 1990): William L. Standard, *Merchant Seamen: A Short History of Their Struggles* (New York: International, 1947).

MARINE FIREMEN, OILERS, WATERTENDERS, AND WIPERS' UNION OF THE PACIFIC COAST (MFOWW), 1883–1953. In the Pacific Coast, the Marine Firemen, Oilers, Watertenders, and Wipers' Union (MFOWW) represented all workers in the engine room except for the engineers, who belonged to the Marine Engineers' Beneficial Association* (MEBA). During the age of coal steamships, the hard, backbreaking task of feeding coal to the furnaces and providing enough steam from the boilers fell to the marine firemen, oilers, watertenders, and wipers, who could easily be provoked into taking radical positions. In particular, these workers wanted their own labor organization that would understand what it meant to toil in the almost hell-like environment of the boilers and engine room. Just as sailors' unions had first appeared on the West Coast rather than on the Atlantic, so the firemen's union appeared first on the Pacific Coast; as a matter of fact, the MFOWW, established in 1883 had preceded by two years the establishment of the Sailors' Union of the Pacific* (SUP), which represented only the deck crew. Jealously among the deck, engine, and steward personnel, the three main departments of the ship, remained strong, and each refused any type of industrial union organization for all workers on the vessel, but the advantages to joint action by all aboard a ship were too evident to be ignored, and thus in 1901 the MFOWW became an affiliate of the newly formed International Seamen's Union* (ISU), which until then had represented only deck crews.

While on the Atlantic the firemen found in militant causes the outlet for their feelings, on the Pacific Coast the members of the MFOWW satisfied their needs by espousing white supremacy attitudes, in particular, by keeping out blacks and Asiatics. Unlike the distinct Marine Firemen, Oilers, Watertenders, and Wipers' Union of the Atlantic and Gulf,* the MFOWW of the Pacific did not experience a dramatic rise in membership during World War I and consequently did not suffer a drastic contraction after the disastrous strike of 1921.* Complacency became the policy of the labor leaders of the MFOWW, who easily adopted the conservative views of the moribund ISU during the 1920s. The Big Strike* of 1934 in San Francisco brought a major upheaval to the MFOWW, and soon radical leaders headed by Earl King gained control of the union. Before the radical leaders could consolidate their grip by recruiting new members, in particular, blacks, as was happening in the Marine Cooks and Stewards' Union,* King and his key collaborators were conveniently framed and convicted to long prison terms in San Quentin in the summer of 1936 on false charges of having murdered the chief engineer of a ship.

The *King* case, along with the Modesto Boys* and the *Harry Bridges* case,* formed the three-pronged legal assault by management to destroy radical influences in the West Coast maritime labor unions. The King conviction was the most successful, because it allowed Vincent J. Malone to become president of the MFOWW, from which position he waged a constant battle to keep radicals, communists, and blacks out of the union. Part of this battle included keeping the MFOWW out of the Congress of Industrial Organizations (CIO): "Two attempts were made to affiliate the union with the CIO, and although in both cases the membership overwhelmingly supported CIO affiliation, the ballots were destroyed." Malone felt the CIO was under too much radical influence, but he also refused to affiliate with the Seafarers' International Union* (SIU), which the American Federation of Labor (AFL) had created to replace the bankrupt ISU. Instead he found a more congenial place for his union in the Maritime Federation of the Pacific* (MFP) because the MFOWW "virtually controlled the balance of power among the seafaring unions' " (Schneider 1958).

Even after the demise of the MFP in 1941, the MFOWW could continue to play off the International Longshoremen and Warehousemen's Union* (ILWU) of Harry Bridges* against the SIU of Harry Lundeberg.* The MFOWW also joined the Committee for Maritime Unity* (CMU), but its collapse in 1947 because of rivalries between the ILWU and the National Maritime Union* (NMU) foreshadowed harsh times for the marine firemen's union. With the expulsion of the ILWU from the CIO in 1950, three rival power blocks appeared on the West Coast waterfront: the ILWU, the SIU, and the NMU. No longer could the MFOWW continue to perform its delicate balancing act, and it might easily find itself crushed in the clash between the giant rivals. Malone was scared of Bridges's supposed radicalism, so the choice boiled down to the SIU or the NMU (the latter ideologically acceptable now that it had expulsed its last communist sympathizers). Malone began negotiations in early 1953 to see which union offered the best terms for the merger of the MFOWW. The industrial structure of the NMU required a full integration into its existing hierarchy, in effect swallowing up the MFOWW into Curran's personal dictatorship. The SIU was more sensitive to the traditional craft feelings and could easily offer the MFOWW "autonomy over selection of officers, finances, negotiations, and ownership of property." A vote in late 1953 approved the merger into the SIU by a two-to-one margin, effectively ending the existence of the MFOWW of the Pacific Coast as an independent union.

Principal Labor Leaders

Earl King	1934?–1936
Vincent J. Malone	1936–1953

References: James C. Healey, *Foc'sle and Glory Hole: A Study of the Merchant Seaman and His Occupation* (New York: Merchant Marine Publishers Association, 1936); Betty V. H. Schneider, *Industrial Relations in the West Coast Maritime Industry* (Berkeley: University of California Press, 1958); Stephen Schwartz, *Brotherhood of the Sea: A History of the Sailors' Union of the Pacific, 1885–1985* (New Brunswick, NJ: Transaction Books, 1986).

MARINE PROPULSION. When humans learned to make efficient engines to move ships across the oceans, the modern shipping industry was born. During previous millennia, shifting winds and to a lesser degree sea currents and human muscle had been the only energy sources available to move the ships. Wooden sailing vessels had many disadvantages, such as slow speed, irregularity, and small size; they also required large crews to constantly tend and adjust the sails to harness the ever-elusive winds. The early steam engines of the first half of the nineteenth century were so rudimentary that no revolution in ocean transport took place, and the early steamers could not even outrace sailing vessels in most services. But when the steam engine was perfected in the second half of the nineteenth century, one of the most important events in the history of ocean transportation took place, and nothing matched its impact until the container* revolution of the second half of the twentieth century.

The effective use of steam power for marine propulsion opened economic and political dimensions whose consequences went far beyond the engine room itself. Nonetheless, the starting point for understanding the dynamics of merchant shipping is to follow the evolution of the engines themselves. The following, roughly chronological list surveys the technological challenges and advances, while separate entries provide further formation on individual engines.

Single-expansion engine*

The single-expansion engine powered the Industrial Revolution in England since the middle of the eighteenth century. This external-combustion engine of massive size required incredible amounts of coal to heat water in a boiler to produce the steam that went into the cylinder to move the piston. The engine was double-acting: a value allowed the steam first to enter one end of the cylinder to push the piston down, and then the other end of the cylinder to push the piston back up; the piston was connected to a crankshaft that rotated. The single-expansion engine produced only slow revolutions and wasted a tremendous amount of steam, so that during decades little demand existed for its application to ocean transportation and then only after many costly experiments eliminated some of the engine's worst drawbacks. In 1807 the American Robert Fulton built and operated the *Clermont*, the first successful river steamboat, and in 1819 the U.S.-flag *Savannah** used steam and sails to cross the Atlantic. In the following years owners installed steam engines aboard their wooden ships to complement the sails, but the huge consumption of coal meant such high operating expenses that not until 1838 did the British *Sirius* become the first ship to cross the Atlantic relying solely on steam power.

All the early ships were side-wheelers because the single-expansion engine could not generate many revolutions. As the cylinder and the boiler became bigger, the heavy weight and high temperatures caused sagging and dry rot in the wooden ships; more iron was used to reinforce the timbers, and in the late 1850s the first iron hulls appeared but did not become the norm until the 1870s. Experiments with the propeller* confirmed its superiority over the side-wheels, but the propeller required for efficient use a higher number of revolutions than what the single-expansion engine could provide; gearing up was a partial solution that again wasted more energy. Ships using the single-expansion engine were so uneconomical that only large government subsidies kept the steamship lines from going bankrupt. The single-expansion engine allowed ships to offer regular scheduled service, but they were slower than most sailing vessels, and the fast clippers easily outran the steamships until the 1860s. Governments could not be expected to subsidize forever such a costly transportation system, and clearly if steam was going to replace sail, a more efficient power unit was needed. How could a better engine be designed?

Compound engine*

In the compound engine, a second larger cylinder received the exhaust steam from the first cylinder, thereby increasing the fuel efficiency as well as the number of revolutions of the engine. This principle had been known in the early nineteenth century but required a steam pressure of sixty pounds per square inch or at least three times higher than the twenty pounds per square inch in the single-expansion engine (the atmosphere at sea level has a pressure of fifteen pounds per square inch). In the more rudimentary stage of metallurgy, pipes and boilers frequently erupted at the higher pressures, sometimes with fatal explosions. Not until the late 1860s did improvements finally permit steamships to use safely the compound engine, whose introduction revolutionized merchant shipping.

With the compound engine, iron hulls and propellers became universal for steamships. Coal consumption was cut in half, although sails still remained standard equipment in case of mechanical failure. The compound engine ran faster and thus turned the propeller shaft directly without having to waste energy in gearing up to faster revolutions, as was required with the single-expansion engine. The savings in fuel and in bunker* space meant that the commercial operation of steamships at last became possible, and with proper scheduling of routes and cargoes, capable management could make profits while governments could afford to reduce or eliminate subsidies in the main routes without fear of endangering steamship services.

The compound engine increased vessel speeds to ten knots, but rarely more than twelve knots. For cargo this speed was satisfactory, but for travelers in a rush, the sailing clippers were faster under favorable winds and still could average fourteen knots and higher in the North Atlantic. Steamships somehow had to meet the demand for fast passenger service, but when engineers experimented with increasing the size and the steam pressures of the compound engine, then too much steam again was wasted, while past a certain point existing metals could not take higher pressures. How could these bottlenecks be overcome?

Triple-expansion engine*

The answer to the limitations of the compound engine was surprisingly simple, namely, add a third cylinder (the largest of the three), so that before the steam cooled, it could be rapidly used three times to produce motion. However, the third cylinder worked effectively only under much higher pressures, and not until the 1880s did the steel mills produce at a low price the better steel required. In 1881 the British launched the *Aberdeen*, the first ship to use the triple-expansion engine. As engineers increased steam pressure to 250 pounds per inch by 1900, the efficiency of the triple-expansion engine increased, and by then it not only had replaced the compound engine but was also rapidly displacing the iron sailing vessels, even for the transport of bulk* cargoes.

The triple-expansion engine was quickly adopted in the United States and the rest of the world because it did allow the faster speed of fourteen knots, but its main attractiveness was the significant reduction of costs. By generating even more movement with less coal, the triple-expansion engine was the most efficient of the steam cylinder engines, but as it approached fourteen knots, energy efficiency began to decline, and consequently it was normally run at lower speeds to achieve the optimal fuel consumption. There was no longer any need to snatch fleeting gusts of air, and the last remaining sails disappeared from the ships. In the 1880s steel replaced iron as the material for the hulls.

The triple-expansion engine remained the most common propulsion for freighters until World War II; in the 1910s most triple-expansion engines in the United States were converted to burn oil, but coal remained the most common fuel in the British ships until World War II. However, the triple-expansion engine had failed to increase travel speeds substantially, leaving unsatisfied the passengers who were willing to pay extra fares for express service across the North Atlantic. Simply increasing the steam pressure had reached the point of diminishing returns: more and more coal was consumed to produce less and less additional speed. In some models the experiments using two cylinders rather than just one for the third expansion suggested important improvements in output. Could anything else be done to enhance the speed of the triple-expansion engine?

Quadruple-expansion engine

"The more the merrier" seemed to be the slogan of engineers, who found a way to obtain more speed by adding a fourth cylinder (again the largest) to the triple-expansion engine. In fact, some of the latter already had four cylinders (two were used for the third expansion), while some of the quadruple-expansion engines reached a maximum of six cylinders. In any case, the performance of the quadruple-expansion engine was mixed at best: speeds of eighteen knots (such as in *Korea** and *Siberia**) and even slightly higher were possible but required enormous consumption of coal. The cylinder steam engines, from the single to the quadruple-expansion, had never been able to turn the shaft fast enough to achieve speeds in the twenty-knot range and higher and thus had never really satisfied the demands of wealthy passengers for fast ocean crossings. Furthermore, the quadruple-expansion engine not only wasted a lot of fuel but was also more complex mechanically than the triple-expansion engine and hence was more expensive to maintain and repair.

The higher costs of the quadruple-expansion engine had to be covered somehow; and although more valuable cargo helped defray part of the expenses, the profitability of the fast passenger liners ultimately depended on the immigrants, whether Europeans or Orientals, who were crammed, often a thousand or more per voyage, in the lower decks in the generally subhuman conditions of steerage* class.

With the quadruple-expansion engine the reciprocating steam engine had reached the point of diminishing returns; a fifth-expansion was out of the question, and within the quadruple expansion six cylinders was the limit. How would marine engineers find a way out of the dead end and into the fast speeds demanded by the wealthy traveling public?

Steam turbine*

Even before the limits of the quadruple-expansion engine had been reached, other engineers were busy at work on a radically different propulsion system. If the cylinder engines had been plagued with the problem of turning the shaft fast enough, why not use the steam turbine, which was capable of an incredibly high number of revolutions? The first steam turbine was successfully used to power a ship in 1894, but the initial excitement soon faded because of two harsh realities. Past a certain number of revolutions, the propeller began to spin in a vacuum and not in water (''cavitation''), thereby sharply reducing its thrusting power. Second, the steam turbines operated best at high speeds. As a matter of fact, for speeds under fourteen knots the triple-expansion engines were more efficient than the turbines. How could a fast turbine move a slow propeller? The only answer was by huge reduction gears, but these necessarily wasted a considerable percentage of energy.

The lower the number of revolutions of the turbine, the higher the waste of energy, so that for speeds of twelve knots and under, the triple-expansion engine remained the economical choice for freighters. But for high speeds, the turbine appeared unbeatable, as the British vessels *Lusitania* and *Mauretania* of the Cunard Line proved in 1907, when they set new world records by steaming across the North Atlantic at twenty-five knots. Unfortunately, steaming at such high speeds required wasting a tremendous amount of energy, and engineers looked for less costly alternatives. The International Mercantile Marine* (IMM) tried the ingenious solution of using two triple-expansion engines in its passenger liners, whose speed was boosted by a third propeller driven by a steam turbine. The three sister ships were capable of twenty-one knots, slower than the Cunard liners, but had much lower fuel costs, and it was hoped that by emphasizing the extremely luxurious facilities aboard, the wealthy passengers could still be lured aboard. Unfortunately the disaster that befell one of the sister ships, the *Titanic*,* totally discredited this alternative as well as other combinations of engines.

Turbines remained the rule for high-speed passenger liners, but after World War I the United Stats also began to install turbines in freighters. Because the steam turbine rotated in only one direction, reverse was an additional problem, unlike the triple-expansion engine, whose motion was easily reversed to move the ship backward; for turbine ships the costly solution required the installation of a second smaller turbine just to move the ship backward. By the 1910s most steamships in the United States had replaced coal with oil, but this change affected only the boiler and did not have implications for the type of engine used until the 1970s. As the horsepower of turbines increased, the greater was the energy loss, unless the gears could somehow be improved. Engineers eventually developed the double reduction gear in 1915, but initially it was not satisfactory for very high horsepower. By the 1930s better double reduction gears had appeared that harnessed less wastefully the high speed of the turbine, but not in a completely satisfactory manner, so engineers continued to search for another solution to the concrete problem of using the high speed of the turbine for marine propulsion.

Turboelectric

Utilities used steam turbines on land to generate electricity; why couldn't the same be done to move ships? In a turboelectric ship (also called one with electric drive), the high-speed steam turbine turned a generator that produced ample electricity to power an electric motor. Unlike the steam turbine, the electric motors could be designed to run at low speeds and therefore transfer the motion directly to the propeller shaft without reduction gears. No second turbine was necessary to move the ship backward, because a flick of the switch reversed the electric motor. In principle and on paper, turboelectric propulsion had solved the problems of the steam turbine, but in practice the results were far from satisfactory.

The installation and maintenance of the additional equipment proved costly, while the waste of energy had really not been avoided because more steps in the process meant loss of energy at each transfer point. Freighters avoided turboelectric as too expensive, but combination passenger-cargo liners, in particular, the *President Coolidge*,* the *President Hoover*,* the *Manhattan*,* and the *Washington* of the early 1930s, employed turboelectric propulsion as a way to attract more passengers. The income from the ships did not justify the greater investment in the additional machinery, so that by the late 1930s the companies concluded that turboelectric propulsion was ill-suited for commercial operations.

Certain warships such as submarines did use turboelectric engines, but gradually the navy grew disenchanted with electric drive for surface vessels. However, if wasting very large amounts of energy was not a consideration, then electric drive was a much smoother means to run a ship than through the noisy and cumbersome reduction gears. The introduction of nuclear energy in the 1960s revived interest in turboelectric propulsion, particularly for warships, but the first nuclear-powered merchant vessel, the *Savannah*,* was a commercial failure.

Diesel engine*

After 1904, as oil began to replace coal as the fuel for the boilers of the triple-expansion engines, the possibility of using the oil-burning internal combustion engine inevitably surfaced. In the internal combustion engine, the fuel ignited and exploded inside each cylinder; the piston was pushed down, thereby producing motion in the crankshaft; usually at least four cylinders and as many as eleven were synchronized in a row. The internal combustion engine eliminated the boiler and ancillary tubes, while the heavy walls of the engine precluded any risk of a fatal explosion.

In the family of internal combustion engines, the diesel soon emerged as the best suited for marine propulsion. There were two types of diesel: one turned the shaft rather rapidly and could be used for trucks and locomotives and even some automobiles, while another was very powerful but turned the shaft very slowly. With a fast shaft, the engineers were back to the old problem of the steam turbine, namely, how to reduce the high speed of the engine to the low speed of the propeller. Clearly it was the second type, called the slow-speed diesel, that intrigued marine engineers as the latest solution to the century-old problem of ship propulsion.

After World War I the Shipping Board* experimented with diesel engines and in 1924 paid to convert twelve freighters to this type of propulsion. The Shipping Board planned to shift the entire U.S. merchant fleet to diesels but was blocked by the powerful steam engine interests, and as a result manufacturers in the United States never acquired the facilities or the technology to produce large numbers of diesel engines. In World War II the U.S. Maritime Commission* wanted diesels for the crash shipbuilding program, but because engine production was so limited, the majority of new ships were fitted with steam propulsion; even turbines were in short supply, so the Liberty* ships used the triple-expansion engine, which was easier and faster to mass-produce and install.

After the war the sale of the surplus vessels perpetuated the grip of steam on U.S. ships for twenty more years. The Maritime Administration* introduced the Mariners* in 1952, a ship design that used steam turbines rather than diesels. For their part, American steamship companies avoided ordering diesels because they were more expensive to buy and to maintain than the steam turbines, while the diesels' lower fuel costs did not seem crucial as long as oil remained cheap. In the engine room the diesel required fewer but better paid men so that some executives felt no significant savings in wages could be expected. Foreign steamship companies had no hesitation about switching massively to the diesel engine after World War II, and the resulting lower operating costs placed U.S.-flag ships at a serious disadvantage.

In effect, the failure to adopt diesel engines was one more factor that contributed to the decline of the U.S.-flag merchant marine. Not until the energy crisis of 1973 did the already vastly reduced ranks of U.S.-flag lines finally turn to diesel engines. There was so much resistance from management, unions, and turbine manufacturers that only the high oil prices could impose the diesels (indeed, when oil replaced coal as the ships' fuel in the 1910s, only the very low oil prices had prevented an earlier adoption of the diesel). However, with coal as a fuel steam turbines could still be competitive, and the steam interests made one last attempt to keep turbines aboard ships when they lobbied for the construction of the coal-burning *Energy Independence** in 1983. The results were not wholly convincing for U.S. merchant shipping companies, and they at last turned to the diesel engine. American President Lines* was the first to order three diesel ships in 1978, Sea-Land* converted seven of its turbine containerships to diesels in 1980, and gradually during the 1980s diesels became the norm for U.S. merchant shipping companies.

Final results

The compound engine rapidly displaced the single-expansion engine in the 1860s, and both were replaced even more swiftly by the triple-expansion engine, which by the 1890s became the accepted norm in world shipping. The real competition in the nineteenth century was not so much one engine against another, but rather against sailing vessels, particularly those with iron hulls. Only with the fuel efficiency and higher speeds of the triple-expansion engine did the sailing vessels finally recede into the rich heritage of the sea.

In the twentieth century triple- and quadruple-expansion engines, steam turbines, and diesels competed for supremacy in ship propulsion. The quadruple-expansion engine was the first casualty and was no longer ordered by the first decade of the twentieth century. For cargo that did not require fast delivery, the triple-expansion engine remained the norm for freighters until after World War II. For passengers and express cargo, the steam turbines became even before World War I the standard propulsion for the fast liners. Turboelectric propulsion in the 1930s failed to reduce the fuel extravagance of the steam turbines, but as long as oil was very inexpensive, steam turbines remained acceptable, and with improvements in the double reduction gear they became the standard propulsion for all new U.S. shipbuilding in the decades after World War II; by the 1960s only the rapidly vanishing U.S.-flag tramps still used triple-expansion engines.

Since the 1920s the major European lines had accepted the diesels as the best choice, and, after World War II, when the United States was building only steam-turbine ships, diesels became the standard propulsion machinery in the rest of the world. Only in the 1980s did the U.S. steamship companies at last replace steam turbines with diesels, but by then the failure to adopt the new marine propulsion had already done tremendous damage and must be considered one of the causes of the decline of the U.S. merchant marine. The lag of fifty years in adopting diesels was nothing less than incredible in a country that traditionally has pushed the introduction of new capital-intensive technologies. When new experimental technologies appear in the next century, hopefully the United States will demonstrate a greater willingness to adopt radical innovations in marine propulsion.

References: Commission on Merchant Marine and Defense, *Third Report: Appendices* (Washington, DC: Government Printing Office, 1988); Gerald S. Graham, "The Ascendancy of the Sailing Ship 1850–1885," *Economic History Review* 9 (1956):74–88; Edwin P. Harnack, *All About Ships and Shipping*, 11th ed. (London: Faber and Faber, 1964); William S. Lindsay, *History of Merchant Shipping and Ancient Commerce*, 4 vols. (New York: AMS Press, 1965); Cedric R. Nevitt, "American Merchant Steamships," John F. Nichols, "The Development of Marine Engineering," and E. H. Rigg and A. J. Dickie, "History of the United States Coastwise Steamers," all in Society of Naval Architects and Marine Engineers, *Historical Transactions, 1893–1943* (Westport, CT: Greenwood Press, 1981); Edward W. Sloan III, "The Machine at Sea: Early Transatlantic Steam Travel," in Benjamin W. Labaree, *The Atlantic World of Robert G. Albion* (Middletown, CT: Wesleyan University Press, 1975); T. W. Van Metre, *Tramps and Liners* (New York: Doubleday, Doran, 1931).

As usual, the suggested publications contain further information, but most readers would find it easier and much more enjoyable in the next family outing to visit the exhibits in the notable museums of the world to actually see the machinery itself and in some cases have hands-on experience! The National Maritime Museum of San Francisco, the National Maritime Museum of Greenwich, England, and the Musée de la Marine in Paris are highly recommended as well as the Smithsonian in Washington, D.C., and the Chicago Museum of Science and Industry. The science museums in most major cities include at least some maritime exhibits, and those in New York City and in Toronto clearly stand out. The Massachusetts Institute of Technology has a museum specialized just in marine propulsion; while the state maritime academies,* including the Merchant Marine Academy,* have a varying number of ship exhibits and machinery on display.

MARINE SERVICE BUREAU, 1919–1935. The Marine Service Bureau of San Francisco was the hiring hall* of the Waterfront Employers' Union* (WEU), a management body. To provide strikebreakers during the 1919 longshoremen's strike, the WEU established the Marine Service Bureau. When the seamen launched the strike of 1921,* the Marine Service Bureau, under the direction of a former police captain, Walter J. Petersen, actively sought scab sailors. After the strike was crushed, the bureau left the tasks of hiring longshoremen to the Blue Book Union.* The Pacific American Steamship Association* (PASSA) and the Shipowners' Association of the Pacific* (SAPC) now decided jointly with WEU to operate the Marine Service Bureau, which now became the only hiring agency for all seafarers on the West Coast.

The seamen first registered, and then to find a job, they came every day to take a number and wait from 7:00 A.M. to 9:00 P.M., the hours the Marine Service was open. "The hall is drafty, dark, and unheated. The furnishings are rude benches" (Hopkins 1935). All seamen were required to carry a "record book" in which the captain wrote his personal opinions of the seaman's performance after each voyage. These record books soon degenerated into "grade books," which effectively blacklisted the seamen, who soon called them "fink books." In case of any mutilation of the fink book, the Marine Service Bureau itself kept card files on each seaman, records that also served the purpose of blacklisting any union activists or radicals: "The prevailing secret mark is a red dot on the upper left-hand corner of the card" (ibid.).

The real function of the bureau was to serve as a strikebreaking agency, and consequently it also maintained current lists of scabs. The staff was composed "of uncompromising union-haters," and the men were "possessed of police authority. . . . All are constantly armed with loaded pistols, and occasionally with night sticks and tear-gas runs" (ibid.). The bitterness of the sailors toward the bureau was "so intense as to be beyond description" (ibid.) and the sailors had nothing but hatred toward what they contemptuously called the "Fink Hall." Nevertheless, "seamen have never protested against the right of a ship's officer to employ whomever they please" (ibid.), so the employer had the privilege of hiring a particular seaman no matter what his waiting number.

After the U.S. Supreme Court in 1926 abolished the requirement of compulsory registration, the number of seamen registered in the Marine Service Bureau declined gradually from 27,000 in 1927 to 9,800 in 1933. In the 1930s union leaders realized that the Marine Service Bureau was an example of how to create a formidable power base, and they struggled to take the hiring hall away from the employers and at the same time fight off attempts to place the employment process in the hands of a more neutral agency of the federal government.

The first order of business was to smash the Marine Service Bureau itself: in the Big Strike* of 1934, the bureau continued to hire strikebreakers, but almost all union seamen boycotted its hiring hall and burned their fink books. As late as February 1935 the bureau was placing thirty or forty men per month in ships, but this number was vastly insufficient to man the ships. The WEU finally disbanded the Marine Service Bureau and agreed to deal directly with the unions to obtain the needed labor force through the union hiring hall,* the real replacement on the West Coast for the Marine Service Bureau. See also Sea Service Bureau.

References: Mary Ann Burki, "Paul Scharrenberg: White Shirt Sailor," Ph.D. diss., University of Rochester, 1971; William S. Hopkins, "Employment Exchanges for Seamen," *American Economic Review* 25 (1935): 250–258; Bruce Nelson, *Workers on the Waterfront* (Urbana: University of Illinois Press, 1990); Walter J. Petersen, *Marine Labor Union Leadership* (San Francisco, 1925).

MARINER CLASS or MARINERS. The Mariners were the first new class of freighters built in the United States after World War II. The U.S. Maritime Commission* designed the Mariners as the replacement for older ships, in particular the Victory* and C-3* classes. A first experimental ship, the *Schuyler Otis Bland*, was operational by 1950, and its success convinced the Maritime Administration* to obtain $350 million from Congress to build thirty-five Mariners. The shipyards delivered the first ship, the *Keystone Mariner*, on 29 February 1952, and by the time the construction program was completed in 1955, the government had sold twenty-nine Mariners to the following firms: nine to United States Lines,* eight to American President Lines* (APL); seven to Pacific Far East lines* (PFEL); two each to Pacific Transport Lines* and Matson Navigation Company;* and one to American Banner Line.* In a curious twist, Matson converted its two mariners into the passenger liners *Monterey** and *Mariposa** in 1956–1957.

The Mariners had an overall length of 564 feet and a beam of 76 feet, and with over 14,000 deadweight* tons they were the biggest freighters in existence during the 1950s. Improvements in hull and marine propulsion* allowed a normal speed of twenty knots, so these efficient steam turbine* freighters were also the fastest in the world. A whole host of engineering and navigational innovations made the Mariners the culmination of sixty years of improvements in break-bulk* vessels. However, the ships were not without drawbacks: their larger size required a bigger crew numbering, fifty-eight persons, while the failure to use the more economical diesel* engine was remarkable. In a move typical of a tradition-bound industry, the steamship companies did not allow the government to incorporate the container* lessons of World War II into the designs.

The steamship companies were satisfied with the Mariner design, and its later versions suggested a pattern of growing by accretion, whereby the extra space went into specialized compartments or into making larger the traditional cargo holds. Modified later versions such as the Master Mariners of APL or the "converted" Mariners of the PFEL had the same dimensions but weighed more.

APL's "Seamasters" of 1967–1968 had even greater weight and had the fast twenty-three-knot speed, but "were all of the basic Mariner design" (Niven 1987). Although the introduction of the fast Mariners into the Far East routes had caused quite a commotion in the mid-1950s, in reality the Mariners looked to the past rather than to the future in ship designs. In the late 1970s most U.S. steamship companies took advantage of new legislation to trade in their Mariners for mothballing in the National Defense Reserve Fleet* in exchange for modest compensation.

References: American President Lines, *Annual Reports* of the 1950s; *American Shipper*, June 1982; René De La Pedraja, *The Rise and Decline of U.S. Merchant Shipping* (New York: Twayne, 1992); Federal Maritime Board, *Decisions*, vol. 4 (Washington, DC: Government Printing Office, 1963); Henry S. Marcus, *Planning Ship Replacement in the Containerization Era* (Lexington, MA: Lexington Books, 1974); John Niven, *The American President Lines and Its Forebears, 1848–1984* (Newark: University of Delaware Press, 1987); Pacific Far East Line, *Annual Reports* of 1950s; White House Central Files, Gerald Ford Presidential Library, Ann Arbor, Michigan.

MARINE WORKERS INDUSTRIAL UNION (MWIU), 1930–1935. The Marine Workers Industrial Union (MWIU) was the labor union created by the Communist party for maritime workers. In 1928 the Communist International (Comintern) urged national communist parties to abandon the policy of "boring from within" the existing labor organizations and instead to organize communist-led unions. After two yeas of organizing and agitating on the waterfront, the Communist party hosted a convention that created the Marine Workers Industrial Union on 26 April 1930. The about 180 delegates were mostly former members of the Marine Transport Workers' Industrial Union, the affiliate of the International Workers' of the World. George Mink* became the first national chairman, and Harry Hynes the first national secretary. The MWIU claimed to represent seamen, longshoremen, and all other port workers, but in fact all attempts to recruit longshoremen failed, and it remained an organization primarily of seamen. Recruiting drives among blacks were disappointing but did begin to awaken a consciousness among black workers that later proved beneficial to the National Maritime Union* (NMU). The MWIU became a catalyst for many workers, both white and black; for example, Joseph Curran* admitted his union experiences began with the communist-led union.

The MWIU carried out a series of highly visible protests and strikes in the early 1930s, but all ended in defeat. A shake-up within the union led to the removal of George Mink and the replacement of Harry Hynes as national secretary by Roy Hudson,* who became the leading figure of the union.

The fortunes of the MWIU appeared to improve when a concerted campaign secured the establishment of a union hiring hall* in Baltimore in February 1934. The success was only temporary, and the seamen in Baltimore were crushed by 2 May. When the Big Strike* began on the West Coast on 9 May 1934, the MWIU eagerly joined the movement and suffered massive repression in the form of constant police raids and arrests. Striking maritime workers appreciated the support, but they also realized that the authorities would never allow the MWIU to operate legally and consequently preferred to operate within the now revitalized International Seamen's Union* (ISU). Over five years of efforts to establish a strong communist-led maritime movement had produced no tangible results, so when the Comintern urged the return to the policy of "boring from within," the Communist party only too eagerly complied and abolished the MWIU in February 1935.

Principal Labor Leaders

George Mink	1930–1933
Harry Hynes	1930–1932
Roy Hudson	1932–1935

References: Howard Kimeldorf, *Reds or Rackets: The Making of Radical and Conservative Unions on the Waterfront* (Berkeley: University of California Press, 1988); Bruce Nelson, *Workers on the Waterfront* (Urbana: University of Illinois Press, 1990); William L. Standard, *Merchant Seamen: A Short History of Their Struggles* (New York: International, 1947).

MARIPOSA, **1931–1947, and** *MONTEREY*, **1932–1947.** The success of the *Malolo** convinced William P. Roth,* president of Matson Navigation Company,* to order more ships for the tourist trade to Hawaii. The *Mariposa* entered service in 1931, and her sister ship, the *Monterey*, in 1932 under the operation of the Matson subsidiary, the Oceanic Steamship Company.* Both ships at 632 feet were longer than the *Malolo* and had the slightly slower speed of twenty knots. The days of the "millionaires' cruises" were over, and although the ships had accommodations for 475 first-class passengers, they also had space for 230 persons in cabin class. To assure passengers for the ships during the whole year, Roth decided to extend the voyages to New Zealand and Australia, with stops in Fiji and other exotic spots. In this way the tourist traffic moving from the United States to Hawaii could be balanced with the Australian and New Zealander passengers wishing to reach England via the United States. The publicity campaign of Matson and the amenities aboard the *Mariposa* and *Monterey* had proven so irresistible to travelers from Australia and New Zealand that the governments of those countries threatened to take reprisals against Matson. The company refused to buckle to the pressure and kept the *Mariposa* and *Monterey* steaming to Australia and New Zealand, but Matson agreed, as a goodwill gesture, to place a third new ship, the *Lurline,** only in the California-Hawaii route. When the United States entered World War II, the *Mariposa* and the *Monterey* were taken over by the government; after the war Matson decided to return to passenger service, but only after extensive renovation of the *Mariposa, Monterey*, and *Lurline*. Frazer A. Bailey* attempted to rebuild the three vessels at Matson's small wartime yard in California, but mounting costs halted work on the *Mariposa* and the *Monterey*, both of which were laid up. The *Mariposa* was sold to Greek owners in 1953 and after operation as a cruise ship was scrapped in 1974; the *Monterey* was sold to the U.S. government in 1952, but the ship gained a new extension on its life as the *Matsonia** in 1956.

References: René De La Pedraja, *The Rise and Decline of U.S. Merchant Shipping in the Twentieth Century* (New York: Twayne, 1992); Frederick E. Emmons, *American Passenger Ships: The Ocean Lines and Liners, 1873–1983* (Newark: University of Delaware Press, 1985); Fred A. Stindt, *Matson's Century of Ships* (Modesto, CA: n.p., 1982); William L. Worden, *Cargoes: Matson's First Century in the Pacific* (Honolulu: University Press of Hawaii, 1981).

MARIPOSA, **1956–1971, and** *MONTEREY,* **1975–present.** Matson Navigation Company* had provided through its subsidiary, Oceanic Steamship Company,* passenger and express freight service from California and Hawaii to Australia and New Zealand before World War II. Matson had wanted to restore the service once the war was over but was not able to return to the route. The interest remained alive, and in 1954 the company confirmed that Australia and New Zealand eagerly welcomed the revival of the Oceanic Steamship Company service; encouraged by this response, Matson ordered the conversion of two Mariner* freighters into the modern fast liners the *Mariposa* and the *Monterey* (the same name of the pre–World War II vessels in the same route). The ships had accommodations for 365 passengers, only in first class, because the forty-two-day cruises were expected to attract only wealthy travelers; the fast ships of twenty-one knots still carried express freight in special holds and in refrigerated spaces.

However, the ships had only a few years' profitable operation after they entered service in 1956–1957, because jet airliners since the late 1950s began to drastically erode passenger traffic, even among wealthy travelers. In the 1960s the company could not book the ships full and increasingly diverted them to make voyages as cruise ships to South America, Mexico, and Alaska. With losses piling up, Matson decided to sell the two liners to Pacific Far East Line* (PFEL) in 1971.

PFEL was now saddled with these money-losing ships, whose poor financial performance contributed to the eventual bankruptcy of the line in 1978. The *Mariposa* and the *Monterey* were laid up and sold. In 1980 a labor union, the International Organization of Masters, Mates and Pilots* (MM&P), purchased the *Monterey* with the intention of refurbishing the vessel and operating her as a U.S.-flag cruise ship in the protected coastwise* service. The task of renovating the *Monterey* required over $30 million, and rumblings among the rank and file produced a crisis within MM&P over whether such a costly overhaul was the best use of union funds when the new vessel would create only ten jobs for its members (the bulk of the cooks, stewards, and waiters were hired through ads in newspapers). In 1987 the MM&P sold the *Monterey* to private investors, who operated the ship in Hawaiian waters from September 1988 until April 1989 when the owners entered bankruptcy proceedings. After failed attempts to find American buyers, the *Monterey* was sold at the auction block in April 1990 for operation as a foreign-flag cruise ship.

References: Frederick E. Emmons, *American Passenger Ships: The Ocean Lines and Liners, 1873–1983* (Newark: University of Delaware Press, 1985); *Journal of Commerce*, 25 March, 30 June, 8 September 1988, 12 March, 3 April 1990; Fred A. Stindt, *Matson's Century of Ships* (Modesto, CA: n.p., 1982); William L. Worden, *Cargoes: Matson's First Century in the Pacific* (Honolulu: University Press of Hawaii, 1981).

MARITIME ADMINISTRATION (MARAD), 1950–present. The Maritime Administration (MARAD), headed by the maritime administrator, has been the government agency in charge of the assistance programs for U.S. merchant shipping companies. The main programs administered by MARAD have been the operating differential subsidy* (ODS) and the construction differential subsidy* (CDS); decisions about both have been taken since 1961 in a special unit within MARAD, the Maritime Subsidy Board* (MSB), composed of three MARAD officials, whose chairman was also the maritime administrator. From 1950 to 1961 the maritime administrator was also the chairman of the Federal Maritime Board* (FMB), whose powers included not only taking subsidy decisions but also performing regulatory functions with regard to rates, services, and other issues of vital concern to shippers.*

Reorganization Plan Number 21 created MARAD and the FMB on 24 May 1950 to replace the discredited but independent U.S. Maritime Commission.* Government reformers wanted a more executive agency under the direction of a cabinet official and hence placed MARAD under a single administrator in the Department of Commerce; the new agency was in charge of all merchant shipping programs except for those under the jurisdiction of the Coast Guard.* To protect the maritime administrator from improper political pressures, decisions about subsidies and regulations were reserved for a more impartial board, the FMB. The three members of FMB were appointed by the president with the consent of the Senate, but since its chairman was also the administrator of MARAD, smooth cooperation between both bodies was expected. As a matter of fact, the same staff was used for both the FMB and MARAD, whose lines of separation were so blurred that both operated in practice as a single agency. Not unexpectedly, shippers felt that MARAD neglected rate regulation, and after the revelations of the Celler Committee,* the shippers secured the transfer of all regulatory functions to a new independent agency, the Federal Maritime Commission* (FMC) in 1961.

Since 1961 MARAD has dealt almost exclusively with the shipowners and has concentrated on the apparently hopeless task of trying to slow down the decline of the U.S. merchant marine. MARAD has been so limited by strict legislative mandates that it has been left largely in the role of hapless witness to the disappearance and bankruptcy of most U.S.-flag merchant shipping companies. Nicholas Johnson* tried in 1964–1966 to change the policies that were driving the merchant marine toward sure extinction, but the bitter opposition of both maritime unions and liner* companies blocked any change in the obsolete subsidy programs of the Merchant Marine Act of 1936.*

In later decades MARAD administrators have increasingly found budget restraints to limit seriously any increases in assistance for the merchant marine. Using the Vietnam War as a way to pressure Congress, another MARAD administrator, Andrew E. Gibson,* united with the shipowners to secure passage of a new law, the Merchant Marine Act of 1970,* which extended the ODS for the first time to bulk* carriers and not just to liner firms as before. Gibson decided that to maintain and secure legislative gains, a broad-based coalition of shipping interests was necessary, and to that effect he created the National Maritime Council* (NMC) in 1971. The NMC during its initial years was an advocacy organization largely dependent for its functioning on MARAD. However, public denunciations in 1978 forced MARAD to withdraw from the NMC, thereby ending the cozy relationships among government, shipowners, shipbuilders, and labor.

The lack of interest by the Department of Commerce was often cited as a major reason for MARAD's lackluster performance, which supposedly would drastically improve under a more sympathetic Department of Transportation. The transfer to Transportation had been proposed since 1966, even before the establishment of that department, and was finally accomplished on 6 August 1981. No dramatic improvement occurred, and in 1989 industry representatives already claimed "that it was probably a mistake to shift MARAD . . . and that the Department of Transportation had not been so great" (*Journal of Commerce*, 28 March 1989).

In 1981 the government announced that no more construction differential subsidies would be awarded, while the last operating differential subsidy contract (usually of a twenty-year duration) was signed in 1982. MARAD still has to enforce the cargo preference* and other laws affecting merchant shipping, but with the constant decline of U.S.-flag merchant shipping, the agency has rapidly been losing its most meaningful missions and soon may lack any role.

Administrators

Admiral Edward L. Cochrane	1950–1952
Albert W. Gatov	1952–1953
Louis S. Rothschild	1953–1955
Clarence G. Morse*	1955–1960
Admiral Ralph E. Wilson	1960–1961
Thomas E. Stakem	1961
Donald W. Alexander	1961–1963
Robert Giles	1963–1964
Nicholas Johnson	1964–1966
James W. Gulick	1966–1968

Andrew E. Gibson	1969–1972
Robert J. Blackwell	1973–1979
Samuel B. Nemirow	1979–1981
Admiral Harold E. Shear	1981–1985
John A. Gaughan	1985–1989
Captain Warren G. Leback	1989–1993
Admiral Albert J. Herberger	1993–present

References: *American Shipper*, February 1979; René De La Pedraja, *The Rise and Decline of U.S. Merchant Shipping in the Twentieth Century* (New York: Twayne, 1992); *Journal of Commerce*, 28 March 1989; Samuel A. Lawrence, *United States Merchant Shipping Policies and Politics* (Washington, DC: Brookings Institution, 1966); Maritime Administration, *Annual Reports*, 1985–1988; *Weekly Compilation of Presidential Documents*, 10 August 1981.

MARITIME FEDERATION OF THE PACIFIC (MFP), 1935–1941. The Maritime Federation of the Pacific (MFP) was the boldest attempt made by sailors, longshoremen, and other shoreside workers to organize a common strike front for the entire maritime industry on the West Coast. Harry Bridges* had proposed the creation of a waterfront organization in February 1934, but the Big Strike* of 9 May–31 July 1934 definitely showed the advantages of common strike action. Momentum for the federation rapidly built up in the fall of 1934, and the new Maritime Federation of the Pacific (MFP) was formally created in Seattle in April 1935; its motto was ''An Injury to One Is an Injury to All.'' The driving personality behind the MFP was Bridges, who had emerged as the real leader of the West Coast longshoremen, and for the first president of the federation he put his support behind Harry Lundeberg,* a patrolman* of the Sailors' Union of the Pacific* (SUP), who was duly elected.

The MFP performed useful functions in quietly concluding an ongoing unsuccessful strike against Standard Oil tankers, and in launching a publicity campaign to draw attention to the unjust imprisonment of the Modesto Boys.* However, disputes soon arose between the sailors and longshoremen, the two main components of the federation. Lundeberg, who owed his job to Bridges's timely support, tried to cooperate but was not about to sacrifice the interests of the sailors. When the longshoremen accepted a renewal in September 1935 of their arbitration award without giving the seamen time to act, a serious breach erupted in the MFP. Lundeberg took his case to the sailors, who overwhelmingly elected him president of the SUP in January 1936, and the next month he stepped down as president of the MFP. The battle lines were drawn on the West Coast for the next twenty years: Lundeberg of the SUP against Bridges of the International Longshoremen's and Warehousemen's Union* (ILWU).

Curiously enough, the MFP was not an immediate casualty of the Lundeberg-Bridges feud, and instead the federation staged the highly successful ''Fall

Strike'' from 30 October 1936 to 4 February 1937. On the West Coast, all strikers obtained gains, although the significant concessions went to the seamen who confirmed the right to the union hiring hall.* On the East Coast and Gulf, the gains were even more dramatic, because for the first time in history, the seamen created a permanent labor organization, the National Maritime Union* (NMU), under Joseph Curran.* Bridges had put all his weight behind the organizing effort of Curran, but Lundeberg did not go beyond having his SUP participate in the strike. Furthermore, he refused to help the East Coast sailors and instead supported the moribund International Seamen's Union* (ISU), which had joined with employers to try to crush Curran and his followers.

Lundeberg justified his inconsistent position on the charges that the NMU was infiltrated with communists, but the real reason was the fear that his smaller SUP would be gobbled by Curran's much larger union. Lundeberg's struggle to defend his labor fief made superfluous membership in the MFP, and in June 1938 the SUP withdrew. The MFP had effectively ended, but it continued to function as an adjunct to the ILWU until July 1941, when the MFP was merged with the Congress of Industrial Organizations (CIO) Maritime Committee. See Maritime Trades Department.

Principal Labor Leaders

| Harry Lundeberg | 1935–1936 |
| Harry Bridges | 1935–1941 |

References: Charles P. Larrowe, *Harry Bridges: The Rise and Fall of Radical Labor in the U.S.* (New York: Lawrence Hill, 1972); Bruce Nelson, *Workers on the Waterfront: Seamen, Longshoremen, and Unionism in the 1930s* (Urbana: University of Illinois Press, 1990).

MARITIME SUBSIDY BOARD (MSB), 1961–present. Reorganization Plan Number 7 of 1961 created the Maritime Subsidy Board (MSB) to decide upon the merits of applications for government assistance to merchant shipping companies, in particular the construction differential subsidy* (CDS) and the operating differential subsidy* (ODS). The Reorganization Plan transferred jurisdiction over subsidies from the Federal Maritime Board,* whose functions had also included the regulation of ocean transportation. In the original proposal, all subsidy functions went directly to the new Maritime Administration* (MARAD), but the Committee of American Steamship Lines* (CASL) objected to this arrangement because it feared that a single official would more likely be swayed by political considerations than a more impartial board. Consequently, in its final version, the Reorganization Plan established the MSB with a membership of three officials from MARAD, one of whom was the maritime administrator himself. Like MARAD, the MSB was within the chain of command of the Department of Commerce (since 1981 under the Department of Transportation), thereby correcting a flaw in the pre-1961 setup. Previously the Federal Maritime Board was ''subject to general policy guidance by the Secretary of Commerce'' (*Public Papers* 1950), but its decisions could not appeal to the secretary of commerce. To avoid the silly task of trying to guess what the secretary of commerce really meant, the new MSB took its determination based on the facts and the legal precedents, but the decisions were subject to reversal or confirmation on appeal to the secretary of commerce (transportation since 1981). In practice, the executive departments have reversed only a small percentage of the decisions of the MSB. Because the same person has been both its chairman and also the maritime administrator, MARAD and the Maritime Subsidy Board have operated as a single unit, but the board system has provided safeguards against any gross violation of accepted legal procedures.

References: Gerald R. Jantscher, *Bread upon the Waters: Federal Aids to the Maritime Industries* (Washington, DC: Brookings Institution, 1975); Samuel A. Lawrence, *United States Merchant Shipping Policies and Politics* (Washington, DC: Brookings Institution, 1966); Maritime Subsidy Board, *Decisions; Public Papers of the President, Harry S. Truman, 1950.*

MARITIME TRADES DEPARTMENT (MTD), 1946–present. The Maritime Trades Department (MTD) has been one of the seven Trade and Industrial Departments within the American Federation of Labor-Congress of Industrial Organizations (AFL-CIO). As early as 1916 and again in 1921, the International Longshoremen's Association* (ILA) had proposed the creation of a ''marine transport department'' within the AFL because ''in the case of closely allied groups . . . our activities can find a more intelligent and concrete expression on an industrial basis'' (Albrecht, 1923), but the bitter opposition of the International Seamen's Union* (ISU), specifically its president, Andrew Furuseth,* who rejected any deviation from craft unionism, blocked any move to coordinate the efforts of seamen and longshoremen within the AFL prior to World War II.

Immobility within the AFL left the field open for the new CIO, which created its own CIO Maritime Committee in July 1937. Under the leadership of Bjorne Halling and Mervin Rathborne, the CIO Maritime Committee strongly supported the spread of the new National Maritime Union* (NMU) on the East Coast and obtained the backing of the International Longshoremen's and Warehousemen's Association* on the West Coast. Smaller maritime unions affiliated as well, but not the Sailors' Union of the Pacific* (SUP) and the Seafarer's International Union* (SIU), both of which remained with the AFL. The Maritime Federation of the Pacific* (MFP) had existed since 1935, but since its primary affiliate remained the ILWU, needless duplication had resulted, and consequently the MFP was fused into the CIO Maritime Committee in July 1941. U.S. entry into World War II halted attempts to coordinate maritime unions until after the war, when the CIO Maritime Committee was replaced by the Committee for Maritime Unity,* a brief experiment that ended in failure in 1947.

Competition from the CIO pressured the AFL to organize at last its own Maritime Trades Department (MTD) in August 1946. The main affiliates were ILA, SIU, and SUP, all of which remained bitterly opposed to the CIO maritime unions. When the AFL-CIO merger finally became a reality in 1955, the MTD became another battleground for the maritime unions, whose former antagonism remained undiminished. Harry Lundeberg,* who headed the SIU and the SUP, became the president of the MTD, which Joseph Curran,* the head of the NMU, refused to join. As a consolation prize to Curran, he headed a newly created Maritime Committee within the AFL-CIO, a highly anomalous situation that resulted in needless duplication and uncoordinated action.

Upon Harry Lundeberg's death in 1957, he was succeeded as head of the MTD by the new SIU president, Paul Hall.* The MTD became a powerhouse of activity under Hall, who carefully cultivated close relations with AFL-CIO president George Meany and in particular through Secretary-Treasurer Lane Kirkland.* MTD competed against the Maritime Committee to see who could have the most effective lobbying campaign in the 1960s to keep federal subsidies flowing into the ever-shrinking U.S.-flag merchant marine. MTD easily drummed up letters, contributions, and votes for congressmen, who learned to respect this powerful lobby. However, the subsidies failed to save U.S.-flag steamship companies, which continued to sink into bankruptcy in the 1970s and 1980s. Upon Hall's death in 1980, he was replaced by the new SIU president, Frank Drozak,* who led the fight to bring veterans' status to World War II merchant seamen and to require U.S. crews for the Kuwaiti tankers registered under the U.S. flag. After the demise of the duplicate Maritime Committee, MTD has remained the main pressure and lobbying arm of organized labor for maritime issues.

Principal Labor Leaders

Harry Lundeberg	1955–1957
Paul Hall	1957–1980
Frank Drozak	1980–1988
Michael Sacco	1988–present

References: AFL-CIO, *Proceedings of the Constitutional Convention*, 1961–1979; Arthur Emil Albrecht, *International Seamen's Union of America: A Study of Its History and Problems*, Bulletin of the Bureau of Labor Statistics, Series No. 342 (Washington, DC: Government Printing Office, 1923); Hyman Weintraub, *Andrew Furuseth: Emancipator of the Seamen* (Berkeley: University of California Press, 1959); *Business Week*, 3 June 1967.

MARVIN, WINTHROP L., 15 May 1863–3 February 1926. Winthrop L. Marvin was the general manager of the American Steamship Owners' Association* from 1919 to 1926, and he was the individual most responsible for the successful operation of the first effective business group for merchant shipping. He was born in Newcastle, New Hampshire, on 15 May 1863 and graduated from Tufts College in 1884. He worked as a reporter in various Boston newspapers and eventually became news editor and chief editorial writer. In 1902 he published the clearly written *The American Merchant Marine*, a book that went through several editions and remains a valuable source for nineteenth-century developments. As an authority on shipping, he was appointed the secretary of the U.S. Merchant Marine Commission* in 1904–1905 and remained involved afterward with shipping interests.

However, his first major position was with the National Association of Wool Manufacturers, whose secretary-treasurer he was from 1909 to 1919. In this position he learned how a business trade group was supposed to function, lessons he applied in 1919, when the American Steamship Association* appointed him its first general manager. The old American Steamship Association had not progressed beyond occasional meetings of company executives, and Marvin now had the task of carrying out the transition to a business association with full-time employees. However, company executives were accustomed to rotate the title of president of ASOA among themselves, so that Marvin was given only the rank of vice president and general manager, the latter suggesting that in reality he was running the organization.

When the steamship executives chose Alfred G. Smith for the first three-year term as president of ASOA, Marvin worked out an arrangement that allowed him to continue as general manager and vice president, while editing at the same time his newspaper, the *Marine Journal*, whose ownership he had obtained. Marvin kept up the grueling work pace for three years, but while on the way from home to his office in Broadway Street, New York, he collapsed and died on 3 February 1926.

References: *New York Times*, 4 February 1926; Record Group 32, National Archives, Washington, DC; *Who Was Who in America, 1897–1942*, vol. 1.

MASTERS, MATES, AND PILOTS, INTERNATIONAL ORGANIZATION OF (MM&P), 1891–present.

The Masters, Mates, and Pilots (MM&P) has been the union for the officers on the bridge of the ship. The initial impetus to create the organization came from the steamship pilots, who felt they had no voice in steamship safety but were then held responsible for any disasters. The first local of the American Brotherhood of Steamship Pilots was founded in New York in 1887, and soon more locals appeared in the same port and in other harbors. Captains (masters) of vessels expressed an interest in joining, and to accommodate them the growing national organization renamed itself the American Association of Masters and Pilots of Steam Vessels in 1891 and in 1900 added the term *mates* to the title.

During its early years, the MM&P concentrated on safety, navigational, and technical issues, as well as mutual aid services. Strike activity was largely ruled out, and it was inconceivable that the smartly uniformed officers would ever take common action with the lowly deck sailors and the dirty engine gangs. The members of MM&P considered themselves "the direct representatives of the employers' interest" (Thor 1965). The master "is in charge of the boat . . . and has the power of discipline . . . his position is somewhat analogous to that of a foreman in a factory'' (ibid.). Not surprisingly the MM&P, along with the marine engineers grouped in the Marine Engineers' Beneficial Association* (MEBA), formed the aristocracy of maritime labor. A first awakening came to the MM&P in 1910, when they struck four New York City harbor companies owned by railroads, over the demand for an eight-hour workday. The strike was a failure, but before the members could convert MM&P into a real fighting union, splinter groups bolted and created two rival organizations, the American Steamship Licensed Officers Association and the Neptune Association.*

The tremendous individualism of the deck officers kept the unions from fully espousing vigorous strike activity. Well educated and accustomed to operate a ship without any interference from others, the deck officers did not easily reach common agreement among themselves. Internal dissension has been a recurrent characteristic of the MM&P and manifested itself in the struggle to affiliate with the American Federation of Labor (AFL). Since 1910 some members had wanted to join the AFL, but others were still reluctant to make the transition from a professional and mutual aid society to a full-fledged trade union. MM&P's application to join AFL had languished until the Neptune Association and the American Steamship Licensed Officers' Association sought recognition from the AFL. MM&P was finally galvanized into action and in 1916 affiliated with the AFL in what ''had the appearance of a forced marriage'' (ibid.). Without the AFL mantle the American Steamship Licensed Officers' Association degenerated into a company union and soon disappeared, but the Neptune Association, which represented the deck officers in transatlantic ships, remained a formidable competitor throughout the 1920s.

Without the ocean officers, 95 percent of the membership of MM&P was composed of deck officers working in tugboats, ferry boats, and pleasure craft. In spite of being confined mainly to the inland seas, MM&P added *National Union of* to its title in 1916, but just like MEBA, it refused to join the International Seamen's Union (ISU), the AFL affiliate that was supposed to represent all seafarers. World War I expanded membership to over 9,000 by 1921, but when the shipping boom ended, MM&P had still not grasped the significance of common action with the rest of the seafarers. The Shipping Board* and the American Steamship Owners' Association* (ASOA) unilaterally declared wage reductions starting on 1 May 1921, but when the ISU unions went on strike, the MM&P, whose contracts expired on 31 July 1921, refused to honor the picket lines. The strike of 1921* was crushed, and MM&P's reverence for the sanctity of contracts backfired when ASOA refused to renew the contract on 1 August 1921, in accordance with the policy it adopted of having ''no signed contract with any of the sea unions'' (ibid.). The Shipping Board did continue to sign contracts with MM&P (and other maritime unions), but ASOA insisted on crushing the still-intact deck officers' organization. Shipowners encouraged the organization of phantom company unions, imposed the open shop, and also backed the Neptune Association in the conscious effort to deepen the divisions among the two rival deck officers' unions. The Great Depression finished off the Neptune Association, and ASOA almost succeeded in driving out of existence the MM&P, whose membership collapsed to barely 2,200 in 1935.

The revival of the MM&P began with the Big Strike* of 1934 in San Francisco. Longshoremen walked off their jobs on 9 May and were soon joined by the sailors. Swept along in the common enthusiasm, the locals of MM&P and MEBA formally decided to join the strike on 19 May, although, on their own, individual members had already joined the picket lines. The strike was a success, and the Pacific Coast locals of MM&P and MEBA proceeded to join the Maritime Federation of the Pacific* (MFP), which won its most spectacular success in the follow-up strike of October 1936–February 1937. Just like MEBA, the MM&P had settled for a modified union hiring hall,* whereby all officers were members of the union, but the company retained the right to appoint the captain and the chief mate.

East Coast locals censured the fraternization of the MM&P with their lowly subordinates on the West Coast, and soon a conservative reaction began. Unlike MEBA, which affiliated with the more radical Congress of Industrial Organizations (CIO), the MM&P safely remained within the more traditional AFL. In July 1938, when the MM&P, together with the Sailors Union of the Pacific* (SUP) and the Marine Firemen, Oilers, Watertenders, and Wipers of the Pacific Coast* (MFOWW), withdrew from the MFP, the conservative reaction was complete. The addition of Canadian locals led to changing the name to International Organization of Masters, Mates, and Pilots in 1954.

From 1938 to Harry Lundeberg's* death in 1957, the MM&P remained strongly under the influence of the Seafarers' International Union, the main AFL affiliate for seamen. After 1949 MM&P agreed to support Lundeberg in his efforts to replace MEBA with his own pet union, the Brotherhood of Marine Engineers. By the time of the 1961 strike, discontent at the pro-SIU policy was rampant in MM&P, and discord raged in the union over whether to support Paul Hall* of the SIU or Joseph Curran of the National Maritime Union* (NMU) in the power struggle for leadership of the maritime movement. Factions continued to tear apart the MM&P in the mid-1960s, with the election of each new president producing unusually intense political struggles. To avoid the entire divisive choice of Hall versus Curran, the MM&P decided in 1971 to become a branch of the International Longshoremen's Association* (ILA), whose conservative policies were highly appealing to most of MM&P's 10,750 members.

The entry into ILA did not bring quiet, because soon another faction condemned the merger and instead wanted to join with MEBA. The struggle raged over the next fifteen years and led to a crisis in 1988, when President Robert Lowlen attempted to follow NMU into a merger with MEBA. A dissident faction within MM&P denounced the move as ploy by Lowlen to avoid elections in the fall and managed to stop any fusion. Lowlen was reelected in the fall of 1988 by a very narrow margin, which dissidents claimed was attained by threatening the crew of the cruise ship *Monterey* (see *Mariposa**) with dismissal if they did not vote for Lowlen. MM&P had purchased and operated the *Monterey* to create jobs for its members, but in reality the union had to hire through newspaper ads the bulk of the crew to work in hotel and restaurant duties.

While MM&P weakened itself by internal strife, management began a determined offensive. In 1984 five tanker companies expelled the MM&P from its ship, and only after granting major cutbacks in wages and benefits did the other companies agree to deal with the union. In 1986 Sea-Land* demanded a return to the 1980 wage levels, and apparently other steamship companies have negotiated similar rollbacks. The decline of MM&P in reality was part of the generalized collapse of the U.S.-flag merchant marine in the last decades of the twentieth century.

References: Gary M. Fink, ed., *Labor Unions* (Westport, CT: Greenwood Press, 1977); Joseph P. Goldberg, *The Maritime Story: A Study in Labor-Management Relations* (Cambridge: Harvard University Press, 1958); Gary Charles Raffaele, "Background and Early History of the International Organization of Masters, Mates, and Pilots (AFL-CIO)," Ph.D. diss., Harvard University, 1973; Record Group 32, National Archives, Washington, DC; Betty V. H. Schneider, *Industrial Relations in the West Coast Maritime Industry* (Berkeley: University of California Press, 1958); Benjamin M. Squires, "Associations of Harbor Boat Owners and Employees in the Port of New York," *Monthly Labor Review* 7 (1918): 45–62; Howard Andrew Thor, "A History of the Marine Engineers' Beneficial Association," M.A. thesis, University of California, Berkeley, 1954; Howard Andrew Thor, "Trade Unions of Licensed Officers in the Maritime Industry," Ph.D. diss., University of California, Berkeley, 1965; Hyman Weintraub, *Andrew Furuseth: Emancipator of the Seamen* (Berkeley: University of California Press, 1959).

MATSON, WILLIAM, 18 October 1849–11 October 1917. Captain William Matson was the founder and first president of the Matson Navigation Company.* His career was remarkable not only because of its success as another rags-to-riches story but also because he was one of the last (if not the last) merchant captains to rise to create his own steamship company. He was born in Lysekil, Sweden, on 18 October 1849, was orphaned at the age of six, and lived afterward with an aunt. He began to ship aboard sailing vessels at the age of ten, but in between voyages he pursued his education in the Swedish schools. In 1863 a voyage brought him to New York City, and he never returned to Sweden. In 1867 he had reached San Francisco and in 1870 was already the captain of a coal schooner. In 1882 he was the captain and partial owner of a schooner he had built expressly for transportation between San Francisco and the Hawaiian islands. The sugar cargoes grew so rapidly that he replaced the smaller schooner with a bigger vessel, and after a few years he owned a variety of sailing vessels.

Matson's fleet was one of several serving the Hawaiian islands, but he decided that the transition to steam power was necessary to remain in the trade. To carry out the conversion to steam, he incorporated the Matson Navigation Company on 9 February 1901, with himself as its first president. However, he did not command the financial resources to build a large enough fleet of steamers, so that American-Hawaiian Steamship Company* (AHSS), with its brand-new fleet of steamers, preempted the trade routes between the United States and Hawaii.

The entry of the AHSS threatened the very survival of his navigation company, but Captain Matson skillfully avoided the danger by investing in the development of oil fields in southern California. The oil not only made him a millionaire but also provided the cargo for Hawaii, allowing his fleet to survive in the face of competition from AHSS. In 1907 Matson further solidified its position by an agreement with Castle & Cooke, whereby the latter invested in the steamship company and, more important, agreed to ship most of its sugar exports aboard Matson's ships. However, the rest of the conglomerates in the islands preferred to ship through AHSS, which continued to carry the majority of the cargo.

The outbreak of World War I in 1914 eliminated several smaller competitors, and in 1916 American-Hawaiian itself announced that it was abandoning the trade of the islands for more lucrative routes in the North Atlantic. Matson Navigation Company had the priceless opportunity to become the main ocean carrier of Hawaii, a possibility that Captain William Matson understood, but unfortunately he did not live to see the culmination of his life's struggle become a reality. He died in San Francisco on 11 October 1917 and left as his heir his only daughter, Lurline. She was married to William P. Roth,* who was already working for the company and became later the real heir of Captain Matson in entrepreneurial boldness and decisions.

References: René De La Pedraja, *The Rise and Decline of U.S. Merchant Shipping in the Twentieth Century* (New York: Twayne, 1992); *National Cyclopedia of American Biography*, vol. 40; Fred A. Stindt, *Matson's Century of Ships* (Modesto, CA: n.p., 1982); William L. Worden, *Cargoes: Matson's First Century in the Pacific* (Honolulu: University of Hawaii Press, 1981).

MATSON NAVIGATION COMPANY, 1901–present. Since the end of World War I Matson Navigation Company has provided the overwhelming majority of the ocean transportation between Hawaii and the mainland of the United States. Captain William Matson,* a Swedish immigrant who owned a fleet of sailing vessels and three steamers he had recently bought, incorporated the company on 9 February 1901. After the annexation of that territory to the United States on 7 July 1898, Congress extended the cabotage* laws to Hawaii, but before Captain Matson could obtain enough ships to carry the cargoes between the mainland and the islands, he was overwhelmed by the arrival in early 1901 of the huge modern fleet that American-Hawaiian Steamship Company* placed in the trade. Matson Navigation survived only because Captain Matson had also invested in California oil fields, and he could still profitably employ his fleet of small steamers and sailing vessels to carry his oil for sale in the islands. In 1907, Matson, already a millionaire, reached an agreement with the sugar firm of Castle & Cooke whereby the later bought a new stock issue of Matson Navigation and, more important, provided part of its sugar cargoes for transportation aboard Matson's ships. However, the rest of the "Big Five" (the main conglomerates in Hawaii) declined to follow Castle & Cooke's lead because they felt American-Hawaiian was sufficiently committed to the welfare of the islands.

When American-Hawaiian suddenly announced the end of service to the islands in 1916, the population of Hawaii was shocked. Now at last the Big Five fully supported Matson Navigation Company, but not until the shipping shortage of World War I ended could the company satisfy the demand for cargo space and become the premier line of the islands. Upon the death of Captain Matson in October 1917, his daughter, Lurline, became the principal stockholder, while management passed to his son-in-law, William P. Roth,* who presided over the expansion of the company. Besides shipping and oil, Matson Navigation invested in sugar mills, real estate, and hotels, the latter as a complement to the passenger business on its ships. To forestall competition, Matson purchased the Los Angeles Steamship Company* in 1930 and assumed its routes between Hawaii and Los Angeles.

Roth's most dramatic move came with the entry into the route between California and New Zealand/Australia, with calls in Hawaii, Fiji, and Tahiti. Freighters began the service in 1928, and in 1932 two specially constructed liners, the *Mariposa** and *Monterey*,* began a luxury passenger and express cargo service. The service was a success but provoked bitter opposition from Australia and New Zealand, particularly from the latter country's Union Steamship Company. The intercession of the governments involved avoided discriminatory measures, and as a concession, Matson did agree not to add to the Australia and New Zealand service a third ship, the *Lurline*,* which instead remained in the Hawaii-California route. When the United States entered World War II, the company's ships were requisitioned by the government, and Matson itself became one of the general agents the War Shipping Administration* used to operate vessels.

Roth also launched Matson into aviation when he created the Air Transport Service on 1 March 1941 to repair navy cargo planes. In 1946 Matson began operating DC-4s, but the continuing refusal of the Civil Aeronautics Board to grant airline routes to steamship companies forced Matson to abandon aviation. To continue in the passenger business and to provide customers for its hotels in Hawaii, the company reconditioned the *Lurline* in 1948 and also converted two Mariner* freighters for passenger service as the *Mariposa* and *Monterey* in 1955. By 1959, however, Matson realized it had invested unwisely in the passenger trade, and it sold the hotels in 1959 and the *Lurline* in 1963. However, no buyer could be found for the *Mariposa* and *Monterey*, which continued to pile up losses, until at last Pacific Far East Line* acquired the two vessels.

Matson knew that its privileged position as the main ocean carrier in the California-Hawaii route exposed the company to charges of monopoly, and to try to keep competitors out and freight rates low, Matson pioneered new transportation methods. The *Hawaiian Motorist*, the first specialized ship for the transport of vehicles, became in 1961 a prototype for the Roll-in/Roll-off* (Ro/Ro) vessels that later formed an important part of the company's regular operations. In 1960 Matson converted the *Hawaiian Citizen* into the first full containership in the Pacific. Other containerships followed, but not before the subsidized American President Lines* (APL) mounted a major offensive during the 1960s to try to enter the lucrative Hawaiian trade. One of the charges used by APL was that since the principal stockholders of Matson were the Big Five, these island conglomerates had secured better rates for themselves than those normally available to other shippers.* To avoid a potentially destructive antitrust suit by the Department of Justice, Alexander & Baldwin, one of the Big Five, agreed to buy the shares of the others, including those of Castle & Cooke. Matson now could turn the antitrust weapon against APL, which at the same time was trying to merge with American Mail Line; to allow this last merger to proceed without interruption, APL abandoned in 1969 its attempt to break into the Hawaiian trade.

That same year the unsubsidized Seatrain* made its first sailing to Hawaii, and bitter competition ensued until the company agreed to sell its ships and route to Matson in 1974. The struggle had convinced Matson to divest itself of its own subsidized Far East Service in 1970, in order to make universal its legal claim that all subsidized lines must be prohibited from entering the Hawaii-U.S. mainland trade.

Since the repulse of the Seatrain challenge, Matson has concentrated on improving its container service and has also acquired Ro/Ro vessels to bring vehicles to the islands. As the main subsidiary of Alexander & Baldwin, Matson prospered in the protected trade and carried the bulk of the cargoes between the U.S. mainland and the islands. Except for new legal attempts by APL since the late 1980s to enter the Hawaiian trade, Matson Navigation has not faced any problems and has continued to provide efficiently and quietly its traditional shipping services.

Principal Executives

William Matson	1901–1917
Edward F. Tenney*	1917–1927
William P. Roth	1927–1945
Frazer A. Bailey*	1945–1947
John E. Cushing*	1947–1950
Randolph Sevier*	1950–1962
Stanley Powell, Jr.	1962–1970
Malcolm H. Blaisdell	1970–1973
Robert J. Pfeiffer	1973–1979
Michael S. Wasacz	1981–1989
C. Bradley Mulholland	1990–present

Some Notable Ships

*Malolo,** 1927–1937; later, *Matsonia,* 1938–1948

Mariposa, 1931–1947

Monterey, 1932–1947; later, *Matsonia,* 1956–1970

Lurline, 1933–1963

Mariposa and *Monterey*, 1956–1971

Hawaiian Citizen

Hawaiian Motorist, 1961–1973

Main Subsidiaries

Oceanic Steamship Company*	1926–1976
Honolulu Oil Corporation	1910–1959
Oceanic and Oriental Navigation Company*	1928–1938

References: Alexander & Baldwin, *Annual Reports*, 1988–1991; Alexander & Baldwin, *Ninety Years a Corporation, 1900–1990*; René De La Pedraja, *The Rise and Decline of U.S. Merchant Shipping in the Twentieth Century* (New York: Twayne, 1992); Fred A. Stindt, *Matson's Century of Ships* (Modesto, CA: n.p., 1982); E. Mowbray Tate, *Transpacific Steam: The Story of Steam Navigation from the Pacific Coast of North America to the Far East and the Antipodes, 1867–1941* (New York: Cornwall Books, 1986); William L. Worden, *Cargoes: Matson's First Century in the Pacific* (Honolulu: University Press of Hawaii, 1981).

MATSONIA, **1956–1963; later** *LURLINE*, **1963–1970.** The sale of the old *Mariposa** and *Monterey,** the latter to the U.S. government in 1952, had drastically reduced the passenger capabilities of the Matson Navigation Company.* The beginning of the tourist boom to Hawaii in the mid-1950s convinced Matson to buy back the *Monterey* from the U.S. government in 1956 and to spend over $20 million in the repair and renovation of the vessel, whose return to passenger took place in 1957 under the new name of the *Matsonia*. The *Matsonia* jumped into the Hawaiian tourist service just as the first Boeing jets were starting their cheaper and faster air trips to the islands, and in a few years the passenger service was causing the company serious losses. Matson began to reduce its passenger fleet, and when it sold off the *Lurline** in 1963, the company changed the name of the *Matsonia* to the *Lurline*. Mounting losses finally forced Matson to sell the *Lurline* in 1970 to a Greek firm for operation under foreign flag as a cruise ship.

References: Frederick E. Emmons, *American Passenger Ships: The Ocean Lines and Liners, 1873–1983* (Newark: University of Delaware Press, 1985); Fred A. Stindt, *Matson's Century of Ships* (Modesto, CA: n.p., 1982); William L. Worden, *Cargoes: Matson's First Century in the Pacific* (Honolulu: University Press of Hawaii, 1981).

MAYAGÜEZ; **formerly,** *SANTA ELIANA*, **1944–1979.** This C-2* freighter, first as the *Santa Eliana* of the Grace Line* and then as the *Mayagüez* of Sea-Land,* was involved in two major international incidents. Under the provisions of the Ship Sales Act of 1946,* the Grace Line purchased the C-2 in 1947, which it renamed the *Santa Eliana*. During ten years the freighter quietly carried cargo between San Francisco and the west coast of South America, until the company made bigger plans for her and her sister ship, the *Santa Leonor*. The Grace Line, normally a very cautious and conservative firm, decided for the first time to take the lead by being the first to use containers* in a foreign trade route. Sea-Land had established commercial container service in the coastwise* trade, but now Grace Line decided to convert the *Santa Eliana* and the *Santa Leonor* to full containerships for service between the United States and Venezuela. A forty-five-foot midsection and special gantry cranes to load and retrieve the containers were installed on the vessels, each of which had a capacity for 476 containers, only 94 of which were carried on the deck, the rest traveling in the holds.

On 29 January 1960 the *Santa Eliana*, "the first all-container ship in the U.S. foreign trade" (Kooiman), sailed from Newark, New Jersey, bound for La Guaira, Venezuela, in a voyage that promised to revolutionize ocean transportation. However, when the vessel reached her destination, longshoremen refused to unload the ship, because they correctly sensed that the containers could increase the unemployment among dockworkers. The Grace Line canceled the sailing of the sister ship, *Santa Leonor*, and after eighteen days of costly waiting, the Venezuelan longshoremen finally agreed to unload the 176 containers on board, but only on the condition that no more vessels of this type come to the port unless a new agreement was signed with the dockworkers. The two sister ships went into layup, and only in October 1962, after arrangements were finally concluded, did the *Santa Eliana* and the *Santa Leonor* attempt to resume container service to Venezuela. As could be expected from any new operation, cargo volumes were initially way below expectations, but the Grace Line* was rapidly running out of patience with the start-up expenses, and after the Maritime Administration* blocked an attempt to make complementary calls in Puerto Rico on the way to Venezuela, the company suspended its foreign container service a year later and laid up the ships.

In October 1964 Sea-Land purchased the two ships and placed them in the route to Puerto Rico and, to reflect the new area, renamed the *Santa Eliana* as the *Mayagüez* and the *Santa Leonor* as the *Ponce*. The *Mayagüez* returned to a tranquil existence on the Puerto Rican service, although occasionally the vessel made voyages to other parts of the world. In one of these voyages the *Mayagüez* was carrying cargo from Hong Kong to Thailand when, while steaming sixty miles off the coast of Cambodia, she was attacked and seized by Cambodian forces on 12 May 1975. After diplomatic steps to secure the release of the crew and the ship failed, President Gerald R. Ford decided to maintain the principle of safe passage through international waters in time of peace and ordered a military rescue mission. On 14 May a combined naval-air-land operation recaptured the vessel and obtained the release of the entire crew, but unfortunately eighteen American soldiers were killed and fifty were wounded during the rescue. The *Mayagüez* was still in condition for a few more years of commercial service, but finally in 1979 she and her sister ship, the *Ponce*, were finally scrapped.

References: René De La Pedraja, *The Rise and Decline of U.S. Merchant Shipping in the Twentieth Century* (New York: Twayne, 1992); Gerald R. Ford, *A Time to Heal* (New York: Harper and Row, 1979); William Kooiman, *The Grace Ships, 1869–1969* (Point Reyes, CA: Komar, 1990); *New York Times*, 22 February 1979.

McCORMACK, EMMET J., 2 September 1880–24 February 1965. Emmet J. McCormack, a steamship executive, was born in Brooklyn, New York, on 2 September 1880. His father was an Irish immigrant who worked as an engineer in a tugboat. Emmet attended public and parochial schools until he was fourteen, when the death of his father forced him to seek work to support the family. Emmet was fascinated with ships, and he began working as an office boy for small firms on the waterfront. He loved to deal with people, and with his remarkable ability to convince persons, he was a born salesman and began to receive contracts to supply ships. By 1913 he owned his own business, the Commercial Coal Company, which specialized in selling and delivering coal to steamships.

McCormack had always wanted to operate and own his own ships, and as a first step toward that goal, he incorporated the Moore-McCormack Company* in 1913 with his friend, Albert V. Moore,* who became president, while McCormack held the position of treasurer. In the early years the company did not own its ships and instead operated chartered* vessels to Rio de Janeiro. Through careful savings and able ship deals, the company slowly began to acquire its own vessels; the big opportunity, however, came with World War I, when the Swedish line (Svenscka Lloyd Line) handed over its ships in the England-Scandinavia route to Moore-McCormack for operation during the duration of the war. With his outgoing personality McCormack developed many Scandinavian contacts that after the war allowed the company to establish regular steamship service between the United States and ports in Scandinavia and the Baltic. The company took advantage of the many opportunities offered by the Shipping Board* to operate government-owned ships and to purchase surplus vessels.

Moore-McCormack became such a profitable company that McCormack was able to divert some of his profits into the establishment in Brooklyn of the Kingsboro National Bank, whose president and later chairman of the board he was for decades. Besides his own holdings in Moore-McCormack, in the 1950s he had also managed to acquire 9 percent of the stock of American Export Lines,* but because of possible legal restrictions he was not able to remain long on the Board of Directors of the later company. Until 1953 McCormack remained as treasurer of the company, and his relationship with Moore stood out as the most solid nonfamily partnership in the history of U.S. steamship companies. With the death of Moore in 1953, his son William replaced him as president, and McCormack became the chairman of the board. The harmonious relationship between the Moore family and McCormack (who had no children of his own) continued without interruption. Probably because of his Irish background, McCormack was a Democrat and participated in numerous political events. Outside the South shipping executives were almost unanimously Republican, and, of course, the Moore family members were staunch Republicans, making all the more notable McCormack's Democratic party affiliation.

McCormack was chairman of the board of Moore-McCormack until 1960, and afterward he remained as chairman of the executive committee until his death in West Palm Beach, Florida, on 24 February 1965.

References: Files of the Maritime Administration, Washington, DC; Robert C. Lee, *Mr. Moore, Mr. McCormack–and the Seven Seas!* (New York: Newcomen Society, 1957); *National Cyclopedia of American Biography*, vol. 52; *New York Times*, 5 September 1955.

McCORMICK, CHARLES R., 6 July 1870–24 February 1955. Charles R. McCormick was the founder and first president of the McCormick Steamship Company* as well as of numerous lumber businesses on the Pacific Coast. He was born in Menominee, Michigan, on 6 July 1870 and studied in the local public schools. His father was a lumberman, and initially Charles began working as a lumberjack in northern Michigan, but in 1901 he moved to Portland, Oregon, and was able to enter into business on his own in 1903 as a lumber broker in San Francisco. He quickly realized that the real profits in lumber sales were made from the shipping, and he began from the start to charter* small sailing vessels, eventually switching to steamers. He acquired his fleet by offering ''interests,'' or a small number of shares in each to investors, and then he placed the vessels in the profitable trade of hauling lumber. The shipping profits financed his acquisition of lumber mills, shipbuilding yards, and timber lands, while the latter in turn provided the cargoes to make his ships even more profitable.

In August 1921 he formally incorporated the McCormick Steamship Company to raise capital by issuing stock and also to direct the operation of his fleet. He continued to buy more properties and companies and on 10 July 1925 came his boldest move, the purchase of Pope and Talbot.* At this point, however, McCormick had overextended himself, and from the start he faced difficulties in meeting the payments to the former owners of Pope and Talbot, who gradually demanded a greater control over his companies to guarantee their outstanding balances. In April 1929 McCormick was replaced as president of Charles R. McCormick Lumber Company but was allowed to remain as chairman of the board, but even this last consolation prize was lost when he was forced to resign on 8 December 1931. ''It was a bitter moment for Charles R. McCormick. He was leaving the companies that he had built up over a period of 27 years'' (Coman 1968).

With his resignation he lost all control over the shipping subsidiary, the McCormick Steamship Company, which, however, continued to operate under that name until it was formally merged with Pope and Talbot in 1940. McCormick devoted himself in the later years of his life to ventures in paper and other forest by-products and finally retired from all business activities in 1954. He died in Portland, Oregon, on 24 February 1955.

References: Giles T. Brown, *Ships That Sail No More: Marine Transportation from San Diego to Puget Sound, 1910–1940* (Lexington: University of Kentucky Press, 1966); Edwin T. Coman, Jr., and Helen M. Gibbs, *Time, Tide and Timber: A Century of Pope and Talbot* (New York: Greenwood Press, 1968); *National Cyclopedia of American Biography*, vol. 45.

McCORMICK STEAMSHIP COMPANY, 1903–1940. The McCormick Steamship Company was one of the large coastwise* firms on the Pacific Coast and by the early 1930s had replaced the Admiral Line* as the most important. In common with other successful steamship companies of the West Coast, the McCormick Steamship Company had its origins in the shipping needs of the lumber business. Charles R. McCormick,* a lumberman and the founder, started in 1901 the company as a partnership with Sidney H. Hauptman to build and operate wooden steam schooners. By 1916 the business had expanded, and McCormick Steamship Company provided service to most ports on the West Coast, although not on a very regular basis, and lumber still formed 80 percent of its cargo. The rapid expansion had been possible because McCormick raised capital by selling "interests," or a small number of shares, on each vessel, a nineteenth-century tradition long since abandoned on the East Coast. Under his careful management the vessels earned profits, allowing him to reinvest into more vessels, lumber mills, or timberlands, to gradually create a large conglomerate.

In 1921 McCormick concentrated the management of the different vessels into a single organization, and he also incorporated formally the McCormick Steamship Company to acquire the "interests" of the holders of shares in individual vessels and to issue stock to raise capital. In that year the company established regular sailings for its growing fleet and began the hard task of securing northbound cargoes to complement the abundant lumber flowing south. In 1925 the company entered the market for fast passenger service but abandoned the attempt in 1927 and henceforth concentrated on cargo, although passengers were enticed to travel aboard the slow freighters by offers of very cheap rates. In 1923 the company concluded that the volume of lumber moving to the East Coast justified a separate service, and consequently McCormick Steamship inaugurated an intercoastal* service as a joint venture with the Munson Line.*

In another important new development for McCormick Steamship, the company became a managing operator* for the Shipping Board's* Pacific Argentine Brazil Line in June 1920, although a regular schedule of sailings did not become a reality until September 1924. Like the intercoastal service, the Pacific Argentine Brazil Line was a joint venture with the Munson Line. When the Shipping Board put the six vessels on the route for sale, McCormick Steamship was the successful bidder for them. In November 1927 McCormick purchased the half interest of Munson in the South American service, and later in 1928 the profitability of the Pacific Argentine Brazil Line was assured by the award of a generous mail contract.

In 1928 McCormick Steamship Company operated one of the largest U.S.-

flag fleets, with twenty vessels owned and twenty-five chartered.* Even more remarkable was the performance of the company during the Great Depression: at a time when all other coastwise and intercoastal companies were retrenching, McCormick was perhaps the only one to expand its services and remain profitable through the 1930s. The only serious blow came when the Merchant Marine Act of 1936* canceled the mail contracts and substituted instead the more modest operating differential subsidies.* In the struggle within the government for a new contract, rival Moore-McCormack* was able to snatch the subsidy away and began service in June 1940, but only temporarily, because after the war McCormick Steamship Company returned to the South American trade under the new name of Pope and Talbot* (P&T).

Charles R. McCormick had purchased P&T on 10 July 1925 but had been delinquent in the payments to the former owners, who gradually acquired a greater role in the management of the McCormick enterprises to guarantee their assets. McCormick was forced to resign as chairman of the board on 8 December 1931, and even before then P&T had been in charge of McCormick Steamship Company. P&T kept the steamship company as a separate entity for nearly ten years and wisely retained its very efficient management. Only on 31 August 1940 was McCormick Steamship Company formally dissolved, and its assets, ships, and personnel merged into the P&T organization, whose involvement in merchant shipping continued after World War II.

References: Giles T. Brown, *Ships That Sail No More: Marine Transportation from San Diego to Puget Sound, 1910–1940* (Lexington: University of Kentucky Press, 1966); Edwin T. Coman, Jr., and Helen M. Gibbs, *Time, Tide and Timber: A Century of Pope and Talbot* (New York: Greenwood Press, 1968).

McLEAN, MALCOM P., 1913–present. Malcom P. McLean was the head of Waterman Steamship Corporation* (WSC), Sea-Land,* and United States Lines* (USL); however, he was generally remembered as the first person who introduced permanent commercial container* service in the United States. McLean was born in North Carolina in 1913, and after completing an eighth grade education, he went to work as a trucker. His small firm grew until in 1940 he organized the McLean Trucking Company of Winston-Salem, which became one of the ten largest trucking companies in the United States. His career already had many of the aspects of a rags-to-riches story, but he still lacked the fame that the sure profits in the comfortable trucking industry would never give him. As he sought a way to expand his business, he discovered that a large number of truck trailers moved from the East Coast to the Gulf of Mexico and calculated that if he could move the trailers by the cheaper water transportation, he could undercut his competitors. McLean's original scheme called for seven ''trailerships'' to carry the trailers to waiting rigs between each port.

He needed ships and soon discovered that Waterman Steamship Corporation was up for sale; however, he hesitated for a moment because the Interstate Commerce Commission (ICC) under existing legislation refused to allow the same company to own two modes of domestic transportation; furthermore, he wanted to buy only Pan-Atlantic Division, which operated the coastwise* services, not all of WSC. A fortuitous set of circumstances provided McLean and his brother James the opportunity to sell at a profit their trucking company, buy with the proceeds from the sale the Pan-Atlantic Division, and then use the latter as collateral for loans to purchase WSC, whose foreign trade routes originally had not interested him but which, he realized now, could be a source of talent and resources to build up the coastwise service for his trailers.

The scheme for the trailerships flopped, and McLean instead decided to revive the discovery of containers by the War Shipping Administration* in World War II. He finally fitted container decks on top of two T-2* tankers and began hauling containers in April 1956, but the service was a loss because the Coast Guard* did not allow him to carry at the same time petroleum in the tanker. Money shortages began to plague McLean, yet he managed to convert freighters to containerships, and to reflect the new type of combined service he was offering to shippers,* he changed the name of the Pan-Atlantic Division to Sea-Land in 1960. His brother James was running Waterman, whose foreign trade routes he had concluded since 1957 could remain profitable only with operating differential subsidies,* but the application at the Maritime Administration* (MARAD) was constantly blocked. In 1962 McLean decided to enter the intercoastal* trade, but soon he was risking a bankruptcy, and after having sold off almost all the assets of WSC, he lacked any other ready source of cash to keep Sea-Land going. McLean attempted to sell WSC to see if he could raise more capital, but only ridiculously low offers were forthcoming; fortunately for McLean, at this time his luck held up, and Daniel Ludwig,* the tanker magnate, appeared to bail out McLean with the purchase of stock in the holding company—McLean Industries—in exchange for stepping aside from the intercoastal service Ludwig wished to start with his American–Hawaiian Steamship Company.*

With this cash infusion, McLean was able to negotiate from a position of strength a fair sale of what was left of WSC to Cornelius Walsh* and his brother in 1965. With this cash McLean now ordered the conversion of other freighters to containerships, and with no other place left in domestic services for the new ships, he began container service to Europe in April 1966. However, he had not been the first to inaugurate container service in the foreign trade, because Moore-McCormack had already done so in February 1966. McLean, who always bitterly opposed government intervention and any form of regulation, was determined to prove that his container service could operate without subsidies but soon saw his early start whittled away as competitors finally began to order containerships. What particularly worried him was USL, whose Lancer* containerships were so much more efficient than McLean's that Sea-Land would be crushed. McLean was again in an exposed position, but once again Ludwig bailed him out by buying more shares in the holding company, and with the new cash McLean ordered construction to begin on the SL-7s,* the newest and fastest generation of containerships in the world. The money was not enough to pay for their full price, but placing the orders gave the impression of a company with a future; McLean capitalized on this temporary good fortune to sell Sea-Land to R. J. Reynolds, the tobacco conglomerate, in May 1969. Ludwig made a tenfold profit on his original investment, and McLean, by now a multimillionaire, received a large chunk of Reynolds stock and a seat on its Board of Directors.

The restless McLean soon was bored and missed the excitement of merchant shipping. Carefully he plotted and executed the steps that, with a lot of good luck, finally brought him control of USL in 1977. As head of USL, he announced plans to build twelve gigantic vessels, later called the Econships,* for a round-the-world* service he proposed to inaugurate. After complex maneuvers USL acquired ten Econships, which began the round-the-world service, but the gamble of McLean did not work; he had ordered the wrong type of ship, and with no Ludwig or anybody else to bail him out, USL went into bankruptcy proceedings in November 1986 and later was liquidated.

Ironically McLean's old company, Sea-Land, bought the Econships at bankruptcy court, but his career in merchant shipping was still not over in spite of his advancing age. When the possibility of buying the government-owned Navieras de Puerto Rico* appeared, McLean stood ready to profit by the purchase, but the bankers vetoed the sale. However, McLean felt there was still an opportunity to enter the trade between the United States and Puerto Rico, and he launched a new venture, Trailer Bridge Co., in 1991. McLean at heart remained a trucker, because the rationale for launching the new company was to have Trailer Bridge Co. use forty-eight-foot highway trailers rather than the more traditional forty-foot containers. Skeptics abound, and whatever the exact outcome of his latest venture, there was no doubt that McLean has been involved, not always with the best results, in some of the key moments in the history of U.S. merchant shipping in the twentieth century.

References: *American Shipper*, August 1991, March 1992; René De La Pedraja, *The Rise and Decline of U.S. Merchant Shipping in the Twentieth Century* (New York: Twayne, 1992); *Journal of Commerce*, 20 May 1988; 12 April 1989; *The Story of McLean Industries, Inc.: Facts for Stockholders* (1956).

MECHANIZATION AND MODERNIZATION AGREEMENT OF 1960 (M&M). This was the name given to the labor contract negotiated between the Pacific Maritime Association* (PMA), representing the employers, and the International Longshoremen and Warehousemen's Union* (ILWU) on the West Coast in 1960. This contract was significant because for the first time the maritime unions accepted the principle of eliminating jobs because of mechanization, in exchange for compensation. The employers agreed to pay a large annual sum each year to the ILWU, which then used the money to encourage early retirement and to increase the benefits and pensions for longshoremen. All hiring continued to be done through the union hiring hall,* but for the first time since the 1930s, the employers regained the right to determine how many men

they wanted working in each gang, within limits specified by the union according to the type of machinery employed. Just in case there was not enough work, all longshoremen were guaranteed thirty-five hours' salary per week even if they were not hired. This last clause was dropped when the contract was renewed in 1966, because the Vietnam War boom guaranteed more than ample employment for the longshoremen. After the strike of 1971–1972, employers agreed to pay a royalty for each container* introduced within a fifty-mile radius of a major port, thereby facilitating the widespread adoption of the containers on the West Coast.

The importance of M&M cannot be overemphasized. On the national level, it paved the way for similar agreements by the International Longshoremen's Association* (ILA) on the East Coast and Gulf of Mexico. The principle of compensating workers for the loss of their jobs was firmly established on the waterfront, thereby clearing the way for the introduction of more productive process. For the ILWU, M&M became a veritable bonanza: the members reaped the high wages and compensation payments, while the union found itself swimming in funds. M&M more than anything else ended whatever lingering traces of radicalism may once have influenced the ILWU, which now became an accepted and wealthy part of establishment institutions on the West Coast.

References: Paul T. Hartman, *Collective Bargaining and Productivity: The Longshore Mechanization Agreement* (Berkeley: University of California Press, 1969); Charles P. Larrowe, *Harry Bridges: The Rise and Fall of Radical Labor in the U.S.* (New York: Lawrence Hill, 1972); Maud Russell, *Men Along the Shore: The ILA and Its History* (New York: Brussel and Brussel, 1966).

MERCHANT FLEET CORPORATION, 1927–1936. The Merchant Fleet Corporation was the new name for the previous Emergency Fleet Corporation.* Although the Merchant Fleet Corporation had the same broad duties as its predecessor, in reality its functions by 1927 had been reduced to the maintenance, supervision, and operation of the remaining government-owned vessels of the wartime fleet. The sale of United States Lines* to private owners in 1929 ended the last direct government operation by the Merchant Fleet Corporation, which, however, still continued to supervise the operation of government-owned vessels in the hands of the dwindling number of managing operators.* Like the Emergency Fleet Corporation, the Merchant Fleet Corporation was owned by the Shipping Board,* which had always been very jealous to preserve full authority over its subsidiary corporation. At the same time as the name change of 1927, the Shipping Board also erected itself as the Board of Trustees for the Merchant Fleet Corporation, thereby eliminating any rival source of power. The commissioners had so discredited themselves, however, that when the Shipping Board at last had full and direct control over the corporation, mounting political pressure paradoxically forced them to leave maximum freedom to the Merchant Fleet Corporation.

Using congressional authority, President Franklin D. Roosevelt transferred to the Department of Commerce the Merchant Fleet Corporation and also the Shipping Board on 10 August 1933, the latter now renamed the Shipping Board Bureau.* Although the Merchant Fleet Corporation was supposed to be liquidated, it remained in existence until Congress, in the Merchant Marine Act of 1936,* finally abolished the Merchant Fleet Corporation and transferred any remaining vessels and duties to the new U.S. Maritime Commission.*

Principal Executives

| Captain Elmer E. Crowley | 1925–1933 |
| James C. Peacock | 1934–1936 |

References: René De La Pedraja, *The Rise and Decline of U.S. Merchant Shipping in the Twentieth Century* (New York: Twayne, 1992); Samuel A. Lawrence, *United States Merchant Shipping Policies and Politics* (Washington, DC: Brookings Institution, 1966); Carroll H. Woody, *The Growth of the Federal Government, 1915–1932* (New York: McGraw-Hill, 1934).

MERCHANT MARINE ACADEMY, 1943–present. The Merchant Marine Academy has been the federal university that trained students to become deck officers and engineers aboard ships. Originally established by the U.S. Maritime Commission,* the Merchant Marine Academy has been under the Maritime Administration* (MARAD) since 1950. The Merchant Marine Academy has been located at Kings Point, Long Island, in the former estate of Walter P. Chrysler.

The need to provide adequate training for officers at a national institution had long been felt, and as a first step the government on 15 March 1938 established the Merchant Marine Cadet corps, which began to function in temporary facilities. When the estate of Walter P. Chrysler came on the market, Admiral Emory S. Land,* the head of the War Shipping Administration* (WSA), felt this was a great opportunity to acquire an ideal place on the coast for a new academy, which was formally inaugurated on 30 September 1943. Eventually other neighboring estates were acquired as well to provide ample grounds for the academy. However, the wartime emergency required the largest number of officers in the shortest time, so the academy did not establish a regular four-year program and instead ran an accelerated course program that graduated 6,634 offices, two-thirds of whom served on merchant ships and the rest of navy ships. Once the war was over, the Merchant Marine Academy formally established a four-year technical college curriculum and was duly accredited.

The temporary training centers of World War II were gradually shut down, leaving the Merchant Marine Academy by the early 1950s as the only federal institution training officers and engineers. Otherwise, students had to seek admission into the four state maritime academies* in California, Maine, Massachusetts, and New York. The Dwight D. Eisenhower administration decided as part of its economy drive to close the Merchant Marine Academy and cleverly orchestrated a political maneuver whereby the remaining cadets and programs of the academy would be transferred to the four existing state maritime academies, on the grounds this measure would result in considerable savings. Congressional defenders of the academy were outraged at this proposal, which would have left candidates from the rest of the country at the mercy of whatever admissions policies these four state maritime academies decided to adopt. After considerable struggle, maritime groups finally secured passage of a law on 20 February 1956 that made permanent the Merchant Marine Academy, which now became the fifth official service academy after those of the army, navy, air force, and Coast Guard.*

The Merchant Marine Academy prospered during the 1960s and 1970s, and because it earned a place among the top 10 percent of universities in the United States, from the start its graduates were in great demand by companies, and not just for seafaring jobs. In 1974 the academy became the first of the service academies to quietly admit women,* and by the late 1980s females were 10 percent of the enrollment, whose presence was handled matter-of-factly; as one male student stated," "We respect them, but don't quote me on that" (*Insight*, 6 June 1988). With the Ronald Reagan administration, the pressure for cuts, if not the outright abolishment of the academy, once again resurfaced, because some felt that the U.S. government could not continue to provide tuition-free education at a time when the U.S. merchant marine was in sharp decline. In response to the budgetary pressures, enrollment gradually declined and only 266 students entered in 1987, a 25 percent drop from the 1982 number.

The Merchant Marine Academy has gradually responded to the new shipping changes by incorporating into the curriculum more business aspects, in particular, the tremendous implications of containers* and intermodalism* for all transportation and not just ocean ships; officers were also finding that even after serving aboard vessels, their later careers increasingly ended in management ranks, and it was the duty of the academy to provide the graduates with these necessary skills. In the otherwise bleak panorama of generally disastrous federal policies toward merchant shipping since 1936, the Merchant Marine Academy stands out as a rare success and one of the wisest investments of tax dollars.

References: *Insight*, 6 June 1988; *Journal of Commerce*, 30 September 1988; *New York Times*, 22, 24 November 1953, 21 February 1956, 18 June 1987; U.S. Senate, Committee on Interstate and Foreign Commerce, *Providing for Maintenance of Merchant Marine Academy* (Washington, DC: Government Printing Office, 1954).

MERCHANT MARINE ACT OF 1891. See Ocean Mail Act of 1891.

MERCHANT MARINE ACT OF 1920. See Jones Act.

MERCHANT MARINE ACT OF 1928. By 1928 the failure of the Shipping Act of 1916* and the Jones Act* to halt the decline of the U.S. merchant marine was becoming obvious, yet Congress could not propose subsidies because they were repugnant at that time to the Democratic party. The spark that galvanized legislative action came when the British Cunard Line decided to place its transatlantic passenger liners in the New York-Havana route during the winter months, in a service that U.S. companies up till then had considered exclusively theirs. Congress avoided the taboo word of *subsidy* and used instead the acceptable term of *mail contract*, while the Merchant Marine and Fisheries Committee* and Senator Wesley Jones* rushed the bill through both houses to secure approval on 22 May 1928. The result was a law hastily drafted with little concern for complications in its application.

U.S. vessels, the majority built after U.S. entry into World War I, were becoming old, and to stimulate the construction of new vessels, as well as to keep alive the U.S. shipbuilding industry, the Merchant Marine Act of 1928 allocated large sums to the Construction Loan Fund, created by the Jones Act, and set very low interest rates for repayment. The Construction Loan Fund, however, was not adequately integrated with the mail contracts, the main measure in the new law. The act established a ranking, whereby the slower vessels received a skimpy mail contract, while those capable of steaming at faster speeds received more generous contracts; to emphasize the military value of these fast vessels, the Navy Department was authorized to assign naval officers to serve on the fast vessels at half pay while receiving the normal salary from the private companies.

The Merchant Marine Act of 1928 created an incredible number of abuses, many of which were later revealed in the hearings of the Black Committee.* The Shipping Board* charged the lowest interest rates for sums borrowed from the Construction Loan Fund and assigned to all the existing lines the maximum payments allowed under the law without any careful examination. When speed tests were run, unscrupulous shipowners merely had to get their slower vessels to run once at the faster speed necessary to qualify for the higher payment. Most of the vessels purchased by private owners had been bought at giveaway prices from the government, and the new shipowners frequently pocketed the funds from the mail subsidies. Only those companies really determined to stay in merchant shipping agreed in their mail contracts to order new vessels with sums borrowed from the Construction Loan Fund, and in general "the program of new construction materialized in a most meager fashion" (Zeis 1938), so that by 1935 only twenty-nine of the ships ordered under the provisions of the mail contracts had been delivered.

The Merchant Marine Act of 1928 launched an era of corruption and mismanagement rarely equaled in the history of the U.S. merchant marine. Waste of public funds became rampant, while private owners rode out the Great Depression on the juicy mail contracts, all the time denouncing the evils of government ownership. The Black Committee finally exposed some of the worst abuses and began the legislative momentum that culminated in the Merchant Marine Act of 1936,* which canceled the ocean mail contracts and largely repealed the Merchant Marine Act of 1928, a disastrous experiment in government support for private enterprise.

References: René De La Pedraja, *The Rise and Decline of U.S. Merchant Shipping in the Twentieth Century* (New York: Twayne, 1992); Samuel A. Lawrence, *United States Merchant Shipping Policies and Politics* (Washington, DC: Brookings Institution, 1966); *U.S. Statutes at Large*, vol. 45; Paul M. Zeis, *American Shipping Policy* (Princeton, NJ: Princeton University Press, 1938).

MERCHANT MARINE ACT OF 1936. For over fifty years, the Merchant Marine Act of 1936 has been the controlling legislation for the subsidy programs for U.S.-flag ships; the act made other changes as well, the most important of which was replacing the Shipping Board Bureau* with a new U.S. Maritime Commission.* The Merchant Marine Act was the direct result of the revelations of the Black Committee,* which exposed the many abuses committed under the mail contracts authorized by the Merchant Marine Act of 1928.* The 1936 act immediately canceled the previous mail contracts, effectively repealing the 1928 act. However, the 1936 act repeated the principles stated since the Jones Act* of maintaining a large fleet of U.S.-flag merchant ships in the foreign trade. Like the previous legislation, the 1936 act did not deal with tramp* vessels or bulk* carriers and covered only the liner* operators; this limitation remained in force for decades until the Merchant Marine Act of 1970* opened the full subsidy program to bulk carriers.

In 1935 intense debates emerged over maritime policy, but in spite of thirty-five drafts, Congress was unable to reach agreement on legislation. A logjam on other bills finally convinced the Senate to pass the bill by voice vote in June 1936, and shortly after it was rushed through the House for final approval on 29 June. Few legislators understood the nature of the measures, while the sponsors of the bill had arranged so many compromises that the bill did not really satisfy any particular group and, at the same time, failed to meet the real public need. The maritime industry was left stuck for over half a century with a law whose impact must be included among the major causes of the decline of the merchant marine in the United States.

The 1936 act introduced the concept of parity or making equal the costs of building and operating U.S.-flag ships. The "scientific" subsidy policy revolved around the difference between the higher U.S. costs and the lower foreign costs; this difference or "differential" would be paid for by the government in order to attain parity. The 1936 act established the two main types of government assistance, the construction differential subsidy* (CDS) to help the shipbuilders and the operating differential subsidy* (ODS) to help shipowners. The twenty-year contracts for the ODS required that only ships built with the CDS could qualify for the ODS, and in this way the 1936 act attempted the nearly impossible task of trying to use the merchant marine to promote shipbuilding as well. The ODS was doomed to a slow, agonizing failure not so much because of the modest sums expended but mainly because of the strict requirements and rigid procedures that neutralized the ability of U.S. shipowners to respond quickly and effectively to changing world conditions. Congress had included the detailed requirements to prevent another orgy of waste and private profiteering as had happened under the mail contracts, but now the government had gone to the other extreme, and during the next fifty years the steamship companies slowly withered under the excessively rigid controls and constant semijudicial proceedings.

The 1936 act did conserve the Construction Loan Fund of the Jones Act as a way to provide low interest loans to steamship companies, but again here the aim was to subsidize the shipbuilder rather than the shipowner. The 1936 act dealt with other issues and contained enough broad statements to have retained for long the title of the Magna Charta of the shipping industry, and in a way it was, because subsidized companies and labor unions based their survival on the 1936 act, whose provisions, however, had been unsound from the very start.

To administer the new subsidy programs, the 1936 act created a new U.S. Maritime Commission to replace the Shipping Board Bureau. Rather than a strong agency responsible to a cabinet official, Congress returned to the discredited commission system and created a new five-member commission, each person with terms of six years, to carry out all the functions of subsidy, as well as the regulatory functions contained in the Shipping Act of 1916.* Of the central provisions of the 1936 act, the first to be repealed was the U.S. Maritime Commission, which in 1950 was replaced by the Maritime Administration* (MARAD), although in fact during World War II the War Shipping Administration* (WSA) had actually carried out most functions affecting the merchant marine, except for shipbuilding.

The act of 1936 was responsible for the particular nature of the decline of the U.S. merchant marine: rather than a spectacular and sudden collapse, the ODS and CDS kept shipyards and steamship companies alive for decades, but without really putting them in a condition to compete effectively. The CDS ended in 1981, no new contracts have been signed for the ODS, and when the last of the existing contracts expire in 2001, the 1936 act will finally finish its own long, agonizing ordeal out of existence.

References: René De La Pedraja, *The Rise and Decline of U.S. Merchant Shipping in the Twentieth Century* (New York: Twayne, 1992); Ernst G. Frankel, *Regulation and Policies of American Shipping* (Boston: Auburn House, 1982); Gerald R. Jantscher, *Bread upon the Waters: Federal Aids to the Maritime Industries* (Washington, DC: Brookings Institution, 1975); Samuel A. Lawrence, *United States Merchant Shipping Policies and Politics* (Washington, DC: Brookings Institution, 1966); Paul M. Zeis, *American Shipping Policy* (Princeton, NJ: Princeton University Press, 1938).

MERCHANT MARINE ACT OF 1970. Since the passage of the Merchant Marine Act of 1936, almost every session of Congress has produced proposals and often legislation to amend one provision or section of the original act, but the first significant change did not come until 1970. The essential structure of the 1936 act remained in force, and the change in 1970 came only because the crew of a foreign-flag ship (but, interestingly enough, not a ship flying flags of convenience*) had refused to transport materials to Vietnam as a protest against that war. In a panic response, Congress approved a bill on 21 October 1970 to try to increase the number of U.S.-flag ships. The Merchant Marine Act of 1970 for the first time extended to bulk* carriers the operating differential subsidy* (ODS) previously limited only to liner* companies. The act wanted U.S.-flag ships to carry 30 percent of U.S. foreign trade by weight and to achieve that goal proposed the construction of a fleet of 300 new vessels.

In spite of the new opportunities the Merchant Marine Act of 1970 provided, the legislation produced meager results. Most bulk carriers were not enthusiastic about shifting from flags of convenience to U.S. registry,* and the Maritime Administration* (MARAD) struggled for years to formulate the guidelines necessary to assign coherently subsidies to the bulk carriers. Between 1973 and 1976 nine bulk companies finally signed ODS contracts, while the three last bulk carriers signed on in 1981, right before MARAD abandoned all efforts to find additional bulk carriers to subsidize. Since the early 1980s MARAD has struggled just to meet the subsidy payments on existing contracts.

References: Ernst G. Frankel, *Regulation and Policies of American Shipping* (Boston: Auburn House, 1982); Gerald R. Jantscher, *Bread upon the Waters: Federal Aids to the Maritime Industries* (Washington, DC: Brookings Institution, 1975); Maritime Administration, *Annual Report 1986*; Clinton H. Whitehurst, Jr., *The U.S. Shipbuilding Industry: Past, Present, and Future* (Annapolis, MD: Naval Institute Press, 1986).

MERCHANT MARINE AND FISHERIES, COMMITTEE ON, 1887– present. The Committee on Merchant Marine and Fisheries of the U.S. House of Representatives was established on 21 December 1887 to handle legislation affecting ocean transportation and the sea; since the 1910s the committee has also supervised the activities of maritime agencies of the federal government. With a large membership and staff, the committee has had the time and resources to carefully study the issues and prepare legislation; and generally, the Commerce Committee* of the Senate has allowed the House committee to take the initiative in legislation. In a major exception, Senator Wesley Jones* rushed through the Merchant Marine Act of 1920,* but the usual procedure has been for the Commerce Committee to serve as a type of ''appeals board'' to revise the work of the House committee.

Unfortunately the diligence and efforts of the House committee have been often wasted, because it simply lacked the political muscle to get the bills through Congress, and in a modern-day indication of importance, television cameras have very rarely bothered to cover its proceedings. The weak performance of the Merchant Marine and Fisheries Committee in its first two decades of existence led President Theodore Roosevelt to suggest the creation of the Merchant Marie Commission,* made up of both representatives and senators, as a way to sidestep the ineffective standing congressional committee. Not until the forceful Joshua Alexander* became chairman did the Merchant Marine and Fisheries Committee at last become a force within the Congress; not only did the committee conduct an intensive investigation into conferences* during 1912–

1914, but it was also largely responsible for the passage of the landmark Shipping Act of 1916.*

The Commerce Committee of the Senate during the years of Wesley Jones largely eclipsed the Merchant Marine and Fisheries Committee. The big legislative success appeared to come when the Merchant Marine and Fisheries Committee teamed up with Senator Jones to secure passage of the Merchant Marine Act of 1928,* but soon this act emerged as one of the worst (if not the worst) maritime law ever approved by Congress. The disaster of the Merchant Marine Act of 1928 and the revelations of the Black Committee* in the Senate overshadowed the House committee, which did not begin to regain status until 1933, when Schuyler Otis Bland* assumed the chairmanship. He served almost continuously until 1950, and under his leadership the Merchant Marine and Fisheries Committee was responsible for the passage of the Merchant Marine Act of 1936,* which totally revamped the system of subsidies for steamship companies. In the 1940s a network of subcommittees emerged within the larger committee, and increasingly the subcommittees, rather that the whole committee, were conducting the inquiries and making the decisions.

Herbert C. Bonner* attempted to continue the work of Bland in the Merchant Marine and Fisheries Committee when he became its chairman in 1955, but by then the decline of U.S.-flag shipping was seriously eroding the power and economic bases of the committee. The committee had become ''one of the less prestigious and less powerful of the twenty standing committees of the House'' (Lawrence 1968); most of the freshmen members had placed other committees as their first three choices and departed as soon as openings in more influential committees appeared. The rapid turnover was not necessarily bad, because the committee usually could count on the support of its former ''alumni'' for votes in the House.

Precisely because it was weak, the Merchant Marine and Fisheries Committee could easily be preempted by other, more powerful bodies in the House, most notably by the Celler Committee,* whose hearings had a disastrous impact on the U.S.-flag merchant marine. The passage of the Merchant Marine Act of 1970* seemed to have restored some prestige to the Merchant Marine and Fisheries Committee, but its reputation was once again tarnished as some of its members wrestled with charges of corruption in the 1970s and 1980s. Rumors have surfaced with alarming frequency that the House leadership planned to root out the problem by simply abolishing the committee, but it has been saved by an unexpected twist: oil spills and environmental damage to ocean waters have put the Merchant Marine and Fisheries Committee back in the forefront of national issues, while Walter B. Jones* as chairman did much to repair the damaged prestige of the committee. In a reflection of the change of emphasis, the committee has gradually shifted its resources and time toward environmental issues and away from the merchant marine, whose jurisdiction, however, the committee must maintain in order to preserve its newfound importance over the ocean environment.

MERCHANT MARINE COMMISSION

Notable Chairmen

Joshua W. Alexander	1911–1919
Schuyler Otis Bland	1933–1947; 1949–1950
Herbert C. Bonner	1955–1965
Edward A. Garmatz*	1965–1973
Leonor K. Sullivan	1973–1977
John M. Murphy*	1977–1981
Walter B. Jones	1981–1992
Jerry E. Studds	1992–present

References: Congressional Quarterly Service, *Congress and the Nation, 1945–1964* and *1985–1988*; Samuel A. Lawrence, *United States Merchant Shipping Policies and Politics* (Washington, DC: Brookings Institution, 1968); Walter Stubbs, *Congressional Committees, 1789–1982: A Checklist* (Westport, CT: Greenwood Press, 1985); Paul M. Zeis, *American Shipping Policy* (Princeton, NJ: Princeton University Press, 1938).

MERCHANT MARINE COMMISSION, 1904–1905. On 28 April 1904 Congress created ''this commission to investigate and to report to the Congress on the first day of its next session what legislation, if any, is desirable for the development of the American merchant marine and American commerce'' (U.S. Congress 1905). The commission, whose chairman was Senator Jacob H. Callinger, was composed of five senators and five representatives; two of the members from each house were of the minority party. The idea for the commission had come from President Theodore Roosevelt, who suggested in his annual message to Congress of 7 December 1903 the creation of a commission composed of members from the executive departments and both houses of Congress; with this diverse membership, Roosevelt had expected a distinterested inquiry, but Congress did not welcome any encroachment upon its investigative powers and created instead merely a special joint committee of both houses. Noteworthy was the way the Congress bypassed its own standing Committee on Merchant Marine and Fisheries,* the first of many usurpations this last committee suffered during the twentieth century.

The Merchant Marine Commission began to take testimony in New York City on 23 May 1904 and then traveled across the country to conduct hearings in the major port cities of the East and West coasts, the Gulf of Mexico, and the Great Lakes. On 22 November the commission began its last set of hearings in Washington, D.C., sifted through all the evidence, and finally issued its report early in 1905. The commission failed to make any new proposals and, while accepting the obvious fact that ships built in the United States cost more than those built abroad, rejected the Democratic appeal for ''free ships''* and simply proposed a subsidy to make American shipbuilding and shipping competitive with foreigners. The protectionist policy of the Republican party precluded any other alternative, and quite naturally the antisubsidy Democrats in Congress blocked passage of the bills that contained the commission's recommendations. The Merchant Marine Commission, although an instructive but ultimately minor episode in the legislative history of the merchant marine, has been remembered mainly because of its monumental *Report.* So many witnesses were heard at the open hearings and so much evidence was gathered that the Merchant Marine Commission provided one of the most complete and intimate views of merchant shipping and certainly the most detailed for the status of U.S. shipping at the dawn of the twentieth century.

References: U.S. Congress, Merchant Marine Commission, *Report*, 3 vols. Report No. 2755, 58th Congress, 3d Session, 1905; Paul M. Zeis, *American Shipping Policy* (Princeton, NJ: Princeton University Press, 1938).

MERCHANTS AND MINERS TRANSPORTATION COMPANY (M&M), 1852–1948. The Baltimore-based Merchants and Miners Transportation Company (M&M) was one of the largest and longest lasting companies providing service along the East Coast of the United States. M&M was incorporated on 25 April 1852 to open service between Baltimore and Boston with steam side-wheelers.* The company added as ports of call Providence in 1858 and Savannah in 1861. The Civil War disrupted the company's activities, yet it managed to keep running the line between Boston and Baltimore. After the war the company introduced screw steamers to resume service with Providence in 1873 and with Savannah in 1876. New stock issues financed M&M's expansion, and in 1907 it purchased the Winsor Line, which had operated a Boston-Philadelphia service since 1872. Except for a brief period of three years after 1879, when M&M had operated a Philadelphia-New York service, the company did not call on New York; this omission not only made M&M unique among the lines in the coastwise* trade but also reflected a tacit division of the market with the New York-based Eastern Steamship Lines,* the only other possible rival.

As part of the arrangement that led to the purchase of the Winsor Line, the New York, New Haven & Hartford Railroad gained a controlling interest in M&M, whose operations remained profitable until December 1912, when the company for the first time in its history suspended dividend payments. In April 1914 the New York, New Haven & Hartford Railroad sold its M&M stock, and a new management team labored to save the steamship company from bankruptcy. After U.S. entry into World War I, the U.S. Railroad Administration requisitioned the company's ships and did not return them until March 1919. In January 1918 M&M had retired the last of its debts and soon felt strong enough to issue new stock, which was quickly subscribed; on 31 December 1921 the company resumed paying dividends.

M&M ordered new vessels from the shipyards for its passenger-cargo services, and in 1929 the company was operating eighteen ships among Baltimore, Boston, Jacksonville, Miami, Norfolk, Philadelphia, Providence, Savannah, and West Palm Beach. The company survived the Great Depression fairly successfully because "it has perhaps more joint through rates with the railroads than any other of the coastwise steamship lines. About 50 percent of its traffic moves in connection with the railroads, and about 50 percent is port-to-port traffic'' (U.S. Congress, 1938). In January 1938 M&M was still operating twenty-one steamships on its traditional routes, but upon the outbreak of World War II the government began to requisition its best vessels, and in January 1942 the company suspended all services. When the surviving vessels were returned after the end of the war, the owners decided to sell them for scrapping. The stockholders did not bother to acquire surplus vessels to try to resume service and instead on 14 March 1948 voted to dissolve M&M.

References: Frederick E. Emmons, *American Passenger Ships: The Ocean Lines and Liners, 1873–1983* (Newark: University of Delaware Press, 1985); *Nautical Gazette*, 23 November 1929; U.S. Congress, House, Committee on Merchant Marine and Fisheries, *Amending Merchant Marine Act, 1936* (Washington, DC: Government Printing Office, 1938).

MERCHANTS' LINE. See New York and Pacific Steamship Company.

METROPOLITAN STEAMSHIP COMPANY, 1866–1911. The Metropolitan Steamship Company was established to provide service between Boston and New York City. The company originally operated wooden side-wheelers* and in 1872 ordered its first iron screw steamer. In 1905 Wall Street financier Charles W. Morse acquired the company and ordered the construction of the two fastest vessels under the American flag, the *Harvard** and *Yale** with steam turbines,* to provide express service between Boston and New York. Unfortunately Morse's shipping combine collapsed in 1907, and he himself ended in a federal penitentiary, leaving the affairs of the Metropolitan Steamship Company in a corporate maze of bankruptcy proceedings. The company, for reasons still unclear today, decided to shift the *Harvard* and *Yale* to the Pacific Coast, where they offered express service between San Francisco and Los Angeles starting in December 1910. In 1916 these two ships were leased to the Admiral Line,* and in 1918 they were purchased by the government for duty in World War I. The career of the two ships resumed after the return of peace, but that of the Metropolitan Steamship Company was over: in 1911 the company entered into the merger proceedings that resulted in the Eastern Steamship Lines,* in what was part of the process of consolidating the coastwise* lines along the East Coast.

Some Notable Ships

Yale and *Harvard*   1906–1949

References: Giles T. Brown, *Ships That Sail No More: Marine Transportation from San Diego to Puget Sound, 1910–1940* (Lexington: University of Kentucky Press, 1966); Frederick E. Emmons, *American Passenger Ships: The Ocean Lines and Liners, 1873– 1983* (Newark: University of Delaware Press, 1985).

MILITARY SEALIFT COMMAND (MSC), 1970–present. On 1 August 1970 the Military Sea Transportation Service* (MSTS), the agency of the navy in charge of ocean cargoes, become the Military Sealift Command (MSC); its first commander, Admiral Arthur R. Gralla, explained the need for this change: "Sealift has a more forceful connotation than transport. It means planning; it means being prepared to operate in wartime or contingency environment which 'sea transportation' just did not connote" (*Maritime*, August 1970). The term also gave the MSC a slight edge to justify its activities against the attacks of the private operators who had always opposed the very existence of this government agency. The big maritime labor organizations such as the Seafarers' International Union* (SIU), if they could not get the government out of shipping, at least wanted to replace the civil service crews with personnel who belonged to their unions; it was revealing to see that the higher wages of these crews were necessary to support the bloated labor organization of big maritime unions. The Gerald Ford administration rejected forcing the MSC to use fewer civil service seamen, but the Jimmy Carter administration, eager to win popularity with organized labor, was more receptive and even wrote to the secretary of the navy to do everything possible to expand the use of non-civil service seamen by the MSC.

Under the Ronald Reagan administration the focus shifted from trying to favor big labor to using the MSC to bail out the private steamships companies, one after another heading toward bankruptcy. Timely charters* from the MSC were publicized as "a helping hand for ailing lines" (*American Shipper*, April 1987) and while the MSC was able to keep alive Waterman Steamship Corporation* and Prudential Lines* in the mid-1980s, United States Lines* (USL) was too big and too far gone to be saved. For the remaining U.S.-flag companies, the contracts to carry cargo for the MSC became a life-or-death issue, and the competitive bidding initiated in the 1960s soon turned very bitter. Fly-by-night outfits appeared to make very low bids that they did not have to fulfill but that served the purpose of lowering prices. MSC was not convinced the rates were so ruinous, because of the comparison with costs on its own ships, but nevertheless the tremendous public outcry finally led to a change in the contract system in 1990, whereby each of the major carriers on each route was guaranteed a share of the cargo, while the bidding procedure merely determined how big the share would be. Just like with the MSTS, the private shipping companies and labor groups have continued to look to the federal government, in this case the MSC, to try to solve their financial woes, instead of letting the MSC operate and own whatever share of its fleet it considered the most appropriate mixture for moving military cargoes.

References: *American Shipper*, April 1987, April 1990; *Journal of Commerce*, 1 September 11 October 1988, 23 February 1989; *Maritime*, August 1970; Presidential Handwriting File, Gerald R. Ford Presidential Library, Ann Arbor, Michigan; White House Central Files, Jimmy Carter Presidential Library, Atlanta, Georgia.

MILITARY SEA TRANSPORTATION SERVICE (MSTS), 1949–1970. The Military Sea Transportation Service (MSTS), under the control of the navy, was the first agency of the government to provide ocean transportation for both the army and the navy. The origins of the MSTS dated back to the Army Transport Service of 1898; prior to that date the army, which only had Indians to fight, did not need more than horses and railroads to reach the enemy, but the Spanish-American War forced the army for the first time to meet overseas commitments, and to avoid the embarrassing unpreparedness in shipping during that conflict, the Military Transportation Act of 1904* specified that 100 percent of military cargoes had to travel aboard U.S.-flag ships. The fact that the army rather than the navy took the lead in providing ocean transportation was easily understood because the army behaved like a proprietary* steamship company: over 90 percent of the cargo needed to support the military overseas was for the army, and the army quite rightly acquired and operated its own fleet of merchant vessels between 1898 and 1950. Originally known as the Army Transport Service, the vessels were handled by a bewildering variety of bureaus, divisions, and services, with such names as Water Transport Branch and Water Division. The vessels were under the general authority of the quartermaster general of the army until 1942, when they were transferred to the Transportation Corps. The creation of the Department of Defense led to attempts to unify common services in one agency, and under the decision that the navy should handle all affairs on water, the Military Sea Transportation Service was created on 1 October 1949, but the army was given until 1 March 1950 to hand over its vessels to the new agency of the Navy Department. The army was not overly pleased with this forced transfer, but on the understanding that the MSTS would handle all army cargoes as if they were of the navy, the MSTS functioned throughout its history to the satisfaction of the army.

The real problem MSTS faced was caused by its very efficient and successful operation of what has frequently been one of the largest, if not the largest, merchant fleets in the United States. Many private steamship companies, unable or unwilling to compete for world trade, made MSTS the scapegoat for their failures and raved during decades about the evils of unfair government competition, charges that the predecessor army service had faced since the first decade of the twentieth century. Private operators, in particular the tramps,* constantly lobbied to deactivate as much as possible of MSTS's fleet so that a greater share of government cargoes would have to travel aboard privately owned vessels. The campaign against the MSTS reached its zenith in 1954 under the pro-business Dwight D. Eisenhower administration. In that year, Congress passed the Cargo Preference Act of 1954,* which specified the half of the military cargoes had to travel aboard *privately* owned U.S.-flag vessels, and the executive branch through the Wilson-Weeks Agreement* agreed to reduce the nucleus fleet of the MSTS to fifty-six transports, thirty-four freighters, and sixty-one tankers.

By these actions, the MSTS was forced to send the military cargoes at a higher cost through private companies, instead of expanding its nucleus fleet, which, manned by civil service crews, had lower operating costs. The U.S. treasury was forced to pay huge sums as one more subsidy to the private companies in order to cover the costs of moving cargoes overseas. When the Vietnam War began, the MSTS was allowed to expand its nucleus fleet, although extreme political pressure was placed on the organization to charter* as many ships as possible from private companies rather than operate them itself. As the Vietnam War dragged on, the MSTS unveiled in 1969 a plan to replace its outdated ships of World War II with a new thirty-freighter fleet, but promptly the American Institute of Merchant Shipping (AIMS) shot down the plan as "the first step in the nationalization of the United States Merchant Marine" (*New York Times*, 30 March 1969). The task of dealing with the hostile private operators, who also bitterly resented competitive bidding for the contracts let out by MSTS, was left to the successor agency, the Military Sealift Command* (MSC).

  References: René De La Pedraja, *The Rise and Decline of U.S. Merchant Shipping in the Twentieth Century* (New York: Twayne, 1992); Wytze Gorter, *United States Shipping Policy* (New York: Council on Foreign Relations, 1956); Gerald R. Jantscher, *Bread upon the Waters: Federal Aids to the Maritime Industries* (Washington, DC: Brookings Institution, 1975); *New York Times*, 30 March 1969; U.S. Senate, Committee on Interstate and Foreign Commerce, *Merchant Marine Study and Investigation*, vol. 5, *Transportation of Cargoes by the Military* (Washington, DC: Government Printing Office, 1950); U.S. Congress, Senate, *Merchant Marine Study and Investigation: Final Report*, Report No. 2494, 81st Congress, 2d Session, 1950; William Joe Webb, "The Spanish-American War and United States Army Shipping," *American Neptune* 40 (1980):167–191.

MILITARY TRANSPORTATION ACT OF 1904. The Spanish-American War had forced the military to hastily charter and purchase merchant vessels to supply overseas operations. Because the cargo needs of the army constituted over 90 percent of military loads, the Army Transport Service was the most important agency. The briefness of the Spanish-American War had prevented any major supply bottlenecks, but in order to be ready for another conflict, Congress agreed with the need to enlarge the U.S.-flag merchant marine and on 28 April 1904 approved the Military Transportation Act, which required all supplies for the army and the navy to be carried aboard U.S.-flag ships. The act allowed exceptions, such as in time of emergencies or if not enough U.S.-flag vessels were available, and already in 1907 for the world tour of the fleet, the navy had to call on tramp* steamers of other nations for coal and other supplies. Nevertheless, the Military Transportation Act operated as a powerful stimulus for the merchant marine. Because the government discovered that it could carry military cargoes at a lower cost aboard its own ships rather than those of private companies, the subsidized companies secured from Congress the Cargo Preference Act of 1954,* which modified the Military Transportation Act of 1904 by stipulating that at least half of the military cargoes had to be carried aboard *privately* owned U.S.-flag ships. In this way the Military Transportation Act, originally a very wise national defense measure, was partially distorted for the sake of generating private profits.

References: Gerald R. Jantscher, *Bread upon the Waters: Federal Aids to the Maritime Industries* (Washington, DC: Brookings Institution, 1975); Transportation Research Board, *Intermodel Marine Container Transportation: Impediments and Opportunities* (Washington, DC: National Research Council, 1992); *U.S. Statutes at Large*, vol. 33 (1904); William Joe Webb, "The Spanish-American War and United States Army Shipping," *American Neptune* 40 (1980):167–191.

MINK, GEORGE, 1899?–1960s? George Mink was the national chairman of the Communist Marine Workers Industrial Union* (MWIU) and became as well a legendary figure on the waterfront. Mystery surrounded Mink's life from the start: his birthplace and birthday of Scranton, Pennsylvania, in 1899 cannot be confirmed. He appeared in Philadelphia, where he may have worked as a taxi driver, and then moved on to the waterfront as a union organizer and member of the Communist party by the mid-1920s. He worked from behind the scenes and soon acquired a reputation as a predatory conspirator. He was helped by his bearing and physical appearance: "brash, tough, shrewd," "an arrogant sort of guy," "his mouth was small and cruel, his teeth irregular, and his eyes had a faint wild-animal glint" (Nelson 1990). When the Communist party created the MWIU in 1930, Mink became the national chairman, but he spent most of the time in secret trips to the Soviet Union and Europe.

Mink was rarely in contact with the seamen, whom he treated with "utter cynicism" (ibid.), and at the headquarters of the Communist party he challenged and threatened the president, Earl Browder. In late 1933 the Communist party removed Mink from his position in the MWIU and left the more cooperative Roy B. Hudson* in charge, while Thomas Ray* henceforth handled relations with the Soviet labor movement; Mink himself was assigned to full-time work with the International Communist (Comintern). His career might be judged a failure, but the Mink legend was just picking up steam: labels as evocative as "the harbor pirate" and "the most dreaded and the most deadly" Moscow agent became associated with his name. Unlike many American communists who died in the Spanish Civil War, Mink survived with his reputation enhanced: "He got the name, 'The Bloody Butcher,' wherever he went men died" (ibid.), and was credited with having murdered over 2,000 persons. His conspiratorial talents had no limits; he appeared to be everywhere but more likely was nowhere: his only verified action was in Denmark, where he was convicted of trying to smuggle anti-Nazi propaganda into Germany in 1935. The intervention of a local communist secured his release from prison, but, more important, the story was transformed by embellishments into a plot to assassinate Adolph Hitler.

Mink was present at the Communist party National Committee meeting at Chicago in September 1936, but this was his last confirmed appearance. Afterward he vanished, but Mink the legend remained a real presence on the waterfront, and anti-communists could be sure to scare rank-and-file seamen with reports that Mink was back and up to his old conspiratorial tricks. As late as the 1950s, Harry Lundeberg* printed wanted posters of "Mink the Fink," denouncing the communist agitator, who had supposedly reappeared.

References: Bruce Nelson, *Workers on the Waterfront: Seamen, Longshoremen, and Unionism in the 1930s* (Urbana: University of Illinois Press, 1990); William L. Standard, *Merchant Seamen: A Short History of Their Struggles* (New York: International, 1947).

MINNESOTA, 1905–1923. The *Minnesota* and the *Dakota** were the two passenger-cargo sister ships that provided service between Seattle and Far Eastern ports. The ships belonged to the Great Northern Steamship Company* (GNSS), whose owner was the railroad magnate James J. Hill. The *Minnesota*, with 22,250 deadweight* tons, length of 622 feet, beam of 73 feet, and accommodations for 200 first-class passengers and at least 1,800 persons in steerage* class, was among the biggest ships of its time, but her maximum speed of thirteen knots was very slow for a passenger liner. Hill insisted on such huge ships in order to achieve "economies of scale" or lower operating costs; he believed low rates would attract large volumes of cargo and make the shipping venture profitable. Until the construction of the *Virginia* in 1928, the *Minnesota* remained the largest ship ever built in an American shipyard, and its cargo capacity was not equaled until 1928, when the Standard Oil Company* built the tanker *C.O. Stillman*. Hill ordered the two ships in 1900, but they did not begin service until 1905, mainly because of his own mistakes. To build what in 1900 would have been the biggest ships in the world, he chose a new shipyard that did not have even a place to work. Further delays resulted from his insistence on trying to insert radical innovations in the ships. Most of his ideas failed, and the ships were plagued with mechanical difficulties during their careers. An interesting feature on both ships was the opium den provided at the rear of the main deck for the convenience of the Chinese passengers.

The *Minnesota* sailed on its first voyage to the Far East on 23 January 1905, while the sister ship *Dakota* finally sailed on 20 September 1905. The liners were so slow that to maintain a semblance of service, the GNSS needed to charter* five other vessels. The volumes of cargo necessary to fill the huge holds failed to materialize, and soon Hill tired of the whole steamship venture. When the *Dakota* was lost off the coast of Japan on 3 March 1907, he refused to replace her and, as a matter of fact, wanted to leave the steamship business altogether. The five smaller ships were easily disposed of, but nobody wanted the *Minnesota* because she was simply too large for any cargo route in the world and too slow for passenger service.

Gradually the GNSS devised a survival strategy for the *Minnesota*. Essentially the ship made four voyages each year and stayed for extended time periods in each of the Far Eastern ports, giving the agents ample time to scrounge for more cargo. As a sort of floating warehouse and quoting the lowest rates, the *Minnesota* collected considerable cargo, and thanks to the use of Chinese crews, income almost covered the ship's operating costs. The small loss was more than offset by the large profits the parent company made once the ship's cargo was transferred to the railroad in Seattle.

The passage of the La Follette Seamen's Act* threatened the Chinese crew of 250 persons, without whose presence the operation of the *Minnesota* was highly unprofitable. Finding a buyer for this white elephant was no easy task, but finally record-high rates on the North Atlantic persuaded the International Mercantile Marine* (IMM) to purchase the vessel in January 1917. IMM operated the *Minnesota* on the Atlantic only from April to October 1917, when she was requisitioned by the Shipping Board* for service in World War I. At last the *Minnesota* found adequate employment, carrying the endless mountains of supplies for the American Expeditionary Forces in Europe. For the first time in her career the ship's huge holds were full, the decks were crammed with freight, and merchandise was suspended even from her rigging. The record-breaking amounts of cargo ended with the return of peace, and after a brief stint with the U.S. Navy in 1919 as the transport *Troy*, the ship was returned to the IMM and basically remained laid up until the *Minnesota* was broken up in 1923.

References: Thomas C. Buckley, "Railroader Afloat: James J. Hill as Ship Builder and Operator," 1993, forthcoming article; René De La Pedraja, *The Rise and Decline of U.S. Merchant Shipping in the Twentieth Century* (New York: Twayne, 1992); Don L. Hofsommer, "The Maritime Enterprises of James J. Hill," *American Neptune* 47 (1987): 193–205; W. Kaye Lamb, "The Transpacific Ventures of James J. Hill," *American Neptune* 3 (1943):185–204; E. Mowbray Tate, *Transpacific Steam: The Story of Steam Navigation from the Pacific Coast of North America to the Far East and the Antipodes, 1867–1941* (New York: Cornwall Books, 1986).

MISSISSIPPI SHIPPING COMPANY. See Delta Line.

MODESTO BOYS. This was the collective name given to the sailors imprisoned because of their participation in the tanker strike against Standard Oil of California in March–April 1935. Two important leaders in the strike were Victor Johnson and Rouel Stanfield, and to eliminate their influence Standard Oil plotted to have them arrested and convicted of wanting to dynamite Standard Oil gasoline stations and a hotel where the company kept strikebreakers. On the testimony of a company agent and a hired spy, a group of seamen, including Johnson and Stanfield, were convicted but only on the one charge of "reckless and malicious possession of explosives" (Schwartz 1986). The men served minimum terms of six months in San Quentin, providing the Maritime Federation of the Pacific* (MFP) with an excellent opportunity for a widespread publicity campaign. Having convicted members serving prison sentences enhanced the status of the maritime unions within the American labor movement. The Modesto Boys proved such a useful rallying cry on the waterfront that to find a substitute, many maritime unions espoused the Harry Bridges' case* with great enthusiasm.

References: Betty V. H. Schneider, *Industrial Relations in the West Coast Maritime Industry* (Berkeley: University of California Press, 1958); Stephen Schwartz, *Brotherhood of the Sea: A History of the Sailors' Union of the Pacific, 1885–1985* (New Brunswick, NJ: Transaction Books, 1986).

MONGOLIA. See *Manchuria* and *Mongolia*.

MONTEREY. See *Mariposa* and *Monterey*.

MOORE, ALBERT V., 21 September 1880–9 January 1953. Albert V. Moore, president of Moore-McCormack,* was born in Hackensack, New Jersey, on 21 September 1880 and attended public schools in his hometown. Although his father was a custom jeweler, his grandfather and uncle had been shipowners, and Moore decided to work as a ship broker* in 1903 after his graduation. He eventually joined the Tweedie Trading Company, whose specialty was shipping with South America and the West Indies, and he rapidly advanced to become the assistant of the owner; in this firm he acquired the initial contacts and knowledge for the South American trade that would subsequently be so important in his career.

Moore wanted to become a shipowner in his own right, but his assets were not enough, so he decided to form a partnership with Emmet J. McCormack* to incorporate Moore-McCormack in 1913. Moore became the president, and McCormack the treasurer, and both nicely complemented each other's abilities. While McCormack loved to deal with people and was a born salesman, Moore was "studious, precise, a believer in research" and "was accustomed to solid, careful planning" (Lee 1957). Moore-McCormack operated in the early years with only chartered,* vessels and the sailings were to Brazil, the area of Moore's expertise. Through careful reinvestment of profits and shrewd ship deals, the company gradually was able to purchase its own ships. The big opportunity, however, came with World War I, when the Swedish line (Svenska Lloyd Line) handed over its ships in the England-Scandinavia route to Moore-McCormack for operation during the duration of the war. With the network of contacts he developed in Scandinavia, Moore-McCormack was well positioned to take a commanding lead in that trade with that region after the war. The opportunity to acquire routes and surplus vessels from the Shipping Board* allowed the company to consolidate its services to ports in South America, Scandinavia, and the Baltic.

Under Moore's methodical manner of operation, Moore-McCormack continued as a very profitable venture until his death in Forest Hills, New York, on 9 January 1953. Some of his heirs sold family stock in the company to R. Stanley Dollar,* who became a director on the board, but his son William retained enough shares and control to replace his father as president of the company.

References: Robert C. Lee, *Mr. Moore, Mr. McCormack–and the Seven Seas!* (New York: Newcomen Society, 1957); *National Cyclopedia of American Biography*, vol. 45; *New York Times*, 16 April 1953.

MOORE, WILLIAM T., 12 August 1913–7 April 1976. William T. Moore, president of Moore-McCormack,* was born in New York City on 12 August 1913. He was the son of the first president and founder of Moore-McCormack, Albert V. Moore.* He studied at Lawrenceville School in New Jersey and attended the University of Virginia until 1935. Afterward his father sent him to the Buenos Aires office of the company and later stationed him at the various offices in Europe prior to his taking a position at headquarters in New York City. In 1939 William became a director in the company, but his ascent was temporarily interrupted by World War II, when he served in the army and reached the rank of lieutenant colonel.

Upon the death of his father in January 1953, William became the president of the company, and except for dwindling guidance from the aging chairman of the board, Emmet J. McCormack* (whom he also replaced in that position in 1960), Moore was now in full charge. While a number of steamship companies were deciding in the 1950s to abandon this highly risky business, Moore felt no such hesitation and boldly purchased the Robin Line* in 1957 as a way to extend Moore-McCormack's South American operations into Africa. An even riskier move was placing orders for the *Argentina* and *Brasil*, the two passenger liners that replaced in 1958 the three overage ships of the Good Neighbor Fleet.* The company bought the two new vessels, unlike the three ships of the Good Neighbor Fleet, which Moore-McCormack had chartered* from the government. Thus, when jet airplane travel was just beginning to make its presence felt in South America, William T. Moore had saddled the company with two passenger liners whose every voyage was soon producing nothing but mounting losses.

Having bungled passenger service, Moore faced the even more difficult decision of choosing the right replacement for the overage World War II break-bulk* vessels of his fleet at a time when the container* revolution was just starting to appear in the very traditional shipping industry. Because of its trade to South America and Africa, Moore concluded that the company could not afford to rush into containerization and instead settled upon a versatile type of vessels suitable for break-bulk, container, and even Roll-on/Roll-off* (Ro/Ro) operations. Unfortunately, these semicontainer vessels proved to be a costly failure and further weakened the rapidly eroding foundations of the company. Belatedly Moore at last realized that the real solution to the company lay in diversifying away from the unpredictable merchant shipping to the more reliable business ventures on land, and in 1965 he created a parent company to handle the new nonshipping business.

In 1971 the stockholders decided that a new young executive with fresh ideas was needed to stop the losses and also to continue the diversification into nonshipping activities, and they chose James R. Barker* to become president and chief executive officer. Moore was named as chairman of the executive committee and remained active in the activities of the Board of Directors until he died of a heart attack in Glen Cove, Long Island, on 7 April 1976.

References: Moore-McCormack Lines, *A Profile of Maritime Progress, 1913–1963*; *National Cyclopedia of American Biography*, vol. J.; *New York Times*, 8 April 1976.

MOORE-McCORMACK, 1913–1982. Moore-McCormack was one of the steamship companies providing service between United States and South America and was also the main U.S.-flag service to ports in Scandinavia and the Baltic. Emmet J. McCormack* and Albert V. Moore,* two rising businessmen connected with shipping, incorporated the company in New York City on 9 July 1913 as a partnership. Initially they owned no ships and began operations by chartering* ships, and the first voyage was to Rio de Janeiro, which had not seen a U.S.-flag ship in twenty-six years. They made some good deals buying and selling ships and also carefully reinvested profits until Moore-McCormack began to acquire its own fleet for the trade between New York and Rio de Janeiro. The biggest break, however, came with the outbreak of World War I, when the Swedish line (Svenska Lloyd Line) handed over its ships in the England-Scandinavia route to Moore-McCormack for operation during the duration of the war. As manager of these Swedish vessels, Moore-McCormack not only increased its service to South America but also developed the network that later allowed the company to become the most important U.S.-flag carrier in the Scandinavian trade.

With the end of World War I, surplus vessels of the Shipping Board* became available for operation as managing operator* or for sale at giveaway prices, and Moore-McCormack was very well placed to take advantage of these opportunities to expand its shipping services. In a first stage of experimentation from 1918 to 1925, Moore-McCormack plunged into the world's sea-lanes and opened services to the Mediterranean, including the Adriatic and the Black Sea, and to India, Cuba, and Ireland. Gradually the company abandoned these exotic routes and concentrated on its original routes to South America and to Scandinavian and Baltic ports. In 1918 Moore-McCormack sent its first ship to Scandinavia and by 1926 was the main shipping line in the trade with Scandinavia, a position further reinforced when Moore-McCormack bought the Scantic Line from the Shipping Board in 1927. With a very generous mail subsidy, the company was able to expand its services in the Baltic, and besides operating services to Russia, it became the shipping agents in the United States for the Russian government. The company, at the request of the Polish government, had been deeply involved in shipping between the United States and Poland and helped with the organization of the new Polish seaport of Gdynia.

Moore-McCormack had continued to increase its sailings to Rio de Janeiro and gradually expanded the service to cover most ports in Brazil. The company then added Montevideo, Uruguay, as a port of call and in 1919 reached for the first time Buenos Aires, initially using on these routes ships chartered from Sweden and later ships of the Shipping Board. The company, however, only briefly obtained control in 1926–1927 of the American Republics Line, the Shipping Board service to South America, although it continued to operate ships without subsidy on that route. The big chance to gain a solid grip on the South American trade came in 1936, when President Franklin D. Roosevelt decided to create U.S.-flag passenger service between South America and the United States. The U.S. Maritime Commission* purchased the *California*,* *Pennsylvania*, and *Virginia* from the International Mercantile Marine* and had them modernized at considerable expense. In 1938 Moore-McCormack made the only charter offer for the three liners (no purchase bids appeared), now renamed the *Argentina*, *Brazil*, and *Uruguay*; the liners operated under the name of the Good Neighbor Fleet.* Along with the three liners, Moore-McCormack at last also acquired the seven freighters of the American Republics Line. In 1940 the company purchased the Pacific Republics Line, which provided service between the West Coast of the United States and eastern South America.

With the outbreak of World War II, the government began to requisition ships until eventually the entire fleet of the company was in government hands. With the end of the war, Moore-McCormack was able to take advantage of the sale of surplus vessels to resume cargo service to South America, Sandinavia, and the Baltic. In 1946 the company owned forty-one ships and chartered the same number from the U.S. Maritime Commission and in 1947 reached the maximum of seventy-one chartered ships. The resumption of passenger service proved more difficult, because the *Argentina*, *Brazil*, and *Uruguay* needed extensive work in the shipyards, so that the Good Neighbor Fleet began to sail again only in January 1948. Shortly after, Moore-McCormack reached the high point of its career, when, taking advantage of the profits from the postwar shipping boom, the company canceled all ships' mortgages and outstanding loans.

On 9 January 1953 Albert V. Moore died, and he was replaced as president by his son William T. Moore.* The other cofounder, Emmet J. McCormack, was over seventy years old, and although he would remain active in the company for ten more years, the time was certainly ripe for a reevaluation of the investment in merchant shipping. Gone forever were the days of running unsubsidized ships to diverse routes, and since the Merchant Marine Act of 1936,* Moore-McCormack had operated only in subsidized trade routes. Furthermore, the World War II ships of the company would face obsolescence by 1960, and vessel replacement loomed as a daunting challenge. Other steamship companies like Farrell* pondered their future, and while some like the Robin Line* wisely decided to abandon risky shipping and invest the proceeds on safer land businesses, Moore-McCormack instead decided to expand and in 1956 acquired the Pacific-Argentine Brazil Line of Pope and Talbot,* whose four ships were integrated into the Pacific Republics Line. The next year Moore-McCormack purchased the Robin Line, thereby acquiring for the first time regular cargo service to Africa.

To replace the three aging liners of the Good Neighbor Fleet, the company ordered the *Argentina* and *Brasil*, whose faster speed of twenty-three knots and over eliminated the need for the third vessel; each of the two new ships carried 550 passengers and express cargo, and they began service in 1958. By then jet airplanes had established regular service to Europe and were soon headed for South America as well, making these two passenger liners obsolete, and soon their losses mounted until by 1967 they came to $2.7 million annually. However, because of subsidy contracts the Maritime Administration* (MARAD) did not allow the lay-up of the vessels until 1969, and the company found a buyer for them only in 1972.

The debacle of the passenger liners was followed by the no less botched-up vessel replacement in the 1960s. The container* revolution was just getting under way, and Moore-McCormack did not want to place all its bets on the untried technology, so it ordered semicontainer vessels that could increase their capacity to carry break-bulk* cargo and containers and even had Roll-on/Roll-off* (Ro/Ro) facilities for vehicles. The company justified the need for this highly versatile vessel on the grounds that South America and Africa, where it conducted most of its business, were still far from entering the container age, but once the transition began in those places, Moore-McCormack believed it would have enough time to order containerships or Ro/Ro vessels as needed.

Moore-McCormack still did not realize it was in dangerous waters, and rather than contracting, it continued to expand. In 1962 the company obtained MARAD permission to operate a subsidized service to Belgium and the Netherlands (the area covered by the North Atlantic Continental Conference*), but not to the United Kingdom. Upon hearing rumors that either United States Lines* or Sea-Land* was on the point of beginning container service, Moore-McCormack decided to jump the gun and started the first container service on the North Atlantic in February 1966. The company loaded 130 twenty-foot equivalent (TEU*) containers on the deck of its new break-bulk freighters, which were subsequently fitted to carry a total of 270 TEUs. To raise funds for the start-up expenses of this new service to Europe, the company sold its Pacific Republics Line to the Grace Line in April 1966. With the extra cash Moore-McCormack did not, however, convert its ships to full containers and instead continued to combine container and break-bulk services on the same ship, producing "two easily predictable results: costs rise and ship efficiency drops" (Marcus 1974). The company hoped to recover after MARAD had approved its application to begin subsidized sailings to France and Germany in 1969, but the next year a rate war broke out in the North Atlantic, and a weakened Moore-McCormack had no choice but to abandon its European services and sell its four freighter-container-Ro/Ro vessels to American Export Lines* in 1970.

Even before the rate war Moore-McCormack was in danger, and to try to stave off the bankruptcy the company had sought unsuccessfully to merge with U.S. Freight in 1966 and with Farrell Lines* in 1969. To try to save the company, the stockholders brought in as president James R. Barker,* who promptly began selling off old ships, including the two passenger liners. With this cash and loans from trusting bankers, Barker intensified a policy begun in 1964 of diversification into land businesses. He decided that Moore-McCormack needed to become a company whose focus was on energy and more generally on natural resources and transportation. As far as shipping was concerned, he saw the future in the Alaska oil trade, protected under the cabotage* laws; since 1969 the company had been wanting to order oil tankers for operation in the coastwise* and intercoastal* trade, but now with funds handy Baker ordered three tankers in July 1973.

When the energy crisis began later in 1973, all of Moore-McCormack's troubles appeared to have disappeared. Barker could continue borrowing from bankers, who were more than eager to lend for his energy ventures. To reflect its new interest in energy, a new company, Moore-McCormack Resources, was incorporated in February 1974, while Moore-McCormack Lines became merely one of its subsidiaries. The fascination of the new energy ventures led Barker to neglect the shipping subsidiary, which, amazingly, was performing well and actually earning profits. In 1980 Moore-McCormack Lines became the sole U.S.-flag service to East and South Africa when it purchased the two vessels of Farrell Line* in that route. Meanwhile shipping to South America remained prosperous. Unfortunately, when the energy bubble burst, the parent company, Moore-McCormack Resources, found itself collapsing, and it desperately sold off assets to try to pay off the mounting debts. In December 1982 Malcom McLean,* president of United States Lines, bought the subsidiary Moore-McCormack Lines, which thereafter lost its independent existence. The parent company, Moore-McCormack Resources, although no longer involved in shipping, continued to struggle to survive as a modest-sized firm.

Principal Executives

Albert V. Moore	1913–1953
Emmet J. McCormack	1913–1965
William T. Moore	1953–1971
James R. Barker	1971–1982

Some Notable Ships

Argentina; formerly, *Pennsylvania*	1938–1958
Brazil; formerly, *Virginia*	1938–1957
Uruguay; formerly, *California*	1938–1958
Argentina	1958–1969
Brasil	1958–1969

Main Subsidiaries

American Scantic Line

American Republics Line

References: René De La Pedraja, *The Rise and Decline of U.S. Merchant Shipping in the Twentieth Century* (New York: Twayne, 1992); Robert C. Lee, *Mr. Moore, Mr. McCormack—and the Seven Seas!* (New York: Newcomen Society, 1957); Henry S. Marcus, *Planning Ship Replacement in the Containerization Era* (Lexington, MA: Lexington Books, 1974); *New York Times*, 23 December 1956, 4 November 1962; Moore-McCormack, *A Profile of Maritime Progress, 1913–1963.*

MORGAN, CHARLES, 21 April 1795–8 May 1878. Charles Morgan had a career in shipping that stretched from the age of sailing vessels to iron steamers with compound engines;* likewise his business practices began in the tradition of a family firm complemented by changing partnerships and gradually advanced until he almost managed to make the transition to a modern corporate structure. He was born in Clinton, Connecticut, to a moderately prosperous farming family on 21 April 1795, and he studied in the local school until 1808, when, along with many other Connecticut men, he left to seek a better fortune in New York City. He did not arrive destitute, however, because two of his brothers had preceded him, and his parents continued to send him money to supplement his meager income working as a clerk in a grocery store. By 1815 he had opened his own store and had become a ship chandler providing supplies for vessels, and in 1819 he began to invest in sailing vessels. He made partial investments in many sailing vessels rather than in just a few, in order to spread the risk around should any ship be lost; he was quite successful with sailing vessels and did not dispose of his last holdings in sail until 1846. By the 1830s he had specialized in ocean transportation, no longer sold supplies or owned cargoes, and instead concentrated on the ownership and management of vessels.

Morgan has been hailed as the "father of coastwise* shipping" because when he and other associates put side-wheel steamers between New York and Charleston in June 1834, this was the first permanent scheduled service along the East Coast. He abandoned this Atlantic service in 1838, but already in 1837 he had placed ships in the routes within the Gulf of Mexico. His fleet of steamers in the Gulf gradually acquired the name of the Morgan Line,* although he had at times incorporated his ships under other company names. The first was the Southern Steamship Company in 1856, but this disintegrated with the impact of the Civil War, and a second attempt came with the incorporation of the Louisiana and Texas Railroad and Steamship Company in 1877, but coming so late in his life, it failed to displace the trade name of Morgan Line.

The Morgan Line was not his only business venture, and in 1850 he created the Morgan Iron Works, which he operated at a profit until 1867, when he sold the factory to naval shipbuilder John Roach. Morgan's shipping investments were not limited to the Morgan Line, and for service to Latin America and to San Francisco, he invested in separate firms, most notably the Empire City Line* and the Accessory Transit Company;* as late as 1877 he continued to move steamers around different trades wherever the demand for cargo was strongest.

Morgan profited tremendously from the Mexican War and the Civil War, and he found a new outlet for his mounting capital in railroads. Beginning with a small acquisition in 1857, Morgan acquired after the Civil War an extensive network of railroads that nicely complemented his steamship services. A very wealthy individual, worth at least $20 million, a fabulous sum for that day, he still wanted to achieve his long-held goal of establishing direct ocean transportation from New York City to the Gulf of Mexico and possibly also wanted one last fight. He ordered four modern steamers with the new compound engines in 1874 and the next year launched the service in ruthless competition against the Mallory Line.* The rate war lasted until 1878 and ended only because of his illness and subsequent death on 8 May. Morgan's talent for seizing the right business opportunity, his flexible deployment of ships to meet market demands, and his ability to understand new technologies were at the root of the extraordinary success of his long career in merchant shipping.

References: James P. Baughman, *Charles Morgan and the Development of Southern Transportation* (Nashville: Vanderbilt University Press, 1968); James P. Baughman, *The Mallorys of Mystic: Six Generations in American Maritime Enterprise* (Middletown, CT: Wesleyan University Press, 1972); Frederick E. Emmons, *American Passenger Ships: The Ocean Lines and Liners, 1873–1983* (Newark: University of Delaware Press, 1985).

MORGAN LINE or SOUTHERN PACIFIC STEAMSHIP COMPANY, 1834–1885. Morgan Line has been a catchall term to refer to the many steamers Charles Morgan* operated on the coastwise* trade of the Atlantic and Gulf coasts of the United States, including calls in Havana, Cuba, then generally regarded as natural extensions of the coastwise service. During his long career, Morgan generally used separate companies for the foreign trade, most notably the Empire City Line* and the Accessory Transit Company,* although he shifted his steamers among the different coastwise and foreign trade routes as the market dictated.

Morgan inaugurated regular coastwise steamship service between the North and the South in 1834, when he decided to place his side-wheel steamers along with those of his associate James P. Allaire in the route between New York and Charleston. Cargoes still traveled cheaper by sailing vessels, so passengers were the main source of revenue, but a series of shipwrecks destroyed the public's confidence in this coastwise service. Morgan withdrew his last steamers on the Atlantic service in 1838 and instead shifted all his steamers to the Gulf of Mexico, where he was already operating.

His side-wheel steamers with the single-expansion engines* of the time could not compete against sailing packets in the route between New York and the Gulf, so Morgan decided to limit his vessels to steaming along ports in the Gulf. His routes from New Orleans to Texas ports, which were expertly managed by his son-in-law Israel C. Harris since 1847, turned out to be the most lucrative both during the period of the Texas Republic and after annexation to the United States. The Mexican War provided a tremendous boost to the Morgan Line, many of whose ships were chartered* by the government, and even after the war was over, his ships were in demand for returning soldiers home. The large profits from the Mexican War gave Morgan the capital to invest in many of his later ventures.

Morgan continued to run his growing fleet of steamers under different loose arrangements and under the vague appellation of the Morgan Line, but in order to centralize operations in a formal structure, he and his associates incorporated the Southern Steamship Company in 1856. He still retained several steamers outside this structure for operation as he saw fit, but the Southern Steamship Company was on the way to becoming his real company until the Civil War shattered its existence.

Morgan profited no less from the Civil War than he had from the Mexican War, and he quickly reconstituted a large fleet of steamers for the coastwise trade once the conflict was over. The death of Harris in 1867 led Morgan to turn to another son-in-law, Charles A. Whitney, to handle not only the Morgan Line but also the new railroad enterprises. Already in 1857 Morgan had inaugurated railways to complement his steamships, and after the Civil War he acquired and built many miles of railroad in the south. His plans gradually moved toward the creation of a rail and ship network throughout the South and with links to Mexico and Cuba. A final consolidation took place in 1877, when the Louisiana and Texas Railroad and Steamship Company was incorporated to handle all of Morgan's assets.

Morgan still wanted to realize his goal of ocean service from New York to the Gulf of Mexico, and in 1874 he ordered four steamships whose new compound engines* were sure to drive out the single-expansion engines the Mallory Line* was still using in that route. When the first Morgan Line steamer began operation in July 1875, a ferocious rate war erupted with the Mallory Line, which the next year ordered new steamers to meet the competition. The rate war raged until March 1878, when Morgan took ill, and his son-in-law Whitney negotiated an agreement to end the bitter dispute and divide the trade among themselves. Henceforth the Morgan Line and the Cromwell Line* divided the cargoes in the New York–New Orleans route, while the Mallory Line monopolized the New York–Galveston route.

When Morgan died on 8 May 1878, Whitney continued as the head of the Morgan Line and its main corporate expression, the Louisiana and Texas Railroad and Steamship Company. When Whitney died on 29 October 1882, no other family member wished to continue the business, and the next year the heirs agreed to sell most of their stock to railroad magnate Collis P. Huntington, whose railroad holdings thus stretched from San Francisco to New Orleans. Huntington merged his properties into the Southern Pacific Company, which henceforth operated the Morgan Line. In 1902 the Southern Pacific added the Cromwell Line to the Morgan Line, which in 1926 operated twenty-three steamships and had just ordered its luxury coastwise liner, the *Dixie*. Although the Morgan Line name was retained as late as 1939, it was increasingly replaced by the new name of Southern Pacific Steamship Company. Shortly after U.S.

entry into World War II, the railroad company abandoned ocean transportation, and the Southern Pacific Steamship Company ceased to exist.

Principal Executives

Charles Morgan	1834–1878
Israel C. Harris	1847–1867
Charles A. Whitney	1867–1882

Some Notable Ships

Creole	1907–1933
Dixie	1938–1941

References: James. P. Baughman, *Charles Morgan and the Development of Southern Transportation* (Nashville: Vanderbilt University Press, 1968); Robert G. Albion, *The Rise of New York Port, 1815–1860* (New York: Scribner's, 1934); James P. Baughman, *The Mallorys of Mystic: Six Generations in American Maritime Enterprise* (Middletown, CT: Wesleyan University Press, 1972); Frederick E. Emmons, *American Passenger Ships: The Ocean Lines and Liners, 1873–1983* (Newark: University of Delaware Press, 1985); *Nautical Gazette*, 14 August 1926.

MORRO CASTLE, **1930–1934.** The worst ocean disaster of a U.S.-flag vessel was the shipwreck of the *Morro Castle* in 1934 (the *Titanic*,* although U.S.-owned, flew the British flag). The *Morro Castle* was a combination cargo-passenger vessel with accommodations for 534 persons (439 first class, 95 tourist); the ship was 482 feet long and had a beam of 71 feet and could reach a speed of twenty knots with her turboelectric drive (see marine propulsion). The Ward Line,* a subsidiary of the Atlantic, Gulf and West Indies Steamship Lines* (AGWI), had obtained government subsidies to build the *Morro Castle* and her sister ship, *Oriente*, for service in the New York-Havana route. Lavish mail subsidies further underwrote the operation of these vessels, which had been designed to compete against the Cunard Line, whose North Atlantic liners since 1929 had started to make winter trips in the New York-Havana route. These inroads or "poaching" on a traditional American preserve had been deeply resented by this AGWI line, which planned to regain its control over the route with the *Morro Castle* and the *Oriente*.

When the two new ships entered service, the company soon realized it had blundered, first because the turboelectric drive proved a bad investment and second because it was difficult to fill the ship with passengers or high-value cargoes. Cut fares and phony propaganda attracted passengers, but only if crew costs were slashed, which meant often hiring incompetent or inexperienced personnel. For cargoes, the ships had to take anything to try to fill the holds, but the steadiest volume of merchandise came from secret arms sales to the Cuban dictators Gerardo Machado, until 1933, and afterward Fulgencio Batista. A major attraction during Prohibition* was serving liquor aboard, which, combined with a publicity campaign aimed at single travelers, conveyed the image of a "love boat," where many could meet and have fun with the opposite sex; unfortunately single females were more numerous than bachelors on most trips, and in the last voyage there were two single women for each bachelor.

In spite of these allurements, AGWI was taking heavy losses mainly because of the *Morro Castle* and the *Oriente*. The challenge from the winter cruises by the British ships proved transient, but even more serious black clouds loomed ahead. Pan American Lines had begun airplane flights to Cuba from the United States, beginning a slow but permanent erosion in those passengers who before had to use the ships because there was no other way to travel between both countries. The repeal of Prohibition on 5 December 1933 eliminated alcohol as a lure to attract passengers, many of whom in any case preferred not to repeat the voyage because of the inferior service generally provided on board.

When the *Morro Castle* left New York City on her 174th voyage on 1 September 1934, she had less than 60 percent passenger occupancy and had her usual secret complement of arms cargo. After arrival in Havana on 4 September, those persons whose final destination was Havana debarked, while new passengers, mostly Cubans traveling to New York, boarded the ship. The cargo was unloaded (including the arms, crated as "sporting goods"), and new merchandise went into the holds, including foul-smelling salted hides; to keep the stench from bothering passengers, Captain Robert Wilmott turned off the ventilation in the holds, thereby automatically disconnecting the smoke detection system. He further ordered that the ventilation system not be turned back on until the last passenger had left the ship in New York City, but because Chief Officer William Warms was not informed of this decision, the latter continued to believe the instruments would report any fire.

At 6:00 P.M. on 5 September the ship left Havana for the return voyage to New York. Captain Wilmott stayed in his cabin most of the time, as he had done during the whole voyage, partly because of illness but also because he feared someone would kill him. On 7 September at 7:48 P.M. Captain Wilmott was found dead in his cabin, and command of the ship passed to Chief Officer Warms. That same night, at 2:50 A.M. on 8 September, smoke was detected in the upper decks.

Both the ship's equipment and the crew were totally unprepared to face the fire, and soon the whole ship was ablaze, with the flames gradually spreading to the lower decks. By 3:15 A.M. the fire was visible from shore and by ships ten miles away, but because the acting captain could not see the fire himself from the bridge and the smoke detection system suggested a very small flame, considerable time elapsed before he finally authorized sending the SOS, right before the radio room was on the verge of being engulfed by flames. By then, panic had seized both the passengers and the ill-trained crew, and unauthorized and inexpert persons had lowered lifeboats into the water. People started jumping into the sea in the vain attempt to try to swim to the distant New Jersey shore, while a bungled rescue operation by the Coast Guard* allowed many to freeze and die in the water. What was most shameful were the lurid accounts of crew members' fleeing to save their lives and leaving most passengers to fend for themselves; of the 316 passengers,

91 died, but of the 230 officers and crew, only 31 died. The stampede was led by the chief engineer himself, who abandoned his post and commandeered a lifeboat for himself and some crew members. Acting Captain Warms had made mistakes, but he was the last person to leave the ship, which by then was completely out of control and shortly after ran aground off Asbury Park in New Jersey. The hazardous fire conditions and shameful performance of the crew reflected negatively on the civilian Bureau of Marine Inspection and Navigation,* whose authority to license officers and inspect ships was severely questioned but not revoked because the Coast Guard's performance had been far from exemplary.

What caused the fire and shipwreck of the *Morro Castle*? The standard accounts have concentrated on the activities of officers and crew aboard the ship, and Chief Radio Officer George Rogers eventually emerged as the main culprit who started the fire. The radio officer suffered from hereditary mental disorders that made his adjustment to life virtually impossible, and his psychological and criminal record before and after the *Morro Castle* shipwreck confirmed his tendency toward violent and destructive actions as a way to obtain necessary recognition. Arson set the ship ablaze, and Rogers later bragged of having started the fire, but was he simply a lone, demented individual?

Since the late 1980s two authors, Frederick R. Asmussen and Robert McDonnell, have been trying through the Freedom of Information Act to obtain the release of secret Federal Bureau of Investigation (FBI) files on the *Morro Castle* shipwreck in order to confirm and detail their preliminary findings. According to these authors, Captain "Wilmott absolutely was not murdered" (*New York Times*, 6 November 1988) and instead died of natural causes. The other hypothesis of a communist plot to stop the flow of arms into Cuba was false, and the authors' conclusion was "that the fire that sank the *Morro Castle* was an insurance fraud plot gone awry" (*Journal of Commerce*, 10 February 1988). The AGWI faced chronic losses as a result of bad management and, specifically, the blunder of ordering the *Morro Castle* and *Oriente*, so there was certainly ample financial motive. If one ship disappeared and the company collected the insurance money, as actually happened, the financial problems of AGWI were postponed for at least ten years. Amateur detectives may pour over the existing accounts of the shipwreck to see how the insurance fraud scam would account for many unexplainable actions and events. However, even if the federal government were to release the files (withheld on the grounds of "national security"), since almost all investigations neglected the company angle, it is very probable that the exact nature of the insurance fraud and how and why the plotters lost full control of events may never be known.

References: *Journal of Commerce*, February 10, 1989; *New York Times*, 6 November 1988; Gordon Thomas and Max M. Witts, *Shipwreck: The Strange Fate of the Morro Castle* (New York: Dorest Press, 1972).

MORSE, CLARENCE G., 7 February 1904–1990s? Clarence G. Morse was head of the Maritime Administration* (MARAD) in 1955–1960 and president of Pacific Far East Lines* (PFEL) in 1960–1962. He was born in Jennings, Louisiana, on 7 February 1904 and studied at the University of California, where he received a B.S. degree in 1926 and a law degree in 1928. He practiced admiralty and regulatory law in San Francisco for many years and later came to Washington, D.C., to become the general counsel for the Federal Maritime Board* (FMB) in 1954. In 1955 he was appointed head of MARAD and brought the agency into close relations with shipowners. As part of his policy of promoting the merchant marine, he adopted self-regulation of conferences* as the best way to reduce the regulatory burden on U.S. steamship companies. The shippers* violently disagreed and promptly sought protection elsewhere, specifically in the Celler Committee,* whose revelations paved the path toward the creation of the Federal Maritime Commission* (FMC) as an institution to protect the interests of shippers and not of shipowners.

Morse resigned in May 1960 to become president of PFEL, whose new owner, Ralph K. Davies, asked him to correct the irregularities Thomas C. Cuffe had left behind in that company. However, the management of PFEL proved vexing for Morse, and Davies had to ask for his resignation after barely eighteen months in office. Morse returned to private law practice in the firm of Graham and Morse in San Francisco, until the Richard Nixon administration appointed him in 1971 to become a commissioner of the FMC. Morse tried to correct the pro-shipper bias in the FMC, and he served as commissioner until 1977. Morse's career illustrated well the revolving door principle of how officials moved back and forth between government and private shipping interests.

References: René De La Pedraja, *The Rise and Decline of U.S. Merchant Shipping in the Twentieth Century* (New York: Twayne, 1992); Samuel A. Lawrence, *United States Merchant Shipping Policies and Politics* (Washington, DC: Brookings Institution, 1966); John Niven, *The American President Lines and Its Forebears, 1848–1984* (Newark: University of Delaware Press, 1987); *Weekly Compilation of Presidential Documents*, 16 August 1971.

MOVIES. Movies contributed to shape the image Americans held about the U.S. merchant marine, but unfortunately Hollywood has rarely shown any deep interest in the subject for the period after the introduction of the steam engine, so that steamships and seamen have served mainly as the backdrops for plot twists that unfold on land and with no real link to the merchant marine. Hundreds of movies have some scenes about ships, but then the plot quickly shifts to activities on land; if the action continued aboard the ships, then the focus was on the private lives and adventures of the passengers on the passenger liners. In almost all cases Hollywood has not considered the merchant vessels and their crews of the post–sailing age as "marketable" enough to make a whole movie, and this neglect has been one more indication of how generally out of mainstream the merchant marine has been regarded; the world of the shipowner and the whole business community that managed the ships has scarcely been noticed in the movies.

Many movies, especially those about pirates, covered the life aboard sailing ships, but the transition to steam somehow dulled, if not ended, the interest of movie directors, unless they could tie the ships into another major theme, in particular, the struggle against the sea as a variation of man against nature. Swashbuckling films about pirates in the sailing age have been a Hollywood staple, but if we believe the movies, piracy ended with the introduction of steel and steam, which has simply not been the case. The classic novels of the sailing age, such as *Billy Budd* (1962) of Herman Melville, have, of course, been brought to the screen, but one novel of the sailing age, *The Sea Wolf* (1941), based on the Jack London novel, was perhaps the only film that suggested the transition from the sailing age to steamships. In the *Sea Wolf* (of which six other film versions exist) the good brother aboard an armed steam vessel tracks down the sadistic Wolf Larsen, the captain of his own sailing ship; the scenes in the film imply the replacement of a more barbaric age of sail and wood by a more placid and civilized age of steam and steel.

''Disaster'' films have been a popular theme for Hollywood in the twentieth century, and the most popular of all have been the films about the *Titanic** tragedy, none of which bothered to inform viewers that the British-flag film was owned by an American corporation, the International Mercantile Marine.* While the 1958 British film *A Night to Remember* provided the best reconstruction and did not engage in the melodramatic accounts of the lives of passengers, Hollywood shifted the focus back to the passengers in the dramatic *Titanic* of 1953, the most spectacular of the many films about the voyage of that ill-fated vessel. Nevertheless the 1953 *Titanic* film did deal with the salient facts, and the combination of reality with fictional characters set the stage for the latter Hollywood development of the ''docudrama'' as a spin-off from the disaster movies.

Until World War II the U.S. merchant marine rarely figured in films, and these few frequently failed to distinguish between American and foreign crewmen; *China Seas* (1935) about the adventures of the captain of a tramp* vessel in China was a rare exception. World War II for the first time brought the U.S. merchant marine to public attention. The impact the war was having on merchant seamen was first brought to the public in *The Long Voyage Home* (1940), one of the masterpieces of director John Ford and based on the plays of Eugene O'Neill. Several other war films about the merchant marine followed, but the one that American seafarers most wished to be remembered by was *Action on the North Atlantic* (1943),* which cast Humphrey Bogart as the chief mate of a vessel in the deadly run to Murmansk, Russia. Alfred Hitchcock's suspense drama, *Lifeboat* (1944), should not be overlooked, because it reflects the fears of so many seafarers of being cast adrift in the middle of the ocean.

After World War II was over, Hollywood again lost interest in the merchant marine, although *Mister Roberts* (1955), a box office hit about a cargo vessel of the Navy Transport Service, provided some glimpses; for example, the captain, who had been accustomed to operate in the merchant marine in a totally arbitrary manner, felt he could treat civilians drafted for the war effort in the same way. *Gun Cargo** (1949), where a shipowner fired his crew and then had to rehire them to deliver the cargo, was the one movie that for the first time dealt squarely with key issues of the merchant marine, but unfortunately the movie was doomed by an atrocious performance. On a lighter note, Walt Disney's *Bon Voyage* (1962), although dismissed by critics as superficial, has the redeeming value that camera crews came aboard the *United States** to shoot the film, thereby capturing on film the rapidly vanishing world of the transatlantic passenger liners to Europe.

In a rare event, Hollywood took a close look at the longshoremen on the docks in the controversial movie *On the Waterfront** (1954), but here again it paralleled the ship movies about the passengers: the docks were just the backdrop for personal drama, and *On the Waterfront* really did not explore the dynamics of longshoremen and often misrepresented or exaggerated the abuses still existing in the early 1950s.

While movies about the sea or the U.S. Navy remained popular with Hollywood, the more specific area of shipping and merchant ships, with the single exception of disasters, seemed to have dropped out from the acceptable repertoire of subjects for directors. The Home Box Office (HBO) decided in 1992 to make a docudrama on another of the disasters of the merchant marine, this time the shipwreck of the *Exxon Valdez.** The resulting film, *Dead Ahead: The Exxon Valdez Disaster,** although not shown in movie theaters, was broadcast repeatedly over the cable network, which had over 17 million subscribers; this last film, more than anything else, has reinforced the public's image of the merchant marine as little more than drunken incompetents, the oil companies as greedy, bumbling fools, and government officials as sly, cowardly politicians.

In the final analysis, the merchant marine has rarely been a subject for movies, so the public at best could obtain only a fragmentary idea about its real activities or problems. Certainly the image could be helped by favorable films such as *Action on the North Atlantic* or hurt by *Dead Ahead: The Exxon Valdez Disaster*, but the underlying problem remained the unspoken assumption by most Americans that the merchant marine was no longer really a part of the mainstream of American life. See also Literature.

References: *Magill's Survey of Cinema* (Englewood Cliffs, NJ: Salem Press, 1980); Jay R. Nash and Stanley R. Ross, *The Motion Picture Guide, 1937–1983* (Chicago: Cinebooks, 1986).

MULZAC, HUGH, 26 March 1886–31 January 1971. Hugh Mulzac was the first person of African origin to command a U.S.-flag merchant ship. As with many of the American black leaders before World War II, Mulzac was a native of the British West Indies, and he was born in Union Island (near Grenada) on 26 March 1886. He completed secondary school in St. Vincent Island before he began to sail aboard wooden vessels and then steam schooners. He saw no future in remaining a simple sailor and decided to invest his savings in studying at the Swansea Nautical College in Wales; eventually he earned the second mate's license. Afterward he served aboard British ships until he finally reached the

United States and became a naturalized American citizen in 1918. He later earned a perfect score on his examinations for master in the United States. Before World War I maritime unions did not allow blacks or persons of other races to join unions, but because of the acute shortage of trained personnel during World War I, he was able to sail as a mate without union papers; once the emergency was over and blacks were no longer needed, Mulzac was left without a job. Mulzac was able to serve as chief officer during Marcus Garvey's attempt to organize the Black Star Line,* but when that ill-fated attempted failed, Mulzac was able to find employment aboard ships only as a cook, because on the East Coast the steward's department had been "reserved" for blacks.

With U.S. entry into World War II, a tremendous shortage of trained seamen again presented itself, and through intensive lobbying efforts from many associations, including the new National Maritime Union* (NMU), Mulzac was at last able to obtain the command of the Liberty* ship the *Booker T. Washington* in 1942. The War Shipping Administration* (WSA) made one last attempt to run a blacks-only ship, but when the NMU guaranteed to provide an integrated crew, Mulzac finally obtained the command of a racially integrated ship. The *Booker T. Washington* served in combat areas and completed twenty-two voyages before being decommissioned after the war ended.

Mulzac had achieved his lifelong desire, but this remarkable triumph did not bring a happy ending. After having served the United States loyally during two world wars, in 1951 the Cold War hysteria unjustly blacklisted Mulzac and another 2,000 American seafarers from service aboard ships. After constant and long appeals, the courts finally overturned the sanction, but by then he and hundreds of other suspects had been permanently driven from the sea. Until the end of his life, Mulzac remained active in causes to promote the welfare of black people and of seamen in particular, and not surprisingly, the House Un-American Activities Committee tried to get him to testify against supposed subversives in 1960. He retired to live in St. Vincent Island in 1962 but returned to New York in December 1970, where he died shortly after on 31 January 1971.

References: W. Augustus Low, *Encyclopedia of Black America* (New York: McGraw-Hill, 1981); Hugh Mulzac, *A Star to Steer By* (New York: International, 1963); *New York Times*, 1 February 1971.

MUNSON, FRANK C., 13 January 1876–24 September 1936. Frank C. Munson was president of the Munson Steamship Company* from 1916 to 1936. He was born in Havana, Cuba, on 13 January 1876; his father, Walter D. Munson,* was running a fleet of sailing vessels to bring Cuban sugar and molasses to New York City. In 1882, when his father moved the company offices to New York City, Frank returned to the United States and graduated from Adelphi Academy in 1895. The next year he began working in his father's company, and after the Munson Steamship Company was incorporated in 1899, he began to climb through positions, becoming vice president upon his father's death in 1908.

Carlos W. Munson, the brother of Frank, became president but for some reason soon tired of the job and in 1916 formally handed over the presidency to Frank, who really had been in charge of the company for some years.

Munson did not take advantage of the sale of surplus World War I vessels to acquire ownership of a large fleet to handle the trade with Cuba and continued to rely on the charter* of foreign-flag vessels to haul the Cuban sugar harvest. He did operate for the Shipping Board* four combination cargo-passenger vessels on the New York–east coast of South America route in 1920–1925 and in that last year bought the four vessels. The company was already having difficulties meeting its mounting debt obligations, and only the granting of very lucrative mail contracts under the Merchant Marine Act of 1928* kept the company afloat. Munson tried to obtain an additional mail contract for the Gulf of Mexico–east coast of South America route, but was beaten in the intense rivalry by the Delta Line.*

The Great Depression further undermined the Munson Line, and in 1934 he was seeking to sell the company to the International Mercantile Marine* (IMM), but the negotiations failed to reach agreement before the Munson Line entered bankruptcy in April 1934. Munson tried desperately to keep his line afloat and managed to continue operations under the protection of bankruptcy proceedings. On 22 September 1936 he suffered an automobile accident and died on 24 September. His brother Carlos returned to the presidency of what was left of the Munson Line, but he could not save the company, which dissolved in 1939.

References: *New York Maritime Register*, 30 September 1936; Record Group 32, National Archives, Washington, DC; *New York Times*, 1 July 1938, 20 November 1939; Vertical File M 100 in G. W. Blunt White Library, Mystic Seaport, Mystic, Connecticut.

MUNSON, WALTER D., 18 February 1843–24 April 1908. Walter D. Munson was the founder of the Munson Steamship Company* and remained its president until his death. He was born in Litchfield, Connecticut, on 18 February 1843 and married before the Civil War began. He enlisted as a private in a Connecticut regiment and reached the rank of captain before the war was over. In 1868 he emigrated with his wife to Havana, where his son Frank C. Munson* was born. Walter engaged in the sugar and molasses business and in 1873 purchases his first sailing ship to carry cargoes from Havana to New York City, and by 1882, when he established his offices in New York City, he owned a fleet of four sailing vessels. In 1893 he purchased his first three steamers, and others followed to provide service to other parts of Cuba, Mexico, and the U.S. Gulf Coast. In 1899, after the Spanish-American War, he incorporated the Munson Steamship Company; his two sons, Frank and Carlos, had already been working with him in the family business. On 24 April 1908 Walter died, and his son Carlos became president of the Munson Line, although the real successor was Frank, who by 1913 had become the head of the company.

References: Frederick E. Emmons, *American Passenger Ships: The Ocean Lines and Liners, 1873–1983* (Newark: University of Delaware Press, 1985); Vertical File M 100 in G. W. Blunt White Library, Mystic Seaport, Mystic, Connecticut.

MUNSON STEAMSHIP COMPANY or MUNSON LINE, 1899–1939. The Munson Line operated in the trade between Cuba and the United States throughout its entire history and also operated other services between the United States and the east coast of South America. After the Civil War, Walter D. Munson* emigrated to Havana to engage in the sugar and molasses business and in 1873 was already chartering* sailing vessels to transport cargoes to the United States. In 1882 he moved his offices to New York City, and in 1893 he purchased his first three steamers, and soon he had a fleet of steamships linking New York City with Cuban, Gulf, and Mexican ports. The Spanish-American War disrupted activities temporarily, but at the same time the expulsion of Spain opened Cuba completely to American enterprises. To take advantage of the new opportunities, in 1899 he incorporated the Munson Steamship Company, or Munson Line, as it was generally called. Its ships stopped on the new sugar ports springing up in the north coast of Cuba and returned either to New York City or Mobile. By 1910 the Munson Line had also begun to haul lumber from Mobile to Argentina and other east coast ports of South America.

The main business of the line, however, remained hauling the sugar harvest of Cuba, a seasonal task that did not keep his ships full the whole year and hence forced the company to adopt measures to remain profitable. In order to reduce the idle time, the Munson Line did not buy new vessels and instead chartered large numbers of foreign-flag ships just for the harvest. The line did everything possible to keep its labor costs low, and in a time of generalized atrocious conditions for seafarers, only the most destitute of sailors worked aboard the line's "hell ships." The Munson Line also used its position in the Cuba trade to negotiate a lucrative arrangement with the Ward Line:* the latter agreed to pay Munson a yearly amount in exchange for staying out of the New York-Havana route.

The Munson Line, under the direction of Frank C. Munson* since 1913, was able to reap large profits during the World War I shipping shortage, but because the company owned so few ships and saw most of its charters canceled, the profits were not as huge as could have been expected if the company had owned a larger percentage of the vessels it operated, and therefore the company missed a great opportunity to increase its capital. In 1920 the Munson Line became a managing operator* and was assigned by the Shipping Board* four combination cargo-passenger vessels (the Pan America Line) for service in the New York-east coast of South American route; in 1925 the Shipping Board, because of continuing losses on that service, sold the Pan America Line to Munson, which hoped to make the service profitable by increasing the refrigerator capacity of the vessels. Meanwhile, in the Cuba sugar trade, the mainstay of the company's business, the Munson Line was starting to show losses because of serious competition from outsiders* such as Hans Isbrandtsen,* who had learned the game of chartering foreign-flag vessels to depress rates during the harvest season.

The generous mail subsidies of the Merchant Marine Act of 1928* bailed out the Munson Line, which already by 1927 was having difficulty surviving a crushing debt burden. Only more mail subsidies could save the company, and President Munson attempted desperately in 1929 to obtain another mail contract, this time for the route in the Gulf of Mexico, only to have Delta Line* receive the award in 1930. President Munson had also established the beginnings of a cruise business to Bahamas and to Bermuda, but these pioneering ventures proved unsuccessful. The Great Depression struck the company very hard, and to try to avert bankruptcy, the Munson family attempted to sell the line to the International Mercantile Marine* (IMM) in January 1934, but the negotiations failed to reach an agreement before the Munson Line fell into bankruptcy in April 1934.

The company continued to operate under the protection of the bankruptcy court, but whatever slim chances the Munson Line had of recovering disappeared when Frank C. Munson died on 24 September 1936 as a result of an automobile accident. His brother Carlos W. Munson (who had managed the firm briefly before) became president and tried hard to impose a reorganization plan that would allow the Munson Line to charter from the government the modernized *California,* *Pennsylvania*, and *Virginia* as replacements for its World War I combination cargo-passenger ships in the South American trade. The plan foundered, the U.S. Maritime Commission* repossessed the remaining vessels of the Munson Line in 1938, and the stockholders had no choice but to accept dissolution of the company in 1939.

Principal Executives

Walter D. Munson	1899–1908
Carlos W. Munson	1908–1913; 1936–1939
Frank C. Munson	1908–1936

Some Notable Ships

American Legion	1921–1938
Pan America	1921–1938
Southern Cross	1922–1938
Western World	1922–1938

References: René De La Pedraja, *The Rise and Decline of U.S. Merchant Shipping in the Twentieth Century* (New York: Twayne, 1992); Frederick E. Emmons, *American Passenger Ships: The Ocean Lines and Liners, 1873–1983* (Newark: University of Delaware Press, 1985); Frank F. Farrar, *A Ship's Log Book* (St. Petersburg, FL: Great Outdoor, 1988); *Journal of Commerce*, 3, 4 January, April 21, 1934; *Nautical Gazette*, 21 November 1925, 29 December 1928; *New York Times*, 1 July 1938, 20 November 1939; Record Group 32, National Archives, Washington, DC; U.S. Congress, House, Committee on the Merchant Marine and Fisheries, *Special Diplomatic and Consular Reports* (Washington, DC: Government Printing Office, 1913).

MURPHY, JOHN M., 3 August 1926–present. John M. Murphy was the chairman of the Merchant Marine and Fisheries Committee* of the House of

Representatives in 1977–1981 and became notorious because of his involvement in several scandals. Murphy was born in Staten Island, New York, on 3 August 1926 and attended public schools and La Salle Military Academy, where he struck up a lifelong friendship with the future dictator of Nicaragua, Anastasio Somoza "Tachito." Murphy served in World War II and in 1946 obtained an appointment to West Point, from which he graduated in 1950, just in time to serve in the Korean War. He returned to civilian life in 1956 and ran various transportation businesses in Staten Island. Eventually he became involved in local Democratic party politics and was elected to the House of Representatives in 1962, where he served continuously until January 1981.

The strong maritime interests of his district made natural his membership in the Merchant Marine and Fisheries Committee, whose chairman he became in January 1977. He had barely taken office when charges surfaced that he had received hefty campaign contributions in exchange for supporting legislation favorable to shipping companies. His friendship with Somoza had blossomed into a deal to construct a refinery in Nicaragua to process shipments of oil from Iran, and although the proposal was later abandoned, Murphy's role in lining up financing was very clear. After the Panama Canal Treaties of 1977, the House had to pass implementing legislation, and for a brief moment Murphy played a central role in national politics as he maneuvered to secure the approval of the Merchant Marine and Fisheries Committee. Originally Murphy had opposed bitterly the Panama Canal Treaties, but accepting defeat in that battle, as a politician, he was willing "to make Panama implementing legislation a hostage in exchange for a revision in the administration's policy toward Nicaragua" (Jorden 1984). The Jimmy Carter administration did soften its policy to Somoza, but Murphy's efforts for his friend were in vain, and the uprising by the Nicaraguan people finally forced the hated dictator to flee in July 1978.

So many allegations about Murphy's dealings continued to float that the Federal Bureau of Investigation (FBI) made him one of the targets for its ABSCAM sting operation. A grand jury indicted him on conspiracy and bribery charges on 18 June 1980, but he still hoped to have the voters vindicate his innocence by his reelection in November. Unfortunately Murphy lost by a landslide to a Republican challenger, and the defeated congressman later was convicted and spent sixteen months in a federal penitentiary. After his release he returned to live in Staten Island, New York, where he has remained involved in various businesses. Murphy's conviction and the accusations against the former chairman of the Committee on Merchant Marine and Fisheries, Edward A. Garmatz,* did considerable public relations damage to merchant shipping, whose public image was not helped by the 1987 conviction on charges unrelated to merchant shipping of Mario Biaggi, the chairman of the House subcommittee on merchant marine.

References: *American Shipper*, November, December 1980; Bernard Diederich, *Somoza and the Legacy of U.S. Involvement in Central America* (Maplewood, NJ: Waterfront Press, 1989); William J. Jorden, *Panama Odyssey* (Austin: University of Texas

Press, 1984); *New York Times*, 18 August 1977; Robert A. Pastor, *Condemned to Repetition: The United States and Nicaragua* (Princeton, NJ: Princeton University Press, 1987); U.S. Congress, *Biographical Directory of the United States Congress, 1774–1989* (Washington, DC: Government Printing Office, 1989).

MYERS, FREDERICK ("BLACKIE"), 17 May 1907–1980s? Frederick Myers was a vice president of the National Maritime Union* (NMU) and made the last serious attempt to reestablish Communist party control over the union. At the time of the Ferdinand Smith* crisis in 1944, the communists had threatened to remove Joseph Curran* from the presidency and to replace him with Myers; the tension intensified during the attempted resignation of NMU treasurer M. Hedley Stone* in 1945, with the union splitting into pro-Curran and pro-Myers factions. The latter was gradually losing ground and also lost the effort to keep the NMU in the brief-lived Committee for Maritime Unity.* For the 1946 election, Myers dropped his threat to run for president and did not even bother to seek reelection as vice president. Shortly after, Myers retired from active life; whatever communist menace may have existed was over. Nevertheless, Curran continued relentlessly his "anticommunist" campaign until 1950, partly to compensate for his long years of collaboration with communists but mainly to eliminate all opposition to his personal dictatorship in the NMU.

References: Richard O. Boyer, *The Dark Ship* (New York: Little, Brown, 1947); Beth McHenry and Frederick N. Myers, *Home Is the Sailor: The Story of an American Seaman* (New York: International, 1948); *Who's Who in Labor, 1946* (New York: Dryned Press, 1946).

N

NANKING. See *Congress.*

NATIONAL BULK CARRIERS. See Ludwig, Daniel K.

NATIONAL DEFENSE RESERVE FLEET (NDRF), 1946–present. The National Defense Reserve Fleet (NDRF) has comprised the merchant vessels that the Maritime Administration* (MARAD) maintained in varying stages of readiness to meet emergencies. The Ship Sales Act of 1946* created the NDRF to keep a number of World War II surplus vessels in usable condition; with the NDRF Congress hoped to avoid the mistake after World War I of selling off too many of the surplus vessels and leaving the government without any reserve stockpile of ships. MARAD took out many ships for the Korean and Vietnam wars, as well as smaller numbers for other international crises, the most recent being the Gulf War. During 1958–1963 the docked ships were used as floating silos to store the record grain surpluses of the United States.

As the smaller ships of World War II were scrapped and replaced by larger vessels that MARAD acquired from U.S. steamship companies through trade-in programs, the number of ships in the NDRF steadily declined from 2,227 in 1950 to 1,027 in 1970. Originally NDRF comprised eight fleet sites, whose number was down to three by 1974. The ships have remained in three places: James River, Virginia, Beaumont, Texas, and Suisun Bay, California. In the late 1970s the Mariners* entered the NDRF, which had become a final stage in the life of commercially obsolete ships prior to the inevitable trip to the scrap yard. In 1976 the government created within the NDRF the Ready Reserve Fleet, whose ships could return to service in no more than ten days' notice; in 1987 the NDRF was down to 205 ships, 96 of which were in the Ready Reserve Fleet.

Already one year after NDRF's creation in 1946, proposals surfaced to transfer its functions to the U.S. Navy for operation as part of the Military Sealift Command,* and turf battles have continued to erupt between MARAD and the Defense Department over the NDRF. Some critics found the performance of the NDRF unsatisfactory during the Gulf War, not so much because of MARAD's fault but because so many of the ships dated back to World War II and were little more than "maritime cadavers." While scrapping the mothballed ships is easy and yields some money, finding modern replacements has such an exorbitant cost that no easy solution is in sight.

References: *American Shipper*, October 1990, September 1991; Ernst G. Frankel, *Regulation and Policies of American Shipping* (Boston: Auburn House, 1982); *Journal of Commerce*, 3 October 1988; Samuel A. Lawrence, *United States Merchant Shipping Policies and Politics* (Washington, DC: Brookings Institution, 1966); Maritime Administration, *Vessel Inventory Report 1987* and *1992*; L. A. Sawyer and W. H. Mitchell, *From America to United States*, 4 vols. (Kendal, England: World Ship Society, 1979–1986); *U.S. Statutes at Large*, vol. 60 (1946).

NATIONAL FEDERATION OF AMERICAN SHIPPING (NFAS), 1944–1953. The National Federation of American Shipping (NFAS) was the only umbrella organization that was ever able to represent virtually all the steamship companies in the United States, including tankers, colliers,* and bulk* carriers. As a federation, its membership consisted of other associations, some of which, however, had been especially constituted so as to qualify for affiliation in NFAS. As World War II came to an end, the disposal of the huge merchant fleet constructed during the war became a vital issue, and the shipowners created NFAS to make sure the government took into account their interests. Almon E. Roth* became the president of the new federation, but the multiplicity of conflicting interests within NFAS greatly hindered any effective lobbying, and consequently the Ship Sales Act of 1946* failed to incorporate key safeguards to protect the U.S.-flag merchant marine against the recuperating foreign fleets. Roth also failed to convince the Civil Aeronautics Board to lift the ban that kept steamship companies from offering aviation services.

When the National Maritime Union* (NMU), the International Longshoremen and Warehousemen's Union* (ILWU), and other labor groups created the Committee for Maritime Unity* (CMU) in 1946, this revitalized NFAS, because management was now forced to maintain a united front against labor's challenge. However, when CMU disintegrated because of interunion rivalry in 1947, NFAS lost a powerful reason to exist. Roth sensed the hopelessness and resigned in 1947 as president.

The federation was too big and unwieldy to accomplish any meaningful results, but more out of inertia than anything else it survived into the early 1950s.

President Frazer A. Bailey* tried in 1952 to rescue the federation: ''As far as results to date, working with the present type organization and without industry unity, they are far from satisfying to me'' (Papers of Robert L. Dennison). He explained that ''in a number of instances, recommendations come through from constituent associations for Federation action on matters of minor importance. . . . We should not dissipate our efforts over too large an area if we are to accomplish worthwhile results on primary matters.'' The solution was straightforward: ''It would seem desirable for us to concentrate upon subjects which are of the greatest importance to the greatest number, as well as those which are of *vital* importance to a lesser *number*'' (ibid.). Bailey's timely warnings went unheeded, while his resignation and retirement on 1 July 1953 unleashed a final round of personal and institutional struggles that resulted in the long-expected collapse of NFAS by September. One of the affiliates, the American Merchant Marine Institute* (AMMI), absorbed the offices and functions of NFAS. AMMI's role as chief lobbyist for shipowners were short-lived, however, because in 1954 the Committee of American Steamship Lines* (CASL), which formerly had existed as a committee within NFAS, assumed independent status to represent the subsidized liner companies. AMMI was left as the voice for most tanker companies and bulk carriers, as well as a few unsubsidized liner firms.

Principal Executives

Almon E. Roth	1944–1947
Frazer A. Bailey	1947–1953

References: *New York Times*, 7 September 1953; Papers of Robert L. Dennison, Harry S. Truman Library, Independence, Missouri; Shipping Policy Files, Record Group 59, National Archives, Washington, DC.

NATIONAL MARITIME COUNCIL (NMC), 1971–1987. The National Maritime Council was an advocacy organization that promoted the revitalization of the U.S.-flag merchant marine. What made NMC so singular in U.S. history was membership by the government, the shipowners, the shipbuilders, and the labor unions; shippers* were also members in an advisory capacity. No wide-ranging maritime coalition had been attempted since the National Merchant Marine Association* of 1919–1925, and the only successful organization for both shipowners and shipbuilders—the American Shipping and Industrial League*— dated back to 1886. In 1970 the founding members finally agreed to create NMC, which was formally organized in 1971. The most important tasks of the new council were to create a spirit of cooperation between labor and management and to induce shippers to utilize U.S.-flag vessels. In the first eight years NMC operated largely as a dependency of the Maritime Administration* (MARAD), which footed most of the bills and provided the support services, including work time from government employees. On 21 July 1978 the House Subcommittee on Commerce, Consumer, and Monetary Affairs blasted the cozy relationship and threatened a Justice Department antitrust investigation as well as criminal charges against MARAD employees. While some considered the relationships to be "incestuous," NMC chairman James R. Barker (also chairman of Moore-McCormack*) defended the cooperation among labor, management, and government as "wholly unique" (*American Shipper*, October 1978). To avoid possible political complications for the Jimmy Carter administration, Secretary of Commerce Juanita Kreps ordered MARAD to withdraw from NMC on 28 July 1978.

Shippers saw in the forced resignation of MARAD an opportunity to expand their role within NMC, because so far the shipper advisers had received "nothing more than a paperweight" and "a free meal" (*American Shipper*, November 1978). Shipowners and labor seized upon MARAD's departure in order to transform NMC into a top-level lobbying organization, with a full-time staff. NMC was soon preparing and distributing recommendations, particularly for a major overhaul of legislation in 1980 (the "Omnibus Bill"), but as NMC took a position on more issues, inevitably cracks appeared in the unwieldy coalition. When NMC supported foreign-built ships as a way to save U.S.-flag steamship companies, the shipyards in protest left the organization in 1983. The deregulatory environment created by the Shipping Act of 1984* persuaded the labor unions to consider withdrawing, and they too left in 1986. That same year came the bankruptcy of United States Lines,* the largest U.S.-flag company and the main financial backer of NMC.

Of the twelve U.S.-flag lines that had belonged in 1971, only four remained in 1987 (Sea-Land,* American President Lines,* Crowley Maritime Corporation,* and Lykes Brothers Steamship*), while the entry of four new members (Navieras de Puerto Rico,* Sea-Barge Group Inc., Totem Express Co., and Rainbow Navigation Co.) did not compensate for the loss of the other original members. Meanwhile the roster of advisory shippers had grown to 500, and a new shippers' committee organized within NMC in early 1987 gave hope that the organization could be saved. Shippers had a long list of grievances about NMC but resisted raising their token dues: "Shippers barely wanted to pay their share of lunch" (*American Shipper*, December 1987). Mounting deficits forced NMC to dissolve in November 1987, thereby ending a unique experiment in cooperation among the private sector. Henceforth each of the groups continued to be represented by its own narrow organization.

References: AFL-CIO, *Proceedings of the Thirteenth Constitutional Convention, 1979*; *American Shipper*, October, November 1978, May, December 1987; Ernst G. Frankel, *Regulation and Policies of American Shipping* (Boston: Auburn House, 1982); Gale Research, *Encyclopedia of Associations*, 1983–1989; *Journal of Commerce*, 14 October, 3 November 1987; *Who's Who in Washington 1983–1984*.

NATIONAL MARITIME UNION (NMU), 1937–1988. The National Maritime Union (NMU) was the principal union for seamen in the East and Gulf coasts and for almost twenty years was also the largest organization for seafarers in the United States. The NMU was during most of its life the personal instrument of its founder, Joseph Curran.* After the successful "fall strike" of 6 November 1936–January 1937, Curran, with the backing of the Communist party, decided to establish the new union. John L. Lewis had promised support from the Congress of Industrial Organizations (CIO) for the new NMU, which was duly founded on 5 May 1937. The majority of officers in the NMU were communists, but Curran remained the president. Membership had already reached 35,000 in July 1937, when an open convention drafted a constitution that guaranteed rights and electoral procedures to all seamen, making the NMU during its early years one of the most democratic unions in the United States. The union periodical, the *Pilot*, published lively debates and opened its columns to the rank and file.

A first divisive struggle erupted in 1938 when a faction led by Jerome King tried to challenge the control by Curran and his communist allies. When it was revealed that King and his followers were on the payroll of steamship companies and had the secret mission of trying to convert the new union into a docile group, the outraged membership blocked this last attempt at direct employer control of the NMU and expelled the divisive faction.

Besides a tremendous respect for democratic procedures, the NMU distinguished itself in the early years by two other causes. First, the NMU actively fought racial discrimination, in sharp contrast to the white supremacy policies of the ISU and its successor, the Seafarers' International Union* (SIU). In its contracts with shipowners, the NMU stipulated that no discrimination would be allowed on the base of race, color, or creed. A major success came when Captain Hugh Mulzac* became the first person of African origin ever to command a U.S.-flag merchant ship. Ferdinand Smith,* another black, was a vice president and later secretary of the union. Second, the NMU adopted a strong commitment to internationalism and proceeded to support workers throughout the world in their struggles. An early manifestation was the opposition to Nazi Germany and other fascist regimes. Aboard ships and on shore seamen were given classes on imperialism and colonialism so that they could understand the atrocious conditions they witnessed in foreign ports. The NMU threw itself wholeheartedly into World War II and to support the U.S. effort fulfilled its pledge of "keep 'em sailing." Once the war was over, the NMU engaged in one last burst of strike activities on behalf of international causes, most notably in Saigon in 1945 to protest the sending of U.S. military equipment to colonialists in French Indochina.

By then the communists' days in the NMU were coming to a end, because Curran was carefully orchestrating the campaign to gain full control over the union. A first skirmish in 1944 over Smith foreshadowed the bigger clash in 1945–1946. Curran cleverly brought over to his side the former communist treasurer of the NMU, M. Hedley Stone,* and now with unrestricted access to union funds, Curran was able to concentrate on eliminating the communist faction around Frederick Myers.* As the Cold War with its wave of hysterical anticommunist began, Curran could hurl charges against the communists to weaken their base; in the 1946 elections they were removed from crucial jobs, and for all practical purposes the communists had been eliminated.

The legacy of democratic practices in the NMU still restricted Curran, who now began a determined campaign to become the undisputed "boss" of the union, which from nearly 50,000 members before World War II had reached the all-time record of 100,000 by the end of the war. Curran had found the anticommunist theme so effective that he decided to continue to use it against any possible opposition groups, until he emerged by 1950 as the undisputed lord of his personal fiefdom. The removal of Jack Lawrenson* silenced the last independent voice and also brought control of the *Pilot* to Curran, who now turned it into a propaganda magazine to extol the virtues of his presidency.

Curran was less successful in dealing with rival unions. The NMU attempted to cooperate first with the Committee for Maritime Unity* (CMU) in 1946–1947 and again with the Conference of American Maritime Unions* (CAMU) in 1954–1955, but both attempts at keeping a truce with rival unions proved short-lived. Curran's own repression was driving members into the rival SIU, which managed to edge the NMU out of the Maritime Trades Department* (MTD) in the newly merged AFL-CIO starting in 1955.

When Curran suffered a heart attack in 1953, he allowed himself to become trapped in a circle of flatterers who were afraid to bring bad news before the union boss. The NMU "degenerated badly in the 1960s—with money scandals, inflated salaries for union officials, and every pretense of rank-and-file democracy stripped away" (*Encyclopedia of the American Left* 1990). The SIU under the aggressive Paul Hall* became an increasingly attractive alternative to many seamen, and by 1971 the SIU with over 80,000 members had surpassed the NMU, which claimed 50,000.

In 1973 Curran retired as president and among other benefits received a million-dollar lump-sump pension that further weakened the NMU's finances. His handpicked successor was Shannon J. Wall,* who struggled to repair the damage of previous decades. Membership continued to shrink, dropping to barely 15,000 in the early 1980s, and worse, the union's pension fund faced insolvency. NMU had barely celebrated its fiftieth anniversary in 1987 when Wall arranged in 1988 a hasty merger with District 1 of the Marine Engineers' Beneficial Association* (MEBA), whose head, C. E. "Gene" DeFries, became the president of the new union. Later it was discovered that Wall had benefited financially from the merger; union leaders claimed he "basically sold his members into political slavery in order to get rich" and that his attitude had been "To hell with the members' interests; put myself first" (*American Shipper*, May 1991). Wall remained as a vice president in the MEBA for a few years, until the outrage at the merger terms forced both his ouster and that of DeFries. As for NMU, both the beginning and the end of its career had been marked by turmoil.

Principal Labor Leaders

Joseph E. Curran ("Joe")   1937–1973

Shannon J. Wall   1973–1988

References: *American Shipper*, May 1991; Richard O. Boyer, *The Dark Ship* (New York: Little Brown, 1947); John J. Collins, *Bargaining at the Local Level* (New York: Fordham University Press, 1974); John J. Collins, *Never Off Pay: The Story of the Independent Tanker Union, 1937–1962* (New York: Fordham University Press, 1964); *Encyclopedia of the American Left* (New York: Garland, 1990); Walter Galenson, *The CIO Challenge to the AFL: A History of the American Labor Movement 1935–1941* (Cambridge: Harvard University Press, 1960); Helen Lawrenson, *Stranger at the Party: A Memoir* (New York: Random House, 1975); National Maritime Union, *This Is the NMU* (New York: William P. Gottlieb, 1954); Bruce Nelson, *Workers on the Waterfront: Seaman, Longshoremen, and Unionism in the 1930s* (Urbana: University of Illinois Press, 1990); William L. Standard, *Merchant Seamen: A Short History of Their Struggles* (New York: International, 1947).

NATIONAL MERCHANT MARINE ASSOCIATION, 1919–mid-1920s. At the end of World War I, the United States was left with a huge surplus fleet of cargo vessels. At a national merchant marine conference in Washington, D.C., in January 1919, the shipowners, shipbuilders, shippers,* and labor leaders united to create the National Merchant Marine Association (NMMA) in order to promote and defend a privately owned U.S.-flag merchant fleet. NMMA was the first such combination since the successful American Shipping and Industrial League* of 1886 and was created in spite of the opposition of the Shipping Board,* which rightly feared that the association would put private interests over national needs. The intent to influence Congress was evident in the election of Senator Joseph Ransdell of Louisiana to be its first president, who fought tirelessly to obtain passage of the Jones Act* of 1920. Only Ransdell's passion for U.S.-flag ships kept the association together, but "this gentleman's enthusiasm for the future of the national merchant marine is such, however, that he frequently advocates measures of relief which would be difficult of realization" (Public Record Office). Among more extreme proposals, in 1923 the NMMA requested that Congress grant preferential customs tariffs when cargo was carried on U.S.-flag ships, but in general the association adopted the positions of the American Steamship Owners' Association* (ASOA). The NMMA foolishly became involved in the struggle within the Shipping Board to favor one steamship line over another, and when the association failed to score any additional legislative successes, shipowners and shipbuilders (the strike of 1921* had crushed the labor unions) allowed NMMA to fold in the mid-1920s.

Nevertheless, its disappearance left a gap, and already in 1928 the Shipping

Board, which in 1919 had been skeptical of the NMMA, was calling for the creation of a new national association to group shipowners, shipbuilders, and "other allied activities." The plea was not heeded until nearly fifty years later when in 1971 the National Maritime Council* (NMC) at last united a broad coalition of maritime groups; until then only the Propeller Club* had partly filled the need for a common front.

Principal Executive

Senator Joseph E. Ransdell   1919–1924

References: Foreign Office 115/2859, Public Record Office, London, England; Adras Laborde, *Ransdell of Louisiana: A National Southerner* (New York: Benziger Brothers, 1951); Record Group 32, National Archives, Washington, DC; *New York Times*, 24 January, 19 March 1919; *U.S. Daily*, 25 April 1928.

NATIONAL SHIPPING AUTHORITY (NSA), 1951–present. The National Shipping Authority (NSA) has been an emergency agency for the acquisition and operation of merchant vessels. The NSA was created within the Maritime Administration* (MARAD) on 28 February 1951 to meet the simultaneous cargo demands of the Korean War and of coal and grain for Europe. Private companies could not provide sufficient cargo space, and in order to fight the Cold War in Europe and the Korean War in Asia, the government had no choice but to take vessels out of the National Defense Reserve Fleet* (NDRF) and place them under the control of the newly created NSA. Since November 1950 the government felt the need for a new organization and regretted the hasty liquidation in 1946 of the War Shipping Administration* (WSA), which now provided the pattern for the new NSA. Like its World War II predecessor, the NSA assigned ships to individual steamship companies for operation as general agents who were responsible for manning and maintaining the vessels at government expense, while NSA itself directly determined their routes, sailings, and cargoes. By August 1951 the NSA has assigned 273 freighters from the NDRF to forty-four general agents and had achieved effectively a rapid mobilization of the required merchant shipping.

The NSA had filled a crucial need, which, however, did not turn out to be permanent as originally expected. The demand for coal and grain cargoes to Europe slackened considerably by April 1952, by which time the needs of the Korean War were more than adequately covered. The NSA had stopped reactivating vessels and now began to return them to the NDRF. By October 1952 the NSA had in operation only 106 ships, after having returned 520 to the NDRF. The activities of the NSA were winding down rapidly in 1953, but MARAD did not allow NSA to be abolished and instead kept the agency as a skeleton organization ready in case of any emergency. During the Vietnam War MARAD did not formally reconstitute NSA because the demands of that conflict did not coincide with any other surge for cargo space. However, NSA was quite handy in providing the legal authorization and framework for reactivating a large number of vessels from the NDRF and their charter* to private operators, without the need to seek additional congressional authorization. In short, since the end of the Korean War NSA has remained as a legal mechanism within MARAD to meet possible shipping emergencies.

References: Samuel A. Lawrence, *United States Merchant Shipping Policies and Politics* (Washington, DC: Government Printing Office, 1966); Maritime Administration, *Annual Report, 1986*; *New York Times*, 30 November 1950, 15 March, 17 August 1951, 26 October 1952; Nicholas Johnson Oral History, Lyndon B. Johnson Presidential Library, Austin, Texas.

NATIONAL UNION OF MARINE COOKS AND STEWARDS. See Marine Cooks and Stewards, National Union of.

NAVIERAS DE PUERTO RICO, 1974–present. Navieras de Puerto Rico has been the U.S.-flag company that has provided ocean transportation for Puerto Rico, a U.S. possession in the Caribbean. Navieras, owned by the Commonwealth of Puerto Rico, has been one of the rare cases of government ownership in the United States and parallels the smaller example of the Alaska Marine Highway,* owned by the State of Alaska. The Commonwealth of Puerto Rico created Navieras on 10 June 1974 in response to the impending departure of Seatrain,* which had announced the cancellation of its services to the islands; in reality, however, the creation of Navieras responded to the long-felt needs of shippers* in the island who had often been neglected or even abandoned by other U.S.-flag companies. The government agreed to purchase the Puerto Rican service of Seatrain, as well as of Sea-Land* and Transamerican, all of whose assets and ships provided the base for Navieras to begin operations in October 1974 under its first director, Esteban Dávila Díaz. To avoid charges of mismanagement or government inefficiency, the actual operation of the company was placed in a private firm, the Puerto Rico Marine Management Inc., therefore combining the long-term stability of government ownership with commercial flexibility of a private business.

Navieras, as the largest company in the trade, stabilized ocean rates between the United States and Puerto Rico. In 1975 Seatrain and Sea-Land decided to return to the island and at least by their presence saved Navieras from charges of being an official monopoly. The return of the other two companies convinced some that Navieras was no longer necessary, and a new governor elected in 1977 attempted to sell off the company. Ironically, privatization failed because the banks that held the loans taken out to purchase the predecessor companies' assets in 1974 did not feel any of the bidders offered sufficient guarantees to meet the loan repayments, and in 1979 the Commonwealth took Navieras off the market.

In 1981 Seatrain suddenly abandoned the Puerto Rican service for the last time, and Navieras was there to fill in the gap in shipping services until transportation to the United States returned to normal. Other U.S. companies, when they had excess ships, were willing to come into the Puerto Rican trade when rates were high, but not always, and consequently most shippers agreed that to stabilize rates and keep them at reasonable levels, the existence of Navieras was essential. In effect, Navieras was in reality a subsidy not to the shippers but to the island consumers, who relied to a large degree on commodities imported from the U.S. mainland, and consequently the shipping company rarely earned profits, and its long-term debt was $250 million in 1991. The purchase of five Lancer-class containerships from the bankrupt United States Lines* (USL) in 1988 at a cost of $44,125,000 had been financed mainly with loans, while another $42.5 million dollars were needed to repair the ships whose maintenance had been neglected by Malcom McLean* in his last years as president of USL. A major political scandal erupted in Puerto Rico over these repair expenses and the purchase of the five ships, even though the company had barely edged out by $125,000 the bid of Sea-Land, which desperately had wanted to purchase those vessels. Nonetheless, the cost overruns on the repairs were used as ammunition to try to force the government to sell off Navieras, but ultimately the shippers concluded that the survival of the shipping company was vital to the island's welfare. The huge debt was a double-edged sword, and although it placed a heavy burden on the company's finances, it also served the valuable function of deterring speculators from trying to privatize the company.

The Commonwealth of Puerto Rico has seen Navieras primarily as a subsidy to the islanders rather than to the shippers, and because the company continues to guarantee a service of vital significance to the island's very survival, Navieras has become a part of Puerto Rico's history and future.

Principal Executives

Esteban Dávila Díaz	1974–1977, 1985–1990
Robert Lugo	1977–1984
Rafael Fábregas	1990–present

References: *American Shipper*, February 1986, June, November 1991, October 1992; René De La Pedraja, *The Rise and Decline of U.S. Merchant Shipping in the Twentieth Century* (New York: Twayne, 1992); *Journal of Commerce*, 3 March 1988, 9 March 1989.

NEPTUNE ASSOCIATION, 1912–1933. The Neptune Association of Masters and Mates of Ocean and Coastwise Steam Vessels was created on 21 March 1912 to represent the deck officers who had bolted from the Masters, Mates, and Pilots (MM&P) after the failure of the 1910 strike. By emphasizing the specific interests of deck officers in the ocean routes as distinct from those in the inland seas, the Neptune Association, in the tradition of craft unionism, was able to carve a special niche for itself, in the process, of course, weakening the bargaining power of the deck officers when they negotiated with management.

The members of the Neptune Association, who commanded the majestic liners in the transatlantic, looked down on the MM&P, whose members handled the small craft in harbors and inland seas. When the AFL renewed the offer of affiliation as a first step in reconciling the two unions for deck officers in 1918, the proud members of MM&P, who identified very closely with the shipowners, rejected the offer, because this meant "taking a back seat and placing the engineers in absolute command of the ship, thus making them dictators as to what the wages of the master and licensed deck officer should be" (Thor 1965).

The World War I shipping boom drove the membership of the Neptune Association to 2,600 members in 1920 (compared with over 9,000 for the MM&P in 1921). When the American Steamship Owners' Association* (ASOA) refused to renew the contract with deck officers when it expired on 1 August 1921, the Neptune Association did not immediately collapse, because the Shipping Board* continued to sign contracts with the deck officers, and some members who had obtained positions within the Shipping Board continued to favor other members of the association when appointing deck officers. Likewise, steamship owners in their own employment bureaus sometimes favored members of the Neptune Association over those of MM&P in order to keep the deck officers divided and weak. The Great Depression struck hard the Neptune Association, which merged on 1 June 1933 with another splinter group, the Ocean Association of Marine Engineers, to create the United Licensed Officers of America, a marginal organization that folded by the late 1930s.

Principal Labor Leaders

Arthur N. McGray	1918–1921
Frederick A. Gainard	1921–1922
John F. Milliken	1922–1930

References: *Handbook of American Trade Unions*, Bulletin of the Bureau of Labor Statistics, No. 618 (Washington, DC: Government Printing Office, 1936); Record Group 32, National Archives, Washington, DC; Benjamin M. Squires, "Associations of Harbor Boat Owners and Employees in the Port of New York," *Monthly Labor Review* 7 (1918): 45–62; Howard A. Thor, "Trade Unions of Licensed Officers of the Maritime Industry," Ph.D. diss., University of California, Berkeley, 1965.

NEW ORLEANS AND SOUTH AMERICAN STEAMSHIP COMPANY (NOSA), 1918–1935. The New Orleans and South American Steamship Company (NOSA), as its title indicated, provided service between New Orleans and the west coast of South America and was a subsidiary of W. R. Grace & Company. The parent company had decided in 1916 to consolidate its separate steamship companies into a single subsidiary, the Grace Line,* but in 1918 had to make an exception to this policy in order to qualify for vessels from the Shipping Board.* According to the law and its own policy, the Shipping Board was supposed to give highest priority to the creation of new steamship companies, and the Grace Line as an old established firm risked being bypassed in favor of previously unknown upstarts. By bringing local investors into NOSA, Grace was able to make a fairly convincing case that this was a genuine attempt to open up direct steamship service between New Orleans and Peru, even though Grace owned a majority of the stock.

In May 1918 NOSA sailed a small chartered* steamer and soon after was able to obtain additional tonnage from the Shipping Board, both chartered and purchased. By 1925 the regular service from New Orleans reached not only Colombia, Ecuador, Peru, and Chile but also the Caribbean, with a range of calls looping from Venezuela to Haiti; this latter service was known as the Aluminum Line. In 1929 NOSA bought three additional vessels from the Shipping Board, whose entry into service coincided with the Great Depression. Cargo volumes dropped off dramatically, and not even an extensive reorganization in 1932–1933 could save this subsidiary. In 1935 the parent company merged NOSA with the Grace Line, and those NOSA ships that did not fit into the remaining routes were sold, bringing to an end this first entry of the Grace Line into the New Orleans-South American trade.

References: Lawrence A. Clayton, *Grace: W. R. Grace & Co. The Formative Years, 1850–1930* (Ottowa, IL: Jameson Books, 1985); William Kooiman, *The Grace Ships, 1869–1969* (Point Reyes, CA: Komar, 1990); Record Group 32, National Archives, Washington, DC.

NEW YORK AND CUBA MAIL STEAMSHIP COMPANY. See Ward Line.

NEW YORK AND PACIFIC STEAMSHIP COMPANY or MERCHANTS' LINE, 1892–1916. The New York and Pacific Steamship Company was incorporated in London in 1892 to establish the first steamship service of the Grace Line.* The commercial house of W. R. Grace & Co. already operated a fleet of sailing ships between New York and Peru known as the ''Merchants' Line,'' but the introduction of the triple-expansion* engine made inevitable the change to steamships even on such long routes. Because shipbuilding costs were drastically lower in England, W. R. Grace ordered the ships from a British shipyard and had them registered under the British flag because, as foreign-built, they did not qualify for U.S. registry.*

The New York and Pacific Steamship Company, a London-based subsidiary, operated the ships and even paid the crew members wages. The first vessel of the company, the *Coya*, departed New York on 4 February 1893, arrived in Callao, Peru, on 8 April, and was back in New York on 18 June, after a voyage of 135 days. Henceforth the New York and Pacific Steamship Company maintained steamers running on regular schedule in the route. When the Panama Canal* opened on 15 August 1914, W. R. Grace shifted the vessels to take advantage of the much shorter route by the new waterway. The outbreak of World War I and the passage of a new law that opened U.S. registry to foreign-built ships allowed W. R. Grace to transfer most of its steamers from British to U.S.-flags, and in any case the tremendous dislocations produced by the war reduced the attractiveness of London as a shipping center. In 1916 the parent company took the decision to begin the consolidation of its separate shipping ventures into a single subsidiary, the Grace Line, and after the end of World War I the New York and Pacific Steamship Company gradually ceased to operate as a separate entity.

References: Lawrence A. Clayton, *Grace: W. R. Grace & Co. The Formative Years* (Ottowa, IL: Jameson Books, 1985); William Kooiman, *The Grace Ships, 1869–1969* (Point Reyes, CA: Komar, 1990).

NEW YORK AND PORTO RICO STEAMSHIP COMPANY. See New York and Puerto Rico Steamship Company.

NEW YORK AND PUERTO RICO STEAMSHIP COMPANY, 1885–1907. In 1873 Archibald H. Bull* began to operate a line of sailing vessels between New York and the Spanish colony of Puerto Rico. Some years later he also put steamers in the route, and soon other competitors appeared. By 1885 all the lines were losing money, and as a solution, they decided to amalgamate into the New York and Puerto Rico Steamship Company in 1885. The company's ships flew the British flag and were built in England; effective management was in the hands of Archibald H. Bull, who was the largest stockholder, although he did not own a majority of the shares.

In 1898 the Spanish-American War made Puerto Rico a U.S. territory, and shortly after, Congress extended the cabotage* privileges to the island, in effect excluding foreign ships from the trade with the U.S. mainland. The New York and Puerto Rico Steamship Company now had to dispose of its British-flag ships and purchase instead a U.S.-flag fleet in order to remain in the trade under the cabotage provisions. The partners in the company, who harbored long-simmering resentments, seized upon this change as a pretext to sell their shares. Bull, who did not have enough funds to buy out his partners, was likewise forced to sell in 1900 because the only buyer insisted on purchasing all the company's shares; furthermore, Bull had to sign a bond to stay out of the steamship service to Puerto Rico for ten years. In 1907 the new owner, John E. Berwind, sold the company to the Consolidated Steamship Lines* of Charles W. Morse. When the Consolidated Steamship Lines went into bankruptcy, its subsidiaries, including the New York and Puerto Rico Steamship Company, became part of a new holding company, the Atlantic, Gulf & West Indies Steamship Lines (AGWI).* Until its sale in 1949 to the Bull Line,* the New York and Puerto Rico Steamship Company continued to operate under its own trade name, although it was under the direct control of the AGWI combine.

References: René De La Pedraja, *The Rise and Decline of U.S. Merchant Shipping in the Twentieth Century* (New York: Twayne, 1992); U.S. House, Committee on Merchant Marine and Fisheries, *Investigation of Shipping Combinations*, 4 vols. (Washington, DC: Government Printing Office, 1913).

NEW YORK AND TEXAS STEAMSHIP COMPANY, 1886–1906. Charles Henry Mallory* incorporated the New York and Texas Steamship Company in

1886 to provide a corporate shell for the maritime assets, including the ships, of his family firm. The New York and Texas Steamship Company name was used on occasion, but the steamship service was more widely known as the Mallory Line.* After the sale of the New York and Texas Steamship Company in 1906, only the name of Mallory Line remained in use.

Reference: James P. Baughman, *The Mallorys of Mystic: Six Generations in American Maritime Enterprise* (Middletown, CT: Wesleyan University Press, 1972).

NONVESSEL OPERATING COMMON CARRIERS (NVOCCs). Nonvessel Operating Common Carriers (NVOCCs) have been essentially cargo consolidators, unlike freight forwarders,* whose main task has been to route the cargo for the shippers.* In reality most of the 1,400 NVOCCs registered with the Federal Maritime Commission* (FMC) in 1989 were also freight forwarders, and foreign countries did not make the distinction between both functions.

Since the introduction of containers* in the 1960s, ocean carriers have quoted significantly lower rates for carrying containers than general or break-bulk* cargo. Most shippers rushed to take advantage of the lower rates, thereby accelerating the conversion to containers for almost all the break-bulk cargo. But what about the small shipper who could not fill a whole container? Some freight forwarders jumped into the new opportunity to make profits by consolidating "less than container loads" (LCL) into "full container loads" (FCL), which thereby qualified for the lower "freight-of-all kind" or FAK rates. The small shippers thus shared but did not receive all the benefits of containers because they still had to pay a higher rate than what the ocean carriers actually received for carrying the single containers.

Ocean carriers have often condemned the NVOCCs as useless intermediaries who first needlessly increased what the shipper actually paid and then abuse their control over many containers to push ocean rates down by pitting one ocean carrier against another. While it was advisable for a shipper with enough cargo to fill a container to check directly with an ocean carrier to obtain the lowest prices, nevertheless, NVOCCs did perform a useful function in providing lower, if not the lowest, rates to small shippers. Furthermore, the hesitant entry of steamship companies into containers had provided the opening for bold and large freight forwarders to start consolidating small lots into full container loads. Congress in the Shipping Act of 1984* gave small shippers another opportunity to obtain low rates by authorizing the creation of shippers' associations,* but the latter's development was less than Congress expected, in large part because the NVOCCs already had a very widespread and effective grip on the cargo. Until merchant shipping companies start to consolidate aggressively less than container loads, the NVOCCs will remain major players in ocean transportation.

References: Advisory Commission on Conferences in Ocean Shipping, *Report to the President and the Congress* (Washington, DC: Government Printing Office, 1992); *American Shipper*, April 1983; Lane C. Kendall, *The Business of Shipping*, 5th ed. (Centreville, MD: Cornell Maritime Press, 1986); Transportation Research Board, *Intermodal Marine Container Transportation: Impediments and Opportunities* (Washington, DC: National Research Council, 1992).

NORTH AMERICAN LLOYD LINE, 1866–1870. The North American Lloyd Line, like the American Steamship Company,* was another of the attempts of the United States to return to steamship service in the North Atlantic after the end of the Civil War. Ruger Brothers of New York organized the North American Lloyd Line in 1866 and acquired the *Atlantic, Baltic,* and the *Ericsson,* ships that had always lost money for the Collins Line* before the Civil War. With these ships, the North American Lloyd Line began service in 1866 to try to tap some of the German immigrant traffic, but did not foresee the ferocity of competition. "A combination was formed by the English and German steamship lines to put on a steamer for New York at the same port, and on the same day that the vessels of this line were advertised to sail, and to take freight and passengers to New York at reduced rates. The result of this combination was death to the line" (Marvin 1902). The outbreak of the Franco-Prussian War disrupted the shipping routes, and soon after the North American Lloyd Line quietly folded.

References: Winthrop L. Marvin, *The American Merchant Marine* (New York: Scribner's, 1902); David B. Tyler, *Steam Conquers the Atlantic* (New York: D. Appleton-Century, 1939).

NORTH AMERICAN STEAMSHIP COMPANY. See Central American Transit Company.

NORTH ATLANTIC CONTINENTAL FREIGHT CONFERENCE, 1922–1985. The North Atlantic Continental Freight Conference controlled sailings, schedules, and rates "from North Atlantic ports of the United States and Canada, in the Hampton Roads/Montreal range, to ports in Belgium, Holland, and Germany (excluding German Baltic)." The conference handled trade moving eastward, while a separate organization, the North Atlantic Westbound Freight Association,* performed the same function for cargoes moving westward.

When originally established in 1920, the North Atlantic Continental Freight Conference had also included French Atlantic ports, but it collapsed when the French lines withdrew. In 1922 the North Atlantic Continental Freight Conference reorganized itself to handle trade only to Belgium, Holland, and North Sea German ports; companies providing service to France created their own organization, which, after a change of name, eventually became the North Atlantic French Atlantic Freight Conference. The third major association for eastbound traffic was the North Atlantic United Kingdom Freight Conference.*

The key members of the North Atlantic Continental Freight Conference during the interwar period were the German lines, specifically Hamburg-America and North German Lloyd. During the 1930s and 1940s, the major issue with the North Atlantic Continental Freight Conference was its reluctance to admit new members. Arnold Bernstein's* company, Black Diamond Steamship Corporation,* and Waterman Steamship Corporation* had to seek the intervention of the U.S. Maritime Commission* to secure admission into the conference, whose membership in 1953 comprised the following firms:

Black Diamond	Holland-America
Cosmopolitan Shipping Company*	Home Lines
Compagnie Générale Belge	Moller-Maersk Line
Compagnie Générale Transatlantique	South Atlantic Steamship Line
Cunard	United States Lines*
Ellerman's Wilson Line	Waterman Steamship Corporation

Shortly after, when the Allies lifted the last controls over occupied Germany, Hamburg-America and North German Lloyd rejoined the conference. In the 1950s the North Atlantic Continental Freight Conference suffered raids by outsider* Hans Isbrandtsen,* who, however, concentrated the brunt of his attacks on the Japan Atlantic & Gulf Conference (JAG)* and the Transpacific Freight Conference of Japan (TPFCJ). The rate war of 1953–1954 on cargo moving from the Continent affected the North Atlantic Westbound Conference but spared the North Atlantic Continental Freight Conference itself. However, a generalized rate war in the North Atlantic began in early 1970 and, until its end in June 1971, had a damaging impact on the member companies. In 1982 the entry of Trans Freight Line into the overtonnaged trades did provoke a rate war, which ended in 1983 when the new company agreed to join the conferences on the North Atlantic.

When the Shipping Act of 1984* legalized superconferences,* the North Atlantic Continental Freight Conference, the North Atlantic French Atlantic Conference, and the North Atlantic United Kingdom Freight Conference were three of the most important associations that merged to crate the new U.S. Atlantic-North Europe Conference (ANEC)* in 1985.

References: Advisory Commission on Conferences in Ocean Shipping, *Report to the President and the Congress* (Washington, DC: Government Printing Office, 1992); *American Shipper*, September 1983, October 1984; Federal Maritime Board, *Decisions*, vol. 4 (Washington, DC: Government Printing Office, 1963); *New York Times*, 4 January 1953, 14 January 1954; Shipping Board, *Decisions*, vol. 1 (Washington, DC: Government Printing Office, 1942); U.S. Maritime Commission, *Decisions*, vol. 2 (Washington, DC: Government Printing Office, 1951).

NORTH ATLANTIC MEDITERRANEAN FREIGHT CONFERENCE (NAMFC), 1904–1985. For U.S. ports between Maine and Hampton Roads, Virginia, essentially New York City, this conference during its long history set rates and services for cargoes moving eastward to the Mediterranean, including the North African coast, but excluding Italy, Spain, Israel, and the French Mediterranean coast. The two world wars interrupted the operation of NAMFC, whose membership in 1964 consisted of nineteen lines, five of which were American. In 1985 it was superseded by a superconference,* the U.S. Atlantic and Gulf Ports/Eastern Mediterranean and North African Freight Conference* (USAGEM).

References: Gale Research, *Encyclopedia of Associations*, 1970, 1985, 1988; US. Congress, House, Committee on Merchant Marine and Fisheries, *Review of Dual-Rate Legislation, 1961–1964* (Washington, DC: Government Printing Office, 1964).

NORTH ATLANTIC UNITED KINGDOM FREIGHT CONFERENCE (NAUK) and NORTH ATLANTIC WESTBOUND FREIGHT ASSOCIATION (NAWFA), 1908–1985. The North Atlantic United Kingdom Freight Conference (NAUK) served the eastbound trade between U.S. ports on the East Coast and those in the United Kingdom, while a separate organization, the North Atlantic Westbound Freight Association (NAWFA) handled the cargoes moving from the United Kingdom to the U.S. East Coast. Steamship companies established both conferences* in 1908, after the ferocious rate war of 1903–1908, in order to return stability to this vital trade route. The most successful period in the history of these conferences was from the late 1940s to the late 1960s; by the latter date, NAUK with ten companies and NAWFA with fifteen were "among the world's oldest and most stable conferences" and their members were "for the most part very old, well-established steamship lines" such as Cunard and United States Lines* (USL) (Federal Maritime Commission 1970). With an average of one eastbound and one westbound sailing every day of the year, shippers* expressed "complete satisfaction with the service," which had enjoyed "an unusual degree of stability in the rates and the service of the conference carriers in both directions" (ibid.).

The cost for such superb service was an extreme overtonnaging in the routes between the United States and the United Kingdom, so that the ships sailed with holds barely 40 percent full. Apparently handling large volumes allowed the companies to survive, but as the containers* appeared in the North Atlantic, a rate war began in early 1970 and lasted until June 1971, while the energy crisis of 1973 sent a further shock through these trades; not unexpectedly companies began to abandon the route or go bankrupt. In 1982 the entry of Trans Freight Line into the overtonnaged trades provoked another rate war, which ended in 1983, when the new company agreed to join the conferences on the North Atlantic. The number of companies declined to six in NAUK and to eight in NAWFC by the early 1980s, and when the Shipping Act of 1984* legalized superconferences,* the advantages of consolidation became irresistible. NAUK joined with other organizations like the North Atlantic Continental Freight Conference* and the North Atlantic French Atlantic Conference to create the new U.S. Atlantic-North Europe Conference* (ANEC) in 1985.

Reference: Advisory Commission on Conferences in Ocean Shipping, *Report to the President and the Congress* (Washington, DC: Government Printing Office, 1922); *American Shipper*, September 1983, October 1984; René De La Pedraja, *The Rise and Decline* *of U.S. Merchant Shipping in the Twentieth Century* (New York: Twayne, 1992); Federal Maritime Commission, *Decisions*, vol. 12, *1968–1969* (Washington, DC: Government Printing Office, 1970).

NORTH   ATLANTIC   WESTBOUND   FREIGHT   ASSOCIATION (NAWFA). See North Atlantic United Kingdom Freight Conference and North Atlantic Westbound Freight Association.

NORTHERN PACIFIC. See *Great Northern* and *Northern Pacific.*

NORTH EUROPE-U.S. ATLANTIC CONFERENCE (NEAC), 1985–1989. NEAC was one of the superconferences* that emerged after the passage of the Shipping Act of 1984.* NEAC combined four previously existing conferences: North Atlantic Westbound Freight, Continental North Atlantic Westbound Freight, Scandinavia-Baltic/U.S. North Atlantic Westbound, and North Europe-U.S. South Atlantic Range Agreement. The consolidation was less dramatic than it seemed, because the same six lines (Atlantic Container Lines, Dart Container Line, Hapag-Lloyd, Sea-Land,* Trans Freight Lines, and United States Lines*) were the only members in the four conferences; furthermore, the same chairman and the same office in New York City had handled the four original conferences. Actually the creation of NEAC, just like of its eastbound counterpart, the U.S. Atlantic-North Europe Conference* (ANEC), was the first part in the restructuring process that culminated in the creation of the North Europe-U.S.A. Rate Agreement* (NEUSARA) and the U.S.A.-North Europe Rate Agreement* (USANERA) in 1989.

References: Advisory Commission on Conferences in Ocean Shipping, *Report to the President and the Congress* (Washington, DC: Government Printing Office, 1992); *American Shipper*, September, October 1984.

NORTH EUROPE-U.S.A. RATE AGREEMENT (NEUSARA), 1989–1992. The creation of the North Europe-U.S. Atlantic Conference* (NEAC) in 1985 was a first major step in consolidating the conferences* in the trade moving across the Atlantic from Northern Europe but did not cover the freight moving in the same direction to the Pacific and Gulf coasts of the United States. The member lines agreed in 1989 to create NEUSARA, and it combined NEAC with the North Europe Gulf Freight Association and the North Europe-U.S. Pacific Freight Conference.

The creation of what truly was a superconference* between Northern Europe and the United States created fears of a monopoly, but the Advisory Commission on Conferences in Ocean Shipping* (ACCOS) found nothing objectionable. In fact the many small conferences were obsolete and reflected "a period when vessels were small and when the countries of Western Europe were not as economically integrated as they are today" (*American Shipper*, October 1984). Superconferences like NEUSARA and its westbound counterpart, the U.S.A.

North Europe Rate Agreement* (USANERA), have become basic to world shipping. The trend toward concentration appears to have no end in sight and, in August 1992, both NEUSARA and USANERA combined to form the Trans-Atlantic Agreement* (TAA).

References: Advisory Commission on Conferences in Ocean Shipping, *Report to the President and the Congress* (Washington, DC: Government Printing Office, 1992); *American Shipper*, September, October 1984; Federal Maritime Commission, *Section 18 Report on the Shipping Act of 1984*, September 1989; *Journal of Commerce*, 2 June 1989.

NOVELS. See literature.

O

OBO or ORE/BULK/OIL. OBOs have been combination vessels for the transportation of ores, oil, and other bulk* commodities like grains and coal. Apparently at the suggestion of the U.S. Maritime Commission,* shipowners began to experiment before World War II with bulk carriers as a way to replace the old colliers,* which carried merely coal. With dry bulk carriers, owners could move ores, grains, and coal, but the transition to a vessel that could also carry liquids was delayed by the World War II surplus vessels, whose ready availability perpetuated the rough division between tankers and dry bulk carriers for over twenty years.

When the Suez Canal closed in 1967, the high tanker rates drove many owners to convert their dry bulk carriers to OBOs in order to take advantage of the favorable market situation, yet without sacrificing their capability to haul other bulk cargoes. In principle the OBOs offered the best of all worlds: they could carry at the same time different types of cargoes to achieve a full load and hence achieve maximum profitability for the owner, or the OBOs could carry only only type of commodity in one direction and make the return voyage loaded with a different cargo. The appeal of the highly versatile vessel proved irresistible but, in an age of specialization, could not be the universal answer to world shipping, so that by the early 1980s OBO construction stabilized. Owners found that tankers and specialized bulk carriers were still needed for many routes in the world where the lack of alternate products precluded combining cargoes for the same voyage or making the return trip fully loaded. Likewise, OBOs did not always reach the lower operating costs or "economies of scale" of the larger specialized vessels. Efforts to achieve maximum flexibility have not flagged, however, and in recent years an additional type of versatile ship has emerged, the PROBO or Product/Bulk/Ore carrier.

OCCIDENTAL AND ORIENTAL STEAMSHIP COMPANY (O&O), 1874–1893. In the transpacific trade, the Occidental and Oriental Steamship Company (O&O) was the first rival to challenge the near-monopoly position of Pacific Mail Steamship Company* (PMSS). The completion of the first transcontinental railroad in 1869 made PMSS a crucial source of eastbound cargo, but the Panama Railroad desperately tried to preserve as much as possible of its previous monopoly and large profits. In 1873 PMSS, "under the influence of the Panama Railroad" (Kemble 1950), refused to unload the ships in San Francisco and instead planned to send all the Far Eastern cargo to Panama for transshipment across the Isthmus to waiting steamers on the Atlantic side. The plan proved unworkable, but the railroads decided never again to risk the chance of losing any major share of freight.

In 1874 the Central Pacific-Union Pacific railroads organized the O&O, which began operations in 1875 with British-flag ships chartered from the White Star Line. British officers directed the Chinese crews, which were also used in the PMSS vessels but under the command of Americans. Spirited competition ensued over the next decade, and PMSS had to replace its older side-wheel steamers with newer screw-driven vessels.

In 1893 the Southern Pacific Railroad gained control of both the larger PMSS and the newer O&O. The transcontinental railroads now had guaranteed their Far Eastern cargo and no longer needed O&O, whose fleet and operations were taken over by PMSS. The house flag and name did not completely disappear until 1908.

References: John H. Kemble, "The Big Four at Sea: The History of the Occidental and Oriental Steamship Company," *Huntington Library Quarterly* 3 (1940): 339–357; John H. Kemble, "A Hundred Years of the Pacific Mail," *American Neptune* 10 (1950): 123–143; E. Mowbray Tate, *Transpacific Steam: The Story of Steam Navigation from the Pacific Coast of North America to the Far East and the Antipodes, 1867–1941* (New York: Cornwall Books, 1986).

OCEANIC & ORIENTAL NAVIGATION COMPANY, 1928–1938. Oceanic & Oriental Navigation Company was a joint venture of American-Hawaiian Steamship Company* and Matson Navigation Company.* In 1926 the Shipping Board* awarded the company Swayne and Hoyt twelve government freighters for operation in the American-Australian and Orient Line, which soon faced difficulties. The Shipping Board then offered to turn over the ships and the routes to American-Hawaiian and Matson; the latter two accepted and to manage the government ships created a new subsidiary, Oceanic & Oriental Navigation Company. In reality Matson handled the freighters on the Australia/New Zealand route, while American-Hawaiian managed those on the China trade. The Shipping Board assigned new government vessels to the services, but even with a large subsidy Oceanic & Oriental Navigation Company was losing money because of foreign discrimination, and only the operation of Matson's express liners *Mariposa** and *Monterey** proved a sound investment. When the government canceled the subsidy in 1937, the Oceanic and Oriental Steamship Navigation Company was dissolved, and the vessels were returned to the government.

References: E. Mowbray Tate, *Transpacific Steam: The Story of Steam Navigation from the Pacific Coast of North America to the Far East and the Antipodes, 1867–1941* (New York: Cornwall Books, 1986); William L. Worden, *Cargoes: Matson's First Century in the Pacific* (Honolulu: University Press of Hawaii, 1981).

OCEANIC STEAMSHIP COMPANY (OSS), 1881–1976.

Oceanic Steamship Company (OSS) provided service from California to New Zealand and Australia via Hawaii. In 1876 Claus Spreckels began to purchase extensive sugar plantations in Hawaii, and to move the raw sugar to his refinery in California, he acquired a fleet of sailing vessels, which soon proved inadequate. In 1881, with his sons, he incorporated the OSS to order from the shipyard and to operate two modern iron steamers, the *Mariposa* and *Alameda*. The steamers proved too large for the available cargo, and to rescue the investment, the Spreckles family lobbied adroitly in Congress to transfer the mail subsidy for the California-Australia/New Zealand service from the Pacific Mail Steamship Company* (PMSS) to OSS in 1885.

The annexation of Hawaii to the United States in 1898 and the subsequent extension of the cabotage* privileges to the islands forced OSS to keep more ships under the U.S. flag; previously most of its ships had been registered under the British or Hawaiian flag. To comply with the provisions of a new mail subsidy from Congress, OSS in 1900 received three new vessels, the *Sonoma*, the *Sierra*, and the *Ventura*; with triple-expansion engines,* they were much faster, and the *Sierra* established the new speed record of nineteen days, seven hours between San Francisco and Sydney.

When Congress failed to renew the mail contract in 1907, OSS laid up its vessels until 1912. When Congress restored the mail contract in 1912, the *Sonoma*, the *Sierra*, and the *Ventura* returned to service, now refitted to burn oil rather than coal as fuel. During World War I the company's ships were requisitioned by the Shipping Board,* but by then the Spreckles family had lost much of its original importance and fortune. A mail contract in 1922 temporarily revived OSS, but when foreign competition stiffened, its old ships began to show large losses. The Spreckes family finally agreed in 1926 to sell the firm to the Matson Navigation Company.*

The independent existence of OSS had ended, but because Matson kept Oceanic as a separate subsidiary, the name remained alive. William P. Roth* assigned to Oceanic the two new liners *Mariposa** and *Monterey,** whose success created considerable international friction with New Zealand and Australia. During 1928–1938 a separate subsidiary, Oceanic and Oriental Navigation Company,* handled the freighters on that route, but after its liquidation in 1938, OSS handled both the freighters and the express liners to Australia and New Zealand.

Oceanic received subsidies for its foreign trade routes, unlike Matson, whose

California-Hawaii service was protected by the cabotage privileges. A major reason Matson decided to liquidate Oceanic was the need to secure legally its service in the Hawaii-California route against challenges from subsidized companies like American President Lines.* In 1970 Matson sold most of the ships of Oceanic (including the passenger liners) and then in 1976 absorbed the three remaining freighters and Oceanic itself, whose existence as a subsidiary finally ended.

Some Notable Ships

Mariposa and *Alameda*	1883–1911
Sierra	1900–1918
Sonoma and *Ventura*	1901–1926
Mariposa and *Monterey*	1931–1947

References: René De La Pedraja, *The Rise and Decline of the U.S. Merchant Shipping Industry* (New York: Twayne, 1992); Frederick E. Emmons, *American Passenger Ships* (Newark: University of Delaware Press, 1985); Fred A. Stindt, *Matson's Century of Ships* (Modesto, CA: n.p., 1982); E. Mowbray Tate, *Transpacific Steam: The Story of Steam Navigation from the Pacific Coast of North America to the Far East and the Antipodes, 1867–1941* (New York: Cornwall Books, 1986); William L. Worden, *Cargoes: Matson's First Century in the Pacific* (Honolulu: University Press of Hawaii, 1981).

OCEAN MAIL ACT OF 1891 or MERCHANT MARINE ACT OF 1891. The Ocean Mail Act of 1891 was the first general subsidy bill passed by Congress since the pre–Civil War period. Previously Congress had approved subsidies for specific steamship services, most notably the United States and Brazil Mail Steamship Company* and the Pacific Mail Steamship Company,* but these had been handled almost as "private" bills, or legislation affecting only one individual or firm. Instead the Ocean Mail Act of 1891 introduced the concept that companies owning a U.S.-built fleet qualified to receive subsidies. In spite of the urgings of the American Shipping and Industrial League,* Congress had rejected a giveaway bill that would have subsidized sailing and steam vessels based on the number of miles of each trip and instead opted on 3 March 1891 only for the Ocean Mail Act, which allowed the Post Office flexibility in accepting or rejecting proposals for contracts of five to ten years' duration as well as on their renewal.

The Ocean Mail Act halted but did not reverse the downward trend in the U.S. merchant marine. The requirement of having to purchase vessels from U.S. shipyards was particularly costly, so only established firms benefited from the subsidy, and not surprisingly the first contract went to the Pacific Mail Steamship Company* (PMSS). The limitations of the act were apparent from the start: when the Post Office asked for bids on fifty-three mail routes, the steamship companies presented proposals only for eleven routes. Nevertheless, the Ocean Mail Act of 1891 did allow a number of firms, such as the Red D Line* and the Ward Line,* to remain under U.S. registry* rather than switch to the lower-cost foreign flags, in particular British registry. Thanks to the Ocean Mail Act, which expired only in 1923, a core of U.S.-flag merchant services survived in the foreign trade routes and with the coastwise* and intercoastal* fleet provided the foundations for the dramatic expansion of the U.S. merchant marine in World War I.

References: John G. B. Hutchins, *The American Maritime Industries and Public Policy, 1789–1914* (Cambridge: Harvard University Press, 1941); U.S. *Statues at Large*, vol. 26 (1891); Paul M. Zeis, *American Shipping Policy* (Princeton, NJ: Princeton University Press, 1938).

OCEAN SHIPPING ACT OF 1978. See Controlled Carriers Act.

OCEAN STEAM NAVIGATION COMPANY. See Bremen Line.

O'CONNOR, THOMAS VENTRY, 9 August 1870–17 October 1935. T. V. O'Connor was president of the International Longshoremen's Association* (ILA) in 1908–1921, and as chairman of the Shipping Board* in 1924–1933, he was one of the few labor leaders to have held high maritime offices in the government. He was born in Toronto, Canada, on 9 August 1870; at age two his family moved to Buffalo, New York, where he made his permanent residence and eventually became a naturalized U.S. citizen. As a marine engineer and a tugboat captain he was active in the tugboat affiliate of the ILA. Daniel Keefe's* sudden resignation from the presidency of ILA in 1908 left O'Connor as one of the few competent members qualified to succeed. As soon as O'Connor was elected, he pruned the ILA of nonmaritime unions and directed the organizing drives toward the longshoremen. The rigid adoption of the craft instead of the industrial principle for the structuring of unions allowed him to enjoy throughout his career the support of Samuel Gompers, the president of the American Federation of Labor, but O'Connor's extreme conservatism (e.g., he claimed never to have sanctioned a strike) made him very unpopular among the rest of maritime labor leaders. O'Connor claimed to be a Democrat until 1920, when he joined the Republican party, and at last he could give free rein to his archconservative views.

Buffalo became the headquarters of the ILA, whose primary focus remained the Great Lakes. In 1912 O'Connor authorized an organizing drive in New York City, thereby beginning the gradual shift of the ILA from the Great Lakes to the East Coast. His initial commitment to promoting workers' rights had given way to a passive acceptance of whatever the employers cared to grant, and in effect by 1915 the ILA was little more than a company union. Discontent spread among the longshoremen, and only with great difficulty did O'Connor fight off the ouster attempt by challenger Thomas Herring of San Francisco. The postelection rift was not healed, and Herring took his San Francisco local out of the ILA and established the separate Longshoremen's Association of San Francisco and the Bay District or the "Blue Book Union"* in

1915. O'Connor's failure to bring the West Coast locals back into the ILA was one of the worst legacies of his presidency, yet he managed to retain his office, thanks to the shipping boom of World War I, which kept ILA members constantly employed at record high wages. Although the shipping boom outlasted the return of peace, O'Connor knew that once the demand for dockworkers slackened, the discontent of longshoremen would erupt again, and he decided to exit gracefully from the ILA presidency by accepting the appointment as a commissioner of the Shipping Board* in June 1921. President Warren Harding had chosen O'Connor because he was one of the very few Republican maritime labor leaders.

Harding's appointment had momentous consequences for the U.S. merchant marine because O'Connor, less than one week after Senate confirmation, secured from the fellow commissioners his election as vice chairman of the Shipping Board, and President Calvin Coolidge appointed him chairman in February 1924, a position he held until 4 March 1933. O'Connor, a master at bureaucratic infighting, made strategic alliances with other commissioners, most notably, Edward C. Plummer, who was vice chairman from 1924 to 1932, until O'Connor had gained enough influence to make the Shipping Board subservient to his own ideas and personal interests. A staunch believer in the free enterprise system, he did everything within his power to drain government funds, vessels, and resources in order to increase the profits of private companies. O'Connor specialized in deals with private steamship companies, and he was in close contact with astute lobbyists like Hardin Arledge* or, if necessary, with the steamship executives themselves, as in the case of R. Stanley Dollar.* The Shipping Board was left to drift, and he cut back its essential technical and administrative services in order to try to reduce the growing deficit in the agency's finances caused by subsidizing the managing operators.* The conversion to diesel* engines, one of the long-range issues of vital importance for the U.S.-flag ships in the 1920s, evoked little interest from O'Connor, who reserved his time and efforts to political maneuvering and hatching new deals for executives who knew how to reward him.

Throughout his long tenure, O'Connor carefully cultivated an image of propriety and staunchly supported the Republican party, so that President Herbert Hoover, who already as secretary of commerce had seen the failings of the Shipping Board, continued to back O'Connor as chairman of the Shipping Board even through its last reorganizations. After the Merchant Marine Act of 1928* authorized the Shipping Board to award mail contracts, O'Connor had a field day assigning the maximum sums allowable under the law to the private companies, irrespective of how well they complied with the other provisions in the laws. Nothing could shake the faith of Hoover in his old Republican backer, but because the Democratic Congress had delayed confirming the reappointment of O'Connor, his recess appointment as chairman expired on 4 March 1933, when Franklin D. Roosevelt became president. O'Connor returned to Buffalo, where he died on 17 October 1935; besides his atrocious record of weakening the position of seafarers and longshoremen, he had been the individual most responsible for wrecking the Shipping Board, and the impact of his career was disastrous on merchant shipping.

References: Gary M. Fink, ed., *Biographical Dictionary of American Labor*, 2d ed. (Westport, CT: Greenwood Press, 1984); *National Cyclopedia of American Biography*, vol. 42; Record Group 32, National Archives, Washington, DC; Maud Russell, *Men Along the Shore: The ILA and Its History* (New York: Brussel and Brussel, 1966); Shipping Board, *Seventeenth Annual Report* (Washington, DC: Government Printing Office, 1933).

OIL POLLUTION ACT OF 1990 (OPA). The Oil Pollution Act of 1990 (OPA) was the most drastic environmental legislation ever passed by Congress to prevent oil spills in U.S. waters. Congress took such extreme measures in reaction to the *Exxon Valdez** shipwreck in Alaska, an environmental disaster particularly embarrassing because the U.S.-flag tanker was operated by an American crew. If this had been a vessel that flew a foreign flag or a flag of convenience,* the blame could have easily been avoided and even turned into a boost for U.S.-flag tankers; instead this accident exposed before public view a shameful behavior right inside the bridge of an U.S.-flag tanker. The *Exxon Valdez* ranked right with the Black Committee* and the Cellar Committee* as one of the worst public relations disasters of the U.S. merchant marine.

The Merchant Marine and Fisheries Committee* had been working quietly on a bill to improve some provisions in the Port and Tanker Safety Act of 1978,* and years of lengthy negotiation had been expected to get the bill through the House and then to secure final passage. The *Exxon Valdez* disaster changed drastically the political situation, and what started out as a transportation bill became an environmental law. Many legislators, who were under extreme public pressure not only to vote for a bill but to make it as tough as possible, added amendments to impose drastic measures, so that when finally passed on 18 August, the Oil Pollution Act of 1990 contained some of the most extreme provisions ever encountered in merchant marine legislation.

The OPA focused on two main areas. The first set of measures extended the authority of the Coast Guard* to review the qualifications of the personnel serving aboard tankers. The 1978 act had made as stringent as possible the actual on-the-job requirements but, because of a deference to privacy laws, had not included provisions to scrutinize an individual's behavior outside the ship. Now the OPA required that the ship personnel be checked for any prior cases of drug and alcohol abuse, and to prevent a repetition of one of the shocking revelations of the *Exxon Valdez* disaster, the OPA excluded individuals who had bad records as automobile drivers from working aboard the tankers. The OPA correctly found in human neglect the cause of the previous disaster and hoped to avoid future accidents by keeping a closer watch on the private and job life of the individuals manning the ships. The oil companies, fearful of the unlimited liability in the law, have adopted the costly precaution of having tugs escort their tankers out of Prince William Sound.

While the most flagrant off-ship violations could be easily detected, only twenty-four-hour surveillance could guarantee that an individual had no habits or tendencies potentially harmful to the operation of a vessel. To reduce to the minimum even the remotest possibility of another oil spill, Congress imposed the requirement of double hulls* on all tankers entering U.S. waters. Since the 1960s seashore communities had frequently wanted double-hull tankers, a request easily ignored because of their high cost, but the public pressure now was too great to be satisfied merely with promises. Although the OPA mandated double-hull tankers, very few then existed, and the law included a detailed time chart that provided a long transition for owners to either discard or refit their older vessels. Older tankers, whose replacement was soon imminent, were allowed fewer years, while newer tankers were granted the most time. Likewise, vessels with either double sides or double bottoms, of which more existed, were given more time to make the transition. However, the absolute limits were the year 2010 for a vessel with only a single hull and the year 2015 for a vessel with either a double bottom or double sides, so that after 1 January 2015 all tankers operating in U.S. waters, whether under foreign or U.S. flags, must be double-hull.

The oil industry has resisted double hulls as a needless expense that will only raise the price of oil, but at least one company, Conoco (owned by Du Pont), decided to gain favorable publicity on prime-time television by being the first to begin the conversion of its entire tanker fleet to double hulls. Barring radical changes in legislation compliance with the double-hull requirement appeared inevitable, and once again the United States may well lead the world in setting standards for vessel safety and performance.

References: *American Shipper*, April 1992; *Pacific Maritime Magazine*, May 1992; *U.S. Statutes at Large*, vol. 104 (1990).

OLANDER, VICTOR A., 28 November 1873–5 February 1949. Victor A. Olander was a high union official and white-shirt* sailor who was involved with the International Seamen's Union* (ISU) for over thirty years. He was born in Chicago on 28 November 1873; even before he completed elementary school, he had joined the crews aboard merchant ships and sailed, mainly in the Great Lakes. He joined the ISU in 1899, and his literacy and organizing abilities soon made him the leader of the Great Lakes sailors. Andrew Furuseth* recognized the talents of Olander and since 1902 began to name him to important positions in the ISU. However, Olander sensed there was more opportunity for him as leader of the labor movement in Chicago, and he declined Furuseth's invitation to become president of ISU in 1909; in many ways Olander's career paralleled that of another white-shirt sailor, Paul Scharrenberg.* Olander continued to rise through the Illinois labor hierarchy until he became the leader of the Illinois State Federation of Labor in 1914, a position he held until his death in 1949.

Statewide labor issues absorbed most of Olander's time, and he had already became a national figure in the circles of the American Federation of Labor, but he continued to head the small Great Lakes local of the ISU. When the secretary-treasurer of the ISU disappeared with almost all the union funds in 1925, President Furuseth asked Olander as a personal favor to accept the vacant job of secretary-treasurer, which he then held until 1935. Olander thus became another excellent example of a white-shirt sailor, namely, a former seaman who had climbed so rapidly in the union hierarchy that he had lost touch with the rank and file. By then he had also absorbed the dress and attitudes of mainstream middle-class Americans, so that when the Great Depression struck, he refused to support the sailors' desperate pleas for emergency food and shelter because the ISU "is not organizing flophouse unions" (Nelson 1990). As part of the labor upheavals of the mid-1930s, Olander came under heavy criticism and left the ISU job in 1935, but he continued as head of the Illinois State Federation of Labor until his death in 1949.

References: Gary M. Fink, ed., *Biographical Dictionary of American Labor*, 2d ed. (Westport, CT: Greenwood Press, 1984); Bruce Nelson, *Workers on the Waterfront: Seamen, Longshoremen, and Unionism in the 1930s* (Urbana: University of Illinois Press, 1990); Hyman Weintraub, *Andrew Furuseth: Emancipator of the Seamen* (Berkeley: University of California Press, 1959).

ON THE WATERFRONT, **1954.** *On the Waterfront* is a powerful film about the lives of longshoremen during their struggle against corrupt and murderous union leaders. Marlon Brando, as Terry Malloy, the ex-boxer turned longshoreman, delivered one of his best performances, winning an Oscar for best actor, while Eva Marie Saint as Edie Doyle won another Oscar as best supporting actress; the film won a total of eight Academy Awards, including best movie of the year. The movie successfully integrated the love story between Edie and Terry into the latter's struggle with his conscience and the search for dignity in his life, while Father Barry, played by Karl Malden in one of his most successful roles, reaffirmed the religious dimension running throughout the film. Terry's love for Edie slowly revived his conscience and finally made him turn against the corrupt union bosses; and in the process he discovered the meaning of his own life. The clear and powerful message that could be read at many levels made the movie a box office success with a profit of over $4 million.

Actually the human drama in the story overshadowed the situation on the waterfront, which really served as a backdrop or stage for the unfolding inner human events, so the film did not provide a complete view of life on the docks and unfortunately left millions of viewers with a highly distorted image of the longshoremen. The film drew on newspaper reporting to re-create the longshoremen's situation as it existed during the bleak years of the Great Depression and at the same time placed in one union local all the imagined and real excesses committed by the International Longshoremen's Association* (ILA) under Joseph Ryan* in the early 1950s. Thus the moving scenes about the men's scrambling for work in the shape-up* were accurate for the 1920s but did not reflect the 1950s. That racketeering existed could not be denied, but the juxtaposition with the situation of the early 1930s, while perhaps allowable as poetic licence, did lend itself for an indictment of the labor movement. Director Elia Kazan, a former communist, had agreed to collaborate with the House Committee on Un-American Activities and, just like Terry in the film, turned stool pigeon on his former acquaintances. For Kazan, the film was a great opportunity to compensate for his communist past and also justify himself, even if it meant tarnishing for decades the reputation of both organized labor and longshoremen throughout the United States.

References: Howard Kimeldorf, *Reds or Rackets: The Making of Radical and Conservative Unions on the Waterfront* (Berkeley: University of California Press, 1988); *Magill's Survey of Cinema* (Englewood Cliffs, NJ: Salem Press, 1980); Jay R. Nash and Stanley R. Ross, *Motion Picture Guide, 1927–1983* (Chicago: Cinebooks, 1986); Maud Russell, *Men Along the Shore: The ILA and Its History* (New York: Brussel and Brussel, 1966).

OPERATING DIFFERENTIAL SUBSIDY (ODS), 1936–present. The operating differential subsidy (ODS) has been one of the two subsidies created by the Merchant Marine Act of 1936* to maintain a strong U.S.-flag merchant fleet and, like the companion construction differential subsidy* (CDS), established the concept of parity or equality of costs between the United States and foreign countries. Historically, U.S.-flag ships have been more expensive to operate than their foreign counterparts, even before the 1930s, when American seamen were paid very low wages. The ODS was supposed to pay the difference between the higher U.S. and the lower foreign costs, in a sense leveling the playing field, so that U.S. companies will not suffer ruinous competition because of large cost disparities.

As with the CDS, the attempt to determine the foreign competitors' exact expenses has rarely been successful, and try as it might, the Maritime Administration* (MARAD) has generally had to make assumptions, generalizations, and approximations to obtain a rough estimate of the foreign competitors' real costs. The foreign competitors' expenses were not static and could fluctuate drastically, thereby rendering outdated the estimates laboriously calculated by MARAD. Furthermore, the ODS imposed upon U.S.-flag companies a whole series of requirements, all of a vexing nature, and some have been outright harmful, such as the requirements for a minimum number of sailings in specified routes. Without flexibility, a company could not meet swiftly changing market conditions in the trade routes. In reality these complex restrictions on the ODS were the backlash from the mail contracts of the Merchant Marine Act of 1928*: at that time Congress had granted shipowners a nearly complete freedom that many had used to pocket the subsidies and reap outrageous profits.

The rigid enforcement of the ODS was supposed to prevent new abuses, and in that sense the program was successful, but the same cannot be said about the primary purpose of the ODS, which was to maintain a strong U.S.-flag merchant marine. The subsidy was too inflexible and too small to save many companies, and since the 1970s bankruptcies and disappearance have been the normal fare for most companies. The Merchant Marine Act of 1970* did not address the real flaws in ODS but did make a major innovation when Congress made bulk* carriers eligible for ODS and not just liner* companies as had been the case since 1936. Over a dozen bulk companies signed agreements to receive the ODS, as the government desperately tried to maintain a U.S.-flag presence in the rapidly expanding overseas bulk trade.

To avoid penalizing the companies for any sudden changes in U.S. government policies, the companies could obtain ODS contracts for a period of as long as twenty years, but when the government halted the CDS in 1981, the ODS program was left without a future beyond the duration of the existing contracts. Furthermore, the ODS required companies to build ships in the United States with the CDS, but without the latter, the companies could not order new ships to keep running their U.S.-flag operations. A special temporary permission allowed the companies to continue receiving the ODS while ordering thirty-two new ships abroad, but attempts to make this permission permanent have failed in Congress. The last ODS contract was signed in 1982, and the last of the twenty-year contracts will expire in the year 2001; since it was unlikely that the federal government would ever have sufficient funds to finance the ODS even if foreign-built ships were allowed to qualify, the end of the ODS, the most complex and rigid maritime program ever devised by the federal government, could be taken for granted. The ODS program was slightly more successful than its counterpart, the CDS, but ultimately both failed to preserve a strong U.S.-flag merchant marine.

References: Ernst G. Frankel, *Regulation and Policies of American Shipping* (Boston: Auburn House, 1982); Gerald R. Jantscher, *Bread upon the Waters: Federal Aids to the Maritime Industries* (Washington, DC: Brookings Institution, 1975); Samuel A. Lawrence, *United States Merchant Shipping Policies and Politics* (Washington, DC: Brookings Institution, 1966); Maritime Administration, *Annual Report 1986*; Transportation Research Board, *Intermodal Marine Container Transportation: Impediments and Opportunities* (Washington, DC: National Research Council, 1992).

OREGON. See *California, Oregon*, and *Panama.*

OREGON RAILWAY AND NAVIGATION COMPANY. See San Francisco and Portland Steamship Company.

OUTSIDER. *Outsider* is a perjorative term used by merchant shipping companies to refer to those lines that operate "outside" the conferences,* usually in open defiance of their rates and agreements, and that do not hesitate to sink the long-range stability of a route for the sake of short-term profits. Outsiders were rare in the pre–World War I period but became more common after that war, when the regulatory principles of the Shipping Act of 1916* began to have an impact on world sea-lanes. The most notorious outsider was Hans Isbrandt-sen,* who did tremendous damage to both U.S. and world shipping.

As the U.S. regulatory system made itself felt after World War II, the benefits of conference membership in the U.S. foreign trade rates declined. Many companies did not want to be openly defiant, and although they remained conference-minded and avoided the excesses of the true outsider, they felt they had to explore opportunities outside the conferences in order to survive. For this latter group of lines, the less pejorative term *independent* has been coined, although this more elegant term has also been appropriated by the real outsiders, who are determined to sink a whole trade route into chaos for the sake of a small immediate profit.

OVERSEAS SHIPHOLDING GROUP (OSG), 1969–present. Overseas Ship-holding Group (OSG), a company specialized in the transport of bulk* and petroleum products, has been the rare case of a success story in the post–World War II period of the United States, while the company's tranquil existence made it something unique in the normally turbulent panorama of merchant shipping in the United States. Raphael Recanati organized OSG in 22 July 1969 out of his small shipping companies, because he had realized he needed to raise capital publicly if he wanted to continue expanding. After the wave of mergers and paper transactions of the 1960s, Recanati's decision to issue stock in 1970 in order to raise capital seemed plainly old-fashioned and simply lacked the excitement of more dramatic Wall Street moves. He was responding, however, to the policy change of the oil companies, which now wished to obtain a greater proportion of their tankers through medium and long-term charters,* although the companies still continued to own large fleets of their own. Recanati realized somebody had to provide those tankers and that if he raised the money in the stock market, OSG could make a profit by ordering new tankers for charter to the oil companies.

From that core business, OSG has expanded into the transportation of bulk* and ore cargoes, for which it ordered the construction of specialized vessels. In 1975 the company owned thirty-eight tanker and bulk vessels of a total of 2.9 million deadweight* tons. The president of OSG, Morton P. Hyman, concluded in 1973 that the company should go beyond the foreign-flag ships built abroad and also enter the protected domestic trade for the transportation of Alaska oil to other ports in the United States. When Alaska oil began to flow in the summer of 1977, OSG was ready with fifteen U.S.-flag tankers built in U.S. shipyards without subsidies; OSG, controlling 20 percent of the domestic fleet, emerged as the largest independent oil tanker operator under the U.S. flag. In the 1980s OSG turned to bulk carriers as the new area for expansion, in order to take advantage of growing demand for steam coal; indeed, throughout its history, the company "has established a record of having the right type of ship at the right time" (*American Shipper*, September 1981). In the 1990s OSG stood ready to replace the fleets of those oil companies that no longer wished to transport the oil themselves because of the unlimited liability contained in the Oil Pollution Act of 1990.* OSG owned forty-nine foreign-flag ships of 5 million deadweight tons in January 1992, and in a business normally associated with wild gyrations and almost recurrent instability, this company under superb management has continued to expand and quietly make substantial profits for stockholders.

Principal Executives

Raphael Recanati	1969–present
Morton P. Hyman	1970–present

References: *American Shipper*, December 1977, September 1981, September 1990; René De La Pedraja, *The Rise and Decline of U.S. Merchant Shipping in the Twentieth Century* (New York: Twayne, 1992); *Forbes*, 1 February 1977; Maritime Administration, *Foreign-Flag Merchant Ships Owned by U.S. Parent Companies*, 1 January 1992; *Moody's Transportation Manual, 1975*.

P

PACIFIC AMERICAN STEAMSHIP ASSOCIATION (PASA or PASSA), 1919–1968. The Pacific American Steamship Association (PASA) represented those shipowners on the West Coast who were primarily engaged in the foreign trade. After several attempts by predecessor organizations dating back to 1907, PASA was finally established on a solid basis in June 1919. Companies in the coastwise* trade had their own separate organization, the Shipowners' Association of the Pacific Coast* (SAPC). In the 1920s PASA's main role was to defend the interests of West Coast shipowners. The real struggle was in Congress, and to adequately present its views, PASA, together with SAPC, decided to open a joint office in Washington, D.C., under James Henry MacLafferty in September 1927; this cooperation was only natural, because both organizations already issued the *Pacific Marine Review* as their official organ.

As was usual with the early shipowner groups, PASA also handled industrial relations and, in conjunction with SAPC, operated the Marine Service Bureau* for sailors. The extraordinary waterfront turmoil beginning with the Big Strike of 1934* required a concerted management response. In 1937 the steamship companies decided to handle all industrial relations with seamen and longshoremen through the newly created Waterfront Employers' Association* (WEA), but by 1946 PASA was again negotiating directly with the seamen's unions.

The shipping boom of World War II revived PASA, which went on to become an affiliate of the National Federation of American Shipping* (NFAS). After the 1940s, the number of member companies began to decline, and when NFAS collapsed in September 1953, a move to fuse PASA with the American Merchant Marine Institute* (AMMI) was on the point of success: ''Five of PASA's twelve lines are also members of AMMI, but they were unable to overcome the Westerners' deep-rooted fear that the big institute in New York would dominate shipping affairs'' (*New York Times*, 29 December 1953). However, PASA agreed to have joint offices in Washington, D.C., with AMMI. Meanwhile the disappearance of coastwise shipping on the Pacific Coast in the late 1950s meant the end of SAPC, leaving PASA as the only organization for shipowners on the West Coast. By the 1960s PASA had become an anachronism that reflected a period in economic history when differences between the two coasts of the United States had been of crucial significance. Member companies continued to go bankrupt, and the reminder chafed at paying double dues to PASA and to AMMI. To make the most of dwindling resources and also to speak with a more unified voice, the member companies dissolved PASA on 31 December 1938 in order to create with two other groups the American Institute of Merchant Shipping* (AIMS) on 1 January 1969.

Principal Executives

James H. MacLafferty	1927–1931
Almon E. Roth*	1937–1939
Lewis A. Lapham*	1945–1946
Robert E. Mayer	1946–1958
Ralph B. Dewey	1958–1968

References: Giles T. Brown, *Ships That Sail No More: Marine Transportation from San Diego to Puget Sound, 1910–1940* (Lexington: University of Kentucky Press, 1966); Gale Research, *Encyclopedia of Associations*, 1956–1968; James C. Healey, *Foc's'le and Glory-Hole: A Study of the Merchant Seaman and His Occupation* (New York: Merchant Marine Publishers Association, 1936); Henrietta Tyler Smith Oral History, Herbert Hoover Presidential Library, West Branch, Iowa; *New York Times*, 29 December 1953; Propeller Club, *American Merchant Marine Conference, 1961*; Official File 810, Harry S. Truman Presidential Library, Independence, Missouri; U.S. Senate, Committee on Interstate and Foreign Commerce, *Decline of Coastwise and Intercoastal Shipping Industry* (Washington, DC: Government Printing Office, 1960).

PACIFIC & EASTERN STEAMSHIP COMPANY, 1915–1920. The Pacific & Eastern Steamship Company was one of the firms that arose in response to the shipping shortages of World War I. In the Pacific Ocean, not only did rates rise dramatically like in the North Atlantic, but services became very scarce; even more ominously, Japanese steamship firms tried to drive out the remaining foreign services. The Pacific Mail Steamship Company* stood ready to overcome any foreign challenges, only to be sabotaged from within by the La Follette Seamen's Act,* which restricted the employment of Chinese crews. Deprived of a safe business environment, the Pacific Mail wisely left the steamship business by chartering* and selling its ships for service on the North Atlantic.

Chinese merchants and government officials wanted to create a merchant shipping company, but the lack of ships and expertise in Asia convinced them to seek U.S. partners who could obtain vessels and suitable management in New

York. Hopefully U.S. investors would materialize, but until then the Chinese were prepared to raise all the initial capital and still have an American general manager to run the line. U.S. embassy officials were enthusiastic about this proposal to strengthen Sino-American trade, but in the United States, no major corporation, whether steamship or railroad, was interested.

The Woodrow Wilson administration needed to find quickly someone for the Chinese, but the only available candidate was Philip Manson, who it later turned out was just "a small-operator with neither the broad experience nor strong financial connections" (Pugach 1975). An "ambitious braggart," Manson had landed the position because "he was a promoter and a jobber, who ingratiated himself with powerful men by advancing their causes" (ibid.). Manson went to China and signed a contract on 29 May 1915; he agreed to create a U.S.-flag steamship company and to operate at least four ships within six months whose purchase would be financed by a bond issue. The Chinese government guaranteed a 6 percent return on the bonds and also agreed to pay for the insurance fees on the ships. On the advice of other American partners, Manson limited the Chinese investment to only half of the bonds, and he promised to raise the rest of the money in New York.

When he returned from China, Manson duly incorporated the Pacific & Eastern Steamship Company on 29 October 1915. Chinese merchants had promptly lined up their half of funds, but New York investors were swamped with too many doubtful wartime schemes to be attracted to the Pacific & Eastern Steamship Co., which seemed to them too dependent on the guarantees of an unstable Chinese government. Manson, rather than immediately buying some ships before their prices rose even more, continued to dally and to watch the initial capital eaten away by the expenses and salaries of the New York office of his largely phantom Pacific & Eastern Steamship Company (he later claimed he had saved the Chinese investors their money by not paying exorbitant prices for any ship).

Tired of waiting, a group of Chinese and Chinese-American investors established the China Mail Steamship Company,* whose first steamer sailed on 30 October 1915. The failure of the Pacific & Eastern Steamship Company proved extremely embarrassing to officials of the Woodrow Wilson administration, who searched for alternatives to Manson, only to find David S. Rose, "an unscrupulous huckster with a tarnished past" who "was generally considered irresponsible in business circles" (ibid.). Nothing was accomplished, and the damage that the Pacific & Eastern Steamship Company did to Sino-American relations was extensive. Many Chinese merchants became disillusioned with American businessmen, while Chinese officials began to question the ability of the U.S. government to move from rhetoric to mutual action.

On another level, the Pacific & Eastern Steamship Company was the clearest warning that any attempt to subsidize the creation of many new U.S. steamship companies was bound to be very expensive and ultimately a disaster. As late as 1920 Manson was trying unsuccessfully to get surplus vessels for the Pacific & Eastern Steamship Co. from the Shipping Board,* which, however, in its rush to find new persons for "managing operators,"* soon harvested a large crop of get-rich-quick speculators and amateurs, who milked the government of funds.

References: Noel H. Pugach, "American Shipping Promoters and the Shipping Crisis of 1914–1916: The Pacific & Eastern Steamship Company," *American Neptune* 35 (1975): 166–182; Jeffrey J. Safford, *Wilsonian Maritime Diplomacy, 1913–1921* (New Brunswick, NJ: Rutgers University Press, 1978); E. Mowbray Tate, *Transpacific Steam: The Story of Steam Navigation from the Pacific Coast of North America to the Far East and the Antipodes, 1867–1941* (New York: Cornwall Books, 1986).

PACIFIC ARGENTINE BRAZIL LINE. See McCormick Steamship Company; Pope and Talbot.

PACIFIC COAST EUROPEAN CONFERENCE (PCEC), 1919–1989. The Pacific Coast European Conference (PCEC) set rates, sailings, and services on ships traveling from the Pacific Coast of the United States to Western European ports. Originally, managing operators* of the Shipping Board* established the conference to try to bring some order into their overlapping and often senseless competition, but by the 1930s the PCEC was heavily dominated by European steamship companies. After World War II the European lines resumed their position in the conference and were joined since the early 1950s by the rapidly growing Japanese companies. U.S.-flag membership continued to dwindle, and in 1957 out of twenty-two regular members, only one, States Marine Corporation,* was American. Because of the overwhelming foreign membership in the conference, it constantly delayed and often succeeded in blocking attempts of the Federal Maritime Commission* (FMC) to obtain evidence that might justify sanctions against the conference.

Much more effective in protecting the shippers* from discriminatory practices was the increasing rivalry among the member lines, and most of them had withdrawn from the conference by the late 1970s to quote rates on their own; in 1983 only three companies remained in the PCEC. Some form of consolidation seemed inevitable after the passage of the Shipping Act of 1984* legalized superconferences,* and in 1989 PCEC joined with the U.S. Atlantic North Europe Conference* (ANEC) and other conferences to form the U.S.A.-North Europe Rate Agreement* (USANERA) in 1989.

References: *American Shipper*, February 1983; Federal Maritime Board, *Decisions*, vol. 5, *1956–1960* (Washington, DC: Government Printing Office, 1964); Federal Maritime Commission, *Decisions*, vol. 7, *1961–1964* (Washington, DC: Government Printing Office, 1965); *Journal of Commerce*, 2 June 1989; U.S. Maritime Commission, *Decisions*, vol. 3, *1947–1952* (Washington, DC: Government Printing Office, 1952).

PACIFIC COAST STEAMSHIP COMPANY, 1877–1916. During forty years the Pacific Coast Steamship Company was the dominant firm in the coastwise* routes along the West Coast of the United States and to Alaska. The company began in 1860 as a partnership between Charles Goodall and Chris Nelson to bring fresh water to ships in San Francisco from springs near the northern part of the Bay; the company prospered and gradually entered coastwise shipping. With the infusion of new capital the partnership was expanded in 1877 into the Pacific Coast Steamship Company, and control of the company eventually passed to eastern investors. The company initially began operations with a modest fleet, which even included four of the obsolete side-wheelers. By the 1880s the company owned the largest coastwise fleet on the Pacific Coast and distinguished itself by the high quality of the service provided to passengers. To maintain its high standards, the company ordered the *Congress,** which, when delivered in October 1912, was the largest coastwise liner* in the United States.

   The Pacific Coast Steamship Company had faced rivals throughout its existence, and by 1910 the competition again intensified. Five lines were challenging the company in 1912, and eleven in 1914; among the most dangerous rivals were the San Francisco and Portland Steamship Company,* the Great Northern Pacific Steamship Company* (both owned by railroads), and the Admiral Line* of Hubbard F. Alexander.*

   By then the eastern investors had tired of waiting for the Pacific Coast Steamship Company to earn decent profits, and rumors of the company's impending sale circulated widely in early 1916. When the *Congress* caught fire at sea on 14 September 1916, the owners used this disaster as a good excuse to announce the sale of the company to the dynamic Alexander, although in fact the sale of the company had been agreed upon at least two weeks before. The small, upstart Admiral Line absorbed the larger organization and fleet of the Pacific Coast Steamship Company, whose existence came to an end.

Notable Ships

Queen of the Pacific (*Queen* after 1890)	1882–1916
President	1907–1916
Congress; later, *Nanking*	1912–1916

   References: Giles T. Brown, *Ships That Sail No More: Marine Transportation from San Diego to Puget Sound, 1910–1940* (Lexington: University of Kentucky Press, 1966); Frederick E. Emmons, *American Passenger Ships: The Ocean Lines and Liners, 1873–1983* (Newark: University of Delaware Press, 1985); John Niven, *The American President Lines and Its Forebears, 1848–1984* (Newark: University of Delaware Press, 1987); E. W. Wright, ed., *Marine History of the Pacific Northwest* (New York: Antiquarian Press, 1961).

PACIFIC FAR EAST LINE (PFEL), 1946–1978. Pacific Far East Line (PFEL) provided transpacific service and was one of the handful of U.S. steamship companies created after World War II. A vice president of American President Lines (APL), Thomas E. Cuffe, had sensed the time was ripe to enter merchant shipping, and in 1946 he created his own company, which initially operated vessels chartered* from the U.S. Maritime Commission* and later pur-

chased them under the provisions of the Ship Sales Act of 1946.* The names
he gave to the ships ended with the word *bear*; for example, in 1948 the company owned the *Pacific Bear, Indian Bear, California Bear, China Bear,* and
the *Philippine Bear.* Quite naturally the house flag consisted of a big bear under
the spaced letters *P F E L.*

Cuffe was a hard-driving and strong-willed executive who pushed to achieve
maximum results. The company prospered and paid out yearly dividends and in
1953 owned eight freighters and chartered additional vessels. PFEL had focused
since 1946 on the carriage of U.S. military cargoes to the Far East, but Japanese
competition was so strong for the rest of the cargoes that after January 1953 the
company needed as well subsidies from the Maritime Administration*
(MARAD).

Unlike the pre–World War II services, PFEL had to meet the large and growing demand for the transport of refrigerated goods and cargo oil. To remain
competitive, PFEL had to order new vessels more suitable to the needs of the
trade and thus was among the first companies to order the new Mariner* class
vessels, which had been designed by MARAD. By 1962 the company, as part
of the replacement program, had traded in the last of its World War II vessels
for modified Mariners with an enlarged capacity for refrigerated and liquid cargoes—and space even for 12- and 24-foot containers.*

The success of PFEL had attracted the attention of oilman Ralph K. Davies,
who, much like Stanley Dollar* before World War II, wanted to create a shipping empire in the Pacific Ocean. Davies already owned the American President
Lines* (APL) and the American Mail Line* (AML), and PFEL was the next
logical acquisition. By 1959 Davies had acquired quietly 40 percent of PFEL's
stock, and a clash with Cuffe, the majority stockholder, seemed inevitable. Unexpectedly on 22 December 1959, Cuffe died of a heart attack, and for a few
months the company "was in disarray" (Niven 1987) until Davies gained full
control.

Davies's assistants soon "discovered major irregularities in the former management," and to correct "the excesses of Cuffe's one-man rule" (Niven 1987),
Davies appointed Clarence G. Morse* as the new president of PFEL. Unfortunately, putting the company in order was not Morse's forte, and in February
1962 he had to be eased out and was replaced by the more aggressive Raymond
Ickes, who quickly had the company operating smoothly. Ickes handled effectively the routine corporate affairs, but he did not know how to cope with the
startling new development of containers. Rather than accepting containers, Ickes
became fascinated with the LASH* (lighter aboard ship) concept. As president
of PFEL he argued strongly for LASH ships, and when Ickes was promoted to
the presidency of APL, he was instrumental in convincing Davies to order LASH
vessels for PFEL.

Too late to change the orders for the nearly completed vessels in the shipyards, Davies finally realized he had made a blunder in ordering the LASH
vessels, and in the time-honored tradition he decided to sell his problems to

somebody else. In 1969 Consolidated Freightways bought PFEL, without realizing what was at stake. Consolidated Freightways was the trucking firm of
William G. White, who already owned an airline, and on paper his acquisition
of PFEL appeared the logical next step to achieve full intermodal* transportation
services. At this moment Matson Navigation Company* wanted to dump its
passenger services and in 1970 found in White the buyer for the money-losing
liners the *Mariposa** and the *Monterey.**

White received a crash course in merchant shipping and soon learned that
PFEL was heading straight to bankruptcy. To avoid mounting losses, he slashed
the price of the company from $24 million to $4 million and then sold the
company to John I. Alioto in 1974. Alioto felt he could succeed where the pros
had failed, and thanks to a short-lived demand for cargo space, he was able to
steer PFEL away from bankruptcy and into high profits. The windfall profits
gave Alioto the chance to convert the LASH vessels to full containers, which
would remain competitive once the brief boom ended. He threw the priceless
opportunity away, and instead in 1975 he decided to provide Roll On/Roll Off*
(Ro/Ro) service to the Middle East, a move that earned PFEL temporary profits
but still left the company without containerships.

Alioto's extraordinary good luck ran out in 1977, and the company began to
pile up heavy losses. He finally ordered the conversion of the three LASH
vessels to containerships, but it was too late, and in February 1978 PFEL filed
for Chapter XI protection. All attempts to revive the company failed, and in
July 1978 the liquidation of the company began. At bankruptcy court APL
purchased the three LASH ships and finished their conversion to containerships.

Principal Executives

Thomas C. Cuffe	1946–1959
Clarence Morse*	1960–1962
Raymond Ickes	1962–1966
Leo C. Ross	1966–1974
John I. Alioto	1974–1978

Some Notable Ships

*Mariposa** and *Monterey**	1970–1978

References: René De La Pedraja, *The Rise and Decline of U.S. Merchant Shipping in
the Twentieth Century* (New York: Twayne, 1992); John Niven, *The American President
Lines and Its Forebears, 1848–1984* (Newark: University of Delaware Press, 1987).

PACIFIC MAIL STEAMSHIP COMPANY (PMSS), 1848–1916. The Pacific
Mail Steamship Company (PMSS), because of its long duration and close relation with the settlement of the Pacific Coast, was probably the most famous
of U.S. steamship companies. PMSS was chartered in April 1848 to take advantage of a U.S. Navy contract that subsidized the operation of fast side-

wheelers (easily converted to naval auxiliaries) between the Pacific side of Panama and the Columbia River in the Oregon territory. News of the discovery of gold in California unleashed in December 1848 a stampede from the East Coast, just as the PMSS was placing its first three steamers, the *California,** *Oregon,** and *Panama,** on the route. Panama was the safest and fastest route to California, and PMSS was ideally placed to reap the greatest windfall profits from the gold rush. After a few years the frenzied excitement died down, but the completion of the railroad across the Isthus of Panama in 1855 guaranteed ample volumes of cargo and passengers for the rapidly growing fleet of eighteen steamers in 1853 and twenty-three in 1869. PMSS provided splendid service to its passengers, and the goodwill it earned was one of the reasons the company outperformed and eventually outlived its early competitors. Until 1867 PMSS paid stockholders annual dividends of 10 to 30 percent, astounding amounts in a period of little inflation; only the profits of the Panama Railroad itself were comparable, making these two firms the most lucrative of U.S. corporations in that period.

The completion of the first transcontinental railroad in 1869 permanently ended the astounding profits, and for the rest of the nineteenth century both PMSS and the Panama Railroad struggled to find a substitute source of income. Even before the completion of the first transcontinental railroad, PMSS had decided to redirect its activities toward transpacific shipping and to reduce to second place the California-Panama route. A mail contract from Congress allowed the company to inaugurate the first regular transpacific service with the sailing of the *Colorado** on 1 January 1867. PMSS ordered four more ships for the route, the *America, China, Great Republic,** and the *Japan,* but all, including the *Colorado,* were obsolete even before they were finished. They were "the largest wooden, ocean-going merchant steamers ever built" (Niven 1987), used wooden side-wheels instead of screws, and for power relied on the single expansion engine* rather than the compound engine,* which had already become standard in new steamship construction. Attractive as was the new technology, PMSS felt that it had not yet reached the distant Pacific Coast, and without modern repair facilities, the company believed it was better off relying on tried-and-proven methods rather than risk embarrassing and costly breakdowns. The lack of coaling stations along the route required the large size, because each vessel had to carry from San Francisco enough coal until the first stop in Japan.

The transpacific line was a success, and starting in 1869 the transcontinental railroads offered to take all the freight coming aboard the vessels, thereby linking for the first time the Far East and the East Coast, the rudimentary beginnings of what in the twentieth century became known as "intermodal"* and "land-bridge"* services. The Panama Railroad, however, was not about to give up without a fight, and in 1873, when it gained influence over PMSS, it attempted to channel all Far East cargoes through the Isthmus of Panama rather than San Francisco. The plan proved unworkable and was largely dropped, but the transcontinental railroads were furious at this attempt to take their cargo away and decided to protect themselves from a similar risk. In 1874 the Central Pacific-Union Pacific railroads organized the Occidental and Oriental Steamship Company* (O&O) to bring freight from the Far East to the Pacific Coast terminals of the railroads. O&O chartered British-flag steamers of the White Star Line, and the arrival of this sharp competition forced PMSS to adopt new vessels of iron hulls and propellers,* which were driven by compound engines. By the early 1880s the company had replaced the last of the wooden side-wheelers.

Mail subsidies from the governments of Australia and New Zealand allowed PMSS to begin a regular service to Sydney and Auckland in 1875. The U.S. government later added its own mail subsidies to the route, but the company was not very interested in this service, which carried only light traffic and did not earn profits. When the U.S. Congress awarded the next mail contract to the Oceanic Steamship Company* (OSS) in 1885, PMSS withdrew its ships from the Australia/New Zealand route.

The last stage in the history of the PMSS began in 1893, when the Southern Pacific Railroad gained control of PMSS and shortly after of O&O. Southern Pacific placed PMSS under a new, dynamic executive, Rennie P. Schwerin,* who gradually absorbed O&O into the PMSS structure. He revitalized the company, which paid dividends in 1897–99 for the first time since 1885. Schwerin promoted the fruit and coffee trade from Central America to generate more cargo for the steamers on the line to Panama, but he knew that the transpacific line remained the most important. He convinced Southern Pacific to invest sums to order in 1898 the *Korea** and the *Siberia*,* and the company received in 1904 the even larger *Manchuria** and *Mongolia*.* Schwerin was convinced that these fast modern steamers could earn profits separate from those the railroad made handling the cargo, but increasingly PMSS faced ruthless competition from the Japanese steamship companies, in particular, Nippon Yusen Kaisha.

Fortunately for PMSS, it had always relied on trained and loyal Chinese crews to man the ships under U.S. officers, so that the company could meet any price competition from the Japanese lines. The deferred rebate* did not become illegal in the United States until 1916 and was a powerful tool that PMSS used to keep cargo coming to its ships. The Japanese lines did receive subsidies, unlike PMSS, but Schwerin was convinced that if he built monster ships to travel from New York through the Panama Canal* to the West Coast and then the Far East, the intercoastal* trade alone guaranteed a profitable venture.

The U.S. Congress had other ideas and, in the Panama Canal Act of 1912,* forbade steamship companies owned by railroads from using the Panama Canal. In a further blow, Congress passed the La Follette Seamen's Act* in 1915, which sharply restricted the use of Chinese crews aboard U.S.-flag vessels. Under these new restrictions, Schwerin considered hopeless any attempt to face the Japanese lines; Southern Pacific agreed and decided to liquidate the fleet and recover its investment. The record-high rates on the North Atlantic convinced the International Mercantile Marine* (IMM) to buy the four giant steamers in August 1915, while the rest of the fleet and the name were sold to the Grace Line* in December. Early in 1916 Schwerin retired, and Grace management took over, although retaining as much as possible the previous PMSS staff; the remaining ships were painted with colors different from their traditional black, but the house flag was retained. The sudden halt of the PMSS transpacific service remained first-page news in the United States for weeks, and the ensuing shipping shortage led the U.S. government to support ventures like the Pacific & Eastern Steamship Company,* but more effective solutions had to wait until the creation of the Shipping Board.*

The Grace Line maintained PMSS as a subsidiary until 1925, but closely integrated with its other steamship services. Unlike Southern Pacific Railway, which had left Schwerin a free hand, Grace closely controlled PMSS, whose independent history definitely ended in 1916. When the Dollar family acquired the PMSS name, house flag, and goodwill from Grace in 1925, the original company had long ceased to function, although the Dollar family could flatter themselves by continuing to tack the PMSS paper shell to small miscellaneous shipping deals as late as 1949.

Principal Executives

William H. Aspinwall	1848–1856
William H. Davidge	1856–1860
Allan McLane	1860–1871
Alden B. Stockwell	1871–1873
Russell Sage	1873–1874
Sidney Dillon	1875–1876
George W. Clyde*	1876–1878
D. S. Babcock	1878–1879
J. B. Houston	1880–1887
George G. Gould	1887–1893
Rennie P. Schwerin	1893–1916

Some Notable Ships

California, *Oregon*, and *Panama*	1848–1870
Colorado	1864–1879
San Francisco	1851–1853
Golden Gate	1853–1862
*Hermann**	1866–1868
Great Republic, *China*, *Japan*, and *America*	1867–1883
*City of Tokyo** and *City of Peking*	1875–1908

Colima	1874–1895
City of Rio de Janeiro	1881–1901
Korea and *Siberia*	1902–1915
Manchuria and *Mongolia*	1904–1915
*China II**	1889–1915

References: René De La Pedraja, *The Rise and Decline of U.S. Merchant Shipping* (New York: Twayne, 1992); John H. Kemble, ''A Hundred Years of the Pacific Mail,'' *American Neptune* 10 (1950): 123–143; John Niven, *The American President Lines and Its Forebears, 1848–1984* (Newark: University of Delaware Press, 1987); E. Mowbray Tate, *Transpacific Steam, The Story of Steam Navigation from the Pacific Coast of North America to the Far East and the Antipodes, 1867–1941* (New York: Cornwall Books, 1986).

PACIFIC MARITIME ASSOCIATION (PMA), 1949–present. The Pacific Maritime Association (PMA) has been since 1949 the employers' association that negotiated with labor on the Pacific Coast. The PMA appeared after the 1948 strike by longshoremen, when management realized that the traditional confrontational tactics were not obtaining results. Steamship companies, terminal operators, and stevedore firms replaced the previous Waterfront Employers' Association* (WEA) with the PMA. The bargaining functions of the Pacific American Steamship Owners' Association* (PASA) were permanently transferred to PMA, but PASA itself survived until 1968 (several published accounts claimed erroneously that PASA merged with the WEA to create PMA). The Shipowners' Association of the Pacific Coast* (SAPC), which represented coastwise* firms, continued to negotiate directly with the sailors' unions and left bargaining with the International Longshoremen and Warehousemen's Union* (ILWU) to the PMA, but these special negotiating arrangements ended when the collapse of coastwise trade led to the disbandment of SAPC.

PMA exemplified the transition from multiservice trade associations to specialized organizations for industrial relations and was in contrast to the practice on the East Coast and Gulf, where the transition began decades later and has never been completed. In practice, PMA has been the counterweight to the ILWU, whose militancy and determination created the need for a similarly solid bargaining employer organization.

Principal Executives

O. W. Pearson	1949–1951
Paul St. Sure	1952–1966

References: Gale Research, *Encyclopedia of Associations*, 1983–1993; Paul T. Hartman, *Collective Bargaining and Productivity: The Longshore Mechanization Agreement* (Berkeley: University of California Press, 1969); Clark Kerr and Lloyd Fisher, ''Conflict on the Waterfront,'' *Atlantic Monthly*, September 1949, pp. 17–23; Charles P. Larrowe, *Harry Bridges: The Rise and Fall of Radical Labor in the U.S.* (New York: Lawrence

Hill, 1972); Maritime Cargo Transportation Conference, *San Francisco Port Study*, 2 vols. (Washington, DC: National Academy of Sciences, 1964).

PACIFIC TRANSPORT LINES (PTL), 1946–1954. Pacific Transport Lines (PTL) was one of the handful of new steamship companies that appeared after World War II. In 1946 PTL was organized by Richard A. McLaren, a veteran operator who had been a vice president of the American-Hawaiian Steamship Company,* and the main investor was Paul I. Fagan, who owned 80 percent of the stock. PTL purchased surplus ships in order to operate a transpacific cargo service from Los Angeles and San Francisco; PTL resembled the Pacific Far East Line* (PFEL), which was organized also in 1946 to provide transpacific service.

PTL's first voyages began in January 1947, and by the end of the year the company owned five vessels. Initially the well-managed company was very successful, but as foreign competition returned to the Pacific Ocean, PTL's prospects began to darken, even before the reentry of Japanese steamship lines in 1951. Along with PFEL, PTL sought and received operating differential subsidies* from the Maritime Administration* after 1950, but this was still not enough to keep the small firm afloat, and it decided to enter the protected Hawaiian trade. PTL was the second company after the Los Angeles Steamship Company* (LASSCO) in the 1920s to try to challenge the near monopoly the Matson Navigation Company* maintained over shipping from the mainland to Hawaii. In July 1950 PTL inaugurated a monthly service to Hawaii "as an extension of its present transpacific service to Japan, China, and the Philippines." PTL "intended to give Matson the toughest kind of competition, but we hope it won't degenerate into a dog fight or a rate war " (*Business Week*, 8 July 1950).

Only cutthroat competition greeted PTL in Hawaii and in the Far East, and as losses piled up, finally Paul I. Fagan decided to get out of the steamship business. In 1954 he sold his stock to the Dant family members, who in 1957 merged PTL with their own shipping firm, the States Steamship Lines.*

References: *Business Week*, 8 July 1950; Maritime Subsidy Board, *Decisions*, vol. 1, *August 1961–September 1964* (Washington, DC: Government Printing Office, 1965); *New York Times*, 8 August 1954; U.S. Congress, House, Committee on Merchant Marine and Fisheries, *Merchant Marine Study and Investigation*, 7 vols. (Washington, DC: Government Printing Office, 1950).

PACIFIC WESTBOUND CONFERENCE (PWC), 1923–1984. In 1923, under the auspices of the Shipping Board,* steamship lines organized the Pacific Westbound Conference (PWC) to set rates, sailings, and other services on cargoes moving westward from the Pacific Coast of North America to the Far East (the Asian countries bordering the Pacific Ocean from Siberia to Indochina, including Japan, Formosa, and the Philippine islands). A separate group of conferences, most notably the Transpacific Freight Conference of Japan* (TPFCJ), established the rates for cargoes moving eastward to the Pacific Coast of the United States.

The PWC functioned effectively until the Great Depression and did not adopt its first dual-rate contract* until 1927. When Hans Isbrandtsen's* ships, starting in 1929, made calls in Los Angeles on their voyage from New York City to the Far East, the PWC faced a first challenge, but soon he saved his most bitter blows for the Far East Conference* (FEC). The real danger to the PWC came in 1932, when the entry of the British firm Ellerman & Bucknall plunged the trade into a long rate war, Only the outbreak of World War II in 1939 ended this British competition, but by then the PWC was totally demoralized and had to await the end of the war to reconstitute itself.

The U.S. occupation of Japan gave U.S. firms privileged control over Japanese cargoes, and soon the PWC was back in operation. The return of Japanese lines in 1951 increased membership, and in 1959 the PWC, besides fourteen associate companies, had the following nineteen regular members:

American Mail Line*	Nissan Kisen Kaisha
American Presidents Line*(APL)	Nitto Shosen Co.
Daido Kaium Kaisha	Osaka Shosen Co.
De La Rama Lines	Pacific Far East Line*
Isthmian Lines*	Pacific Orient Express Line
Java Pacific & Hoegh Lines	States Marine Corp.*
Klaveness Line	States Steamship Lines*
Knutsen Line	Waterman Steamship Corp.*
Mitsubishi Shipping Co.	Yamashita Kisen Kaisha
Nippon Yusen Kaisha	

During the 1960s and 1970s a relatively tranquil existence resulted in a bloated and soft bureaucracy for the conference, which was ill-prepared to face the series of rate wars that broke out in the early 1980s. Membership shrunk to ten lines, and twenty other lines were quoting rates outside the conference. Korea Marine Transport Co. resigned in May 1984, and when Sea-Land* offered in August a special discount plan to shippers,* the other lines were furious. After attempts to reach an agreement failed, APL resigned, and the other nine lines did the same, so that the memberless PWC officially dissolved on 1 November 1984. The trade route of PWC, along with the routes of six other outbound conferences, went into the Transpacific Westbound Rate Agreement* (TWRA), one of the superconferences* that emerged after the passage of the Shipping Act of 1984.*

References: *American Shipper*, June and November 1984; René De La Pedraja, *The Rise and Decline of U.S. Merchant Shipping in the Twentieth Century* (New York: Twayne, 1992); U.S. Congress, House, Committee on Merchant Marine and Fisheries,

Steamship Conference Study, 3 vols. (Washington, DC: Government Printing Office, 1959).

PALMER, LEIGH CARLYLE, 11 January 1873–26 February 1955. Leigh Carlyle Palmer was a naval officer who served as president of the Emergency Fleet Corporation* (EFC) in 1924–1925 and who was vice president of the American South African Line* and the Farrell Line* from 1927 to 1950. Palmer was born on 11 January 1873 in Saint Louis, Missouri, and graduated from the U.S. Naval Academy in 1896. As a naval officer, he actively sought the command of ships and flotillas, where he distinguished himself, but his most important work came as chief of its Bureau of Navigation in 1916–1918, where he successfully organized the recruiting and training of personnel for the World War I navy. He resigned from the navy in 1920 and went to the Far East on business.

The Shipping Board,* under pressure from President Calvin Coolidge to reduce expenses, called Palmer back to assume the presidency of the Emergency Fleet Corporation on 7 January 1924; his appointment, however, was so unpopular with the commissioners that Chairman Thomas V. O'Connor* had required that Palmer file a signed resignation for possible use in the future. Palmer's main task was to consolidate the overlapping and conflicting routes so that a smaller number of firms could provide adequate services at lower cost to the Shipping Board. It was inevitable that the firms slated for elimination would resent Palmer's attempt to consolidate the routes, while the Shipping Board resented any encroachment on its powers. In one swift power play, the Shipping Board dismissed Palmer on 6 October 1925, an action that further weakened the public image of that government agency; even president Calvin Coolidge was so angry that he considered abolishing the Shipping Board.

Palmer was out of a job, but James A. Farrell, Sr.,* the president of United States Steel Corporation, soon had a proposal: his son, James A. Farrell, Jr.,* had just begun to operate a new company, the American South African Line,* and needed an experienced hand to steer him through the business. John M. Franklin* was temporarily lending a hand, but his heart was really in the International Mercantile Marine* (IMM), whose leadership soon he would assume. Palmer accepted the offer and in July 1926 began to work for the American South African Line; in April 1927, when Franklin left, Palmer became the vice president.

As the right hand of John J. Farrell, Palmer proved instrumental in the successful operation of the company. Naval officers, because they know about the sea and ships, often were considered ideal candidates to run a merchant fleet, but this has usually not been the case, because the complexities of operating a profitable merchant shipping firm required talents in addition to those of a good naval officer. Rennie Schwerin* of Pacific Mail Steamship Company* and Palmer were examples of naval officers who succeeded in the business of shipping. Palmer continued as vice president until 1950, by which time the company had changed its name to the Farrell Line. Although he remained a member of the Board of Directors, he had retired and moved to California, where he died on 26 February 1955.

References: Robert G. Albion, *Seaports South of Sahara: The Achievements of an American Steamship Service* (New York: Appleton-Century-Crofts, 1959); *National Cyclopedia of American Biography*, vol. 46.

PANAMA. See *California, Oregon,* and *Panama.*

PANAMA CANAL, 1914–present. The Panama Canal joins the Atlantic and Pacific oceans at the Isthmus of Panama. As one of the engineering wonders of the twentieth century, it has had a tremendous impact on the U.S. merchant marine. For centuries the dream of building the canal had existed, and after an initial attempt by the French, it was left to the U.S. government to build the canal, which was opened for navigation on 15 August 1914. Unfortunately in obtaining the territory for the canal, the United States had broken international treaties and supported a separatist revolt in Panama as a way to obtain the rights for the canal, which Colombia appeared to have refused to grant. In reality the whole Panama coup had been an episode hatched by the stockholders of the French Panama Canal Company, who wanted to recover their initial investment by selling the company to the U.S. government.

The French company had failed because it underestimated the challenge. It believed that construction would not be much harder than for the Suez Canal, which was built at the sea level over generally flat terrain. Moving whole mountains proved much harder in Panama, as U.S. builders likewise discovered: even after years of vigorous excavation, the opening of the canal, which originally was expected for 1913, had to be postponed until 15 August 1914 because of unusual difficulties in digging through the mountains, particularly in what became known as Culebra Cut. The opening of the canal, although clouded by the outbreak of World War I in Europe, had fueled the plans of many companies to enter shipping, as was the case with the Isthmian Line,* while other firms, such as American-Hawaiian Steamship Company* and Grace Line,* which previously had used the longer route around South America through the Straits of Magellan, now shifted to the Panama Canal. However, barely a year later new landslides blocked Culebra Cut on 13 September 1915. General George Goethals, who was in charge of the construction, decided to remove large sections of the mountain to avoid any future closings, and finally on 15 April 1916 the Panama Canal resumed service without any further interruptions from nature. However, smaller landslides have made constant dredging necessary to keep the waterway navigable.

The canal consists of a systems of locks, Gatun Lake, and the canal channel itself. The dimensions of the locks, 1,000 feet long by 110 feet wide, determined the size of the ships, and while the whole work was a colossal achievement, one of the few things that the original planners could be criticized for was not making the locks wider; already in the original design the width of the canal was increased from 100 to 110 feet at the insistence of the navy, which had on the drawing board a battleship 98 feet wide. Not too much vision was required to realize that 12 feet was a very small margin of space to leave for a century of growth in marine architecture.

The United States had full control over the canal and over a strip on land on each side of the waterway known as the Canal Zone. Upkeep and maintenance of the canal were the main concerns until the middle of the twentieth century, and once shippers* were convinced that the canal was a reliable route, the volume of traffic (necessarily slack during World War I) increased and ten years after the opening had equaled the volume of the Suez Canal. Tolls financed the operation of the canal, and no major changes occurred until the installation of channel lights made possible night transits for small and medium-sized vessels. The volume of traffic increased steadily after World War II, and by the early 1970s a ship was passing the canal every hour every day of the year.

The oil crisis of 1973 sharply reduced volume because tankers had been major users of the canal. Oil from Alaska gave a temporary boost until the completion of a pipeline across Panama in 1982 virtually eliminated tankers from the canal and sent traffic volumes down again. However, new cargoes appeared; for example, vessels loaded with Japanese cars for East Coast ports provided a temporary boost in the 1980s, while bulk* cargoes have remained a solid core of volume for the canal. Moreover, for the countries of Chile, Peru, Ecuador, and even Colombia, their location on the Pacific coast of South America has made the canal vital for their links with the United States and Europe, so that those South American countries comprised the largest users of the canal.

The Panama Canal Treaties of 1977 appeared to bring political clouds over the operation of the waterway, and it was feared that once the United States has completed its pullout from the isthmus on 31 December 1999, political instability would reduce the efficiency of the canal. When dictator Manuel Noriega decided upon a confrontation with the United States, the fears about the canal and about the Panamanian flag of convenience* appeared confirmed, but the waterway continued in operation. Only with the U.S. invasion of Panama on 20 December 1989 was transit briefly interrupted, but it resumed after, at most, a five-day delay to the nearly 100 vessels backed up, waiting for transit. Most shippers, swamped by intense competitive pressures, do not even want to think what will happen when Panama regains full control over the canal in 2000.

An even more serious challenge for the canal has been the landbridge* system across the United States and, in particular, the introduction of double-stack* trains in 1984. Many prophesied that the all-water route through the canal to the East Coast was doomed, and initially the predictions seemed to be borne out. However, by 1988 many shippers who wanted the lowest rates for their containers* and were not overly concerned about speed continued to rely on the canal. The authorities at the canal, to make the waterway more attractive, decided to begin in 1992 an expansion program to speed up passage. Normally transit time was twenty-four hours, at least half of it spent waiting for the order to proceed to the next step, but, by widening the Culebra Cut, a wider channel will make possible two-way traffic through the waterway for Panamax* and also night transits, just like for the smaller vessels. With these steps the Panama Canal hoped to remain competitive and to attract more vessels beyond its core group of bulk carriers, South American countries, and some Far Eastern lines. Numerous plans have been proposed to enlarge the existing waterway, and whatever decision is finally reached, no doubt remained about the need for world shipping to build a bigger canal either in Panama or perhaps even in another site, most probably Nicaragua or Colombia.

References: *American Shipper*, March, September 1991; William J. Jorden, *Panama Odyssey* (Austin: University of Texas Press, 1984); *Journal of Commerce*, 25 January, 14 March 1988; David McCullough, *The Path Between the Seas: The Creation of the Panama Canal, 1870–1914* (New York: Simon & Schuster, 1977).

PANAMA CANAL ACT OF 1912. As the construction of the Panama Canal* neared completion, the U.S. government felt the need to stipulate clearly the rules "for the opening, maintenance, protection, and operation of the Panama Canal, and the sanitation and government of the Canal Zone" (*U.S. Statutes at Large* 1912). From the international perspective, the act of 24 August 1912 ratified previous treaty commitments that had opened the canal to the world's commerce during peacetime to the ships of all nations, without any discrimination in rates or services. As an additional goodwill gesture, the United States also opened its registry* to new foreign-built ships, whose operation was allowed only in the foreign trade routes and excluded from domestic shipping protected by the cabotage* privileges.

For the U.S. merchant marine, the most significant clauses dealt with internal matters unrelated to other nations. The Panama Canal Act prohibited absolutely the ownership by the railroads of any ship that would use the new canal. The Southern Pacific Railroad owned the Pacific Mail Steamship Company* (PMSS), which now had to abandon its plans to build huge ships in time for the opening of the Panama Canal in 1914. Furthermore, the act prohibited railroads from owning steamship companies at all unless the Interstate Commerce Commission* (ICC) granted approval, and the result of these clauses was that most railroads gradually divested themselves of their shipping services, and worse, a hostility emerged between railroads and merchant shipping unknown before that time.

The Panama Canal Act was supposed to bring competition to the ocean trades by reducing the role of the railroads, but in reality most of the steamship lines could survive only as feeder services for the railroads, so that many coastwise* firms gradually disappeared in the following decades. In the competition for the intercoastal* trade and the remaining coastwise cargoes, the railroads after World War II launched such fierce competition that domestic ocean shipping practically disappeared.

The Staggers Rail Act of 1980 removed most restrictions on railroad ownership of other modes of transportation, including merchant shipping companies, and the ICC in its rulings has approved the acquisition by the railroads of firms in other transportation modes. In a major case in 1986, when a railroad, CSX, purchased Sea-Land,* the ICC declared it had no jurisdiction over the merger; nevertheless, to avoid even the remotest possibility of a violation of the Panama Canal Act, Sea-Land, which did not have any plans to use the Panama Canal, sold a foreign-flag joint venture on the grounds the latter might someday consider using that waterway. While the greater acceptance of the ICC toward ownership of different types of transportation by the same company has encouraged the spread of intermodalism,* the anachronistic Panama Canal Act of 1912 has continued to bar railroads from owning ships that use the canal, a law that has undermined and weakened the U.S. merchant marine.

References: *American Shipper,* July 1986, March 1987; René De La Pedraja, *The Rise and Decline of U.S. Merchant Shipping in the Twentieth Century* (New York: Twayne, 1992); Ernst G. Frankel, *Regulation and Policies of American Shipping* (Boston: Auburn House, 1982); John G. B. Hutchins, *The American Maritime Industries and Public Policy, 1789–1914* (Cambridge: Harvard University Press, 1941); Samuel A. Lawrence, *United States Merchant Shipping Policies and Politics* (Washington, DC: Brookings Institution, 1966); Transportation Research Board, *Intermodal Marine Container Transportation: Impediments and Opportunities* (Washington: DC: National Research Council, 1992); *U.S. Statutes at Large,* vol. 37 (1912).

PANAMA RAILROAD STEAMSHIP COMPANY or PANAMA STEAMSHIP COMPANY or PANAMA LINE, 1889–1981. The Panama Steamship Company carried cargo and passengers from the United States to Panama and back. The French company that had been building a canal across the isthmus was no longer satisfied with the shipping services on the Atlantic side (on the Pacific Coast the Pacific Mail Steamship Company* provided adequate schedules), and decided in 1889 to charter its own vessels, which originally it ran under the name of the Columbian line because Panama at that time belonged to Colombia. In 1894 the French company purchased three steamers and in 1896 changed the name from Columbian line to Panama Railroad Steamship Company.

After Panama became independent through U.S. intervention, the United States received the Canal Zone, a strip of territory extending ten miles on each side of the proposed canal route. The U.S. government also purchased the bankrupt French canal company, and among the latter's assets came the three ships of the Panama Railroad Steamship Company. The Isthmian Canal Commission, the agency in charge of the Canal Zone and of the construction work on the waterway, soon realized that more vessels were needed to bring the workers and materials for the new canal and purchased three more combination passenger-cargo ships. These were still not enough, and the Isthmian Canal Commission added two more, the *Ancón* and the *Cristóbal,* in 1908. With the completion of the work for the Panama Canal* in August 1914, the demand for cargo space slackened considerably, and the Panama Railroad Steamship Company gradually settled down to the routine of carrying supplies and passengers for the upkeep and maintenance of the installations in the Canal Zone.

In the 1920s businessmen eager to make quick profits at the expense of long-range national interests began to attack the Panama Railroad Steamship Company with charges of unfair government competition with private enterprise, but the U.S. Army, which by then operated most installations in the Canal Zone, including the line, managed to head off the attacks. When the Black Committee* exposed how private businessmen had shamelessly and wantonly milked the Shipping Board* for private profits, in sharp contrast to the exemplary government operation of the Panama Line—as it was most frequently called since the late 1930s—the attacks against government ownership abated for several decades. The Panama Line was a proprietary* company of the Canal Zone government, which in the tradition of similar large enterprises did not want to trust the carriage of its cargoes to outside firms; furthermore, not only were the operations of the Panama Line successful, but in the route from the Canal Zone to New York, the government line had also slowly and carefully built up the trade with Haiti.

During the Dwight D. Eisenhower pro-business administration, private shipping companies made numerous attacks on the Panama Line, which, as a government-owned line, was a convenient scapegoat to blame for the ills of the merchant marine without having to dig deeper into the real causes for the decline of U.S.-flag shipping. After a long, dragged-out bureaucratic battle, President Eisenhower ordered on 21 December 1960 that the two remaining ships of the Panama Line be placed in the National Defense Reserve Fleet* and that all cargoes henceforth travel aboard private companies, in particular, the Grace Line.* The incoming John F. Kennedy administration felt this measure was too extreme and countered in April 1961 with a more modest proposal that left the *Cristóbal* in service but only for the carriage of government cargoes. With only one ship, the Panama Line could not maintain the New York route and the Haitian calls and limited itself to the Canal Zone-New Orleans route. By this action the Panama Line was crippled, but the fortunes of the Grace Line were in no way appreciably improved. The Grace Line dropped out of merchant shipping in 1969, and in contrast the Panama Line continued service with its lone ship until 1981, when the Panama Canal treaties ended not only the Canal Zone itself but many of the obligations the United States previously had shouldered to maintain the railroad and the canal in proper condition.

Notable Ships

Cristóbal and *Ancón*	1909–1939
Panama	1939–1956
Ancón	1939–1961
Cristóbal	1939–1981

References: Commission on Organization of the Executive Branch of the Government, *Transportation: A Report to the Congress* (Washington, DC: Government Printing Office, 1955); René De La Pedraja, *The Rise and Decline of U.S. Merchant Shipping in the Twentieth Century* (New York: Twayne, 1992); Frederick E. Emmons, *American Passenger Ships: The Ocean Lines and Liners, 1873–1983* (Newark: University of Delaware Press, 1985).

PANAMAX. Panamax stands for Panama Canal Maximum, or the largest containerships that could still pass the Panama Canal.* The dimensions of the locks in the Panama Canal, 1,000 feet long and 110 feet wide, have been a bottleneck for builders of merchant and naval ships for decades. Oil tankers were the first large vessels built that could not pass through the Panama Canal, but steamship companies had expected break-bulk* freighters to continue using the Panama Canal far into the twenty-first century.

The container* revolution totally transformed cargo service and required bigger ships because containers occupied more space than most break-bulk cargo. As ship sizes grew, the limitations of the Panama Canal became more evident. The term *Panamax* applied to the ships that just barely fit through the canal; the most famous in that generation were the Econships,* whose length of 950 feet and beam of 106 feet made them the biggest containerships in the world. The more containers a ship could carry, the lower the operating costs, and these "economies of scale" because of larger size have convinced companies to construct Post-Panamax* vessels of even bigger container capacity.

References: American Bureau of Shipping, *History 1862–1991: Journal of Commerce*, 26 August 1988; *American Shipper*, December 1986; Transportation Research Board, *Intermodal Marine Container Transportation: Impediments and Opportunities* (Washington, DC: National Research Council, 1992).

PATROLMAN. The patrolmen have been the crucial link between the shoreside union officials and the union crews aboard ships. Already in the last two decades of the nineteenth century patrolmen had emerged as full-time salaried officials in the Sailors' Union of the Pacific (SUP) and the International Seamen's Union* (ISU). A patrolman would be at the pier when the ship docked and sailed, in each case ready either to receive the latest news from the voyage or to impart last-minute instructions. Patrolmen would try to solve whatever issues the sailors raised and, if important enough, would refer them to the port agent, who was the highest-ranking union representative in that particular port; normally a number of patrolmen (who were walking or "patrolling" from ship to ship) worked under one port agent.

With the expansion of sailors' unions after the late 1930s, the patrolmen rose in importance within the growing union bureaucracy, even though their influence was soon eclipsed as a few top union leaders gained autocratic power by the early 1940s. Nevertheless, the union bosses needed the patrolmen to transmit orders to the rank and file, while the multiplication of beefs* by the ships' committees* kept the patrolmen more than busy. After World War II the patrolmen also participated in the union efforts to elect candidates friendly to maritime labor. In the 1980s and 1990s the rapid disappearance of most U.S.-flag ships sharply reduced the number of patrolmen, who may even be fused with the port agent in regions of less traffic.

References: Richard O. Boyer, *The Dark Ship* (New York: Little, Brown, 1947); Joseph P. Goldberg, *The Maritime Story: A Study in Labor-Management Relations* (Cambridge: Harvard University Press, 1958); National Maritime Union, *This Is the NMU* (New York: William P. Gottlieb, 1954); Hyman Weintraub, *Andrew Furuseth: Emancipator of the Seamen* (Berkeley: University of California Press, 1959).

PAUL, JOSEPHINE BAY, 10 August 1900–6 August 1962. Josephine Bay Paul was the largest stockholder of the American Export Line* (AEL) in 1955–1960 and, as chairman of the board in 1959–1960, has been the first and only woman ever to head a major steamship company in the United States. She was born in Anamosa, Iowa, on 10 August 1900; her maiden name was Josephine Perfect, and her father was a real estate agent. She studied in private schools and also attended Colorado College in 1918–1919. Afterward she was involved in ventures that revealed her ability to excel in business deals. In the 1920s she organized with her sister Tirzah Perfect a Christmas card business ("Tirzah Perfect Cards"); the sister designed the cards, while Josephine handled with great success the marketing and distribution of the cards throughout the United States. The Christmas card business came to an end after Tirzah's marriage; nonetheless, Josephine was already launched in other highly successful ventures.

When Josephine married multimillionaire stockbroker Charles U. Bay in 1942, she plunged with great gusto into her husband's financial investments. In 1946 her husband (the son of a Norwegian immigrant) secured the appointment of U.S. ambassador to Norway, and she participated actively in the social life of the Oslo embassy until 1953. Shortly after their return to the United States, Bay died in December 1955, and Josephine was faced with the decision of what to do with her husband's sizable holdings in the brokerage house of A. M. Kidder & Co. and in AEL.

Rather than promptly sell off the assets, as was traditional with widows, she decided to become the chairman of A. M. Kidder & Co. in 1956, the first woman ever to head a Wall Street firm of the New York Stock Exchange. With AEL she proceeded more cautiously and assumed only the chairmanship of the Executive Committee of the Board of Directors, leaving the rest of the management team in place.

In January 1959 she married the Russian immigrant C. Michael Paul, who had made his own fortune in commerce and the oil business. Josephine's second marriage resulted in a drastic change in the corporate affairs; first, her husband replaced her as head of A. M. Kidder & Co., and second, in February 1959 she assumed the chairmanship of the Board of Directors of AEL. However, her tenure as the first woman to head a major steamship company was short-lived, because it appears that from the beginning it was the intention of the Pauls to dispose of their one-third stockholding in AEL. With her acute business sense Josephine had no trouble putting together her last business deal, and she soon had Jakob Isbrandtsen* bidding against a rival buyer. She sold the stock at an inflated price on 3 October 1960, although she later faced a lawsuit from minority stockholders who claimed they had been deprived of the opportunity to participate in this highly profitable transaction.

Josephine retired from business affairs and henceforth concentrated on philanthropic duties as she and her husband distributed part of the vast fortune they had accumulated. As a Democrat, Josephine had also been a rarity among shipowners, who, except in the deep South, have traditionally belonged to the Republican party. The high point in her public image came in December 1961, when she and her husband lent their Palm Beach mansion for the Christmas vacation of President John F. Kennedy and his wife, Jacqueline. She died on 6 August 1962.

References: *Current Biography 1957*; René De La Pedraja, *The Rise and Decline of U.S. Merchant Shipping in the Twentieth Century* (New York: Twayne, 1992); *National, Cyclopedia of American Biography*, Current vol. I; *New York Times*, 26 February 1959; *Time*, 15 December 1961; *Who Was Who*, vol. 4.

PENINSULAR & OCCIDENTAL STEAMSHIP COMPANY, 1900–1967.

The ships of the Plant Line* and those of railroad magnate Henry Flagler were combined to create the Peninsular & Occidental Steamship Company in July 1900. The new line, owned by the railroads, provided service from Tampa, Miami, and Key West to Havana. When the Florida East Coast Railroad reached Key West in 1912, the Peninsular & Occidental Steamship Company reduced its ports of call to only Tampa, Key West, and Havana. The company plied quietly this route during the next decades and in 1931 ordered the turbine liner *Florida*, whose fast speed of nineteen knots and capacity for 612 passengers in first class and 130 in second class were needed to meet the growing demand for travel to Cuba during the winter.

After World War II competition from airplanes began to make serious inroads into the passenger business as well as the express cargo that was the majority of the freight the company handled. The harsh fact was that the *Florida* was obsolete as a passenger liner and lacked the amenities of a cruise ship. To try to postpone the inevitable, the company shifted to Liberian registry in 1955, in the hope that the moderately lower wages of Cuban, compared with U.S., crews would keep the service profitable. The Seafarers' International Union* (SIU) intervened and obtained in 1958 a decision from the National Labor Relations Board that allowed the union to organize the Cuban crew members to seek wages equal to those of American seamen. The *Peninsular and Occidental* ruling helped galvanize other American owners of foreign-flag ships to create the American Committee for Flags of Necessity* to defend their interests, but not in time to save Peninsular & Occidental, which was soon overtaken by more misfortunes.

When the Cuban revolution began in January 1959, the number of tourists visiting Cuba dropped precipitously, and the company had no choice but to sell one of its old vessels for scrapping. To avoid another heavy loss, rather than sell the *Florida*, the company decided to operate the vessel in cruise voyages between Miami and Nassau, Bahamas, but the results were very modest at best. The aging *Florida* could no longer compete with the newer, specially designed cruise ships and was sold in 1967 for use as a floating hotel (and renamed *Le Palais Flottant*) at the Montreal World Exposition in 1967, and the next year she was scrapped. Peninsular & Occidental attempted to continue the cruise service to Bahamas by chartering foreign-flag ships, but new safety requirements of the Coast Guard* forced the owners to suspend its weekly voyages from Miami to Nassau in December 1967, and the long career of the company came to an end.

A Notable Ship

Florida 1931–1967; later, *La Palais Flottant* 1967–1968

References: Rodney P. Carlisle, *Sovereignty for Sale: The Origins and Evolution of the Panamanian and Liberian Flags of Convenience* (Annapolis, MD: Naval Institute Press, 1981); René De La Pedraja, *The Rise and Decline of U.S. Merchant Shipping in the Twentieth Century* (New York: Twayne, 1992); Frederick E. Emmons, *American Passenger Ships* (Newark: University of Delaware Press, 1985); *Florida Journal of Commerce*, February 1968; *New York Times*, 21 June 1958.

PENNSYLVANIA. See *California, Pennsylvania,* and *Virginia.*

PLANT LINE, 1885–1900. Henry B. Plant, the railroad tycoon, created this line, whose steamers operated among Tampa, Key West, and Havana. When Plant's railroad reached Tampa in 1884, he decided to convert the sleepy little town into the starting point for a profitable tourist trade to exotic Cuba. His trains brought the tourists, who stayed in the plush Tampa Bay Hotel prior to boarding the *Mascotte* and the *Olivette*, the two fast steamers with triple-expansion* engines he ordered built for this route. Winter, when tourists sought comfort in the warm climate of Cuba, was the heaviest season for the Plant Line, but the line provided service during the rest of the year on a reduced schedule. Plant was making so much money that besides chartering* additional ships, he decided to order a bigger steamer, *La Grande Duchesse*, which would combine winter service on the Havana-Tampa route with summer voyages to Canada. When the ship was delivered in 1896, mechanical problems prevented adequate performance in the planned routes.

Before Plant could decide how to deal with the setback of *La Grande Duchesse*, he died in July 1899, and his heirs decided to dissolve the Plant Line. Meanwhile the railroad magnate Henry Flagler had been operating his own line on the Miami-Key West route, and it was decided to combine the ships of Flagler's line and those of Plant's former line into the new Peninsular & Occidental Steamship Company* in July 1900. *La Grande Duchesse* did not enter the new company and was sold off as unsuitable for the service; the vessel, after passing through several owners and undergoing major transformations, finally was acquired in 1905 by the New York and Puerto Rico Steamship Company* and renamed the *Carolina*. The *Carolina* remained in the service of that company until June 1918, when the ship was sunk by a German U-boat.

Principal Executive

Henry B. Plant   1884–1899

Notable Ship

La Grande Duchesse; later,   1896–1918
    Carolina

References: *Dictionary of American Biography*, vols. 6 and 14; Frederick E. Emmons, *American Passenger Ships* (Newark: University of Delaware Press, 1985); Edward A. Mueller, articles in *Florida Journal of Commerce*, May, June, July 1975.

PLAYS. See Literature.

PLIMSOLL MARK. See load line.

POPE AND TALBOT (P&T), 1849–1916, 1930–1961. Pope and Talbot (P&T) was one of the lumber firms of the Pacific Northwest that from the start had to develop their own fleet of vessels to carry lumber to market; Robert Dollar* and Charles R. McCormick* were examples of other lumbermen who likewise entered merchant shipping because of their needs for cargo space for their lumber. P&T's involvement with merchant shipping fell into two stages, 1849–1916 and 1930–1961.

The first stage consisted of sailing vessels. P&T gradually acquired a large fleet of sailing vessels of all sizes for the shipment of lumber cargoes not only down the coast to California, but ultimately to all parts of the world. Hawaii and Australia became important markets for P&T, while the company had established a regular intercoastal* service around Cape Horn to supply lumber to the East Coast of the United States. The company had acquired a commanding position in merchant shipping but foolishly frittered its lead away by stubbornly refusing to purchase steam schooners after the 1880s. After the introduction of the triple-expansion engines,* the days of the sailing vessels were numbered, but P&T refused to make the transition to steam, in the process leaving a large opportunity for bolder entrepreneurs like Robert Dollar and Charles R. McCormick, whose steam schooners could sail up many rivers and bays to pick up lumber on a regular schedule, something the sailing vessels could never do. Fortunately for P&T, the critical shipping shortage created a demand for anything that could float, and in 1916 it sold its last four sailing vessels at a profit, bringing to an end the first stage in the company's experience with merchant shipping.

P&T afterward did not need to worry about transportation, because in 1917 lumber companies formed the Douglas Fir Export Company, through which all the companies received their foreign orders, and although the primary reason for its creation was to prevent foreign buyers from trying to get each lumber company to underbid another, among its other services the Douglas Fir Export Company chartered* whatever vessels were necessary to carry the lumber to its destination. When on 10 July 1925 McCormick bought almost all the assets of P&T, the latter's lumber cargoes increasingly began to travel aboard the vessels of the McCormick Steamship Company.* McCormick proved derelict in meeting the payments for the purchase of P&T, and consequently the former owners of P&T, in order to safeguard their assets, began to take greater control over McCormick's properties; McCormick himself was removed from the presidency of his holding company in April 1929 and was forced to resign as chairman of the board on 8 December 1931. Normally the buyer absorbed the purchased company, but in this very unusual case, the tables were turned, and the purchased company ended up absorbing the buyer's assets.

Thus began a second stage in P&T's involvement with merchant shipping, because now P&T inherited the McCormick Steamship Company, whose management it wisely decided to conserve. Although providing supervision, P&T kept McCormick Steamship Company as a separate entity until 31 August 1940, when it was dissolved. Before P&T could make any major innovations with its fleet of twenty-six vessels, U.S. entry into World War II suspended operations, and not until after the return of peace could P&T again manage its own ships. During the war it had operated as many as fifty-seven vessels for the War Shipping Administration* (WSA) under general agency agreements, but as early as August 1943 the company had begun an advertising campaign to remind the public that it would return to merchant shipping once the war was over. Using vessels chartered from the WSA, the company resumed intercoastal service in October 1945 and next year added a call in Puerto Rico; the company eventually placed in the intercoastal trade three C-3* vessels purchased from the government. In February 1946 P&T, with chartered WSA ships, also resumed coastwise service, which initially was prosperous because of pent-up demand during the war, but in June 1948 growing competition from trucks and low rates from railroads forced P&T to abandon the separate coastwise route, which henceforth was merged into the intercoastal service.

An important goal of P&T had been to reestablish the service McCormick Steamship Company had provided from the West Coast to Argentina and Brazil, and as soon as P&T purchased two C-3 surplus vessels in March and June 1947, it reopened this route to South America and soon purchased two more ships for this initially very profitable service. By the middle of 1948 foreign competitors had sharply reduced the profits in the South American service, and P&T applied for an operating differential subsidy,* which, after overcoming bitter opposition from Moore-McCormack,* was finally approved on 27 January 1949. Competition from foreign lines remained just as strong, and P&T finally decided to sell its fleet and route in the South American trade to Moore-McCormack in December 1956.

P&T was left with the intercoastal run as its only remaining shipping service, but it too faced difficulties. In July 1955 the call in Puerto Rico was dropped, and from 1955 through 1960 the company was earning barely 1 percent on its vessel investment. Management expected a loss of $1 million for 1961, because of lower rail rates approved by the Interstate Commerce Commission* and rising wages for unions because of the Seamen's Strike of 1961.* Only a large federal subsidy could keep the company's five remaining vessels as "the last surviving intercoastal service operating as a common carrier both eastbound and westbound" (White House Central Files), but because no federal aid was forthcoming, P&T had no choice but to suspend permanently its last shipping operation in October 1961.

References: Edwin T. Coman, Jr., and Helen M. Gibbs, *Time, Tide and Timber: A Century of Pope and Talbot* (New York: Greenwood Press, 1968); *New York Times*, 2 July 1955, 23 December 1956, 26 October 1961; U.S. Senate, Committee on Interstate and Foreign Commerce, *Merchant Marine Studies*, 2 vols. (Washington, DC: Government Printing Office, 1954); White House Central Files, John F. Kennedy Presidential Library, Boston.

POPEYE. For many Americans the comic strip character *Popeye the Sailor* has remained the most readily available visual image of the seafarer. It is not known exactly why its creator, Elzie C. Segar, adopted the sailor motif for the character, and in any case the cartoonist, who had begun his regular comic strip *Thimble Theatre* in 1919, did not introduce Popeye for the first time until January 1929. The character, "the first serious fighting man in the comics" (Becket 1959), was an instant success, and the reading audiences constantly demanded more adventures from this sailor, and in July 1933 Popeye appeared in the first of many film cartoons. The comic strip character became a part of Americana and introduced such lasting words into the vocabulary as *jeep* and *wimpy*. Segar retained a nautical flavor and background in the strip, but it was clear that he and, in particular, his successors after his death in 1938 used the character to act out many fantasies of the audience. While entertainment was the main goal of Popeye, the comic strip did contribute to the image of the sailor as a good, hardworking, and generous individual, and with exciting adventures in the sea and through mysterious islands, it certainly must have contributed to attract young Americans to join the merchant marine in the critical years of World War II.

References: Stephen Becket, *Comic Art in America* (New York: Simon and Schuster, 1959); *Buffalo News*, 26 January 1992; Maurice Horn, ed., *World Encyclopedia of Cartoons* (New York: Chelsea House, 1980).

PORT AND TANKER SAFETY ACT OF 1978. The Port and Tanker Safety Act of 17 October 1978 reflected a shift by Congress toward strict measures to prevent environmental damage by oil spills. The existing legislation, most notably the Tank Vessel Act of 1936 and the Ports and Waterways Safety Act of 1972, likewise reflected environmental concerns, but the primary purpose of the earlier laws had been to mandate national standards, whose enforcement had proved impossible on the part of private companies and local government. The urgency in the 1978 act reflected the *Sansinena** and *Argo Merchant* disasters in U.S. waters, and in order to safeguard the marine environment, Congress was determined to take strong but not extreme measures.

Essentially the act increased the powers and authority of the Coast Guard* over vessels and personnel in U.S. waters. Tankers were subjected to additional inspections, while the Coast Guard kept a special computerized record on the activities of all vessels so as to be able to detect problems and, if necessary, prevent the entry into U.S. waters of dangerous vessels. The act imposed civil and criminal penalties upon offenders and also authorized proceedings to seize the ship as part of the liability against damages for oil spills. The act imposed a new set of qualifications for tanker personnel, who had to take examinations and inspections in addition to those normally required of all seafarers. The act detailed the procedures for certification for American seafarers, but if the Coast Guard was not satisfied that the personnel aboard foreign ships met comparable standards, the act authorized the Coast Guard to take a variety of actions against foreign ships and, if necessary, could forbid their entry into U.S. ports. In the Port and Tanker Safety Act of 1978 Congress expected that rigorous enforcement would prevent future oil spills. The optimism proved unfounded, and the *Exxon Valdez** disaster forced Congress to take even more drastic measures in the Oil Pollution Act of 1990.*

References: Ernest G. Frankel, *Regulation and Policies of American Shipping* (Boston: Auburn House, 1982); *U.S. Statutes at Large*, vol. 92 (1978).

POST-PANAMAX. The term Post-Panamax refers to the latest generation of containerships whose size exceeds the dimensions of the Panama Canal.* The term in theory could apply to tankers too large to use the Panama Canal, such as the VLCC* and ULCC,* but in practice Post-Panamax has referred only to containerships. Experience with containers* convinced shipowners that the larger the size of the ship, the lower the operating costs per container. Thus the ships of 1,000 twenty-foot equivalent units or TEUs* of the late 1960s gave way to the containerships of over 4,000 TEUs of the 1970s. With such large capacities, the Panama Canal became a serious limitation, and designers of the Panamax* generation wrestled with the problem of how to squeeze the vessels through the canal.

The next step was to build containerships bigger than what the Panama Canal could handle, and hence the latest generation of containerships were called Post-Panamax. American President Lines* (APL), whose *President Truman*, completed in mid-1988, was the first Post-Panamax containership in the world, discovered that a wider vessel meant lower operating costs because of shallower draft, greater stability, and almost no need for ballast. Hence a Post-Panamax vessel was shorter but had a bigger beam than a Panamax ship of similar capacity, and because length was the most expensive dimension in shipbuilding, the Post-Panamax was also 5 percent cheaper to build.

With no apparent limits in size, Post-Panamax vessels of 5,000 TEUs and more are expected to appear in ocean shipping, each one further reducing the competitiveness of the Panama Canal. The economical performance of the Post-Panamax vessels has been one of several factors contributing to the tremendous success of intermodal* and landbridge* service in the United States.

References: Commission on Merchant Marine and Defense, *Third Report: Appendices* (Washington, DC: Government Printing Office, 1988); John Niven, *The American President Lines and Its Forebears, 1848–1984* (Newark: University of Delaware Press 1987); Transportation Research Board, *Intermodal Marine Container Transportation: Impediments and Opportunities* (Washington, DC: National Research Council, 1992).

***PRESIDENT COOLIDGE*, 1931–1941.** The *President Coolidge* and the *President Hoover** were the two combination passenger-cargo ships the Dollar Steamship Company* used for the route between San Francisco and the Far East starting in 1931; they were also the only two ships the company ever ordered from shipyards, because otherwise the Dollar Line's fleet was composed of surplus or used vessels. The two combination cargo-passenger vessels were large ships, with an overall length of 654 feet and a beam of 81 feet. With twin screws and turboelectric engines the ships had a cruising speed of twenty-one knots, making them the fastest in the Pacific Ocean. Normally the ships steamed much slower to conserve fuel, but in 1937 the *President Coolidge* ran at full power and lowered the transpacific record (held since 1905 by the *Siberia**) to nine days, nine hours.

Besides huge holds for cargo, the *President Coolidge* and the *President Hoover* had accommodations for a total of 988 passengers distributed in first class, tourist or "special class," third class, and steerage.* Two outdoor swimming pools, a large gym, and cinema halls were some of the many amenities scattered throughout the broad decks and spacious rooms. Forced ventilation reached all public areas and passenger staterooms, providing the best temperature comfort possible prior to the age of air-conditioning. Each passenger room had a telephone, and art deco graced all the interior spaces of the two modern liners.

In spite of these and many other amenities, the two ships came on the market just as the world was feeling the full weight of the Great Depression. For years the passenger traffic failed to materialize, and the ships sailed half empty at best. Only in the late 1930s, when the economy started to rebound, did passenger and cargo traffic rise, but by then the Dollar Line was on the verge of bankruptcy. On 6 March 1937 as the *President Coolidge* was passing through dense fog in the Golden Gate, she rammed and sank the tanker *Frank H. Buck*; after repairs the liner returned to service and joined the fleet of American President Lines* (APL) in 1938.

In June 1941 the army took over the *President Coolidge* as a transport. On

26 October 1942, the ship struck a minefield and sank in an hour and a half. The ship was crammed with over 5,100 men, but the officers and crew organized the evacuation so effectively that only two of those on board lost their lives.

References: John Niven, *The American President Lines and Its Forebears, 1848–1984* (Newark: University of Delaware Press, 1987); E. Mowbray Tate, *Transpacific Steam: The Story of Steam Navigation from the Pacific Coast of North America to the Far East and the Antipodes, 1867–1941* (New York: Cornwall Books, 1986).

PRESIDENT HARRISON, 1923–1941. The *President Harrison* was one of the seven 502s (a surplus combination cargo-passenger type of the wartime construction program and so named because 502 was the number of feet in the length of the vessel) that the Dollar Steamship Company* purchased from the Shipping Board* for the round-the-world* service. After extensive festivities in San Francisco, the ship inaugurated the round-the-world service on 5 January 1925. The combination passenger-cargo service was a success, and to handle the greater than expected number of travelers, the *President Harrison* was one of the four 502s whose capacity for first-class passengers was enlarged from 87 to 175 persons in 1929.

In 1938 the *President Harrison* was transferred, along with the rest of the Dollar Line fleet, to the newly created American President Lines* (APL), and the ship continued to ply the round-the-world route, which, however, was increasingly subject to schedule modifications because of the Japanese militaristic adventures in the Far East. In January 1941 the government had begun to requisition the ships of the APL, and by December of that year eight of its thirteen vessels were under government control. The *President Harrison* and the *President Madison* were in the Philippines under military control, and they had just finished evacuating a marine battalion from China to Manila on 4 December 1941. Apparently the U.S. government did not want to give the appearance of too hasty an abandonment of U.S. interests in China and had refused to evacuate at the same time the legation guards at Beijing and Tientsin. On second thought, the military changed its mind and sent the *President Harrison* back to China to withdraw the legation guards, so that ship was heading north on the China Sea when Japan attacked Pearl Harbor on 7 December 1941. The ship had been under constant Japanese surveillance, and at dawn on 8 December a Japanese plane ordered the ship to stop. The plane strafed the *President Harrison*, and a little later a fast Japanese destroyer appeared on the horizon. Captain Orel Pierson knew escape was impossible, and he headed at full speed toward the reefs, in an attempt to tear off the ship's bottom. Unfortunately, damage proved lighter than expected, and diligent Japanese work crews had the liner sailing under a Japanese name in six weeks. The *President Harrison* had been the only U.S. liner captured by the Japanese, because the *President Madison* had escaped safely, and all the other round-the-world vessels were in American ports on Pearl Harbor day. The captured crew and officers of the *President Harrison* went to prison camps and received barbaric treatment; all suffered tremendously, and sixteen died. In September 1944, the *President Harrison*, under the Japanese flag, was torpedoed, and she sank with heavy loss of life; paradoxically the ship was carrying American and Allied prisoners of war to Japan, a fact that the U.S. submarine did not know.

References: Frederick E. Emmons, *American Passenger Ships: The Ocean Lines and Liners, 1873–1983* (Newark: University of Delaware Press, 1985); John Niven, *The American President Lines and Its Forebears, 1848–1984* (Newark: University of Delaware Press, 1987); E. Mowbray Tate, *Transpacific Steam: The Story of Steam Navigation from the Pacific Coast of North America to the Far East and the Antipodes, 1867–1941* (New York: Cornwall Books, 1986).

PRESIDENT HOOVER, **1931–1937.** The *President Hoover* and the *President Coolidge** were the two combination passenger-cargo ships the Dollar Steamship Company* used for the route between San Francisco and the Far East starting in 1931; they were also the only two ships the company ever ordered from shipyards, because otherwise the Dollar Line's fleet was composed of surplus or used vessels. The two combination cargo-passenger vessels were large ships, with an overall length of 654 feet and a beam of 81 feet. With twin screws and turboelectric engines the ships had a cruising speed of twenty-one knots, making them the fastest in the Pacific Ocean, but normally the ships steamed much slower to conserve fuel.

Besides huge holds for cargo, the *President Coolidge* and the *President Hoover* had accommodations for a total of 988 passengers distributed in first class, tourist or "special class," third class, and steerage.* Two outdoor swimming pools, a large gym, and cinema halls were some of the many amenities scattered throughout the broad decks and spacious rooms. Forced ventilation reached all public areas and passenger staterooms, providing the best temperature comfort possible prior to the age of air-conditioning. Each passenger room had a telephone, and art deco graced all the interior spaces of the two modern liners.

In spite of these and many other amenities, the two ships came on the market just as the world was feeling the full weight of the Great Depression. For years the passenger traffic failed to materialize, and the ships sailed half empty at best. Only in the late 1930s, when the economy started to rebound, did passenger and cargo traffic rise, but by then the Dollar Line was on the verge of bankruptcy.

When Japan launched a full-scale invasion of China in July 1937, the hostilities forced modifications in the schedule of the Dollar Line, but not enough to avoid a first incident later that year when the Chinese air force, in a vain attempt to stop the Japanese warships, mistakenly bombed the *President Hoover* and nearby ships. Over 900 Chinese died in the nearby ships, and aboard the *President Hoover* many were injured, but only one crewman died. Because of U.S. sympathy for the Chinese side in that war, the mistaken bombing was largely ignored in the press reporting, and the U.S. government decided not to make any major diplomatic moves over the incident, which it rapidly declared closed.

The *President Hoover* returned for repairs and soon was back in service. In December 1937 the liner was in Kobe, Japan, when she received instructions to skip the call in Shanghai because heavy fighting between Japanese and Chinese forces had closed the port. The captain of the ship, rather than travel through the well-known route between mainland China and Formosa, "decided to cut time and distance" (Niven 1987) by sailing east of Formosa, whose eastern shoreline he believed had ample navigational lights, according to his detailed charts. Upon reaching the eastern coast of Formosa, the captain discovered that the Japanese had extinguished or removed the navigational aids, while bad weather reduced visibility. The captain did not slow down but continued to steam at twenty knots until at midnight on 11 December the *President Hoover* struck the shoals off Hoishito Island near Formosa. At daybreak the passengers were safely disembarked, but accusations of drunkenness and insubordination among the crew tarnished the rescue operation. The ship lost half of its plate bottoms and could not be refloated, and eventually Japanese salvagers reduced the vessel to scrap on the spot. The loss of this ship deprived the company of needed revenues just when passenger traffic was at last reviving and hastened the bankruptcy of the Dollar Line. The deficient performance of U.S. seamen and officers in the *President Hoover* and in other incidents like the shipwreck of the *Morro Castle** in 1934 provided ammunition for those who wished to take the authority to license officers and inspect ships away from the Bureau of Marine Inspection and Navigation* and place it instead in the hands of the Coast Guard.*

References: John Niven, *The American President Lines and Its Forebears, 1848–1984* (Newark: University of Delaware Press, 1987); E. Mowbray Tate, *Transpacific Steam: The Story of Steam Navigation from the Pacific Coast of North America to the Far East and the Antipodes, 1867–1941* (New York: Cornwall Books, 1986); Barbara W. Tuchman, *Stilwell and the American Experience in China 1911–1945* (New York: Bantam, 1972); Milton H. Watson, *Disasters at Sea* (Northamptonshire, England: Patrick Stephens, 1987); U.S. Congress, House, Merchant Marine and Fisheries Committee, *Amend the Merchant Marine Act, 1936* (Washington, DC: Government Printing Office, 1938).

PROHIBITION, 17 January 1920–5 December 1933. Prohibition was the attempt by the federal government to try to stop the production, sale, and consumption of alcoholic beverages in the United States. Of the vast field of prohibition, several aspects had an effect on the merchant marine. The Coast Guard,* as a federal police force, labored to stop the smuggling of liquor into the United States and waged an ultimately unsuccessful campaign against the rum runners, the boats of the smugglers. But it was not those more colorful exploits at sea that left the lasting legacy on the merchant marine. When the Volstead Act enforcing the constitutional amendment on Prohibition went into effect on 17 January 1920, the question of whether the prohibition of alcoholic beverages extended to U.S.-flag vessels remained open, but since many of the ships belonged to a government agency, the Shipping Board,* an even stronger case existed for extending the prohibition. However, if U.S. ships refused to serve alcohol aboard, what about foreign ships? The rest of the countries of the world had wisely decided to pass the chance to participate in the "great experiment," and foreign ships with the support of their governments refused to observe the Volstead Act except when within the three-mile territorial waters then claimed by the United States. The great majority of passenger travel would shift to foreign-flag vessels if U.S. ships were not allowed to serve alcohol, thereby crippling the Shipping Board's attempts to develop passenger, as well as cargo, services.

In an initial ruling, Attorney General Harry Daugherty issued a prohibition against serving alcohol on any U.S.-flag ship, whether private or government-owned. Albert D. Lasker,* the chairman of the Shipping Board and an advertising tycoon himself, devised a number of new means to keep passengers happy aboard U.S.-flag ships. He began showing recent movies aboard the ships and recruited big name bands to provide the very best night club entertainment on board. With other amenities, such as unlimited caviar for first-class passengers and the novelty of telephone service between the ship and land, he hoped to make the passengers forget the absence of alcohol. The many novelties of Lasker managed to keep passengers coming aboard U.S.-flag ships, at least until the Supreme Court ruled on 30 April 1923 that Prohibition applied to ships of all flags only when they were within the territorial waters of the United States. At last U.S. ships could compete for passengers on even terms with foreign-flag ships, with the sole restriction of locking up all alcoholic beverages when inside the three-mile limit of the United States.

The superior entertainment and dining did not disappear with the Supreme Court ruling, and many of these services became standard, not just for first class but also for the growing tourist class. The greatest legacy of Prohibition for the merchant marine, however, was the birth of the cruise business; up to the 1920s people had used ships for travel because there was no other way to cross the oceans, but with Prohibition the distinct possibility emerged that people who really had no particular destination just wanted to board to enjoy the benefits of sea travel, which then included alcoholic beverages. Soon Americans began to charter* vessels just to travel beyond the three-mile territorial limit, but the British, whose transatlantic liners were underused in the winter months, went further and now shifted them for voyages between the United States and the British Caribbean. Other operators simply announced what were dubbed the "voyages to nowhere": ships sailed from a port and, after steaming at sea for days and perhaps a week, returned back to the same port. While the advertising brochures emphasized the invigorating effect of the fresh sea air and the benefits of repose from hard work on land, most passengers seemed quite content just to enjoy the liberal consumption of alcohol. American lines decided to place new passenger ships on the intercoastal* service, because while most passengers had normally traveled by the transcontinental railroads, the ocean trip between the two coasts of the United States suddenly became more attractive aboard the ships serving alcohol than on the "dry" railroads.

When the superior entertainment and dining of the early years of Prohibition were combined with Caribbean voyages, the cruise ship industry was born. If people were willing to go on voyages with only occasional calls in exotic islands, then the trip itself, not just the destination, became the main goal of the passengers, unlike the passenger travel before the 1920s, when the quickest way across the Atlantic had remained the highest priority. The demand for speed on the transatlantic voyages never abated and was responsible for the rapid switch to airplanes since the 1950s; but by then, a separate demand for passenger travel, in which a pleasurable time aboard the ship itself was the main goal, had appeared. When Prohibition was finally repealed in the United States on 5 December 1933, the demand for intercoastal passenger services slackened considerably and among other problems left the International Mercantile Marine* stuck with the money-losing *California,* *Pennsylvania,* and *Virginia,* but these were inevitable problems of the transition back to a legally alcohol-consuming world. Many steamship companies began to cater their passenger services toward pleasure travelers, and the cruise industry was solidly launched; unfortunately for the U.S. merchant marine, although cruise ships under the U.S. flag do exist, most notably the converted passenger liners the *Constitution* and the *Independence,* the cruise industry has largely been monopolized by foreign companies using ships registered mainly under flags of convenience.

References: Rodney P. Carlisle, *Sovereignty for Sale: The Origins and Evolution of the Panamanian and Liberian Flags of Convenience* (Annapolis, MD: Naval Academy Press, 1981); John Gunther, *Taken at the Flood: The Story of Albert D. Lasker* (New York: Harper and Brothers, 1960); Jerry Shields, *The Invisible Billionaire: Daniel Ludwig* (Boston: Houghton Mifflin, 1986).

PROPELLER. Wooden side-wheels placed on each side toward the middle of the ship ("amidships") moved all the early steamers across the ocean. The inventor John Ericsson fitted a propeller to a steamer for the first time in 1838, and a tug-of-war between two steamers in 1845 convinced the Royal Navy that propellers were vastly superior to side-wheels. However, controversy continued to rage over the benefits of each, and as late as the 1860s the Pacific Mail Steamship Company* (PMSS) was still ordering side-wheelers (*Great Republic,* *China, Japan,* and *America*), some of which remained in service until the early 1880s.

The main obstacle to the adoption of the propeller was the single-expansion engine,* which ran at 14 to 18 revolutions per minute, while the propeller needed at least 150 revolutions per minute to thrust the ship forward. The only way to achieve this high number of revolutions was to "gear up": the slow engine was connected to a huge gear that made the small gears of the propeller shaft spin rapidly. In making this transfer to faster revolutions, considerable motion was lost, and the single-expansion engine with its extravagant consumption of coal could not afford this additional waste of energy. Instead a low number of revolutions was best for the side-wheels, which thus fitted well with the slow rotations of the engine.

The propeller had other disadvantages. A more complex longitudinal shaft had to be developed to carry the motive power from the engine in the center of the ship to the propeller in the rear or stern. Instead the side-wheels were located to the sides of the center of the ship, and a transverse shaft sufficed to carry the motion from the engine. The noise and vibration of the propeller affected the already cramped passenger quarters, which, according to maritime tradition, were located in the rear of the vessel. Travelers often felt unsure about the propeller, which did its mysterious work underwater and out of sight, unlike the easily seen and understood side-wheels.

Even with the single-expansion engine, some shipowners realized the propeller was more economical. The propeller took up less room than the side-wheels and consequently made available space for fuel and cargo in the otherwise cramped steamer. The propeller had less drag than the side-wheels under sail and hence could make better use of the wind to compensate partly for the high coal consumption of the single-expansion engine.

Soon after the introduction of the compound engine* in 1865, the propeller rapidly replaced the side-wheel in new ocean steamers. The compound engine turned the shaft faster and hence dispensed with the cumbersome gears that had wasted so much energy. In particular, the compound engine cut in half coal consumption and the size of the bunkers,* thereby releasing ample space for cargo and travelers. The passengers' quarters were relocated in the late 1860s to spacious and comfortable accommodations in the center of the ship, away from the noise of the propeller, whose vibrations were considerably reduced as well.

The triple-expansion engine* drove ships faster and, because it was also the most economical of the steam engines, was best suited for cargo vessels. For passenger ships, the steam turbine was necessary to attain speeds of twenty knots and higher. However, the steam turbine presented the propeller with the opposite problem of the single-expansion engine: while the latter had turned the shaft too slowly, the former was too fast for the propeller. Gears were again necessary, but now to reduce the speed, rather than, as previously, to increase the speed. In the passenger liners of the 1930s, the reduction gears lowered the 1,800 revolutions per minute of the steam turbine to the 180 revolutions per minute of the propeller.

For the most economical operation possible, cargo vessels generally have only one propeller; for faster travel speeds the larger passenger liners have been built with two, three, and even four propellers.

References: Gerald S. Graham, "The Ascendancy of the Sailing Ship 1850–1885," *Economic History Review* 9 (1956): 74–88; John F. Nichols, "The Development of Marine Engineering," in Society of Naval Architects and Marine Engineers, *Historical Transactions, 1893–1943* (Westport, CT: Greenwood Press, 1981); Edward W. Sloan III, "The Machine at Sea: Early Transatlantic Steam Travel," in Benjamin W. Labaree, *The Atlantic World of Robert G. Albion* (Middletown, CT: Wesleyan University Press, 1975).

PROPELLER CLUB, 1927–present. The Propeller Club has been since 1927 the educational, social, and public relations arm of the U.S. merchant marine. To complement the very exclusive India House,* which was eminently social and just for company executives, the first Propeller Club was established in New York in 1922, and soon more were organized in other cities. On 9 November 1927 the shipowners saw the advantage of creating a national organization that would serve as a "mutual meeting ground where competitors could get together" (*Fortune*, September 1937) and also foster public relations. New York City became the headquarters, and the individual clubs were called "ports" of the national Propeller Club. The organization spread rapidly throughout the United States and took permanent root under the dynamic leadership of Arthur M. Tode, a consulting engineer, who was its president from 1931 to 1935.

Commander Tode was "a skillful publicist in his own right, a forceful speaker" who "travelled to every key city in the United States . . . his contagious enthusiasm in the cause of American shipping soon won not only the support of thoughtful personalities in the maritime industry, but the friendship and help of many prominent men throughout the United States" (*Who's Who in the Maritime Industry, 1946*). The Propeller Club had forty-five ports in 1937, including eleven abroad, and a membership of around 6,000. Commander Tode remained an honorary president and lived to see the wartime boom expand the Propeller Club to ninety-seven ports in the world, claiming more than 12,000 members in 1946. By that date the Propeller Club was no longer comprised mainly of persons from management and the government; instead the bulk of the membership of the individual ports now came from labor unions.

A very important function of the Propeller Club has been organizing and hosting the annual American merchant marine conference. The Shipping Board* had started the conferences and organized them until January 1933, when budgetary limits ended this activity, which subsequently became the responsibility of the Propeller Club. The annual conferences have convened without interruption, providing a forum for experts, executives, and government officials, while congressional figures were often the keynote speakers; after the reunion was over, the Propeller Club published most speeches in its annual proceedings. As in most conventions, the formal events provided the necessary stage for behind the scenes contacts among the participants.

Amidst the instability and frequent changes in owners' organizations since World War II, the Propeller Club has provided a degree of continuity and has gradually assumed a greater role in the public relations campaigns of U.S. merchant shipping. The Propeller Club also prepares "positions" that are widely circulated among congressional and other government officials, but the need to reach consensus among all its members severely restricted this lobbying function. To enhance the lobbying role the national headquarters moved from New York City to Washington, D.C., in 1974. However, a serious blunder took place in October 1978, when the Propeller Club was persuaded to denounce the temporary transfer of a vessel to U.S. registry* without first having secured the approval of all the delegates to its annual convention; henceforth the Propeller Club has been extremely reluctant to become involved in situations where members might have "adversary positions."

Since the 1930s the Propeller Club has also chartered ports in universities with maritime programs; in 1991 there were twenty-four of these "student ports," which included the U.S. Merchant Marine Academy* and the five state maritime academies.* The Propeller Club also has cooperated with schools by means of the annual Maritime Essay Competition and the adopt-a-ship program for individual classes. In conclusion, the Propeller Club has performed a very useful role in providing meeting grounds and channels to link management, government, labor, the universities, and even the schools.

References: *American Shipper*, November 1978; *Fortune*, September 1937; Propeller Club, *American Merchant Marine Conference: Proceedings*, 1962, 1980; Propeller Club letter of 12 August 1991 to author from vice president J. Daniel Smith and materials; Record Group 32, National Archives, Washington, DC; *Who's Who in the Maritime Industry 1946*.

PROPRIETARY COMPANIES or INDUSTRIAL CARRIERS. Proprietary companies or industrial carriers have been giant corporations that own the majority of the cargo carried aboard their ships. For proprietary companies ocean transportation has been one more step in the long process of production and distribution of their finished products. The pure case of proprietary companies has been best illustrated by the fleets of oil companies like Standard Oil,* whose ships carry only the parent company's oil products. The exact opposite were the liner* and tramp* firms, which did not own the cargo aboard their ships but instead obtained their cargo from shippers.*

In between, however, was a large gray area in which it was not always easy to determine when a firm ceased to be a proprietary company. A clear-cut case has been firms that carry proprietary cargoes in one direction and then compete for return cargo in the opposite direction; Calmar* and Weyerhaeuser* have been good examples of this practice. Other companies, like the Dollar Line,* began in the same pattern of proprietary cargoes in one direction but eventually evolved until the proprietary cargoes ceased to be the majority of the company's business. In the case of the Grace Line,* the company's cargo formed a "core" around which other shippers' merchandise was added in increasingly greater amounts to assure the profitability of the shipping operations. At what point did a company cease to be a proprietary company? Only a case-by-case examination of long-term trading patterns could provide a precise categorization for companies in the gray areas, but as a minimum guideline, if less than a third of the cargo belonged to the company, then its shipping operations, if continued for long with this ratio, were rapidly losing their proprietary nature. Shipping has always been dynamic, and ultimately the parent company, like in the case of United Fruit Company,* could make decisions to reduce or drastically increase its cargo, in the latter case thereby restoring its nature as a proprietary company.

References: René De La Pedraja. *The Rise and Decline of U.S. Merchant Shipping in the Twentieth Century* (New York: Twayne, 1992); Grover G. Huebner, *Ocean Steamship Traffic Management* (New York: D. Appleton, 1920); Lane C. Kendall, *The Business of Shipping*, 5th ed. (Centreville, MD: Cornell Maritime Press, 1986).

PRUDENTIAL LINES, 1933–present. Prudential Lines has provided cargo service between the United States and the Mediterranean during most of its existence. The company was established by the Greek immigrant Stephan Stephanidis in 1933 and began originally as a tramp* outfit operating one coal-burning freighter with a triple-expansion* engine. By 1939 Prudential owned three ships, and during World War II it was one of the general agents that operated government vessels for the War Shipping Administration* (WSA). After the return of peace the company purchased three surplus Victory* vessels, but something went wrong with this opportunity, and in 1954 Prudential faced bankruptcy. Only a cash infusion from Spyros P. Skouras, the owner of the movie studio Twentieth-Century Fox, saved the company. Shortly after, Stephanidis died, and full control of Prudential fell to Skouras, who handed over its management to his son, Spryos S. Skouras.

The son took a long time to learn the shipping business and even the operations of his father's company, but gradually Prudential Lines expanded through the acquisition of new vessels. The big break came in December 1969, when W. R. Grace & Co., desperate to abandon shipping, agreed to sell the Grace Line* at a slashed price to the Prudential Lines. By this one move, Skouras now headed not just a small firm in the Mediterranean trade but also the largest U.S.-flag steamship company in the Latin American routes. He soon realized that the passenger services of the former Grace Line had no future, and less than one year later in November 1970 Prudential Lines announced the end of cruise service to the Caribbean; shortly after, the *Santa Rosa* and the *Santa Paula* were laid up and subsequently sold.

Even before the Grace purchase, Skouras had doomed Prudential Lines because of his 1965 decision to order the Lighter Aboard Ship or LASH* vessels, essentially barge carriers to raise barges from the water and lower them into the water. Prudential received its first LASH vessel in 1970 and by 1974 had five altogether in operation, but the company never came close to the commercial success of Central Gulf Lines* with this new technology. Unexpected complications with the handling of the vessels resulted in delays in service, and typically one or more of the LASH vessels remained idle because of lack of cargo for the barges. Losses continued to pile up, but Skouras was so devoted to the LASH concept that rather than dispose of these money-losers, he instead sold off the Latin American services of the former Grace Line to the Delta Line* in 1977. Because of oil exports from Venezuela and Ecuador, most of the Latin American routes were booming during the years of the energy crisis, so the decision to sell off the profitable services to try to save the LASH routes seriously undermined Prudential's position. Skouras now could have invested in safer land ventures, and indeed he had recovered most of the money of the original Grace Line purchase, but instead he decided to use the proceeds to extend his Mediterranean services into the Middle East, hopefully to take advantage of the huge cargo volumes moving to that region in the wake of the energy crisis.

When the oil bubble burst in 1981, cargo to the Middle East sharply declined, and since 1981 rumors began to circulate about the impending bankruptcy of Prudential Lines, whose fleet dwindled down to three vessels by 1986. In May of that year creditors seized the vessels in New York and Italy, but soon Prudential was back in operation under the protection of bankruptcy proceedings. A contract from the Military Sealift Command* (MSC) in 1989 kept his vessels busy hauling government cargoes, but in spite of several reorganization attempts, the latest in 1990, Skouras has so far been unsuccessful in attempts to operate without the protection of bankruptcy court.

Principal Executive

Spyros S. Skouras   1960–present

Some Notable Ships

Santa Paula and *Santa Rosa*	1970–1971
Santa Magdalena, Santa Mariana, Santa María, and *Santa Mercedes*	1970–1977

References: *American Shipper*, October 1990; René De La Pedraja, *The Rise and Decline of U.S. Merchant Shipping in the Twentieth Century* (New York: Twayne, 1992); William Kooiman, *The Grace Ships, 1869–1969* (Point Reyes, CA: Komar, 1990).

R

RAY, THOMAS WELCH, 7 February 1905–1980s? Thomas W. Ray was a communist organizer and ideologue of the National Maritime Union* (NMU) and subsequently became an anticommunist. Born in Portland, Maine, on 7 February 1905, he graduated from high school and was continuously at sea until around 1929, when he joined the Communist party. He threw himself into party work, and his educational level made him a candidate for important tasks. He became well respected in international communist circles and was a frequent guest at labor conferences in Moscow. More important, he became the link between the Communist party and waterfront activities. He had his greatest success when he led the communists, who enthusiastically supported the founding of the NMU. To assure the success of the new union, Ray carefully guided President Joseph Curran* in the early years, if necessary, even writing his speeches. Curran appreciated this help, and a long friendship emerged. Already during World War II, Ray's analytical mind had begun to question many of the policies of the Communist party, so that in 1945 he was more than ready to bolt the party, along with M. Hedley Stone* and Jack Lawrenson.* Ray's defection deprived the Communist party of its most direct link to the NMU and made inevitable the failure of Frederick ("Blackie") Myers* campaign to unseat Joseph Curran from the presidency. Unlike Lawrenson, however, Ray realized the struggle was not over communism but over power. Curran rewarded Ray's timely support and allowed him to remain as research director of the NMU until his retirement.

References: Joseph H. Ball, *The Government-Subsidized Union Monopoly: A Study of Labor Practices in the Shipping Industry* (Washington, DC: Labor Policy Association, 1966); National Maritime Union, *This Is the NMU* (New York: William P. Gottlieb,

1954); Bruce Nelson, *Workers on the Waterfront: Seamen, Longshoremen, and Unionism in the 1930s* (Urbana: University of Illinois Press, 1990).

RAYMOND, HARRY HOWARD, 16 December 1864–27 December 1935.
H. H. Raymond was for nearly twenty years the head of the Atlantic Gulf & West Indies Steamship Lines* (AGWI). He was born in Yarmouth, Nova Scotia, on 16 December 1864. He studied at the Yarmouth Seminary and afterward began to work as a clerk in the steamship company that served the Yarmouth-Boston route. He came to the United States in 1884 and obtained U.S. citizenship in 1892. He became a purser in a Mallory Line* ship in 1885 and rapidly rose through the ranks until in 1899 he became general superintendent at the New York headquarters. He worked closely with Henry Rogers Mallory,* and their personal relationship resembled the previous one of Charles Henry Mallory* with Captain Elihu Spicer, Jr.

When the Mallory Line became a subsidiary of the Consolidated Steamship Lines* in 1907, Raymond's position was threatened, but the bankruptcy of the Consolidated Steamship Lines allowed both Henry Rogers and Raymond to stage a swift power play to take over the different subsidiaries. Atlantic Gulf & West Indies Steamship Lines emerged in 1908 as the new holding company, with Henry Rogers as president of it as well as of each of the subsidiaries. At the same time Raymond was appointed the vice president of the Mallory Line and of the Clyde Line, in effect becoming their real head. The power play of 1907–1908 had been decisive for Raymond, because since he was not a major shareholder, he had to create his independent power base within the corporate hierarchy.

When Henry Rogers retired in 1915, Raymond was promoted to president of both the Mallory Line and the Clyde Line, titles that reflected more accurately the real power he had held since 1908. When the United States entered World War I, he was one of the steamship executives who helped the Shipping Board* deliver troops and supplies to Europe. With the end of the war, he realized that surplus ships and subsidies were readily available to create new steamship firms, but not to support old, established combines like AGWI. Raymond rose to the challenge, and he concocted a scheme whereby the new Colombian Steamship Company* was owned through dummy corporations of AGWI. This indirect tapping of government subsidies proved extremely lucrative, although when exposed during the Black Committee* hearings of 1933–1934 it generated a tremendous uproar and negative publicity.

In 1927 the stockholders elected Raymond the head of AGWI, and he left the running of the subsidiaries to younger men. He remained formally as chairman until his death on 27 December 1935; however, because of ill health, he spent the last years of his life in virtual retirement at his summer home in Yarmouth, Nova Scotia.

References: James P. Baughman, *The Mallorys of Mystic: Six Generations in American Maritime Enterprise* (Middletown, CT: Wesleyan University Press, 1972); *Dictionary of American Biography*, Supp. 1; U.S. Senate, Special Committee on Investigation of Air Mail and Ocean Mail Contracts, *Hearings*, 9 vols. (Washington, DC: Government Printing Office, 1933–1934).

RED D LINE, 1838–1938. The Red D Line provided ocean transportation between the United States and Venezuela during a century. In 1823 the Philadelphia merchant John Dallett went to Venezuela right after the country had gained its independence from Spain, and he established an alliance with John Boulton, whose commercial house remained influential in the country for over a century. Dallett soon returned to Philadelphia and began to supply merchandise for Boulton in Caracas; by 1838 the cargoes had become large enough to charter* sailing vessels, and the Dallett family gradually increased its fleet until it was carrying a large share of the trade between Venezuela and the United States. The fleet needed a house flag, and Dallett chose a white color with a red D in the center for his name, but instead of being known as the Dallett Line, the name of "Red D" stuck throughout the company's history.

In 1879 the Red D Line introduced three new steamers, which provided departures from New York every twelve days; their average speed of fourteen knots drove the sailing vessels from the trade, and not until 1889 did Dutch, Spanish, and German lines attempt to contest the trade. Only the Dutch line (Koninklyke West-Indische Maildienst), because of its obligation to provide service to the Dutch island of Curaçao right off the coast of Venezuela, remained for long in the trade, but only with old steamers. By 1912 an arrangement was in place whereby the Dutch line, whose steamers needed sixteen days to make the trip from New York to Venezuela, would not set rates lower than 90 percent of those charged by the Red D line, whose faster steamers made the same trip in ten to eleven days.

Except for a brief period after 1879 under the British flag, the Red D Line kept its steamers under the U.S. flag. Its ships were designed specially to cross the Venezuelan shoals, so the U.S. government did not requisition any during the Spanish-American War or World War I. The Red D Line received mail subsidies from the U.S. government, starting with the Ocean Mail Act of 1890,* and also began to provide passenger service. The company ordered two combination cargo-passenger vessels in the 1920s, the *Carabobo* and the *Caracas*, with accommodations for 87 and 137 passengers, respectively. The Red D Line retained a link with the Boulton merchant house and at least until the early twentieth century continued to have a share in some of the merchandise carried aboard its ships. At the same time the line developed a very close relationship with Venezuelan shippers* and generally tried to anticipate their needs for cargo space so as not to provoke any complaints. In a sense Venezuela and the Red D Line had "adopted" each other in a manner similar to the Clyde Line* with the Dominican Republic or Matson Navigation Company* with Hawaii.

When the Merchant Marine Act of 1936* ended the mail contracts and substituted the operating differential subsidy,* the latter's rigid and less favorable terms convinced the Red D Line to abandon shipping altogether. In October

1937 the owners sold the company to the Grace Line,* which disposed of the fleet, dropped the Red D name, and incorporated the New York-Venezuela route into its other Latin American routes. Once the special relationship between Venezuela and the Red D was broken, try as it might, the Grace Line never quite acquired the same network of contacts or acceptance among local shippers, so that the departure of the Red D Line was one more factor that helped convince Venezuelans that they needed their own merchant fleet.

References Frederick E. Emmons, *American Passenger Ships: The Ocean Lines and Liners, 1873–1983* (Newark: University of Delaware Press, 1985); Mark H. Goldberg, *Going Bananas: 100 Years of American Fruit Ships in the Caribbean* (Kings Point, NY: American Merchant Marine Museum, 1993); Winthrop L. Marvin, *The American Merchant Marine* (New York: Scribner's, 1902); *Mast Magazine*, January 1951; *Nautical Gazette*, 24 September 1927; *New York Times*, 6 October 1937; U.S. Congress, House, Committee on the Merchant Marine and Fisheries, *Special Diplomatic and Consular Reports* (Washington, DC: Government Printing Office, 1913).

RED STAR LINE, 1872–1937. The Red Star Line was the trade name of the International Navigation Company, which was organized in 1872 by American investors to operate Belgian-flag ships between Antwerp and Philadelphia. Oil exports from the Pennsylvania fields were the main cargo, but soon the focus shifted to New York, and by 1883 six of the company's ships steamed between that port and Antwerp, while only four remained in the Philadelphia route. The driving force behind the Red Star Line was the millionaire Clement Acton Griscom,* one of the wealthiest Americans of his day. In 1884 he purchased the American Line,* a U.S.-flag venture that the Pennsylvania Railroad had operated since 1873, and in 1886 he also acquired a British-flag line. Griscom kept the three lines as separate subsidiaries of the International Navigation Company, but when the British government withdrew subsidies from two of his ships, the *City of New York* and the *City of Paris*, he maneuvered an exemption to U.S. laws that allowed him to transfer the foreign-built ships to U.S. registry* as the *New York* and the *Paris* in 1893. However, Congress specified the condition that the American Line must build in U.S. shipyards two comparable passenger liners; with the completion of the *St. Louis** and the *St. Paul*,* which entered service in 1895, Griscom fulfilled the requirement.

The two vessels were the first modern liners built in the United States since those of the pre–Civil War Collins Line,* but the operation of the *St. Louis* and the *St. Paul* under the American flag proved disappointing, in spite of subsidies under the Ocean Mail Act of 1891.* While the British-flag line and the Belgian-flag Red Star Line were profitable, in effect they were subsidizing the losses of the U.S.-flag operation. When foreign companies planned bigger and faster liners for the transatlantic trade, Griscom faced the problem of how to match the competition. A first solution was to merge with the only other U.S.-owned company, the Atlantic Transport Company* of Bernard N. Baker.*

The merger took place as part of complex maneuvers that culminated in the creation of the International Mercantile Marine* (IMM) under Wall Street magnate J. P. Morgan in 1902. In the new shipping combine, the International Navigation Company gradually disappeared, but its Belgian-flag subsidiary, the Red Star Line, retained its name and its existence as a separate entity, although with considerable exchanges of ships among the different subsidiaries of IMM. After 1902 the activities of the Red Star Line were largely indistinguishable from the corporate existence of IMM, and only when the latter decided to dispose of its last foreign-flag holdings did it sell the Red Star Line in 1935 to the German Arnold Bernstein, who began to merge his new acquisition into his own Bernstein Lines. The Nazi government intervened and confiscated Bernstein's assets in 1937 and briefly restored the Red Star Line's name prior to its subsequent sale to the Dutch line, the Holland-America, bringing at last to a close the career of the Red Star Line.

Principal Executives

Clement A. Griscom	1872–1902
Arnold Bernstein	1935–1937

References: John G. B. Hutchins, *The American Maritime Industries and Public Policy, 1789–1914* (Cambridge: Harvard University Press, 1941); Winthrop L. Marvin, *The American Merchant Marine* (New York: Scribner's, 1902); *National Cyclopedia of American Biography*, vol. 56; Thomas R. Navin and Marian V. Sears, "A Study in Merger: Formation of the International Mercantile Marine Company," *Business History Review* 28 (1954) 291–328; *New York Times*, 25 November 1937.

REGISTRY, U.S. or SHIP'S REGISTRY, U.S. Registry has been the system whereby a ship was allowed to fly the flag of a country provided the shipowner met a number of conditions, which at the very least included paying fees and taxes. Until the late nineteenth century the nationality of the shipowner and that of the vessel were generally the same. From 1789 to 1912 the main requirement to qualify for U.S. registry was that the ship had to be built in the United States or, conversely, that foreign-built ships could not fly the U.S. flag. Minor exemptions were foreign ships captured as prizes during war or shipwrecked foreign ships that had been largely rebuilt in U.S. shipyards.

After the Civil War, on 10 February 1866, Congress prohibited the repatriation of U.S.-built ships registered under foreign flags in order to "punish" those shipowners who had adopted the British flag to avoid capture by Confederate raiders. A more counterproductive measure could hardly have been imagined, because many American shipowners who wanted to return to U.S. registry were forced by their own government to continue flying foreign flags, particularly the British, whose many benefits they soon discovered and began to enjoy.

Meanwhile, with U.S.-flag shipping declining, the protectionist measures that prohibited bringing foreign-built ships under U.S. registry came under attack during the last decades of the late nineteenth century, and the Democratic party led the fight for "free ships,"* in other words, allowing the registration of more cheaply built foreign vessels under the U.S. flag. In 1892 Congress made an exception and authorized the registration of the British-built *City of New York* and *City of Paris*. After the annexation of Hawaii in 1898, Congress accepted all ships of Hawaiian flag into U.S. registry; since the annexation of the islands had been expected for some time, a number of companies, including Pacific Mail Steamship,* had transferred British-built ships to the Hawaiian flag in the, certainty that they would later be brought into U.S. registry, as actually happened.

It was not, however, until the Panama Canal Act of 1912* that for the first time Congress opened U.S. registry to new ships built abroad. By then the benefits of operation under foreign flags (principally British), were so manifest that not a single shipowner bothered to bring his ships into U.S. registry.

After the outbreak of World War I, the vessels of the belligerent countries abandoned their prewar routes, and the United States suffered a shipping crisis. Fear that England would requisition all American-owned vessels flying the British flag convinced Congress on 18 August 1914 to pass the Ship Registry Act, whose more open provisions, as well as the pressures of war, at last convinced many companies to transfer their ships to the U.S. flag. Although modifications in U.S. registry have taken place, the principle that foreign-built ships may freely be registered under the U.S. flag has remained valid. However, enough restrictions remain on foreign-built vessels to make their transfer to the U.S. flag highly undesirable for shipowners. The cabotage* laws of the United States were not repealed by the Panama Canal Act of 1912, so that a ship built abroad could not serve the coastwise* and intercoastal* routes, a prohibition the Jones Act* of 1920 reaffirmed. Second, ships built abroad do not qualify to receive direct government aid, in particular, the operating differential subsidy* (ODS). The Merchant Marine Act of 1936* further tightened the restriction and excluded a company that operated foreign-built ships from qualifying for any subsidies. However, this restriction was waived in the early 1980s, so that the rest of the U.S.-flag fleet of the company could still qualify for subsidies.

Lastly, with the U.S. flag came a series of tax, labor, and regulatory requirements that significantly increased the cost of operating a U.S.-flag vessel. A 1961 amendment tried to further limit the benefits from the cargo preference* statutes by requiring a three-year waiting period for foreign-built ships to qualify for these cargoes; however, a good attorney could usually set up a dummy corporation to bypass this last requirement. Some companies, for example, Sea-Land* and, even earlier, States Marine Corporation,* insisted on operating foreign-built ships under U.S. registry, but the practice has become less frequent as shipowners overwhelmingly turn to flags of convenience.*

References: George W. Dalzell, *The Flight from the Flag: The Continuing Effect of the Civil War upon the American Carrying Trade* (Chapel Hill: University of North Carolina Press, 1940); John G. B. Hutchins, *The American Maritime Industries and Public Policy, 1789–1914* (Cambridge: Harvard University Press, 1941); Gerald R. Jantscher, *Bread upon the Waters: Federal Aids to the Maritime Industries* (Washington, DC: Brookings Institution, 1975); Samuel A. Lawrence, *United States Merchant Shipping*

Policies and Politics (Washington, DC: Brookings Institution, 1966); Transportation Research Board, *Intermodal Marine Container Transportation: Impediments and Opportunities* (Washington, DC: National Research Council, 1992); *Statues at Large*, vol. 37 (1912), vol. 38 (1914).

RIVER PLATE AND BRAZIL CONFERENCES, 1923–1967. The River Plate and Brazil Conferences was the coordinating body and the collective name for a number of smaller conferences and agreements in the trade between the East and Gulf coasts of the United States and the east coast of South America. The appearance of several managing operators* of Shipping Board* vessels had thrown the trade into confusion, and to try to stabilize rates the steamship companies crated the River Plate and Brazil Conferences in 1923. The member lines in that year were American Republics Line, Booth Steamship Company, Delta Line,* Lloyd Brasileiro, Lamport and Holt, Osaka Shoshen Kaisha, Prince Line, Pan America Line, and Wilhelmsen Steamship Line. The River Plate and Brazil Conferences set rates that Brazilian shippers considered too high, and, in response, Lloyd Brasileiro, the line owned by the Brazilian government, frequently either left or threatened to leave the conferences in order to keep rates low from the 1920s to the mid-1930s. With the outbreak of World War II in 1939, Delta Line and Lloyd Brasileiro were left as the only conference members and the only lines providing service.

The River Plate and Brazil Conferences resumed normal operations after World War II and continued to set rates for this trade, which was particularly valuable because of coffee exports from Brazil and Argentine imports from the United States. By the early 1960s this conference structure proved rather unwieldy, and it was eventually replaced in 1967 by the Inter-American Freight Conference* (IAFC).

Principal Executive

George F. Foley   1930–early 1960s

References: René De La Pedraja, *The Rise and Decline of U.S. Merchant Shipping in the Twentieth Century* (New York: Twayne, 1992); Gilbert M. Mellin, ''The Mississippi Shipping Company,'' Ph.D. diss., University of Pittsburgh, 1955; U.S. Congress, House, Committee on Merchant Marine and Fisheries, *Steamship Conference Study*, 3 vols. (Washington, DC: Government Printing Office, 1959).

ROBIN LINE, 1920–1957. The Robin Line was the main subsidiary of the Seas Shipping Company, a holding company established in 1920 by Arthur R. Lewis, Sr., in conjunction with the Farrell family. The Robin Line, so called because the names of its ships always began with the word *Robin*, operated in the intercoastal* trade as a type of reserve fleet for the other maritime ventures of the Farrell family, most notably, the American South African Line,* in which Lewis also had a stake. In 1933, as a result of a bitter feud between both families, the ownership and management of all the firms were completely separated, so that the Farrells controlled American South African Line, and the Lewises the Robin Line. Shortly after Lewis, Sr., died, his son Arthur R. Lewis, Jr.,* became the president of the Robin Line.

Lewis continued to operate the lein's four ships in the intercoastal trade until Sylvester J. Maddock, an employee fired by the Farrells, convinced Lewis to bring the Robin Line into the African trade in 1935. Maddock knew the ports and shippers* in Africa and thus was able to build up the cargo volumes for the Robin Line at the expense of the American South African Line, and soon one of the most bitter rate wars in the history of U.S. merchant shipping had begun (see U.S.A.-South Africa Conference*). The rate war ended only in 1937, and the next year the U.S. Maritime Commission* awarded subsidy contracts to both the Robin Line and the American South African Line. During World War II, the vessels of both lines were requisitioned, and they both operated government ships for the War Shipping Administration,* but after the return of peace the two lines resumed their bitter rivalry.

In hearings before the U.S. Maritime Commission, the Robin Line, because of the opposition from the Farrell Line*, lost the subsidies on the route from U.S. Atlantic ports to West Africa in 1947. However, when Farrell declined to handle the unusually large volume of automobile exports to South Africa, the Robin Line did provide the service and won lasting goodwill among the automobile exporters. The personal and commercial rivalry was taking a toll on the middle-aged president of Robin Line, Lewis, Jr., who died on 16 March 1954. None of the family members wished to follow his crushing life-style, and instead they elected Winthrop O. Cook as the new president. As president, Cook had to replace the company's old wartime surplus vessels, but the heirs wisely decided to avoid the problem, and instead they sold the Robin Line to Moore-McCormack* in March 1957.

Principal Executives

Arthur R. Lewis, Sr.	1920–1933
Arthur R. Lewis, Jr.	1934–1954
Winthrop O. Cook	1954–1957

References: Robert G. Albion, *Seaports South of Sahara: The Achievements of an American Steamship Company* (New York: Appleton-Century Crofts, 1959); Federal Maritime Board, *Decisions*, vol. 4, *1952–1956* (Washington, DC: Government Printing Office, 1963); *New York Times*, 1 April 1954, 7 March, July 19, 1957; U.S. Maritime Commission, *Decisions*, vol. 3, *1947–1952* (Washington, DC: Government Printing Office, 1963).

ROLL-ON/ROLL-OFF (RO/RO). Roll-on/Roll-off (Ro/Ro) vessels specialized in the transportation of trucks, automobiles, and other vehicles; as the name suggested, the vehicles were driven on and off the ship, avoiding the costly and time-consuming lifting and packing that had been the rule with break-bulk* freighters. Ro/Ro vessels have been in reality huge floating barges, with a ramp usually at the rear that, when lowered, allowed driving on or off the vehicles. Ro/Ro vessels started to appear in the 1950s, but because their gradual introduction coincided with the container* revolution of the 1960s and 1970s, the failure of management to distinguish between the potential of each type meant bankruptcy for several companies. Ro/Ro vessels have become the standard means to move large volumes of vehicles, and because they required no cranes or other shoreside equipment, Ro/Ro vessels not only meant a faster turnaround time for the ship but also allowed bypassing any congestion or backlog at the part. Specialization has not stopped, however, and next to the versatile vessels able to carry most vehicles, at least since the 1980s, a specific type has also emerged, the PCC or Pure Car Carrier, whose employment has been widespread in the transportation of automobiles from Japan to the United States.

ROOSEVELT, KERMIT, 10 October 1889–4 June 1943. Kermit Roosevelt was president of the Roosevelt Steamship Company* in 1920–1930 and a vice president of the International Mercantile Marine* (IMM) in 1930–1938. Kermit was born at Oyster Bay, Long Island, New York, on 10 October 1889 and was the second son of president Theodore Roosevelt. Politics never appealed to Kermit, and as a quiet, dreamy child he did not seem to fit the dynamic pattern of his family. At Groton school (1902–1908) he developed a lifelong interest in languages and literature and in outings with his father developed a passion for hunting and rough adventure; throughout his whole life he was driven by these two opposite forces, the contemplative versus the adventuresome. He graduated from Harvard but declined a secure job in New York and instead accepted a position with the Brazil Railroad Company. While in Brazil, he joined his father's expedition to explore one of the Amazon's tributaries. After marriage on 11 June 1914, he settled with his wife, Belle Wyatt Willard, in Buenos Aires, Argentina, where he accepted a position with the branch of the National City Bank. His early business experiences, although interesting at first, soon seemed dull, and when the United States entered World War I, he immediately jumped at the opportunity to participate in combat. He fought alongside British forces in Mesopotamia (present-day Iraq); these battle experiences formed the nucleus of his first book, *War in the Garden of Eden*, which he published in 1919 after additional service with American forces in France.

He was back in the United States in 1919, and he was one of the well-to-do Americans, such as Basil Harris,* and W. Averell Harriman, who became fascinated with merchant shipping. Roosevelt joined with George Goethals to organize the American Ship and Commerce Corporation, which tried to establish a joint venture with the German line Hamburg-America. Harriman preempted the action and in a swift power play gained control of the American Ship and Commerce Corporation, which he then consolidated into his United American Lines.* Goethals and Roosevelt had been unceremoniously kicked out, but they fought back, and their attacks on Harriman's links with the former German enemies did contribute to undermine United American Lines.

For Roosevelt another more successful venture came when the Shipping Board* appointed him managing operator* of the Roosevelt Steamship Company, which he founded in 1920. Initially the company operated vessels to London, then experimented with numerous services, but finally settled down to the operation of the route between United States and India, to which service the Shipping Board later added the Australia-U.S. route. In the bustle and rivalry of merchant shipping Roosevelt at last had found himself, and he thoroughly enjoyed power plays, rate wars, challenging and beating the British, as well as traveling to exotic India and Central Asia to attract shippers* and also to engage in some much deserved hunting and adventures. Travel books were the inevitable sequels to his principal exploring expeditions, and running his own steamship company offered him the right mixture of excitement, income, and free time for travel and writing.

He joined with his friends John Franklin* and Basil Harris in 1930 in their successful attempt to gain control of IMM, then the largest steamship company in the United States, and although Roosevelt became a vice president of IMM, his own company was merged into the shipping combine. His last big challenge came in 1931 with the struggle against rivals to acquire United States Lines* (USL). Afterward IMM, now in control of USL, settled down to a more routine existence, gradually boring Kermit, who soon became restless as a name within a tradition-bound hierarchy. The revelations of the Black Committee* destroyed whatever prestige merchant shipping had enjoyed in previous decades and necessarily weakened Kermit's commitment to the business. In 1938, when the threat of a revived Germany guaranteed another war, Kermit jumped at the chance to escape from boredom and resigned from all his posts in IMM. He went to England to join British forces, eventually participating in the Norway campaign of 1940. With U.S. entry into World War II, he returned to work in army intelligence and was assigned to Alaska, where he died on 4 June 1943. Roosevelt was among those very few upper-class Americans who have been attracted to merchant shipping; in his individual case he was ultimately disillusioned by the innate conservatism of a very traditional business.

References: Rudy Abramson, *Spanning the Century: The Life of W. Averell Harriman, 1891–1986* (New York: William Morrow, 1992); René De La Pedraja, *The Rise and Decline of U.S. Merchant Shipping in the Twentieth Century* (New York: Twayne, 1992); *Dictionary of American Biography*, Suppl. 3; Kermit Roosevelt Papers, Library of Congress, Washington, DC.

ROOSEVELT STEAMSHIP COMPANY, 1920–1940. The Roosevelt Steamship Company operated principally in the routes from the United States to India and Australia. Kermit Roosevelt* established the company on 19 October 1920, and he remained its head until 1938. The company, which initially experimented with different routes, was a managing operator* for the vessels of the Shipping

Board.* Kermit discontinued a service to London when it proved very unprofitable, and the Shipping Board rewarded his honesty by giving the Roosevelt Steamship Company the route between New York and India on 22 October 1924. The service to India became the backbone of the Roosevelt Steamship Company, and in 1926 the company also received from the Shipping Board a valuable complement, the ships and the route from New York to Australia. The company successfully integrated the Australia and India services, so that ships coming from New York after they dropped off cargoes in Australia picked up return cargoes for the voyage back home via the Suez Canal. From 1927 to 1932 the Roosevelt Steamship Company participated aggressively in numerous rate wars that plagued the service to India prior and during the Great Depression and emerged victorious. From the experience in these long routes, Kermit soon recognized the advantages of diesel* engines, at a time when the conventional wisdom in the tradition-bound shipping industry remained committed to steam engines.

In 1930 Kermit merged the Roosevelt Steamship Company into the International Mercantile Marine* (IMM), which henceforth controlled the operations of this subsidiary, but since Kermit had became a vice president of IMM, through his position he remained in control of the Roosevelt Steamship Company, whose activities, however, were increasingly circumscribed by those of the parent combine. Kermit eventually became bored in IMM and resigned in 1938 to join British forces preparing to do battle against a rearming Germany. Just a few years after his departure, IMM shifted to another subsidiary, United States Lines* (USL), the remaining vessels of the Roosevelt Steamship Company, which became inactive in 1940.

References: René De La Pedraja, *The Rise and Decline of U.S. Merchant Shipping in the Twentieth Century* (New York: Twayne, 1992); *Moody's Transportation, 1940*; Record Group 32, National Archives, Washington, DC.

ROTH, ALMON E. ("AL"), 31 July 1886–1 January 1964. Almon E. Roth was the president of the Waterfront Employers' Association* (WEA) in 1937–1942 and the National Federation of American Shipping* (NFAS) in 1944–1947. Roth was born in Crandon, South Dakota, on 31 July 1886; at age four his parents moved to California, and he was raised in Mendocino County. He studied at Stanford University, where he supported himself by working as a waiter; he was active in college sports and was president of the student body in his senior year. He graduated in 1909 and began to work for Stanford University as the first dean of men, at the same time studying for his law degree, which he received in 1912. Afterward he worked as an attorney in San Francisco until he returned to Stanford in 1919 to become the university's business manager.

After the Big Strike* of 1934, San Francisco became synonymous with labor unrest, and Roth felt he could make a contribution to restore labor peace to the city. The moment was propitious, because many shipowners had tired of repeated confrontations with the International Longshoremen and Warehousemen's Union* (ILWU) and wondered whether some sort of accommodation could be worked out with Harry Bridges.* The shipowners created a new organization, the Waterfront Employers' Association (WEA), and Roger D. Lapham* convinced them the new association needed as head a strong independent dynamic figure like Roth, who accepted the position in 1937. Roth's greatest success came then, because he managed to restore labor peace to the waterfront and reconciled shipowners to Bridges, whom he managed to turn away from his radical past. Roth's success became legendary, and other business leaders wanted to benefit from his conciliatory talent, and they established the San Francisco Employers' Council in 1939 to solve labor problems in other industries of the city. His success brought him national recognition, and when the United States entered World War II, he was called to be one of the industry representatives in the National War Labor Board.

Roth decided to intensify his activities in Washington, and in 1944 he resigned from the National War Labor Board to become the first president of the National Federation of American Shipping (NFAS). He was a very effective advocate for the merchant marine in its relations with Congress and the executive branch, but after 1945 he saw his work weakened by the constant carping among the different factions in maritime business. Roth, who had achieved miracles in bringing management and labor together, finally met his match in the shipping executives: try as he might, he could not get the warring factions to support a coherent policy. Frustrated with Washington politics, he quietly resigned in 1947 and returned to the scene of his earlier triumphs to resume his old job as president of the San Francisco Employers' Council. He left that position in 1951 to return to private law practice. He died in Palo Alto, California, on 1 January 1964.

References: *Current Biography 1946*; *Forbes*, 15 February 1941; *National Cyclopedia of American Biography*, vol. 51; Roger D. Lapham Oral History, Bancroft Library, University of California, Berkeley, 1957; *Who's Who in the Maritime Industry 1946*.

ROTH, WILLIAM P., 23 July 1881–24 February 1963. William P. Roth was president of Matson Navigation Company* from 13 May 1927 to 16 March 1945 and then became chairman of the board, a position he held until 1962. His father was from Austria, and Roth was born on 23 July 1881 in Honolulu, where he studied in local schools, and then he attended Stanford University. He returned to Honolulu, where he held several jobs until he set up his own stock brokerage firm. In 1912 Captain William Matson's* only daughter, Lurline, met Roth during one of her trips to the island, and a romance ensued that resulted in their marriage on 27 May 1914. Captain Matson had approved the marriage only on the condition that Roth come to live in San Francisco and work for Matson Navigation Company.

A propitious marriage had certainly enhanced Roth's career, but he quickly showed himself to have keen business talent. In 1916 he had already become secretary-treasurer of the firm, and after Captain Matson's death on 11 October

1917, Roth became the vice president and general manager of the company. The elder Edward D. Tenney,* who represented the Matson stock owned by Castle & Cooke, became president of Matson, but because he stayed mainly in Honolulu, most of the time Roth ran the company from the head offices in San Francisco. When old age convinced Tenney to step down as president on 13 May 1927, it was a formality to have Roth recognized as the new president of the company.

Roth had decided to plunge Matson into the passenger traffic in a big way. In 1927 the *Malolo*,* a new liner he had ordered, started bringing tourists to Hawaii, where they stayed in the Royal Hawaiian, a plush hotel the company had built in Waikiki. In 1932 two new ships, the *Mariposa** and *Monterey*,* inaugurated passenger service to New Zealand and Australia from California, with calls in Hawaii and other Pacific islands; the launching of this new route was a potentially risky move, which, however, proved such a resounding success with the traveling public that the governments of Australia and New Zealand threatened to take reprisals against Matson. To avoid shipping discrimination, Roth agreed to keep a third ship, the *Lurline*,* in the Hawaii-California service, rather than adding the new passenger liner to the New Zealand-Australia service as originally intended.

Under Roth's presidency, Matson successfully weathered the Great Depression and continued to expand and prosper. With U.S. entry into World War II, the company's ships were requisitioned by the War Shipping Administration,* but already Roth was looking for new areas to expand, and in March 1941, as a first step toward entering commercial aviation, he established the Air Transport Division to repair navy planes.

On 16 March 1945 Frazer A. Bailey* became the new president, replacing Roth, who became chairman of the board, a position he held until 1962. He died in San Mateo, California, on 24 February 1963.

References: Alexander & Baldwin, *Ninety Years a Corporation 1900–1990* (Honolulu: Alexander & Baldwin, 1990); René De La Pedraja, *The Rise and Decline of U.S. Merchant Shipping in the Twentieth Century* (New York: Twayne, 1992); *National Cyclopedia of American Biography*, vol. 55; Fred A. Stindt, *Matson's Century of Ships* (Modesto, CA: n.p., 1982); E. Mowbray Tate, *Transpacific Steam* (New York: Cornwall Books, 1986); William L. Worden, *Cargoes: Matson's First Century in the Pacific* (Honolulu: University of Hawaii Press, 1981).

ROUND-THE-WORLD SERVICE, 1920–1986. Regularly scheduled steamship service around the world by U.S. companies began in 1920 and continued with some intervals until 1986; unlike the rest of the routes that started and finished at different ports, in the round-the-world service the terminus and the point of departure were the same port.

Previously, many U.S. ships had circumnavigated the globe; the first was the *Columbia*, which left Massachusetts in 1787 and completed an epic three-year voyage. Other sailing vessels followed, and the *Columbia* itself completed a second circumnavigation in 1793. However, the immense distances and times involved precluded any regular service, and sending sailing vessels around the world remained a highly risky venture reserved only for the boldest of speculators.

With the introduction of steamships in the late nineteenth century, travel times were drastically slashed, and voyages could be measured in months and no longer in years; undoubtedly some U.S. steamship tramps* found themselves drifting around the world as they searched for cargoes, but which U.S. steamer vessel first circumnavigated the globe remains unknown in the present state of research. What is known is that no U.S. steamship company even attempted to establish a regular round-the-world service before 1920. The simplest market analysis revealed that to be profitable, a round-the-world service had to join directly Asia, Europe, and the United States. The opening of the Suez Canal in 1869 linked directly Asia and Europe for the first time, but this route, which became the lifeline of the European empires in Asia, was heavily tonnaged and tightly controlled by British lines, such as Peninsular and Oriental (P&O). No U.S. challenge was possible until the opening of the Panama Canal* in 1914 eliminated the long and costly trip around South America.

Once World War I was over, the possibilities of a round-the-world service appeared irresistible, and two firms, the Dollar Line* and W. R. Grace & Co., through its subsidiary the Pacific Mail Steamship Company* (PMSS), began to send steamers around the world to explore the market possibilities. The voyage results were disappointing, but W. R. Grace & Co. concluded that the trade could be built up and went ahead to establish a regular round-the-world freight service, with the first sailing on 3 March 1920. The risk was small, because the company was operating government-owned vessels whose expenses were covered by the Shipping Board.* The service prospered while the postwar shipping boom lasted, but as more normal peacetime conditions returned in 1921, the service piled up impressive losses. European competitors were fighting for every cargo load, W. R. Grace & Co. had failed to enter the Asian and European markets, and its area of greatest strength, the west coast of South America, was irrelevant for the round-the-world service. After the last sailing by its PMSS subsidiary in July 1921, W. R. Grace & Co. quietly dropped the round-the-world service.

The Dollar Line had been at work trying to organize its own round-the-world service, and it was much better positioned than Grace to succeed. The Dollar Line had over twenty years' experience in the transpacific trade and already enjoyed a network of agents and contacts in Asia. Traditionally ships sailed with full loads to the Far East, but return cargoes for the West Coast of the United States remained scarce, and as the volume of U.S. exports to Asia increased, some means had to be found to fill the ships on the return leg of their voyages. The round-the-world service offered an ingenious way out of the deficit: all ships steamed west with the U.S. exports, but the return cargoes were concentrated on those ships serving only the transpacific route; the rest of the ships continued to steam westward, picking up whatever cargoes were available along the way for delivery to the East Coast of the United States.

The Dollar Line inaugurated the combined passenger-freight service with the sailing of the *President Harrison* from San Francisco on 5 January 1924; henceforth every two weeks until 1941 a ship sailed from San Francisco on the round-the-world service. The Dollar Line settled upon a 112-day schedule for the circumnavigation of the world; the normal route was for the ships to steam from San Francisco to Honolulu, then make calls at Kobe, Shanghai, Hong Kong, Manila, and Singapore, a route basically duplicated by the company's transpacific ships. The round-the-world ships went on to make calls in the Indian subcontinent and then entered the Mediterranean via the Suez Canal to make stops in Alexandria, Naples, Genoa, Marseille, and Barcelona; the ships steamed to Boston and New York City and, after a call in Havana, crossed the Panama Canal to return to San Francisco after a stop in Los Angeles.

The Dollar Line had begun the service with seven 502s (combination cargo-passenger vessels so named because of their length) and gradually added more vessels to the profitable route, whose income came to equal that of the regular transpacific service. The Dollar Line was successful because it found there was a lot of high-value cargo ready to be carried in the various legs of the voyage, for example, from China to India or from India to the Mediterranean. Of course, there was always considerable cargo for the East Coast of the United States, and once in New York, the ships could be easily filled with intercoastal* cargo for California; indeed, the intercoastal business became so profitable that the company ran separate ships for that service from roughly 1928 to 1935.

When the Dollar Line went bankrupt in 1938, the round-the-world service was inherited by its successor, the American President Lines* (APL). However, the outbreak of the Sino-Japanese War in 1937 and of World War II in 1939 forced numerous reroutings and modifications in the schedule. A major change came in June 1940, when Italy's entry into World War II closed the Mediterranean and forced the ships to steam in the long route around Africa via the Cape of Good Hope. To maintain the profitable service, APL ordered more ships, but from early 1941 until December, "the government took over eight of the thirteen vessels that APL was operating, including all its new ships" (Niven 1987). The biweekly sailing scheduled was disrupted, but somehow APL managed to make the sailings until the last departure on 11 October 1941 marked the end of the first stage of the round-the-world service.

After the end of World War II, APL reestablished the round-the-world service in 1946, initially with sailings every two months, but by 1947 the company had restored the biweekly schedule. However, of the prewar combination passenger-cargo vessels, only the *President Monroe* and the *President Polk* returned to the round-the-world service, so that although the biweekly schedule was met, it usually meant only freighter service. APL had ordered three new passenger-cargo vessels, but they were still in the shipyards when the Korean War broke out and the U.S. Navy finished them as troop transports, which never joined the APL fleet.

The Isbrandtsen Steamship Company* opened its own round-the-world service in 1949, but unlike APL, Isbrandtsen's ships sailed *eastward*. Taking advantage of the shipping turmoil after World War II, Hans Isbrandtsen,* the owner of the company, had begun in 1947 a service between New York and Japan via the Suez Canal. In 1949 he ordered his freighters to continue steaming eastward from Japan back to New York via the Panama Canal. Isbrandtsen's round-the-world service was exclusively for cargo and remained profitable as long as occupied Japan was forbidden from operating a merchant marine. In 1951 Japanese lines, led by the formidable Nippon Yusen Kaisha, began to restore their prewar services, and in 1953 and 1954 Isbrandtsen Steamship Company suffered heavy losses. Finally in 1954 Jakob, the son and heir of Hans, suspended the eastbound round-the-world service.

APL continued its own service and by 1957 had placed a new generation of freighters, the Mariners,* in the route. Refrigerated and liquid cargoes had become much more important than in the pre–World War II service; for example, the Mariner vessels had about fifteen sections of deep tanks, compared with three or four in the older ships. The *President Monroe* and the *President Polk* continued to provide combination passenger-cargo service until 1965, when both ships were sold; henceforth APL carried only cargo.

A brief closure of the Suez Canal in 1956 had been inconsequential, but in 1967 the Six-Day War closed the waterway for over five years. The company had to send its vessels on the long trip around Africa, and the long interruption disrupted cargo flows. To cut costs, APL established a feeder service in 1973 to bring the cargoes of the Indian subcontinent to Singapore for transfer aboard the transpacific vessels of the company. The company still wanted to reestablish the round-the-world service, and once the Suez Canal reopened, APL resumed sending ships via that waterway in August 1975. The nature of the cargo flows had changed so much by then that the service was a losing proposition, and APL, which decided to focus its efforts on the booming Pacific Basin trade, suspended the round-the-world service in 1977.

The idea was not yet dead, however, and after Malcom McLean* purchased United States Lines* (USL), he made the round-the-world service the center of his world strategy for his gigantic Econships.* He operated the first of these ships in the Far East-U.S. East Coast trade starting in July 1984, and when the Korean shipyards had delivered enough vessels, he resumed U.S.-flag round-the-world service in 1985. The delivery of the last Econoship in early 1986 allowed USL to offer shippers* weekly sailings, but filling the Econships proved harder than expected. On 24 November 1986 USL filed for bankruptcy and promptly suspended this last attempt to revive U.S.-flag round-the-world service in the twentieth century.

References: *American Shipper*, August 1975, September 1984; René De La Pedraja, *The Rise and Decline of U.S. Merchant Shipping in the Twentieth Century* (New York: Twayne, 1992); Frederick E. Emmons, *American Passenger Ships* (Newark: University of Delaware Press, 1985); John H. Kemble, "A Hundred Years of the Pacific Mail," *American Neptune* 10 (1950): 123–143; *Moody's Transportation Manual*, 1975; John Niven, *The American President Lines and Its Forebears, 1848–1984* (Newark: University of Delaware Press, 1987); Record Group 32, National Archives, Washington, DC; *New York Times*, 1 December 1957, 17 January 1987; E. Mowbray Tate, *Transpacific Steam: The Story of Steam Navigation from the Pacific Coast of North America to the Far East and the Antipodes, 1867–1941* (New York: Cornwall Books, 1986).

RUNAWAY FLAGS. *Runaway flags* has been a derogatory expression used by the labor unions since the 1950s to refer to ships flying flags of convenience.* The term contained only a grain of truth: while it cannot be denied that the transfers from U.S. registry* (distinct from bona fide sales to foreign buyers) to flags of convenience have occurred, the term overlooked two fundamental realities. First, U.S. companies in the foreign trade, unless they have been heavily subsidized or otherwise favored by the U.S. government, have traditionally operated since the beginning of the twentieth century with foreign flags, so the companies could not "run away" from something that had never been the norm in the foreign trade. Second, the overwhelming majority of the U.S.-owned ships registered under flags of convenience went straight from foreign shipyards to registry under those flags, because their operation under the U.S. flag meant enormous losses. It is safe to conclude that during the last fifty years these ships would not have been built under the U.S. flag, once again refuting the runaway ships claim. See also flags of convenience.

RYAN, JOSEPH PATRICK ("JOE"), 11 May 1884–26 June 1963. Joe Ryan was the president of the International Longshoremen's Association* (ILA) from 1927 to 1953. He was born on 11 May 1884 in the Long Island town of Babylon, but shortly afterward his family moved to the Chelsea district of New York City, where he attended a Catholic school until he was twelve years old. After trying his hand at odd jobs, he ended up working in the docks in 1912. He quickly rose through the union hierarchy and in 1916 was a full-time officer. In 1918 he was elected vice president of the ILA as an ally of Thomas Ventry O'Connor,* but a bitter struggle against rival F. A. Paul Vaccerelli allowed Anthony Chlopek to become the next ILA president when O'Connor resigned in 1921 to accept the appointment as a commissioner of the Shipping Board.* Ryan continued to seek the presidency, and as a very effective speaker his support among longshoremen increased until he was elected president of the ILA in 1927.

The Ryan presidency, among other things, meant the final transfer of the ILA's base from the Great Lakes to the East Coast. Ryan had become popular with longshoremen because he promised not to recentralize power in the hands of the president, as has been the rule under Daniel Keefe* and, to a lesser degree, under O'Connor. Locals were free to negotiate their own contracts with employers, but Ryan soon felt the need to exercise some control, at least when the

RYAN, JOSEPH PATRICK ("JOE")

employers desired his cooperation. Soon Ryan had fully adopted tuxedo union-ism* as he paraded himself in elegant suits that included painted neckties and boasted that "next to myself, I like silk underwear best" (Nelson 1990). After a pleasant meal at an exclusive New York restaurant, he liked to pass by the waterfront to show off his latest outfit and, if necessary, to pass out dollar bills in the manner of a Mafia godfather.

Elegant fund-raisers and a high salary made him wealthy and provided ample resources to buy off many longshoremen opponents. Ryan worked closely with the local politicians and became one more boss in the political machines. He claimed to rehabilitate former criminals by giving them jobs on the waterfront, but in reality he created "a racketeers' jungle run wild" (ibid.). Ryan controlled squads of hardened thugs ready to do his bidding, and those longshoremen who could not be bribed were crushed. To justify his dictatorial rule, Ryan adopted a fanatical anticommunism that conveniently allowed him to label all dissidents or opponents as communists. When fighting the imaginary communists, Ryan did admit that "some of these fellows with the bad criminal records were pretty handy out there when we had to do it the tough way" (Nelson 1990). He capped his dictatorship in 1943, when the ILA elected him president for life, and his grip over the East Coast and Gulf of Mexico appeared unshakable.

On the West Coast the ILA had never established a strong base, and this gap ultimately proved Ryan's undoing. When the Big Strike* erupted in San Fran-cisco in 1934, desperate employers brought Ryan to impose a settlement, which was unanimously rejected at a meeting after one longshoreman shouted "This guy's a fink and he's trying to make finks out of us. Let's throw him out!" (ibid.). Ryan's mixture of company unionism and racketeering was rejected by the San Francisco dockworkers, who instead backed the creation of the Inter-national Longshoremen and Warehousemen's Union* (ILWU) under the leftist Harry Bridges.* The ILWU went on to achieve dramatic breakthroughs for long-shoremen, including the replacement of the infamous shape-up* by the union hiring hall.* In 1943 ILA longshoremen demanded conditions comparable to those on the West Coast, in particular, the end of the shape-up, and in 1945 and 1946 these insurgents went on wildcat strikes to back their demands, but Ryan sided with the employers and sent his thugs to crush all opposition to his still solid control.

In the post–World War II years Ryan's fiefdom was gradually undermined and finally shaken by a combination of forces. The press mounted a steady campaign of revelations about corruption and racketeering, and soon the state and federal governments began criminal investigations. In this tense situation Ryan miscalculated when he tried to ram an unfavorable contract through the rank and file in October 1951, but his attempt triggered a wildcat strike by the insurgents, who now counted among their ranks the clever vice president Tho-mas Gleason.* After the longshoremen returned to work, a bitter tug-of-war raged within the ILA. The American Federation of Labor delivered the final blow in August 1953, when it expelled the ILA because of corruption. Finally at a special emergency convention on 16 November 1953, Ryan resigned in the face of mounting public, press, government, and labor opposition. Ryan still had to face a long legal battle to escape going to jail. He was convicted, but because he had kept poor records and had relied on untraceable cash for payments, his lawyers were able to overturn the conviction on appeal. He died on 26 June 1963.

References: *Current Biography 1949*; Gary M. Fink, ed., *Biographical Dictionary of American Labor*, 2d ed. (Westport, CT: Greenwood Press, 1984); Bruce Nelson, *Workers on the Waterfront: Seamen, Longshoremen, and Unionism in the 1930s* (Urbana: University of Illinois, 1990); Maud Russell, *Men Along the Shore: The ILA and Its History* (New York: Brussel and Brussel, 1966); Harold Seidman, *Labor Czars: A History of Labor Racketeering* (New York: Liveright, 1948); *Who's Who in the Maritime Industry 1946*.

S

SAFETY OF LIFE AT SEA CONVENTIONS (SOLAS). The huge loss of life when the *Titanic** sank on 14 April 1912 convinced world opinion that action was necessary to prevent another similar tragedy. The U.S. Congress passed a resolution calling for a meeting to set international standards, and the British government duly convoked the reunion, which finished its labors in January 1914. The 1914 Safety of Life at Sea Convention or SOLAS established international standards for safety equipment such as rafts and life preservers and also mandated drills and other training exercises to prepare both passengers and crew for any emergency. The outbreak of World War I delayed the ratification of the 1914 SOLAS convention by most countries, and in the United States labor leader Andrew Furuseth* blocked U.S. ratification because he felt that the provisions of SOLAS could be used to reduce seamen to a state of servitude. Congress felt the need for action, however, and in the La Follette Seamen's Act* wrote into law detailed requirements for protecting the lives of passengers and crew aboard the ships.

Once World War I ended, the need for an international convention to establish universal standards remained no less pressing, but with changes and improvements in both vessels and lifesaving equipment, the British government felt another meeting was necessary to write up-to-date requirements into a new convention, which was completed in May 1929. Ratification in the United States again proved difficult, because Furuseth still was opposed to SOLAS on the grounds that by international conventions American seamen might lose the rights previously acquired in the La Follette Seamen's Act. In particular, Furuseth and his International Seafarers' Union* (ISU) attacked the flexible manning requirements aboard foreign vessels, because the SOLAS convention left to other foreign countries the determination of what constituted "sufficient and efficient manning.'' The ISU wanted inserted in the convention the stipulations that 75 percent of the crew must know the language of the officers and that at least 65 percent of the crew must be able-bodied seamen* (AB). The *Morro Castle** disaster convinced Congress that whatever the merits of additional safety requirements, at the very least the SOLAS convention of 1929 had to be ratified, which Congress finally did in 1936.

Controversy over SOLAS has receded, and the conventions of 1948, 1960, and 1974 have been ratified without any complications. Indeed, since the 1960s, partly because of the almost total shift to airplanes for passenger travel and partly because of a greater awareness of the environment, public opinion has largely lost interest in saving the ships or the lives of those on board and has instead concentrated on the damage that the vessels may inflict on the environment by oil spills and the escape of dangerous or toxic cargoes.

References: U.S. Department of State, *Treaties and International Agreements*; Rudolph W. Wissmann, *The Maritime Industry: The Role of Federal Regulation in Establishing Labor and Safety Standards* (New York: Cornell Maritime Press, 1942).

SAILORS' UNION OF THE PACIFIC (SUP), 1891–present. The merger of the Coast Seamen's Union* (CSU) and the Steamship Sailors' Protective Union* created the Sailors' Union of the Pacific (SUP) on 29 July 1891. The merger had been the result of patient effort by Andrew Furuseth,* who had been elected president of the CSU in April 1891 on a platform of ending the wave of graft, the most recent episode of which was the treasurer's disappearance with all the union funds. Furuseth cleaned up the CSU, and engineered the merger with the Steamship Sailors' Protective Union, and at the close of his term in February 1892 he returned to the sea. The SUP could not survive without him, and two months later the members asked for his return; in June 1892 he resumed the presidency, which he held until 1936.

With a membership of 2,317, the SUP went on strike in 1893, but it was no match for the Shipowners' Association of the Pacific Coast* (SAPC), which, to crush the strike, hired a clever manipulator who was fleeing from arrest. A clever propaganda campaign turned public opinion against the SUP while the economic depression of that year allowed the shipowners to hire replacements among the thousands of unemployed. The mysterious explosion of a bomb in the boardinghouse of a crimp* was blamed on the union, and although Furuseth did his best to refute the charge, the strike was lost.

SAPC refused to accept the existence of the union, and it took the 1899 strike to convince shipowners to negotiate verbally with Furuseth, although they still rejected any written agreement. After one last citywide attempt to break all the waterfront unions in 1901, finally in 1902 the shipowners agreed to sign a written contract with SUP and the Marine Firemen's Union of the Pacific Coast,* both at last recognized as labor organizations. The 1906 strike brought wage increases to sailors for the first time, and SUP's membership rose to 5,100 in 1907.

SUP created and kept functioning the International Seamen's Union* (ISU), a labor federation for all seamen in the United States. Furuseth now began to devote most of his time to ISU affairs in Washington, D.C., and after 1910 he returned to the West Coast only for occasional inspection trips. Furuseth's absence was a double loss: not only was the SUP deprived of the dynamic presence of a dedicated leader, but the time Furuseth devoted to ISU did not result in the creation of powerful unions on the East Coast. Specific West Coast factors made union organizing easier for the SUP. There was no permanent oversupply of labor as in the eastern cities of the United States, teaming with immigrants, so that, traditionally, West Coast sailors (and workers in general) commanded higher wages. The many isolated ports from which hides and, in particular, lumber were carried required very skilled seamen who could also unload the ships when a local force of longshoremen was not available. Thus the craft skills in the coastwise* trade on the Pacific Coast accounted for this early success story and was reinforced by the Scandinavian ethnic background of the overwhelming majority of coastwise sailors in the Pacific. Unfortunately, the SUP attained ethnic cohesion at the price of blatant racism against Orientals and later against blacks as well.

The ISU affiliates on the East Coast started the strike of 1921* and were joined by SUP, which managed to sustain the struggle against the employers. Out of the disastrous defeat in that strike, Furuseth was able to salvage something for the SUP, but he insisted on keeping out of the union any new ideas. On the false charges of harboring sympathy for the International Workers of the World (IWW), Furuseth expelled J. Vance Thompson, the editor of SUP's periodical, *The Seamen's Journal*. Furuseth kept the union in the hands of old-time loyalists, but since he himself remained in Washington, D.C., concerned mainly with ISU issues, apathy and demoralization had spread through the declining membership of SUP. Nothing could be done that went against the inflexible and absolute principles of Furuseth, by the early 1930s few members attended the weekly meetings, and even in the biggest local, San Francisco, "things here are slow" and could even become "exceedingly slow" (Nelson 1990).

When the Big Strike* erupted in 1934, the SUP leaders were caught by surprise and failed to understand the nature of the rank-and-file revolt among seamen who on 15 May voted to join with striking longshoremen to stop cargoes in San Francisco and most ports of the West Coast. Furuseth returned from Washington to try to control the seamen, but only when the longshoremen and teamsters returned to work did the SUP consider halting the strike. Furuseth seized the opportunity to regain leadership by organizing a bonfire to burn the seamen's hated "fink" book on 29 July, and the next day the men returned to work.

The Big Strike had not been a failure, because although workers obtained few concessions, they had learned the power of coordinated action and had revived the long-forgotten strike techniques. Waterfront workers united to create the

Maritime Federation of the Pacific* (MFP) in April 1935; and longshoreman Harry Bridges* picked SUP patrolman* Harry Lundeberg* to be the federation's first president, but soon the two men became rivals. While Lundeberg began to build a power base in SUP, Paul Scharrenberg,* the editor of *The Seamen's Journal*, continued to defend the anachronistic policies of Furuseth. Drawing on the rank-and-file resentment against the conservative policies of the old leadership, Lundeberg secured the expulsion of Scharrenberg from the SUP in July 1935. Lundeberg now had himself elected head of SUP in January 1936, overcoming the opposition of a faction supported by Bridges. The next month Lundeberg stepped down as president of MFP and in effect put more distance between himself and Bridges.

Lundeberg, however, could not quit the MFP, because he still needed Bridges's support against a last challenge from the ISU. On 27 January 1936 Furuseth responded to Lundeberg's election by expelling the SUP from the ISU. The American Federation of Labor (AFL) backed ISU's efforts to seize SUP's assets and remove its new leadership, but because of support by the MFP and support from the rank-and-file seamen, Lundeberg kept control of SUP. Cooperation of longshoremen and seamen appeared to have reached the highest level when the MFP went on strike on 30 October 1936. As San Francisco prepared for a convulsion similar to the Big Strike of 1934, cracks started to appear in the union front. Lundeberg was on the verge of taking the SUP out of the strike because he had already reached a long-term understanding with the shipowners, who now ceased to attack him; however, he decided not to abandon the strike as the longshoremen had done in 1934 and instead continued the fight until 4 February 1937, when he obtained the crucial concession of union hiring halls* for the seamen.

The SUP was still not sure where exactly to throw its lot, but the rise of Joseph Curran* as an East Coast union leader during the 1936–1937 strike made Lundeberg afraid of being swallowed up by Curran's movement, which was later called the National Maritime Union.* April 1937 was the turning point for Lundeberg: a personal meeting with Curran failed to reach any understanding, while that same month Bridges joined the Congress of Industrial Organizations (CIO), in effect preempting any larger role for Lundeberg within the CIO. For about a year Lundeberg tried to keep the SUP alive as an independent union, but without powerful allies, his union risked isolation and possible setbacks. In June 1938 Lundeberg ended all pretense of cooperation with the longshoremen when he withdrew the SUP from the MFP. In October the SUP found a new home when it rejoined the AFL on very advantageous terms. The AFL agreed to abolish the old discredited ISU and in its place created the Seafarers' International Union* (SIU), with the SUP as its main affiliate; Lundeberg remained the head of SUP and also became the president of SIU.

With AFL financial and political support, the SIU now began its fifty-year fight against the NMU; in this nationwide struggle gradually the center of power shifted to the SIU and away from its main affiliate, the SUP. Lundeberg never gave up his position in the SUP, just like Furuseth, whose real successor he was, but unlike Furuseth, Lundeberg succeeded in gradually constructing a powerful and permanent power base in the SIU. As the long-term power shift toward the SIU unfolded, the SUP lost its independence and merely followed the orders coming from the top leadership. By 1942, when the SUP assumed the authority to appoint the previously elected ship's representatives, thereby depriving the ship's committees* of any real voice in union affairs, the transition to rule by the clique around Lundeberg was complete. "While men who engaged in militant action aboard ship were increasingly characterized as drunks, those who offered more than an occasional gripe at union meetings were labeled commies." If "guys talk off the point, to stir up trouble" and did not heed the warnings to be quiet, then "a couple of guys throw them out" (Nelson 1990)— in one case a sailor received forty stitches. Lundeberg participated personally in violent actions, thereby setting an example for his followers, who did not hesitate to impose discipline upon the rank and file by force.

Lundeberg's drive to power was aided by his full acceptance of white supremacy doctrines, so that members of the SUP could trust him to keep blacks, Orientals, and other minorities out of the union. As late as 1972 a government report found that the SUP's racial practices and composition of the membership had not changed. Lundeberg himself had begun the accommodation with shipowners and by 1940 had turned against the New Deal, although he did make sure that the SUP received very favorable wage contracts, thereby making shipowners pay heavily to secure labor peace aboard the ships.

To maintain support from the seamen, Lundeberg maintained the fiery language of the 1930s, and to give an appearance of radicalism, he also welcomed into the SUP during the 1936–1937 strike Trotskyists, who provided an effective counter to the denunciations by the Communist party. The Trotskyists provided the radical rhetoric and ideological bulwarks, and in return Lundeberg supported their causes and gave them jobs and influence within the SUP. In the mounting power struggle against the Communist party and Bridges's ILWU, Lundeberg did not overlook any possible ally, and he welcomed the remnants of the Marine Transport Workers' Union No. 510 of the International Workers of the World, or Wobblies, into the SUP.

On the West Coast the bitter rivalry between Lundeberg and Bridges was postponed during World War II. With the war over, both leaders resumed their traditional feuding, and each tried to obtain better concessions from the shipowners. Bridges made a bold move by joining with the NMU to create the Committee for Maritime Unity* (CMU), and this show of force by seamen and longshoremen brought employer concessions. Lundeberg countered by sending the SUP and the SIU on strike in August 1946, and after twenty-one days his unions secured better conditions in one more case of whipsawing.* CMU had meanwhile joined the strike but obtained mixed results, and soon jealousy between Curran and Bridges brought the collapse of CMU, thereby ending this last threat to Lundeberg's position in the SUP.

The Cold War was already raging, and Lundeberg's fanatical anticommunism gave him the opportunity to try to destroy Bridges, whose leftist record appeared to provide an easy target. Confident of success and wishing to appear without any trace of radicalism, Lundeberg purged the SUP of his Trotskyist allies in 1949–1950. The expulsion of the Trotskyists deprived Lundeberg of the last ideological justification and exposed as mere power plays his moves to take over the Marine Firemen, Oilers, Watertenders, and Wipers' Union of the Pacific Coast* (MFOWW) and the National Union of Marine Cooks and Stewards* (NUMCS). After constant and sometimes bitter struggles, Lundeberg gained control of these two unions, which he placed under the direct control of the SIU, but not of the SUP, whose position was somewhat weakened.

Lundeberg never had a chance to launch the final assault on Bridges because of an internal challenge. Obsessed with the struggle against communism and Bridges, Lundeberg had neglected the internal situation, in particular, the new forces in the SIU districts on the East Coast and Gulf. The center of power was shifting decisively from the SUP to the SIU, but a new rising star, Paul Hall,* made Lundeberg fear for his own position. In a desperate move to find allies to neutralize the Hall challenge, Lundeberg decided to end his violent hostility toward Joseph Curran, who was suffering himself from Hall's raiding drives against the NMU. The result was the creation of the Conference of American Maritime Unions* (CAMU) in 1954 as a stop-Hall organization. Curran made the Herculean effort of controlling his autocratic tendencies and began to co-operate, but before CAMU could engage in any significant action, the more hotheaded Lundeberg exploded and pulled his unions out of CAMU in 1955. A fuming Lundeberg could not only watch helplessly as Hall consolidated his power and Bridges remained as defiant as ever within the ILWU. Lundeberg was mercifully spared of more disagreeable news when he died in 1957, and power now swiftly passed to the new SIU president, Paul Hall, who among other changes ended the feuding with Bridges and the ILWU.

The centralization of power was now so complete in the SIU that, unlike Furuseth and Lundeberg, Hall did not even bother to head the SUP but instead left it in the hands of Morris Weisberger,* who was a longtime friend of Hall's. The real foundation of the ISU was not the SUP, which now no longer held an independent position and saw its activities reduced to purely local affairs. On all issues of importance, orders came from the top ISU leadership and flowed down to the bottom ranks of the SUP through the system of tight discipline that Lundeberg had previously established. The SUP went on strike in 1962 against the Pacific Maritime Association* (PMA), but in part because the federal government imposed a truce, the key decisions on the strike were taken by Hall at SIU headquarters in Washington, D.C., until a satisfactory agreement with PMA was negotiated.

Ill health forced Weisberger to retire in 1978, and he was replaced by Paul Dempster.* By then SUP's main problem was the same as that of all other seamen's unions, namely, the rapid decline of U.S.-flag shipping. The collapse of Pacific Far East Lines,* States Steamship Lines,* and Prudential Lines* was a major blow to the union. Some of Prudential's ships were sold to Delta Line,* which, however, won a court battle to man them with NMU crews, thereby inflicting an additional setback to the SUP. In the 1980s SUP developed a close working relationship with the ILWU. In the late 1980s and early 1990s, SUP's main efforts have been to try to survive amidst the virtual disappearance of U.S.-flag shipping.

Principal Labor Leaders

Andrew Furuseth	1891–1936
Paul Scharrenberg	1901–1936
Harry Lundeberg ("Lunchbox")	1936–1957
Morris Weisberger	1957–1978
Paul Dempster	1978–1990
Gunnar Lundeberg	1990–present

References: CIO Files of John L. Lewis, Part I: Correspondence with CIO Unions, Microfilm, University Publications of America; Bruce Nelson, *Workers on the Waterfront: Seamen, Longshoremen, and Unionism in the 1930s* (Urbana: University of Illinois Press, 1990); Betty V. H. Schneider, *Industrial Relations in the West Coast Maritime Industry* (Berkeley: Institute of Industrial Relations, 1958); Stephen Schwartz, *Brotherhood of the Sea: A History of the Sailors' Union of the Pacific, 1885–1985* (New Brunswick, NJ: Transaction Books, 1986); Hyman Weintraub, *Andrew Furuseth, Emancipator of the Seamen* (Berkeley: University of California Press, 1959); Stan Weir, "The Informal Work Group," in Alice Lynd and Staughton Lynd, eds., *Rank and File: Personal Histories by Working-Class Organizers* (Boston: Beacon Press, 1973), pp. 177–200.

***ST. LOUIS* and *ST. PAUL*, 1895–1923.** The *St. Louis* and the *St. Paul* were the first large passenger ships built in the United States since the *Adriatic* of 1857, the last Collins* liner. With an overall length of 554 feet and a beam of 63 feet, the ships carried 320 passengers in first class, 220 in second, and 800 in steerage* or third class. The quadruple-expansion engines allowed the ships to reach a speed of twenty knots, and double screws eliminated permanently any lingering need to rely on sails. The ships "represented about the average in size and speed of the Atlantic greyhounds of that era" (Nevitt 1981); nonetheless the *St. Louis* and *St. Paul* were involved in key events in the maritime history of the United States.

The two ships belonged to the International Navigation Company,* an American firm that also owned British- and Belgian-flag tonnage. After a very heated controversy, the company had obtained special permission from Congress to bring the two British-flag vessels, the *City of Paris* and the *City of New York*, into U.S. registry* in 1892, so that they could qualify for subsidies under the Ocean Mail Act of 1891.* However, Congress in exchange had imposed upon the company the obligation to build in U.S. shipyards two modern passenger liners, so that the four vessels could provide continuous U.S.-flag passenger service across the Atlantic. The William Cramp shipyards duly constructed the *St. Louis* and *St. Paul*, which entered into service in 1895.

The U.S. Navy requisitioned the ships as auxiliary cruisers in the Spanish-American War. The *St. Louis* cut underwater Spanish cables near Puerto Rico and, to accomplish the same task near Santiago de Cuba, engaged in duels with shore batteries. The *St. Paul* underwent one of the earliest destroyer attacks, but good aim managed to destroy the Spanish torpedo boat, the *Terror*, before it could inflict any damage. The *St. Paul* and the *St. Louis* returned after the war to the International Navigation Company. The *St. Paul* was the first ship in the world to have a wireless telegraph aboard: Guglielmo Marconi made the installations in November 1899, and this innovation gradually revolutionized the movements of ocean ships, including the tramp* vessels.

By the time the United States entered World War I, the two ships were showing their age and could not be expected to repeat the gallant feats of the era of the Spanish-American War. When the U.S. Navy took over the ships for conversion to transports, the *St. Paul*, on the eve of the first naval voyage, capsized at the pier; by the time the vessel was ready again, the war was over, and the navy returned the ship to her owners. The *St. Paul* managed to provide passenger service from 1920 until 1923, when the vessel was scrapped. The *St. Louis* did serve as a transport during World War I and had several encounters with German U-Boats. The navy returned the vessel to the company, but a fire in 1920 precluded any resumption of passenger service, and the *St. Louis* was finally scrapped in 1924. No comparable passenger liners were built again in the United States until the *President Hoover** of 1931 and the *Manhattan** of 1932.

References: Frank O. Braynard, *Famous American Ships* (New York: Hastings House, 1956); Frederick E. Emmons, *American Passenger Ships: The Ocean Lines and Liners, 1873–1983* (Newark: University of Delaware Press, 1985); John G. B. Hutchins, *The American Maritime Industries and Public Policy, 1789–1914* (Cambridge: Harvard University Press, 1941); Winthrop L. Marvin, *The American Merchant Marine* (New York: Scribner's, 1902); Cedric R. Nevitt, "American Merchant Steamships," in Society of Naval Architects and Marine Engineers, *Historical Transactions, 1883–1943* (Westport, CT: Greenwood Press, 1981).

ST. PAUL. See *St. Louis* and *St. Paul*.

SAN FRANCISCO AND PORTLAND STEAMSHIP COMPANY or THE BIG THREE, 1879–1924. The San Francisco and Portland Steamship Company or the ''Big Three''—so called because of the three big ships it attempted to operate during most of its existence on the West Coast—was originally known as the Oregon Railway and Navigation Company, which had operated steamboats along the Columbia River, but when the railroad track united Portland to the Pacific Coast in 1882, the company, under the direction of the bold financier

Henry Villard, expanded into the coastwise* trade. In 1904 the company was acquired by the Union Pacific Railroad, which renamed it the San Francisco and Portland Steamship Company to reflect the railroad's goal of tapping the California trade. The Big Three, as it preferred to be called, had extended its service to the south beyond San Francisco and as far as Los Angeles in 1910, and the company appeared to have obtained a secure place in the coastwise trade of the Pacific Coast.

Railroad magnate James J. Hill crashed into the business when he established the Great Northern Pacific Steamship Company* in 1913 to place two modern, fast liners in direct competition with the older and slower ships of the Big Three, which failed to counter with its own fast ships. After U.S. entry into World War I, the company was left with only one vessel, the *Rose City*, and after the war it chartered one vessel, the *Alaska*, to try to restore a more adequate service. After barely nine months in operation, the *Alaska* was shipwrecked with the loss of forty-two lives out of the 220 persons aboard on 6 August 1921. The company had been plagued with shipwrecks and accidents throughout its history, and to remedy the bad public image, the Big Three announced plans to build three new ships, subsequently reduced to only two, to try to regain a competitive position in the coastwise trade. Nothing came of these plans, and the *Rose City* remained as the company's sole ship until 1924, when the railroad decided to suspend operations and sell the ship to the McCormick Steamship Company.*

Some Notable Ships

*Columbia**	1880–1907
Rose City	1908–1924
Alaska; formerly, *Kansas City*	1920–1921

References: Giles T. Brown, *Ships That Sail No More: Marine Transportation from San Diego to Puget Sound, 1910–1940* (Lexington: University of Kentucky Press, 1966); Frederick E. Emmons, *American Passenger Ships: The Ocean Lines and Liners, 1873–1983* (Newark: University of Delaware Press, 1985); E. W. Wright, ed., *Marine History of the Pacific Northwest* (New York: Antiquarian Press, 1961).

SANSINENA, **1958–1976.** The *Sansinena*, a tanker of 66,000 deadweight* tons built in the United States in 1958, was the object of a bitter political maneuver known as the "*Sansinena* affair" during the administration of Richard Nixon. The tanker originally was under U.S. registry* but later had been placed under the Liberian flag of convenience.* The *Sansinena* was one of the two tankers that belonged to the Barracuda Tanker Corporation (headquarters in Bermuda), which was owned by executives and attorneys of the Union Oil Company of California. Barracuda Tanker Corporation was already notorious as the owner of the tanker *Torrey Canyon*, whose shipwreck in the English Channel on 15 March 1967 had produced a massive oil spill over the coasts of southern England

and northern France. A stockholder of Barracuda Tanker Corporation and also its president, Peter M. Flanigan in 1969 came to work in the Nixon White House.

Since mid-1967 the Union Oil Co. of California had sought to obtain a waiver from the government to allow the operation of this Liberian-flag tanker in the domestic trades normally reserved under the cabotage* laws to U.S.-built and U.S.-flag vessels. One powerful motivation for the transfer was to safeguard the *Sansinena* from arrest orders by both the British and French governments, which wanted to collect claims on the huge damage caused by the *Torrey Canyon* oil spill. In comparison to foreign tankers, the *Sansinena* was small in size, but in the domestic trade where most vessels averaged 25,000 deadweight tons, the tanker would rank as the sixth largest ship. For some unknown reason, Union Oil and Barracuda did not attempt to return the tanker first to U.S. registry,* a difficult but not impossible procedure, given that the ship had been built in a U.S. shipyard, apparently without construction subsidies (whose refund was then mandatory). Among other possible motivations for the transfer was that the value of the tanker, as soon as the ship was approved for service in the domestic trade, climbed from zero to over $18 million, in comparison to its value of $4.5 million in the foreign market—and this without deducing the combined British-French claims of over $15 million. Barracuda's position was that an American company would own the vessel, whose flag eventually would be shifted to U.S. registry, but initially could find no agency to buy this argument. Finally through patient and constant lobbying Barracuda found an opening in the pliant Department of the Treasury, which, without listing any specific reason, granted an open-ended waiver on 2 March 1970, an extraordinary measure normally justified only in times of national emergency.

The Department of Defense had not provided any national security grounds for the waiver, while the Maritime Administration* (MARAD), with the authority to grant temporary waivers when U.S.-flag vessels or services were not available, had likewise refused the request of Barracuda. A congressional investigator found that White House aide Flanigan, the former president of Barracuda, had performed some discreet inquiries on behalf of Barracuda; but before any impropriety could be uncovered, on 10 March the Treasury Department revoked its earlier decision, while very effective cooperation between senators and the White House managed to silence the whole episode. The *Sansinena* affair revealed the intensity of feeling among shipyards and domestic operators who felt mortally threatened by the introduction of Liberian-flag ships. The affair was also a preview of later scandals that rocked and finally toppled the Nixon administration, but because the *Sansinena* affair had been so hurriedly halted and hushed, public opinion did not have the opportunity to hear this early warning about politics and business in the Nixon administration.

The *Sansinena* remained under the Liberian flag, and Barracuda eventually settled the claims with the British and French governments so that the tanker could travel freely around the world. The eventful career of the tanker was not yet over, however: the *Sansinena* exploded on 17 December 1976 in Los Angeles harbor while docked near the Union Oil Co. refinery; fortunately, most of the fuel oil aboard had been pumped out, but enough remained aboard to produce an explosion that split the ship in half and caused an oil spill. At least four died, over fifty were wounded, and the blast shattered windows twenty-one miles away. This disaster, coming just a few days after the *Argo Merchant* ran aground near Nantucket Island on 15 December and spilled massive amounts of oil, convinced Congress that existing laws for the protection of the environment were too weak and in response to these calamities enacted the Port and Tanker Safety Act of 1978.*

SAVANNAH, 1818–1821. The *Savannah* was the first true steamship for ocean transportation, as distinct from the more modest steamboat* of inland waters. Up to 1819 engines had been limited to steamboats for rivers, but in 1818 the *Savannah* was built to carry a single-expansion engine* to move the paddle wheels on the sides of her wooden hull. On 22 May 1819 the *Savannah* sailed from Savannah, Georgia, on a pioneer voyage that for the first time brought steam to the world's oceans. The day is still commemorated as National Maritime Day in the United States, and that voyage—although sail supplemented steam power—began a revolution in world trade.

The *Savannah* had sailed without cargo or passengers, and upon her return no one was interested in purchasing the steamship; her promoters finally sold her for operation as a sailing packet once her machinery was removed. On 3 November 1821, now operating just as a sailing packet in the coastwise* trade, she ran aground and was a total loss. The sad fate of the *Savannah* herself was indicative of the experience of the United States with new marine technology. A blind faith in technology as the key to business success in ocean shipping often led many Americans to ignore the commercial realities of ocean transportation. From the *Savannah* to the containers* of the 1960s, U.S. lines have introduced innovations only to have them rapidly adopted by foreign competitors, who then took a commanding lead. Thus it was with the *Savannah*, whose successful experiment with steam navigation became the foundation of a huge British, rather than American, merchant marine for over a hundred years.

References: Robert G. Albion, *The Rise of New York Port, 1815–1860* (New York: Scribner's, 1939); Erik Heyl, *Early American Steamers*, 6 vols. (Buffalo, 1953–1969); William S. Lindsay, *History of Merchant Shipping and Ancient Commerce*, 4 vols. (New York: AMS Press, 1965); David B. Tyler, *Steam Conquers the Atlantic* (New York: D. Appleton-Century, 1939).

SANTA ELIANA. See *Mayagüez.*

SAVANNAH, 1959–1970. The *Savannah* was the first nuclear-powered merchant vessel in the world and was named in honor of the original *Savannah*, the first ship to use steam power to cross the Atlantic, in the hope that the later *Savannah* would likewise usher in a new era in ocean transportation. In 1955,

initially with great enthusiasm, President Dwight D. Eisenhower had proposed
nuclear-powered ships as part of his "Atoms-for-Peace" campaign intended to
show the world, locked in the Cold War and fearful of nuclear weapons, that
atomic energy could really help humanity. Congress embraced the idea and
approved in 1956 the funds to build and operate an experimental ship, whose
keel was laid on National Maritime Day, 22 May 1958. The *Savannah* was
launched on 21 July 1959, and "then the long and intensive testing of the
nuclear power plant began" (Atomic Energy Commission 1965). Only on 21
December 1961 did a low-power chain reaction begin, and many more tests and
sea trials were necessary before the ship was finally delivered to the States
Marine Corporation* on 1 May 1962, not for commercial operation but as a
demonstration ship to tour ports in the United States. The ship was 595 feet
long, had a beam of 78 feet and cabins for sixty passengers, and required a
gigantic crew of 110; the cruising speed was twenty-one knots, and the ship in
size and design belonged to the Mariner* class.

In spite of this apparent success, long before then the career of nuclear-
powered merchant ships had been cut short, at least for the twentieth century.
The pressurized-water reactor in the *Savannah* could never compete with ships
powered by conventional fuels, and while some valuable experience could be
gained from the ship, any chance of developing a vessel for commercial operation lay not with this break-bulk* ship but with a tanker using a boiling-water
reactor. In 1958, when the Maritime Administration (MARAD) proposed
installing a boiling-water reactor in a tanker under construction, the Eisenhower
administration, whose earlier enthusiasm for nuclear merchant ships as a way
to win the Cold War propaganda battle had waned considerably, declined to
support the proposal, in effect killing any hopes for a fleet of nuclear-powered
merchant vessels to survive without massive subsidies.

In early 1963 the engineers of States Marine Corporation left the *Savannah*
idle because of a labor dispute, and in July 1963 MARAD decided to solve the
impasse by handing over the vessel to a new operator, the American Export
Lines* (AEL). The ship continued to tour ports and generate goodwill, and by
the end of 1965, 1,389,000 visitors had come on board. In August 1965 the
Savannah entered commercial service, carrying cargo for AEL across the Atlantic to Europe and the Mediterranean, but because of the much higher operating costs of the vessel, the ship could remain in service only because of lavish
subsidies, which allowed AEL to reap a modest profit as well. Already in 1968
the government wanted to suspend the voyages of this vessel because all possible
experimental and publicity potential had been exhausted, but Congress retained
the subsidies until 1970. Finally in July 1970 the vessel was laid up, and in
April 1971 the nuclear core was removed; the *Savannah*, however, fell into a
legal limbo as MARAD held the vessel, but without formally entering her into
the National Defense Reserve Fleet,* until the government could decide upon
the final disposition. In 1976 "the secondary cooling system was drained of
contaminated fluids" and thus "will effectively preclude any further operation

of the vessel as a nuclear ship'' (John March Files). The *Savannah* was an early candidate for preservation in a maritime museum, and after delays and false starts, the vessel finally was opened to the public in Charleston, South Carolina.

In spite of all the experiments, the *Savannah* failed to answer the vital question of whether any type of nuclear power was justified for commercial operations, and not surprisingly the vessel did not launch a revolution comparable to that begun by the first *Savannah* with the introduction of steam into ocean transportation in 1819. A major part of the blame for the failure of the nuclear-powered *Savannah* rested with the Eisenhower administration, whose preference for short-term gains in the propaganda battle of the Cold War sacrificed the long-term development of the merchant marine.

References: Atomic Energy Commission, *Nuclear Power and Merchant Shipping*, 1965; Norman J. Brouwer, *International Register of Historic Ships* (Annapolis, MD: Naval Institute Press, 1985); *Congressional Record*, 24 August 1970; John March Files, Gerald Ford Presidential Library, Ann Arbor, Michigan; Official File, Dwight D. Eisenhower Presidential Library, Abilene, Kansas; *Public Papers of the Presidents, Dwight D. Eisenhower, 1955* (Washington, DC: Government Printing Office, 1959).

SCHARRENBERG, PAUL, 1877–27 October 1969. Paul Scharrenberg, a California labor leader, was one of the officials who helped Andrew Furuseth* maintain control over the Sailors Union of the Pacific* (SUP); during nearly twenty-five years Scharrenberg was also the editor of its official publication, the *Coast Seamen's Journal.* He was born in Hamburg, Germany, in 1877 and came from a family that for three generations had gone to the sea, and soon the young boy himself was fascinated with the sea. The unexpected death of his father ended his family's comfortable middle-class life-style, and Scharrenberg had to abandon his education and ship out to sea at age twelve. He came to New York City, where he began to improve his English and continued to make voyages until the vessel he was sailing on shipwrecked near San Francisco in 1898. He was immediately fascinated with San Francisco, found a wife, and decided to make the city his home port while he sailed on coastwise* voyages. The next year he joined the SUP and met Andrew Furuseth,* with whom he developed a lifelong relationship. In the strike of 1901, Scharrenberg was injured by a blow from the police, and, no longer able to stand in the picket line, he was given the job of assistant manager of the *Coast Seamen's Journal.* "By the chance occurrence of this injury'' (Burki 1971) he abandoned the sea, devoted all his time to the union, and became an excellent example of the white-shirt* sailor. His link with the *Coast Seamen's Journal* continued, and in 1913 he became its editor.

Scharrenberg realized that the SUP would always remain the personal domain of Furuseth, and while a clash with the latter was inconceivable, Scharrenberg sought to have his own separate organization where he could play a major role in labor politics. The big break came when he secured his election as head of the California State Federation of Labor in 1909, not necessarily a major step up since that organization, with only 25,000 members, was still insignificant, but now he had the base upon which to build and expand his activities. By 1921 the federation reached the high number of 104,000 persons, and more remarkably, he was able to maintain membership near those levels during the 1920s, perhaps the most difficult decade for labor in U.S. history. Scharrenberg achieved success mainly because of his very effective work as a lobbyist in Sacramento. He enjoyed the political maneuvering and organized the labor lobbyists in the state legislature to work as a team. He was at home in dealing with men of power and was a natural among politicians. In the early 1910s he changed his registration from Democrat to Republican, although he did vote for Woodrow Wilson and later, Franklin D. Roosevelt. In the 1910s Scharrenberg, an unabashed white supremacist, already had acquired a middle-class life-style, belonged to exclusive clubs, and cultivated carefully friendships with businessmen.

Not unexpectedly, Scharrenberg had lost touch with the rank and file of SUP, but while the prosperity of World War I lasted, the discontent among the sailors was muted by the high wages. As the postwar boom started to collapse, Scharrenberg, as perhaps the most conservative of labor leaders, began to receive mounting criticism from seafarers, and he was ousted as editor of the *Coast Seamen's Journal* in January 1921, but after the disastrous strike of 1921,* Furuseth regained a strong grip over the SUP and reinstated Scharrenberg as editor in September.

By then the SUP had been largely destroyed as an effective organization for the rest of the 1920s, and while Furuseth concentrated on the lobbying activities of the International Seamen's Union* (ISU) in Washington, D.C., Scharrenberg devoted most of his time to the California State Federation of Labor and the political lobbying in Sacramento he loved so much. Scharrenberg's only change was the intensification of his anti-Oriental biases, and he did much to fan an emotional hatred for the Japanese, who, unlike the Chinese, posed not even the remotest menace to California labor. When the Big Strike* erupted in 1934, Scharrenberg was caught totally by surprise and vainly attempted to dismiss the movement as a radical plot hatched by communists. To try to discredit Harry Lundeberg* and Harry Bridges,* Scharrenberg collected doubtful evidence of their supposed communist participation, setting the base for the extremely long and agonizing *Bridges* case.* However, not even hurling charges of communism could save Scharrenberg, who was expelled from the SUP in June 1936 after a rank-and-file revolt.

Furuseth tried one last time to save Scharrenberg by having the ISU revoke the charter of the SUP, but nothing could save Scharrenberg, who had become to all seamen the visible symbol of reactionary and pro-business leadership. To remain as secretary of the California State Federation of Labor, he had to ram his membership application through a minor union, but holding the state office while being repudiated by the rapidly growing SUP left him in a very awkward position. He decided to accept the offer to replace the aging Furuseth in Washington, D.C., as the lobbyist for the ISU in January 1936 and left California still clinging to the editorship of the *Seamen's Journal* but no longer as head of the State Federation of Labor. When the ISU collapsed in 1937, Scharrenberg was almost left without a job, but American Federation of Labor president William Green kept him as a paid lobbyist in the nation's capital. Good luck did not abandon the fallen labor leader, who in 1943 was recalled by Republican governor Earl Warren to become the head of the California Department of Industrial Relations, a position he held until his retirement in 1955. He devoted the remaining years of his life to writing manuscripts about his many experiences in the labor movement; he died on 27 October 1969.

References: Mary Ann Burki, "Paul Scharrenberg: White Shirt Sailor," Ph.D. diss., University of Rochester, 1971; Bruce Nelson, *Workers on the Waterfront: Seamen, Longshoremen, and Unionism in the 1930s* (Urbana: University of Illinois Press, 1990); Hyman Weintraub, *Andrew Furuseth: Emancipator of the Seamen* (Berkeley: University of California Press, 1959).

SCHWERIN, RENNIE PIERRE, 8 August 1858–11 January 1936. From 1893 to 1915 Rennie P. Schwerin was the dynamic executive of the Pacific Mail Steamship Company* (PMSS). Schwerin was born on 8 August 1858 in New York City, raised in Schenectady, New York, and graduated from the U.S. Naval Academy at Annapolis. He began his service in the navy in 1874 and rose to the rank of lieutenant. He caught the attention of railroad magnate Collis P. Huntington, who called Schwerin back to civilian life with a job as chief purchaser for the Southern Pacific Railroad in 1892. When Southern Pacific acquired PMSS in 1893, Huntington placed Schwerin in charge of the moribund company. PMSS "had only one first-class steamship, the *China*,* in the transpacific trade, its other vessels being old, out of repair and unfit for the Oriental service; the company was graft-ridden and its treasury practically empty" (*National Cyclopedia of American Biography*).

By his tremendous driving power and organizational abilities, Schwerin saved the bankrupt company, which paid dividends in 1897 for the first time since 1885. He ordered new ships for the fleet, the *Korea* and *Siberia** in 1902 and the *Manchuria** and the *Mongolia** in 1904. With the fastest and largest vessels in the Pacific Ocean, PMSS had become the most important transpacific firm, while its reliance on Chinese crews allowed the company to compete on equal terms with other competitors, most notably the Japanese, who were feverishly building their merchant marine.

To halt the Japanese advance, Schwerin obtained the financing to build four gigantic ships, which would provide intercoastal* service from New York City to California, as well as serve the transpacific routes. When in 1912 the U.S. Congress passed the Panama Canal Act,* which closed the Panama Canal* to steamship lines owned by railroads, he had to abandon the plan. The passage in 1915 of the La Follette Seamen's Act,* whose avowed aim was to outlaw Chinese crews, was the last straw for Southern Pacific, which decided to sell

PMSS in 1915; Schwerin himself felt betrayed by his own government and gave up the struggle to maintain a U.S.-flag presence in the Pacific Ocean.

In spite of its tragic ending, Schwerin's rescue and revival of PMSS remained the greatest success of his career. After 1915 Schwerin participated in other businesses, generally assuming control of a bankrupt company, whether in oil, telegraphs, or wool manufacture, and nursing it back to record profits. Highly profitable as were his later ventures, none equaled the success he had achieved during his years at PMSS. He died in San Francisco on 11 January 1936.

References: René De La Pedraja, *The Rise and Decline of U.S. Merchant Shipping in the Twentieth Century* (New York: Twayne, 1992); John H. Kemble, "A Hundred Years of the Pacific Mail," *American Neptune* 10 (1950): 123–143; *National Cyclopedia of American Biography*, vol. 26.

SCULLY, JOHN JAMES JOSEPH, 10 February 1867–5 April 1947. John James Joseph Scully was born on 10 February 1867 in South Amboy, New Jersey, and studied at private and public schools. He took university courses to become a marine pilot and then joined the Organization of Masters, Mates, and Pilots* (MM&P), the main association for deck officers. After World War I Scully became secretary-treasurer of MM&P and retained that position until his retirement in 1945. He also edited the magazine of the union, the *Master, Mate and Pilot*, and was a Democrat. He died on 5 April 1947.

References: Gary M. Fink, ed., *Biographical Dictionary of American Labor*, 2d ed. (Westport, CT: Greenwood Press, 1984); *Who's Who in Labor, 1946* (New York: Dryden Press, 1946).

SEAFARERS' INTERNATIONAL UNION (SIU), 1938–present. The Seafarers' International Union (SIU) was the seamen's union created by the American Federation of Labor (AFL) to counter the threat from the National Maritime Union* (NMU). The AFL realized that the International Seamen's Union* (ISU) was almost totally discredited and decided to replace that bankrupt organization with the new SIU on 14 October 1938. The main affiliate of the new SIU was the Sailors' Union of the Pacific* (SUP), whose ranking officer, Harry Lundeberg,* also became the first president of the SIU. Besides an almost permanent hostility to the NMU of the East Coast, the SIU under Lundeberg easily adopted the policies of white supremacy and fanatical anticommunism, in contrast to the NMU, which was open to all races and in the early years also to communists.

Until the end of World War II it appeared that the SIU would remain a largely paper front for the SUP, in a sense duplicating the pattern of the former ISU under Andrew Furuseth.* Even the AFL had stopped pouring money into the SIU's organizing drives on the Gulf and East Coast, because the best Lundeberg could find were notorious characters like former associates of "Emperor" David Grange;* not surprisingly, the 50,000 members of the NMU vastly exceeded those of the SIU. The situation began to change when Paul Hall* began organizing drives on the East Coast and Gulf during World War II, and by 1948 these new districts had acquired considerable influence, and to represent them Hall was elected vice president of the SIU, whose total membership now equaled that of the rival NMU. In 1948 Lundeberg decided to bring the National Union of Marine Cooks and Stewards* (NUMCS) into the SIU, thereby setting off a long, bitter battle against Harry Bridges* and his International Longshoremen and Warehousemen's Union Association.* Finally in 1955 by recourse to voting tricks, the NUMCS was forcibly incorporated into the SIU. Meanwhile, Hall's influence in the SIU had been quietly spreading, and to try to halt it, Lundeberg attempted to call off the struggle against the NMU and joined in forming the Conference of American Maritime Unions* (CAMU) with NMU president Joseph Curran* in 1954. The rivalry between the two leaders was too strong, and CAMU collapsed the next year. Lundeberg had no choice but to see Hall confirmed as his heir apparent, and upon Lundeberg's death in 1957, Hall became the new president of the SIU.

Besides the incorporation of the NUMCS in 1955, the Marine Firemen, Oilers, Watertenders, and Wipers of the Pacific Coast* (MFOWW) had abandoned their independent status and decided to join the SIU rather than the NMU in 1953. MFOWW members had been convinced by the greater sensitivity of the SIU to the craft feelings of shipboard personnel, and this more receptive attitude continued to be a powerful weapon in the organizing drives against NMU unions, which had seen their industrial organization gradually transformed into a source of absolute power for Curran's personal rule. The expulsion of communists from the NMU had weakened that union and had been followed by the even harsher drive to concentrate all power in the hands of Joseph Curran and a few associates. Dissatisfaction grew within the NMU, and many members preferred to join the SIU. Even in Lundeberg's last years, he had begun to edge out Curran as the main spokesman for seamen, in particular, when he obtained the presidency of the Maritime Trades Department* of the AFL. The lead over the NMU increased under Hall, as the SIU rose to become the most important seamen's labor organization in the United States and Hall, the real spokesman. Thus the period from 1938 to 1957, when labor leadership had been divided between Curran's NMU and Lundeberg's SIU (in contrast to the previous unity under Andrew Furuseth), gave way to leadership under Hall's SIU, which reported 80,000 members in 1973.

Hall pushed aggressively for government subsidies for the companies and in turn pressured management for maximum benefits for the seamen. The apparent success of this policy could not hide the constant decline of U.S.-flag merchant shipping, while cooperation with the NMU over a common policy toward the flags-of-convenience* problem proved impossible; for example, the brief-lived experiment with the International Maritime Workers' Union (IMWU) collapsed because of jurisdictional squabbles. Diversification away from the maritime sector had also helped the SIU in its rivalry against the NMU. Since the 1950s, the SIU had attempted to expand into nonmaritime areas and created the United Industrial Workers as the affiliate for members who worked on land. Of the

SIU's 80,000 members, 25,000 were employed in activities such as taxi drivers, cannery workers, and maintenance personnel. The SIU's entry into land employment paralleled a similar policy by many steamship companies, which were diversifying into nonshipping activities since the 1950s.

Upon Hall's death in June 1980, his successor as SIU and MTD president, Frank P. Drozak,* attempted to reverse the decline of the U.S.-flag merchant fleet by adopting a more pro-business policy. Also, Drozak proposed the consolidation of the many maritime unions, and right before his death in 1988, District 2 of the Marine Engineers' Beneficial Association merged with the SIU. Drozak was replaced by Michael Sacco as the new SIU president.

Principal Labor Leaders

Harry Lundeberg	1938–1957
Paul Hall	1957–1980
Frank P. Drozak	1980–1988
Michael Sacco	1988–present

References: Joseph H. Ball, *The Government-Subsidized Union Monopoly* (Washington, DC: Labor Policy Association, 1966); Walter Galenson, *The CIO Challenge to the AFL: A History of the American Labor Movement, 1935–1941* (Cambridge: Harvard University Press, 1960); Joseph P. Goldberg, *The Maritime Story: A Study in Labor-Management Relations* (Cambridge: Harvard University Press, 1958); Samuel A. Lawrence, *United States Merchant Shipping Policies and Politics* (Washington, DC: Brookings Institution, 1966); Bruce Nelson, *Workers on the Waterfront: Seamen, Longshoremen, and Unionism in the 1930s* (Urbana: University of Illinois Press, 1990).

SEA-LAND, 1960–present. Since 1960 one of the largest merchant shipping companies in the United States has been Sea-Land. Originally the company was a subsidiary of the Waterman Steamship Corporation* and was known as Pan-Atlantic Steamship Corporation, whose services covered the coastwise* trade and Puerto Rico. Sea-Land adopted its present name in 1960.

The history of Sea-Land was closely intertwined with the activities of Malcom McLean,* who had bought the Pan-Atlantic Steamship Corporation and Waterman Steamship in 1955. Through Pan-Atlantic Steamship McLean tried to introduce containers* into the coastwise trade, and after 1960 he likewise used Sea-Land as the instrument to expand container service within the routes protected by the cabotage* laws of the United States. In 1962 Sea-Land restored the nearly vanished intercoastal* service and, encouraged by the reliability of the offshore domestic trade to Puerto Rico, bought the Alaska Freight Lines in 1964. Sea-Land has remained the main carrier providing ocean transportation between the mainland United States and Alaska, and this offshore domestic trade and a continuing presence in Puerto Rico have been two solid foundations behind the company's survival.

The profits from Waterman Steamship Corporation were financing the expansion of Sea-Land, but when billionaire Daniel K. Ludwig* decided to order large containerships for the intercoastal trade, McLean had no choice but to seek an accommodation with the new rival. McLean left the intercoastal trade to Ludwig's American-Hawaiian Steamship Company* in exchange for a cash infusion from the billionaire in the form of a stock purchase. To finish financing the expansion of Sea-Land, McLean sold Waterman Steamship Corporation in 1965; the former subsidiary began a life of its own that was soon to eclipse the impressive achievements of the original parent company.

The only place left for his containerships was the North Atlantic routes, but he needed to convert more vessels in order to offer a regular container service. Furthermore, he was haunted by Grace Line's* attempt to introduce containers to Venezuela in 1960, a fiasco that set back the introduction of containers into foreign trade routes. As a way of gaining confidence with creditors, McLean had announced since 1965 his plans to inaugurate container service to Europe, but when Sea-Land finally began the service in April 1966, Moore-McCormack* already had initiated the service two months before in February. But worse was in store for Sea-Land: United States Lines* (USL) had been very carefully and methodically planning the transition to container service and after several changes had ordered from the shipyards the first generation of containerships, the Lancers.* In speed, capacity, and ease, McLean's old, converted World War II freighters and tankers were no match, and he knew that Sea-Land was finished once USL's Lancers entered the European service.

Billionaire Ludwig again rescued McLean by buying more Sea-Land shares with shipbuilding funds the Maritime Administration had released from the otherwise defunct American-Hawaiian. McLean now could order the next generation of containerships, and the faster and bigger SL-7s* were sure to crush the Lancers of USL. Favorable as the situation seemed, McLean knew Sea-Land was broke and was kept going only by military cargoes to Vietnam and in no case could finish paying for the construction of the new ships. Fortunately for McLean, the outward appearances sufficed to convince R. J. Reynolds, the tobacco conglomerate, to buy Sea-Land in May 1969. Ludwig made at least a fivefold profit on his original investment, while the chunk of tobacco shares McLean received as payment gave him a seat on the Board of Directors of R. J. Reynolds.

The tobacco conglomerate easily covered the costs of the eight SL-7s, and these monster ships entered Sea-Land's service in the summer of 1972, supposedly guaranteeing the company's future now that Vietnam War cargoes were declining. With their large capacity and record speed of thirty-three knots, the fuel-guzzling ships were expected to drive out the Lancers and regain superiority in the North Atlantic from USL. Sea-Land's success was short-lived, however, because the energy crisis struck the next year in 1973, and with spiraling oil prices, the company was forced to run the ships at twenty-six knots and lower, and even at these reduced speeds the operation of the SL-7s remained uneconomical. McLean had left these "white elephants" as his legacy to Sea-Land,

and nobody in the business world wanted them; fortunately for the company, when the Cold War intensified for the last time after 1979, the navy decided to acquire the vessels, whose high speed made them suitable for military transports after extensive reconstruction in U.S. shipyards.

In another step to reduce losses, in January 1978 Sea-Land suspended its last coastwise and intercoastal sailings but maintained the lucrative Alaska and Puerto Rico services. Sea-Land was still able to draw one last time on the largesse of R. J. Reynolds to finance the construction of a new generation of twelve containerships, the D-9s, equipped with the fuel-efficient, slow-speed diesel* engines. R. J. Reynolds, however, was already becoming restless with this very expensive subsidiary, and the tobacco conglomerate, itself in mounting difficulties, announced no further capital outlays and began to demand high annual profits of at least 15 percent from Sea-Land. As early as 1980, R. J. Reynolds publicly stated that it had wanted to sell off the merchant shipping subsidiary and that in the future Sea-Land would have to finance out of its own revenues any future vessel replacement program.

Until 1976 Sea-Land had assured its competitive position in Asia and Europe by offering secret rebates to shippers,* but when a Securities and Exchange Commission investigation revealed these illegal practices, R. J. Reynolds management ordered a halt to further rebating. Sea-Land saw its market share decline after 1976 because conference* members were meeting the prices of independents* by continuing to offer secret rebates, something Sea-Land could no longer do. President Charles I. Hiltzheimer had tried since 1978 to get the Pacific conferences to reduce their rates to keep cargo from going to the independents, but block voting by the Japanese lines had kept the conferences from lowering rates.

As soon as the twelve D-9s were delivered in 1980, Hiltzheimer placed ten in the Pacific routes and promptly had Sea-Land resign from all the Pacific conferences. The Diesel-powered D-9s were more economical than any Japanese vessels, and in the ensuing rate war Sea-Land regained its market share of transpacific cargoes. Finally in 1981 the rate war ended when the Japanese lines agreed to Sea-Land's conditions to reenter the conferences. Likewise in the Atlantic, similar aggressive action by Hiltzheimer had restored the position of the company in the European routes.

However, these successes had not impressed R. J. Reynolds, which finally made up its mind to sell Sea-Land, but finding a buyer was no easy task. McLean, who by now owned USL, promptly stepped forward with a scheme to merge Sea-Land with USL, but R. J. Reynolds, fooled in 1969 into buying a bankrupt Sea-Land from McLean, had learned its lesson and now demanded $1 billion in cash for any deal. McLean quietly faded away, and with no other buyers in sight, R. J. Reynolds had no choice but to spin off Sea-Land as a separate company in 1974; stockholders of the old R. J. Reynolds company now received new shares distributed between those for the tobacco company and those for Sea-Land. To prevent panic selling of the new shares, R. J. Reynolds tried to reassure stockholders by maintaining minor links with the new company; most notably, R. J. Reynolds appointed one of its best executives, Joseph F. Abely, as the new president, while Hiltzheimer was supposed to step down to an important but subordinate position within the now independent Sea-Land. Unfortunately, a very disgruntled Hiltzheimer resigned in protest because he had opposed the spin-off plan and felt slighted by the offer of a subordinate position. Undaunted by this setback, the new president, Abely, began to plan in 1984 for a new generation of containerships once the D-9s had lost their competitive advantage. Meanwhile, Hiltzheimer had been plotting to recapture his president's seat by advising Dallas investor Harold C. Simmons on how to gain control of Sea-Land. Simmons did not need much urging, and he had already engineered a number of hostile takeovers and was not afraid to engage in questionable practices to gain control of a target company during the takeover frenzy of the 1980s. Sea-Land management and Simmons (with 40 percent of the shares) had reached a temporary truce prior to the final clash, when the railroad company CSX appeared as a "white knight" and bought out both Simmons and the remaining stockholders of Sea-Land at inflated prices. Analysts promptly lowered the credit rating of CSX out of fear that the Sea-Land acquisition would bankrupt the railroad; Wall Street does not read history, so the contribution steamship companies had made before World War I to their railroad owners had been overlooked, while the immense possibilities that intermodalism* offered for service and profits had still not been grasped.

CSX could absorb the high purchase price of Sea-Land, but more questionable was the latter's decision to acquire USL's Econships,* the last creation of McLean. USL had entered bankruptcy proceedings in November 1986, and the liquidators had appointed Hiltzheimer as president of USL in the belief that through his many contacts with his former employer he could awaken Sea-Land's interest in the Econships. Sea-Land finally made a successful bid for the twelve Econships and purchased as well other containerships of USL, including some of the Lancers. Sea-Land attempted to rename the Econships "Atlantic Class," and early in 1988 Sea-Land placed the slow Econships in the North Atlantic trade and hoped that by carrying only 3,400 rather than 4,400 twenty-foot equivalent units or TEUs,* the faster ship speed would make possible a modestly profitable operation. However, the Econships were too big to be kept profitably filled all the time, and their operation proved a permanent challenge to the company, which had to invent ever more ingenious arrangements to avoid a drain on income. The military cargoes for the Gulf War helped Sea-Land tremendously, but the revenue benefits were only temporary, and on 29 June 1993 the company announced plans to begin the transfer of its U.S.-flag ships to flags of convenience.*

As long as CSX considered Sea-Land a crucial link in the intermodal network, the survival of the merchant shipping company was assured. Hopefully when Sea-Land orders the next generation of containerships, the legacy of McLean will at last disappear, because the company has too often turned out to be the playground or dumping site for his failed ideas.

Principal Executives

Malcom McLean	1960–1969
Michael R. McEvoy	1969–1976
Charles I. Hiltzheimer	1975–1983
Joseph F. Abely, Jr.	1983–1987
Robert I. Hintz	1987–1988
Alex J. Mandl	1988–1991
John P. Clancey	1991–present

Some Notable Ships

SL-7s	1972–1981
D-9s	1980–present
Econships	1988–present

References: *American Shipper*, December 1976, November 1980, June, September 1984, January, February, June 1986, March, June 1987, September 1991, September 1992, August 1993; *Business Week*, 29 April 1972, 4 February 1980, 24 October 1983; René De La Pedraja, *The Rise and Decline of U.S. Merchant Shipping in the Twentieth Century* (New York: Twayne, 1992); *Florida Journal of Commerce*, May 1974; *Fortune*, 1 June 1981; *Journal of Commerce*, 4 February, 25 March, 1 November 1988; Henry S. Marcus, *Planning Ship Replacement in the Containerization Era* (Lexington, MA: Lexington Books, 1974); *Moody's Transportation Manual 1968; New York Times*, 28 February 1980.

SEAMEN'S ACT. See La Follette Seamen's Act.

SEAMEN'S CHURCH INSTITUTE (SCI), 1834–present. The Seamen's Church Institute (SCI) of New York, a branch of the Episcopal church, has been the most important of the religious organizations tending the needs of seamen. The SCI rose to prominence among the rest of the organizations doing social work for seamen during the long tenure of the Rev. Archibald Romaine Mansfield. From 1896 to 1934 he consecrated himself to improving the organization until with the help of contributors the SCI "erected the largest and most comprehensive building in the world exclusively for seamen" (Healey 1936). For a modest fee the seaman obtained a bed, a hot meal, and a place to store his belongings. Originally the SCI also provided a health clinic and, prior to unionization, also operated a hiring hall* where seamen could be hired without having to suffer the abuses of the crimps.* However, to many seamen the hiring hall made the SCI seem like just a disguised crimp joint, and soon some were calling the SCI the Dog House because of its too close association with ship-owners. In the midst of the Great Depression, with thousands of seamen un-employed and living in the streets, the expenditures of the SCI on salaries for officials, religious literature, and stained glass for the chapel made many sea-farers angry and not really welcomed, who instead looked to have a place where they could really feel at home.

After the wave of unionization of the late 1930s restored basic civil rights to seafarers, the SCI has concentrated on a variety of social services within a religious framework. Besides a "Personal Problem Service" and "Missing Sea-men Bureau," the SCI provides seamen, who tend to be very lonely people, many personal services, like ship visiting, hospitality, information, and, of course, chaplaincy. When the SCI established the first Alcoholics Assistance Clinic for seamen in the late 1940s, the SCI took the initiative and has remained in the forefront of dealing with a very serious problem among many mariners. Besides hotel rooms and recreational services, the SCI has also provided a wide range of courses and educational opportunities to the seamen. In another new direction, the SCI established the Center for Seafarers' Rights in 1982 to im-prove the quality and quantity of legal advice that the seamen were receiving. Already in 1992 representatives of foreign governments have come to observe the SCI to see how to establish similar institutions in their home countries. The SCI has always been open to seamen of all nations, and with the rapid decline of the U.S. merchant marine, foreign sailors have constituted an ever increasing majority of the persons the SCI attempts to serve.

References: Frank F. Farrar, *A Ship's Log Book* (St. Petersburg, FL: Great Outdoors, 1988); Gale Research, *Encyclopedia of Associations*, 1993; James C. Healey, *Foc's'le and Glory-Hole: A Study of the Merchant Seaman and His Occupation* (New York: Merchant Marine Publishers Association, 1936); *Journal of Commerce*, 15 October 1992; Bruce Nelson, *Workers on the Waterfront: Seamen, Longshoremen, and Unionism in the 1930s* (Urbana: University of Illinois Press, 1990); Marian G. Sherar, *Shipping Out: A Sociological Study of American Merchant Seamen* (Cambridge, MD: Cornell Maritime Press, 1973).

SEAMEN'S STRIKE OF 1961. The Seamen's Strike of 1961 was unique in the merchant marine and probably also in the labor history of the United States as the only strike called *against* higher wages. The Seamen's Strike also un-derlined not only the failures of the subsidy policy of the U.S. government but also the extremes to which selfish labor leaders were willing to go to win their power plays. The Seafarers' International Union* (SIU) represented on the Gulf and East coasts the crews on nonsubsidized ships, while the National Maritime Union* (NMU) represented those on the subsidized companies. When the latter granted the NMU a very favorable contract, the whipsawing* or "catching- up" problem took a new twist: SIU felt that many nonsubsidized companies could not make comparable offers and would have to go out of business, thereby costing seafarers many jobs. The SIU gained the support of the Marine Engineers' Beneficial Association* (MEBA), and these two unions struck the ships under the NMU in 16 June 1961 on the grounds that the wage concessions granted were inflationary and had to be rolled back to the levels of what SIU had granted. The NMU immediately joined the strike, demanding from the companies that the agreements extend to their foreign-flag ships. The strike, one of the most disruptive since World War II, was suspended by federal injunction on 3 July; the final settlement, which largely returned to the situation existing before the strike, came only in October.

The need to improve upon "an almost chaotic form of collective bargaining and labor-management relationships" (White House Central Files) was pressing, and the experience of the Independent Tanker Unions* (ITUs) suggested that better alternatives existed. As part of the settlement of the strike, labor and management agreed to create the American Maritime Association* under J. Max Harrison* as a way to promote the interests of the nonsubsidized companies and also to try to stop U.S. corporations from using flags of convenience* rather than ships under U.S. registry.*

References: Joseph H. Ball, *The Government-Subsidized Union Monopoly: A Study of Labor Practices in the Shipping Industry* (Washington, DC: Labor Policy Association, 1966); John J. Collins, *Never Off Pay: The Story of the Independent Tanker Union, 1937–1963* (New York: Fordham University Press, 1964); Samuel A. Lawrence, *United States Merchant Shipping Policies and Politics* (Washington, DC: Brookings Institution, 1966); White House Central Files, John F. Kennedy Presidential Library, Boston, Massachusetts.

SEARACERS. The Searacer was the name of a particular type of combination-break-bulk*-container* ship that entered the fleet of the American President Lines* (APL) in 1961. Only two of them were built, the *President Lincoln* and *President Tyler*, and these semicontainer ships were significant because they captured one moment in the difficult transition from break-bulk to container vessels.

With accurate hindsight, the Searacers have been condemned as a "costly error" and as a "mistake" (Niven 1987), yet a closer analysis revealed that the decision was justified on many grounds. Up to that time Sea-Land* and Matson Navigation Company* had used containers only in the domestic routes protected by the cabotage* privilege, but for APL, whose operations were almost exclusively in the foreign trade routes, the risks were much greater. The Grace Line* had suffered an embarrassing setback when it tried to introduce containers in its service to Venezuela, and initial soundings by APL revealed that the introduction of containers faced many obstacles in the Far East. When the Searacers were ordered in 1958, the remarkable expansion of the Pacific Rim countries was still some years away; the boom of Japan was clear to all, but the Japanese lines had declared war on containers, whose introduction they tried to block in every way possible. Computers that would allow the calculation of how containers affected the cost and speed of handling cargo under different scenarios were still not available, and it seemed desirable to acquire some hard data from direct experience before risking the entire APL fleet on the costly and risky conversion to containers. Lastly, containers might turn out to be just one more "add-on," similar to the refrigerated spaces and deep liquid cargo holds that gradually had been added to the Mariner* freighters without affecting the basic function of carrying break-bulk cargo.

The Searacers, with a length of 564 feet, had the same dimensions as the Mariner class, and the steam turbine* reached the same speed of twenty knots, but the Searacers could carry slightly more cargo. In the design of some hatches and holds the company made adjustments for containers but left most of the ship suited for the usual break-bulk cargo. When put into service in 1961, the two ships "never operated efficiently" because the two systems of handling cargo "simply got in the other's way, slowing down rather than speeding up the loading and unloading process" (ibid.). APL had experimented with containers in the foreign trade and had learned the expensive lesson that they could not be combined in the same ship with break-bulk cargo: a ship could handle either break-bulk cargo or containers, but not both. The company now had to decide whether to order containerships or wait still a few more years, and after a ferocious internal battle among warring factions, the anticontainer advocates gained the upper hand. The result was a truly colossal blunder, nothing less than the decision to order for the next generation the Master Mariners, essentially larger break-bulk freighters, which were delivered in 1965–1966. These ships, an attempt to stop the march of history, were obsolete even before they were launched. As for the two Searacers, the *President Lincoln* and *President Tyler*, they were converted to full containerships in 1968 with a capacity of 378 twenty-foot equivalent units (TEUs*) and were expanded in 1971 to 410 TEUs in 1971; even with the enlargements they were too small to face world competition, and in 1979 the company traded them to the Maritime Administration* for the National Defense Reserve Fleet.*

References: René De La Pedraja, *The Rise and Decline of U.S. Merchant Shipping* (New York: Twayne, 1992); John Niven, *The American President Lines and Its Forebears, 1848–1984* (Newark: University of Delaware Press, 1987); Henry S. Marcus, *Planning Ship Replacement in the Containerization Era* (Lexington, MA: Lexington Books, 1974).

SEA SERVICE BUREAU, 1917–1934. On 29 May 1917 the Shipping Board* established a recruiting service to hire and train the crews and officers desperately needed during World War I. The number of graduates from the training schools was so large that the Shipping Board on 8 July 1917 authorized the creation of a department called the Sea Service Bureau to place the new personnel on the vessels. The Sea Service Bureau performed effectively during the war, and with the return of peace in November 1918, the recruiting service began to wind down its activities, most of which ended in 1919. The last of the training schools closed in 1921, but the Sea Service Bureau did not disappear and actually entered the most controversial period of its existence.

The Shipping Board operated its government-owned vessels long after World War I had ended, and the Sea Service Bureau continued to man those vessels. Andrew Furuseth* tried to salvage something out of the disastrous Strike of 1921* by claiming that only the unions knew the workers well enough to keep out the radicals intent on sabotage and disruptions. To avoid any need for even a modified union hiring hall,* the Sea Service Bureau rejected Furuseth's gambit and made its screening methods even more stringent to keep out all subversives. After 1921 Furuseth's union, the International Seamen's Union* (ISU), charged that the Sea Service Bureau had gone too far and was deliberately using extensive blacklists in a persecution campaign to punish seamen by denying them employment aboard any vessel. Organized labor explained that whatever recruitment functions were still necessary by law belonged to the shipping commissioners, and hence the continued operation of the Sea Service Bureau, besides being harmful to sailors, was also redundant. By the late 1920s the sailors had developed an intense dislike of the Sea Service Bureau, which they equated with the company-run hiring halls like the Marine Service Bureau.* With the coming of the New Deal, organized labor finally achieved in 1934 the abolition of the hated Sea Service Bureau, whose remaining functions and surviving records were transferred to the Bureau of Marine Inspection and Navigation.*

References: *Congressional Record*, 12 February 1929; James C. Healey, *Foc'sle and Glory Hole: A Study of the Merchant Seaman and His Occupation* (New York: Merchant Marine Publishers Association, 1936); Record Group 32, National Archives, Washington, DC; U.S. National Archives, *Guide to the National Archives of the United States* (Washington, DC: Government Printing Office, 1974).

SEAS SHIPPING COMPANY. See Robin Line.

SEATON, W. BRUCE, 1 April 1925–present. Bruce Seaton was president of American President Lines* (APL) in 1977–1992 and was responsible for the remarkable turnaround that saved the company from decline and probably even its demise. Seaton was born in Philadelphia on 1 April 1925 and graduated with a degree in business administration from the University of California at Los Angeles in 1949. Shortly after, while already employed, he earned the title of Certified Public Accountant. He worked for Douglas Oil Company in 1953–1966 and for Occidental Petroleum Company in 1966–1970 and had become an expert in the oil business, where he seemed headed to make a major contribution. Not surprisingly, Seaton's entry into shipping came through an oil firm, Natomas, the parent company of American President Lines (APL). Ralph Davies, the owner of Natomas, was finally convinced to hire a financial expert, and in 1970 Seaton joined the management team at Natomas, where among other functions, he became familiar with the balance sheet of APL.

From very early Seaton became the most vocal advocate of selling off APL, whose activities he quite rightly considered a drain on the oil company. Ironically, Natomas's new chief, Dorman Commons, asked Seaton to head APL in 1977, and the latter accepted but only on the condition that he could return to his old job at the oil company. Seaton embarked on a twofold strategy to save APL. First, he seized every opportunity to reduce the operating expenses of ocean transportation, whether by cutting back routes or building the economical diesel* containerships of post-Panamax* size. Second, Seaton followed the pattern of other U.S.-flag companies of diversifying into land ventures, but he made an innovation by organizing on a solid footing a new business on land, namely, moving containers across the country under the control of a merchant shipping company. To handle the railroad cars, containers,* and land terminals required to move the cargo from Japan to New York by the landbridge,* APL ended up creating a separate subsidiary to manage the domestic operations. In one further step, APL under Seaton introduced the double-stack* trains in 1984, so that henceforth two containers, rather than just one as before, were stacked on the railroad cars.

When Natomas became the object of a hostile takeover, APL was spun off as an independent company in 1983, with Seaton continuing as its president. APL under Seaton had become an independent company and, after the collapse of United States Lines* (USL) in 1986, was the only merchant shipping company whose shares were publicly traded in the stock market. Independence had its high price, and Seaton had to take numerous precautions, including buying back stock, to prevent a hostile takeover of APL by some bold Wall Street raider. At least during Seaton's watch APL did not face any takeover attempt, and the company prospered by recourse to the proper exploitation of fortuitous events. Seaton stepped down as president on 2 January 1992 and was replaced by his handpicked successor, John M. Lillie.

References: American President Companies, *Annual Report*, 1992; John Niven, *American President Lines and Its Forebears, 1848–1984* (Newark: University of Delaware Press, 1987); *Who's Who, 1992–1993*.

SEATRAIN, 1928–1981. Seatrain, as its name suggests, originally specialized in carrying railcars aboard ships in the coastwise* trade and between the United States and Cuba; in the mid-1960s Seatrain became a conglomerate involved in a variety of activities, such as tanker operations, shipping to many parts of the world, and even shipbuilding. Graham M. Brush established Seatrain in 1928 to put into practice his new idea of carrying railcars in the holds of oceangoing vessels. He was a civil engineer and fitted the ships with decks and equipment that permitted the transfer of the railcars from the tracks in the docks to the holds of the ships. Carrying the railcars was cheaper than moving them by land, so that Seatrain was a financial success since the inauguration of its first service between New Orleans and Havana in December 1928. The operation also avoided the costly loading of merchandise by longshoremen and thus was an important precursor of the containers,* but few in the tradition-bound shipping industry realized the immense possibilities behind the labor and time that Seatrain saved in port. The company expanded its operations to provide similar railcar service to ports in New York, Florida, the Gulf, and Cuba. During its first thirty years the company's history was uneventful, and only a suit by Graham Brush against the stockholders who had taken control of the company away from him in 1958 briefly disturbed management.

A more serious crisis came when U.S. opposition to the Cuban Revolution halted all trade with Cuba in 1960, and Seatrain was left with excess ships. Quite naturally the company tried to place the vessels from the Cuba route into its coastwise* service, but the railroad companies had decided to eliminate this potential rival, and their low rates undermined Seatrain's financial position. Seatrain had spurned an offer in 1959 to merge with Malcom McLean's* Sea-Land* and instead decided in 1963 to redeploy its ships to Puerto Rico to try to achieve with that small island the long-term success it had enjoyed with the ten-times-larger island of Cuba. Since 1963 interested buyers wished to acquire Seatrain, and finally in 1965 Joseph Kahn and Howard Pack, two ex-furriers who were tired of the fur business and wanted something more exciting, bought the company, whose history now entered its most hectic phase.

Kahn and Pack had bought Liberty* ships in 1950 and soon were buying and chartering* tankers until the Seatrain purchase was just the next logical step. The timing of the purchase was great, because all of Seatrain's excess ships were soon needed to take military cargoes to Vietnam, and as long as that conflict lasted, the finances of the company remained solid. The tanker operations remained profitable, and Seatrain was eager to try new ideas in oil transport; for example, the company fitted the *Manhattan*,* for many years the largest U.S.-flag tanker, with icebreaking capabilities in order to try to open the Northwest Passage in 1969 to bring oil from Alaska. Although the *Manhattan*'s historic voyage was successful, the economics of the operation ruled out that route. The company's long history with railcars made it realize the immense advantages of containers,* and by 1969 it had decided to convert its cargo vessels into containerships. Seatrain had not bungled vessel replacement as many other companies had done, but its mounting debt of $100 million to finance the expansion was a serious drain on the company's income.

Seatrain received its first four containerships in 1971 and afterward went on to establish the "landbridge"* across the United States. Merchandise from New York was sent in containers aboard special express rails to the West Coast for loading aboard the company's ships for delivery to the Far East. Travel time was cut by one-third, and delivery that normally took thirty days via the Panama Canal now was accomplished in twenty days. With the landbridge in place, Seatrain was at the center of a world transportation network, as its ships served Europe, the Far East, Puerto Rico, and Hawaii. Seatrain was poised to become the largest merchant shipping company in the United States but soon found itself struggling to survive its growing debt of $244 million in 1973.

The landbridge operation of Seatrain had some flaws, but the source of the problem was not this, but rather Kahn and Pack's decision to enter into shipbuilding in January 1969. Rather than concentrating all their resources into containers and the landbridge, Seatrain was lured by offers of city and federal government to open a commercial shipyard in the site of the Brooklyn Navy Yard in New York City. The shipyard was supposed to convert the hard-core poor among blacks and Puerto Ricans in the city into skilled workers, and this educational task generated enormous cost overruns. The company lost $20 million on the construction of its first two tankers but fortunately was reimbursed by the Maritime Administration* (MARAD). The problems of the sprawling conglomerate were becoming hard to follow for Kahn and Pack, who decided in 1974 to bring in a financial expert, Steve Russell, to keep even the income and expense flows.

Russell decided to diversify Seatrain into other areas, and taking advantage of the energy crisis of the 1970s, he borrowed money to purchase coal fields and one oil refinery. He immediately realized that the real problems of Seatrain were caused by the shipyard and decided that once the two tankers in the ways, the *Bay Ridge* and *Stuyvesant*, were finished, the company would abandon shipbuilding altogether. He first had to negotiate complex arrangements to secure the funds to finish the tankers, but when the *Bay Ridge*, the last of the four tankers Seatrain built, was finished in May 1979, he shut down the shipyard.

It was too late for Seatrain: the shipyard had eaten out the company from the inside, and although its container and landbridge operations were posting profits and becoming lucrative, the debt of Seatrain climbed to $270 million. Russell concluded that only if the company's containerships steamed full could the company earn enough to pay off the debt, and he decided to make one last attempt to save the doomed Seatrain by starting a rate war in the North Atlantic on 1 February 1980. The foreign competitors saw a great opportunity to eliminate one more rival, and in three months it was over for Seatrain, whose losses of $30 million forced the company to sell off its ships in the Atlantic service in August.

In December 1980 Seatrain tried to gain time from creditors by selling off its ships in the Pacific, but it was useless, as the company was rapidly collapsing. Russell himself bailed out in the first week of February 1981 into a small Caribbean subsidiary he had spun off as a safe refuge, and the accountant who then became president had no choice but to file for protection under Chapter 11 bankruptcy proceedings on 12 February 1981. Seatrain was finished, and although successive reorganization plans attempted to revive the cadaver, all to no avail, no alternative was left but to liquidate the company in 1982.

Principal Executives

Graham M. Brush, Sr.	1929–1958
John L. Weller	1958–1965
Joseph Kahn	1965–1981
Howard Pack	1965–1981
Steve Russell	1974–1981

Some Notable Ships

Manhattan	1962–1987
Stuyvesant	1977–present
Bay Ridge	1979–present

References: James P. Baughman, *The Mallorys of Mystic: Six Generations in American Maritime Enterprise* (Middletown, CT: Wesleyan University Press, 1972); René De La Pedraja, *The Rise and Decline of U.S. Merchant Shipping in the Twentieth Century* (New York: Twayne, 1992); *Nautical Gazette*, 15 September 1928; *New York Times*, 20 May, 12 August 1959; Seatrain, *Thirtieth Annual Report* (1960).

SERVICE CONTRACTS, 1984–present. The Shipping Act of 1984* created service contracts as a legal substitute to the dual-rate* system, which had never recovered from the *Isbrandtsen** decision of 1958. In essence, service contracts authorized conferences* and ocean carriers to charge lower rates to shippers* who needed to move large quantities of cargo. While the relation between larger volume and lower rate was implicit in the dual-rate contracts, the emphasis had been on loyalty to the conferences, and hence even small shippers could qualify for dual-rate contracts, provided they agreed to send all their shipments through conference lines. The Shipping Act of 1984 specified that the conference or ocean carrier had to make public the requirements to obtain a service contract, so that any shipper who reached the requisite volume automatically qualified for the lower rate, independent of whether the shipper for the rest of his merchandise wished to patronize another conference.

The idea of discounts for large shipments has been widely accepted in the United States but did risk leaving small and medium-sized shippers at a disadvantage. Congress agreed to authorize shippers' associations,* so that small and medium-sized shippers could combine their cargoes and hence share in the benefits of service contracts.

The Shipping Act of 1984 triggered an explosion of service contracts, with nearly 32,000 signed during 1984–1991, but because the act had also encouraged individual ocean carriers to bolt the conferences and offer their own rates (''independent action''), only 30 percent of the service contracts were with conferences, and 70 percent were with independent lines that rushed to reach agreements with their favorite shippers. Conferences, in order to prevent further deterioration of their position, have begun since 1989 to adopt service contracts whose individual appendices list for each line the rate and schedules offered for large volumes.

References: Advisory Commission on Conferences in Ocean Shipping, *Report to the President and the Congress* (Washington, DC: Government Printing Office, 1992); Federal Maritime Commission, *Section 18 Report on the Shipping Act of 1984*, September 1989; Lane C. Kendall, *The Business of Shipping*, 5th ed. (Centreville, MD: Cornell Maritime Press, 1986).

SEVIER, RANDOLPH ("JOE"), 6 June 1897–20 September 1966. Randolph Sevier was president of Matson Navigation Company* in 1950–1962. He was born in Eureka, California, on 6 June 1897 and studied at the agricultural college of the University of California. In 1923 he began working as a clerk aboard Matson's vessels and after three years was promoted to handle land transportation for tourists visiting the Hawaiian islands. In 1930 he went to work for Castle & Cooke (then a major stockholder of Matson) and concentrated on solving problems on the waterfront.

In 1948 Sevier was back in Matson as vice president and as the likely successor to the aging John E. Cushing.* As vice president Sevier had his greatest impact in convincing Matson and the executives of other lines to negotiate with Harry Bridges* in order to end costly confrontations like the longshoremen's strike of 1948. Sevier was instrumental in abolishing the intolerant Waterfront Employers Association* and replacing it with the more flexible Pacific Maritime Association,* which maintained labor peace on the waterfront of Hawaii and the West Coast until 1971.

On 30 June 1950 Sevier succeeded the retiring Cushing as president of Matson. Endowed with a great personality and a tremendous talent for organization, he had earned a reputation as a superb operational executive who always achieved results. All his personality was required just to keep harmony among the members of the Board of Directors, who, as major stockholders themselves, had the most diverse ideas on which way the company should go. In an early decision, Sevier agreed that Matson had to remain in the passenger service and ordered the conversion of two fast Mariner* freighters into two new liners, which also kept alive the old names of *Mariposa** and *Monterey.** Soon after these two liners entered service, the mistake of investing in passenger service became obvious, but by then the company was stuck with two money-losing vessels. In 1959 the company decided to concentrate on merchant shipping and sold off its hotels (later considered a blunder) and also liquidated what was left of its subsidiary the Honolulu Oil Corporation.

The setbacks were more than compensated for by Sevier's grasp of the significance of containers* for ocean transportation. Because of his long experience on the waterfront, Sevier instinctively knew that the problems of shipping were no longer at sea but in the docks with the slow and costly handling of the cargo. Sevier authorized the creation in early 1956 of a research department to study precisely the introduction of containers. In 1957 Sevier accepted the recommendations of beginning first with carrying containers on deck and regular cargo in the holds and then moving to full containerships. In August 1958 the first freighter converted to carry containers on the deck sailed, and the results almost immediately led Sevier to shift to full containerships, the first of which was completed in 1960. Sevier at Matson rather than Malcom-McLean* at Sea-Land really earned the merit of placing the commercial operation of containers on a solid base.

With containers Sevier expected to cut costs and reduce freight rates, but only if the longshoremen accepted the changes; Matson and other employers of the Pacific Maritime Association secured the dockworkers' approval with the Mechanization and Modernization Agreement* of 1960. The reductions in costs came just in time to allow Matson to face a wave of new challenges in the 1960s, but these tasks were left to the next president, Stanley Powell, Jr., because Sevier retired at age sixty-five to the less hectic position of chairman of the board. He resigned as chairman in 1965 but remained on the board until his death in Sonoma, California, on 20 September 1966.

References: Charles P. Larrowe, *Harry Bridges: The Rise and Fall of Radical Labor in the U.S.* (New York: Lawrence Hill, 1972); *Nation's Business*, April 1952; William L. Worden, *Cargoes: Matson's First Century in the Pacific* (Honolulu: University Press of Hawaii, 1981); *Who Was Who in America*, vol. 4.

SHANGHAIING. Shanghaiing was the practice of kidnapping sailors to complete the crews for long voyages. The term *shanghai* referred to the Chinese port city of Shanghai, already a distant-enough destination but in reality worse because the ships sailing from San Francisco did not return home after reaching Shanghai but continued to circumnavigate the world. The sailors were drugged or intoxicated with alcohol, and when they finally woke up, they would be miles out to sea aboard the vessel. In the United States shanghaiing virtually came to an end in 1872, when Congress passed the Shipping Commissioner's Act,* which prohibited a vessel from leaving port until the crew had first been brought before a shipping commissioner. As a substitute for shanghaiing, the crimps* became the normal suppliers of crews for the ships. Nevertheless, isolated cases of shanghaiing still occurred, even in the United States. In foreign ports with a strong British presence the practice was more frequent: for centuries the British had been accustomed to impress persons for their ships, but by the late nineteenth century the British had largely reduced the practice to shanghaiing Irish for the engine and boiler rooms. Consequently, any stray and careless U.S. sailor in a foreign port could easily be caught in the net of a shanghaiing party, but by the first decade of the twentieth century the overabundance of unemployed seamen had limited the practice largely to the folklore of the sea.

References: Stephen Schwartz, *Brotherhood of the Sea: A History of the Sailors' Union of the Pacific, 1885–1985* (New Brunswick, NJ: Transaction Books, 1986); William L. Standard, *Merchant Seamen: A Short History of Their Struggles* (New York: International, 1947).

SHAPE-UP. In shape-up, a method of hiring maritime workers, the men "shaped-up" in a circle around the manager, foreman, or vessel officer, who then picked those he needed by calling out "You! No, not you. *You!*" For longshoremen the shape-up had been traditional since far back into the nineteenth century. For sailors the shape-up had begun much later, specifically after the crushing of the strike of 1921;* previously the crimps* had enrolled the sailors without recourse to the shape-up. For both longshoremen and seamen the movement begun with the Big Strike* of 1934 eliminated the shape-up from the waterfront.

In San Francisco longshoremen went down to the Embarcadero at six in the morning to try their daily luck at a job. Usually hiring did not begin until 7:30 A.M., but enough foremen needed to start earlier to make it worthwhile for longshoremen to be milling around from six in the morning in any kind of weather. In New York City snow and ice were additional hardships, but in San Francisco a worse insult was reserved for the men: at eight in the morning those still not hired were pushed aside by police, who needed to clear a path for the white-collar workers coming on the ferry from East Bay. Hiring resumed afterward, but as there were always many more men than available jobs, a few would remain lingering around until noon, hoping that replacements might be needed; most had to hope that next day they would have better luck. Extreme favoritism was the rule in choosing longshoremen, and many had to offer kickbacks to the foremen in order to be hired. The men had no rights: ''We were hired off the streets like a bunch of sheep'' (Larrowe 1972).

While longshoremen had not known any other system of hiring, for sailors the start of the shape-up system in the early 1920s proved a bitter shock: ''It's no more than a goddam slave block'' (McHenry and Myers 1948). The end of the crimps had not proven the magic answer, and now sailors had to shape-up after they had turned in their papers at the company's hiring office in the pier. The lucky ones whose names were called out quickly clambered on board, assuming, of course, that they had not been blacklisted for any reason, whether union activism or subversion of any stripe. The rest stayed milling around, ready to shape-up as soon as a foreman appeared to complete the crew or to replace sailors who had been disqualified by management or who had left the ship at the last moment. After the bitter strikes of 1934–1937, the shape-up was replaced by the union hiring hall* for most maritime workers; however, in the Gulf and East coasts, longshoremen continued to be hired by the shape-up until the mid-1950s; the movie *On the Waterfront** (1954) dramatized the shape-up of the early 1950s, in some scenes more accurately depicting the situation in the early 1930s.

References: Joseph H. Ball, *The Government-Subsidized Union Monopoly: A Study of Labor Practices in the Shipping Industry* (Washington, DC: Labor Policy Association, 1966); Richard O. Boyer, *The Dark Ship* (New York: Little Brown, 1947); Charles P. Larrowe, *Harry Bridges: The Rise and Fall of Radical Labor in the U.S.* (New York: Lawrence Hill, 1972); Beth McHenry and Frederick N. Myers, *Home Is the Sailor: The Story of an American Seaman* (New York: International, 1948); William W. Pilcher, *The Portland Longshoremen: A Dispersed Community* (New York: Holt, Rinehart, and Winston, 1972).

SHIP BROKERS. The ship broker has corresponded roughly to the real estate agent on land in that both perform the same functions of selling, renting, and leasing, but while the real estate agent dealt with properties on land, the ship broker handled vessels. The chartering,* rather than the selling of ships, constituted the majority of the brokers' business, and here they performed their most valuable service to world commerce by putting together the shipper,* who needs to carry the cargo to the marketplace, with the tramp* operator, who earns his livelihood by carrying the cargo. The ship broker could also supervise the loading, discharging, and operation of the chartered vessel while in port, although most large charterers generally had already made separate arrangements for these services. During most of the twentieth century ship brokers were influential and respected figures who operated quietly and efficiently in the background of the more visible liner* and tramp firms, but the reputation of ship brokers has fallen somewhat into disrepute since the late 1980s because of the adoption by some unscrupulous operators of practices more akin to those of used car salesmen.

References: *American Shipper*, March 1990; Grover G. Huebner, *Ocean Steamship Traffic Management* (New York: D. Appleton, 1920); Lane C. Kendall, *The Business of Shipping*, 5th ed. (Centreville, MD: Cornell Maritime Press, 1986).

SHIP OPERATORS AND OWNERS' ASSOCIATION, 1942–circa 1951.
The Ship Operators and Owners' Association was the trade organization that represented those tramp* companies in existence prior to World War II but not those new tramp outfits that had appeared for the first time during the war. Until 1947 it was generally known as the Ship Operators' Association and should not be confused with the 1920s organization of the same name, which had represented liner* companies and not tramp vessels. When the United States entered the conflict, the War Shipping Administration* (WSA) decided to tap the experience of the existing tramp companies and assigned to each about twenty-five war-built ships, the maximum number the WSA felt a small organization could run effectively. WSA agreed to pay a fee to each firm for operating the vessels, under these "general agency agreements." To deal with many common problems facing these operators of government vessels, twenty-six companies agreed, in consultation with the WSA, to create the Ship Operators' Association in 1942. Jacob Barstow Smull, the driving force behind the creation of the Ship Operators' Association, became its first president; he himself was vice president and manager of J. H. Winchester & Co. The practice of doubling up as head of the trade organization and executive of a company was the norm for the tramp associations.

Once World War II ended, the question of what to do with the surplus vessels became a primary concern for the Ship Operators' Association, which was well aware that the comfortable wartime arrangements could not continue indefinitely. The WSA was abolished in 1946, and its remaining functions were taken over by the U.S. Maritime Commission,* which in early 1947 substituted bareboat* charters* for the fee arrangement previously in force. The members of the association in 1947, all of whom were bareboating their tramp vessels from the U.S. Maritime Commission, were:

American Foreign Steamship Co.

American-Hawaiian Steamship Co.*

Blidberg Rothchild Co.

Boland and Cornelius

A. H. Bull and Co.*

A. L. Burbank and Co.

Cosmopolitan Shipping Co.*

Dichmann, Wright and Pugh, Inc.

Eastern Steamship Lines*

Fall River Navigation Co.

Marine Transport Lines

R. A. Nicol and Co.

North American Shipping and Trading
   Co.

North Atlantic and Gulf Steamship Co.

Norton-Lilly Management Corp.

Parry Navigation Co.

Ponchelet Marine Corp.

Prudential Lines*

William J. Rountree Co.

Shepard Steamship Co.

Sieling and Jarvis

U.S. Navigation Co.

Wessel, Duval and Co.

J. H. Winchester and Co.

The U.S. Maritime Commission stressed to these companies that they were expected to take advantage of the Ship Sales Act of 1946* to purchase vessels; to reflect this new requirement, the organization used since 1947 the longer name of Ship Operators and Owners' Association. Lengthening the name was easier than convincing the members to buy vessels, because most of the member companies had invested wartime income into more profitable ventures on land and were reluctant to return to the high risks and low profits of tramping in the high seas. Already a few operators had used the shift from fees to bareboating in 1947 as a good pretext to abandon tramping. When in 1948 the U.S. Maritime Commission refused to charter to firms that had not already bought U.S.-flag vessels, more companies decided to abandon the sea altogether.

Membership in the Ship Operators and Owners' Association was down to fourteen companies in 1950, and previously five of the older companies had swallowed their pride and shifted their membership to the Committee for Promotion of Tramp Shipping under American Flag in Foreign Commerce,* the organization that also included the upstart tramp firms. The Ship Operators and Owners' Association was inactive by 1951.

References: *New York Times*, 26 January 1948, 23 September 1948; President's Advisory Commission on the Merchant Marine, Harry S. Truman Presidential Library, Independence, Missouri; U.S. Congress, Senate, Committee on Interstate and Foreign Commerce, *Merchant Marine Study and Investigation*, 7 vols. (Washington, DC: Government Printing Office, 1950); *Who's Who in the Maritime Industry 1946*.

SHIP OPERATORS' ASSOCIATION, 1942–circa 1951. See Ship Operators and Owners' Association.

SHIPOWNERS' ASSOCIATION OF THE PACIFIC COAST (SAPC), 1886–circa 1963. The Shipowners' Association of the Pacific Coast (SAPC) represented the owners of vessels engaged in the coastwise* trade on the West Coast. During its initial decades the organization was for owners and managers of sailing vessels and was called the Shipowners' Association of San Francisco. The association was created in direct response to the appearance of the first permanent labor union for seamen on the West Coast, the Sailors' Union of the Pacific* (SUP). For ships in the foreign trade, owners could draw upon an apparently inexhaustible supply of Oriental seamen from the Far East, but for the coastwise trade the necessity of having to find crews in U.S. ports gave a slight opening to coastwise sailors who tried to bargain through the SUP.

The association easily defeated a first strike by the SUP in 1886, but when the seamen regrouped and prepared a stronger strike effort in 1893, the association countered by hiring G. C. Williams, of Michigan, who later turned out to be a fugitive from justice, to crush SUP. Williams, with prior experience in bribing state legislators, led numerous intrigues to discredit the union in the press, and the timely explosion of a bomb in a crimp's* boardinghouse allowed Williams to make the seamen the scapegoats. The 1893 strike soon folded, another victory for the SAPC, which did not hesitate to win at any price.

Another strike in 1899 convinced the shipowners to negotiate verbally with union president Andrew Furuseth,* but they still refused to sign a formal written contract. One last citywide attempt to crush the waterfront unions of San Francisco in 1901 failed, and finally in 1902 the shipowners signed the first written contract with SUP, thereby recognizing the right of the union to exist. In February 1904 the association merged with the Steam Schooner Owners' Association and adopted the name of Shipowners' Association of the Pacific Coast to represent owners of both sailing and steam vessels. In spite of this stronger management unity, SUP still won the next strike in 1906 and secured for the first time wage raises. Subsequently the Shipowners' Association enjoyed labor peace until after World War I. Timely concessions by SAPC kept the 1919 strike from affecting the Pacific Coast, but for the strike of 1921,* the situation changed drastically.

The American Steamship Owners' Association* (ASOA) took the lead in crushing the strike of 1921, but SAPC was no less instrumental in reducing the SUP to virtual helplessness. For over ten years the association did not have to worry about labor and simply dictated whatever terms the companies wanted; the hiring of sailors was done through the Marine Service Bureau,* operated in conjunction with the newly created Pacific American Steamship Association* (PASA). With fifty-two coastwise companies as members in 1923, the association appeared strong, but really the 1920s revealed early symptoms of decline for SAPC. The companies in the foreign trade rose in prominence and created their own separate organization (PASA), which soon made government relations in Washington, D.C., its first priority. SAPC agreed to open a joint office in Washington with PASA in 1927, and although both issued the *Pacific Marine*

Review as their official organ, clearly the initiative was passing to the foreign trade companies. The most threatening aspect was the slow but certain decline in coastwise trade in the 1920s and 1930s: unless SAPC could mobilize a sustained effort to revive shipping along the U.S. Pacific Coast, the association risked losing its entire membership through attrition.

The rapid spread of unions on the waterfront starting with the Big Strike of 1934* forced the member companies of SAPC to cooperate closely with the Waterfront Employers' Association* (WEA) to face seamen and longshoremen temporarily united in the Maritime Federation of the Pacific* (MFP). The collapse of the MFP allowed SAPC to regain independence, and it resumed direct contacts with the SUP but kept negotiations with the longshoremen in the hands of the WEA. When the Pacific Maritime Association* (PMA) replaced the WEA in 1949, the arrangement remained in force during the 1950s, but by then only a handful of coastwise companies (with usually only a few ships each) remained in SAPC, whose staff declined to one part-time secretary. After the bankruptcy in 1960 of the last coastwise company on the West Coast, the end of SAPC was inevitable, although it lingered on until 1963 in the vain hope of a revival.

References: Clarence E. Bonnet, *History of Employers' Associations in the United States* (New York: Viking Press, 1957); Giles T. Brown, *Ships That Sail No More: Marine Navigation from San Diego to Puget Sound, 1910–1940* (Lexington: University of Kentucky Press, 1966); Gale Research, *Encyclopedia of Associations*, 1956–1964; Record Group 32, National Archives, Washington, DC; Stephen Schwartz, *Brotherhood of the Sea: A History of the Sailors' Union of the Pacific* (New Brunswick, NJ: Transaction Books, 1986); Hyman Weintraub, *Andrew Furuseth, Emancipator of the Seamen* (Berkeley: University of California Press, 1959).

SHIPPERS. The shipper is the customer or client who pays for carrying the cargo aboard a vessel. The shippers who own the cargo they pay to move are called direct shippers, and these are generally large corporations with their own traffic departments. The shippers that do not own the cargo fall into three categories: freight forwarders,* the oldest; Nonvessel Operating Common Carriers* (NVOCCs) since the 1960s; and shippers' associations* since 1984. The shippers' central aim has been to obtain the lowest rate possible for the safe delivery of their goods on schedule. The shippers constantly shopped around for the lowest price possible and generally have had no loyalty to individual ship companies, except in island trades like Hawaii and Puerto Rico, where some shippers have learned they could not survive without ample ocean services. For ocean lines, on the other hand, cargo services have been not the end but the means to assure at the very least their institutional survival and hopefully also some profits (although usually not the highest profits, as less risky ventures on land normally offered higher profits). In the trade routes that did not touch U.S. ports, conferences traditionally used deferred rebates,* dual rates,* loyalty contracts,* and other mechanisms to keep the shippers from turning to nonconference lines.

The shippers have thus been the permanent antagonist of the ocean carriers and in particular of the conferences,* which set the rates. The tension between shippers and liner companies was one of the results of specialization in the middle of the nineteenth century. Originally the shippers had owned not only the cargo but also the sailing ships (and sometimes doubled up as captains of the vessels). Gradually during the second half of the nineteenth century the shippers reduced their investment in the vessel and preferred to pay either the liner* company or the tramp* vessel to transport the merchandise. About a hundred shippers called proprietary companies* never made the transition to hiring vessel space and continued to operate large fleets of their own to carry mainly oil, bananas, and ores. Because of the convenience and often the absolute need to have complete control over the sailing schedules, these proprietary companies have not hesitated to operate their fleets, if necessary, at a loss, although generally their operation has been profitable.

Most shippers, however, have preferred to ship their cargo through liner companies, and the tension between carriers and shippers has been an inevitable and permanent consequence. The image of shippers as millions of small producers may appear valid; for example 100,000 U.S. manufacturing firms exported overseas in 1987, but in reality 400 shippers controlled 80 percent of U.S. exports in the last decades of the twentieth century; this concentration resulted from consolidation by freight forwarders and the existence of the proprietary companies. While it was natural for shippers always to be looking for a better deal, the ocean carrier who anticipated and met the valid needs of the shippers will always have the advantage over the competitors, and, after all, it was only because shippers have had cargo to transport that the whole merchant shipping industry has existed.

References: Advisory Commission on Conferences in Ocean Shipping, *Report to the President and the Congress* (Washington, DC: Government Printing Office, 1992); René De La Pedraja, *The Rise and Decline of U.S. Merchant Shipping in the Twentieth Century* (New York: Twayne, 1992); Federal Maritime Commission, *Section 18 Report on the Shipping Act of 1984*, September, 1989; Transportation Research Board, *Intermodal Marine Container Transportation: Impediments and Opportunities* (Washington, DC: National Research Council, 1992).

SHIPPERS' ASSOCIATIONS or COUNCILS, 1984–present. Congress, in the Shipping Act of 1984,* decided to extend antitrust immunity to the previously prohibited shippers' associations or councils, which henceforth could consolidate or distribute freight on a nonprofit basis for its members, as well as negotiate directly with conferences* in order to secure lower rates for ocean transportation. The extreme fear of monopolistic practices had long kept the prohibition on shippers' associations in spite of the fact they were simply cooperatives, otherwise widely accepted throughout American society. The Shipping Act of 1984 also had legalized service contracts* by which shippers* of large volumes obtained lower rates, but the only way small and medium-sized shippers could benefit from lower rates was by combining their cargoes through shippers' associations, which Congress at last legalized in the act.

The encouragement provided by the Shipping Act of 1984 was not enough, and "there are not as many shippers' associations operating in the marketplace today as had been anticipated" (Advisory Commission 1992). The modest growth of shippers' associations contrasted with the dramatic expansion of "mega" or superconferences* and revived fears of monopolistic practices. However, the failure of shippers' associations to expand more rapidly was more the result of the pervasive coverage of freight forwarders* and Nonvessel Operating Common Carriers* (NVOCCs), which, through efficient and sharp competition, already controlled the overwhelming bulk of the freight. Three port authorities created shippers' associations in an attempt to attract cargo to their ports, and others may follow the example. Generally when the same product (e.g., beverages, cotton, wool, meats) also enjoyed a minimal regional concentration, the nonprofit shippers' associations could be a low-cost alternative to freight forwarders and NVOCCs.

References: Advisory Commission on Conferences in Ocean Shipping, *Report to the President and the Congress* (Washington, DC: Government Printing Office, 1992); Transportation Research Board, *Intermodal Marine Container Transportation: Impediments and Opportunities* (Washington, DC: National Research Council, 1992).

SHIPPING ACT OF 1916. The Shipping Act of 1916 initiated government regulation of ocean transportation and also established the Shipping Board,* the first government agency devoted to defend and promote the U.S. merchant marine. Congress passed the shipping act in response to fears of monopoly and the shipping shortage caused by World War I. With antitrust sentiment rising in the United States, Congress was particularly sensitive to the charges of American shippers* that they were being discriminated against by the monopoly practices of conferences* and foreign lines. The Alexander Committee* had thoroughly examined the conferences and found that although they were necessary to stabilize ocean rates, the Interstate Commerce Commission* (ICC) should regulate the conference system to avoid the many abuses already detected. A second problem was the shipping shortage caused by the start of World War I in 1914, a scarcity that moved a reluctant public opinion in the United States to accept some sort of government involvement as necessary to provide adequate shipping for the foreign trade. After several attempts in previous legislative sessions had failed, Congressman Joshua Alexander* finally obtained passage of the shipping act on 7 September 1916.

The previous work of the Alexander Committee allowed the new act to specify regulations for many aspects of ocean transportation, and more than half of the act was devoted to shipper concerns. The act outlawed the fighting ship* and the deferred rebate* and required all conferences in the U.S. foreign trades to file with the Shipping Board all their rate and service agreements; otherwise the latter would not be valid. Once the Shipping Board approved the agreements, they were exempt from prosecution under the antitrust laws of the United States. The Shipping Board retained the right to reject agreements it felt were unjustly discriminatory to any shipper and also had the authority to impose penalties for violations. The act was badly written in parts; for example, certain clauses appeared to outlaw the dual-rate* contracts, while other clauses gave the Shipping Board broad authority to approve dual-rate contracts; the Shipping Board usually accepted dual-rate contracts as valid, until the Supreme Court in the *Isbrandtsen** case declared them illegal. The act also introduced into world shipping the concept of ''open'' conferences, namely, that any company could enter or leave at will, in contrast to the traditional practice in the rest of the world that membership in the conferences was by invitation only. The act applied only to liner* shipping and specifically exempted ocean tramps* from its provisions. In the final analysis, the Shipping Act of 1916 ''was an anomaly both in terms of international practice and domestic antitrust policy'' (ibid.), while its many gaps and badly written passages guaranteed conflicts and contradictions in its implementation.

No other nation had ever before attempted to regulate conferences, but the pro-shipper bias in the act came out most clearly in those provisions that authorized the Shipping Board to set maximum rates on coastwise* and intercoastal* shipping but said nothing about minimum rates to protect the survival of the carriers. The omission of minimum rates was a crucial factor in the bitter commercial conflicts that ultimately destroyed most of the companies in the Coastwise Conference* and the United States Intercoastal Conference.*

The act established a Shipping Board of five commissioners, each one serving staggered six-year terms; no more than three commissioners could be from the same political party, and they had to represent the principal geographic divisions of the country. The president nominated the commissioners, but once they were confirmed by the Senate, the Shipping Board was truly independent and even elected its own chairman and vice chairman. This independence had been strongly urged by shippers, who wanted an impartial body to decide on the merits of the conference agreements and other regulatory issues of ocean transportation. Because of the wartime shipping crisis, the board was authorized to form ''one or more corporations for the purchase, construction, equipment, lease, charter, maintenance, and operation of merchant vessels in the commerce of the United States'' (*U.S. Statutes at Large* 1916); the board soon used this authority to establish the Emergency Fleet Corporation* (EFC) to build and operate a huge amount of tonnage for the wartime emergency. However, opposition to government ownership and operation was so strong that the act specified that five years after World War I was over, whatever corporations the Shipping Board had created must be dissolved.

The Shipping Act of 1916 had created one agency to handle the separate functions of regulating ocean transportation and supporting the U.S. merchant marine. The act strongly suggested that shipper concerns should be the main occupation of the new government agency, but with U.S. entry into World War I, the Shipping Board found itself absorbed body and soul in the wartime crash effort to build and operate a merchant fleet. With the return of the peace, Congress in the Jones Act* decided to make the creation and support of the U.S.-flag merchant marine the primary duty of the Shipping Board, whose characteristics and duties were redefined and restructured. However, the Division of Regulation within the Shipping Board expanded and continued to investigate and take action on the complaints of shippers. The successor agencies continued to enforce the shipper provisions of the Shipping Act of 1916, whose essential clauses suffered no major modifications until the passage of the Shipping Act of 1984.*

References: Advisory Commission on Conferences in Ocean Shipping, *Report to the President and the Congress* (Washington, DC: Government Printing Office, 1992); René De La Pedraja, *The Rise and Decline of U.S. Merchant Shipping in the Twentieth Century* (New York: Twayne, 1992); Grover G. Huebner, *Ocean Steamship Traffic Management* (New York: D. Appleton, 1920); Jeffrey J. Safford, *Wilsonian Maritime Diplomacy, 1913–1921* (New Brunswick, NJ: Rutgers University Press, 1978); *U.S. Statutes at Large,* vol. 39 (1916); Paul M. Zeis, *American Shipping Policy* (Princeton, NJ: Princeton University Press, 1938).

SHIPPING ACT OF 1984. The Shipping Act of 1984 was the first major legislation in sixty-eight years affecting the regulation and antitrust immunity of conferences.* Supreme Court decisions, partial legislative remedies, actual practice, and, above all, changing technological and economic conditions had made the previous law, the Shipping Act of 1916, not only obsolete, but also "a major constraint retarding the evolution of the industry" (Advisory Commission 1992). The legislative struggle to pass the shipping act began in 1980, although the origins of many provisions dated back to earlier legislative attempts. The rivalry between shippers* and ocean carriers resulted in "difficult, sometimes even bitter, debate and negotiation," and it was "somewhat of a minor miracle" (ibid.) that the law was passed at all on 20 March 1984.

The act ratified and expanded the previous antitrust immunity of conference agreements; for example, they now could cover the inland portion of intermodal* rates. In a significant departure, the act shifted the burden of proof to those challenging the antitrust provisions of these agreements. In a clause initially little noticed, the 1984 act also granted antitrust immunity to "interconference agreements," whose definition remained somewhat vague.

To compensate the shippers, the 1984 act prohibited conference practices such as dual-rate contracts,* deferred rates,* and fighting ships.* To encourage competition within the conferences, the act recognized the right of any member line to offer a different rate on ten days' notice; this "independent action" was intended to spark rivalry inside the conference. The 1984 act repeated the prohibition on closed conferences and instead mandated "open" conferences, whereby member lines could resign and reenter at will without any penalty, a concept introduced in the 1916 legislation. The 1984 act also wrote into law the "neutral body" as a mechanism by which the conferences policed themselves.

The categoric elimination of dual-rate contracts penalized those shippers who could no longer obtain discounts for sending large volumes of cargo, and to remedy this omission, the Shipping Act of 1984 created the legal instrument of service contracts,* whereby any shipper who handled a large volume automatically qualified to receive the publicly available lower rates. So as not to penalize unduly the small and medium-sized shippers, they could consolidate their cargoes into larger lots by means of shippers' associations,* whose activities received in the act antitrust immunity.

As a final safeguard, Congress stipulated the convocation of the Advisory Commission on Conferences in Ocean Shipping (ACCOS)* five and a half years later to review the impact of the Shipping Act of 1984. At the moment of the passage of the act, it was "seen as substantially limiting conference power" (ibid.), but in reality the law has allowed the conferences in U.S. foreign trade routes to survive, in particular, through the consolidation into "mega" or "superconferences." The growth of shippers' associations has not been as vigorous as originally expected, while service contracts have dramatically expanded. In 1992 ACCOS could not reach any agreement on changing the Shipping Act of 1984, whose provisions will remain the law in the 1990s and probably for decades to come.

References: Advisory Commission on Conferences in Ocean Shipping, *Report to the President and the Congress* (Washington, DC: Government Printing Office, 1992); Lane C. Kendall, *The Business of Shipping*, 5th ed. (Centreville, MD: Cornell Maritime Press, 1986); Transportation Research Board, *Intermodal Marine Container Transportation: Impediments and Opportunities* (Washington, DC: National Research Council, 1992).

SHIPPING ARTICLES. Shipping articles have been the contract each seaman must read and sign before sailing and as soon as he returned from each voyage. To prevent the shanghaiing* of sailors, Congress stipulated in the Shipping Commissioners' Act of 1872* that the shipping articles must be signed before a shipping commissioner. During the age of sailing vessels, when voyages easily could last over a year, the shipping articles provided a convenient way to begin and end the labor relationship between the captain (who often had a financial stake in the vessel or its cargo) and the sailors. With the introduction of steam and steel, traveling time was dramatically reduced, and now the concern of sailors became not the excessive length of their voyage, but how long they would have to wait until they could ship out again. Management enjoyed the advantage of abundant and cheap labor and preferred to discharge the crew at the end of each voyage and then select a new one for the next trip, rather than try to build up a nucleus of permanent seamen, hence the shipping articles remained in use under the vastly changed circumstances of the steamship age.

Management abused its advantageous position until the 1930s, when the labor union resurgence turned the tables and made organized labor the dominant partner. Labor leaders could have abolished the shipping articles and substituted semester or year contracts, but they soon realized this would eliminate a major reason to have the union in the first place. In the Military Sea Transportation

Service* (MSTS) and in the Independent Tanker Unions,* where continuity in employment was the rule for seamen, labor unions always faced the toughest opposition to organize and remained the weakest, and sometimes they were little more than thinly disguised company unions. Instead the shipping articles kept the job offers flowing through the union hiring hall,* which became the foundation of the maritime labor movement. Men would have to wait weeks and sometimes even a few months before they were able to ship out again, while a larger number of workers were kept in this industry than the actual job opportunities warranted. In the hiring hall the rotary system spread the income around by giving first opportunity to the man who had been longest waiting for a ship. The sailor would wait around for so long only if the job was extremely well paid to cover for the long time he was not earning wages, and hence the labor leaders knew they were under tremendous pressure to drive wages and benefits as high as possible. The survival of the Shipping Articles of the sailing age gave a meaningful function to the hiring hall, and thus they formed a vital cog in the machinery that generated considerable power for the union leaders during many decades. Finally on 3 December 1979 Congress abolished the office of shipping commissioner, and the duty of having seamen sign on and off the shipping articles fell to the ship captains, who now follow a set of rules and regulations prepared by the Coast Guard.*

References: Joseph H. Ball, *The Government-Subsidized Union Monopoly: A Study of Labor Practices in the Shipping Industry* (Washington, DC: Labor Policy Association, 1966); John J. Collins, *Never Off Pay: The Story of the Independent Tanker Union, 1937– 1962* (New York: Fordham University Press, 1964); Joseph P. Goldberg, *The Maritime Story: A Study in Labor-Management Relations* (Cambridge: Harvard University Press, 1958); James C. Healey, *Foc'sle and Glory Hole: A Study of the Merchant Seaman and His Occupation* (New York: Merchant Marine Publishers Association, 1936); Martin J. Norris, *The Law of Seamen*, 4th ed. (Rochester: Lawyers' Cooperative, 1985); William L. Standard, *Merchant Seamen: A Short History of Their Struggles* (New York: International, 1947).

SHIPPING BOARD, 1916–1933. The Shipping Board, the first government agency charged with the task of promoting and regulating merchant shipping, had a lasting impact on the development of the U.S. merchant marine. The Shipping Act of 1916* created the Shipping Board, composed of five commissioners appointed by the president with the consent of the Senate for six-year terms; the new board was completely independent of the executive branch and even elected its own chairman and vice chairman. Congress had passed the Shipping Act to deal with two separate problems. The first was the need forcefully documented by the Alexander Committee to regulate conferences* so that shippers* would be protected from discriminatory or unfair rates for cargo. The second was the tremendous shipping shortage caused by the outbreak of World War I in 1914, and this crisis had finally forced Congress to grant the Shipping

Board authority to organize separate corporations to build, buy, charter, and operate vessels until five years after the end of the war.

The Shipping Board was a novel adventure for the United States, and with so many possible interpretations as to what its proper activities should be under the badly written Shipping Act of 1916, not surprisingly controversies surrounded the Shipping Board during its entire life and even before it began operations. President Woodrow Wilson encountered unusual difficulties in finding and keeping commissioners, so that although the Shipping Act had been passed on 7 September 1916, the Shipping Board did not actually constitute itself until January 1917. William Denman, an admiralty lawyer, became the first chairman, but the Shipping Board still was not an effective body and consequently was quite unprepared when the United States declared war on Germany on 6 April 1917. In great haste, the Shipping Board created the Emergency Fleet Corporation* (EFC) on 16 March to begin a vast shipbuilding program whose direction was placed the next month under General George Goethals, the builder of the Panama Canal.* The unclear lines of authority between the Shipping Board and the EFC soon resulted in a bitter rivalry between Denman and Goethals, and not until President Wilson accepted the resignation of both men on 24 July did the Denman-Goethals controversy finally end.

To try to make up for the lost time, Wilson appointed a successful businessman with prior government experience, Edward N. Hurley,* to head the Shipping Board, whose primary functions now had become the construction and the operation of merchant vessels to support the American Expeditionary Force in France. Hurley placed Charles Piez in charge of the EFC, and finally both organizations began to function effectively and in harmony. The Shipping Board kept the supply lines flowing to Europe with the ships requisitioned in U.S. waters, including the interned German vessels. The Shipping Board not only delivered many new vessels from its massive shipbuilding program but also trained the personnel necessary to put the new ships immediately into service. In what was an example of mobilization for total war, the Shipping Board, through its Shipping Control Committee headed by P.A.S. Franklin,* controlled the movement of all the ocean transportation of the United States.

Hurley drove the Shipping Board hard to produce the tonnage necessary to fulfill President Wilson's promise to the Allies of eighty American divisions for the final offensive against German forces in the spring of 1919, but when Germany unexpectedly collapsed in November 1918, the EFC was left with a large number of vessels in various stages of construction and planning. In a momentous decision, Hurley decided to complete almost the entire original shipbuilding program, and since only 470 ships had been delivered by Armistice Day, this meant that nearly three times more vessels were completed in peacetime than during the war. Unfortunately Hurley decided not to remain to deal with the consequences of his decision, and after he accompanied President Wilson to the Paris Peace Conference, Hurley resigned in May 1919. The task of converting the wartime fleet to commercial peacetime use fell to another chairman, Admiral

William S. Benson.* Benson found a kindred soul in Senator Wesley Jones,* who rushed through Congress the Jones Act,* which enacted the policy of creating a strong, privately owned U.S. merchant marine. Although the Shipping Board was no longer required to cease the ownership and operation of vessels five years after the end of World War I, the act was very clear in ratifying Admiral Benson's decision to create U.S.- flag lines in every conceivable trade route of the world.

Since other, more controversial measures in the Jones Act never went into effect, the main policy instrument the Shipping Board applied to create a strong U.S.-flag presence was to pay "managing operators"* to run its vessels, although notable cases of direct government operation, like United States Lines* (USL), proved unavoidable during 1921–1929. The price of paying these managing operators, soon numbering over 200, was huge, and as the shipping market started to collapse in 1921, the Shipping Board faced the prospect of massive losses. Because the Wilson administration had failed to push the nomination of Benson as chairman of the Shipping Board (although later he was confirmed as a commissioner), the Republican administration of Warren G. Harding was left free to appoint the new chairman and eventually settled in June 1921 on Albert D. Lasker,* a successful advertising executive. As a businessman Lasker quickly saw the root of the problem and had the solution at hand: the government should sell all the ship lines to the managing operators, who on their own would have to make the lines into paying propositions, but if any managing operators declined to buy the ships, then the government should either suspend or operate itself the lines, as the Shipping Board was already doing with several routes, in particular, USL. After two frustrating years that left him permanently embittered toward official Washington, Lasker resigned in January 1923 without having solved the merchant shipping problems, and the Shipping Board continued on its path of raking up huge deficits to cover the mounting losses of the managing operators.

The Shipping Board had been trying to cut back on the managing operators, whose numbers had reached a high of over 200 in early 1920 and finally dropped to 25 in 1923, but the commissioners, who had developed close relationships with many of the remaining private lines, did not want to take any more drastic measures. President Calvin Coolidge attempted to solve the problem by bringing new people to the board, and, in particular, he secured the appointment of Admiral Leigh C. Palmer* as president of the EFC in January 1924 to see how costs could be reduced. Palmer very efficiently began to reduce the waste among the managing operators and also continued the consolidation of lines, moves that angered the Shipping Board, which in a cunning power play removed Palmer from office in October 1925. The usual shady deals between managing operators and the Shipping Board continued, and although President Coolidge considered abolishing the Shipping Board, in accordance with the prevailing philosophy of the 1920s, he quietly dropped the idea of antagonizing any group of businessmen.

Coolidge found his solution to the Shipping Board in the discreet Thomas V. O'Connor,* its vice chairman since 1921 and chairman since 1924. Without creating public controversy, O'Connor did everything possible to help private companies and was not above cooking special deals for individual companies. The Shipping Board continued its policy of subsidizing private individuals with government funds, yet Congress, in a wave of nationalistic feeling, placed in the hands of these discredited commissioners the administration of the ocean mail contracts authorized by the Merchant Marine Act of 1928.* The Shipping Board duly assigned the maximum payments to any private company that applied and in general gave private steamship companies every conceivable benefit so that they could reap huge profits at government expense.

During the pro-business 1920s the waste of the Shipping Board did not arouse any particular objections, because the government money was going into the pockets of influential businessmen. Once the Great Depression made its impact felt, at last public opinion began to question the propriety of these continued subsidy payments under the mail contracts, and finally the Black Committee* undertook an intensive investigation, which exposed some, but far from all, of the most blatant cases of abuses and excessive favoritism under the Merchant Marine Act of 1928. President Herbert Hoover had felt the need to reform the Shipping Board and, as a first step, declined to fill the vacancy created when vice chairman Edward C. Plummer died in March 1932, and later the president used the authority in the Economy Act of 30 June 1932 to reduce the number of commissioners from seven to three. However, it was left to President Franklin D. Roosevelt to abolish the Shipping Board on 10 August 1933, when its functions were transferred to a new Shipping Board Bureau* placed in the Department of Commerce.

Chairmen

William Denman	1917
Edward N. Hurley	1917–1919
John B. Payne	1919
Admiral William S. Benson	1920–1921
Albert D. Lasker	1921–1923
Edward P. Farley*	1923
Thomas V. O'Connor	1924–1933
Admiral Hutch I. Cone	1933

Notable Vice Chairmen

Thomas V. O'Connor	1921–1924
Edward C. Plummer	1924–1932

References: Paul V. Betters and Darrel H. Smith, *The United States Shipping Board. Its History, Activities and Organization* (Washington, DC: Brookings Institution, 1931); René De La Pedraja, *The Rise and Decline of U.S. Merchant Shipping in the Twentieth Century* (New York: Twayne, 1992); Mary Klachko, *Admiral William S. Benson: First Chief of Naval Operations* (Annapolis, MD: Naval Institute Press, 1987); Record Group 32, National Archives, Washington, DC; George C. Thorpe, *Federal Departmental Organization and Practice: The Executive Departments, Bureaus and Independent Establishments of the United States Government* (Kansas City: Vernon Law Book, 1925); Carroll H. Woody, *The Growth of the Federal Government, 1915–1932* (New York: McGraw-Hill, 1934).

SHIPPING BOARD BUREAU, 1933–1936. President Franklin D. Roosevelt created the Shipping Board Bureau on 10 August 1933 to continue the operation of the government's maritime programs, including the Merchant Fleet Corporation,* until Congress decided upon a more permanent institution. Dissatisfaction with the predecessor Shipping Board* had been growing since the mid-1920s, President Herbert Hoover had indicated his desire to abolish that board many times, and he had refused to appoint a successor to fill the vacancy created by the death of Vice Chairman Edward C. Plummer on 20 March 1932; later the president used the authority in the Economy Act of 30 June 1932 to reduce the number of commissioners from seven to three. However, the task of formally abolishing the independent Shipping Board and creating a new Shipping Board Bureau within the Department of Commerce was left to President Franklin D. Roosevelt, who accomplished the change on 10 August 1933.

The Shipping Board Bureau became an interesting experiment in a commission form of government within a cabinet department. Admiral Hutch I. Cone, the last chairman of the Shipping Board, initially became the head of the Shipping Board Bureau and continued as one of the three remaining commissioners. The secretary of commerce, Daniel C. Roper, was determined to bring the new bureau under his direct control, although his initial appointment of Henry H. Heimann as director flopped when the latter decided to return to private business after only four months in office. With the appointment of James C. Peacock on 25 August 1934 as director, the secretary at last gained a firm control over the Shipping Board Bureau, whose actions could start to mesh into the general foreign trade policies of the United States.

Most subsidized steamship companies soon resented what they considered the extreme control of Secretary Roper over the Shipping Board Bureau, and they longed for the predecessor Shipping Board they had easily manipulated and duped without the risk of any intervention from high officials in the executive branch. President Franklin D. Roosevelt, Secretary Roper, and most officials in the Department of Commerce were satisfied with the organizational arrangements for the Shipping Board Bureau and felt that Congress should make changes primarily in the subsidy legislation. Unfortunately, in the hastily passed Merchant Marine Act of 1936,* Congress discarded the recommendations of the executive branch and, rather than confirm the Shipping Board Bureau, created instead the U.S. Maritime Commission,* which in effect meant a return to the totally discredited system of an independent agency for merchant shipping. The Shipping Board Bureau experiment, although brief, was not forgotten, and the possibilities of improving administration by making ingenious combinations of government by commission and by a single official later resurfaced in the Federal Maritime Board* and in the Maritime Subsidy Board.*

Principal Executives

Admiral Hutch I. Cone	1933–1936
Henry H. Heimann	1934
James C. Peacock	1934–1936

References: Samuel A. Lawrence, *United States Merchant Shipping Policies and Politics* (Washington, DC: Brookings Institution, 1966); Official File, Franklin D. Roosevelt Presidential Library, Hyde Park, New York; Carroll H. Woody, *The Growth of the Federal Government, 1915–1932* (New York: McGraw-Hill, 1934).

SHIPPING COMMISSIONERS. See Shipping Commissioners' Act of 1872.

SHIPPING COMMISSIONERS' ACT OF 1872. The Shipping Commissioners' Act of 1872 was a first attempt by Congress to end the shanghaiing* of sailors and to control the worst abuses of the crimps.* The act required all sailors to sign shipping articles* in front of a shipping commissioner appointed by the nearest federal circuit court before they could begin and end a voyage. Determined crimps could avoid the control by having someone else sign the name of the poor sailor, who had already been delivered to the ship in a drugged sleep, but by the end of the nineteenth century the active presence of the shipping commissioners made impossible any serious evasion, in effect reducing shanghaiing to very rare cases in U.S. ports. The shipping commissioners were placed under the Bureau of Navigation* in 1884, and their functions were transferred to Coast Guard* personnel in 1942. The emergence of a very powerful maritime labor movement had made the Shipping Commissioners superfluous by then, but they were not formally abolished until 3 December 1979. Since then ship captains sign on and discharge seamen in accordance with a set of rules and regulations provided by the Coast Guard.

References: James C. Healey, *Foc'sle and Glory Hole: A Study of the Merchant Seaman and His Occupation* (New York: Merchant Marine Publishers Association, 1936); Martin J. Norris, *The Law of Seamen*, 4th ed. (Rochester: Lawyers' Cooperative, 1985); Lloyd M. Short, *The Bureau of Navigation: Its History, Activities and Organization* (Baltimore, MD: Johns Hopkins University Press, 1923); William L. Standard, *Merchant Seamen: A Short History of Their Struggles* (New York: International, 1947); Hyman Weintraub, *Andrew Furuseth: Emancipator of the Seamen* (Berkeley: University of California Press, 1959).

SHIP SALES ACT OF 1946. The end of World War II found the United States with a fleet of over 4,000 merchant ships, and Congress decided not to repeat the mistakes after World War I, when the Shipping Board* had paid unprepared and in many cases unscrupulous individuals to run the government ships. The Ship Sales Act of 1946 established two main principles for the disposition of the wartime fleet; first, the vessels would be sold or chartered* with preference always given to purchasers rather than charterers, and second, a core of surplus vessels, plus any others that could not be sold, would be set aside in the National Defense Reserve Fleet* for possible reactivation in case of an emergency. Congress passed the act on 8 March 1946 and granted the U.S. Maritime Commission* authority to sell or charter ships until 31 December 1947, and by later legislation it extended the deadline for U.S. citizens until 15 January 1951.

The original act gave U.S. citizens priority over noncitizens in the purchase of the ships but left the U.S. Maritime Commission enough flexibility to determine who was the best individual buyer. Rivalries among U.S. merchant shipping companies and the temporary ascendancy of shipyard interests in the U.S. Maritime Commission resulted in foreign buyers' obtaining the largest number and the best of the vessels available for sale, so that while noncitizens purchased more than 1,100 ships by 31 December 1947, U.S. citizens, even after the extensions, until January 1951 had acquired only 823 ships. Furthermore, the number of ships bought by U.S. citizens in reality was lower, because some U.S. citizens had set up dummy corporations to acquire ships for foreigners after the expiration of the 31 December 1947 deadline. U.S. shipyards had foolishly hoped to dump the ships in the world market to destroy their foreign competitors and to create a demand for ships of the quality built in the United States, but the result of trying to help domestic shipyards was to create ferocious competition for U.S. merchant shipping companies while the foreign orders for U.S. shipyards never materialized. Foreigners could not be blamed for taking advantage of the opportunities provided by the contradictions in U.S. maritime policy, and consequently failure of a long-term program to dispose of the surplus fleet meant that the Ship Sales Act of 1946 and its implementation greatly contributed to undermine U.S. merchant shipping in the next two decades.

References: Congressional Quarterly Service, *Congress and the Nation, 1945–1964*; René De La Pedraja, *The Rise and Decline of U.S. Merchant Shipping in the Twentieth Century* (New York: Twayne, 1992); Samuel A. Lawrence, *United States Merchant Shipping Policies and Politics* (Washington, DC: Brookings Institution, 1966); Jerry Shields, *The Invisible Billionaire: Daniel Ludwig* (Boston: Houghton Mifflin, 1986); *U.S. Statutes at Large*, vol. 60 (1946).

SHIPS' COMMITTEES. Even in the nineteenth century union members held meetings at sea, sometimes secretly, but except for the West Coast, ships' committees with regular union meetings were mainly a product of the 1930s union organizing drives. On the West Coast sailors had discussed their problems with their patrolman* or had dropped by the local union office, but with the creation of the National Maritime Union (NMU)* in 1937, the need for a more formal union organization aboard the ships became evident. During World War II the ships' committees—and there was at least one aboard each ship—held regular meetings for all members, conducted classes, established subcommittees, and in general made the union presence felt. From among its members the committee selected one to be the ships' delegate, who spoke for the crew when talking with officers aboard and union officials ashore.

Certainly the most delicate task was bringing charges against fellow sailors for drunken or illegal behavior, for example, petty racketeering. After the war was over, preparing beefs* against the companies became the preferred task, and it seemed that the ships' committees were going to make management pay for the previous decades of exploiting sailors. Coordinating the crew for strike action once the ship docked was also another duty. As the idealism of the 1930s gave way to business unionism, the ships' committees became merely a cog in the rigid union power hierarchy. Shipboard democracy received a fatal blow in 1942 when the Sailors' Union of the Pacific* (SUP) decided to appoint the ships' delegates, who no longer were concerned with representing rank-and-file sentiment but instead concentrated on making sure that the orders coming down from the union bosses were carried out. The ships' committees lost the right to elect the union delegate for the ship, who henceforth was appointed by the patrolman or the port agent, while meetings aboard ship became infrequent. Clearly the earlier dynamism had been lost, while for the union delegate aboard the ship, the committee became a step in the ladder toward more important positions within the union hierarchy on shore. The ships' committees lost even more influence in the NMU, but there the change took place more discreetly to disguise Joseph Curran's* personal dictatorship.

References: Richard O. Boyer, *The Dark Ship* (New York: Little, Brown, 1947); Joseph P. Goldberg, *The Maritime Story: A Study in Labor-Management Relations* (Cambridge: Harvard University Press, 1958); National Maritime Union, *This Is the NMU* (New York: William P. Gottlieb, 1954); Bruce Nelson, *Workers on the Waterfront: Seamen, Longshoremen, and Unionism in the 1930s* (Urbana: University of Illinois Press, 1990).

SIBERIA **and** *KOREA*, **1902–1930.** In 1898 the Pacific Mail Steamship Company* (PMSS) was at a crossroads. Except for the *China II** (1889) it had not ordered any ships since 1875, and its existing fleet was virtually obsolete. The company either had to abandon merchant shipping, or it had to order a new generation of modern, fast steel steamers to maintain its transpacific services. Rennie Schwerin,* the chief executive of PMSS, convinced the parent railroad company to invest in new ships, and consequently in 1898 he ordered for PMSS two new ships, the *Korea* and the *Siberia*. Construction proceeded slowly, and they were not completed until 1902.

The *Korea* and *Siberia* were the largest vessels then existing in the transpacific trade. With quadruple-expansion engines (see marine propulsion), two screws each, and a speed of eighteen knots, they were also the fastest vessels in the Pacific and had made the eastbound crossing in ten days, ten hours from Yokohama to San Francisco, a record that held until broken by the *President Coolidge** in 1937. The immediate success of these ships convinced PMSS to order two more large steamers, the *Manchuria** and the *Mongolia.**

When PMSS decided to abandon merchant shipping in August 1915, the company sold the *Korea* and *Siberia*, along with the *Manchuria, Mongolia*, and the *China II*, to the International Mercantile Marine* (IMM). Upon closer inspection, IMM realized that the old and slow *China II* was unsuited for transatlantic service and promptly sold the vessel to the China Mail Steamship Company;* *Korea* and *Siberia* operated briefly in the Atlantic, but for unspecified reasons IMM likewise found the ships unsatisfactory and sold them to Toyo Kisen Kaisha in May 1916. That the two fastest steamers in the Pacific ended their careers under the operation of Japanese lines was one more indication of how shipping supremacy in the Pacific was gradually slipping from the United States to Japan. In 1926 Nippon Kisen Kaisha acquired the two vessels and, after a few years of service, scrapped them in 1930.

References: René De La Pedraja, *The Rise and Decline of U.S. Merchant Shipping in the Twentieth Century* (New York: Twayne, 1992); John H. Kemble, ''A Hundred Years of the Pacific Mail,'' *American Neptune* 10 (1950):123–143; John Niven, *The American President Lines and Its Forebears, 1848–1984* (Newark: University of Delaware Press, 1987); E. Mowbray Tate, *Transpacific Steam: The Story of Steam Navigation from the Pacific Coast of North America to the Far East and the Antipodes, 1867–1941* (New York: Cornwall Books, 1986).

SIDE-WHEELS or SIDE-WHEELERS. See Propeller.

SINGLE-EXPANSION ENGINE, 1819–1870s. Since the middle of the eighteenth century the single-expansion engine had powered the Industrial Revolution in England. This external-combustion engine of massive size required huge amounts of coal to turn the water in the boiler into the steam that moved the piston inside the engine's cylinder. The engine was double-acting because a valve led the steam first into one end of the cylinder to push the piston down, then to the other end of the cylinder to push the piston back up; the piston was connected to a crankshaft that rotated. The single-expansion engine could produce only slow speeds and was very expensive to operate because it wasted massive amounts of steam.

Nevertheless, the potential for ocean transportation was there, but only after many costly experiments improved the single-expansion engine. In 1807 the American Robert Fulton built and operated the *Clermont*, the first successful river steamboat, and in 1819 the U.S.-flag *Savannah** crossed the Atlantic using steam and wind power. In the following years owners installed steam engines aboard their wooden ships to complement the sails, but the huge consumption of coal meant such high operating expenses that not until 1838 did the British *Sirius* become the first ship to cross the Atlantic relying solely on steam power.

In 1838 steamships inaugurated regular transatlantic service, with announced departure and arrival schedules, the latter being something the sailing packets had never been able to offer. The British Cunard Line entered the service in 1840 and remained the main firm in this route throughout the nineteenth century;

the only U.S. company that briefly attempted to compete against the British was the Collins Line.* The fast steamers of the latter attracted many passengers, and the number of Americans crossing the Atlantic increased from 5,330 in 1850 to 32,631 in 1854. However, the success of the single-expansion engine was more apparent than real, because the steamship services were a luxury possible only with government subsidies.

Aboard the steamships passengers found only cramped and dark cabins that made the modest accommodations of the sailing ships look roomy. Without public rooms or any other distractions, the passengers had to loiter in the deck, generally exposed to the elements. Concentration for reading or writing was difficult because of the racket and vibrations of the engine, while the introduction of the propeller initially made the situation worse, because the passengers' cabins, in the time-honored tradition of the sea, were located in the rear of the ship. Only in the late 1860s did designers finally take the revolutionary step of placing passengers' quarters along the center sides of the vessel (''amidships''), but no such shift was possible with the single-expansion engine because it left no room for spacious quarters anywhere in the ship.

The tiny passenger quarters simply reflected the lack of space aboard the early steamers. The massive size of the machinery and the need to carry a huge supply of coal left little room for passengers or income-producing cargo. These steamers always carried more coal than cargo, in many cases twice as much, if not more. Most sailing vessels were faster than the early steamers, and in one revealing episode, when a robber boarded a steamer bound for Liverpool, the authorities managed to arrest him upon his arrival by sending a fast sailing vessel, which reached the port of destination before the steamer arrived. Steamships maintained full rigging for sails, and this meant higher labor costs, because besides the engine crew, the ship needed the regular complement to tend the sails. Lastly, steamships cost three times more to build than sailing vessels, while the engine caused sagging and dry rot in the ship's timbers, requiring major overhauls in dry dock at least every three years. Clearly, wooden steamships using the single-expansion engine could not be commercially successful, and only generous government subsidies allowed the regularly scheduled service across the Atlantic to continue as a luxury form of transportation.

Gradual improvements in the single-expansion engine and the keen desire to have a regularly scheduled service sustained the hope that one day the steamship could be a commercial success. Steam pressures in the first engines had begun very low at five pounds per inch but by the 1850s had risen to twenty pounds per inch; the higher pressure did improve the speed, but not the fuel consumption of the vessel. The wooden hull was braced and reinforced with more iron, but the shift to iron hulls was not completed until 1870. Making the ship larger did not create more space, because then a bigger engine and even more coal were needed, and sailing vessels remained necessary to carry the coal to the refueling stations of the steamers.

Thanks to the enthusiasm and perseverance of the early promoters, the single-expansion engine remained in use for ocean travel. However, unless the engineers came up with a more efficient propulsion, the steamers could never become a commercial proposition and risked being shunted aside or confined to specialized tasks. Not until sailing vessels lost their grip over ocean transportation could modern merchant shipping emerge as a business. See also marine propulsion.

References: Gerald S. Graham, "The Ascendancy of the Sailing Ship 1850–1885," *Economic History Review* 9 (1956): 74–88; William S. Lindsay, *History of Merchant Shipping and Ancient Commerce*, 4 vols. (New York: AMS Press, 1965); John F. Nichols, "The Development of Marine Engineering," in Society of Naval Architects and Marine Engineers, *Historical Transactions, 1893–1943* (Westport, CT: Greenwood Press, 1981); Edward W. Sloan III, "The Machine at Sea: Early Transatlantic Steam Travel," in Benjamin W. Labaree, *The Atlantic World of Robert G. Albion* (Middletown, CT: Wesleyan University Press, 1975).

SL-7s, 1972–present. The SL-7s (*SL* stands for Sea-Land* and 7 for its seventh generation of ships) have been the fastest containerships ever built in the world. At the time the eight ships were completed they were also the largest containerships in the world, and with a length of 946 feet and a beam of 105 feet they barely squeezed through the Panama Canal* and hence were Panamax* vessels. The ships had a capacity for 1,096 containers (896 that were thirty-five feet long and 200 forty feet long), but the most distinctive characteristic of the SL-7s was their high operating speed of thirty-three knots. In sea trials and using only 80 percent of her power the *Sea-Land Galloway* hit thirty-five knots, and on 6 October 1972 the vessel effortlessly regained the "Blue Ribbon" for the United States by setting for cargo vessels the transatlantic speed record, which still stands today. Sea-Land had not run the vessel to maximum power, perhaps out of deference to the passenger liner *United States*, whose speed record of thirty-five knots still stands, or more likely because the outlandish fuel consumption at such high speeds meant such high costs even in a period of cheap oil.

Sea-Land had ordered the SL-7s, the monster ships of their day, for three main reasons. First, in the late 1960s competition from air cargo services was threatening to take away the most valuable freight from ships, and the company hoped to retain its appeal among shippers* by means of high-speed ships racing across the Atlantic. Second, Sea-Land was engaged in deadly competition against United States Lines* (USL), whose containerships, the Lancers,* had almost destroyed Sea-Land earlier; the latter now hoped to strike the final blow against the Lancers, whose twenty-four-knot speed was no match for the thirty-three knots of the SL-7s. Lastly, Sea-Land hoped to ratify its long-standing policy of never receiving subsidies, because supposedly its huge technological lead would push it far ahead of foreign competitors and reap as well substantial profits. Although Sea-Land placed the ships under U.S. registry,* the fact that they had been built in low-cost shipyards permanently disqualified them from receiving any subsidies, a limitation that originally had not concerned the company.

Even before the first of the ships entered service in October 1972, the reasons underlying their construction began to crumble one by one. For example, as far as air competition was concerned, shippers had chosen airplanes not because of the slowness of the Atlantic crossing but because of the endless delays, complications, and pilfering at the ports, but once containers dramatically speeded up turnaround time at the docks, the need for faster vessels largely vanished. In any case, the experiment with the SL-7s never had a real chance, because the energy crisis of 1973 quadrupled fuel prices at one blow, and the prices continued to rise during the 1970s. Sea-Land had no alternative but to lower the vessels to twenty-six knots, but the lower speed merely reduced the losses, which continued to pile up. The company hoped the oil prices would come down again and, if not, hoped that the oil prices would become high enough to justify conversion (at government expense) to nuclear power,* but neither of these two scenarios materialized.

The SL-7s were more victims of bad luck and bad timing but were not such a colossal blunder as the Econships,* whose failure had been predicted from the start. No foreign or domestic company wished to buy the SL-7s, and Sea-Land labored to find an alternative to scrapping the vessels. Fortunately for the company, the Cold War heated up on last time, and the U.S. Navy feverishly prepared to mobilize a fleet for what was then considered the inevitable clash with the Soviet Union. The high speeds of the vessels made them ideal for military transports, but when the navy attempted to buy them, U.S. shipyards and U.S. shipyard unions bitterly opposed the move on the grounds that this set the dangerous precedent of building abroad the ships for the U.S. Navy. Sea-Land lobbied furiously for the purchase, while the U.S. Navy emphasized that with military conflicts impending, the immediate availability of the vessels was the determining factor. Finally in May 1981 the U.S. Congress passed special legislation to authorize the purchase of the vessels by the U.S. Navy; the conversion of most of the eight ships to Roll-on/Roll-off* (Ro/Ro) vessels was a consolation prize for the domestic shipbuilding industry.

The navy considered the ships "invaluable assets" and wanted to order at least four more, and the SL-7s did prove particularly useful during the Gulf War. However, with the end of the Cold War, it was not clear whether the navy will continue to maintain on active duty these ships, whose high costs of operation made them candidates for mothballing in the National Defense Reserve Fleet.*

References: *American Shipper*, March 1980; *Business Week*, 29 April 1972, 4 February 1980; René De La Pedraja, *The Rise and Decline of U.S. Merchant Shipping in the Twentieth Century* (New York: Twayne, 1992); *Florida Journal of Commerce*, December 1971, November 1972, May 1974; *Journal of Commerce*, 3 October 1988.

SLATER, JOHN E., 11 August 1891–1980s? John E. Slater was the president of American Export Lines* (AEL) in 1949–1956 and had been vice president since 1935. Slater, whose father was a traveling salesman, was born in Somerville, Massachusetts, on 11 August 1891. He attended private schools and graduated from Harvard University in 1913 with a degree in engineering. Except for active duty during World War I, he worked for railroads from 1913 to 1925. In 1929 he joined the consulting firm of Coverdale in New York City. In 1934 Coverdale became the head of AEL, and the next year he called Slater to join him in the extremely difficult task of saving AEL from bankruptcy. Slater's most notable accomplishment was in working effectively with Coverdale to save AEL, which otherwise would have folded, as had happened to almost all of the steamship firms created after World War I.

With the completion of the remarkable rescue of AEL, Slater was free to participate actively in a new aviation subsidiary, the American Export Airlines. Although the aviation venture was profitable, the Civil Aeronautics Board's decision in 1945 to forbid ownership of airplane services by steamship firms ended American Export Airlines. However, Slater was among the first steamship executives to realize and sound publicly the warning that airplanes were going to drastically impact passenger travel aboard ships. Specifically Slater told steamship executives first in 1944 and again in 1946 that all travelers wishing speed would soon prefer airplanes and that only by concentrating on the narrow luxury market of persons who preferred ocean travel could shipowners hope to remain in the passenger business. Slater's warnings were prophetic and, although heeded in some foreign countries, were largely ignored in the United States, starting with Slater himself, who in 1948 fell into the rush to order new passenger liners, most notably the *Constitution** and *Independence*. When they entered into service in 1951, Slater was already the president of AEL, and he faced the problem of making the vessels pay. He reached the conclusion that the conversion of four navy attack transports into a second generation of the Four Aces* had been a mistake and that henceforth the company would build either cargo or passenger ships, no more combination vessels like the Four Aces. Slater as late as 1956 was thinking of ordering a third express liner in the vain attempt to make the operation of the *Constitution* and *Independence* profitable, when the introduction of jet travel dashed the last hopes for ocean passenger travel for U.S.-flag vessels.

In 1954 AEL passed its first dividend payment in eighteen years, a warning of future problems, and the next year, when the main stockholder of AEL, Charles Ulrich Bay, died, his widow, Josephine Bay Paul,* began to take a closer look at the company's sagging finances, and she decided to change management. John E. Slater retired on 31 December 1956, ending his active involvement in merchant shipping.

References: *Current Biography*, 1951; *New York Times*, 18 August 1949, 2 September 1954, 22 March 1956, 21 September 1956.

SMITH, FERDINAND CHRISTOPHER, 3 May 1893–16 August 1961. Ferdinand Christopher Smith was the first black seaman to hold a high union position in a racially integrated maritime labor organization. Born in Jamaica on 3 May 1893, he entered the United States at New Orleans in 1918. When he requested naturalization as a U.S. citizen in 1927, his application was rejected because he lacked the visa status of permanent resident. Smith continued to work on vessels serving the Gulf of Mexico, but when he tried to organize fellow seamen to improve their conditions, he found that his skin color was a barrier to joining the lily-white locals of the ISU;* no such color prejudices blocked his entry into the Communist party of the United States, which he joined around 1936. The establishment of the National Maritime Union* (NMU) represented the big push by the Communist party to break into maritime labor, and Smith, along with President Joseph Curran,* was one of the original founders in 1937. In order to attract black sailors, the Communist party had Smith elected vice president in 1938 and national secretary in 1939.

In 1944 the NMU faced its first internal crisis when newspapers reported that Smith was a member of the Communist party and did not have American citizenship. How such personal information was leaked to the press is open to question, and in any case the crisis marked Joseph Curran's first clash with the Communist party over control in the NMU. Curran wanted to drop Smith, but the communists insisted he be kept as a symbol to blacks. Curran backed down, and Smith was able to keep his office until 1948, when Curran's backers soundly defeated his reelection bid. That same year the Immigration and Naturalization Service began long and complex deportation proceedings. To avoid deportation, he left the United States on 15 August 1951. The Federal Bureau of Investigation (FBI) reported that in October 1951 he was employed in Vienna, Austria, by the World Federation of Trade Unions, a communist front. Afterward he returned to his native Jamaica, where he died on 16 August 1961.

References: Richard O. Boyer, *The Dark Ship* (New York: Little, Brown, 1947); Rayford W. Logan and Michael R. Winston, *Dictionary of American Negro Biography* (New York: W. W. Norton, 1982); *New York Times*, 16 August 1961; *Who's Who in Labor, 1946* (New York: Dryden Press, 1946).

SOUTHERN PACIFIC STEAMSHIP COMPANY. See Morgan Line.

SOUTH EUROPE-UNITED STATES FREIGHT CONFERENCE (SEUSA), 1985–present. The South Europe-United States Freight Conference (SEUSA) has been one of the superconferences* created after the passage of the Shipping Act of 1984.* SEUSA replaced four previous conferences,* and it has controlled the trade moving from Italy, Portugal, Spain, and the Mediterranean coast of France to the United States. Originally in 1985 it was called the Mediterranean United States Freight Conference or MEDUSA but was renamed more accurately as SEUSA in 1987. Out of a membership of seventeen companies, only two—Farrell Lines* and Lykes Brothers Steamship Company*— were U.S.- flag. The counterpart of SEUSA for cargoes moving from the United States to Italy, Portugal, Spain, and the Mediterranean coast of France has been the U.S. Atlantic and Gulf Western Mediterranean Agreement (AGWM), which was created from the merger of two older conferences in 1985.

References: Advisory Commission on Conferences in Ocean Shipping, *Report to the President and the Congress* (Washington, DC: Government Printing Office, 1992); Federal Maritime Commission, *Carrier Agreements in the U.S. Oceanborne Trades*, September 1990; Federal Maritime Commission, *Section 18 Report on the Shipping Act of 1984*, September 1989.

STANDARD FRUIT AND STEAMSHIP COMPANY (SFS), 1899–present.
Standard Fruit and Steamship Company (SFS) was the main competitor of United Fruit Company* until 1973, when SFS became the largest supplier of bananas to the U.S. market. SFS began as a small family firm of the three Vaccaro brothers (Joseph, Luca, and Felix) and the son-in-law of Joseph Vaccaro, Salvador D'Antoni, and although the firm grew to become a large corporation, it remained in family hands until the 1960s, when all the heirs declined to stay in the prosperous business. The firm was based in New Orleans, and the founders vigorously developed the market for bananas in the U.S. South. The main source for bananas remained Honduras, one of the few areas that United Fruit had not monopolized. In 1899 the family members established more formally their operations and also decided to charter* their first ship, in order to guarantee the safe delivery of bananas from Honduras to New Orleans. SFS wanted to purchase ships as an added guarantee but lacked the capital for such outlays and had to content itself with chartering ships under British, Norwegian, and Honduran flags. An important infusion of capital came in 1903, when United Fruit purchased a half interest in the company so that SFS could build a crucial railroad in Honduras, but once the railroad was built, SFS returned the full amount and in 1908 was completely free of any United Fruit influence.

SFS continued to prosper through the World War I years and apparently took advantage of the sale of surplus ships after the war to acquire a fleet of its own steamers. The company had become very profitable and began to diversify into other areas and, among other acquisitions, purchased the Grunewald Hotel in New Orleans in 1921. Large sums of money were accumulating in the banks, and the company decided to expand into areas beyond Honduras, which had remained until then the company's sole source of bananas. SFS reorganized itself as a public corporation in 1923, with most of the stock held by family members, although for the first time outsiders had a chance to buy small lots of shares. As the fleet expanded to bring bananas from many new points, the company decided to enter the passenger business, and cruises to Mexico began in 1924 and to the Caribbean in 1926. The ships were fitted with large staterooms able to carry comfortably around fifty passengers, and while the company emphasized the wonders of travel into the exotic tropical regions, Prohibition* more than guaranteed ample travelers, because once the ships left the U.S. three-mile territorial limits, alcohol could be freely served and consumed aboard and in the countries along the route. Passenger service aboard the SFS ships lasted until the 1950s, when the company decided to limit itself to the by then much simpler and more profitable banana trade.

The fleet of banana boats continued to expand even during the Great Depression, and in an unusual acquisition, the company purchased four destroyers from the navy, which, after removal of armor and the replacement of steam turbines* with diesel* engines, made valuable additions to the SFS fleet, which numbered thirty-five ships in 1935. The outbreak of World War II in 1939 disrupted the company's activities, and its three British-flag ships were soon requisitioned by the English government; when the United States entered the conflict, the War Shipping Administration* (WSA) requisitioned all but the slowest and oldest vessels of the company. Later SFS, just like almost all other steamship companies in the United States, operated for the WSA government-owned vessels under the general agency agreements.

The government returned the requisitioned vessels after the war, but SFS made little, if any, use of the liberal provisions of the Ship Sales Act of 1946,* and as a matter of fact the company decided in 1949 to abandon the policy of owning ships and henceforth to rely only on bareboat* charters. By 1962 the company had disposed of its fleet of old steamers and instead operated directly foreign-flag vessels chartered as needed. In another change, the company had also shifted from carrying bananas by the stem, the pattern since the nineteenth century, to using cardboard boxes with air holes and handles; this change had proven necessary because of the replacement of the old Gros Michel variety with the new disease-resistant Cavendish banana, which, however, was more sensitive to bruising.

SFS was very prosperous in the 1960s, and majority ownership by the family precluded takeover attempts; nevertheless the company needed direction for the coming decades. None of the family members wished to remain in the business, and the widowed matriarch of the family, Mary Vaccaro D'Antoni, had to decide what to do. At this moment Castle and Cooke (called Dole since 1991) had sold its stock interest in Matson Navigation Company* and was looking for a substitute long-term investment. The food conglomerate believed SFS fit right into their operations and made a bid, and then a group of Wall Street speculators made a higher offer. Some negotiations followed, but finally Mary decided to take the lower offer of Castle and Cooke as the best way to avoid the dismemberment of SFS.

The initial stock purchases began in 1964, and the merger of SFS into Castle and Cooke was not completed until December 1968. In 1974 SFS ordered two ships and three more in the late 1980s, but it has continued to ship the bulk of its bananas aboard chartered vessels. The cardboard boxes have proved so efficient that the company has concluded that the shift to containers* would not bring any appreciable savings. The bananas of SFS were marketed under the label "Cabana" until 1972 and have since been labelled "Dole."

References: *American Shipper*, December 1978; René De La Pedraja, *The Rise and Decline of U.S. Merchant Shipping in the Twentieth Century* (New York: Twayne, 1992); Mark H. Goldberg, *Going Bananas: 100 Years of American Fruit Ships in the Caribbean* (Kings Point, NY: American Merchant Marine Museum, 1993); Thomas L. Karnes, *Trop-

ical Enterprise: The Standard Fruit and Steamship Company in Latin America (Baton Rouge: Louisiana State University Press, 1978); Maritime Administration, *Foreign-Flag Merchant Ships Owned by U.S. Parent Companies*, 1 January 1991.

STANDARD OIL COMPANY OF NEW JERSEY or ESSO or EXXON, 1911–present. During its existence the Standard Oil Company of New Jersey, later called Esso and today, Exxon, owned the largest tanker fleet in the Western Hemisphere and fought with Royal Shell to have the largest tanker fleet in the world. When the U.S. government ordered the breakup of John D. Rockefeller's Standard Oil Company, then the largest in the world and also the owner of the largest tanker fleet in the world, several independent Standard Oil companies appeared in 1911, the most important of which was Standard Oil of New Jersey, which henceforth for simplicity's sake will be referred to by its later names of Esso and today of Exxon. An urgent task for Esso was the acquisition of a new fleet, because the breakup had left the majority of the tankers in the hands of what was now an independent company, Standard Oil of New York, and Esso had to find the tankers to move the oil in the United States and abroad. Esso established in 1911 under David T. Warden the Foreign Shipping Department to cope with the shortage of tankers "that threatened to become acute" by 1912. The Foreign Shipping Department began busily chartering* every available tanker on the market, but the rising tanker rates also forced Esso to order the construction of new tankers.

By 1913 the worldwide tanker shortage eased, and the Foreign Shipping Department could turn to deal with a dangerous imbalance in tanker ownership: the twenty-three tankers of the German subsidiary Deutsche-Amerikanische Petroleum Gessellschaft (DAPG) formed the bulk of Esso's fleet, an unusual circumstance caused by the somewhat haphazard way in which the U.S. government had at random distributed foreign affiliates and assets among the companies that emerged in 1911 out of the former Standard Oil. Five of the DAPG tankers were sold or transferred to other affiliates, but since that fleet continued to grow, Esso found itself in a potentially vulnerable position when World War I began in August 1914. Fortunately for the company, the majority of the DAPG fleet was near or in U.S. waters, and the war found only nine of its tankers in German ports. Under a new law Esso transferred those German tankers in U.S. ports to U.S. registry.* As for the nine tankers in German ports, Esso regained them temporarily after the war, but in spite of a long and bitter campaign to keep them, the company had to return them to the French and English as part of their war reparations.

With its shipbuilding program advancing, Esso had expanded its fleet until in 1919 its seventy-one tankers made it the second largest fleet in the world and the biggest in the Western Hemisphere, and this command over ships gave the company a distinct advantage over other U.S. oil companies. In spite of this incredible achievement, for some reason Esso management was not satisfied with the performance of Worden, who left the company and was replaced as head of the Foreign Shipping Department, also newly renamed as the Marine Department, by the colorful Robert L. Hague.* He centralized all authority in himself and ran the Marine Department much as a one-man show, totally rejecting the layers of corporate management Standard Oil was rapidly piling on in other departments. The Marine Department kept the tankers running full and on time, and although it chartered in 1927 vessels to move 36 percent of its oil cargoes, Esso continued to expand the fleet with even bigger tankers. The *John D. Archbold* of 22,600 deadweight* tons was the world's biggest tanker for a number of years after she was delivered in 1921, and the company ordered an even bigger one in 1928, the *C. O. Stillman* of 24,185 deadweight tons. The company wished to order more of the "supertankers" of that day but was deterred, first, by the shipyards, which did not have ways large enough to build such big ships, and second, by the lack of sufficient depth in most U.S. ports, which were too shallow for the deep draft of the larger tankers. Hague also recognized the cost advantages of diesel* engines and demanded this type of marine propulsion for all tankers subsequently ordered by Esso. His many successes gave him sufficient influence to convince upper management after the tanker strike of 1923 to pay the personnel aboard the tankers adequate wages. His policy toward labor was very effective, and he continued to instill dynamism and raise morale among the men, and by the late 1930s he also came to support the personnel's right to belong to the Independent Tanker Unions* (ITUs).

In 1927 the company decided to create for its fleet a separate subsidiary, Standard Shipping Company, but because of changes in the income tax law, the subsidiary was reabsorbed into the parent company in 1934 as the Marine Department, and, of course, through these changes Hague remained firmly in control of all tanker operations. His biggest challenge was the Great Depression, and he desperately halted charters, including those from his friend Clifford D. Mallory,* but to no avail, and in 1930 for the first time tankers of Esso lay idle, not just because of the decline of volume but also because the shipyards were still delivering tankers ordered in the boom years of the late 1920s. In spite of reducing the vessels' speed to spread the work around and reduce costs, by 1932 Esso had laid up twenty-seven vessels. At last in 1934 business began to recover, and gradually all the company's tankers returned to full-time duty, and eventually Standard needed to order more vessels. Hague convinced the company to order in 1938 twelve new fast tankers ("Cimarron" class), whose higher speed of eighteen knots and other defense features were covered by the government, and these new tankers proved invaluable to the navy during World War II.

During the war the Standard Oil fleet was controlled by the War Shipping Administration* (WSA), and once the government returned the fleet to private control, the postwar shortage of tankers guaranteed ample employment until early 1949, when a new slump appeared. The tanker market revived again in 1950 partly because of the outbreak of the Korean War. In 1945 Millard G. Gamble* became the head of the Marine Department, which the company reconstituted in 1950 as a separate entity, Esso Shipping Company, only to be reabsorbed by the parent company again in 1958. Other transformations oc-curred, until eventually Exxon Shipping had emerged by the late 1970s. (Esso adopted the new name of Exxon in 1972.)

The two main concerns of the shipping subsidiary have been first, to adjust the fleet size to the fluctuations of market demand, essentially increasing the number of tankers when demand was high, disposing or laying up vessels when demand dropped. To achieve smooth adjustment, the company has worked out numerous arrangements with its ITUs to minimize the adverse effect of layoffs on the tanker personnel, while at the same time to retain a pool of experienced individuals ready for the next expansion. As far as the operations themselves, a structural shift took place in the 1970s, as the flow of oil from the Gulf of Mexico to the East Coast declined, and instead the movement of Alaska oil to mainland United States became the principal occupation of the U.S.-flag tankers. For the transport of oil from abroad, as well as for the needs of its foreign subsidiaries, the company has continued the traditional practice of relying on a separate fleet of vessels either under flags of convenience* or under the registry of the host country.

Environmental precautions have been the second major concern of manage-ment, which at all costs wanted to avoid oil spills or other major environmental damage. When the tanker *Exxon Valdez** shipwrecked off the port of Valdez, Alaska, on 24 March 1989, 11 million gallons leaked into Prince William Sound. The fact that the tanker was U.S.-flag and built in the United States did not allow shifting the blame to foreign operators, and the disaster was particularly costly and embarrassing for both Exxon and the U.S. merchant marine. Exxon, however, as one of the wealthiest corporations in America, has survived this disaster, and as long as the demand for oil remains strong, Exxon will continue to need tankers to bring oil to the markets and to maintain its preeminent po-sition among the oil companies of the world.

References: John J. Collins, *Bargaining at the Local Level* (New York: Fordham University, 1974); René De La Pedraja, *The Rise and Decline of U.S. Merchant Shipping in the Twentieth Century* (New York: Twayne, 1992); George S. Gibb and Evelyn H. Knowlton, *The Resurgent Years, 1911–1927* (New York: Harper and Brothers, 1956); Evelyn H. Knowlton, Henrietta M. Larson, and Charles S. Popple, *New Horizons, 1927–1950* (New York: Harper and Row, 1971); Bennett H. Wall, C. Gerald Carpenter, and Gene S. Yeager, *Growth in a Changing Environment, 1950–1975* (New York: McGraw-Hill, 1988).

STATE MARITIME ACADEMIES, 1874–present. For over a century the state maritime academies have trained persons to become deck officers and en-gineers aboard ships. The state maritime academies, whose number, mission, and characteristics have changed over time, provide a revealing glimpse not only of the evolution of the merchant marine in the United States but also of the division of functions between the federal and the state governments.

The shortage of American seamen had become acute by the 1870s, and to try to encourage American boys to return to the sea, Congress passed a law in 1874 authorizing the U.S. Navy to lend naval vessels as training ships to any states that decided to establish nautical schools. By this act, Congress began the permanent tradition of having the federal government provide the training ships and some of the instructors for the state institutions. New York, as the shipping center of the United States, promptly established in 1874 its nautical school under the management of the Board of Education of the city. The New York Nautical School received on loan the sloop-of-war *St. Mary's* from the navy, and the vessel served as dormitory, recreation hall, and classroom for the boys, who spent all their time aboard the ship, irrespective of whether the *St. Mary's* was at sea or simply docked. Apparently only a grade school education was required for admission to the two-year program, while the law of 1874 had stipulated that no one could be sentenced to attend as a punishment. All students who graduated qualified as seamen, while the more studious ones went on to take courses elsewhere or to study on their own to prepare for the examinations they had to pass to earn licenses as deck officers (see American Shipmasters' Association).

The other states had not been as quick as New York to take advantage of navy vessels; only in 1889 did Pennsylvania establish its state nautical school, and Massachusetts organized its own in 1891. Because the Massachusetts Nautical Training School received a steam vessel (the cruiser *Enterprise*) from the navy and not just sailing ships like the other schools, Massachusetts was until 1908 the only school able to offer an engineering program. In 1911 Congress passed the first of many laws that authorized the federal government to make annual subsidy payments to each of the nautical schools, in addition to the training ships and the officers that the navy continued to furnish. The federal aid was not enough for the local Board of Education, which refused to provide funding for the New York Nautical School in 1913, and consequently the state government took over the institution, whose new name became the New York State Nautical School.

The three nautical schools dramatically expanded their enrollments to try to meet the labor needs of World War I, but the slump in shipping after 1920 postponed the plans of other states to establish their own nautical schools. The lack of training facilities on the West Coast was acute, and the Pacific American Steamship Association* finally convinced the state government to establish a school in California in 1929. The California State Nautical School changed its name to California Maritime Academy in 1936 and has remained the only institution of its kind on the West Coast. In Maine, the Propeller Club* of Portland vigorously pushed during the 1930s for an institution to train Maine citizens to be merchant marine officers, until in 1941 the legislature established the Maine Nautical Training School. Virginia considered establishing its own maritime academy, but only as part of another "school up in the mountains"; as Congressman Schuyler O. Bland* observed, "It is the most absurd thing I ever saw," and it never did materialize (U.S. Congress, House, 1935).

Gradually the idea gained ground in the 1930s that rather than more state academies, what was needed was a national merchant marine academy run and funded exclusively by the federal government. Proponents of big government eagerly embraced the idea and proposed taking over the state academies and putting them all under the Department of Commerce, and in this way all U.S. citizens, not just those from the coastal states, would have equal access to a maritime education. The defenders of state maritime academies countered that the federal government should not waste money educating people from inland, because "they would soon drift back home" while those "whose homes are near the ports that their ships touch are the ones most likely to continue to follow the sea" (ibid.). A deadlock was reached, and the federal government could not proceed with its plans for a national academy in the 1930s, but fortunately the emergency of World War II allowed the U.S. Maritime Commission* to circumvent the opposition and establish the Merchant Marine Academy* in Kings Point, Long Island, New York. The resulting political and educational compromise nicely balanced federal and state government involvement to provide the students with a wide choice of alternatives for maritime education. Of course, while World War II lasted, the federal government virtually ran the schools and imposed accelerated programs in order to graduate the largest possible number of officials for the wartime emergency.

The acute shipping shortage lasted several years after World War II, but by the late 1940s the gradual decline of U.S.-flag shipping had begun its apparently irreversible course. Meanwhile, the merchant marine had become a much more complex and technically challenging task than before, and the maritime academies had to decide what type of education to provide for the changing and shrinking marketplace. Pennsylvania decided to avoid the problem altogether, and in 1947 the state scuttled its nautical school, abruptly ending a tradition of nearly sixty years and more than 2,000 graduates. Massachusetts began to require in 1919 a high school degree for admission into its nautical school (whose name was changed to Massachusetts Maritime Academy in 1942, when it moved out of Boston), and the rest of the nautical schools gradually accepted this more selective standard. A grammar school education was no longer sufficient, and, more significantly, maritime training was for the first time pushed into the realm of higher education. Slowly the schools began to make the transition from dealing with impressionable "boys" to attracting young adults who were taking conscious decisions about their career choices for life.

The New York State Nautical School was the first to realize that the standard two-year program for training officers simply did not have a future in higher education because of the low status generally associated with degrees from two-year institutions. Expansion was the only answer, and the New York school became the first to acquire extensive shore facilities when it moved to its present location near Fort Schuyler in 1938; subsequently in 1940 the school announced its long-planned decision to begin a three-year program as the next step toward the inevitable four-year program in the future. World War II temporarily suspended these plans, but with the return of peace the school resumed its three-year curriculum in 1946 and in 1948 became the first school to offer a four-year program leading to a bachelor's degree. In 1949 the school, as the newly named New York State Maritime College, joined the recently created State University of New York system and soon after became the first of the maritime academies to gain accreditation as a four-year college.

California tried to catch up with New York, but for the other academies, "merchant marine education is a closed book . . . the tendency is to leave the conduct of these academies to the governing authority of a board of ancient mariners who live in the past and who are not progressive" (Record Group 59). One academy wanted a return to the days of sail, another insisted on running the ship like the navy before 1845, while "two resent any guidance from the federal government, insist on state monopoly, and refuse to develop along modern lines" (ibid.). Progress gradually came as the other state maritime academies moved to four-year programs; for example, the Maine Maritime Academy graduated its first four-year class in 1964. As a next step, the academies proceeded to meet the standards necessary to receive accreditation as institutions of higher learning. An important requirement was to have adequate shore facilities and not just training ships, a particularly challenging task for the Massachusetts Maritime Academy, which had lost all its shore facilities when it moved from Hyannis to its present location in Buzzards Bay in 1949. The cadets resumed the old pattern of living and studying aboard the training ship, until the construction program begun in the 1960s finally provided the academy with dormitories and other buildings on land; in 1974 the Massachusetts Maritime Academy received the indispensable accreditation.

The state maritime academies traditionally applied the strictest military discipline and accepted for admission only single males. The marital requirements were the first to quietly fade, and later the gender barriers also came down. The Maine Maritime Academy admitted its first female student in 1974, and all now have as students a small percentage of women, ranging from a high of 15 percent at the California Maritime Academy to 8 percent at the Massachusetts Maritime Academy. In the tradition of the sea, cadets (as the students generally are called) sometimes earned a not always deserved reputation for "riotous living in foreign cities" when they went abroad on the mandatory cruises in the training ships. Apparently the entry of females as students and faculty has multiplied the number of incidents of sexual improprieties, some of which were lurid enough to catapult the Maine Maritime Academy into television tabloids such as "A Current Affair."

A recurrent task for the academies has been their struggle to secure and preserve federal assistance. The Dwight D. Eisenhower administration was the first to attempt in 1955–1956 to halt all federal support for maritime education, and only a vigorous lobbying campaign convinced Congress to restore the funds. When federal assistance became more generous in the 1960s, two states decided to open their own maritime academies. In 1962 Texas A&M University established as one of its branches the Texas Maritime Academy in Galveston. The new academy was able to draw on the rich resources and traditions of higher education in that state and soon was operating successfully. In the late 1960s the Great Lakes Maritime Academy began to operate on a modest scale in Traverse City, Michigan, with the more limited goal of providing some training for students who would serve only on Great Lakes vessels. The struggles over federal funding resumed under the Ronald Reagan administration, so that no replacements were possible for the training ships, the newest built in 1962 and the oldest in 1940. "Our cadets are being trained on equipment they will never see again. . . . We can't get parts. None are diesel* powered. . . . I think it is a national disgrace" (Commission on Merchant Marine and Defense).

Although the demand for ship officers has proven surprisingly strong, the decline of the U.S. merchant marine was making inroads on enrollment, and the academies devised strategies to survive. The most important was to expand into related areas of the sea, whether the management aspects of shipping or the many fields of marine biology and oceanography. The Maine Maritime Academy acquired a research vessel to conduct oceanographic research, while the California Maritime Academy likewise has branched out into other marine sciences. With these additions to the course offerings, the maritime academies have become more like colleges rather than the military institutions they originally were, and consequently the many students who do not plan to work aboard a merchant vessel no longer find the military discipline useful for their later careers. The Maine and California maritime academies have gone the furthest in accommodating students who want "optional life-styles" different from those of the highly regimented military system. All still maintain some dress code, while the Massachusetts Maritime Academy continues to require that the students wear uniforms every day and participate in traditional military activities such as flag formation.

While the military connection has declined in the academies, the cadets can still follow a naval science program that will qualify them to receive a commission in the naval reserve after graduation, and some cadets may even have the option to serve on active duty in one of the branches of the armed forces, so that the academies still remain a source of military officers. The public, however, has often failed to realize that the state academies continue to provide meaningful functions, and calls to close them altogether have not been lacking. The late 1980s witnessed a move to merge the Massachusetts Maritime Academy with another state university, and the early 1990s saw attempts to abolish altogether the New York Maritime Academy. It would indeed be tragic if the accumulated talent and experience in the state maritime academies and the Merchant Marine Academy were sacrificed because of the blunders the United States has committed in its merchant shipping policy.

References: James M. Aldrich, *Fair Winds—Stormy Seas: 50 Years of Maine Maritime Academy* (Stonington, ME: Penobscot Books, 1991); Commission on Merchant Marine and Defense, *Public Hearings February 1987–July 1987* (Washington, DC:

Government Printing Office, 1987); William B. Hayler, "Our Imperiled State Maritime Academies," *U.S. Naval Institute Proceedings* 98 (1972): 50–57; *Journal of Commerce*, 18 July 1988; Maritime Administration, *Vessel Inventory Report as of July 1, 1992*; Record Group 59, Shipping Policy Files, National Archives, Washington, DC; U.S. Congress, House, Committee on Merchant Marine and Fisheries, *To Develop an American Merchant Marine* (Washington, DC: Government Printing Office, 1935); U.S. Congress, Senate, Committee on Interstate and Foreign Commerce, *Merchant Marine Training and Education* (Washington, DC: Government Printing Office, 1956).

STATES MARINE CORPORATION, 1930–early 1980s. Henry D. Mercer created the States Marine Corporation in 1930, and the next year he brought in Cornelius S. Walsh* as secretary, who later became an investor in the company as well. They did not have enough funds to purchase vessels, so they chartered* foreign-flag tonnage, which they placed wherever there was a demand for cargo space. States Marine operated initially as a tramp* and gradually developed liner* services in more stable routes, but the company always retained the policy of switching ships to whatever routes were more profitable. From the proceeds of each voyage, the owners plowed back profits until at last in 1940–1941 they were able to purchase five U.S.-flag vessels, which, however, were soon after requisitioned for service in World War II.

After the war States Marine bought twenty surplus vessels at low prices from the U.S. Maritime Commission* and continued to charter both U.S. and foreign-flag tonnage. States Marine retained its prewar policy of moving its ships among different routes and trades in order to maximize profits; likewise the company continued to rely on chartered ships to move a large percentage of the cargo, so that the company could easily cut back or expand its fleet as the market demanded. Also, the company was expanding into the bulk* trades, an area where it continued to operate as a tramp. Unlike the other famous nonsubsidized company, Isbrandtsen Line,* States Marine did not engage in costly wars against conferences* and instead joined those that were in its interest and operated as an outsider* in other routes. In perhaps the best example of its international perspective, the company bought in 1947 a controlling interest in the South African Marine Corporation (Safmarine), the national shipping company of South Africa.

States Marine's approach for a while seemed to hold in store the future for U.S. shipping, and as part of its expansion the company began to acquire other firms. In 1954 States Marine took over the management of the Bloomfield Steamship Company* and eventually gained control of this firm, whose name, however, continued in use into the early 1960s for trade purposes. In March 1956 States Marine purchased the Isthmian Steamship Line* from U.S. Steel, an acquisition that hit shipping circles "like a bombshell" partly because it was "the biggest single shipping purchase in memory" (*New York Times*, 7 March 1956). By this transaction States Marine added twenty-four vessels to its fleet and became the largest unsubsidized U.S.-flag firm and came close to challenging in size United States Lines* (USL).

However, the purchase of Isthmian marked a change toward a policy of operating only U.S.-flag vessels. In 1954 States Marine had filled its first application to qualify for subsidies, and the company had purchased the U.S.-flag fleet of Isthmian as a way to bolster its standing to qualify for subsidies. The Maritime Administration* (MARAD) required that States Marine dispose of any foreign-flag holdings as a condition to receive subsidies, and consequently in 1959 the company sold its very profitable 54 percent stake in Safmarine, and the proceeds from this sale were also needed to pay for the loans taken out to buy Isthmian. However, the Committee of American Steamship Lines* (CASL) represented the subsidized companies and conducted an all-out campaign to keep States Marine from joining that very exclusive club, so that the years dragged by without any decision on the subsidy application. As a first step toward disposal of its foreign-flag holdings, States Marine had created in 1959 a separate subsidiary, Global Bulk Transport, to receive all the foreign-flag ships that would continue to be operated until a suitable buyer could be found; the company was regretting the sale of Safmarine and did not wish to suffer any more losses on hasty sales.

Why did States Marine insist on shifting to subsidized U.S.-flag operation? The very stressful and constantly changing challenges of running tramps and liner services across the world were proving exhausting for Mercer and Walsh, who aspired to a more relaxed operation in the subsidized routes. Furthermore, by the 1960s they knew that their aging fleet of World War II vintage had to be replaced, probably by containerships, and they mistakenly believed that operation under subsidies would make the task of vessel replacement easier.

By 1965 it was clear that the member lines of CASL would never allow States Marine to receive subsidies, so that Walsh decided to sell his stake in the company to Mercer and with the proceeds to purchase a subsidized line, Waterman Steamship Corporation.* Walsh was finally operating a subsidized U.S.-flag company, but what about States Marine? Mercer threatened to transfer his remaining U.S.-flag ships to foreign flags if MARAD did not approve the subsidy, but MARAD administrator Nicholas Johnson* merely responded to the ultimatum by noting that it was ''of particular interest.'' States Marine was left with no choice but to continue transferring its vessels to foreign flags, although in 1969 Mercer almost managed to dump the whole problem on the Santa Fe International Corporation, which rashly had made a purchase offer in exchange for $101 million in its stock—but backed down in time.

After a very long life in stressful merchant shipping, Mercer felt he could do no more, and he retired as chairman of States Marine in November 1970. The family and heirs proceeded to gradually liquidate their investment in ships during the 1970s. States Marine was still sailing to Europe in 1971, but increasingly the remaining shipping operations were in the hands of the subsidiary Global Bulk Transport, which still owned in 1975 ten ships with a total of 366,000 deadweight* tons. In 1978 Global Bulk Transport was down to two vessels owned jointly with Republic Steel with a total of 94,000 deadweight tons but by 1982 was no longer listed as an owner, so both Global Bulk and presumably States Marine, long before, had ceased active operations. States Marine had pioneered the daunting road of operating simultaneously both U.S.- and foreign-flag shipping but had failed to make the transition into the bulk trades, like the very successful Overseas Shipholding Company.*

References: *Business Week,* 6 September 1958; Maritime Administration, *Foreign-Flag Merchant Ships Owned by U.S. Companies,* 1975–1982; *New York Times,* 5 January 1954; 7 March 1956, 26 May and 6 September 1959, 3 June 1965, 4 February 1969, 25 November 1970; Official File, Harry S. Truman Presidential Library, Independence Missouri; *Wall Street Journal,* 21 March 1969, 22 July 1971.

STATES STEAMSHIP LINES (SSS), 1921–1979. Charles E. Dant of Portland, Oregon, organized the States Steamship Lines in 1921 to handle his lumber schooners and the Shipping Board* vessels of the Columbia Pacific Steamship Company (CPSS). The CPSS had been created in 1919 to send government-owned vessels from the Columbia River to Europe and later to operate a second line to the Far East. In 1920 Dant gained control of CPSS, which continued to operate the government vessels; however, he placed those ships purchased from the Shipping Board in SSS. By 1928 the name CPSS had been dropped, and SSS remained as the sole owner and operator of steamship vessels.

Under the generous mail contracts, SSS was so successful that it decided to venture into passenger service. The company obtained three passenger-cargo ships from the United Fruit Company* in 1932 and initially operated them profitably. However, the *Morro Castle** disaster had forced the government to raise safety standards considerably, and in 1936 Congress abolished the mail contract system, so that SSS concluded that the cost of remodeling the three ships ruled out any future profits from passenger service and in 1937 returned the vessels to United Fruit Company.

The direct service to Europe had ended by the early 1930s, but SSS continued to operate a profitable Far East service, whose core was the route to the Philippines. Besides the Japanese lines, SSS faced fierce competition from the Dollar Line, which was determined to corner all American shipping in the Pacific Ocean. During World War II the vessels of the SSS were requisitioned by the government but were replaced after the war with surplus vessels. The postwar shipping boom, the Korean conflict, and operating differential subsidies* from the Maritime Administration* kept the company in a satisfactory condition until the late 1950s.

The survival of small companies like SSS was becoming increasingly doubtful as foreign competitors became fiercer, and sensing the danger, in 1954 the Dant family decided to grow by purchasing the Pacific Transport Lines* (PTL), which was merged with SSS in 1957. The World War II vessels were starting to show their age, and SSS placed in 1960 the first orders in its gradual vessel-replacement program; in 1965 the company had received six new Mariners* and in total owned thirteen ships, one of the smallest of the subsidized fleets.

By the late 1960s the container* revolution was beginning, but SSS refused to accept the change and, rather than shifting to containerships, placed orders for the traditional freighters. In the 1970s, as one competitor after another shifted to containers, SSS found itself tied to the dwindling share of break-bulk* cargo. The company finally ordered five Roll on/Roll off* vessels, but never the containerships, and in any case was stuck with a huge investment in the obsolete traditional freighters. The energy crisis of 1973 with its high fuel prices further weakened SSS, which was kept afloat only by cash infusions from the Dant family. A last-minute attempt to find a buyer for SSS in 1978 failed, and the next year SSS went into bankruptcy for eventual liquidation.

References: René De La Pedraja, *The Rise and Decline of the U.S. Merchant Shipping Industry* (New York: Twayne, 1992); Henry S. Marcus, *Planning Ship Replacement in the Containerization Era* (Lexington, MA: Lexington Books, 1974); E. Mowbray Tate, *Transpacific Steam: The Story of Steam Navigation from the Pacific Coast of North America to the Far East and the Antipodes, 1867–1941* (New York: Cornwall Books, 1986).

STEAMBOAT and STEAMSHIP. *Steamboat* and *steamship* were the principal terms used to describe the two main types of vessels driven by steam engines. The word *steamboat* referred to craft in rivers, sounds, bays, or other inland waterways and was the oldest of the two terms. The earliest form of steam travel was in these inland waterways, so consequently when the government established the earliest agency to inspect these vessels, it was called the Steamboat Inspection Service* and retained that title until 1936 in an anachronistic manner, even though long before the majority of its activities involved ocean vessels. For ocean navigation the term *boat* was considered too modest, and instead the loftier term of *steamship* was coined and entered into widespread use. The word *steamer* was often used to refer to both steamboats and steamship during the nineteenth century but gradually came to be reserved principally for the oceangoing steamships. The term *steamboat* started to fall into disuse with the introduction of gasoline and diesel motorboats and largely disappeared after World War II. The word *steamship* has proved more lasting, in part because U.S.-flag ships continued to use the fuel-costly turbine* engines into the 1980s and also because no adequate term has been found in English to refer to the vessels powered by diesels.*

STEAMBOAT INSPECTION SERVICE, 1852–1932. The Steamboat Inspection Service was the first agency of the U.S. government created to supervise the merchant marine, specifically, the inspection of steamships and the certification of officers for the vessels. The origins of the Steamboat Inspection Service dated back to the act of Congress of 7 July 1838, which authorized federal district courts to appoint inspectors to examine steam vessels upon the request of shipowners; the latter paid a flat fee to have each hull or boiler inspected and then declared safe in a certificate. These first inspectors were officers of the court, but as the rapidly growing number of steamships increased the volume of inspections, the need to have a permanent agency under the executive and not the judiciary branch became obvious. Congress agreed, and in the act of 30 August 1852 formally created the Steamboat Inspection Service, composed of nine supervising inspectors appointed by the president with the consent of the Senate. Each of the supervising inspectors had his own territory and within his jurisdiction appointed local inspectors, with the approval of the secretary of the treasury, to examine the vessels and issue certificates of seaworthiness. The inspectors also issued licenses certifying that engineers and officers were competent to handle the steamships. Shipowners and officers greeted the newly created Steamboat Inspection Service with "rather prevalent hostility and opposition" (Short 1922) as needless government interference in a private business, but finally by 1862 they had come to accept the utility of the inspection laws in saving lives and property and had also established by then comfortable and even cozy relationships with their nearest supervising inspector and his local agents.

Although the nine supervising inspectors were required to meet annually as a board to set common rules, in practice the act of 1852 had created nine separate inspection services: "The system is at present without an efficient head . . . a body without a head is a monster, and so likewise is a body with nine heads" (ibid.). Because the secretary of the treasury had only very limited powers over the Steamboat Inspection Service, it was at that time the only government agency not accountable to either the president or a cabinet officer, and as such "the board of supervising inspectors is an anomaly" (ibid.). Congress by the act of 28 February 1871 placed the Steamboat Inspection Service under the secretary of the treasury and created the new position of supervising inspector general, who was appointed by the president with the consent of the Senate. The supervising inspector general now became the chairman of the board of the nine supervising inspectors, who met as a group at least once a year, while its rules and regulations, once approved by the secretary of the treasury, had the force of law. Around the time of the passage of the law, all the supervising inspectors resumed the duty of examining officers and engineers for the purpose of issuing licenses. The Steamboat Inspection Service had suspended license examinations for masters and mates (but not engineers) in 1860, and the service was then provided by the American Shipmasters' Association,* which continued to administer its own exams and issue licenses for masters and mates until 1900, when the Steamboat Inspection Service became the sole authority for licensing all officers on board.

The Marine Engineers' Beneficial Association* (MEBA) became the watchdog organization of the Steamboat Inspection Service after the latter's reorganization in 1871; in particular, MEBA pressured extensively at the national and local level for adequate enforcement of the steamship safety laws. Ferocious political struggles raged over the appointments of the local inspectors, as MEBA, the shipowners, and the politicians tried to impose their favorite candidate.

While the Steamboat Inspection Service could be very lax in enforcing rules, and many inspectors sold licenses to anybody who could pay the fee, the Steamboat Inspection Service was quick to revoke engineers' licenses whenever shipowners wanted to crush any MEBA strike. The appointment of George Uhler, a former president of MEBA, as supervising inspector general in 1903 appeared to have ended the revocation of licenses as an antistrike tactic, but when he stepped down from the job in 1913, the Steamboat Inspection Service resumed its antilabor practices. Only the passage of Hardy Act in 1915 finally recognized the engineers' right to strike without fearing license revocation at the hands of the Steamboat Inspection Service.

The poor results of the Steamboat Inspection Service were evident, and as a way to improve performance, a proposal surfaced in 1882–1883 to transfer all bureaus involved in maritime affairs, including the Steamboat Inspection Service, to a new Bureau of Mercantile Marine in the Navy Department, under the idea that they would function more efficiently under military authority. Congress and the chiefs of the civilian bureaus found repulsive the idea of having an armed branch of the government enforce laws over civilians, and although the proposal died, it reappeared under a modified form in the 1940s. The Steamboat Inspection Service realized its performance had to improve and took measures such as abolishing the charging of fees in 1886 and bringing all employees except the supervising inspectors under the civil service in 1896. An act of Congress of 14 February 1903 transferred the Steamboat Inspection Service from the Treasury Department to the newly created Department of Commerce and Labor, and when the latter split into two departments on 4 March 1913, the Steamboat Inspection Service remained within the Department of Commerce. The already low prestige of the service suffered a major blow when the *General Slocum* burned in the East River, New York, with the loss of 957 persons, mostly women and children, on 15 June 1904. President Theodore Roosevelt appointed a special commission, which laid the blame for the tragedy squarely on the Steamboat Inspection Service and made numerous recommendations to prevent another maritime disaster. Congress accepted the recommendations and passed additional legislation on 3 March 1905; the new changes included paying fixed salaries to the employees, whose pay previously had been determined by the number of vessels inspected: "a substantial premium was thus actually placed on lax inspection" (Thor 1965).

In the 1920s the Steamboat Inspection Service still was not working as an effective agency, and while its small central office in Washington, D.C., depended on other offices of the Department of Commerce for its support services, the supervising inspectors, whose number had increased to eleven and who were still appointed by the president with the consent of the Senate, continued to lord over their respective territories. Essentially the supervising inspector general had no formal powers over the other eleven, while recourse to the always busy secretary of commerce was possible only in the most extreme cases. The result was a "rather unusual scheme of organization and administration" (Short 1922) that gave tremendous freedom at the local level, but as long as the ships were safe and the officers competent, the arrangement lasted, and Congress failed to approve proposals to take the eleven supervising inspectors out of politics by placing them too under civil service.

The Great Depression forced the government to take stringent economy measures. As a way to reduce expenditures, Congress on 30 June 1932 consolidated the Steamboat Inspection Service and the Bureau of Navigation into a new Bureau of Navigation and Steamboat Service, whose name was changed by Congress on 27 May 1936 to the Bureau of Marine Inspection and Navigation.*

Notable Executive

George Uhler   1903–1913

References: *Congressional Record*, 14 December 1928; Lloyd M. Short, *Steamboat Inspection Service: Its History, Activities and Organization* (New York: D. Appleton, 1922); Howard A. Thor, "Trade Unions of Licensed Officers in the Maritime Industry," Ph.D. diss., University of California at Berkeley, 1965; *U.S. Statutes at Large*, vol. 47 (1932); Carroll H. Woody, *The Growth of the Federal Government, 1915–1932* (New York: McGraw-Hill, 1934).

STEAMSHIP SAILORS' PROTECTIVE UNION, 1886–1891. The Steamship Sailors' Protective Union was an excellent example of how the gradual introduction of new technologies could create deep divisions and long-lasting resentments among workers engaged in the same labor tasks. The establishment of the Coast Seamen's Union* (CSU) in San Francisco in 1885 had left out not only those men working aboard sailing vessels in the foreign trade but also all sailors manning steam vessels, whether in the foreign or coastwise* trade. Men of sailing vessels considered steamships sailors not real seamen, and the latter reciprocated the hostility, so that in the United States relations between both groups remained tense from the 1880s into the first decade of the twentieth century. On the West Coast, shipowners were gradually converting their sailing vessels to steam, creating as a by-product the new group of steamship sailors, whose interests were not protected by the CSU. The new steam sailors organized the Steamship Sailors Union in San Francisco in May 1886, and it was soon locked in bitter jurisdiction fights with the CSU, which charged the new organization with being a company union. As more owners shifted to steam, the CSU claimed its members had the right to man the vessels. Andrew Furuseth,* the leader of the CSU, abandoned the attempt to destroy the Steamship Sailors' Union and instead began negotiations in 1889 to combine both unions. Resentment ran deep, and not until 29 July 1891 did Furuseth obtain the agreement that fused the Steamship Sailors' Union and the CSU into the new Sailors' Union of the Pacific* (SUP).

This was not the end of the story, however: the steam sailors still felt ill at ease in the new organization and, taking advantage of several strike setbacks, gradually drifted away from the SUP, so that in 1899 only a handful remained out of the more than a thousand who had joined in 1891. Furuseth put Nick Jortall, the former secretary of the Steamship Sailors' Union, in charge of a new membership drive to bring the steam sailors back to the SUP. The steam sailors were afraid they would be required to pay four or more years of back dues, but the SUP compromised and allowed them to rejoin upon payment of one year's dues. The SUP remained as the sole voice of West Coast sailors, and in any case the start of the twentieth century had made clear to all that steamships had permanently replaced sailing vessels on the seas. The rivalry between both types of sailors had become in reality meaningless, although seamen who had served in sailing vessels at the beginning of their careers continued for decades afterward to consider themselves superior to those who knew only steamships.

References: Stephen Schwartz, *Brotherhood of the Sea: A History of the Sailors' Union of the Pacific, 1885–1985* (New Brunswick, NJ: Transaction Books, 1986); Hyman Weintraub, *Andrew Furuseth: Emancipator of the Seamen* (Berkeley: University of California Press, 1959).

STEAM TURBINES, 1894–1990s. The steam turbine was first used to power a ship in 1894, and turbines pushed the Cunard Liners *Lusitania* and *Mauretania* across the North Atlantic to set new world records of twenty-five knots. It seemed that high speeds had come permanently to ocean transportation and that in just a short time turbines would become universal for marine propulsion. In 1906 the *Creole* was the first ship fitted out with turbines in the United States, and other followed for the passenger trade, most notably, the sister ships the *Harvard** and *Yale** in 1907 and the *Great Northern** and *Northern Pacific** in 1915. However, the early interest in turbines was premature, and in a revealing reversal, the pioneering *Creole* had its turbines replaced by triple-expansion engines* because the latter were more economical for a cargo vessel.

The reason the turbines had failed to gain a more widespread acceptance was their high fuel consumption. In the basic turbine design, high pressure steam from a boiler hit the blades in the turbines, which then rotated at high speed. For generating electricity this design was optimal, but not for turning a propeller that operated best at a lower number of revolutions. Some earlier types of turbines slowed down the steam so that it would not hit the blades as hard and hence produce the lower number of revolutions, but the resulting waste of fuel proved prohibitive. No other way existed to cross the oceans rapidly, so passenger liners driven by the travelers' demand for speed had no choice but to adopt the wasteful steam turbines. Instead, cargo vessels generally were not under such time pressures and relied until after World War I almost exclusively on the triple-expansion engine, which was vastly more economical in fuel consumption but could not attain high speeds.

In the period between the two world wars, engineers continued to try to solve the problem of how to reduce the high speed of the turbine to the low speed of the propellers. A first way was to have the turbine turn a generator, and the electricity then powered a motor whose speed was easily adjusted to the needs of the propeller. The *President Coolidge*,* the *President Hoover*,* the *California*,* the *Pennsylvania*, the *Virginia*, the *Morro Castle*,* and the *Oriente* were some of the combination passenger-cargo liners that used turboelectric propulsion, but by the late 1930s companies ceased to place new orders because it was commercially unsuccessful.

The second way was by improving the reduction gear so that the many revolutions could be reduced to the number suitable for the propeller without an excessive waste of energy; the gradual perfection of the double reduction gear by the late 1930s was instrumental in making the steam turbine the standard propulsion for U.S. ships until the 1980s. The additional electrical equipment in the turboelectric ships proved a costly investment, and consequently United States Lines* (USL) ordered steam turbines for the *America** of 1940. Shortages of turbines forced the installation of triple-expansion engines in many of the ships built in World War II, but after the war all new U.S. ships, whether passenger or cargo, used the steam turbine for propulsion. The oil-guzzling steam turbines put the post–World War II passenger liners at a serious disadvantage: to compete against airplanes, the passengers liners had to travel faster, but this meant increasing fuel consumption and costs. Once permanent jet airline service began across the Atlantic in October 1958, the failure to replace the steam turbine with more efficient diesel engines hastened the withdrawal from service of the obsolete passenger liners.

Aboard freighters the diesel* engine had become the rule in marine transportation, but the United States did not finally move away from steam turbines until the late 1970s, when the energy crisis finally forced the adoption of the fuel-efficient diesel for cargo vessels.

References: *American Shipper*, June, October 1980; Frank O. Braynard, *The Big Ship: The Story of the S.S. United States* (Newport News, Virginia, Mariners' Museum, 1981); Cedric R. Nevitt, ''American Merchant Steamships,'' and John F. Nichols, ''The Development of Marine Engineering,'' in Society of Naval Architects and Marine Engineers, *Historical Transactions, 1893–1943* (Westport, CT: Greenwood Press, 1981); T. W. Van Metre, *Tramps and Liners* (New York: Doubleday, Doran, 1931).

STEERAGE or STEERAGE CLASS. Steerage class referred to the passengers who paid the lowest fare to travel in the worst conditions, originally near the steering mechanism of the ship, hence the word *steerage*, which subsequently applied to a much larger part of the ship. Steerage roughly corresponded to third-class passengers and sometimes applied to a fourth class as well. Not all ships had second class; for example, in the routes of the Pacific Mail Steamship Company* (PMSS) and the Dollar Line,* the word *Asiatic* (in reference to primarily to Chinese and Filipinos) was often used instead of steerage. The overwhelming majority of immigrants coming into the United States from Europe and Asia until World War I were steerage passengers; in spite of the glamour and luxury of first-class travel aboard the transatlantic liners, the real profits for steamship companies came from the persons in steerage class who were stuffed into any corner of the ship and treated in wretched conditions often likened to those of the slave trade. When the United States imposed immigration restrictions in 1920, the flow of immigrants from Europe dried up, and steamship companies were faced with the task of finding a substitute for what previously had been their most profitable source of income. Cargo then assumed a new importance, and to try to replace the wretched immigrants, the companies attempted since the 1920s to increase and improve second-class facilities without raising fares; eventually the companies devised a new ''tourist'' class as a way to lure modestly well-off but not wealthy passengers aboard the liners in a vain attempt to replace the very lucrative steerage trade.

References: René De La Pedraja, *The Rise and Decline of U.S. Merchant Shipping in the Twentieth Century* (New York: Twayne, 1992); Francis E. Hyde, *Cunard and the North Atlantic, 1840–1973* (Atlantic Highlands, NJ: Humanities Press, 1975); Robert J. Schwendinger, *Ocean of Bitter Dreams: Maritime Relations Between China and the United States, 1850–1915* (Tucson: Westernlore Press, 1988).

STONE, M. HEDLEY, 1897–1970. M. Hedley Stone was the treasurer of the National Maritime Union* (NMU) and one of the former communists who had abandoned the party and instead supported Joseph Curran's* drive for personal dictatorship. The switch had taken place in late 1945, when Stone presented his resignation to Curran, on the grounds that fellow communist Frederick ''Blackie'' Myers* was using union funds to build up his political base, and Stone as treasurer did not want the embarrassment of having to expose him. Curran immediately saw the opportunity to strike a fatal blow at Communist party influence over his union and convinced Stone to stay at his job and proceed with the denunciations. The charges were devastating for the Myers faction, which for all practical purposes had been eliminated as a rival; furthermore, Stone's support gave Curran full control over the treasury. Stone continued to denounce former and supposed communists; for example, in the 1950s he was a prosecution witness in the trials of the *Bridges* case.* Stone remained a key element in the autocratic NMU, because just like Curran, the lure of power and wealth had proven irresistible and had replaced any earlier idealism.

References: Joseph P. Goldberg, *The Maritime Story: A Study in Labor-Management Relations* (Cambridge: Harvard University Press, 1958); Helen Lawrenson, *Stranger at the Party: A Memoir* (New York: Random House, 1975).

STRIKE OF 1921. The strike of 1921 was the strike that crushed seamen's unions and kept them powerless until the Big Strike* of 1934. Membership in the International Seamen's Union* (ISU) had swollen during World War I, spreading for the first time to the Atlantic and Gulf, not just the West Coast, the base of the Sailors' Union of the Pacific* (SUP), which traditionally had been the most important union in the ISU. Because freight rates remained high after the war, the unions won easily the 1919 strike, which gave the new union members an exaggerated sense of their power. By January 1921 freight rates had collapsed from the wartime highs, but when the Shipping Board* and the American Steamship Owners' Association* proposed a 15 percent reduction in wages and the end to overtime, the unions balked at any compromise. To stop the mounting losses, the chairman of the Shipping Board, Admiral William Benson, announced that the new wage conditions would go into force for all government-owned vessels on 1 May 1921. President Warren Harding ignored a last-minute appeal by Andrew Furuseth* to arbitrate, so the strike began on 1 May.

While the government wanted to reduce its losses, the private owners saw in the strike the golden opportunity to strike a fatal blow against labor unions. Because many sailors were already unemployed, it was easy for the companies to find scabs to work the ships, but the decisive battle was over the marine engineers, whose participation in the strike kept the ships from sailing. Cleverly, the owners offered a better deal to the Marine Engineers Beneficial Association* (MEBA), and with its defection, the strike was over and the unions had been smashed by 15 June. The Shipping Board stuck to its original intent and put into practice the conditions of the 1 May ultimatum, but the private companies could not resist taking advantage of the victory to dictate worse conditions. Since the Shipping Board was trying to withdraw from the steamship business, the harsh conditions of the private companies became the rule for seamen. The ISU never regained strength after the 1921 strike, while its affiliates, including the once-powerful SUP, could survive only as thinly disguised company unions.

References: Bruce Nelson, *Workers on the Waterfront: Seamen, Longshoremen, and Unionism in the 1930s* (Urbana: University of Illinois Press, 1990); Stephen Schwartz, *Brotherhood of the Sea: A History of the Sailors' Union of the Pacific, 1885–1985* (New Brunswick, NJ: Transaction Books, 1986); Hyman Weintraub, *Andrew Furuseth: Emancipator of the Seamen* (Berkeley: University of California Press, 1959).

SUPERCONFERENCES, 1984–present. Superconferences or ''megaconferences'' have been one result of the Shipping Act of 1984,* which granted them antitrust immunity, but the reasons for their rapid spread lay in an earlier period. At least as early as 1959, shippers* were denouncing superconferences, when liner* companies were trying to reduce the excessive number of conferences* (118 existed in that same year). The Shipping Board* after World War I had spawned not only over 200 new steamship companies but also a large number of conferences, whose number exceeded 100. The majority of the new steamship firms had disappeared by the late 1930s, but consolidating the conferences, most covering the trade of only one U.S. port or a very specific trade route, exposed the companies, at the least, to cumbersome legal proceedings.

In the 1950s the liner* companies began to combine the conferences in a process whereby the same staff, often the same official, handled the affairs of several conferences, in one case as many as fifteen conferences. In this way the individual conferences could join these emerging ''superconferences,'' which provided for coordinated action among the members. At the same time changes in transportation technology, most notably, containers,* had finished making the old conferences largely obsolete, and liner companies were waiting for the opportunity to make the conference system conform in law to the new economic and technological realities.

The Shipping Act of 1984 authorized "interconference agreements" and thus apparently without intention provoked a wave of amalgamations. All the functions of the previous conferences were absorbed by the new superconferences, which now covered a larger geographic area (e.g., the entire U.S. East Coast rather than specific ports as before). The Shipping Act of 1984 had also extended antitrust immunity to shippers' associations,* which were supposed to balance the "interconference agreements," whose proliferation, however, has vastly outstripped that of the shippers' associations. Because superconferences eliminated the possibility of competition between conferences serving neighboring areas, shippers denounced the superconferences "as nothing more than Goliath-type cartels that will require some strong Davids in Congress to eradicate . . . conferences have finally revealed what they truly represent" (Advisory Commission 1992). In 1992 the liner companies kept the Advisory Commission on Conferences in Ocean Shipping from making any recommendations against the superconferences, and in any case it was not clear how Congress could try to turn the clock back to the vanished conference system of the 1920s.

References: Advisory Commission on Conferences in Ocean Shipping, *Report to the President and the Congress* (Washington, DC: Government Printing Office, 1992); Federal Maritime Commission, *Section 18 Report on the Shipping Act of 1984*, September 1989.

SVENSKA **CASE or** *SVENSKA* **STANDARD** *(Federal Maritime Commission v. Aktiebolaget Svenska Amerika Linien).* In this 1968 decision of the *Svenska* case, the Supreme Court upheld the general principle that dual-rate contracts* were "contrary to the public interest" unless the ocean carrier or the conference could show there was an overwhelming need for such practices. The Court had shifted the burden of proof to the carriers and the conferences, and not surprisingly "there has been a chilling effect on the number filed with the Federal Maritime Commission"* (Advisory Commission 1992). The *Svenska* standard prevented U.S. steamship companies from using the dual-rate system to try to remedy their worsening situation, but in the trade routes beyond U.S. jurisdiction foreign companies continued to sign dual-rates contracts. Only with the Shipping Act of 1984* was a way found around the *Svenska* standard, as the new law created the legal instrument of the service contract.* However, the "public interest" standard of *Svenska* was not completely buried and briefly reappeared in arguments of early 1992, when Philadelphia tried to make the North Atlantic conferences preserve its status as an alternate port of call.

References: Advisory Commission on Conferences in Ocean Shipping, *Report to the President and the Congress* (Washington, DC: Government Printing Office, 1992); *American Shipper*, January 1992.

T

T-2 TANKER. The T-2 tanker was the most famous and numerous tanker type ever built in the world, and its significance has resided in two factors. The T-2 tanker was one of the vessel types designed by the U.S. Maritime Commission* and formed a major part of the crash shipbuilding program of World War II. The T-2 tanker of 16,600 deadweight* tons was 514 feet long and had a beam of 68 feet; it had a draft of 30 feet and a speed of 14.5 knots; one type of T-2s, the thirty-four Mission tankers (so-named after California missions) had the very high speed for a nonpassenger ship of 16.5 knots. The U.S. Maritime Commission mass produced 481 in 1942–1945 as part of its emergency program, and the tankers were one of the decisive factors contributing to the Allied victory in World War II.

The T-2s became the basis of the world tanker fleet for nearly twenty years, and because they had been so numerous that almost every country, company, and route in the world had some T-2s in operation, these tankers acquired a second significance as a measurement for tanker capacity. In tanker circles the expression ''T-2 equivalent tankers,'' generally shortened to T-2s and more recently referred to as ''standard tankship,'' became the basic unit for measuring and calculating tanker volumes and rates, as the equivalent of 16,600 deadweight tons. Long after the last of the T-2s finally left service, they have continued to exist in the minds of the personnel who keep the oil flowing across the oceans.

References: John A. Culver, *Ships of the U.S. Merchant Fleet*, rev. ed. (Weymouth, MA: Denison Press, 1965); Walter W. Jaffee, *The Last Mission Tanker* (Sausalito, CA: Scope, 1990); Frederick C. Lane, *Ships for Victory: A History of Shipbuilding Under the U.S. Maritime Commission in World War II* (Baltimore: Johns Hopkins University Press, 1951); Paul Stevens, ed., *Oil and Gas Dictionary* (New York: Nichols, 1988); U.S. Congress, Senate, Committee on Interstate and Foreign Commerce, *Merchant Marine*

Study and Investigation, 7 vols. (Washington, DC: Government Printing Office, 1949–1950).

TACOMA ORIENTAL STEAMSHIP COMPANY, 1928–1936. When the Dollar family purchased the five passenger-cargo ships of the American Mail Line* from the Shipping Board* in 1926 and subsequently moved the company's home office from Seattle to San Francisco, Washington state interests were outraged at the loss of local control. However, the American Mail Line still operated seven government-owned freighters, and when these came on sale in 1928, powerful lobbying by the Northwest delegation to the U.S. Congress convinced the Shipping Board to accept the bid of the newly organized Tacoma Oriental Steamship Company* rather than that of the Dollar family.

The Tacoma Oriental Steamship Company, whose owners were Tacoma and Seattle businessmen, received a splendid ten-year mail subsidy to provide service to the Far East. The owners placed the management of the vessels in the experienced hands of the States Steamship Lines* (SSS), and in the first two years the Tacoma Oriental Steamship Company was a profitable service. However, R. Stanley Dollar* had never accepted this upstart company, and when the onset of the Great Depression lowered cargo volumes in the routes of the Dollar Line,* he decided to place six of his freighters in direct competition with the ships of the Tacoma Oriental Steamship Company. The owners of the Tacoma Oriental Steamship Company saw losses pile up and began to sell their stock until by 1931 Dollar controlled the majority of the shares. In 1932 he had the American Mail Line take full control of the company (SSS promptly lost its management contract), and it seemed that Dollar had lived up to his reputation as the shipping octopus of the Pacific Coast.

Dollar's vaunted empire was tottering, however, and already in 1931 he had requested from the Shipping Board a moratorium for the debts of the Dollar Line and the American Mail Line. In the shaky Dollar conglomerate, the Tacoma Oriental Steamship Company was the weakest link, and it was the first company to seek bankruptcy and cease operations in 1936. Its ships were sold, and the company was dissolved in 1937, but this had just been the opening act in the collapse of the Dollar shipping empire.

References: John Niven, *The American President Lines and Its Forebears, 1848–1984* (Newark: University of Delaware Press, 1987); E. Mowbray Tate, *Transpacific Steam: The Story of Steam Navigation from the Pacific Coast of North America to the Far East and the Antipodes, 1867–1941* (New York: Cornwall Books, 1986).

TAYLOR, FRANK J., 1883–7 May 1958. Frank J. Taylor was the first president of the American Merchant Marine Institute* (AMMI) and was largely responsible for its initial success. Taylor was born in New York City in 1883; he was orphaned at the early age of seven and was adopted by the Taylor couple, whose family name he kept as his own. He finished elementary school and began to work at age twelve and soon was working in the shipyards of New York

City. He soon found his true interest in politics and beginning in 1912 had himself elected to positions in city government, culminating with his election as controller in 1934. His bid for reelection to that job failed, and in 1938 he decided to become the last president of the American Steamship Owners' Association* (ASOA), at that moment torn by dissention among factions.

Taylor ended the strife and in June 1938 convinced the members to change the name of the organization to the American Merchant Marine Institute, whose first president he became. As a Democrat, Taylor was quite effective in dealing with government officials of the Democratic administrations in Washington, D.C. Taylor's skills as a politician also provided invaluable in keeping the membership of AMMI working harmoniously, particularly during the turbulent years of the National Federation of American Shipping* (NFAS). In late 1951 Taylor retired and was replaced as president of AMMI by Walter E. Maloney, who had worked closely with Taylor as the organization's chief attorney for years. Taylor died in New York on 7 May 1958.

References: *New York Times*, 8 May 1958; *Who's Who in the Maritime Industry 1946*.

TELEVISION. See movies.

TENNEY, EDWARD DAVIES, 26 January 1859–29 April 1934. From 1917 to 1927 Tenney was the president of Matson Navigation Company.* In spite of the long term of his office, he was essentially a transitional figure between the founder, Captain William Matson,* and the dynamic third president, William P. Roth.* Upon Matson's death, Tenney, as the representative of the major stockholder Castle and Cooke, was elected president on 25 October 1917, but William P. Roth was also elected vice president at the same time, and the latter gradually assumed a growing control over the daily management of Matson. As Tenney became older, he preferred to devote most of his time and efforts to the sugar and real estate operations of Castle and Cooke, whose presidency he had held since 1916. Full control of Matson passed to Roth on 13 May 1927, when Tenney became its chairman of the board, a mainly honorific position he held until his death on 29 April 1934.

References: *National Cyclopedia of American Biography*, vol. 36; Fred A. Stindt, *Matson's Century of Ships* (Modesto, CA: n.p., 1982); William L. Worde, *Cargoes: Matson's First Century in the Pacific* (Honolulu: University of Hawaii Press, 1981).

TEU. TEU stands for twenty-foot equivalent units and is a measurement for containers;* for example, the Econships* of United States Lines* (USL) had a capacity of 4,482 TEUs. The containers were eight feet high by eight feet wide, but for length a variety of sizes remained necessary to handle diverse cargo. Common container lengths were ten, twenty, thirty-five, and forty feet, but of these the twenty-foot length was the most widely used. A measurement was needed to quickly describe the capacity of containerships, and already by the late 1970s the TEU was in widespread use. For twenty-foot containers, the TEU is simply their number; to obtain the TEU of other sizes, the number of containers is multiplied by their length, and the result is divided by twenty. As examples, ten twenty-foot containers have ten TEUs, while five forty-foot containers also have ten TEUs. See also FEU.

References: *Jane's Freight Containers*, 1986 or other annual issues; Lane C. Kendall, *The Business of Shipping*, 5th ed. (Centreville, MD: Cornell Maritime Press, 1986).

TEXTRON, INC., 1956–1959. Textron Inc., a large modern corporation, was the third company that attempted to challenge the Matson Navigation Company* in the Hawaii-California route. Textron lacked experience in the field, but a group of steamship people agreed to run the operation; to earn high profits effortlessly, all Textron had to do was provide the bulk of the capital for the Hawaiian Steamship Company, which was incorporated in 1956. The promoters did not burden Textron with inconvenient historical facts such as the failure of the previous challengers, the Los Angeles Steamship Company* and the Pacific Transport Lines.*

The Hawaiian Steamship Company bought the passenger liner *La Guardia* from American Export Lines,* and the ship, renamed the *Leilani*, made its first voyage in the Los Angeles-Honolulu run on 5 February 1957; two chartered* freighters completed the company's service to Hawaii. The Hawaiian Steamship Company piled up incredible losses, and Textron, to save some of its investment, repossessed the *Leilani* and the two charters; these three ships then became in December 1957 the assets of a new company, Textron Hawaiian, which was operated directly by Textron.

After one year of direct hands-on experience in the Hawaiian trade, Textron decided to leave the steamship business and write off its investments in Textron Hawaiian as a loss. "We have decided to stay in business where we are successful," explained the president of Textron (*New York Times*, 7 January 1959). The charters of the two freighters were allowed to lapse, while the *Leilani* was repossessed by the Maritime Administration* and subsequently resold to the American President Lines* for operation as the *President Roosevelt*.

References: Frederick E. Emmons, *American Passenger Ships* (Newark: University of Delaware Press, 1985); *New York Times*, 7, 14 January 1959.

TITANIC, 1912. The *Titanic*, the second of the trio of ships built by the International Mercantile Marine* (IMM) for transatlantic crossings, suffered one of the worst disasters in maritime history. To meet the competition from the German liners and, in particular, those of Cunard, the British-flag White Star Line, the main subsidiary of the U.S.-owned IMM, ordered the *Olympic*, the *Titanic*, and the *Gigantic* from shipyards in the United Kingdom. The *Olympic* entered service in 1911 and was followed by the *Titanic* in 1912, while the *Gigantic* (whose name was later changed to the less arrogant *Britannic*) was expected in 1914. While Cunard had emphasized the speed of the *Lusitania* and the *Mauretania*, IMM for public relations purposes stressed the luxury and comfort aboard its vessels, but by the time the *Titanic* entered service, J. Bruce Ismay, the president of the White Star Line, belatedly realized that passengers preferred speed over luxury. To try to minimize negative consequences, he was determined to drive the *Titanic*, at least on her maiden voyage, to the maximum of the engines' capability.

Unlike the *Lusitania* and the *Mauretania*, whose 25-knot speed was made possible by steam turbines,* which wasted a tremendous amount of energy, the *Titanic* used the more economical triple-expansion engines* for two of its propellers, while a steam turbine connected to the third propeller gave the vessel an extra push. The vessel's normal cruising speed was 21 knots, but she could do 22 knots, and on the night of the fatal accident was making 22.5 knots.

To try to catch up with the competition, IMM also emphasized the safety of the ship, and when a shipbuilding journal stated that the watertight compartments made the ship "practically unsinkable," the public relations experts stressed only the "unsinkable" in the publicity campaigns. In reality the vessel lacked double sides or even a double bottom,* and although the latter would have been useless in this accident, the former could possibly have saved the *Titanic* and at the very least most of those aboard.

The *Titanic* began her maiden voyage to New York on 10 April 1912; aboard the ship was not only Ismay himself but also a celebrity crowd drawn from the richest and wealthiest families in the United States and Great Britain; for Ismay, whose management of the White Star Line was already under question by the American stockholders, it was imperative that the ship make a media splash upon both departure and arrival in order to draw away passengers from the Cunard liners. When telegraph reports of icebergs ahead poured in with alarming frequency, Ismay persuaded the captain not to shift course to the warmer waters to the south because this would mean a longer voyage; instead Ismay convinced the captain to increase power to cross at the fastest speed possible the iceberg-infested waters (but without posting any special lookouts), so that the ship would arrive ahead of schedule at New York and thereby guarantee favorable publicity.

At 11:40 P.M. on 14 April 1912, at last a lookout detected an iceberg in front of the ship, and although the bridge gave orders to change course, not enough time was left to turn away, and the *Titanic* struck the iceberg. The high-speed collision flooded six of the watertight compartments, when according to specifications the ship could expect to remain afloat with a maximum of four flooded compartments. The exact nature of the damage caused by the iceberg cannot yet be determined because the underwater cameras of today can observe the top of the sunken ship but not the damaged bow side buried in the mud of the ocean floor. It appears that only double sides (very rare at the time) could have saved the ship, or at least slowed down the sinking (by preventing the flooding of one or two more compartments), thereby gaining time for the *Carpathia* to arrive and rescue the passengers. The latest study in 1993 finds brittle steel a major culprit, and claims that the iceberg did not rip a gash in the hull, but instead the steel plates broke under the impact of the crash; presumably a different grade of steel would have prevented the flooding of so many watertight compartments and gained time for rescue vessels to reach the *Titanic* before she sank.

Whatever the exact explanation, the ship was doomed, and the captain sent the SOS distress signal by wireless radio still in its infancy, so that the freighter *California*, probably no more than a half hour's steaming time away, had turned off her radio equipment for the night. The old Cunard liner *Carpathia* did receive the message, but she was over four hours' steaming time away even when driving her old engines beyond their maximum capacity. The rest of what followed aboard the *Titanic* captured the public imagination and has formed subject matter not only for articles and books but also for many movies* and television shows. For the 2,206 persons aboard, the lifeboats had space only for 1,178, but a bungled evacuation because of the lack of drills on the part of the crew and passengers rendered useless many of the lifeboats, while survival in the icy sea was impossible. The *Titanic* sank at 2:20 A.M., and about two hours later the *Carpathia* arrived to rescue the 703 persons on the lifeboats.

The *Carpathia* took the passengers to New York City and returned the lifeboats of the *Titanic*, all that was left of the doomed ship, to the White Star Line. The captain of the *Titanic* bravely went down with his ship, but Ismay himself escaped alive to witness a publicity spectacle bigger than any he could have imagined. Thoroughly disgraced, Ismay was removed from all positions in the White Star Line and IMM. Costly litigation ensued, but IMM managed to avoid the large payments that in any case would have bankrupted the company. The advantages of foreign-flag ownership and multiple corporate layers became obvious, because since the *Titanic* flew the British flag and had a British crew, its American ownership was easily hidden and thus diverted attention away from IMM, whose problems were more than compounded by the loss of the *Titanic*. IMM could not match the weekly sailings of Cunrad with vessels of comparable size and comfort, and was left only with the single *Olympic*, while the *Britannic* was not delivered until 1914. IMM could continue running older liners, but Cunrad had clearly won the the struggle for supremacy on the North Atlantic. Worse, because of the *Titanic* loss IMM was not able to participate in the record shipping profits of 1912, thereby weakening the financial position of the company, which drifted into bankruptcy when World War I began.

The *Titanic* disaster did produce changes, because at last governments adopted comprehensive measures to protect the lives and the cargo aboard ships. The La Follette Seamen's Act of 1915* included a large number of safety requirements for ocean vessels, while the Safety of Life at Sea Conventions* (SOLAS) established international standards for the protection of lives and property at sea. In the United States the Steamboat Inspection Service* and the American Bureau of Shipping* assumed the task of certifying that the U.S.-flag vessels met the required safety standards. Not until the *Morro Castle* in 1934 did the United States face a comparable maritime disaster.

References: James Bisset, *Tramps and Ladies: My Early Years in Steamers* (New

York: Criterion Books, 1959); René De La Pedraja, *The Rise and Decline of U.S. Merchant Shipping in the Twentieth Century* (New York: Twayne, 1992); John Maxtone-Graham, *The Only Way to Cross* (New York: Macmillan, 1972); *New York Times*, 17 September 1993; Milton H. Watson, *Disasters at Sea: Every Ocean-Going Passenger Ship Catastrophe Since 1900* (Northamptonshire, England: Patrick Stevens, 1987).

TRAILER MARINE TRANSPORT (TMT) 1954–present. Trailer Marine Transport (TMT) has provided Roll-on/Roll-off* (Ro/Ro) service between Puerto Rico and mainland United States, and since the 1980s has also established branch routes from Puerto Rico to the Dominican Republic, other islands in the Caribbean, and Colombia. TMT was organized in September 1954 and began service to Puerto Rico with surplus Landing Ship Tanks (LSTs); although the demand for trailer service to Puerto Rico was growing, the company fell into bankruptcy in 1957. TMT continued to operate under the protection of the Federal District Court of Miami, and although the company earned small annual profits, TMT was never able to work itself out of receivership.

In 1971 Thomas B. Crowley* decided to send many of his idle tugs and barges of the Alaska trade to try to earn some money in Puerto Rico, and he organized Caribe Hydro-Trailer (inspired after his Alaska Hydro-Train*) to compete against TMT. Crowley soon found that TMT, in spite of its older equipment, had a very loyal following of shippers* who felt Crowley had just showed up to make some quick profits and then abandon the island as other shipowners had done before. In 1972 Crowley found a better business alternative in leasing some equipment to TMT, and consequently he disbanded Caribe Hydro-Trailer.

Even with the new equipment TMT could still not extricate itself from receivership, and finally in 1974 Crowley decided to buy the bankrupt company, settle all its pending accounts, and invest funds to make TMT into a major carrier. Crowley made the barges of TMT double-decked and later triple-decked and also lengthened them to handle the growing volume of traffic, so that by the late 1970s, TMT was the largest Ro/Ro operator in the Caribbean. In 1988 TMT was operating nine monster Ro/Ro barges as well as two trailer ships on the Puerto Rico–U.S. mainland trade. Smaller feeder barges provided service from Puerto Rico to the Dominican Republic, Haiti, and other islands in the Caribbean, as well as to Colombia. Under Crowley management, TMT has pushed into innovative uses of barges as a way to transport speedily growing volumes of trailers at low rates, thereby opening previously unsuspected possibilities in merchant shipping for the combination of tugs and giant barges.

References: *American Shipper*, May 1990, May 1992; "Celebrating a Century of Service," *Journal of Commerce*, 5 August 1992; "Crowley Maritime Corporation," Special Supplement, *Journal of Commerce*, 1988; *Florida Journal of Commerce*, December 1974; *Moody's Transportation Manual 1958*.

TRAMPS or TRAMP VESSELS, 1880–present. Tramps have been the most direct manifestation of the market mechanism at work in ocean shipping, because they chased around the world from port to port scrounging whatever cargoes were available to fill their holds. If a sudden demand for vessel space materialized in a certain port or country, the tramps rushed to that place in order to benefit from the higher rates, while when business was slow the tramps must accept rates below costs just to move the ship nearer to more lucrative cargo offerings. The tramps revealed the ceaseless interplay of demand and supply, and they also charged what the market would bear; often, however, tramps have been older and slower vessels that have not always been maintained in top condition.

While liner* service for high-value cargoes appeared with the compound engine* in the late 1860s, for ores, grains, and coal—all bulk* commodities that did not require fast delivery schedules—iron sailing vessels remained a slower and more economical alternative. The tramps really appeared with the introduction of the triple-expansion engine* after 1880. Steamers at last could compete for bulk cargoes with iron sailing vessels, whose replacement had become inevitable by the 1900s.

The tramp steamers not only could chase after any cargoes throughout the world, but upon reaching a port, the captain received by telegraph messages of where the demand for vessel space was greatest. The news might be old by then, but the introduction of the wireless telegraph in the 1910s allowed constant communication with the captain and solidly established the tramp vessels as another essential element in the world shipping of the twentieth century. While the vessel was on the high seas, a shipper* negotiated with a ship broker,* and the tramp was easily diverted to pick up merchandise in a certain port, and by the time this load was delivered, the vessel was already booked to pick up cargoes somewhere else.

The attitude of liner firms to the tramps has remained relatively unchanged since the nineteenth century: "They are like flies around a lump of sugar . . . that travel around preying on any decent business that any man has. If you have got a good business the tramp will come along and spoil it. . . . They prey upon anybody and everybody" (U.S. Congress 1890). The introduction of faster and better liner services in the twentieth century has led to occasional but false predictions about the demise of the tramps, whose activities have remained vital to world transportation.

References: René De La Pedraja, *The Rise and Decline of U.S. Merchant Shipping in the Twentieth Century* (New York: Twayne, 1992); Grover G. Huebner, *Ocean Steamship Traffic Management* (New York: D. Appleton, 1920); Lane C. Kendall, *The Business of Shipping*, 5th ed. (Centreville, MD: Cornell Maritime Press, 1986); U.S. Congress, House, Committee on Merchant Marine and Fisheries, *American Merchant Marine in the Foreign Trade*, Report No. 1210, 51st Congress, 1st Session, 1890.

TRANS-ATLANTIC AGREEMENT (TAA), 1992–present. The Trans-Atlantic Agreement has been the biggest of the superconferences* to have emerged after the passage of the Shipping Act of 1984.* The Federal Maritime

Commission* (FMC), in a precedent-setting move, authorized TAA to begin functioning on 31 August 1992. The new agreement replaced the two previous superconferences in the North Atlantic, the North Europe-U.S.A. Rate Agreement* (NEUSARA) and U.S.A.-North Europe Rate Agreement* (USANERA). Ship lines saw in TAA a way to raise rates in order to offset the heavy losses in those overtonnaged routes, and even the FMC realized that without higher rates only a few firms would survive, and a near-monopoly situation could not possibly be favorable to shippers.* In other innovations, TAA required that shippers carry an annual minimum of 250 twenty-foot equivalent units or TEUs* in order to qualify for service contracts.* As a way to raise income, the tariff system for the rates also placed a price on each specific service: "just as a restaurant reaps greater returns when diners order a la carte, so too should TAA's member lines"—whose plans did not include offering "a lot of blue plate specials" (*American Shipper*, January 1993).

The members of TAA in 1993 were:

Atlantic Container Line	Neptune Orient Line
Cho Yang Shipping Company	Nippon Yusen Kaisha
DSR/Senator Joint Service	Orient Overseas Container Line
Hapag-Lloyd	P&O Containers
Mediterranean Shipping Company	Polish Ocean Line
A. P. Moller-Maersk Line	Sea-Land*
Nedlloyd Lines	

TAA had such great success in raising rates, that two lines, Neptune Orient Line and Nippon Yusen Kaisha, originally not among the founding members in 1992, joined the superconference in March 1993, and some of the independents* still outside may well join as well. While the FMC has continued to monitor carefully TAA, the European regulatory body (the Commission of the European Communities) has so far declined to give its formal approval to TAA. European shippers almost succeeded in securing a halt to TAA's continued operation, and while the shipowners mounted their own aggressive lobbying campaign, as of December 1993 the final outcome was still in doubt. It was indeed ironic that Europe, throughout its history more receptive to conferences,* should have revived the antitrust fears traditionally an obsession of the United States.

References: *American Shipper*, October 1993, January, June, December 1993; Federal Maritime Commission, *31st Annual Report, Fiscal Year 1992* (Washington, DC: Government Printing Office, 1993).

TRANSPACIFIC FREIGHT CONFERENCE OF JAPAN (TPFCJ). See Japan Atlantic & Gulf Conference (JAG)

TRANSPACIFIC WESTBOUND RATE AGREEMENT (TWRA), 1985–present. The collapse of the Pacific Westbound Conference* (PWC) in 1984 led the member lines to combine in its trade route with those of other six conferences into a new superconference,* the Transpacific Westbound Rate Agreement (TWRA), which originally included nineteen ocean carriers. Because TWRA covered all trade from the United States to Asia, including Japan, the Asia jurisdiction of the conference was broader than the eastbound counterpart, the North America Rate Agreement* (ANERA), which did not cover cargoes moving east from Japan.

Since 1989 TWRA has pioneered a novel form a service contract,* which "is unique in that rate structures, service schedules, and rules governing these provisions are set forth in individual appendices to the contract, each of which applies to a particular carrier member" (Advisory Commission 1992). In 1990 TWRA extended its authority to cover cargoes moving from the United States to Bangladesh, Burma, India, Pakistan, and Sri Lanka; however, by the end of the year its membership was down to eight lines, the same companies that also belonged to ANERA.

References: Advisory Commission on Conferences in Ocean Shipping, *Report to the President and the Congress* (Washington, DC: Government Printing Office, 1992); *American Shipper*, November, December 1984, January, December 1990; Federal Maritime Commission, *Section 18 Report on the Shipping Act of 1984*, September 1989.

TRIPLE-EXPANSION ENGINE, 1881–1960s. The introduction of the triple-expansion engine in 1881 brought the ship's reciprocating steam engine to its highest level of fuel efficiency. The compound engine* had introduced the principle of recycling the exhaust steam; the goal was to convert as much as possible of the steam to motion before it was lost as useless heat through the walls of the engine. The compound engine had achieved a twofold improvement in fuel economy by adding a larger low-pressure cylinder to harness the exhaust steam from the small high-pressure cylinder but had still not achieved sufficient efficiency to challenge iron sailing vessels in the bulk* trades. The triple-expansion engine was the logical next step, with a third cylinder added to receive the exhaust steam from the second intermediate-pressure cylinder; the third cylinder was the largest in size but the lowest in pressure.

Further experiments tried to improve the triple-expansion engine, and in one variation two cylinders of the same size received the exhaust steam from the second cylinder. Soon, however, the triple-expansion engine was recognized as the culmination of that particular system of obtaining motion to drive a ship's propeller. The economy in fuel consumption and the simplicity of the engine explain its long duration in the world's sea-lanes. Its fuel efficiency finally displaced the iron sailing vessels from the carriage of bulk* cargoes, the last refuge of sail. The triple-expansion engine pushed speeds permanently past the ten-knot mark, but fourteen knots was generally the maximum so that fast passenger liners wishing to travel at twenty knots or more needed a different system of marine propulsion. For cargo vessels, the triple-expansion engine remained widespread in world shipping until the 1950s, and their extreme economy means that they are still in use in many of the poorer corners of the world. See also marine propulsion.

References: Gerald S. Graham, "The Ascendancy of the Sailing Ship, 1850–1885," *Economic History Review* 9 (1956):74–88; Edwin P. Harnack, ed., *All About Ships & Shipping*, 11th ed. (London: Faber and Faber, 1964); John F. Nichols, "The Development of Marine Engineering," in Society of Naval Architects and Marine Engineers, *Historical Transactions, 1893–1943* (Westport, CT: Greenwood Press, 1981); T. W. Van Metre, *Tramps and Liners* (New York: Doubleday, Doran, 1931).

TURBINES. See Steam Turbines.

TUXEDO UNIONISM. Tuxedo unionism consists of labor leaders' dressing themselves in the most exquisite clothes available in order to show off their newly found wealth and position. Clothes were only one of the visible aspects of tuxedo unionism, which generally also included chauffeur-driven limousines and a retinue of armed followers. Any union that had fallen into tuxedo unionism inevitably was run by a dictator who controlled the rank and file through sham elections and gangs of armed thugs. Links with the mob, racketeers, and the criminal underworld were another inevitable sequel. Unfortunately for the American labor movement, tuxedo unionism has repeatedly surfaced throughout the twentieth century with distressing frequency, although since the late 1980s tuxedo unionism has no longer been evident.

The International Longshoremen's Association* (ILA) has been a bastion of tuxedo unionism, but nonmaritime unions, in particular the Teamsters, have also suffered the same problem. Labor leaders sometimes avoided wearing the tuxedo to disguise the true nature of their autocratic control; such was the case with Harry Lundeberg* of the Sailors' Union of the Pacific* (SUP), who continued to dress as a sailor and relished participating in the violent street clashes but who lived in splendor in one of the best neighborhoods of San Francisco. Among maritime unions, intellectualism and middle-class origins have been anathema to the rank and file, who have generally preferred leaders with working-class background. The results at best have been white-shirt sailors,* but all too often a passion for social climbing and nouveau rich behavior degenerated into tuxedo unionism.

References: Howard Kimeldorf, *Red or Rackets? The Making of Radical and Conservative Unions on the Waterfront* (Berkeley: University of California Press, 1988); Bruce Nelson, *Workers on the Waterfront: Seamen, Longshoremen, and Unionism in the 1930s* (Urbana: University of Illinois Press, 1990); Maud Russell, *Men Along the Shore: The ILA and Its History* (New York: Brussel and Brussel, 1966).

U

ULCC or ULTRALARGE CRUDE CARRIERS. ULCC has been the abbreviation used to refer to the largest oil tankers in existence, those over 320,000 or 350,000 deadweight* tons. The upper limit was set by the largest tankers afloat, which have reached 550,000 deadweight tons. The driving force toward the construction of these monster tankers was the same as for the smaller very large crude carriers (VLCCs*): the larger the tanker, the lower the operating costs per barrel of oil, what was called "economies of scale." In the case of tankers, bigger appeared to be better, but limitations already present for the VLCCs have so far halted the rush to even bigger ULCCs. The economies of scale worked to the maximum only if the tanker was fully loaded, so that they could be used only in routes moving large amounts of crude. With such behemoths, the problem of the depth or draft of the ports posed another restriction, and even if enough channels were widened, deepened, and maintained, not too many countries had that amount of capital ready to invest. For some ports the ULCC has to pump its oil offshore through a pipeline or to another smaller tanker, with a corresponding loss of benefits. In the late 1970s Daniel Ludwig* had planned to build million-ton tankers, but he later abandoned the idea. There was only so much demand and room for the monster ULCCs, and the majority of the world's oil travels aboard VLCCs and tankers in the range of 45,000 to 159,000 deadweight tons.

UNITED AMERICAN LINES, 1920–1926. For a brief period in 1920–1922, United American Lines was not only the largest U.S.-flag merchant fleet but also one of the biggest in the world. United American Lines was the first independent business venture of W. Averell Harriman, the son of railroad magnate Edward H. Harriman, and Averell was determined to make himself known on his own right and not just as a reflection of his father. Harriman had gone into the steamship business through shipbuilding: the shortage of ships had convinced him in January 1917 to buy the Chester, Pennsylvania, shipyard that had belonged to the naval entrepreneur John Roach, and after U.S. entry into World War I in April, he also assumed the management of another new shipyard for the government. When World War I abruptly ended in November 1918, Harriman was among the many who wanted to operate his own fleet of merchant vessels. His ambition was more far-reaching than that of most others, however, because he visualized a maritime conglomerate combining ship operations with shipbuilding, engineering, financing, and insurance, all not as ends in themselves but as a means to enter successfully into international trade.

Harriman first bought old, established U.S. flag firms, starting with American-Hawaiian Steamship Company* (AHSS) in April 1919 and the Coastwise Transportation Company, which operated ten colliers* along the East Coast. While the firms were valuable acquisitions, they were only a start for his shipping empire: to try to obtain the expertise and contacts in foreign trade, he went to Germany and negotiated in April 1920 an agreement with the Hamburg-America, the powerful pre–World War I German line whose ships had all been confiscated by the Allies. The young, inexperienced Harriman was bamboozled by the clever Germans, who seized this opportunity to regain an entry into merchant shipping; in the joint venture, Hamburg-America and Harriman agreed to provide half the tonnage for a service between the United States and Germany and to act as agents in their respective countries. The Shipping Board* had to provide Harriman with the vessels but would not do so until the rival claim of American Ship and Commerce Corporation had been settled. This last corporation, organized by George Goethals and Kermit Roosevelt,* had also been trying to negotiate a more equitable agreement with the Germans, who quite naturally had preferred the much more favorable terms of Harriman. In a swift power play, Harriman obtained enough shares of the American Ship and Commerce Corporation to gain control and drive out Goethals and Roosevelt in May 1920. The venture with Hamburg-American could not proceed, and Harriman now attempted to consolidate his different steamship ventures into a single organization, the United American Lines.

As the news of the takeover of American Ship and Commerce and the alliance with the Germans leaked out, Harriman made it on his own to the front pages as the ''steamship king'' and for the first time had escaped his father's shadow, although both his shipbuilding and shipping ventures had been heavily financed by his mother's money. On the negative side, the alliance with Hamburg-America destroyed Harriman's reputation for years, because the public and many of his friends who had fought the Germans during the war could not understand why to make money he had decided to join the United American Lines with the former enemies of the United States. Harriman countered with a campaign against the bad publicity, and his interviews and the release in October 1920 of the text of the agreement with Hamburg-America temporarily calmed the public outcry.

Equally serious was the collapse of the postwar shipping boom in 1920. The glut of ships in the market hit first shipbuilding, and the cancellation of orders for new ships forced him to abandon the shipyard later that year. Harriman became a managing operator* for Shipping Board vessels, and while the cargo vessels steaming to all corners of the world did well under the very generous government payments, the attempts to enter passenger service, although initially successful, soon ran into problems. United American Lines began passenger service on Christmas Day, 1920; the real profits were in steerage* class, but when Congress imposed in 1921 quota restrictions on foreign immigrants, the volume of traffic necessarily slowed down and offered little future for expansion. United American Lines acquired vessels for first-class passenger operation in early 1922, but when initially it seemed that Prohibition* would not allow the serving of alcohol aboard U.S.-flag ships, Harriman disposed of his passenger services and by 1923 was becoming so impatient with the problems of merchant shipping that he wished to get out of the business altogether.

United American Lines had been losing money during most of its existence, several millions, according to Harriman's mother, who continued to make cash infusions so that her son would not suffer a traumatic failure so early in his business career. Harriman himself had stopped pressuring the Shipping Board for more routes and had gradually begun to dismantle United American Lines, which always had been an unwieldy organization. The attempt to run the AHSS through United American Lines had quickly been abandoned, and now Harriman separated the two companies, thereby giving him time to gradually dispose of his stockholdings in AHSS during the late 1920s. He continued to sell off vessels to reduce his exposure in shipping. The most embarrassing outcome came from the joint venture with Hamburg-America, which, as many Americans had feared, had simply used United American Lines as a stepping-stone to restore its own operations; now that the U.S. company was not useful to the Germans, they pushed it aside in the manner typical of the savage, almost Darwinian competition in merchant shipping. In 1926 the Germans wanted to buy out the joint venture, and Harriman was able to recover some of his losses in a sale to Hamburg-America, which he claimed was "considerably better than I expected" (Abramson 1992). By August 1926 the remaining assets of United American Lines passed under the control of Hamburg-America, and the new owner transferred the remaining ships to the German flag.

Harriman slowly had been disposing of his other shipping assets, and during the 1920s he sold off the rest of his stock in the other steamship companies he had bought. There was no doubt that Harriman had taken heavy losses with United American Lines, but it had been his real business apprenticeship, and he had sharpened his ability to seize profit opportunities, while business trips abroad for United American Lines did bring him into international trade, where he later reaped substantial profits. Many other managing operators* who did not have a wealthy mother to bail them out likewise failed to establish solid steamship companies, but all, like Harriman, received their baptism by fire in business, and the skills, experience, and in most cases capital many managing operators acquired later served them well to establish other commercial ventures on land.

References: Rudy Abramson, *Spanning the Century: The Life of W. Averell Harriman, 1891–1986* (New York: William Morrow: 1992); Walter Isaacson and Evan Thomas, *The Wise Men: Six Friends and the World They Made; Acheson, Bohlen, Harriman, Kennan, Lovett, McCloy* (New York: Simon and Schuster, 1986); *Nautical Gazette*, 14 August 1926; Jeffrey J. Safford, *Wilsonian Maritime Diplomacy*, 1913–1921 (New Brunswick, NJ: Rutgers University Press, 1978).

UNITED FRUIT COMPANY or GREAT WHITE FLEET, 1899–present.

The United Fruit Company has operated since 1899 a large fleet of ships to bring tropical products, in particular, bananas, to the United States. For United Fruit, its vessels, collectively called "Great White Fleet" because of the color the ships were painted, were merely one more chain in the operation of totally integrated business enterprise, beginning with the ownership of plantations in Latin America and reaching into the final marketing of the bananas in the United States and Europe. As a proprietary company* that owned the bulk of the cargo, United Fruit was primarily concerned with bringing the bananas safely to markets; however, in order to reduce shipping costs, the company during most of its history has also carried cargo for shippers.* Unlike the Grace Line,* whose proprietary cargoes gradually diminished, for United Fruit its own products remained the majority of the cargo.

The predecessor companies of United Fruit had relied on chartered* vessels, but after 1900 United Fruit began to purchase its own ships (refrigerated starting in 1903) so as to be able to guarantee delivery of the bananas without any interruption or spoilage. With British-flag ships exempted from U.S. requisition, the company could guarantee that the bananas always arrived in safe condition and in sufficient quantities. With the supply guaranteed, the company could begin in the 1900s a marketing campaign, finally completed successfully in the 1920s, to convince Americans to eat bananas on a regular basis. For periods of peak demand, the company throughout its history chartered additional vessels to supplement the vessels it owned. Until 1960 the operations of the fleet were complicated by the need to ship sugar from its sugar plantations on the island of Cuba to the company's refinery near Boston; when the sugar mills were confiscated during the Cuban Revolution, the company was not only deprived of the highly profitable sugar cargoes but also left with excess ships.

In reality the company had been facing declining profit margins since the late 1940s, so that the confiscation of the sugar mills was an additional heavy blow for the company, which, nonetheless, decided to diversify away from Latin America and from bananas to try to survive. The old and conservative management did not press hard the diversification program and, worse, allowed the value of the stock to remain very low; after a very bitter takeover fight, former rabbi Eli M. Black gained control of the company in 1968. United Fruit now became a subsidiary and lost its status as an independent company. At the same time, competition intensified, first, because its main rival, Standard Fruit and Steamship Company,* merged into the conglomerate Castle and Cooke (Dole since 1991) in 1968, and second, because as part of a settlement of an antitrust suit, United Fruit was required to sell its Guatemalan properties to another food conglomerate, the Del Monte Corporation. When the energy crisis struck in 1973, the fuel bills of the ships further contributed to the woes of the company, and apparently despairing of any solution, Eli M. Black jumped out of the forty-fourth-story offices of the company in the Pan American building in New York in February 1975.

The suicide of the chief executive plunged the company into a turmoil, and even today the company still has not overcome the legacy of problems of the 1960s and 1970s. The number of refrigerated ships of United Fruit continued to decline, and the fleet was soon overtaken in size by those of Dole and Del Monte. However, since the late 1980s United Fruit Company has been busily trying to expand its fleet again and has positioned itself to carry shipper's cargo southbound besides its own northbound shipments of bananas. In 1990 the parent company, Chiquita Brands, a producer, processor, and distributor of food product, decided to dissolve United Fruit Company and to call instead the shipping unit with the traditional name of Great White Fleet.

References: *American Shipper*, October 1990; René De La Pedraja, *The Rise and Decline of U.S. Merchant Shipping in the Twentieth Century* (New York: Twayne, 1992); Mark H. Goldberg, *Going Bananas: 100 Years of American Fruit Ships* (Kings Point, NY: American Merchant Marine Museum, 1993); Thomas P. McCann, *An American Company: The Tragedy of United Fruit* (New York: Crown, 1976); John H. Melville, *The Great White Fleet* (New York: Vantage Press, 1976).

UNITED SEAMEN'S SERVICE (USS), 1942–present. The United Seamen's Service has provided rest, relaxation, and recreation to seamen in the more informal manner of a clubhouse. As a home away from home, the USS also has handled currency exchange, held and mailed letters, and helped seamen temporarily in difficulties. The need for these services was always present, but only when World War II made the need acute did the War Shipping Administration* (WSA) take action. The war had put seafarers under massive stress, and the men needed special attention before they could be sent back to the ships; some seamen even developed ''convoy fatigue,'' whose cure often required being left a few days or even a few weeks in quiet and comfortable surroundings. Private organizations like the Seamen's Church Institute* were already overworked, and in any case many seafarers wanted an organization that would not have religious or philanthropic overtones. Because union leaders had foolishly opposed the government's plan to consider the merchant sailors and officers as military personnel during the war, they did not qualify for admission into United Service Organizations (USO), whose services were reserved for enlisted personnel. The

WSA then proposed to create a separate organization for seafarers and, rather than another government agency, chose the format of a nonprofit voluntary association like USO.

The USS, whose funds came mostly from the government, was operating in September 1942 and enjoyed the support of shipowners, shipbuilders, and social workers; originally all the labor unions supported USS, but Harry Lundeberg,* the head of the Seafarers' International Union* (SIU), turned against USS in February 1943 and made his opposition the official policy of the SIU, whose members, however, voted with their feet and not only used but supported the activities of USS.

USS expanded dramatically during the war and established many overseas centers, as well as a network of hotels and restaurants in the major ports of the United States. Although seamen paid for their rooms and meals, there was always a gap in operating expenses, and after World War II ended, the problem of covering overhead expenses become more pressing as the government gradually cut back its funding. Even labor organizations like the National Maritime Union* (NMU) were not willing to commit large resources to USS, whose headquarters decided to conduct polls among 30,000 seamen to determine if they wished to see the organization dissolved like so many of the other wartime agencies. The seamen replied overwhelmingly that they wanted USS to continue operating like a clubhouse run by a helpful staff and that they were willing to make contributions to help defray the expenses. However, financing proved a major problem, and USS headquarters tried to reduce costs by gradually reducing the number of centers, but finally on 31 December 1947 it was left with no option but to close all centers in the United States. USS struggled to keep the overseas centers open, but out of nineteen in 1947, twelve were left in 1948, and by the fall of 1949 only four survived, Yokohama, Bremerhaven, Caripito, and Amuay Bay (the last two in Venezuela). Seamen had attempted to raise private funds and in the case of the two centers in Venezuela had been successful because Standard Oil Company of New Jersey* had agreed to cover the deficit in the operating costs because it felt those facilities were so beneficial to the tanker crews that they enhanced the latter's performance. In 1950 the Italian government provided in Naples rent-free space to open a center, which has survived until the present. In spite of these local achievements, it was really the outbreak of the Korean War that saved USS, which once again enjoyed government support.

Not even the Korean War could reopen the domestic centers, leaving a huge gap in the services for seamen that was in marked contrast with the practices of many foreign governments like Norway, France, England, and Sweden. The gap has been too big for religious organizations like the Seamen's Church Institute (SCI) to fill, and two partial substitutes have emerged since the demise of USS's domestic facilities. The first has been the union hiring halls* themselves, which have served as a natural meeting ground for seamen. The labor unions, however, have failed to realize the need to provide counseling and other family services for their members, while the atmosphere necessarily has been too work-related to provide sufficient relaxation. The second partial substitute has been the seamen's bars, which sprang up in every U.S. port. The owner, usually a former sailor or otherwise closely connected with maritime labor, has catered to the psychological and personal needs of the sailor, but at the high price of having the sailor spend large some on liquor in the bar. While the seamen's bars continue to provide a necessary service in the men's constant transition from shore to ship and back again, the price of increasing alcoholism does seem too high and makes all the more notable the lack of domestic centers run by the USS.

USS expanded again during the Vietnam War, and its centers in Vietnam were the last U.S. installations to abandon that country; equally important, that conflict led to the passage of the Seamen's Service Act on 31 December 1970, which authorized the Department of Defense at its discretion to fund or otherwise support USS. The civilian personnel of the Military Sea Transportation Service* (MSTS), later, the Military Sealift Command* (MSC), had long participated in USS, which now was officially opened to all military personnel who happened to be near one of the centers. Coast Guard* personnel likewise have continued to use the USS facilities.

The USS has been nearly self-supporting and has obtained 80 percent of its income from the sale of supplies and services at the overseas centers. To make up the difference, the USS has organized fund-raisers, most notably the annual Admiral of the Ocean Sea Award (AOTOS) banquet. In 1970 USS instituted this highly coveted annual award, named after Christopher Columbus, to recognize outstanding business, labor, and government leaders in the field. The activities of the USS were enhanced when the American Merchant Marine Library Association* (AMMLA) became an affiliate in 1973. The USS, in the tradition of the brotherhood of the sea, has also opened its overseas centers to seafarers of allied nations, in particular, to those too poor to provide similar services to their own seamen; by 1989 six out of ten seafarers using USS were foreigners. Until the present, the USS has struggled to the limit of its resources to meet in overseas centers the needs of mariners peculiar to their occupation, which has characteristics so different from those of employment on land.

References: Joseph P. Goldberg, *The Maritime Story: A Study in Labor-Management Relations* (Cambridge, MA: Harvard University Press, 1958); Elmo P. Hohman, *History of American Merchant Seamen* (Hamden, CT: Shoe String Press, 1956); *Journal of Commerce*, 25 May 1989; Marian G. Sherar, *Shipping Out: A Sociological Study of American Merchant Seamen* (Cambridge, MD: Cornell Maritime Press, 1973); United Seamen's Service, *49th Annual Report 1991*, and *USS Reports: Anniversary Issue 1992*.

UNITED SHIPOWNERS OF AMERICA (USA), 1987–1990. The United Shipowners of America (USA) represented the U.S.-flag companies and was the successor to the Council of American-Flag Ship Operators* (CASO), which had represented only the *subsidized* U.S.-flag companies. CASO's membership had declined to three subsidized firms in 1987, and its disappearance seemed inevitable. The nonsubsidized U.S.-flag firms Crowley Maritime Corp.* and Sea-Land* agreed in November 1987 to join with the three remaining members of CASO to create a successor organization, USA, whose founding companies were American President Lines,* Crowley Maritime Corporation, Farrell Line,* Lykes Brothers Steamship Co.,* and Sea-Land.

The offices and most of the staff of CASO went to USA, which declared its top priority to be "the reform of the operating differential subsidy"* (*Journal of Commerce,* 18 November 1987). USA was never able to overcome the underlying rivalry between the subsidized and unsubsidized companies, and the organization collapsed in 1990, when Lykes Brothers charged that its efforts to obtain subsidies to operate foreign-built ships had been blocked by Sea-Land, which did not receive subsidies. In 1991 the former members of USA, with the exception of Lykes Brothers, had joined the American Institute of Merchant Shipping* (AIMS).

Principal Executives

James L. Holloway	1987
Albert E. May	1987–1989
William P. Verdon	1990

References: *American Shipper,* August 1991, March 1992; *Journal of Commerce,* 13, 18 November 1987.

UNITED STATES, **1952–1969.** The *United States* was the biggest passenger liner built in the United States and also set the existing record for fastest transatlantic crossing. John M. Franklin,* president of United States Lines* (USL), was determined to build "the fastest, safest and greatest passenger vessel" (Braynard 1981) in the world. Franklin strongly believed that passenger ships had a long future, and of more immediate concern, he also needed a new ship to replace the obsolete *Washington,* then on charter* from the U.S. government. Franklin, the National Maritime Union* (NMU), and the shipbuilders lobbied intensively to obtain the subsidies necessary to build the very expensive ship; the Department of Defense fully backed the project because until the late 1950s it believed that troopships were necessary to deploy armed forces aboard.

Congress agreed to provide the special funding for this superliner, whose construction began in the Newport News Shipbuilding and Dry Dock Company at Virginia in 1949. The famed naval architectural firm of Gibbs & Knox had developed the plans for the vessel's design, which also incorporated many national defense features. Gibbs & Knox had wanted to construct a superliner in the United States since the 1910s, and the firm had frequently updated its plans, while the construction of the *America** in 1940 had been excellent preparation for the *United States.* Even though the ship was intended for commercial use only in the North Atlantic, the military's insistence that the *United States* fit through the Panama Canal* (or be a Panamax* vessel) limited the ship to a length of 990 feet and a beam of 101 feet; this limitation also meant that in size and weight the superliner would never be the biggest ship afloat. The decoration was not outstanding either, largely because of the desire to eliminate all wood on board to prevent any repetition of the fires that gutted the *Morro Castle.** The recreational facilities aboard were adequate for tourists who wished to rest prior to reaching Europe or who wanted to recover from an exhausting tour of the continent.

What really made the *United States* outstanding was its high speed, and the ship still holds the record for fastest transatlantic crossing. Gibbs & Knox reduced the weight of the vessel by design innovations, which, among other changes, called for the construction of many sections with light-weight aluminum, whose use had already begun in the *America*. Further developments in double-reduction gear and in the use of high steam pressures (925 pounds per square inch) allowed Gibbs & Knox to reduce the weight and space of the turbine and equipment while obtaining more propulsion. Unfortunately, any savings in propulsion costs were totally lost by the military's requirement of four propellers and two separate engine rooms.

The *United States* made its maiden voyage on 3 July 1952 and in August crossed the Atlantic at an average speed of thirty-five knots. Since 1852, when the *Baltic* of the Collins Line raced across the Atlantic, the United States had not held the speed record for fastest transatlantic crossing. Actually, in its trial run the ship had reached a maximum of thirty-eight knots. No passenger liner subsequently came close to the speed of the *United States*, but in 1972 the SL-7s,* the containerships of Sea-Land, although operating at only 80 percent of power, effortlessly passed thirty-four knots and set the record for cargo vessels, which still stands today. Perhaps out of deference to the *United States*, or more likely because of the exorbitant fuel consumption at such high speeds, the management of Sea-Land decided not to break the speed record of the passenger liner.

Even before the ship was completed, warnings that this was a "white elephant" had started to appear. In addition USL was entangled in a long legal battle over the subsidies, because some government officials felt this was an outrageous waste of taxpayers' money in what smacked of a pork-barrel project. Was the *United States* a paying proposition once the government had covered the high shipbuilding costs? Unlike the liners of the early twentieth century that had made profits by packing poor immigrants from Europe into steerage* class and returning with any type of cargo, the *United States* was the last stage in the evolution of a liner specializing exclusively in middle- and upper-class passengers. The reductions in machinery released space to carry nearly 2,000 passengers (871 first, 508 cabin, and 549 tourist) but only by a clever distribution of rooms that did not meet the real needs of the travelers. The passengers were no longer the wretched immigrants who could be stuffed anywhere, so that from the start the ship rarely carried more than 1,700 persons, and empty beds meant less income from each voyage. Nevertheless, thanks to a very effective public relations campaign, the ship became a symbol for many Americans in the 1950s; even a children's book on the ship was widely distributed, while the vessel itself served as scenario for about a third of the plot in the Walt Disney film *Bon Voyage*, which captured the romance of the rapidly disappearing transatlantic liners.

The fascination with ocean travel was so great that USL had planned from the start to order a sister ship for the *United States* to replace the aging *America*. Not even the inauguration of regular jet plane service to Europe in October 1958 could dampen the enthusiasm, and in response to a vigorous lobbying campaign, Congress passed in 1958 the legislation authorizing the construction of a sister ship. However, the Eisenhower administration refused to place in the federal budget the funds authorized by Congress, so that actual construction never began. At last by 1960 the idea was dawning that ocean passenger travel belonged to a glorious past and had no future, but by then it was too late for USL, which began to pile up losses because of its passenger operations.

Disposal of the older *America* was easier, and after its last voyages in 1963 were canceled, the ship was sold back to the government in 1964; it was hoped that by eliminating the *America*, its previous passengers would now seek, instead, accommodations aboard the *United States*. However, because of competition from jet airplanes and foreign liners whose lower operating costs meant tempting fares for travelers, the volume of passengers aboard the *United States* continued to decline.

Besides extensive advertising, USL took numerous steps to try to save the *United States*. Since 1961 the company obtained authorization to use the ship on subsidized voyages during the winter off-season months to the Caribbean, a practice that drew protests from other subsidized lines in the trade, such as the Grace Line.* Operation on the cruise trade soon revealed that the ship lacked the many recreational facilities by then essential aboard cruise vessels, but the major overhaul required to make the huge vessel suitable for the cruise trade cost as much as ordering a new vessel. Meanwhile competition from the *France* was threatening to take away the tourist-class passengers of the *United States*, the only class that consistently had been booked solid. To try to maintain its market share, the company decided in 1964 to improve the tourist accommodations, but at the cost of reducing that class by forty-three passengers—and charging higher fares.

Labor problems, in particular the Seamen's Strike of 1961,* had forced the cancellation of voyages, hurting irreparably the ship's image as a reliable form of transportation. During the last years of operation, jurisdictional disputes between rival unions continued to plague the operation of the ship, but for USL it was clear that with or without labor disputes the ship was tremendous drain not only on the funds of the company but also on its time and talent. Management, rather than boldly plunging into the new world of containers,* hesitated too long, in part, by the distraction of the passenger service, so the *United States* was one of the factors that contributed to the decline of USL, and in retrospect the vessel should never have been built.

So much symbolism and prestige surrounded the superliner that only a change of management finally made possible laying up the *United States*, whose last voyage ended on 7 November 1969. In 1972 the government formally purchased the ship, which henceforth was maintained in lay-up by the Maritime Administration* as part of the National Defense Reserve Fleet* (NDRF) in spite of the fact that the military was no longer interested in vessels to take troops abroad. Repeated attempts to sell the vessel failed to elicit any satisfactory bids until 1979, when the vessel was sold for operation as a cruise ship. Although special legislation allowed the operation of the ship between California and Hawaii, the deal collapsed, and the *United States* went back to the NDRF. By the early 1990s the liner was deteriorating, and the government decided to sell the vessel for scrap; however, in early 1992, a Turkish group offered $2.6 million, a price higher than scrap value for the vessel. The Turkish investors planned to spend $140 million to convert the rusting vessel into a modern cruise ship, but their plans will take at least three years to become reality.

References: Frank O. Braynard, *The Big Ship: The Story of the S.S. United States* (Newport News, VA: The Mariners' Museum, 1981); René De La Pedraja, *The Rise and Decline of U.S. Merchant Shipping in the Twentieth Century* (New York: Twayne, 1992); Files of the Maritime Administration, Washington, DC; *Journal of Commerce*, 28 April 1992.

UNITED STATES AND BRAZIL MAIL STEAMSHIP COMPANY, 1865–1893. Under the same name of United States and Brazil Mail Steamship Company, three different companies operated between the United States and Brazil in 1865–1875, 1878–1881, and 1883–1893.

First, in 1864 the U.S. Congress approved a ten-year subsidy to operate a steamship mail service to Brazil. The United States and Brazil Mail Steamship Company offered the lowest bid and was awarded the subsidy. Service began in October 1865 with discarded naval auxiliaries hastily converted for commercial transportation. Wooden hulls and the inefficient single-expansion engines* characterized the fleet, and until the end the company operated the obsolete sidewheelers. Poor service meant losses, and to offset them the company attempted in 1872 to have Congress increase its subsidy but failed. The government refused to renew the ten-year contract, so that when it expired in 1875, the company discontinued operations.

Second, only a shipbuilder could believe that the problems of the first United States and Brazil Mail Steamship Company were solely the result of running inferior ships. John Roach decided to build new vessels in his shipyards for the second United States and Brazil Steamship Company. Charles Henry Mallory,* out of a deep friendship for Roach, put up 10 percent of the investment, but no other backers appeared. Roach did not enjoy a subsidy from the U.S. government but had obtained a one-year mail contract from the emperor of Brazil in 1877, with promise of more help once the Brazilian Chamber of Deputies approved a bill; furthermore, Roach counted on eventually convincing the U.S. Congress to subsidize his service.

The *City of Rio de Janeiro** built at the Roach yards made the first voyage to Brazil in May 1878 and was followed a month later by the *City of Pará*, also from the Roach yards. These vessels had iron hulls, propellers,* and compound engines,* and had first-class staterooms luxuriously fitted for ninety-six first-class passengers and space for at least 500 persons in steerage* class, as well as ample cargo holds. Technically the ships were among the best in their day and certainly were the best in that route; however, the capacity of the ships was too big for the small trade then existing between the United States and Brazil, while the statesrooms rarely carried more than thirty first-class passengers.

When Roach tried to solicit cargo for his vessels, he ran against the vicious competition of British firms. England controlled the trade of Brazil and was not about to let the United States into areas vital to British commerce. The return cargoes were mainly coffee, and British steamship companies timed their ships to depart with the coffee right before the arrival of Roach's vessels. Brazilians were accustomed to British products, so Mallory, the New York agent for Roach, could find little southbound cargo. The British controlled the coal supply in Brazilian ports and charged Roach's ships more for fuel to drive his costs higher. British firms manipulated the Brazilian Chamber of Deputies into refusing a mail contract for Roach's firm, and when the U.S. Congress balked at providing a subsidy, he could no longer bear the losses and made the last sailing in May 1881.

Third, both Mallory and Roach promised never again to be involved in the trade with Brazil, but only the former kept his word. Barely a year later, in June 1882, Roach joined with Collis P. Huntington to revive for a third time the United States and Brazil Mail Steamship Company. The stimulus was the subsidy granted by the Brazilian Chamber of Deputies, which at last realized it had been duped by the British and now wanted U.S. steamship services to counter the British monopoly. As the general manager of the company explained, "We are in existence today by the aid of a foreign government" (U.S. Congress 1890). Roach himself was more cautious because he had finally learned that the operation of a shipyard and a steamship firm were two different endeavors. For this venture he confined his investment to the company's first three ships also built in his yards (*Finance*, *Advance*, and *Reliance*) and avoided any role in the management of the steamship firm.

The British, however, were not about to give up their Brazilian markets and put up a ferocious resistance. To counter the Brazilian subsidy, the Royal Mail West Indies Company received a subsidy from the British government that allowed the British company to place better ships in competition with those of the U.S. firm. In a desperate attempt to regain cargoes, the United States and Brazil Mail Steamship Company ordered two large luxury ships in 1890, but the company merely repeated Roach's mistake and found itself with excess capacity and finally went into bankruptcy in 1893. The British emerged triumphant, and until after World War I, passengers, cargo, and mail could only reach Brazil by first going through England.

References: Frederick E. Emmons, *American Passenger Ships* (Newark: University of Delaware Press, 1985); Winthrop L. Marvin, *The American Merchant Marine* (New York: Scribner's 1902); Leonard A. Swann, *John Roach, Maritime Entrepreneur: The Years as Naval Contractors, 1862–1886* (Annapolis, MD: U.S. Naval Institute Press, 1965); Frank J. Taylor, "Early American Steamship Lines," in Society of Naval Architects and Marine Engineers, *Historical Transactions 1893–1943* (Westport, CT: Greenwood Press, 1981); U.S. Congress, House, Committee on Merchant Marine and Fisheries, *American Merchant Marine in the Foreign Trade*, Report No. 1210, 51st Congress, 1st Session, 1890.

UNITED STATES INTERCOASTAL CONFERENCE, 1920–1934. Companies in the intercoastal* trade organized the United States Intercoastal Conference to set rates, to pool revenues, and also to equalize the services to ports. This conference covered the trade between Pacific and Atlantic ports, excluding, however, the Gulf of Mexico, which had its own separate organization, the Gulf Intercoastal Conference.* Since legislation required filing with the Shipping Board* only the maximum, but not the minimum, rates, this intercoastal conference operated largely outside the regulatory framework. The stormy history of vicious and destructive competition was ably summarized as follows:

The conference . . . was never able to enroll or keep within its fold all the carriers operating in this trade and otherwise it did not have a happy existence. It was organized on 5 August 1920, and functioned until June 1922. This period was followed by a severe rate war lasting until the conference was again organized on 1 August 1923. From that date it continued, as stated by a witness, "in a somewhat hit-and-miss fashion" until 31 July 1927. Reorganized on 1 August 1927, it fell apart on 13 February 1931, when a "pretty savage" rate war ensued during which each line made its own quotations. Organized once more it functioned for only seven months, or from 1 March to 30 September 1932. A new agreement became effective on 1 October 1932, and in modified form the conference continued from time to time until last disbanded on 31 July 1934. (Shipping Board, 1942)

When the conference disintegrated, the member lines were American-Hawaiian (AHSS),* Argonaut Line,* Arrow, Dollar Line,* Grace Line,* Isthmian Line,* Luckenbach,* McCormick,* Nelson, Panama Pacific (a subsidiary of the International Mercantile Marine* or IMM), Quaker, Weyerhaeuser,* and Williams (a subsidiary of AHSS); outside the conference also operated the States Steamship Lines,* Shepard Steamship Company, and Calmar* (a subsidiary of Bethlehem Steel).

Passage of the Intercoastal Shipping Act of 1933, which allowed the government to set minimum as well as maximum rates, came too late to save the United States Intercoastal Conference. After a few years, however, the intercoastal lines felt they needed another organization, this time mainly to present a common front on rate matters before the federal government, and consequently the companies created the Intercoastal Steamship Freight Association* in 1936.

References: *Journal of Commerce*, 15 December 1933; *Nautical Gazette*, 28 July 1928; Shipping Board, *Decisions*, vol. 1 (Washington, DC: Government Printing Office, 1942).

UNITED STATES LINES (USL), 1921–1986. During most of its existence, United States Lines (USL), whose operations were concentrated in the North Atlantic, was the largest and most prestigious merchant shipping company in the country. The Shipping Board* established the government-owned company in August 1921 to operate the former German liners, in particular, the *Leviathan*;* the Shipping Board refused to hand the vessels over to the International Mercantile Marine* (IMM), while the remaining American companies proved unable to operate successfully the large passenger liners. USL was expected to quickly go broke, but when it prospered under government ownership, inevitably speculators sought to bring the company under private control because supposedly the ships would be run more efficiently. After several unsuccessful attempts to sell the line, the Shipping Board finally found a buyer in Paul W. Chapman, who became the owner of USL on 20 March 1929. Chapman ordered two new superliners, the *Manhattan** and the *Washington*,* from the shipyards, but the supposed efficiency of private ownership proved an illusion, and to prevent a bankruptcy, the Shipping Board had no choice but to take over the company in 1931.

Bowing to the inevitable, the Shipping Board sold the company to a consortium headed by the IMM and the Dollar* family in October 1931. By 1934 the Dollar family had withdrawn, leaving full ownership in the hands of IMM. The *Manhattan* and the *Washington* entered into service in 1932 and 1933, respectively, while the overage *Leviathan* ended operations in 1934. To keep U.S.-flag passenger service at a satisfactory level, USL ordered a third vessel, the *America*,* which was completed in 1940. By then World War II was already raging in Europe, and the company suffered the greatest disruptions in its sailing schedules. Government aid and the requisitioning of most of the fleet for wartime service once again bailed out the company, which had been staring at bankruptcy in 1941.

Since the early 1930s IMM had been disposing of its foreign-flag vessels as a way to placate the mounting nationalist criticism in the United States, but management felt a further visible step was necessary and replaced the foreign-sounding name of International Mercantile Marine with the thoroughly American designation of United States Lines in May 1943. In effect the subsidiary had swallowed up the original holding company.

Once World War II was over, USL operated profitably a large number of surplus freighters for its cargo services in the North Atlantic and to Australia and the Far East, but passenger services demanded more costly solutions. In

1945 the government had totally reconstructed the *America*, which the company bought at a bargain price and placed in service in 1946, while the old *Washington* returned to passenger service briefly in 1948–1951. However, the president of the company, John M. Franklin,* wanted to build the fastest and most modern passenger liner and after considerable lobbying obtained government financing to build the *United States*,* which entered service in July 1952. The company decided to seek similar government assistance to build a replacement for the rapidly aging *America*, but the Eisenhower administration balked at the proposal, and USL was finally forced to retire the ship in 1964.

By the late 1950s USL was likewise looking to replace its World War II freighters. The initial steps in vessel replacement had been easy, because the company only needed to order the Mariner* class ships that the Maritime Administration* (MARAD) had designed. The first of the fast Mariners entered the Pacific routes in 1957, and by 1960 the company owned nine. But the Mariners were the last generation of commercial ships the government designed, and the pro-business Eisenhower administration decided that ship design and planning were best left in the hands of the supposedly more efficient private sector. In the early 1960s the containers* were starting to reveal their potential, and they in turn enormously complicated the vessel replacement program of companies like USL.

USL dragged out the study on containerization, and not until December 1964 did it order five ships able to carry both the regular break-bulk* cargo and 228 containers. To finance this new vessel replacement program, USL sold its Australia trade route to the Farrell Line* in 1965. When Sea-Land* launched container service in the North Atlantic in April 1966, USL reacted by changing twice its shipyard orders until the new design of the Lancers* emerged. The Lancers, the fastest and largest containerships of their day, had a service speed of twenty-two knots and carried 1,178 containers, and they could be counted upon not only to crush Sea-Land's small converted containerships but also to regain market shares lost to foreign competitors.

Before the Lancers could reach their full potential, USL became a prey of the takeover mania of the late 1960s. After a relatively smooth hostile takeover, the investment firm of Walter Kidde and Company gained control of USL in January 1968 and installed John McMullen, a minor stockholder, as the new president. Soon Walter Kidde and Company regretted having acquired USL, and McMullen struggled to set the company on a true course. He retired the money-losing *United States* in November 1969, thereby ending passenger service, and in an attempt to simplify operations, he chartered* the entire container fleet of USL to Sea-Land, now owned by R. J. Reynolds, in October 1969. Antitrust considerations blocked what would have been the largest peacetime maritime charter in history, and Walter Kidde decided to dispose of the problem by selling USL to Sea-Land in November 1970, but this proposed sale only aggravated the antitrust problem. Both the Federal Maritime Commission* and the antitrust division of the Justice Department refused to approve the sale, so that the new owner, R. J. Reynolds, had no control over USL, while Walter Kidde, nominally in charge, wanted only to get rid of the property. The sale to R. J. Reynolds was retracted in 1976, and Walter Kidde at last in September 1977 found a buyer acceptable to the government, none other than Malcom McLean,* the popularizer of containers.

USL had suffered grievously since 1968, and it was up to McLean to take drastic remedial action to save the company, whose Lancers were no match for the SL-7s* Sea-Land had introduced as the largest and fastest containerships in the world. McLean decided to gamble the whole future of USL on one grand play, a new generation of containerships, the Econships,* which would have the lowest operating costs per container in the world and, although built in Korea, would still fly the U.S. flag through a special congressional dispensation. The monster ships had a capacity for 4,380 twenty-foot equivalent units (TEUs*) and were of the Panamax* class because they still managed to fit through the Panama Canal. The diesel* engines provided significant economies in fuel, but at the cost of a speed of only sixteen knots.

Analysts had calculated that these ships could cover expenses if only half full, while large profits were possible with cargo loads of 80 percent. To keep the ships running with full loads all the time proved a staggering task, and when the ships began to arrive from the Korean shipyard in 1984, McLean placed them in a new round-the-world* service, and by early 1986, when the last of the Econships were delivered, USL offered shippers* weekly sailings on the round-the-world service. To provide "feeder" routes into the round-the-world service, USL acquired the fleet of Moore-McCormack* in January 1983 and Delta Line* in December 1984, as part of a strategy to create a worldwide ocean transportation network.

Early in 1986 USL began to pile up huge losses, and the company itself entered bankruptcy in November of that year. The revival of the company proved impossible, McLean was removed from the presidency, and the liquidation of USL was only delayed by the tremendous difficulty of finding a buyer for the Econships. USL, the direct heir of the International Mercantile Marine, had come to a disastrous end.

Principal Executives

John M. Franklin	1931–1967
Basil Harris	1931–1948
W. B. Rand	1960–1966
John McMullen	1968–1970
Malcom McLean*	1977–1986

Some Notable Ships

Leviathan	1921–1934
Manhattan and *Washington*	1932–1951
America	1940–1964

United States	1952–1969
Mariners*	1956–1970s
Lancers*	1968–1989
Econships*	1986–1989

References: Frank O. Braynard, *The Big Ship: The Story of S.S. United States* (Newport News, VA: Mariners' Museum, 1981); René De La Pedraja, *The Rise and Decline of U.S. Merchant Shipping in the Twentieth Century* (New York: Twayne, 1992); Frederick E. Emmons, *American Passenger Ships: The Ocean Lines and Liners, 1873–1983* (Newark: University of Delaware Press, 1985).

UNITED STATES MAIL STEAMSHIP COMPANY, 1847–1859. The settlement of the Oregon dispute with England convinced the U.S. government of the need to establish closer links between that new territory and the eastern seaboard of the United States. Based on authority granted by Congress, the Navy Department awarded two very generous mail contracts, one to the United States Mail Steamship Company to provide service on the Atlantic side from the East and Gulf coasts of the United States to Panama and another to the Pacific Mail Steamship Company* (PMSS) to provide service on the Pacific side from Panama as far as Oregon. The contract with United States Mail included the requirement that the company use for commanders and watch officers naval personnel on leave of absence as a way to familiarize them with the operation of steamers.

On 1 December 1848 the first vessel of United States Mail, the *Falcon*, sailed from New York, almost two months after the first steamer of the PMSS, the *California*,* had left for the long trip around Cape Horn to position itself for its permanent route in the Pacific Ocean; the plan calculated that by the time the passengers of the *Falcon* crossed the Isthmus of Panama after scheduled stops in Havana and New Orleans, the *California* would be waiting on the Pacific side to pick them up and take them to Oregon. The news of the California gold rush overtook the *Falcon* in New Orleans, and the steamer dropped a full load of passengers in Panama, while the *California* in even more crowded conditions delivered the passengers to California.

The owners of United States Mail, George Law and Marshall O. Roberts, were reaping huge profits from the flood of fortune seekers heading to California as well as from those returning to the East with their newly obtained wealth. However, in 1850 the owners decided they wanted an even greater share of the profits, and when they placed vessels on the Pacific side as well, a full-scale rate war erupted with PMSS. The latter company retaliated by ordering more steamers from the shipyards and placing competing vessels on the Atlantic side to challenge United States Mail in its home ground. Mounting losses convinced the owners of United States Mail to end the rate war in January 1851; by the terms of the agreement, PMSS bought the Pacific fleet of United States Mail, which did the same with the Atlantic ships of PMSS. Each company agreed to stay henceforth within its respective ocean and to work "in close harmony" to facilitate through connections for passengers and shippers* of cargo. United States Mail now redeployed its ships into two routes, a direct service from New York to the Isthmus of Panama, and another from New York with calls at Havana and New Orleans before reaching Panama.

Meanwhile Law had shifted his money into streetcars, leaving the other owner, Roberts, without sufficient backing to acquire new ships. When the mail contract expired in 1859, Roberts discontinued the operations of United States Mail, but that same year he placed its ships as his share of the investment in the Atlantic and Pacific Steamship Company,* a new venture he created with Cornelius Vanderbilt.*

References: Robert G. Albion, *The Rise of New York Port, 1815–1860* (New York: Scribner's, 1939); David I. Folkman, Jr., *The Nicaragua Route* (Salt Lake City: University of Utah Press, 1972); Wheaton J. Lane, *Commodore Vanderbilt: An Epic of the Steam Age* (New York: Alfred A. Knopf, 1942); John Niven, *The American President Lines and Its Forebears, 1848–1984* (Newark: University of Delaware Press, 1987).

UNITED STATES STEEL. See Isthmian Line.

URUGUAY. See Good Neighbor Fleet.

U.S. ATLANTIC AND GULF PORTS/EASTERN MEDITERRANEAN AND NORTH AFRICAN FREIGHT CONFERENCE (USAGEM), 1985– present. The U.S. Atlantic and Gulf Ports/Eastern Mediterranean and North African Freight Conferences (USAGEM) emerged from the fusion of smaller conferences such as the North Atlantic Mediterranean Freight Conference* (NAMFC). USAGEM supposedly was one of the superconferences* that appeared after the passage of the Shipping Act of 1984,* but even after the merger only five companies were members: Farrell Lines,* Levant Line, Lykes Brothers Steamship Company,* Pharos Lines, and Waterman Steamship Corporation.* USAGEM has set rates and services for cargoes moving eastward from the Atlantic and Gulf coasts of the United States to ports in the eastern Mediterranean and North African.

References: Federal Maritime Commission, *Carrier Agreements in the U.S. Oceanborne Trades*, September 1990; Gale Research, *Encyclopedia of Associations*, 1989– 1993.

U.S. ATLANTIC-NORTH EUROPE CONFERENCE (ANEC), 1985–1989. The U.S. Atlantic-North Europe Conference (ANEC) was one of the superconferences* that emerged after the passage of the Shipping Act of 1984.* ANEC combined five previously existing units: the North Atlantic United Kingdom Freight Conference* (NAUK), the North Atlantic French Atlantic Freight Conference, the North Atlantic Continental Freight Conference,* and the North Atlantic Baltic Freight Conference. The merger was less dramatic than it seemed, because at the time those five conferences had as members the same six lines: Atlantic Container Lines, Dart Container Line, Hapag-Lloyd, Sea-Land,* Trans Freight Lines, and United States Lines.* The five original conferences had the same chairman and the same office in New York City. In reality the creation of ANEC, just like of its westbound counterpart, the North Europe U.S. Atlantic Conference* (NEAC), was the first part in the restructuring process that culminated in the creation of the U.S.A.-North Europe Rate Agreement* (USA-NERA) and the North Europe-U.S.A. Rate Agreement* (NEUSARA) in 1989.

References: Advisory Commission on Conferences in Ocean Shipping, *Report to the President and the Congress* (Washington, DC: Government Printing Office, 1992); *American Shipper*, September, October 1984.

U.S. COAST GUARD. See Coast Guard.

U.S. MARITIME COMMISSION, 1936–1950. The Merchant Marine Act of 1936* created the U.S. Maritime Commission to replace the Shipping Board Bureau.* The act established the new commission as an independent regulatory agency composed of five members (no more than three from the same party) appointed by the president with the consent of the Senate for six-year terms; the president also appointed the chairman, who lacked any special powers and received the same salary as the other commissioners. With this act the Congress had rejected the executive branch's proposal to maintain control in the hands of a single cabinet officer and had returned to a commission type of government like the original Shipping Board,* whose many mistakes Congress hoped to avoid by the strict legislative requirements written into the operating differential subsidy* (ODS) and the construction differential subsidy* (CDS).

Franklin D. Roosevelt had a difficult time finding somebody to head the new commission and finally convinced Joseph P. Kennedy* to accept the position. The Merchant Marine Act of 1936 had canceled the mail contracts of the Merchant Marine Act of 1928,* and the shipowners could be expected to file costly lawsuits in what had obviously been a blatant breach of the contracts. Fortunately for the government, the shipowners themselves had violated most of the provisions of their contracts, as the revelations of the Black Committee* amply demonstrated, so that the U.S. Maritime Commission was ready to go into court with its own set of claims. Kennedy, a businessman himself, was ideally suited to negotiate settlements between the shipowners and the commission, so that the government, instead of having to pay over $166 million in claims, was able to settle the mail contracts for 1 percent of their value. Roosevelt rewarded this accomplishment by appointing Kennedy, after just ten months in office, to be the U.S. ambassador to Great Britain in 1938.

By then the possibility of war in Europe was becoming very real, and Roosevelt, who did not want to go again through the ordeal of having to convince a qualified civilian, appointed Admiral Emory S. Land,* who already was a commissioner, to be chairman; Roosevelt likewise appointed more naval officers to the commission as vacancies appeared. Kennedy had been too diligent in canceling mail contracts, and it was left to Land to find solutions to problems like that of the Baltimore Mail Line* and also to take decisions regarding the bankruptcies of the Munson Line* and the Dollar Line.* The U.S. Maritime Commission made arrangements to establish the Good Neighbor Fleet* for passenger service to South America and also purchased the Dollar Line, now renamed the American President Lines,* to avoid any interruptions in freight and passenger services to the Far East.

The outbreak of World War II in 1939 and U.S. entry into the conflict in December 1941 had a dramatic effect on the activities of the U.S. Maritime Commission. Even with naval officers as a majority of the commissioners, Land felt hindered by the slow deliberations and complex proceedings of the agency and pleaded with President Roosevelt to establish control by one official. The president agreed and created the War Shipping Administration* (WSA) on 7 February 1942 under Admiral Land to operate not only the existing ships in the U.S. merchant marine but also all ships coming off the shipyards in the crash construction program. The U.S. Maritime Commission received one last chance to redeem itself by carrying out the shipbuilding program, with the understanding that if bureaucratic procedures delayed ship deliveries, the president could immediately transfer all construction work to the WSA. The U.S. Maritime Commission rose to the challenge and did fulfill its shipbuilding functions, but officials deeply resented the concentration of powers in the hands of Chairman Land.

When Admiral Land resigned as chairman on 15 January 1946, the U.S. Maritime Commission was left without leadership, and soon all the commissioners who had served during the war likewise resigned. The situation was made worse by the transfer to the U.S. Maritime Commission of the remaining functions of the WSA upon the latter's premature dissolution on 1 September 1946. Already in October of that year the new chairman "had lost control" because the new commissioners were concerned only with preserving their own individual power and wanted at all costs to avoid the emergence of a strong chairman; they even went so far as to abolish the executive director's job, which had functioned until 1946 as the operating arm of the chairman. The commissioners bogged themselves down in every minute detail and quite naturally lost sight of the crucial issues. "The commission was agonizingly slow in arranging sales of tankers to alleviate Europe's critical fuel needs, it proved powerless to quell the industry's serious labor problems, it failed in an abortive attempt to reestablish coastwise* and intercoastal* freight and passenger services" while the rivalries among the commissioners meant that "the agency was unable to carry out its duties properly" (Lawrence 1966). Worse, the U.S. Maritime Commission found itself involved in maritime scandals, as slick operators managed to profit by violating the clauses of the Ship Sales Act of 1946,* while some commissioners hatched deals to help their friends in the private companies.

The U.S. Maritime Commission had fallen into the abuses of the Shipping Board, and unable to keep its own house in order, the calls for drastic change became more insistent. The U.S. Maritime Commission failed to heed the warnings, and only after repeated denunciations did it at last adopt in 1948 a plan to establish for its bureaus clear lines of authority under a general manager responsible to the commissioners. The action came too late for both Congress and the Hoover Commission on the Organization of the Executive Branch of the Government; and consequently Reorganization Plan Number 21 of 1950 abolished the U.S. Maritime Commission, whose functions were transferred to two new bodies, the Maritime Administration* and the Federal Maritime Board,* both in the Department of Commerce.

Chairmen

Admiral Henry A. Wiley	1936–1937
Joseph P. Kennedy	1937–1938
Admiral Emory S. Land	1938–1946
Admiral William W. Smith	1946–1948
General Philip B. Fleming	1949–1950

References: René De La Pedraja, *The Rise and Decline of U.S. Merchant Shipping in the Twentieth Century* (New York: Twayne, 1992); Samuel A. Lawrence, *United States Merchant Shipping Policies and Politics* (Washington, DC: Government Printing Office, 1966); Official File, Franklin D. Roosevelt Presidential Library, Hyde Park, New York; Official File, Harry S. Truman Presidential Library, Independence, Missouri; U.S. Commission on Organization of the Executive Branch of the Government, *Task Force Report on Regulatory Commissions, Appendix N* (Washington, DC: Government Printing Office, 1949).

U.S. SHIP OPERATORS' ASSOCIATION, 1919–early 1930s. When the Shipping Board* decided in 1919 to pay private individuals for the operation of government-owned vessels, a new class of steamship executives was born. The new executives did not own the ships and hence did not qualify to join the American Steamship Owners' Association, which in any case looked down on the new upstarts. These new executives were totally dependent on the government, and to try to defend their interests, they established the U.S. Ship Operators' Association in October 1919. There was no possibility of charging significant dues, and without a permanent staff, the association was more a committee for shifting coalitions of members. The president in 1919–1924 was Charles H. Potter, who was also president of the Potter Transportation Company.

The membership of the association was highest during 1919–1920, the years when the Shipping Board was busily creating many competing companies. Starting in 1921, when the Shipping Board suspended tramp* operations and began to consolidate the liner* services in overlapping routes into a smaller number

of companies, the membership of the association began to decline. The U.S.
Ship Operators' Association was a way station for persons who either rose to a
long-standing position within U.S. merchant shipping or else dropped out altogether. Membership in 1924 comprised the following forty firms:

Baltimore Oceanic Steamship Co.	John A. Merritt & Co.
Black Diamond Steamship Co.*	Moore & McCormack Co.*
Barber Steamship Line	Munson Steamship Company*
W. A. Blake & Co.	McAllister Bros.
A. H. Bull & Co.*	Potter Transportation Co., Inc.
Callaghan Atkinson & Co.	Daniel Ripley & Co.
Carolina Co.	Rogers & Webb
Columbia Pacific Shipping Co.	S. Sgitcovich & Co.
Consolidated Navigation Co.	South Atlantic Maritime Co.
Cosmopolitan Shipping Co.*	Strachan Shipping Co.
Delta Line*	Struthers & Barry
East Baltic Line, Inc.	Swayne & Hoyt, Inc.
Export Steamship Corp.*	Tampa Inter Ocean Steamship Co.
Export Transportation Co.	Terminal Shipping Co.
General Navigation Co.	Trosdal, Plant & LaFonta
Geyelin & Co.	M. H. Tracy & Co.
Hasler & Co.	U.S. & A Lines, Inc.
International Freighting Corp.	Waterman Steamship Corp.*
Lykes Brothers Steamship Co.*	Wessel, Duval & Co.
C. D. Mallory & Co.*	J. H. Winchester & Co.

At the end of 1924 the prospects looked "somewhat dubious" because "the
Shipping Board has ignored the Association and that it has no future" (Record
Group 32) but in January 1925 the association, under new president Winchester
Noyes, took over the Standing Committee of Managing Agents, a body for
coordination with the Shipping Board. The association appeared to have regained a meaningful function, and the standing committee held meetings once
every month. However, all pertinent issues had been resolved when the last
meeting with Shipping Board officials was held in December 1926, and because
of lack of items for the agenda all subsequent meetings of the Standing Committee were canceled by mutual accord.

When the Shipping Board began to require the purchase of the vessels in
order to qualify for subsidies, the ranks of the operators thinned even more
rapidly. The U.S. Ship Operators' Association was still active at the end of
1929, but shortly after, Lykes Brothers Steamship Co., which had become a
large enterprise, decided to transfer its membership to the more prestigious and

powerful American Steamship Owner's Association. Once the operators had become owners, no further reason remained to keep alive the U.S. Ship Operators' Association, which quietly folded in the early 1930s.

Principal Executives

Charles H. Potter	1919–1924
Winchester Noyes	1925–1928?

References: James P. Baughman, *The Mallorys of Mystic: Six Generations in American Maritime Enterprise* (Middletown, CT: Wesleyan University Press, 1972); *New York Times*, 10 October 1919, 28 June 1921; Record Group 32, National Archives, Washington, DC; Waterman Steamship Corporation Papers, Mobile Public Library, Mobile, Alabama.

U.S. SHIPPING BOARD. See Shipping Board.

U.S. SHIPPING BOARD BUREAU. See Shipping Board Bureau.

U.S.A.-NORTH EUROPE RATE AGREEMENT (USANERA), 1989–1992. The creation of the U.S. Atlantic North Europe Conference* (ANEC) in 1985 had been a first major step to consolidate the conferences* in the trade moving across the Atlantic from the U.S. Atlantic Coast to Northern Europe but left out the cargo moving in the same direction from the Pacific and Gulf coasts of the United States. The member lines finally agreed in 1989 to create the U.S.A.-North Europe Rate Agreement (USANERA) and it combined ANEC with the Gulf European Freight Association* and the Pacific Coast European Conference* (PCEC). USANERA's membership in 1990 consisted of seven lines, of which only one, Sea-Land,* was U.S.-flag.

The creation of this superconference* between the United States and Northern Europe aroused fears of a monopoly, but the Advisory Commission on Conferences in Ocean Shipping* (ACCOS) found nothing to condemn. The many small conferences were in fact obsolete and reflected "a period when vessels were small and the countries of Western Europe were not as economically integrated as they are today" (*American Shipper*, October 1984). Superconferences like USANERA and its eastbound counterpart, the North Europe–U.S.A. Rate Agreement* (NEU-SARA), have become basic to world shipping. The trend toward concentration appears to have no end in sight and, in August 1992, both USANERA and NEUSARA combined to form the Trans-Atlantic Agreement* (TAA).

References: Advisory Commission on Conferences in Ocean Shipping, *Report to the President and the Congress* (Washington, DC: Government Printing Office, 1992); *American Shipper*, September, October 1984; *Journal of Commerce*, 2 June 1989.

U.S.A.-SOUTH AFRICA CONFERENCE, 1924–1960s. When the Shipping Board* successfully established direct service between the United States and

South Africa, the British lines, which before had provided at best only a trian-
gular service via England, also entered the trade. To avoid destructive competition, the lines agreed in 1924 to establish the U.S.A.-South Africa Conference
to set rates, routes, and number of sailings. This was an outward conference
with jurisdiction only over cargoes leaving the United States; the lines created
a separate body, the South Africa-U.S.A. Conference, with jurisdiction over the
inbound cargoes coming from South Africa to the United States. Although South
Africa was the center of the trade, the conference, in spite of its title, held an
undefined jurisdiction for decades over the east and west coasts of Africa, as
far north as the Azores and the Canary Islands; only after World War II with
the creation of the American West African Freight Conference* did jurisdictional borders become clearer.

   The U.S.A.-South Africa Conference was particularly famous for the ferocious rate war that raged between the Robin Line* and the American South African Line* in 1935–1937. Other rate wars, such as those of Hans Isbrandtsen*
in the Pacific Ocean, involved more companies and larger sums of money, but
few if any could match the ferocity and personal vindictiveness of the 1935–
1937 rate war in the South African trade. The Robin Line and the American
South African Line had been jointly owned and managed by the Farrell and
Lewis families, but because of a sudden bitter clash, the family members completely separated their interests in the two companies. The Farrells retained the
American South African Line, and the Lewises the Robin Line; this latter was
engaged mainly in the intercoastal* trade but in 1935 shifted its four vessels to
the South African route in an attempt to strike a blow against the Farrell family.

   To try to drive the Robin Line from the trade, the U.S.A.-South Africa Conference reduced its rates from twenty dollars to eight dollars a ton, and eventually to four dollars; this last figure barely covered half of the operating costs,
so that the companies were taking heavy losses on each voyage. The Robin Line
did not collapse, however, because it was shipping for Chrysler and Ford large
volumes of automobiles to South Africa. When the Robin Line applied for
membership in the conference as a way of ending the rate war, the Farrell family
had the application rejected. The American South African Line had the advantage of a mail subsidy, yet even without it the Robin Line managed to survive
until 1937, when a reduction in the government subsidy at last forced the Farrell
family to call off the extremely bitter rate war.

   In 1938 the Robin Line managed to secure its own subsidy from the U.S.
Maritime Commission,* and the next year World War II temporarily halted the
destructive competition. Although the two lines remained rivals, they preferred
to respect the agreements of the U.S.A.-South Africa Conference. In 1955 the
last of the British lines withdrew from the route, leaving as active members of
the conference only the Robin Line and the Farrell Lines.* When Moore-
McCormack* bought the Robin Line in 1957, the new owner made other arrangements for the vessels of the former Robin Line, and with only the Farrell

Line as a member, the U.S.A.-South Africa Conference quietly folded in the early 1960s.

References: Robert G. Albion, *Seaports South of Sahara: The Achievements of an American Steamship Service* (New York: Appleton-Century Crofts, 1959); Lane C. Kendall, *The Business of Shipping*, 5th ed. (Centreville, MD: Cornell Maritime Press, 1986); U.S. Maritime Commission, *Decisions*, vols. 2–3, *1938–1952* (Washington, DC: Government Printing Office, 1951–1963).

V

VANDERBILT, CORNELIUS ("COMMODORE") 27 May 1794–4 January 1877. Cornelius Vanderbilt was a millionaire businessman who engaged in numerous shipping ventures. He was born on 27 May 1794 in Port Richmond, Staten Island (today part of New York City). His ancestors had come from Holland in the late seventeenth century, and his father complemented farming in Staten Island with providing boating services. Cornelius was big and strong and at the age of thirteen became his father's helper handling small vessels; he did not study beyond the age of eleven. Vanderbilt built a ferry business hauling passengers and cargo between Staten Island and New York City and gradually expanded his fleet until he was providing sailing services in nearby sounds and also in the coastwise* trade. He had married on 19 December 1813, and his wife, Sophia Johnson—a cousin, the daughter of his father's sister—operated a very successful tavern and hotel in New Brunswick, and this business helped raise part of the initial capital he needed to expand his fleet. Vanderbilt appeared headed toward entering ocean shipping first in the coastwise and then the foreign trades, but instead he made the first of the abrupt changes that characterized his business career.

In 1818 he sold all his sailing vessels and became a steamboat* captain for Thomas Gibbons in the inland waters of New York State, and in 1829 he opened his own steamboat business, whose center of activities was the Hudson River. He managed to amass a fortune in bitter competition with other steamboat rivals and later established service on Long Island Sound and later to Rhode Island and Boston. He attracted passengers by providing sumptuous steamboats with all the luxuries then available. By the 1850s, however, he was withdrawing from the steamboat business, perhaps tired of its by then routinized operations, or more likely he needed to find a newer challenge for his boundless energies and competitive drive.

The California gold rush gave him the opportunity to make money carrying eager passengers, but finding that the Pacific Mail Steamship Company* (PMSS) and the United States Mail Steamship Company* had monopolized the route via Panama, he proceeded to open up a new and shorter route through Nicaragua. Vanderbilt organized the Accessory Transit Company* to convey efficiently the passengers across Nicaragua, and his steamers brought the passengers from New York and then picked them up on the Pacific side for the trip to San Francisco. Actually the Accessory Transit Company was part of his larger scheme to build a canal across Nicaragua, but the failure of British investors to provide financing forced him to abandon the canal project as beyond the reach of even his growing wealth. The Nicaragua route was full of complications, including wars and political intrigues, but Vanderbilt thoroughly relished the fight against ruthless competitors. He finally abandoned the Nicaragua route in 1858 after having increased his personal fortune enormously.

In 1854 he organized the Vanderbilt European Line* to provide service between New York and Europe. The withdrawal of British ships from the North Atlantic because of the Crimean War had opened this possibility to make profits, even in competition with the heavily subsidized Collins Line,* whose collapse in February 1858 favored the Vanderbilt European Line. However, Vanderbilt failed to obtain a mail contract, and although he managed to avoid losses in the North Atlantic service, the dwindling profits cooled his enthusiasm for this route, so that when the Civil War broke out, he promptly suspended the sailings of the European Vanderbilt Line.

He transferred the ships of the Vanderbilt European Line to the Atlantic and Pacific Steamship Company,* which he had organized in 1859 and which turned out to be his last venture in ocean transportation. The Atlantic and Pacific Steamship Company was another attempt to tap into the profits of the passenger travel between New York and California; this time Vanderbilt chose the Panama route and engaged in a very bitter fare war with PMSS. By 1860 both companies had decided to reach an agreement, whereby PMSS operated only in the Pacific side, and the Atlantic and Pacific Steamship Company only in the Atlantic. His reputation suffered considerably in this last steamship venture, because "the service of the Vanderbilt ships was dammed along with the ships themselves, the crowded conditions on board, and the food" (Kemble 1943). In 1864 Vanderbilt sold his holdings in the Atlantic and Pacific Steamship Company, thereby severing his last direct link with ocean transportation.

Vanderbilt, a millionaire many times over, could afford to sit back and relax during the last years of his life, and although rapidly approaching seventy years of age, he plunged into the new and exciting field of railroad acquisitions. He began buying his first railroad in 1862, gained control of the New York Central in 1867, and by 1873 controlled an integrated system of railways stretching from New York to Chicago and reaching even into Canada. He continued expanding his railroad empire almost until the time of his death on 4 January 1877, but his only major work of philanthropy was a large donation to a university in Nashville, Tennessee, which subsequently adopted the name of Vanderbilt University in honor of its main benefactor.

References: Robert G. Albion, *The Rise of New York Port, 1815–1860* (New York: Scribner's, 1939); *Dictionary of American Biography*, vol. 19; David I. Folkman, Jr., *The Nicaragua Route* (Salt Lake City: University of Utah Press, 1972); John H. Kemble, *The Panama Route 1848–1868* (Berkeley: University of California Press, 1943); Wheaton J. Lane, *Commodore Vanderbilt: An Epic of the Steam Age* (New York: Alfred A. Knopf, 1942).

VANDERBILT EUROPEAN LINE, 1854–1861. The Vanderbilt European Line was one of the steamship ventures of Cornelius Vanderbilt.* When the start of the Crimean War forced the British government to requisition some Cunard vessels in the North Atlantic, Vanderbilt saw the opportunity to make money with his own ships. He ordered two new steamships in 1854 from the shipyard; the wooden side-wheeler *North Star* began service from New York to Le Havre on 21 April 1855 and was followed by the *Ariel* in May. The Vanderbilt European Line was successful while the Crimean War shipping shortage lasted, but the fast ships of the Collins Line* continued to attract the bulk of the passenger traffic. Cornelius decided to order a fast ship, the *Vanderbilt*, to compete in speed with the Collins Line; the *Vanderbilt* began service in July 1856, and Cornelius hoped the vessel, perhaps the largest in the North Atlantic, would also receive a mail subsidy. The government did not grant Vanderbilt the subsidy, but because Congress revoked the mail contract of the Collins Line, which promptly collapsed, the Vanderbilt European Line could continue to operate now that its main U.S.-flag competitor had vanished.

Using single-expansion* engines and without any government subsidy, the Vanderbilt European Line had to be very aggressive to survive. The company changed its routes as needed to maximize profits; for example, it entered the New-York-Bremen route in 1857 to obtain profits, and although it drove the Bremen Line* out of existence, the Vanderbilt European Line dropped that service in 1859 in the face of strong German competition. Another survival strategy of the company was to lay up its vessels in winter, when passenger traffic traditionally declined; in this way the company saved the expense of running nearly empty ships. Likewise the company placed these vessels on the route to Panama whenever it was profitable. Passengers complained about the somewhat irregular service of the Vanderbilt European Line, yet it managed to carry a significant percentage of the travelers crossing the North Atlantic.

By 1860 the British lines were starting to place vessels with iron hulls and propellers* in the trade, and no matter how attached Vanderbilt and other Americans remained to wooden side-wheelers, it was clear a new generation of U.S.-flag vessels was needed to compete against the English. When the Civil War began in April 1861, the Vanderbilt European Line suspended service to Europe, and Vanderbilt transferred the vessels to the fleet of the Atlantic and Pacific Steamship Company,* his last venture in ocean transportation.

References: Erick Heyl, *Early American Steamers*, 6 vols. (Buffalo: 1953–1969); Wheaton J. Lane, *Commodore Vanderbilt; An Epic of the Steam Age* (New York: Alfred A. Knopf, 1942); David B. Tyler, *Steam Conquers the Atlantic* (New York: D. Appleton Century, 1939).

VICTORY SHIPS. The Victory was one of the two emergency ship designs the U.S. Maritime Commission* mass-produced in response to the needs of World War II. The commission had always opposed the other, the Liberty* ship, and at last in 1944, after a ferocious bureaucratic battle, the U.S. Maritime Commission finally obtained the authorization to shift the shipbuilding priorities away from the Liberty and toward the new Victory. The Victory was derived from the commission's excellent C-2* design (its formal designation was "VC2") and essentially was a stripped-down version of the latter to allow for more rapid construction and delivery. The Victory at a length of 455 feet was 5 feet shorter than the C-2, and its beam was 1 foot less than the C-2's 63 feet but had a draft 3 feet deeper than the 26 feet of the C-2; in deadweight* tons the Victory's 10,700 was larger than the 8,800 of the C-2 but smaller than the 12,500 of the larger C-3,* whose speed of 16.5 knots was the same as the Victory's.

Admiral Emory S. Land* insisted on the Victory not only to help win the war but also because as a superior ship the Victory was well suited to commercial operation in the postwar trades. However, the Liberty ship program had gained such momentum that it could not be stopped, so that by the time the building program of the U.S. Maritime Commission ended after the war, the 414 Victory ships (whose deliveries had begun only in 1944) were dwarfed by the final output of 2,708 Liberty ships. The Victories were in great demand by buyers who took advantage of the Ship Sales Act of 1946* to acquire them, and many remained in service until the early 1960s.

References: John A. Culver, *Ships of the U.S. Merchant Fleet* (Weymouth, MA: Denison Press, 1965); René De La Pedraja, *The Rise and Decline of U.S. Merchant Shipping in the Twentieth Century* (New York: Twayne, 1992); Frederick C. Lane, *Ships for Victory: A History of Shipbuilding Under the U.S. Maritime Commission in World War II* (Baltimore: Johns Hopkins University Press, 1951).

VIRGINIA. See *California, Pennsylvania,* and *Virginia.*

VLCC or VERY LARGE CRUDE CARRIERS. VLCC has been the abbreviation used to refer to oil tankers in the approximate range of 160,000 to 319,000 deadweight* tons. Competition between the American Daniel Ludwig* and the Greek shipowners Aristotle Onassis and Stavros Niarchos in the 1950s and 1960s gradually pushed upward the size of the tankers until the VLCC had far surpassed the venerable T-2s* of World War II. The drive toward these monster ships was fueled by ''economies of scale'': essentially, the bigger the tanker, the lower the operating costs per barrel of oil carried, provided that the VLCC was fully loaded. The push to reduce costs drove shipbuilders to create the next category, ULCC,* for the biggest tankers of all.

W

WALL, SHANNON J., 1919–present. Shannon J. Wall was the second and last president of the National Maritime Union* (NMU). He was born in Seattle, Washington, in 1919 and studied in public schools. He was a student in the University of Washington when the Japanese attacked Pearl Harbor, and he decided to join the merchant marine and soon became active in the ship's committee.* He continued to serve aboard ships until 1951, when he was elected a patrolman.* Wall quickly learned the way to advancement: "The secret of getting elected in the NMU is to be on the administration slate, which I've always been" (Quaglieri 1989). This translated into blind obedience and loyalty to Joseph Curran,* the real ruler of the NMU. In 1966 Curran made Wall part of the inner team when he had him elected secretary-treasurer, from which position Wall was ready to become the next president when Curran retired because of ill health in March 1973.

The NMU was in deep turmoil because of rank-and-file resentment at Curran's autocratic methods, yet Wall did not attempt any opening, much less, reforms, within the rigid union hierarchy. Meanwhile the Seafarers' International Union* (SIU) in membership had surpassed the NMU, which continued to decline. Wall continued the relentless campaign of Curran against "runaway ships," but with little success, so as U.S.-flag shipping dwindled, the union became more concerned with handling its portfolio of investments. Wall convinced members that their pension fund lacked solvency and that only a quick merger with the more solid pension fund of the Marine Engineers' Beneficial Association* (MEBA) District 1 could save their retirement payments.

Wall received a huge severance payment and a large pay raise as soon as he became a vice president in the newly created NMU/MEBA-1. The demotion of Wall and the merger were particularly embarrassing because the NMU had just finished celebrating its fiftieth anniversary, but soon the former NMU members had more complaints: the pension funds had not been merged, while their votes in the union convention were reduced by half, giving MEBA full control over the new union. Union leaders claimed that Wall had "sold the NMU members into political and economic slavery" (*American Shipper*, May 1991). In 1991 Wall himself took a long leave of absence from NMU/MEBA-1 to try to organize seamen on foreign ships owned by U.S. corporations; he was trying to repeat the attempt of the International Maritime Workers Union.* Possibly to avoid U.S. jurisdiction over funds and elections, he registered the new union, the International Organization of Professional Seamen, in the Cayman Islands. Philip J. Loree of the Federation of American Controlled Shipping* was struck by the ironic twist in Wall's latest career move: "So the union leader who spent most of his career castigating 'runaway ships' is now the 'runaway president' of his own 'runaway union' " (ibid.). Wall's new union folded soon after.

References: *American Shipper*, December 1987, May 1991; Philip L. Quaglieri, ed., *America's Labor Leaders* (Lexington, MA: Lexington Books, 1989).

WALSH, CORNELIUS S. ("NEIL"), 27 December 1907–present. Cornelius S. Walsh was president of States Marine Corporation* in 1953–1965 and of Waterman Steamship Corporation* in 1965–1988. He was born in New York City on 27 December 1907; his father was an Irish immigrant who worked in trucking. Walsh received his initial education in public schools and then attended Eastman-Gaines School during 1918–1924. He began working as a typist in Dyson Shipping Co., a freight forwarder* firm. He quickly mastered the business and was promoted to vice president. In 1931 he became the secretary of the States Marine Corporation, a new steamship company just crated the previous year by Henry D. Mercer. Walsh eventually became an important investor in States Marine and in 1953 assumed the presidency, a position he held until his retirement in 1965.

As president, Walsh pushed the application of States Marine to qualify for government subsidies, but the unrelenting opposition of the subsidized companies grouped in the Committee of American Steamship Lines* (CASL) prevented its approval by the Maritime Administration* (MARAD). In 1965 Walsh sold his investment in States Marine to Mercer and with the proceeds from the sale acquired Waterman Steamship Corporation (WSC), whose president he became that same year. At last Walsh owned a subsidized line, but operation of WSC proved more difficult than expected; in particular, the transition to containerships demanded huge cash outlays, which Walsh could not gather without putting at risk his control over the company. WSC was in bankruptcy proceedings by 1984, and in 1988 International Shipholding Corporation* agreed to buy the company. After MARAD approved the sale in 1988, Walsh resigned as president.

References: *American Shipper*, January 1984, August 1986; *Journal of Commerce*, 17 October 1988, 31 March 1989; *National Cyclopedia of American Biography*, current vol. L; *Who's Who in America, 1992–1993*.

WARD, JAMES EDWARD, 25 February 1836–24 July 1894. James E. Ward was the founder and first president of the Ward Line* also called the New York and Cuba Mail Steamship Company. He was born on 25 February 1836 in New York City, and his father James Otis Ward operated sailing ships to a number of foreign ports. James Ward continued in the family business, but he decided to specialize in the trade of one region, unlike his father, who sent ships anywhere there was cargo. Ward picked the Cuba trade as the most promising for a New York shipping man, and in 1856 he established the Ward Line to provide regular sailing service between Havana and New York City, the route that remained the backbone of the Ward Line's operations throughout its history.

In 1866 Ward took Henry P. Booth as a partner, and with this increased financial backing he placed the first wooden steamships in the route. Ward was among the first executives to realize the superiority of steam, and in 1881 he had replaced all his sailing vessels with iron steamships. This complete change was possible because he accepted timely investment in the Ward Line by John Roach, in whose shipyard many of the new vessels were constructed. As steamships became bigger and faster, the Ward Line regularly placed orders for new vessels to improve its fleet. The Alexandre Line,* which served mainly the Mexican ports, had begun to enter the Cuba trade, until it was purchased in 1888 by the Ward Line, which also acquired the ships and routes to the Caribbean ports of Mexico. The Ward Line was a prosperous and successful enterprise when Ward died on 24 July 1894. His only direct heir was a daughter, but neither she nor her husband showed any interest in the shipping business, so that Ward's partner, Henry P. Booth, became the president of the Ward Line.

References: *National Cyclopedia of American Biography*, vol. 6; *Nautical Gazette*, 25 February 1928; Frank J. Taylor, ''Early American Steamship Lines,'' in Society of Naval Architects and Marine Engineers, *Historical Transactions 1893–1943* (Westport, CT: Greenwood Press, 1981).

WARD LINE or NEW YORK AND CUBA MAIL STEAMSHIP COMPANY, 1856–1959. The Ward Line provided cargo and passenger service from New York City to Cuba and the Caribbean ports of Mexico. In 1856 James E. Ward* established in New York City a line that provided regular service to Havana on sailing vessels. After the Civil War he took Henry P. Booth as a new partner, and with the new funds the Ward Line began in 1866 the permanent scheduled steamship service to Havana with two vessels of wooden hulls. Ward was among the first steamship executives to realize that the future was in iron and steam and not in wooden sailing vessels, and in 1877 he contracted with the shipbuilder John Roach to build two iron steamships, the *Saratoga* and the *Niagara*, which were the most advanced craft under the U.S. flag.

Roach became a larger investor in the Ward Line, which in 1881 received from his shipyard the *Santiago* and the *Newport*; the latter luxury vessel was the fatest and most splendidly equipped then existing under the U.S. flag and reduced travel time to four days, one hour southbound and three days, nine hours northbound, speed records that held for a number of years in the Havana route. In 1881 the Ward Line disposed of the last of its sailing vessels and became exclusively a metal and steam fleet, a remarkably early switch because most other lines still retained at least some wooden sailing vessels.

Unfortunately for the Ward Line, the growing Havana trade still could not support such a large ship as the *Newport*, which had to be sold to the Pacific Mail Steamship Company* (PMSS) in 1886. The proceeds from the sale and other profits did allow the company to buy out its main competitor, the Alexandre Line,* in 1888 and to take over the latter's routes to the Caribbean ports of Mexico. As the volume of trade with Cuba and Mexico grew, the Ward Line increased its fleet to nine ships and ordered faster and bigger steamships fitted with the new triple-expansion* engines. The subsidy provided under the Ocean Mail Act of 1891* allowed the company to operate successfully against the Spanish line, which, in any case, suspended operations a few years before the Spanish-American War of 1898; except for the inevitable forays of tramp* vessels, the Ward Line was relatively free of foreign competitors during the rest of its existence.

When James Ward died in 1894, Henry P. Booth became the president, and he continued the traditional policies of the line. In April 1907 Booth and the other stockholders agreed to sell the Ward Line to Charles W. Morse, who made it one of the subsidiaries of his holding company, the Consolidated Steamship Lines.* When the latter collapsed in 1908, it was replaced by the Atlantic, Gulf & West Indies Steamship Lines (AGWI),* whose ownership of the Ward Line lasted until 1954. During 1908–1954 the activities of the Ward Line formed part of the larger history of the parent firm.

The Ward Line resumed a more independent existence in 1954, when AGWI during its liquidation sold this subsidiary to the investor Richard Weininger, who put steamship executive Thomas J. Stevenson in charge of the Ward Line. Like the AGWI stockholders, Weininger and Stevenson refused the government's conditions to receive operating differential subsidies,* so that by the end of 1954 the Ward Line had sold its six U.S.-flag C-2* freighters. The Ward Line did not disappear but continued its service by means of foreign-flag chartered* ships; as a matter of fact, in October 1954 the company resumed the pre–World War II service to eastern Cuba and, in a further attempt to find enough cargo for this revived route, added calls to Haiti.

Running foreign-flag ships to Cuba and Mexico was moderately profitable, but not enough, in Weininger's opinion, to justify buying vessels. Instead he spent the assets of the Ward Line in February 1956 to purchase a controlling interest in the Martin-Parry Corporation, manufacturer of metal partitions and vacuum cleaners, and in the Prosperity Company, manufacturer of commercial laundry and dry cleaning equipment. In March a new holding company was created, Ward Industries, with Weininger as chairman, and Stevenson continued as head of the Ward Line. The diversification to businesses on land or "coming ashore'' revealed clearly how unstable and unrewarding shipping really was. The failure of the revived service to eastern Cuba was the last straw for Weininger, who in mid-1956 sold the Ward Line (but not all of its assets) to Compañía Naviera García, a Cuban firm that promptly renamed itself the Ward-García Line to capitalize on the goodwill of both lines.

Ward-García was in financial trouble by 1958, while Ward Industries on second thought considered that its sale of the Ward Line had been hasty and made an offer to repurchase the line in June 1959, but before the transaction was completed, the deal fell through. Without a cash infusion, Ward-García ended the New York service in July 1959, and the Ward Line name gradually disappeared from merchant shipping. Jakob Isbrandtsen* by 1960 had become the majority stockholder in Ward Industries, which did operate ships directly for a few more years, although it too disappeared in 1963.

Principal Executives

James E. Ward	1856–1894
Henry P. Booth	1894–1907

(for 1908–1954, see Atlantic, Gulf & West Indies Steamship Lines)

Thomas J. Stevenson	1954–1960
Richard Weininger	1954–1960

Some Notable Ships

Saratoga	1878–1906
Newport	1880–1886

References: Winthrop L. Marvin, *The American Merchant Marine* (New York: Scribner's, 1902); *National Cyclopaedia of American Biography*, vol. 6; *Nautical Gazette*, 25 February 1928; *New York Times*, 16 January, 1 June, 4 and 14 October 1954, 1 February, 16 March, 19 October 1956, 1 July 1959; Frank J. Taylor, ''Early American Steamship Lines,'' in Society of Naval Architects and Marine Engineers, *Historical Transactions, 1893–1943* (Westport, CT: Greenwood Press, 1981); U.S. Congress, House, Committee on Merchant Marine and Fisheries, *American Merchant Marine in the Foreign Trade*, Report No. 1210, 51st Congress, 1st Congress, 1st Session, 1890; U.S. Congress, *Report of the Merchant Marine Commission*, 3 vols., Report No. 2755, 58th Congress, 3d Session, 1905.

WAR SHIPPING ADMINISTRATION (WSA), 1942–1946. The War Shipping Administration (WSA) was in charge of the American merchant marine during World War II. The government had begun to requisition privately owned vessels even before U.S. entry into World War II on 7 December 1941, but the slow and cumbersome board proceedings of the U.S. Maritime Commission* were far from ideal to meet the rapidly changing needs of the wartime crisis. President Franklin D. Roosevelt used his authority under the War Powers Act to create a separate agency, the WSA, on 7 February 1942. To ensure ample coordination with the U.S. Maritime Commission, the president appointed its chairman, Admiral Emory S. Land,* to be the administrator of the WSA. Land entrusted various aspects of shipping to fellow commissioners: the shipbuilding program to Admiral Howard L. Vickery and seafaring personnel to Captain Edward Macauley, both of whom also received appointments as deputy administrators of the WSA. The U.S. Maritime Commission retained control of the shipbuilding program, but with the understanding that if the two civilian commissioners or any of the civilian staff hindered or failed to fully support Admiral Vickery, then the president at any moment could transfer the entire shipbuilding program to the WSA, an option that never proved necessary.

Admiral Land did not move as fast in dealing with the central issue of cargo allocation, and to fill the void, President Roosevelt appointed Lewis W. Douglas as deputy administrator of the WSA and largely independent of Land. Douglas was instrumental in setting up efficient procedures to route cargoes around the world, and soon he had created an efficient organization with very competent officials. Douglas also was extremely effective in negotiations with the British on common shipping problems and succeeded in avoiding the rivalries present in other areas of the Anglo-American wartime alliance. However, day-to-day operations bored Douglas, whose autonomous position Admiral Land strongly resented; when Douglas failed to land the position of under secretary of state in the summer of 1943, he gradually withdrew from WSA, and in February 1944, even before his formal resignation a few months later, he had, in fact, been replaced by Captain Granville Conway, who enjoyed excellent relations with Admiral Land.

WSA concentrated on the most efficient allocation of space aboard the ships in order to carry the largest amount of cargo. The WSA wisely delegated the actual manning and upkeep of the ships at government expense to general agents, who initially were the U.S. steamship companies existing before World War II. As the flood of wartime construction flowed out of the shipyards, the WSA assigned vessels to tramp* operators and, when these were not enough, also called on steamship agents and freight forwarders* to handle vessels; for many in the latter two groups this was their first exposure to steamship operations, and some attempted to remain in the business after the war was over.

At headquarters in Washington, D.C., the WSA received the requests to carry cargoes and then allocated the available space to try to satisfy as much as possible the demand, quite naturally rerouting or changing the voyages of the ships to enhance the cargo-carrying capacity of the vessels. Given that large numbers of seamen were dying because of the enemy attacks on the convoys and that merchant mariners suffered the highest percentage of casualties among the military services, the WSA and President Roosevelt prepared to extend military status to the seafarers, a proposal bitterly rejected and finally blocked by the maritime labor leaders in one of their worst mistakes.

The WSA struggled continuously during the war to convince the army, which generated over 90 percent of the military cargoes, of the need to combine military cargoes with civilian cargoes in one single pool. The Joint Chiefs of Staff supported the WSA's control over all civilian cargoes, but when it came to military cargoes, they acted like proprietary* companies and insisted on having their own merchant ships to carry only military cargoes. The WSA did not question the military's right to have priority for its cargoes and simply wanted to have the opportunity to use the freighters to carry other cargoes both before and after the trips carrying the military cargoes. While the military was determined to have delivery of their goods at any cost, the WSA had the priority of keeping the ships running full all the time, thereby saving time and money and ultimately requiring fewer ships for the war.

Gradually the military began to accept the wisdom of the WSA position, although never completely. The WSA continued to perform with clockwork precision and was one of the more successful government agencies dealing with merchant shipping. Among its many accomplishments, the WSA was responsible for one breakthrough of monumental proportions. Trucking specialists brought into the WSA discovered that the delays in ocean transportation were caused not by the time at sea, but rather by the many days wasted in port loading and unloading the vessel. To end this bottleneck the WSA pressed for changes in vessel design to expedite cargo handling and soon developed the totally novel system of containers* as the fastest way to move cargo. The WSA was amazed at the savings in time achieved by containers and was preparing to shift the operations of all the general agents to containers, but before final action could be taken, World War II ended, and the rush to demobilize killed any chance of an early shift to containers in U.S. merchant shipping.

The WSA published its container findings to no avail, because merchant shipping, one of the most tradition-bound businesses, has stubbornly resisted innovations. The huge fleet built during the war did require immediate government attention to make an orderly transition to peacetime shipping, but when the Ship Sales Act* was passed in March 1946, the adopted policy of selling off the surplus ships left little room for the WSA, whose end was rapidly approaching. The government and the country in the rush to demobilize were not about to allow the WSA to become another Emergency Fleet Corporation* nor the U.S. Maritime Commission another Shipping Board.* Prematurely the WSA was dissolved in 1 September 1946, and its remaining functions were transferred to the U.S. Maritime Commission. The liquidation of WSA was so complete that not even a skeleton organization was left behind to cope with any future emergencies, and consequently when the Korean War broke out, the government in haste had to create a new agency, the National Shipping Authority* (NSA), patterned after the WSA.

Principal Executives

Admiral Emory S. Land	1942–1946
Lewis W. Douglas	1942–1943
Granville Conway	1944–1946

References: Robert P. Browder and Thomas G. Smith, *Independent: A Biography of Lewis W. Douglas* (New York: Alfred A. Knopf, 1986); René De La Pedraja, *The Rise and Decline of U.S. Merchant Shipping in the Twentieth Century* (New York: Twayne, 1992); Frederick C. Lane, *Ships for Victory: A History of Shipbuilding Under the U.S. Maritime Commission in World War II* (Baltimore: Johns Hopkins University Press, 1951).

WASHINGTON. See *Manhattan* and *Washington.*

WATERFRONT EMPLOYERS' ASSOCIATION (WEA), 1937–1949. The Waterfront Employers' Association was created in 1937 in direct response to the growing power of the labor movement on the Pacific Coast. Seamen and longshoremen's unions had united to create the Maritime Federation of the Pacific* (MFP), and management had to counter this challenge. The Pacific American Steamship Association* (PASA) had negotiated only with seamen, while the Waterfront Employers' Union* (WEU) had dealt with longshoremen, but now PASA agreed to transfer its bargaining authority to WEA, which also replaced the WEU.

The new association required a full-time president with adequate staff, unlike the previous WEU, whose presidency had been rotated on an annual basis among executives of the member companies. Roger Lapham* wanted a president from outside the industry "who would have access to the principal executives of the Waterfront Employers Association, the companies that make it up, and who could go in and meet them face to face and tell them why this was wrong or that" (Roger Lapham Oral History). Almon E. Roth,* the comptroller of Stanford University, accepted the offer to become president of WEA in 1937. Roth soon negotiated contracts with Harry Bridges* and Harry Lundeberg;* gradually labor peace began to return to the previously turbulent waterfront of the Pacific Coast.

Roth's tact and diplomatic ability were not immediately missed when he left the position in 1939, because for the duration of World War II, government accords kept the docks quiet. The end of the war led WEA to believe that hostility could reduce the unions to their pre-1934 impotence, but the longshoremen fought back and won the successful strikes of 1946 and 1948. Confrontation with the unions had only served to disrupt operations on the waterfront, and to prevent further strikes, the steamship companies disbanded the discredited WEA. In its place, management crated a new organization, the Pacific Maritime Association* (PMA), to pursue more conciliatory tactics with Bridges.

Principal Executives

Almon E. Roth	1937–1939
Frank Foisie	1939–1949

References: Clark Kerr and Lloyd Fishers, "Conflict on the Waterfront," *Atlantic Monthly*, September 1949; Charles P. Larrowe, *Harry Bridges: The Rise and Fall of Radical Labor in the U.S.* (New York: Lawrence Hill, 1972); Roger Lapham Oral History, University of California, Berkeley.

WATERFRONT EMPLOYERS' UNION (WEU), 1914–1937. In spite of the word *union*, the Waterfront Employers' Union was an organization of steamship owners and not of workers on the West Coast. The WEU was established in 1914 in response to the attempts by the International Longshoremen's Association* (ILA) to create branch unions on the Pacific Coast. The employers wanted a showdown with labor, but the disruptions associated with World War I postponed the confrontation until after the war. In September 1919 the WEU struck hard to crush once and for all any independent labor movement in the docks of San Francisco. The longshoremen were in an isolated position because they had bolted from the ILA and had not united with the seamen or other labor groups. The strikers made radical demands that allowed the WEU to brand the longshoremen as Bolsheviks who wanted another Russian Revolution. To crush the strike, WEU established the Marine Service Bureau* to recruit nonunion workers. The shipowners went so far as to hire armed strikebreakers, and although the longshoremen fought back with violence, finally WEU emerged victorious. The independent union of the longshoremen disappeared and was replaced by the Blue Book Union,* a company union that enforced management policies among the workers. However, the victory in the San Francisco Bay Area did not automatically mean management control over the entire West Coast, and WEU had to fight a battle in each of the ports and, in the case of Portland, Oregon, did not achieve full management control until 1922.

When the seamen began the Strike of 1921,* the Marine Service Bureau of WEU immediately began to hire scabs to keep the ships running. After the strike was crushed, the WEU decided to rationalize its hiring, and henceforth all longshoremen were hired through the Blue Book Union, while the Marine Service Bureau handled only seamen. The Pacific American Steamship Association* (PASA) and the Shipowners' Association of the Pacific Coast* (SAPC) agreed to make the Marine Service Bureau their only hiring hall for seamen. The Shipping Board did continue to operate the parallel Sea Service Bureau* to hire the crews for government-owned vessels.

Once the seamen and longshoremen had been crushed, the WEU did not have much to do, and in effect it became lax and unprepared to face the renewed wave of labor unrest that erupted in the 1930s. The loyal and obedient Blue Book Union was the first casualty in 1933, while the Big Strike of 1934* saw the collapse of the Marine Service Bureau. The WEU itself almost disappeared and was saved only by timely backing from the entire business community of San Francisco. In 1935 seamen and longshoremen united to form the Maritime Federation of the Pacific (MFP), a formidable labor coalition that WEU was in no condition to face. To replace the weakened WEU, the owners needed a more dynamic organization, and in 1937 they created the Waterfront Employers' Association* (WEU) to defend the owners' interests and conduct collective bargaining.

References: Giles T. Brown, *Ships That Sail No More: Marine Transportation from San Diego to Puget Sound, 1910–1940* (Lexington, University of Kentucky Press, 1966); William S. Hopkins, "Employment Exchanges for Seamen," *American Economic Review* 25 (1935): 250–258; Bruce Nelson, *Workers on the Waterfront* (Urbana: University of Illinois Press, 1990); William W. Pilcher, *The Portland Longshoremen: A Dispersed Urban Community* (New York: Holt, Rinehart, and Winston, 1972).

WATERMAN, JOHN B., 1866–30 April 1937. John B. Waterman was the founder and first president of the Waterman Steamship Corporation* (WSC), one of the most successful firms in the years between the two world wars. Waterman was born in New Orleans in 1866 and from very early developed what became his lifelong ambition of owning a merchant shipping company. Although of a good family, he lacked the resources to set himself up in business and began working for railroads, first the Illinois Central in Mississippi and later the Texas Pacific. Rather than continue to advance as a railroad executive, he decided to return to New Orleans to enter the steamship business, but he found that the tightly closed circles in that city had no need for additional talent. Undaunted, he moved to nearby Mobile, Alabama, in 1902 and became a manager for Elder Dempster & Co. and later was able "to operate as a private charterer* on his own account" (*Nautical Gazette*, 10 October 1931). However, the lack of funds precluded formal entry into steamship ranks, but in preparation for any eventual opportunity, he carefully cultivated links with local businessmen in the hopes of organizing a shipping venture.

When the Shipping Board* announced after World War I the policy of paying managing operators* to handle government vessels, Waterman immediately saw the opportunity of a lifetime. He quickly organized the WSC on 9 June 1919 and secured the backing of local promoters to try to convince the Shipping Board to assign him vessels for operation from Mobile to foreign ports. Waterman's application was quickly accepted, and soon he was operating a small fleet of government vessels, but in this he did not differ from the over 200 other managing operators who in their overwhelming majority were only interested in milking the Shipping Board to make quick profits. For Waterman, who had that rare sentimental attachment to the business of merchant shipping, profits were not the end but merely the means to construct a maritime enterprise of the first magnitude. He had a vision for the company and gradually extended routes, purchased ships, and expanded into shoreside activities like stevedoring, repairs, and eventually ownership of a shipyard, stretches of land, and the Grand Hotel across Mobile Bay.

As he later explained, "the development of this company has been the climax of my life's efforts" (De La Pedraja 1992). He surrounded himself with an extremely competent team of new executives, and he imposed the policy of plowing back the profits into the company rather than into wasteful expenses, as had been the case with many of the managing operators,* or even into conspicuous consumption, as did Henry Herbermann* of American Export Lines.* His emotional attachment to merchant shipping when he could make more money more easily on land (he rejected offers to sell out) did not blind him to the cruel competition prevalent in the field, and to protect himself he hired Hardin Arledge,* one of the most influential lobbyists in Washington, D.C., during the 1920s and 1930s. Waterman had really taken to heart the task of providing excellent shipping to the Gulf of Mexico, a region neglected by most companies before World War I. He cooperated closely with the Delta Line* to maintain ample steamship services to the Gulf of Mexico, but the last years of his life were frustrated by the bitter discovery that his company, already one of the most successful of U.S. steamship companies, had been secretly hindered and blocked for decades by Lykes Brothers Steamship Company,* which wanted to acquire a virtual monopoly over all shipping in the Gulf of Mexico. John B. Waterman died in Mobile, Alabama, on 30 April 1937.

References: René De La Pedraja, *The Rise and Decline of U.S. Merchant Shipping in the Twentieth Century* (New York: Twayne, 1992); *Nautical Gazette*, 10 October 1931; *New York Times*, 1 May 1937; Waterman Steamship Corporation Records, Mobile Public Library, Mobile, Alabama.

WATERMAN STEAMSHIP CORPORATION (WSC), 1919–present. The Waterman Steamship Corporation (WSC) provided ocean transportation from the Gulf of Mexico to Europe until the 1970s and since then has provided shipping services from New York to various places in the world. John B. Waterman* organized the company on 9 June 1919 to provide adequate steamship service to Mobile, Alabama, a port that had been usually eclipsed by New Orleans. The company was a managing operator* for the vessels of the Shipping Board* and, like many other managing operators, sent vessels throughout many places in the world, until it finally settled down in 1923 upon its most promising route, from the Gulf to ports in England and Northern Europe. The Florida Boom convinced the company to purchase three vessels in 1925 for the coastwise* trade, but the collapse of the Florida Boom in 1927 almost bankrupted the company until it shifted its own three vessels into the Puerto Rico trade, a service the company continued to provide until it was transferred to Sea-Land* in 1964.

When the Shipping Board began to reduce drastically the number of managing operators in the early 1920s, WSC had to wage a constant battle to escape consolidation into the other firms in the Gulf of Mexico, particularly Lykes Brothers Steamship Company,* which had formed a pattern of destroying or absorbing its Gulf rivals. WSC, because it was so well managed, survived intact the attacks of Lykes Brothers, while the help of the master lobbyist Hardin B. Arledge* allowed WSC to survive the shifting political alliances at the Shipping Board. After a long bureaucratic battle, the Shipping Board at last agreed in 1931 to sell the ships in the East Gulf-United Kingdom route to WSC, whose position as the second most important carrier in the Gulf of Mexico was thus confirmed. Because the volume of coastwise cargo was increasing, Waterman Steamship Corporation decided in 1933 to create a new subsidiary, the Pan-Atlantic Steamship Company, to run the service from the Gulf to New York, Philadelphia, and Boston.

John B. Waterman reinvested the profits into the company and related activities such as stevedoring and in 1937 also acquired a shipyard to perform repair work on its vessels. With U.S. entry into World War II, the company's vessels were requisitioned for wartime duty, but once the conflict was over, WSC acquired enough surplus vessels to make its fleet the third largest under the U.S. flag. Chairman E. A. Roberts even attempted from 1945 to 1947 to establish Waterman Airlines, but this aviation venture, although initially successful, had to be abandoned because the Civil Aeronautics Board did not want steamship companies to provide regular airplane service. The company reaped high profits in the immediate postwar years because of the shipping shortage, but by 1948, when the first warning signs of impending troubles were evident, Chairman Roberts, who concentrated on his other personal ventures, did not change policies. Only the outbreak of the Korean War and the need to send cargoes to French Indochina saved the company from drastic cutbacks, and although the company eventually rebounded, shortly after, Roberts convinced the stockholders to sell, not just because of the mounting difficulties in merchant shipping but also to escape the payment of the federal inheritance tax. About this time Malcom McLean* was looking to buy a coastwise company so that he could carry out his experiment of hauling truck trailers aboard ships, and he agreed in January 1955 to buy the coastwise subsidiary, the Pan-Atlantic Steamship Company, with borrowed money and the proceeds from the sale of his trucking firm; one month later bankers convinced him to put the Pan-Atlantic Steamship Company as collateral for a loan so that he could buy all of WSC as well, and he quickly agreed to such a favorable transaction.

McLean placed his brother James in charge of WSC, while he himself concentrated on the Pan-Atlantic Steamship Company in order to apply his concept of "trailerships." Soon McLean realized that carrying truck trailers was unprofitable, and he decided instead to adopt the container* system developed by the War Shipping Administration* (WSA) during World War II. Even here McLean committed the mistake of trying to carry the containers on top of T-2* tankers, which would continue to carry petroleum from the Gulf to the East Coast. McLean's learning experience with containers was extremely expensive, and gradually WSC was drained of most of its resources and assets. In 1960 McLean changed the name of the Pan-Atlantic Steamship Company to Sea-Land, which remained the focus of his activities. His brother James had realized since 1957 that WSC could not continue to operate in the foreign trade routes unless it first received operating differential* subsides, but the application constantly was blocked. However, through carefully manipulated moves, McLean managed to position himself strongly enough to negotiate a favorable sale of WSC to the brothers Cornelius S. Walsh* and Edward P. Walsh in May 1965. To save a nearly bankrupt WSC, the Walsh brothers obtained in 1966 capital from U.S. Freight Company (later, Transway), which acquired a 50 percent stake in the steamship company. Headquarters moved to New York, and with this cash infusion Waterman survived until finally the Maritime Administration* awarded three contracts for operating-differential subsidies. However, Waterman still could not find funds to order the construction of new vessels to replace the aging ships and was forced to allow two of its subsidy contracts to lapse, one in 1977 and the second in 1984 because the contracts required the construction of new vessels. Seeing the danger, the company decided to file for bankruptcy in November 1983 in the hope that while it was still strong Waterman could somehow recover under the Chapter 11 protection of the bankruptcy court. At that time the company was operating seven LASH* vessels between New York and ports in the Far East and Middle East and no longer served the Gulf of Mexico, although it still maintained some administrative offices in Mobile to take advantage of lower salaries and costs in the South.

The company went into a complex reorganization, which culminated in the acquisition of Waterman by the International Shipholding Corporation* (ISH) in October 1988. The offices of Waterman in Mobile were consolidated with those of ISH in New Orleans, while the New York offices moved to ISH headquarters in the same city. Waterman under International Shipholding Corporation continued to operate its U.S.-flag ships with subsidies and since has focused on the trade to the Middle East, India, and Indonesia.

Principal Executives

John B. Waterman	1919–1937
Edward A. Roberts	1928–1955
Norman G. Nicholson	1933–1955
Malcom McLean	1955–1965
James McLean	1955–1965
Cornelius S. Walsh	1965–1988
Niels W. Johnsen*	1988–present

References: *American Shipper*, July 1977, January 1984, March, August 1990; René De La Pedraja, *The Rise and Decline of U.S. Merchant Shipping in the Twentieth Century* (New York: Twayne, 1992); International Shipholding Corporation, *Annual Report, 1990; Journal of Commerce*, 28 October 1988, 13 March 1989; Maritime Subsidy Board, *Decisions*, vol. 4 (Washington, DC: Government Printing Office, 1980); *Mobile Register*, 7 August 1986; *New York Times*, 12 May 1965; *Wall Street Journal*, 2 June 1966.

WEIR, STAN, 1921–present. Stan Weir was a gifted labor organizer whose rejection of bureaucracy and authoritarianism deprived him of high union positions. He was born in Los Angeles of working-class parents in 1921 and graduated from public high school in 1940. He attended college one year but then dropped out of the University of California at Los Angeles because the courses did not offer "the truth" he had been expecting since junior high. Weir also thirsted for a life of action but had become so cynical that he could not stand the discipline in the armed forces during World War II; as a compromise, he joined the merchant marine as a cadet in uniform but quickly discovered that the combination of hard work and outward laxness characteristic of sailors was more suited for his temperament. He resigned as a cadet (forsaking the certainty of rising to officer rank) and instead joined the Sailors' Union of the Pacific* (SUP). As a sailor he was exposed to socialist and Marxist ideas that balanced his otherwise anarchist tendencies.

Weir had great talent to lead the seamen, and he was routinely elected to be a member of the ship's committee.* His abilities called the attention of Harry Lundeberg,* who chose Weir to organize the crews aboard the tankers of Standard Oil of California in 1943–1944. Weir completed the task, but he lost all enthusiasm when he learned that the SUP tolerated the blatantly racist policies of some officials because, as Lundeberg explained about a specific individual, "the man's doing a good job for us over there and we have to overlook some of his faults" (Weir 1973).

Weir had become a militant and had gone sour on bureaucracies, which he felt did nothing but cover up mistakes and flaws. After an attempt to challenge SUP policies in 1945, Weir left the merchant marine, disillusioned because the union would not allow any meaningful social change. From 1945 to 1959 Weir held a series of jobs in automobile factories and trucking firms, and in each place he repeated his attempts to challenge union leadership, and in the case of the gangster-controlled Teamsters he was quite justified. This period was significant for the full development of his ideas, because Weir found in the dynamics of the "informal work group," or the dozen or so workers in the shop who work together, the key to reconcile his rejection of bureaucracy and authoritarianism with his ideas of a socialist democracy.

A layoff from the automobile factory in 1956 raised the more mundane problem of having to earn a living, no easy task because "he had picked up a reputation as a troublemaker." Like many other rebellious persons, he eventually drifted into the more tolerant International Longshoremen and Warehousemen's Union* (ILWU) and began to work as a longshoremen in 1959, a job he liked enough to decline the offer to return to the former auto plant. The ILWU had hired him as one of 743 "B-men" (60 percent of them black) who received whatever work was left after the union hiring hall* had exhausted the supply of "A-men" (regular union members). Normally the B-men came up for promotion to A-men after a year or so, but the Mechanization and Modernization Agreement of 1960* left the B-men in a probationary period. Inevitably Weir, the perpetual rebel, emerged as the spokesman of the B-men, and he began to advocate their case inside and outside union circles, and soon Harry Bridges,* the president of the ILWU, saw in Weir not so much a political rival as more a deadly danger to the ILWU who could easily destroy the organization that longshoremen had so painfully constructed over decades.

In 1963 a joint committee of the Pacific Maritime Association* (PMA) and the ILWU* agreed to promote 500 men to ''A'' rank, and since the original number of 743 had declined to only 561, the committee had to make the painful choice whom to fire and retain. In the frequent manner of executives in companies, Bridges took advantage of the procedure to dismiss Weir, whom he felt posed a permanent danger to the organization. Weir fought against his expulsion by organizing a defense committee and among other charges claimed that racism had been responsible for the firing of the B-men because many were black. Weir afterward became an instructor at the University of Illinois and authored a number of influential articles, in particular ''USA: The Labor Revolt.''

References: Gary M. Fink, ed., *Biographical Dictionary of American Labor*, 2d ed. (Westport, CT: Greenwood Press, 1984); Stan Weir, ''The Informal Work Group,'' in Alice Lynd and Staughton Lynd, eds., *Rank and File: Personal Histories by Working-Class Organizers* (Boston: Beacon Press, 1973), pp. 177–200.

WEISBERGER, MORRIS, 10 August 1907–23 September 1987. Morris Weisberger was the head of the Sailors' Union of the Pacific* (SUP) from 1957 to 1978. Weisberger was born in Cleveland, Ohio, on 10 August 1907 and became a seaman in 1926. He entered the union bureaucracy as front office clerk of the SUP in 1936. Weisberger replaced Harry Lundeberg* as head of the SUP, but not as president of the Seamen's International Union* (SIU) because the latter position went to Paul Hall,* who held the real power. This was the first time in the twentieth century that the leader of the SUP did not also head a national seamen's organization and reflected a long-term shift in the center of power. As a matter of fact, Weisberger had obtained the SUP leadership because he had become a supporter of Hall. The highly centralized power structure inherited from Lundeberg made the SUP a pliable instrument for communicating to the rank and file the orders coming down from the SIU hierarchy. Weisberger led the SUP in a 1962 strike against the Pacific Maritime Association,* but the real decisions about the strike were taken by Hall in SIU headquarters. Weisberger joined with Hall in ending the bitter hostility that had existed under Lundeberg between the SUP and the International Longshoremen and Warehousemen's Union* (ILWU). Because of health reasons, Weisberger retired in 1978 and was succeeded by Paul Dempster.* Weisberger died in San Francisco on 23 September 1987.

References: Bruce Nelson, *Workers on the Waterfront: Seamen, Longshoremen, and Unionism in the 1930s* (Urbana: University of Illinois Press, 1990); Stephen Schwartz, *Brotherhood of the Sea: A History of the Sailors' Union of the Pacific, 1885–1985* (New Brunswick, NJ: Transaction Books, 1986); *West Coast Sailors*, 19 October 1990.

WESTWOOD SHIPPING LINES. See Weyerhaeuser Company.

WEYERHAEUSER COMPANY, 1923–1968; 1981–present. Weyerhaeuser dated back to 1900 and, as one of the largest forest products companies in the United States, has frequently operated its own merchant ships. In 1923 the company entered the intercoastal* trade because it was having a hard time booking enough space to send its lumber from the Pacific Northwest to the East Coast. The company's ships were surplus World War I vessels, and after World War II the company resumed the intercoastal service again with surplus vessels; generally the company's lumber provided the eastbound cargoes, but competition for westbound cargoes were increasingly tough, not from other steamship companies but because of the low rates of the railroads.

By 1960, with one intercoastal steamship company folding after another, the parent company considered buying new vessels a risky proposition and instead opted for rehabilitating six of its excellently maintained ships to prolong their life for another fifteen years. The rehabilitation was completed in April 1962, but the fifteen years proved unnecessary, because the company completely abandoned the intercoastal service and sold its U.S.-flag ships in 1968.

Foreign-flag tonnage and chartered* ships carried the lumber to foreign ports until 1991, when Weyerhaeuser decided to return to the direct management of its own vessels. The parent company created a separate subsidiary, Westwood Shipping Lines, to operate foreign-flag vessels on long-term charter. The two main services for Westwood were from the Pacific Coast to the Far East and to Europe. Westbound cargoes were lumber products primarily for Korea and Japan, but for the return voyage, Westwood Shipping had to compete furiously for eastbound cargoes by charging rates 5 to 10 percent below those of eastbound conferences.* The shipping subsidiary was so profitable that Weyerhaeuser decided to order five vessels in 1986 and 1987, all operated under long-term charter to the company.

In 1989 Westwood decided to suspend its service to Europe as not essential to the export of the parent company's lumber products. The shipping services to the Far East remained profitable, and when Weyerhaeuser decided in 1990 to cut back on many of its businesses and other ventures, Westwood survived intact. Weyhaeuser's shipping operations have been interesting because of the mix the company has achieved between pure proprietary* operation, when the company owned the cargo carried aboard its vessels, and liner* service, when the company allowed shippers* to send cargo aboard its ships at lower rates during certain legs of the voyage.

References: *American Shipper*, July 1977, May 1981, March 1990, July 1992; Ralph W. Hidy, Frank E. Hill, and Allan Nevins, *Timber and Men: The Weyerhaeuser Story* (New York: Macmillan, 1963); Propeller Club, *American Merchant Marine Conference: Proceedings 1962.*

WHIPSAWING. Whipsawing has been union tactic to drive up wages and increase benefits. The original meaning of *whipsaw* is a long saw with a handle at each end: as each man pushes the saw, this allows the other to push even harder to cut the log. What this has meant in union practice is that each union leader wants to obtain a contract for his workers as good as that of the other maritime unions, but once negotiations were rolling favorably, he could not resist "showing off" and getting just a bit more than the other labor leaders had obtained. When the contracts of the other unions were up for renewal, they also wanted to achieve parity with the other union, but once attained, they could not resist pushing management for a few added concessions, and consequently the process repeated itself as labor costs spiralled out of control.

The interunion power struggle was the driving force behind the labor leaders who were afraid of losing their membership to rival unions. Whipsawing affected negatively all of the U.S. merchant marine from the late 1930s to the 1960s and bore a large share of the responsibility for the collapse of coastwise* shipping services in the United States. The precarious financial position of most U.S. steamship companies made them capitulate to whipsawing rather than risk the potentially fatal "job action"* on the part of the unions.

References: Joseph H. Ball, *The Government-Subsidized Union Monopoly* (Washington, DC: Labor Policy Association, 1966); René De La Pedraja, *The Rise and Decline of U.S. Merchant Shipping* (New York: Twayne, 1992); Joseph P. Goldberg, *The Maritime Story: A Study in Labor-Management Relations* (Cambridge: Harvard University Press, 1958).

WHITE-SHIRT SAILOR. *White-shirt sailor* is a term that described those union leaders who were former sailors but had gradually assumed the attitudes and manners of conservative Americans on land. The union officials, with the notable exception of Andrew Furuseth,* abandoned the traditional sailors' garments for the office dress of business executives, hence the term *white shirt.* As early as 1900, Ed Rosenberg made this justification: "I did not want to play to the dungaree sailor element by pretending that I was one of them. Their filthy language, their beastly carousing, their dirt, I despise, and I shall always say so. It is evil and it should be fought against. I am no saint nor holier than thou person, only a 'white shirt sailor' and it is the white shirt sailors who have made the union what it is today" (Weintraub 1959).

To run the unions white-shirt sailors such as Paul Scharrenberg* were necessary, but unlike unions representing workers on land, the leaders could not easily drop in on the factory floor or workplace, and thus they easily lost touch with the rank and file. Only the Independent Tanker Unions,* because of the continuous nature of their workers' employment, have escaped the problems of white-shirt sailors. In its most extreme case, white-shirt sailors degenerated into "Tuxedo unionism,"* with the labor leaders dressed in the finest clothes money could buy and surrounded by gangs of thugs that kept the union under control

by the liberal use of force and threats of violence; ''Emperor'' David E. Grange*
was the most notorious example of a white-shirt sailor turned Tuxedo unionist.

References: Mary Ann Burki, ''Paul Scharrenberg: White Shirt Sailor,'' Ph.D. diss.,
University of Rochester, 1971; Stephen Schwartz, *Brotherhood of the Sea: A History of
the Sailors' Union of the Pacific, 1885–1985* (New Brunswick, NJ: Transaction Books,
1986); Hyman Weintraub, *Andrew Furuseth: Emancipator of the Seamen* (Berkeley:
University of California Press, 1959).

WILSON-WEEKS AGREEMENT OF 1954. The Wilson-Weeks Agreement
established policies that severely restricted the activities of the Military Sea
Transportation Service* (MSTS) in order to favor private steamship companies.
The agreement was signed during the pro-business Dwight D. Eisenhower administration between secretary of defense Charles E. Wilson and secretary of
commerce Sinclair Weeks on 1 July 1954. By the term of this agreement, the
government agreed to limit the size of the MSTS fleet, often referred to as the
''nucleus fleet,'' to fifty-six transports, thirty-four cargo ships, and sixty-one
tankers except in times of emergency. The agreement also specified the priority
MSTS was to follow to obtain additional shipping: First, U.S.-flag liner* service;
then, chartering* U.S.-flag vessels; then, taking out vessels from the National
Defense Reserve Fleet;* and only lastly, using space or vessels under foreign
flags. This order of priority had already been established in a previous Memo-
randum of Agreement between the Department of Defense and the Department
of Commerce on 15 August 1951. The innovation in the Wilson-Weeks Agreement was the severe limitation on the fleet size of the MSTS, thereby guaranteeing private operators a substantial share of military cargoes the government
otherwise would have carried much more cheaply aboard its own ships. Not
only did the government have to pay more to carry the military cargoes, but the
merchant shipping companies were reinforced in their dependent attitude of
looking toward the government for cargo and for profits, when they should have
been devoting their efforts to reduce costs and improve services as part of an
aggressive campaign to attract foreign and American shippers.* The Wilson-
Weeks Agreement also marked one of the two high points in the pro-business
Eisenhower administration's policy of favoring private merchant shipping; the
second high point came less than two months later in the Cargo Preference Act
of 1954.*

References: Wytze Gorter, *United States Shipping Policy* (New York: Council on
Foreign Relations, 1956); Gerald R. Jantscher, *Bread Upon the Waters: Federal Aids to
the Maritime Industries* (Washington, DC: Brookings Institution, 1975); Samuel A.
Lawrence, *United States Merchant Shipping Policies and Politics* (Washington, DC:
Brookings Institution, 1966); U.S. Congress, Committee on Merchant Marine and Fisheries, *Cargo for American Ships*, 2 vols. (Washington, DC: Government Printing Office,
1972).

WOMEN. The U.S. merchant marine has generally been closed to women, and
even after formal barriers have come down since the 1960s, the shrinking world

of merchant shipping has remained one of the few essentially male bastions at a time when women have made their presence felt in almost every activity in the United States. While the exclusion of women was initially deliberate, actions of an unintentional or accidental nature have been no less decisive in more recent decades.

During the days of sail the wives and daughters of captains often lived aboard the ships, but when the introduction of steam brought an almost complete separation between the functions of captain and shipowner, this tradition died out in the United States, although it has survived in Europe. Except for the female passengers, the crews and officers of ships were males, and on the docks the longshoremen (many of whom were sailors who wished to settle down) were also all males. Among the shipping executives, the situation was no different, and while attitudes toward women have ranged from the deferential in the South to arrogance by those owners who considered their wives as ships to be owned and showed off, the consensus was that females had no role in the management of shipping firms.

The exhausting work of handling coal for the engines and loading the ships argued for keeping these hardship tasks in the hands of men, but in countries of the former Soviet bloc throughout the twentieth century women were used as stevedores on the docks and carried aboard ships for harsh tasks, often deliberately as a way to exploit the female labor force, so that the severity of the work did not fully explain the lack of female participation. Studies suggest that a large proportion of seamen could not or more likely did not want to work on land and that they have created a special seafarers' culture and community precisely because they have not been able to integrate themselves into the society on land. The word *marginal* has been used to refer to seamen in the sense that they belonged to the margins of society, and hence because they did not fit into the mainstream, they found in the seafaring life an acceptable outlet. Apparently U.S. society since the nineteenth century has produced large numbers of individuals who felt marginalized and find a solution or an escape in the life of a seaman; females, on the other hand, traditionally considered very sociable and constantly striving to create and belong to social groups, have not experienced the same need to find in seafaring an alternative to life on land.

Thus deck and engine personnel have remained exclusively male until very recently, but for the steward's department, the exclusion of females seemed more an imposition of those land values regarding what the proper role of women should be. As passenger services improved since the 1920s, the need to provide better services to a larger percentage of the travelers and not just to those in first class, as was the case up to World War I, meant a tremendous expansion in the stewards' department. Finally the Grace Line* took the inevitable step in 1929 of introducing waitresses aboard the vessels, a practice that initially was disconcerting to some who felt discipline would suffer because of jealousies over the females. The rivalries by the crewmen over women were rare, and eventually other steamship companies began to use waitresses in their passenger vessels. Gradually, companies offering passenger services have come to expect as normal a large number of females engaged in the serving and handling of food, as maids, as tourist and travel directors, and even as clerical help aboard the ships. However, with the disappearance of U.S.-flag passenger services everywhere except in the domestic trades protected by the cabotage* laws, the transition to females in the stewards' department has largely continued in foreign-owned ships that generally had never quite broken the tradition of having females on board.

Shipping executives, the companies, organizations, and clubs remained male preserves, often in accordance with charters. The question of giving some role at least to the wives of executives appeared in the 1930s and culminated in the establishment of the Women's Organization for the Advancement of the American Merchant Marine in 1937. Although established as an independent organization, it operated as a women's auxiliary to the Propeller Club,* whose membership remained closed to females. The Propeller Club transferred some of its social functions to the Women's Organization, in particular, the "adopt-a-ship-program" whereby boys—but not girls—in schools adopted a ship of the U.S. merchant marine and followed its progress through correspondence and the press. The Women's Organization also hosted charitable events to raise funds for the Society for Seamen's Children and the Merchant Marine Library Association.* Occasionally the Women's Organization supported the trade associations by sending its own pleas to the government, asking for greater support for the merchant marine. With U.S. entry into World War II, the wives of the executives shifted the focus of their activities to the United Seamen's Service.* The massive expansion of the merchant marine did not bring the entry of women into the field, and no "Sally the Sailor" emerged, in sharp contrast to the shipbuilding industry, where the large-scale use of female labor ("Rosie the Riveter") marked a watershed in changing women's role in society.

With a return of peace the executives' wives organized in 1945 a national association that they called the Women's National American Merchant Marine Organization to resume the traditional functions. However, by the 1950s a new generation of women was starting to emerge and was demanding more direct participation in the merchant marine. When Josephine Bay Paul* became chairman of the board of American Export Lines in 1959, the first time a woman had ever held such a position, this sent a clear message to women who sought a greater role. The Propeller Club at last relented on its males-only policy and accepted as members the first six females, including Congresswoman Leonor K. Sullivan and Helen D. Bentley,* who later was elected to Congress. Other females in government and public positions joined, and eventually most other organizations in the maritime sector opened their ranks to females. Quietly in 1974 the Merchant Marine Academy* became the first of the five service academies to admit female students.

Aboard ships and on the docks, however, the introduction of laborsaving devices was not opening opportunities for women. While automatization aboard and containers on the docks removed a great deal of the harshness from maritime work, the sharp reduction in the size of crews and dock gangs meant that a shrinking labor force could not offer spaces for women to join. However, a federal judge felt women had been unfairly excluded, and ordered the International Longshoremen and Warehousemen's Union* to hire 300 female stevedores in 1990. Fears of insufficient candidates proved groundless, and over 3,000 women applied for the positions. On the ships, the continuing decline of the U.S.-flag merchant fleet made the primary concern trying to save the jobs in a shrinking industry rather than attracting new female personnel. However, at least a few women dreamed of becoming captains of vessels, and in 1988 one, Lynn Korwatch, became the first woman in the modern history of the U.S. merchant marine to reach the rank of master, in her case of a vessel of the Matson Navigation Company* in the late 1980s.

While the formal and technical barriers to the entry of women into the merchant marine no longer exist, the industry has remained one of the last predominantly male preserves in the United States. No other female executive has emerged since Paul's brief tenure at AEL, and although women in government and public positions have continued to play important roles, until a revival of merchant shipping takes place, no large-scale expansion of women's roles can be expected.

References: Alexander & Baldwin, Inc., *Ninety Years a Corporation, 1900–1990* (Honolulu: Alexander & Baldwin, 1990); Julia C. Bonham, "Feminist and Victorian: The Paradox of the American Seafaring Woman of the Nineteenth Century," *American Neptune* 37 (1977): 203–218; *Congressional Record*, 4 February 1957, p. 1455, 22 January 1970, p. 881; *Journal of Commerce*, June–July 1990; William Kooiman, *The Grace Ships, 1869–1969* (Point Reyes, CA: Komar, 1990); *New York Times*, 27 January, 8 May 1938; Propeller Club, *American Merchant Marine Conference Proceedings*, 1961, 1980; Mariam G. Sherar, *Shipping Out: A Sociological Study of American Merchant Seamen* (Cambridge, MD: Cornell Maritime Press, 1973).

Y

YALE and HARVARD, 1906–1949. The *Yale* and the *Harvard* were the fastest ships under the U.S. flag when they were launched, and these two express passenger liners were built to carry passengers between Boston and New York. Each ship had three propellers drive by turbines,* had a speed of twenty-two knots (the *Yale* could sometimes reach twenty-four knots), and originally were built to carry 987 overnight passengers. The Metropolitan Steamship Company,* then part of the shipping combine of Wall Street financier Charles W. Morse, had ordered the two vessels, but the collapse of Morse's empire in 1907 threw into confusion the Metropolitan Steamship Company. For reasons that have never been discovered, the two ships were transferred to the Pacific Coast, where they began an express service between San Francisco and Los Angeles in December 1910 and later added a call in San Diego. The Metropolitan Steamship Company itself was merged into the Eastern Steamship Lines,* and this latter company in July 1916 leased the *Yale* and *Harvard* to the Admiral Line,* which continued to operate them until they were purchased by the navy in March 1918 for wartime service.

After the war the promoters of the Los Angeles Steamship Company* (LAS-CO) purchased the two vessels, which returned to their express service among San Francisco, Los Angeles, and San Diego, but only after they had been rebuilt to carry only 466 passengers in greater comfort and room than before. On 30 May 1931 the *Harvard*, while traveling at high speed, ran aground off Point Arguello, California, and although all on board were safely disembarked, the ship was declared a total loss. The *Yale* was laid up in July 1935 and was purchased to serve as a floating dormitory for defense construction workers in Alaska in 1941. She was recommissioned by the navy at the end of World War

II to carry passengers among the Aleutian Islands and was finally scrapped in 1949.

References: Frank O. Braynard, *Famous American Ships* (New York: Hastings House, 1956); Giles T. Brown, *Ships That Sail No More: Marine Transportation from San Diego to Puget Sound, 1910–1940* (Lexington: University of Kentucky Press, 1966).

APPENDICES

Appendix A
Chronology of Selected Events

1807 August 21	Robert Fulton placed the steamboat *Clermont*, the world's first steam vessel in the world, in regular service on the Hudson River between New York and Albany; the *Clermont* was soon followed by many other steamboats in U.S. and foreign rivers.
1815 March 21	The steamer *Fulton* began service between New York City and New Haven, Connecticut.
1819 May 24	The side-wheeler *Savannah** left the port of that same name in Georgia on the first transatlantic crossing using steam; since the late 1930s, the United States has celebrated 24 May as National Maritime Day.
1834 June	James P. Allaire and Charles Morgan* started a line between New York City and Charleston, the first regularly scheduled coastwise* steamship service between the North and the South.
1838 April 22	Arrival of British-flag *Sirius* and *Great Western* marked the beginning of permanent transatlantic steamship service for New York City.
1838 July 7	Congress authorized federal district courts to appoint inspectors who had the power to certify whether steam vessels were safe.

1846	Annexation of Texas completed U.S. coastline in the Gulf of Mexico. Great Britain recognized U.S. control over Oregon territory—the future states of Washington and Oregon.
1846 May–1848 February	Mexican War; U.S. acquired California and territories to east as far as Texas; Pacific coastline of mainland United States reached its present extension.
1847 June 1	The Bremen Line,* with the departure of the *Washington*, inaugurated the first regularly scheduled U.S.-flag steamship service across the North Atlantic.
1848 January 24	Discovery of gold in California and gold rush starting in March gave tremendous boost to Pacific Mail Steamship Company* and other steamship services using the Panama route.
1849	Havre Line* was organized to provide U.S.-flag steamship service between New York and Le Havre, France.
1850 April 27	Collins Line* inaugurated service from New York City to Liverpool with the side-wheel steamer *Atlantic*.
1850 December 27	Accessory Transit Company* of Cornelius Vanderbilt* began steamship service from New York to California via Nicaragua.
1851 January	Pacific Mail Steamship Company* agreed to operate only on Pacific side of Panama route, and United States Mail* agreed to operate only on Atlantic side of Panama route.
1852 August 30	Congress created the Steamboat Inspection Service.*
1854 September 27	Collins Line's* *Arctic* shipwrecked with the loss of 318 lives.
1855 January 28	Opening of Panama railroad reaffirmed steamship route via Panama as the fastest way to travel between New York and California.
1856 January	*Pacific* of Collins Line* disappeared in North Atlantic with forty-five passengers and the crew of 141.
1857 June	Bremen Line* halted services and dissolved itself.

1858 February	Collins Line* suspended transatlantic service; remaining ships sold at auction in April.
1858 December	Accessory Transit Company* suspended steamship service to California via the Nicaragua route.
1861 April	Havre* and Vanderbilt* lines discontinued transatlantic steamship service after outbreak of Civil War. Confederate raiders forced many U.S.-flag ships to seek protection under foreign registry; none were allowed to return to U.S. registry* after return of peace.
1861 October 24	Inauguration of transcontinental telegraph; steamships on Panama route were no longer the fastest way to communicate news between New York and California.
1865	Discovery of petroleum in western Pennsylvania marked the beginning of what became after some decades the single most important cargo in world shipping.
1865 April	End of Civil War.
1865 October	United States and Brazil Steamship Company* began its first attempt to establish permanent scheduled steamship service between both countries.
1865–1869	Compound engine* and propeller* became universal in steamships.
1866	North American Lloyd Line* began U.S.-flag steamship service from New York City to Germany and England. Ward Line* began its U.S.-flag steamship service between New York and Havana.
1867 January 1	For the first time in the world's history, Pacific Mail Steamship Company* inaugurated scheduled transpacific service between San Francisco and the Far East with the *Colorado*,* which was joined later in the year by the *Great Republic** and the *China*.
1867 April 9	U.S. purchased Alaska from Tsarist Russia; only fitful and seasonal steamship service between mainland United States and Alaska in initial decades of U.S. occupation.
1867 May 10	Completion of the first transcontinental railroad in United States immediately reduced the importance

	of Panama route for passenger travel; although five transcontinental railroads were in operation by 1890, permanent landbridge* service across United States did not appear until late 1970s.
1867 August	American Steamship Company* began service from Boston to Liverpool but ceased to operate by end of year.
1867 November 17	Inauguration of Suez Canal.
1870	North American Lloyd Line* discontinued operations. Iron hulls replaced wooden ships in U.S. shipbuilding.
1872 June 7	Congress passed the Shipping Commissioners* Act to assure that seamen were properly signed on and discharged.
1875	First conference* in world established for the England-India trade; gradually conference system spread throughout world trade routes.
1875 February 23	Marine Engineers' Beneficial Association,* the first permanent maritime union, was organized in Cleveland, Ohio.
1875 July 15	Occidental and Oriental Steamship Company* became the first U.S. firm to compete against Pacific Mail Steamship Company* in the transpacific service.
1875 October 8	Pacific Mail Steamship Company* began service to Australia and New Zealand.
1877	Pacific Coast Steamship Company,* the largest coastwise* firm on the West Coast during forty years, began operations.
1878 May	Mallory Line* and Morgan Line* agreed to divide coastwise* routes between New York and Gulf of Mexico in arrangements that lasted until 1902.
1880	Steel hulls replaced iron in new vessel construction. Tramp* steamers appeared in large numbers and ever since have remained a basic element in world shipping.
1880 May	Thomas A. Edison installed lights on *Columbia,* first ship in the world to have electricity aboard.
1881	Introduction of triple-expansion engine,* which rapidly replaced the compound engine.* Atlantic

Transport Company* organized to provide steamship service between Baltimore and London.

1883 July — Oceanic Steamship Company* began its scheduled steamship service to Hawaii from San Francisco.

1884 June 26 — Bureau of Navigation* established to direct the shipping commissioners.*

1885 March — Establishment of Coast Seamen's Union,* the first permanent maritime labor union on the Pacific Coast of the United States.

1885 November 21 — Oceanic Steamship Company* replaced Pacific Mail Steamship Company* in service to Australia and New Zealand.

1886 June 16 — First specially designed tanker was launched; soon Standard Oil Company* owned largest tanker fleet in the world.

1887 December 21 — Merchant Marine and Fisheries Committee* established in the House of Representatives of U.S. Congress.

1891 March 3 — Congress approved Ocean Mail Act of 1891.*

1891 July 29 — Sailors' Union of the Pacific* created from merger of Coast Seamen's Union* and the Steamship Sailors' Protective Union.*

1892 — International Longshoremen's Association created.

1893 — Last attempt of the United States and Brazil Steamship Company* to establish direct service between both countries failed.

1893 February 4 — Grace Line* inaugurated steamship service between New York and Peru.

1895 June 5 — The *St. Louis*,* the first passenger liner built in the United States in nearly forty years, began service to England.

1897 January 25 — Supreme Court ruled in the *Arago** decision that seamen were not covered by the constitutional guarantees of the Thirteenth Amendment.

1897–1899 — Rate war in the New York-Gulf of Mexico coastwise* routes.

1898 April–August — Spanish-American War; United States acquired Philippines and Puerto Rico, but cabotage* privileges extended only to latter.

1898 July 7	Annexation of Hawaii to United States.
1899 March 7	American-Hawaiian Steamship Company* incorporated; George S. Dearborn* first president.
1899 November	Gughielmo Marconi installed the first wireless telegraph aboard an ocean vessel, the *St. Paul.* *
1899 December	Andrew Furuseth* organized the International Seamen's Union,* the first national labor organization for seamen.
1900 December	J. P. Morgan purchased Atlantic Transport Line* and the Red Star Line* in the first step toward the creation of the International Mercantile Marine.*
1901 January	American-Hawaiian Steamship Company* started service between New York and Hawaii via the Straits of Magellan.
1902 October 1	International Mercantile Marine* formally incorporated.
1903 February	Rate war in North Atlantic began.
1904 April 28	Military Transportation Act* reserved military cargoes for U.S.-flag vessels.
1904 April	American Hawaiian Steamship Company* successfully operated *Nebraskan* with oil burner; U.S. companies began a rapid process of conversion from coal to oil as the fuel for their steamers.
1905 January 23	*Minnesota* * entered the transpacific service of the Great Northern Steamship Company* and was followed by her sister ship, the *Dakota,* * on 20 September.
1907 January	American-Hawaiian Steamship Company* shifted vessels to the Tehuantepec Railroad in Mexico for the New York-Hawaii service.
1907 January 2	Wall Street Financier Charles W. Morse incorporated the Consolidated Steamship Lines.*
1907 March 3	Shipwreck of *Dakota* * dashed James J. Hill's hopes for a transpacific shipping empire.
1908 April	Rate war in North Atlantic ended; North Atlantic United Kingdom Freight Conference* established.
1908 November 25	Atlantic, Gulf, and West Indies Steamship Lines* incorporated after the collapse of Charles W. Morse's financial empire.

1910	U.S. Steel organized the Isthmian Line* in London.
1911	First merchant ship was built with diesel engine,* whose widespread application to shipping began after World War I.
1912 April 12	*Titanic** of the International Merchantile Marine* sunk; campaign for passenger protection culminated in Safety of Life at Sea Convention.*
1912 August 24	Panama Canal Act* excluded lines owned by railroad from using the new waterway.
1912–1914	Alexander Committee* investigated conferences* and recommended they be regulated.
1913 July 9	Moore-McCormack* incorporated.
1914 August 4	Outbreak of World War I began acute shipping shortage.
1914 August 15	Opening of Panama Canal; American-Hawaiian Steamship Company,* Grace Line,* and other firms abandoned Straits of Magellan route to use the new waterway.
1915 March 4	La Follette Seamen's Act* restored rights lost by *Arago** decision.
1915 March 23	*Great Northern** inaugurated express coastwise* service between Oregon and San Francisco for the Great Northern Pacific Steamship Company.*
1915 August	Pacific Mail Steamship Company* decided to abandon ocean transportation, and its fleet was purchased by the International Mercantile Marine* and the Grace Line.*
1915 September 13	Landslides at Culebra Cut closed Panama Canal;* ships forced to return to Straits of Magellan route around South America.
1916 April 15	Panama Canal* resumed transit and has never again been closed because of natural causes.
1916 September 7	Shipping Act of 1916* began regulation of ocean transportation and created the Shipping Board.*
1916 September	American-Hawaiian Steamship Company announced the suspension of services to Hawaii.
1916 April 6	United States declared war on Germany, thereby entering World War I.
1917 April 16	Shipping Board* established the Emergency Fleet Corporation.*

1918 November 11	Armistice Day, end of World War I.
1919	Shipping Board* began to assign vessels to managing operators,* of whom over 200 soon existed.
1919 March 24	Delta Line* incorporated to provide steamship service between New Orleans and the east coast of South America.
1919 June 9	Waterman Steamship Corporation* organized to provide service for the port of Mobile, Alabama.
1919 November	American Steamship Owners' Association* created out of the previous American Steamship Association.*
1920 March 3	W. R. Grace & Co. through its Pacific Mail Steamship Company* began the first U.S.-flag round-the-world* cargo service, which ended in July 1921.
1920 April	United American Lines* organized joint venture with Hamburg-America Line.
1920 June 5	Jones Act* reaffirmed cabotage* privileges.
1921	Standard Oil Company of New Jersey* received the *John D. Archbold*, the world's biggest tanker.
1921 May 1	Seamen's strike of 1921* began and was smashed by 15 June.
1921 August	Shipping Board* established the government-owned United States Lines.*
1924 January 5	With the departure of the *President Harrison*,* the Dollar Line* inaugurated its permanent round-the-world* service, which continued without interruption until World War II.
1926 August	W. Averell Harriman sold ships of United American Lines* to the Hamburg-America Line.
1928	Standard Oil Company of New Jersey* received the *C.O. Stillman*, then the world's biggest tanker.
1928 May 22	Merchant Marine Act* established the ocean mail contracts.
1928 December	Seatrain* inaugurated service between New Orleans and Havana for the transportation of railroad cars aboard specially designed vessels.
1929 October 29	Stock market crashed; Great Depression began.

1931	American Export Lines* placed in service the Four Aces,* its first combination passenger-cargo liners. Hans Isbrandtsen* began rate war against Far East Conference.*
1931 July 1	Baltimore Mail Line,* the last firm organized to bring cargo steamship service for a specific port, began sailings to Europe.
1931 August 28	Dollar Line* placed in service the *President Hoover*,* which was joined by sister ship *President Coolidge*` in November.
1931 October	International Mercantile Marine* purchased United States Lines* from the Shipping Board.*
1932 June 3	Bureau of Marine Inspection and Navigation* created out of consolidation of Steamboat Inspection Service* and Bureau of Navigation.*
1932 August 10	Maiden voyage of *Manhattan*,* joined next year by sister ship *Washington*.
1932–1939	Rate war in jurisdiction of Pacific Westbound Conference.*
1933 August 10	Independent Shipping Board* was abolished and replaced by Shipping Board Bureau* in Department of Commerce.
1933–1936	Black Committee* exposed scandalous abuses in ocean mail contracts.
1934 April	Henry Herbermann* removed from presidency of American Export Lines, and new president William H. Coverdale* began rescue of company from bankruptcy. Rate war in jurisdiction of Far East Conference* subsided.
1934 May 9	Big Strike* began in San Francisco.
1934 September 8	Burning and shipwreck of *Morro Castle*.*
1935–1937	Rate war in U.S.A.-South Africa trade between Robin Line* and American South African Line.*
1936 June 1	Daniel K. Ludwig* organized National Bulk Carriers.
1936 June 29	Merchant Marine Act* created the U.S. Maritime Commission* to administer the construction differential subsidy* and the operating differential subsidy.*
1937 May 5	Joseph Curran* organized the National Maritime Union.*

1937 December 11	*President Hoover** shipwrecked off Formosa and declared a total loss.
1938 June	American Merchant Marine Institute* replaced American Steamship Owners' Association.*
1938 August 15	U.S. Maritime Commission* purchased the Dollar Line,* which it renamed the American President Lines.*
1938 September 8	Good Neighbor Fleet* began service to east coast of South America.
1938 October 14	American Federation of Labor created the Seafarers' International Union* to replace the discredited International Seamen's Union.*
1939 September 1	Germany invaded Poland; World War II began.
1939 November 4	Neutrality Act forbade the entry of U.S.-flag ships into almost all European ports.
1940 August 10	United States Lines* placed the *America** in service.
1941 December 7	Japanese attack on Pearl Harbor brought United States into World War II.
1942 February 7	War Shipping Administration* created.
1942 February 28	Bureau of Marine Inspection and Navigation* placed under Coast Guard.*
1943 May 21	United States Lines* absorbed the International Mercantile Marine,* whose namer ceased to be used.
1944 February	National Federation of American Shipping* organized.
1944–1945	War Shipping Administration* developed and used for first time containers,* whose adoption was rejected by private companies after the war.
1945	After extensive litigation and appeals, the Civil Aeronautics Board prohibited operation by steamship companies of regular airplane services; firms like Waterman Steamship Corporation,* American Export Lines,* and Matson Navigation Company* divested themselves of airline subsidiaries.

1945 August 15	Surrender of Japan and end of World War II.
1945 November 5	R. Stanley Dollar* began the Dollar Line case.*
1946 March 8	Ship Sales Act* created National Defense Reserve Fleet.*
1946 May 6	Longshoremen and seamen created the Committee for Maritime Unity,* their last attempt to organize joint strike action.
1946 May 16	Reorganization Plan No. 3 abolished the Bureau of Marine Inspection and Navigation,* whose functions were permanently transferred to the Coast Guard.*
1946 September 1	War Shipping Administration* was dissolved, and remaining functions transferred to U.S. Maritime Commission.*
1947 November	*Natalie O. Warren*, the first LPG* vessel, entered service.
1948	American Export Lines* received the new Four Aces* for combination passenger-cargo service.
1950 May 24	Reorganization Plan No. 21 abolished the U.S. Maritime Commission* and created the Maritime Administration* and the Federal Maritime Board.*
1950 June 25	Korean War began.
1951	American Export Lines* placed the *Constitution** and *Independence* in transatlantic passenger service.
1952 February 29	Shipyards began the delivery of the Mariner* class of break-bulk* freighters with the *Keystone Mariner*.
1952 March	Out-of-court settlement of Dollar Line case.*
1952 July 3	Maiden voyage of *United States*.*
1952 October 29	Oilman Ralph K. Davies acquired American President Lines,* whose years under government ownership and operation ended.
1953 March	Far East rate war began. American-Hawaiian Steamship Company discontinued intercoastal* service.
1953 July 27	Korean War ended.
1953 September	National Federation of American Shipping* collapsed.

1953 October 14	Stockholders of the Atlantic, Gulf, and West Indies Steamship Lines* voted to begin liquidation.
1954 January	Seamen's unions established the Conference of American Maritime Unions* in one last attempt to try to coordinate their actions.
1954 July 1	Wilson-Weeks Agreement* drastically curtailed the fleet of the Military Sea Transportation Service.*
1954 August 26	Cargo Preference Act* reserved 50 percent of government cargoes for *privately* owned vessels.
1955	After a very bitter takeover battle, Daniel K. Ludwig* gained control of American-Hawaiian Steamship Company and soon sold all its shipping assets.
1955 March	Using as collateral the Pan-Atlantic Steamship Company he had bought in January, Malcom McLean* borrowed the sums to buy the Waterman Steamship Corporation.*
1956 March	States Marine Corporation* bought the Isthmian Line* from U.S. Steel.
1956 April	The Pan-Atlantic Line of Malcom McLean* began container* service along the East Coast of the United States.
1957 March	Moore-McCormack* bought the Robin Line.*
1958 April	Far East rate war ends.
1958 May 19	Supreme Court in *Isbrandtsen** decision declared dual-rate* contracts illegal.
1958 October 26	Pan American Airlines inaugurated permanent jet airplane service across the Atlantic; ocean passenger liners became obsolete.
1959 January 1	Cuban Revolution began and gradually caused disruptions in U.S. shipping to that island.
1959 January 31	*Methane Pioneer*, the first LNG* vessel, began service.
1959 February	Josephine Bay Paul* assumed chairmanship of the Board of Directors of American Export Lines* and became the first and only woman ever to head a steamship company.
1959 November	Bankruptcy of the American Banner Lines,* the last steamship venture of Arnold Bernstein;* passenger liner *Atlantic* purchased by American Export Lines.*

1959–1960	Celler Committee* investigated practices of conferences.*
1960 March	The last common carrier providing coastwise* service along the West Coast of the United States suspended service.
1960 August	Last sailings of Lykes Brothers Steamship Company,* Seatrain,* and other U.S.-flag firms to Cuba.
1960 October 3	Josephine Bay Paul* sold her controlling share of stock in American Export Lines* (AEL) to Jakob Isbrandtsen.*
1961 March 22	Luckenbach Steamship Company* made the last sailing on its intercoastal* service.
1961 June 16	Seamen's strike* began; ended by federal injunction on July 3.
1961 August 12	Reorganization Plan No. 7 abolished the Federal Maritime Board* and created the Federal Maritime Commission.*
1961 October	American Maritime Association* was organized after settlement of Seamen's Strike of 1961;* J. Max Harrison* its first president.
1962 January 10	*Manhattan,* then the world's largest tanker, entered service.
1962 June	U.S. government approved merger of Isbrandtsen Lines* into American Export Lines.*
1963 February 18	Supreme Court in *Incres-Hondureña* cases recognized the right of U.S. corporations to use flags of convenience.*
1964 October	Castle and Cooke (Dole since 1991) purchased Standard Fruit and Steamship Company.*
1965 March 8	Landing of American combat troops marked beginning of Vietnam War for United States.
1966 February	Moore-McCormack* began container service on North Atlantic to Europe and was followed later in year by Sea-Land* and United States Lines.*
1968 January	Walter Kidde and company gained control of United States Lines* after a bitter takeover fight.
1968 May	United States Lines* received the *American Lancer,* first of the Lancers,* the first ships built expressly to carry containers.*

1969 January 1	American Institute of Merchant Shipping* replaced the American Merchant Marine Institute.*
1969 January	Seatrain* leased Brooklyn Navy Yard from federal government to build tankers.
1969 March	American Export Lines* laid up the *Independence*,* the last of its three passenger liners.
1969 July 22	Overseas Shipholding Group* incorporated.
1969 October	Central Gulf Lines* began operation of the world's first LASH* vessel.
1969 November 7	Last voyage of *United States*,* ended.
1969 December	Prudential Lines* purchased Grace Line.*
1970 January–June 1971	Rate war in the North Atlantic.
1970 March	The *Sansinena*,* affair: attempt to introduce a Liberian-flag tanker into the U.S. domestic trades failed.
1971	Seatrain* established the first landbridge* service across the United States.
1971 June	Jakob Isbrandtsen* was removed from the presidency of American Export Industries, the holding company for American Export Lines.*
1972 October 6	Sea-Land* received the first of SL-7s,* the fastest containerships in the world.
1973 January 27	Paris Peace Accords ended U.S. involvement in Vietnam War.
1973 October	Arab oil embargo began energy crisis; rise in fuel prices crippled many steamship companies.
1974 June 10	Commonwealth of Puerto Rico created the U.S.-flag Navieras de Puerto Rico* to provide service with mainland United States.
1974 December 30	Gerald Ford vetoed the Energy Transportation Act of 1974, which required 30 percent of U.S. oil imports to come aboard U.S.-flag tankers.
1977	American President Lines* ended its round-the-world service.*
1977 July	Bankruptcy of American Export Lines,* whose remaining ships were auctioned in bankruptcy court and purchased by Farrell Lines.*

1977 September	Malcom McLean* purchased United States Lines.*
1978 January	Sea-Land,* the last common carrier between the East Coast and the Gulf of Mexico, suspended its coastwise* service.
1978 February	Pacific Far East Line* filed for bankruptcy.
1980 January	Sea-Land* received D-9s, containerships that began the long overdue transition of the U.S. merchant marine from steam turbines* to diesel* engines.
1980 February 1	Seatrain* started rate war in North Atlantic that lasted until August.
1980 February	Withdrawal of Sea-Land* from conferences* set off a series of rate wars in the Pacific that did not subside until 1984.
1981	Price of oil fell, end of energy crisis.
1981 January 12	Seatrain* filed for bankruptcy protection.
1981 May	U.S. Navy purchased the SL-7s* from Sea-Land* and converted most of them into Roll-on/Roll-off* vessels.
1982 December	United States Lines* bought Moore-McCormack Lines,* whose independent existence as a shipping entity came to an end.
1982–1983	Rate war in North Atlantic.
1984	American President Lines* began double-stack* service, which was soon adopted by its competitors.
1984 March 20	Congress passed Shipping Act of 1984,* which authorized superconferences,* shippers' associations,* and service contracts.*
1984 July 22	*American New Yorker,** first of Econships,* finished maiden voyage from Far East; when her sister ships were delivered, United States Lines* inaugurated round-the-world service.*
1984 November 1	Collapse of Pacific Westbound Conference.*
1985–1989	Superconferences* appeared in almost all the foreign trade routes of the United States.
1986 May	Creditors seized ships of Prudential Lines,* which, however, has continued to operate under protection of bankruptcy court.

1986 24 November	United States Lines* filed for bankruptcy and suspended the round-the-world service.*
1988	National Maritime Union* merged into Marine Engineers' Beneficial Association* to form MEBA/NMU.
1989 March 29	*Exxon Valdez** ran aground in Price William Sound, Alaska, and caused worst oil spill in the history of the United States.
1989 December 20	U.S. invasion of Panama; Panama Canal* closed briefly for first time in its history because of political events rather than actions by nature.
1990 August 1	Iraqui invasion of Kuwait started U.S. buildup for the Gulf War.
1990 August 18	Oil Pollution Act* required double hulls* for tankers.
1991 February 27	Gulf War ended.
1992 April 10	Advisory Commission on Conferences in Ocean Shipping* in its report tacitly accepted value of Shipping Act of 1984,* including the superconferences.*
1992 August	Creation of the Trans-Atlantic Agreement* (TAA) the biggest of the superconferences.*
1993 February 26	World Trade Center terrorist explosion disrupted offices of many ocean transportation firms, including American Bureau of Shipping.*
1993 June 29	Sea-Land* announced plans to begin transfer of its fleet to flags of convenience.*
1993 July	Lykes Brothers Steamship Company* abandoned plans to operate simultaneously flags-of-convenience* ships and those under subsidy contracts.
1993 July 16	American President Lines* (APL) filed application to begin transfer of its ships out of U.S. registry.*

**Appendix B
Diagrams of Government Agencies**

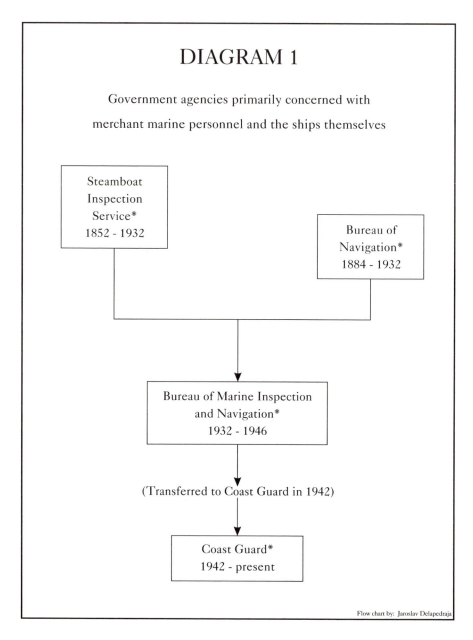

DIAGRAM 1

Government agencies primarily concerned with
merchant marine personnel and the ships themselves

Steamboat
Inspection
Service*
1852 - 1932

Bureau of
Navigation*
1884 - 1932

Bureau of Marine Inspection
and Navigation*
1932 - 1946

(Transferred to Coast Guard in 1942)

Coast Guard*
1942 - present

Flow chart by: Jaroslav Delapedraja

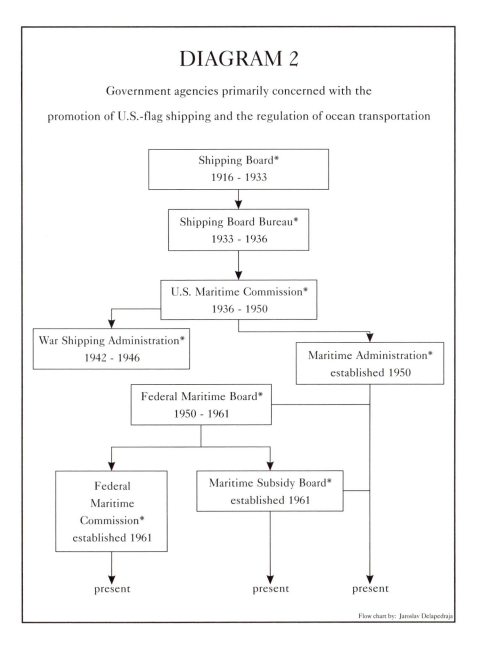

DIAGRAM 2

Government agencies primarily concerned with the

promotion of U.S.-flag shipping and the regulation of ocean transportation

Shipping Board*
1916 - 1933

Shipping Board Bureau*
1933 - 1936

U.S. Maritime Commission*
1936 - 1950

War Shipping Administration*
1942 - 1946

Maritime Administration*
established 1950

Federal Maritime Board*
1950 - 1961

Federal
Maritime
Commission*
established 1961

Maritime Subsidy Board*
established 1961

present   present   present

Flow chart by: Jaroslav Delapedraja

Appendix C
Principal Maritime Labor Unions and Business Groups (by date of founding)

LABOR UNIONS

1875–present	Marine Engineers' Beneficial Association*
1883–1953	Marine Firemen, Oilers, Watertenders, and Wipers Union of the Pacific Coast*
1885–1891	Coast Seamen's Union*
1886–1891	Steamship Sailors' Protective Union*
1891–present	Masters, Mates, and Pilots, International Organization of*
1891–present	Sailors' Union of the Pacific*
1892–present	Longshoremen's Association, International*
1899–1937	International Seamen's Union*
1901–1937	Marine Cooks and Stewards' Association of the Atlantic*
1901–1955	Marine Cooks and Stewards, National Union of*
1902–1937	Marine Firemen, Oilers, Watertenders, and Wipers Union of the Atlantic and Gulf*

1912–1933	Neptune Association*
1930–1935	Marine Workers Industrial Union*
1935–1941	Maritime Federation of the Pacific*
1937–present	Longshoremen and Warehousemen's Union, International*
1937–1988	National Maritime Union*
1938–present	Seafarers' International Union*
1959–1961	International Maritime Workers' Union*

BUSINESS GROUPS

1886–1891	American Shipping and Industrial League*
1886–circa 1963	Shipowners' Association of the Pacific Coast*
1905–1919	American Steamship Association*
1914–1937	Waterfront Employers' Union*
1919–1938	American Steamship Owners' Association*
1919-mid 1920s	National Merchant Marine Association*
1919–1968	Pacific American Steamship Association*
1919-early 1930s	U.S. Ship Operators' Association*
1937–1949	Waterfront Employers' Association*
1938–1968	American Merchant Marine Institute*
1942–1962	Association of American Shipowners*
1942-circa 1951	Ship Operators and Owners' Association*
1944–1953	National Federation of American Shipping*
1946–1949	American Tramp Shipowners' Institute*
1949–1953	Committee for Promotion of Tramp Shipping under American Flag in Foreign Commerce*
1949–present	Pacific Maritime Association*
1953–circa 1970	American Tramp Shipowners' Association
1954–1968	Committee of American Steamship Lines*
1959–1973	American Committee for Flags of Necessity*
1961–present	American Maritime Association*

1969–present	American Institute of Merchant Shipping*
1974–present	Federation of American-Controlled Shipping*
1971–1987	National Maritime Council*
1978–1987	Council of American-Flag Ship Operators*
1987–1990	United Shipowners of America*

BIBLIOGRAPHIC ESSAY

In addition to the references that follow the individual entries in this dictionary, the following pages provide suggestions for further reading. While this essay includes important older works, it emphasizes readily available publications containing the latest research. The goal has been to alert the reader to the most informative books used during the course of preparing this dictionary, but not to survey the entire field, a task that would require a whole volume in itself. The standard bibliographies are Robert G. Albion, *Naval & Maritime History: An Annotated Bibliography*, 4th ed. (Mystic, CT: Marine Historical Association 1972), and Benjamin W. Labaree, *A Supplement (1971–1986) to Robert G. Albion's Naval & Maritime History: An Annotated Bibliography* (Mystic, CT: Mystic Seaport Museum, 1988). For abstracts of periodical articles, consult Charles R. Schultz, *Bibliography of Maritime and Naval History: Periodical Articles* (College Station: Texas A & M Press, 1972–present), a publication that appears every two years. Also very convenient is Susan K. Kennell and Suzanne R. Ontiveros, *American Maritime History: A Bibliography* (Santa Barbara, CA: ABC-CLIO, 1986).

The bibliographies make clear that scholarly writings do not cover all the major topics in the U.S. merchant marine, while no surge of forthcoming academic works is visible. Consequently, publications by enthusiasts of maritime history—sometimes called by the now derogatory term *amateur*—often are the only published sources available. In maritime history a healthy tradition of publication by enthusiasts or buffs, many with shipboard experience, has long thrived. If even during periods of abundant financial resources too many topics within maritime history remained unresearched, in a time of shrinking budgets it is unrealistic to expect professional historians to exhaustively research the whole field. The enthusiasts, whether from a love of the sea, of ships, or of their individual company or labor union, have made valuable contributions to both the preservation and diffusion of information, and this essay mentions some of their more notable publications.

For greater ease for the reader, the bibliographic comments appear under the main topical headings of government publications; government, legislation, and public policies; business; labor; ships; and marine propulsion and technology. There are really no general books that cover in one volume the topics included in this historical dictionary, and the nearest to general treatments are the usually multivolume publications of the U.S. government. The often-neglected government publications do provide comprehensive coverage, and this essay begins with a discussion of some of the most important ones.

GOVERNMENT PUBLICATIONS

Since the late 1910s the Merchant Marine and Fisheries Committee* of the House of Representatives has issued annually a growing mass of hearings, while its Senate counterpart, the Commerce Committee,* has contributed to the flood of publications, particularly since World War II. The executive branch was initially slow to issue reports, but since the establishment of the Maritime Administration* in 1950, this and other agencies—and without mentioning special commissions and task forces—have routinely distributed many interesting government reports. For quasi-judicial functions, the Maritime Administration has issued its *Decisions* in printed volumes since 1950, and the Federal Maritime Commission has its own set of *Decisions* since 1961; both of these publications are ongoing series.

Among the over 1,000 government publications on the merchant marine, almost all contain something of value; nonetheless, a small number tower above the rest as indispensable references. For the often-confusing government publications on the merchant marine in the nineteenth century, J.G.B. Hutchins, *The American Maritime Industries and Public Policy, 1789–1914* (Cambridge: Harvard University Press, 1941) contains a detailed list, while Paul M. Zeis, *American Shipping Policy* (Princeton, NJ: Princeton University Press, 1938) continues the list of the most famous government publications down to 1938. Of the nineteenth-century publications, the best is probably *American Merchant Marine in the Foreign Trade*, Report No. 1210, 51st Congress, 1st Session, 1890. Often referred to as the "Farquhar Report" after the chairman of the House Merchant Marine and Fisheries Committee who conducted the hearings, it contains valuable information, but perhaps because of briefness it left out important developments in the merchant marine at that time. Some of the gaps in the Farquhar Report were filled by Merchant Marine Commission, *Report*, 3 vols., Senate Report No. 2755, 58th Congress, 3d Session, 1905, which not only gave extensive attention to events of the early twentieth century but also gathered considerable testimony on the late nineteenth century. The Merchant Marine Commission held hearings throughout the United States and quite effectively captured regional feelings about the merchant marine; the commission, under the influence of the dynamic Winthrop L. Marvin,* did its work so carefully that for a number of events and institutions it is the only known published source.

The *Investigation of Shipping Combinations*, 4 vols. (Washington, DC: Government Printing Office, 1913) by the House Merchant Marine and Fisheries Committee, was the first extensive inquiry of steamship conferences.* The Alexander Committee,* as this inquiry has generally been called, made the first formal recommendation for government regulation of ocean transportation. The report overflows with a wealth of data on U.S. and foreign shipping, and is one of the landmark sources for the period before World War I. The first three volumes contain the hearings, while volume 4 has diplomatic and consular reports on "the methods and practices of steamship lines engaged in the foreign carrying trade of the U.S."

During the 1920s private companies developed very cozy relationships with the Shipping Board* and the maritime committees of Congress, and soon accusations of fraud and corruption surfaced. To make an independent investigation of the relations between government and the private companies, the Senate created a Special Committee on Investigation of Air Mail and Ocean Mail Contracts, whose *Hearings*, 9 vols. (Washington, DC: Government Printing Office, 1933–1934) are indispensable for shipping events between the two world wars. Unfortunately the Black Committee,* as it was generally called, did not press home its attacks and failed to pursue aggressively numerous leads, so that the many revelations in these volumes should not lull the reader into concluding that the committee had exposed all the abuses. The failure to make a full diagnosis of the problems of the merchant marine quieted the demands for a radical transformation in the sector, so that the many changes Congress enacted into law in the Merchant Marine Act of 1936* did not challenge the assumption that subsidizing private companies was the best possible government policy.

After the dramatic expansion of World War II was over, the U.S. merchant marine resumed its slow and steady decline, and innumerable reports vainly tried to find a solution. The most useful of the sympathetic publications was Senate Interstate and Foreign Commerce Committee, *Merchant Marine Study and Investigation*, 7 vols. (Washington, DC: Government Printing Office, 1950). Senator Warren Magnuson* gathered and published valuable documents and useful testimonies but generally avoided the hard questions about the real problems of the U.S. merchant marine. In contrast to the excessive deference of the Magnuson report was the extreme hostility of the most important government publication of the second half of the twentieth century: U.S. House, Committee of the Judiciary, *Monopoly Problems in Regulated Industries: Ocean Freight Industry*, 7 vols. (Washington, DC: Government Printing Office, 1960). The shippers* were determined to obtain the lowest rates for carrying their merchandise and convinced the Committee of the Judiciary to conduct a searching investigation into steamship conferences. The Celler Committee,* as it was generally known, unearthed and published the largest and richest amount of information ever on the U.S. merchant marine and exposed better than any other published source the brutal competition, often of a very vindictive and ferocious nature, that normally reigns in ocean transportation. While the evidence gathered by the Celler Committee was necessarily slanted against the merchant shipping companies and in favor of the shippers, the hearings printed so many internal documents of the companies that the researcher literally has in these ''portable archives'' a veritable treasure trove on the 1950s.

Nothing comparable to the Cellar Committee has since appeared, and in general government publications after the 1960s have not lived up to the standards set by the predecessors. One of the most useful for an overall view is Office of Technology Assessment, *An Assessment of Maritime Trade and Technology* (Washington, DC: Government Printing Office, 1983) whose supplement appeared in 1985. The most disappointing government effort was the Commission on Merchant Marine and Defense, whose confusing series of reports and hearings appeared in 1987 and 1988. Professional lobbyists presented carefully tailored statements for the Commission on Merchant Marine and Defense, which really did not move into any aggressive information gathering, although occasionally the commission received some valuable reports that it published in appendix volumes. Of the special investigatory efforts on the merchant marine in the twentieth century, this commission clearly ranked near the bottom.

Much more successful was the Advisory Commission on Conferences in Ocean Shipping, whose *Report to the President and the Congress* (Washington, DC: Government Printing Office, 1992) is well organized and generally clearly written. The publication of an appendix volume with testimony and documents would have put this report in the class of the great government publications on the U.S. merchant marine, and in any case the *Report* has joined the list of standard references on the workings of conferences and government regulation.

GOVERNMENT, LEGISLATION, AND PUBLIC POLICIES

No up-to-date survey exists covering government policy toward the merchant marine in the twentieth century, and the many studies that do exist tend to concentrate on the recent period immediately preceding their publication. For the period up to 1914 the standard reference is J.G.B. Hutchins, *The American Maritime Industries and Public Policy, 1789–1914*, published in 1941 and reprinted in 1969. Unfortunately the book is very tough going, and the deadening prose is sure to scare away all but the most dedicated. For the few who persevere, the rewards do not justify the efforts, and the reader will have to go somewhere else to understand the dynamics of merchant shipping. A good index allows locating some facts, while the most valuable part of the book is the detailed listing of the sometimes confusing-to-locate government publications of the nineteenth century. Readers are better off beginning with Paul M. Zeis, *American Shipping Policy* (Princeton, NJ: Princeton University Press, 1938). Zeis, the rare economist with both a historical sense and a grasp of merchant shipping, covers the period up to the Merchant Marine Act of 1936* in one-third the number of pages of Hutchins's book, in clear prose, and with a sharp analytical understanding. The Zeis book, a minor classic, is the best one-volume introduction to the historical development of government policy toward the merchant marine in the United States.

On the average, every ten years a new study comes out providing an account of recent changes in government policy, but the next really major study after Zeis in 1938 did not come until 1966, when Samuel A. Lawrence published *United States Merchant Shipping Policies and Politics* (Washington, DC: Brookings Institution, 1966). As far as understanding the politics of how interest groups in Washington, D.C., shape and capture government policies, Lawrence's work remains unrivaled, and it also contains detailed discussions of all major policy initiatives and government agencies since the Merchant Marine Act of 1936. Incisive observations fill this book, which could have been written only by an insider with unparalleled access to official workings. The individual sections and chapters of the book are easy to read, but unfortunately the book does not flow well as a whole and, although highly recommended, is best savored after some familiarity with the topic. Lawrence gives the impression of always having more information and inside accounts at the tip of his pen, but unfortunately he could not play up this information, and frequently he tucked away precious nuggets of information deep within footnotes or in odd places in his book.

Historians have not given maritime policy the attention it deserves. A major exception is Jeffrey J. Safford, *Wilsonian Maritime Diplomacy, 1913–1921* (New Brunswick, NJ: Rutgers University Press, 1978), which covers carefully a vital period. For the years before or after the period covered in Safford's book, nothing comparable exists. Robert G. Albion, *Seaports South of the Sahara: The Achievements of an American Steamship Service* (New York: Appleton-Century-Crofts, 1959), although a company history of the Farrell Lines,* also provides considerable discussion of government policies. René De La Pedraja, *The Rise and Decline of U.S. Merchant Shipping in the Twentieth Century* (New York: Twayne, 1992), although a business history, provides capsule accounts of the principal government agencies and their policies.

For the advanced reader, another book by an economist, Gerald R. Jantscher, *Bread Upon the Waters: Federal Aids to the Maritime Industries* (Washington, DC: Brookings Institution, 1975), contains some of the most polished and penetrating comments on government policy toward the merchant marine. Jantscher first discusses the exact meaning and intent of the legislation and then uses economic analysis to draw conclusions about the effectiveness of the laws in the light of statistical data. While always challenging, the book does have its flaws, most notably, the failure to grasp the commercial, as distinct from the military, significance of the U.S. merchant marine. The latest scholar to have discussed government policy is Clinton H. Whitehurst, Jr., whose *The U.S. Merchant Marine: In Search of an Enduring Policy* was published by the U.S. Naval Institute Press in 1983. If the ten-year average I have detected for the frequency of books on government policy holds up, a publication on recent government maritime policies should soon be appearing.

BUSINESS

For business history the reader is fortunate to have an up-to-date survey in René De La Pedraja, *The Rise and Decline of U.S. Merchant Shipping in the Twentieth Century* (New York: Twayne, 1992), which covers the evolution of the main merchant shipping companies, including tramps* and tankers. Although that book contains a longer discussion of the principal sources for business history, at least some of the more important titles may be mentioned here. For nineteenth-century developments, perhaps the two most important books are John H. Kemble, *The Panama Route, 1848–1869* (Berkeley: University of California Press, 1943), and David B. Tyler, *Steam Conquers the Atlantic* (New York: D. Appleton-Century, 1939). The single most important company history published so far for the merchant marine is John Niven, *The American President Lines and Its Forebears, 1848–1984* (Newark: University of Delaware Press, 1986). Niven's well-written book remains the only inside account of the operations of a U.S. company in the age of containers, but this invaluable book at times leaves the reader hungry for more information and explanations about the crucial transition from steam freighters to diesel containership.

Other excellent company histories are James P. Baughman, *The Mallorys of Mystic: Six Generations in American Maritime Enterprise* (Middletown, CT: Wesleyan University Press, 1972), which contains a wealth of information; Robert G. Albion, *Seaports South of Sahara: The Achievements of an American Steamship Company* (New York: Appleton-Century Crofts, 1959), which used a relatively small company as the starting point to study larger policy questions; Lawrence A. Clayton, *Grace: W. R. Grace & Co. The Formative Years, 1850–1930* (Ottawa, IL: Jameson Books, 1985) explains how a merchant house established a major steamship company; William L. Worden, *Cargoes: Matson's First Century in the Pacific* (Honolulu: University of Hawaii Press, 1981) very effectively traces the special link between Hawaii and the Matson Navigation Company.*

The major regional study of shipping is Giles T. Brown, *Ships That Sail No More: Marine Transportation from San Diego to Puget Sound, 1910–1940* (Lexington: University of Kentucky Press, 1966), while Rodney P. Carlisle explores an important topic affecting many companies in *Sovereignty for Sale: The Origins and Evolution of the Panamanian and Liberian Flags of Convenience* (Annapolis, MD: Naval Institute Press, 1981). Business manuals should not be overlooked as a way to obtain a "feel" for the operations of merchant shipping; although older ones exist, the reader might want to begin with Carl E. McDowell and Helen M. Gibbs, eds., *Ocean Transportation* (New York: McGraw-Hill, 1954), which is straightforward and widely available. For the rest of the twentieth century, the reader can profitably trace the evolution of practices in the successive revisions of Lane C. Kendall, *The Business of Shipping*, 5th ed. (Centreville, MD: Cornell Maritime Press, 1986); the publisher has promised a final, revised edition for 1994.

LABOR

No survey of maritime labor history from the rise of the first organizations to the present exists; most accounts stop their coverage around World War II, and very few venture beyond the 1950s. Hyman Weintruab, *Andrew Furuseth: Emancipator of the Seamen* (Berkeley: University of California Press, 1959) set a high standard for scholarship on maritime labor history; his book is carefully researched, well organized, and easy to read and is the logical starting point for anyone trying to understand the history of maritime labor from the 1890s to the 1930s. New findings for the 1920s and 1930s are contained in Bruce Nelson, *Workers on the Waterfront: Seamen, Longshoremen, and Unionism in the 1930s* (Urbana: University of Illinois Press, 1990). Nelson's book is much broader than its title suggests and may be taken as a history of the maritime labor movement since its inception, but unfortunately the book stops with World War II and promises no sequel for the crucial post-1945 years.

Two books are vital for the emergence of "big labor" movement in the maritime unions after World War II: Joseph P. Goldberg, *The Maritime Story: A Study in Labor-Management Relations* (Cambridge: Harvard University Press, 1958), and Joseph H. Ball, *The Government-Subsidized Union Monopoly: A Study of Labor Practices in the Shipping Industry* (Washington, DC: Labor Policy Association, 1966). Both are highly critical of the unions and help to understand the corruption, abuses, and power struggles that so perverted the original idealism of the maritime labor movement. The idealism and spirit of sacrifice of the early labor movement are well captured in accounts such as the still-useful study by William L. Standard, *Merchant Seamen: A Short History of Their Struggles* (New York: International, 1947). Stephen Schwartz, *Brotherhood of the Sea: A History of the Sailors' Union of the Pacific, 1885–1985* (New Brunswick, NJ: Transaction Books, 1986) is the rare history of a single union. Unfortunately the difficult reading of *Brotherhood of the Sea* is not made any easier by the author's curious ideological mix, while the book shies away from the bitter power struggles of the union bosses after World War II.

The primary emphasis in all the above books is on the unlicensed seamen, and the books generally neglect the officers and engineers on board. For the most complete and readable account of officers' unions, the reader will have to consult Howard A. Thor, "Trade Unions of Licensed Officers in the Maritime Industry," Ph.D. diss. Berkeley, 1965. For the independent tankers unions,* two books by John J. Collins, *Never Off Pay: The Story of the Independent Tanker Union, 1937–1962* (New York: Fordham University Press, 1964), and *Bargaining at the Local Level* (New York: Fordham University Press, 1974) provide a full account of their origin and development. The thoughtful books by Collins are also highly recommended because of the insights they provide into the dynamics of maritime labor in general and their challenging of accepted assumptions, which make for stimulating reading.

As for longshoremen, Bruce Nelson provides considerable information in his book

Workers on the Waterfront. For longshoremen on the Pacific Coast, Charles P. Larrowe, *Harry Bridges: The Rise and Fall of Radical Labor in the U.S.* (New York: Lawrence Hill, 1972) is the standard source, while additional insights on Bridges may be gained from the documentary "Harry Bridges" broadcast by public television stations in September 1993. Maud Russell, *Men Along the Shore: The ILA and Its History* (New York: Brussel and Brussel, 1966) is good for the early decades of the longshoremen's movement on the East Coast, but in the later chapters the book degenerates into an apology for the excesses of some of the union bosses. William W. Pilcher, an anthropologist and former longshoreman, has provided a fascinating account of the work and lives of dockworkers in *The Portland Longshoremen: A Dispersed Urban Community* (New York: Holt, Rinehart, and Winston, 1972). The sociologist Howard Kimeldorf brings the perspective of his discipline and new information to bear on the topic in his valuable recent study, *Reds or Rackets: The Making of Radical and Conservative Unions on the Waterfront* (Berkeley: University of California Press, 1988).

While most of the books on maritime unions contain extensive information on the lives of the seamen, a few books focus exclusively on the human side of living and working aboard ships and the difficulties of constantly having to readjust to society on land. James C. Healey, *Foc's'l and Glory Hole: A Study of the Merchant Seaman and His Occupation* (New York: Merchant Marine Publishers Association, 1936) is a very human book that captures the plight of the seamen in the vanished period just prior to the appearance of powerful maritime unions. Elmo Paul Hohman, in two books, *History of the American Merchant Seamen* (Hamden, CT: Shoestring Press, 1956) and *Seamen Ashore* (New Haven, CT: Yale University Press, 1952), took into account the changes in seamen's lives brought about by unionization. Great insight into the personal and psychological situation of seamen comes from reading Mariam G. Sherar, *Shipping Out: A Sociological Study of American Merchant Seamen* (Cambridge, MD: Cornell Maritime Press, 1973), probably the study in print that best captures the feeling of being an unlicensed seaman. For the legal aspects of life and work aboard the ships, Martin J. Norris, *The Law of Seamen*, 4th ed. (Rochester: Lawyers' Cooperative Publishing, 1985) is the standard source, while the first three editions allow the reader to follow the changes in the legal provisions affecting seafarers.

SHIPS

Numerous books provide accounts of ships, in particular, the luxury transatlantic liners. These publications chronicle the careers of ships in the hallowed tradition of the sea as if the ships were actual living beings that are born, grow, and finally die, but not without first passing through all sorts of adventures, generally memorable. For the nineteenth-century steamships, Erik Heyl, *Early American Steamers*, 6 vols. (Buffalo NY: 1953–1969) is the essential source; not only is *Early American Steamers* easy to consult, but the publication also provides the assurance of knowing there will be an entry for whatever ship the reader has in mind. No one has attempted the perhaps impossible task of continuing Heyl's monumental work for the decades after the 1880s, so that the reader wishing information on less well-known vessels has no choice but to turn to the official publications of the U.S. government, in particular, *Merchant Vessels of the United States* (published annually since 1867) for statistical specifications on all ships under U.S. registry.* The annual *Record of the American Bureau of Shipping* is similarly helpful, but for the period before 1920, when most U.S.-flag ships were classified by Lloyd's of London, consult the latter's annual publication, the *Lloyd's Register of Shipping*.

Readers wishing a more easily available, more complete, and certainly more readable account of individual ships than what is found in the official registers have a wide selection to choose from. Frank O. Braynard, *Famous American Ships* (New York: Hastings House, 1956), is a good place to start, while for passenger ocean liners, Frederick E. Emmons, *American Passenger Ships: The Ocean Lines and Liners, 1875–1983* (Newark: University of Delaware Press, 1985), is encyclopedic in its coverage and provides the most useful of the recent publications. The difficulty of finding information applies mainly to the freighters, tankers, and containerships, whose activities have generally been slighted because of the appeal of the more glamorous ocean passenger liners. For transpacific navigation until 1941, E. Mowbray Tate has written an extremely useful book, *Transpacific Steam: The Story of Steam Navigation from the Pacific Coast of North America to the Far East and the Antipodes, 1867–1941* (New York: Cornwall Books, 1986). David B. Tyler, *Steam Conquers the Atlantic* (New York: D. Appleton-Century, 1939), covers ships and navigation in the North Atlantic only until the 1880s and forms a very readable complement to the biographies of individual ships found in Heyl.

A number of authors have written books on the fleets of individual steamship companies. The most important are William Kooiman, *The Grace Ships, 1869–1969* (Point Reyes, CA: Komar, 1990), Fred A. Stindt, *Matson's Century of Ships* (Modesto, CA: n.p., 1982), and John H. Melville, *The Great White Fleet* (New York: Vantage Press, 1976). The histories of individual companies should also be consulted because they all contain a good amount of information on the ships themselves; three business histories, because in addition they offer detailed biographical lists of the individual ships, should be singled out: John H. Kemble, *The Panama Route, 1849–1869* (Berkeley: University of California Press, 1943), Giles T. Brown, *Ships That Sail No More: Marine Transportation from San Diego to Puget Sound, 1910–1940* (Lexington: University of Kentucky Press, 1966), and John Niven, *The American President Lines and Its Forebears, 1848–1984* (Newark: University of Delaware Press, 1986).

Thanks to the fascination of Frank O. Braynard with ships, readers are able to enjoy the books he has published on individual vessels, starting with six volumes on *The World's Greatest Ship: The Story of the Leviathan*, published from 1972 to 1978, and the more manageable one volume, *The Big Ship: The Story of the S.S. United States* (Newport News, VA: Mariners' Museum, 1982).

Other authors have concentrated on the history of a particular ship type, beginning with the solid work by John Gorley Bunker, *The Liberty Ships: The Ugly Ducklings of World War II* (Annapolis, MD: Naval Institute Press, 1972), while Walter W. Jaffee is rescuing information on other ship types, most notably in his *The Last Mission Tanker* (Sausalito, CA: Scope, 1990). L. A. Sayer and W. H. Mitchell, *From America to United States* 4 vols. (Kendal, England: World Ship Society, 1979–1986), have surveyed the shipbuilding program of the U.S. Maritime Commission,* and provide information not only on the ship types, but also on the individual vessels themselves. However, the most ambitious undertaking so far is that of Mark H. Goldberg who plans to write the biography of apparently every merchant and passenger ship of the U.S. fleet. He has already published *The Hog Islanders: The Story of 122 American Ships* (Kings Point, NY: American Merchant Marine Museum, 1991), *Caviar & Cargo: The C-3 Passenger Ships* (Kings Point, NY: American Merchant Marine Museum, 1992), and *Going Bananas: 100 Years of American Fruit Ships in the Caribbean* (Kings Point, NY: American Merchant

Marine Museum, 1993). He promises at least nine more volumes, and if completed, the series will surely rank as a monumental accomplishment.

MARINE PROPULSION AND TECHNOLOGY

Although no historical survey of the technical evolution of ships exists, the American Bureau of Shipping has mentioned the principal highlights in its illustrated official *History 1862–1991*. Several writers have also taken considerable pains to explain the technical functioning of a ship as clearly as possible to the lay reader. The many excellent essays contained in Society of Naval Architects and Marine Engineers, *Historical Transactions, 1893–1943*, reprinted by Greenwood Press in 1981, constitute a good starting point. All the authors were highly knowledgeable in their fields, and many were actual participants who strove to present clearly the salient facts. While the *Historical Transactions* volume is not overly technical, the reader wishing livelier prose can begin with T. W. Van Metre, *Tramps and Liners* (New York: Doubleday, Doran, 1931), whose sketches and illustrations help to explain many aspects of marine propulsion. For developments since 1943 no comparable survey exist, and the reader must piece together the story from several sources. Two recent and most useful accounts are found in the Commission on Merchant Marine and Defense, *Third Report: Appendices* (Washington, DC: Government Printing Office, 1988) and Transportation Research Board, *Intermodal Marine Container Transportation: Impediments and Opportunities* (Washington, DC: National Research Council, 1992). The reader wishing the most complete technical information will wish to consult the monthly periodical *Marine Engineering/Log*, called *Marine Log* since 1987; persons less technically oriented will probably be satisfied with the reporting in the monthly *American Shipper* and the newspaper the *Journal of Commerce*.

Most of the books on ships and many on business history also contain information on the engineering aspects of shipping. On containers, besides the recent study by the Transportation Research Board, the reader should consult the classic study by Henry S. Marcus, *Planning Ship Replacement in the Containerization Era* (Lexington, MA: Lexington Books, 1974).

INDEX

The page numbers in **boldface** indicate the location of the main entry.

Company, compared with, 10; and
American-Hawaiian Steamship
Company, 31, 169, 302; and business
groups, 52, 141; and Castle and Cooke,
578; and containers, 42, 113, 150; and
labor strife, 346; and Los Angeles
Steamship Company, 320; and
Mariners, 365, 368; and Oceanic &
Oriental Navigation Company, 450–
451; and Oceanic Steamship Company,
45; and Pacific Transport Lines, 474;
presidents of, 67, 166, 378, 512–513,
551–552, 601; sale of passenger liners,
469; ships of, 330, 367–369; and
women, 663
Matsonia (1938–1948), **341–342**
Matsonia (1956–1963), 368, **382**
Mauretania, 265, 360, 593, 602–603
May, Albert E., 141, 618
Mayagüez, 107, 229, **382–383**
Mayer, Robert E., 464
McAdoo, William, 41, 45
McAllister, Breck P., 24,
McAllister, Charles A., 23,
McAllister Bros., 632
McAuliffe, John, 278
McCormack, Emmet J., **384–385**, 407,
408, 409–412
McCormick, Charles R., **385–386**, 486–
487
McCormick, Eugene F., 234
McCormick Steamship Company, 130,
385, **386–387**, 487; and conferences,
623
McEvoy, Michael R., 542
McFee, William, 310–311
McGray, Arthur N., 439
McLane, Allan, 472
McLaren, Richard A., 474
McLean, James, 388, 654, 655
McLean, Malcom P., 152, 172, **387–389**,
548, 552; and Econships, 188–189,
233; and Daniel K. Ludwig, 327; and
Moore-McCormack Steamship, 412;
and round-the-world service, 516; and
Sea-Land, 538–542; and United States
Lines, 438, 626; and Waterman
Steamship Corporation, 654–655

McLean Industries, 388
McMullen, John, 625, 626
McNeil, Wilfred J., 228, 229
Meany, George, 244, 293, 374
Mechanization, 89
Mechanization and Modernization
Agreement of 1960 (M&M), 223, 315,
389–390; and Harry Bridges, 93, 656–
657; and business groups, 552
Mediterranean, shipping services to, 499–
500, 576; from New York, 444–445
Mediterranean Line, 338
Mediterranean Shipping Company, 607
Mekong river, 303
Melville, Herman, 309, 420
Memoirs (Robert Dollar), 175
Men and Machines, 223
Mercantilism, 112, 286
Mercer, Henry D., 586–587, 644
Merchant Fleet Corporation, 191, 192,
390–391, 567
Merchant Marine Academy, 87, 292, 364,
391–392; creation of, 298, 583; and
Propeller Club, 498; and State
Maritime Academies, 583–584; and
women, 662
Merchant Marine Act of 1891. *See* Ocean
Mail Act of 1891
Merchant Marine Act of 1920. *See* Jones
Act
Merchant Marine Act of 1928, 48, 285,
392–394; backlash against, 458; and
Baltimore Mail Line, 68–69;
investigation of mail contracts, 78–79,
394, 397; and managing operators,
343, 566
Merchant Marine Act of 1936, 53, 69,
148–149, **394–395**; and Committee of
American Steamship Lines, 140–141;
failure of, 370; and mail contracts,
290; and Merchant Fleet Corporation,
391; passage of, 857; and Red D Line,
503–504; and Shipping Board Bureau,
567–568; and subsidies, 79, 227–228,
397, 410; subsidy program of, 458–
459; and United States Lines, 214. *See
also* Construction differential subsidy;
Operating differential subsidy

Troy, U.S.S., 406
Trucking firms, 387–388, 649
Truman, Harry S., 299
Tugs, 159, 161. *See also* Barges
Tung, C. Y., 148
Turbines. *See* Steam Turbines.
Turboelectric drive, 110, 176, 177, 190, 345; and passenger liners, 360–361, 416, 490, 492, 594
Turkish investors, 621
Turman, Solon B., 331, 333
Turner Networks, 6
Tuxedo Unionism, 317, 328, **609**, 659; among longshoremen, 518–519
Tweedie Trading Company, 407
Twentieth-Century Fox, 499

Uhler, George, 349, 352, 591, 592
ULCC or Ultra Large Crude Carriers, 489, 611, 641
Un-American Activities Committee of the U.S. House of Representatives, 252, 422, 458
Union Oil Co. of California, 52, 210, 529–531
Union Pacific Railroad, 529
Union Sulphur Co., 52
United American Lines, 509–510, **611–614**; and American-Hawaiian Steamship Co., 31
United Fruit Company or Great White Fleet, 52, 498, 588, **614–615**; and Colombian Steamship Company, 136; and flags of convenience, 24, 210, 256; and Standard Fruit and Steamship Co., 577–578
United Industrial Workers, 537–538
United Licensed Officers of America, 439
United Mine Workers, 318
United Philippine Lines, 198
United Seamen's Service (USS), 40, **615–617**, 662
United Service Organizations, 615
United Shipowners of America (USA), 33, 156, **617–618**
United States, 215, 306, 421, **618–621**, 625, 627; and *America*, 20; speed record, 573

United States and Brazil Mail Steamship Company, 123, 340, 452, **621–623**
United States Freight Company, 154
United States Intercoastal Conference, 238, 321, 560, **623–624**
United States Lines (USL), 52, 72, 81, 82, **624–627**; and *America*, 19–20, 345; and American Merchant Line, 38; and Australia, 200–202; and business groups, 141, 156, 432; and conferences, 198, 444–446, 629; and containers, 150, 388–389, 539; and Delta Line, 160, 172; and Econships, 40–41, 188–189, 333, 389, 541–542; under government operation, 192, 306, 390, 565; and intercoastal service, 152; and International Mercantile Marine, 266, 267; and *Manhattan* and *Washington*, 345–346; and Mariners, 365; and Military Sealift Command, 401; and Moore-McCormack, 72, 412; officials of, 214–216, 244–245, 387–389; and Roosevelt Steamship Company, 510–511; and round-the-world service, 516; and Sea-Land, 539–542, 573–574; and *United States*, 618–621
United States Mail Steamship Company, 60, 193, **627–628**; and Cornelius Vanderbilt, 4–5, 638
United States Standard Steamship Owners, Builders, and Underwriters Association, 21
United States Steel, 48, 57, 111, 277–278. *See also* Isthmian Line
Universal Negro Improvement Association, 79, 82–83
Universe Tankships, 327
Uruguay, 224, 410
U.S. & A Lines, Inc., 632
U.S. & Australian Steamship Company, 48
U.S. Army. *See* Army
U.S. Atlantic and Gulf Ports/Eastern Mediterranean and North African Freight Conference (USAGEM), **628**
U.S. Atlantic and Gulf Western Mediterranean Agreement (AGWM), 576

About the Author

RENÉ DE LA PEDRAJA is Associate Professor of History at Canisius College and the author of *The Rise and Decline of U.S. Merchant Shipping in the Twentieth Century* (1992), which *Choice* selected as an Outstanding Academic Book in 1994. Other recent books cover the history of energy policies and industries in South America.

ISBN 0-313-27225-5

90000>

EAN

9 780313 272257

HARDCOVER BAR CODE